BANKRUPTCY AND
INSOLVENCY ACCOUNTING

Subscriber Update Service

BECOME A SUBSCRIBER!

Did you purchase this product from a bookstore?

If you did, it's important for you to become a subscriber. John Wiley & Sons, Inc. may publish, on a periodic basis, supplements and new editions to reflect the latest changes in the subject matter that you *need to know* in order to stay competitive in this ever-changing industry. By contacting the Wiley office nearest you, you'll receive any current update at no additional charge. In addition, you'll receive future updates and revised or related volumes on a 30-day examination review.

If you purchased this product directly from John Wiley & Sons, Inc., we have already recorded your subscription for this update service.

To become a subscriber, please call **1-800-225-5945** or send your name, company name (if applicable), address, and the title of the product to:

mailing address: **Supplement Department
John Wiley & Sons, Inc.
One Wiley Drive
Somerset, NJ 08875**

e-mail: **subscriber@wiley.com**
fax: **1-732-302-2300**
online: **www.wiley.com**

For customers outside the United States, please contact the Wiley office nearest you:

Professional & Reference Division
John Wiley & Sons Canada, Ltd.
22 Worcester Road
Rexdale, Ontario M9W 1L1
CANADA
(416) 675-3580
Phone: 1-800-567-4797
Fax: 1-800-565-6802
canada@jwiley.com

John Wiley & Sons, Ltd.
Baffins Lane
Chichester
West Sussex, PO19 1UD
ENGLAND
Phone: (44) 1243 779777
Fax: (44) 1243 770638
cs-books@wiley.co.uk

Jacaranda Wiley Ltd.
PRT Division
P.O. Box 174
North Ryde, NSW 2113
AUSTRALIA
Phone: (02) 805-1100
Fax: (02) 805-1597
headoffice@jacwiley.com.au

John Wiley & Sons (SEA) Pte. Ltd.
37 Jalan Pemimpin
Block B # 05-04
Union Industrial Building
SINGAPORE 2057
Phone: (65) 258-1157
Fax: (65) 463-4604
csd_ord@wiley.com.sg

Bankruptcy and Insolvency Accounting

PRACTICE AND PROCEDURE

Volume 1

Sixth Edition

GRANT W. NEWTON, CIRA, CPA, CMA

Professor of Accounting

Pepperdine University

JOHN WILEY & SONS, INC.

New York • Chichester • Weinheim • Brisbane • Singapore • Toronto

**To Valda, Aaron,
Paul, and Danae**

This publication is designed to provide accurate and authoritative
information in regard to the subject matter covered. It is sold with
the understanding that the publisher is not engaged in rendering
legal, accounting, or other professional services. If legal advice or
other expert assistance is required, the services of a competent professional person should be sought.

Library of Congress Cataloging-in-Publication Data:

Newton, Grant W.
    Bankruptcy and insolvency accounting / by Grant W. Newton.—6th ed.
      p.   cm.
    ISBN 0-471-33144-9 (cloth set : alk. paper)—ISBN 0-471-33143-0 (vol. 1 : alk. paper)
    —ISBN 0-471-33142-2 (vol. 2 : alk. paper)
      1. Bankruptcy—United States. 2. Bankruptcy—United States–Forms. 3.
    Bankruptcy—United States—Accounting.   I. Title.

    KF1527 .N49 2000
    346.7307'8'0269–dc21   00-043296

Printed in the United States of America.

10 9 8 7 6 5 4 3 2 1

About the Author

GRANT W. NEWTON, Professor of Accounting at the Graziadio School of Business and Management at Pepperdine University, Malibu, California, is a coauthor with Gilbert D. Bloom author of *Bankruptcy and Insolvency Taxation*, 2nd edition (1994; updated annually), also published by John Wiley & Sons. He is also the editor and a contributing author of *CMA Review*, published by Malibu Publishing Company. His articles have appeared in a large number of professional periodicals. A CIRA, CPA, and CMA, he received a Ph.D. degree from New York University, a Master's degree from the University of Alabama, and a B.S. degree from the University of North Alabama.

Dr. Newton was a member of the AICPA's Task Force on Financial Reporting by Entities in Reorganization Under the Bankruptcy Code, which resulted in the issuance of AICPA Statement of Position 90-7. He has served as a consultant to national and regional CPA firms on bankruptcy and insolvency matters. He has spoken on the subjects of bankruptcy and insolvency accounting and management accounting to many professional groups, including AICPA, state societies of CPAs, American Bankruptcy Institute, Institute of Management Accountant, Practising Law Institute, American Bar Association, California Bar, and Arizona Bar.

Acknowledgments

Many individuals provided invaluable assistance during the writing of this book, particularly the members of the Committee on Development of a Manual of Bankruptcy and Insolvency Procedures of the New York Society of Certified Public Accountants, who provided support, encouragement, and timely assistance on many occasions during the writing of the first edition.

Although it is not possible to recognize all of the persons to whom thanks are due, acknowledgment for providing assistance for the earlier editions is gratefully given to Robert A. Adams, Dan E. Williams, Bernard L. Augen, Louis Klein, Milton Mintzer, Irving Rom, Kermit Easton, Walter J. Henning, Jerry Klein, Professor Joseph E. Lane, Jr., Professor Norman Martin, Professor Jeremy Wiesen, Elliot Meisel, Alexander E. Slater, Jerry Toder, Burton D. Strumpf, Edward A. Weinstein, Jack A. Cipra, John A. Flynn, Andrew A. Krinock, Russel A. Lippman, and Howard C. White.

I am especially grateful to Professor Kenneth N. Klee of School of Law, UCLA, for his assistance in helping me interpret the provisions of the new bankruptcy law, and for reviewing the legal parts of early editions of the book.

The careful manuscript review by Joseph A. Laurion of Kay, Fialkow, Richmond & Rothstein was most helpful. Also, I am grateful for his assistance in helping me practically apply many of the provisions of the new law.

I am especially grateful to Donald E. Condit for assisting me with Chapter 13, along with R. Todd Neilson, for helping me to obtain a large amount of practical experience. The support and the assistance of the faculty and staff of Pepperdine University are gratefully acknowledged.

I am grateful to Dr. Lee J. Seidler for introducing me to the area of bankruptcy accounting and for the many valuable suggestions he provided during the writing of the first edition of the book.

Finally, I thank Valda L. Newton for her editorial assistance and for her patience and understanding while I revised this edition.

G.W.N.

Preface

This work is designed to provide a broad range of practical guidance for accountants, financial advisors, lawyers, bankruptcy trustees, referees, and creditors of business enterprises in financial straits. It is presented in two volumes. Volume 1, Practice and Procedure, consists of text material that describes the economic, legal, accounting, and tax aspects of bankruptcy proceedings. Volume 2, Forms and Exhibits, contains examples of various forms and exhibits that are used by accountants, financial advisors, and other professionals in bankruptcy cases and out-of-court workouts. Both volumes are updated annually.

The role of the accountant and financial advisor is viewed against a background of economic, legal, and management considerations, and the interdependence of the various interests involved is clearly delineated.

From informal adjustments made out of court through full court proceedings under chapter 11 jurisdiction, the book discusses alternative courses of action, working procedures, and statutory requirements applicable to the particular situation. The accountant is shown the type of information required by the debtor attorney for the bankruptcy petition and how to prepare operating statements to be filed with the court. He is aided in formulating a plan of reorganization that will gain acceptance by creditors and at the same time allow the client to operate a business successfully. The means by which the accountant can help the creditors' committee exercise adequate control over the debtor's activities are also described.

The bankruptcy and insolvency special investigation is explored in detail, with emphasis on the detection of irregularities and procedures to be performed if irregularities exist. The types of reports often required of the accountant are illustrated, and advice is offered on the special problems encountered in reporting on a company in financial difficulty. The reader is taken step by step through a typical bankruptcy audit, including preparation of requisite forms and issuance of the audit report.

Taxes, which often impose undue hardship on the bankrupt during the administration period, are dealt with in a separate chapter. Instructions are given for tax minimization, filing returns, treatment of income during bankruptcy, and dealing with the varied tax planning and compliance problems peculiar to bankruptcy. The tax coverage is limited. For a detailed and current discussion of tax issues faced by the debtors having financial trouble, see *Bankruptcy and Insolvency Taxation*, written by Grant W. Newton and Gilbert D. Bloom, also published by John Wiley & Sons, and updated annually.

This sixth edition has been revised to include the most recent amendments to the Bankruptcy Code and court decisions based on the Bankruptcy Code.

Included are decisions dealing with preferences, automatic stay, fees, and property of the estate. A new section on lender liability has been added.

Revised Federal Rules of Bankruptcy Procedure were issued and became effective August 1, 1991, and subsequent modifications have been made to several rules. The rules that affect the accountant the most are those in the first four parts which deal with the filing of a petition, the administration of the case, claims and equity interests, and the debtor. The Rules from these four parts including revisions, are included in Appendix B. The Bankruptcy Code appears in Appendix A.

The Bankruptcy Reform Act of 1994, effective generally for petitions filed after October 22, 1994, represents the largest number of revisions to the Bankruptcy Code since it became effective 15 years ago. Generally, this revision benefited creditors. Major changes welcomed by most creditors included the repeal of the *DePrizio* doctrine dealing with insider preference; a limitation on the time a single-asset real estate property or project with a value of less than $4 million can remain in bankruptcy without payments on the debt; repeal of the provision that left unimpaired a claim that was satisfied as of the effective date of the plan with payments equal to the value of the claim; and the granting of the right for creditors to elect a trustee in chapter 11 cases. Among other provisions, the Act provided for the appointment of a commission to study bankruptcy law and practice and to recommend changes to the Bankruptcy Code. Sections of the text that have been impacted by the Bankruptcy Reform Act of 1994 are identified in this edition.

Accountants and financial advisors are taking a more active role in helping companies identify business problems and in working with these troubled companies to turn them around, often without use of the bankruptcy court. A new chapter (3) dealing with the turnaround process is included in this edition. Chapter 7 has been revised to make the practitioner aware of the guidelines issued by the Executive Office of the U.S. Trustee.

The valuation analysis in Chapter 11 has been expanded to include areas other than valuations related to a plan. Recent cases dealing with valuation of the business and property of the debtor and with valuation problems associated with partnership bankruptcies are given in Chapter 11.

Key provisions of Statement of Position (SOP) 90-7, *Financial Reporting by Entities in Reorganization under the Bankruptcy Code*, issued by the Accounting Standards Executive Committee of the AICPA in November 1990, are examined. This Statement of Position affects how debtors in chapter 11 will report financial results during the reorganization and upon emergence from chapter 11. An important part of this Statement of Position is the requirement that all companies that emerge from chapter 11, where the reorganization value of the entity as a whole is less than the liabilities before confirmation and there is a more than 50 percent change in the shareholders of the new entity, adopt fresh-start reporting.

The provisions in SOP 90-7 relating to how the financial position and results of operations are reported during the proceeding are applicable to all companies that file chapter 11 and are described in chapters 13 and 14. A copy of SOP 90-7 is in Appendix C.

The literature prior to the issuance of SOP 90-7 provided very little guidance for financial reporting by companies that were in chapter 11. As a result, the reporting practices were very diverse. Volume 1 of *Bankruptcy and Insolvency Accounting* includes detailed discussion of related practices and issues, such as accounting for professional fees, accruing prepetition liabilities after the petition is filed (such as claims for lease rejection), reporting liabilities on emergence from chapter 11 (discounted or not discounted), classifying liabilities during the proceeding, reporting deferred taxes, adoption of quasi-reorganization accounting, and so on. SOP 90-7 dealt with all of these issues.

In April 1991, the American Bankruptcy Institute released a study dealing with professional compensation in bankruptcy cases. Several aspects of this study are described in this volume.

In addition to the issuance of revised Federal Rules of Bankruptcy Procedure, the official forms, both for schedules and statement of financial affairs, were completely revised. Several forms have been integrated into others. A complete set of the revised forms is included in Appendix A of Volume 2.

Several examples of sections of the disclosure statement and financial statements in 10-K's that applied provisions of SOP 90-7 are included in Volume 2.

In addition to the coverage of practical procedure and statutory provisions, the book views the history of financial failure. It is hoped, therefore, that the work overall will serve the advancement of understanding and competence in this essential but sometimes neglected area of accounting.

Comments from users are welcomed.

GRANT W. NEWTON

Medford, Oregon
June 2000

Contents

Bankruptcy and Insolvency Environment

1

Accountant's Role in Perspective

§ 1.1 Introduction

Thousands of businesses fail each year in the United States, and the number grew considerably in the 1980s and early 1990s. The liabilities associated with these failures escalated in the first part of the 1990s, but declined in the late 1990s. In 1998 over 1.4 million bankruptcy petitions were filed. Almost 97 percent of these filings were by consumers, representing the largest number of petitions ever filed in a 12-month period. This increase in filings took place during a period of over eight straight years of economic growth. In 1998, business filings of 44,367 decreased by 18 percent over the filings in 1997. The number of business filings for the year ending June 30, 1999 was only 39,934. For the first time in five years, the number of total filings in 1999 declined. For the year ending June 30, 1999 *1,391,964* petitions were filed. It was estimated in 1970 that one out of every five Americans had been involved in bankruptcy proceedings as a bankrupt or a creditor, or was acquainted with someone who had become bankrupt.[1] The number involved today is much higher.

At one time or another, almost all accountants will find that one or more of their clients are experiencing some type of financial difficulty. Because accountants are often the first professional persons to realize that a financial problem exists, they are in a position to render very valuable services. Before accountants can give useful advice to a financially troubled client, they must be thoroughly familiar with the various alternatives available to the client and the ramifications of each alternative.

The purpose of Volume 1 is to analyze in detail the accountant's role in bankruptcy and insolvency procedures, and to provide a practice guide that will assist accountants in rendering professional services in the liquidation and rehabilitation of financially troubled debtors in and outside of bankruptcy court. This volume describes those aspects of bankruptcy and insolvency proceedings of which accountants must be aware, delineating their functions and duties and the procedures they must follow in the auditing inquiry and in the preparation of the various financial statements and reports that are required by the courts. It presents the accounting methods, procedures, and techniques

---

[1] David T. Stanley et al., *Bankruptcy: Problems, Process, Reform* (Washington, DC: The Brookings Institution, 1971), p. 1.

that may be used and explains the applicability of generally accepted accounting principles (GAAP) and generally accepted auditing standards (GAAS) to bankruptcy and insolvency proceedings. This volume explains how most of the services rendered in bankruptcy and out-of-court workouts fall under the litigation consulting guidelines rather than the attestation standards or accounting and review services guidelines. Finally, it discusses the conflicts and problems in principles and practice.

Volume 2 consists of examples of various aspects of bankruptcy proceedings, including samples of schedules and forms with which accountants and other professionals must be familiar in order to effectively serve their clients and easily handle the administrative aspects of a case.

It is hoped that this work will also benefit nonaccountants, such as trustees, judges, and attorneys, in clarifying the purposes, nature, and limitations of the services of the accountant. Although the primary effort in the development of these books has been directed to the accountant in an explanation of "how to do it" and in a discussion of the ethical problems and responsibilities involved, the coverage of the economic and legal aspects of bankruptcy and insolvency should be of value to other professionals involved in these proceedings.

§ 1.2 Scope of Coverage

The scope of these volumes is, deliberately, fairly broad. The various accounting procedures to be followed under each alternative remedy for business failure are analyzed in detail. To provide a complete and realistic description of the environment within which the accountant must work, the discussion incorporates the economics and the legal aspects of business liquidations and rehabilitations.

The economics of bankruptcy and insolvency proceedings is most important when considering the various causes of financial difficulties. Once the causes have been ascertained, the most appropriate remedy may then be determined. Economic considerations are also important when analyzing what remedies have proven most successful in particular circumstances.

The legal aspects of bankruptcy permeate the entire book, for the Federal Bankruptcy Code (title 11) establishes the framework within which anyone concerned with insolvency must work. As a result, the Bankruptcy Code is explicitly cited in the descriptions of the petitions, forms, and schedules that must be filed; the alternatives and rights available to all parties involved, including the creditors; the requirements of the debtor; and the treatment of the various transactions and property of the debtor, both before and after the proceedings. Bankruptcy and insolvency proceedings cannot be correctly handled unless everyone involved has a thorough understanding of the legal aspects of the case.

Only about 3 percent of the bankruptcy court petitions are filed by businesses. The majority are filed by wage earners; however, it is primarily the business bankruptcy and insolvency proceedings that require the services of an accountant. The book is therefore directed toward business bankruptcies. Although the emphasis is on incorporated businesses, materials covered are applicable to partnerships and proprietaries because the remedies available are basically the same.

ACCOUNTING SERVICES

§ 1.3   Need for Accountants' Services

The accountant can provide various kinds of services that can be effective in helping the debtor overcome its financial problems and again operate profitably, and that can also assist the creditors and their committees in deciding on the type of action they should take. The accountant may become a party to insolvency and bankruptcy proceedings while serving a client who is having financial problems. Before resorting to judicial proceedings, the debtor may attempt to negotiate a moratorium or settlement of its debt with unsecured creditors. Accountants may be retained by the debtor and/or creditors' committee to perform accounting services.

Reorganization of a corporation under chapter 11 of the Bankruptcy Code involves many parties who may need the assistance of accountants. First, the debtor, who remains in possession, has the right to retain an accountant to perform necessary accounting functions, to develop a business plan that will help turn the business around, and to develop and negotiate the terms of a plan of reorganization. Others include attorneys, trustee, examiner, creditors, security holders, and stockholders.

In liquidation proceedings under chapter 7 of the Bankruptcy Code, the accountant often assists in accounting for the distribution of the debtor's assets. If the liquidation proceedings are initiated involuntarily, the petitioning creditors will need the assistance of an accountant in establishing a case of insolvency, and the debtor will need an accountant's assistance in trying to prove a defense of solvency. An investigation may be required for specific purposes, such as by the debtor to defend a turnover proceeding or by a third party to defend a suit by the trustee alleging a preferential transfer.[2]

The trustee as the appointed or elected representative of the creditors in a bankruptcy court proceeding most frequently finds it necessary to employ an accountant to examine the debtor's books and records and to investigate any unusual or questionable transactions. A corporation's past transactions may need investigation to determine whether any assets have been concealed or removed or any preferences, fraudulent conveyances, or other voidable transactions committed. Often, the debtor may have kept inadequate books and records, further complicating the situation. The accountant may help the trustee develop a business plan, and may negotiate the terms of a plan of reorganization.

Under section 1103 of the Bankruptcy Code, the creditors' committee is permitted to employ such agents, attorneys, and accountants as may be necessary to assist in the performance of its functions. The accountant can provide valuable assistance to the committee by reviewing the business plan and the plan of reorganization of the debtor. At times, the accountant may help the committee develop a plan. The committee may also retain its own accountant to examine the debtor's books and records and to investigate the activities of the debtor. The creditors' committee is expected to render an opinion on the plan

---

[2] Asa S. Herzog, "CPA's Role in Bankruptcy Proceedings," *Journal of Accountancy*, Vol. 117 (January 1964), p. 59.

of reorganization, and to do so it must have knowledge of the debtor's acts and property. It must know the value of the debtor's assets in liquidation and the nature of the transactions entered into by the debtor before proceedings began. Because accountants are most qualified to establish these facts, they are often engaged to perform an investigation of the debtor's operations so that the committee will be able to give an informed opinion on the actions to take, such as a search for preferences or fraudulent transfers.

The debtor's internal accounting staff is also actively involved in the proceedings. Staff members often provide information or advice that assists the debtor in selecting the appropriate remedy. They also provide the debtor's attorneys with the accounting information needed to file the bankruptcy court petition.

Accounting and financial advising services are needed by a large number of participants in both out-of-court and bankruptcy proceedings. See 1.1 of Volume 2, *Bankruptcy and Insolvency Accounting*, for a list of these parties.

§ 1.4 "Accountants" Defined

It is not unusual to see several accountants or financial advisors involved in bankruptcy court proceedings. There may be independent accountants for the debtor, internal accountants of a debtor company, independent accountants for the trustee, and independent accountants or financial advisors representing the creditors' committee or individual holder of claims. Many of the accounting functions may be performed by more than one accountant. For example, each of the accountants will want to determine the underlying causes of failure. The term "accountants" is used here to refer to any accountant involved in the proceedings; where the service must be rendered by a particular accountant, the type of accountant or financial advisor is identified either in the text or at the beginning of the chapter. Many individuals who provide financial advice to companies in financial trouble are not CPAs and many of the boutique firms that provide business turnaround, bankruptcy, and restructuring services do not practice as CPA firms, even though a large number of their professional staff are CPAs.

TOPICAL OVERVIEW

§ 1.5 Economic Causes of Business Failure

The first topic discussed in Chapter 2 is the economic causes that lead to business failure. A knowledge of the common causes of financial trouble can often enable the accountant to identify a potential problem, and corrective action can be taken before the situation becomes too serious. Methods of detecting failure tendencies are also described.

§ 1.6 Business Turnaround

Two critical aspects of the process of making a business with problems profitable again involve solving the operational problems and restructuring the debt and equity of the business. In this book, *turnaround* is used to mean the process of solving the operation problems of a business. It involves improving the position of the business as a low-cost provider of increasingly differentiated products and services and nurturing a competent organization with industry-oriented technical expertise and a general sense of fair play in dealing with employees, creditors, suppliers, shareholders, and customers.[3] Chapter 3 describes the business turnaround process.

Restructuring will be used to mean the process of developing a financial structure that will provide a basis for turnaround. Some entities in financial difficulty are able to solve their problems by the issuance of stock for a large part of the debt; such is the case where the company is overleveraged. Others are able to regain profitability by improving cost margins through reduction of manufacturing costs and elimination of unprofitable products. However, the majority of businesses require attention to operating problems as well as changes to the structure of the business. Chapter 4 describes the process of restructuring the business out-of-court and Chapter 6 deals with the process of restructuring the business in the bankruptcy court. The business aspect of the restructuring process is discussed throughout the text.

§ 1.7 Alternatives Available to a Financially Troubled Business

In order to render services effectively in bankruptcy and insolvency proceedings, the accountant must be familiar with the Federal Bankruptcy Code (title 11 of the United States Code). Chapter 5 begins with a discussion of the history of the bankruptcy law in the United States, and the provisions of the Bankruptcy Code are described throughout Chapters 5 and 6.

The debtor's first alternatives are to locate new financing, to merge with another company, or to find some other basic solution to its situation, in order to avoid the necessity of discussing its problems with representatives of creditors. If none of these alternatives is possible, the debtor may be required to seek a remedy from creditors, either informally (out of court) or with the help of judicial proceedings. To ensure that the reader is familiar with some of the alternatives available, they are briefly described in the paragraphs that follow. The general provisions of an assignment for the benefit of creditors are described in greater detail in Chapter 5. Often, debtors prefer to work out their financial problems with creditors by mutual agreement out of court; these settlements are described in Chapter 4. A chapter 11 reorganization, the second major rehabilitation device for a debtor, is analyzed in Chapter 6 and throughout this book.

(a) Out-of-Court Settlements

The debtor may request a meeting with a few of the largest creditors and one or two representatives of the small claimants to effect an informal agreement. The function of such a committee may be merely to investigate, consult, and give advice to the debtor, or it may involve actual supervision of the business or liquidation of the assets. An informal settlement usually involves an exten-

---

[3] Frederick M. Zimmerman, *The Turnaround Experience* (New York: McGraw-Hill, 1991), p. 11.

sion of time (a moratorium), a pro rata settlement (composition), or a combination of the two. The details of the plan are worked out between the debtor and creditors, the latter perhaps represented by a committee. Such extralegal proceedings are most successful when there are only a few creditors, adequate accounting records have been kept, and past relationships have been amicable. The chief disadvantage of this remedy is that there is no power to bind those creditors who do not agree to the plan of settlement.

(b) Assignment for Benefit of Creditors

A remedy available, under state law, to a corporation in serious financial difficulties is an "assignment for the benefit of creditors." In this instance, the debtor voluntarily transfers title to its assets to an assignee who then liquidates them and distributes the proceeds among the creditors. Assignment for the benefit of creditors is an extreme remedy because it results in the cessation of the business. This informal (although court-supervised in many states) liquidation device, like the out-of-court settlement devised to rehabilitate the debtor, requires the consent of all the creditors or at least their agreement to refrain from taking action. The appointment of a custodian over the assets of the debtor gives creditors the right to file an involuntary bankruptcy court petition.

Proceedings brought in the federal courts are governed by the Bankruptcy Code. It will normally be necessary to resort to such formality when suits have already been filed against the debtor and its property is under garnishment or attachment, or is threatened by foreclosure or eviction.

(c) Chapter 11—Reorganization

Chapter 11 of the Bankruptcy Code replaces Chapters X, XI, and XII of the Bankruptcy Act, which applied only to cases filed before October 1, 1979.[4] Chapter 11 can be used as the means of working out an arrangement with creditors where the debtor is allowed to continue in business and secures an extension of time, a pro rata settlement, or some combination of both. Or, chapter 11 can be used for a complete reorganization of the corporation affecting secured creditors, unsecured creditors, and stockholders. The objective of the reorganization is to allow the debtor to resume business in its new form without the burden of debt that existed prior to the proceeding.

One important aspect of the proceedings under chapter 11 is to determine whether the business is worth saving and whether it will be able to operate profitably in the near future. If not, then the business should be liquidated without incurring further losses. The new law allows the debtor—if it is determined that the business should be liquidated—to propose a plan that would provide for the orderly liquidation of the business without conversion of the proceedings to chapter 7 (the successor to straight bankruptcy). Another aspect

---

[4] Prior law (Bankruptcy Act) used "Chapter" and roman numerals (Chapter VII, Chapter XI, and so on) for chapter identification; the new law (Bankruptcy Code) uses "chapter" and arabic numbers (chapter 7, chapter 11, and so on). Chapters in this book are cross-referenced as Chapter 7, Chapter 11, and so on.

of the new chapter 11 is that the debtor will in most cases be allowed to operate the business while a plan of reorganization is being proposed.

There has been a major increase in the number of prepackaged chapter 11 plans that are filed with the bankruptcy court. Before filing for chapter 11, some debtors develop a plan and obtain approval of the plan by all impaired claims and interests. The court may accept the voting that was done prepetition, provided that the solicitation of the acceptance (or rejection) was in compliance with applicable nonbankruptcy law governing the adequacy of disclosure in connection with the solicitation. If no nonbankruptcy law is applicable, then the solicitation must have occurred after or at the time the holder received adequate information as required under section 1125 of the Bankruptcy Code.

It is necessary for a chapter 11 plan to be filed for several reasons, including:

- Income from debt discharge is taxed in an out-of-court workout to the extent that the debtor is or becomes solvent. Some tax attributes may be reduced in a bankruptcy case, but the gain from debt discharged is not taxed.
- The provisions of section 382(1)(5) and (6) dealing with preserving net operating losses apply only to bankruptcy cases.
- Some bond indenture agreements provide that amendments cannot be made unless all holders of debt approve the modifications. Because it is difficult, if not impossible, to obtain 100 percent approval, it is necessary to file a bankruptcy plan to reduce interest or modify the principal of the bonds.

The professional fees and other costs of a prepackaged plan, including the cost of disrupting the business, are generally much less than the costs of a regular chapter 11. A prepackaged bankruptcy may therefore be the best alternative.

A prepackaged plan is generally thought to be most appropriate for debtors with financial structure problems (often created by leveraged buyouts [LBOs]), rather than operational problems. However, a prepackaged plan may be used in most situations where an out-of-court workout is a feasible alternative. Recently, there has been an increase in the number of prepackaged plans filed. If a prepackaged plan is going to be effective in solving operational problems, it is important that early action be taken before operations deteriorate to the point where a bankruptcy petition must be filed in order to prevent selected creditors from taking action against the debtor that would preclude any type of reorganization. In situations where a petition must be filed in order to obtain postpetition financing to operate the business (such as in a retail operation), a petition will have to be filed before any type of plan can be developed.

(d) Chapter 12—Adjustment of Debts of Family Farmers

To help farmers resolve some of their financial problems, Congress passed chapter 12 of the Bankruptcy Code. This chapter became effective November 26, 1986, and became law under a provision that allows the law to expire unless the expiration time-period is extended by Congress. Congress allowed the law to expire October 1, 1998, but subsequently retroactively extended the expiration date to October 1, 1999, so that farmers can continue to use chapter 12. While it is expected that Congress will eventually make chapter 12 permanent, Congress extended the expiration date to July 1, 2000, in October 1999. A family farmer may use this chapter if his total debt does not exceed $1.5 million. Chapter 12 is designed to give family farmers an opportunity to reorganize and keep their land. Through bankruptcy, the farmers have the protection they need while they attempt to resolve their financial problems. At the same time, the law was passed for the purpose of preventing abuse of the system and ensuring that farm lenders receive a fair repayment of their debts.

(e) Chapter 13—Adjustment of Debts of an Individual with Regular Income

The new law allows some small businesses to use chapter 13, which, under prior law, had been used only by wage earners. However, as initially passed, only businesses that are owned by individuals with unsecured debts of less than $100,000 and secured debts of less than $350,000 may use this chapter. Effective for petitions filed on or after October 22, 1994, the Bankruptcy Reform Act of 1994 increased the debt limits for the filing of a chapter 13 petition as follows: for unsecured debt, from $100,000 to $250,000; for secured debt, from $350,000 to $750,000. On April 1, 1998, and at each three-year interval thereafter, the dollar amounts for the debt limits for a chapter 13 petition are to be increased, beginning on April 1, to reflect the change in the Consumer Price Index for All Urban Consumers that has occurred during the three-year period ending on December 31 of the immediately preceding year. The amounts are to be rounded to the nearest $25 multiple. Effective through March 31, 2001, the unsecured debt limit is *$269,250* and the secured debt limit is *$807,750*.

Debtors must have income that is stable and reliably sufficient to enable them to make payments under the chapter 13 plan. As in a chapter 11 proceeding, the debtor will be allowed to operate the business while a plan is being developed that will, it is hoped, provide for the successful operation of the business in the future. The chapter 13 proceeding, a streamlined rehabilitation method for eligible debtors, is also discussed in Chapter 6.

(f) Chapter 7—Liquidation

Chapter 7 of the Bankruptcy Code is used only when the corporation sees no hope of being able to operate successfully or to obtain the necessary creditor agreement. Under this alternative, the corporation is liquidated and the remaining assets are distributed to creditors after administrative expenses are paid. An individual debtor may be discharged from his or her liabilities and entitled to a fresh start.

The decision as to whether rehabilitation or liquidation is best also depends on the amount to be realized from each alternative. The method resulting in the greatest return to the creditors and stockholders should be chosen. The amount to be received from liquidation depends on the resale value of the firm's assets minus the costs of dismantling and legal expenses. The value of the firm after rehabilitation must be determined (net of the costs of achieving the remedy). The alternative leading to the highest value should be followed.

Exhibit 1-1   Schedule of Alternatives Available

Unsuccessful Action	Alternatives Available
Out-of-court settlement	Chapter 13 (small businesses only)
	Chapter 11—reorganization
	Assignment for benefit of creditors (state court)
	Chapter 7—liquidation
Chapter 13 (small businesses only)	Chapter 11—reorganization
	Assignment for benefit of creditors (state court)
	Chapter 7—liquidation
Assignment for benefit of creditors (state court)	Chapter 7—liquidation
Chapter 11—reorganization	Chapter 11—reorganization (liquidation plan)
	Chapter 7—liquidation

Financially troubled debtors often attempt an informal settlement or liquidation out of court, but if it is unsuccessful they will then initiate proceedings under the Bankruptcy Code. Other debtors, especially those with a large number of creditors, may file a petition for relief in the bankruptcy court as soon as they recognize that continuation of the business under existing conditions is impossible.

Exhibit 1-1 summarizes the most common alternatives available to the debtor in case the first course of action proves unsuccessful.

§ 1.8   Comparison of Title 11 of the United States Code with the Bankruptcy Act

The new bankruptcy law, signed by President Carter on November 6, 1978, and applicable to all cases filed since October 1, 1979, contained many changes from prior law. The new law is codified in title 11 of the United States Code, and the former title 11 is repealed. Exhibit 1-2 summarizes the changes brought about by the first major revision of bankruptcy law in the past 40 years and compares the provisions of the prior law with the new law as amended.

§ 1.9   Retention of the Accountant and Fees

Accountants must be retained by order of the court before they can render services in bankruptcy court proceedings for the trustee, creditors' committee, or debtor-in-possession. For out-of-court settlements, the accountant obtains a signed engagement letter. Chapter 7 of this book describes and provides examples of the formal and informal retention procedures, and illustrates how independent accountants must clearly set forth the scope of their examination and not deviate from it. The chapter also enumerates the factors to consider in estimating fees and keeping time records, and describes the procedure for filing a petition for compensation.

Exhibit 1-2 Comparison of the Provisions of Title 11 of the United States Code with the Bankruptcy Act

Item	Bankruptcy Act (old law) Chapter XI	Bankruptcy Act (old law) Chapter X	Bankruptcy Code (new law) Chapter 11
Filing petition	Voluntary	Voluntary and involuntary	Voluntary and involuntary
Requirements for involuntary petition		Must commit an act of bankruptcy	Generally not paying debts as they become due or custodian appointed in charge of debtor's property
Nature of creditors' committee	Three to eleven members elected by creditors	Usually not appointed	Seven largest holders of unsecured claims
Operation of business	Usually debtor-in-possession (at time receiver appointed)	Usually by trustee	Most cases debtor-in-possession
Appointment of trustee	Not appointed	Required if debts exceed $250,000	May be appointed (or elected) on petition after notice and an opportunity for hearing
Appointment of an examiner	No provision	No provision	(1) On request and after a notice and a hearing or (2) if unsecured debts exceed $5,000,000 after request. Purpose is to examine the affairs of the debtor
Preferences Time period	Four months prior to petition date	Four months prior to petition date	Ninety days prior to petition date (time period extended to one year for insiders)
Insolvency at time of payment	Required	Required	Required, but for 90-day provision insolvency is presumed
Exception for payments for business purposes and terms	No provision	No provision	Provided
Creditors receiving payment required to have knowledge of debtor's insolvency	Required	Required	Not required for 90-day requirement and required for payments to insiders

Exhibit 1-2 (*continued*)

Automatic stay	Provided for	Provided for	Provided for with some modifications regarding use of property
Setoffs	Allowed	Allowed	Allowed with new restrictions
Plan Submission	By debtor-in-possession	Normally, by trustee	Normally, by debtor-in-possession. However, if plan not submitted in 120 days or trustee appointed, trustee or creditors may submit plan
Coverage	Unsecured debt	All debt and equity interest	All debt and equity interest
Acceptance	Majority in amount and in number of each class of unsecured creditors	Two-thirds in amount of debt and majority in amount for equity interest	Two-thirds in amount and majority in number of holders in each class of those voting and two-thirds in amount of stockholders voting
Disclosure statement	Not required	Formal statement filed with SEC	Required before can solicit votes for plan
Confirmation requirements	Best interest of creditors, feasible	Fair and equitable, feasible	Class not impaired or accept plan, best interest of creditors, feasible

§ 1.10 Accounting Services

In addition to the usual accounting services performed for the debtor, the accountant provides information needed to negotiate with creditors or to file a petition in bankruptcy court, prepares operating statements, assists in formulating a plan, and provides management advising services. Chapters 8 and 9 provide information concerning the nature of these services.

The creditors' committee often needs an accountant to assist it in protecting the creditors' interest and supervising the activities of the debtor. Some of the services rendered by the accountant, which are described in Chapter 10, include assisting the committee in exercising adequate supervision over the debtor's activities, performing an investigation and audit of the operations of the business, and assisting the committee in evaluating the proposed plan of settlement or reorganization. Additional services rendered by accountants relating to the valuation of the business or its component assets are discussed in Chapter 11.

A list of the services often rendered by accountants in the bankruptcy and reorganization area is presented in 1.2 of Volume 2, *Bankruptcy and Insolvency Accounting*.

§ 1.11   Special Investigation and Financial Reporting

Reporting on insolvent companies requires the application of procedures that vary somewhat from those used under normal circumstances. Emphasis in Chapter 12 of this book is on special procedures that differ from those used under normal conditions and on procedures that assist in the discovery of irregularities and fraud. Chapter 13 describes financial reporting during a chapter proceeding and Chapter 14 describes how to report on the emerging from chapter 11. Chapter 15 describes the nature of the accountant's opinion associated with the reports.

§ 1.12   Tax Awareness

Chapter 16 covers the tax areas that the accountant should consider when rendering services for a debtor or creditor of a troubled company and points out how proper tax planning can preserve and even enlarge the debtor's estate.[5]

Beyond the scope of this book are nonuniform provisions under state or common law for judicial receivership proceedings and specialized provisions of the Bankruptcy Code for municipality, stockbroker, commodities broker, and railroad proceedings.[6]

RESPONSIBILITIES OF INDEPENDENT ACCOUNTANT

§ 1.13   Responsibilities in General

Independent accountants are aware that their responsibilities to clients often extend beyond merely auditing the books and giving an opinion on the financial statements. They frequently give management an opinion on the progress of the business, its future, and avenues of improvement, not only in the system of record keeping, but in the overall management of the enterprise. The intensity of involvement required depends on several factors, including an individual judgment to be made by the accountant.

Independent accountants owe some degree of responsibility to third parties interested in their clients' affairs. This includes the duty to remain independent so that an unbiased opinion can be rendered. The accountant is also relied on to reveal all those facts that might be relevant and important to other persons. This again involves judgment as to the level of disclosure that is appropriate. (See Chapter 8.)

---

[5] Wiley also publishes *Bankruptcy and Insolvency Taxation*, written by this author and Gilbert D. Bloom. The book covers in more detail the tax aspects of bankruptcy, and is supplemented annually or more often, if needed.

[6] A receiver may be an official appointed by a state court judge to take charge of, preserve, administer, or liquidate property designated by the court. The Commonwealth of Massachusetts specifically confirms the power of its judges to exercise this equitable remedy to appoint liquidating receivers at the request of creditors of dissolved or terminated corporations or of creditors of corporations that have failed to satisfy outstanding judgments against them. See, for example, Mass. Gen. Laws Ann. ch. 156B, §§ 104–05.

The accountant's position and responsibilities as they relate to a client experiencing financial difficulties and to third parties interested in the proceedings will be introduced in the remaining sections of this chapter.

§ 1.14 Observation of Business Decline

The first and most crucial step in any situation involving a business in financial trouble is recognizing that a problem exists. This is important because corrective action should be taken as soon as possible, to halt any further deterioration in the firm's position.

Many people normally maintain close contact with a business—management, employees, lawyers, accountants, customers, competitors, suppliers, owners, and the government, to list only the most obvious ones. Few of these persons, however, would be in a position to recognize when the enterprise is headed for trouble. Normally, this requires someone who intimately works with the financial data and is trained in analyzing such information. Usually, only the financial managers of the business, such as the treasurer and controller, or the independent accountants employed by the firm have these qualifications.

Some independent accountants who conduct only an annual audit and do not maintain close contact with their client throughout the year are often of little assistance in recognizing a potential problem. However, in many small and medium-size businesses, the accountants not only conduct the annual audit but review quarterly and monthly statements and render various types of advisory services. In these situations, the accountants are aware of what has been occurring in the major accounts, and in the firm as a whole and, because of their education and experience in business finances, they should be able to identify when an enterprise is headed for trouble and alert management to their suspicions. Thus, because of the nature of both the type of work they do and the ability they possess, accountants are in an excellent position to identify any tendencies to failure.

As an example, the independent accountants of a New York garment business had served as auditors for the company for many years. The company had been operative through successive generations of the same family for approximately ninety years. As a consequence of changing fashion styles, the company experienced a few consecutive years of operating losses. The accountants noticed that the company was not taking any action to correct the loss trend— the president, in fact, seemed incapable of reversing the situation. Although there was still some working capital and net worth that might have enabled the company to obtain credit and continue in business, the accountants suggested that the following actions be taken:

- Discontinue placing orders for raw materials for the upcoming season, other than to permit completion of orders on hand.
- Start terminating personnel in the areas of design, production, and administration.
- Offer the plant facilities for sale.

- Liquidate inventories in an orderly fashion.
- Meet with creditors to explain the situation.

The accountants' suggestions were followed and the plants were sold, resulting in a settlement with creditors at 87.5¢ on the dollar. The stockholders received payment in full on a mortgage loan they had made to the company. Had the accountants' suggestions not been followed, further substantial operating losses would most probably have been incurred; the creditors would have been fortunate to receive a distribution of 15 percent; and it is doubtful that the mortgage loan would have been paid in full.

To be able to recognize a potential problem, accountants need to have an understanding of the definition of financial failure, the nature of insolvency, and the most common causes of financial difficulties. They must have a familiarity with the characteristics of business decline, which include lower absolute sales and slower growth in sales, poorer cash flow and weak cash position, deteriorating net income, insufficient working capital, large incurrence of debt, and high operating costs and fixed expenses. These symptoms are normally found in the accounting records, and the accountant is most likely to be first to recognize them.

§ 1.15 Responsibility to Client

At the very first suspicion of pending financial trouble, accountants have a duty to alert management to the situation, submit as much supporting information as is possible, describe the various alternatives available to reverse the deterioration, and advise on what avenue should be chosen as a remedy. All these measures are taken to implore the client to begin corrective action before the situation becomes more serious, and the accountant should be concerned with pointing out to the client ways of avoiding insolvency. The responsibility of the independent accountant where fraud is involved is described in Chapter 12.

Should the situation become serious enough to warrant some type of remedy outside the usual business corrective measures, the accountant must make a thorough analysis to determine the most appropriate action to be taken (Chapter 2). This involves an investigation into the causes of financial difficulty and steps that will correct the trouble. The accountant must therefore be familiar with the various alternatives available and when they are most appropriate. This involvement by the accountant should aid the debtor in adopting the rehabilitation procedure most likely to be successful.

It is also the accountant's responsibility to know the procedures required under each alternative remedy. In an out-of-court settlement, this involves awareness of the methods that have proven successful in particular situations. For example, in an informal composition, the accountant should know when it is best to have all creditors meet and under what circumstances only a representative group is more advisable. When formal proceedings are initiated, it is imperative that the accountant know what information is required on the bankruptcy court petition and what schedules must be filed. Otherwise, it would not be possible to converse with the debtor's attorney, a failure that could conceivably delay the settlement and cause further deterioration in the client's position.

Timing is crucial in a situation involving insolvency. Should the accountant fail to alert the debtor to the situation and urge some action, the creditors might move first and attempt legally to seize the assets. Speed is then important if the debtor wishes to file a chapter 11 petition and remain in possession of the business.

§ 1.16   Advice on Selection of Attorneys

One of the first steps of a debtor faced with financial difficulties is the employment of legal counsel. When a company realizes that it will be unable to continue profitable operations or pay liabilities as they become due, it should quickly seek a lawyer to help effect a compromise or an extension of the indebtedness. Because the independent accountant is often the first professional the client contacts concerning financial difficulties, the accountant is frequently asked for advice as to the selection of a special bankruptcy attorney.

There are many advantages to the accountant's involvement at this point. Frequently, accountants are aware of those attorneys most familiar with bankruptcy and insolvency cases, and can recommend someone with adequate experience and knowledge. By suggesting a lawyer of known reputation, the accountant and the debtor's creditors are assured of working with someone in whom full confidence can be placed. It is imperative that the accountant and attorney be able to work well together. The accountant should be present at the meetings with the debtor and provide the counsel with an overall view of the debtor's financial condition and the events that preceded it, including the basic facts and information about the business, its history, and the causes of its present difficulties.

Because they are most familiar with the attorneys best qualified in this field and will be required to work with the lawyer chosen by the debtor, accountants have good reason to be involved in the selection process. However, the situation may give rise to questions concerning an accountant's independence. If an attorney is recommended more on the basis of friendship with the person than on qualifications, the accountant is not being fair to the client. The accountant must be very careful not to have a vested interest in any attorney suggested. Disregarding this situation, the accountant is a logical person for the debtor to turn to for help in choosing legal counsel.

§ 1.17   Other Steps to "Manage" the Proceedings

Accountants are often intimately involved in every aspect of a bankruptcy or insolvency case. They may "manage" the case from the initial discovery of financial trouble, suggesting the best remedy to seek, advising regarding any necessary alterations or modifications of the plan chosen, and monitoring the operations of the debtor by reviewing the operating results during the proceedings. They maintain close contact with the creditors, working with their committee in an effort to find the most advantageous settlement for them. They then provide all the financial information concerning the debtor's progress and make sure all interested parties are aware of what is occurring. Accountants can help determine the going concern value of the business. This value is then used to determine the amount of debt that the entity emerging from bankruptcy can service and also help the interested parties agree on the terms of a plan. Accountants representing the creditors may also be involved in helping the creditors determine the value of the debtor's business. If all parties involved can reach an agreement about the value of the business, the first major step toward agreeing on the terms of the plan has been accomplished. Possibly more than any other outside party, the accountant is responsible for the smooth and successful rehabilitation of the debtor. This is primarily because of a close involvement with all the interested parties, including the debtor, creditors, attorney, trustee, and governmental agencies.

PROFESSIONAL CERTIFICATION

§ 1.18 Certified Insolvency and Restructuring Advisors (CIRA)

The Association of Insolvency and Restructuring Advisors (AIRA) has developed an educational program covering an appropriate common body of knowledge designed specifically for those who specialize in the area of bankruptcy and troubled business. This educational program covers a wide range of subjects, preparatory to a written examination. Completion of the course of study and passing of the examination, in combination with a comprehensive experience requirement, will lead to certification by the AIRA as a Certified Insolvency and Restructuring Advisors (CIRA).

(a) Purpose

The purpose of the CIRA program is to recognize by public awareness and by certification those individuals who possess a high degree of specialized, professional expertise in the area of business bankruptcy and insolvency. Such experience includes accounting, taxation, law, finance, and management issues related to business bankruptcy and reorganization.

In addition, the CIRA Certification will:

- Provide a special recognition standard for the public, the bankruptcy court system, governmental agencies, and other professionals.
- Differentiate certified specialists from those persons who do not possess the required experience, education, and technical skills.
- Serve as a credential to support the qualifications of those who possess this special certification.
- Promote a higher degree of specialized skills.

(b) Requirements for Certification

To be eligible to enroll in the course of study and take the examination, the candidate must:

- Be a regular member in good standing in the AIRA.

- Satisfy one of the following requirements:
  - Be a continued license holder as a Certified Public Accountant, Chartered Accountant (or equivalent license), or Certified Management Accountant.
  - Possess (at least) a bachelor's degree from an accredited college or university and complete four years of accounting or financial experience.[7]

To obtain the certification, the following three requirements must be satisfied:

1. Complete five years of accounting experience, or financial experience.[8]
2. Complete 4,000 hours, within the previous eight (8) years, of specialized insolvency and reorganization experience.
3. Complete the course of study and pass the uniform written examination.

(c) Course of Study

The course of study is divided into three parts:

1. Managing turnaround and bankruptcy cases
2. Plan development
3. Accounting, financial reporting, and taxes

Each part consists of a 2½-day course and a 3-hour examination taken during the last half-day of attendance.

Additional information about the CIRA program can be obtained by contacting the Association of Insolvency and Restructuring Advisors, 132 W. Main Street, Suite 200, Medford, OR, 97501, (541)858-1665.

---

[7] Relevant experience includes public accounting, crisis management, consulting, investment banking, credit management, loan workout or applicable government experience (e.g. financial analyst with Office of the U.S. Trustee, Pension Benefit Guarantee Corporation, FBI and SBA, etc.).
[8] *See* note 7.

2

Economic Causes of Business Failures

§ 2.1 Introduction

Business failures have been with us as long as businesses have existed, and their end is not in sight. A failure may be in the form of a small retail store owner closing his door because he cannot pay his rent or it may be a large corporation that is forced to liquidate because of continuously mounting losses.

It is crucial for accountants to understand the material presented in this chapter because a knowledge of the common causes of financial troubles will enable accountants to identify a potential problem, alert management to their suspicions, and assist management in taking corrective action before the situation becomes too serious. Accountants can often point out to their clients ways of avoiding failure.

DEFINITION OF SUCCESSFUL AND UNSUCCESSFUL BUSINESS

§ 2.2 Failure Defined

Terms indicative of financial difficulties are used indiscriminately in discussion and often fail to convey the legal or even the generally accepted meaning of the word.

"Failure" is defined by Webster as "the state or fact of being lacking or insufficient, 'falling short.'" All businesses plan to be successful, but not all of them accomplish their objective. The fact that many firms fail to achieve success is evidenced to some extent by the increasing number of businesses that discontinue operations each year. All of the discontinued businesses could not be defined as failures. No doubt several were discontinued because they were successful in that they had accomplished their objective.

Dun & Bradstreet has adopted the term "failure" to refer to those businesses that ceased operations following assignment or bankruptcy; ceased doing business with a loss to creditors after such actions as foreclosure or attachments; voluntarily withdrew leaving unpaid debt; were involved in court action such as reorganization under chapter 11; or voluntarily compromised with creditors. The Department of Commerce stopped the reporting of new businesses and discontinued businesses in 1962; however, for each year from 1940 to 1962 the

Exhibit 2-1   Comparison of Business Failures with Business Bankruptcy Petitions Filed, 1970–1995

Year	Failure Record (1) Number	(2) Percentage of Change	Business Bankruptcy Petitions Filed (3) Number	(4) Percentage of Change
1970	10,748		16,197	
1971	10,326	−4	19,103	18
1972	9,566	−7	18,132	−5
1973	9,345	−2	17,490	−4
1974	9,915	6	20,746	19
1975	11,432	15	30,130	45
1976	9,628	−16	35,201	17
1977	7,919	−18	32,189	−9
1978	6,619	−16	30,528	−5
1979	7,564	−14	29,500	−3
1980	11,742	55	45,857	55
1981	16,794	43	66,006	44
1982	25,346	51	69,207	5
1983	31,334	24	62,412	−10
1984	52,078	—	64,214	3
1985	57,253	10	71,277	11
1986	61,616	8	81,235	14
1987	61,111	−1	82,446	1
1988	57,098	−7	63,853	−23
1989	50,361	−12	63,235	−1
1990	60,747	20	64,853	2
1991	88,140	45	71,549	10
1992	97,069	10	70,643	−1
1993	86,133	−11	62,304	−11
1994p	71,558	−17	52,374	−16
1995p	71,128	−1	51,959	−1
1996	71,931	—	53,549	3
1997p	83,384	16	54,027	1
1998p	—	—	44,367	−18

Calendar year was used for failures. Fiscal year was used for bankruptcy petitions, between 1970 and 1981; calendar year used since 1982.
p = preliminary.
Sources: Column (1): *Business Failure Records* (New York: Dun & Bradstreet, Inc., 1998), p. 2; column (3): Administrative Offices of the U.S. Courts, *Bankruptcy Statistics* (mimeographed).

number of failures reported by Dun & Bradstreet amounted to only 3 or 4 percent of the total businesses discontinued. Exhibit 2-1 shows the number of failures for selected years as reported by Dun & Bradstreet. It should be pointed out that the failures include only the type of firms registered in Dun & Bradstreet's Reference Book for years prior to 1984. Specific types of businesses not included for years prior to 1984 are financial enterprises, insurance and real estate companies, railroads, terminals, amusements, professionals, farmers, and many small single-owner services. From 1984 on, all industries in the

United States are represented in Dun & Bradstreet's coverage, including agriculture, forestry, and fishing; finance, insurance, and real estate; and the service sector in its entirety. Thus, data prior to 1984 are not directly comparable to subsequent years.

A business is also known as a failure when it can no longer meet the legally enforceable demands of its creditors. If the debtor is unable to reach some type of an arrangement with the creditors, it may be necessary to file for relief under the provisions of the Bankruptcy Code. Under conditions where there is not only a certain degree of lack of success but an official recognition of it, legal failure exists. "Bankruptcy" is the term most commonly used to refer to legal failure. Although, technically, there are no more "bankrupts" nor "bankruptcies" under the new Bankruptcy Code (for cases filed on or after October 1, 1979), when the term "bankruptcy" is used in this book it refers to the formal declaration by a firm in a federal court.

§ 2.3   Business Failure Statistics

Exhibit 2-1 also compares the Dun & Bradstreet failure record with the business bankruptcy petitions filed for the past several years. Because many firms that filed petitions with the bankruptcy court were not registered with Dun & Bradstreet, the number of business bankruptcy petitions filed prior to 1984 is much greater than the number of failures. The number of business failures began to increase in the early 1990s and peaked in 1992 at an all time high of 97,069 failures, as noted in Exhibit 2-1. As the economy continued to improve in 1993 through 1995, the failures continued to decline, until there was a slight increase in 1996, but in 1997 there was a material increase of 16 percent to 83,384. In 1998, that number is expected to remain up. Exhibit 2-1 compares the number of business failures (columns 1 and 2) with the number of business bankruptcy petitions filed (columns 3 and 4), as reported by Dun & Bradstreet for the years 1970–1998.

The number of business bankruptcy filings had a similar pattern starting with a decline in filings in 1991 and continuing to decline until 1996. In both 1996 and 1997, there were slight increases in the number of petitions filed. However, in 1998, the number of business petitions filed declined by 18 percent to the lowest level of filing in 20 years of only 44,367 petitions. This decline followed the beginning of at least eight years of economic growth.

CAUSES OF FINANCIAL DIFFICULTY

§ 2.4   Introduction

It is not easy to determine the exact cause or causes of financial difficulty in any individual case. Often, it is the result of several factors leading up to one event that immediately brings failure. A fundamental cause may not be at all obvious from the evidence at hand. Exhibit 2-2, which is based on data prepared by Dun & Bradstreet, sets forth the causes of failure for the year 1993. According to Dun & Bradstreet, the major causes of business failures are finance and economic causes. For example, 47 percent of the failures were

Exhibit 2-2 Causes of Business Failures—1993p

	Agriculture, Forestry & Fishing	Mining	Construction	Manufacturing	Transportation & Public Utilities	Wholesale Trade	Retail Trade	Finance, Insurance & Real Estate	Services	Total
Neglect Causes	**4.4%**	**11.1%**	**6.2%**	**4.0%**	**4.5%**	**4.7%**	**3.7%**	**9.5%**	**1.7%**	**3.9%**
Business conflicts	2.2%	11.1%	3.3%	3.0%	3.6%	2.2%	1.9%	9.5%	1.1%	2.5%
Family problems	0.0%	0.0%	1.6%	0.3%	0.0%	1.1%	0.6%	0.0%	0.4%	0.6%
Lack of commitment	0.0%	0.0%	0.8%	0.7%	0.0%	0.7%	0.5%	0.0%	0.1%	0.4%
Poor work habits	2.2%	0.0%	0.5%	0.0%	0.9%	0.7%	0.7%	0.0%	0.1%	0.4%
Disaster	**2.2%**	**0.0%**	**4.9%**	**8.1%**	**1.8%**	**8.3%**	**13.1%**	**4.8%**	**2.3%**	**6.3%**
Fraud	**0.0%**	**3.7%**	**1.4%**	**3.7%**	**6.4%**	**9.0%**	**3.1%**	**11.9%**	**2.4%**	**3.8%**
Economic Factors Causes	**47.8%**	**77.8%**	**36.6%**	**45.2%**	**46.3%**	**48.3%**	**38.4%**	**14.3%**	**32.0%**	**37.1%**
High interest rates	0.0%	0.0%	0.0%	0.0%	0.0%	0.0%	0.0%	0.0%	0.0%	0.0%
Inadequate sales	0.0%	0.0%	2.2%	2.4%	2.7%	8.3%	2.8%	0.6%	0.5%	2.2%
Industry weakness	37.0%	22.2%	19.5%	19.9%	23.6%	16.6%	17.7%	8.3%	28.0%	21.6%
Insufficient profits	8.6%	48.2%	14.6%	20.2%	17.3%	18.4%	15.1%	4.8%	3.4%	11.6%
Inventory difficulties	0.0%	0.0%	0.0%	0.3%	0.0%	1.4%	0.3%	0.0%	0.0%	0.2%
Not competitive	2.2%	0.0%	0.3%	0.7%	0.9%	2.9%	1.2%	0.0%	0.0%	0.7%
Poor growth prospects	0.0%	3.7%	0.0%	1.4%	1.8%	0.7%	0.6%	0.6%	0.0%	0.5%
Poor location	0.0%	3.7%	0.0%	0.3%	0.0%	0.0%	0.7%	0.0%	0.1%	0.3%
Experience Causes	**0.0%**	**0.0%**	**0.5%**	**1.0%**	**0.0%**	**1.5%**	**1.1%**	**0.6%**	**0.2%**	**0.6%**
Lack of business knowledge	0.0%	0.0%	0.0%	0.7%	0.0%	1.1%	0.5%	0.6%	0.1%	0.3%
Lack of line experience	0.0%	0.0%	0.0%	0.3%	0.0%	0.0%	0.3%	0.0%	0.0%	0.1%
Lack of managerial experience	0.0%	0.0%	0.5%	0.0%	0.0%	0.4%	0.3%	0.0%	0.1%	0.2%
Finance Causes	**43.4%**	**7.4%**	**47.4%**	**36.3%**	**40.1%**	**26.8%**	**39.8%**	**58.9%**	**61.0%**	**47.3%**
Burdensome institutional debt	8.7%	7.4%	3.0%	8.1%	8.2%	2.5%	3.0%	3.0%	2.5%	3.6%
Heavy operating expenses	34.7%	0.0%	41.1%	19.8%	24.6%	18.9%	33.3%	54.1%	57.6%	40.5%
Insufficient capital	0.0%	0.0%	3.3%	8.4%	7.3%	5.4%	3.5%	1.8%	0.9%	3.2%
Strategy Causes	**2.2%**	**0.0%**	**3.0%**	**1.7%**	**0.9%**	**1.4%**	**0.8%**	**0.0%**	**0.4%**	**1.0%**
Excessive fixed assets	0.0%	0.0%	0.0%	0.0%	0.0%	0.0%	0.0%	0.0%	0.1%	0.0%
Overexpansion	2.2%	0.0%	0.0%	0.0%	0.9%	0.0%	0.5%	0.0%	0.1%	0.2%
Receivables difficulties	0.0%	0.0%	3.0%	1.7%	0.0%	1.4%	0.3%	0.0%	0.2%	0.8%

Results based on primary reason for failure.

p = preliminary.

Source: *Business Failure Record* (New York: Dun & Bradstreet, Inc., 1994), p. 19.

Exhibit 2-3   Failure Trends since 1940 (Selected Years)

Year	Number of Failures	Total Failure Liabilities ($000)	Failure Rate per 10,000 Listed Concerns	Average Liability per Failure
1940	13,619	$166,684	63	$12,239
1945	809	30,225	4	37,361
1950	9,162	248,283	34	27,099
1955	10,969	449,380	42	40,968
1960	15,445	933,630	57	60,772
1965	13,514	1,321,666	53	97,800
1966	13,061	1,385,659	52	106,091
1967	12,364	1,265,227	49	102,332
1968	9,636	940,996	39	97,654
1969	9,154	1,142,113	37	124,767
1970	10,748	1,887,754	44	175,638
1971	10,326	1,916,929	42	185,641
1972	9,566	2,000,244	38	209,099
1973	9,345	2,298,606	36	245,972
1974	9,915	3,053,137	38	307,931
1975	11,432	4,380,170	43	383,150
1976	9,628	3,011,271	35	312,762
1977	7,919	3,095,317	28	390,872
1978	6,619	2,656,006	24	401,270
1979	3,564	2,667,362	28	352,639
1980	11,742	4,635,080	42	394,744
1981	16,794	6,955,180	61	414,147
1982	24,908	15,610,792	88	626,738
1983	31,334	16,072,860	110	512,953
1984	52,078	29,268,647	107	562,016
1985	57,253	36,937,369	115	645,160
1986	61,616	44,723,992	120	725,850
1987	61,111	34,723,831	102	568,209
1988	57,097	39,573,030	98	693,084
1989	50,361	42,328,790	65	840,507
1990	60,747	56,130,074	74	923,996
1991	88,140	96,825,314	107	1,098,539
1992	97,069	94,317,500	110	971,653
1993	86,133	47,755,514	109	554,438
1994p	71,558	28,977,866	86	404,956
1995	71,128	37,283,551	82	524,175
1996	71,931	29,568,732	80	411,071
1997p	83,384	37,436,935	88	448,970
1998	—	—	—	—

Due to statistical revision, data prior to 1984 are not directly comparable with those for later years.

p = preliminary.

Source: *Business Failure Record* (New York: Dun & Bradstreet, Inc., 1999), p. 2.

attributable to finance causes, of which 40 percent were caused by heavy operating expenses. Another 37 percent of the failures were attributable to economic factors. Insufficient profits accounted for over 11 percent of failures attributable to the economic factors. Only 1 percent of the failures were directly attributable to a lack of experience, and only 4 percent were attributable to fraud. It might appear that at least some of the failures attributable to insufficient profits and heavy operating costs could have as their underlying cause a lack of good managerial decision making in the business. Because Dun & Bradstreet discontinued publishing the table describing the causes of failures in *Business Failure Record* in 1993, the table reflects data for that year.

Why does a particular business fail? The answer can be very simple or exceedingly complex. In many cases, the determination of the cause of failure of a particular business involves only a basic examination of the financial statements and records. Accountants and others who have experience in analyzing financially troubled companies can identify the underlying cause of the failure and determine whether some aspects of the business might support a turnaround in a relatively short time period. In other cases, fewer in number, an intensive investigation may be needed to ascertain the cause of the problem and the prospects for future profitable operations.

§ 2.5 Size of Business Failures

Both the number of business failures and the total liabilities associated with each failure have increased tremendously. Exhibit 2-3 summarizes the failure trends since 1940, several of which are significant. The failure rate per 10,000 concerns increased in 1993 to 110, which is the highest rate since 1986. After 1993, the failure rate per 10,000 concerns began to decline substantially to 80 failures per 10,000 concerns in 1996. However, in 1997 that number increased to 88 failures per 10,000 concerns. A failure rate of 88 failures per 10,000 concerns is high and indicates that a large number of businesses are still having financial problems.

In 1979, the rate per 10,000 concerns increased for the first time since 1975 and the rate continued to rise, reaching 110 per 10,000 concerns in 1983. In 1986 the rate per 10,000 concerns increased to 120, but dropped off in 1987. The 1986 rate of 120 failures per 10,000 concerns represents the highest failure rate per 10,000 concerns since 1932, when the rate was 154.

The average liability per failure has also followed an increasing trend since 1940. The average increased to $383,150 in 1975 from only $97,654 in 1968. In 1991, the average liability per failure was over $1 million, which represents the highest level to date. The average liability, reflecting a decline in the large company failures in 1992, dropped by 10 percent. Part of this increase is due to the rise in prices, which is reflected in larger asset and liability balances, but most of this change has been caused by a greater number of large companies having financial difficulties, impacted by the large number of leveraged buyouts (LBOs).

By 1994, the average liability per failure had dropped to $404,956, the lowest level since 1980. In 1995 the average liability per failure increased to $524,175, but declined again in 1996 to $411,071 and increased in 1997 to $448,970. The average liability per failure in 1998 was expected in increase also.

Exhibit 2-4   Failure Distribution by Liability Size, 1940–1997 (Selected Years)

Year	Under $5,000 No.	%	$5,000 to $25,000 No.	%	$25,000 to $100,000 No.	%	$100,000 to $1 Million No.	%	Over $1 Million No.	%
1940	6,891	50.6	5,442	40.0	1,067	7.8	209	1.5	10	0.1
1945	270	33.4	343	42.4	146	18.0	45	5.6	5	0.6
1950	2,065	22.5	4,706	51.4	1,975	21.6	407	4.4	9	0.1
1955	1,785	16.3	5,412	49.3	2,916	26.6	820	7.5	36	0.3
1960	1,688	10.9	6,884	44.6	5,078	32.9	1,703	11.0	92	0.6
1965	1,007	7.5	5,067	37.5	5,266	39.0	2,005	14.8	169	1.2
1966	932	7.1	4,569	35.0	5,332	40.8	2,042	15.7	186	1.4
1967	814	6.6	4,434	35.9	4,896	39.6	2,045	16.5	175	1.4
1968	481	5.0	3,332	34.6	4,016	41.7	1,686	17.5	121	1.2
1969	416	4.6	3,000	32.8	3,776	41.2	1,807	19.7	155	1.7
1970	430	4.0	3,197	29.7	4,392	40.9	2,450	22.8	279	2.6
1971	392	3.8	2,806	27.2	4,413	42.7	2,423	23.5	292	2.8
1972	394	4.1	2,497	26.1	4,149	43.4	2,236	23.4	290	3.0
1973	285	3.0	2,434	26.1	3,908	41.8	2,375	25.4	343	3.7
1974	304	3.1	2,150	21.7	4,279	43.1	2,755	27.8	427	4.3
1975	292	2.5	2,226	19.5	4,986	43.6	3,459	30.3	469	4.1
1976	122	1.3	1,750	18.2	4,304	44.7	3,029	31.4	423	4.4
1977	102	1.3	1,283	16.2	3,476	43.9	2,708	34.2	350	4.4
1978	76	1.2	928	14.0	2,708	40.9	2,593	39.2	314	4.7
1979	62	0.8	954	12.6	2,914	38.5	3,216	42.5	418	5.6
1980	72	0.6	1,243	10.6	4,367	37.2	5,417	46.1	643	5.5
1981	118	0.7	1,862	11.1	6,253	37.2	7,648	45.6	913	5.4
1982	141	0.6	2,789	11.2	8,579	34.4	11,737	47.1	1,662	6.7
1983	1,065	3.4	4,167	13.3	19,340	33.0	13,851	44.2	1,911	6.1
1984	16,095	30.9	5,489	10.5	11,943	22.9	15,723	30.2	2,828	5.4
1985	19,028	33.2	5,287	9.2	12,236	21.4	17,359	30.3	3,343	5.8
1986	21,694	35.2	4,579	7.4	12,635	20.5	19,013	30.9	3,695	6.0
1987	23,215	38.0	4,185	6.8	11,549	18.9	18,593	30.4	3,569	5.8
1988	23,356	40.9	4,259	7.5	10,685	18.7	15,659	27.4	3,138	5.5
1989	19,152	38.0	3,707	7.4	10,453	20.8	14,245	28.3	2,804	5.6
1990	25,292	41.6	3,881	6.4	11,660	19.2	16,368	26.9	3,546	5.8
1991	38,542	43.7	5,930	6.7	16,328	18.5	22,654	25.7	4,686	5.3
1992	44,889	46.2	6,428	6.6	17,085	17.6	24,329	25.1	4,338	4.5
1993	40,885	47.5	5,594	6.5	14,787	17.2	21,481	24.9	3,386	3.9
1994p	32,630	45.6	4,967	6.9	13,273	18.5	18,254	25.5	2,434	3.4
1995	31,398	44.1	4,472	6.3	13,669	19.2	19,353	27.2	2,236	3.2
1996	30,959	43.1	4,171	5.8	14,546	20.2	20,495	28.5	1,742	2.4
1997p	34,041	40.8	4,340	5.2	17,669	21.2	25,649	30.8	1,685	2.0
1998	—	—	—	—	—	—	—	—	—	—

Due to statistical revision, data prior to 1984 are not directly comparable with those for later years.

p = preliminary.

Source: *Business Failure Record* (New York: Dun & Bradstreet, Inc., 1999), p. 3.

Exhibit 2-4, which presents the failure distribution by liability size, indicates the increased number of large companies that are having financial problems. The number of failures with liabilities in excess of $1 million increased from 155 in 1969 to 469 in 1975. The number dropped in the next few years, but by 1980 the number of failures with liabilities in excess of $1 million was up to 643 and was over 1,900 in 1983. With the expansion to include other industries in the *Business Failure Record*, the number jumped to 2,828 in 1984 and (based on comparable data) increased to 3,695 in 1986. Dun & Bradstreet reported that there were particularly high failures per 10,000 concerns in agriculture (production of both crops and livestock); forestry; mining, including metals and coal; manufacturing of food and kindred products, textile mill products, and industrial machinery and equipment; apparel and drug wholesale trade; and furniture and home furnishing stores in retail trade. The number of failures during the late 1980s began to decline; however, with the current economic conditions, the trend reversed in 1990. Note that the number of business failures with liabilities over $1 million increased in 1990 and 1991, but declined slightly in 1992. The number of failures with liabilities over $1 million has continued to decline in number and in failures as a percent of total failures. For example, in 1993, the number of failures with liabilities over $1 million as a percent of total failures declined from 4 percent in 1993 to only 2 percent in 1997. Also, the actual number of failures with liabilities over $1 million declined from 3,386 in 1993 to 1,685 in 1997. This decline in the percentage of large company failures is most likely first attributable to a decline in the number of LBOs that filed chapter 11 petitions or attempted an out-of-court workout. A major cause of the decline is attributable to the fact that the United States has experienced over eight consecutive years of economic growth since 1991.

The large numbers of failures of small businesses annually act as a deterrent to others who might be considering starting their own business. For example, a study completed by Professor Namaki, Director of the Netherlands International Institute for Management,[1] discovered that 71 percent of local ventures by entrepreneurs in Singapore fail within five years of start-up. Failure rates of this magnitude discourage others from wanting to start their own businesses. In Singapore, only 12 out of every 100 persons in the workforce elect to start their own businesses. In South Korea, the figure is almost 28 (of every 100); in Indonesia it is 42.[2] The failure rate of small businesses in the United States has continued to rise in recent years. For example, in 1992, over 50 percent of all business failures were of firms with liabilities under $25,000, as shown in Exhibit 2-4.

The increase in business failures, especially among small businesses, has not been restricted to the United States. For example, company liquidations in the United Kingdom more than doubled after 1987, reaching nearly 24,500 in 1992. As in the United States, small companies are responsible for a large percentage of the business failures. In the United Kingdom, small companies, employing fewer than 15 people, account for more than four-fifths of the failures.[3]

---

[1] Ven Sreenivasan, "Singapore's Entrepreneurs: Enterprise and Management," *Business Times* (United Kingdom), July 26, 1993, p. 23.

[2] *Id.*

[3] Ian Cowie, "Management Causes Failure," *The Daily Telegraph*, April 21, 1993, p. 22.

Exhibit 2-5   Failures in 50 U.S. Cities, 1996–1997p

	1991		1992p	
City	Number	Liabilities	Number	Liabilities
1. New York, NY	1,383	$5,605,387,986	2,225	$17,776,647,580
2. Chicago, IL	550	581,067,044	538	405,888,808
3. Los Angeles, CA	795	2,773,029,383	1,411	1,164,768,951
4. Philadelphia, PA	560	225,225,663	607	3,117,308,359
5. Houston, TX	1,164	1,295,206,635	1,314	784,425,221
6. Detroit, MI	242	100,886,331	248	69,382,152
7. Dallas, TX	729	1,810,957,135	763	196,339,647
8. San Diego, CA	903	253,509,810	981	231,415,314
9. Phoenix, AZ	729	1,607,031,840	780	182,188,794
10. Baltimore, MD	324	178,055,964	422	103,168,365
11. San Antonio, TX	498	296,877,214	545	166,831,155
12. Indianapolis, IN	491	1,069,376,346	398	668,117,998
13. San Francisco, CA	441	413,501,699	535	570,149,087
14. Memphis, TN	295	35,660,339	262	35,176,679
15. Washington, DC	198	64,143,206	210	105,959,115
16. Milwaukee, WI	223	31,703,592	214	17,177,646
17. San Jose, CA	312	117,266,041	404	160,811,639
18. Cleveland, OH	342	163,477,312	376	416,333,949
19. Columbus, OH	220	147,620,933	169	131,771,395
20. Boston, MA	181	1,167,252,259	154	184,413,651
21. New Orleans, LA	146	75,195,358	121	43,715,978
22. Jacksonville, FL	212	731,873,626	193	48,318,661
23. Seattle, WA	292	1,610,078,094	357	225,200,462
24. Denver, CO	515	154,651,305	435	799,509,487
25. Nashville, TN	265	61,860,095	246	73,420,805
26. St. Louis, MO	379	54,632,662	358	135,062,406
27. Kansas City, MO	198	258,366,479	258	540,837,471
28. El Paso, TX	107	16,835,624	149	30,909,254
29. Atlanta, GA	677	481,021,778	576	192,018,808
30. Pittsburgh, PA	205	710,202,385	254	1,090,862,498
31. Oklahoma City, OK	504	152,890,415	298	207,510,301
32. Cincinnati, OH	319	672,369,343	302	59,831,430
33. Fort Worth, TX	345	108,489,212	302	118,284,384
34. Minneapolis, MN	447	103,637,408	366	50,291,853
35. Portland, OR	313	90,108,437	299	101,042,928
36. Honolulu, HI	43	31,718,820	129	59,514,074
37. Long Beach, CA	114	94,755,563	196	716,487,607
38. Tulsa, OK	194	40,387,596	276	113,862,031
39. Buffalo, NY	210	45,102,989	223	28,332,354
40. Toledo, OH	100	128,562,630	114	16,185,203
41. Miami, FL	683	11,068,777,067	671	2,722,218,533
42. Austin, TX	472	3,840,639,346	431	207,247,207
43. Oakland, CA	165	132,037,024	219	58,674,524
44. Albuquerque, NM	210	68,607,762	202	11,026,879
45. Tucson, AZ	364	2,170,763,422	239	338,159,587
46. Newark, NJ	99	117,966,285	93	3,452,456,246
47. Charlotte, NC	231	107,003,923	256	47,459,550
48. Omaha, NE	200	18,554,483	170	16,951,299
49. Louisville, KY	223	55,261,903	204	15,443,706
50. Birmingham, AL	178	48,069,941	164	36,849,042
Total 50 Cities	**18,990**	**$41,187,657,707**	**20,657**	**$38,045,960,073**
Balance of country	69,150	$55,637,657,034	76,200	$53,243,418,980
Total United States	**88,140**	**$96,825,314,741**	**96,857**	**$91,289,379,053**

Includes data for city limits, not metropolitan area.

p = preliminary.

Source: *Business Failure Record* (New York: Dun & Bradstreet, Inc., 1993), p. 5.

§ 2.6 Geographic Distribution of Business Failures

For years, New York City has had more business failures than any other American city. For example, in 1996, the failures in New York City accounted for 19 percent of the total liabilities for all failures reported by Dun & Bradstreet. This large percentage is due in part to the large number of firms that have corporate offices in New York. However, in 1997, the liabilities associated with failures in New York City declined by over 70 percent. In 1997, Chicago had the largest liabilities associated with failures of almost $5 billion. Obviously, fluctuations from year to year can be materially due to the failure of a very large business located in one of the large cities. Exhibit 2-5 summarizes the failures in 50 large cities in the United States for a two-year period. Business failures in the 50 largest cities account for almost 20 percent of the number of failures and over 30 percent of the liabilities associated with the failures. The liabilities associated with failures in the 50 largest cities as a percent of total liabilities have declined in recent years.

In 1981, Michigan, Tennessee, California, Washington, and Oregon were the states that had the largest failure rate per 10,000 listed concerns. With the problems with real estate and in the defense industry, California experienced 169 failures per 10,000 concerns in 1992. Georgia also had 169 failures per 10,000 concerns, which was a decline from 203 failures per 10,000 concerns in 1991. Arizona had 164 failures per 10,000 concerns. In 1997 the three states with the highest failures per 10,000 concerns were Colorado (183 per 10,000 concerns), California (176 per 10,000 concerns), and Hawaii (173 per 10,000 concerns). Other states with over 130 failures per 10,000 concerns were Kansas, Arkansas, Oklahoma, and Idaho.

§ 2.7 Age of Business Failures

One of the most consistent bankruptcy court statistics is the age at which companies fail. For the past 30 years, except for a few years, 40 to 50 percent of the businesses that failed were in their first five years of operation. In 1996, this statistic was 42 percent, and the proportion of casualties coming from operations in the six- to ten-year range was over 24 percent. In 1996, the businesses that failed during their first five years of operation increased to over 40 percent. In 1998, the businesses that failed during the first five years were ____ percent of the total number of concerns that failed. In recent years that has been a slight increase in the number of failures of concerns in operation for more than 10 years. However, in 1997, that number declined to under 32 percent. In 1998, the number of failures in operation for more than 10 years decreased slightly over 1996. Exhibit 2-6 shows the age of failures by industry for 1998. The retail industry has consistently had a larger percentage of failures in the first five years of operation than the other industries. In agriculture, forestry, and fishing, in 1992, almost 55 percent of the failures came from concerns that had been in business for over ten years. This rate for farming is more than 20 percentage points higher than the rate for most other industries and is another statistic illustrating the financial difficulty farmers faced in the 1980s and 1990s. By 1997, that number had dropped to 43 percent. Refer to the most recent supplement for business failures for various industry categories from 1998 and later.

Exhibit 2-6 Age of Failed Businesses by Function—1997p

	Agriculture, Forestry, & Fishing	Mining	Construction	Manufacturing	Transportation & Public Utilities	Wholesale Trade	Retail Trade	Finance, Insurance, & Real Estate	Services	Total
One year or less	0.9%	1.9%	0.8%	1.7%	1.9%	1.2%	1.8%	2.7%	2.5%	1.7%
Two years	3.6	3.4	3.4	6.4	5.9	5.9	8.1	4.9	7.1	6.2
Three years	4.5	8.4	6.6	10.7	10.7	9.5	12.7	7.0	9.8	9.9
Total Three Years or Less	**9.0%**	**13.6%**	**10.7%**	**18.9%**	**18.4%**	**16.6%**	**22.6%**	**14.5%**	**19.4%**	**17.8%**
Four years	5.4%	6.2%	7.7%	10.6%	9.0%	8.9%	10.7%	7.7%	9.5%	9.4%
Five years	4.2	10.2	8.5	9.4	9.4	8.5	9.4	7.1	8.4	8.7
Total Five Years or Less	**18.5%**	**30.0%**	**27.0%**	**38.9%**	**36.9%**	**34.0%**	**42.7%**	**29.3%**	**37.3%**	**35.9%**
Six years	7.7%	6.8%	8.3%	7.9%	8.2%	8.6%	8.0%	8.0%	8.6%	8.2%
Seven years	5.4	4.6	8.1	6.6	8.5	7.9	6.5	8.6	7.7	7.4
Eight years	5.2	7.7	6.8	5.5	5.7	5.8	5.4	8.0	6.5	6.1
Nine years	4.2	5.6	5.5	4.5	4.7	5.0	4.4	5.6	4.7	4.8
Ten years	4.3	6.8	4.4	3.6	4.0	4.0	3.5	4.3	3.8	3.9
Total Six to Ten Years	**26.8%**	**31.6%**	**33.1%**	**28.1%**	**30.9%**	**31.3%**	**27.9%**	**34.6%**	**31.4%**	**30.4%**
Over ten years	54.7%	38.4%	39.9%	33.0%	32.2%	34.7%	29.4%	36.1%	31.3%	33.7%
Total	**100.0%**	**100.0%**	**100.0%**	**100.0%**	**100.0%**	**100.0%**	**100.0%**	**100.0%**	**100.0%**	**100.0%**

p = preliminary.
Source: *Business Failure Record* (New York: Dun & Bradstreet, Inc., 1998), p. 17.

§ 2.8 Business Failures and Economic Conditions

As would be expected, the number of business failures does increase as a result of a contraction of economic activity. The mild recessions of 1948–1949, 1953–1954, 1957–1958, 1960–1961, 1969–1970, 1974–1975, 1980, 1981–1982 and 1990–1991 have all resulted in an increase in the number of business failures. For example, the slowdown in economic activity that began in 1974 had its impact on the number of failures. As evidenced by the filing of a bankruptcy petition, the number was 28,969 for 1975, which represents an increase of approximately 46 percent over the number for 1974, and there was another increase of 18 percent in 1976. Also, the Securities and Exchange Commission (SEC) reviewed 117 bankruptcy petitions in fiscal 1974, 2,003 in 1975, and 2,221 in 1976. The recessions in the early 1980s and 1990–1991 significantly increased both the number of failures as reported by Dun & Bradstreet and the number of bankruptcy petitions filed by businesses. The number of failures increased by over 400 percent between 1979 and 1983 and by almost 100 percent between 1989 and 1992. The number of petitions increased over 300 percent, from 29,500 petitions in 1979 to 95,439 in 1983 and over 16 percent, from 62,534 in 1989 to 72,650 in 1992. During periods of expansion, the failure rate has almost always decreased. However, in 1985 through 1988, the number of business failures continued to be strong even though we were not in a recession. The problems in agriculture, oil, and financial areas, especially savings and loan, contributed significantly to the large number of failures during this period.

It is very difficult to determine the impact of inflation on the number of failures. As reported by Dun & Bradstreet, the number of failures decreased for the years 1971, 1972, and 1973, when the rate of inflation was the highest since the inflationary period following World War II. It should be noted, however, that the number of bankruptcy petitions filed in the fiscal year ending June 30, 1972, increased by 18 percent over the number filed in fiscal 1971. We also experienced, in the 1974–1976 period (following the years of high inflation), one of the largest increases in business bankruptcies since the Great Depression. During 1979, when the inflation rate was 13 percent, the number of petitions filed increased by 12 percent. As the inflation rate increased in 1980 and 1981, the number of failures also increased. No doubt inflation does have an unfavorable effect on the operations of some firms, but it tends to assist others.

With the decline in the inflation rate in the 1990s and with eight consecutive years of economic growth, the business failures have declined some, but have not reached the level of 65 failures per 10,000 concerns that existed in 1989.

The key causes of business failure are discussed in the following sections.

§ 2.9 Characteristics of the Economic System

The economic structure within which a firm must exist acts as a cause of failure that originates outside the business itself and is not a result of acts of management. Management must accept the changes that occur in our economic system and attempt to adjust the firm's operations to meet these changes.

One characteristic of the American economic system is freedom of enterprise—the absolute right of all individuals to engage in any business regardless of their personal qualifications. This permits the entry of people who lack experience and training in their chosen business and who are thus more susceptible to failure. Galbraith suggested that there are two parts to the economy. One is the small and traditional proprietors and the other consists of the world of the few hundred technically dynamic, massively capitalized, and highly organized corporations.[4] The smaller firms are the ones most susceptible to failure. The large firms can tolerate market uncertainty much better than the smaller firms. Galbraith further stated, "Vertical integration, the control of prices and consumer demand and reciprocal absorption of market uncertainty by contracts between firms all favor the large enterprise."[5]

Frequently given as a cause of failure is intensity of competition; however, an efficient management is a tough foe for any competitor. Some new businesses do fail because of a lack of adequate ability, resources, and opportunity to meet successfully the existing competition. Also, established concerns may be unable to match the progressive activities of new and better qualified competition.

Analogous to intense competition is the challenge offered by business changes and improvements and shifts in public demand. Companies that fail in the transition to modern methods of manufacturing and distribution, or are unable to adapt to new consumer wants, are not successful.

Business fluctuations are another characteristic of a free economic system such as ours. Adverse periods marked by maladjustment between production and consumption, significant unemployment, decline in sales, falling prices, and other disturbing factors will have some effect on the number of business failures. However, a temporary lull in business activities is not usually found to be a fundamental cause, although it does at least accelerate movement toward what is probably an inevitable failure.

The freedom of action characteristic of our society may result in actions by third persons that prove detrimental to a business firm. The demands of labor unions and organized actions by community and other special interest groups have in recent years contributed to the failure of some businesses. Government actions—for example, the enactment of new tax legislation, lowering or elimination of tariffs, wage and hour laws, court decisions, price regulations, and the like—occasionally result in the failure of some companies. As an example, several small manufacturers have been forced out of business because they were unable to meet the pollution standards established by the federal government.

Professor Namaki, using World Bank data for the 1980–1990 period, determined that problems relating to finance, rather than economic conditions, are increasingly the cause for small businesses' failure in high-income economies.[6]

§ 2.10   Casualties

The causes of trouble occasionally may be entirely beyond the control of the business. Some of these causes are known as "acts of God" and this category is found in all societies regardless of their particular economic system. Included

---

[4] John Kenneth Galbraith, *The New Industrial State* (Boston: Houghton Mifflin Co., 1967), pp. 8–9.
[5] *Id.*, p. 32.
[6] Sreenivasan, *supra* note 1.

are such things as fires, earthquakes, explosions, floods, tornadoes, and hurricanes, all of which may certainly cause the downfall of some businesses.

Thus, the limits within which a business must function prove to be an important determinant of its success. The challenge to management is to meet and adapt to changing conditions in such a manner that they do not prove to be adverse. A company cannot change the environment; it must be able to use it to its benefit.

§ 2.11 Inside Underlying Causes

Internal causes of failure are those that could have been prevented by some action within the business; they often result from an incorrect past decision or the failure of management to take action when it was needed. Management must assume the responsibility for any business difficulties resulting from internal factors.

(a) Overextension of Credit

One inside cause of failure is the tendency of businesses to overextend credit and subsequently become unable to collect from their debtors in time to pay their own liabilities. Manufacturers overextend credit to distributors so that they may increase their sales. Distributors, to be able to make payments to their manufacturers, must then overextend credit to their customers. These buyers must in turn continuously keep bidding lower and lower to be able to keep their equipment busy and meet their commitments. In this manner, a chain of credit is developed, and if one link defaults there is trouble all the way down the line. The failure to establish adequate credit margins thus may result in business crises.

The obvious answer is to expand credit investigations and, possibly, restrict sales made on account. However, many businesses feel that their volume of sales will fall as a result, perhaps more than offsetting the credit losses they are now experiencing. One unusual default could cause serious financial trouble for a firm and might have been avoided by a more careful credit policy. A manager's decision to grant credit indiscriminately means a risk of a company's own financial stability. Unusual credit losses may so greatly weaken the firm's financial structure that it is no longer able to continue operation.

(b) Inefficient Management

Businesses often fail because of managers' lack of training, experience, ability, adaptation, or initiative. Indications of probable failure of an enterprise include management's inability or failure to remain current with technological changes, lack of educational training, and lack of experience in the particular line of business that is being pursued. Inefficient management has been found to be the cause of the majority of business failures.

Included in this category is neglect on the part of managers to coordinate and effectively communicate with specialists. With the great complexity and vast specialization of business, complete harmony and cooperation become crucial. All management services must be integrated for maximum profitability. Often, it has been found that a business failure could have been avoided by the proper use of effective managerial control.

Dun & Bradstreet's analyses show that in 1992 approximately 24 percent of business failures were due to finance causes. In 1993, the percent of failures due to finance causes increased to 47 percent. In 1992, over 64 percent of the business failures were caused by economic factors, with over 60 percent of these attributable to insufficient profits. Were the insufficient profits caused by economic conditions or by the incompetence of management? Earlier studies completed by Dun & Bradstreet would suggest that most of the insufficient profits were due to the incompetence or inexperience of management.[7] These studies show that incompetence and inexperience were evidenced to a large extent by management's inability to avoid conditions that resulted in inadequate sales and competitive weakness.

Every accountant interviewed in the course of preparing this book listed inefficient management as the number-one cause of business failures. Both earlier and later studies have also confirmed the analysis that deficient management is primarily responsible for the failure of business. The Bureau of Business Research of the University of Pittsburgh made a detailed study of ten unsuccessful manufacturing plants in western Pennsylvania between 1954 and 1956.[8] The firms that failed were contrasted with ten conspicuously successful firms to determine points of contrast that might explain the reasons for failure. These differences were as follows:

- The unsuccessful firms had very poor records and record-keeping procedures. One firm shipped $10,000 of oil burners to a customer who was bankrupt. The shipments continued over nine months, during which time no payments were received.
- The successful firms spent time and money on product development while several unsuccessful firms ignored this need.
- Several unsuccessful firms allowed themselves to go beyond the technical depth of their management.
- Executives of unsuccessful firms neglected market analysis and selling. Unsuccessful plants displayed a lack of organization and of efficient administrative practices.

The results of the analysis were summarized in the following statement:

> None of the failures studied occurred because the firm was small. They all occurred because of a very obvious, easily identified management error. The management error might have occurred because one man was saddled with too much, and didn't have time to devote to his various responsibilities, a situation indirectly associated with smallness, but in the last analysis, the failure was occasioned by a management error which could have been avoided.[9]

---

[7] *Business Failure Record*, 1982–1983 (New York: Dun & Bradstreet, Inc., 1985), pp. 14–15.
[8] A. M. Woodruff, *Causes of Failure*, undated pamphlet reporting address by Dr. Woodruff and distributed by the Small Business Administration in 1957.
[9] *Id.*, p. 11.

The Society of Insolvency Practitioners (United Kingdom) reported that bad management and slack demand during recession cause more companies to fail than banks' "pulling the plug." Its survey of 1,700 businesses that collapsed during 1992 found that management failure was the single largest cause of insolvency in the United Kingdom, accounting for more than one-third of the total. Loss of market, at 31 percent, followed. By contrast, loss of long-term finance caused only 3.5 percent of corporate failures, and lack of working capital accounted for an additional 18.5 percent.[10]

A common situation involves managers who are experts in their particular fields, such as engineering, but lack the simple tools necessary to control their finances or administer a going concern. In this instance, it is often found that they fail to restrain salaries or benefits and are unable to maintain a close rapport with their accounting staff.[11] Effective and efficient management is partially dependent on adequate accounting records that will reveal inefficiencies and act as a guide in formulating policies. Several of the accounting firms actively involved in bankruptcy audits have estimated that at least 90 percent of the financially troubled businesses they examine have very inadequate accounting records. Although poor accounting information or records may not be the underlying cause of failure, their inadequacy does prevent the business from taking corrective action in many cases.

Inefficient management is often evidenced by its inability to avoid circumstances that have resulted in the following conditions.

(i) Inadequate Sales   This may be a result of poor location, an incompetent sales organization, poor promotion, or an inferior product or service. This obviously means that the firm will be unable to make a sufficient profit to stay in business.

(ii) Improper Pricing   In relation to its costs, the firm is charging too low a price, accepting either a loss on the item or very little profit.

(iii) Inadequate Handling of Receivables and Payables   Billings for products sold or services rendered should not be delayed. Because of the importance of getting jobs completed, there may be a tendency to perform other functions besides sending out bills. The failure to take large discounts and the failure to pay crucial creditors on time can create problems that could have been avoided with careful planning as to the timing of payment and selection of the creditors to be paid.

(iv) Excessive Overhead Expenses and Operating Costs, and Excessive Interest Charges on Long-Term Debt   All these act as fixed charges against revenue, rather than varying with the volume of goods produced. The firm's break-even point is high: it must sell a relatively large volume of goods before it begins earning a profit.

---

[10] Cowie, *supra* note 3.
[11] R. A. Donnelly, "Unhappy Ending? Chapters 10 and 11 of the Bankruptcy Act Don't Always Tell the Story," *Barron's*, July 12, 1971, p. 14.

(v) Overinvestment in Fixed Assets and Inventories   Both types of investment tie up cash or other funds so that they are no longer available to management for meeting other obligations. As a company expands, there is a need for
greater investment in fixed assets. It becomes profitable for the company at the
current production level to reduce labor costs by investing in additional equipment. If the company can continue to operate at this capacity, profits will continue; however, if production drops significantly, the company is in a difficult
position. Fixed assets are not used fully and, as a result, the depreciation charge
against net income is unduly high for the level of production. These costs are
committed and little can be done in the short run to affect their total. If the
reduction in production is not temporary, action must be taken, very quickly,
to eliminate some of the unprofitable divisions and dispose of their assets.
Under some conditions, it may be best to liquidate the business. (See § 1.6.)
The objective thus becomes to have the optimum level of investment and
maximum utilization of the available capacity.

Carrying a large amount of inventories results in excessive storage costs,
such as warehouse rent and insurance coverage, and the risk of spoilage or
obsolescence. Thus, in addition to tying up the use of funds, overinvestment in
fixed assets or inventories may create unnecessary charges against income.

(vi) Insufficient Working Capital, Including a Weak Cash Position   Inadequate working capital is often the result of excessive current debt due to acquisition of fixed assets through the use of short-term credit; overexpansion of
business without providing for adequate working capital; or deficient banking
facilities, resulting in high cost of borrowing current funds. An unwise dividend policy may use up funds that are needed for operating the business. A
weak working capital position, if not corrected, will eventually cause a delay
in the firm's payment of debt.

***(vii) Unbalanced Capital Structure—An Unfavorable Ratio of Debt to Cap-
ital***   If the amount of capital secured through bonds or similar long-term liabilities is relatively high, fixed charges against income will be large. This is
advantageous when the firm is earning a healthy profit and the residual after-
interest charges accrue to the owners. But where the business is experiencing
financial difficulties, this interest burden acts to drag down earnings. Alternatively, a high percentage of capital obtained through equity has a high intrinsic
cost to the firm because the owners demand a rate of return higher than the
interest rate given on debt, to compensate them for their risk. It must also be
remembered that, to attract investors, earnings per share must be maintained.

Leveraged buyouts (LBOs) may end in failure a few years after the buyout is
completed, because of insufficient working capital and an unbalanced capital
structure. Very little capital and limited sources for increasing the capacity to
borrow for working capital needs are typical conditions. Thus, if sales decrease
because of unfavorable economic conditions, or a competitor introduces a new
product that competes favorably with the LBO company, or other developments
require extra working capital, the LBO may end up in chapter 11 because the
cash from the decreased sales level cannot fund the large debt payments. For
example, in the case of Revco, the company's debt was increased from less than
$700 million to over $1.5 billion, leaving the company with very little equity.

The total amount of the stockholders' equity, after the assets were almost doubled as a result of the LBO's being recorded as a purchase, was less than $25 million. The leverage buy-out transaction was completed at the end of 1986. Eighteen months later, Revco filed a chapter 11 petition. (Revco is discussed further in 2.1 of Volume 2 of *Bankruptcy and Insolvency Accounting*.)

(viii) Inadequate Insurance Coverage   If a business is not compensated for losses such as fire and theft, it might very well be forced to close its doors.

(ix) Inadequate Accounting Methods and Records   Management will not have the information it needs to identify problem areas and take preventive action.

(x) Uncontrolled, Poorly Managed, or Excessive Growth   Growth that is too rapid creates demands for cash and other resources that the company cannot satisfy in a short time period. Under these conditions, additional cash is obtained only at an excessive cost. Unmanageable interest cost, too much debt, and a lack of support for sales and production efforts result in inefficient use of resources and, eventually, failure. Businesses that start out slowly often have a much better chance of success than those that start out at a rapid pace.

(xi) Excessive Concentrations of Risk   Companies that have relatively few customers may be forced to file a chapter 11 petition if one of the accounts is lost or if a single customer files bankruptcy. It is not unusual for the delay in receiving payment for an account from a chapter 11 debtor to cause the supplier to file a chapter 11 petition.

The existence of any one of these factors may be an indication of potential trouble caused by management's inability or inefficiency. The accountant is in an excellent position to discover any of these conditions and alert management to their existence and possible consequences.

(c) Insufficient Capital

As previously mentioned, insufficient capital may be thought to be an inside cause of business failures. When business conditions are adverse and there is insufficient capital, the firm may be unable to pay operating costs and credit obligations as they mature. However, the real cause of difficulty is often not insufficient capital, but a lack of ability to manage effectively the capital that is available for use or to convert merchandise and receivables into cash with which to pay the firm's debts.

§ 2.12 Dishonesty and Fraud: Planned Bankruptcies, Sham

Premeditated bankruptcy fraud has been found to be the cause of a small number of bankruptcy proceedings. The reasons for fraudulent bankruptcies include the desire of many credit grantors to maintain their sales volume at any cost, the neglect of creditors to investigate bankruptcy causes, and the ability of dishonest persons to utilize profitably the benefits of the bankruptcy courts without fear of prosecution.

§ 2.13 Outside Immediate Causes

Normally, the immediate action that leads to failure is not the fundamental reason for failure. Some of the outside immediate causes that are responsible for the inevitable end of the firm include threatened or actual suits, involuntary bankruptcy court petitions, execution levies, tax levies, and setoffs by lending institutions.[12] Many companies delay the filing of the bankruptcy petition until they are forced to do so by their creditors in the form of a suit filed to collect an outstanding debt. Or, they may be forced into bankruptcy by an involuntary petition filed by the creditors. Banks have the right to set off money in their possession against a claim that is past due. If a company has a past-due note or installment payment, the bank may take funds on deposit in the firm's account to cover the debt owed the bank. Normally, banks will not take this type of action unless a business is very weak financially. Thus, setoffs and other creditors' actions such as foreclosure or eviction may become the precipitating cause of a bankruptcy petition.

STAGES OF FINANCIAL FAILURE

§ 2.14 Introduction

The general activity in firms that are failing includes lower sales, a slower growth in sales, poorer cash flow and net income positions, and large incurrence of debt. These factors combine to cause marked deterioration in the firm's solvency position. Unsuccessful firms also experience higher major operating costs, especially excessive overhead costs, than the average for similar successful firms. As the firm suffers losses and deteriorates toward failure, its asset size is reduced. Assets are not replaced as often as during more prosperous times, and this, along with the cumulative losses, further reduces the prospects for profitable operations.[13]

The stages of financial failure may be analyzed in four distinct phases: (1) period of incubation, (2) cash shortage, (3) financial insolvency, and (4) total insolvency. The time period associated with each stage will differ depending on many factors. Although most failures will follow the stages in the order listed, some companies may proceed through a later stage first. For example, some troubled businesses may be totally insolvent before they run out of cash.

§ 2.15 Period of Incubation

A business does not suddenly or unexpectedly become insolvent. Any business concern having financial difficulty will pass through several transitional stages before it reaches the point where it is necessary to file a bankruptcy petition. An ailing business has been compared with an individual suffering at the

---

[12] David T. Stanley et al., *Bankruptcy: Problems, Process, Reform* (Washington, DC: The Brookings Institution, 1971), p. 111.

[13] Edward I. Altman, "Financial Ratios, Discriminant Analysis and the Prediction of Corporate Bankruptcy," *Journal of Finance*, Vol. 23 (September 1968), pp. 590–97.

start from a minor ailment, such as a common cold, which if not remedied, in due time could develop into a serious disease like pneumonia and result in death.[14] During the period of incubation, one or even a number of unfavorable conditions can be quietly developing without being recognizable immediately by outsiders or even by management. For example, a company whose major source of revenue came from steel fabrication work in connection with highway construction failed to take action two years previously, when it was obvious that interstate highway construction would be reduced in the company's market area. As a result, the company was forced to file a petition in bankruptcy court. Some of the types of developments that may be occurring in the incubation period are:

- Change in product demand
- Continuing increase in overhead costs
- Obsolete production methods
- Increase in competition
- Incompetent managers in key positions
- Acquisition of unprofitable subsidiaries
- Overexpansion without adequate working capital
- Incompetent credit and collection department
- Lack of adequate banking facilities

It is often in the incubation stage that an economic loss occurs: the return realized on assets falls below the firm's normal rate of return. At this stage of failure, management should give careful consideration to the cause. If the cause cannot be corrected, management must look for alternatives. It is best for the company if the problem is detected at this stage, for several reasons. First, replanning is much more effective if initiated at this time. Second, the actions required to correct the causes of failure are not nearly so drastic as those required at later stages. Third, the public confidence is less likely to be impaired if corrective action is taken at this stage. This is critical because if public confidence is shaken, the charges for funds will increase and the firm will be in a position where would-be profitable projects must now be rejected.

It is possible that, under certain conditions, the economic loss may not occur until the enterprise is in the second stage, experiencing a shortage of cash.

§ 2.16 Cash Shortage

A business, for the first time, may be unable to meet its current obligations and in urgent need of cash, although it might have a comfortable excess of physical assets over liabilities and a satisfactory earning record. The problem is that the assets are not sufficiently liquid and the necessary capital is tied up in receivables and inventories.

---

[14] Helene M. A. Ramanauskas, "How Close to Bankruptcy Are You?," *Woman CPA*, Vol. 28 (October 1966), p. 3.

The cash shortage is generally not the underlying cause of the financial problems faced by a failing company, but the shortage is often identified as the principal cause. Thus, action taken in this stage often focuses on obtaining additional cash without looking to the real underlying cause of the financial difficulty.

§ 2.17 Financial or Commercial Insolvency (Equity Definition)

In this stage, the business is unable to procure through customary channels the funds required to meet its maturing and overdue obligations. Management will have to resort to more drastic measures such as calling in a business or financial specialist (often a CPA), appointing a creditors' committee, or resorting to new financing techniques. However, there still exists a good possibility for survival and for future growth and prosperity if substantial infusions of new money and financing can be obtained and the underlying cause of the financial difficulty is identified and corrected.

§ 2.18 Total Insolvency (Bankruptcy Definition)

At this point, the business can no longer avoid the public confession of failure, and management's attempts to secure additional funds by financing generally prove unsuccessful. Total liabilities exceed the value of the firm's assets. The total insolvency becomes confirmed when legal steps, involuntary or voluntary, are taken by filing a petition under the federal Bankruptcy Code.

§ 2.19 Bankruptcy or Turnaround Activity

The question is often asked: At what stage should a troubled company file a chapter 11 petition or attempt a workout out of court? Action should be taken early—at the incubation stage, when problems begin to develop. The sooner corrective action is taken in the form of a bankruptcy filing or an out-of-court workout, the greater the prospects for successful turnaround of the business.

Even after a chapter 11 petition is filed, companies may continue to move through these stages until the plans developed during the chapter 11 proceedings are implemented. However, the filing of a petition or the obtaining of a moratorium on debt payments in an out-of-court workout reduces the impact of a cash shortage and allows the debtor to use existing cash for operations rather than debt service.

Often, companies will allow the business to proceed through all four stages before taking any action to correct the financial problems; unfortunately, many businesses then liquidate, which might be described as the fifth stage.

DETECTION OF FAILURE TENDENCIES

§ 2.20 Introduction

Effective management cannot wait until the enterprise experiences total insolvency to take action, because at this final stage the remedies available are rather restricted. There are several tools that may be used to diagnose business failures, but they will not necessarily reveal the cause of failure. It is the cause that must be determined and corrected; it is not enough just to correct the symptoms. For example, a constantly inadequate cash position is an indication that financial problems are developing, but the problem is not solved by management's borrowing additional funds without determining the real cause for the shortage. However, if the cause of the shortage is ascertained and corrected, management can then raise the necessary cash and be reasonably certain that the future cash inflow will not be interrupted in such a manner as to create a similar problem.[15]

External and internal methods may be used to detect failure tendencies. The most common sources of external data are trade reports and statistics, and economic indicators published by the federal government and by private organizations.

Many internal methods are simply extensions of the work done by accountants. During their audit investigation, the preparation of their reports, and the performance of other services, most accountants become aware of what has been occurring in the major accounts and in the firm as a whole. Because of their training and experience in business finances, they often are able to identify when the enterprise is headed for trouble and alert management to these suspicions. Thus, because of the nature of both the type of work they are doing and the ability they possess, accountants are in an excellent position to identify any tendencies toward failure.

§ 2.21 Trend Analysis

(a) Historical Date

One of the most frequently used methods of examining data from within a firm is an analysis of the financial statements over a period of years so that trends may be noted. Using a certain year as base, a trend analysis of the important accounts is developed on a monthly or quarterly basis. The balance sheet trends will generally reveal the following failure tendencies:

- Weakening cash position
- Insufficient working capital
- Overinvestment in receivables or inventories
- Overexpansion in fixed assets
- Increasing bank loans and other current liabilities
- Excessive funded debt and fixed liabilities
- Undercapitalization
- Subordination of loans to banks and creditors

---

[15] *Id.*

The income account changes that may disclose additional failure tendencies are:

- Declining sales
- Increasing operating costs and overhead
- Excessive interest and other fixed expenses
- Excessive dividends and withdrawals compared to earning records
- Declining net profits and lower return on invested capital
- Increased sales with reduced mark-ups

(b) Actual versus Forecast

An effective way to evaluate the performance of management is to compare actual results with management's projections. Some aspects of the effectiveness of a corporation's management, based on publicly available information, can be evaluated by examining the plans described by the chief executive officer in management's letter accompanying the annual report, and comparing them with the actions that were subsequently taken. A trend may become evident, indicating that very few of management's plans were in fact implemented.

Among the comparisons that might be helpful are:

- Actual/standard costs per unit
- Actual/planned production
- Actual/planned fixed manufacturing cost
- Actual/budgeted gross margin
- Actual/planned sales volume
- Actual/planned sales and administrative costs
- Actual/budgeted capital expenditures
- Actual/budgeted research and development expenditures

The comparisons over a period of several years may reveal factors that will help identify the underlying cause of the company's financial problems.

(c) Comparison with Industry

A comparison of a company's operating results, financial conditions, ratios, and other characteristics with those of companies of similar size in the same industry may indicate problem areas. This comparison measures the company against an industry norm. When using industry data for comparison purposes, however, the use of different accounting methods and practices, operating methods, objectives, ownership styles, and so on, all of which can impact the results, must be taken into account.

Industry data are available from several sources, including trade associations for the industry in which the debtor operates. Other general sources include Dun & Bradstreet and Robert Morris Associates. For example, Robert

Morris Associates publishes, on an annual basis, key asset, liability, income, and ratio information for a large number of categories in manufacturing, wholesaling, retailing, and service industries as well as data from contractors. These data are presented for at least six different categories, based on the book value of the asset and dollar sales.

§ 2.22 Analysis of Accounting Measures

In conjunction with the trend analysis, certain ratios or accounting measures are of benefit in indicating financial strength. The current and liquidity ratios are used to portray the firm's ability to meet current obligations. The efficiency in asset utilization is often determined by fixed asset turnover, inventory turnover, and accounts receivable turnover. The higher the turnover, the better the performance, because management will be able to operate with a relatively small commitment of funds.

The soundness of the relationship between borrowed funds and equity capital is set forth by certain equity ratios. The ratios of current liabilities, long-term liabilities, total liabilities, and owners' equity to total equity assist in appraising the ability of the business to survive times of stress and meet both its short-term and long-term obligations. There must be an adequate balance of debt and equity. When the interest of outsiders is increased, there is an advantage to the owners in that they get the benefit of a return on assets furnished by others. However, there is in this advantage an increased risk. By analyzing the equity structure and the interest expense, insight can be gained as to the relative size of the cushion of ownership funds creditors can rely on to absorb losses from the business. These losses may be the result of unprofitable operations or simply due to a decrease in the value of the assets owned by the business.[16] Profitability measures that relate net income to total assets, net assets, net sales, or owners' equity assist in appraising the adequacy of sales and operating profit. An analysis of the various measures and relationships for a given year may be of limited value, but when a comparison is made with prior years, trends can be observed that may be meaningful.

In using ratios, it should be realized that there is an expected difference in the ratios, not only among companies in different industries (such as the profit margin ratio of a grocery store compared with that of a clothing store), but among companies within the same industry. For example, differences in methods of accounting (LIFO versus FIFO), methods of operations, methods of financing, and so on, can result in ratios that are justifiably different.

Common ratios may be given several different classifications. Some analysts classify all of the financial ratios into either profitability or liquidity ratios. Robert Morris Associates uses five basic classifications for their analysis:[17]

1 Liquidity ratios
2 Coverage ratios

---

[16] Ramanauskas, *supra* note 14, p. 12.
[17] *RMA Annual Statement Studies*, 1993 (Philadelphia: Robert Morris Associates, 1993), pp. 10–15.

3 Leverage ratios
4 Operating ratios
5 Expense to sales ratios

Ratios under the first four classifications used by Robert Morris Associates are described below. Relevant expense to sales ratios are included under operating ratios. The ratio analysis is followed by description of a model for predicting corporate bankruptcy.

(a) Liquidity Ratios

Liquidity ratios measure the quality of current assets and their adequacy to satisfy current obligations. The key liquidity ratios are discussed in the following sections.

(i) Current Ratio

$$\frac{\text{Current assets}}{\text{Current liabilities}} = \text{Current ratio}$$

The current ratio is an indicator of the entity's ability to meet its short-term obligations, on an ongoing basis, with its current assets.

A rule-of-thumb standard of 2:1 (current assets to current liabilities) is sometimes suggested as a minimum desired ratio, on the grounds that the resources that will become available during the operating cycle will be adequate to just cover obligations coming due during the same period. This standard implies that the greater the ratio of current assets to current liabilities, the better. Although this may be true to some extent, one must view a very high current ratio with a certain amount of suspicion. Perhaps the ratio is indicative of an excess amount of idle cash on hand, an obsolete or overstocked inventory, a large amount of overdue accounts receivable, or a failure to use current "leverage" effectively (see section (c)).

(ii) Acid Test Ratio

$$\frac{\text{Current assets} - (\text{Inventories} + \text{Prepaid expenses})}{\text{Current liabilities}} = \text{Acid test or quick ratio}$$

The acid test (or quick) ratio is a measure of the entity's ability to meet its short-term obligations more or less immediately with the assets most easily converted into cash.

Because it is an indicator of the firm's ability to meet its currently maturing obligations out of its most liquid assets, the quick ratio is especially appropriate in distress situations or in highly volatile businesses. A rule-of-thumb standard of 1:1 (quick assets over current liabilities) is often prescribed as the minimum desired quick ratio, but the interpretation of this ratio is subject to the same problems outlined for the current ratio.

(iii) Working Capital to Total Assets Ratio

$$\frac{\text{Working capital}}{\text{Total assets}} = \text{Liquidity of total assets}$$

The ratio of working capital to total assets is a measure of the liquidity status of an entity's total assets. It relates the firm's short-term liquidity status to its overall financial position. Although there is no widely accepted rule-of-thumb standard regarding the relationship between working capital and total assets, historical and industry comparisons that would indicate excessive buildups or deficiencies in working capital can be made.

(iv) Accounts Receivable Turnover Ratio

$$\frac{\text{Net credit sales}}{\text{Average accounts receivable}} = \text{Accounts receivable turnover}$$

Accounts receivable turnover is an indicator of the number of times per period the entity fully collects (turns over) its accounts receivable.

A relatively slow turnover (low ratio value) indicates an inability on the part of the firm to collect its accounts receivable on a timely basis (and perhaps the existence of significant uncollectible accounts). This could signify potential and/or existing cash flow problems. On the other hand, a turnover rate much in excess of the standard may also signal problems, such as a too stringent credit policy (causing lost sales to potential customers who cannot meet the firm's overly restrictive credit requirements), and/or excessive early payment incentives (such as overly generous—and costly—cash discounts). Thus, a slow turnover of accounts receivable (in relation to the chosen standard—for example, the firm's own credit terms and/or industry averages) should be considered unhealthy, but a very rapid turnover must also be investigated for potential problems.

Several points should be made regarding this ratio. Net credit sales (the numerator of the ratio) is sales on account minus sales returns and allowances and write-offs of uncollectible accounts. Sales returns and allowances and write-offs of uncollectible accounts should be deducted because they are, in effect, reductions to sales. Failure to exclude allowances and bad-debt write-offs would overstate the turnover of accounts receivable. Cash sales are also excluded: they were never recognized as receivables, and to include them would introduce an upward bias (overstatement) in accounts receivable turnover.

Average accounts receivable (the denominator) is used to eliminate the effect of fluctuations in accounts receivable balances. However, the average used is generally a simple average of beginning and ending balances ((beginning inventory ÷ ending inventory) ÷ 2), rather than a weighted or moving weekly, monthly, or even quarterly average. (The additional computational effort required by these more sophisticated averaging procedures is seldom justified by the incremental precision derived.)

It is usually not difficult to determine net sales: the sales figure is reported in the income statement net of allowances and write-offs of uncollectible accounts, or the allowances and write-offs are disclosed separately in the statement. Determining credit sales from published financial statements, on the other hand, is probably impossible because few published financial statements distinguish between cash and credit sales. However, the dollar volume of cash transactions in U.S. business operations is negligible, and, therefore, consistent use of net sales (as opposed to net credit sales) does not, as a general rule, significantly bias the accounts receivable turnover figure.

As for averaging accounts receivable in the denominator, the analyst may or may not wish to follow this practice. Averaging reduces the effects of temporary fluctuations in accounts receivable on the accounts receivable turnover statistic, but it also tends to obscure, or at least delay, recognition of long-term trends in accounts receivable balances. (The average always lags behind the most recent data.) Because the balance in accounts receivable is determined at the same point in the company's operating cycle year after year, increases or decreases in that balance (at least for established businesses) generally reflect long-term trends rather than temporary fluctuations. The current environment of the business, of course, may indicate otherwise, so caution is advised for those who would accept this generalization at face value.

(v) Age of Accounts Receivable Ratio

$$\frac{\text{Number of days in accounting period}}{\text{Accounts receivable turnover}} = \text{Average age of accounts receivable}$$

By dividing the accounts receivable turnover statistic (computed in section (iv)) into the number of days in the period covered by the net credit sales figure, the analyst can determine the average length of time it takes the company to collect its accounts receivable.

The average age of accounts receivable is interpreted in a manner similar to accounts receivable turnover. Unduly old accounts receivable indicate collection difficulties, and relatively young accounts might suggest other problems.

(vi) Inventory Turnover Ratio

$$\frac{\text{Cost of goods sold}}{\text{Average inventory}} = \text{Inventory turnover}$$

Inventory turnover is an indicator of the number of times the business liquidates (turns over) its inventory in the period covered by the cost-of-goods-sold figure. Previous comments regarding the use of averages in the denominator when computing accounts receivable turnover apply equally to the computation of inventory turnover. However, the reader should be reminded that several generally accepted inventory cost flow assumptions exist that may produce significantly different amounts for inventories and cost of goods sold. Consequently, as demonstrated by the following tabulation, significant differences in inventory turnover may exist solely because of the differences in cost flow assumptions employed:

	Company A (LIFO)	Company B (FIFO)	Company C (Average)
Beginning inventory (5 units @ $10)	$ 50	$ 50	$ 50
Purchases (5 units @ $20)	100	100	100
Available for sale (10 units)	150	150	150
Ending inventory (5 units)	50	100	75
Cost of goods sold (5 units)	$100	$ 50	$ 75
Inventory turnover	2 times	.5 times	1 time

Comparison of the three firms—without knowledge of their respective inventory cost flow assumptions—would suggest that Company A (a LIFO company) is the most efficient firm in its inventory management. Its inventory turnover is double that of Company C (an "average" company), and four times that of Company B (a FIFO company). If true, these results would be highly significant; however, in reality, all three companies' experiences are identical and the "significant" difference is spurious.

For manufacturing businesses, inventory turnover statistics can be computed for all three types of inventory (raw materials, work-in-process, and finished goods) by relating the particular inventory to its counterpart in the income statement, as follows:

1 For raw materials:

$$\frac{\text{Cost of raw materials used}}{\text{Average raw materials inventory}}$$

2 For work-in-progress inventory:

$$\frac{\text{Cost of goods manufactured}}{\text{Average work-in-process inventory}}$$

3 For finished goods inventory:

$$\frac{\text{Cost of goods sold}}{\text{Averaged finished goods inventory}}$$

A relatively slow inventory turnover indicates potentially excessive (and perhaps obsolete) inventories. Excessive inventories portend obsolescence difficulties and perhaps unreasonably high inventory carrying charges. A relatively high turnover, however, may be indicative of burdensome opportunity costs in the form of lost sales caused by lack of inventory. In either case, inventory turnovers higher or lower than the standard should be investigated for potential problems.

(vii) Age of Inventory Ratio

$$\frac{\text{Number of days in accounting period}}{\text{Inventory turnover}} = \text{Average age of inventory}$$

By dividing the appropriate inventory turnover statistic (computed in section (vi)) into the number of days in the period covered by the income statement, the analyst can determine the average length of time it takes the entity to turn over its inventories.

The average age of inventories is interpreted in the same manner as the inventory turnover ratio (section (vi)). Old inventory suggests overstocking and possible obsolescence; a very young inventory suggests the possibility of inadequate supplies to achieve the firm's potential sales level.

(viii) Length of Operating Cycle Ratio

$$\frac{\text{Average age of}}{\text{accounts receivable}} + \frac{\text{Average age of}}{\text{inventory}} = \frac{\text{Approximate length of}}{\text{firm's operating cycle}}$$

This statistic gives an indication of the length of time that it would take for cash, put into inventory, to be converted first into accounts receivable and then back into cash. For short-term borrowing situations, knowing the length of the borrowing company's operating cycle is crucial because it indicates the minimum length of time (on the average) required for cash to be generated from operations and hence be available for repayment of the short-term loan. A 60-day inventory loan to a firm with a 90-day operating cycle would, other considerations aside, be ill-advised. In attempting to turnaround a business in financial difficulty, the length of operating cycle is critical.

(b) Coverage Ratios

Coverage ratios measure the ability of firms to service debt. Debt service involves both interest and required principal repayments. The key coverage ratios are described here.

(i) Times Interest Earned Ratio

$$\frac{\text{Net income} + \text{Annual interest expense} + \text{Income taxes}}{\text{Annual interest expense}} = \frac{\text{Times interest}}{\text{earned ratio}}$$

The times interest earned ratio is a measure of the enterprise's ability to pay its interest charges out of earnings. Interest expense is added back into the numerator because interest costs were already covered by operations in arriving at net income. Income taxes are added back into the denominator because interest is paid out of pretax income (that is, it is deductible in arriving at taxable income). The smaller the times interest earned ratio, the greater the risk of business failure caused by inability to meet periodic interest payments. Sudden downturns in operations, even if temporary, could be disastrous for a firm with "thin" interest coverage.

(ii) Times Preferred Dividends Earned Ratio
As a practical matter, when analyzing financial statements, preferred stockholders and long-term creditors are concerned with many of the same factors. Unless the preferred stock is convertible into common stock, preferred stock generally has more in com-

mon with debt securities than it does with equity securities; that is, the preferred stock stipulates certain preferences (preferred as to a specified dividend, or as to assets in liquidation, and so on) that are not found in common stocks. As a result, preferred stockholders' information requirements are largely concerned with the risk inherent in the investment. On the basis of that risk, they are concerned that an appropriate purchase price be established for the stock in light of the fixed dividend rate. Among the statistics particularly relevant to a preferred stockholder are the following:

$$\frac{\text{Net income}}{\text{Preferred dividend requirement}} = \frac{\text{Times preferred dividends}}{\text{earned ratio}}$$

The times preferred dividends earned ratio is a measure of the enterprise's ability to meet stipulated preferred dividend commitments out of current earnings. Note that income taxes are not added back to net income here as they were in the times interest earned ratio because preferred dividends, being nondeductible for tax purposes, are paid out of after-tax income. The ratio merely indicates the ability of the enterprise to meet dividend requirements out of after-tax earnings—it does not mean that such dividends will necessarily be declared by the board of directors. Because, legally, preferred stocks are equity securities, declaration of dividends on them is left to the discretion of the board of directors. As a general rule, however, preferred dividend payments are relatively assured either by cumulative provisions or by tradition.

(iii) Cash Flow to Debt Repayments Ratio

$$\frac{\text{Cash flow from operations}}{\text{Debt repayments}}$$

This ratio measures the ability of the debtor to make debt payments after all other payments have been made. Cash flow from operations should be calculated after interest and taxes.

The ratios above may be combined into one fixed coverage ratio consisting of the net income from operations before interest and taxes divided by both interest expense and principal repayments.

(c) Leverage Ratios

Leverage ratios measure the ability of a firm to survive a business downturn. Key leverage ratios are described in the following sections.

(i) Relationship of Debt to Equity Ratio
Like short-term creditors, long-term creditors, in their analysis of financial statements, are primarily concerned with the debt-paying ability of the enterprise. Consequently, even though the debt is outstanding for a longer time period, the immediate debt-paying ability of the enterprise—as indicated by the statistics presented in the previous section—is a vital concern to the long-term creditor as well. In addi-

tion to those short-term statistics are the following, which relate primarily to the information needs of long-term creditors:

$$\frac{\text{Total debt}}{\text{Total assets}} = \text{Debt ratio}$$

$$\frac{\text{Total owners' equity}}{\text{Total assets}} = \text{Equity ratio}$$

$$\frac{\text{Total debt}}{\text{Total owners' equity}} = \text{Debt-to-equity, or debt/equity ratio}$$

All three of these statistics are measures of the same thing, that is, the extent of "leverage" in the enterprise's financial structure. Leverage means using debt and/or preferred stock financing at a fixed interest/dividend rate to improve the rate of return on common stockholders' equity.

To illustrate, a company that has total assets of \$400,000 and no liabilities, and is earning \$80,000 before taxes of 50 percent, would be returning 10 percent on invested capital as follows:

$$0.5(\$80,000) \div \$400,000 = 10\%$$

If that same company had total debt of \$200,000, which carried an 8 percent interest rate, it would be returning 16 percent on invested capital as follows:

$$0.5(\$80,000 - (0.08 \times \$200,000)) \div \$200,000 = 16\%$$

As long as the company is successfully covering its fixed interest charges, trading on the equity (another term for leverage) is a positive factor for common stockholders. For creditors, however, highly leveraged companies represent a greater risk than nonleveraged companies, for three reasons:

1   The interest payments represent a fixed cash commitment, and any sudden downturn in the business's operations might find the enterprise, because of insufficient cash inflows, unable to make interest payments and, therefore, vulnerable to bankruptcy.

2   Greater leverage means the cushion between solvency and insolvency is correspondingly reduced, and assets must be spread over a greater number (or at least a larger amount) of claims in the case of business failure.

3   There is a feeling, at least for smaller, closely held enterprises, that with less of their own capital invested in the company, residual stockholders might be less committed to the success of the business.

In any case, an analyst would have no reason to compute all three of the above debt and equity ratios, because computation of any one of them indicates the extent to which enterprise assets are financed with debt and/or equity capital. The evaluation of these ratios depends on whether the evaluator is a potential long-term creditor grantor or an equity investor.

(ii) Fixed Assets to Owners' Equity Ratio

$$\frac{\text{Net fixed assets}}{\text{Total owners' equity}}$$

This ratio measures the extent to which the owners of a company have invested in the property, plant, and equipment. A high ratio would indicate that most of the equity of the business has been invested in fixed assets and very little cushion may be left for the equity holders if the business liquidates.

(d) Operating Ratios

The operating ratios measure the performance of the company. They examine the relationships of profit to sales and profit to investment. Key ratios include the following.

(i) Return on Sales Ratio

$$\frac{\text{Net income}}{\text{Sales}} = \text{Return on sales}$$

This "component percentage" is an indicator of enterprise efficiency. The greater the percentage, the more efficient the enterprise. Improvements in operating efficiency may be achieved by (1) reducing costs and expenses of operations while holding sales constant, or (2) increasing sales while holding costs and expenses constant (or at least increasing costs and expenses at a slower rate than sales are increasing). In either case, the issue is one of obtaining greater amounts of output relative to input.

(ii) Asset Turnover Ratio

$$\frac{\text{Sales}}{\text{Total assets}} = \text{Asset turnover}$$

This cross-financial statement ratio is indicative of operating effectiveness. It measures the number of times total assets are covered by operating revenue. It is an effectiveness measurement in that asset turnovers of different companies can be compared to determine the extent to which the enterprise is effectively employing its assets. (A high turnover would generally be considered favorable; a low turnover would generally be considered unfavorable.)

(iii) Return on Investment Ratio

The ultimate operating success or failure of an enterprise is a function of both efficiency and effectiveness, as reflected in the return on investment (ROI) statistic.

$$\text{Return on investment} = \frac{\text{Net income}}{\text{Investment}} = \frac{\text{Net income}}{\text{Sales}} \times \frac{\text{Sales}}{\text{Investment}}$$

The "investment" amount may be total assets—as in the asset turnover ratio—or it may be common stockholders' equity. The former definition is appropriate to determine return on total assets committed to enterprise operations; the latter reflects the rate of return on common stockholders' equity, taking into account the effect of leverage.

In either case, return on investment may be improved by (1) improving operating efficiency (increasing return on sales), (2) improving operating effectiveness (increasing investment turnover), or (3) a combination of efficiency and effectiveness improvements.

As an example, assume that Alpha Co. had a return on sales of 10 percent and an investment turnover of two times per year, as follows:

$$\text{Return on sales} = \frac{\text{(Net income) \$150,000}}{\text{(Sales) \$1,500,000}} = 10\%$$

$$\text{Investment turnover} = \frac{\text{(Sales) \$1,500,000}}{\text{(Investment) \$750,000}} = 2 \text{ times}$$

Alpha Co.'s return on investment would be:

$$\frac{\text{(Net income) \$150,000}}{\text{(Investment) \$750,000}} = 20\% \text{ (or 10\% return on sales} \times \text{investment turnover of } 2 = 20\%)$$

If we know (by examining the performance of other firms in the industry) that an ROI of 30 percent is more in line with industry performances, we can compare Alpha's return on sales and investment turnover to ascertain the source of its problem(s).

To improve Alpha's ROI performance, we could either improve its return on sales to 15 percent—for example, by cutting costs, and thereby increasing net income while maintaining constant sales; or we might be able to improve its asset turnover to three times per year—for example, by reducing the amount of investment while maintaining constant sales. Either strategy would bring Alpha's ROI in line with industry performance. Note, however, that unless improvements are made in one or both of the component ROI ratios (return on sales and investment turnover), increasing sales will not improve return on investment!

By way of example, assume that Alpha Co. could increase its sales by 33⅓ percent (or $500,000) over its current sales level if it spent $250,000 to renovate its production facility. Because the company is already operating at peak efficiency, it is unlikely that the firm's return on sales would increase above the present 10 percent level. If Alpha successfully completed the necessary renovations and achieved the anticipated sales level, its return on investment would be unchanged, as follows:

$$\frac{\text{(Net income) \$200,000}}{\text{(Investment) \$1,000,000}} = 20\%$$

Return on sales was not improved and the increased investment negated the effect of the sales increase, leaving the investment turnover unchanged:

$$\frac{\text{(Sales) } \$1,500,000 \div \$500,000}{\text{(Investment) } \$750,000 \div \$250,000} = 2 \text{ times per year}$$

Indeed, if Alpha had to borrow to finance the renovation, its return on sales (after interest expense) and, therefore, its return on investment would decline.

Increasing sales is almost always much easier said than done. Failure to meet the projected sales increase after increasing the investment base would negate, to some extent, any gains that might have been made in operating efficiency.

(iv) Earnings per Share Ratio   Of all the various financial ratios, none has received the attention that has been afforded the earnings per share (EPS) statistic. Arguments abound in the accounting and finance literature regarding the significance of EPS; yet, because of its presumed importance to investors in common stock, earnings per share is the only financial ratio for which the computation has been meticulously prescribed by the designated standard setting authority for financial reporting.

The essence of the earnings per share statistic is reflected in the computation of EPS for the "simple capital structure" situation, as follows:

$$\frac{\text{Net income} - \frac{\text{Dividends on non-common-stock-equivalent senior securities}}{}}{\text{Weighted average number of outstanding common shares}} = \frac{\text{Earnings per}}{\text{share (EPS)}}$$

EPS, then, is significant to the investor in common stock in that it reflects the amount of enterprise earnings attributable to each share of residual (common) stock. As such, the EPS statistic provides some information about the dividend-paying ability of the company (although the amount of dividends actually distributed, if any, is left to the discretion of the board of directors). Also, because there is a presumed relationship between the earning capacity of the stock and its value, the statistic can be used to evaluate the current selling price of the stock.

In evaluating the current selling price of the stock, the EPS statistic itself is used as a component of another widely used statistic—the price/earnings (P/E) ratio.

(v) Price/Earnings Ratio

$$\frac{\text{Current market price per share of stock}}{\text{EPS}} = \text{Price/earnings (P/E) ratio}$$

The price/earnings multiple reflects the number of dollars investors are willing to pay per dollar of earnings for that particular stock. Comparing the computed P/E ratio with the P/E ratios of other companies in the same industry and/or with industry average P/E ratios provides the investor with a means to evaluate the current selling price of the stock. A low P/E ratio (other things being equal) relative to the ratios compared would be conducive to investment (that is, the security is said to be underpriced); a high P/E ratio, using similar reasoning, would be considered not conducive to investment.

In addition to EPS and the P/E ratio, another ratio, book value per share, is often computed in connection with common stock investments, although its significance is relatively limited.

$$\frac{\text{Total assets} - \text{Total liabilities} + \text{Claims of senior equity securities}}{\text{Number of common shares outstanding}} = \text{Book value per common share}$$

There is seldom any reason for computing book value per common share unless the analyst is interested in determining the availability of enterprise assets to residual stockholders in liquidation. However, because enterprise assets are usually valued, in accordance with generally accepted accounting principles, at historical cost, it is unlikely that the amount of book value per common share (computed for a going concern) is sufficiently informative for this purpose to warrant its computation. If, on the other hand, liquidation of the enterprise is imminent and assets have been revalued accordingly, the common stockholder's cash planning efforts might very well benefit from such a statistic.

The amounts of total assets and total liabilities, and the number of outstanding common shares in the ratio are self-explanatory. Claims of senior equity securities include the liquidation value of outstanding preferred shares as well as any specified cumulative and participative preferences. Thus, if assets have been revalued accordingly, the numerator of the ratio reflects the value of assets available to common stockholders after satisfying claims of creditors and senior equity security holders in liquidation. If assets have not been revalued, and the call price of preferred stock (rather than its liquidation value) is deducted in the numerator, the resultant book value figure roughly measures common stockholders' equity in the going concern on a per-share basis.

(vi) Gross Margin Ratio

$$\frac{\text{Gross Margin}}{\text{Sales}}$$

The gross margin, sometimes called gross profit, is the difference between sales and the cost of goods sold. For a manufacturing concern, it represents the difference between sales and the manufacturing cost for the goods sold. For many companies in financial difficulty, the gross margins are often out of line with other firms within the same industry.

(e) Altman's Model

In a model designed by Altman,[18] five basic ratios were used in predicting corporate bankruptcy. The five ratios selected from an original list of twenty-two are as follows:

[18] Edward I. Altman, "Corporate Bankruptcy Prediction and Its Implications for Commercial Loan Evaluation," *Journal of Commercial Bank Lending,* Vol. 53 (December 1970), pp. 10–19.

1 Working capital/Total assets (X_1)
2 Retained earnings/Total assets (X_2)
3 Earnings before interest and taxes/Total assets (X_3)
4 Market value equity/Book value of total debt (X_4)
5 Sales/Total assets (X_5)

The model may be defined as follows:

$$Z = 1.2X_1 + 1.4X_2 + 3.3X_3 + .6X_4 + .99X_5$$

The values for X_1, X_2, X_3, X_4, and X_5 are calculated from the five ratios listed above. Firms that have a Z-score greater than 2.99 clearly fall into the non-bankrupt sector, while a Z-score less than 1.81 would indicate bankruptcy. Those that have a Z-score between 1.81 and 2.99 are in a gray area because of susceptibility to error classification. Further analysis by Altman suggests that the Z-score that best discriminates between the bankrupt firm and the non-bankrupt firm is 2.675. However, some analysts prefer to use the 1.81 and 2.99 scores as the classification criteria where users have the greatest confidence, and they have doubts about those firms with a Z-score between 1.81 and 2.99.[19]

The fourth variable is the relationship of market value of equity to the book value of total debt. This model was designed for public companies; it is difficult to determine the market value for private companies. The market value, according to Altman, appears to be a more effective predictor of bankruptcy than the commonly used ratio of net worth to total debt.[20] To calculate the Z-score for privately held companies, book value may be used; however, Altman's research suggests that if book value of equity is substituted for market value, the coefficients should be changed. Altman revised the model for private firms to the following:

$$Z' = .717X_1 + .847X_2 + 3.107X_3 + .420X_4 + .998X_5$$

Also, the Z'-score indicating bankruptcy now has a value of 1.23 (as compared to 1.81) and the nonbankrupt Z'-score is 2.9 (as compared to 2.99), creating a larger gray area.[21]

Based on the results of his research, Altman suggested that the bankruptcy prediction model is an accurate forecaster of failure up to two years prior to bankruptcy and that the accuracy diminishes substantially as the lead time increases. Exhibit 2-7 summarizes the predictive accuracy, using the model, of the initial sample of 33 manufacturing firms that filed petitions under Chapter X during the period 1946–1965. Each firm's financial statement was examined each year for five years prior to bankruptcy. The n value is less than 33 for the second to fifth years prior to bankruptcy because some of the firms in the sample were not in existence for five years before they went bankrupt.

---

[19] Edward I. Altman, *Corporate Financial Distress* (New York: John Wiley & Sons, 1983), pp. 108, 119–20.
[20] *Id.*, p. 108.
[21] *Id.*, pp. 120–24.

Exhibit 2-7   Five-Year Predictive Accuracy of the Multiple Discriminant Analysis
Model (Initial Sample)

Years Prior to Bankruptcy	Hits	Misses	Percentage Correct
1st $n = 33$	31	2	96%
2nd $n = 32$	23	9	72
3rd $n = 29$	14	15	48
4th $n = 28$	8	20	29
5th $n = 25$	9	16	36

Source: Edward I. Altman, "Corporate Bankruptcy Prediction and Its Implications for Commercial Loan Evaluation," *Journal of Commercial Bank Lending*, Vol. 53 (December 1970), p. 18.

Altman also selected a second sample of 33 firms that were solvent and still in existence in 1968. This sample was taken to test for the possibility of a Type II error (the classification of a firm in the bankruptcy group when in fact it did not go bankrupt). The Type II error from the sample was only 3 percent.

These five ratios selected by Altman showed a deteriorating trend as bankruptcy approached, and the most serious change in the majority of these ratios occurred between the third and second years prior to bankruptcy.

In Volume 2 of *Bankruptcy and Insolvency Accounting*, 2.1 contains the calculation of Altman's Z-score for Revco for two years—the year that ended just before the leveraged buyout (June 1, 1985) and the year that ended just after the leveraged buyout (May 31, 1986). The Z-score declined from 5.47 in 1985 to 1.86 in 1986.

An analysis of accounting measures or predictions of failure by Beaver indicated that the nonliquid asset measures predict failure better than the liquid asset measures. The evidence also indicated that failed firms tend to have lower, rather than higher, inventory balances as is often expected.[22]

The Failing Company Model was an outgrowth of the Supreme Court decision in the case of *International Shoe v. F.T.C.*[23] in 1930, but gained wide acceptance only after Congress expressly approved the Failing Company Doctrine during hearings on the Celler-Kefauver amendments in 1950. The model, shown in Exhibit 2-8, incorporates twelve measures divided into three categories underlying the cash-flow framework: liquidity, profitability, and variability.

Blum used discriminant analysis to test the model, finding that it distinguished failing from nonfailing firms with an accuracy of approximately 94 percent of the first year before failure, 80 percent at the second year, and 70 percent at the third, fourth, and fifth years before failure.[24] Beaver's best predictor, cash flow/total debt ratio, was again found to have a generally high ranking among the variables, although overall relative importance could not be determined. Predictions of failed firms not to fail (Type II error) is very low, in contrast to Beaver's research, and the model appears to be less susceptible to manipulation than a single ratio.

[22] William H. Beaver, "Financial Ratios as Predictors of Failure," in *Empirical Research in Accounting: Selected Studies 1966*, 1st University of Chicago Conference (May 1966), p. 121.
[23] *International Shoe v. F.T.C.*, 280 U.S. 291 (1930).
[24] Marc Blum, "Failing Company Discriminant Analysis," *Journal of Accounting Research*, Vol. 12 (Spring 1974), pp. 1–25.

Exhibit 2-8   Failing Company Model

I	Liquidity		
	A Short-run liquidity		
		Flow:	1 The "quick flow" ratio
		Position:	2 Net quick assets/inventory
	B Long-run liquidity		
		Flow:	3 Cash flow/Total liabilities
		Position:	4 Net worth at fair market value/Total liabilities
			5 Net worth at book value/Total liabilities
II	Profitability		6 Rate of return to common stockholders who invest for a minimum of three years
III	Variability		7 Standard deviation of net income over a period
			8 Trend breaks for net income
			9 Slope for net income
		10–12	Standard deviation, trend breaks, and slope of the ratio, net quick assets to inventory; variables 10, 11, and 12 are only used at the first and second year before failure

A financial consulting firm, Zeta Services Inc., has developed a computerized credit-scoring model with the aid of E. I. Altman, based on his previous work.[25] Negative Zeta scores are used as warning of a firm's financial ill health. This model is made up of seven weighted financial ratios, with retained earnings, total assets given the heaviest weight. Other measures include leverage, earnings stability, return on total assets, fixed charge coverage, liquidity, and asset size. In 1980, *Business Week* presented an analysis of 24 major corporations, selected for having comparatively low Zeta scores, using this computer model. A cursory review of the companies indicates that a significant number of them have filed a chapter 11 petition or obtained relief from creditors out of court. Among the companies listed were Itel, Sambo's, Fed-Mart, White Motor, and Chrysler.

Scott[26] compared several of the leading empirical models that have been developed in terms of their observed accuracies and their adherence to Scott's own conceptual bankruptcy framework. Included in Scott's analysis were the models of Beaver, and the two models of Altman (Z-score and ZETA) mentioned above. Scott concluded:

Of the multidimensional models, the ZETA model is perhaps most convincing. It has high discriminatory power, is reasonably parsimonious, and includes accounting and stock market data as well as earnings and debt variables. Further it is being used in practice by over thirty financial institutions. As a result, although it is unlikely to represent the perfect prediction model, it will be used as a benchmark for judging the plausibility of the theories discussed in the following sections.[27]

[25] "The Economic Case Against Federal Bailouts . . . and Who May Need Them," *Business Week* (March 24, 1980), pp. 104–07.

[26] J. Scott, "The Probability of Bankruptcy: A Comparison of Empirical Predictions and Theoretical Models," *Journal of Banking and Finance*, Vol. 5 (September 1981).

[27] *Id.*, pp. 324–25. For a more detailed discussion of how empirical models can be used to predict bankruptcies, see Altman's *Corporate Financial Distress: A Complete Guide to Predicting, Avoiding, and Dealing with Bankruptcy* (New York: John Wiley & Sons, 1983).

Exhibit 2-9 Long-Term Liquidity Ratios
by Years Prior to Bankruptcy

Years Prior to Bankruptcy	Long-Term Liquidity Ratio
7	0.00002
6	0.00038
5	0.00567
4	1.0
3	0.86545
2	1.0
1	1.0

A public accounting firm used a long-term liquidity ratio as a means of projecting possible liquidity problems within the next five years. This overall liquidity ratio was developed because other widely used ratios depicting financial health, such as current ratio, are effective only as shorter-range predictors of illiquidity. They do not reflect trends in the depletion of noncurrent assets and the increase of long-term obligations to finance current operations.

The long-term liquidity ratio measures the trend by using a mathematical model that determines the nature of year-to-year changes in the liquidity of a company. The model then computes the probability of the trend's continuing until a point is reached when available resources will be depleted. A ratio of 1 indicates that, unless the trend is altered, an illiquid position is probable within a five-year period. The result of an analysis of one company in bankruptcy for a period of seven years prior to bankruptcy is presented in Exhibit 2-9. Note that this unfavorable trend was developing four years prior to bankruptcy, yet management was not aware of or was unable to respond to it.

§ 2.23 Analysis of Management

Certain characteristics giving evidence of inefficient and ineffective management also serve as warning signals to potential trouble. Those concerned with a firm's viability should be on the alert if it is known that management lacks training or experience in basic business methods, such as interpreting financial data, managing funds, scheduling production and shipping, coordinating departmental activities, and any other management functions. In a common situation, a manager may be an expert in a technical field, such as designing, but have little managerial ability for directing the activities of the business.

Indications that management is ineffective and that trouble may result include the presence of any of the following: inefficient and inadequate information systems, disregard for operating and financial data supplied, lack of interest in maintaining an adequate sales volume, large fixed charges resulting from excessive overhead and operating expenses or large debt in the capital structure, or illogical pricing schemes. Other conditions pointing to inefficient management certainly are possible, and all such factors should alert those interested to the possible existence of later trouble.

§ 2.24 Importance of Forecasts

The debtor's accountant can assist in the detection of financial failure tendencies by preparing, or in some cases reviewing, for management the forecasts and projections of operations and cash flow for the next accounting period. These forecasts often highlight problems at a very early point in time, which permits corrective action to be taken. Forecasts, if prepared realistically, should answer these questions for management:

- Can the profit objective be achieved?
- What areas of cost and expenses will create a drag on profitability and should be watched?
- Are financial resources adequate?

It is also important that interim financial statements be prepared, in a meaningful manner, and that the company have year-end certified audits.

§ 2.25 Other Factors

The following events may also indicate to the accountant that financial difficulties are imminent:

- Factoring or financing receivables, if they are normally handled on an open account basis
- Compromise of the amount of accounts receivable for the purpose of receiving advance collections
- Substitution of notes for open accounts payable
- Allowing certain key creditors to obtain security interests in the assets
- Inability of the firm to make timely deposits of trust funds such as employee withholding taxes
- Death or departure of key personnel
- Unfavorable purchase commitments
- Lack of realization of material research and development costs
- Change in accounting methods by client, primarily designed to improve the financial statements

PART TWO

Legal Aspects of Bankruptcy and Insolvency Proceedings

3

Turnaround Process

STAGES OF TURNAROUND PROCESS

This chapter begins with the stages that are necessary to turn a business around and with the characteristics of an effective turnaround manager.

§ 3.1 Stage 1: Management Change

The objectives of the management change stage are to put in place a top management team that will lead the turnaround and to replace any top management members who will hinder the turnaround effort. Studies suggest that in most turnaround situations, top management is replaced, and that in most successful turnarounds, top management was generally replaced with outsiders rather than insiders. Bibeault suggests that in 90 percent of successful turnarounds, where the downturn was caused by internal problems, top management was replaced with outsiders.[1]

Leadership changes are made for both symbolic and substantive reasons. Replacing managers has stimulated change by unfreezing current attitudes, breaking mindsets conditioned by the industry, removing concentrations of power, and providing a new view of the business and its problems.[2] Replacing leadership may in fact create the level of stress or tension needed to stimulate change. Because a majority of business failures and the need for business turnaround are related to poor management, there are obviously substantive reasons for leadership change.

Many writers suggest that the turnaround leader should be both a turnaround professional and an individual with industry experience, or at least operating experience. However, Hoffman notes that around 75 percent of the turnarounds are handled by growth-oriented and entrepreneurial managers rather than turnaround specialists.[3]

Efforts are made in some cases to select a high-profile CEO to serve as the leader of the turnaround. A leader with a good reputation in turning around troubled business helps instill both creditor and management confidence in

---

[1] Bibeault, *Corporate Turnaround: How Managers Turn Losers into Winners* (New York: McGraw-Hill, 1982).
[2] Richard C. Hoffman, "Strategies for Corporate Turnarounds: What Do We Know About Them?," *Journal of General Management* (Spring 1989), p. 59.
[3] *Id.*

the process, especially at the beginning. It may also provide for a longer "honeymoon" period. However, in the final analysis, the success will depend on many factors, including the leadership actually provided by the CEO.

(a) Replacing Existing Management

Often the creditors will insist that there be a change in management before they will work with the debtor out of court or in a chapter 11 case. A management change might take the form of replacing existing top management with new management experienced in the debtor's type of operations. However, in many out-of-court situations, a workout specialist is engaged to locate the debtor's problems and see that the business is preserved. Once operations are profitable, the workout specialist moves on to another troubled company. These individuals are generally given the freedom to run the companies they take over as they see fit. Managers perceived as being competent and those the specialist feels comfortable working with will be retained. The other managers are let go. Compensation paid these specialists will vary; some want, in addition to a salary, a stake in the ownership or other forms of bonuses if their efforts prove successful. These workout specialists, in addition to running the business, work with the creditors' committee in developing the plan of settlement. The key management positions in the company are staffed under the direction of the specialist so that, once the operations are again profitable, the workout specialist can move on. If the companies involved are relatively small, the workout specialist may be supervising the operations of several businesses at one time. These specialists are also the same individuals who specialize in managing companies in bankruptcy.

(b) Replacing Board Members

Members of the board of directors who do not actively participate or who, for various reasons, are not contributing members should be replaced. The majority of the board should be outsiders. Individuals who are insightful, studious, and fair, and who have some understanding about the business, should be invited to join the board of directors.[4] Appointments for which a conflict of interest might arise should be avoided. As a general rule, the turnaround leader should avoid making reciprocity appointments.

§ 3.2 Stage 2: Situation Analysis

The objectives of the second stage are to determine that the "bleeding" can be stopped and that the business is viable; to identify the most appropriate turnaround strategy; and to develop a preliminary action plan for implementation.

(a) Nature of Turnaround Situation

The turnaround situation can vary from one where the problems are just beginning and the impact has not been fully recognized to situations where the

---

[4] Frederick M. Zimmerman, *The Turnaround Experience* (New York: McGraw-Hill, 1991), p. 278.

business is in danger of complete failure. The sooner action is taken—often with the appointment of a specialist to turn the business around or the selection of a consultant to work with the debtor—the greater the possibility of a successful turnaround. Broad categories of the situations a turnaround leader may face may be described as follows:

- *Declining business*—decreasing market share, operating and gross margins, market leadership, product quality, and so on.
- *Substantial or continuing losses*—but survival not threatened.
- *Danger of failure.* The company may already be in chapter 11 or on the verge of filing.

Unless immediate and appropriate action is taken, liquidation is the only alternative. The situation that the business is in will impact the nature, as well as the speed, of the actions needed to stabilize the business and begin the process of turning it around.

(b) Preliminary Viability Analysis

One of the first roles of the turnaround leader is to make a preliminary assessment of the viability of the business. The factors considered in the assessment include:

- *An identification of the business unit or units that appear to be viable*—business units that have a potential for profitable future operations. These units, which serve as the core for the turnaround, may not always be the original core of the business. In the study by Bibeault,[5] only two-thirds of the cores that appeared to be the viable part of the businesses were the founding businesses.
- *The availability of interim financing*—financing needed during the turnaround period. The turnaround leader must determine if there is support from existing lenders and if funds are available from other credit sources.
- *The adequacy of organizational resources.* This determination may involve a preliminary and broad assessment of the strengths and weaknesses of the business.

See 3.1 of Volume 2, *Bankruptcy and Insolvency Accounting,* for an example of the type of analysis that might be completed during the first few weeks of the assignment.

(c) Strategic and Operating Turnarounds

Some turnaround approaches deal with strategic areas that need to be considered, such as diversification, divestment, expanding to new markets, and vertical integration. Operating turnarounds deal with operating efficiency, plant expenditures, product quality, and so forth. Dividing turnarounds

---

[5] Bibeault, *supra* note 1, p. 207.

between these major categories is questionable for two basic reasons. First, only a small percentage of turnarounds might be defined as basic strategic turnarounds. For example, the strategic approach is not applicable to most mature businesses that are in financial difficulty. Second, in most cases some combination of both strategic and operational approaches must be considered. For example, a determination that 60 percent of the existing product line should be eliminated might free more capacity and require a strategic decision as to whether it would be profitable to expand sales into another region or country.

(d) Detailed Viability Analysis: Strengths and Weaknesses

Determining the strengths and weaknesses of the company may appear to be a very simple task, but in fact it needs careful analysis. The answer, according to Drucker,[6] is usually anything but obvious. The evaluation should include an analysis of at least some of the following:

- Organizational structure
- Market capability
- Production capabilities
- Engineering and research and development
- Administration

(i) Organizational Structure   Focusing on the questions listed here will help in analysis of the organizational structure:

- What is the present structure?
- Does this structure lend itself to the creation of new operating divisions and profit centers?
- Is there sufficient depth in top management so that management of new facilities can come from within, or will it be necessary to hire from outside the firm?
- Has management policy on recruitment and development of new employees been successful?

(ii) Market Capability   In making an evaluation of the market position of the company, the following factors would be considered:

- In what market (both geographical and product) has the firm been involved in the last three years or so? Is there a pattern of success and failure?
- What market share has the company had in the last three to five years?
- What new products have been introduced (especially during the last three years)?
- What promotional activities are used or have been used by the firm in the last three years?

[6] Peter F. Drucker, *The Practice of Management* (New York: Harper & Row, 1959), p. 49.

- What channels of distribution are used or have been used by the firm in the last three years?

To effectively evaluate the market capability, the turnaround leader needs to know historical information regarding the items mentioned, reasons for change in market share, and the assumptions that are being made about future size of market, product trends, and likely competitive moves.[7]

Once the market position has been assessed, Bibeault[8] suggests that effectiveness in the marketing area be evaluated. Two key sources of information for this evaluation come from observing people in the organization and from reviewing their responses to information requests. The evaluation should, at a minimum, include answers to the following questions:

- Does management acknowledge the primacy of the marketplace and of customer needs in shaping company plans and operations?
- Does marketing management generate innovative strategies and plans for long-run growth and profitability?
- Is the marketing organization staffed and integrated so that it will be able to carry out marketing analysis, planning, implementation, and control?
- Are marketing plans implemented in a cost-effective manner, and are the results monitored for rapid corrective action?
- To monitor results, does management receive the kind and quality of information needed to conduct effective marketing?

It is also helpful to make several customer calls to determine the customers' attitudes and opinions about the company's performance. Selected calls to major customers that are dissatisfied with the company's performance can, in addition to revealing more about customers' attitudes toward the company, have a major impact on the attitudes of the employees toward customers.

(iii) Production Capabilities   Information about the production facilities might be collected by looking at the following questions:

- What types of production processes have been used in the past?
- How modern are the production facilities?
- Where are the facilities located?
- Does surplus capacity exist in the firm?
- What technical skills do the workers possess? Can these skills be applied to other products?
- Are labor relations favorable?

Assessments in the short run should be made in at least three areas:

1 *Manufacturing cost*—Is the cost to manufacture in line with competition?

---

[7] Bibeault, *supra* note 1, p. 222.
[8] *Id.*, pp. 222–23.

2 *Short-term replacement*—Are there facilities that must be replaced for the business to continue in the short term?

3 *Facilities available for disposal*—Are there facilities that can be sold in the short run to generate additional cash?

(iv) Engineering and Research and Development Businesses must be assessed in terms of their technological capabilities. Hofer[9] suggests that the following dimensions be evaluated:

- Basic research and development on new product concepts
- Major product improvements
- Product modifications
- Process improvements

Each of these dimensions should be assessed in terms of whether the company is a leader, a follower, or not involved. The assessments should be checked against the product/market segment evolution in which the firm finds itself. For example, has the firm properly planned for new products or product improvements when they are available, or are plans for new products inconsistent with research and development policy? From the production perspective, will the capacity be available to make new products, or are there plans to increase the capacity?

(v) Administration

- Is management given the information it needs?
- Could the present administration handle a major acquisition?
- Are the lines of communication well defined and operational?
- Does the company have a data processing system that is able to handle present needs?
- What changes would be necessary to handle additional requirements?

This list is not intended to be all-encompassing, as each business in financial difficulty will have differing requirements. The important point is that questions such as these must be answered before making decisions about the direction the company should take as it completes reorganization and moves ahead.

(e) Detailed Viability Analysis: Environment and Competitive Ability Assessment of Environmental Forces

In analyzing the environment, issues such as the following must be studied and answered.

1 *The market*—What is total demand? Is it increasing? Is it decreasing?

2 *The customers*—What are their needs, expectations, values, and resources?

---

[9] Charles W. Hofer, "Turnaround Strategies," *Journal of Business Strategy* (Summer 1980), p. 23.

3 *The competition*—Who? Where? What are their strengths and limitations?

4 *Suppliers*—Are they there? For example, sugar beet factories in Maine went bankrupt in part because farmers did not plant enough beets.

5 *The industry*—Is there surplus capacity? A shortage of capacity? What is the distribution system?

6 *Capital market*—How and at what costs and conditions can capital be raised?

7 *Government and society*—What demands are society and government making on the firm?

The current answers to these questions can be obtained from historical data. However, trying to answer these same questions in terms of the situation five to ten years from now is extremely difficult. The techniques now used for forecasting environmental factors are extremely weak and thus not highly reliable or accurate. However, it is generally conceded that it is better to have a somewhat inaccurate prediction of the future environment than no prediction at all. See 3.2 of Volume 2, *Bankruptcy and Insolvency Accounting*, for an example of a situation analysis checklist. The checklist covers in-depth situation analysis of general operational review, review of assets and liabilities, environmental and land-use information, creditor composition, financial structure, profit analysis, and much more.

In terms of competitive ability:

- Does the firm know what its actual competition is?
- Has past forecasting of the competitors' likely market strategies been accurate? How quickly has the firm been able to react to unexpected moves by competitors?

There are several sources the accountant might use to assist the debtor in developing the business plan. One approach receiving considerable attention is the competitive strategy framework developed by Porter,[10] which concentrates on the analysis of five competitive forces that drive industry structure:

1 Threat of new entrants
2 Threat of substitute products
3 Bargaining power of buyers
4 Bargaining power of suppliers
5 Rivalry among current competitors

In analyzing the competitive ability of the company, it is necessary to first understand the industry structure and the company's competitive position in that industry. After the structure and competitive position have been assessed, Porter suggests that the focus shift to converting this knowledge into competitive advantage. Porter defines *competitive advantage* as follows:

---

[10] Michael E. Porter, *Competitive Advantage* (New York: Free Press, 1985), p. 5.

Competitive advantage grows out of value a firm is able to create for its buyers that exceeds the firm's cost of creating it. Value is what buyers are willing to pay, and superior value stems from offering lower prices than competitors for equivalent benefits or providing unique benefits that more than offset a higher price. There are two basic types of competitive advantage: cost leadership and differentiation.[11]

As noted part of the environmental analysis involves evaluating competitors or peer groups. See 3.3 of Volume 2, *Bankruptcy and Insolvency Accounting*, for an example of a peer group analysis.

(f) Overall Viability Assessment

In summary, the ability of the debtor to survive will be determined through the process of developing or attempting to develop a business plan. This decision might be expressed in terms of the factors that determine the viability of the business, including:

- Industry in which debtor operates
- Debtor's position in the industry
- Debtor's management
- Debtor's cost structure
- Debtor's capital structure

§ 3.3 Stage 3: Design and Selection of Turnaround Strategy

After an analysis has been made of the business, a strategy to turn the business around must be developed. The elements of an effective strategic plan are:

- Specific goals and objectives
- Sound corporate and business strategies
- Detailed functional action plans

(a) Types of Turnaround Strategies—Operating

Operating strategies generally focus on revenue increases, cost reduction, asset reduction and redeployment, and competitive repositioning strategies. It may be that a combination of strategies is needed to effectively turn the business around.

(i) Revenue-Increasing Strategies
In a typical revenue-increasing strategy, the focus is on existing product lines. However, existing product lines may be supplemented by products that have been temporarily discontinued, provided these products can be reintroduced quickly and will be profitable. Existing products that might be discontinued in the long run may continue to be produced if they will increase short-term utilization of facilities and add to short-term cash flow. Special efforts are made to stimulate existing sales, often

---

[11] *Id.* at 3.

through price reduction, increased advertising, and increased direct sales effort. Under this strategy, there is generally a low ratio of research and development to sales, these costs often being reduced in the short run. Although very little focus is placed on long-term strategies during this stage, it is critical that the skills and resources needed to implement long-term goals be identified. Action taken in the short run should not negatively affect these resources or the long-term strategy of the company.

(ii) Cost-Reduction Strategies   Hofer[12] suggests that firms that are close to their current breakeven point, with high fixed costs, high labor costs, or limited financial resources, may find it necessary to focus on cost-reduction strategies. Often moderately large short-term decreases in cost are possible. Cost-reduction strategies usually produce results more quickly than revenue-increasing or asset-reduction strategies.

(iii) Asset-Reduction and Redeployment Strategies   If current sales are less than a third of breakeven sales, Hofer[13] concludes that the only viable option in most cases is a program of asset reductions. Decisions must be made as to which assets to sell and which assets to keep. Unless liquidation is imminent, sales over a period of time will generate more cash than forced sales.

(iv) Competitive Repositioning Strategies   In some turnaround situations, the company, for various reasons, has lost its competitive position. For the turnaround to be successful, that competitive position must be reestablished. Zimmerman[14] indicates that one characteristic of most successful turnarounds has been product differentiation. Companies that no longer have a product that is different from their competitors' will have difficulty surviving. The reestablishment of the product differentiation, by redeveloping features that make the product different, improving reliability and performance, or improving product quality, will help the company regain its competitive position.

(v) Combination Strategies   When a company's current sales are between 50 to 80 percent of breakeven sales, a combination of strategies may be used.[15] Under the combination approach, a balance between other strategies, such as revenue increases, cost reduction, and asset reduction, may be achieved as the strategies are pursued simultaneously. For example, while measures to increase revenue are being considered, costs that do not add value to operations may be eliminated; an asset-reduction strategy implemented in conjunction with reduction of costs may result in a substantial improvement in cash flow.

As a general rule, a combination of strategies, effectively implemented, will result in a cash flow greater than would be generated by the adoption of only one strategy. However, there is one major problem in the adoption of a combination strategy: it may be more difficult to implement action under a combi-

[12] Hofer, *supra* note 9, p. 25.
[13] *Id.*, p. 27.
[14] Frederick M. Zimmerman, "Managing a Successful Turnaround," *Long Range Planning*, Vol. 22 (June 1989), p. 117.
[15] Hofer, *supra* note 9, p. 28.

nation strategy. It is better to focus on only one strategy when it is obvious that a single clear and pervasive goal (such as increasing revenue or reducing costs) will better motivate and guide organizational action. One major problem often faced by companies in financial difficulty is inability to focus on important tasks. Under the adoption of a combination of strategies, according to Hofer,[16] a number of individuals will focus on relatively unproductive tasks because of the absence of a single, clear-cut goal.

(b) Establishment of Framework for Integration of Strategy into Business Plan

Often a company does not have any type of business or strategic plan at the time it attempts to work out an arrangement with creditors out of court or in a chapter 11 proceeding. Up until the date the petition is filed, management has devoted most of its time to day-to-day problems and has not analyzed the major financial problems faced by the business. Management has failed to ask questions that are most important for the survival of the business, such as:

- What products are most profitable?
- What are the strengths and weaknesses of the company?
- What areas should be expanded? liquidated?
- In what areas does the real potential for this business lie?
- What direction should this business take?

The greater the financial problems, the more time management tends to devote to day-to-day details; thus, almost no time is spent on providing direction for the company. After the petition is filed, it is then frequently left to the bankruptcy court and the creditors to make strategic decisions that significantly influence the future of the business. They may decide which operations to eliminate and which products to discontinue. These decisions are made on a quasi-intuitive basis. For example, selected equipment may be sold or retained based on the influence of particular creditors rather than on the basis of an overall business plan.

To effectively turn the business around, it is necessary that the debtor develop a business plan. Once the business plan has been developed, it will serve as the basis for the development of a reorganization plan and will facilitate the process of obtaining creditor approval of the steps the turnaround leader wants to take. It is difficult to develop a viable reorganization plan without having developed a business plan first.

In rendering advisory services to help develop a business plan, the accountant examines all the available information, analyzes it (taking future prospects into consideration), and develops recommendations. These recommendations may involve closing unprofitable units, replacing poor management, changing the information system, and revising the marketing approach. Some of the recommendations are implemented while the company is in chapter 11 proceedings and the effect is known immediately (e.g., closing some

---

[16] *Id.*

unprofitable operating units). Other strategic actions have very long-range effects, but still have an impact on the nature of the company as it comes out of the proceedings. A business plan allows all interested parties to have a better idea of what parts of the operations are salvageable and provides for better understanding of the plan proposed by the debtor.

The analysis required to make reasonable recommendations must involve an assessment of the environmental forces (past, present, and future) influencing the business and an evaluation of the strengths and weaknesses of the company.

§ 3.4   Stage 4: Emergency Action Stage

Once a strategy or combination of strategies has been carefully selected, immediate action must be taken to start the process of turning the business around. The objectives of the emergency action stage are to:

- Take whatever actions are necessary to enable the organization to survive.
- Establish a positive operating cash flow as quickly as possible.
- Raise sufficient cash to implement the chosen turnaround strategy.
- Protect and develop the resources that will be needed for future profitability and growth.

(a) Taking Charge

The nature of the action that the turnaround leader takes will depend on the seriousness of the problems. The more serious the problems, the quicker and more decisive the action that must be taken.

One aspect of taking charge is to get the attention of both management and employees. There are several ways to achieve this. In smaller companies, it often begins with a meeting of all the employees. In larger companies, it may be a meeting with upper management and a video presentation to the rest of the employees. At this meeting, it must be established that the turnaround leader is in charge. On a video that was distributed to NCR employees, Bibeault relates the following comments made by William Anderson: "Complacency and apathy—these are NCR's greatest sins. Until we return to profitability, something akin to martial law will be in effect in Dayton."[17] Various styles are used by turnaround leaders. Some leaders think this is necessary to shock the system, sometimes in the form of a sacrificial lamb (e.g., terminate one executive to establish a tough policy). Others prefer to move gradually, establish policy and guidelines, and deal swiftly and forcefully with those who violate the guidelines.[18] Most writers suggest that the turnaround leader must be more authoritarian than in most businesses, especially at the beginning of the turnaround process.

Bibeault[19] indicates that it is important for the turnaround leader to serve as a model of tough self-discipline, placing emphasis on businesslike, neat, and

---

[17] Bibeault, *supra* note 1, p. 167.
[18] *Id.*, p. 168.
[19] *Id.*, p. 166.

orderly activity in every respect. Often turnaround leaders take selected actions immediately to get the attention of the managers and staff. Designed to set the stage for change, these opening moves are reversible, do not necessarily relate to the core problems, and may not actually contribute a lot to the bottom line. Examples of opening moves include:

- Elimination or reduction of temporary help
- Restrictions on hiring
- Elimination of all first-class air travel
- Limitations on travel (may require CEO approval of all foreign travel)
- Limitations on redecoration of offices and other facilities
- Requirement of top management approval of all capital expenditures above a dollar limit
- Restrictions on entertainment and similar expenses

(b) Control of Cash and Cash Flows

Critical to the turnaround process is control of cash inflows and outflows and the elimination of negative cash flows from operations. Action must be taken immediately to ascertain the principal reasons for poor cash flows and to correct the problem as swiftly as possible. As noted earlier, an important part of the stabilization process is to eliminate the "bleeding" of the firm's liquidity. Once the cash flows are stabilized, the turnaround leader must monitor the cash flows on a daily basis. There are several approaches to monitoring cash flows, including daily reports of cash inflows and outflows. Detailed weekly cash flow reports should also be prepared. Larger companies should have a centralized cash management system. The turnaround leader may want to see daily reports providing information critical to cash management. The nature as well as the type of report will depend on several factors, including the industry and type of company (service, manufacturing, etc.). For example, the turnaround leader might want to see daily reports on collections and goods shipped.

Often, when a turnaround leader takes control of the business, the information that has been given to creditors has been questionable. They have very little confidence in financial statements, especially cash flow projections, and other promises that were made previously by the company. One of the first objectives is to reestablish confidence in the debtor's operations and in the information given to creditors. One way to help develop this confidence is to prepare three to four months of cash flow projections. Then every possible effort should be made to meet those projections. If the projections are met, then the creditors will begin to develop renewed confidence in the company.

See 3.4 of Volume 2, *Bankruptcy and Insolvency Accounting*, for an example of a cash flow analysis. The objectives of the cash flow analysis is to identify the potential for a future cash crisis, to evaluate the adequacy of cash flows for meeting a company's needs and plans and to evaluate and measure such items as financial performance, profitability, liquidity and adequacy of current and projected cash flows. Since cash flow analysis is involved in almost all aspects of a the turnaround process, this analysis goes beyond the emergency action stage.

(c) Financial Management

The financial officer assists in turning the business around by contributing to the following areas.

(i) Debt Restructuring   In almost all turnaround situations, there must be some type of debt restructuring. For a discussion of some of the issues associated with debt restructuring, see the subsequent sections on "debtor-in-possession financing" and "postconfirmation financing." Cost reduction, sale of assets, and other measures may represent a source of repayment of part of the debt.

(ii) Working Capital Improvements   As companies grow, the working capital needs often increase faster than increases in total revenue. Special analysis should be made of areas that might improve working capital, such as reduction in inventory and more effective collection of receivables (in many turnaround situations, the average collection period is too long). It is critical to look at the underlying causes of the unfavorable impact on working capital. For example, a delay in the collection of receivables may be caused by failure to mail invoices on a timely basis and/or by failure to deliver the goods on a timely basis. Customers receiving late deliveries might delay payment to see if the goods can be sold (and if not sold, they will be returned). Thus, it is critical to find and correct the underlying cause of the delay in remittance before any significant improvement can be made. There are many examples where a more aggressive approach to collections has resulted in a major decrease in the collection period.

The growth in working capital should be compared to the growth in sales. Any future planning should relate additional working capital requirements to increases in sales. Working capital can be significantly improved by increasing the inventory turnover period. Zimmerman[20] noted that inventory turnovers were approximately one-third higher in the successful turnarounds than in the unsuccessful firms he studied. Zimmerman pointed out that it was during the period of turnaround that the successful firms learned how to handle inventory much more effectively.

(iii) Cost Reduction Analysis   Zimmerman[21] concluded that the three key factors in successful turnarounds are low cost operation, product differentiation, and appropriate turnaround leadership. Consequently, a lot of focus must be placed on cost reduction. In examining the successful turnarounds in the agricultural equipment and automotive industries, Zimmerman noted that successful firms focus on reducing cost relative to present revenue levels to increase profitability, not on increased revenue. In other words, it is important to bring existing operations in line with proper cost-to-revenue ratio, rather than attempting to improve this ratio by increasing revenue. To become a low-cost producer, a company should focus on at least three major areas:

1   *Operational efficiency*—According to Zimmerman,[22] the following are practical lessons on operational efficiency:

---

[20] Zimmerman, *supra* note 14, p. 107.
[21] Zimmerman, *supra* note 4, pp. 12–14.
[22] *Id.*, p. 57.

- Successful firms concentrate on efficiency first, products second, and then on marketing and sales. Revenue expansion based on inefficient operations results in severe operating losses.
- Successful companies reduce cost relative to present revenue levels. Unsuccessful companies attempt to increase revenue to cover existing costs.
- Successful companies implement proven efficiencies immediately, but work through people.
- Successful firms achieve scale economies at the component or process level, not at the level of the overall business unit.
- Top managers who know how to achieve efficiencies in the particular industry being served are retained or recruited.
- Successful companies work productively with suppliers to reduce product cost.
- Successful managers make investments to sustain and improve efficiency, but understand processes well enough to know what really pays off.

2 *Modest overhead*—Many companies in financial difficulty spend too much on items unrelated to the product sold or services rendered. During the turnaround process, costs unrelated to the cost of goods must be reduced as a percentage of sales. The following table shows the non-cost-of-sales expense (excluding tax) as a percent of revenue for the successful and unsuccessful cases examined by Zimmerman.[23]

	Preturnaround	Crisis	Recovery
Successful cases	10.03%	15.21%	9.53%
Unsuccessful cases	7.76%	11.24%	14.01%

3 *Lowering cost through design*—The design of the delivery system should be the concern of both manufacturing and nonmanufacturing industries. In fact, the design of low-cost delivery systems for service companies is as important as it is for manufacturing. Many successful turnarounds result from the design of products that can be produced at lower costs, balanced with efficiency in manufacturing.

(iv) Profitability Analysis   The following lists several types of profitability analysis that must be considered by the turnaround leader:

- *Contribution by segment or line of business*—In determining the profit by segment (i.e., division).
- *Contribution by product line*—Product lines that do not contribute enough profit for overhead analysis should be eliminated unless changes can be made to make them profitable.

[23] *Id.*, p. 75.

- *Contribution by products*—Even if a product line is profitable, the profit might be improved significantly if some of the products in the line were eliminated. Thus, it is critical in most cases to know the profitability of each individual product. Concluding that selected products, even though they are not profitable, should be included because they are the basis for other sales should not be accepted until proof has been presented. Some companies have improved profit considerably by eliminating a large percentage (as high as 60 to 80 percent) of their products. Often 20 to 30 percent of the products will contribute around 80 percent of the profit.
- *Contribution by customer*—A calculation of the profit made on each customer can be quite revealing. In making this analysis, all costs should be considered from the time the orders are placed to the collection of the cash from the sales.

(v) Sale of Nonproducing Assets   Assets that will not be used during the near future and are not a part of the long-term plans of the company should be sold through an orderly process.

(d) Marketing Management

In many turnaround situations, the focus is on reducing sales by eliminating unprofitable markets. Some of the factors to be considered in marketing management during the emergency stage include:

- *Correcting serious pricing problems*—It is not unusual, in a turnaround situation, to see the price of selected products materially below that of competitors. Prices of these products must be increased. In other cases, the pricing error (either over- or underpricing) may be due to poor pricing strategy or theory. As noted earlier, a pricing policy that provides for an increase in volume to cover more of the fixed costs generally results in more losses. As a general rule, prices should not be reduced below the level needed to recover both variable and fixed costs. Bibeault[24] suggests that pricing products at a level where the price does not cover their share of fixed overhead is dangerous.
- *Product line pruning*—The process of adding large numbers of products to a line of products and adding large numbers of product lines is a characteristic of many companies in trouble. As noted, a complete analysis of product lines, as well as products within a product line, is necessary. Elimination of more than 50 percent of the number of products is not uncommon.
- *Weeding out weak customers and distributors*—An analysis of profitability of each customer can indicate those customers for which the price must be increased, order size changed, average number of days for account turnover materially reduced, or other improvements made. If corrective action is not feasible, then the sales to this customer should be discontinued.

[24] Bibeault, *supra* note 1, p. 285.

- *Getting sales and marketing costs in line with industry averages*—Costs of this nature that are not comparable with costs incurred by other companies in the industry should be reduced.

(e) Manufacturing/Operations Management

Some of the actions that are pursued during the emergency stage include:

- *Eliminate unprofitable operations*—Operations that will not be part of the core businesses that will survive the turnaround should be shut down.
- *Reduce the workforce*—Most troubled companies have excessive labor costs, especially in nonproduction areas. Nonessential overhead and service-type costs must be eliminated.
- *Reduce inventories*—Many companies in financial difficulty have excess inventory and inventory shortages. Excess inventory is generally found in slow-moving finished goods and in raw materials of unprofitable products. Inventory shortages often exist in fast-moving items and in critical raw materials.
- *Control purchases*—Purchase only items that are needed immediately and arrange for delivery as they are needed. Move toward establishment of a just-in-time inventory system.
- *Increase productivity*—Find improved ways to manufacture the products, including the elimination of most costs that do not add value to the final product.

(f) Engineering and Research and Development

During the emergency stage, resources available for research and development activity are obviously very limited. As a result, the focus should be on accelerating high-potential projects and shutting down tangential projects for the present. As discussed earlier, effort should be directed toward lowering cost through design.

(g) Changing the Culture

Most turnarounds will be unsuccessful unless the company's workers are also "turned around." In the effort to stabilize a business, including eliminating inefficiencies to provide for the short-term survival of the organization, the needs of its employees often are forgotten. Special effort must be made to get all employees involved in the turnaround and to fully understand how their jobs relate to the turnaround efforts. For many troubled organizations, there must be a change in the organizational culture. Some of the items that might be considered during the emergency stage include challenging and developing ways to change the status quo, rewarding those who change, and terminating those who do not adjust to changing needs.

§ 3.5 Stage 5: Business Restructuring Stage

The major objectives of the business restructuring stage are to enhance profitability through more effective and efficient management of current operations and to reconstruct the business for increased profitability and enhancement of the value of the shareholders' equity.

(a) Financial Management

During the restructuring stage, the focus is on:

- Improving liquidity, including providing enough working capital to allow the business to operate effectively—but do not let inefficient use gradually work its way back into the business.
- Restructuring the balance sheet—Work with the team that is restructuring the financial aspects of the business to develop a capital structure that will support the operations.
- Developing control systems to adequately protect the assets of the business, to evaluate operational efficiency, and to help prevent the organization from returning to its old ways of excessive overhead and the like.
- Creating a managerial accounting system (including, when appropriate, the development of an activity-based cost system) that accurately reflects the costs of products manufactured and provides relevant data to management to guide product selection and related decisions.

(b) Marketing Management

Efforts during this stage focus on:

- Reassessing product lines and competitive pricing practices
- Exploiting existing products and developing new products
- Improving the customer and distribution mix
- Improving sales and marketing productivity and effectiveness
- Improving profit per customer

(c) Manufacturing/Operations Management

Manufacturing and operations management are focused, during the restructuring stage, on:

- Developing ongoing productivity improvement programs
- Developing a cost system to effectively determine the cost of products or services and to provide the type of information that managers need to effectively perform their jobs
- Conducting overhead value analysis periodically to ensure that overhead is being effectively controlled and used
- Establishing ongoing profit improvement programs

(d) Management of Engineering and Research and Development

During the restructuring stage, the focus should be on making the new product development process market- and customer-oriented; making low-cost products and rendering services at reduced costs through design; and building an economic value-added orientation into process engineering practices.[25]

(e) People and Organizational Management

During the restructuring stage of the turnaround, a lot of attention must be focused on developing a team that is motivated and focused toward the company's objectives. Among the tasks that receive special efforts during this phase are:

- Improving the people mix of the business
- Restructuring the organization for competitive effectiveness
- Developing reward and compensation systems that reinforce the turnaround efforts and are based on improvements in shareholder value

§ 3.6 Stage 6: Return-to-Normal Stage

The focus of the return-to-normal stage is to institutionalize an emphasis on profitability and enhancement of shareholder value; that is, to build within the organization controls and attitudes that help prevent the organization from reverting to its old ways. The organization must continue to look for opportunities for profitable growth and build the competitive strengths the business needs to take advantage of such opportunities.

(a) Marketing Management

The focus in this stage is on increasing revenue growth and profit growth by exploring new markets and customer segments, examining industry restructuring opportunities, pursuing value-added chain restructuring opportunities, and considering synergistic diversification opportunities.

By the time the return-to-normal stage is reached, the promotional activities should be at a peak and the company should be positioned for continued growth.

(b) Manufacturing/Operations Management

As the company begins to return to normal, the focus on low-cost provider and product differentiation should continue. Costs that do not add value to the product should continue to be minimized if the company expects to remain competitive. The company should develop strategic alliances with selected major suppliers, continue to stress operational efficiency and the elimination of costs (tasks) that do not add value to the product, and continue to restructure the manufacturing process to effectively compete as a low-cost provider.

(c) Engineering and Research and Development

Although the focus of the company in the return-to-normal stage relating to product development and research should become more long-term, the funda-

---

[25] *Id.*, pp. 311–313.

mentals learned during the turnaround should not be ignored. The company should continue to be a lower-cost provider through product design; establish advanced technology monitoring systems to ensure that research and development activities are properly directed; seek strategic leverage in all engineering and research and development activities; and seek ways to avoid complacency.[26]

(d) Financial Management

The financial function in return to normal stage does begin to resemble that of a normal company. There are, however, several activities that are critical, including:

- Development of strategic accounting and control systems that provide timely and relevant information in both conventional and nonconventional formats, especially relating to cost of products or services
- Maintenance of the tight financial disciplines that were learned during the turnaround process
- Restructuring the business's long-term financing to maximize shareholder value

(e) People and Organizational Management

As the business begins to return to normal, the following changes should take place:

- Institutionalize continuous, ongoing employee and management development programs.
- Restructure the organization and its systems periodically to reflect changing strategies and environmental conditions. Return the organization to a less highly centralized style.
- Modify management and employee compensation plans to be at least partly based on the increase in shareholder value, and not necessarily to reflect the typical corporate forms.[27]

CHARACTERISTICS OF EFFECTIVE TURNAROUND MANAGERS

Most writers in the area of turnaround management agree that it is difficult to generalize about the characteristics of a "typical" turnaround leader. This section describes some of the qualities most often observed in turnarounds.

§ 3.7 Organizational Leader

Good turnaround leaders usually evince:

- *Personal leadership ability.* The extent to which the turnaround professional is a leader may be more important than having a particular style.

---

[26] *Id.*, p. 312.
[27] *Id.*, pp. 327–32.

The leader's ability and personal style contribute more to company performance, character, and tone during a turnaround than at any other time
in corporate life.[28] Andrews notes that business leaders generally are
characterized by drive, intellectual ability, initiative, creativity, social
ability, and flexibility.[29] He further concludes that these qualities permit
a fairly wide range of style so long as the style is dynamic and energetic.

- *Self-confidence.*[30]
- *The ability to attract good people*—may be more inclined to be "people
  users" rather than "people-oriented."
- *Toughness and competitiveness.* The turnaround manager was described
  by Bibeault[31] as "[t]he tough-minded man who demands facts, a blueprint
  for action, and realistic controls, yet is impatient to get something done."
- *Enormous energy to drive the organization and themselves to task completion.*
- *The chemistry and charisma that builds and links the team of managers
  together.*

§ 3.8   Ability to Develop and Implement Strategy

Not only must turnaround leaders be designers of strategy, but, according to
Bibeault,[32] most importantly they must also be implementers of strategy. They
must supply organizational strategy, promote and defend it, integrate the conflicting interests that arise around it, see to it that the essential needs of the
company are met, and judge the results.

§ 3.9   Entrepreneurial Instincts

Entrepreneurial skills are needed by the turnaround manager in almost
every part of the process to devise, search out, and seize opportunities. According to Bibeault,[33] entrepreneurial instinct, along with good professional management skills, is one of the most critical characteristics of an effective leader.

§ 3.10   "Hands-On" Operating Experience

Most turnaround situations require the leader to have hands-on experience.
The professionals involved must have had operating responsibilities at some
point in their careers. Evidence tends to support the belief that successful turnarounds are often led by individuals with extensive experience in the industry.
For example, Zimmerman[34] notes that an examination of eight successful
turnarounds in the agricultural equipment and automotive industries found
that six were headed by individuals with manufacturing background. The sev-

---

[28] *Id.,* p. 150.
[29] Kenneth Andrews, *The Concept of Corporate Strategy* (Homewood, IL: Dow-Jones-Irwin, 1971),
p. 236.
[30] Bibeault, *supra* note 1, p. 150.
[31] *Id.,* p. 151.
[32] *Id.,* p. 149.
[33] *Id.,* pp. 153–54.
[34] Zimmerman, *supra* note 14, p. 115.

enth company, Chrysler, was headed by Iacocca, who had an initial background in engineering. The eighth turnaround, that of Deere & Co., was also led by an engineer with extensive product experience. Most of the unsuccessful cases were headed by individuals with sales or financial background.

§ 3.11   Effective Negotiating Skills

The ability to negotiate is another critical attribute of turnaround professionals. Skill in this area is needed to deal with, among others:

- Existing creditors
- New lenders
- Suppliers
- Labor unions
- New investors, including merger partners or acquirers

At times, major negotiations will be undertaken before the turnaround professional will accept the assignment. Bibeault[35] reports that, prior to accepting the position as CEO of Memorex, Robert Wilson (with the help of a colleague) negotiated the following:

- Required Bank of America and other banks to convert $40 million of $150 million in debt to equity
- Lowered the interest rate to 4 percent on the balance owed to banks and extended the payment schedule
- Obtained a new line of credit from Bank of America of $35 million

§ 3.12   Good Interviewing Skills

Most companies that are in trouble have inadequate information systems. Thus, to ascertain what is really happening within the company, the turnaround professional must have excellent interviewing skills.

§ 3.13   Action Orientation

Many effective turnaround managers enter the process with lots of enthusiasm and action orientation that help motivate other individuals involved. They must be able to build a team and have the chemistry and charisma to bind the team together. Bibeault[36] suggests that the renowned football coach, Vince Lombardi, was a great turnaround professional. Although they bring lots of energy into the situation, turnaround professionals often become restless after the business has been turned around. Some turnaround managers attempt to stay with the company and build it up, but additional turnaround opportunities often have a magnetic appeal for them.[37]

---

[35] Bibeault, *supra* note 1, p. 155.
[36] *Id.*, p. 153.
[37] *Id.*, p. 161.

§ 3.14 Trustworthiness and Fairness

Zimmerman[38] notes that, although evidence is difficult to obtain, there is some support for the opinion that successful turnarounds exhibit greater fairness than unsuccessful turnarounds in dealing with employees, creditors, stockholders, and customers. In his conclusion, Zimmerman states:

> Most of the successful turnaround people were from rather humble origins. They were not attracted to high salaries or fancy offices or heavy involvement in high society. They didn't drink very much and they enjoyed wholesome personal reputations. They worked hard, knew their jobs and fostered an atmosphere of trust. They tended to appreciate the contribution of others—even those who may have been a part of the company when the problems began. The successful turnaround agents allowed others in the organization to be recognized. It takes more than one person to turn a company around. The successful chief turnaround agents were people who could share center stage.[39]

TECHNIQUES USED IN BUSINESS TURNAROUNDS

§ 3.15 Introduction

Accountants, financial advisors, and turnaround specialists must be aware of and adapt to the major changes occurring in the manufacturing and non-manufacturing environments. The objective of this section is to discuss a few of the basic developments, including just-in-time, activity-based costing, retail store "four-walls" analysis, and business process reengineering.

§ 3.16 Just-In-Time

Just-in-time (JIT) is the philosophy that activities are undertaken only as needed or demanded. Foster and Horngren have identified four characteristics of JIT:[40]

1 Elimination of all activities that do not add value to a product or service
2 Commitment to a high level of quality
3 Commitment to continuous improvement in the efficiency of an activity
4 Emphasis on simplification and increased visibility to identify activities that do not add value

In a cost system where JIT purchasing is adopted, Foster and Horngren[41] suggest five changes that would be realized:

---

[38] Zimmerman, *supra* note 14, p. 114.
[39] *Id.*, p. 117.
[40] George Foster and Charles T. Horngren, "JIT: Cost Accounting and Cost Management Issues," *Management Accounting*, June 1987, p. 19.
[41] *Id.*, p. 21.

1 *Increase in direct traceability of costs.* In a traditional cost system many
   of the materials handling and warehouse costs are incurred for multipur-
   pose facilities that service many product lines. Thus, these costs are
   often considered indirect costs. In a JIT environment, warehouse and
   materials handling facilities would be more decentralized, often serving
   a single retail or production area. Thus, these costs would now be direct
   costs of a retail area or production line.

2 *Changes in the cost pools used to accumulate costs.* For example, the
   pool used to allocate materials handling costs discussed above would be
   eliminated.

3 *Changes in the bases used to allocate indirect costs to production
   departments.* Under the traditional cost system, costs such as materials
   handling and warehouse costs might be allocated based on warehouse
   space. Dollar value of materials or number of deliveries may "better cap-
   ture the cause and effect relationship between purchasing/materials handling activities and indirect cost incurrance."[42]

4 *Reduced emphasis on individual purchase price variance information.*
   Companies in a JIT environment often have long-term agreements to
   achieve price reduction. Thus, there is no need to record price variance in
   the accounts. Emphasis is placed on total cost of operations. Quality and
   availability are important considerations in selecting a supplier.

5 *Need to reduce the frequency or detail of reporting of purchase deliveries in the internal accounting system.* The number of deliveries in a JIT
   environment is large. Foster and Horngren identify two ways to reduce
   entries.[43] One is to use batching and only record the aggregate of deliveries for a set time period, such as weekly. Another is to use an electronic
   transfer system where the initial purchase order (or delivery schedule)
   automatically sets up the data transfer at the delivery date and then
   transfers the funds at the payment date.

In JIT production "each component on a production line is produced immediately as needed by the next step in the production line. The production line
is run on a demand-pull basis, so that activity at each work station is authorized by the demand of downstream work stations."[44]

In a JIT environment, emphasis is placed on reducing the time it takes once
the production has started until the product leaves the production line. This is
also referred to as cycle time. If a problem develops in the manufacturing
process, such as a defective product, the production line is stopped until the
problem is corrected. No value is created by building up inventories on the other
parts of the production line. Since there is no inventory buildup on the production line, a problem discovered on the production line results in a smaller quantity to be reworked or discarded.

Companies that adopt JIT production often rearrange the layout of their
plants to provide for very little materials handling. The objective is to elimi-

---

[42] *Id.,* p. 21.
[43] *Id.,* p. 22.
[44] *Id.*

nate as much as possible of the cost of production that does not add value to the product, such as materials handling and carrying cost for inventories. The production lines are often U-shaped, where the raw materials are delivered directly to the start of the production line as they are needed. The materials move, often by the use of conveyor belts, from one station to another until the product is finished near the point where the process started. The finished products are then available for direct shipment to the customer.

In summary, a just-in-time production system allows companies to be customer oriented and minimizes non-value-added costs. Orders, not inventory size, drive the production process. Goods are not produced until they are needed for shipment to the customer. Zero inventory should be a major objective of a manufacturing firm.

§ 3.17 Activity-based Costing (ABC)

For years, manufacturing firms used direct labor hours (DLH) as the primary cost driver to apply overhead costs to products. A cost driver is the activity that causes the cost to be incurred. In today's manufacturing process, a single firm produces hundreds or thousands of products. With plants becoming highly automated, direct labor is no longer an adequate cost driver. Direct labor was realistic when labor cost accounted for the majority of the production costs. Currently, labor cost is often less than 10 percent of the total manufacturing cost. Even machine-hours and raw material content, when applied to all parts of the factory, are too simplistic.

To better control cost, many firms have adopted activity-based costing (ABC). Activity-based costing has been designed for firms that manufacture numerous products and want accurate product costing. The emphasis of ABC is to trace the overhead cost to the product that benefited for the cost. Johnson and Kaplan identify activity-based costing as a two-step process.[45] The first step requires tracing costs according to their activities, dividing them into homogeneous pools, and determining appropriate cost drivers. Following are some examples:

Activity	Cost Driver
Material handling	Number of components
Purchasing raw materials	Quality of materials used in production
Packing and shipping	Number of orders
Special works	Number of new products

The second step requires applying the costs of these activities to the product by calculating a rate for the cost driver for each pool. To illustrate the second step, assume the Packaging Department uses the number of orders processed as a cost driver and that $100,000 was spent for 10,000 orders being processed. The pool rate would be $10 per order processed ($100,000/10,000). Similar calculations would be made for other overhead costs using appropriate cost drivers.

---

[45] H. Thomas Johnson and Robert S. Kaplan, *Relevance Lost: The Rise and Fall of Management Accounting* (Boston: Harvard Business School Press, 1987), p. 238.

To contrast activity-based costing with direct labor cost allocation, assume that Oaks Publishing Corporation publishes three books: *Urban Farming, Exercising for Fun,* and *How to Be Your Own Boss.* The following data have been accumulated for each product to estimate setup costs:

	Urban Farming	Exercising for Fun	How to Be Your Own Boss
Units produced	2,000	40,000	100,000
Typical batch size	200	1,000	20,000
Number of setups	10	40	5
Total direct labor hours	400	8,000	18,000
Urban Farming (10 × $300)	$ 3,000		
Exercising for Fun (40 × $300)	12,000		
How to Be Your Own Boss (5 × $300)	1,500		
Setup costs	$16,500		

In this example, direct labor hours for all three books totals 28,400 hours; therefore, using direct labor hours as the cost driver results in each unit printed being assigned setup costs at the rate of $.625 direct labor ($16,500/26,400 DLH). Using ABC, the setup cost per unit for each book varies from $.015 to $1.50 per unit:

	Urban Farming	Exercising for Fun	How to Be Your Own Boss
Total setup cost (a)	$3,000	$12,000	$1,500
Units produced (b)	2,000	40,000	100,000
Cost per unit (a/b)	$1.50	$.30	$.015

A comparison between total setup costs for the two cost drivers is shown below:

	DLH	ABC
Urban Farming:		
400 DLH @ $.625	$250	
10 setups @ $300		$3,000
Exercising for Fun:		
8,000 KLH @ $.625	5,000	
40 setups @ $300		12,000
How to Be Your Own Boss		
18,000 DLH @ $.116	11,250	
5 setups @ $300		1,500
	$16,500	$16,500

Activity-based costing is an effective approach to properly assigning cost and it is not limited to manufacturing overhead. Administrative expenses also can be allocated to the product using this approach. Activity-based costing may help management focus on costs that don't add value.

For example, purchasing could have some of its costs allocated to the product based on the number of unusual parts ordered. This would encourage more standardization of parts. A car manufacturer's engineering department might be influenced to redesign the air filter space so that fewer filter configurations would have to be purchased, if the cost of storage is traced and attached to engineering.

Activity-based costing, like other methods, has its strengths and weaknesses. Kaplan, in defending ABC, wrote, "ABC systems provide valuable economic information to companies, especially companies active in process improvement and customer satisfaction."[46] He added,

> ABC models provide an economic model of the organization that enables managers to set priorities, make tradeoffs, determine the extent of the investment they are willing to undertake for improvements, and, at the end of the day . . . learn whether these programs have increased profits.[47]

In an article criticizing the overselling of ABC, Johnson conceded that ABC succeeded in increasing profits and reducing cost. However, he concluded that ABC failed to make businesses more responsive to their customers, especially in light of what the global competition was doing.[48] In his concluding comments, he summarized his thoughts:

> Activity-based cost drivers information overcomes distortions inherent in traditional cost accounting information. . . . Activity-based information, however, does not help companies achieve continuous improvement of globally competitive operations.[49]

(a) Major Trends

Howell and Soucy identify six major trends that are taking place among leading U.S. manufacturers:[50]

1 *Higher quality*—Foreign competitors have provided markets with higher-quality goods at competitive prices than U.S. manufacturers. U.S. companies have also realized that poor quality is a significant cost driver. For example, poor-quality materials, the lack of highly trained employees, and the failure to properly maintain equipment have resulted in lower-quality products. At the same time, the cost to manufacture these products has been high because of the increased cost of nonquality items such as scrap, rework, excess inventories and equipment breakdowns, field service, and product warranty claims.

---

[46] Robert S. Kaplan, "In Defense of Activity-Based Cost Management," *Management Accounting*, Nov. 1992, p. 58.
[47] *Id.*
[48] H. Thomas Johnson, "It's Time to Stop Overselling Activity-Based Concepts," *Management Accounting*, September 1992, p. 33.
[49] *Id.*
[50] Robert A. Howell and Stephen Soucy, *Factory 2000+* (Montvale, NJ: Institute of Management Accounting, 1988), pp. 2–6.

2 *Lower inventory*—Inventory has been reduced because it required too much capital, encouraged inefficiencies, and failed to provide a basis for properly controlling quality.

3 *Flexible flow lines*—Flexible flow lines represent the path a product takes through the manufacturing process from the receipt of raw materials to the shipment of the product. Manufacturers are shortening cycle time. To accomplish this, all of the equipment needed in the manufacturing process is brought together (thus, large groups of similar equipment are split up) and "mini" product lines are created. This layout significantly reduces the materials handling cost and the amount of funds needed for inventory. This process allows the product to flow through the process in a very short time and reinforces quality and employee identification with the end product. With the short cycle time, customer demand then is responsible for pulling the product through the process as discussed above.

4 *Automation*—By developing flexible flow lines, the manufacturer automation, if it is cost effective, is directed toward the part of the process that adds value rather than focusing on items that do not add value such as automation of materials handling. In evaluating automation, the focus, in addition to direct cost savings, should be on improved quality, delivery service, and flexibility, reduced product development time, and improved competitive position. In fact, the manufacturer should attempt to quantify these factors in making automation decisions.

5 *Product line organization*—There should be a scaling down of centralized service departments and reassignment of people to the product lines.

6 *Efficient use of information technology*—Integrated systems are being developed that allow companies to exercise more control over the factory floor. A single database is needed that allows use for both operating control and financial reporting purposes.

(b) Updated Cost Systems

In the new manufacturing environment, the measures used in the traditional accounting system (labor utilization, standard versus actual performance, and overhead absorption) are inadequate. The cost accountant must look at key factors critical to each particular process. These factors will vary from one process to another. The reporting of key factors by the accountant will allow the workers to more efficiently manage the process for which they are responsible. Five operating measures that could serve as the basis for reporting are classified by Howell and Soucy as follows:[51]

1 Quality
2 Inventory
3 Material/scrap
4 Equipment/maintenance
5 Delivery/throughput

[51] *Id.*, pp. 15–21.

These factors along with several measures that might be used to evaluate performance are presented in Exhibit 3-1.

§ 3.18 Retail Store "Four-Wall" Analysis[52]

Another technique that is often used in the retail industry is a *four-wall analysis* of each store. The most common problems found in analyzing the operating performance of retail stores are:

- Accounting data insufficient to properly measure store level profitability; frequently, accounting systems are adequate for supporting the preparation of financial statements but are inadequate for supplying management

[52] Adapted from Maureen A. Donahoe, "Retail Store 'Four Wall' Analysis," *Proceedings 13th Annual Bankruptcy and Reorganization Conference* (Medford, OR: Association of Insolvency and Restructuring Advisors, 1997), pp. 1–10. Used by permission.

Exhibit 3-1   Operating Measures

OPERATING MEASURES IN THE NEW MANUFACTURING ENVIRONMENT

Quality	Inventory
Customers complaints	Turnover rates by location
Customer surveys	Raw materials
Warranty claims	Work-in-process
Quality audits	Finished goods
Vendor quality	Composite
Cost of quality	Turnover rates by product
Scrap	Cycle count accuracy
Rework	Space reduction
Field service	Number of inventoried items
Warranty claims	
Lost business	

Material/Scrap	Equipment/Maintenance
Quality—incoming material inspection	Equipment capacity/utilization
Material cost as a percentage of total cost	Availability/downtime
Actual scrap loss	Machine maintenance
Scrap by part/product/operation	Equipment experience
Scrap percentage of total cost	

Delivery/Throughput
On-time delivery
Order fill rate
Lead time—order to shipment
Waste time—lead time less process time
Cycle time—material receipt to product shipment
Setup time
Production backlog (in total and by product)

Source: Robert A. Howell and Stephen Soucy, *Factory 2000+* (Montvale NJ: Institute of Management Accounting, 1988), p. 21.

with useful data for running the business (financial accounting versus management accounting).

- Too many expenses allocated where ability to specifically identify exists/should exist.
- No precise criteria for defining minimum tolerable performance levels.
- Evaluation criteria frequently is inconsistent with corporate objectives as well as store operations incentive compensation arrangements; for example:

Issue	*Performance Criteria*
Store Evaluation	Earnings
Corporate Objectives	Return on Investment
Incentive Compensation Criteria	Sales

- Companies frequently fail to consider working capital requirements, cost to supervise remote locations, capital expenditure requirements, and so on.
- Focus frequently on store earnings without consideration for return or investment.

(a) Overview of Four-Wall Contribution Analysis Data Requirements

A four-wall analysis will usually include an analysis of sales and expenses. Sales is generally not difficult to determine because sales by store location are typically properly captured in the Company's accounting records. However, the expense analysis is often more difficult. Because it is desirable that the four-wall contribution approximately equate to cash flow, the calculation should exclude depreciation and other noncash items. Additionally, expenses may include certain allocations. Therefore, all expenses must be analyzed to determine if they are (1) direct, (2) assignable, or (3) allocable.

Direct expenses are those that are incurred by, or within, a specific location, without regard to whether they are controllable. These expenses should be charged directly to each individual store location. Examples of such expenses include payroll, rent (if property is leased) or debt payments (if owned), and utilities.

Expenses that can be identified with specific locations should be assigned based on workload, usage, benefit, or some other logical basis. Frequently we have found that these expenses are generally accumulated in the expense center where they are generated and not allocated. Examples of such expenses include advertising, centralized mailings, freight-in expense, and merchandise handling.

The third category of expenses are those that cannot be identified with any specific location but are incurred for the benefit of the total organization. Some companies allocate these expenses to store locations. Typically, these expenses are initially accumulated in the central expense centers, and then allocated based on predetermined criteria such as the proportion of the net sales of each location to total net sales. Examples of such expenses include corporate management, accounting, data processing, and public relations.

Since one of the objectives of a four-wall analysis is to develop data that indicate how much each individual store generates or uses cash, allocating expenses that don't vary (in the short-term) to changes in store population should be excluded.

(b) Treatment of Expense Allocations

The starting point for this analysis is typically the basic financial data from the Company's books and records, including sales, margins, and direct expenses of each store for the period to be analyzed. Company store-level accounting records may already include allocations, by store, of various expense items. For purposes of this analysis, each allocated expense should be analyzed to determine the appropriateness of its inclusion. When possible and practical, the allocations of fixed corporate/home office costs should be excluded.

On the other hand, expenses that could be assignable or are otherwise deemed properly allocable should be added to the analysis. These expenses could include the following:

- Variable distribution center costs, market-specific advertising
- Field supervision
- Interest expense allocable to owned locations
- Property-specific security (asset protection) costs

This process of determining allocation methods requires the identification of "cost drivers," described in § 3.17. For example, variable distribution costs may be appropriate to allocate based on quantities shipped. This process will result in comparative operating results for each store location that will more accurately reflect actual individual store results.

(c) Sales and Margins

Sales typically come directly from the Company's books and records without further adjustment. For accounting purposes, gross margin may include allocations of certain items among all the stores, which can be specifically identified on a store-by-store basis.

The following allocations are descriptions of specific adjustments made to gross margin that we have seen in practice. These allocations, if made by the Company and included in the general ledger balances, should be identified, removed, and replaced by actual store results on an individual store basis:

- *Allowance adjustment*—This represents additional vendor allowances provided by vendors post-closing. These allowances are allocated to each store based on sales levels and will affect the net gross margin.
- *Market price*—Some companies identify and allocate certain competitive repricing initiatives. This represents the impact to gross margin from a store's direct competition, that is, a store that competes with a Wal-Mart may have pricing that generates a smaller gross margin than a store that does not compete with a Wal-Mart. The market pricing data is captured by the cash register, totaled for the chain, and then this total is allocated among all the stores. This allocation should be removed for the four-wall contribution analysis.

- *Clearance centers adjustment*—Sometimes retail chains will operate clearance centers at certain locations that will lower those stores' total gross margins. To appropriately measure the four-wall contribution by store, the effect of having a clearance center should be removed from those stores having such centers and allocated to those stores not having clearance centers. The rationale for this is because if no clearance centers existed in the chain, each store would realize lower gross margins because they would have to liquidate the inventory themselves.

- *Transportation haul adjustment*—Sometimes freight expense gets allocated by store based on sales. This adjustment should remove the allocation and input the actual freight expense computed by actual mileage and number of cartons delivered to the store.

- *Other year-end or periodic adjustment*—Book-to-physical inventory adjustments, based on the physical counts obtained at each location, should be recorded and will impact the individual stores' gross margin and the chain's gross margin by the net amount of the book-to-physical adjustment.

The revised gross margin by store will include the sum of the general ledger gross margin plus adjustments and reallocations identified in the process.

(d) Reallocation of Direct Expenses

Companies may also allocate certain selling, general, and administrative expenses to the stores instead of posting the direct expense incurred at the store level. The allocations of the following expenses should be removed and the actual direct expense of the store input. The following allocations are descriptions of specific adjustments made to direct expenses that we have seen in practice:

- *Step rent*—This represents the incremental cash impact of leases where the accounting treatment of the lease expense may reflect a different amount.

- *Leased capital adjustment*—This may represent the costs of operating leases for items such as telephone systems, cash registers, and copy machines, which are allocated to each store as a percentage of sales. This adjustment should remove the allocation and input the actual direct expense of the individual stores.

- *Rent adjustment*—This may represent the impact of negotiated rent concessions received from landlords that had not been posted yet.

- *Clearance Centers*—This would represent the incremental payroll expense incurred by the stores that operate clearance centers, as discussed above.

The revised expenses by store will include the sum of the direct expenses, plus adjustments and reallocations. These expenses are deducted from the recalculated gross margin by store, calculated above to yield the four-wall contribution by store.

(e) Using the Four-Wall Contribution Information

The information from the four-wall contribution analysis may be used for the following purposes:

- *Evaluation process*—The resulting four-wall contribution by store can be used by management to evaluate each store's performance. Stores should be categorized as good and therefore retained, watch list and requiring further evaluation, or poor and therefore candidates for closure.
- *Rank stores by lowest to highest contribution*—First, the resulting four-wall contribution should be sorted by largest four-wall loss to greatest four-wall contribution. This ranking will enable management to focus on poor performers. At this point, management must establish a minimum performance level threshold. All stores performing below the minimum four-wall contribution performance level should then be analyzed in detail to determine the underlying causes of the losses.
- *Minimum performance thresholds*—This is established to identify stores that require management's attention. Minimum performance thresholds should consider (1) minimum tolerable contribution margins necessary to fund corporate overhead, debt service, capital expenditures, and shareholder returns, and (2) minimum return on working capital invested.

Criteria may be two-tier to further refine the evaluation process:

1 The first performance threshold may be reflective of a "model store." Stores that meet or exceed this performance level have earnings and cash flow such that, together with all other stores, management's long-term performance objectives could be achieved.

2 The second threshold may equate to a break-even concept whereby the store's earnings, at a minimum, are sufficient to fund the cost or working capital deployed. Such stores may be "keepers" short-term, since (1) they are not draining working capital, and (2) subject to analysis, operational improvements may be achievable.

Stores below the second threshold should be considered closure candidates.

(f) Nonqualitative Considerations

The rationale for retaining stores that do not meet minimal performance levels may include:

- Extraordinary expenses may have been incurred during the year.
- The location may be close to break-even and management has developed plans to increase profitability, which may include obtaining rent concessions from the landlord, a change in store management, remerchandising the store, and remodeling the location.

- A competitor has announced plans to close a competing location, which may in turn increase sales at the Company location.

Alternatively, the rationale for the closing of certain marginal stores may include:

- New competition coming into the area.
- Significant planned changes to traffic patterns that will make the location undesirable.
- Cost to remodel is deemed to be too high versus expected return.

(g) Identify Markets that Should Be Exited

After the initial determination of stores to be closed, management should reevaluate the remaining store locations on a market-by-market basis. Advertising and marketing expenditures are typically market driven, not store driven. The reduction of stores in a given market may incrementally increase the advertising and marketing expenditures for the remaining stores, thus causing the remaining stores, on a pro forma basis, to generate negative four-wall contribution. Certain markets may no longer contain sufficient stores to warrant merchandise deliveries to that area or marketing expenditures within the market; thus the markets should be reevaluated after the initial store closures are determined and, if necessary, the remaining stores in the market should also be closed.

(h) Compute the Cost of Capital and Return on Investment

Another aspect of the profitability of each location is the expected return on investment. This aspect is typically overlooked by management in their analysis of a store's contribution. Retailers typically have a significant investment in inventory at each location. The carrying cost of this inventory should be considered in the evaluation process. Similarly, the capital expenditures required to remodel the location, if necessary, should be evaluated in light of the expected sales and margin growth. The anticipated return on investment for the capital expenditures should be considered.

Other investments may include new registers, new signage, new fixtures to remerchandise the inventory, and the cost of exiting certain lines of merchandise.

(i) Other Items to Examine

Other items that may require analysis in completing the four-wall contribution analysis include:

- Store closing costs
- Lease termination costs
- Lease rejection costs
- Competition

- Going-out-of-business (GOB) sales
- Use of GOB proceeds
- Regional/market-specific advertising contracts
- Fixed corporate overhead costs, lag in reducing SG&A after closure
- Possible effect on pricing due to volume reductions with vendors

§ 3.19 Business Process Reengineering

Business process reengineering (BPR) is an approach designed to accomplish several important, overall objectives in a turnaround situation. These include building a team and getting buy-in, reducing cost structures of the company, and the maximization of available resources. BPR also emphasizes building a focus on the future and the development of a "story" for parties-in-interest and potential investors.

The basic tenets and definition of business process reengineering are its focus on business process, continuous improvement, quality, root cause analysis, prevention versus failure, and measurement.

BPR involves coordination in five major areas: organization and people, cross-functional work flows, information technology, physical infrastructure, and policies and regulations. In the first of these areas—organization and people—BPR objectives are to reduce the number of distinct departments or groups; organize into teams emphasizing development of multiskilled workers; provide appropriate incentives for employees; empower individuals; and measure performance in relation to process.

In the area of cross-functional work flows, BPR seeks to eliminate bottlenecks, move work in a continuous flow, organize work in parallel processes, and move activities closer to the customer. For information technology, BPR objectives include improvement of quality and timeliness of information, as well as the streamlining of process work flows.

With respect to physical infrastructure, BPR focuses on modification of physical facilities to facilitate material movements; matching equipment capabilities to changes in work flow; and improvement of tools and work areas to fit skills and responsibilities. Finally, in policies and regulations, BPR seeks to change the rules to fit the needs of the restructured business.

Critical advantages of BPR are its focus on improved cost structures, establishing priorities, and rebuilding the management team. In contrast to operations in a stable business environment, BPR provides special strategies for the turnaround environment, most notably focus on functional improvement, short-term duration, incremental improvement in productivity, identifying and working with "low-hanging fruit"; and identifying and seeking break-even opportunities.

BPR lists the following as key elements in successful turnaround: management change, development of detailed action plans, establishment of accountabilities, clarification of organizational responsibilities, an ongoing cycle of communication and follow-up, and the setting of measurable targets and deadlines.

SUMMARY AND RECOMMENDATIONS

§ 3.20   Summary

Zimmerman concludes his book by making the following recommendations for the future:[53]

Recommendations for Businesses Involved in Turnarounds

- Find managers who understand the business.
- Be respectful of the people who are involved in the company.
- Cultivate both formal and informal forecasting techniques.
- Ensure that the entire organization is part of the turnaround process.
- Examine the environment on the basis of essential information.
- Hire and retain people partly on the basis of character traits.
- Get efficient first-sell later.
- Use efficiency savings to differentiate the products and improve quality.
- Systematically withdraw resources to improve performance.
- Make small, incremental improvements constantly.

Recommendations for Board of Directors

- Cultivate the acceptability of voting conscience and judgment.
- Upgrade and round out the Board of Directors.
- Be alert to strategic conflicts of interest.
- Retest the forecasts.
- Hold board meetings at reasonable places.
- Remedy obvious ethical problems when they occur.
- Get realistic as to executive compensation.
- Help formulate public policy.

---

[53] Zimmerman, *supra* note 4, pp. 274–79.

4

Out-of-Court Settlements

§ 4.1 Introduction

The number of agreements reached out of court between financially troubled debtors and their creditors rose considerably during the past 20 years. Not only is the number of such agreements growing, but the kinds of businesses seeking this type of remedy have also increased. At one time, the informal out-of-court agreement was used frequently only in selected areas, such as in New York City's garment industry, but its popularity has now spread to other industries and locations. There are more agreements reached each year out of court than through the bankruptcy courts. In fact, some attorneys specializing in bankruptcy work estimate that there are at least five out-of-court settlements for each reorganization of a business in chapter 11. In most situations where it appears that the business could be rehabilitated, out-of-court settlement should at least be considered because it may, in fact, be the best alternative.

Because of the cost associated with a chapter 11 filing, the number of debtors reaching out-of-court settlements continues to increase as a percent of total settlement in and out of chapter 11. Creditors are realizing that many provisions of the Bankruptcy Code are available to them in an out-of-court agreement or settlement. Thus, because a settlement can generally be approved in a shorter time period, with less cost to administer and greater returns to creditors in the long run, its popularity has increased.

An informal settlement effected between a debtor and his or her creditors is normally one of three possible types of agreement:

1 *Moratorium* (extension)—an extension of time with eventual full payment in installments or stock
2 *Pro rata cash settlement* (composition)—payment on a proportional basis, in cash and/or stock, in full settlement of claims
3 *Combination*—payment of part of the debts in cash or stock at the time of the settlement and agreement to make further installment payments[1]

Certain conditions are normally advantageous to a successful out-of-court agreement. The debtor company should be a good moral risk so that creditors

[1] John E. Mulder, "Rehabilitation of the Financially Distressed Small Business—Revisited," *The Practical Lawyer*, Vol. 11 (November 1965), p. 40.

may have some assurance it will be true to its word. The debtor should have the ability to recover from financial difficulties. General business conditions should be favorable to a recovery.[2]

§ 4.2 Nature of Proceedings

The informal settlement is an out-of-court agreement that usually consists of an extension of time (stretch out), a pro rata cash payment for full settlement of claims (composition), an exchange of stock for debt, or some combination. The debtor, through counsel or credit association, calls an informal meeting of the creditors for the purpose of discussing his or her financial problems. In many cases, the credit association makes a significant contribution to the out-of-court settlement by arranging a meeting of creditors, providing advice, and serving as secretary for the creditors' committee. A credit association is composed of credit managers of various businesses in a given region. Its functions are to provide credit and other business information to member companies concerning their debtors, to help make commercial credit collections, to support legislation favorable to business creditors, and to provide courses in credit management for members of the credit community. At a meeting of this type, the debtor will describe the causes of failure, discuss the value of assets (especially those unpledged) and unsecured liabilities, and answer any questions the creditors may ask. The main objective of this meeting is to convince the creditors that they will receive more if the business is allowed to operate than if it is forced to liquidate, and that all parties will be better off if a settlement can be worked out.

In larger businesses, it may take months, or even years, to develop an agreement that will provide the type of relief the debtor needs. For example, International Harvester had been working with its creditors for several years before its out-of-court plan was finalized. In these situations, the negotiations are generally between the debtor's counsel, who should be experienced in bankruptcy and "workout" situations, and counsel who represents major creditors or committees of creditors.

§ 4.3 Importance of an Early Meeting Date

To be successful in any attempt to work out an agreement with creditors, the debtors must obtain, very early during the time period when financial problems develop, the cooperation of some of the largest creditors and those with the most influence over other creditors.

It is difficult for a debtor to admit that it cannot pay debts and continue profitable operations. As a result, decisions to call a meeting of creditors or to file a petition under the Bankruptcy Code often are postponed until the last minute. This delay benefits no one, including the debtor. A debtor may place the last penny of his or her life's savings in the business, even when the possibility is remote that this last investment will actually provide the corrective action. Where the product is inferior, the demand for the product is declining, the distribution channels are inadequate, or other similar problems exist that cannot

---

[2] Fred Weston, *Managerial Finance* (Hinsdale, IL: The Dryden Press, 1978), pp. 897–98.

be corrected, either because of the economic environment or management's lack of ability, it is normally best to liquidate the company immediately.

For several reasons, it is advisable to call a meeting of creditors as soon as it becomes obvious that some type of relief is necessary:

- The debtor still has a considerable asset base.
- There is a tendency for many of the key employees to leave when they see unhealthy conditions developing; early corrective action may encourage them to stay.
- Prompt action may make it possible for the debtor to maintain some of the goodwill that was developed during successful operating periods.

The fact remains that in many cases no kind of action is taken, and the creditors force the debtor to call an informal meeting or file a bankruptcy court petition.

§ 4.4   Preparation for the Creditors' Meeting

The creditors will almost always be represented by professionals who have handled many cases and are true specialists in negotiating settlements. The debtor must select counsel who is adequately prepared for the meeting with creditors. The independent accountant can, more than anyone else, assist the debtor in this preparation. It is advisable that the debtor's legal counsel be experienced in bankruptcy and insolvency proceedings and be especially familiar with problems associated with out-of-court settlements. After counsel has been engaged and before the creditors' meeting is called, it is necessary, even when the meeting is called on short notice, for both the accountant and counsel to consult with the debtor.

At this conference, the attorney obtains sufficient background information about the debtor's operations so that the attorney can present the facts to the creditors, knowledgeably discuss the situation with them, and explain why the debtor is in difficulty and why a settlement out of court would be advantageous to all parties. Also, various types of financial information similar to that needed for a chapter 11 proceeding must be supplied to the attorney. The first kind of information needed is a summary of the major causes of failure and the possible corrective action that can be taken. To prepare this type of summary, the accountant must analyze the past activities of the debtor, compare the financial statements for the past three or four years, and determine what caused the cash shortage. The attorney will need a copy of the most recent balance sheet, income statement, and statement of changes in financial position, as well as a list of the debtor's creditors and executory contracts. The attorney also should have some idea of the liquidation value of the assets and know the nature of the liabilities (that is, those secured, unsecured, and contingent), and be familiar with the changes that have occurred in inventory and the reasons for the changes. The debtor's independent accountant should make sure the attorney knows of any sales made below cost, or considerably below the normal price, and of any preferential payments, fraudulent transfers, or setoffs.

It is often advisable, provided there is enough time, for the accountant and the attorney to assist the debtor in preparing a suggested plan of settlement so it can be presented and discussed at the first meeting with creditors. Typically, only the largest creditors and a few representatives of the smaller creditors are invited, to avoid having a group so large that little can be accomplished.

Counsel may also prefer to meet individually with the major institutional lenders and several of the larger trade creditors. In these meetings, counsel for the debtor can explain the problem, the action the debtor is taking to attempt to locate the cause of the financial trouble, and the type of relief and support that is needed. The debtor also seeks advice and input from the major creditors concerning the type of action they might consider at least partly acceptable. As a result of these meetings, the debtor may be able to obtain some support for the action the company is taking.

At a typical meeting, the debtor will provide the creditors with copies of the latest financial statements and other pertinent financial information. These statements will be reviewed by the creditors, and the liquidating values of the various assets will be discussed. If the debtor has developed a suggested plan of settlement, this also will be discussed by the creditors, who may accept it or, under certain conditions, ask for another plan or recommend that the debtor file a petition in bankruptcy court. If a debtor is well prepared by its accountant and attorney and has a good opportunity of being rehabilitated at a reasonable cost, it can avoid being forced involuntarily into bankruptcy court.

§ 4.5 Appointment of Creditors' Committee

To make it easier for the debtor to interact and work with the creditors, a committee of creditors is normally appointed during the initial meeting of the debtor and its creditors—if the case is judged to warrant some cooperation by the creditors. It should be realized that the creditors are often as interested in working out a settlement as is the debtor. There is no set procedure for the formation of a committee. Ideally, the committee should consist of four or five of the largest creditors and one or two representatives from the smaller creditors. A lot of unnecessary time wasted on deciding the size and composition of the committee would be saved at creditors' meetings if the committees were organized in this manner. However, there are no legal or rigid rules defining the manner in which a committee shall be formed. Although a smaller creditor will often serve on a committee, there are committees on which only the larger creditors serve, either because of lack of interest on the part of the smaller creditors or because the larger creditors override the wishes of others.

The debtor's job of running the business while under the limited direction of the creditors' committee can be made easier if the creditors selected are those most friendly to the debtor.

§ 4.6 Duties and Functions of Creditors' Committee

The creditors' committee is the liaison between creditors and debtor and is also the representative and bargaining agent for the creditors. Once a settlement has been arranged, it is the responsibility of the committee to solicit the acceptance of the creditors. Honesty and good faith are requirements in the performance of all committee functions. Committee members must recognize that their interests are the same as those of the other creditors; they must not allow their own interests to be brought into conflict with those of the body of creditors and must completely refrain from seeking personal gain.[3]

The creditors' committee serves as the bargaining agent for the creditors, observes the operation of the debtor during the development of a plan, and solicits acceptance of a plan once it has been approved by the committee. Generally, the creditors' committee will meet as soon as it has been appointed, for the purpose of selecting a chairperson and counsel. The committee also will engage an independent accountant to review the books and records of the debtor and the operations to see if there is a basis for future profitable operations.

At the completion of the investigation, the creditors' committee will meet to discuss the results. If it is revealed that the creditors are dealing with a dishonest debtor, the amount of settlement that will be acceptable to the creditors will be increased significantly. It becomes very difficult for a debtor to avoid a bankruptcy court proceeding under these conditions. On the other hand, if the debtor is honest and demonstrates the ability to reverse the unprofitable operations trend and reestablish his or her business, some type of plan may eventually be approved.

As to the independent accountant who may be engaged by the creditors' committee, he or she can assist the committee in monitoring the debtor's business while a plan of settlement is being developed and during the period when installment payments are being made under the terms of the plan. The objective is to see that assets of the debtor are conserved and, once agreement has been reached on a plan of settlement, to see that all terms of the plan are being followed. The auditor will establish controls to ascertain that all cash receipts from sales, collections on account, and other sources are deposited intact, and that disbursements are for a valid purpose. Also, he or she will either prepare or review cash flow statements. Procedures must be established to ensure that all liabilities incurred after the first creditors' meeting are paid promptly so that the debtor can become reestablished in the credit community.

"In non-bankruptcy matters the functions of a committee have run the gamut from investigation, consultation, and advice to supervision and liquidation."[4] All these functions include supervision of the activities of the debtor, ensuring that all possible steps are taken to collect and preserve the assets, guard against careless acts of the debtor, and receive information from creditors as to the conduct of the debtor. This can amount to the debtor's submission of its business and financial affairs to the supervising committee (but see § 4.8).

Creditors' committees should, however, be very careful about the extent to which they take over the management of the business. Along with this function come responsibilities that most creditors are not willing to assume. For example, they can be liable for withholding taxes if they are not properly remitted to the government. They will be classified as insiders if the debtor ends up in bankruptcy court, and may find that they are not in as good a position as

---

[3] Chauncey Levy, "Creditors' Committees and Their Responsibilities," *Commercial Law Journal,* Vol. 74 (December 1969), p. 360.
[4] *Id.,* p. 359.

those creditors that did not get involved in the out-of-court activities. They may have additional liability under the 1933 and 1934 securities laws.

§ 4.7 Workout Specialist

Often, the creditors will insist that there be a change in management before they will work with the debtor out of court. A management change might introduce new management, experienced in the debtor's type of operations, to replace existing top management. However, in many out-of-court situations, a workout specialist is engaged to attempt to locate the debtor's problems and see that the business is preserved. Once operations are profitable, the workout specialist moves on to another troubled company. These specialists are generally given the freedom to run the companies they take over as they see fit. Managers perceived as being competent, and those the specialists feel comfortable working with, will be retained. The other managers will be let go. Compensation paid these specialists will vary; some want, in addition to a salary, a stake in the ownership or other forms of bonuses if their efforts prove successful. Workout specialists, in addition to running the business, work with the creditors' committee in developing the plan of settlement. The key management positions in the company are staffed under the direction of the specialist so that, once the operations are again profitable, the workout specialist can move on to the next troubled company. If the companies are relatively small, the workout specialist may be supervising the operations of several businesses at one time. These specialists are the same individuals who specialize in managing companies in bankruptcy.

§ 4.8 Committee Management

Under conditions where the creditors elect committee management, an agreement is entered into between the debtor and the creditors, whereby supervision of the business is turned over to a committee of the creditors. The use of this approach has declined in recent years because of the disadvantageous position a creditor can be in if control is exercised over the debtor and a petition is subsequently filed. (See § 10.14.) The debtor, in doing this, normally executes an assignment for the benefit of creditors, which is held in escrow by the committee. If it becomes necessary, the creditors can liquidate the debtor's assets or use the assignment to bring the debtor into bankruptcy court. The directors and officers of the debtor corporation tender resignations, which the committee also holds in escrow. The stockholders often endorse all shares of stock in blank, to be held in escrow by the committee. The committee can operate the business itself, bring in an outside business expert, or use a present officer of the company. Usually included in the agreement is a provision for existing creditors to grant extensions or subordinate their claims in return for new financing. New funds can then be obtained from banks and others to provide the company with working capital. Usually, the internal organization of the company is not changed; alterations are made only as necessary to effect efficiency and economies in operation.

After the business has operated for a short time under the plan designed by the creditors' committee, those in charge of managing the company determine whether recovery under the new regime is possible, or whether reorganization or liquidation is necessary. If recovery seems possible, the agreement normally continues for a given period of time or until the creditors' claims have been paid or adjusted out of the proceeds realized under the management of the committee. When reorganization appears necessary, the committee may assist management in designing a plan. If the only alternative is liquidation, the committee may supervise the process.

(a) Management Control Problems

In attempting to work with the debtor in an out-of-court proceeding, the creditors must be aware of the additional liability they may incur if they elect to exercise direct control over the debtor's operations. There is a fine line between counseling the debtor and controlling the debtor's operations.

If creditors do exercise control, they may be considered as insiders if a bankruptcy petition is subsequently filed (see discussion at § 10.14), have their debt subordinated to other creditors, and be liable for the losses suffered by the other creditors attributable to interference by the controlling creditors. The creditor who obtains control of the debtor may be liable under the federal securities laws. For example, adverse consequences could result from a failure to obtain requisite regulatory approvals before and after assuming control of corporations in regulated industries such as insurance.[5] The failure to collect and remit taxes withheld from the wages of a debtor's employees can result in the creditors' being liable for these taxes if they are in control of the debtor's operations.

Douglas-Hamilton suggested that creditors might consider the following recommendations to avoid being in control of the debtor:

1 Avoid any interference with the management of the debtor; the lender, not the debtor's management, should run the company.

2 Carefully examine the lender's collateral security position with regard to the stock of the debtor and the debtor's subsidiaries.

3 Exercise extreme caution in making and securing new loans, to be certain there is no breach of the rights of existing creditors. (For example, the taking of collateral that is controlling stock of a subsidiary in exchange for a loan to a solvent subsidiary upstreamed to the parent in exchange for debts of questionable value may result in the subordination of this loan to other creditors.)

4 Take care in seeking to improve the lender's position with respect to its outstanding loans, to avoid charges by third parties or other creditors that the lender induced the debtor to breach their contractual rights or aided and abetted or conspired with the debtor in leading others along.[6]

---

[5] Margaret Hambrecht Douglas-Hamilton, "Troubled Debtors: The Fine Line Between Counseling and Controlling," *Journal of Commercial Bank Lending*, Vol. 60 (October 1977), p. 33.
[6] *Id.*, pp. 34–35.

PREPARATION OF A PLAN OF SETTLEMENT

§ 4.9 Introduction

There is no set pattern for the form a plan of settlement proposed by the debtor must take. It may call for 100 percent payment over an extended period of time, payments on a pro rata basis, in cash, for full settlement of creditors' claims, an exchange of stock for debt, or some combination. A carefully developed forecast of projected operations, based on realistic assumptions developed by the debtor with the aid of his or her accountant, can help creditors determine whether the debtor can perform under the terms of the plan and operate successfully in the future.

Generally, for creditors to accept a plan, the amount they will receive must be at least equal to the dividend they would receive if the estate were liquidated. This dividend, expressed as a percent, is equal to the sum of a forced-sale value of assets, accounts receivable, cash, and prepaid items, minus priority claims, secured claims, and expenses of administration divided by the total amount of unsecured claims.

The plan should provide that all costs of administration, secured claims, and priority claims, including wages and taxes, are adequately disposed of for the eventual protection of the unsecured creditors.[7] If the debtor's plan includes a cash down payment, in full or partial settlement, the payment should at least equal the probable dividend the creditors would receive in bankruptcy. It is not likely that creditors will accept under an agreement anything less than they would get in chapter 7 liquidation proceedings.

In Volume 2 of *Bankruptcy and Insolvency Accounting*, 4.1 contains suggestions as to how an out-of-court settlement might be drafted. The draft agreement provides several suggestions, in document form, for specific items that should be included.

§ 4.10 Conditions of Agreement

When an agreement calls for future installment payments, the creditors may insist that these payments be secured, for example, by notes or a mortgage on real estate. The debtor may execute an assignment for the benefit of creditors to be held in escrow and to become effective only if the debtor defaults in performance of the plan. The creditors may require that their own accountant make frequent reviews of the controls and operating activities of the business (§ 10.12). Also, creditors may require that a workout specialist be allowed to operate the business during the period when the plan is being carried out (§ 4.7).

An example of an actual out-of-court settlement that was approved by the creditors and implemented is presented as 4.2 in Volume 2. The agreement provided for the payment of 20 percent of the allowed claim of unsecured creditors over a period of 18 months. The agreement was accompanied by a combination solicitation letter and disclosure statement of the debtor.

---

[7] Leon S. Forman, *Compositions, Bankruptcy, and Arrangements* (Philadelphia: The American Law Institute, 1971), p. 13.

An out-of-court plan granting various security to creditors for the performance of the plan can be accompanied by a combination solicitation letter and disclosure statement of the debtor. (Readers are urged to study § 6.26, regarding the content of a disclosure statement.) By including information that meets the disclosure requirements, the debtor may be able to use this acceptance as the approval of the plan if it becomes necessary to file a chapter 11 plan. The integration of Schedule A and Schedule B in the agreement shown as 4.2 in Volume 2, and the integration of Schedule B in the agreement in 4.1 of Volume 2, indicates the creditor's approval of the chapter 11 plan if the debtor files such a plan. (See § 6.26.) If "adequate information" is not disclosed at the time the debtor solicits the approval of the plan of settlement, the bankruptcy court will not accept the vote.

After the creditors' committee approves a plan, it will notify all of the other creditors and recommend to them that they accept it. Even if a few creditors do not agree, the debtor should continue with the plan. Such creditors will eventually have to be paid in full, and the plan may even provide for full payment to small creditors, thus destroying "the nuisance value of the small claims."[8] When a plan is agreed on, the debtor should "either make out the checks for the initial payment and turn them over to counsel for the creditors' committee, or deposit with such counsel the funds for that purpose."[9] The funds to be deposited by the debtor must usually be sufficient to pay priority claims, secured claims, and administrative costs.

In an informal agreement, where there is no provision binding on the minority of creditors to accept the will of the majority, the consent of the members of the committee must be obtained for the plan to work. "These methods of friendly adjustment out of court are feasible only where the debtor corporation and substantially all the creditors are disposed to take a cooperative and realistic attitude and to work harmoniously toward a solution of the problem."[10] Creditors' committees have had success in "prevailing upon creditors to withhold institution of actions or the prosecution of pending actions."[11] If the firm does not begin to recover under the aegis of the committee, it can be liquidated.

Volume 2, *Bankruptcy and Insolvency Accounting*, 4.3, contains an actual settlement agreement providing for a 60 percent payment to creditors, limited note payments to the owner, and partial payment of an insider note. Included are negative and affirmative covenants, and definition of committee roles during negotiations and after the agreement becomes effective.

§ 4.11   Out-of-Court Agreement Prior to Chapter 11 (Prepackaged Bankruptcy)

As noted above, if in an out-of-court workout the debtor does not obtain the large percent of acceptance desired, it may file a chapter 11 petition using the balloting of the out-of-court workouts for chapter 11 approval. In some

---

[8] *Id.*, p. 15.
[9] *Id.*
[10] William J. Grange et al., *Manual for Corporation Officers* (New York: The Ronald Press Co., 1967), p. 340.
[11] Levy, *supra* note 3, p. 357.

cases, the debtor may solicit acceptance of the plan with the intent, if approval is obtained, to file a petition. Crystal Oil Company, in a disclosure statement filed with its creditors and stockholders on July 9, 1986, stated that the company was not currently a debtor in chapter 11, but if the plan was approved a chapter 11 petition would be filed. On October 1, 1986, the company filed its chapter 11 petition and, on December 31, 1986, the plan was confirmed. Thus, in a period of three months after filing, the debtor was out of bankruptcy. Crystal Oil had total assets of approximately $140 million when it issued the disclosure statement. One major advantage of reaching agreement out of court is that it reduces the professional fees substantially. At the same time, when a chapter 11 petition is filed, the debtor obtains all of the benefits of a bankruptcy filing. Crystal was one of the first companies to follow the process of obtaining approval of the plan prior to filing the petition which later became known as "prepackaged bankruptcy." Since Crystal's plan was confirmed a large number of companies have elected the "prepackaged bankruptcy" and have been in bankruptcy for a period as short as 38 days.

ADVANTAGES AND DISADVANTAGES

§ 4.12 Advantages

The following are a few of the reasons why the informal settlement is often used in today's environment:

- The out-of-court settlement is less disruptive of a business that continues operation.
- The debtor can receive considerable benefits from the advice of a committee, especially if some of the committee members are businesspeople, preferably but not necessarily in the same line of business.
- The informal settlement avoids invoking the provisions of the Bankruptcy Code and, as a result, more businesslike solutions can be adopted.
- Frustrations and delays are minimized because problems can be resolved properly and informally without the need for court hearings.
- An agreement can usually be reached much faster informally than in court proceedings.
- The costs of administration are usually less in an out-of-court settlement than in a formal reorganization.

§ 4.13 Disadvantages

The weaknesses of informal composition settlements are as follows:

- A successful plan of settlement requires the approval of substantially all creditors, and it may be difficult to persuade distant creditors to accept a settlement that calls for payment of less than 100 percent.

- The assets of the debtor are subject to attack while a settlement is pending. (The debtor can, of course, point out to the creditor that if legal action is taken, a petition in bankruptcy court will have to be filed.)
- The informal composition settlement does not provide a method to resolve individual disputes between the debtor and creditors.
- Executory contracts, especially leases, may be difficult to avoid.
- There is no formal way to recover preferences or fraudulent transfers.
- Certain tax law provisions make it more advantageous to file a bankruptcy court proceedings.
- Priority debts owed to the United States under Revised Statute section 3466 must be paid first.

From the above, it is obvious that, for several reasons, it is often best for the debtor to seek assistance out of court. But this avenue can be lost if the debtor is not cautious in its actions.

5

Nature of Bankruptcy and Insolvency Proceedings

HISTORICAL ORIGIN

§ 5.1 Introduction

An accountant or financial advisor who understands the scope and nature of bankruptcy and insolvency engagements and is technically competent is capable of representing a client in the proceedings. Part of the accountant's background must consist of some familiarity with the legal aspects of bankruptcies and insolvencies. This chapter and the next two provide the accountant with the legal background needed to represent effectively a client in various situations involving financial difficulties. The objective of this chapter is threefold: (1) to describe the origin of our current bankruptcy law, (2) to discuss the legal meaning of insolvency, and (3) to set forth the various alternatives available to debtor and creditor when failure appears imminent. Two of these alternatives—assignment for benefit of creditors and chapter 7 liquidation under the Bankruptcy Code—are discussed in detail.

In early times, the proverb "He who cannot pay with his purse, pays with his skin" had a ruthlessly literal application. The law of ancient Rome (450 B.C.) declared that the borrower was *nexus* to his creditors, which meant that his own person was pledged for repayment of the loan. If the borrower failed to meet his obligation, the creditor could seize him. The creditor then publicly invited someone to come forth to pay the debt, and if no one did, the creditor killed or sold the debtor.[1] A number of Biblical references testify to the fact that one could be enslaved for the nonpayment of debt. In II Kings 4: "... a certain woman of the wives of the sons of the prophets cried out to Elisha, 'Your servant my husband is dead, and you know that your servant feared the Lord; and the creditor has come to take my two children to be his slaves.' Elisha said, 'Go, borrow vessels at large for yourself from all your neighbors.' From one jar of oil she filled all the vessels that had been borrowed. Elisha said to her, 'Go, sell the oil and pay your debt, and you and your sons can live on the rest.' " In ancient Greece, under the criminal code of Draco (623 B.C.), indebtedness was classified with murders, sacrilege, and other capital crimes. Solon, during his reign, ordered that the debts that

---

[1] George Sullivan, *The Boom in Going Bust* (New York: Macmillan, 1968), p. 25.

remained after an attempt at restitution should be forgiven, but that the debtor and his heirs had to forfeit their citizenship.[2]

The first English bankruptcy law, passed in 1542, was a law against the debtor. Only the creditor could, under certain conditions, initiate bankruptcy action and divide up the assets of the debtor. If there were liabilities that the debtor was unable to pay with his assets, he was sent to prison. The 1542 law applied only to traders, but in 1570 it was amended to include merchants.[3] It was not until 1705 that the English law provided for discharge of the debtor from his debts.

§ 5.2 United States

Physical punishment, imprisonment, and other similar practices, which were common in England and in some of the American Colonies and which were seen by many as being totally ineffective, influenced American lawmakers to see the need for a national bankruptcy law. However, it was not considered until a very late date in the proceedings of the Federal Convention. On August 29, 1787, Charles Pinckney of South Carolina moved to give the federal government the power to establish uniform laws on the subject of bankruptcy as a part of the Full Faith and Credit Clause (Article XVI). On September 1, 1787, John Rutledge recommended that in Article VII, relating to the Legislative Department, there be added after the power to establish uniform rule of naturalization a power "to establish uniform laws on the subject of bankruptcies." On September 3, 1787, this clause was adopted after very little debate. Only the State of Connecticut opposed the provision; its representative, Roger Sherman, objected to any power that would make it possible to punish by death individuals who were bankrupt. In the final draft, the power to establish uniform bankruptcy laws was inserted after the provision to regulate commerce in Section 8 of Article I.[4]

The wording of the provision is: "Congress shall have the power . . . to establish . . . uniform Laws on the subject of Bankruptcies throughout the United States." Although the right was granted, the states were so opposed to it that national bankruptcy laws existed intermittently for only about 17 years prior to 1900.[5] The meaning and scope of the term "bankruptcy" as used by the framers of the Constitution are unclear. The English law in existence at the time this provision was added to the Constitution used the word "bankruptcy" as an involuntary proceeding applying only to traders. However, at this time, some states had laws that used the term to apply to all classes of persons and all forms of insolvency. The intent of the writers in using the term "bankruptcy" served as a focal point of debate each time a bankruptcy law was proposed, for a period of over 80 years.

---

[2] *Id.*

[3] Louis Levinthal, "The Early History of Bankruptcy Law," *University of Pennsylvania Law Review*, Vol. 66 (1917–1918), p. 224n.

[4] Charles Warren, *Bankruptcies in United States History* (Cambridge, MA: Harvard University Press, 1935), pp. 4–5.

[5] Charles Gerstenberg, *Financial Organization and Management of Business* (Englewood Cliffs, NJ: Prentice-Hall, Inc., 1959), p. 532.

Under the authority granted, Congress passed three bankruptcy acts prior to 1898. The first act, passed in 1800 and repealed three years later, applied to traders, brokers, and merchants, and contained no provisions for voluntary bankruptcy. The first act was finally passed as a result of a financial crash brought about by overspeculation in real estate. Many rich and prominent traders were in prison because they were unable to pay their creditors. Robert Morris, the great financier of the Revolution, was in the Prune Street Jail in Philadelphia with liabilities of about $12 million. James Wilson, a Justice of the United States Supreme Court, went to North Carolina just before his death, to avoid imprisonment for debts he owed in Pennsylvania.[6]

The first act, by its terms, was limited to five years, but it lasted only three years because of several factors. First, there was the difficulty of travel to the distant and unpopular federal courts. Second, very small dividends were paid to creditors. One reason for this was that most of the debtors forced into bankruptcy were already in prison. Third, the act had been largely used by rich debtors, speculators, and, in some cases, fraudulent debtors to obtain discharge from their debts.[7] Among the debtors who were released as a result of this act was Robert Morris.

The second act, passed in 1841, applied to all debtors, contained provisions for voluntary bankruptcy, and allowed a discharge of the unpaid balance remaining after all assets were distributed to creditors. The second act was not really given an opportunity to succeed. The bill was defeated in the House on August 17, 1841, by a vote of 110 to 97. Because of some maneuvering, the bill was reconsidered the next morning and passed by a vote of 110 to 106. Opponents of the bill started working toward its repeal and the bill was revoked by a vote of 140 to 71 in the House and 32 to 13 in the Senate after it had lasted just over one year.

The financial problems created by the Civil War caused Congress to consider a third act, which became law in 1867 and was repealed in 1878. This act marked the beginning of an attempt by Congress to permit the debtor to escape the stigma associated with bankruptcy by allowing a composition of his debts without being adjudicated a bankrupt.

The Bankruptcy Act passed in 1898, as amended, applies to all cases that were filed before October 1, 1979. The act was thoroughly revised by the Bankruptcy Act of 1938, commonly known as the Chandler Act, which added to the basic law the chapter proceedings. The most profound of all developments in bankruptcy law must have been the passing of the Chandler Act, which gave the courts the power to regulate the disposition of all debtors' estates—individuals as well as business, agriculture, railroads, municipalities, and real estate, whether in liquidation, rehabilitation, or reorganization. The most frequently used of the chapter proceedings created by the Chandler Act was Chapter XI, which was established to provide rehabilitation of the honest debtor with a maximum of speed and a minimum of cost.[8]

---

[6] Warren, *supra* note 4, p. 13.

[7] *Id.*, pp. 19–20.

[8] George Ashe, "Rehabilitation under Chapter XI: Fact or Fiction," *Commercial Law Journal*, Vol. 72 (September 1967), p. 260.

It is interesting to note how the economic philosophy of bankruptcy has changed over the past 400 years. The first laws in Great Britain and the United States were for the benefit of creditors only. Later laws gave consideration to the debtor by allowing discharges in exchange for their cooperation. They also gave the debtor some protection against haphazard seizure by creditors; however, this provision became law primarily to protect the interest of other creditors. Very little consideration seems to have been given to the public in the United States until 1933 when section 77 was added to the 1898 act granting railroads the right to reorganize.[9]

The Bankruptcy Act of 1898, as amended in 1938, consisted of fourteen chapters. The first seven dealt with the basic structure of the bankruptcy system and set forth all of the proceedings of so-called straight bankruptcy. Chapter VIII dealt with the reorganization of railroads, and Chapter IX concerned the composition of debts of certain public authorities. Chapter X set forth in great detail the rules for reorganizing corporations with secured debts and often publicly held stock. Chapter XI covered arrangements with unsecured creditors primarily for business debtors and for other persons who were not wage earners. Provisions for wage earners were described in Chapter XIII. Chapter XII covered debts that are secured by liens on real property, and Chapter XIV dealt with maritime liens. Chapters VIII, IX, and XIV were used very infrequently. During the last half of the 1970s, the number of Chapter XII proceedings that were filed increased substantially. Most of this increase was caused by the large number of limited partnerships involving real property ownership that had financial problems.

Bankruptcy law, as it has evolved during the past 90-plus years, was intended not only to secure equality among creditors and to provide relief to debtors by discharging them from their liabilities and allowing them to start a new economic life, but also to benefit society at large.

§ 5.3 Insolvency and Bankruptcy Laws Today

The term "bankruptcy laws" is used only in reference to federal laws because of the power given to Congress to establish these laws in the U.S. Constitution. The term "insolvency laws" is used to refer to the enactments of the various states. Insolvency laws may be used as long as they do not conflict with the federal laws, except for municipal insolvency, which cannot bind dissenters.

During the final days of the 95th Congress, the Bankruptcy Reform Act of 1978 was passed. President Carter signed it on November 6, 1978. This legislation repealed the Bankruptcy Act of 1898 and its amendments (including the Chandler Act of 1938) and applies to all cases filed on or after October 1, 1979. Two years later, Congress passed the Bankruptcy Tax Bill of 1980, which was effective generally as of October 1, 1979. The Bankruptcy Reform Act deals with all of the proceedings in the bankruptcy court except for federal taxes. The tax bill establishes the procedures to follow regarding the determination of federal income taxes. In July 1984, Congress passed the Bankruptcy Amend-

---

[9] Gerstenberg, *supra* note 5.

ments and Federal Judgeship Act of 1984 which changed the bankruptcy court system and several provisions of the Bankruptcy Code.

In October 1986, Congress passed the Bankruptcy Judges, United States Trustees, and Family Farmer Bankruptcy Act of 1986. This Act, in addition to authorizing the appointment of 52 new bankruptcy judges, established a U.S. trustee system throughout the United States and created a chapter 12 for a family farmer that has financial problems. Chapter 15 of the Bankruptcy Code was repealed; however, its provisions were incorporated in the other chapters. In addition to making substantial modifications to the Bankruptcy Code, the Bankruptcy Reform Act of 1994—the third major revision to the Bankruptcy Code—authorized the establishment of a Bankruptcy Review Commission. The Commission, after two years of work, issued its final report in 1997.

The Supreme Court began, in 1973, to submit to Congress for its approval the Federal Rules of Bankruptcy Procedure, to supplement the provisions of the Bankruptcy Act regarding matters of form, practice, and procedures. These rules often coexisted with local rules of each judicial district governing local matters. After Congress enacted the Bankruptcy Reform Act, the Advisory Committee on Bankruptcy Rules of the U.S. Judicial Conference concluded that a complete revision of the existing rules could not be completed by October 1, 1979. They drafted a set of interim rules that would be helpful in applying the original rules of the new law where possible and in filling the gaps where not. These interim rules were effective until August 1, 1983. On April 25, 1983, the U.S. Supreme Court prescribed new Bankruptcy Rules that were reported to Congress and became effective on August 1. Minor revisions were made to the Bankruptcy Rules in 1987, and in 1991 there was a major revision of the rules and the forms. Again, in 1993, minor revisions were made to the Federal Rules of Bankruptcy Procedure. These rules supplement, but may not contradict, the provisions of the Bankruptcy Code. Each bankruptcy court may adopt local bankruptcy rules, as long as they are not inconsistent with the Bankruptcy Rules, by action of a majority of its judges. The Bankruptcy Rules are presented in Appendix B of this volume.

At the time the Bankruptcy Rules were prescribed, the Judicial Conference also prescribed official bankruptcy forms. These forms are to be observed and used with alterations as may be appropriate in filing the petition and other reports required by the Bankruptcy Code. Selected official bankruptcy forms are included in Appendix A of Volume 2.

§ 5.4   Current Bankruptcy Statistics

Bankruptcy filings increased in 1998 to an all-time high of over 1.44 million petitions. Most of this increase was attributable to an increase in chapters 7 and 13 filings. While the number of petitions continued to increase, the rate of increase declined in 1998 and, for the first time since 1994, the number of bankruptcy petitions filed during the 12-month period ending December 31, 1999, declined by over 8 percent. The decrease occurred in all chapters.

From October 1, 1979—the date the Bankruptcy Code became effective— through the next 20 years, except for 1984, 1993, 1994, and 1999, the number of bankruptcy filings has increased over the previous year. Bankruptcy filings are now four times the level of filings recorded fifteen years ago. The increase in filings has occurred during a period of over eight years of constant economic growth. This increase, however, is attributable to consumer filings and not business filings.

Exhibit 5-1 summarizes by circuit and by chapter the number of business and nonbusiness petitions that were filed during the 12-month period ending December 31, 1999. The number of business bankruptcy petitions filed continued to decline from 44,367 for the calendar year 1998 to 37,884 for the fiscal year ending December 31, 1999. Business filings as a percent of total filings is at its lowest level. For the fiscal year ending December 31, 1999 business filings constituted only 2.9 percent of the total filings, down from 3.1 percent in 1998, and well below the 18 percent for 1983 and 1984. Approximately 23 percent of the business filings were filed under chapter 11.

NATURE OF INSOLVENCY

§ 5.5 Types of Insolvency

Accountants and financial advisors must know and understand the technical meaning of insolvency because they play an important role in proving insolvency or solvency, as the case may be. The accountant may be retained by the debtor or by the creditors to prove solvency on a given date. The accountant or financial advisor is requested not only to establish insolvency, but to establish it as of a given date or dates, sometimes as far back as a year prior to the filing of the petition.

Insolvency in the equity sense refers to the inability of the debtor to pay obligations as they mature. In this situation, the test is the corporation's present ability to pay, and the concern is primarily with equity for the protection of creditors.

The bankruptcy sense of insolvency is the definition contained in section 101(32) of the Bankruptcy Code:

> Insolvent means . . . financial conditions such that the sum of . . . [the] entity's debts is greater than all of such entity's property, at a fair valuation, exclusive of (i) property transferred, concealed, or removed with intent to hinder, delay, or defraud such entity's creditors and (ii) property that may be exempted from property of the estate under section 522.

This is also referred to as legal insolvency or the balance sheet test.

Other definitions of insolvency have been devised to apply to special situations. The Uniform Fraudulent Conveyance and Transfer Act, which was incorporated into the Bankruptcy Act, used a slightly different definition. Found in section 67d(1)(d) of the prior law and used only for the purposes of section 67d regarding fraudulent transfers, it stated that a person is "insolvent" when the present fair salable value of his property is less than the amount required to pay his debts. Section 548 of the 1978 Bankruptcy Code includes a similar provision for the avoidance of fraudulent transfers; however, insolvency is defined the same way here as in the paragraph above.

The Uniform Commercial Code also contains, in section 1-201(23), a definition of insolvency that incorporates both the equity and the bankruptcy

Exhibit 5-1 Bankruptcy Cases Commenced* During the Year Ended December 31, 1999, by Chapters of the Bankruptcy Code for Business and Nonbusiness

Circuit and District[†]	Total Filings	Business					Nonbusiness			
		Total	Chapter 7	Chapter 11	Chapter 12	Chapter 13	Total	Chapter 7	Chapter 11	Chapter 13
Total	1,319,465	37,884	22,510	8,609	834	5,903	1,281,581	904,564	706	376,311
District of Columbia	2,718	81	34	38	—	9	2,637	1,771	4	862
First	49,850	1,433	958	296	4	171	48,417	32,689	20	15,708
Second	80,698	2,097	1,080	725	32	250	78,601	65,099	99	13,403
Third	89,320	4,401	1,375	2,781	15	229	84,919	58,726	112	26,081
Fourth	116,174	2,522	1,641	457	40	383	113,652	73,454	62	40,136
Fifth	105,093	3,092	1,635	723	108	622	102,001	56,617	39	45,345
Sixth	158,385	2,912	1,725	649	61	477	155,473	105,245	47	50,181
Seventh	120,692	2,714	1,934	347	115	317	117,978	91,283	34	26,661
Eighth	77,736	2,843	1,958	204	212	471	74,893	56,518	17	18,358
Ninth	283,921	10,365	6,840	1,422	92	2,006	273,556	220,586	163	52,807
Tenth	71,184	2,334	1,614	253	95	372	68,850	55,018	16	13,816
Eleventh	163,694	3,090	1,718	714	60	596	160,604	87,558	93	72,953

*Cases commenced reflect initial filings, not subsequent transfers that may have occurred during the year from one chapter of the act to another.

[†]States or jurisdictions within each Circuit are as follows:

First Circuit: Maine, Massachusetts, New Hampshire, Rhode Island, Puerto Rico.

Second Circuit: Connecticut, New York, Vermont.

Third Circuit: Delaware, New Jersey, Pennsylvania, Virgin Islands.

Fourth Circuit: Maryland, North Carolina, South Carolina, Virginia, West Virginia.

Fifth Circuit: Louisiana, Mississippi, Texas.

Sixth Circuit: Kentucky, Michigan, Ohio, Tennessee.

Seventh Circuit: Illinois, Indiana, Wisconsin.

Eighth Circuit: Arkansas, Iowa, Minnesota, Missouri, Nebraska, North Dakota, South Dakota.

Ninth Circuit: Alaska, Arizona, California, Hawaii, Idaho, Montana, Nevada, Oregon, Washington, Guam.

Tenth Circuit: Colorado, Kansas, New Mexico, Oklahoma, Utah, Wyoming.

Eleventh Circuit: Alabama, Florida, Georgia.

Source: United States District Courts.

senses. A person is insolvent who either has ceased to pay his debts as they become due or is insolvent within the meaning of the Federal Bankruptcy Code. This definition is intended to be used for both the buyer's right to the delivery of goods on the seller's insolvency, and the seller's remedy in the event of the buyer's insolvency.[10]

§ 5.6 Equity versus Bankruptcy Meanings of Insolvency

It is important to make a clear distinction between the equity and bankruptcy meanings of insolvency. Under the 1867 Bankruptcy Act, the equity test was used to determine insolvency. The balance sheet approach replaced the equity test in the 1898 Act. The test of insolvency was important under this Act because it was a necessary element in proving three of the six acts of bankruptcy.[11] In two of the acts—making or suffering a preferential transfer while insolvent, and failing to discharge a judgment lien while insolvent—the balance sheet approach was used to prove insolvency.[12] A third act—suffering or permitting the appointment of a receiver while insolvent—required that the debtor be insolvent only in the equity sense; however, the balance sheet test as defined in section 1(19) of prior law may have been used as an alternative for the equity test.[13]

The Bankruptcy Code primarily makes use of the balance sheet test for insolvency. This law eliminates the "acts of bankruptcy" and allows the creditors to force the debtor into bankruptcy court under the condition that the debtor is generally not paying its debts as they become due. Thus, a petition may be allowed, even though the debtor is not bankrupt in the equity sense, under conditions where the debtor has the current funds to pay its debts but is generally not paying them. The balance sheet test as defined above in § 5.5 will be used as a condition for certain transfers that may be considered fraudulent or preferential.

It is quite possible for a firm to be temporarily unable to meet its current obligations but also be legally solvent. A business with a temporary shortage of liquid assets may be at the mercy of its creditors, regardless of whether its total position shows an excess of assets over liabilities. On the other hand, a debtor may be insolvent in the bankruptcy sense, with liabilities greater than the fair value of its assets, but temporarily paying its currently maturing debts. In this situation, creditors are normally unaware of the debtor's financial distress but, even if they were, they would be unable to organize and initiate proceedings to protect their interests.

§ 5.7 Determination of Assets and Liabilities

The Bankruptcy Act required that the fair value of the firm's assets exceed its liabilities for the firm to be considered solvent. Section 101(32) of the Bank-

---

[10] Sydney Krause, "What Constitutes Insolvency," *Proceedings, 27th NYU Institute on Federal Taxation* (1969), pp. 1085–86.

[11] Bankruptcy Act, § 3a(1–6).

[12] Thomas H. Burchfield, "Balance Sheet Test of Insolvency," *University of Pittsburgh Law Review*, Vol. 23 (October 1961), p. 6.

[13] *Id.*, pp. 6–7.

ruptcy Code explicitly excludes any property the debtor may have conveyed, transferred, concealed, removed, or permitted to be concealed or removed, with intent to defraud, hinder, or delay its creditors from its assets. Intangible property, such as trade names, patents, and property rights, has often been included. The total assets used in the balance sheet test for an individual also exclude the debtor's exempt property—that is, the assets that are expressly excluded by law from the payment of debts. The liabilities used in determining insolvency are defined in section 101(12) as "liability on a claim." The meaning of claim is defined in section 101(5) and discussed in § 5.31 and in § 11.21.

§ 5.8 Valuation of Assets

The method of determining the fair value of assets may also give rise to controversy. Two approaches are generally found in use by the courts today. First is the fair market value. Courts that use the fair value method have generally emphasized that it does not mean the amount that would be received for the assets at a forced sale. It also does not represent the value that could be received under ideal conditions during the normal course of business.[14] It is defined as "such a price as a capable and intelligent businessman could presently obtain for the property from a ready and willing buyer."[15] In valuation literature this approach is referred to as the *market* approach. This definition does not give any insight into whether the courts assume the assets will be sold separately or as a unit.[16] Second is the use value of the assets to the debtor, which is based on the future earning power of the business and assumes that the firm will continue to be operated by the debtor rather than be liquidated.[17] In valuation literature, this approach is referred to as the *income approach* and involves the use of either an earnings or cash flow multiple or the discounting of future cash flows. Since 1980, the discounting of future cash flows has been used most frequently. The first approach is used for situations where a business is being liquidated or under conditions where the business will reorganize and there are comparative market values available for individual assets such as real estate or similar businesses. The second is used under chapter 11 reorganization proceedings where the debtor expects to continue the operations of the business. Valuation literature also refers to a third approach—*cost*—that is based on the cost to replace the assets. At times this approach may be used in bankruptcy cases. Chapter 11 contains a detailed discussion of the approaches that are used to value businesses in financial trouble.

§ 5.9 Insolvency and the Bankruptcy Code

The various definitions of insolvency assumed importance in the different proceedings under the 1898 Bankruptcy Act. In Chapter XI arrangement proceedings, the petition had to be voluntarily filed and the debtor must have been

---

[14] *Duncan v. Landis*, 106 F. 839 (1901).
[15] *In re Ouellette*, 98 F. Supp. 941 at 943 (1951).
[16] Burchfield, *supra* note 12, p. 12.
[17] *Id.*, pp. 11–13.

insolvent in either the equity or bankruptcy sense. Corporate reorganization, as provided for in Chapter X, was voluntarily or involuntarily initiated, and also required insolvency in one of the two alternatives. However, which situation governed was of supreme importance to stockholders. Should the corporation be insolvent in the bankruptcy sense, the shareholders were not allowed to retain any interest in the reorganized corporation. On the other hand, the stockholders were included in the plan of reorganization if the corporation was insolvent only in the equity sense. Voluntarily to begin liquidation under prior law, the debtor did not need to be insolvent in any manner. For creditors to begin liquidation proceedings against the debtor, insolvency in the bankruptcy sense was necessary for the filing of a petition after the commission of an act of bankruptcy. There were two exceptions to this: a general assignment for the benefit of creditors, or an admission in writing of the debtor's inability to pay its debts and its willingness to be adjudicated bankrupt.

To force the debtor into involuntary bankruptcy under the Bankruptcy Code, insolvency is not a requirement. It is only necessary for the debtor to be not paying its debts as they become due or to allow the appointment of another custodian for all or substantially all of its assets.

Insolvency is not necessary for a voluntary chapter 11 or a chapter 13 petition; however, petitions filed by a debtor where equity or balance sheet test of insolvency does not exist may be dismissed. Very few chapter 11 business petitions have been dismissed because the debtor may be solvent. As long as there is some indication of financial problems, judges generally will not dismiss the petition. For example, the bankruptcy court ruled in *In re Johns-Manville*[18] that the elimination of the prior law's insolvency requirement was intentional and to be followed, and that reorganization was to be encouraged. Manville filed a bankruptcy petition in August 1982. At that time, it was a very solid company with operating profits and a positive net worth. One reason for the filing of the petition was the large number of asbestos victims' claims. The asbestos litigants claimed that the bankruptcy petition was filed in bad faith and was the result of pure fraud. The bankruptcy court held that the filing of the petition by Manville was not an abuse of the court's jurisdiction: a corporation was not created for the filing to defraud others, a legitimate operating history was not lacking, there was no absence of creditors or crushing debt, and there was no attempt to avoid taxes or foreclosure.

Lewis,[19] in analyzing the judge's decision, indicated that the opinion rests on three central ideas. First, Manville was facing both a short-term financial crisis—the accounting need to book reserves for future asbestos claims—and a long-term financial crisis in the predicted size of the future claims. The alternative to chapter 11 was liquidation, which would destroy Manville's ability to operate and preclude the profits necessary to pay later asbestos claimants. Second, the court held that, notwithstanding the potential difficulty in characterizing future asbestos victims as existing creditors, the Bankruptcy Code required that they be treated by the court equitably with other claimants to the

---

[18] 36 B.R. 727 (Bankr. S.D.N.Y. 1984).
[19] Daniel M. Lewis, "Corporate Bankruptcy Rulings Did Not Pry Open the Floodgates," *Los Angeles Daily Journal*, March 20, 1984, p. 4.

estate. Third, chapter 11 protections and procedures, including fundamental financial restructuring, were going to be used by the debtor in satisfying asbestos claims and preserving an operating entity.[20]

§ 5.10   Should There Be a Threshold Test?

The economic and social philosophy underlying the U.S. bankruptcy laws has changed significantly since this country was founded. Following the Great Depression and until the 1980s, the business community and the general public believed that the purpose of the federal bankruptcy law was to allow businesses and individuals in financial trouble to liquidate or reorganize. However, healthy and solvent companies have recently been using the bankruptcy system to resolve problems that are primarily legal. This has been to the detriment of public interest and, according to some, needs to be remedied by changing the current bankruptcy law.

As noted above, the first bankruptcy laws were for the benefit of creditors only. Later, consideration was given to debtors by allowing their debts to be discharged in exchange for cooperation. Public interest was given very little consideration in bankruptcy law until the 1930s. In 1933, modifications were made to allow railroads to reorganize and, in 1938, reorganization was made available to other businesses and to individuals. Reorganization served public interest better than liquidation because it allowed customers to continue receiving goods and services, enabled employees to keep their jobs, provided larger and more equitable distributions to creditors, and gave many stockholders the opportunity to receive larger returns on their investments.

Until recent years, bankruptcy carried a stigma that prevented most public companies from filing a bankruptcy petition unless it was the only viable solution to their financial problems. Thus, bankruptcy petitions were typically filed as a last resort by troubled businesses overburdened by debt that could only be restructured through the bankruptcy courts.

Currently, the stigma associated with bankruptcy has diminished and bankruptcy laws are used in many ways that are not consistent with the original purpose of the law. Some view bankruptcy as a vehicle for avoiding union contracts (this use was somewhat limited by an amendment to the bankruptcy law in 1984), obtaining access to overfunded pension plans, avoiding or delaying class action suits, or delaying or reducing liabilities for judgments.

Because current bankruptcy law does not preclude these misuses, the responsibility for protecting the integrity of the bankruptcy system rests with the courts. However, the courts have been reluctant to dismiss bankruptcy cases filed without "good faith" or evidence that the bankruptcy court is needed to solve the company's financial problems. Thus, apparently healthy, solvent companies are allowed to continue their use of bankruptcy courts to resolve legal problems and disputes. In the awareness of business and the general public, this has greatly increased confusion and lack of confidence regarding the U.S. bankruptcy system.

---

[20] *Id.*

The Texaco bankruptcy petition illustrates why there is so much confusion over the nature and purpose of federal bankruptcy law. Texaco filed its bankruptcy petition on April 12, 1987. In its annual report for the year ending December 31, 1986, Texaco reported total assets of approximately $35 billion with total stockholders' equity of just under $14 billion. The price of Texaco stock during the proceeding ($40 per share most of that time), which had to have been somewhat discounted due to a possible payment to Pennzoil, suggested that the stockholders' equity was worth approximately $10 billion. Security analysts had computed a value of over $70 per share (ignoring the Pennzoil judgment) for a total equity value of $17 billion. Furthermore, Texaco paid a $120 million dividend to common stockholders 33 days prior to filing the bankruptcy petition. Texaco also paid $10 billion for Getty, whose oil reserves alone were subsequently determined to be worth around $17 billion.

These facts would certainly suggest to some that Texaco did not need to use the bankruptcy court to survive, even if it had to pay the full judgment of over $10 billion. Ironically, in a court document filed prior to its bankruptcy, Texaco stated that it could find a way to pay the entire amount of the Pennzoil claim if it lost the case. Pennzoil made two offers to Texaco prior to the filing of the bankruptcy petition that would have required Texaco to pay much less than $10 billion to settle the judgment. After Texaco filed the petition, Pennzoil also indicated that it would settle the judgment for just over $4 billion and subsequently settled for $3 billion.

The Bankruptcy Code does not specifically preclude healthy, solvent companies from filing a bankruptcy petition, and the courts are reluctant to limit their jurisdiction to companies experiencing financial difficulty. It has therefore been suggested by several writers that Congress needs to revise the Bankruptcy Code. This revision may take the form of a threshold test that must be met before an individual, corporation, or other entity uses the bankruptcy court to resolve its debt problems. Such a threshold requirement would preclude healthy, solvent companies from using the bankruptcy courts, thus freeing additional court time for companies that are in actual financial difficulty and in need of the services of the court to effectively reorganize. Precluding viable companies from using the bankruptcy courts may also encourage them to resolve their problems sooner, through negotiations. Perhaps Texaco would have changed its strategy if it had been unable to file a bankruptcy petition.

Bankruptcy laws in the United States have enabled many companies that otherwise would have gone out of business to reorganize and operate profitably. As a result, many employees have kept their jobs and creditors have received greater payments than would have been received if these businesses had liquidated. According to some, action needs to be taken to prevent the misuse of our bankruptcy laws before the public becomes so disillusioned with the system that it overreacts, causing many truly beneficial provisions to be discarded in an attempt to eliminate the abuses. However, since Texaco, it would appear that public companies not in financial difficulty have made limited use of the bankruptcy courts, thus limiting, at least temporarily, the need for a threshold test.

§ 5.11 Alternatives Available to a Financially Troubled Business

When a corporation finds itself heading toward serious financial difficulties and unable to obtain new financing or to solve the problem internally, it should seek a remedy vis-à-vis its creditors either informally (out of court) or with the help of judicial proceedings. Under either method, the debtor has several alternatives to choose from as to the particular way it will seek relief. The method selected depends on the debtor's history, size, and future outlook, and on the creditors' attitudes, types, and size of claims. In studying the alternatives that face a financially troubled company, two issues are important:

1   Should the company liquidate or reorganize?
2   Should the liquidation or reorganization take place out of court or in bankruptcy court?

The first alternative is to liquidate the business. This can be done in most states through an assignment under state or common law for the benefit of creditors or through a liquidation under chapter 7 of the Bankruptcy Code. This chapter describes these liquidation proceedings. Because it will be helpful to understand assignments before looking at chapter 7 liquidation, these are described in the next section of this chapter.

Where it is desirable for the business to continue, and it appears that the business has the possibility of again resuming profitable operations, rehabilitation proceedings can be pursued either out of court or under the Bankruptcy Code. Chapter 4 is devoted to a discussion of out-of-court settlements. Proceedings to rehabilitate the business under the bankruptcy law must proceed through either chapter 11 or 13 of the Bankruptcy Code, the topic of discussion in Chapter 6.

ASSIGNMENT FOR THE BENEFIT OF CREDITORS (STATE COURT)

§ 5.12   Introduction

Under an assignment for the benefit of creditors, the debtor voluntarily transfers title to all his or her assets to a trustee or assignee who then sells or otherwise liquidates the assets and distributes the proceeds among the creditors on a pro rata basis. An assignment provides an orderly method of liquidation and prevents the disruption of the business by individual creditors armed with attachments or executions acquired subsequent to the assignment. Most statutes uphold assignments against the attack of particular creditors.

The board of directors usually has the power to make an assignment for the benefit of creditors when the corporation is insolvent. However, when a going concern sells a large share of its assets, such action typically must be approved by the stockholders.

§ 5.13   Duties, Functions, and Procedures of Assignee

The debtor initiates the action by executing an instrument of assignment, which is recorded in the county where executed. This recordation serves as notice to all third parties. Most statutes have no prohibition against the choice of the debtor's representative as the assignee. Thus, the proceeding is of a quasi-judicial nature: the corporation may select anyone it prefers to act as the assignee, but the person chosen is subject to the control of the court in states where judicial supervision exists.[21] Attorneys are generally selected as the assignees. The statutes in New York[22] and in California,[23] as in many other states, are very comprehensive and contain detailed regulations covering the proceedings, which include specifications of the duties and powers of each assignee. The assignee supervises the proceedings, including the sale of the assets and the distribution of the proceeds. This procedure results in a quick disposition of assets and avoids creditors' attaching claims to the assets or the debtor's wasteful use of the assets. But if the facts warrant a finding of misconduct or incompetence on the part of the debtor and/or assignee, the creditors could petition for a substitution of the assignee or file an involuntary petition in bankruptcy within a short time (four months) after the assignment under prior law. Under the new law, the time period is 120 days (section 303(h)(2)).

Assignees are trustees for all the unsecured creditors and will be held personally liable to the creditors if they fail to exercise the care and diligence required of trustees. To further ensure the protection of the creditors, assignees may be required to post a bond. The duties of assignees generally include taking charge of, inventorying, collecting, and liquidating the assets transferred to them. Liquidation is usually done at a public sale, although a private sale may be held upon specific authorization by court order. Assignees also collect any money owed the debtor, solicit additional claims, and distribute the proceeds from the liquidation to the creditors on a pro rata basis, giving preference to any claims that are legally entitled to priority, such as secured claims, taxes, and wages. Assignees in some states must have their accounts approved and their bond discharged by the court.

It may be advantageous to continue the business for a short period if it appears that the amount realized from liquidation will be greater if the business is phased out gradually rather than liquidated immediately. Also, if the necessary adjustments can be made to the operations so that there is a net cash inflow, the business may continue long enough to satisfy all, or at least a large percentage, of the creditors' claims. It will be necessary under these conditions for the assignee to take, on advice of counsel, the action necessary to ensure that he will not be held personally liable for any losses that occur. Any profits earned accrue to the benefit of the creditors.

§ 5.14 Discharge of Debts

State assignment laws do not discharge debts; thus, this remedy does not offer a means of canceling the debts of the corporation. The creditors may receive their pro rata dividends and still have a valid claim against the debtor. Thus, the individual debtor must still file a bankruptcy court petition and obtain a discharge if he or she wants to be relieved of his or her debts. This limitation is of lesser consequence because a corporation or partnership cannot obtain a discharge in chapter 7 according to section 727(a)(1) of the new Bank-

---

[21] William J. Grange et al., *Manual for Corporation Officers* (New York: The Ronald Press Co., 1967), p. 391.
[22] New York Debtor and Creditor Law, §§ 2–24.
[23] California Civil Code, §§ 3448–71.

ruptcy Code. Although the debtor is not automatically discharged through the proceedings of an assignment, it may in some states discharge itself by writing on the dividend check the necessary legal language to make the payment a complete discharge of the obligation.[24] Essentially, this is a statement that endorsement of the check represents full payment for the obligation.[25] As a practical matter, this is not generally done because it is the assignee who issues the dividend checks.

For an assignment to be successful, consent of nearly all the creditors must be obtained, or at least they must refrain from filing an involuntary petition. If only a few creditors object, they may be paid off. In most states, formal acceptance is not legally required and all creditors are not necessarily asked for their consent. However, if any three unsecured creditors with claims totaling at least $5,000 are opposed to the assignment and desire to file a bankruptcy petition based on the assignment, they are free to do so within 120 days after the assignment. In most states, if no creditor action is taken within 120 days, the assignment is then binding on all creditors. Because it is a federal statute, the Bankruptcy Code is superior in authority to the state laws governing assignments. Therefore, when a petition in bankruptcy is filed, the assignee must surrender control and turn the assets over to the trustee[26] in bankruptcy. If the debtor is unable to obtain the support of nearly all the creditors, it should file a petition under the Bankruptcy Code because it will be impossible to arrange an assignment for the benefit of the creditors.

Assignments may also be used as a condition of an out-of-court settlement to continued negotiations, to become effective upon default of the debtor to the terms of the agreement, the failure of the debtor to negotiate fairly, or the happening of other events set forth in the settlement or assignment.[27] Thus, an assignment is used as an "escrow document" where the collateral is deposited with the creditors' committee; in the event of a default by the debtor in making payments, the creditors can liquidate the debtor's assets through the assignment or use the assignment to force the debtor into bankruptcy court.[28]

§ 5.15 Advantages

An assignment for the benefit of creditors has the advantage of being quicker, simpler, and less expensive than bankruptcy court proceedings. It is simpler to initiate and less time-consuming to consummate. It is also preferred by debtors because they are able to select their own liquidators. Under this procedure, creditors usually receive a larger percentage of their claims because more time is available to find good buyers, a foreclosure sale is not necessary,

---

[24] For example, this does not apply in Massachusetts. *See Foakes v. Beer*, 9 App. Cas. 605 (England, 1884).

[25] Fred Weston, *Managerial Finance* (Hinsdale, IL: Dryden Press, 1978), pp. 905–06.

[26] 11 U.S.C. § 543.

[27] Sydney Krause, "Insolvent Debtor Adjustments under Relevant State Court Status as against Proceedings under the Bankruptcy Act," *The Business Lawyer*, Vol. 12 (January 1957), p. 189.

[28] 11 U.S.C. § 303(h)(1). *See* Benjamin Weintraub, Harris Levin, and Eugene Sosnoff, "Assignment for the Benefit of Creditors and Competitive Systems for Liquidation of Insolvent Estates," *Cornell Law Quarterly*, Vol. 39 (1953–1954), pp. 4–6.

and court and legal costs are greatly reduced.[29] An additional advantage to the debtor is that its self-image suffers less damage than if it were to experience the stigma associated with bankruptcy. Less publicity is involved and a future credit rating may suffer less. Assignments have also been successful in preserving assets for the benefit of creditors. If any creditor attempts to take action before any of the other creditors, the debtor may effect an assignment so that all the creditors will be treated equally. Under such circumstances, a vindictive creditor does not have an advantage, because there is no property in the hands of a debtor on which a judgment must rest as a lien.[30]

§ 5.16 Disadvantages

If certain preferences must be set aside or liens invalidated, bankruptcy court proceedings are essential for the creditors. Some states do not allow any preferences, others have very limited provisions, and a few have fairly detailed provisions. For example, New York has a preference law and California allows an assignee to avoid preferences. Federal tax claims in insolvency proceedings are governed by section 3466 of the Revised Statutes[31] where "debts due to the United States shall be first satisfied." If the claims are not satisfied, personal liability is imposed on the assignee.[32] Section 3466 of the Revised Statutes does not apply in a case under title 11 because of an amendment made in the 1978 legislation.

Satisfaction of federal tax claims is required only after administrative expenses are paid, but they do have priority over state and local taxes and wages.[33] In general, "the assignee's armory is rather weak compared with the trustee's arsenal."[34] There are, however, some states, such as California and New York, where the assignment law is very strong.

A disadvantage often cited for the debtor is the possibility of dissenting creditors or an inability to compel the creditors to assent to the assignment. This is found to be inconsequential in the case of a corporation, however, because following the realization of the assignment no assets will remain for such creditors to pursue.

An assignment would be inappropriate in any case involving fraud and requiring intensive investigation. Such situations should be handled in the bankruptcy courts. It should also be realized that there are often major differences between the procedures under state court statutes and the Bankruptcy Code, and the various classes of creditors should be aware of the distinctions in the order of priority in state assignments and the Bankruptcy Code.

Even though the appointment of an assignee to liquidate the business may be used by the creditors as the basis for a petition in involuntary bankruptcy,

---

[29] Elvin F. Donaldson, John K. Pfahl, and Peter L. Mullins, *Corporate Finance*, 4th ed. (New York: The Ronald Press Co., 1975), p. 615.
[30] Gerstenberg, *supra* note 5, p. 516.
[31] 31 U.S.C. § 191.
[32] 31 U.S.C. § 192.
[33] *Kennebec Box Co. v. O.S. Richards Corp.*, 5 F.2d 951 (2d Cir. 1925).
[34] Richard A. Kaye, "Federal Taxes, Bankruptcy and Assignments for the Benefit of Creditors—A Comparison," *Commercial Law Journal*, Vol. 73 (March 1968), p. 78.

it is still commonly used, especially in the New York City area. Assignment is a less expensive but effective means of orderly liquidation in situations where there is no particular need for bankruptcy proceedings. Indeed, the court may, under section 305, abstain from handling a case if it determines that the interests of creditors would be better served by the dismissal or suspension of the proceedings.

PROVISIONS COMMON TO ALL PROCEEDINGS

§ 5.17 Introduction

Title 11 of the U.S. Code contains the major part of the Bankruptcy Reform Act of 1978. It consists of eight chapters:

Chapter 1: General Provisions

Chapter 3: Case Administration

Chapter 5: Creditors, the Debtor, and the Estate

Chapter 7: Liquidation

Chapter 9: Adjustment of Debts of a Municipality

Chapter 11: Reorganization

Chapter 12: Adjustments of Debts of a Family Farmer with Regular Annual Income

Chapter 13: Adjustment of Debts of an Individual with Regular Income

Chapters 1, 3, and 5 apply to all proceedings except chapter 9 under the Code. The provisions of chapter 9 regarding municipalities and chapter 11 regarding railroad reorganizations are, in their specific detail, beyond the scope of this book.

The Bankruptcy Reform Act also contains several provisions that modify other statutes. Included are the addition of chapters 6, 50, and 90, dealing with bankruptcy courts, and chapter 39, establishing the pilot U.S. trustee system under title 28 of the U.S. Code. These statutes and the Bankruptcy Code (title 11) were modified by the Bankruptcy Amendments and Federal Judgeship Act of 1984.

Another modification was made in October 1986, when Congress passed the Bankruptcy Judges, United States Trustees, and Family Farmer Bankruptcy Act of 1986. This Act, in addition to authorizing the appointment of 52 new bankruptcy judges, established a U.S. Trustee system throughout the United States and created a chapter 12 for a family farmer who has financial problems. Chapter 15 of the Bankruptcy Code was repealed; however, the provisions of this chapter were incorporated in the other chapters. Chapter 12 was scheduled to be repealed as of October 1, 1993, unless Congress voted to extend this date or to repeal the limitations on the life of this chapter. Public Law 103-65, enacted August 6, 1993, extended the use of chapter 12 to October 1, 1998. Two subsequent amendments have extended the use of chapter 12 to July 1, 2000.

§ 5.18 Bankruptcy Courts

The Bankruptcy Reform Act of 1978 established a bankruptcy court in each judicial district, with jurisdiction to decide almost any matter that related to the estate. This jurisdiction included the traditional "case matters," such as objections to discharge or claim, as well as affirmative actions against third parties who may have filed a claim against the estate such as preferential transfers or fraudulent transfer actions. The court also had the jurisdiction to hear matters related to antitrust actions, personal injury claims, wrongful deaths claims, and any other matter related to the bankruptcy case. Each bankruptcy court consisted of the bankruptcy judge or judges for the district.[35] The judges were appointed for a term of 14 years at a salary of $50,000 subject to annual adjustments.[36] It was these latter two provisions that caused the Supreme Court, in June 1982, to rule that the broad jurisdictional power granted to these judges was unconstitutional.[37] "Article III judges" should have a salary of $75,000, not $50,000 subject to annual adjustment, and life tenure, not a 14-year term. The Supreme Court delayed the effective date of its decision until December 24, 1982, to give Congress time to correct the constitutional problems mentioned above. Congress did not act and the bankruptcy court operated under an emergency resolution whereby the bankruptcy judges continued to act under the supervision of the district judges.

On July 10, 1984, President Reagan signed the Bankruptcy Amendments and Federal Judgeship Act of 1984.[38] This Act states that the district court *may* provide that any or all cases under title 11 and any or all proceedings arising under title 11 shall be referred to the bankruptcy judges for the district. Thus, the Act gives some discretion to the district court to retain some cases or other bankruptcy matters.[39]

Section 157(b) of title 28 provides that the bankruptcy judge may hear and decide all cases and all "core proceedings" arising in a case referred to the bankruptcy court by the district court. The term "core proceedings" as used in the Act is much broader than in the past. Generally, "core proceedings" includes such matters as allowance of claims, objections to discharge, confirmation of plans, and the like. The definition of "core proceedings" used in the Act includes, but is not limited to, the following:

1 Matters concerning administration of the estate.
2 Allowance or disallowance of claims and determination of exemption claims.
3 Counterclaims by the estate against persons filing claims.

---

[35] 28 U.S.C. § 151.
[36] *Id.*, §§ 153 and 154.
[37] *Northern Pipeline Construction Co. v. Marathon Pipe Line Co.*, 102 S. Ct. 2858 (1982).
[38] The author acknowledges the assistance provided by Bronson, Bronson, and McKinnon, in San Francisco, in summarizing the provisions of the sections of the Act that relate to the new bankruptcy court system.
[39] 28 U.S.C. § 157.

4   Orders relating to obtaining of credit.

5   Orders relating to turnover of property of the estate.

6   Proceedings to determine, avoid, or recover preferences.

7   Motions to terminate or modify the automatic stay.

8   Proceedings to determine, avoid, or recover fraudulent conveyances.

9   Determination as to dischargeability of debts.

10   Objections to discharge.

11   Determinations of the validity, extent, or priority of liens.

12   Confirmation of plans.

13   Orders approving the use or lease of property, including the use of cash collateral.

14   Orders approving the sale of property of the estate.

15   Other proceedings affecting the liquidation of the assets of the estate or the adjustment of the debtor–creditor or the equity–security holder relationship, except personal injury tort or wrongful death claims.

The Bankruptcy Amendments and Federal Judgeship Act of 1984 provided that personal injury tort and wrongful death claims are to be heard in the district court in the district where the bankruptcy case is pending or in the district where the claim arose, as determined by the district court where the bankruptcy case is pending. Except for personal injury and wrongful death claims, the bankruptcy judge may claim the matter is a core proceeding under this broad definition. This will be an area of future litigation.

If the bankruptcy judge determines that it is a noncore proceeding, the proceeding may still be heard in the bankruptcy court. However, the bankruptcy judge may submit findings of fact and conclusions of law to the district court for a final order after reviewing the proposed findings and conclusions and any matter to which a party specifically objected. If prior practice continues, the district court will rely heavily on the findings of the bankruptcy court.

Under the new Act, bankruptcy appeals are to go to the district court or to a bankruptcy appellate panel consisting of three bankruptcy judges.

Appeal from the decision of the district court or the appellate panel is to the appropriate circuit court of appeals. Prior to the Bankruptcy Reform Act of 1994, only the Ninth Circuit had established bankruptcy appellate panels. The 1994 Act provides that section 158(b) of title 28 of the United States Code is amended to create bankruptcy appellate panels in each judicial circuit. The panels are to consist of sitting bankruptcy judges who serve in place of the district court in reviewing bankruptcy court decisions. Under this provision, each judicial council of each circuit must establish the appellate panel unless the council finds that insufficient judicial resources are available in the circuit or that establishment would result in undue delay or increased cost to the parties. In circuits where bankruptcy appellate panels are established and operating, all appeals from the bankruptcy court are to be heard by the appellate panel unless a party makes a timely election to have the appeal heard by the district court. Bankruptcy appellate panels are currently operating in the First, Second, Sixth, Eight, Ninth, and Tenth Circuits.

§ 5.19 U.S. Trustee

Chapter 39 of title 28 of the U.S. Code provides for the establishment of the U.S. trustee program. The Attorney General is responsible for appointing one U.S. trustee in each of the 21 regions and one or more assistant U.S. trustees when the public interest requires such an appointment. The U.S. trustees perform the supervisory and appointing functions formerly handled by bankruptcy judges. They are the principal administrative officers of the bankruptcy system. The U.S. trustees and assistant U.S. trustees are appointed to serve five-year terms. The U.S. trustee, subject to the Attorney General's approval, may appoint and supervise standing trustees to handle the administration of chapter 12 and 13 cases. See § 9.3 for a discussion of the involvement of the U.S. trustee in chapter 11 cases.

The Bankruptcy Judges, United States Trustees, and Family Farmer Bankruptcy Act of 1966 expanded the U.S. trustee system throughout the United States. Prior to this Act, the system applied to only ten pilot programs covering 18 judicial districts. Once the U.S. trustee system is operating in all regions, there will be a U.S. trustee in the following 21 regions composed of federal judicial districts:

1 The judicial districts established for the states of Maine, Massachusetts, New Hampshire, and Rhode Island.

2 The judicial districts established for the states of Connecticut, New York, and Vermont.

3 The judicial districts established for the states of Delaware, New Jersey, and Pennsylvania.

4 The judicial districts established for the states of Maryland, North Carolina, South Carolina, Virginia, and West Virginia, and for the District of Columbia.

5 The judicial districts established for the states of Louisiana and Mississippi.

6 The Northern District of Texas and the Eastern District of Texas.

7 The Southern District of Texas and the Western District of Texas.

8 The judicial districts established for the states of Kentucky and Tennessee.

9 The judicial districts established for the states of Michigan and Ohio.

10 The Central District of Illinois and the Southern District of Illinois; and the judicial districts established for the state of Indiana.

11 The Northern District of Illinois; and the judicial districts established for the state of Wisconsin.

12 The judicial districts established for the states of Minnesota, Iowa, North Dakota, and South Dakota.

13 The judicial districts established for the states of Arkansas, Nebraska, and Missouri.

14 The District of Arizona.

15 The Southern District of California; and the judicial districts established for the state of Hawaii, and for Guam and the Commonwealth of the Northern Mariana Islands.

16   The Central District of California.

17   The Eastern District of California and the Northern District of California; and the judicial district established for the state of Nevada.

18   The judicial districts established for the states of Alaska, Idaho (exclusive of Yellowstone National Park), Montana (exclusive of Yellowstone National Park), Oregon, and Washington.

19   The judicial districts established for the states of Colorado, Utah, and Wyoming (including those portions of Yellowstone National Park situated in the states of Montana and Idaho).

20   The judicial districts established for the states of Kansas, New Mexico, and Oklahoma.

21   The judicial districts established for the states of Alabama, Florida, and Georgia, and for the Commonwealth of Puerto Rico and the Virgin Islands of the United States.

The U.S. trustee will establish, maintain, and supervise a panel of private trustees who are eligible and available to serve as trustee in cases under chapter 7 or 11. Also, the U.S. trustee will supervise the administration of the estate and the trustees in cases under chapter 7, 11, 12, or 13. It is not intended that the U.S. trustee system will replace private trustees in chapter 7 and chapter 11. Rather, the system should relieve the bankruptcy judges of certain administrative and supervisory tasks and thus help to eliminate any institutional bias or the appearance of any such bias that may have existed in the prior bankruptcy system.[40]

The Bankruptcy Judges, United States Trustees, and Family Farmers Bankruptcy Act of 1986 provided that the judicial districts of Alabama and North Carolina were not to be a part of the expansion of the U.S. Trustee program until October 1, 1992. The Judicial Improvements Act of 1990 (P.L. 101-650, signed by President Bush on December 1, 1990) extended to October 1, 2002, the time period in which these districts must be a part of the system. However, any of the six districts affected by this exception may elect to become a part of the U.S. Trustee program prior to that date.

(a) Functions of U.S. Trustee

Under the provisions of the 1986 amendments, the panel of trustees that is appointed by the U.S. trustee will now be extended to all regions. The Attorney General will promulgate rules that establish qualifications for membership on the panel. The regulations to be issued may not require that members of the panel be restricted to attorneys. Section 586(a) of title 28 of the U.S. Code lists the following functions of the U.S. trustee:

1   Monitor applications for compensation and reimbursement for officers filed under section 330 of title 11 and, whenever the U.S. trustee deems it to be appropriate, file with the court comments with respect to any of such applications.

---

[40] *CCH Bankruptcy Reports,* ¶ 14,001.

2   Monitor plans and disclosure statements filed in cases under chapter 11 and file with the court comments with respect to such plans and disclosure statements.

3   Monitor plans filed under chapters 12 and 13 of title 11 and file with the court comments with respect to such plans.

4   Take such action as the U.S. trustee deems to be appropriate to ensure that all reports, schedules, and fees required to be filed under title 11 and this title by the debtor are properly and timely filed.

5   Monitor creditors' committees appointed under title 11.

6   Notify the appropriate U.S. attorney of matters that relate to the occurrence of any action that may constitute a crime under the laws of the United States and, on the request of the U.S. attorney, assist the U.S. attorney in carrying out prosecutions based on such action.

7   Monitor the progress of cases under title 11 and take such actions as the U.S. trustee deems to be appropriate to prevent undue delay in such progress.

8   Monitor applications filed under section 327 for the retention of accountants and other professionals and, whenever the U.S. trustee deems it to be appropriate, file with the court comments with respect to the approval of such applications.

9   Perform other duties that the Attorney General may prescribe.

As described previously, the trustee program will be expanded to all districts. A task force consisting of representatives from the Administrative Office of the U.S. Courts and the U.S. Trustee's Executive Office was formed to discuss the implementation throughout the United States. The task force proposed "Interim Transitional Guidelines" to describe how the duties and responsibilities of the U.S. trustee will be accomplished as the program is expanded. In October 1991, the task force developed a memorandum of understanding pertaining to the closing of cases and the monitoring of chapter 11 cases after confirmation. This memorandum, presented as Exhibit 5-2, replaces the guidelines previously issued.

Although it will have a more direct impact on attorneys, this memorandum will give accountants who have not previously worked with the U.S. trustee's office an indication of how the U.S. trustee's office interfaces with professionals and a description of the role of U.S. trustees.

§ 5.20   Sovereign Immunity

Effective for all petitions filed after October 22, 1994, and for all petitions pending as of that date, the Bankruptcy Reform Act of 1994 modified section 106 of the Bankruptcy Code to provide for a waiver of sovereign immunity by governmental units with respect to monetary recoveries as well as declaratory and injunctive relief. This modification was designed to overrule two Supreme Court decisions holding that the states and the federal government are not deemed to have waived their sovereign immunity under the prior wording of section 106 of the Bankruptcy Code. For example, the Supreme Court held, in

Exhibit 5-2 Memorandum of Understanding between the Executive Office for United States Trustees and the Administrative Office of the United States Courts Regarding Case Closing and Postconfirmation Chapter 11 Monitoring

The purpose of this memorandum is to set forth the responsibilities and procedures pertaining to the closing of cases and the monitoring of chapter 11 cases after confirmation.

I. Background

Upon the implementation of the United States trustee program nationwide pursuant to Pub. L. 99-554 (1986), the Executive Office for United States Trustees (EOUST) and the Administrative Office of the United States Courts (AO) meet periodically to discuss matters of mutual concern. Representatives of the bankruptcy courts and United States trustees participate in such meetings.

1. The administration of a particular estate is entrusted to private individuals, whether a trustee under chapters 7, 11, 12, and 13 of the Bankruptcy Code, or the debtor itself under chapter 11. Ensuring efficient and effective administration of the case is the responsibility of both the United States trustee and the court. As the degree of creditor participation in a chapter 7 liquidation case is generally limited, review by the United States trustee of how a particular estate is administered is important. Additionally, ensuring the final resolution of a chapter 11 case, after the plan has been confirmed, so that the court may close the case, is an important element of effective case administration.

2. Pursuant to 28 U.S.C. section 586, the United States trustee has the responsibility to appoint private trustees, oversee their performance, and generally supervise the administration of estates.

3. Pursuant to 11 U.S.C. section 350, and 28 U.S.C. section 151 *et seq.*, the court's responsibility includes adjudicating disputes arising in a case and approving certain actions of debtors and trustees. Under 11 U.S.C. section 350, the court has the responsibility to close a case and discharge the trustee.

4. Pursuant to 28 U.S.C. section 156(b) and FRBP 5001, the clerk of the court (clerk) is the recipient and repository of all court records. The clerk also assists the court in carrying out its duties.

5. The court, the clerk, and the United States trustee all have a responsibility to ensure that cases move expeditiously, efficiently and properly through the system.

6. In March 1988 the Judicial Conference of the United States directed that clerks' offices not perform or duplicate the case closing review function performed by the United States trustee. *See* Resolution of the Judicial Conference, Conf. Rpt. at pp. 9–10 (March 1988).

7. Effective August 1, 1991, FRBP 5009 creates a presumption that a panel or standing trustee has fully administered an estate under chapters 7, 12, and 13 of the Bankruptcy Code, absent a timely objection by a party in interest or the United States trustee to the panel or standing trustee's final report and certification.

8. Also addressed in this memorandum are responsibilities regarding chapter 11 cases subsequent to confirmation but prior to the closing of the case. The responsibilities have been structured in terms of FRBP 3022.

II. Duties of the United States Trustee in Case Closing—The United States trustee shall undertake the following efforts with regard to case closings in chapters 7, 12, and 13 cases.

Exhibit 5-2 *(continued)*

A. Review of chapter 7 asset reports—The trustee will submit a proposed final report (wherein the trustee proposes a distribution or payment of dividend from the estate) to the United States trustee. The United States trustee will review within 60 days of receipt all proposed final reports in chapter 7 asset cases utilizing the following procedures:

The United States trustee will conduct a thorough review of all asset case reports. This involves determining that all assets in the estate were properly administered (*i.e.,* examination of exemptions, abandonments, sales, or other liquidations). All reports will be reviewed to ensure the inclusion of court orders approving employment, payment of compensation, sales (if applicable) and other actions taken by the trustee in the case. All fee requests and expense reimbursement requests filed on behalf of the trustee and/or other professionals or agents will be reviewed for compliance with the Bankruptcy Code and Rules. All calculations in the trustee's final report, including the calculation of the trustee's fee and proposed dividends to creditors, will be reviewed for correctness. Based upon a review of case documents received by the United States trustee, a determination will be made that the trustee has reviewed and properly dealt with all claims. The United States trustee will rely on the trustee's certification that all claims have been reviewed. If deemed necessary by the United States trustee, the trustee's certification will be verified by further review of the documents on file with the clerk. Deficiencies in the trustee's administration or other problems or mistakes will be brought to the trustee's attention for corrective action.

The United States trustee will file the proposed final report or an amended proposed final report with the clerk, noting that the report has been reviewed, at or before the end of the 60 day review period, if all deficiencies are resolved. The filing of the proposed final report will constitute the case trustee's final report. If the case trustee does not agree with the United States trustee's position that the report is deficient, the United States trustee shall file the proposed final report with the clerk by the end of the 60 day review period, indicating his objection to the final report pursuant to FRBP 5009. The United States trustee may also file a motion for an extension of time to obtain an amended or corrected final report or make such other request for remedial action.

The United States trustee will place responsibility on the panel trustees, in accordance with FRBP 5009, to certify that the estate has been properly administered, including documenting the disposition of assets, expenditures, review of claims and final distribution and may rely on such certification, as appropriate. Upon the completion of distribution, the trustee will submit a proposed final account and application for final decree and discharge of the trustee to the United States trustee. The United States trustee will review the trustee's proposed final account for accuracy. Upon completion of the review and the correction of any deficiencies, the United States trustee will file within 30 days of receipt the proposed final account and application for final decree and discharge of the trustee with the court. This will constitute the trustee's final account and application for final decree and discharge of the trustee.

It will be the United States trustee's responsibility to see that adequate procedures are in place in all offices to ensure an effective and efficient case closing procedure. The court will not be involved in the review process other than hearing objections, should they be filed.

Exhibit 5-2 *(continued)*

B. Review of chapter 7 no asset cases—Pursuant to 11 U.S.C. section 704(9), the trustee will file a final report and account (report of no distribution) with the court with a copy to the United States trustee, within 60 days of the meeting required by 11 U.S.C. 341. In order to assure proper filing of the report, the clerk and United States trustee will periodically exchange a list of those no asset reports each has received.

Because of the nature and volume of no asset cases, a detailed review of each case is not feasible. The United States trustee's review will be based on an evaluation of a random sample of reports of no distribution submitted by each trustee. In those cases selected for review, the schedules will be examined to determine that all assets listed were properly exempted or of no value to the estate. If it appeared that assets were available for liquidation, the minute report or the section 341 meeting tape will be reviewed to see if it explains the failure to liquidate. If it does not, the trustee will be required to provide an explanation. If the deficiencies are of such magnitude that the United States trustee believes that the court should reopen the cases, the United States trustee will make such a motion to the court. Errors, omissions or a clear failure to perform will result in a more thorough review of that trustee's work product and, if deemed appropriate, action will be taken by the United States trustee. In addition to this process, a verification letter will be sent to the debtor in the sampled cases as a further substantiation that assets were not turned over to the trustee.

C. Review of chapter 12 and 13 cases—With regard to chapter 12 and 13 case closings, the United States trustee's review will be based on the supervision of the standing trustees through reporting requirements, budget approvals and on site visits as well as an annual audit by an independent certified public accounting (CPA) firm. If the standing chapter 12 and 13 trustee falls below the threshold amount for the hiring of an independent CPA, an annual review will be conducted by the United States trustee's office or other office of the Department of Justice. During an audit, selected cases will be reviewed in depth for the accuracy of receipts and disbursements. Internal controls and procedures will also be scrutinized. The annual audit will be made available to the court if requested.

In conformance with these procedures, the chapter 12 and 13 standing trustees will incorporate "a certification that the estate has been fully administered" in their final report in order to comply with the provisions of proposed changes in FRBP 5009.

If warranted, the United States trustee will object to the trustee's final report and account based upon the utilization of these review procedures in conformance with FRBP 5009 as amended.

If the caseload has not warranted the appointment of a standing chapter 12 or 13 trustee, those chapter 12 and 13 cases will be processed on a case by case basis in the manner established for chapter 7 asset cases.

III. **Court and Clerk**—The court and clerk shall undertake the following efforts.

A. Chapter 7 Asset Cases

1. The clerk will receive all final reports and final accounts and certifications that the estate has been fully administered. The clerk shall have the responsibility to see that all docket entries are accurate and complete. The clerk's office will bring to the attention of the United States trustee any discrepancies or deficiencies discovered in the course of its statistical

Exhibit 5-2 *(continued)*

processing so that such can be resolved. Staff of the clerk's office, however, should not be used to perform or duplicate the United States trustee's responsibilities.

   2. Pursuant to FRBP 3009, the court will enter an Order for Distribution and, upon submission of a final account and application for final decree and discharge of trustee, close the case pursuant to 11 U.S.C. section 350.

  B. Chapter 7 No Asset Cases

   1. Upon receiving the final report and account (report of no distribution) in a no asset case, the clerk shall proceed to close the case and undertake the process to pay the case trustee, upon the expiration of both the time limits (pursuant to FRBP 5009) for filing objections to the case trustee's report and for filing objections to the debtor's discharge (pursuant to FRBP 4004(a)).

   2. The court, pursuant to 11 U.S.C. section 350 and FRBP 5009, will enter an order to discharge the trustee and close the case after the expiration of the 30 day period set forth in FRBP 5009.

  C. Chapter 12 and 13 Cases

   1. The court, pursuant to 11 U.S.C. section 350 and FRBP 5009, after submission by the standing trustee of the final report and account and certification that an estate has been fully administered, shall close the case.

   2. In judicial districts where no standing trustee has been appointed, chapter 12 and 13 cases shall be processed and closed in the manner established for chapter 7 asset reports.

IV. Post Confirmation Chapter 11 Cases

  A. Background

   1. The AO and EOUST agree that the issue of ensuring that a plan of confirmation is implemented to the degree necessary to allow the court to close the case is a challenge to efficient and effective case administration. In this regard, the following efforts shall be undertaken.

    a. Court and Clerk—As part of the confirmation of a debtor's plan, the court generally provides that a debtor shall certify to the court that disbursements pursuant to the plan have been undertaken, *i.e.*, file a final report with a motion for a final decree. If available in an automated format, the clerk will periodically provide the United States trustee a list of those cases where a final report has not been timely filed.

    b. United States trustee—The United States trustee will review any application for a final decree and report(s) required by the order of confirmation pursuant to his overall responsibility to monitor the case, the debtor-in-possession or trustee. If deemed appropriate, the United States trustee will object to such motion and report(s). If no objection has been filed within 30 days of the filing of the report(s), a presumption can be made that the estate has been properly administered. Where no timely final report has been filed, the United States trustee will undertake efforts to secure the filing of the final report, or seek the appropriate remedy from the court.

V. Implementation and Follow-Up—The responsibilities that are set forth herein require resources and the establishment of procedures. It will require time to obtain resources and the full implementation of the standards set forth herein.

Exhibit 5-2   *(continued)*

Efforts should be undertaken to implement the necessary procedures to reflect the intent of this memorandum as soon as possible. The standards set forth herein, and the efforts to implement these standards, are a foundation toward improving the administration of bankruptcy cases. All parties are committed to this goal, and the need to continually examine policies and procedures so that they can be refined. Comments, questions, or problems regarding this memorandum and its implementation should be directed to the Working Group established by the AO and the EOUST.

AGREED TO:

Secretary to the Judicial Conference	Executive Office for United States Trustees United States Department of Justice

Date: _____October 7, 1991_____   Date: _____October 9, 1991_____

Hoffman v. Connecticut Department of Income Maintenance,[41] that even if the state did not file a claim, the trustee in bankruptcy may not recover a money judgment from the state. In *United States v. Nordic Village, Inc.,*[42] the Court would not allow a trustee to recover a postpetition payment by a chapter 11 debtor to the Internal Revenue Service. Although the modification will allow the trustee or debtor-in-possession to recover money judgments, preferences, postpetition transfers, and the like, it will not allow the court to enter an award for punitive damages. In awarding fees or costs under the Bankruptcy Code or under Bankruptcy Rules, the award is subject to the hourly rate limitations contained in section 2412(d)(2)(a) of title 28 of the United States Code.

The Bankruptcy Reform Act of 1994 also amended section 106(d) of the Bankruptcy Code by allowing a compulsory counterclaim to be asserted against a governmental unit only if the unit has actually filed a proof of claim in the bankruptcy case.

§ 5.21   Commencement of Cases

(a) Voluntary

As under prior law, a voluntary case is commenced by the filing of a bankruptcy petition under the appropriate chapter by the debtor. The format for the petition is shown as Form 1 in Appendix A of Volume 2 of *Bankruptcy and Insolvency Accounting.* The form would be modified for the appropriate chapter. For example, a petition under chapter 11 would state that a plan is enclosed

---

[41] 492 U.S. 96 (1989).
[42] 112 S. Ct. 1022 (1992).

or will be submitted at a future date. Also, local rules and practices may require that additional information be included in the petition. In the districts of Maine, Massachusetts, New Hampshire, and Rhode Island, a chapter 11 petition contains a statement as to whether the debtor's fixed, liquidated, or unsecured debts, other than debts for goods, services, or taxes, or debts owed to an insider, exceed or do not exceed $5 million. In Volume 2, the example in 5.1 contains the chapter 11 petition, along with the accompanying schedules and other information, filed by Standard Brands Paint Company. This petition represents the type of information that is generally included in a voluntary petition.

(b) Involuntary

An involuntary petition can be filed by three or more creditors (if eleven or fewer creditors, only one creditor is necessary) with unsecured claims of at least $10,775 and can be initiated only under chapter 7 or 11.

Effective for all petitions filed after October 22, 1994, the Bankruptcy Reform Act of 1994 increased (from $5,000 to $10,000) the amount of unsecured debt needed to file an involuntary petition against the debtor. On April 1, 1998, and at each three-year interval thereafter, the dollar amount of the unsecured debt needed to file an involuntary petition is to be increased, beginning on April 1, to reflect the change in the Consumer Price Index for All Urban Consumers that has occurred during the three-year period ending on December 31 of the immediately preceding year. The amounts are to be rounded to the nearest $25 multiple. The amount of debt needed to file remains at $10,775 through March 31, 2001.

An indenture trustee may be one of the petitioning creditors. Under prior law, before proceedings could commence, it was necessary for the debtor to have committed one of the acts of bankruptcy. The Bankruptcy Reform Act eliminates the acts of bankruptcy and permits the court to allow a case to proceed only (1) if the debtor generally fails to pay its debts as they become due, provided such debts are not the subject of a bona fide dispute; or (2) within 120 days prior to the petition a custodian was appointed or took possession. The latter excludes the taking of possession of less than substantially all property to enforce a lien.

The requirement that the debtor must not be generally paying its debts as they become due is similar to the equity meaning of insolvency, but ability to pay is not a factor. A debtor who has the current resources to make payment and is thus solvent in the equity sense may still be forced into bankruptcy if he or she is not generally paying debts as they become due. There is no requirement that the debtor be insolvent in the bankruptcy sense where the total value of the assets is less than the liabilities. An alternative to determining whether the debtor is not paying his or her debts is the appointment of a custodian or the taking of possession of the assets by the custodian within the past 120 days. This is commonly the assignment for the benefit of creditors or a receiver appointed by a state court to operate or liquidate a business. Passage of more than 120 days since the custodian took possession of the debtor's assets does not preclude the creditors from forcing the debtor into bankruptcy but, rather, suggests that the creditors will have to prove that the debtor is generally not paying its debts as they mature.

Only a person (individual, partnership, or corporation) can be forced into bankruptcy. Governmental units, estates, and trusts cannot have an involuntary petition filed against them. Section 303(a) provides that neither a farmer nor a nonprofit corporation can be forced into bankruptcy. One major change brought about by the new law is that creditors now have a choice when it comes to forcing the debtor into bankruptcy. Under prior law, other than straight bankruptcy, the only chapter under which involuntary proceedings could be started was Chapter X. Thus, large businesses that were not corporations and many small businesses could be forced only into straight bankruptcy, but under the new law can be proceeded against in involuntary chapter 11 proceedings.

The Supreme Court has held that the plain language of the Bankruptcy Code permits individual debtors not engaged in business to file for relief under chapter 11.[43]

The holding of the *Toibb* case gives an individual not engaged in business one more option in bankruptcy. Chapter 13 relief is available only to individuals whose unsecured debts amount to less than $100,000 and whose secured debts are less than $350,000. Chapter 11 contains no comparable limit. As Justice Stevens noted in dissent, it takes time and money to determine whether a chapter 11 plan will provide creditors with benefits equal to those available through liquidation, and still more time and money to find out whether such a predictive decision turns out to be correct or incorrect. The "complex" chapter 11 process will almost certainly consume more time and resources than the "simpler" chapter 7 procedures.

If the creditors are able to prove the allegations set forth in the involuntary petition (or if they are not timely contested), the court will enter an order for relief and the case will proceed. If the creditors are unable to prove their allegations, the case will be dismissed. This may, however, not be the end of the creditors' action. To discourage creditors from filing petitions that are unwarranted, section 303(i) provides that the court may require the petitioners to cover the debtor's costs and reasonable attorney's fees, compensate for any damages resulting from the trustee's (if one was appointed) taking possession of the debtor's property, and, if filed in bad faith, for any damages caused by the filing, including punitive damages.

Section 303 provides that one condition necessary for an involuntary petition to be filed against the debtor is that the debtor generally fails to pay its debts as the debts become due, provided the debts are not subject to a bona fide dispute.

Although the definition of a bona fide dispute is not clear from the statute, case law has settled on a definition. In *In re Lough*[44] and later cases, the courts have stated that a bona fide dispute exists if there is either: (1) a genuine petitioning for involuntary bankruptcy, or (2) a meritorious contention as to application of law to undisputed facts. See also *In re Norris Brothers Lumber Co., Inc.*[45] If such a dispute exists, the involuntary case must be dismissed.

---

[43] *Toibb v. Radloff,* 111 S. Ct. 2197 (1991).
[44] 57 B.R. 993 (Bankr. E.D. Mich. 1986).
[45] 133 B.R. 599 (Bankr. N.D. Tex. 1991).

§ 5.22   Filing and Quarterly Fees

A debtor filing a chapter 11 petition must pay both a filing fee and a quarterly fee based on disbursements for each case until the plan is dismissed or the case is converted to another chapter. On January 26, 1996, Congress modified the quarterly fees for chapter 11 cases that were confirmed so that quarterly fees would continue to be paid after confirmation and until the case is dismissed.[46] Prior law provided that the quarterly fees were not assessed after confirmation.

On October 3, 1991, the House and Senate approved H.R. 2608 (Commerce and Related Agencies Appropriations bill for fiscal year ending September 30, 1992), which includes a provision that would increase filing fees and quarterly fees in chapter 11 cases. President Bush signed the bill (P.L. 102-140) on October 28, 1991, and it became effective on December 27, 1991. The fees were again modified by Congress on September 30, 1996.[47] These modifications increase the fees for several levels of payments and increase the cap of $5,000 for disbursements of $3,000,000 or more to $10,000 for disbursements of $5,000,000 or more. The rates as of October 1999 are:

Total Disbursements per Quarter	Quarterly Fees
Less than $15,000	$ 250
$15,000 or more, but less than $75,000	500
$75,000 or more, but less than $150,000	750
$150,000 or more, but less than $225,000	1,250
$225,000 or more, but less than $300,000	1,500
$300,000 or more, but less than $1,000,000	3,750
$1,000,000 or more, but less than $2,000,000	5,000
$2,000,000 or more, but less than $3,000,000	7,500
$3,000,000 or more, but less than $5,000,000	8,000
$5,000,000 or more	10,000

The costs of filing a bankruptcy petition are as follows:

Chapter	Filing Fees
7	$ 130
9	300
11 (nonrailroad)	800
11 (railroad)	1,000
12	200
13	130
Conversion from chapter 7 or 13 to 11	400

Part of the funds collected from this program will be used to fund the U.S. trustee program. Based on 1990 data, the increase in fees should result in an

---

[46] P.L. 104-99 (January 26, 1996).
[47] P.L. 104-208 (September 30, 1996).

increase of approximately $24 million in funding of the trustee program. The above fees also reflect the increase provided in P.L. 103-121.

These Acts amend section 1930(a) of title 28 of the U.S. Code.

In September 1992, the Judicial Conference approved a $30 miscellaneous administrative fee under section 1930 of title 28 of the U.S. Code. The fee will be added to the cost of a filing under chapter 7 or chapter 13. This is not a filing fee, but is described as a miscellaneous fee that will be charged at the same time as the filing fee. The miscellaneous fee replaces the 50 cent per notice fee that was previously charged.

§ 5.23   Partnership

A partnership is considered a person by the Bankruptcy Code and thus may file a petition in chapter 7 or 11. A petition will be considered voluntary if all the general partners are part of the petition. Bankruptcy Rule 1004 indicates that all general partners must consent to the filing of a voluntary petition, but it is not necessary that they all execute the petition. Exactly what will be the status if fewer than all of the partners file is not clear where the partnership agreement provides for the right of an individual partner to file on behalf of the partnership. Section 303(b)(3) indicates that fewer than all of the general partners may commence an involuntary case. The partners filing the petition are treated as creditors for the provisions of the law applicable to involuntary petitions, such as the statutory liability for wrongfully filing a petition or the posting of an indemnity bond. Furthermore, if all of the general partners are in bankruptcy court proceedings, any general partner, general partner's trustee, or creditor of the partnership can file a petition on behalf of the partnership.

§ 5.24   Meeting of Creditors

Section 341(a) and Bankruptcy Rule 2003 provide that, within a period of 20 to 40 days after the order for relief in any bankruptcy court proceedings, there will be a meeting of creditors. Subsection (b) states that the court may also order a meeting of any equity security holders. The court may not preside at, nor attend, any meetings called under section 341.

Rule 2003 of the Federal Rules of Bankruptcy Procedure provides that the U.S. trustee will preside over a meeting of creditors under section 341(a) and may also convene a meeting of equity security holders. If a meeting of equity security holders is convened, the U.S. trustee will preside. The Bankruptcy Reform Act of 1994 provides that, in the judicial districts where the bankruptcy system is administered by a bankruptcy administrator (currently, those in Alabama and North Carolina), the administrator's power to preside at creditors' meetings and conduct examinations of the debtor will be equal to that of a U.S. trustee.

Rule 2003 also provides that the meeting will be held at the regular place for holding court or at any other place designated by the U.S. trustee. For example, in some of the larger cases, the meetings are held in a large hotel. At a meeting under section 341(a), the debtor is to appear and submit to examination under oath. Creditors, an indenture trustee, or a trustee or examiner, if appointed, may examine the debtor.[48] Section 343 is modified by the 1986 amendments to provide that the U.S. trustee can administer the oath for the examination. The meetings under section 341 are often adjourned from time to time by announcement at the meeting. No vote will be taken at a meeting under section 341 in a chapter 11 case. In a chapter 7 case, a trustee and/or creditors' committee can be elected.

Effective for petitions filed after October 22, 1994, the Bankruptcy Reform Act of 1994 added subsection 341(d) of the Bankruptcy Code, which provides that a trustee in a chapter 7 case, prior to the conclusion of the meeting of creditors or equity holders, must orally examine the debtor to ensure that the debtor is aware of:

1 The potential consequences of seeking a discharge in bankruptcy, including the effects on credit history.
2 The ability to file a petition under a different chapter.
3 The effect of receiving a discharge of debts.
4 The effect of reaffirming a debt, which requires knowing the provisions of section 524(d) of the Bankruptcy Code.

Legislative history suggests that, in view of the information that must be disclosed and the limits on available time for meetings of creditors, trustees, or courts may provide written information on these topics at or in advance of the meeting, and the trustee may ask questions to ensure that the debtor is aware of the information.

The section 341(a) hearing is often criticized for being short on content. While the debtor is required to attend and the creditors are allowed to ask questions on a broad range of topics, the debtor is often instructed by counsel not to answer many of the questions asked by the creditors or their committee. For example, in a chapter 7 case, questions may deal with the issues of dischargeability and disposition of assets prior to the filing of the petition. In a chapter 11 case, the questions might center around the feasibility of reorganization and liquidation values. Creditors' committees can, however, often obtain more information from the debtor in a Rule 2004 examination, which is the bankruptcy court equivalent to a deposition. During an examination under Rule 2004, the creditors can, for example, conduct discovery into all aspects of the debtor's financial history.

§ 5.25 Meeting of Equity Security Holders

Section 341(b) also allows the U.S. trustee to order a meeting of the stockholders of the debtor corporation. At this meeting, the U.S. trustee or designee will preside.

§ 5.26 Adequate Protection

In instances where a creditor's security interest is in an asset that is endangered, depreciating, or being dissipated by the debtor's actions, the creditor

---

[48] 11 U.S.C. § 343.

may move the court for adequate protection.[49] A creditor who seeks adequate protection is asking the court to ensure that the status quo will be maintained throughout the duration of the stay.[50] The court has broad discretion in the method it chooses to remedy adequate protection problems.

The legislative history indicates the process by which Congress intended to resolve adequate protection problems. First, the trustee or debtor-in-possession should propose a method for providing adequate protection. The creditor can then accept, object, or negotiate an alternative solution. If the parties cannot reach an agreement, the court will step in to resolve the dispute.

Although a creditor may enter an adequate protection motion with the desire to continue a foreclosure action or stop the debtor from granting an additional lien on property in which the creditor holds a security interest, an alternative remedy may be the result of the above process. The court may require the debtor-in-possession to make cash payments to a creditor in instances where the value of the collateral is decreasing or where the amount of any security cushion is eroding as interest accrues. The court may also choose to grant relief from stay in order to allow the creditor to seize assets in which the creditor holds a security interest. The court must balance the danger to the interests of the creditor against the necessity of the property to the debtor in the reorganization.

Adequate protection may be required under three Bankruptcy Code sections:

1 *Section 362, dealing with the automatic stay*—For example, unless the security interest of the debtor is adequately protected, the court may remove the stay.

2 *Section 363, dealing with the use (including the use of cash collateral), sale, or lease of property of the debtor*—For example, the court may not approve the release of cash collateral until it has been determined that the impacted creditors are adequately protected.

3 *Section 364, dealing with the obtaining of credit*—For example, before the court might approve the granting of a senior or equal lien under the priming of a secured creditor, the court must ascertain that the creditor is adequately protected.

Adequate protection, according to section 361 of the Bankruptcy Code, may be provided by:

1 Requiring the trustee or debtor in possession to make cash payments to the extent that the stay under section 362 or the use, sale, or lease under section 363, or the grant of a lien under section 364 results in a decrease in the value of the entity's interest in such property.

---

[49] A motion for adequate protection under section 361 can be brought under Bankruptcy Code section 362 (relief from the automatic stay), section 363 (motion to halt the use of cash collateral), or section 364 (regarding the granting of liens on previously encumbered property).

[50] There are three seminal cases in the adequate protection area: (1) *In re American Mariner Industries, Inc.*, 734 F.2d 426 (9th Cir. 1984); (2) *In re Briggs Transportation Co.*, 780 F.2d 1339 (8th Cir. 1985); and (3) *United Savings Association v. Timbers of Inwood Forest Association*, 484 U.S. 365 (1988).

2 Providing an additional or replacement lien to the extent that the stay, use, sale, lease, or grant results in a decrease in the value of the entity's interest in such property.

3 Granting such other relief, other than entitling such entity to an administrative expense, that will result in the realization by such entity of the indubitable equivalent of the entity's interest in such property.

Adequate protection for the purposes of section 363(c) of the Bankruptcy Code (dealing with the use of cash collateral and other soft collateral such as inventory and accounts receivable) should be determined based on the manufacturing cycle of the business. Thus, adequate protection exists if it appears that the level of collateral that supports a floating lien will be restored within the projected business cycle, even though there may be a decline at some given point in the cycle.[51] A third-party guarantee may constitute adequate protection, depending on the guarantor's financial strength.[52] An unsecured junior creditor is entitled to adequate protection to the extent that accruing interest on the senior lien reduces the collateral that is available to the junior creditor.[53]

An undersecured creditor is not entitled to the provisions of adequate protection unless it is shown that the collateral is at risk of depreciating in value.[54]

In *In re Elmira Litho, Inc.*,[55] the bankruptcy court held that lack of adequate protection for equipment pledged as security is proved by showing an actual or threatened decrease in the value of the collateral. The court noted that persuasive proof of declining value is shown by quantitative evidence, such as an appraisal, that shows the property was either worth more prebankruptcy or will be worth less in the future. Qualitative proof, such as proof that a debtor failed to make postpetition payments, may not be adequate if there is still equity in the equipment.

In *In re Delta Resources, Inc.*,[56] the Eleventh Circuit held that an oversecured creditor is not entitled to have its "equity cushion" in the underlying collateral maintained at its prepetition level. The oversecured creditor moved for relief from the automatic stay so that it could foreclose on the equipment it had financed. The bankruptcy court denied the motion, but ordered the debtor to pay adequate protection on a monthly basis for the deteriorating value of the equipment. The creditor argued that because interest was accruing on its debt, its "equity cushion" was being depleted, and that it should also receive interest payments as part of its adequate protection. The district court, on appeal from the bankruptcy court, ordered the debtor to pay both the depreciation and interest. The Eleventh Circuit reversed the district court's decision, noting that secured creditors have several protections under the Bankruptcy Code against unreasonable debtor delay other than the payment of depreciation and interest.

---

[51] *In re Dynaco Corp.*, 162 B.R. 389 (Bankr. D. N.H. 1993).
[52] *In re Swedeland Development Group, Inc.*, 16 F.3d 552 (3d Cir. 1994).
[53] *Matter of Rupprect*, 161 B.R. 48 (Bankr. D. Neb. 1993).
[54] *In re Immenhausen Corp.*, 164 B.R. 347 (Bankr. M.D Fla. 1994).
[55] 174 B.R. 892 (Bankr. S.D.N.Y. 1994).
[56] 54 F.3d 722 (11th Cir. 1995).

When the request for adequate protection has been made, there has been considerable uncertainty as to the date when the value of the collateral should be determined. The Ninth Circuit Bankruptcy Appellate Panel (BAP) looked at the issue in *In re Deico Electronics, Inc.*[57] and concluded that the value of the collateral should be determined as of the date on which the protection is sought. Any protection to which the creditor is entitled would then be calculated from this date rather than from the date the petition was filed.

Courts have not agreed on the meaning of indubitable equivalent, and the term was not defined in the Bankruptcy Code. Section 361(3) of the Bankruptcy Code provides that the granting of an administrative expense may not be used to satisfy this requirement. The indubitable equivalent requirement has been satisfied by the use of substitute collateral. Section 361(3) indicates that the realization of the indubitable equivalent standard is measured against the entity's interest in such property and not the value of the property. Thus, it might be acceptable to substitute another collateral as long as the value of the collateral is at least equal to the interest that the creditor has in the property (the amount of the debt). As noted above, some courts may also require that an equity cushion be provided. Courts considering the issue of what is acceptable as substitute collateral have found that (1) promissory notes secured by deeds of trust given in exchange for a creditor's release of a deed of trust against a debtor's property and (2) securities given in lieu of cash may satisfy the indubitable equivalent requirement.[58]

(a) Equity Cushion

One issue that has not been resolved is the extent to which an equity cushion or other forms of assurance are required in determining whether the secured lender is adequately protected.[59] An equity cushion is the value in the property, above the amount owed to the creditor with a secured claim,

---

[57] 139 B.R. 945 (9th Cir. BAP 1992); *see In re Best Products Co., Inc.*, 138 B.R. 155 (Bankr. S.D.N.Y. 1992).

[58] *See In the matter of Sun Country Developers, Inc.*, 764 F.2d 406, 409 (5th Cir. 1985); *In re San Felipe at Voss, Ltd.*, 115 Bankr. 526, 531 (S.D. Tex. 1990).

[59] Courts that have argued that the equity cushion theory is questionable include: *In re A. J. Lane*, 108 B.R. 6 (Bankr. D. Mass. 1989); *In re McCombs Properties VI, Ltd.*, 88 B.R. 261 (Bankr. C.D. Cal. 1988); *In re Triplett*, 87 B.R. 25 (Bankr. W.D. Tex. 1988); *In re Alyucan Interstate Corp.*, 12 B.R. 803 (Bankr. D. Utah 1981). Courts arguing for the theory include: *In re Pitts*, 2 B.R. 476 (Bankr. C.D. Cal. 1979); *In re Rogers Development Corp.*, 2 B.R. 679 (Bankr. E.D. Va. 1980) (value of $130,000 over the $620,000 mortgage was adequate); *In re Mellor*, 734 F.2d 1396 (9th Cir. 1984) (20 percent equity cushion considered adequate); *In re Plaza Family Partnership*, 95 B.R. 166 (E.D. Cal. 1989) (50 percent equity cushion adequate); *In re Cardell*, 88 B.R. 627 (Bankr. D.N.J. 1988) (cushion of almost 50 percent adequate); *In re Jug End in the Berkshires, Inc.*, 46 B.R. 892 (Bankr. D. Mass. 1985) (equity cushion of, at most, 8 percent deemed inadequate); *In re Smithfield Estates, Inc.*, 48 B.R. 910 (Bankr. D.R.I. 1985) (collateral valued at $4.5 million to $5.0 million deemed insufficient to provide an adequate equity cushion for $4.7 million debt; debtor required to commence monthly interest payments and cure arrearage); *In re Hagendorfer*, 42 B.R. 13 (Bankr. S.D. Ala. 1984), *aff'd, Hagendorfer v. Marlette*, 42 B.R. 17 (S.D. Ala. 1984) (equity cushion of 9.3 percent to 12.2 percent inadequate); *In re Schaller*, 27 B.R. 959 (W.D. Wis. 1983) (cushion of 17 to 18 percent inadequate); *In re Tucker*, 5 B.R. 180 (Bankr. S.D.N.Y. 1980) (7.4 percent cushion inadequate).

that will shield that interest from loss due to any decrease in the value of the property during the time an automatic stay remains in effect. Equity, on the other hand, is the value, above all secured claims against the property, that can be realized from the sale of the property for the benefit of the unsecured creditors. Thus, if property with a value of $50 is secured by a first lienholder with a claim of $30, and a second lienholder with a claim of $25, there is an equity cushion of $20 in reference to the first lienholder, and there is no equity in the property because the total debt of $55 is greater than the value of the property.

Courts that hold that an equity cushion is necessary would evaluate the amount of the equity cushion to determine whether some form of adequate protection is necessary to remove the stay, to approve a cash collateral order, or to allow the priming of a lien. Courts that do not accept the equity cushion theory would claim that the creditor is adequately protected as long as the collateral does not decline in value to create a deficiency. For the above property valued at $50, no adequate protection is required for the first lienholder as long as the value of the collateral exceeds the claim of $30.

According to *In re McKillips*,[60] case law almost uniformly concludes that: (1) an equity cushion of 20 percent or more constitutes adequate protection; (2) an equity cushion of less than 11 percent is insufficient; and (3) a range of 12 percent to 20 percent has divided the courts.

In *Ahlers v. Norwest Bank*,[61] the Eighth Circuit found that the starting date for adequate protection should not be when the petition is filed, but rather when the secured creditor seeks either possession of the collateral or adequate protection.

Most courts since *United Sav. Ass'n of Texas v. Timbers of Inwood Forest Assocs., Ltd.*[62] have focused on the date adequate protection is sought.[63]

In *In re Craddock-Terry Shoe Corp.*,[64] the bankruptcy court held that a creditor was entitled to adequate protection from the date of the debtor's petition. In *In re Ritz-Carlton of D.C., Inc.*,[65] the court also ruled that the calculation should be made from the petition date but cautioned that adequate protection should not run from a date earlier than when debtor could reasonably anticipate that it would be required. One reason why courts suggest the use of the date action was taken is that adequate protection analysis requires the bankruptcy court to first determine when the creditor would have obtained its state law remedies had bankruptcy not intervened. Presumably, that will be after the creditor first seeks relief, and the court must then determine the value of the collateral as of that date.

---

[60] 81 B.R. 454 (Bankr. N.D. Ill. 1987).

[61] 794 F.2d 388, 395 n. 6 (8th Cir. 1986), *rev'd on other grounds. Norwest Bank v. Ahlers*, 485 U.S. 197 (1988).

[62] 484 U.S. 365 (1988).

[63] See *In the Matter of Continental Airlines, Inc.* 146 B.R. 536 (D. Del. 1992) (Suggested that a pre-Timbers decision, *In re Monroe Park*, 17 B.R. 934 (D. Del. 1982) that used the period between the petition date and the confirmation would no doubt have been decided differently today.)

[64] 98 B.R. 250, 255 (Bankr. W.D. Va. 1988).

[65] 98 B.R. 170, 173 (S.D.N.Y. 1989).

(b) Analysis of Specific Risks

Not all courts, however, have endorsed the use of the equity cushion method of measuring adequate protection.[66] In *In re LNC Investment* the district court noted that recent decisions in the Second Circuit have rejected the equity cushion approach in favor of a more individualized analysis of the specific risks threatening the collateral. Even when applying equity cushion analysis and concluding that 65 percent equity cushion provides adequate protection, the bankruptcy court acknowledged that "this quantitative approach may have the salutary effect of giving precise guidance as to the standard to be used, but it does seem to be inconsistent with the Congressional intent that each case is to be judged on its own facts."[67] In *In re Alyucan Interstate Corp.*, 12 Bankr. 803, 813 (Bankr. D. Utah 1981), the bankruptcy court noted that cushion analysis "is not fully alert to the legislative directive that the facts, in each hearing under Section 362(d), will determine whether relief is appropriate under the circumstances."

Thus, rather than focusing on the equity cushion as the method to use to determine adequate protection, emphasis is often placed on actual or likely diminution in the value of the collateral during the time between the petition date and the confirmation of the plan. The district court in *LNC Investment, Inc.*, referred to several other cases considered in establishing the fact that courts are adopting alternative approaches to determining adequate protection.[68]

Also in *LNC Investment, Inc.* the district court concluded that the approach of evaluating the merits of a lift stay motion is supported by the Supreme Court decision in *United Sav. Ass'n of Texas v. Timbers of Inwood Forest Assocs., Ltd.*[69] Here the Court recognized that a creditor is entitled to adequate protection payments if the security has depreciated during the term of the stay.

§ 5.27 Automatic Stay

A petition filed under the Bankruptcy Code results in an automatic stay of the actions of creditors. The automatic stay, one of the fundamental protections provided the debtor by the Bankruptcy Code, dates back to an 1880 case where it was stated that "[T]he filing of the petition is a caveat to all the world,

---

[66] *LNC Investment, Inc. and Charter National Life Insurance Co. v. First Fidelity Bank, et al.*, 1995 U.S. Dist. LEXIS 5065 (S.D.N.Y. 1995); *In re Snowshoe Co., Inc.*, 789 F.2d 1085, 1090 (4th Cir. 1986).

[67] *In re San Clemente Estates*, 5 Bankr. 605, 610 (Bankr. S.D. Cal. 1980).

[68] *See In re Lane*, 108 B.R. 6, 9–10 (Bankr. D. Mass. 1989) (creditor not adequately protected when equity cushion is eroding); *In re 1606 New Hampshire Ave. Assocs.*, 85 B.R. 298, 309 (Bankr. E.D. Pa. 1988) (adequate protection is largely a function of movements in value of collateral); *In re Hagendorfer*, 42 B.R. 13, 16 (Bankr. S.D. Ala.) (secured creditor entitled to protection even when there is ample equity, if value of lien decreased following bankruptcy), *aff'd, Hagendorfer v. Marlette*, 42 B.R. 17 (S.D. Ala. 1984); *Alvucan*, 12 B.R. at 809 (adequate protection warranted if value of creditor's interest in property is declining, regardless of equity cushion). Attention is focused on shifts in the ratio of the debt to the value of the collateral, rather than on the absolute size of the equity cushion, which serves as merely one element in a multifactored analysis. *In re Johnson*, 90 B.R. 973, 979 (Bankr. D. Minn. 1988).

[69] 484 U.S. 365 (1988).

and in effect an attachment and injunction. . . ."[70] In a chapter 7 case, it provides for an orderly liquidation where all creditors are treated equitably. For business reorganizations under chapter 11 and chapter 13, it provides time for the debtor to examine the problems that forced it into bankruptcy court and to develop a plan for reorganization. As a result of the stay, no party, with minor exceptions, having a security or adverse interest in the debtor's property can take any action that will interfere with the debtor or his property, regardless of where the property is located, until the stay is modified or removed. Section 362(a) provides a list of eight kinds of acts and conduct subject to the automatic stay. The stay operates against:

1　The commencement or continuation of a judicial, administrative, or other action or proceeding against the debtor, including the issuance or employment of process, that could have been commenced before the petition date or would be commenced to recover a claim that arose prior to the commencement of the case in the bankruptcy court. (Note that the stay does not apply to postpetition claims or proceedings involving postpetition transactions or conduct of the debtor.)

2　The enforcement against the debtor, or against property of the estate, of a judgment obtained before the commencement of the case.

3　Any act to obtain possession of property of the estate or of property from the estate or to exercise control over the property of the estate.

4　Any act to create, perfect, or enforce any lien against property of the estate.

5　Any act to create, perfect, or enforce against property of the debtor any lien to the extent that such lien secures a claim that arose before the commencement of the case.

6　Any act to collect, assess, or recover a claim against the debtor that arose before the commencement of the case.

7　The setoff of any debt owing to the debtor that arose before the commencement of the case against any claim against the debtor.

8　The commencement or continuation of a proceeding before the United States Tax Court concerning the debtor.

A creditor that accepts or deposits a check of the debtor given in payment of a prepetition claim violates both item 3 (any act to obtain possession of the debtor's property) and item 6 above (any act to collect or recover a prepetition claim) even though the creditor's conduct is of a passive nature.[71] The automatic stay does not prevent a creditor from furnishing information concerning the debtor to a credit reporting agency.[72] In *Johnson v. Garden State Brickface and Stucco Co.,*[73] the district court held that a postpetition claim can be pursued to judgment without violating the automatic stay.

---

[70] *International Bank v. Sherman,* 101 U.S. 403 (1880).
[71] *In re Germansen Decorating, Inc.,* 149 B.R. 517 (Bankr. N.D. Ill. 1992).
[72] *Hickson v. Home Federal of Atlanta,* 805 F. Supp. 1567 (N.D. Ga. 1992).
[73] 150 B.R. 617 (E.D. Pa. 1993).

A creditor's prosecution of a suit to recover the fraudulent transfer under nonbankruptcy law does not violate the automatic stay under section 362(a)(3) of the Bankruptcy Code against interfering with the property of the estate, because, until the property is recovered, it is not property of the estate.[74]

Section 362(a)(8) of the Bankruptcy Code states that the filing of a bankruptcy petition operates as a stay against the commencement or continuation of a proceeding before the U.S. Tax Court. However, the Ninth Circuit concluded that section 362(a)(8) has no application to appeals following the termination of proceedings in the Tax Court before the bankruptcy petition was filed.[75]

Courts have generally held that an insurance company cannot unilaterally cancel a chapter 11 debtor's insurance policy without court approval. Such cancellation violates the automatic stay provisions of section 362. In situations where the policy has been canceled, courts have reinstated the coverage.

Section 362(b) contains a number of limitations on the operation of the stay described above. Among the items listed are the following:

1 The commencement or continuation of a criminal action or proceeding against the debtor.

2 The establishment or modification of an order for, or the collection of, alimony, maintenance, or support from property that is not property of the estate.

3 Any act to perfect an interest in property to the extent that the trustee's rights and powers are subject to such perfection under section 546(b) within the time period provided in section 547(e)(2)(A).

4 The commencement or continuation of an action or proceeding by a governmental unit to enforce such governmental unit's police or regulatory power.

6 The setoff of any mutual debt and claim that are commodity futures contracts, forward commodity contracts, leverage transactions, options, warrants, rights to purchase or sell commodity futures contracts or securities, or options to purchase or sell commodities or securities.

7 The setoff of any mutual debt or claim for a margin or settlement payment arising out of repurchase agreements against cash, securities, or other property held by or due from such repo participant to margin, guarantee, secure, or settle repurchase agreements.

8 The commencement of any action by the Secretary of Housing and Urban Development to foreclose a mortgage or deed of trust on property consisting of five or more living units held by the Secretary that is insured or was formerly insured under the National Housing Act.

9 An audit by a governmental unit to determine the tax; the issuance by a governmental unit of a notice of tax deficiency; a demand for tax returns; or the making of an assessment for any tax and issuance of a

---

[74] *In re Colonial Realty Co.,* 980 F.2d 125 (3d Cir. 1992); *Matter of Thielking,* 163 B.R. 543 (Bankr. S.D. Iowa 1994).

[75] *William P. Cheng v. Commsissioner,* 938 F.2d 141 (9th Cir. 1991). See *Roberts v. Commissioner,* 175 F. 3d 889 (8th Cir. 1999). (Decision not final until 90 days later).

notice and demand for payment of the assessment (but any tax liens that would otherwise attach to property of the estate due to the assessment shall not take effect unless the tax is a debt of the debtor that will not be discharged in the case and such property or its proceeds are transferred out of the estate or to the debtor).

10 Any act by a lessor under a lease of real nonresidential property that has terminated by the expiration of the terms of the case before the petition is filed or during the case to obtain possession of the property.

11 The presentment of a negotiable instrument and the giving of notice of and protesting dishonor of such an instrument.

12 After 90 days after filing the commencement or continuation and conclusion to the entry of final judgment of a chapter 11 debtor brought by the Secretary of Transportation to foreclose a preferred ship or fleet mortgage, or security interest in a vessel held by the Secretary of Transportation under the Merchant Marine Act.

13 After 90 days after filing the commencement or continuation and conclusion to the entry of final judgment of a chapter 11 debtor brought by the Secretary of Commerce to foreclose a preferred ship or fleet mortgage in a vessel or security interest in a fishing facility held by the Secretary of Commerce under the Merchant Marine Act.

14 Any action by an accrediting agency regarding the accreditation statutes of the debtor of an educational institution.

15 Any action by a state licensing body regarding the licensure of the debtor of an educational institution.

16 Any action by a guaranty agency under the Higher Education Act of 1965 or the Secretary of Education regarding the eligibility of the debtor to participate in programs authorized under such Act.

17 Selected setoffs by swap participants.

18 Creation or perfection of a statutory lien for property taxes by the District of Columbia or a political subdivision of a state, if such tax comes due after the filing of the petition.

Effective for petitions filed after October 22, 1994, the Bankruptcy Reform Act of 1994 modified section 362(d) of the Bankruptcy Code to provide another limitation on the operation of the stay, bringing to eighteen the total provisions that are dealt with under the exceptions to the automatic stay. This newest limitation provides that the creation or perfection of a statutory lien for property taxes that becomes due after the filing of the petitions will not be subject to the automatic stay.

Limitation 2, dealing with the collection of alimony, maintenance, or support, has been expanded for petitions filed after October 22, 1994. Modifications to section 362(b)(2) of the Bankruptcy Code now provide that the stay does not operate against (1) the commencement or continuation of an action or proceeding for the establishment of paternity or the establishment or modification of an order for alimony, maintenance, or support, and (2) the collection of alimony, maintenance, or support from property that is not property of the debtor.

Effective for petitions filed after October 22, 1994, the Bankruptcy Reform Act of 1994 modified section 362(b)(9) of the Bankruptcy Code to provide that the automatic stay is not applicable to a tax audit, a demand for tax returns, or the issuance of a notice and demand for payment for such assessment. The amendment provides that, for a notice and demand for payment, any tax lien that would otherwise attach to property of the estate by reason of such assessment will not take effect unless the tax is a type that will not be discharged and the property or proceeds are transferred to the debtor.

The Bankruptcy Reform Act of 1994 also amended sections 362(b)(3) and 546(b) of the Bankruptcy Code to clarify that, pursuant to the Uniform Commercial Code, certain actions taken during bankruptcy proceedings to maintain a secured creditor's position as it was at the commencement of the case do not violate the automatic stay. These actions, including the filing of a continuation statement or of financial statements, are taken to ensure continued perfection that maintains the status quo and does not improve the position of the secured lender.

(a) Duration of the Stay

The stay of an act against the property of the estate continues, unless modified, until the property is no longer the property of the estate.[76] The stay of any other act continues until the case is closed or dismissed, or the debtor is either granted or denied a discharge. The earliest occurrence of one of these events terminates the stay.[77]

In *In re Reisher*,[78] the bankruptcy court held that, according to section 1141(d) of the Bankruptcy Code, the postponement of the effect of the discharge until completion of the performance under the plan will also leave the automatic stay in effect.

A proceeding to obtain compensation from willful violation of the automatic stay under section 362(h) of the Bankruptcy Code may continue, even though the bankruptcy case has been dismissed or terminated.[79]

(b) Relief from the Stay

The balance of section 362 deals with the procedures to follow to obtain relief from the stay. Section 362(d) provides that, for relief to be granted, it is necessary for a party to institute action with the bankruptcy court. The court may grant relief, after notice and hearing, by terminating, annulling, modifying, or conditioning the stay. The court may grant relief for cause, including the lack of adequate protection of the interest of the secured creditor. With respect to an act against property, relief may be granted under chapter 11 if the debtor does not have an equity in the property and the property is not necessary for an effective reorganization.

---

[76] 11 U.S.C. § 362(c).
[77] Frank R. Kennedy, "Automatic Stays under the New Bankruptcy Law," *University of Michigan Journal of Law Reform*, Vol. 12 (Fall 1978), p. 38.
[78] Adv. N.D. 1-92-0347 (Bankr. M.D. Pa. 1992).
[79] *Price v. Rochford*, 947 F.2d 829 (7th Cir. 1991); *In re Kearns*, 161 B.R.

The Bankruptcy Reform Act of 1994, effective for petitions filed after October 22, 1994, added a third reason for the relief of the stay, where single-asset real estate is involved. Section 362(d)(3) of the Bankruptcy Code provides that, in the case of a single-asset real estate, the court may grant relief from the stay unless the debtor, within 90 days of the order for relief: (1) has filed a plan of reorganization that has a reasonable possibility of being confirmed within a reasonable time period or (2) has commenced monthly payments to each creditor whose claim is secured by the real estate, other than a claim secured by a judgment lien or by an unmatured statutory lien. Payments should at least be equal to interest at a current fair market rate, based on the value of the creditor's interest in the real estate.

A single-asset real estate is defined in section 101 of the Bankruptcy Code to mean real property constituting a single property or project, other than residential real property with fewer than four residential units, which generates substantially all of the gross income of a debtor and on which no substantial business is being conducted by a debtor other than the business of operating the real property, and activities thereto having aggregate, noncontingent, liquidated secured debts that do not exceed $4 million. This provision will not have the impact that earlier drafts might have had: it is limited to single real estate properties or projects with debts of $4 million or less.

There is a conflict of opinion on the issue of whether the $4,000,000 applies to the amount of the note or to the value of the collateral. Two courts have held that it is the amount of the debt.[80] Oceanside Mission Associates used the amount of the note rather than the value of the collateral, in part because a determination dependent on a valuation of the collateral under Code section 506(a) could lead to undue delay in the very class of cases that Congress had targeted to receive expeditious treatment under section 362(d)(3) of the Bankruptcy Code.[81]

In *In re Pensignorkay, Inc.*,[82] the court noted that section 506(a) of the Bankruptcy Code provided that the allowed claim of a creditor holding a lien on property of the estate is a secured claim only "to the extent of the value of such creditor's interest in the estate's interest in such property . . . , and is an unsecured claim to the extent that the value of such creditor's interest . . . is less than the amount of such allowed claim." The court concluded that the determination of the extent to which a debt is secured depends on the value of the collateral to which the creditor's lien attaches.

In *In re Philmont Development Co.*,[83] the bankruptcy court held that a general partner's chapter 11 case was not a single-asset case where its assets were limited partnership interests in three limited partnerships and two undeveloped building lots. However, the court held that the limited partnerships were single-asset cases. The limited partnerships had a series of semidetached houses, and the court held that these constituted a "single project." As a result, they were considered single-asset real estate. As a result of this decision, for

---

[80] *In re Oceanside Mission Associates*, 192 B.R. at 236–38 and *In re Standard Mill Ltd. Partnership*, 1996 Bankr. LEXIS 1120, 1996 WL 521190 (Bankr. D. Minn. 1996).

[81] *In re Oceanside Mission Associates*, 192 B.R. at 238.

[82] 204 B.R. 676, 683 (Bankr. E.D. Pa. 1997).

[83] 181 B.R. 220 (Bankr. E.D. Pa. 1995).

each of the limited partnerships, the mortgagee was held to be entitled to relief from the automatic stay when the limited partnerships had not filed chapter 11 reorganization plans within 90 days after entry of the orders for relief.

In another decision, *In re Kremko, Inc.*,[84] based on the definition of a single asset real estate case under section 101(51)(B), as provided for by the Bankruptcy Reform Act of 1994, the bankruptcy court also held that any residential real property with more than four residential units is certainly single-asset real estate. The *Kremko* court concluded that apartment buildings and residential projects are within the scope of section 101(51)(B).

Section 361 identifies three acceptable ways of providing the adequate protection that is required. First, the trustee or debtor may be required to make periodic cash payments to the entity entitled to relief as compensation for the decrease in value of the entity's interest in the property resulting from the stay. Second, the entity may be provided with an additional or replacement lien to the extent that the value of the interest declined as a result of the stay. Finally, the entity may receive the indubitable equivalent of its interest in the property. (See § 5.26.)

During the initial 120-day period in which debtors have an exclusive right to file a plan of reorganization, the bankruptcy courts apply a lesser standard in determining whether the burden of showing "a reasonable possibility of a successful reorganization within a reasonable time" has been satisfied.[85] Determination that property is not necessary to an effective reorganization due to the lack of feasibility should not be favored in the early stages of a bankruptcy because no one knows whether the debtor can survive until it has done what chapter 11 affords it occasion to do. Since this time is needed to clean house and work out a plan, uncertainties should be resolved in the debtor's favor during the period in which the debtor is entitled to file a plan of reorganization.[86]

The amount of evidence that must be presented for the court to determine that a plan meets the confirmation requirements of section 1129 is generally not required to show that a plan has a reasonable chance of being confirmed. "The difference between a section 362(d)(2) analysis and a section 1129 analysis is in the level of scrutiny to which Debtor's feasibility evidence is subjected, not in the factors to be considered in assessing feasibility."[87] Section 1129 can, however, provide guidance in analyzing the feasibility of the plan, for if the proposed plan cannot meet confirmation standards, it cannot form the basis for finding a reasonable possibility of a successful reorganization as required by the Bankruptcy Code.[88]

While it is true that a party advocating reorganization need not show at the section 362(d)(2) hearing that its plan is confirmable, that party does bear the burden of showing that the proposed things to be done after confirmation can be done as a practical matter.[89]

---

[84] 181 B.R. 47 (Bankr. S.D. Ohio 1995).

[85] *In the Matter of Apex Pharmaceuticals*, 203 B.R. 432 (N.D. Ind. 1996).

[86] *In re 6200 Ridge, Inc.*, 69 Bankr. at 837 (Bankr. E.D. Pa. 1987).

[87] *Edgewater Walk Apts.*, 162 Bankr. 490, 499 (N.D. Ill. 1993).

[88] *In re Cho*, 164 Bankr. 730 at 733 (Bankr. E.D. Va. 1994)

[89] See *In re 160 Bleecker St. Assocs.*, 156 B.R. at 411; *In re Ritz-Carlton of D.C., Inc.*, 98 B.R. at 172.

Commenting on the plan proposed in *In re Nattchase Associates Limited Partnership*,[90] the bankruptcy court noted that the debtor has not proposed in the tendered plan to adequately deal with the debt due the secured creditor other than through a sale of the property within one year from the effective date of the plan. Additionally, the plan does not meet the requirements of the Bankruptcy Code in satisfying the priority claim for real estate taxes or the secured claim, and allows for the retention of ownership of the debtor's property by the principals of the debtor without paying all superior classes in full, and is therefore not confirmable in its present state. The court's brief review of the debtor's proposed treatment of various classes of its creditors indicated that the suggested plan will not meet the requirements of section 1129 of the Bankruptcy Code for confirmation. The Court was unable to conclude that there is a reasonable possibility of a successful reorganization within a reasonable time.[91]

The bankruptcy court in *In re Nattchase Associates Limited Partnership* noted that in determining whether there is a reasonable possibility of a successful reorganization, the Court must look to the financial prospects of the property in question. However, the relief from stay hearing is not the time for the Court to determine the ultimate accuracy of financial projections.[92] Courts have generally found that unless the projections are shown to be highly inaccurate, or are fixed in a manner that makes operation of the property unfeasible, the projections need only show that reorganization is possible, or likely.[93] However, a reasonable possibility for reorganization cannot be grounded solely on speculation, and a "mere financial pipe dream" is insufficient to meet the requirements of section 362(d)(2).[94] Further, "to determine that there can be an effective reorganization of the debtor's business, the debtor must persuade the Court that the operation of the business will generate sufficient income to pay debt service."[95] The plight of the single-asset debtor is unique, for an integral component of the ability to reorganize turns on the ability to utilize the property for income-producing purposes.

A large number of courts have held that when a creditor requests relief from the stay in the early stages of a bankruptcy case, the burden on the debtor is less stringent than it would be later in the proceeding.[96] It is true that a section 1129 analysis is premature; however, it can provide guidance in analyzing the feasibility of a plan. If the plan proposed cannot meet confirmation standards, it cannot form the basis for finding there to be a reasonable possibility of a successful reorganization as required by section 362(d)(2) of the Bankruptcy Code.

---

[90] 178 B.R. 409 (E.D. Virg. 1994).

[91] See *In re L & M Properties, Inc.*, 102 B.R. 481 (Bankr. E.D. Va 1989).

[92] *In re Nattchase Associates Limited Partnership*, 178 B.R. at 409 (Bankr. E.D. Va 1994).

[93] *See In re Northgate Terrace Apts., Ltd.*, 126 Bankr. 520, 524 (Bankr. S.D. Ohio 1991).

[94] *In re L & M Properties, Inc.*, 102 Bankr. at 484 (citing *In re Dublin Properties*, 12 Bankr. 77, 81 (Bankr. E.D. Pa. 1981)).

[95] *In re L & M Properties*, 102 Bankr. at 485.

[96] *See Timbers of Inwood Forest*, 484 U.S. 365, 376 (1988); *Edgewater Walk Apartments*, 162 B.R. 490, 499–500 (N.D. Ill. 1993); *In re 160 Bleecker St. Assocs.*, 156 B.R. 405 (S.D. N.Y. 1993); *In re Holly's, Inc.*, 140 B.R. 643, 701–02 (Bankr. W.D. Mich. 1992); *In re Ashgrove Apartments of DeKalb County, Ltd.*, 121 B.R. 752, 756 (Bankr. S.D. Ohio 1990); *In re Grand Sports, Inc.*, 86 B.R. 971, 974 (Bankr. N.D. Ind. 1988).

In considering the evidentiary burden of the debtors, the cases intimate a lesser burden during the exclusivity period and a greater burden in the later stages.[97]

However, the district court noted that it was unable to find any reported decision in which a court has held that the same approach applies to creditors who submit proposed plans of reorganization after the debtor's exclusive period has ended.[98] To apply the "sliding scale" analysis to a creditor's proposed plan of reorganization after the expiration of the 120-day initial period would serve no comparable purpose and, according to the district court, could conceivably lead to the creditor's plan being examined under a lighter burden of proof than that which would be applied to any plan submitted by the debtor at that point.

The granting of relief when the debtor does not have any equity in the property was added to solve the problem of real property mortgage foreclosures where the bankruptcy court petition is filed just before the foreclosure takes place. It was not intended to apply if the debtor is managing or leasing real property, such as a hotel operation, even though the debtor has no equity, because the property is necessary for an effective reorganization of the debtor.[99]

The automatic stay prohibits a secured creditor from enforcing its rights in property owned by the debtor until the stay is removed. Without this prohibition, a creditor could foreclose on the debtor's property, collect the proceeds, and invest them and earn income from the investment, even though a bankruptcy petition has been filed. Because the Bankruptcy Code does not allow this action to be taken, the creditor loses the opportunity to earn income on the proceeds that could have been received on the foreclosure. The courts refer to this as creditor's opportunity costs. Four circuit courts have looked at this concept of opportunity cost. Two circuits (Ninth and Fourth) have ruled that the debtor is entitled to opportunity cost, the Eighth Circuit ruled that under certain conditions opportunity costs may be paid, and the Fifth Circuit ruled that opportunity cost need not be paid. In January 1988, the Supreme Court held, in *In re Timbers of Inwood Forest Associates*,[100] that creditors having collateral with a value less than the amount of the debt are not entitled to interest during the period when their property is tied up in the bankruptcy proceeding. Because of the extended time period during which the creditors' interest in the property is tied up in bankruptcy proceedings, this decision will most likely encourage creditors to be sure that their claim is properly collateralized and may in limited ways restrict the granting of credit. (See § 6.11 for additional discussion of *Timbers*.)

The legislative history indicates that the reasons found in the statute are not the causes for relief. For example, in a case where the debtor is the prosecutor or administrator of another estate, the proceedings should not be delayed; these activities are not related to the bankruptcy case. Postpetition activities of the debtor also need not be stayed because they bear no relationship to the purpose of the stay.[101]

---

[97] *Timbers*, 484 U.S. at 376.
[98] *In the Matter of Apex Pharmaceuticals*, 203 B.R. 432 (N.D. Ind. 1996).
[99] 124 Cong. Rec. H11,092-93 (daily ed. September 28, 1978) (statement of Rep. Edwards).
[100] 484 U.S. 365 (1988).
[101] H.R. Rep. No. 95-595, 95th Cong., 1st Sess. 343–44 (1977). See *supra* note 57.

Subsection (e) of section 362 provides that, unless the court acts after the relief is requested, the relief is automatic. The court has 30 days to rule on the stay request, but in more complex cases the court is required to have only a preliminary hearing within the 30-day period and then conclude the final hearing within another 30-day period. The court may continue the stay after a preliminary hearing only if there is a reasonable likelihood that the relief will not be granted at the final hearing. Legislative history suggests that compelling circumstances justifying an extension include bona fide illness of any party or of the judge, or the occurrence of an event beyond the parties' control.[102]

Section 362(f) allows the court to grant relief from the stay without a hearing, provided immediate action is needed to prevent irreparable damage to the interest in property and such damage would occur before there is an opportunity for notice and a hearing. Bankruptcy Rule 4001 provides additional information about procedures that must be followed to obtain immediate relief from the stay, including how notices of the order granting relief are to be distributed.

If relief from the stay is granted, a creditor may foreclose on property on which a lien exists, may continue a state court suit, or may enforce any judgment that might have been obtained before the bankruptcy case.[103]

Subsection (g) places the burden of proof on the requesting party where the request for relief alleges that the debtor has no equity in the property. On all other issues, the party opposing the relief requested has the burden of proof.

A creditor has no standing to appeal an order lifting the automatic stay if the debtor-in-possession or trustee elects not to do so, unless the court authorizes the creditor to make the appeal in the name of the estate.[104]

In *United States v. Edwin Paul Wilson*,[105] the Fourth Circuit held that the lifting of a stay does not preclude bankruptcy court jurisdiction. In 1983, the Internal Revenue Service (IRS) issued notices of deficiency against Edwin Wilson for almost $30 million in taxes, interest, and penalties. Wilson filed a petition for redetermination in the U.S. Tax Court. Late in 1984, he filed a chapter 11 petition and the bankruptcy court subsequently lifted the stay on the Tax Court case.

The trustee and the IRS reached a settlement of the tax claim that limited the IRS's recovery to the assets of the estate. To obtain court approval of the settlement, the IRS moved to have the stay of the Tax Court proceeding reinstated and asked for a determination of Wilson's tax liabilities. The trustee filed with the bankruptcy court a stipulation containing the terms of the settlement agreement. Wilson objected to the settlement, claiming that the bankruptcy court lacked subject matter and personal jurisdiction and that the settlement violated due process. The bankruptcy court did not reinstate the automatic stay, but it did approve the settlement. On appeal, the district court affirmed the decision of the bankruptcy court.

The Fourth Circuit has affirmed the district court's decision, holding that the bankruptcy court had jurisdiction to resolve Wilson's tax liability even

---

[102] H.R. Rep. No. 103–835 103d Cong., 2d Sess. Sec. 101 (1994).
[103] *CCH Bankruptcy Law Reports*, ¶ 8606.
[104] *American Ready Mix, Inc.*, 14 F.3d 1497 (10th Cir. 1994).
[105] 974 F.2d 514 (4th Cir. 1992).

though the same issue was before the Tax Court and the automatic stay had been lifted. The court held that the bankruptcy court and the Tax Court enjoyed concurrent jurisdiction once the stay had been lifted, and that the Tax Court case did not limit the bankruptcy court's jurisdiction because the matter had not been adjudicated before the petition was filed.

In *John E. Sanford III v. Commissioner,*[106] the Tax Court held that Sanford's Tax Court petition was not filed in violation of the automatic stay because it was filed after the bankruptcy court had entered an order discharging Sanford from all dischargeable debts. The court noted that "the automatic stay was terminated on that date [discharge] by virtue of the express terms of 11 U.S.C. section 362(c)(2)(C)."

§ 5.28 Use of the Estate's Property

Section 363 permits the trustee or debtor to use, sell, or lease property (other than cash collateral) in the ordinary course of business without a notice or hearing, provided the business has been authorized to operate in a chapter 7, chapter 11, or chapter 13 proceeding and the court has not restricted the powers of the debtor or trustee in the order authorizing operation of the business. As a result of this provision, the debtor may continue to sell inventory and receivables and use raw materials in production without notice to secured creditors and without court approval. The use, sale, or lease of the estate's property other than in the ordinary course of business is allowed only after notice and an opportunity for a hearing.

The new law gives the greatest protection to creditors with an interest in *cash collateral,* consisting of cash negotiable instruments, documents of title, securities, deposit accounts, and any other cash equivalents. Included as cash collateral are proceeds from noncash collateral such as inventory, accounts receivable, products, offspring, rents, or profits of property subject to a security interest, if converted to proceeds of the type defined as cash collateral. To use cash collateral, the debtor must obtain the consent of the secured party or the authorization of the court after notice and an opportunity for a hearing.

Additional requirements regarding the use of the estate's property, including cash collateral, and the obtaining of new credit are described in §§ 6.12–6.14.

§ 5.29 Executory Contracts and Leases

Section 365(a) provides that the debtor or trustee, subject to court approval, may assume or reject any executory contract or unexpired lease of the debtor. Contracts are executory which are "so far unperformed that the failure of either [the bankrupt or nonbankrupt] to complete performance would constitute a material breach excusing the performance of the other."[107] Countryman's definition seemed to have been adopted by Congress when it stated that

---

[106] T.C. Memo. 1992-182.
[107] Countryman, "Executory Contracts in Bankruptcy," *Minnesota Law Review,* Vol. 57 (1973), pp. 439, 460.

"executory contracts include contracts under which performance remains due to some extent on both sides."[108]

(a) Assumption and Assignment

Before a contract can be assumed, subsection (b) of section 365 indicates that the debtor or trustee must:

1 Cure the past defaults or provide assurance they will be promptly cured.
2 Compensate the other party for actual pecuniary loss to such property or provide assurance that compensation will be made promptly.
3 Provide adequate assurance of future performance under the contract or lease.

Effective for petitions filed after October 22, 1994, the Bankruptcy Reform Act of 1994 modified section 365(b)(2) of the Bankruptcy Code: a contract provision that allows or charges a penalty rate to cure defaults, or a similar provision relating to a default, is not enforceable in bankruptcy. Thus, a lease can be cured at a nondefault rate.

A chapter 11 debtor may extend leases without first curing default to preserve for the debtor the ability to assume leases, even though leases provided that the renewal was conditioned on the absence of defaults.[109] The Ninth Circuit stated: "If the Bankruptcy Court could not allow a debtor to renew a lease without first curing defaults, section 365's basic purpose would be frustrated. The debtor would be denied the benefit of section 365's 'suspension of time' in order to determine whether to assume or reject the lease."

To be rejected, the contract must still be an executory contract. For example, the delivery of goods to a carrier, under terms that provided that the seller's performance is completed upon the delivery of the goods to the carrier, before the petition is filed would not be an executory contract in chapter 11. Furthermore, the seller's claim would not be an administrative claim. On the other hand, if the terms provide that the goods are received on delivery to the buyer, the seller, under section 2-705 of the Uniform Commercial Code, would have the right to stop the goods in transit and the automatic stay would not preclude such action. If the goods are delivered, payment for such goods would be an administrative expense.[110]

A debtor may assume or reject a lease under section 365 of the Bankruptcy Code only if the lease was effective as of the petition date.[111] A franchise agreement and a lease have been held to be a single contract for purposes of a decision to assume or reject.[112]

If the other party can demonstrate that the debtor does not have the financial capacity to make payments under the contract or lease, then the court

---

[108] See S. Rep. No. 95-989, 95th Cong., 2d Sess. 2266 (1977).
[109] In re Circle K Corp. 127 F.3d 904, 911 (9th Cir. 1997), cert. denied, 118 S. Ct. 1166 (1998).
[110] See In re Nevins Ammunition, Inc., 79 B.R. 11 (Bankr. D. Ida. 1987).
[111] In re King, 162 B.R. 86 (Bankr. E.D.N.Y. 1993).
[112] In re Karfakis, 162 B.R. 719 (Bankr. E.D. Pa. 1993).

would direct that the contract be rejected. Some debtors may make the few months' delinquent payments and easily establish that they have the financial capability to meet the monthly payments. The court will look at a debtor's financial projections before deciding whether the debtor can be expected to meet the terms of the contract or lease. Under other conditions, it may take considerable effort on the part of the debtor to convince the court that it has the ability to make future payments. For example, section 365(b)(3) of the Bankruptcy Code states that, in the case of a lease of real property in a shopping center, it would be necessary to show adequate assurance:

1   Of the source of rent and other considerations due under the lease. In the case of an assignment, adequate assurance that the financial condition and operating performance of the proposed assignee and its guarantors, if any, are similar to those of the debtor and its guarantors, if any, at the time the debtor became the lessee.
2   That any percentage due would not decline substantially.
3   That assumption or assignment of the lease would not breach substantially any provision such as radius, location, use, or exclusivity rights granted to other tenants.
4   That the assumption or assignment of the lease will not disrupt substantially any tenant mix or balance in the shopping center.

The requirement of adequate assurance for the payment applies only to contracts or leases where there were prior defaults. If the contract is to be assigned and sold, like any other property right of the debtor, to a third party, then section 365(f)(2)(B) requires that adequate assurance be provided, even though there has not been a default in the contract or lease. Section 365(l), added by the Bankruptcy Amendments and Federal Judgeship Act of 1984, provides that, if an unexpired lease is assigned by the debtor, the lessor may require a deposit or other security for the performance of the debtor's obligation that is substantially the same as would have been required upon the initial leasing to a similar tenant.

Section 365(b)(2) provides that clauses that automatically cause the contract or lease to terminate in the event of bankruptcy are invalidated and are thus not considered a default of the contract or lease. The prohibition against an insolvency or bankruptcy clause or the prohibition against appointing a trustee does not apply to financing agreements or contracts under which applicable state law excuses a party from accepting substitute performance, such as personal performance contracts. Thus, any funds obtained during the reorganization will depend on the debtor's ability to convince lenders to make adequate financing available.

Section 365(b)(4) provides that, before assumption of a lease in default, other than because of bankruptcy or insolvency of a debtor, the lessee cannot require a lessor to provide services or supplies unless the lessor is properly compensated according to the terms of the lease. Section 365(l) allows the lessor of a lease assigned by the debtor to require a deposit or other security for the performance of the debtor's obligation, as would have been required upon the initial leasing to a similar tenant.

(b) Meaning of "Sixty-Day" Assumption

Bankruptcy Code section 365(d) provides that, in chapter 7 liquidation, the trustee must assume the contract or lease within 60 days after the order of relief (or in an additional period if the court, for cause, extends the time) or the contract or lease is deemed rejected; in the case of nonresidential real property, the property is to be immediately surrendered to the lessor. No time limit is set in chapter 11 or chapter 13, except for nonresidential real property, provided the contract or lease is accepted or rejected before the confirmation of the plan. However, if the other party requests the court to fix a time, the court may establish a set time within which the debtor or trustee must act. In the case of nonresidential real property, Section 365(d)(4) provides that if the debtor does not assume the unexpired lease within 60 days (or an additional period, if authorized by the court) after the order for relief, the lease is deemed rejected and the property is to be immediately surrendered to the lessor. In a chapter 11 case, the debtor may assume the lease at this time and then later provide for rejection of the lease in the plan.

The Bankruptcy Reform Act of 1994 added paragraph (10) to section 365(d) of the Bankruptcy Code. It states that, 60 days after the order for relief, the debtor must perform all obligations under a personal lease, such as an equipment lease, unless the court orders otherwise because of the equities of the case. Under prior practice, the lessors were permitted to petition the court to require the lessee to make lease payments to the extent that the lease payments benefited the estate. The responsibility of bringing a motion now has shifted to the debtor. At the same time, the debtor is given sufficient time to make an informed decision about the lease. This change should remove some of the inequities in prior practice.

A split in the cases has developed over the issue of whether an extension of the 60-day period must be actually granted by the court during the 60-day period or whether the filing of a motion for extension before the expiration of the period will preserve the right to an extension, assuming the court subsequently grants the extension.

Generally courts are granting the extension as long as the motion for extension is filed before the end of the 60-day period or a prior extended period.[113] Since the statute indicates that the extension of the initial 60-day period be fixed within 60 days, it may be advisable to file for the extension before the last minute to give the court time to act within the 60-day period, even though it may not always be necessary. There is also an issue as to what constitutes an assumption during the period.

In *In re Victoria Station, Inc.*,[114] the Ninth Circuit Court of Appeals held that a debtor-tenant's motion to assume a lease was in accordance with the section 365(d)(4) 60-day requirement when it was served on the lessor within the 60-day period, even though it was not filed with the court until a few days after the 60-day period had expired. The rationale was that section 365(d)(4) does not limit the time in which the court must approve the

---

[113] *See In re Southwest Aircraft Services, Inc.*, 831 F.2d 848 (9th Cir. 1987); *In re American Healthcare Management, Inc.*, 900 F.2d 827 (5th Cir. 1990).
[114] 840 F.2d 682 (9th Cir. 1988).

assumption if the motion to assume was within the period. The *Victoria* case followed the earlier Ninth Circuit case of *In re Southwest Aircraft Services, Inc.*[115] Generally, the conduct of the parties will not result in the assumption of the lease. The cases support the conclusion that, without a motion during the 60-day period, in general, the conduct of the parties will not result in an assumption of the lease.[116] However, the case of *In re Casual Male Corp.*[117] stands for the proposition that leases may be assumed by unequivocal conduct of the lessor.

In *In re Ho's Ltd.*,[118] the court held that the lease was deemed rejected by operation of law when the debtor failed to file a motion to assume the lease within 60 days of the filing of the petition, even though the parties had reached an understanding that the debtor would be able to file a motion to assume the lease outside the 60-day period.

When a lease has been rejected because the time to assume the lease has expired, the bankruptcy court may order the surrender of the premises.[119]

In *In re Pier 5 Management Co., Inc.*,[120] the court found that, because the landlord failed to provide the debtor the promised construction cost information necessary to calculate the rent, the landlord was stopped from asserting the forfeiture. Thus, even though Pier 5 did not assume the lease, the landlord was unable to obtain possession of the property.[121]

The rejection of an executory contract or lease (that has not been assumed) constitutes a breach of the contract or lease as of the date immediately preceding the filing of the petition. Thus, the rejections are treated as prepetition claims. In determining the allowed amount of the claim postpetition, payments must be discounted to their present value.[122]

In *In re Hunan Rose, Inc.*,[123] the bankruptcy court held that the debtor-in-possession must assume the lease (or request an extension) even though the landlord had moved for a declaration that the lease had been terminated before the petition was filed. The court held that the action by the landlord did not toll the 60-day period; thus, the lease was assumed rejected at the end of the 60-day period under section 365(d)(4).

---

[115] 831 F.2d 848 (9th Cir. 1987). *See also In re Wedtech Corp.*, 72 B.R. 464 (Bankr. S.D. N.Y. 1987) and *In re Bon-Ton Restaurant and Pastry Shop, Inc.*, 52 B.R. 850 (Bankr. N.D. Ill. 1985).

[116] *See In re BDM Corp.*, 71 B.R. 142 (Bankr. N.D. Ill. 1987) (statement by chapter 11 debtor's president that debtor intended to honor existing lease and lessor's acceptance of lease payments did not result in effective assumption of the lease); *In re Treat Fitness Center, Inc.*, 60 B.R. 878 (9th Cir. BAP 1986) (lease cannot be assumed by conduct); *In re Chandel Enterprises, Inc.*, 64 B.R. 607 (Bankr. C.D. Cal. 1986) (acceptance of postpetition rent did not constitute waiver by owner; lease can be assumed only by timely formal motion); *In re Re-Trac Corp.*, 59 B.R. 251 (Bankr. D. Minn. 1986) (rent accepted after 60-day period was not payments under the lease, but payments made for reasonable use of premises).

[117] 120 B.R. 256 (Bankr. Mass. 1990).

[118] 82 B.R. 342 (Bankr. M.D. Pa. 1988).

[119] *In re Elm Inn, Inc.*, 942 F.2d 630 (9th Cir. 1991); *see In re King*, 162 B.R. 86 (Bankr. E.D. N.Y. 1993).

[120] 83 B.R. 392 (Bankr. E.D. Va. 1988).

[121] For additional discussion of section 365(d)(4), see *Distressed Business and Real Estate Newsletter* (August–September, 1988), pp. 5–6.

[122] *In re Cochise College Park, Inc.*, 703 F.2d 1339 (9th Cir. 1983).

[123] 146 B.R. 313 (Bankr. D. D.C. 1992).

The Ninth Circuit, in *In re Arizona Appetito's Stores, Inc.*,[124] held that the bankruptcy court did not have to approve the debtor's rejection, which was made within the 60-day period specified by Bankruptcy Code section 365(d)(4), in order that the automatic rejection provisions of section 365(d)(4) would come into effect. The debtor had a change of heart after the 60-day period and filed a motion to assume the lease. The court noted that the legislative purpose of section 365(d)(4) is to avoid delays in assumption or rejection of executory contracts and that a lease is deemed rejected where a motion to reject is filed within the 60-day period and no other motion is filed within the 60-day period.

The Rail Safety Enforcement and Review Act, signed into law by the President on September 3, 1992 (Public Law 102-365), amends section 365(d) of the Bankruptcy Code to protect lessors of aircraft terminals or aircraft gates when the lessee is a debtor in a case under title 11. Such leases will be terminated, unless assumed within five days after a "termination event," that is, the filing of or conversion to a chapter 7 case or when the lessor gets relief from the automatic stay (unless the property is found not to be necessary to an effective reorganization).

Section 365(c) was amended by adding new paragraphs, which required assumption and assignment of all aircraft terminal or aircraft gate leases to the same person unless the airport operator consents to a partial assignment. After a termination event, section 365(f)(1) will not permit a bankrupt lessee to assume and assign the lease of an aircraft terminal or aircraft gate.

The purpose of this change in the Bankruptcy Code, which was initially effective September 3, 1992, was to avoid in the city of St. Louis a repetition of Kansas City's experience with Braniff, wherein unused gates were tied up in court for months. The legislation placed Lambert Airport of St. Louis in a very strong position to secure unused TWA gates and attract a new carrier, should TWA cease to operate.

Although designed for Lambert Airport, this amendment applied to all large airports where a single airline has at least 65 percent of the gates. If the airline ceases to operate, the airport will be able to reclaim its gates from the trustee of the bankrupt airline within five days. The only way the trustee could retain gates is by assuming the full lease obligations for the lease term, including payment of all rent due and other obligations, which is unlikely unless the trustee has an airline to operate the gates.

Section 363(e) of the Bankruptcy Code was amended by the Bankruptcy Reform Act of 1994 to clarify that the lessor's interest in personal property is subject to adequate protection.

Section 354(d)(4) provides that the bankruptcy court may extend the 60-day period if the debtor makes a timely motion and establishes cause. While the Bankruptcy Code does not define cause, case law has developed a list of items that should be considered, including the following:[125]

---

[124] 893 F.2d 216 (9th Cir. 1990).

[125] *In re 611 Sixth Avenue Corp.*, 191 B.R. 295; (Bankr. S.D.N.Y. 1996); *See Theatre Holding Corp. v. Mauro*, 681 F.2d 102, 105–06 (2d Cir. 1982); *Escondido Mission Village L.P. v. Best Products Co.*, 137 Bankr. 114, 117 (S.D.N.Y. 1992); *In re Babylon Ltd. Partnership*, 76 Bankr. 270, 274 (Bankr. S.D.N.Y. 1987); *In re Wedtech Corp.*, 72 Bankr. 464, 471–72 (Bankr. S.D.N.Y. 1987).

1 The significance of the lease to the debtor's business and the plan

2 Whether reversion will produce a windfall to the landlord

3 Whether the debtor has had sufficient time to appraise its financial situation and the potential value of the lease to the formulation of its plan

4 The complexity of the case and number of leases it involves

5 The need for a judicial determination as to whether a lease exists

6 The failure to pay postpetition use and occupancy or comply with other lease obligations

7 Whether the landlord has suffered damage that is not compensable under the Bankruptcy Code

8 Inability to formulate a plan within sufficient time

9 Any other facts showing the lack of a reasonable time to decide whether to assume or reject

(c) Acceptance and Rejection

If the trustee assumes and later rejects an executory contract, all of the damages resulting from the rejection are considered administrative expenses and would include any interest or attorney's fees that are part of the damages.[126]

(d) Lease Rejection

A debtor-in-possession choosing to reject an executory contract or a lease is subject to an action for breach of contract that will be treated as a prepetition claim. The power to reject burdensome contracts is significant because it allows the debtor to relegate the claim for breach to the same status as unsecured claims and possibly pay off the claimant at less than the face value of the claim through a plan. Often the cost of rejection is less than the cost of assumption. If the lease is a real property lease the damages will be limited to a cap that is described below.

A lease provision that permits the landlord to pass to its tenants the operating costs of the property and is referred to in the lease as "additional rent" was considered rent.[127] The bankruptcy court used the maintenance and operating costs rates in effect as of the petition date for all years, rather than the actual space maintenance rates that were later identified. The landlord argued that the actual rates for future years should have been used to allocate the additional rent. The district court concluded that section 506(b) provides that the bankruptcy court is to determine the amount of claims "as of the date of the filing of the petition." Thus the rates in effect as of the petition date must be used by the bankruptcy court.[128]

Reference to state law regarding lease termination is contemplated by the bankruptcy code. "[T]he Bankruptcy Code was written with the expectation that it would be applied in the context of state law and that federal courts are

---

[126] *In re Frontier Properties, Inc.*, 979 F.2d 1358 (9th Cir. 1992).
[127] *In re Allegheny Int'l, Inc.*, 145 B.R. 823 (W.D. Pa. 1992).
[128] *Id.*

not licensed to disregard interests created by state law when that course is not clearly required to effectuate federal interests . . . absent a countervailing federal interest, the basic federal rule is that state law governs" (citations omitted).[129]

Generally state court judgments arising from the cancellation of a lease are considered a part of the damages claim because "once a state court judgment becomes final and is no longer subject to appeal, it may not be collaterally attacked by the parties in subsequent litigation, either in the state court or in a federal court".[130] Thus, damage from the termination of a real property lease determined by state court judgment must be included in the amount that is compared to the section 502(b)(6) cap as described below.

Under section 502(b)(6) damages are computed on the earlier of (1) the date of the filing of the petition or (2) the date on which such lessor repossessed, or the lessee surrendered, the leased property. "The date upon which the leased premises were either 'repossessed' or 'surrendered' for purposes of section 502(b)(6)(A)(ii) is that date upon which the lease was terminated under state law."[131]

In *Evans, Inc. v. Tiffany & Co.*, the district court allowed the rental damages from a breach of a commercial lease in Illinois to be determined by calculating the lessor's total rental deficiency and discounting that value to the present by using the prevailing 6 percent statutory rate of judgment interest.[132] By accepting the statutory rate, the court noted that the statutory rate was appropriate because it "fairly ascertains the amount which, if awarded as a lump sum on which Evans can earn interest, will produce an award equivalent to the losses suffered during the term of the lease."[133]

The Sixth Circuit rejected an approach approved by the district court and advocated by the unsecured creditors' committee that allowed the use of different discount rates based on the respective credit ratings of the debtor and the new landlord.[134] Thus a higher discount rate was advocated for the debtor (24 percent) than the new lessor (11.5 percent) to determine the value of future rental stream under each lease. By using the higher discount the district court determined that there were no damages and thus no claim for lease rejection. In rejecting the district court's approach, the Sixth Circuit allowed the rent deficiency approved by the bankruptcy court that was discounted at 9 percent, which was the prevailing Illinois statutory judgment rate at the time of the evidentiary hearing.

Selected types of cost may be allowed as claims for damages, but may not be considered in the cap, such as attorney's fees, liquidation damages, and late fees.[135]

---

[129] *See Integrated Solutions, Inc. v. Service Support Specialties, Inc.*, No. 124 F.3d 487, (3d Cir. 1997).

[130] *In re Kovalchick*, 175 B.R. 863, 871 (Bankr. E.D. Pa. 1994). *See In re Eric J. Blatstein.* 1997 U.S. Dist LEXIS 13376 (E.D. Pa. 1997); *In re Fifth Ave. Jewelers, Inc.*, 203 B.R. 372, 382 (Bankr. W.D. Pa. 1996)

[131] *Fifth Ave.*, 203 B.R. at 380.

[132] 416 F. Supp. 224, 242 (N.D. Ill. 1976).

[133] *Id.*

[134] *In re Highland Superstores, Inc.*, 154 F.3d 573; (6th Cir. 1998).

[135] *See In re PPI Enterprises, Inc.*, 228 B.R. 339 (Bankr. D. Del. 1998).

(e) Real Property Cap

Section 502(b)(6) limits the amount of the damages that will be allowed on the rejection of a lease to the following:

(6) if such claim is the claim of a lessor for damages resulting from the termination of a lease of real property, such claim exceeds—

(A) the rent reserved by such lease, without acceleration, for the greater of one year, or 15 percent, not to exceed three years, of the remaining term of such lease, following the earlier of—

(i) the date of the filing of the petition; and

(ii) the date on which such lessor repossessed, or the lessee surrendered, the leased property; plus

(B) any unpaid rent due under such lease, without acceleration, on the earlier of such dates.

The legislative history of section 502(b)(6) of the Bankruptcy Code states that this provision is "designed to compensate the landlord for his loss while not permitting a claim so large as to prevent other general unsecured creditors from recovering a dividend from the estate."[136] The legislative history of section 502(b)(6) also indicates that the cap for allowable claims of lessors of real property was based on two considerations. First, the amount of the damages owed to the lessor on breach of a real estate lease was considered contingent and difficult to prove. Second, in a true lease of real property, the lessor retains all the risk and benefits as to the value of the real estate at the termination of the lease. Thus, it has been for an extended time period considered equitable to limit the claims of a real estate lessor.[137]

Courts that have applied section 502(b)(6)'s framework for determining the allowable amount of a lessor's total rejection damage claim (the cap) generally employ a four-step process.

1   The court calculates the total rents due under the lease from the earlier of the date of filing or the date on which the lessor repossessed or the lessee surrendered the leased property.

2   The court determines whether 15 percent of that total is greater than the rent reserved for one year following the debtor's filing.

3   The 15 percent amount is compared to the rent reserved under the applicable lease for three years following the filing.

4   Finally, the court, on the basis of the foregoing calculations, arrives at the total allowable amount of the landlord's rejection damages.[138]

The Ninth Circuit BAP[139] concluded that in order for an additional charge, other than for rent, to be included in the cap it must meet the following requirements:

---

[136] 4 *Collier on Bankruptcy* P 502.03[7][a].
[137] *In re Episode USA, Inc.*, 202 B.R. 691, 693 (S.D.N.Y. 1996).
[138] *See, e.g., In re Financial News Network, Inc.*, 149 B.R. 348, 351 (Bankr. S.D.N.Y. 1993); *In re Atlantic Container Corp.*, 133 B.R. 980, 989 (Bankr. N.D. Ill. 1991).
[139] *In re McSheridan*, 184 B.R. 91, 99–100 (9th Cir. Bankr. App. 1995); *See Fifth Ave.*, 203 B.R. at 381

(1) ... the charge must: (a) be designated as "rent" or "additional rent" in the lease; or (b) be provided as the tenant's/lessee's obligation in the lease;

(2) The charge must be related to the value of the property or the lease thereon; and

(3) The charge must be property classified as rent because it is a fixed, regular or periodic charge.

In the case of *In re Lindsey*, the section 502(b)(6) statutory cap was calculated as follows:

> Rent reserved for one year would be $5,779,000. This figure is calculated by adding together rent ($3,725,000), real estate taxes ($24,000), insurance ($30,000), and the yearly capital improvement fee ($2,000,000). The full rental obligation from the petition date to the end of the lease term is approximately $26 million. Fifteen percent of that amount is only $3,900,000. The larger number of these two figures is the amount of rent reserved for one year, $5,779,000. Thus, this is the applicable amount of the statutory cap on the claim of the lessor.[140]

Courts have reached different conclusions as to the meaning of 15 percent of the remaining payments—is the 15 percent multiplied by the time remaining term or by the total remaining rent? A majority of the cases support the position that the 15 percent cap must be calculated with reference to the total amount of the rent remaining due, as opposed to the total amount of time remaining under the lease.[141]

The minority position concludes that it should be based on the term because section 502 generally speaks in terms of time periods for which rent is due after termination of the lease. The "statute provides that claims cannot exceed the greater of one year, or 15 percent, not to exceed three years, of the remaining term, following the earlier of the date of the filing of the petition and the date surrendered. The statute is written in terms of time. The bankruptcy court's analysis of the legislative history demonstrates that Congress intended the phrase 'remaining term' to be a measure of time, not rent."[142] For example, in the case of *Allegheny Int'l, Inc.*,[143] the bankruptcy court reviewed the plain language in light of the legislative history of the statute and related case law, and concluded that the "or 15 percent" cap applies to the next succeeding term remaining in the lease.

The use of 15 percent of the remaining time period will often result in a lower cap since par of all of future rent increases will not be considered.

The Ninth Circuit BAP and other courts, however, have determined that the bankruptcy courts must make an independent determination of what consti-

---

[140] 199 B.R. 580, 586 (E.D. Va. 1996).

[141] *See In re McLean Enterprises, Inc.*, 105 B.R. 928 (Bankr. W.D. Mo. 1989); *In re Communicall Cent., Inc.*, 106 B.R. 540 (Bankr. N.D. Ill. 1989); *In re Q-Masters, Inc.*, 135 B.R. 157 (Bankr. S.D. Fla. 1991); *In re Bob's Sea Ray Boats, Inc.*, 143 B.R. 229 (Bankr. D.N.D. 1992); *In re Financial News Network, Inc.*, 149 B.R. 348 (Bankr. S.D.N.Y. 1993); *Today's Woman of Florida, Inc.*, 195 B.R. 506, 507 (Bankr. M.D. Fla. 1996); *In re Gantos*, 176 B.R. 793 (W.D. Mich. 1995)

[142] *In re Eric J. Blatstein*; 1997 U.S. Dist LEXIS 13376 (E.D. Pa. 1997). *See In re Allegheny Int'l, Inc.*, 145 B.R. 823, 828 (W.D. Pa. 1992); *In re Iron-Oak Supply Corp.*, 169 B.R. 414, 420 (Bankr. E.D. Ca. 1994).

[143] 136 B.R. 396, 403 (Bankr. W.D. Pa. 1991); *aff'd*, 145 B.R. 823 (W.D. Pa. 1992)

tutes "rent reserved" because labels alone may be misleading.[144] Other courts have taken a strict interpretation of the meaning of rent. For example, in the case of *In re Conston Corp., Inc.*,[145] the bankruptcy court held that appendages to pure rent are allowable as rent reserved under section 502(b)(6) only if the lease expressly so provides and the charges in question are properly classifiable as rent because they are regular, fixed, periodic charges payable in the same way as pure rent. Amortized improvement cost was considered "rent" under the lease where a regular charge was paid to the landlord as part of monthly payments. The cap, once determined, should not be reduced to net present value.[146]

The Ninth Circuit BAP,[147] as noted above established standards to determine if for an additional charges other than for rent, may be included in the cap.

Generally claims by landlords for unpaid rent are subject to the limitations of section 502(b)(6) regardless of whether the action is filed by a landlord against a tenant or a guarantor of a lease.[148] In *In re Danrik*, the debtor was a guarantor who had paid all other creditors in full and had sufficient monies to pay the landlord in full. The bankruptcy court using its equitable powers held that section 502(b)(6) did not limit the landlord's claim under these facts.[149]

The claim allowed under section 502(b)(6) is to be reduced by the security deposit. "Although section 502(b)(6) does not speak to the point, the comments by both the House of Representatives and the Senate make clear that the vitality of Oldden v. Tonto Realty Co.[, 143 F.2d 916 (2d Cir. 1944)] remains undiminished at least insofar as that case held that the amount of security held by a landlord was to be deducted from the allowable claim under Section 63a(9) of the 1898 Bankruptcy Act."[150]

Thus, the landlord will not be able to offset the security deposit against actual damages unless actual damages are less than the cap, but rather will be required to offset the deposit against the cap. If the security deposit exceeds the cap, the landlord will be required to remit the balance because such balance is property of the estate.

For example, if the claim for damages is $10,000, the cap (15 percent of the remaining term applies) is $6,000, and the security deposit is $5,000, the cap of $6,000, which becomes the allowed claim, would be offset by the security deposit of $5,000. The offset would leave a prepetition claim for lease rejection

---

[144] *See In re Fifth Ave. Jewelers, Inc.*, 203 B.R. 372, 381 (Bankr. W.D. Pa. 1996); *In re Rose Stores, Inc.*, 179 B.R. 789, 790 (Bankr. E.D.N.C. 1995); *In re Heck's, Inc.*, 123 B.R. 544, 546 (Bankr. S.D.W. Va. 1991); *In re Eric J. Blatstein*, 1997 U.S. Dist LEXIS 13376 (E.D. Pa. 1997).

[145] 130 B.R. 449 (Bankr. E.D. Pa. 1991).

[146] *In re Allegheny Int'l, Inc.*, 145 B.R. 823, 828 (W.D. Pa. 1992).

[147] See *supra* note 139.

[148] *See In re Rodman*, 60 Bankr. 334 (Bankr. D. Colo. 1986); *In re Thompson*, 116 Bankr. 610 (Bankr. S.D. Ohio 1990); *In re Interco, Inc.*, 137 Bankr. 1003 (Bankr. E.D. Mo. 1992); and *In re Farley*, 146 Bankr. 739 (Bankr. N.D. Ill. 1992).

[149] *In re Danrik*, Ltd., 92 Bankr. 964 (Bankr. N.D. Ga. 1988).

[150] 4 *Collier on Bankruptcy* P 502.03[7][a]. See *In re All For a Dollar, Inc.*, 191 B.R. 262, 264 (Bankr. D. Mass. 1996); *In re Atlantic Container Corp.*, 133 B.R. 980, 989 (Bankr. N.D. Ill. 1991); *Conston*, 130 B.R. at 452; *Communicall*, 106 B.R. at 544; *In re Danrik, Ltd.*, 92 B.R. 964, 967–68 (Bankr. N.D. Ga. 1988); *See, e.g., In re Handy Andy Home Improvement Centers, Inc.*, 222 B.R. 571, 574–75 (Bankr. N.D. Ill. 1998); *Blatstein*, 1997 U.S. Dist LEXIS 13376 (E.D. Pa. 1997).

of $1,000 ($6,000 – $5,000). If the security deposit were $8,000, the landlord would owe the estate $2,000 ($6,000 – $8000). If the cap were $14,000, then the security deposit would be offset against the $10,000 claims for damages (since the claim is less than the cap), leaving a prepetition claim of $5,000 ($10,000 – $5,000).

There is some misunderstanding as to the extent to which attorney fees of the landlord can be awarded over and above the cap. For example, in *In re Lindsey*[151] the district court allowed the additional fee noting that the bankruptcy court correctly awarded attorneys' fees independently from the statutory cap of 15 percent. However, the district court in *In re Blatstein* refused to award these costs stating the following:[152]

> Section 502(b)(6) applies to the "claim" of the lessor for damages resulting from lease termination. Here, the Complaint . . . attached to [landlord's] Proofs of Claim delineates attorneys' fees as an item of damages in addition to past and accelerated rent. . . . As such, attorneys' fees are nothing more than a component of the lessor's "claim" and are subject to the section 502(b)(6) cap. The cap represents the maximum amount recoverable as a result of the termination of the lease, thereby precluding the payment of attorneys' fees as additional damages.

A large number of courts have allowed claims for deferred maintenance damages resulting from the debtor prior to the filing of the petition as a prepetition claim, and because they did not arise due to the termination of the lease the claims were not considered a part of the cap. It appears that most of the cases that have disallowed the damages have done so because the claim arose because of the termination of the lease. These claims were considered part of the rent.[153]

(f) Employment Contracts

The cancellation of an employment contract may result in severance pay being held as a administrative expense by some courts, but other courts may view it differently. For example, in *In re Child World, Inc.,*[154] the bankruptcy court relied on *In re W. T. Grant Co.*[155] to hold that a postpetition rejection of an executory employment contract with a provision for severance pay results in an administrative expense. However, the First Circuit ruled that the rejection related to a wage continuation obligation rather than an obligation for severance pay; as a result, the claim was prepetition and unsecured.[156]

(g) Rents Prior to Rejection of Lease

Section 365(d)(3), added to the Bankruptcy Code by the Bankruptcy Amendments and Federal Judgeship Act of 1984, provides that the trustee or debtor-

---

[151] *Lindsey,* 199 B.R. at 586.
[152] 1997 U.S. Dist LEXIS 13376 at 45.
[153] *See In re Best Products Co., Inc.,* 229 B.R. 673; (E.D. Va. 1998) for a detailed discussion of the issues and additional citations.
[154] 23 Bank. Ct. Dec. (CRR) 1054 (S.D.N.Y. 1992).
[155] 620 F.2d 319 (2d Cir. 1980).
[156] *In re Mammoth Mart, Inc.,* 536 F.2d 950 (1st Cir. 1976).

in-possession is to timely perform all the obligations of the debtor until the nonresidential real property lease is assumed or rejected. Exceptions are: obligations related to the breach of a provision or to the financial conditions of the debtor, or actions taken (such as the filing of a bankruptcy petition) that arise from and after the order of relief. Under section 365(d)(3) of the Bankruptcy Code, the landlord is entitled to the rent at the contract rate, even though this rate may be more than the current market rate during the period that begins when the petition is filed and ends on the date of actual rejection or deemed rejection—and regardless of whether the landlord demanded payment. The postpetition rent is an administrative expense but does not have priority over other administrative expenses.[157] Rent expense incurred when the lessee remains in possession after the rejection of the lease will be allowed, to the amount provided under section 503(b)(1)(A) of the Bankruptcy Code.[158] The Ninth Circuit has held that, during the time period before the lease was rejected, the landlord is entitled to an administrative claim for the amount of the accrued rent, regardless of the actual value conferred by the lease on the estate.[159]

The trustee or debtor-in-possession only has an obligation to pay the taxes that are provided for in the lease and that are properly allocated to the period after the issuance of the order for relief and before the rejection. Taxes that are allocated to the period prior to the issuance of the order for relief are not an administrative expense under section 365(d)(3) of the Bankruptcy Code, even though they did not become due until after the order for relief.[160]

There is uncertainty as to the items that should be included in the calculation of the damages under the limitations of section 502(b)(6) of the Bankruptcy Code for the rejection of real property leases. The majority view[161] is that a claim for damages applies to all damages occasioned by the rejection of the lease, including damages caused by the debtor's breach of a covenant to repair and maintain the premises. However, in *In re Atlantic Container Corp.*,[162] the bankruptcy court held that the limitation applied only to the lease cancellation and not to a contractual obligation to maintain and repair the property.

(h) Rejection by Lessor

A debtor may reject the lease as a lessee or as a lessor. Effective for petitions filed after October 22, 1994, the Bankruptcy Reform Act of 1994 modified section 365(h) of the Bankruptcy Code to mandate that a landlord in bankruptcy cannot strip away the rights of the lessee appurtenant to its leasehold, including the rights regarding the amount and timing of payment of rent or other amounts payable by the lessee; the rights to use, possess in quiet enjoyment, sublet, or assign the lease that are in or appurtenant to the real property for the

---

[157] *In re Dawson*, 162 B.R. 329 (Bankr. D. Kan. 1993).
[158] *Id.*
[159] *In re Pacific-Atlantic Trading Co.*, 27 F.3d 401 (9th Cir. 1994).
[160] *In re Child World, Inc.*, 161 B.R. 571 (S.D.N.Y. 1993).
[161] *See In re Mr. Gatti's, Inc.*, 162 B.R. 1004 (Bankr. W.D. Tex. 1994).
[162] 133 B.R. 980 (Bankr. N.D. Ill. 1991).

balance of the term of such lease, and for any renewal or extensions, provided such rights are enforceable under applicable nonbankruptcy law. This change will overrule the courts that have interpreted the rights to only relate to those of possession. For example, in *Home Express, Inc. v. Arden Associates, Ltd.*,[163] the tenant was prevented from enforcing restrictive covenants in the lease. Section 365(h)(1)(C) also provides that for shopping center provisions relating to radius, location, use, exclusivity, or tenant mix or balance will survive the lease rejection. Since the amendment did not provide that the lessee may retain all of its rights, litigation will most likely continue in those areas not provided for in the revision to section 365(h).

§ 5.30 Utility Service

Section 366 provides that a utility may not refuse, alter, discontinue service to, or discriminate against, the trustee or debtor solely because it has not made timely payment for services rendered before the order for relief. This injunction, for example, prohibits the utility from cutting off or reducing the service or charging telephone numbers. But the trustee or debtor must, within 20 days after the order for relief, furnish adequate assurance of payment for services after that date. This can often be resolved by negotiation with the utility and can be in the form of a deposit or other security. Some utilities may initially demand a fairly large deposit. Often, by negotiating with the utility, the deposit can be reduced to a reasonable period, such as six weeks.

In some situations adequate assurance has been provided by the fact that postpetition usage is an administrative expense. However, a bankruptcy court has determined that an administrative expense priority did not constitute adequate assurance of payment.[164]

Courts, while not required to do so, have often looked to state public utility commissions to determine the nature, amount, and purpose of a deposit. Generally courts will not allow discrimination. Thus, if new customers are not required to provide a deposit, the utility could not require the chapter 11 company to provide a deposit. Also, a utility cannot demand a deposit from a debtor that is current with its payments solely because of the filing.[165] On request of a party in interest and after notice and hearing, the court may order reasonable modifications of the amount necessary to provide adequate assurance of payment.

A utility that terminated service to the debtor prior to the filing of the petition is not obligated to automatically restore service. Before the service is restored, the utility has the right to demand adequate assurance of payment under section 366(b).

§ 5.31 Allowance of Claims or Interests

Section 501 permits a creditor or indenture trustee to file a proof of claim and an equity holder to file a proof of interest. Bankruptcy Rule 3002 pro-

---

[163] 152 B.R. 971 (Bankr. E.D. Cal. 1993).
[164] *In re Stagecoach Enters Inc.*, 1 C.B.C.2d 293 (Bankr. M.D. Fla. 1979).
[165] *In re Heard*, 84 B.R. 454 (Bankr. W.D. Tex. 1987).

vides that an unsecured creditor or an equity holder must file a proof of claim or interest for the claim or interest to be allowed in a chapter 7 or chapter 13 case. A secured creditor needs to file a proof of claim for the claim to be allowed under section 502 or 506(d), unless a party in interest requests a determination and allowance or disallowance. In a chapter 7 or chapter 13 case, a proof of claim is to be filed within 90 days after the date set for the meeting of creditors under section 341(a). For cause, the court may extend this period and the court will fix the time period for the filing of a proof of claim arising from the rejection of an executory contract. The filing of the proof of claim is not mandatory in a chapter 9 or chapter 11 case, provided the claim is listed in the schedule of liabilities. However, if the claim is not scheduled or the creditor disputes the claim, a proof of claim should be filed. It is generally advisable to file a proof of claim even though the claim is scheduled. See Rule 3003. A proof of claim filed will supersede any scheduling of that claim in accordance with section 521(l). In a chapter 12 case, the proof of claim must be filed within 90 days after the date is set for the meeting of creditors under section 341(a).

According to Bankruptcy Rule 1019(4), claims that are filed in a superseded case are deemed filed in a chapter 7 case. Thus, in a case that is converted from chapter 11 to chapter 7, it will not be necessary for the creditor to file a proof of claim in chapter 7 if one was filed in the chapter 11 case. However, if the debt was listed on the schedules in a chapter 11 case and a proof of claim was not filed, it will be necessary to file a proof of claim if the case is converted to chapter 7. Bankruptcy Rule 1019 was amended in 1987 to require the proof of claim. This amendment changed the results of the Third Circuit Court's decision in *In re Crouthamel Potato Chip Co.*,[166] where it was held that a proof of claim was not necessary in a conversion to chapter 7 if the debt was properly listed on the schedules accompanying a chapter 11 petition. The Advisory Committee Note to Rule 1019 indicates that the reason for the change is that it is unfair to the chapter 7 trustee and creditors to require that they be bound by schedules that may not be subject to verification.

To be allowed, a proof of claim does not have to be formal. A proof of claim can be amended after the bar date for filing the proof of claim, provided evidence of the claim exists prior to the bar date. It is, however, necessary for the holder of the claim to state an explicit demand showing the nature and the amount of the claim and some evidence of an intent to hold the debtor liable for the debt.[167] In another Ninth Circuit decision, the court held that a well-documented request for relief of the stay, stating the nature and the contingent amount of the claim, is an amendable informal proof of claim.[168]

Section 501(c) also gives the debtor or trustee the power to file a claim on behalf of the creditor, if the creditor did not file a timely claim. Thus, for debts that are nondischargeable, such as tax claims, the debtor may file a proof of claim to cause the creditor to receive some payment from the estate and avoid having to pay all of the debt after the bankruptcy proceedings are over.

---

[166] 786 F.2d 141 (3d Cir. 1986).
[167] *In re Sambo's Restaurants,* 754 F.2d 811 (9th Cir. 1985).
[168] *Pizza of Hawaii,* 761 F.2d 1374 (9th Cir. 1985); *See In re Herbert L. Holm,* 931 F.2d 620 (9th Cir. 1991).

If the tax authority files a tax claim that is different from the amount of tax that the debtor believes is due, the creditor may file an objection to the claim. In *In re Richard J. Morrell*,[169] the IRS filed tax claims and the creditors' committee objected to the tax claims and filed notice with the Director of the IRS in San Francisco. At the hearing, because the U.S. Government was not represented, the objections of the creditors' committee were sustained and the claims disallowed. Rules 9014 and 7004(b) provide that the U.S. Attorney for the district in which the action is brought and the U.S. Attorney General must be notified. On appeal, the district court ruled that because the creditors' committee failed to properly notify the U.S. Attorneys, the tax claims must be considered on their merits and reversed the bankruptcy court's disallowance of the claims.[170]

Generally a secured creditor need not file a proof of claim; however, it may be advisable for a claim to be filed. If a secured creditor fails to file a proof of claim, it appears that the debtor is not required to deal with the claim in the bankruptcy. The creditor does, however, retain its lien.[171] Also in no-asset liquidating cases, a proof of claim is generally not necessary. However, if a trustee recovers or receives property and the chapter 7 filing becomes an asset case, a proof of claim must be filed. The trustee should notify the creditor of the asset discovery and have the court establish a bar date for the proof of claims to be filed.

The proof of claim according to section 502(a) that is filed with the court is deemed allowed unless a party in interest objects. Claims may be disallowed for nine basic reasons, as set forth in section 502(b). They are:

1 A claim will be disallowed if it is unenforceable against a debtor for any reason other than because it is contingent or unliquidated. Contingent or unliquidated debts will be liquidated by the bankruptcy court. (This is a departure from prior law, in which these claims were generally not provable.)

2 Claims for unmatured interest will be disallowed. Postpetition interest that is not yet due and payable and any portion of prepaid interest that represents an original discounting of the claim are included as disallowed interest. Thus, present law is retained in that interest stops accruing on unsecured claims when the petition is filed (unless the debtor is solvent), and bankruptcy works as the acceleration of the principal amount of all claims.

3 To the extent that a tax claim assessed against property of the estate exceeds the value of the estate's interest in such property, the claim will be disallowed.

4 Claims by an insider or attorney for the debtor will be disallowed if they exceed the reasonable value of those services. This permits the court to examine the attorney's claim independently of any other section, and prevents overreaching by the debtor's attorney and the concealing of assets by the debtor.

[169] 87-1 USTC ¶ 9142 (N.D. Ga. 1986).
[170] *See In re F.C.M. Corp.*, 1987 U.S. Dist. LEXIS 15275 (S.D. Fla. 1987).
[171] *See In re Thomas*, 883 F.2d 991, 996–998 (11th Cir. 1989), *cert. denied*, 497 U.S. 1107 (1990).

5   Postpetition alimony, maintenance, or support claims are disallowed because they are nondischargeable and will be paid from the debtor's postbankruptcy property.

6   The damages allowable to the landlord of a debtor from termination of a lease of real property are limited to the greater of one year or 15 percent, not to exceed three years, of the remaining portion of the lease's rent due for the period beginning from the earlier of the date of the filing or surrender of the property plus the prepetition unpaid rent. This formula compensates the landlord while not allowing the claim to be so large as to hurt other creditors of the estate.[172]

7   The damages resulting from the breach of an employment contract are limited to one year following the date of the petition or the termination of employment, whichever is earlier. (This is a new addition to the area of disallowed claims.)

8   Certain employment tax claims are disallowed. Specifically, this relates to a federal tax credit for state unemployment insurance that is disallowed if the state tax is paid late. Now, the federal claim for the tax would be disallowed as if the credit had been allowed on the federal tax return.[173]

9   When debt for a proof of claim is not timely filed, the only exceptions possible are: (a) when the tardy filing is permitted under paragraph (1), (2), or (3) of section 726(a) of the Bankruptcy Code or under the Federal Rules of Bankruptcy Procedure, or (b) when the claim is a debt of a governmental unit, in which case it is considered timely filed if it is filed within 180 days after the order for relief (or a later date that might be provided by Federal Rules of Bankruptcy Procedure).

Item 9 was added by the Bankruptcy Reform Act of 1994 to help clarify the extent to which the Internal Revenue Service or other taxing authorities can file a proof of claim after the bar date. The Act also modified section 726(a) of the Bankruptcy Code to allow a priority tax as long as the proof of claim is filed prior to the date on which the trustee begins to distribute the property of the estate.

Claims are disallowed if they arise from a rejection of an executory contract or lease that was not assumed. Upon the recovery of setoff or voidable transfer (for example, preferences or fraudulent transfer), such a claim is treated as though the claim had arisen prior to the filing of the petition.[174] Tax claims that arise after the filing of the petition and are eighth-priority tax claims are to be treated as though the claim had arisen prior to the petition date.[175] For example, the assessment of additional income taxes resulting from an audit of a tax return due within three years before the petition date would be generally considered a prepetition eighth-priority claim even though the assessment was made after the petition was filed.

---

[172] Derived from prior law as set out in *Oldden v. Tonto Realty Co.*, 143 F.2d 916 (2d Cir. 1944).
[173] *CCH Bankruptcy Law Reports*, ¶ 9006.
[174] 11 U.S.C. § 502(g) and (h).
[175] *Id.*, § 502(i).

(a) Secured Claims

The Bankruptcy Act referred to creditors as either secured creditors or unsecured creditors. The Bankruptcy Code refines this distinction and refers to creditors as holders of secured and unsecured claims. Section 506(a) states:

> An allowed claim of a creditor secured by a lien on property in which the estate has an interest, or that is subject to setoff under section 553 of this title, is a secured claim to the extent of the value of such creditor's interest in the estate's interest in such property, or to the extent of the amount subject to setoff, as the case may be, and is an unsecured claim to the extent that the value of such creditor's interest or the amount so subject to setoff is less than the amount of such allowed claim.

Thus, an undersecured creditor's allowed claim is separated into two parts. A secured claim exists to the extent of the value of the collateral, and the balance is unsecured. A secured claim must, first, be an allowed claim; second, it must be secured by a lien on the property; and, third, the debtor's estate must have an interest in the property secured by the lien or it must be subject to setoff. (See Chapter 11 for a discussion of the section 506 valuation.)

A creditor may prefer to have the entire claim classified as unsecured. The creditor may think that the collateral will not be able to withstand probable attacks and may prefer to renounce the collateral and have the entire claim considered unsecured. The Bankruptcy Code does not specifically state that the creditor has the right to renounce the collateral, but the principle was well settled under the practice of the prior law.[176] (See § 6.16.)

In *In the matter of Laymon*,[177] the Fifth Circuit held that equities in the case determine whether an oversecured creditor is entitled to interest at the contractual predefault rate or at the higher default rate (if one is stipulated in the contract). The court held that the Supreme Court did not address the issue of interest rate in *United States v. Ron Pair Enterprises, Inc.*[178]

§ 5.32 Expense of Administration

The actual, necessary costs of preserving the estate, including wages, salaries, and commissions for services rendered after the commencement of the case are considered administrative expenses. Any tax (including fines or penalties) is allowed unless it relates to a tax-granted preference under section 507(a)(7). Compensation awarded a professional person, including accountants, for post-petition services is an expense of administration. (See § 7.6.) Expenses incurred in an involuntary case subsequent to the filing of the petition but prior to the appointment of a trustee or the order for relief are not considered administrative expenses. They are, however, granted second priority under section 507.

Effective for petitions filed after October 22, 1994, the Bankruptcy Reform Act of 1994 modified section 503(a) of the Bankruptcy Code to allow a claim to be tardily filed for administrative expenses, if permitted by the court for cause.

---

[176] *Collier Bankruptcy Manual*, 3d ed., ¶ 506.02[3]. *See also In re Tiger*, 109 F. Supp. 737 (D.N.J. 1952), *aff'd*, 201 F.2d 670 (3d Cir. 1953).
[177] 958 F.2d 72 (5th Cir. 1992).
[178] 489 U.S. 235 (1989).

§ 5.33   Priorities

The 1978 Bankruptcy Code and subsequent amendments modified to a limited extent the order of payment of the expenses of administration and other unsecured claims. Section 507 provides for the following priorities:

1   Administrative expenses.
2   Unsecured claims in an involuntary case arising after commencement of the proceedings but before an order of relief is granted.
3   Wages (including sales commission of independent contractor as described below) earned within 90 days prior to filing the petition (or the cessation of the business) to the extent of $4,300 per individual.
4   Unsecured claims to employee benefit plans arising within 180 days prior to filing the petition limited to $4,300 times the number of employees covered by the plan less the amount paid in priority 3 above and the amount previously paid on behalf of such employees.
5   Unsecured claims of grain producers against a grain storage facility or of fishermen against a fish produce storage or processing facility to the extent of $4,300.
6   Unsecured claims of individuals to the extent of $1,950 from deposits of money for purchase, lease, or rental of property or purchase of services not delivered or provided.
7   Allowed claims for debts to a spouse, former spouse, or child of the debtor, for alimony to, maintenance for, or support of such spouse or child, in connection with a separation agreement, divorce decree, or other order of the court, or property settlement agreement. The priority would not apply to the extent that such debt is assigned to another entity or includes a liability designated as alimony, maintenance, or support unless such liability is actually in the nature of alimony, maintenance, or support.
8   Unsecured tax claims of governmental units:

   Income or gross receipts tax provided tax return due (including extension) within three years prior to filing petition, provided tax was assessed within 120 days or tax is assessable.

   Property tax last payable without penalty within one year prior to filing petition.

   Withholding taxes (no time limit).

   Employment tax on wages, and so forth, due within three years prior to the filing of the petition.

   Excise tax due within three years prior to the filing of the petition.

   Customs duty on merchandise imported within one year prior to the filing of the petition.

   Penalties related to a type of claim above in compensation for actual pecuniary loss.
9   Allowed unsecured claims based upon any commitment by the debtor to a Federal depository institutions regulatory agency (or predecessor to such agency) to maintain the capital of an insured depository institution.

Beginning April 1, 1998, and at each three-year interval thereafter, the dollar amounts for priorities under section 507(a) of the Bankruptcy Code are increased to reflect the change in the Consumer Price Index for All Urban Consumers that has occurred during the three-year period ending on December 31 of the immediately preceding year. The amounts are rounded to the nearest $25 multiple. The priority amounts above reflect changes through March 31, 2001.

Effective for petitions filed after October 22, 1994, section 507(a)(3) of the Bankruptcy Code has been modified to allow, as a priority for wages, the sales commissions earned by an individual, or a corporation with only one employee, who acted as an independent contractor in the sale of goods or services for the debtor in the ordinary course of the debtor's business. To qualify, at least 75 percent of the amount the individual earned by acting as an independent contractor during the past 12 months has to be earned from the debtor.

The fourth priority was added by the Bankruptcy Reform Act of 1978, but note that it is limited to the amount of unused wage priority. The wage priority amount has been increased to $4,300 from the $2,000 amount in the Bankruptcy Reform Act of 1978. Only $600 was allowed under prior law. Salary claims are included, as are vacation, sick leave, and severance pay. The fifth priority applies in cases filed on or after October 8, 1984. The sixth priority provides for payments up to $1,950 for each individual consumer who has deposited or made partial payment for the purchase or lease of goods or services that were not delivered or provided by the debtor prior to the date of bankruptcy. Taxes were granted a fourth priority under prior law but are now entitled to eighth priority. Priority 9 was added by the Crime Control Act of 1990.[179] It provides that commitments made by the debtor to maintain the capital of an insured depository institution are a priority item.

Section 507(b) provides that a holder of a claim secured by a lien on property of a debtor that received adequate protection under section 361 shall be given priority over all other priorities if the adequate protection granted proves to be inadequate.

In *United States v. Cardinal Mine Supply Co. Inc.*,[180] the Sixth Circuit held that a proof of claim that was filed late would be allowed as a priority claim because the creditor failed to receive timely notice of the bar date. The district court in *United States v. Vecchio*[181] held that a late-filed proof of claim for a priority claim is subordinated under section 726(a)(3). The court limited that application of *Cardinal Mine Supply* to cases where the creditor was not properly notified. In *In re Mantz*,[182] the Ninth Circuit BAP, disagreeing with the Sixth Circuit in *Cardinal Mine Supply*, held that a priority tax claim holder that did not receive notice of the filing until too late to file was to be treated as a general creditor and share in the distribution with these creditors under section 726(a)(2)(C). The Ninth Circuit BAP also held that, to the extent that the late-filed claim included a penalty, it was to be subordinated and distributed under the provisions of section 726(a)(4).

---

[179] Pub. L. No. 101-647.
[180] 916 F.2d 1087 (6th Cir. 1990); *see In re Rago*, 149 B.R. 882 (Bankr. N.D. Ill. 1992); *but see In re Stoecker*, 24 Bank. Ct. Dec. (CRR) 10 (Bankr. N.D. Ill. 1993).
[181] 147 B.R. 303 (E.D.N.Y. 1992).
[182] 151 B.R. 928 (9th Cir. BAP 1993).

In *In re Chateaugay Corporation (LTV)*,[183] the district court ruled that the claim of the Pension Benefit Guaranty Corporation (PBGC) does not have priority under section 507 of the Bankruptcy Code. The claim is considered unsecured and not an administrative expense.

The officials at the PBGC were concerned over this decision and attempted to convince Congress to change the law and allow the claim as a priority item. An argument can also be made that if these claims are allowed as a priority, unsecured creditors will, in many cases, receive very little and their desire to help the debtor reorganize will be substantially reduced. In fact, in many such cases it may be best for the debtor to liquidate. The current and future payments that will be required if the PBGC claims are granted priority will take most of the future cash flows from operations of the business and leave very little cash for trade and other unsecured creditors.

In another related case the Tenth Circuit[184] held that the PBGC's claim against the debtor for failing to make minimum funding contributions was also not a priority tax claim or an administrative priority claim except for part of the claim for postpetition services of employees. The claim was considered an unsecured claim that was reduced to its present value based on the "prudent investor" method instead of the PBGC's actuarial method resulting in a claim of $124 million that was $76 million less than the amount advocated by the PBGC.

§ 5.34 Exemptions

Prior law allowed an individual to exempt any property so stipulated as being exempt under applicable state law where the petition was filed. The Bankruptcy Code provides an individual debtor with an option to exempt from the estate either the federal exemption or the property stipulated by state law unless a state passes a law to the contrary. Over one-half of the states have adopted a law that requires debtors in those states to follow state laws only. Under joint cases filed under section 302 or individual cases that are jointly administered under Bankruptcy Rule 1015(b), one spouse cannot use the state exemption and the other the federal. If they cannot agree on the alternative to be elected, unless prohibited by state law, they shall adopt the federal exemption as required by section 522(b).

Based on states' laws, the exemption for a residence will vary significantly. For example, in New York, the exemption is $10,000; in California, it is $75,000 for a family home and $50,000 for a single occupancy. Texas, Florida, and a few Plains and Midwestern states have no cap on the homestead exemption. Florida has received considered publicity because several homesteads with equity in excess of $1 million have to be excluded from the property of the estate.[185]

Included in the federal exemption under section 522(d) are the debtor's interests in the following:

---

[183] 130 B.R. 690 (S.D.N.Y. 1991).
[184] *In re CF&I Fabricators*, 150 F.3d 1293 (10th Cir. 1998), *cert. denied.* 143 L.Ed.2d 1032 (1999).
[185] Larry Rohter, "Rich Debtors Finding Shelter under a Populist Florida Law," *New York Times* (July 25, 1993), sec. 1, p. 1.

1 Real property or personal property used as a residence, not to exceed $16,150.

2 One motor vehicle, not to exceed $2,575.

3 Household items and wearing apparel for personal use, not to exceed $425 in any particular item or $8,625 in aggregate value.

4 Personal, family, or household jewelry, not to exceed $1,075.

5 Any property identified by the debtor, not to exceed $850 plus the unused portion of the exemption in (1) above, not to exceed $8,075.

6 Professional books or tools of trade, not to exceed $1,625.

7 Unmatured life insurance contract (excluding credit life insurance).

8 Accrued dividend, loan value, and so forth, of unmatured life insurance contract, not to exceed $8,625.

9 Professionally prescribed health aids.

10 Right to receive selected payments such as social security, unemployment benefits, retirement benefits, veterans benefits, disability benefits, alimony, compensation for certain losses, and the like. Some of these are exempted only to the extent reasonably necessary for the support of the debtor and his or her dependents.

11 Rights to receive, or property traceable to, an award under a crime victim's reparation law, a payment due to wrongful of an individual or under a life insurance contract of whom the debtor was a dependent for reasonable support, a payment, not to exceed $16,150 due to personal body injury, and a payment due to loss of future earnings for reasonable support.

Beginning April 1, 1998, and at each three-year interval thereafter, the dollar amounts under section 522(d) of the Bankruptcy Code are increased to reflect the change in the Consumer Price Index for All Urban Consumers that has occurred during the three-year period ending on December 31 of the immediately preceding year. The amounts are rounded to the nearest $25 multiple. The exemption amounts above reflect changes through March 31, 2001.

This change will, in most states, result in less property being available for distribution to creditors. Whether a debtor may acquire or improve its exempt assets in contemplation of a bankruptcy petition is thoroughly discussed by Resnick.[186]

The Supreme Court held that a chapter 7 trustee could not contest the validity of a claim exemption after the 30-day period for objecting (as provided by Rule 4003(b) of the Federal Rules of Bankruptcy Procedure) had expired and no extension had been obtained, even though the debtor had no credible basis for claiming the exemption.[187] The trustee apparently could have made a valid objection under section 522(l)—which provides, *inter alia*, that "property claimed as exempt . . . is exempt . . . [u]nless a party in interest objects," but

---

[186] Alan N. Resnick, "Prudent Planning or Fraudulent Transfer: The Use of Nonexempt Assets to Purchase or Transfer Property on the Eve of Bankruptcy," *Rutgers Law Review*, Vol. 31 (December 1978), pp. 615–54.

[187] *Taylor v. Freeland*, 112 S. Ct. 1644 (1992).

does not specify the time for objecting—if he had acted promptly under Rule 4003(b), which establishes the 30-day objections period for trustees and creditors "unless, within such period, further time is granted by the court."[188] The court stated, "To the extent that the various Code and Rules provisions aimed at penalizing debtors and their attorneys for improper conduct fail to limit bad-faith exemption claims, Congress, rather than this Court, may rewrite 522(l) to include a good-faith requirement."[189]

Section 522(f) of the Bankruptcy Code allows the debtor to avoid the fixing of a lien on an interest of the debtor in property, to the extent that such a lien impairs an exemption to which the debtor would have been entitled under section 522(b) of the Bankruptcy Code. Such a lien must be (1) a judicial lien or (2) a nonpossessory, non-purchase-money security interest in: household furnishings, household goods, wearing apparel, appliances, books, and so on, held primarily for the personal, family, or household use of the debtor; implements, professional books, or tools of trade; or professionally prescribed health aids. Under the Bankruptcy Reform Act of 1994, effective for petitions filed after October 22, 1994, section 522(f)(1) of the Bankruptcy Code was amended to prohibit the debtor from avoiding a judicial lien that secures a debt for alimony, maintenance, or support in connection with a separation agreement, divorce decree, or other court order.

The Bankruptcy Reform Act also modified section 522(f) of the Bankruptcy Code to clarify the meaning of the words "impair an exemption." Because the Bankruptcy Code does not currently define the meaning of the words "impair an exemption" in section 522(f), several court decisions have reached varied results. This amendment provides a simple arithmetic test to determine whether a lien impairs an exemption, based upon a decision, *In re Brantz*,[190] that was favorably cited by the Supreme Court in *Owen v. Owen*.[191] For example, a lien is considered to impair an exemption to the extent that the sum of the lien, all other liens, and the amount of the exemption that the debtor could have if there were no liens on the property, exceeds the value of the debtor's interest in the property if there were no liens. Thus, if another lien is senior to a judicial lien of $40,000 on a house worth $40,000, the judicial lien could be avoided. Legislative history suggests that if the debtor has a $10,000 homestead exemption and the value of the property is $50,000 with a first mortgage of $40,000, a $20,000 judicial lien could be avoided. A judicial lien may also be avoided in situations where the judicial lien is senior to a nonavoidable mortgage, the value of which exceeds the value of the property. The net impact of this change is that, if there is no equity in the property—considering the exemption and without considering the judicial lien—the judicial lien can be avoided.

Supporting the Fifth Circuit ruling in *In re Henderson*,[192] the amendment to section 522(f) of the Bankruptcy Code would allow the debtor to avoid a lien that impaired the homestead exemption, even if the lien cannot be enforced through an execution sale.

---

[188] *Id.*, 1647–48.
[189] *Id.*, 1647–49.
[190] 106 B.R. 62 (Bankr. E.D. Pa. 1989).
[191] 111 S. Ct. 1833, 1838, n.5. (1991).
[192] 18 F.3d 1305 (5th Cir. 1994); for a contra ruling, *see In re Dixon*, 885 F.2d 327 (6th Cir. 1989).

Section 522(f) of the Bankruptcy Code was also modified to provide that, to the extent that state exemption laws apply, the debtor may not avoid a fixing of a lien on an interest of the debtor or a dependent of the debtor in property, if the lien is a nonpossessory, non-purchase-money security interest in implements, professional books, tools of the trade, farm animals, or crops, to the extent that the value of such items exceeds $5,000.

§ 5.35 Discharge of Debts

Section 523 lists several debts that are excepted from a discharge of an individual debtor. These debts are exempted from a filing under chapters 7, 11, and 12, but chapter 13 has special provisions. The items listed in subsection (a) include:

1 A tax with priority under section 507(a)(2) or 507(a)(8) or that was willfully evaded.

2 Debts from which money, property, services, or a renewal of credit was obtained by false pretenses, false representations, or actual fraud. This includes materially false statements in writing concerning the debtor's financial condition, on which the creditor reasonably relied, and the debtor's issuance of financial statements with the intent to deceive. Also exempt from discharge are consumer debts of individuals, if more than $1,075 is owed to a single creditor for "luxury goods or services," that were incurred within 60 days before the order for relief, and cash advances of more than $1,075 that are extensions of consumer credit under an open-end credit plan obtained by an individual.[193]

3 Debts that were not scheduled in time to permit timely action by the creditors to protect their rights, unless they had notice or knowledge of the proceedings.

4 Debts for fraud or defalcation while acting in a fiduciary capacity, or for embezzlement or larceny.

5 Alimony, maintenance, or support obligations.

6 Debts due to willful and malicious injury to another entity or its property.

7 Debts for fines, penalties, and forfeitures that are not compensation for actual pecuniary loss payable to a governmental unit, except a penalty relating to a nondischargeable tax or to a tax due when the transaction occurred more than three years prior to bankruptcy.

8 Most educational loans, unless the loan first became due more than five years prior to the petition date or an undue hardship would be imposed (see Public Law 96-56).

9 Debts from judgments or consent decrees resulting from the operation of a motor vehicle while legally intoxicated.

---

[193] The dollar amount here was adjusted on April 1, 1998, and will be at each three-year interval thereafter, to reflect the change in the Consumer Price Index for All Urban Consumers that has occurred during the three-year period ending on December 31 of the immediately preceding year. The amounts are rounded to the nearest $25 multiple. The dollar amount reflects changes through March 31, 2001.

10 Debts owed that were or could have been listed in a prior bankruptcy case if the debtor waived a discharge or had been denied a discharge for a statutory reason other than the six-year limitation bar.

11 Judgment or settlement agreement resulting from fraud or defalcation while acting in a fiduciary capacity at bank or credit union.

12 Debt due to malicious or reckless failure to fulfill commitment to government to maintain the capital of a bank.

13 Payment of an order of restitution under title 18, United States Code.

14 Debt incurred to pay a tax to the United States that would be nondischargeable.

15 Debt not of the kind described in item 5 above [dealing with alimony, maintenance, and support debts] that is incurred by the debtor in the course of a divorce or separation agreement or in connection with a separation agreement, divorce decree, or other order of a court of record, unless: (a) the debtor does not have the ability to pay such debt from income or property not necessary for the support of the debtor or a dependent of the debtor, or, if the debtor is engaged in a business, for expenditures necessary for the operation of the business; or (b) the discharge would result in a benefit to the debtor that outweighs the detrimental consequences to a spouse, former spouse, or child of the debtor.

16 Debts for a fee or assessment that becomes due and payable, after the order for relief, to a membership association with respect to the debtor's interest in a dwelling, in condominium ownership, or in a share of a cooperative housing corporation, provided the debtor occupied the unit or rented it and received rental payments.

Section 523(c) provides that a creditor who is owed a debt that might be exempted from discharge as a result of false statements; fraud, embezzlement, or larceny; or willful or malicious injuries, as specified above, must initiate proceedings to obtain the exception to discharge. Otherwise, the discharge of those debts will be granted unless the debtor's entire discharge is denied. Section 523(d) provides that, if a creditor requests a determination of the dischargeability of a consumer debt on the grounds that such debt was incurred by the issuance of false financial statements or under false pretenses and the court discharges the debt, the creditor may be liable for the cost of such proceedings—including attorney's fees. As stated above, section 523(a)(2) provides that it is necessary, in the case of financial statements, for the creditor to have relied on the statements and for the debtor to have issued them with the intent to deceive, before a discharge of those debts will be denied. The effect of these changes is to limit the requests for a denial of a discharge on the basis of false financial statements to those situations where material, intentional errors are involved.

The Supreme Court has held that the Bankruptcy Code did not preclude a mortgagor from doing serial filings where a chapter 7 is first filed to discharge the mortgagor's liability and thereafter a chapter 13 is filed to restructure the mortgage. The Court did not reach the question of whether such filings met the Code requirement that filing must be in good faith.[194]

---

[194] *Johnson v. Home State Bank*, 111 S. Ct. 2150 (1991).

The holding of the *Home State Bank* case represents a major setback for creditors. It does not, however, resolve the question of whether the debtor has the right to do serial filings, because the Court did not address the question of good faith. Serial filings (the filing of a chapter 7 followed by the filing of a chapter 13), referred to as "a chapter 20," have been subjected to much abuse by debtors. Objectives of serial filings have been: to achieve the reimposition of the automatic stay; to discharge, with a nominal payment in a chapter 13, a debt that was nondischargeable in a chapter 7; and to obtain a discharge of a home mortgage by filing a chapter 7 and thereafter filing a chapter 13 to cure the mortgage that was discharged under chapter 7.

The Bankruptcy Code (section 524(c)) also provides that any dischargeable debt that is reaffirmed—namely, the debtor agrees to pay notwithstanding its discharge—must be reaffirmed before the discharge is granted and only after the debtor has had at least 60 days to rescind the agreement. If it is a consumer debt of an individual, the reaffirmation must be approved by the court. A separate hearing is not mandatory in order to reaffirm a debt where the debtor is adequately represented by counsel.

§ 5.36 Property of the Estate

The commencement of a case under chapter 7, 11, 12, or 13 of the Bankruptcy Code creates an estate. The estate is composed of the debtor's property wherever it may be located.[195] All of the debtor's interest in property, legal or equitable, becomes property of the estate. It covers both tangible and intangible property, causes of action, and property that is out of the debtor's control but is still its property.[196] Property that the trustee recovers as a result of his or her avoiding powers, such as recoveries from preferences or fraudulent transfers, is considered property of the estate. Inherited property, property received from a settlement with the debtor's spouse, or beneficiary proceeds from a life insurance policy that are property of the debtor at the date of filing or that the debtor acquires or is entitled to acquire within 180 days after the filing are considered property of the estate.

The Seventh Circuit Court of Appeals has held that a bona fide purchaser at a bankruptcy sale received good title despite the fact that a lienholder did not receive notice prior to the sale.[197]

A creditor, holding a second mortgage on a chapter 7 debtor's property, moved to vacate a bankruptcy court's order confirming sale of property to a third party and subsequently filed an adversary complaint seeking determination that the second mortgage had priority over other liens against the property. The bankruptcy court dismissed both the motion and complaint. In affirming the bankruptcy court and the district court, the Court of Appeals held that the adversary complaint could not invoke jurisdiction of the bankruptcy court because the property at issue had passed outside the court's control when it was sold free and clear of all liens and the bona fide purchaser at the bankruptcy sale acquired good title to the debtor's property,

---

[195] 11 U.S.C. § 541(a).
[196] *CCH Bankruptcy Law Reports,* ¶ 9501.
[197] *In re Edwards,* 926 F.2d 641 (7th Cir. 1992).

even though the mortgagee had not received notice of sale until more than one year later.

Section 541(b) indicates four items that are not considered property of the estate. They are:

1   Power that the debtor may exercise solely for the benefit of an entity other than the debtor.

2   Interest of the debtor under a nonresidential real property lease that terminated at the expiration of the stated terms of such lease before the commencement of the bankruptcy case, and ceases to include any interest of the debtor as a lessee under a lease of nonresidential real property that has terminated at the expiration of the stated term of such lease during the case.

3   Eligibility of the debtor to participate in programs authorized under the Higher Education Act of 1965 or an accreditation status or state licensure of the debtor as an educational institution.

4   Interest of the debtor in liquid or gaseous hydrocarbons that the debtor has transferred or is obligated to transfer pursuant to a farmout agreement.

5   Proceeds from money orders sold within 14 days of the filing of the bankruptcy petition, pursuant to an agreement prohibiting the commingling of such sales proceeds with property of the debtor. To benefit from the change, the money order issuer must have acted, prior to the filing of the petition, to require compliance with commingling prohibition.

(a) Farmout Agreements

Item 4 above would not exclude from the estate any consideration the debtor retains, receives, or is entitled to receive for transferring an interest in liquid or gaseous hydrocarbons pursuant to a farmout agreement. A farmout agreement as defined under section 101(21A) means a written agreement in which the owner of a right to drill, produce or operate liquid or gaseous hydrocarbons on property agrees or has agreed to transfer or assign all or part of such rights to another entity that agrees, as consideration, to perform drilling, reworking, testing, and so on, to develop or produce liquid or gaseous hydrocarbons on the property.

The farmout exclusion was in the Energy bill (P.L. 102-486) that was passed by both the Senate and House during the last days of the 102nd Congress and signed by the President on October 24, 1992. The bill was effective upon enactment; however, it does not apply to bankruptcy cases commenced before the date of enactment.

(b) Pensions

The Supreme Court held in *Patterson v. Shumate*[198] that retirement funds under the terms of the Employee Retirement Income Security Act (ERISA) are not part of an individual's bankruptcy estate.

---

[198] 112 S. Ct. 2242 (1992).

Shumate was president, chairman of the board, and the majority shareholder of a highly leveraged corporation that filed bankruptcy approximately 19 months before Shumate did. Shumate was the plan sponsor and had the legal power to cause the corporation to distribute his pension benefits to him at any time, even though the bank that lent on the leveraged buyout—with the loan guaranteed by Shumate personally—would have strenuously objected. The corporation's pension plan was terminated as part of its bankruptcy and Shumate had a benefit of approximately $250,000. Should this benefit have been considered property of his estate or exempt property?

The Bankruptcy Code has a very comprehensive definition of property of the estate of a debtor; section 541(a) includes in the estate all legal and equitable interests of the debtor, wherever located and by whomever held.

Section 541(c)(1) states that property of the debtor will be included in the estate, notwithstanding any provision in an agreement or applicable nonbankruptcy law that restricts or conditions such a transfer, including those that provide that property reverts to a creditor upon the bankruptcy, financial condition, or insolvency of the debtor.

One exception to this treatment in section 541(c)(2) states that "a restriction on the transfer of a beneficial interest of the debtor in a trust that is enforceable under applicable nonbankruptcy law is enforceable in a case under this title." The legislative history of the Bankruptcy Code indicates that this exception was intended to keep the assets of any spendthrift trust of which the debtor was a beneficiary out of the debtor's estate, in recognition of the wishes of the settlor.

Although section 522 allows the debtor to retain certain exempt assets, these assets go into the estate. Under section 522, a decision has to be made as to whether the property qualifies for one of the exemptions under section 522 or under applicable state law. Under section 522(b), the debtor may elect to use the federal exemptions provided for in section 522(d) or the exemptions allowed by the state, unless the state of domicile of the debtor requires the state law exemptions to be followed. Shumate lived in Virginia, which does not allow the debtor to make an election but requires the use of the State of Virginia's exemptions.

The district court held that the trust could not be considered a spendthrift trust under Virginia law and thus the benefits were property of the estate. Shumate was an insider and was both settlor and beneficiary of the pension trust. The Fourth Circuit reversed the decision.

The Fourth Circuit held, as have the Third, Sixth, and Tenth Circuits,[199] that the phrase "applicable nonbankruptcy law" encompasses any and all transfer restrictions under state or federal law, and thus would include ERISA's "antialienation clause." ERISA section 206(d)(1) states that "each pension plan shall provide that the benefits provided under the plan may not be assigned or alienated." Thus, the individual retains the benefit.

The Second, Fifth, Ninth, and Eleventh Circuits had interpreted section 541(c)(2) to include only state spendthrift trust law. For example, in *Goff v. Taylor*,[200] the Fifth Circuit noted that Congress intended for section 541(c)(2) to

---

[199] *In re* Moore, 907 F.2d 1476 (4th Cir. 1990); *Creasy v. Coleman Furniture Corp.*, 943 F.2d 362 (4th Cir. 1991); *Velis v. Kardanis*, 949 F.2d 78 (3d Cir. 1991), 924 F.2d 597 (6th Cir. 1991).
[200] 706 F.2d 574 (5th Cir. 1983).

continue the prior law exclusion for spendthrift trust assets. The court did not see any reason to expand it or to assume that Congress had overlooked ERISA.

The Eighth Circuit, in *Samore v. Graham*,[201] noted that debtors using the federal exemptions are subject to the limited exemption for pension benefits in section 522(d)(10)(E) and that Congress could not have meant to create a blanket exclusion for ERISA for all debtors in section 541(c)(2).

The Supreme Court held that the phrase "applicable nonbankruptcy law" in section 541(c)(2) encompasses any and all transfer restrictions under state or federal law, and thus would include ERISA's "antialienation clause" (each pension plan shall provide that the benefits provided under the plan may not be assigned or alienated).

The Supreme Court noted that its interpretation of section 541(c)(2) ensures that the treatment of pension benefits will not vary based on the beneficiary's bankruptcy status, which gives effect to ERISA's goal of protecting pension benefits and ensures uniform national treatment of pension benefits. Justice Scalia stated that he found it mystifying that three Courts of Appeals could have thought the term "applicable nonbankruptcy law" was synonymous with "state law."

(c) Lender Liability

One source of property for the debtor's estate and for the benefit of creditors is the recovery of property in the form of preferences or fraudulent transfers. Another source in some cases is recovery for wrongful actions committed against the debtor. The liability of creditors to their borrowers has resulted in some jury verdicts in favor of debtors; however, the number and amount of awards has not reached the level predicted by some. Rosen suggests the following guidelines to help avoid lender liability:[202]

1 *Do not deviate suddenly from loan agreements or normal lending practices.* In *K.M.C., Inc. v. Irving Trust Co.*,[203] a grocery store established a line of credit for up to $3.5 million with Irving Trust. The store needed an $800,000 advance to cover checks that would be presented to the bank the next day. Irving Trust denied the store's request, claiming that the financing agreement gave the bank sole discretion over the line of credit. Even though the bank was notified that the store would collapse if the $800,000 request was not paid on time, Irving Trust refused to advance the money. The court concluded that the bank had breached its duty to act in good faith by such an abrupt change in the loan arrangement. To have acted in good faith, Irving Trust would have had to allow the store enough time to find alternative financing.

2 *Be honest in business dealings.* In *State National Bank of El Paso v. Farah*,[204] the creditors threatened to bankrupt the company by declaring

---

[201] 726 F.2d 1268 (8th Cir. 1985).
[202] J. Philip Rosen, "Ten Commandments of Avoiding Lender Liability in a Workout," *Real Estate Finance Journal* (Winter 1992), pp. 5–10.
[203] 757 F.2d 752 (1984).
[204] 678 S.W.2d 661 (Tex. Ct. App. 1984).

a default if the current executive officers were reinstated. The creditors, however, had no intention of doing so but were trying to manipulate the election of officers, which they succeeded in doing. The court found the bank guilty of fraud and warned the bank that the truth is of paramount importance, especially in the workout context.

3 *Do not run the borrower's company.* The creditor is responsible only for overseeing the loan, not taking control of the company's management. If a creditor in effect operates the debtor's business, the creditor is likely to be perceived as a fiduciary. In cases where a bankruptcy petition is filed, the creditor may be construed as an "insider" and have its claims subordinated to the other creditors. In addition, the lender's liability under various state and federal environmental laws may be increased. For example, see *United States v. Fleet Factors Corporation*[205] and the Environmental Protection Agency's interpretative rules[206] related to *Fleet Factors*, for an indication of the extent to which creditors may be liable for environmental claims.

4 *Keep promises made in the loan agreement.* In *Robinson v. McAllen State Bank*,[207] the borrowers obtained two loans from McAllen; each was secured by a mortgage on real estate. Robinson paid off one loan, expecting the mortgage on that property to be released. Instead, the bank retained the mortgage as extra collateral for the remaining loan. As a result, Robinson could not secure financing to finish construction of its store and subsequently filed a bankruptcy petition. The jury determined that McAllen had violated its agreement by not releasing the mortgage to Robinson on the property that was paid off.

5 *Do not waive rights during the workout discussion.* If a bank is having trouble collecting on a loan and is considering restructuring the loan, the bank should require that the borrower sign a preworkout agreement. This document recognizes the bank's entitlements under the previous loan agreement by having the borrower acknowledge default and the amount of the debt.

6 *Hire workout experts to represent the lender during the workout.* The lender needs a workout banker to act as a third-party mediator. The workout banker had no part in the making of the loan, so he or she adds an element of independence. The workout banker is also able to offer an unbiased, unemotional opinion on the possible solutions to the workout. Rather than wasting time criticizing either side, the expert can more readily pursue a logical approach to correcting the situation.

7 *Avoid the compulsion to assume an air of superiority.* When the loan was originally made, the creditor supposedly had the ability to hold the borrower to conditions set forth in the loan agreement. However, once a debtor's financial condition has declined to the point where a workout is necessary, the threat exists that the debtor will file a bankruptcy petition. Thus, the bank's advantage diminishes and the two parties must

[205] 901 F.2d 1550 (11th Cir. 1990).
[206] 40 C.F.R. pt. 300, subpart L.
[207] No. C-1948-84-D (Tex. 1987).

negotiate as equals. If the bank exhibits arrogance during the workout, the likelihood increases that the borrower may instigate and win a lawsuit. For example, Richard Gotcher reports that the CEO of European American Bank stated that he "approaches each loan individually, looking for the best way to resolve woes without meting out punishment."[208] European American Bank previously had a reputation of being the first in line for collections, as well as the "first to foreclose, the first to sue against personal guarantees and the first to make bankruptcy an attractive alternative for borrowers.[209]

8 *Maintain clean files for use as evidence in case of a trial.* Significant discussions with the borrower should be well documented in internal memoranda. Each memo should be accurate, impersonal, and to the point so that the lender's intentions are clearly stated.

9 *Stay on a professional level with the borrower.* Any correspondence with the borrower must be conducted in a businesslike fashion. The bank should be sure not to create any unfavorable impressions of its actions. If the bank's loan officer and the borrower experience a personality clash, the loan officer should be replaced. Interacting professionally with the borrower is crucial to preventing accusations of bad faith.

10 *Be reasonable and flexible during the workout.* Almost always, both the borrower and the lender will have to make concessions in order to cut their losses. Rather than rigid concern with the borrower's obligation under the loan agreement, the lender must reassess the situation and tailor its demands to the current realities.

The Seventh Circuit held that a bankruptcy trustee could use assets held in an IRA for the benefit of the debtor's creditors.[210] Also, the trustee is responsible, under section 408(f) of the Internal Revenue Code, for penalty tax due on the distribution of the IRA funds as well as the income tax that might be owed, as was held in a later hearing.[211] A bankruptcy court[212] also held that a corporation that maintains an Employee Stock Ownership Plan (ESOP) for its employees must turn over the distributable portion of an employee's interest in the ESOP to a trustee where the debtor had filed a chapter 7 petition.

§ 5.37 Avoiding Power of Trustee

The Bankruptcy Code grants the trustee (or debtor-in-possession) the right to avoid certain transfers made and obligations incurred. They include the trustee's powers as successor to actual creditors, as a hypothetical judicial lien creditor, and as a bona fide purchaser of real property. In addition, the trustee has the power to avoid preferences, fraudulent transfers, statutory liens, and certain postpetition transfers.

---

[208] *Turnarounds & Workouts,* Vol. 6 (October 1992) p. 2.
[209] *Id.,* pp. 1–2.
[210] *In re Richard L. Kochell,* 732 F.2d 564 (7th Cir. 1984).
[211] *In re Richard L. Kochell,* 804 F.2d 84 (7th Cir. 1986).
[212] *In re Charles James Lawson,* 67 B.R. 94 (Bankr. M.D. Fla. 1986).

The trustee needs these powers and rights to ensure that actions by the debtor or by creditors in the prepetition period do not interfere with the objective of the bankruptcy laws, and to provide for a fair and equal distribution of the debtor's assets through liquidation—or rehabilitation, if this would be better for other creditors involved.

(a) Trustee as Judicial Lien Creditor

Section 70(c) of the Bankruptcy Act, referred to as the "strong-arm clause," gave the trustee the right of a hypothetical creditor with a judicial lien on all the assets of the debtor as of the date of bankruptcy. The purpose of this provision was to allow the trustee to avoid unperfected security interests under statutes similar to article 9 of the Uniform Commercial Code, and other interest in the debtor's property that is not valid against a creditor obtaining a judicial lien as of the date of bankruptcy.[213]

Section 544(a) of the Bankruptcy Code, recodifies the strong-arm clause. The new law clarifies some of the prior law's provisions. It makes it clear that the trustee relies on a hypothetical creditor that extends credit at the time of the commencement of the case and obtains the judicial lien at the same time.

(b) Trustee as Purchaser of Real Property

Section 544(a)(3) of the Bankruptcy Code expands the trustee's strong-arm powers by giving the trustee the rights and powers of a bona fide purchaser of real property other than fixtures from the debtor, against whom applicable law permits the transfer to be perfected. Thus, unrecorded real estate transfers by way of a grant or security that is not valid as against a bona fide purchaser but is good against a judicial lien creditor, will now be voidable by the trustee as a hypothetical bona fide purchaser. Teofan and Creel indicate that:

> Equitable interests of beneficiaries under unperfected express or implied trusts, resulting trusts and constructive trusts will also fall before the attack of the trustee as a bona fide purchaser. In addition, the trustee will cut off equities created by mutual mistake, fraud, or similar situations for which equitable relief is afforded by state law. This new strong-arm status may well be the "coup de grace" in bankruptcy court proceedings to all nonpossessory equitable interests in real property which are not disclosed in a written instrument properly recorded prior to the commencement of the proceedings.[214]

(c) Trustee as Successor to Actual Creditors

Section 70(e) of the Bankruptcy Act gave the trustee the powers and rights of an actual creditor to avoid transfers made or obligations incurred by the debtor that are avoidable under state law. Section 544(b) of the Bankruptcy Code contains this basic concept.

---

[213] Richard B. Levin, "An Introduction to the Trustee's Avoiding Powers," *American Bankruptcy Journal*, Vol. 53 (Spring 1979), p. 174.

[214] Vernon O. Teofan and L. E. Creel III, "The Trustee's Avoiding Powers under the Bankruptcy Act and the New Code: A Comparative Analysis," *St. Mary's Law Journal*, Vol. 11 (1979), p. 319.

The trustee may avoid any transfer of an interest of the debtor in property or any obligation incurred by the debtor that is voidable under applicable law by a creditor holding an unsecured claim that is allowable under section 502 of this title or that is not allowable only under section 502(e) of this title.

Two major changes are made. First, the claim must be unsecured, whereas under prior law it probably could be either secured or unsecured. Second, the Bankruptcy Code eliminates the requirement that the creditor on whom the trustee relies must have a provable claim. Provability itself has been eliminated under the Code.

§ 5.38   Reclamation

One area where the avoiding power of the trustee is limited is in a request for reclamation. Section 546(c) provides that, under certain conditions, the creditor has the right to reclaim goods if the debtor received the goods while insolvent. To reclaim these goods, the seller must demand in writing, within 10 days after their receipt by the debtor, that the goods be returned. If the 10-day period expires after the petition is filed, the time allowed for reclamation is now 20 days. For example, if the goods were delivered 7 days before the petition was filed, the creditor has 20 days from the date of delivery to reclaim the goods in writing. On the other hand, if the goods were delivered more than 10 days before the petition was filed, and the request was not made within the 10-day period, the goods may not be reclaimed.

Thus the conditions for the debtor to reclaim the goods under section 546(c) are:

1   A statutory or common law right to reclaim the goods
2   The debtor's insolvency when it received the goods
3   A written reclamation demand made within 10 days after the debtor received the goods[215]

The demand must be made while the goods are in the possession of the debtor. In *In re Charter Co.,*[216] the bankruptcy court concluded that a seller's right to reclaim goods under section 546(c) is implicitly conditioned on a showing that the goods were identifiable and in the debtor's possession when it received the reclamation demand. The burden of proof that the goods were in the possession of the debtor at the time of the demand is on the seller.[217]

The court can deny reclamation, assuming the right is established, only if the claim is considered an administrative expense or if the claim is secured by a lien. There are some problems that a creditor faces in attempting to reclaim goods. One is that the request must be made within 10 days. Requests made after this time period will be denied. For example, in *In re First Software Corp.,*[218] the bankruptcy court held that the 10-day period began when the

---

[215] See *In re Rawson Food Serv.,* 846 F.2d 1343 (11th Cir. 1988) and *In re New York Wholesale Distributors Corp.,* 58 B.R. 497, 500 (Bankr. S.D. N.Y. 1986).
[216] 54 B.R. 91, 92 (Bankr. M.D. Fla. 1985).
[217] See *In re Rawson Food Serv.,* 846 F.2d 1343 (11th Cir. 1988) and cited cases.
[218] 72 B.R. 403 (D. Mass. 1987).

goods were delivered by the seller and not when the title later passed and the goods were installed.

While the Bankruptcy Code provides for the seller to reclaim goods, that right may not be asserted to defeat the interests of previously perfected inventory lien creditors, including floating liens. The right of reclamation is subordinate to those of previously perfected lien creditors.[219]

Another problem is that the Uniform Commercial Code right of reclamation under section 2-702 is basically a right to obtain the physical return of particular goods in the hands of the debtor. If the goods have been sold or used, the ability to obtain the goods may be limited. For example, the seller could not reclaim goods that were sold by the debtor to a purchaser in good faith who had no knowledge of the debtor's financial problems. Also, the reclamation rights of the seller are subject to any superior right of other creditors, which most likely would include the good faith purchaser or buyer in the ordinary course of business. If before reclamation is demanded the goods are manufactured or processed into a finished product, the seller has no right to reclaim the goods, as held in *In re Wheeling-Pittsburgh Steel Corp.*[220] Fungible goods may, however, be reclaimed if the seller can trace them into an identifiable mass containing goods of that kind.

Section 2-702(2) of the U.C.C. provides that the 10-day prior notice requirement is waived if the buyer fraudulently misrepresents its solvency to the seller within three months prior to the receipt of the goods. No such provision is provided for in the Bankruptcy Code. While the demand for reclamation must be in writing under section 546(c), the Uniform Commercial Code does not require a written demand.[221]

The Bankruptcy Reform Act of 1994 added subsection (h) to section 546 of the Bankruptcy Code. The subsection provides that, within 120 days after the order for relief, with the consent of a creditor, the trustee or debtor can make a motion to have goods returned that are not subject to reclamation and were delivered before the commencement of the case. The court may grant the motion if it determines that a return is the best interest of the estate. The purchase price of the goods will be offset against the claim of the creditor. If a manufacturing concern has raw materials that are no longer needed because the product line that used the materials has been eliminated, the manufacturer may find that the liquidation value of the goods is worth much less to the estate than would be realized by returning the goods to the supplier that has access to markets for the raw materials.

§ 5.39 Preferences

Section 547 provides that a trustee or debtor-in-possession can avoid transfers that are considered preferences. The trustee (debtor-in-possession) may avoid any transfer[222] of an interest of the debtor in property, as described in section 547(b):

---

[219] *In re Fairfield Lumber & Supply,* 214 B.R. 441 (Bankr. D. Conn. 1997); *In re Coast Trading Co., Inc.*
[220] 74 B.R. 656 (W.D. Pa. 1987).
[221] *See In re Rawson Food Serv.* 846 F.2d 1343 (11th Cir. 1998) and *In re Flagstaff Foodservice Corp.,* 14 B.R. 462, 467 (Bankr. S.D. N.Y. 1981).
[222] Section 101(54) of the Bankruptcy Code defines a transfer as "every mode, direct or indirect, absolute or conditional, voluntary or involuntary, of disposing of or parting with property or with an interest in property, including retention of title as a security interest and foreclosure of the debtor's equity of redemption."

1 To or for the benefit of a creditor.

2 For or on account of an antecedent debt owed by the debtor before such transfer was made.

3 Made while the debtor was insolvent.

4 Made—
   A on or within ninety days before the date of the filing of the petition. Or
   B between ninety days and one year before the date of the filing of the petition, if such creditor, at the time of such transfer was an insider.

5 That enables such creditor to receive more than such creditor would receive if—
   A the case were a case under chapter 7 of this title.
   B the transfer had not been made.
   C such creditor received payment of such debt to the extent provided by the provisions of this title.

One change brought about by the Bankruptcy Code is that the time period when a transfer will be considered preferential has been reduced from four months to 90 days. Added, however, was the provision that if the creditor is an "insider" the debtor can go back an entire year to void the transfer.

(a) Insolvency

In order to void a preferential transfer, section 547(b)(3) requires that the transfer must have been made while the debtor was insolvent. *Insolvent* is defined in section 101(32) as total liabilities exceeding the entity's property at fair valuation. Fair value, in the context of a going concern, is determined by the fair market price of the debtor's assets that could be obtained if sold in a prudent manner within a reasonable period of time to pay the debtor's debts.[223] Thus, historically this definition has been interpreted to mean that insolvency is determined by looking at the balance sheet and comparing the value of the assets with the liabilities.[224] Case law generally interprets "fair valuation" for purposes of solvency analysis to mean fair market value— amount realized between willing buyers and sellers if sold in a prudent manner in current market conditions. See Chapter 11 for a discussion of how to determine fair market value.[225]

In determining the solvency or insolvency of the debtor the liabilities should be measured at their face value rather than market.[226]

There is considerable uncertainty as to the premise that should be used for the purpose of determining insolvency for potential preference. Some courts suggest that liquidation values should be used and others suggest that going-concern values should be used. The status of the financial condition at the

---

[223] *See Rubin v. Manufacturers Hanover Trust Co.*, 661 F.2d 979, 995 (2d Cir. 1981); *Syracuse Engineering Co., Inc. v. Haight*, 110 F.2d 468, 471 (2d Cir. 1940); *Coated Sales, Inc. v. First Eastern Bank, N.A. (In re Coated Sales, Inc.)*, 144 Bankr. 663, 666–67 (Bankr. S.D. N.Y. 1992); *see also Briden v. Foley*, 776 F.2d 379, 382 (1st Cir. 1985).

[224] *See In re Healthco Int'l Inc.*, 208 B.R. 288 (Bankr. D. Mass 1997).

[225] *Lamar Haddox Contractors*, 40 F. 3d 118 (5th Cir. 1994).

[226] *In re Trans World Airlines, Inc.* 134 F.3d 188 (3d Cir. 1998).

time of the transfer may impact which method should be used. For example, in *In re Miller & Rhodes, Inc.*,[227] the court held that liquidation rather than going-concern values should be used. Another bankruptcy court held that, in determining whether the debtor is insolvent, the going-concern or fair-market basis is to be used unless the debtor is on its deathbed at the time of the questionable transfer.[228] Generally accepted accounting principles (GAAP) may be relevant to the solvency or insolvency analysis, but they are not controlling.[229]

When there is evidence to suggest that the debtor is a going concern, evidence related to subsequent values received on liquidation may not be enough evidence to prove that the debtor was insolvent at the time of the transfer. For example, in *Jones Trucking*, rather than present evidence of a negative going concern value on April 15, the debtor relied on postbankruptcy liquidation values of assets later sold by a broker and attacked its own financial statements, including its equity because of a planned conversion of debt to preferred stock that did not occur and its liabilities because they understated a substantial liability. The Eighth Circuit noted that "[w]e are inclined to agree with . . . the [creditor] that Jones's evidence on this issue was contrary to the principles of going concern valuation. But more to the point, the evidence on the question of insolvency was conflicting, and the jury was not required to credit Jones's evidence, or to find that Jones had met its burden of proof."[230]

Another change of the new law is that section 547(f) provides that the debtor is presumed to be insolvent during the 90-day period. This presumption requires the adverse party to present some evidence to rebut the presumption. The burden of proof, however, remains with the party (trustee or debtor-in-possession) in whose favor the presumption exists.

Though a debtor is presumed insolvent during the preference period, if the creditor produces evidence of solvency, the debtor has the ultimate burden of proof.[231] Generally a financial statement showing positive net worth is sufficient to rebut the presumption of insolvency.[232]

To overcome the section 547(f) presumption that the debtor is insolvent, the defendant must produce "evidence sufficient to cast into doubt the statutory presumption";[233] however, evidence that the debtor is current on its bill, unaudited pretransfer financial statement with positive equity, and other inaccurate financial reports or opinions of the defendants' credit manager indicating the debtor was solvent, have all been insufficient to overcome the presumption.[234]

In *In re Mangold*,[235] the bankruptcy court held that a negative balance sheet, but not cash flow or liquidity problems, raises an inference of insolvency. Unverified operating reports or opinions were held to be insufficient to overcome the presumption of insolvency.[236] The debtor's schedules, unless easily

---

[227] 146 B.R. 950 (Bankr. E.D. Va., 1992).

[228] *In re Coated Sales, Inc.* 144 B.R. 663 (Bankr. S.D.N.Y. 1992).

[229] *In re Parker Steel Co.*, 149 B.R. 834 (Bankr. N.D. Ohio 1992).

[230] *Jones Trucking*, 83 F. 3d 253, 259 (8th Cir. 1995).

[231] *Clay v. Traders Bank*, 708 F.2d 1347, 1351 (8th Cir. 1983).

[232] *Jones Trucking Line, Inc.*, *supra* note 230. *See In re Almarc Mfg., Inc.*, 60 B.R. 584, 586 (Bankr. N.D. Ill. 1986).

[233] *In re Emerald Oil Co.*, 695 F.2d 833 (5th Cir. 1983).

[234] *See In re World Financial Services Center, Inc.*, 78 B.R. 239 (9th Cir. BAP 1987).

[235] 145 B.R. 16 (Bankr. N.D. Ohio 1992).

[236] *In re Tuggle Pontiac-Buick-GMC, Inc.*, 31 B.R. 49 (Bankr. E.D. Tenn. 1983).

shown to be incorrect, rebut the presumption of insolvency under section 547(b)(3) of the Bankruptcy Code.

In determining the solvency of a partnership debtor in the context of a preference action against nonrecourse creditor, section 101(32)(B) of the Bankruptcy Code requires that the net assets of a general partner be counted, even though the debtor will not have access to the assets because the debt is nonrecourse.[237] See § 11.4 for a discussion of valuation issues.

(b) Determination

Under prior law, for there to be a preferential transfer the creditor had to be preferred over other creditors in the same class. The class requirement has been eliminated; to be a preferential transfer, the creditor must only receive more than would be received by such creditor in a chapter 7 liquidation. The Bankruptcy Code eliminates the "reasonable-cause-to-believe-insolvency" requirement of prior law. Thus, in order to avoid a transfer, it is now not necessary to prove that the creditor has reasonable cause to believe that the debtor was insolvent at the time the transfer was made. This change was made to provide for a more equitable distribution of the assets of the debtor. It is now easier for the trustee or debtor to recover payments to creditors that are considered preferences. In summary, section 547 contains six conditions that must be satisfied before the transfer will be considered a preference:

1 A transfer of the debtor's interest in property must be made,
2 To or for the benefit of a creditor,
3 For or on account of an antecedent debt,
4 While the debtor is insolvent,
5 Within 90 days before the petition (one year for insiders),
6 The creditor receiving the transfer must receive more than would have been realized in a liquidation case without the transfer.

As noted above, in order for the debtor to recover a preferential transfer, the debtor must have an interest in the property. Generally the debtor looks to state law to determine whether property is an asset of the debtor's estate.[238] In determining whether a particular transfer involved property, courts have looked at the impact the transfer had on the debtor's estate, such as whether the transfer diminished the debtor's estate.[239] A debt is generally considered to be an antecedent debt if it is incurred before the transfer, and thus a transfer that preceded the debt is not a preference.[240]

In the majority of instances, the preference rules are construed as strictly as the language of section 547 will allow. For example, a payment from funds that would otherwise be exempt has been held to constitute a waiver of the exemption and a preference.[241] Additionally, one court found a preferential payment

[237] In re Union Meeting Partners, 169 B.R. 229 (Bankr. E.D. Pa. 1994).
[238] In re Maple Mortgage, Inc. 81 F.3d 592 (5th Cir. 1996).
[239] See In re Union Sec. Mortgage Co., 25 F.3d 338 (6th Cir. 1994).
[240] See Ledford v. Fort Hamilton Hughes Memorial Hosp., 15 B.R. 573 (Bankr. S.D. Ohio 1981).
[241] In re Rundlett, 149 B.R. 353 (S.D.N.Y. 1993).

occurred when a portion of the prepetition purchase price of assets of the debtor consisted of payment to one of the debtor's creditors.[242]

The perfecting of a security interest in property within 90 days (one year for insiders) is also a preference. For example, in *In the matter of R & T Roofing Structures and Commercial Framing*,[243] the court held that the levy upon and seizure of the debtor's general bank account within 90 days prior to bankruptcy pursuant to a tax lien for trust funds (a seventh priority) was an avoidable preference. The assets of the debtor were not sufficient to pay all administrative expenses and priority wages. The court also held that the exception under section 547(c)(6) (fixing of statutory lien) did not apply. The court stated that this exception applies to the fixing of the lien, not to a seizure that satisfies the lien.

In determining whether payment was made within 90 days, the Ninth Circuit court held, in *In re Wolf & Vine*,[244] that if a check is honored within 30 days, the delivery date is the same as the payment date; if the check is not honored within 30 days, the date the check is honored is the payment date. Thus, a check delivered as payment of an antecedent debt more than 90 days prior to the filing of the petition may be a preference if the check is not honored within 30 days after it is received but is presented for payment within the 90-day period prior to bankruptcy.

The Supreme Court held, in *Barnhill*, that the date the bank honors the check is the date of transfer for purposes of determining whether the transfer is avoidable under section 547(b) of the Bankruptcy Code.[245] This case is significant because of the frequent occurrence of the problem and because there was a split in the lower court decisions. The Court reasoned that an unconditional transfer of the debtor's interest in property did not occur before the honoring of the check, because receipt of the check gave the creditor no right in the funds the bank held on the debtor's account. No transfer of any part of the debtor's claim against the bank occurred until the bank honored the check, at which time the bank had the right to "charge" the debtor's account, and the creditor's claim against the debtor ceased. The Court noted that honoring the check left the debtor in the position that it would have occupied had it withdrawn cash from its account and handed it over to the creditor. Thus, it was not until the debtor directed the bank to honor the check and the bank did so, that the debtor implemented a "mode . . . of disposing . . . of property or . . . an interest in property" under section 101(58) and a "transfer" took place.

The Supreme Court reviewed a Tenth Circuit decision, *In re Antweil*,[246] holding that a "transfer" through check will be deemed to have occurred when the check is honored by the drawee bank, rather than when the check is delivered to the payee. The Tenth Circuit joined the Seventh and Eleventh Circuits in adopting a date of honor rule, and disagreed with Sixth and Ninth Circuit decisions that had adopted a date of delivery rule.[247]

---

[242] *In re Interior Wood Products Co.*, 986 F.2d 228 (8th Cir. 1993).

[243] 79 B.R. 22 (D. Nev. 1987).

[244] 825 F.2d 197 (9th Cir. 1987).

[245] *Barnhill v. Johnson*, 112 S. Ct. 1386 (1992).

[246] 931 F.2d 689 (10th Cir. 1991).

[247] *Nicholson v. First Inv. Co.*, 705 F.2d 410 (11th Cir. 1983); *Fitzpatrick v. Philco Finance Corp.*, 491 F.2d 1288 (7th Cir. 1974); *but see In re Belknap, Inc.*, 909 F.2d 879 (6th Cir. 1990); *In re Kenitra, Inc.*, 797 F.2d 790 (9th Cir. 1986).

The Tenth Circuit reasoned that deeming a transfer to occur when the check is honored is consistent with Uniform Commercial Code section 409(1), which states that a check does not of itself operate as an assignment of any funds available to the drawee for payment until the drawee accepts the check. Additionally, the date of honor rule is capable of easier proof than is the date of delivery. Finally, the Court concluded that a contrary result was not mandated by the fact that the date of delivery rule applies when determining whether a preferential transfer comes within the ordinary course of business exception to the trustee's avoiding powers under section 547(c) of the Bankruptcy Code.

In *In re Freedom Group Inc. v. Lapham-Hickey Steel Corp.*,[248] the Seventh Circuit held that it is not the date on which the creditor obtains a judgment against the debtor in state court and enters the notice of garnishment against the debtor, but the date of transfer (the date of final order of attachment) that should be used in determining if the obtaining of the garnishment is a preference. In *Freedom Group*, the judgment was obtained on the 91st day prior to the filing of the petition, and the final order of attachment was issued two days later. The court ruled that the garnishment was a preference because the order of attachment was issued within 90 days. The Seventh Circuit cited the Supreme Court decision in *Barnhill v. Johnson*,[249] wherein the Court held that the date for the preference was the date that the check was honored, not the delivery date. Layden notes that other courts have held that a transfer occurs, for preference purposes, when the creditor's interest in property is perfected.[250]

The timing of the preference period in consolidated cases raises the issue of whether the preference period relates to the earlier or the later petition. In cases that are substantively consolidated—not simply consolidated administratively under Rule 1015—the preference period must be calculated from the date of the earliest petition.[251]

Listed below are examples of items examined to determine the extent to which they may be preferences:

1 A foreclosure sale conducted within 90 days prior to the filing of the petition to enforce an unperfected security interest was a preference.[252]

2 The return, within the preference period! of funds from a down payment on a contract for the purchase of equipment that was repudiated, was a preference.[253]

3 A check issued to a creditor and paid by the bank even though there were no funds in the account was considered an avoidable preference.[254]

---

[248] 50 F.3d 408 (7th Cir. 1995).

[249] 112 S. Ct. 1386 (1992).

[250] Angela K. Layden, "Preferential Transfers under Section 547—Defining Transfer," 14 *ABI Journal* No. 6 (July/August 1995), p. 26. *See Matter of T.B. Westex Foods Inc.*, 950 F.2d 1187 (5th Cir. 1992); *In re Howes*, 165 B.R. 270 (E.D. Mo. 1994); *Matter of Aztec Concrete Inc.*, 143 B.R. 537 (S.D. Iowa 1992).

[251] *In re Baker & Getty Financial Services, Inc.*, 974 F.2d 712 (6th Cir. 1992).

[252] *In re PC Systems, Inc.*, 163 B.R. 382 (Bankr. S.D. Fla. 1994).

[253] *In re Cybermech, Inc.*, 13 F.3d 818 (4th Cir. 1994).

[254] *In re Kemp Pacific Fisheries, Inc.*, 16 F.3d 313 (9th Cir. 1994).

4 Funds that were deposited in the debtor's own bank account by mistake, but should have been sent to its client, were held to not be a preference because applicable state law imposed a constructive trust on the funds.[255]

Section 547(b)(5) required a comparison of what the creditor actually received with what would have been received under a chapter 7 distribution. To make this determination the court must determine the creditor's class and the distribution that creditor would have received. The test is made as of the petition date and not the date of the transfer.[256] Also the determination of what the debtor would have received in a liquidation should be based on the actual effect of the payment as determined when bankruptcy resulted and not on what the situation would have been if the debtor's assets had not been liquidated.[257] Administrative expense claims should be considered in determining the distribution the creditor would have received. Superpriority administrative expense claims should not be considered.[258]

(c) Insider Guarantee

The Bankruptcy Reform Act of 1994 amended section 547 of the Bankruptcy Code to overrule *Deprizio* and limit payments to noninsiders to the 90-day period. Under *Deprizio*, the trustee or debtor-in-possession was able to recover, as preferences, payments made to noninsiders if such payments benefited an insider during the period beginning one year prior to bankruptcy and ending 90 days prior to bankruptcy. Thus, if the debtor made a payment to a bank on a loan personally guaranteed within that period, the payment could be recovered by the trustee or debtor-in-possession. However, for petitions filed after October 22, 1994, the Bankruptcy Reform Act of 1994 provides that payments made to noninsiders within the period beginning one year prior to bankruptcy and ending 90 days prior to bankruptcy are not subject to recovery action under section 547 of the Bankruptcy Code. Insiders that benefit from the transfers are still subject to recovery action for the one-year period.

In *Levit v. Ingersoll Rand Financial Corp.* [Deprizio],[259] the court held that outside creditors who deal at arm's length with a debtor are subject to the year-long preference recovery period. This was followed by the Tenth Circuit in *In re Robinson Brothers Drilling, Inc.*[260] and Sixth Circuit in *In re Cartage Co. Inc.*[261]

It is common for banks and other creditors to require guarantees from insiders, such as officers of the debtor. The rationale for these decisions is that any payment made to the outside creditor may reduce the potential liability of the insider on the guarantee. The insider/guarantor is construed to be a "creditor" because if the guarantor has to pay on the guarantee, the guarantor then has a "claim" against the debtor under Bankruptcy Code section 1(4)(A). Therefore,

---

[255] *In re Unicom Computer Corp.*, 13 F.3d 321 (9th Cir. 1994).
[256] *See In re Chattanooga Wholesale Antiques, Inc.*, 930 F.2d 458 (6th Cir. 1991).
[257] *In re Finn*, 909 F.2d 903 (6th Cir. 1990).
[258] *See In re Tenna Corp.* 801 F.2d 819 (6th Cir. 819).
[259] 874 F.2d 1186 (7th Cir. 1989).
[260] 892 F.2d 850 (10th Cir. 1989).
[261] 899 F.2d 1490 (6th Cir. 1990).

the payment to the outside creditor is ". . . for the benefit of a creditor . . ." (the insider), according to Bankruptcy Code section 7(b)(1).

For the payment to be a preference avoidable for a year, the debt must be unsecured or undersecured. If the creditor were fully secured, then the creditor would receive payment up to the full value of the collateral in a chapter 7 liquidation, and hence the requirement of section 7(5) would not be met. However, unsecured and undersecured creditors generally contest these preference issues.

For the preference period to be extended to one year, the payments must result in a benefit to the guarantor. For example, in *In re Erin Food Services, Inc.*,[262] the First Circuit held that where there was not tangible benefit to the insider, the preference period was not extended to one year. Here, payments were made on the note guaranteed by the insider, but the total amount of the note was $61.7 million and the insider's personal nonrecourse guaranty was for only $19.35 million. Thus, the payments made did not benefit the insider and were not a preference that could be extended to one year. In a situation where an insider has guaranteed all of the debts of a debtor or is personally liable for all debts as a general partner, *Deprizio* would not apply. The insider received no benefit from the preferential transfer because the insider is liable for all debts,[263] and a general partner that is liable for all the debts of the partnership receives no benefit when the debtor pays a claim that was guaranteed by the general partner.[264]

(d) Exceptions

As under prior law, there are a number of exceptions to the power the trustee has to avoid preferential transfers. Section 547(c) of the new law contains seven exceptions.

(i) Contemporaneous Exchange A transfer that is intended by the debtor and creditor to be a contemporaneous exchange for new value given to the debtor, and is in fact a substantially contemporaneous exchange, is exempted. The purchase of goods or services with a check would not be a preferential payment, provided the check is presented for payment in the normal course of business, which section 3-503(2)(a) of the Uniform Commercial Code specifies as 30 days.[265] In *In re Wolf & Vine*,[266] the court applied the 30-day rule for determining whether the payment by check is a contemporaneous exchange. If the check is honored within 30 days of payment, the delivery date of the check is the payment date. However, if the check is not honored within 30 days, the honored date is used and the transaction is not a contemporaneous exchange.

Several courts have held that replacement checks given for bounced checks that were issued for COD purchases are considered contemporaneous exchanges.[267]

---

[262] 980 F.2d 792 (1st Cir. 1992).
[263] *In re Sprint Mortgage Bankers Corp.*, 164 B.R. 224 (Bankr. E.D. N.Y. 1994).
[264] *In re Broad Street Associates*, 163 B.R. 68 (Bankr. E.D. Va. 1993).
[265] H.R. Rep. No. 95-595, 95th Cong., 1st Sess. 373 (1977).
[266] 825 F.2d 197 (9th Cir. 1987).
[267] *See, e.g., In re Old Electralloy Corp.*, 164 B.R. 501 (Bankr. W.D. Pa. 1994).

(ii) Ordinary Course of Business   The second exemption protects payments of debts that were incurred in the ordinary course of business or financial affairs of both the debtor and the transferee, when the payment is made in the ordinary course of business according to ordinary business terms. For bankruptcy petitions filed prior to October 8, 1984, there is a condition that requires that, to be exempt, payments must be received within 45 days of the date the debt was incurred. The Bankruptcy Amendments and Federal Judgeship Act of 1984 repealed this 45-day provision. "Ordinary course of business" was deliberately left undefined. With the elimination of the 45-day period, a key area of litigation centers around "according to ordinary course of business" and "ordinary business terms." Open accounts that normally have a payment period of over 45 days will now fall within the exception.

The definition that has become a standard for defining *ordinary business terms* is found in *In re Tolona Pizza Products Corp.*[268] The Seventh Circuit defined "ordinary business terms" as the general practices of similar industry members, and that "only dealings so idiosyncratic as to fall outside that broad range should be deemed extraordinary and therefore outside the scope of subsection C."[269] Under this standard, a creditor must show that the business terms of the transaction in question were within the outer limits of normal industry practices.[270] Thus it is not necessary to show that similar late payments represent a majority of the industry's transactions, or that the late payment is a significant percentage of specific customers.[271] Only when a payment is ordinary from the perspective of the industry will the ordinary course of business defense be available for an otherwise voidable preference. "Defining the relevant industry is appropriately left to the bankruptcy courts to determine as questions of fact heavily dependent upon the circumstances of each individual case."[272] *Roblin* noted that Courts of Appeals for the Third and Fourth Circuits adopted a modified test by linking the extent to which the terms of a transaction may permissibly deviate from industry practice to the duration of the relationship between debtor and creditor.[273]

Courts have often looked to industry standards to determine whether a payment was (1) incurred by the debtor in the ordinary course of its affairs with the creditors, (2) for a transfer made during the ordinary course of these affairs, and (3) for a transfer made according to ordinary business:

> [W]e adopt the following rule of construction as an aid to resolving these problems: the more cemented (as measured by its duration) the preinsolvency relationship between the debtor and the creditor, the more the creditor will be allowed to vary its credit terms from the industry norm yet remain within the safe harbor of section 547(c)(2). . . . In sum, we read subsection c [of section 547] as establishing a requirement that a creditor prove that the debtor made its prepetition preferential transfers in harmony with the range of terms prevailing as some relevant industry's norm. That is, subsection c allows the creditor consid-

---

[268] 3 F.3d 1029 (7th Cir. 1993).
[269] *Id.*, 3 F.3d at 1033.
[270] *In re Roblin Industries, Inc.* 78 F.3d 30 (2d Cir. 1996).
[271] *ABI World, supra* note 17, p. 3.
[272] *Supra* note 1, p. 40.
[273] *See Advo-System*, 37 F.3d at 1050; *Molded Acoustical*, 18 F.3d at 225.

erable latitude in defining what the relevant industry is, and even departures from that relevant industry's norms which are not so flagrant as to be "unusual" remain within [the] subsection's protection. In addition, when the parties have had an enduring, steady relationship, one whose terms have not significantly changed during the pre-petition insolvency period, the creditor will be able to depart substantially from the range of terms established under the objective industry standard inquiry and still find a haven in subsection c.

Thus, in order to determine if a transfer was made in the ordinary course of business, consideration must be given to relevant industry standards as well as the course of business between the two parties, according to additional cases in the Second, Fourth, Sixth, Seventh, Eighth, Ninth, Tenth, and Eleventh Circuits. The circuits that have considered the issue agree that the language of subsection (c)(2)(C) requires bankruptcy courts to consult industry standards in classifying a disputed transfer.[274] These cases emphasize that an interpretation of section 547(c)(2)(C) that focuses exclusively on the relationship between the creditor and the debtor would deprive subsection (c)(2)(C) of any independent meaning because subsection (c)(2)(B) already requires that the payment be evaluated in the context of the ongoing relationship between the debtor and the creditor.

While industry standards are the norm, there is some uncertainty as to whether industry standards apply to a troubled or to a healthy company. Recent cases have tended to focus on how the industry treats healthy, rather than moribund, customers.[275]

The Seventh Circuit noted that the comparison to industry standards serves the evidentiary function of providing a basis to evaluate the parties' self-serving testimony that an extraordinary transaction was in fact intended as a preference to a particular creditor and held that a rather liberal comparison with industry norms was critical in determining the meaning of ordinary business terms.

In *In re Fred Hawes Organization, Inc.,*[276] the Sixth Circuit held that late payments (between 31 and 90 days) made to a creditor were not in the ordinary course of business where (1) late payments were not usual between these parties and the terms of the agreement required timely payments (subjective prong), and (2) no creditable proof existed that late payments are the norm in the industry (objective prong). The court noted that both subjective and objective elements must be met in order to obtain the benefits of section 547(c)(2)

---

[274] *In re Roblin Industries, Inc.,* 78 F.3d 30, 41 (2d Cir. 1996); *In re Molded Acoustical Prods.,* 18 F.3d 217, 225 (3d Cir. 1994); *Advo-System, Inc. v. Maxway Corp.,* 37 F.3d 1044, 1048 (4th Cir. 1994); *In re Fred Hawes Org., Inc.,* 957 F.2d 239, 244 (6th Cir. 1992); *In re Tolona Pizza Prods. Corp.,* 3 F.3d 1029, 1032–33 (7th Cir. 1993); *In re U.S.A. Inns of Eureka Springs, Arkansas, Inc.,* 9 F.3d 680, 684 (8th Cir. 1993); *In re Food Catering & Hous., Inc.,* 971 F.2d 396, 398 (9th Cir. 1992); *In re Meridith Hoffman Partners,* 12 F.3d 1549, 1553 (10th Cir. 1993); *In re A.W. & Associates, Inc.,* 136 F.3d 1439 (11th Cir. 1998).

[275] *See In re Molded Products, supra* note 10, p. 227; *In re Thompson Boat Company,* 199 B.R. 908, 916 (Bankr. E.D. Mich. 1996); *but see U.S.A. Inns of Eureka Springs, supra* note 10 (it is appropriate to examine the manner in which similarly situated creditors in the industry deal with their delinquent customers, and whether that is the industry norm) (Thompson Boat Company expressly rejected *U.S.A. Inns of Eureka Springs*); *see* Lisa Sommers Gretchko, "Sharpening and Polishing the 'Objective Prong' of section 547(c)(2)" (abiworld.org, September 1, 1998), p. 2.

[276] F.2d 239 (6th Cir. 1992).

of the Bankruptcy Code. Thus, it would appear that, in the Sixth Circuit, both debtor history and industry norms are important in attempting to recover preferences.

The Ninth Circuit held, in *In re Grand Chevrolet*,[277] that there is no per se rule regarding delays in payments. In a situation where the creditor regularly received late payments and there was no evidence that the creditor was taking advantage of the debtor's deteriorating financial condition, the transaction was ordinary as between the two parties. The Ninth Circuit held, in *In re Food Catering & Housing, Inc.*,[278] that payments made to a supplier, consisting of more than 20 invoices that were over 90 days late, were not in the ordinary course of business because, in the normal course of dealing between the parties, payments were never more than 60 days late and consisted of no more than 8 invoices. The court also noted that industry practice requires payment within 60 days.

Courts have generally held that, when creditors pressure debtors to pay bills more rapidly, and when debtors use unusual methods of payments, the payments are not in the ordinary course of business.[279] However, where payments were similar to the late-payment history of the debtor and where there was no pressure for payment, the bankruptcy court has held that such payments were in the ordinary course of business.[280]

In *In re Youthland, Inc.*,[281] even though payments were ordinary between the two parties, those payments that were outside the industry norm were not made in the ordinary course of business.

The "ordinary course" exception was designed to cover ordinary trade intended to be paid in full within a short period of time. Earlier court decisions supported this position. For example, the bankruptcy court held, in *In the matter of Sweetapple Plastics, Inc.*,[282] that the exception is limited to trade credit that is kept current or other transactions that are paid in full within the initial billing cycle, although a late payment is not automatically outside this exception.[283] In *Steel Improvement*,[284] the bankruptcy court held that to establish that a late payment is an exception to a preference, it must be shown that (1) the manner and timing of the payment were consistent with the previous dealings between the creditor and debtor and (2) the manner and timing were consistent with the ordinary course of business in the industry.

As noted below, recent courts have exported the exceptions to nontrade debt. In *In re Bishop, Balwin, Rewald, Dillingham Wong*,[285] the Ninth Circuit ruled that payments made to an innocent investor by a debtor who conducted a Ponzi scheme would not qualify as an ordinary course exception.

---

[277] 1994 App. Lexis 10198 (9th Cir. 1994).

[278] 971 F.2d 396 (9th Cir. 1992).

[279] *See In re Tennessee Chemical Co.*, 159 B.R. 501 (Bankr. E.D. Tenn. 1993).

[280] *In re Matters*, 99 B.R. 314 (Bankr. W.D. Va. 1989).

[281] 160 B.R. 311 (Bankr. S.D. Ohio 1993).

[282] 77 B.R. 304 (M.D. Ga. 1987).

[283] *See In re Craig Oil Co.*, 785 F.2d 1563 (11 Cir. 1986); *In re Steel Improvement Co.*, 16 BCD 855 (E.D. Mich. 1987).

[284] *In re Steel Improvement Co.*, 16 Bank. Ct. Dec. (CRR) 855 (E.D. Mich. 1987).

[285] 819 F.2d 214 (9th Cir. 1987).

In another Ninth Circuit case, *Henderson v. Buchanan*,[286] it was held that payments made pursuant to a Ponzi scheme did not come within the ordinary course of business exception because such a scheme is not a business within the meaning of section 547(c)(2) of the Bankruptcy Code.

The Ninth Circuit Court of Appeals held that interest payments made on long-term debts can be avoided as preferences and do not fall within section 547(c)(2) of the Bankruptcy Code for payments made "in the ordinary course of business" of the debtor.[287] Payments made within 90 days of bankruptcy can be avoided as preferential payments if all of the requirements of section 547 are met. However, an exception found in section 547(c)(2) provides that the trustee may not avoid under section 547 a transfer:

(2) to the extent that such transfer was—
   (A)   in payment of a debt incurred by the debtor in the ordinary course of business or financial affairs of the debtor and the transferee;
   (B)   made in the ordinary course of business or financial affairs of the debtor and the transferee; and
   (C)   made according to ordinary business terms;

The issue is whether interest payments on long-term debt are "made in the ordinary course of business." The Circuit Court of Appeals examined the legislative history and the precedents and concluded that the primary purpose of the exception was to encourage trade creditors to continue dealing with a financially shaky purchaser.

In *In re Bourgeois*,[288] the first case to squarely address this issue in its holding, the court held that principal and interest payments by the debtor to a bank on long-term loans were not intended by the 1984 amendment to fall within the section 547(c)(2) exception to avoidance of preferential transfers. The court noted that Congress did not intend to change the spirit of the section, that is, the exemption from avoidance of trade credit transactions that are substantially contemporaneous exchanges. The court felt that the reasoning of the *Bourgeois* case and the cases following it is sound. It would be against the congressional policy of pro rata distribution to let a long-term creditor who has had the foresight or power to demand monthly interest or principal payments to receive three payments in full while those creditors who are awaiting quarterly interest or principal payments receive nothing (or only whatever percentage all unsecured creditors receive upon distribution).

The court believed that it does not foster the congressional policy of encouraging creditors to engage in short-term and trade credit transactions to allow long-term creditors to make use of the section 7(c)(2) exception. A bank is unlike a supplier, because it analyzes a debtor's creditworthiness before it agrees to make the loan. Allowing a bank to exempt payments on long-term debt will not encourage it to do business with the debtor because the bank will have already made the decision to do business with the debtor.

---

[286] 95 F.2d 1021 (9th Cir. 1993).
[287] *CHG International, Inc. v. Barclays Bank (In re CHG International)*, 897 F.2d 1479 (9th Cir. 1990).
[288] 58 B.R. 657 (Bankr. W.D. La. 1986).

The Supreme Court, however, held, in *Union Bank v. Wolas*,[289] that payments on long-term as well as short-term debt qualify for the ordinary course of business exception. During the 90-day period preceding its filing of a petition under chapter 7 of the Bankruptcy Code, ZZZZ Best Co., Inc. (debtor) made two interest payments and paid a loan commitment fee on its long-term debt to Union Bank. After Wolas was appointed trustee of the debtor's estate, he filed a complaint against the bank to recover those payments as voidable preferences under section 547(b) of the Bankruptcy Code. The Bankruptcy Court held that the payments were transfers made in the ordinary course of business pursuant to section 547(c)(2) and thus were excepted from section 547(b). The District Court affirmed, but the Court of Appeals reversed, holding that the ordinary course of business exception was not available to long-term creditors.

The Supreme Court determined that payments on long-term debt, as well as those on short-term debt, may qualify for the ordinary course of business exception to the trustee's power to avoid preferential transfers. The Court noted that section 547(c)(2) contains no language distinguishing between long- and short-term debt and, thus, provides no support for Wolas's contention that its coverage extends only to short-term debt.

Section 547(c)(2), as originally enacted, was limited to payments made within 45 days of the date a debt was incurred. In 1984, Congress deleted the time limitation entirely. The Court noted that Congress may have intended only to address particular concerns of specific short-term creditors in the amendment or may not have foreseen all of the consequences of its statutory enactment as insufficient reason for refusing to give effect to section 547(c)(2)'s plain meaning.

The question of whether the Bankruptcy Court correctly concluded that the debtor's payments qualify for the ordinary course of business exception remains open for the Court of Appeals on remand.

The Tenth Circuit held, in *In re Meridith Millard Partners*,[290] that payments made to a finance company were not in the ordinary course of business because the parties had not previously used a lockbox arrangement or escrow account and the arrangement was not common in the industry unless the lender was preparing to foreclose. The Tenth Circuit noted that the arrangement was an unusual debt collection policy that came into being only after the partners were insolvent and in default.

In *In re Faleck & Margolies, Inc.*,[291] the district court held that payments to a gem wholesaler were not in the ordinary course of business where the debt instrument was a note rather than an invoice, and where the payments were made on a timely basis although the debtor and the industry traditionally made late payments on the invoices.

In *In re U.S.A. Inns of Eureka Springs, Arkansas, Inc.*,[292] the Circuit Court held that, for a bank, each of the elements of the ordinary course of business exception must be met, including objective proof of industry practice. The bank was able to present sufficient objective proof that it worked with delin-

---

[289] 1991 U.S. LEXIS 7174.
[290] 12 F.3d 1549 (10th Cir. 1993).
[291] 985 F.2d 1021 (9th Cir. 1993).
[292] 9 F.3d 680 (8th Cir. 1993).

quent customers as long as some type of payments were forthcoming, thereby convincing the court that this practice was common industry practice. Payment to a fully secured lender is not a preference.[293]

Payments of principal and interest were held not to be preferences due to the ordinary course of business exception, even though the senior managers were the subject of criminal investigation because of an issuance and sale of debentures.[294] The district court relied on *Union Bank v. Wolas.*

(iii) Purchase Money Security Interest The third exception exempts security interests granted in exchange for enabling loans when the proceeds are used to finance the purchase of specific personal property. For example, a debtor borrowed $75,000 from a bank to finance a computer system and subsequently purchased the system. The "transfer" of the system as collateral to the bank would not be a preference, provided the proceeds were given after the signing of the security agreement, the proceeds were used to purchase the system, and the security interest was perfected within 20 days after the debtor received possession of the property.

Most courts have held that creditors that fail to perfect their security interest within the relevant grace period, 20 days, may not claim that such payments are not preferences because of a contempraneous exchange.[295]

(iv) New Value This exception provides that the creditor is allowed to insulate from preference attack a transfer received to the extent that the creditor replenishes the estate with new value. For example, if a creditor receives $10,000 in preferential payments and subsequently sells to the debtor on unsecured credit goods with a value of $6,000, the preference would be only $4,000. The new credit extended must be unsecured and can be netted only against a previous preferential payment, not a subsequent payment.

In *In re Toyota of Jefferson, Inc.,*[296] the new value exception applied to all but the last payment. The court noted that the new value exception is narrower than the old net result rule.

For purposes of the new value exception under section 547(c)(4), the Ninth Circuit held that the transfer occurs at the time the check is delivered, but the date the check is honored is used if there is more than a ten-day delay in honoring the check.[297] Outside of the Ninth Circuit, courts do not apply section 547(e) to transactions falling under section 547(c)(4), and the date of delivery is generally conclusive regardless of whether the bank honors the check within ten days.[298] As discussed above in reference to section 547(b) dealing with determination of 90 days prior to bankruptcy the Supreme Court held that the date the bank honors the check is the date of transfer.

---

[293] *In re Pineview Care Center, Inc.,* 152 B.R. 703 (D.N.J. 1993).

[294] *In re American Continental Corp.,* 142 B.R. 894 (D. Ariz. 1992).

[295] *In re Tressler,* 771 F.2d 791 (3rd Cir. 1985); *In re Holder,* 892 F.2d 29 (4th Cir. 1989); *In re Davis,* 734 F.2d 604 (11th Cir. 1984); *but see In re Burnette,* 14 B.R. 795 (Bankr. E.D. Tenn. 1981); *In re Martella,* 22 B.R. 649 (Bankr. D. Colo. 1982).

[296] 14 F.3d 1088 (5th Cir. 1994).

[297] *In re Wadsworth Building Components, Inc.,* 711 F.2d 122 (9th Cir. 1983).

[298] *See In re Antwell,* 931 F.2d 689 n. 2 (10th Cir. 1991); *In re Metro Produce, Inc.,* 80 B.R. 570 (Bankr. N.D. Ga. 1987); *In re Fasano/Harriss Pie Co.,* 43 B.R. 871 (Bankr. W.D. Mich.).

(v) Inventory and Receivables   This exception allows a creditor to have a continuing security interest in inventory and receivables (or proceeds) unless the position of the creditor is improved during the 90 days before the petition. If the creditor is an insider, the time period is extended to one year. An improvement in position occurs when a transfer causes a reduction in the amount by which the debt secured by the security interest exceeds the value of all security interest for such debt. The test to be used to determine whether an improvement in position occurs is a two-point test: the position 90 days (one year for insiders) prior to the filing of the petition is compared with the position as of the date of the petition. If the security interest is less than 90 days old, then the date on which new value was first given is compared to the position as of the date of the petition. The extent of any improvement caused by transfers to the prejudice of unsecured creditors is considered a preference.

To illustrate this rule, assume that on March 1 a bank made a loan of $700,000 to a debtor secured by a so-called floating lien on inventory. The inventory value was $800,000 at that date. On June 30, the date the debtor filed a bankruptcy petition, the balance of the loan was $600,000 and the debtor had inventory valued at $500,000. It was determined that 90 days prior to June 30 (the date when the petition was filed) the inventory totaled $450,000 and the loan balance was $625,000. In this case, there has been an improvement in position of $75,000 (($600,000 – $500,000) – ($625,000 – $450,000)) and any transfer of a security interest in inventory or proceeds could be recovered to that extent.

To be considered a preference, there must be a transfer. For example, if a loan of $100,000 is secured by $70,000 in inventory of jewelry 90 days prior to bankruptcy and at the date of bankruptcy the same items are worth $90,000, there would not be a preference because there has not been a transfer. Furthermore, section 547(c)(5) provides that the improvement in position must be to the prejudice of other unsecured creditors. The problem of determining improvement in position becomes more difficult when dealing with work-in-process. If the $100,000 loan was secured by raw materials worth $70,000 and the raw materials are assembled, they now have a value as of the date of the petition of $90,000 because of the work of the employees who were paid for their efforts. It could be argued that there is "prejudice" to the estate, but has a transfer occurred?[299] Also associated with the exemption is a valuation problem: the difference is based on the value of the inventory, which may not necessarily be book value.

(vi) Fixing of Statutory Lien   This exception states that a statutory lien that is valid under section 545 is not voidable as a preference.

(vii) Alimony, Maintenance, or Support Payments   Effective for petitions filed after October 22, 1994, the Bankruptcy Reform Act of 1994 added a new seventh exception to the right to recover preferences. (The prior seventh exception is renumbered as the eighth exception.) The new seventh exception provides that, to the extent that a transfer was a bona fide payment of a debt to a spouse, former spouse, or child of the debtor, for alimony, maintenance, or sup-

---

[299]Barkley Clark, "Preferences under the Old and New Bankruptcy Acts," *Uniform Commercial Code Law Journal*, Vol. 12 (Fall 1979), p. 180.

port of such spouse or child in connection with a separation agreement, divorce decree, or other order of a court of record, it will not be subject to recovery as a preference.

(viii) **Consumer Debts**   The final exception, added by the Bankruptcy Amendments and Federal Judgeship of 1984, provides that in the case of an individual debtor whose debts are primarily consumer debts, the transfer is not voidable if the aggregate value of the property affected by the transfer is less than $600.

Legislative history indicates that if creditors can qualify under any one of the exceptions, they are protected to that extent. If they can qualify under several, they are protected by each to the extent they can qualify under each.[300] Thus, by using the cumulative effect of these exceptions, creditors may obtain greater protection than could be obtained under any one exception.

§ 5.40   Fraudulent Transfers

Modern fraudulent conveyance law has its roots in the ancient English statutes that provided a remedy against debtors who conveyed their property in such a manner as to deliberately defraud creditors. The Statute of 13 Elizabeth, enacted in 1570, codified 200 years of common law and provided for the avoidance of such transfers.

Fraudulent conveyances may be attacked under the Bankruptcy Code or under state law. Section 548 of the Bankruptcy Code allows transfers within one year prior to filing of a petition to be avoided.

(a) State Laws

State laws are generally based on one of three provisions:

1 *Uniform Fraudulent Conveyance Act (UFCA).* The UFCA, drafted in 1918, applies in no more than 12 states and is similar to section 548. It has no "reach-back" provisions, but incorporates the state statutes of limitations that run from one to six years.

2 *Uniform Fraudulent Transfer Act (UFTA).* The UFTA, drafted in 1984 to replace the UFCA, has been adopted in over 20 states and has a reach-back of four years. The UFTA was designed to harmonize the UFCA with section 548 of the Bankruptcy Code. Under the UFTA, the definition of solvency is similar to that used in the Bankruptcy Code. However, section 2(b) provides that a rebuttable presumption exists that a debtor that is generally not paying its debts as they become due is insolvent.

3 *Statutory and common law.* For states without the UFTA or the UFCA, an American version of Statute of 13 Elizabeth has been adopted. The statute of limitations for fraud will most likely apply from one to six years.

Actions brought under the UFCA, the UFTA, or state statutes are based on section 544(b), which allows action to be taken to recover transfers based on

[300]H.R. Rep. No. 95-595, 95th Cong., 1st Sess. 372 (1977).

state fraudulent conveyance laws. Generally, any action brought under state laws requires a claim by at least one creditor that existed at the time of the transfer, before action can be taken. However, the recovery is not limited to the claim of the creditor, and the entire transfer may be avoided.

(b) Time to Bring Action

According to section 546(a) of the Bankruptcy Code the period in which action can be taken under sections 544, 545, 547, 548 and 553 of the Bankruptcy Code is the earlier of (1) the later of: two years after the order for relief or one year after the appointment or election of a trustee if such appointment or election occurs within two years after the entry of the order for relief; or (2) the time the case is closed or dismissed. Because of this time restriction, it is often difficult for the debtor to take the necessary action to reserve the right to later recover fraudulent transfers while the debtor and the creditors are in the process of negotiating the terms of a plan. The debtor may request the court to extend the time period, to avoid having to file a suit against creditors that might have been involved in a fraudulent transfer while the debtor is trying to convince them to vote for a plan.

Generally, a trustee or debtor has standing to bring action in the form of a suit to set aside a fraudulent transfer. Creditors have been permitted to sue in certain cases, usually where the debtor is not taking action or does not have the funds to take action for recovery of the transfer.

Section 548 of the Bankruptcy Code is a federal codification of the Uniform Fraudulent Conveyance Act, as was section 67(d) of the Bankruptcy Act. Although there are few changes in the new law, it should be noted that section 548(a) does not require that an actual creditor exist before the trustee may avoid a transfer or obligation. To be voidable, all fraudulent transfers and obligations must have been made or incurred within one year before the date of the filing of the petition. Fraudulent transfers are voidable under section 548 because they are made with the intent to defraud or they are construed to be fraudulent. Transfers of property of the debtor or obligations incurred by the debtor with the actual intent to hinder, delay, or defraud either existing or future creditors are voidable as fraudulent transfers. Thus, to be voidable under this provision, the debtor must have intended to hinder, delay, or defraud existing or real or imagined future creditors.

Intent must be more than the desire to prefer one creditor over another;[301] however, specific malice against creditors is not required.[302] Often, intent is established from a pattern of actions.[303] There may be a presumption of intent where there are transfers to relatives or business associates or obligations incurred to related parties.[304] Proof of insolvency is not required[305] and transfers are voidable even if made for full value.

Three kinds of constructively fraudulent transfers are voidable under the Bankruptcy Code. The constructively fraudulent transfers must have been

---

[301] *Prisbrey v. Noble*, 505 F.2d 170 (10th Cir. 1974).
[302] *In re Independent Clearing House Co.*, 77 B.R. 843 (D. Utah 1987).
[303] *In re Freudmann*, 495 F.2d 816 (2d Cir. 1974).
[304] *In re Checkmate Stereo & Electronics, Ltd.* (Bankr. E.D.N.Y. 1986).
[305] *See In re Vaniman International Inc.*, 22 B.R. 166 (Bankr. E.D.N.Y. 1982).

made for less than reasonably equivalent value, whereas an actual fraudulent transfer can be voidable even if made for full value. The trustee may void a transfer of less than equivalent value (1) if the debtor was insolvent or has become insolvent as a result of the transfer, (2) if the debtor was engaged in business or in a transaction and after the transfer the capital remaining was unreasonably small, or (3) if the debtor intended to or believed that it would incur debts that would be beyond the debtor's ability to pay as they matured.

In constructively fraudulent transfers there is another change from section 67(d) of the Bankruptcy Act. "Fair consideration" was used as a requirement rather than the phrase "reasonably equivalent value" in the new law. The phrase "fair consideration" included the requirement of good faith as well as fair equivalent value.[306] Thus, under prior law a transfer could have been considered fraudulent even if made for full consideration if the consideration was not given in good faith. The Bankruptcy Code eliminates the good faith requirement and requires only equivalent value.

The fact that the transfer was made in "good faith" does not preclude the transfer from being recovered under section 548. However, the debtor is entitled to value to the extent that was given to the debtor for the transfer under section 548(c). On the other hand, an insider would not be protected by this provision if the insider had reasonable cause to believe that the debtor was insolvent at the time of the transfer, as indicated by section 550(b) of the Bankruptcy Code.

A major change was made in this section in that it does not require that the value be present value. Thus, the satisfaction of an antecedent debt that occurred prior to 90 days before the date of the petition will be adequate value under the new law and will protect the transfer from being totally voidable. Value is defined to mean "property, or satisfaction or securing of a present or antecedent debt of the debtor," but does not include an unperformed promise to furnish support to the debtor or to a relative of the debtor.[307]

Section 548(b) provides that a transfer of partnership property to a general partner when the partnership is insolvent is deemed to be fraudulent and voidable by the trustee.

(c) Meaning of Transfer

Section 101(58) of the Bankruptcy Code defines transfers as every mode, direct or indirect, absolute or conditional, voluntary or involuntary, of disposing of or parting with property or with an interest in property, including retention of title as a security interest and foreclosure of the debtor's equity of redemption. The Supreme Court, in *Segal v. Rochelle*,[308] defined property under the Bankruptcy Act to include anything of value—anything that has debt-paying or debt-securing power.

Under section 548(d)(1) of the Bankruptcy Code, the transfer is considered made at the time of its perfection. If the transfer is not recorded before the petition is filed, then the transfer is deemed to have occurred just before the

---

[306] Levin, *supra* note 126, p. 181.
[307] 11 U.S.C. § 548(d)(2)(A).
[308] 382 U.S. 375 (1966).

petition was filed. In *In re Oesterle*,[309] the transfer was made beyond one year prior to filing, but was recorded two days after the filing. The transfer was thus deemed to have been made immediately before the petition was filed. This provision allows insolvency to be determined at a later date and also allows provisions of section 548 to apply that otherwise would not be applicable. The purpose of this provision is to discourage secret or unperfected liens.

Transfers, among other activities, may include:

1   A pledge of assets to secure a letter of credit[310]
2   An execution on a judgment lien[311]
3   A renewal of a loan and payments thereunder[312]
4   A termination of a lease[313]
5   A rescission of a profitable contract[314]
6   A payment of a dividend[315]
7   A purchase of treasury stock[316]
8   The incurring of an obligation.

In determining the insolvency of the debtor for purposes of section 548, publicly traded debt should be measured at its face value and not its market value.[317] It would also appear that the same situation would apply to nonpublic debt.

In *In re Richels*,[318] the bankruptcy court determined that the debtor, a stockholder, was a corporation's *alter ego*. The court permitted the trustee of the debtor's bankruptcy to attempt to avoid a fraudulent transfer made by the corporation.

(d) Reasonable Equivalent Value

Reasonable equivalent value is a question of fact and is determined on a case-by-case basis.[319] In determining reasonable equivalent value, the court must focus on what the debtor received in return for what was surrendered.[320] In *In re Ewing*,[321] a transfer was held not voidable if the transfer results from the enforcement of a security interest in compliance with Article 9 of the Uniform Commercial Code.

---

[309] 2 B.R. 122, 124 (Bankr. S.D. Fla. 1979).
[310] *In re Richmond Produce Co.*, 118 B.R. 753 (Bankr. N.D. Cal. 1990).
[311] *In re Frank*, 39 B.R. 166 (Bankr. E.D.N.Y. 1984).
[312] *In re B.Z. Corp.*, 34 B.R. 546 (Bankr. E.D. Pa. 1983).
[313] *In re Queen City Grain, Inc.*, 51 B.R. 722 (Bankr. S.D. Ohio 1985).
[314] *Wilson v. Holub*, 202 Iowa 549, 210 N.W. 593 (1926).
[315] *In re Dondi Financial Corp.*, 119 B.R. 106 (Bankr. N.D. Tex. 1990).
[316] *In re Roco Corp.*, 701 F.2d 978 (1st Cir. 1983).
[317] *In re Trans World Airlines, Inc.*, 134 F.3d. 188 (3d Cir. 1998).
[318] 163 B.R. 760 (Bankr. E.D. Va. 1994).
[319] *In re Ozark Restaurant Equipment Co.*, 850 F.2d 342 (8th Cir. 1988); *In re Join-In Int'l (U.S.A.) Ltd.*, 56 B.R. 555 (Bankr. S.D.N.Y. 1986).
[320] *In the matter of Bundles*, 856 F.2d 815 (7th Cir. 1988).
[321] 33 B.R. 288 (Bankr. W.D. Pa. 1983), *rev'd.*, 36 B.R. 476 (W.D. Pa. 1983), *aff'd*, 746 F.2d 1465 (3d Cir. 1984).

(e) Insolvency or Small Capital

As noted above, section 548 provides that a transfer for less than equivalent value may be avoided if the debtor was insolvent at the time of the transfer, or became insolvent as a result of the transfer, or was left, as a result of the transfer, with an unreasonably small amount of capital. The insolvency test is based on an examination of the balance sheet under section 101(32) of the Bankruptcy Code, where the debtor's liabilities exceed its assets at a fair valuation, excluding exempt property and fraudulently transferred property.[322] In the case of a partnership, the sum of the general partner's nonpartnership assets (excluding exempt property) less the general partner's nonpartnership debt is also considered in determining insolvency.

In *In re CRS Steam, Inc.*,[323] the bankruptcy court held that a constructive trust was a fiction that created no property interest.

Evidence that the debtor was constantly behind in paying its debts or continued its business under financial risk may indicate an unreasonably small amount of capital.[324] The Uniform Fraudulent Transfer Act focuses on whether the amount of all of the assets retained was inadequate in light of the needs of the debtor.[325]

(f) Foreclosure as Fraudulent Transfer

In *Durrett v. Washington National Insurance Co.*,[326] the court held that a noncollusive, regularly conducted foreclosure sale was a fraudulent transfer where the foreclosure sale was held while the debtor was insolvent and within one year prior to the filing of a bankruptcy petition, and where the sales price was for less than fair consideration. This decision was based on the Bankruptcy Act, but similar language exists in section 548 of the Bankruptcy Code. From this decision, a generally accepted standard of less than 70 percent consideration has developed. This standard implies that the transfer may be subject to fraudulent transfer rules if the sales price is less than 70 percent of the property's value. This decision is not based on actual fraud but on constructive fraud, where fraud is presumed without looking at the intent of the transfer. Many other cases have followed *Durrett*.

The *Durrett* rule was rejected in *In re Winshall Settlor's Trust*.[327] The Sixth Circuit ruled that a foreclosure sale should be deemed to be for reasonably equivalent value. The *Durrett* rule has been inapplicable in at least two cases where it was held that the date of transfer was not the foreclosure date, but the time when the mortgage was recorded, resulting in the transfer taking place outside the one-year period prior to bankruptcy. For example, see *Calairo*[328] and *In re Madrid*.[329]

---

[322] *See In re Roco Corp.*, 701 F.2d 978 (1st Cir. 1983). See also § 11.4.

[323] 225 B.R. 833 (Bankr. D. Mass. 1998).

[324] *See New York Credit Men's Adjustment Bureau, Inc. v. Adler*, 2 B.R. 752 (S.D.N.Y. 1980); *In re Tuller's Inc.*, 480 F.2d 49 (2d Cir. 1973).

[325] *In re Vadnais Lumber Supply Inc.*, 100 B.R. 127 (Bankr. D. Mass. 1989).

[326] 621 F.2d 201 (5th Cir. 1980).

[327] 758 F.2d 1136 (6th Cir. 1985).

[328] 746 F.2d 1465 (3d Cir. 1984), *cert. denied*, 105 S. Ct. 1189 (1985).

[329] 725 F.2d 1179 (9th Cir. 1984), *cert. denied*, 105 S. Ct. 125 (1984).

In *In re Ristich*,[330] the bankruptcy judge stated that a sale to a third-party purchaser is presumptively for a reasonably equivalent value absent a showing of actual fraud or collusion recognized by Illinois law. This view was adopted in *In re Bundles*,[331] but reversed by the seventh circuit. The 1984 amendments to the Bankruptcy Code provided that a foreclosure is a transfer to be tested under section 548(a) of the Bankruptcy Code. This change was effected by including in the definition of transfer in section 101(50) not only involuntary transfers, but also "foreclosure of the debtor's equity of redemption." As a result of this change, it would appear that courts should take specific steps to ensure that reasonably equivalent value is obtained. In fact, some bankruptcy courts have required that certain steps be taken to ensure that the foreclosure sale is not a fraudulent conveyance. One rule was fashioned by Judge Lavien in *Ruebeck v. Attleboro Savings Bank (In re Ruebeck)*,[332] to ensure that the foreclosure sale was reasonable. *Ruebeck* required, among other things, that the secured creditor obtain a presale appraisal, advertise in the real estate section of a newspaper, and give notice to real estate brokers within a limited radius of the property.

The *Durrett* rule could have a very negative impact on the real estate market if it was to become generally accepted. It would limit third-party bidding at foreclosure sales, limit financing to the most creditworthy borrowers, and restrict the extent to which nonrecourse financing is used.

Case law continued to evolve on this subject, but with each new case the courts seemed to be moving further away from the test established in *Durrett*, until the Supreme Court ruled in 1994. In *In re BFP*,[333] the Ninth Circuit held that a price "which is received at a noncollusive, regularly conducted foreclosure sale" establishes reasonably equivalent value as a matter of law. The Supreme Court[334] affirmed the decision of the Ninth Circuit and held that when a real estate foreclosure sale is in compliance with applicable state law, the reasonable equivalent value is the price that is in fact received from such sale and no further analysis is needed.

The Ninth Circuit Court of Appeals held that a mortgagee has not received a voidable preference when, within 90 days prior to the debtor's bankruptcy, the mortgagee nonjudicially foreclosed, purchased the property by bidding the amount due, and resold the property for a profit.[335]

In the *Ehring* case, all of the elements of a preferential transfer were met with the possible exception that the creditor must receive "more" than in a chapter 7 liquidation. The Bankruptcy Code, section 7(b)(5), requires that the transfer to the creditor be a transfer:

(5) that enables such creditor to receive more than such creditor would receive if—

(A) the case were a case under chapter 7 of this title;

[330] 57 B.R. 568 (N.D. Ill. 1986).
[331] 78 B.R. 203 (S.D. Ind. 1987), *rev'd* 856 F.2d 815 (7th Cir. 1988).
[332] 55 B.R. 163 (Bankr. D. Mass. 1985).
[333] 974 F.2d 1144 (9th Cir. 1992).
[334] *BFB v. Resolution Trust Corp.*, 511 U.S. 512 (1994).
[335] *Ehring v. Western Community Moneycenter (In re Ehring)*, 900 F.2d 184 (9th Cir. 1990).

Because the creditor appears to have received value greater than the debt that was secured, the debtor argued that the creditor received "more" from the foreclosure than it would have under a chapter 7 liquidation. The court rejected this argument, apparently on the grounds that the mortgagee was entitled to bid in at the sale.

(g) Leasehold Assignment as Fraudulent Transfer

In many cases, the most valuable asset of a debtor is equity in its leasehold. The debtor may have been unsuccessful at running the business, but while the individual tried, the value of the leasehold increased. In need of cash, the debtor may have assigned or sublet the property. The purchaser of the assigned lease is in a strong bargaining position and obtains a good price on the lease. If the debtor subsequently files a bankruptcy petition or if the creditors bring an action under the Uniform Fraudulent Conveyance Act or a similar state statute, this transfer may be considered fraudulent. The result could be that the debtor's creditors could have the leasehold sell again at a higher price. Usually, the purchaser would have a lien on the leasehold for what he paid the debtor. However, depending on the "lack of good faith" of the purchaser, the court could eliminate the purchaser's lien on the leasehold for "value" given and for any "improvements" that purchaser may have made.[336] This would leave the "bad faith" purchaser with no lease, no lien, and an unsecured claim for the purchase price and the cost of the improvements.[337]

Aaron suggests that a similar problem can occur when the debtor, because of personal guarantees or for other reasons, transfers the lease back to the owner in exchange of the termination of the lease. The transfer back to the landlord, when the value of the improvements and the unexpired leasehold have a value in excess of the past due rents and future rents, may constitute a fraudulent transfer.[338]

Thus, when dealing with a distressed debtor, it is important that the transfer be for fair value, made in good faith, and properly documented.

(h) Leveraged Buyout as Fraudulent Transfer

The leveraged buyout (LBO) is considered a fraudulent transfer because the buyout group, rather than the company being acquired, receives the consideration for the interest in assets that is granted to the lender. A transfer where a third party receives the benefit is not generally considered to be for equivalent value.

Several forms are used in an LBO. The facts from one of the better known cases, *United States v. Tabor Court (Gleneagles)*,[339] will be used to illustrate one form of the buyout.

---

[336] 11 U.S.C. §§ 548(c) and 550(d)(1). *See In re 716 Third Avenue Corp.*, 225 F. Supp. 268 S.D.N.Y., *rev'd* 340 F.2d 42 (2nd Cir 1964).

[337] Kenneth E. Aaron, "Fraudulent Conveyance and Leaseholds," *Distressed Business and Real Estate Newsletter* (October–November, 1987), p. 8.

[338] *Id.*, pp. 8–9; *see Fashion World, Inc.* 44 B.R. 754 (D. Mass. 1984); *In re Ferris*, 415 F. Supp. 33 (W.D. Okla. 1976).

[339] 803 F.2d 1288 (3d Cir. 1986).

An LBO was defined by the court in *Gleneagles* as "a short-hand expression describing a business practice wherein a company is sold to a small number of investors, typically including members of the company's management, under financial arrangements in which there is a minimum amount of equity and a maximum amount of debt."[340]

In *Gleneagles*, an investment group formed a holding company, Great American Coal Company, which purchased the stock of the Raymond Group—a group of coal companies. A total of $6.2 million in cash and $500,000 in unsecured notes was paid to the shareholders of Raymond. The Institutional Investors Trust loaned approximately $8.5 million to the Raymond Group, advancing $7 million in cash, and keeping a reserve of $1.5 million. The companies that borrowed the funds gave Institutional Investors Trust a first lien on their assets and the part of the Raymond Group that did not borrow the funds gave the lender a second lien on their assets.

Raymond Group transferred $4 million to the Great American Coal Company in return for an unsecured note and transferred $2.9 million to Chemical Bank which held a lien on some of the assets of Raymond. The mortgage payable to Institutional Investors Trust was assigned to third parties.

The Raymond Group did not have funds to cover routine operating expenses and real estate taxes. Within six months after the LBO transaction was completed, the company ceased its mining operations.

The district court held (and was affirmed by the Third Circuit) that the mortgages of the Institutional Investors Trust were fraudulent conveyances under the actual fraud provisions of the FTCA because Institutional Investors Trust was aware of the financial conditions of the Raymond Group and of the intended use of the proceeds.

In *Kupetz v. Wolf*,[341] the Ninth Circuit declined to analyze leveraged buyout under the constructive fraud provisions of the California UFCA, on the theory that it would be "inappropriate to utilize constructive intent to brand most, if not all, LBOs as illegitimate."

In *Jeannette Corp. v. Security Pacific Business Credit, Inc.*,[342] the Third Circuit held that Security Pacific Business Credit had not engaged in a fraudulent conveyance of Jeannette Corp. Coca-Cola agreed to sell Jeannette Corporation, a manufacturer of solid glass, ceramic, china, plastic and candle houseware products in the United States and Canada, for $12.1 million to group investors. The investors acquired Jeannette in a leveraged buyout that was financed by Security Pacific. Less than a year and a half after the LBO, Jeannette filed a chapter 11 petition.

The bankruptcy trustee brought action to set aside the advance made and obligations incurred in connection with the acquisition. The trustee alleged that the leveraged buyout constituted a fraudulent conveyance under the Pennsylvania Uniform Fraudulent Act and was therefore avoidable under section 544(b) of the Bankruptcy Code. The defendant did not contest the finding that the LBO was made without fair consideration. Thus, it was up to the defendant to prove that Jeannette was neither rendered insolvent nor left with an unreasonably small amount of capital.

[340] *Id.* at 1291.
[341] 845 F.2d 842 (9th Cir. 1988).
[342] 971 F.2d 1056 (3d Cir. 1992).

The Third Circuit found that Jeannette was not rendered insolvent because the present fair salable value of the company's total assets exceeded its liabilities by between $1 million and $2 million. The Third Circuit held that the district court properly valued the company's assets on a going-concern basis because bankruptcy was not clearly imminent on the date of the LBO.

In determining whether Jeannette was left with an unreasonably small amount of capital, the Third Circuit held that the district court properly considered the availability of Jeannette's line of credit with Security Pacific and focused on the reasonableness of the parties' projections. The projections were based on a historical analysis of Jeannette's performance and a month-by-month assessment of the company's ability to operate successfully in the year following the acquisition. It was also determined that the company's actual performance in the five months after the leveraged buyout supported the finding that the projections were reasonable. The Third Circuit upheld the district court's findings that the projections of Jeannette were reasonable.

The Third Circuit agreed with the district court that the extent of the decline in sales in 1982 resulted from increased foreign and domestic competition that was not foreseeable at the time of the leveraged buyout. The Third Circuit concluded that Jeannette's failure was caused by the decline in sales rather than a lack of capital.

The Third Circuit held that the district court did not err in finding that the defendants did not intend to defraud the creditors of Jeannette. Even assuming that parties are deemed to have intended the natural consequences of their actions, it follows that if Jeannette's demise was not clearly imminent as of the date of the LBO and the LBO was not constructively fraudulent, the LBO was not intentionally fraudulent.

§ 5.41 Postpetition Transfers

Section 549 of the Bankruptcy Code allows the trustee to avoid certain transfers made after the petition is filed. Those that are avoidable must be transfers that are not authorized either by the court or by an explicit provision of the Bankruptcy Code. In addition, the trustee can avoid transfers made under sections 303(f) and 542(c) of the Bankruptcy Code even though authorized. Section 303(f) is the section that authorizes a debtor to continue operating the business before the order for relief in an involuntary case. Section 549 does, however, provide that a transfer made prior to the order for relief is valid to the extent of value received. Thus, the provision of section 549 cautions all persons dealing with a debtor before an order for relief has been granted to evaluate carefully the transfers made. Section 542(c) explicitly authorizes certain postpetition transfers of real property of the estate made in good faith by an entity without actual knowledge or notice of the commencement of the case.

In *Hellums*,[343] the court held that the automatic stay provisions prohibited the continuance of payroll deductions that were used to make payments on prepetition debt.

---

[343] 772 F.2d 379 (7th Cir. 1985).

There is still considerable uncertainty as to whether a check that was delivered prior to bankruptcy, but not cashed until after the petition is filed, is a postpetition transfer. In the Ninth Circuit, courts have held that the date of delivery is the date to use, provided the check clears within a reasonable time period. Thus, the payment is not a postpetition transfer, but might be recoverable as a preference. Other reported decisions, including the Supreme Court, hold that the date the check clears determines whether the payment is a postpetition transfer (§ 5.39(b)).

§ 5.42 Postpetition Effect of Security Interest

Generally, property acquired by the debtor after the commencement of the case is not subject to any lien resulting from any security agreement entered into by the debtor before the commencement of the case. Thus, an agreement that allows a creditor to have a continuing security interest in accounts receivable would not apply to receivables that arise after the petition is filed. A few exceptions to this rule generally relate to cash collateral or the limited situations where the right to perfect a security interest after the petition is filed is allowed.[344]

Section 552 of the Bankruptcy Code, as amended by the Bankruptcy Reform Act of 1994, provides that if the debtor enters into a security agreement that otherwise would not be avoidable, such as a preference, before the commencement of the case, and if the security interest created by such security agreement extends to property of the debtor acquired before the commencement of the case and to amounts paid as rents of such property, or the fees, charges, accounts, or other payments for the use or occupancy of rooms and other public facilities in hotels, motels, or other lodging properties, then such security interest extends to the rents, fees, and so on, acquired by the estate after the commencement of the case, to the extent provided in the security agreement, unless the court, after a notice and a hearing, orders otherwise.

§ 5.43 Setoffs

"Setoff is that right which exists between two parties to net their respective debts where each party, as a result of unrelated transactions, owes the other an ascertained amount."[345] The right to setoff is an accepted practice in the business community today. When one of the two parties is insolvent and files a bankruptcy court petition, the right to setoff has special meaning. Once the petition is filed, the debtor may compel the creditor to pay the debt owed and the creditor may in turn receive only a small percentage of the claim—unless the Bankruptcy Code permits the setoff.

The Bankruptcy Code contains the basic rules followed under prior law, which give the creditor the right to offset a mutual debt providing both the

---

[344] 11 U.S.C. § 552.
[345] Carmelita J. Hammon, "Setoff in Bankruptcy: Is the Creditor Preferred or Secured?" *University of Colorado Law Review,* Vol. 50 (Summer 1979), p. 511.

debt and the credit arose before the commencement of the case.[346] There are, however, several exceptions:

1 Claims that are not allowable cannot be used for offsets.
2 Postpetition claims transferred by an entity other than the debtor or incurred for the purpose of obtaining a right of setoff against the debtor are disallowed for offsets.
3 Claims transferred to the creditors within 90 days before the filing of the petition and while the debtor was insolvent are precluded. Also, section 553(c) provides that, for setoffs, the debtor is presumed to have been insolvent on and during the 90 days immediately preceding the filing of the petition. The new law does not require, as was necessary under prior law, that the creditor have reasonable cause to believe that the debtor was insolvent at the time the transfer was received.

Another major restriction on the use of setoffs prevents the creditor from unilaterally making the setoff after a petition is filed. The right to a setoff is subject to the automatic stay provisions of section 362 and the use of property under section 363. Thus, before a debtor may proceed with the setoff, relief from the automatic stay must be obtained (§ 5.27(b)). This automatic stay and the right to use the amount subject to setoff will be possible only if the trustee or debtor-in-possession provides the creditor with adequate protection. If adequate protection—normally in the form of periodic cash payments, additional or replacement collateral, or other methods that will provide the creditor with the indubitable equivalent of his interest—is not provided, then the creditor may proceed with the offset as provided in section 553.

If the creditor had a right to a setoff under section 553(a) of the Bankruptcy Code, the court may deny the setoff because the debtor violated the automatic stay by withholding or imposing a freeze on money it owed the debtor.[347]

The bankruptcy court held that a setoff is an exercisable prerogative, not a natural right conclusively established because the parties have claims against one another. The court refused to allow the U.S. Customs Department to follow through with the setoff because Customs had previously entered into an agreed order with the trustee settling its claim.[348]

Section 553(b) contains a penalty for those creditors who elect to offset their claim prior to the petition when they see the financial problems of the debtor and threat of the automatic stay. The Bankruptcy Code precludes the setoff of any amount that is a betterment of the creditor's position during the 90 days prior to the filing of the petition. Any improvement in position may be recovered by the debtor-in-possession or trustee. The amount to be recovered is the amount by which the insufficiency on the date of offset is less than the insufficiency 90 days before the filing of the petition. If no insufficiency exists 90

---

[346] 11 U.S.C. § 553.
[347] *In re Ionosphere Clubs, Inc.* 25 BCD 465, USTC (CCH) ¶ 75,770 (Bankr. S.D.N.Y. 1994).
[348] *In re Holder*, 182 B.R. 770 (Bankr. M.D. Tenn. 1995). *See In re De Laurentiis Entertainment Group Inc.*, 963 F.2d 1269 (9th Cir. 1995); *In re Stephenson*, 84 B.R. 74 (Bankr. N.D. Tex. 1988).

days before the filing of the petition, then the first date within the 90-day period where there is an insufficiency should be used. "Insufficiency" is defined as the amount by which a claim against the debtor exceeds a mutual debt owing to the debtor by the holder of such claim. The amount recovered is considered an unsecured claim.

In *In re Crabtree*,[349] the bankruptcy court held that where the IRS did not obtain permission to set off a tax refund it owed the debtor against taxes owed for other years, the IRS was not allowed to offset the tax after the plan was confirmed. The plan provided that all taxes were to be paid in accordance with the plan provisions of section 1129(a)(9)(c). The IRS's action to freeze and retain a debtor's refund is a setoff and is in violation of the automatic stay.[350] In other cases courts have allowed the setoff even though the request was not made before the setoff took place.[351]

To illustrate the offset provision, consider the following situation where the creditor is a bank and the debtor has a checking account and a loan with the bank.

Days prior to petition:	90	70	45	1
Balance in checking account	$ 600	$ 500	$ 850	$ 300
Loan balance	1,000	1,000	1,000	1,000
Insufficiency	$ (400)	$ (500)	$ (150)	$ (700)

If the bank sets off one day prior to the filing of the petition, there is no recovery because the insufficiency at this date ($700) is not less than the insufficiency 90 days prior to the petition date ($400). However, $250 could be recovered if the setoff was made 45 days prior to the petition date ($400 – $150). Improvement in position rules may encourage financial institutions to set off upon the first indication of debtor insolvency rather than encourage them to work with the debtor hoping that he or she will ultimately be able to meet his or her obligations.

A payment that was made on a debt that would ordinarily be a preference is not a preference if a right of setoff existed at the date of the filing of the petition. This would be true even though the payment was made before the creditor had become obligated to the debtor. For example, see *Braniff Airways, Inc., v. Exxon Co., U.S.A.*[352] The extent to which the preference can be avoided must be tested against the improvement in position under section 553(b), as discussed above.

In *David L. Morgan et al. v. United States*,[353] the district court held that the setoffs did not constitute a levy prohibited by section 6703(c)(1). The court

---

[349] 76 B.R. 208 (M.D. Fla. 1987).

[350] *United States v. Reynolds*, 764 F.2d 1004 (4th Cir. 1985).

[351] *In re Gribben*, 158 B.R. 920 (S.D.N.Y. 1993) and *In re Rush-Hampton Industries, Inc.*, 159 B.R. 343 (Bankr. M.D. Fla. 1993).

[352] 814 F.2d 1030 (5th Cir. 1987).

[353] 1991 U.S. Dist. LEXIS 11810 (E.D. Ark. 1991).

noted that a levy would involve an IRS action to acquire possession of a tax-payer's property, while a setoff is the application of funds already in the government's possession against a taxpayer's outstanding tax liability.

CHAPTER 7 LIQUIDATION

§ 5.44 Filing the Petition

Chapters 1, 3, and 5 of the Bankruptcy Code deal with the provisions that apply to all chapters. Chapter 7 is concerned with the liquidation of a debtor in financial trouble and contains provisions for the appointment of the trustee, liquidation of the business, distribution of the estate to the creditors, and discharge of the debtor from its liabilities. Collier stated:

> It is the purpose of the Bankruptcy Act to convert the assets of the bankrupt into cash for distribution among creditors, and then to relieve the honest debtor from the weight of oppressive indebtedness and permit him to start afresh, free from the obligations and responsibilities that have resulted from business misfortunes.[354]

The same objective applies to chapter 7 of the Bankruptcy Code.

All persons[355] are eligible to file a petition under chapter 7 except railroads, domestic insurance companies and banks (including savings and loan associations, building and loan associations, credit unions, and so forth) and foreign insurance companies and banks engaged in the insurance and banking business in the United States. Foreign insurance companies and banks not engaged in such business in the United States could file a petition. Although farmers and nonprofit corporations may file voluntary petitions, their creditors may not bring them involuntarily into the bankruptcy court.

The person filing voluntarily need not be insolvent in either the bankruptcy or equity sense; the essential requirement is that the petitioner have debts. When a corporation is insolvent, shareholder approval or authorization to the filing of a petition is in some situations unnecessary; the board of directors may have the power to initiate proceedings. However, the power to initiate the proceedings depends on state corporate law, the articles of incorporation, and the bylaws of the corporation. The filing of a voluntary petition under chapter 7 constitutes an order for relief, which is the equivalent of being adjudged a bankrupt under the Bankruptcy Act. The debtor corporation's property is then regarded as being in the custody of the court and "constitutes the assets of a trust for the benefit of the corporation's creditors." For an involuntary petition that is not timely converted, the court, under chapter 7, will only after trial order relief if it finds that the debtor is generally not paying its debts as they become due, or that within 120 days a custodian took possession of all or substantially all of the debtor's assets.

The debtor can convert a chapter 7 case to a chapter 11 or chapter 13 case at any time, and this right cannot be waived. In addition, on request of a party in

---

[354] *Collier on Bankruptcy,* 13th ed., p. 6.
[355] Individuals, partnerships, or corporations, but not a governmental unit (11 U.S.C. § 101(35)).

interest, after notice and a hearing, the court may convert the chapter 7 case to a chapter 11 case.

§ 5.45 Trustee

As soon as the order for relief has been entered, the U.S. trustee will appoint a disinterested person from a panel of private trustees to serve as the interim trustee. If a person was serving as trustee in an involuntary case prior to the order for relief, he or she may also be appointed as interim trustee.[356] The function and powers of the interim trustee are the same as those for a trustee. If none is willing to serve, then the U.S. trustee may serve in this capacity. In situations where the schedules of assets and liabilities disclose that there are unlikely to be any assets in the estate, the U.S. trustee may serve as the interim trustee and as the trustee if one is not elected by the creditors.

(a) Election of Trustee

At a meeting of creditors called under section 341, a trustee may be elected if an election is requested by at least 20 percent in amount of qualifying claims. Creditors who (1) hold an allowable, undisputed, fixed, liquidated, unsecured claim, (2) do not have an interest materially adverse to the interest of all creditors, and (3) are not insiders may vote. To elect a trustee, holders of at least 20 percent of the qualifying claims must vote and the candidate must receive a majority in amount of those voting. If a trustee is not elected, the interim trustee will serve as the trustee.[357] If the U.S. trustee is the interim trustee and no trustee is elected, then he or she will serve as the trustee.

The provision that the creditors may elect the trustee may result in different trustees being appointed for a partnership and the individual partners in the proceedings. If, of course, they have the same creditors, a common trustee would most likely be elected. The election of multiple trustees would probably cost more, but might result in a more equitable distribution of the estate. Conflicts of interest can arise in situations where there is a common trustee for the individual partners and the partnership.

(b) Duties of Trustee

Section 704 identifies the following as duties of the trustee:

1 Collect and reduce to money the property of the estate for which such trustee serves, and close up such estate as expeditiously as is compatible with the best interest of parties-in-interest.
2 Be accountable for all property received.
3 Ensure that the debtor performs his or her intention as to the surrender or redemption of property used as security for consumer debts or as to the reaffirmation of debts secured by such property. See section 521(2).

---

[356] 11 U.S.C. § 701(a).
[357] *Id.*, §§ 702 and 703(c).

4 Investigate the financial affairs of the debtor.

5 If a purpose would be served, examine proofs of claims and object to the allowance of any claim that is improper.

6 If advisable, oppose the discharge of the debtor.

7 Unless the court orders otherwise, furnish such information concerning the estate and the estate's administration as is requested by a party-in-interest.

8 If the business of the debtor is authorized to be operated, file with the court and with any governmental unit charged with responsibility for collection or determination of any tax arising out of such operation, periodic reports and summaries of the operation of such business, including a statement of receipts and disbursements, and such other information as the court requires.

9 Make a final report and file a final account of the administration of the estate with the court.

In addition to filing various reports with the court, the trustee must file copies of the operating statements and other reports on the administration of the estate with the U.S. trustee. See Chapter 9.

The duties set forth are very similar to those of prior law. One of the most important duties of the trustee is to reduce the property to money and close up the estate in a manner that will allow the interested parties to receive the maximum amount. For some businesses, it may be best for the trustee to operate the business for a short time so that the liquidation can be carried out in an orderly fashion. This is likely when the completion of work-in-process or the retail sale of inventory is likely to bring the highest value on liquidation. Authority to operate the business must, however, come from the court.[358] If the trustee does operate the business, periodic operating reports, including a statement of receipts and disbursements, must be filed with the court and the U.S. trustee. Additional information may be required by local rules, by the court, and by the U.S. trustee.

(c) Compensation of Trustee

For petitions filed after October 22, 1994, the Bankruptcy Reform Act of 1994 increased the trustee fees. The new rates are: 25 percent on $0 to $5,000, 10 percent on $5,000 to $50,000, 5 percent on $50,000 to $1,000,000, and reasonable compensation (not to exceed 3 percent) on an amount in excess of $1,000,000 of all funds disbursed or turned over by the trustee to parties in interest—excluding the debtor, but including holders of secured claims.

The Bankruptcy Reform Act of 1994 allowed the Judicial Conference of the United States to prescribe additional fees of $15 for trustees in chapter 7 cases. This would bring to $60 the amount that a trustee might receive in no-asset cases. The $15 fees would be deducted by trustees or other entities making distributions from the moneys payable to creditors, thus constituting user fees charged to those who receive distributions in bankruptcy cases. Legislative

---

[358] *Id.,* § 721.

history notes that, because the fees are payable by the creditors from funds to be distributed to them, such deductions would not affect the application of the best-interest-of-creditors tests for confirmation of plans in chapters 11, 12, or 13. The Judiciary Committee intended that the funds for this increase were not to be borne by the Federal Treasury or by debtors in chapter 7 or 13. After October 22, 1995, these fees would be payable to the trustee after trustees' services are rendered.

§ 5.46 Creditors' Committee

At the meeting of creditors under the provisions of section 341(a), in addition to voting for a trustee they may vote to elect a committee of not fewer than three and no more than 11 creditors. Each committee member must hold an allowable unsecured claim, to be eligible to serve.[359] The committee's function will be to consult with the U.S. trustee and the trustee administering the estate, make recommendations to the trustee regarding the performance of his or her duties, and submit to the court any questions affecting the administration of the estate.[360] The committee may also make recommendations to the U.S. trustee regarding the performance of the trustee and submit to the U.S. trustee, as well as to the court, any questions affecting the administration of the estate. Unlike chapter 11 cases, where creditors' committees are appointed by the U.S. trustee in every case where there are creditors willing to serve, a creditors' committee will not serve in a chapter 7 liquidation unless the creditors elect one.

§ 5.47 Partnerships

Section 723(a) provides that if the property of the partnership is insufficient to satisfy in full the claims of the partnership and if a general partner is personally liable, a claim exists against the general partner for the full amount of the deficiency. According to section 723(b), the trustee is required to seek recovery first from the general partners that are not debtors in a bankruptcy case. The court has the authority to order the general partners to provide assurance that the partnership deficiency will be paid or may order general partners not to dispose of their property.

Section 723 of the Bankruptcy Code is modified to provide that the trustee's or debtor's claim against a general partner is limited to the amount that, under applicable nonbankruptcy law, the general partner is personally liable for. Thus, in the case of a limited liability partnership, the partner will not be liable for more than he or she would be under state law.

Under prior law, nonadjudicated partners were required to file schedules of assets and liabilities and the partnership trustee had the prerogative to collect, evaluate, preserve, liquidate, and otherwise manage the separate estates of the nonadjudicated partners. Hanley's[361] analysis of the legislative intent and of

---

[359] *Id.,* § 705(a).
[360] *Id.,* § 705(b).
[361] John W. Hanley, Jr., "Partnership Bankruptcy under the New Act," *Hastings Law Journal,* Vol. 31 (September 1979), pp. 162–66.

the development of these broad powers in the first place suggested that the powers should be reduced. He, however, concluded:

> Despite this analysis, in light of the broad discretion of the court under the new Act, partnership trustees probably will continue to seek a variety of managerial orders regarding the estates of nonadjudicated partners. The rules will continue to require the filing of a schedule of assets and liabilities, which arguably is necessary to determine whether security for a deficiency is required. In some circumstances, particularly after the rendition of a judgment against the partner, a court may grant the trustee's request for a turnover order, although it is doubtful that one should ever apply to the assets of an exempt partner. Finally, the legislative history of the Act suggests that the court's authority to enjoin a partner's creditor from levying on the separate property of the partner is continued.[362]

Section 723(c) gives the partnership trustee the right to file a claim against the general partners in bankruptcy court. This section states:

> Notwithstanding section 728(c) of this title, the trustee has a claim against the estate of each general partner in such partnership that is a debtor in a case under this title for the full amount of all claims of creditors allowed in the case concerning such partnership. Notwithstanding section 502 of this title, there shall not be allowed in such partner's case a claim against such partner on which both such partner and such partnership are liable, except to any extent that such claim is secured only by property of such partner and not by property of such partnership. The claim of the trustee under this subsection is entitled to distribution in such partner's case under section 726(a) of this title the same as any other claim of a kind specified in such section.

If the trustee is unsuccessful in recovering the full amount of the deficiency of the partnership from the general partners not in a bankruptcy proceeding, a claim may be asserted against the general partner in bankruptcy court. Note that the claim against the partners is not subordinated to the claims of the individual partners, as was done under prior law. The purpose of this section has been to provide that partnership creditors and partner creditors would be treated alike in the proceedings. This section also provides that only one claim will be allowed where creditors have filed claims against the partnership and against individual partners in bankruptcy proceedings. It would thus appear that holders of claims against both the partnership and the partners would have duplicate claims, which they had filed against individual partners, disallowed.

If the trustee recovers from general partners in a bankruptcy proceeding a greater amount than is necessary to satisfy in full the claims of the partnership, the court, after notice and hearing, will determine an equitable distribution of the surplus.[363]

Section 727(a)(1) provides that only an individual may obtain a discharge. Thus, it is not possible for a partnership to obtain a discharge. As with corporations, this provision would make it undesirable to make continued use of a particular partnership shell following the liquidation of the partnership.

---

[362] *Id.*, p. 166.
[363] 11 U.S.C. § 723(d).

An individual partner can, of course, obtain a discharge from debts. This individual partner must, however, satisfy the requirements for a discharge in section 727.

One provision that can have an effect on partnership proceedings is that an individual discharge can be denied if the debtor commits one of the listed offenses in connection with another case concerning an insider.[364] Because a general partner is an insider, an unacceptable action of the general partner with respect to the partnership's property or financial statements could prevent a subsequent discharge of the individual partner from his or her debts. These provisions respecting the complete denial of an individual's discharge are discussed in § 5.50.

§ 5.48 Treatment of Tax Liens

In a chapter 7 liquidation, the provision of prior law in which tax liens were subordinated to administrative expenses and wage claims is codified in section 724(b). According to this section, distribution is made first to holders of liens senior to the tax lien. Administrative expenses, wage claims, and consumer creditors granted priority are second—limited, however, to the extent of the amount of the allowed tax claim secured by the lien. If the entire claim has not been used up, the tax claimant has third priority to the extent that the priority claims did not use up the tax claim due to the lien. Fourth are junior lienholders, and the fifth distribution would go to the tax claimant to the extent he or she was not paid in the third distribution. Any remaining property goes to the estate.[365]

In addition, section 724(a) gives the trustee the right to avoid a lien that secures a fine, penalty, forfeiture, or a multiple, punitive, or exemplary damages claim to the extent that the claim is not for actual pecuniary loss suffered by the holder and occurred before the order for relief or the appointment of a trustee in the case.

§ 5.49 Liquidation of Assets

After the property of the estate has been reduced to money and the secured claims to the extent allowed have been satisfied, the property of the estate shall be distributed to the holders of claims in a specified order. Unless a claim has been subordinated under the provisions of section 510, section 726(a) provides that the balance is distributed in the following order:[366]

1 To the holders of priority claims as set forth in section 507 for which a proof of claim is timely filed or tardily filed before the date on which the trustee commences distribution under section 726(a) of the Bankruptcy Code.

---

[364] *Id.*, § 727(a)(7).
[365] *CCH Bankruptcy Law Reports,* ¶ 10,108.
[366] *But see* §§ 364(c) and 507(b).

2 To the holders of general unsecured claims who timely filed proof of claim or those who filed late because of a lack of notice or knowledge of the case.

3 To the holders of general unsecured claims filed late.

4 In payment of an allowed secured or unsecured claim, not compensation for actual pecuniary losses, for fines, penalties, forfeitures, or damages suffered by the claim holder.

5 In payment of interest on the above claims, at the legal rate, from the date of filing the petition.

6 Any balance to the debtor.

Section 726(b) provides for claims within a particular classification to be paid on a pro rata basis when there are not enough funds to satisfy all of the claims of a particular classification in full. There is one exception to this policy. If there are not enough funds to pay all administrative expenses, and part of the administrative expenses related to a chapter 11 or chapter 13 case prior to conversion, then those administrative expenses incurred in chapter 7 after conversion will be paid first. Thus, accountants whose fees in a chapter 11 case were not paid before the conversion could find that they would not receive full payment if funds are not available to pay all administrative expenses in a subsequent chapter 7 case.

Subsection (c) of section 726 sets forth the provisions for distribution of community property.

After the assets have been liquidated and the proceeds distributed in the proper order, the trustee will make a final report and file a final accounting of the administration of the estate with the court. At this time, the trustee will be discharged from further responsibility.

The Federal Deposit Insurance Corporation (FDIC), as the receiver of a bank, is not entitled to priority over claims of shareholders against officers, directors, and other parties alleged to have caused the bank's failure.[367]

The issue before the Eleventh Circuit Court was whether the FDIC was entitled to priority, either through its status as insurer of the failed Park Bank or through general principles of priority following insolvency, over the shareholders for claims against solvent third parties. The court held that the FDIC was not entitled to priority under either basis.

The court found that the Federal Deposit Insurance Act contains no indication of an intention to create an absolute priority rule in favor of the FDIC, and reversed the district court's finding, which was based on policy considerations to protect the insurance fund.

The FDIC argued that if it is not entitled to a priority under the statutory scheme, the court should consider fashioning a federal common law absolute priority rule by analogy to the absolute priority rule in bankruptcy where creditors are paid before shareholders. The court declined to create such a rule.

The absolute priority rule evolved out of the bankruptcy principle that a debtor receives distribution only after all creditors have been satisfied. The

---

[367] *Federal Deposit Insurance Corp. v. Jenkins*, 888 F.2d 1537 (11th Cir. 1989).

rule applies to equity contributions in corporations by requiring that the providers of the equity (the stockholders) not seek recovery of corporate assets until general creditors' claims have been satisfied.[368] "Secured creditors get first priority according to their rank and the unsecured creditors follow."[369] "All members of a higher priority class must be paid in full before lower priority classes can be paid."[370]

The court noted that, in the present case, however, the shareholders were not attempting to collect on assets of the failed bank. Rather, they were proceeding against solvent third parties in nonderivative shareholder suits.

§ 5.50 Discharge

Section 727 states that a discharge will be granted to the debtor unless one of ten conditions is encountered (see below). In that case, the discharge will be denied. The grounds for denial are very similar to those of prior law with two exceptions. The first exception deals with the issuance of false financial statements. Under prior law, a discharge of all debts was barred by the obtaining of credit through the use of false financial statements, but this provision was omitted from the Bankruptcy Code. As noted in paragraph 105, the use of false financial statements can result in a debt obtained by such false statements not being discharged. Thus, the issuance of false financial statements to obtain business credit will now only prevent a discharge for that particular debt rather than bar a discharge of all debts. The second exception is that failure to pay the filing fee is no longer a basis to deny discharge. Instead, Bankruptcy Rule 1006 states that every petition shall be accompanied by the prescribed fee. It further implies that no petition shall be *accepted* by the bankruptcy court clerk unless accompanied by the fee or a proper application to pay the fee in installments. In addition, sections 707 and 1307 provide that for nonpayment of fees the court may dismiss a case after notice and a hearing.

It should be noted that section 523 contains a list of specific debts that may be excepted from the discharge provision; section 727 provides for a denial of a discharge of all debts. A denial of a discharge benefits all creditors. An exception to a discharge primarily benefits only the particular creditor to which the exception applies.

The other interesting change in the new law relates to the discharge of a corporation. Under prior law, corporations in straight bankruptcy being liquidated could receive a discharge of debts and the remaining corporate structure (called its shell) could be used for certain tax benefits. The new law, however, allows only individuals to obtain a discharge under chapter 7 liquidation. Corporations will not be reluctant to use these shells because any assets eventually received by the shell are subject to attack for payment of prepetition debts.

The ten statutory conditions that will deny the debtor a discharge are that the debtor:

---

[368] *In re Perimeter Park Investment Associates*, Ltd., 697 F.2d 945, 952 n. 8 (11th Cir. 1983).
[369] *Id.*
[370] *Id.*

1 Is not an individual.

2 Within one year prior to the filing of the petition, or after filing, transferred, destroyed, or concealed, or permitted to be transferred, destroyed, or concealed, any of his or her property with the intent to hinder, delay, or defraud creditors.

3 Failed to keep or preserve adequate books or accounts or financial records.

4 Knowingly and fraudulently made a false oath or claim, offered or received a bribe, or withheld information in connection with the case.

5 Failed to explain satisfactorily any losses of assets or deficiency of assets to meet his or her liabilities.

6 Refused to obey any lawful order or to answer any material questions in the course of the proceedings after being granted immunity from self-incrimination.

7 Within one year prior to the filing of the petition, committed any of the above acts in connection with another bankruptcy case concerning an insider.

8 Within the past six years, received a discharge in bankruptcy under chapter 7 or chapter 11 of the Bankruptcy Code or under the Bankruptcy Act.

9 Within the past six years, received a discharge under chapter 13 of the Bankruptcy Code or Chapter XIII of prior law, unless payments under the plan totaled 100 percent of the allowed unsecured claims or at least 70 percent of such claims under a plan proposed in good faith and determined to have been performed according to the debtor's best effort.

10 The discharge will be denied if, after the order for relief, the debtor submits a written waiver of discharge and the court approves it.

These provisions are strictly construed in favor of the debtor. Nevertheless, one bankrupt under prior law was denied his discharge for failure to list as an asset on his schedule his collection of Superman comic books.[371]

Section 727(c) provides that the U.S. trustee, a creditor, or the trustee can object to the court's granting the debtor a discharge under section 727(a). Subsection (d) provides that, on request of the trustee, a creditor, or the U.S. Trustee, and after a notice and hearing, the court may revoke the discharge if:

1 The discharge was obtained through fraud of the debtor and the requesting party did not know of the fraud until after the discharge was granted.

2 The debtor acquired or was entitled to acquire property that is or should have been property of the estate and knowingly and fraudulently failed to report or deliver the property to the trustee.

3 The debtor refused to obey a lawful order of the court or to respond to material questions approved by the court.

---

[371] *In re Ruben Marcelo*, 5 Bank. Ct. Dec. (CRR) 786 (S.D.N.Y. Aug. 7, 1979). (The collection was valued at $2,000.)

(a) Avoidance of Liens

The Supreme Court held in *Dewsnup v. Timm*[372] that chapter 7 debtors could not void the portion of the lien secured by real property that exceeded the value of the property. The Third Circuit had ruled that the portion of the lien that exceeded the value of the property could be voided, even though the property had not been administered by the estate and debtors had no equity in the property.[373] This is the first Court of Appeals to so directly hold in a liquidation case in which the debtor has no equity in the property.

The debtors filed a chapter 7 petition, listing their residence as their sole asset of any value. After they received their discharge, they started an adversary proceeding in the bankruptcy court to avoid liens. The debtors alleged that the property had a value of $34,000 and was subject to a first mortgage, with a balance of $28,873.50, and a second mortgage, with a balance of more than $200,000, with the Small Business Administration (SBA) as the junior mortgagee. Relying on section 506(d) of the Bankruptcy Code, the debtors sought an order voiding the SBA's security interest in excess of $5,126.50—the property's claimed value less the balance of the first mortgage. The District Court, affirming an order of the bankruptcy court, held that the debtors could not avoid the portion of secured liens that exceeded the value of the underlying property, because the property was not administered in the bankruptcy proceeding. The Third Circuit reversed the lower courts and under section 506(d) of the Bankruptcy Code allowed the debtors to void the junior mortgagee's lien in excess of the $5,126.50.

The issue in the case is the interpretation of the meaning of Bankruptcy Code section 506(d). Does it allow the debtor under chapter 7 to liquidate and obtain a discharge and thereafter void a junior mortgagee's unsecured lien and redeem the property by paying the junior the value of the secured lien? Can the debtor obtain a more favorable result under chapter 7 than under chapter 11 or chapter 13? The meaning of section 506(d) is not clear. By allowing the debtor to void the unsecured portion of the lien, the court apparently thought the policy favoring the debtor's "fresh start" more important than preserving the mortgagee's rights in the unsecured portion of the lien. The case gives the debtor an additional route to follow in bankruptcy.

Section 506(a) and 506(d) of the Bankruptcy Code provides, in relevant part:

> (a) An allowed claim of a creditor secured by a lien on property in which the estate has an interest, . . . is a secured claim to the extent of the value of such creditor's interest in the estate's interest in such property, . . . and is an unsecured claim to the extent that the value of such creditor's interest . . . is less than the amount of such allowed claim. Such value shall be determined in light of the purpose of the valuation and of the proposed disposition or use of such property, and in conjunction with any hearing on such disposition or use or on a plan affecting such creditor's interest.

> (d) To the extent that a lien secures a claim against the debtor that is not an allowed secured claim, such lien is void, unless—(emphasis added)

The court relied on what was contended to be the plain meaning of section 506(a) and 506(d). It asserted that section 506(a) bifurcates a secured creditor's claim into a secured and an unsecured component, with the claim secured to

---

[372] 112 S. Ct. 773 (1992).
[373] *Gaglia v. First Fed. Savings & Loan Ass'n (In re Gaglia)*, 889 F.2d 1304 (3d Cir. 1989).

the extent that the creditor may look to the underlying collateral. The SBA junior mortgagee would therefore have a secured claim for the difference between the market value of the property and the remaining amount of the first mortgage, with the rest of its claim unsecured. The unsecured portion is then void under section 506(d). The court contended that the SBA would receive the same amount if the property were liquidated and that lien avoidance simply duplicates the results.

The court rejected the reasoning of *In re Maitland*,[374] that section 506 was intended to apply only to property administered under the Code, not to property abandoned or released from the estate. The SBA, relying on the language of section 506(a), argued that because the debtors have no equity in the property and the property will not be administered, the estate has no "interest" in it. The SBA contended that section 506(d) is designed only to facilitate the administration and distribution of the estate. Hence, the SBA asserted that the debtors should not be able to use section 506 to their advantage. The Court of Appeals rejected this argument by noting that when a debtor files a chapter 7 petition, all of the debtor's right and title to property, legal as well as equitable, passes to the estate.[375] This includes the legal title to property secured by a mortgage. The court concluded that, even though the debtors had no equity in the property, the estate had an interest in it.

The court also rejected the premise that voiding the unsecured lien would create a conflict with section 362(d)(2) of the Bankruptcy Code. That section states that a court shall, after notice and hearing, grant a party-in-interest relief from the automatic stay if the debtor has no equity in the property and the property is not necessary to an effective reorganization. According to the bankruptcy court, this section requires the stay to be lifted at a secured creditor's request so that he "may pursue his remedy against the liened property for whatever benefit he may perceive," a purpose that would be frustrated if a debtor could use section 506 of the Bankruptcy Code to avoid the undersecured portion of a lien and "redeem" the property at market value. The bankruptcy court reasoned that the debtor's interpretation of section 506(d) was too drastic a change from practice under the Bankruptcy Act to stand in the face of the inclusion of section 362(d)(2), which indicated to the court that Congress wanted to balance debtors' rights in over-encumbered assets against the interest of the lenders.

Bankruptcy Code section 722 allows a debtor to redeem "personal property" from a lien securing a dischargeable consumer debt. The Court of Appeals rejected the lower court's conclusions that section 506(d) applied only to property sold by the estate and that permitting a debtor to void liens on real property under section 506(d) and thereafter redeem the property would render section 722's limitation to personal property meaningless,[376] in which the court held that lien avoidance under section 506 would render section 722 totally surplus.

The court thought that voiding the unsecured lien under section 506(d) places the SBA in the same position as if the property had been liquidated. In liquidation, the SBA would have received the difference between the sale price and the balance remaining on the first mortgage. Under section 506, the SBA has a secured claim to the extent the fair market value of the property, as deter-

---

[374] 61 B.R. 130 (Bankr. E.D. Va. 1986).

[375] 11 U.S.C.A. § 362(d)(2).

[376] *See In re Mahaner*, 34 B.R. 308, 309 (Bankr. W.D.N.Y. 1983).

mined by the bankruptcy court, exceeds the balance on the first mortgage. The SBA may foreclose on the property to realize the value of its secured claim. If it does, it should receive the same amount as liquidation would have produced. The SBA is no worse off than if the property were sold, but the debtors may realize significant benefits from lien avoidance. They may be better able to negotiate a repayment schedule with the SBA for the reduced amount of the secured claim. Thus, they have an increased chance to retain their homestead. The court noted that, if section 506 is not applied and the property is not liquidated, the SBA will hold a mortgage exceeding $200,000 on property allegedly worth $34,000. The debtors would have little incentive to remain on the property, because they could get a good title only after paying far more than the amount the property is worth. Finally, the court said the debtors may use section 506 because they fear that a lienor might hang back till the debtor has been discharged, and then foreclose and obtain a deficiency judgment. This tactic might impede the debtor's "fresh start"; and section 506(d), read together with section 501(c), enables the debtors to avoid the tactic.

The case had disturbing implications for secured creditors:

1 Outside of bankruptcy, the undersecured mortgagee can foreclose, bid in at the sale, and hope that the property will appreciate in value. In bankruptcy, if the debtor can liquidate and redeem by paying the undersecured creditor the value of the secured lien, this gives the liquidating debtor the potential for the appreciation.

2 It is submitted that section 362(d)(2) of the Bankruptcy Code indicates that Congress did not intend to let a chapter 7 debtor remain in the debtor's home as part of the debtor's fresh start.

3 Allowing lien avoidance in chapter 7 would discourage the use of chapter 11 and chapter 13 in favor of chapter 7. Under section 1322(b)(2) of the Bankruptcy Code, a chapter 13 debtor may not modify a claim secured only by the debtor's residence. Voiding the unsecured portion of the lien certainly appears to be a modification.[377]

4 Allowing debtors to use section 506 will improperly discourage them from using chapter 11. This effect results because title 11, section 1111(b)(1) of the U.S. Code permits certain creditors to elect to have their claims treated as secured to the extent they are allowed, notwithstanding section 506(a).

The Bankruptcy Appellate Panel (BAP) of the Ninth Circuit followed the Tenth Circuit case of *Dewsnup v. Timm (In re Dewsnup)*,[378] rather than the Third Circuit case of *Gaglia v. First Federal Savings and Loan Association (In re Gaglia)*,[379] in holding that a chapter 7 debtor may not use the provision of Bankruptcy Code section 506 (allowing bifurcation of a claim into secured and unsecured portions) in order to avoid the unsecured portion of a lien on real property.[380]

In *Dewsnup*, the Tenth Circuit noted, among the various reasons stated for denying relief under section 506: (1) that abandoned property is not administered

---

[377] *But see In re Hougland*, 1989 WL 114163 (9th Cir. 1989) (allowing modification of unsecured portion of lien).

[378] 908 F.2d 588 (10th Cir. 1990).

[379] *Supra* note 232.

[380] *State of Oregon v. Lange*, 120 B.R. 132 (9th Cir. BAP 1990).

by the estate and therefore has no application; (2) that allowing this relief inequitably gives debtors more in a chapter 7 liquidation than they would receive in the reorganization chapters; and (3) that allowing lien avoidance pursuant to section 506(d) renders the redemption provision found in section 722 meaningless.[381]

The BAP stated that, on balance, it found that the analysis of *In re Dewsnup* and its progeny better reconciles the various provisions of the Bankruptcy Code.[382] In *Dewsnup*, the Tenth Circuit articulated two reasons for rejecting the Third Circuit approach. "First," the court said, "we reject the notion that section 506(d) must be read in isolation."[383] Rather, the Tenth Circuit reasoned that courts should look to the provisions of the whole law, and to its object and policy. "Second," the court noted, "the Third Circuit's rationale does not adequately recognize the [e]ffect of abandonment with its resulting consequences, including reversion of the property to pre-bankruptcy status."[384]

The court reasoned that to permit strip-down (avoiding the unsecured portion) after abandonment would defeat the purpose behind the abandonment provision and run counter to the plain language of the Bankruptcy Code.

The Supreme Court affirmed the decision of the Tenth Circuit. In *Dewsnup v. Timm*,[385] the Court held that, after a property has been abandoned by the trustee, a debtor cannot use section 506(a) and 506(d) to strip down an undersecured creditor's lien on real property to the value of the collateral.

The Supreme Court's rationale for not allowing a strip-down of the lien to the secured portion is confusing. The Court primarily rejected strip-down for policy reasons. It was not convinced that Congress, in enacting the 1978 Bankruptcy Code, intended to depart from the pre-Code rule that liens pass through bankruptcy unaffected. The Court stated:

> The practical effect of petitioner's argument [to void the unsecured lien] is to freeze the creditor's secured interest at the judicially determined valuation. By this approach, the creditor would lose the benefit of any increase in the value of the property by the time of the foreclosure sale. The increase would accrue to the benefit of the debtor, a result some of the parties describe as a "windfall."

> We think, however, that the creditor's lien stays with the real property until the foreclosure. That is what was bargained for by the mortgagor and the mortgagee. The voidness language [of Section 506(d)] sensibly applies only to the security aspect of the lien and then only to the real deficiency in the security. Any increase over the judicially determined valuation during bankruptcy rightly accrues to the benefit of the creditor, not to the benefit of the debtor and not to the benefit of other unsecured creditors whose claims have been allowed and who had nothing to do with the mortgagor-mortgagee bargain.

> . . . The "fresh-start" policy cannot justify an impairment of respondents' property rights, for the fresh start does not extend to an in rem claim against property but is limited to a discharge of personal liability.[386]

The decision in *Dewsnup* has not resolved the issues associated with strip-down of mortgages. For example, in a chapter 13 case, the Second Circuit

---

[381] 908 F.2d at 589–90.
[382] 120 B.R. 132, 135.
[383] 908 F.2d at 591.
[384] *Id.*
[385] *Supra* note 231.
[386] *Supra* note 231, p. 775.

Court of Appeals held that, although section 1322(b)(2) of the Bankruptcy Code bars the modification of the rights of holders of claims secured by a debtor's principal residence, this does not preclude modification of a mortgage lender's rights with regard to the unsecured portion of an undersecured mortgage.[387]

Section 1322(b)(2) provides that a chapter 13 plan of reorganization may modify the rights of holders of secured claims (other than a claim secured only by a security interest in real property that is the debtor's principal residence) or of holders of unsecured claims.

The issue is whether, when a mortgagee holds a mortgage that is undersecured, these Code provisions mean (1) the debtor can first use section 506(a) to bifurcate the mortgage into secured and unsecured portions and then modify the unsecured portion, or (2) section 1322(b)(2) prohibits the modification of any portion of the claim that is secured by the debtor's residence.

The Second Circuit followed prior cases, which held the former; that is, the debtor can strip down the lien and treat the undersecured portion as an unsecured lien. This was the first court of appeals decision after the Supreme Court's *Dewsnup* decision.

The court of appeals in *Bellamy* distinguished *Dewsnup* based on the facts and said that Code provisions other than section 506(a) were involved in the two cases. The court seemed to ignore the policy arguments made by the Supreme Court in *Dewsnup*.

The Supreme Court subsequently examined the issue in *Nobelman v. American Savings Bank*[388] and held that section 1322(b)(2) of the Bankruptcy Code prohibits a chapter 13 debtor from relying on section 506(a) to reduce an undersecured homestead mortgage to the fair market value of the mortgaged residence.

§ 5.51   Discharge of Environmental Claims

The Supreme Court, in *Ohio v. Kovacs*,[389] ruled that the environmental consent orders issued to an individual, which constitute requests for payment of money, are liabilities subject to discharge under section 727(b). According to the ruling, the discharge would not shield the individual from criminal prosecution and, if the clean-up order resulted in fines and penalties prior to bankruptcy, such claims are not dischargeable under section 523(a)(7).

The Supreme Court, in *In re Quanta Resource Corp.*,[390] upheld a Third Circuit decision[391] that would not allow Quanta to abandon two contaminated waste sites by using a balancing test that took into consideration the public interest. Thus, while section 554(a) of the Bankruptcy Code appears to give the trustee an unqualified right to abandon burdensome assets, the Third Circuit stated that "[i]f trustees in bankruptcy are to be permitted to dispose of hazardous waste under the cloak of the abandonment power, compliance with environmental protection laws will be transformed into government clean-up by default."[392]

---

[387] *Bellamy v. Federal Home Loan Mortgage Corp. (In re Bellamy)*, 962 F.2d 176 (2d Cir. 1992).
[388] 113 S. Ct. 2106 (1993).
[389] 105 S. Ct. 705 (1985).
[390] 106 S. Ct. 755 (1986).
[391] 739 F.2d 912 (3d Cir. 1984).
[392] *Id.* at 921.

These two decisions leave considerable uncertainty as to the extent to which bankruptcy laws can be used to avoid environmental responsibilities. *Kovacs* suggests that environmental consent orders, which constitute requests for the payment of money, are liabilities or claims and are therefore subject to discharge. On the other hand, the *Quanta* decision indicates that a trustee in bankruptcy may not abandon a toxic waste site in contravention of a state statute designed to protect the public health.

SIPC LIQUIDATION

§ 5.52   Introduction

A special type of liquidation for which accountants may render services is the liquidation of a stockbroker. The liquidation of a stockbroker or stock dealer is governed by the Securities Investor Protection Act of 1970 (SIPA), as amended, and by sections 741–752 of chapter 7 of the Bankruptcy Code. The Securities Investor Protection Corporation (SIPC) is responsible for the liquidation of a troubled stockbroker. The membership of SIPC—a nonprofit corporation—consists of all persons registered as brokers or dealers under section 15(b) of the Securities and Exchange Act of 1934. Through an annual assessment from its members, SIPC establishes a fund to cover the costs to customers of a stockbroker who is being liquidated.

Section 6(a) of the SIPA provides that the purpose of a SIPC liquidation proceeding is:

1   As promptly as possible after the appointment of a trustee in such liquidation proceeding, and in accordance with the provisions of this Act—

   A   to deliver customer name securities to or on behalf of the customers of the debtor entitled thereto as provided in section 8(c)(2); and

   B   to distribute customer property and (in advance thereof or concurrently therewith) otherwise satisfy net equity claims of customers to the extent provided in this section;

2   to sell or transfer offices and other productive units of the business of the debtor;

3   to enforce rights of subrogation as provided in this Act; and

4   to liquidate the business of the debtor.

§ 5.53   Determination of Need of Protection

The SEC or any other self-regulatory organization should notify SIPC if it becomes aware of facts that indicate a stockbroker may be having financial difficulty. Section 5(a) of the SIPA provides that SIPC may, upon notice to the member having financial difficulty, file an application for protective decree with a court of competent jurisdiction if it is determined by SIPC that:

1   A member of SIPC (or a member within 180 days prior to this determination) has failed or is in danger of failing to meet its obligations to customers and

2   One or more of the conditions necessary for the court to issue a protective decree exists.

Once the court receives the application from SIPC, it will issue a protective decree if the debtor consents to or fails to contest the application. If the application is contested, section 5(b) of the SIPA provides that the court—before it may issue the protective decree—must find that the debtor:

1   Is insolvent within the meaning of section 101 of title 11 of the U.S. Code or is unable to meet its obligations as they mature;
2   Is the subject of a proceeding pending in any court or before any agency of the United States or any State in which a receiver, trustee, or liquidator for such debtor has been appointed;
3   Is not in compliance with applicable requirements under the 1934 Act or rules of the SEC or any self-regulatory organization with respect to financial responsibility or hypothecation of customers' securities; or
4   Is unable to make such computations as may be necessary to establish compliance with such financial responsibility or hypothecation rules.

§ 5.54   Appointment of Trustee

As soon as the court issues a protective decree, a trustee is appointed to liquidate the broker or dealer. An attorney for the trustee is also appointed. The trustee and attorney may be associated with the same firm. In most cases, the trustee in an SIPC liquidation is an attorney, but accountants have also served in this capacity. The trustee is appointed by the court in which the protective decree is issued. The SIPC may appoint itself or one of its examiners as trustee when the unsecured general creditors and subordinated claims appear to total less than $750,000 and the debtor's customers appear to number fewer than 500.

§ 5.55   Bankruptcy Court Jurisdiction

Section 5(b)(4) of the SIPA provides that, once the protective decree has been issued and the trustee appointed, the liquidation proceeding is transferred to a bankruptcy court.

§ 5.56   Powers and Duties of Trustee

The trustee in a SIPC case has the same powers and rights as a trustee in a bankruptcy case. In addition, the trustee may, with the approval of SIPC but without any need for court approval:

Hire and fix the compensation of all personnel (including officers and employees of the debtor and of its examining authority) and other persons (including accountants) who are deemed by the trustee necessary for all or any purposes of a liquidation proceeding.

Utilize SIPC employees for all or any purposes of a liquidation proceeding.

Manage and maintain customer accounts of the debtor for the purposes of section 8(f).

The duties of the trustee are also similar to those in a chapter 7 liquidation case (see § 5.45), except that the trustee has no duty to reduce to money securities that are customer property or that are in the general estate of the debtor. Additionally, as provided in SIPA section 6(b), 6(c), and 6(d), the trustee is to:

1 Deliver securities to or on behalf of customers to the maximum extent practicable in satisfaction of customer claims for securities of the same class and series of an issuer.

2 Subject to the prior approval of SIPC but without any need for court approval, pay or guarantee all or any part of the indebtedness of the debtor to a bank, lender, or other person if the trustee determines that the aggregate market value of securities to be made available to the trustee upon the payment or guarantee of such indebtedness does not appear to be less than the total amount of such payment or guarantee.

3 Make to the court and to SIPC such written reports as may be required of a trustee in a case under chapter 7, and include in such reports information with respect to the progress made in distributing cash and securities to customers. The report should present fairly the results of the liquidation proceeding in accordance with section 17 of the Securities Exchange Act of 1934, taking into consideration the magnitude of items and transactions involved in connection with the operation of a dealer or broker.

4 Investigate the actions of the debtor. The trustee shall:
   a As soon as practicable, investigate the acts, conduct, property, liabilities, and financial condition of the debtor, the operation of its business, and any other matter, to the extent relevant to the liquidation proceeding, and report thereon to the court.
   b Examine, by deposition or otherwise, the directors and officers of the debtor and any other witness concerning any of the matters referred to in paragraph (a).
   c Report to the court any facts ascertained by the trustee with respect to fraud, misconduct, mismanagement, and irregularities, and any causes of action available to the estate.
   d As soon as practicable, prepare and submit to SIPC and to such other persons as the court designates, and in such form and manner as the court directs, a statement of the investigation of matters referred to in paragraph (a).

§ 5.57 Satisfaction of Claims

The key objective of the trustee is to satisfy customer accounts as quickly as possible and in an orderly manner. Claims of customers in a stockbroker liquidation are satisfied in one of two ways. If the records appear to be in reasonable order, the trustee may—with SIPC approval—transfer the customers' accounts to another broker. In connection with this transfer, the trustee may waive or modify the need to file a written statement of claim, and enter into an agreement with the broker receiving the accounts to cover shortages of cash or securities in customer accounts sold or transferred. SIPC funds are made available to cover any cash or security shortages.

The second approach involves direct settlement of accounts with the customers. A claim form is mailed to each customer. The amount shown on the stockbroker's books is compared with the proof of claim. Once these have been reconciled, a check and/or securities is sent to satisfy the customers' accounts. This approach takes much more time than the transfer of the customers' accounts to another broker. However, the direct settlement approach is generally used for the liquidation of small brokers or of brokers with very poor customer account records.

To provide for prompt payment and satisfaction of customer accounts, SIPC advances to the trustee funds for each customer (not to exceed $500,000) as may be required to pay or satisfy claims. Section 9(a) of the SIPA provides the following limitations:

1 If all or any portion of the net equity claim of a customer in excess of his or her ratable share of customer property is a claim for cash, as distinct from a claim for securities, the amount advanced to satisfy such claim for cash shall not exceed $100,000 for each such customer.

2 A customer who holds accounts with the debtor in separate capacities shall be deemed to be a different customer in each capacity.

3 If all or any portion of the net equity claim of a customer in excess of his or her ratable share of customer property is satisfied by the delivery of securities purchased by the trustee to satisfy claims for net equities, the securities so purchased shall be valued as of the filing date for purposes of applying the dollar limitations of this subsection.

4 No advance shall be made by SIPC to the trustee to pay or otherwise satisfy, directly or indirectly, any net equity claim of a customer who is a general partner, officer, or director of the debtor, a beneficial owner of 5 percent or more of any class of equity security of the debtor (other than a nonconvertible stock having fixed preferential dividend and liquidation rights), a limited partner with a participation of 5 percent or more in the net assets or net profits of the debtor, or a person who, directly or indirectly and through agreement or otherwise, exercised or had the power to exercise a controlling influence over the management or policies of the debtor.

5 No advance shall be made by SIPC to the trustee to pay or otherwise satisfy any net equity claim of any customer who is a broker or dealer or bank, other than to the extent that it shall be established to the satisfaction of the trustee that the net equity claim of such broker or dealer or bank against the debtor arose out of transactions for customers of such broker or dealer or bank, in which event each such customer of such broker or dealer or bank shall be deemed a separate customer of the debtor.

In addition, SIPC may advance funds to complete the close-outs as of the filing date that are allowed by SIPC rules and to cover administrative expenses to the extent the general estate of the debtor is not sufficient to pay them.

6

Rehabilitation Proceedings under the Bankruptcy Code

§ 6.1 Introduction

Bankruptcy court proceedings are generally the last resort for the debtor whose financial condition has deteriorated to the point where it is impossible to acquire additional funds. When the debtor finally agrees that bankruptcy court proceedings are necessary, the liquidation value of the assets often represents only a small fraction of the debtor's total liabilities. If the business is liquidated, the creditors get only a small percentage of their claims. The debtor is discharged of its debts and is free to start over; however, the business is lost and so are all the assets. Normally, liquidation proceedings result in serious losses to the debtor, the creditor, and the business community. Arrangement proceedings were enacted in 1938, as a part of the Chandler Act, to reduce these losses. When the Bankruptcy Code of 1978 went into effect, it combined the arrangement proceedings of Chapter XI with real property arrangements under Chapter XII and Chapter X corporate reorganizations into one rehabilitation chapter known as chapter 11 reorganization.

A timely filed chapter 11 petition can give the debtor an opportunity to reorganize its business, provide a larger payment to creditors than would have been received in a liquidation, eliminate the unprofitable aspects of the business, focus on that part of the business that can be profitable, preserve the jobs for its employees, and emerge from chapter 11 as a very competitive, viable business.

This chapter describes in summary form the provisions of chapter 11 of the Bankruptcy Code and briefly discusses chapters 12 and 13.

§ 6.2 Purpose of Chapter 11

Under the Bankruptcy Reform Act, chapter 11 is designed to accomplish the same objective as Chapters VIII, X, XI, and XII of prior law: provide the debtor with court protection, allow the debtor (or trustee) to continue the operations of the business while a plan is being developed, and minimize the substantial economic losses associated with liquidations. The new chapter 11 attempts to provide for the flexibility of prior Chapter XI, yet it contains several of the protective provisions of prior Chapter X. It is designed to allow the debtor to use different procedures, depending on the nature of the debtor's problems and the needs of the creditors. Agreements under this chapter can affect unsecured creditors, secured creditors, and stockholders. It would, however, be expected that an agreement that would affect only unsecured creditors, which could have been arranged under prior law, could still be resolved under the Bankruptcy Code in a similar manner. The more complicated cases, requiring adjustment of widely held claims, secured creditors' claims, and stockholders' interest in a public case, can also be resolved under chapter 11. Chapter 11 of the Bankruptcy Code provides a basis for these public cases to be resolved without necessarily going through the formal process of determining the going-concern values of the business and the extent to which various classes of creditors and stockholders can participate in the plan. The Reform Act was designed to prevent some of the uncertainty connected with whether proceedings could remain in Chapter XI or be forced into Chapter X, and to avoid unnecessary litigation cost to determine the specific chapter under which a case should proceed.

OPERATING UNDER CHAPTER 11

§ 6.3 Role of the Court

As noted in Chapter 5, a voluntary or involuntary petition can be filed in chapter 11. Upon the filing of an involuntary petition, the court may, on request of an interested party, appoint a trustee. This appointment is not mandatory and the debtor may, in fact, continue to operate the business as if a bankruptcy petition had not been filed, except that certain transfers may be avoided under section 549(a) of the Bankruptcy Code. If the creditors prove the allegations set forth in the involuntary petition, an order for relief is entered and the case will then proceed in a manner identical to a voluntary case.[1]

One of the major changes of the Bankruptcy Code was to relieve bankruptcy judges of administrative functions and let their primary function be to settle disputes. The 1986 amendments to the Bankruptcy Code expanded the U.S. trustee pilot program, established in 1979, to all areas except Alabama and North Carolina. Thus, as the U.S. trustee system became operational in each of 21 regions, the judges will be relieved of administrative duties and completely free to adjudicate disputes.

Many chapter 11 cases have taken much longer than some have considered necessary to reorganize. As a result, these cases have incurred substantial administrative expenses. The Bankruptcy Reform Act of 1994 attempts to resolve some of the causes of this delay by providing for status conferences by the bankruptcy judge. Section 105 of the Bankruptcy Code provides that the bankruptcy court, or any part in interest, may move for a status conference and issue an order to facilitate the case's being handled expeditiously. A date may be established for the debtor to accept or reject executory contracts and leases. The Bankruptcy Reform Act of 1994 also modifies section 105 of the Bankruptcy Code to provide that, in a chapter 11 case, the court may:

---

[1] J. Ronald Trost, "Business Reorganization under Chapter 11 of the New Bankruptcy Code," *Business Lawyer*, Vol. 34 (April 1979), p. 1313.

1   Set the date for the trustee or debtor to file the disclosure statement and plan.

2   Set the date by which the trustee or debtor must solicit acceptances of the plan.

3   Set the date for which a party in interest may file a plan.

4   Set the date for which a proponent, other than a debtor, must solicit acceptance of a plan.

5   Fix the scope and format of the notice for the hearing for approval of the disclosure statement.

6   Provide that the hearing on the disclosure statement may be combined with the hearing for the confirmation of the plan.

§ 6.4   U.S. Trustee Administration

In the federal districts, except those in Alabama and North Carolina, the U.S. trustee is responsible for the administration of cases. They will appoint the committees of creditors with unsecured claims and also appoint any other committees of creditors or stockholders authorized by the court. If the court deems it necessary to appoint a trustee or examiner, the U.S. trustee makes this appointment (subject to court approval) and may also petition the court to authorize such an appointment. See § 5.19 for a more detailed discussion of the functions performed by the U.S. trustee.

§ 6.5   Consolidation of Chapter 11 Petitions

An issue that often arises when a corporation has several subsidiaries, or several corporations have common ownership, is whether these companies should be consolidated. In general, proceedings may be substantively consolidated or consolidated for administrative purposes only.

(a) Substantive Consolidation

Under substantive consolidation, the assets and liabilities of different juridical entities are consolidated as if the assets and liabilities were those of a single entity.[2] Generally, included in substantive consolidation is a request that (1) all claims of each individual case be considered those of the consolidated class, (2) all duplicate claims filed with more than one individual case be removed, (3) all intercompany claims be disallowed, (4) a single set of schedules be filed, and (5) one consolidated plan be proposed.[3] Because the Bankruptcy Code does not contain a specific provision for substantive consolidation, authority is derived from section 105(a), which allows the court to issue any order, process, or judgment necessary to carry out the provisions of the Code. Because of all of the procedural problems and the potential inequities found when one creditor group must share with another, substantive consolidation is an unusual occurrence.

---

[2] *Collier Bankruptcy Manual,* 3d ed., ¶ 1100.06[1].
[3] *Id.*

The most common use of substantive consolidation is by affiliated debtor corporations.[4] Situations that tend to suggest that consolidation is justified include:

1 Creditors of the affiliates acted as though there was one economic unit and did not rely on separate entities in extending credit.
2 Activities of the affiliates are so entangled that it is too costly to deal with them separately.
3 The separate legal identities of affiliates have not been preserved.
4 The creditors of any single affiliate are not significantly harmed from substantive consolidation.

It is also possible to consolidate the debtor and nondebtor corporations, especially where assets were transferred for the purpose of hindering, delaying, and defrauding creditors.[5] However, it is more difficult to obtain an order for substantive consolidation where some of the affiliates have not filed a petition. A more common occurrence is action to recover the assets that were fraudulently transferred, under the provisions of section 544 or 548.

Often, debtor corporations may find it much easier to file a consolidation plan of reorganization: the debtors request that the creditors approve the substantive consolidation of the affiliated corporations. Unless the plan receives unanimous approval, the court will still have to look at the substantive consolidation issue. For example, the court must at least determine that creditors not approving the plan receive as much as would be received in a chapter 7 liquidation of the respective debtor entities.[6]

Court decisions suggest that the proponents of substantive consolidation must establish that there is a need for substantive consolidation and that the benefits outweigh the harm that may be experienced by objecting creditors. For example, the Second Circuit, in *In re Augie/Restivo Baking Co., Ltd.*,[7] would not allow substantive consolidation where it was determined that an unsecured creditor that relied on separate credit of one entity would have been prejudiced on its deficiency claim as a result of the consolidation. The court noted that, when an objecting creditor relies on separate credit and financial condition of an entity in extending credit, that creditor is generally entitled to the distribution that would be received for the entity's separate assets without consolidation, unless the financial affairs of the entity are so "hopelessly commingled" with others that the attempt to unscramble them threatens the realization of any net assets for the benefit of all creditors, or no accurate identification or allocation of assets is possible.

In a Tenth Circuit case based on the Bankruptcy Act, the order allowing the consolidation was reversed, even though there were control and accounting difficulties, because creditors relied on the separate credit of one entity.[8] However, the First Circuit approved a consolidation of chapter 7 estates when it

[4] *Id.*
[5] *Sampsell v. Imperial Paper Corp.*, 313 U.S. 215 (1941).
[6] 11 U.S.C. § 1129(a)(7).
[7] 860 F.2d 515 (2d Cir. 1988).
[8] *In re Gulfco Investment Corp.*, 539 F.2d 921 (10th Cir. 1979).

was determined, on balance, that substantive consolidation fostered a net benefit among creditors.[9]

In *In re Vecco Construction Industries, Inc.,*[10] the bankruptcy court listed seven factors that might be applied when weighing the equities to determine whether a case should be consolidated:

1 The difficulty of segregating and ascertaining the individual assets and liabilities of each corporation;
2 The presence or absence of consolidated financial statements;
3 The profitability of consolidation at a single physical location;
4 The commingling of assets and business functions;
5 The unity of interests and ownership between the various corporate entities;
6 The existence of intercorporate guaranties of loans;
7 The transfer of assets without formal observance of corporate formalities.

Poulin-Kloehr and Feldstein[11] noted that several decisions have characterized the applicable standard as a "balancing test" where the party seeking the substantive consolidation must show that any prejudice resulting from consolidation is outweighed by greater prejudice in its absence.[12]

Poulin-Kloehr and Feldstein[13] described the effects of substantive consolidation:

1 *Elimination of duplicate claims.* A creditor is allowed only one claim against the consolidated estates, even where more than one debtor was liable, either primarily or by way of a guaranty on the debt. Without substantive consolidation, creditors may be allowed more than one claim where debts were cross-collateralized or guaranteed by another entity.
2 *Elimination of intercorporate liabilities.* All intercompany accounts and obligations, as well as continuing obligations under intercompany leases and agreements, are eliminated.
3 *Pooling of assets and liabilities.* All assets of all debtors become available for distribution to all creditors of all debtors, which facilitates classification of claims under a plan.
4 *Expansion of "reach back" periods for avoiding power actions.* Transfers made by all debtors for the preference and fraudulent transfer periods, measured from the earliest filed case, can be examined.

---

[9] *In re Hemingway Transport, Inc.,* 954 F.2d 1 (1st Cir. 1992).
[10] 4 B.R. 407, 410 (Bankr. E.D. Va. 1980).
[11] L. Poulin-Kloehr and H. R. Feldstein, "Substantive Consolidation," *Proceedings of 9th Annual Reorganization and Bankruptcy Conference* (Westlake Village, CA: Association of Insolvency Accountants, 1993), p. 3.
[12] *In re Hemingway Transport, Inc.,* 954 F.2d 1 (1st Cir. 1992); *In re Tureaud,* 59 B.R. 973, 976 (N.D. Okla. 1986); *Holywell Corp. v. Bank of New York,* 59 B.R. 340, 347 (S.D. Fla. 1986); *In re DRW Property Co.,* 54 B.R. 489, 495 (Bankr. N.D. Tex. 1985).
[13] *Supra* note 11 at 4.

5 *Elimination of certain avoiding power actions.* Provision of "new value" or "fair consideration" to one debtor entity becomes a defense to an action by another debtor entity to avoid a transfer.

In Volume 2 of *Bankruptcy and Insolvency Accounting,* 6.1 provides a checklist for determining the extent to which substantive consolidation may be appropriate. The checklist deals with the financial and management issues as well as the legal factors to consider when deciding whether an effort should be made for substantive consolidation of the entities in chapter 11.

(b) Administrative Consolidation

If substantive consolidation is not feasible, the case may be consolidated for administrative purposes. A single docket is used, for example, for the parent and its filed subsidiaries, for matters occurring in the administration of the estate, including the filing of claims, combining of notices mailed to creditors, and other purely administrative matters, to expedite the case. Administrative consolidation does not in any way impact the rights of creditors.

§ 6.6 Creditors' and Equity Holders' Committees

Section 1102 of the Bankruptcy Code provides that a committee of creditors holding unsecured claims shall be appointed as soon as practicable after the order for relief is granted. The trustee has the responsibility for appointing the committee without any authorization from the court (section 1102(a)).

Section 1102 provides that, on the request of a party-in-interest, the court may order the U.S. trustee to appoint additional members to the creditors' committee or equity security holders' committee.

(a) Creditors' Committee

The unsecured creditors' committee will ordinarily consist of the seven largest creditors willing to serve, or, if a committee was organized before the order for relief, such committee may continue provided it was fairly chosen and is representative of the different kinds of claims to be represented. Under prior law, the creditors elected their own committee. At times, this election process was quite controversial, primarily because creditors or their legal representatives attempted to serve their own personal interests. The requirement that the court appoint the creditors' committee eliminated the problems associated with electing a committee.

Note that section 1102(b) of the Bankruptcy Code states that the committee "shall ordinarily consist of . . . ," thus leaving some discretion to the U.S. trustee so that a committee can be selected that will be willing to serve. The committee would not necessarily have to consist of seven members if a small committee would be more efficient in the existing circumstances. In other cases, the U.S. trustee might find it necessary to appoint a committee larger than seven members, to be sure that the interests of all of the unsecured creditors are properly represented on the committee. In *In re A. H. Robins Com-*

pany,[14] the district court indicated that the size of the creditors' committee is immaterial in determining whether statutory requirements of representativeness are satisfied under section 1102 (b)(1).

Section 1102(b) of the Bankruptcy Code provides that persons are to be appointed to the committee. Prior to the Bankruptcy Reform Act of 1994, a person was defined in section 101(41) of the Bankruptcy Code to include individuals, partnerships, and corporations, and to exclude governmental units, unless a governmental unit acquired the assets from a person as a result of a loan guarantee agreement or as a receiver or liquidating agent of a person. Effective for petitions filed after October 22, 1994, the Bankruptcy Reform Act of 1994 modified section 101(41) of the Bankruptcy Code to allow the Pension Benefit Guaranty Corporation and state employee pension funds to be considered persons for the purposes of section 1102 of the Bankruptcy Code. As a result of this amendment, representatives from these organizations will be allowed to serve on chapter 11 creditors' committees or equity holders' committees.

An unsecured creditor that is a competitor of the debtor may not be appointed to the committee, even though it may be one of the 20 largest creditors.[15]

The Third Circuit, in *In re Altair Airlines, Inc.,*[16] held that the collective bargaining representative had a right to payment of unpaid wages within the meaning of a claim under section 101(4). Thus, the pilots' association, which was the exclusive bargaining agent for the pilots employed by the debtor, was entitled to appointment to the unsecured creditors' committee.

The Bankruptcy Code does not set forth any requirements that must be met to satisfy the condition that a previously elected committee may continue only if fairly chosen. Rule 2007 does suggest that the conditions necessary for the committee to continue may consist of the following:

1   The committee was selected by majority in number and amount of unsecured creditors at a meeting where creditors with claims over $1,000, or the 100 largest unsecured creditors, had at least five days' notice in writing, and written minutes of the meeting reporting the names of creditors present or represented were kept and were available for inspection.

2   All proxies voted were solicited in accordance with the conditions of Rule 2006, and the lists and statements (for example, a statement that no consideration has been paid or promised by the proxyholder for the proxy) of subdivision (e) thereof have been transmitted to the U.S. trustee.

3   The organization of the committee was in all other respects fair and proper.

Although the requirement is that the committee must consist of creditors with unsecured claims, this does not prohibit the U.S. trustee from appointing

---

[14] 65 B.R. 160 (E.D. Va. 1986).

[15] *See In re Wilson Foods Corporation,* 31 B.R. 272 (Bankr. W.D. Okla. 1983).

[16] 727 F.2d 88 (3d Cir. 1984).

one or more persons to the committee who have both secured and unsecured claims. If some of the unsecured creditors object to the fact that there are too many creditors on the committee who also hold secured claims, they could petition the court to change the composition of the committee. Under section 1102(a) of the Bankruptcy Code, the U.S. trustee may also appoint additional committees of creditors and of equity security holders as the U.S. trustee deems appropriate or as the court may order based on the request of a party-in-interest. In small cases, only one committee may be necessary, but, for large companies that are publicly held, some may argue that there is a need for several committees.

The appointment of a single unsecured committee is considered by some courts to be the norm.[17] Because of the cost associated with the operation of more than one committee, some judges have refused to appoint more than one unsecured committee. For the purpose of developing a plan and getting its acceptance, one committee may be an advantage. For example, having one committee that has representatives from the trade, senior bondholders, junior bondholders, undersecured creditors, and other classes of creditors may result in these groups' discussing plan issues with each other much earlier, because they are on the same committee. Thus, rather than having the committees meet separately for an extended time period and then having representatives from the committee negotiate a plan, the members of the single committee are forced to deal with some of the plan issues much earlier and may reach a decision sooner than would otherwise be possible.

The appointment of one committee rather than several will generally result in fewer professional fees.

Once the committee has been appointed, the official relationship of the U.S. trustee ends, because the Bankruptcy Code does not provide that the U.S. trustee is to supervise the activities of the committee. The U.S. trustee is, however, responsible for the administration of the case and of the trustee (where one is appointed) in chapter 11 cases. Thus, if the U.S. trustee ascertains that a committee is not functioning properly or that one or more members of the committee are not representing the creditors as a whole but are interested only in serving their own interests, he or she may take a more active role in evaluating the debtor's operations or even remove the member from the committee and exercise the option to replace that member. The amendments to the Bankruptcy Code in 1986 deleted section 1102(c), which gave the bankruptcy judge authority to remove a member from the committee, and left that authority with the U.S. trustee. In *In re Wheeler Technology, Inc.*,[18] the Ninth Circuit Bankruptcy Appellate Panel (BAP) held that the bankruptcy court could not use section 105(a) of the Bankruptcy Code to circumvent the congressional intent to leave decisions regarding committee membership to the U.S. trustee. Other bankruptcy courts, however, continue to review the appointments of committee members.[19]

---

[17] *In re* Transworld Airlines, Inc., 22 Bank. Ct. Dec. (CRR) 1236 (Bankr. D. Del. 1992); *In re Sharon Steel Corp.*, 100 B.R. 767 (Bankr. W.D. Pa. 1989).
[18] 139 B.R. 235 (9th Cir. BAP 1992).
[19] *See, e.g., In re Plabell Rubber Products*, 140 B.R. 179 (N.D. Ohio 1992).

It would not be expected that the U.S. trustee would take action to change the nature of the committee when he or she merely disagrees with the decisions and actions of the committee. The responsibility that the U.S. trustee has for the administration of the case can be relaxed to some extent when one or more committees are actively functioning. In fact, the committee or committees share the U.S. trustee's role in the administration of the case and in seeing that the debtor's operations are properly controlled.

Members of the creditors' committee are not paid for serving on the committee. However, the cost of food, lodging, and transportation for individual members of the official creditors' committee is considered an administrative expense and is subject to reimbursement under Rule 2016.

Section 1103 of the Bankruptcy Code, as originally passed, did not deal with the question of whether the committee or its members are to receive reimbursement from the estate for expenses incurred while performing committee duties. Section 330 does not authorize the reimbursement of such expenses. The provisions of section 503 expressly excluded expenses incurred by an official chapter 11 creditors' committee. However, the Advisory Committee Note to Bankruptcy Rule 2016(a) indicates that a committee, or its members, may seek reimbursement of expenses. However, the Bankruptcy Reform Act of 1994 amended section 503(b)(3)(F) of the Bankruptcy Code to provide that a member of a committee appointed under section 1102 of the Bankruptcy Code may be reimbursed for actual, necessary expenses incurred in the performance of duties of the committee. The reimbursement for expenses would apply to all committees appointed, including equity holders' committees. Most courts previously approved the requests for reimbursement of expenses by the members of the committee, but there was no provision in the Bankruptcy Code that specifically provided for the reimbursement.

The reported cases prior to the 1994 amendment, as would be expected, are split on this issue. An American Bankruptcy Institute (ABI) survey[20] noted that the cases break down into three basic areas of authority. First, many cases emphasize the exclusionary clause of section 503, or the lack of express authority for reimbursement. Leading this group is *In re UNR Industries*,[21] a case that relied on the absence of any authority for such reimbursement in section 1103 and 330 as justification for not allowing any such expense.

The second area of authority involves cases that allowed reimbursement but required a showing that the committee or its members made a "substantial contribution" to the case. The "substantial contribution" standard eliminated reimbursements for routine committee functions.

The third approach allowed reimbursement of committee expenses without showing "substantial contribution" in the case. The courts used many methods of reasoning to come to this conclusion, but usually relied on policy considerations, as the Sixth Circuit did in *In re George Worthington Co.*[22]

---

[20] American Bankruptcy Institute, *National Report on Professional Compensation in Bankruptcy Cases* (Washington, DC: American Bankruptcy Institute, 1991), p. 218–221.

[21] 736 F.2d 1136 (7th Cir. 1986).

[22] 921 F.2d 626 (6th Cir. 1990).

(b) Equity Security Holders' Committee

As mentioned above, section 1102(a)(2) of the Bankruptcy Code provides that the court may authorize the appointment of an equity security holders' committee. Section 1102(b)(2) states that the committee, appointed by the U.S. trustee, shall ordinarily consist of the persons, willing to serve, who hold the seven largest amounts of equity securities (of the kind represented on the committee) of the debtor. More than one equity security holders' committee may be appointed where more than one class of stock (such as preferred and common) is involved.

Recently, the courts have been reluctant to authorize the appointment of a committee of equity security holders. Some courts elect not to authorize such an appointment in order to keep the costs for professional services at a minimum. In general, courts may find it difficult to justify the appointment of such a committee when the debtor is insolvent because, technically, the equity security holders are not required to be party to the proceedings. Even in a cram down, they may not receive any consideration when the debtor is insolvent. For example, in *In re Wang Laboratories, Inc.*, the bankruptcy court held that the court should not generally appoint an equity security holders' committee when the debtor was hopelessly insolvent.[23]

§ 6.7 Appointment or Election of Trustee

The new law provides that a trustee can be appointed or elected in certain situations based on the facts in the case and not related to the size of the company or the amount of unsecured debt outstanding. The trustee is appointed or elected only at the request of a party-in-interest after a notice and hearing. A party-in-interest includes the debtor, the trustee (in other contexts), creditors' or stockholders' committees, creditors, stockholders, or indenture trustees.[24] A U.S. trustee, although not a party-in-interest, may petition the court for an appointment of a trustee.[25] The SEC may also be heard on the issue (but has no right of appeal) and could thus express its desires about the appointment of a trustee.[26]

Section 1104 provides that the U.S. trustee can request the court to order the appointment of a trustee or an examiner. If the court orders such an appointment, then the U.S. trustee, after consultation with parties-in-interest and subject to court approval, will appoint a trustee (unless one is elected by the creditors) or an examiner. The U.S. trustee will also appoint another trustee or examiner if the previously appointed trustee dies, resigns, or is removed.

The Bankruptcy Reform Act of 1994 provides, for petitions filed after October 22, 1994, that in a chapter 11 case the creditors may elect a trustee. On the request of a party in interest, within 30 days after the court orders the appoint-

---

[23] 149 B.R. 1 (Bankr. D. Mass. 1992); *see In re Emons Industries, Inc.*, 50 B.R. 692 (Bankr. S.D.N.Y. 1985).
[24] 11 U.S.C. § 1109(b).
[25] *Id.*, § 1104(a).
[26] *Id.*, § 1109(a).

ment of a trustee, the U.S. trustee is to convene a meeting of creditors for the purpose of electing one disinterested person to serve as the trustee. The election is conducted in the same manner as for a chapter 7 trustee. Creditors that (1) hold an allowable, undisputed, fixed, liquidated, unsecured claim; (2) do not have an interest that is materially adverse, other than an equity interest that is not substantial in relation to such creditor's interest; and (3) are not insiders, may vote in the election. To be elected, a trustee must receive a majority of the votes from those that were entitled to vote and did indeed vote. At least 20 percent of the holders of the dollar amount of the unsecured claim described above must vote in the election. If a trustee is not elected, the interim trustee will serve as the trustee. Creditors that previously would not have moved for the appointment of a trustee, primarily because of the uncertainty as to the trustee that might be appointed by the U.S. trustee, may more actively push for such an appointment because they can elect the trustee that will serve. Most of the U.S. trustees will now consult with the creditors prior to appointing a chapter 11 trustee, to be sure that the trustee appointed is acceptable to the creditors and to minimize the number of chapter 11 trustees that are elected to replace interim trustees. In one case a representative from the office of the U.S. trustee attended presentations made by professionals seeking the appointment of trustee to a group of creditors.

In *In re Plaza De Diego Shopping Center,*[27] the First Circuit reversed a district court decision that had held that the court had the right to instruct the U.S. trustee to present to the court three individuals to be appointed as trustees. Section 1104(c) provides that if the court orders the appointment of a trustee or examiner, then the U.S. trustee, after consultation with the parties-in-interest, shall appoint, subject to the court's approval, one disinterested person other than the U.S. trustee to serve as trustee in the case. The district court concluded that this section is not meant to preclude the submission of more than one qualified candidate so as to expedite the procedure in a particularly urgent case. On reversal, the First Circuit stated that the plain meaning of this language, its legislative history, and the interpretation given to this provision by the courts all dictate a reversal of the district court's decision. The court also found that the bankruptcy court's equity powers under section 1104(c) are insufficient to provide an independent ground for affirming the district court's order. The First Circuit noted that the 1978 legislative history[28] showed that Congress had decided to shift the power of appointment from judges to the U.S. trustees for two reasons: (1) to free bankruptcy judges from burdensome administrative tasks and, more importantly, (2) to avoid the possibility or appearance of a conflict of interest necessarily arising when a judge must decide matters litigated between a trustee of his or her own selection and other parties to the bankruptcy.

The court can order the appointment of the trustee for cause or if the appointment is in the best interest of the creditors, stockholders, or any other interests of the estate. Section 1104(a) states that a trustee is to be appointed:

1   For cause, including fraud, dishonesty, incompetence, or gross misman-
    agement of the affairs of the debtor by current management, either before

---

[27] 911 F.2d 820 (1st Cir. 1990).
[28] H.R. Rep. No. 595, 95th Cong., 2d Sess. 88–89 (1978).

or after the commencement of the case, or similar cause, but not including the number of holders of securities of the debtor or the amount of assets or liabilities of the debtor; or

2 If such appointment is in the interests of creditors, any equity security holders, and other interests of the estate, without regard to the number of holders of securities of the debtor or the amount of assets or liabilities of the debtor.

The Third Circuit held that extreme acrimony between the debtor-in-possession and a major creditor was cause for the appointment of a neutral trustee to facilitate reorganization.[29]

In *In re Sidco, Inc.*,[30] the court noted that a debtor-in-possession is unlikely to take any action contrary to the interest of its principal or principals, and that the conduct of the debtor's attorney will reflect that reality. The court concluded that the relationship between a debtor-in-possession and its principals is best addressed by considering whether a trustee should be appointed. The appointment of a trustee is also appropriate when the board of directors or the partners of a debtor are at an impasse.[31]

The U.S. trustee is responsible for the appointment of the trustee from a panel of qualified trustees, once the appointment has been authorized by the court. It would also appear that the U.S. trustee would have the right, subject to court approval, to replace trustees who fail to perform their functions properly.

The legislative history recognized the inefficiency of requiring a trustee in every case because of the need for the trustee to learn the business. During this time of learning, the business is without real guidance at a time that is most important for the business's survival. Unless there is some tangible contrary reason, the debtor should be allowed to operate the business during the period when the plan is being developed.[32] Even in some of the larger cases where there has been mismanagement, there may not be a need to appoint a trustee if the corporation has obtained new management.[33] Under these conditions, if any appointment is necessary, an examiner might be most appropriate.

The following duties of the trustee for a chapter 7 case are also required in chapter 11 proceedings:

1 Be accountable for all property received.

2 If a purpose would be served, examine proofs of claims and object where a claim is improper.

3 Unless the court directs otherwise, furnish the information requested by a party-in-interest concerning the estate and the estate's administration.

4 File, with the court and taxing authorities, periodic reports and summaries of the operation of the business, including a statement of cash receipts and disbursements and other information required by the court.

---

[29] *In re Marvel Entertainment Group, Inc.* 140 F.3d 463 (3d Cir. 1998). *See also In re Cajun Elec. Power Coop.* 74 F.3d 599 (5th Cir. 1996) *cert. denied*, 117 S. Ct. 51 (1966).

[30] 162 B.R. 299 (Bankr. E.D. Cal. 1993).

[31] 156 B.R. 525 (Bankr. E.D. La. 1993).

[32] H.R. Rep. No. 95-595, 95th Cong., 1st Sess. 233 (1977).

[33] *But see In re La Sherene, Inc.*, 3 B.R. 169 (Bankr. N.D. Ga. 1980).

5 Make a final report and file a final account of the administration of the estate with the court.

Other duties of the chapter 11 trustee are:

1 File the list of creditors, schedules, and statements required with or subsequent to the filing of the petition, if not previously filed.
2 Unless the court orders otherwise, investigate the acts, conduct, assets, liabilities, and financial condition of the debtor, the operation of the debtor's business, the desirability of the continuation of the business, and any other matter relevant to the case or to the formulation of a plan.
3 As soon as practicable, file a statement of the investigation conducted, including any fact ascertained pertaining to fraud, dishonesty, incompetence, misconduct, mismanagement, or irregularity in the management of the affairs of the debtor, or to a cause of action available to the estate, and transmit a copy or a summary of any such statement to any creditors' committee or equity security holders' committee, to any indenture trustee, and to such other entity as the court designates.
4 As soon as practicable, file a plan, file a report of why the trustee will not file a plan, or recommend conversion of the case to a case under chapter 7, chapter 12, or chapter 13 of this title, or dismissal of the case.
5 File tax returns and information required by taxing authorities.
6 After confirmation of a plan, file such reports as are necessary or as the court orders.

§ 6.8 Appointment of Examiner

Under the Bankruptcy Code, the trustee performs two major functions: (1) operating the business and (2) conducting an investigation of the debtor's affairs. Under certain conditions, it may be best to leave the current management in charge of the business without resolving the need for the investigation of the debtor. The Code provides for the appointment of an examiner to perform this function. Section 1104(b) states that, if a trustee is not appointed:

> . . . [O]n request of a party in interest, and after notice and a hearing, the court shall order the appointment of an examiner to conduct such an investigation of the debtor as is appropriate, including an investigation of any allegations of fraud, dishonesty, incompetence, misconduct, mismanagement, or irregularity in the management of the affairs of the debtor of or by current or former management of the debtor, if—
>
> 1 such appointment is in the interests of creditors, any equity security holders, and other interests of the estate; or
>
> 2 the debtor's fixed, liquidated, unsecured debts, other than debts for goods, services, or taxes, or owing to an insider, exceed $5 million.

Note that, in the second situation (unsecured debts exceed $5 million), the court has no discretion; an examiner must be appointed upon request. However, in *In re Shelter Resources*,[34] the court refused to appoint an examiner even though the unsecured debt exceeded $5 million because such appointment would cause undue delay in the administration of the estate. Also, the court felt the appointment would most likely cause the debtor to incur substantial and unnecessary costs, detrimental to the interest of creditors and other parties-in-interest.

In *In re Rutenberg*,[35] the court refused to appoint an examiner even though it was apparently mandatory under section 1104(b)(2) of the Bankruptcy Code. When the debtor made the request, the court perceived it as a delaying tactic.

In *In re Revco D.S., Inc.*,[36] the bankruptcy court refused to appoint an examiner even though the liabilities of Revco exceeded $5 million. The Sixth Circuit, concluding that section 1104(b)(2) requires the appointment of an examiner, reversed the decision of the bankruptcy court.

Any party in interest, including the debtor, may petition the court for the appointment of an examiner under section 1104(b) of the Bankruptcy Code. The appointment of an examiner is not dependent on the bankruptcy court's refusal to appoint a trustee.[37]

The phrase "other than debts for goods, services, or taxes" leaves debts owing to institutions or public debt as those that count. "Goods" refers to inventory and not "goods" in an economic sense. The U.S. trustee will appoint the examiner subject to court approval. Section 321(b) states that an examiner cannot serve as a trustee in the same case or, if the chapter 11 petition is converted to a chapter 7 petition, in the converted chapter case. Also, section 327(f) provides that the trustee (debtor-in-possession) may not employ a person who served as an examiner in the case.

Considerable discussion has centered around who can be appointed as examiner. The Bankruptcy Code does not state who may serve, nor does it provide for the examiner to retain professionals such as attorneys or accountants and financial advisors. Based on the functions to be performed by the examiner, it would appear that accountants would be the most logical choice for this position, because most of the investigation centers around financial information (§ 8.21). Several accountants and financial advisors have been appointed as examiners. In some districts, the percentage of accountants and financial advisors used is much higher than in others. However, in most districts, attorneys still continue to be appointed much more frequently than accountants and financial advisors.

The examiner's scope of examination is broader than civil discovery under Rule 2004. The examination may be as broad as appears proper to the examiner. The information collected by the examiner is not available to the public until it is filed with the court or emerges in judicial documents in some other way.[38]

The function of the examiner is to conduct an investigation into the actions of the debtor—including fraud, dishonesty, mismanagement of the financial

---

[34] 35 B.R. 304 (Bankr. N.D. Ohio 1983).
[35] 58 B.R. 230 (Bankr. M.D. Fla. 1993).
[36] 898 F.2d 498 (6th Cir. 1990).
[37] *In re Keene Corp.*, 164 B.R. 844 (Bankr. S.D.N.Y. 1994).
[38] *In re Ionosphere Clubs, Inc.*, 156 B.R. 414 (S.D.N.Y. 1993).

condition of the debtor, and of the operation of the business—and the desirability of the continuation of the business. The report is to be filed with the court and given to any creditors' committee, stockholders' committees, or other entities designated by the court. These duplicate two of the functions of the trustee (§ 6.7). In addition to these two provisions, section 1106(b) states that an examiner may perform other functions as directed by the court. In some cases, the court has expanded the role of the examiner. For example, the bankruptcy judges may prefer to see additional controls exercised over the management of the debtor, but may not see the need to incur the costs of the appointment of a trustee. These functions are assigned to the examiner.

The court in *In re John Peterson Motors, Inc.*[39] ruled that if the bankruptcy court finds that there are sufficient grounds to appoint a trustee but decides that the appointment would be unfair to the debtor, then an examiner may be appointed to carry out all of the functions of a trustee except those that the court elects to leave with the debtor. If, after the investigation and related report of the examiner, the court authorizes the appointment of a trustee, the examiner could not be appointed as the trustee because section 327(f) precludes a party serving as an examiner from subsequently being appointed as the trustee. In *In re International Distribution Centers, Inc.*,[40] the district court reversed the bankruptcy court's approval to expand the role of the examiner. The bankruptcy court ordered the appointment of an examiner after the creditors' committee had moved for the appointment of a trustee. Subsequent to the appointment of the examiner, the creditors' committee (joined by the U.S. trustee) filed an oral application for the examiner's powers to be expanded to encompass those of a trustee. The court granted the application and specifically delegated to the examiner the powers of the trustee. Although the court realized the need to fashion the examiner's powers as circumstances require, it stated that to render the examiner a "pseudo-trustee" is beyond the bankruptcy court's discretion.

Thus, it would appear that the role of the examiner may be expanded by the court, but such expansion may be successfully challenged where the court completely assigns to the examiner the powers of the trustee or where the expansion is made after the examiner's report is issued.

Another role of the examiner that should be given careful consideration is the use of the examiner as a mediator. In *In re Public Service Company of New Hampshire*,[41] the court appointed an examiner to foster plan negotiations after exclusivity had been terminated and it appeared that multiple plans would be filed. The court gave the parties a 60-day negotiation period to develop a plan, if possible, and directed the examiner to use the data and analysis developed during the case, mediate the efforts, and prepare a report for the court at the conclusion of the 60-day period.

Section 473 of title 28 of the U.S. Code, as amended by the Judicial Improvements Act of 1990, directs each federal district court to implement a "civil jus-

---

[39] 47 B.R. 551 (Bankr. D. Minn. 1985).
[40] 74 B.R. 221 (S.D. N.Y. 1987).
[41] 99 B.R. 177 (Bankr. D. N.H. 1989); *see In re Apex Oil Co.,* 101 B.R. 92 (Bankr. E.D. Mo. 1989); *In re UNR Industries, Inc.,* 72 B.R. 789 (Bankr. N.D. Ill. 1987); *In re Eagle Bus Manufacturing, Inc.,* 134 B.R. 584 (Bankr. S.D. Tex. 1991).

tice expense and delay reduction plan" aimed at expediting and improving litigation management and the resolution of civil disputes. Several bankruptcy
courts have implemented some form of alternative dispute resolution procedures, such as mediation.

At the request of a major creditor, a court may refuse to appoint an examiner
to act as a mediator, but may instead appoint another individual to serve as a
mediator. An actual request for appointment of an examiner, which the court
refused to grant, appears as 6.2(a) in Volume 2. The subsequent history—a supplemental motion to appoint either an examiner or a mediator, and an order
issued by the court, appointing a mediator—is presented as 6.2(b) and 6.2(c)
respectively, in Volume 2.

Since the Bankruptcy Code became effective, a large number of examiners
have been appointed. As noted above, in a case where the unsecured debts
exceed $5 million, the court must appoint an examiner if requested. In addi-
tion, an examiner might be appointed instead of a trustee. For example, the
court may find it easier to appoint an examiner to investigate the operations of
the debtor rather than proceed at the present time with hearings to determine
whether the appointment of a trustee is necessary. Then, if the examiner's
investigation reveals that there is fraud or gross mismanagement on the part of
the debtor, a trustee can be appointed.

§ 6.9 Operation of the Business

No order is necessary under the Bankruptcy Code for the debtor to operate the
business in chapter 11. Sections 1107(a) and 1108 grant the debtor all of the
rights, powers, and duties of a trustee, except the right to compensation under
section 330, and provide that the trustee may operate the business unless the
court directs otherwise. Thus, the debtor will continue to operate the business
unless a party-in-interest requests that the court appoint a trustee. Until action
is taken by management to correct the problems that caused the adverse financial condition, the business will most likely continue to operate at a loss. If the
creditors believe new management is necessary to correct the problem, they will
press for a change in management or the appointment of a trustee. In most large
bankruptcies as well as in many smaller cases, the old management is replaced.
In large cases, management may be replaced by turnaround specialists—individuals who specialize in taking over troubled companies. They often eliminate the
unprofitable aspects of the company's operations, reduce overhead, and find additional financing as part of the turnaround process. Once the plan has been confirmed, turnaround specialists frequently move on to other troubled companies.
In small cases, where management is also the stockholders, creditors are apt to be
uncomfortable with existing management, which may have created the problems in the first place. Creditors may want a trustee appointed unless management is willing to have workout or turnaround specialists exercise some type of
control over operations. This could involve temporarily turning the management
function over to the specialists, or having existing management work with the
specialists in resolving financial problems and developing a plan. There are some
CPAs who serve as specialists but, as a result, they are no longer independent.

From the debtor's perspective, one of the major advantages of Chapter XI
over Chapter X of prior law was that, under Chapter XI, a receiver was not

automatically appointed. Under Chapter X, the appointment of a trustee was mandatory when liabilities exceeded $250,000. The Bankruptcy Code provides for more flexibility by allowing the debtor to maintain possession of its property and operate the business unless the court orders otherwise. For cause, including fraud, dishonesty, incompetence, or gross mismanagement of the business, the court, upon request, will hold a hearing and appoint a trustee; the court may also appoint a trustee if it is determined that such action is in the best interest of creditors and stockholders.

The debtor-in-possession is required to perform all the functions specified for the trustee (§ 6.7) except conducting an investigation of its own acts, conduct, and financial affairs, and filing a statement of investigation.[42] Section 1107 also states that the rights are subject to any limitations or conditions the court may prescribe. Thus, the court has the power to set conditions that the debtor must abide by in operating the business. For example, the court might require that a given business pay all ongoing bills before the expiration of 30 days. The creditors are constrained from filing a plan during the first 120 days or longer, if the court directs, subsequent to the date of the order for relief when the debtor remains in possession.

§ 6.10 Automatic Stay

The immediate objective of the debtor (or trustee, if appointed) is to keep the business operating. To maintain the critical assets of the business intact and to prohibit the creditors from continuing to harass the debtor, the Bankruptcy Code provides for an automatic stay of the actions of creditors. The need for the stay can be seen by looking at the conditions existing in an average case. The debtor will be in default on loan agreements and leases; secured parties, through court action or self-help, will be accelerating efforts to take possession of their collateral; the debtor's vendors will have substantially reduced, if not halted, credit to the debtor and may have already commenced suits to collect amounts past due; and the debtor will be without cash. In addition, the major assets needed to run the business will be subject to security interests or charges of one kind or another.[43] The stay, in effect, gives the debtor time to make some crucial operating decisions. See § 5.27 for a discussion of the type of actions that are subject to the stay and the process necessary to remove stays.

§ 6.11 Impact of *Timbers*

In *In re Timbers*,[44] the Supreme Court examined the issue as to whether an undersecured creditor in a chapter 11 case is entitled to compensation for the delay, caused by the automatic stay, in its right to foreclose on the collateral. As noted in § 5.27, *Timbers* resolved a conflict that existed in several circuits by holding that the undersecured creditor is not entitled to interest on its collateral during the stay to ensure adequate protection.

---

[42] 11 U.S.C. § 1107(a).
[43] Trost, *supra* note 1, p. 1317.
[44] 484 U.S. 365 (1988).

It may appear that the *Timbers* decision was a victory for debtors, but the Court emphasized that undersecured creditors retain substantial rights with respect to their collateral, including the right under section 362(d)(1) as to adequate protection against any decline in the value of the collateral, and the right under section 362(d)(2) to relief from the stay unless the debtor can show that the collateral is necessary for an effective reorganization. The Court stated: "This requirement is not merely a showing that if there is conceivably to be an effective reorganization, this property will be needed for it; but that the property is essential for an effective reorganization that is in prospect. This means . . . that there must be reasonable possibility of a successful reorganization within a reasonable time." Prior to *Timbers*, there was disagreement as to the proper standard for determining whether the collateral was needed for effective reorganization. *Timbers* seems to have resolved this problem by requiring that there must be a reasonable possibility of a successful reorganization. For example, in lifting the stay based on *Timbers* even before the 120-day exclusivity period ended, another court stated:

> [t]he debtors' hopes and aspirations for reorganization, although well-intended, have not been supplemented by a showing that a reorganization is possible, let alone reasonably likely within a reasonable period of time.[45]

Timbers has been used to restrict the extent to which the secured creditor may be entitled to revenue from the collateral. For example, in *In re Prichard Plaza Associates Limited Partnership*,[46] *Timbers* was cited in support of a decision that would not turn over rentals previously received by the debtor to the creditor (or allow the creditor rights to current rents), absent a showing that the collateral was declining in value. Based on *Timbers*, in *In re Conroe Forge & Manufacturing Corp.*,[47] the court denied a creditor's request for the receipt of proceeds for the sale of the collateral in advance of the plan confirmation.

§ 6.12 Use of Collateral

The debtor or trustee must be able to use a secured party's collateral, or in most situations there would be no alternative but to liquidate the business. Section 363(c) gives the trustee or debtor the right to use, sell, or lease property of the estate in the ordinary course of business without a notice and a hearing.

The debtor can use or lease any other property of the estate as long as the action taken is in the ordinary course of business. To stop the debtor from using, in the ordinary course of business, property for which a creditor has a security interest, the creditor must petition the court for relief from the automatic stay or for a specific order preventing the debtor from using the property. To use, sell, or lease property other than in the ordinary course of business requires notice and opportunity for a hearing.[48]

---

[45] *In re Diplomatic Electronics Corp.*, 82 B.R. 688, 693 (Bankr. S.D.N.Y. 1988).
[46] 84 B.R. 289 (Bankr. Mass. 1988).
[47] 82 B.R. 781 (Bankr. W.D. Pa. 1988).
[48] 11 U.S.C. § 363(b). *See* 11 U.S.C. § 102(1).

§ 6.13   **Use of Cash Collateral**

One restriction is, however, placed on the trustee or debtor to use the property of the estate where cash collateral is involved. Cash collateral is cash, negotiable instruments, documents of title, securities, deposit accounts, or other cash equivalents where the estate and someone else have an interest in the property. Also included would be the proceeds of noncash collateral, such as inventory and accounts receivable and proceeds, products, offspring, rents, or profits of property subject to a security interest, if converted to proceeds of the type defined as cash collateral, provided the proceeds are subject to the prepetition security interests.

To use cash collateral, the creditor with the interest must consent to its use, or the court, after notice and hearing, must authorize its use. The court may authorize the use, sale, or lease of cash collateral at a preliminary hearing if there is a reasonable likelihood that the debtor-in-possession will prevail at the final hearing. The Bankruptcy Code also provides that the court is to act promptly for a request to use cash collateral.[49] In some situations, there may not be enough time for a hearing, and the court may release cash collateral immediately—for example, in situations where the debtor must meet a payroll or needs cash immediately to preserve perishable inventory. In this case, the procedures discussed in § 5.26 are followed. A creditor is entitled to adequate protection of its security interest under section 361 when the court uses its cash collateral. Thus, cash in bank accounts subject to setoff or collections from pledged receivables and inventory prior to the filing of the petition are not available for use until the consent of the appropriate secured creditor or of the court is obtained. In many bankruptcy cases that are filed, nearly all of the cash and cash equivalents will be considered cash collateral and barred from use. For example, a small car rental agency might well continue to lease its automobiles on a day-to-day basis without the permission of the bank for which the fleet is collateral, but the agency must be careful of its use of the car rental payments received if the bank has a security interest in the proceeds of the agency's accounts receivable that existed as of the date the petition was filed. One of the first orders of business once the petition has been filed will be to obtain the release of the cash collateral. Courts have in general released cash collateral on relatively short notice to provide debtors with the cash necessary to operate the business.

Because the debtor must obtain the release of the cash collateral within the first few days after the petition is filed, the first order is usually for a relatively short time period such as seven to 14 days. Some orders have been for periods of only three days. Depending on the conditions of the debtor's operations, the second and future cash orders may also be restricted to a relatively short time period. Often, the debtor requests the use of the cash collateral for a short time period during which the debtor attempts to obtain debtor-in-possession financing. The secured creditor will often restrict the use of the cash to the acquisition of needed inventory and the payment of immediate and necessary expenses, including payroll and payroll expenses. The items for which cash may be used, along with the maximum amount, may be attached to the cash

---

[49] 11 U.S.C. § 363(c)(3).

collateral order. In situations where the debtor had negotiated a cash collateral agreement with a bank or other secured lender, the time period is often longer.

As noted above, the court must provide for adequate protection for the creditor prior to approving the order. Examples of the types of provisions that are found in cash collateral agreements to give adequate protection include:

1 Security interest in and lien on all of the property of the debtor, including postpetition inventory and receivables.

2 A continuing security interest in and lien on the collateral and proceeds thereof, with the lien subordinated only to the extent necessary to pay postpetition wages.

3 Release of all cash collateral, which becomes a postpetition claim (administrative expense) with priority over all other administrative claims in the case, except for unpaid wages and professional fees not to exceed a stipulated amount.

Adequate protection should be determined based on the manufacturing cycle of the business. Thus, adequate protection exists if it appears that the level of collateral that supports a floating lien will be restored within the projected business cycle, even though there may be a decline at some given point in the cycle.[50]

Cash collateral agreements often provide that the security interest that is part of the agreement must be properly perfected without filing the generally needed statements. Some creditors also want a statement from the debtor that all prepetition security interests are perfected and that the debtor agrees not to assert any defense, offsets, claims, or counterclaims with respect to the existing obligations, liens, or prepetition transactions between the bank and the debtor. Statements of this nature are more often found in debtor-in-possession (DIP) financing agreements than in the use of cash collateral orders.

An example of an order authorizing the use of cash collateral is presented as 6.3 in Volume 2. This particular order, covering nine days, contains a list of the items for which the cash collateral may be used. This list usually is limited to payroll and related costs, inventory that must be acquired, and other expenditures that are absolutely necessary. The order provides that the bank will have an administrative expenses priority claim over other administrative expenses claims except for postpetition payroll and professional fees not to exceed $500,000. The cash collateral order perfects security interest in inventory, accounts receivable, and other property, without having to perfect security interest in the normal manner.

When there are both senior and junior security interests in cash collateral, approval for the use of the cash collateral by the senior lienor is insufficient. Approval of the court is necessary, pursuant to section 363(c)(2)(B) of the Bankruptcy Code.[51] However, as a general rule, no notice or hearing is required under section 363(c)(2)(A) of the Bankruptcy Code when the debtor-in-possession has the consent of the secured creditor to use the cash collateral.[52]

[50] *In re Dynaco Corp.*, 162 B.R. 389 (Bankr. D.N.H. 1993).
[51] *In re Nemko, Inc.*, 143 B.R. 980 (Bankr. E.D.N.Y. 1992).
[52] *Armstrong v. Norwest Bank*, Minneapolis, N.A., 964 F.2d 797 (8th Cir. 1992).

The Second Circuit held that a mortgage with an assignment of rents, which had not taken the enforcement or sequestration step required by state law prior to the filing of the bankruptcy petition, has an inchoate interest in the rents that makes them cash collateral under section 363(a) of the Bankruptcy Code.[53] The court also noted that the bankruptcy court might strip the creditor of some of its rights under the "equities of the case" exception of section 552(b) of the Bankruptcy Code, to prevent the creditor from obtaining a windfall. In an earlier decision, the Ninth Circuit BAP also held that the interest in rents where enforcement action was not taken was cash collateral.[54] However, in *In re Wiston XXIV Ltd. Partnership*,[55] the bankruptcy court held that rents do not become cash collateral where enforcement steps were not taken prior to the filing of the bankruptcy petition.

Another example authorizing the use of cash collateral is presented as 6.4 in Volume 2.

§ 6.14 Obtaining Credit

In most chapter 11 proceedings, the debtor must obtain additional financing in order to continue the business. The debtor was allowed to obtain credit under prior law, but the power granted to the debtor under the Bankruptcy Code is broader. Section 364(a) allows the debtor to obtain unsecured debt and to incur unsecured obligations in the ordinary course while operating the business. This right is automatic unless the court orders otherwise. Also, the holder of these claims is entitled to first priority as administrative expenses.

It is important for the creditor to be sure the granting of credit is in the ordinary course of doing business. For example, in *In re Garofalo's Finer Foods, Inc.*,[56] the bankruptcy court held that the bank's postpetition extensions of overdraft credit to the debtor were not ordinary course of business transactions. On appeal the district court directed the bankruptcy court to determine the extent to which over-draft extensions post-petition compared to pre-petition practice and consider such payments made in ordinary course of business. Failure to obtain court approval under section 364 of the Bankruptcy Code resulted in the claims that were not made in ordinary course of business not being classified as administrative expenses. Repayment by applying postpetition deposits was held to be avoidable as an unauthorized postpetition transfer under section 549 of the Bankruptcy Code and was subject to recovery under the provisions of section 362 of the Bankruptcy Code as a violation of the automatic stay.

If the debtor is unable to obtain the necessary unsecured debt under section 364(a), the court may authorize the obtaining of credit and the incurring of debt by granting special priorities for the claims. These priorities may include the following:

1 Giving priority over any or all administrative expenses.
2 Securing the debt with a lien on unencumbered property.
3 Securing the debt with a junior lien on encumbered property.

---

[53] *In re Vienna Park Properties*, 976 F.2d 106 (2d Cir. 1992).
[54] *In re Tucson Industrial Partners*, 129 B.R. 614 (9th Cir. BAP 1991).
[55] 141 B.R. 429 (Bankr. D. Kan. 1992).
[56] 164 B.R. 955 (Bankr. N.D. Fld. 1994); *aff'd* in part and *rev'd* in part, 186 B.R. 414 (N.D. F11, 1995).

For the court to authorize the obtaining of credit with a lien on encumbered property that is senior or equal to the existing lien, the debtor must not be able to obtain credit by other means and the existing lienholder must be adequately protected. However, in *In the matter of Stratbucker*,[57] the court held that the farmer could grant a senior lien to creditors for working capital to plant crops. Mortgage holders were adequately protected because the value of the real estate was greater than the debt, and, unless the crops were planted, the lien-holders would have no interest to be protected.

Credit obtained other than in the ordinary course of business must be authorized by the court after notice and a hearing. Where there is some question whether the credit is related to the ordinary course of business, the lender should require court approval. Ordinary course of business is determined by reference to two tests.[58] The first is the creditor expectation test, which looks at whether a hypothetical creditor of the debtor would expect the debtor to incur the type of debt contemplated as part of doing business. For example, a creditor of a debtor construction company would probably expect the construction company to incur short-term debt when purchasing lumber for a project. The second test is whether similar businesses generally take on the type of debt contemplated.

Chemical Bank has been the leader in offering DIP financing, starting in the early 1980s. Several years later, other banks became interested. With a proper assessment of the financial conditions of the debtor, DIP financing arrangements are a relative low risk. In fact, in many of the larger bankruptcies, Chemical and other banks often have not lent any or have lent only a very small amount of the funds to the debtor. Once the DIP financing arrangement is in place, trade creditors may begin shipping inventory on regular credit terms; with no payments required on debt except oversecured debt, additional cash requirements are needed for only a short time period. In fact, some creditors have been critical of the debtor for establishing, in a DIP financing agreement, a line of credit that is too low and too costly to the estate.

Section 364(c) allows the debtor-in-possession the flexibility to grant super priority, secured, or junior-secured status if he or she cannot otherwise obtain credit on an unsecured basis. To obtain credit under this provision, there must be notice and a hearing. Courts analyze such requests carefully because of the danger that any increase in postpetition debt will decrease the amount available for the unsecured creditors if the debt is not used in a way that increases the debtor's total value. In instances where the court feels the credit will only serve to prolong an inevitable liquidation, the motion under this section will be denied.

The provisions in section 364(c) allow primarily for the increasing use of larger DIP loans and lines of credit. The debtor-in-possession has the sometimes difficult task of finding a source of credit to meet the needs of the estate. Generally, the debtor-in-possession can either approach the prepetition lender or use an institution with a department that deals specifically with DIP financing.[59]

---

[57] 4 B.R. 251 (Bankr. D. Neb. 1980).
[58] *In re Dant-Russell, Inc.*, 853 F.2d 700 (9th Cir. 1988).
[59] In the past, Chemical Bank, Salomon Brothers, and First Boston Corporation have all dealt with these types of lending.

Using the prepetition lender may hinge on whether the debtor maintained a positive working relationship with the lender prior to the filing. If the relationship is intact at the commencement of the case, then it is normally much simpler to continue to utilize the same lender. Problems frequently will arise when attempting to negotiate postpetition financing. The lender will often want the debtor-in-possession to agree to several concessions, such as waiving prepetition claims against the bank, stipulating to the validity of the bank's security interests, and cross-collateralizing the bank's prepetition debt with postpetition collateral. A debtor-in-possession must carefully weigh the cost of such concessions against the use of a new lender.

Choosing to utilize the services of a new lender gives a debtor-in-possession several valuable advantages. A new lender can be brought in quietly during prebankruptcy planning and allow for a smooth transition into the reorganization process by assuring unsecured creditors of the continued creditworthiness of the business. The use of a new lender can also strengthen management relative to the prepetition lenders. From the perspective of a new lender, extensive analysis is required to determine the availability of unencumbered assets and the possibility of an effective reorganization.

In summary, Siskin identified the following items that suggest that DIP loans may be safer:[60]

- Many uncertainties are indeed removed from the credit-granting process.
- Collateral values and therefore lending advances are enhanced through super-priority liens and court orders permitting going-out-of-business sales.
- Covenants, rules of conduct, and related remedies are preapproved by the court, which leads to greater certainties of lender action upon defaults.
- Financial statement misrepresentations and inappropriate actions by management are treated more severely in bankruptcy venue.
- Involvement of outside accountants and turnaround advisors provides additional assurances of financial integrity.
- Lender can sometimes ascertain the continued support of the trade vendors through negotiations with the unsecured creditors' committee.

Siskin also identified the following items that are negative rather than positive in determining if DIP loans are safer:[61]

- Total fees in bankruptcy cases and related carveouts reduce borrowing base availability and limit financial resources that are needed by the company to restructure.
- Lack of uniformity by the courts in defining the criteria and time frames to grant the lender a request for an emergency hearing creates uncertainties.

---

[60] Edward J. Siskin, "Exit and Postpetition Financing," *16th Annual Bankruptcy and Reorganization Conference* (Medford, OR: Association of Insolvency and Restructuring Advisors, 1999), p. 3.
[61] *Id.*, p. 4.

- Requirement to deal with creditors' committee and landlords who object leads to additional expenses and compromises on the part of the DIP lender that are not required in non-DIP loans.
- Trustees can introduce themselves into cases at the tail end and hold up payments to the lender for long periods of time. If viewed by lender as inappropriate, it will discourage future DIP loans in that jurisdiction unless acted upon quickly by the judge.
- Success fees (i.e., warrant kickers) to reward lenders for helping a troubled company turn around its business are usually not part of DIP pricing.

(a) Priming Prepetition Liens

In instances where the debtor-in-possession cannot obtain postpetition financing on an unsecured basis or secured by a junior lien, a creditor may obtain a lien that primes prepetition liens. Under section 364(d), such an arrangement can be made after notice and a hearing. The court must first determine that credit cannot otherwise be obtained and that the holder of the previous lien is adequately protected. The debtor-in-possession has the burden to prove that the prior lienholder will be adequately protected.

Under section 364(d) of the Bankruptcy Code, adequate protection cannot be demonstrated unless the creditor is furnished with additional collateral or guarantees, and so on, that do not currently exist.[62] For a discussion of the meaning of adequate protection, see § 5.26 of the main text.

Prepetition loans may be primed in several different ways. For example, in a case where there is only one property of significant value, the court may allow a new lender to have a first-lien security interest in property where the prepetition creditor held a first priority lien. Consider a situation where a $15 million loan was secured with property having a value of $27 million. The court may allow a new lender to obtain a first security interest in the property as long as the prepetition lender is adequately protected. Using the figures above, the court might approve a $6 million loan from a new lender secured with a first priority lien, leaving the prepetition creditor with a second lien on the property with an equity of $19 million and an equity interest of $15 million. As discussed in § 5.26, some courts, before approving the priming of the loan, may want an equity cushion or a cushion to cover potential risks during the proceeding.

A more common way to prime a prepetition creditor where there are several separate assets is to allocate some of the property to the first-lien creditor and the balance to a new lender. Again using the facts in the above example, assume that there are two assets—one with a value of $19 million and the other with a value of $8 million. The court may approve a postpetition financing arrangement where the new lender is given a first lien in the $8 million property for a $6 million loan and a second lien in the other property. Excerpts from a postpetition financing agreement that involved the priming of the prepetition lien can be found in 6.5 of Volume 2.

---

[62] *In re Swedeland Development Group, Inc.*, 16 F.3d 552 (3d Cir. 1994).

(b) Cross-Collateralization

Cross-collateralization agreements are often requested by prepetition lenders as a requirement for the extension of DIP financing. There are generally two types of cross-collateralization agreements. The first is not the subject of much question or dispute: A lender takes a lien on property acquired prepetition in order to secure a postpetition loan, effectively changing a postpetition unsecured administrative claim into a postpetition secured claim.[63] The second type of cross-collateralization has been the subject of some debate and is the type most prepetition lenders attempt to negotiate. A prepetition lender acquires a security interest in postpetition assets to secure prepetition unsecured debt. This is in exchange for DIP financing.

This second type of cross-collateralization should be entered into with care. There is potential for the courts to avoid a transfer if the option to enter into the cross-collateralization agreement is not accompanied by a noticed hearing and the option for other prepetition creditors to obtain similar favorable terms. Cross-collateralization should not be the debtor's first choice for financing; rather, it is an extraordinary measure to be utilized only as a last resort. The courts generally require proof that absent cross-collateralization the company's survival would be in question. For a creditor, a cross-collateralization agreement may sound good; but if the court later finds that the arrangement was in bad faith, the court can invalidate the agreement, possibly leaving the creditor worse off than it was prior to the agreement.

In *In the matter of Saybrook Manufacturing Co., Inc.*,[64] the Eleventh Circuit held that cross-collateralization of prepetition claims with postpetition assets violates the fundamental priority scheme laid out in the Bankruptcy Code and was therefore invalid.

Several Districts have issued orders or guidelines of facts that should be considered in preparing motions relating to financing agreements. Contained in 6.6 of Volume 2 are general orders/guidelines from the Districts of Delaware, Central District of California, Northern District of California, Eastern District of California, and District of Oregon.

(c) Other Issues

Section 364(e) of the Bankruptcy Code provides that the reversal or modification on appeal of an authorization under section 364 to obtain credit or incur debt, or the grant of a priority or a lien does not impact the validity of the debt incurred or priority or lien granted unless such authorization is stayed pending appeal. A postpetition order that is granted under section 364(d) allowing the priming of the prior lender cannot be overturned unless the objecting party obtains a stay of the order while the petition is under appeal.[65] Additionally,

---

[63] The authority for providing what may appear to be preferential treatment is found in the provisions of section 364(c), which allows the court to grant the debtor authority to grant security agreements to gain funds necessary for the reorganization.

[64] 963 F.2d 1490 (11th Cir. 1992).

[65] *In re Swedeland Development Group, Inc.* 9 F.3d 111 (3d Cir. 1993).

section 364(e) prevents reversal of a cross-collateralization clause unless a stay is obtained pending appeal or the creditor acted in bad faith by lending with the purpose of securing a prepetition loan.[66]

The Eleventh Circuit also held that the use of section 105(a) of the Bankruptcy Code to justify the granting of the lien on the basis that it will further the goal of reorganization could not be invoked.

It is important that any DIP financing arrangement under section 364 of the Bankruptcy Code be approved by the court before credit is granted. In *In re E-Tron Corp.*,[67] the bankruptcy court held that such approval should be granted *nunc pro tunc* only under extraordinary circumstances, and then only if the court would have authorized the loan if the request had been timely filed.

The court may approve special financing fees or other consideration in order for the debtor-in-possession to obtain financing. For example, in *In re Defender Drug Stores, Inc.*,[68] the debtor-in-possession and the lender agreed to an additional "10 percent enhancement fee" and the court approved the arrangement. The court held that, under section 364 of the Bankruptcy Code, the court is authorized to approve lender incentives for postpetition financing beyond the priorities and liens, including conditions where objections to the lender's prepetition security interest are waived.

An arrangement whereby a debtor received new value in exchange for an administrative expense and a security interest that covered both prepetition and postpetition debt was held to be a preference and in violation of section 364, which allows a priority or a lien only on debts incurred after the petition is filed.[69]

An example of a debtor-in-possession (DIP) financing agreement for Standard Brands Paint Company is given as 6.7 in Volume 2. The financing in this example was by a new lender, Foothill Capital—a company specializing in making DIP loans. In 6.7(a), there is indication that the funds will be used to cover ordinary operating expenses such as payroll, raw materials, capital expenditures, and administrative expenses including professional fees. The agreement provides that the maximum amount that will be loaned, which will include up to $5 million in the form of letters of credit and letter-of-credit guarantees, will be $17 million. Section 2.1 of 6.7(b) indicates that the funds loaned will be up to 70 percent of the eligible trade receivables, 25 percent of the eligible inventory, $.6 million based on the value of rolling stock, and $2 million to $6 million based on the value of real property.

Section 2.8 of 6.7(b) indicates the fees that will be paid to Foothill Capital under the DIP agreement.

Another example of a motion for an order authorizing DIP financing is presented in 6.8 of Volume 2 by Mellon Bank to Consolidated Stainless, Inc. Among the standard provisions, the motion establishes a time period for an objection to the priority of the prepetition claim and the validity or perfection of the Mellon's liens and security interest in the prepetition collateral.

Listed below are examples contained in a DIP financing agreement:

---

[66] *In re Adams Apple, Inc.* 829 F.2d 1484 (9th Cir. 1987).
[67] 141 B.R. 49 (Bankr. D. N.J. 1992); *see In the matter of Grant Valley Sport & Marine, Inc.*, 23 Bankr. Ct. Dec. (CRR) 493 (Bankr. W.D. Mich. 1992).
[68] 145 B.R. 312 (9th Cir. BAP 1992).
[69] *In re Monarch Circuit Industries, Inc.*, 41 B.R. 859 (Bankr. E.D. Pa. 1984).

1 First-priority perfected lien and security interest obtained in substantially all of the debtor's property, including inventory, receivables, accounts, equipment, contracts, leaseholds, trademarks, patents, etc.,

2 All parties-in-interest, including the committee of unsecured creditors, precluded from asserting any claim or contention relating to the granting of the security interest, to the contrary. Any party-in-interest given until ____ (less than 90 days), to commence an adversary proceeding, contested matter, or other form of legal proceeding against the bank, with respect to the prepetition transactions.

3 Debtor agrees to waive, release, and agree not to assert any defenses, offsets, claims, or counterclaims with respect to the existing obligations, liens, or prepetition transactions between the bank and the debtor.

4 New loan to replace prepetition debt (except term loan), subject to any claims, rights, or actions commenced before ____.

5 New loan to take priority over other administrative expenses except: wages and related benefits not to exceed $____; chapter 11 fees; and professional fees not to exceed $____.

6 Prepetition debt to be secured with postpetition assets.

The data checklist for DIP financing that is in section 6.9 of Volume 2, includes the items that should be considered when reviewing a motion for a DIP financing agreement.

In summary, Siskin identified the following factors that are risks and issues that need to be considered in postconfirmation financing (financing on emergence from chapter 11):[70]

- Many companies emerge prematurely due to bankruptcy and competitive pressures
- Management team may be new and relatively unfamiliar with company's business or with operating a fragile company
- Many second-line, seasoned employees may have left during bankruptcy process
- Difficult to ascertain projected levels of trade support outside bankruptcy, particularly without a creditors' committee
- Super-priority lien status and related benefits of DIP loan protection are gone (i.e., assignment of leases, landlord waivers, etc.)
- Difficult to close locations or void other contracts if not fully taken care of in bankruptcy.
- Team of turnaround advisors no longer available to support company with a weak financial infrastructure

The strengths that are attributable to extending credit to a company on emergence from chapter 11 as identified by Siskin are as follows:[71]

---

[70] *Supra* note 60, p. 5.
[71] *Id.*, p. 6.

- Stronger company able to meet competition and marketplace challenges
- New or improved management team able to meet the financial challenges ahead
- Fresh start—elimination of many contingent liabilities and obligations
- Trade often an owner, or has a term note
- If company should file again, usually not successful in preventing liquidation of collateral
- Lender can negotiate upside rewards in the form of warrants, which are not available in DIP loans

§ 6.15 Claims and Interests

A proof of claim or interest is deemed filed in a chapter 11 case provided the claim or interest is listed in the schedules filed by the debtor, unless the claim or interest is listed as disputed, contingent, or unliquidated. A creditor is thus not required to file a proof of claim if it agrees with the debt listed in the schedules submitted. It is, however, advisable for creditors to file a proof of claim in most situations. (See § 5.31.) Creditors who for any reason disagree with the amount admitted on the debtor's schedules, such as allowable prepetition interest on their claims, or creditors desiring to give a power of attorney to a trade association or lawyer, should always prepare and file a complete proof of claim. Special attention must also be devoted to secured claims that are undersecured.

(a) Application of OID to Debt Exchanges

Judge Liffland held, in *In re Chateaugay Corporation, Reomar, Inc.,*[72] that original issue discount (OID) rules apply to situations where the creditor exchanges its debt for another debt instrument. The district court affirmed the bankruptcy court's decision and Valley appealed. The Second Circuit[73] reversed by holding that, for purposes of section 502(b)(2), no new OID is created by a face value debt-for-debt exchange in a consensual workout.

As of December 1, 1982, LTV had issued a total face amount of $150,000,000 in debentures due December 1, 2002. LTV received a total of $133,002,000 for these bonds. On May 1, 1986, LTV offered to exchange $1,000 face amount of additional notes and 15 shares of LTV stock for each $1,000 principal amount of the original debentures offered for exchange. A total of $116,035,000 face amount of original debentures was exchanged for the new notes as of June 1, 1986.

LTV and 66 of its subsidiaries filed for reorganization under chapter 11 of the Bankruptcy Code on July 17, 1986. The debtors have continued management of their own businesses as debtors-in-possession, pursuant to sections 1107 and 1108 of the Code. In turn, on November 27, 1987, Valley Fidelity filed proofs of claim on behalf of the holders of both the original debentures and new notes, to which the debtors objected. The U.S. Bankruptcy Court has jurisdic-

---

[72] 109 B.R. 51 (Bankr. S.D.N.Y. 1990).
[73] *The LTV Corp. v. Valley Fidelity Bank & Trust Co.,* 961 F.2d 378 (2d Cir. 1992).

tion of this matter pursuant to the "core proceedings" section of title 28, section 157 of the U.S. Code.

LTV moved for partial summary judgment on the grounds that the unamortized OID in Valley Fidelity's claims was not allowable under the guidelines of section 502 of the Bankruptcy Code. These were the issues:

1   Whether Valley Fidelity is the proper party-in-interest in this action.
2   Whether a claim for unamortized OID shall be allowed pursuant to section 502(b)(2) of the Bankruptcy Code.
3   Whether the unamortized discount should be calculated using the constant interest method.
4   Whether the amounts of unamortized discount on the two claims of Valley Fidelity are both readily calculable.

The bankruptcy court began with a statement in regard to the granting of summary judgments. A summary judgment may be proper when the movant demonstrates that there are no genuine issues of material fact to be tried. However, this decision should be made with great caution. Any ambiguities must be resolved, and reasonable inferences must be drawn in favor of the nonmovant.

In this instance, the submissions of the parties establish a sufficient record for the court to grant LTV's motion as to the issues relating to the proper party-in-interest, the allowance of unamortized OID, and the proper method of calculating unamortized OID. However, the issue of the amount of unamortized OID applicable to Valley Fidelity's claim on the new notes is a disputed issue that cannot be decided on summary judgment.

Allowance of OID   The Bankruptcy Code provides that the court shall determine the amount of a creditor's claim and allow the claim, except to the extent that the claim is for unmatured interest (section 502(b)(2)). This required disallowance is determined without reference to any *ipso facto* clause of the agreement creating the claim. The amount disallowed includes any portion of prepaid interest that represents an original discounting of the claim that would not yet have been earned as of the date of bankruptcy.

It has become an acceptable practice under the Bankruptcy Code that, in general, the amount of the claim is represented by the amount of cash received from the issue. For example, if a 10-year, $1,000 bond with a stipulated interest rate of 10 percent is issued for $788, the claim at the time of issuance is $788 because section 502(b)(2) provides that a claim for unmatured interest is not allowed. Interest is earned on the carrying value of the debt and not paid by the debtor, so the principal amount of the debt increases. Because the bond sold for $788, the effective interest rate is actually 14 percent rather than the 10 percent rate stated on the face of the bond. The effective rate of interest determines the amount for which the bond will sell. The bankruptcy court noted that the issuance of debenture bonds with a face value greater than the cash or other consideration received is very common in today's financial markets. Some of these bonds are zero coupon bonds that are issued at large discounts, and others are "junk bonds"—the stated rate does not fully reflect the risk of nonpayment, resulting in the bonds being issued at a discount.

In the above example, the proceeds of $788 on the issuance of the $1,000 face bond results in an effective interest rate of 14 percent, because this is the rate that yields $788 when the value of the payments of the principal (10 years from now) plus the semiannual interest payment of $50 ($1,000 × .10 percent × .5) for the next 10 years are discounted to the present as shown below:

Present value of principal payments of $1,000 at end of 10 years at 14%	$258
Present value of 20 semiannual interest payments of $50 at 14%	$530
Value of bond at time of issuance	$788

Proceeds of less than $788 would indicate an effective rate of interest that is greater than 14 percent; for proceeds greater than $788, the effective rate of interest is less than 14 percent.

The OID process can be illustrated by the following journal entries:

Cash	$788	
Bonds payable		$788

To record the issuance of the bond.

Interest expense (.5 × 14% × $788)	$ 55	
Cash (.5 × 10% × $1,000)		$ 50
Bonds payable		5

To record the first semiannual interest payment.

Interest expense (.5 × 14% × ($788 + $5))	$ 56	
Cash		$ 50
Bonds payable		6

To record the second payment.

If a bankruptcy petition were filed one year after the bond was issued and all interest was paid, the amount of the claim would be $799 ($788 + $5 + 6). The method for amortizing the premium is known as the *effective interest rate method* or the constant interest method, because the interest expense is always the effective interest rate multiplied by the carrying value of the bond. Thus, during the early years when the bond is outstanding, the increases in carrying value will be less than those near the maturity date of the bond.

The Second Circuit noted that section 502(b)(2) of the Bankruptcy Code provides that a claim shall be allowed "except to the extent that . . . such claim is for unmatured interest." The Circuit Court held that unamortized OID is "unmatured interest" within the meaning of section 502(b)(2). In arriving at this conclusion, the Circuit first noted that "[a]s a matter of economic definition, OID constitutes interest."[74] The Second Circuit also noted that the Bank-

---

[74] *United States v. Midland-Ross Corp.*, 381 U.S. 54, 57 (1965) (treating OID for tax purposes as income, not capital).

ruptcy Code's legislative history makes inescapable the conclusion that OID is interest within the meaning of section 502(b)(2). The House committee report on that section explains:

> Interest disallowed under this paragraph includes postpetition interest that is not yet due and payable, and any portion of prepaid interest that represents an original discounting of the claim, yet that would not have been earned on the date of bankruptcy. For example, a claim on a $1,000 note issued the day before bankruptcy would only be allowed to the extent of the cash actually advanced. If the original issue discount was 10% so that the cash advanced was only $900, then notwithstanding the face amount of the note, only $900 would be allowed. If $900 was advanced under the note some time before bankruptcy, the interest component of the note would have to be pro-rated and disallowed to the extent it was for interest after the commencement of the case.[75]

Cases that have considered the issue under section 502(b)(2) and have held that unamortized OID is unmatured interest and therefore unallowable as part of a bankruptcy claim include *In re Public Service Co. of New Hampshire*[76] and *In re Allegheny Int'l, Inc.*[77] (See also *In re Pengo Industries Inc.*[78]) In *In re Radio-Keith-Orpheum Corp.*,[79] a case under the Bankruptcy Act, the court allowed debentures issued at a discount for full face amount. The Second Circuit in *LTV* cited the *Public Service* court: "The word 'interest' in the statute is clearly sufficient to encompass the OID variation in the method of providing for and collecting what in economic fact is interest to be paid to compensate for the delay and risk involved in the ultimate repayment of monies loaned."[80]

Consensual Workouts   In the case of an original issue, the OID rules apply. The amount of the debt is based on the value of the cash received. The issue faced in *LTV* was: Should the OID rules also apply to an exchange of one debt instrument for another? To illustrate, assume that one year after the issuance of the bond the debtor has financial difficulty and the holder of the bond agrees to accept a new bond with an interest rate of 8 percent and with covenants that are not as restrictive as those of the prior issue. At the time of the exchange offer, the old bond is selling for $560.

Shortly after the exchange takes place, the debtor files a bankruptcy petition. What is the amount of the claim? In *LTV*, the bankruptcy court ruled that the amount of the claim is only $560 and not $799. The value of the consideration received by the debtor when the new bond was issued in exchange for the old was $560, which was the value of the old bond. The court is suggesting that the difference between the carrying value of the old bond of $799 and the market price of $560 is a gain that should be recognized on the exchange, and that

---

[75] H.R. Rep. No. 595, 95th Cong., 1st Sess. 352–353 (1977), reprinted in 1978 U.S. C. C.A.N. 5963, 6308–09.
[76] 114 B.R. 800, 803 (Bankr. D. N.H. 1990).
[77] 100 B.R. 247, 250 (Bankr. W.D. Pa. 1989).
[78] 129 B.R. 104, 108 (N.D. Tex. 1991).
[79] 106 F.2d 22, 27 (2d Cir. 1939), *cert. denied*, 308 U.S. 622 (1940).
[80] 114 B.R. at 803.

the carrying value of the new bond should be reported at $560, which is the amount of the allowed claim.

The bankruptcy court stated that the Financial Accounting Standards Board (FASB) has detailed guidelines to force the issuer and purchaser to reflect the underlying economic substance of original issue discounts. At the time the original bond is issued, Accounting Principles Board Opinion No. 21 would require that the original issue be reflected at the value of the consideration received (discounted to reflect the effective interest rate of 14 percent), which was $788 in the example. However, under FASB Statement No. 15, the debtor would not recognize any gain on the exchange of the old bond for the new one and the carrying value of the old bond of $799 would be the basis of the new bond. FASB Statement No. 15 states that no gain will be recognized by the debtor unless the carrying value of the old bond ($799 in the example) exceeds the total future cash payments (in the example, this would include interest at the rate of 8 percent for 9 years, or $720 plus the principal payment of $1,000) specified by the new terms. Thus, because $1,720 is greater than the carrying value of $799, no gain would be recognized. Several accountants do not agree with the conclusions of the FASB and would prefer that the new bond be reflected on the books of the debtor at its discounted present value of $560, as suggested by the bankruptcy court.

If the restructuring had taken place in chapter 11, SOP 90-7 rules or in a quasi-reorganization or corporation readjustment with which a troubled debt restructuring coincided and the debtor "restate[d] its liabilities generally," FASB Statement No. 15 would not apply (see footnote 4 to FASB Statement No. 15, and FASB Technical Bulletin 81-6). Under conditions where FASB Statement No. 15 does not apply or conditions where SOP 90-7 applies, the liabilities will be shown at their discounted value, which in the example would be at $560.

In an earlier decision,[81] the bankruptcy court also held that the OID rules apply to debt exchanges.

The bankruptcy court dismissed Valley Fidelity's argument that the exchange of the notes was merely a bookkeeping entry to which no economic significance should be attached. The court reasoned that changed maturity dates, different interest rates, and further requirements destroyed the validity of this contention. In response to the argument that by not allowing such claims courts would create a devastating impact on debtors attempting a "workout," the court simply said that the contentions were unfounded and that the parties were merely overreacting. Finally, the bankruptcy court returned to the original premise of interest—money paid to the lender as compensation for risk, length of time, and loss of purchasing power. The discount in this case is of the same nature. A court must apply section 502(b)(2) of the Bankruptcy Code with an eye toward the particular facts, specifically the underlying economic substance of the transaction. In the situation presented by this case, the claim for such unmatured interest must be disallowed under section 502(b)(2).

The Second Circuit also examined the issue of the applicability of section 502(b)(2) to the new notes issued in a debt-for-debt exchange offer as part of a

---

[81] *In re Allegheny International, Inc.*, 100 B.R. 247 (Bankr. W.D. Pa. 1989).

consensual workout, and held that no new OID is created by a face value debt-for-debt exchange in a consensual workout.

The Second Circuit noted that a debtor in financial trouble may seek to avoid bankruptcy through a consensual out-of-court workout. Such a recapitalization, when it involves publicly traded debt, often takes the form of a debt-for-debt exchange, whereby bondholders exchange their old bonds for new bonds. As a result of the exchange, the debtor hopes that default will be avoided by changing the terms of the debt. On their part, the bondholders hope that the exchange will benefit them as well, by increasing the likelihood of payment on their bonds. The court also noted that both the debtor and its creditors "share an interest in achieving a successful restructuring of the debtor's financial obligations in order to avoid the uncertainties and daunting transaction costs of bankruptcy."

The court stated that the exchange can be either a fair market value exchange or a face value exchange. In a fair market value exchange, "an existing debt instrument is exchanged for a new one with a reduced principal amount, determined by the market value at which the existing instrument is trading." Through a fair market value exchange, the debtor seeks to reduce its overall debt obligations. This type of exchange, the court said, is usually sought only by companies in severe financial distress.

In contrast, a face value exchange "involves the substitution of new indebtedness for an existing debenture, modifying terms or conditions but not reducing the principal amount of the debt. A relatively healthy company faced with liquidity problems may offer a face value exchange to obtain short-term relief while remaining fully liable for the original funds borrowed."

The bankruptcy court and the district court held that a face value exchange generates OID. The bankruptcy court concluded that, "by definition, OID arises whenever a bond is issued for less than its face amount, and that in LTV's debt-for-debt exchange, the issue price of the New Notes was the fair market value of the Old Debentures."[82]

> The bankruptcy court's reasoning leaves us unpersuaded. While its application of the definition of OID to exchange offers may seem irrefutable at first glance, we believe the bankruptcy court's logic ignores the importance of context, and does not make sense if one takes into account the strong bankruptcy policy in favor of the speedy, inexpensive, negotiated resolution of disputes, that is an out-of-court or common law composition. See H.R. Rep. No. 95-595, 95th Cong.; 1st Sess. 220 (1977), reprinted in 1978 U.S.S.C.A.N. 5963, 6179–80; see also In re Colonial Ford, Inc., 24 B.R. 1014, 1015–17 (Bankr. D. Utah 1982) ("Congress designed the Code, in large measure, to encourage workouts in the first instance, with refuge in bankruptcy as a last resort.").

The Second Circuit noted that, because unamortized OID is disallowed and if an exchange of debt increases the amount of OID, creditors will be disinclined to cooperate in a consensual workout that might "otherwise have rescued a borrower from the precipice of bankruptcy." The court also stated, "We must consider the ramifications of a rule that places a creditor in the position

---

[82] *In re Chateaugay Corp., supra* note 58, pp. 56–57.

of choosing whether to cooperate with a struggling debtor, when such cooperation might make the creditor's claims in the event of bankruptcy smaller than they would have been had the creditor refused to cooperate." The court noted that the bankruptcy court's position unreversed would place creditors in a position that would likely result in fewer out-of-court debt exchanges and more chapter 11 filings.

The Second Circuit criticized the bankruptcy court for finding that the exchange created new OID and reduced LTV's liabilities when no such reduction was required on LTV's balance sheet.

The Second Circuit held that a face value exchange of debt obligations in a consensual workout does not, for purposes of section 502(b)(2) of the Bankruptcy Code, generate new OID. The court noted that an exchange does not change the character of the underlying debt, citing *In re Red Way Cartage Co.*,[83] where in context of preferential transfers, a settlement agreement did not create new debt but only reaffirmed the antecedent debt; *In re Magic Circle Energy Corp.*,[84] where the court stated: "We do not accept the proposition that the consolidation of debt into a long-term promissory note wrought a metamorphosis wherein the nature of the debt was alleged."; and *In re Busman*,[85] where the court noted that "the rule of section 502(b)(2) is clearly not entrenched as an absolute."

The Circuit Court stated that "[i]n the absence of unambiguous statutory guidance, we will not attribute to Congress an intent to place a stumbling block in front of debtors seeking to avoid bankruptcy with the cooperation of their creditors. Rather, given Congress's intent to encourage consensual workouts and the obvious desirability of minimizing bankruptcy filings, we conclude that for purposes of section 502(b)(2), no new OID is created in a face value debt-for-debt exchange in the context of a consensual workout."

The Circuit Court noted that the cases on which the bankruptcy court relied in reaching a contrary conclusion are distinguishable. For example, the bankruptcy court found support for its conclusion by looking to tax cases. Under the Internal Revenue Code, an exchange offer generates new OID. For example, in *Cities Service Co., v. United States*,[86] it was held in tax context that OID arose on exchange because the face amount of the issue exceeded the consideration. The Circuit Court reasoned that the tax treatment of a transaction, however, need not determine the bankruptcy treatment. For example, in *In re PCH Associates*,[87] an agreement structured as a ground lease for tax benefits was treated as a joint venture under the Bankruptcy Code.

In *In the matter of Pengo Industries, Inc.*,[88] the Fifth Circuit held that a debt-for-debt face value exchange in an out-of-court workout does not result in additional OID and thus reduce the allowed amount of the claim. The court held that the fact that the market value of the note was less than the face amount of the debt was not relevant, but expressly declined to rule as to the extent that OID might be realized if the old debt is exchanged in a fair market

---

[83] 84 B.R. 459, 461 (Bankr. E.D. Mich. 1988).
[84] 64 B.R. 269, 273 (Bankr. W.D. Okla. 1986).
[85] 5 B.R. 332, 336 (Bankr. E.D.N.Y. 1980).
[86] 522 F.2d 1281, 1288 (2d Cir. 1974), *cert. denied*, 423 U.S. 827 (1975).
[87] 55 B.R. 273 (Bankr. S.D.N.Y. 1985), *aff'd*, 60 B.R. 870 (S.D.N.Y.), *aff'd*, 804 F.2d 193 (2d Cir. 1986).
[88] 962 F.2d 543 (5th Cir. 1992).

exchange where the new debt has a lower face amount than the old or where the old debt involved a debt-for-equity exchange.

The Circuit Court also pointed out that *In re Allegheny International, Inc.*[89] is distinguishable because the exchange is debt-for-equity and not debt-for-debt. The court in LTV noted:

> That case, however, involved a debt-for-equity exchange, not a debt-for-debt exchange. The debtor in *Allegheny* offered to exchange debt instruments for previously issued preferred stock. *Id.* at 248. Thus, the stockholders had no claim against the debtor prior to the exchange, and the debtor's balance sheet reflected an increase in overall liabilities from the exchange. We need not decide whether *Allegheny* was correct. Whether or not its reasoning is sound in the context of a debt-for-equity exchange, it is inapplicable to a debt-for-debt exchange such as LTV's.

Calculation of OID   The bankruptcy court then considered the proper method to be used in calculating unamortized OID that is not part of an allowed claim pursuant to section 502(b)(2). The Bankruptcy Code suggests that a claim for OID may be maintained only to the extent that OID has been "earned" by the creditor. The Internal Revenue Code mandates that for debentures issued subsequent to July 1, 1982, the constant interest method (also known as yield-to-security, effective interest, and economic accrual) must be employed in such a situation. The straight-line method of valuation is not a proper method of measuring the interest costs to the insurer. The OID bond allows for larger deductions in early years than would be possible for borrowing the same amount in ordinary loans. Also, the constant interest method has been required for accounting purposes in cases involving OID since 1972. The bankruptcy court concluded that the constant interest method of proportionality, allocating OID over the entire life of the debenture, is the method that best conforms with both congressional intent and the economic realities of the situation.

The Second Circuit agreed with the bankruptcy court in holding that the methodology for calculating OID amortization is the constant interest method (effective interest method). Valley argued that the proper method for calculating unamortized OID under the Bankruptcy Code is the straight-line method, by which the amount of the discount is spread equally over the duration of the maturation of the note. LTV argued, in contrast, that the constant interest method (also referred to as the yield-to-maturity, effective interest, or economic accrual) should be used. Under the constant interest method, the Circuit Court noted that OID is amortized on the assumption that interest is compounded over time and that the amount of interest that accrues each day increases over time.

The bankruptcy court and district court also held that the constant interest method should be used, noting that the constant interest method comports more closely than the straight-line method with economic reality.

In *Allegheny*,[90] the bankruptcy court held that OID should be calculated by the straight-line method for purposes of Bankruptcy Code section 502(b)(2).

---

[89] 100 B.R. 247 (Bankr. W.D. Pa. 1989).
[90] *Supra* note 89, p. 254.

The Second Circuit pointed out that the bankruptcy court noted that the legislative history of section 502(b)(2) provides that unmatured interest should be "prorated," and assumed without analysis that the prorating must be done so that the increases are constant through time, rather than so that the *rate* of increase is constant through time.

Thus, the old OID is carried over to the new debt and must be amortized based on the life of the new debt, employing the constant interest method. If the maturity date of the new note (as in *LTV*) is earlier than the old debt, then the amount of the claim that will be allowed in bankruptcy will also be greater than the amount that is allowed for those that did not participate in the workout.

Valuation of Old Debt   Last, the bankruptcy court explored the calculation of OID, for which the value paid for the debenture must be determined. The value given in an exchange transaction like the one above is the fair market value of the property given up in exchange. The date of valuation of property given in exchange is the date of the exchange. For these reasons, the court found that the amount of the unamortized OID on the original notes could be readily calculated by applying the aforestated principles. However, the amount of unamortized OID on the new notes given in exchange cannot be calculated until the value of the original on the exchange date, which is subject to factual dispute, is determined by further proceedings.

Conclusion   Some of the reasoning used by the Second Circuit is similar to the logic used by the FASB in its Statement No. 15 to justify the reporting of no gain or loss on the exchange of debt instruments by troubled companies under certain circumstances. The logic and conclusions of the FASB have been questioned by many accounting theorists since its issuance. The Circuit Court noted that such "an exchange does not change the character of the underlying debt, but reaffirms and modifies it." The Second Circuit concluded that the concept of realization as used by the Internal Revenue Code does not apply in the bankruptcy context. It seems that the Circuit Court, as well as the FASB, has ignored that an exchange has occurred and that the debtor is most likely better off economically as a result of the new agreement.

As a result of the Second Circuit ruling, the fear that it will be more difficult to obtain an out-of-court agreement with bondholders has been eliminated.

Citing *In re Pittsburgh Rys Co.*,[91] the district court held that the fact that a claim was acquired at a discount does not affect the allowable amount of the claim or the creditor's voting power.

(b) Pension Claims

The Supreme Court ruled that the Pension Benefit Guaranty Corporation (PBGC) was within its rights in attempting to restore to LTV underfunded defined benefit pension plans that the company had surrendered to the PBGC while it was in bankruptcy.[92] LTV could not voluntarily terminate two of its three defined benefit plans because they had been negotiated in collective bar-

---

[91] 159 F.2d 630 (3d Cir. 1946).
[92] *Pension Benefit Guaranty Corporation v. LTV Corporation*, 110 S. Ct. 2668 (1990).

gaining. As a result, LTV attempted to have the PBGC terminate the plans. The PBGC involuntarily terminated three plans. Participants' benefits under the PBGC were less than the benefits that had been negotiated between the company and unionized workers. The workers sued. LTV subsequently negotiated a settlement of the lawsuit filed by the workers covered under the plan. LTV agreed to pay plan participants the difference between the benefits available from the prior plans and the amount paid by the PBGC.

The PBGC objected to the agreements negotiated. The PBGC characterized the plans as "follow-on" plans—designed to wrap around the insurance benefits provided by the PBGC in such a way as to provide both retirees and active participants substantially the same benefits as they would have received had no termination occurred. The PBGC considers follow-on plans "abusive" and structured to have the PBGC subsidize employers' pension plans. The bankruptcy court approved LTV's plans. The PBGC issued a restoration order, which LTV ignored. The PBGC sued in district court to enforce its order.

The district court vacated the PBGC's order, finding that the agency had exceeded its authority under section 4047 of ERISA. The Second Circuit affirmed. The Supreme Court ruled that ERISA section 4047 grants the PBGC the authority to reinstate follow-on plans.

It is estimated that this decision should save the PBGC about $2.5 billion. PBGC Executive Director James B. Lockhart praised the Supreme Court's decision, indicating that, although the PBGC is currently operating with a net worth deficit of $1 billion and faces an uncertain future, the agency is certainly more secure in light of the LTV decision.

Lockhart also indicated that the PBGC will begin immediately to work with LTV to return responsibility for the pension plans to the company. Agency officials also will work with LTV to ensure smooth administration of benefit payments to nearly 60,000 retirees and 40,000 workers and resumption of legally required funding of the plans.

To enhance the PBGC's position in relation to uninsured creditors in future bankruptcy situations, the PBGC has made a number of recommendations in the form of proposed changes in the Bankruptcy Code and other statutes to provide incentives to companies not to terminate their plans, including giving the PBGC priority in cases of bankruptcy and providing minimum funding standards.

The Court further held that the PBGC is not required to consider bankruptcy or labor law principles in deciding to restore pension plans.

In *In re Chateaugay Corporation (LTV)*,[93] the district court held that the claim of the PBGC does not have priority under section 507 of the Bankruptcy Code. The claim is considered unsecured and not an administrative expense (see § 5.32).

(c) Rejection of Collective Bargaining Agreements

Section 1113 of the Bankruptcy Code describes the procedures that must be followed for rejection or modification of an existing collective bargaining

---

[93] 130 B.R. 690 (S.D.N.Y. 1991).

agreement. Subsequent to filing the petition and prior to attempting to reject or modify an agreement, the debtor-in-possession or trustee must:

1   Make a proposal to the union, based on the most complete and reliable information available at the time. The proposal should provide for the modifications in the employee benefits and protections that are necessary to permit the reorganization of the debtor and should ensure that all creditors, the debtor, and all of the affected parties are treated fairly.
2   Provide the representative of the employees (usually, a union) with relevant information that is necessary for evaluation of the proposal.

During the period that begins with presentation of the proposal and ends on the date when the court will hear a request for rejection of the collective bargaining agreement, the debtor-in-possession or trustee should meet with the union representative, confer in good faith, and attempt to reach mutually satisfactory modifications of the agreement.

After seeing that the above requirements are satisfied, the court will rule on the rejection of the collective bargaining agreement. No damages are allowed when a labor contract is rejected under section 1113 of the Bankruptcy Code because section 365 of the Bankruptcy Code is inapplicable when the provisions of section 1113 of the Bankruptcy Code govern.[94]

§ 6.16   Special Provisions for Partially Secured Creditors

Section 1111(b) allows a secured claim to be treated as a claim with recourse/nonrecourse against the debtor in chapter 11 proceedings (that is, where the debtor is liable for any deficiency between the value of the collateral and the balance due on the debt) whether or not the claim is nonrecourse by agreement or applicable law. This preferred status terminates if the property securing the loan is sold under section 363 or is to be sold under the terms of the plan, or if the class of which the secured claim is a part elects application of section 1111(b)(2).

To illustrate this provision, consider the following. A corporation owns a building that is encumbered by a first mortgage of $8 million, a nonrecourse second of $4 million, and a nonrecourse third of $2 million. The debtor files a chapter 11 petition. The plan proposed by the debtor calls for interest and principal payments to be made to the first mortgage holder, and a reduction, by $1 million, of the amount to be paid to the second mortgage holder. The third mortgagee will receive nothing, because it is estimated that the value of the property is only $11 million. The second and third mortgagees reject the plan. As a result, there is a valuation of the building and it is determined to be worth $9 million. The allowed secured claims would be only $1 million for the second mortgagee and zero for the third mortgagee. However, because of section 1111(b), the nonrecourse mortgage is considered recourse and the provision of 502(b), which disallows claims that are not enforceable, does not apply. Three million dollars of the second mortgage and the entire amount of the third

---

[94] *In re Blue Diamond Coal Co.,* 160 B.R. 574 (E.D. Tenn. 1993).

mortgage ($2 million) would be unsecured claims. If, however, the property is sold for $9 million under section 363 or as a part of the plan, the second mortgagee would receive only $1 million and the third mortgagee nothing; they would not have unsecured claims for their deficiency in collateral.

Another selection is available under section 1111(b). A class of creditors can elect to have its entire nonrecourse claim considered secured. A class of creditors will normally be only one creditor. Multiple-member classes may, however, exist where there are publicly issued debentures, where an indenture trustee holds a lien on behalf of the debenture holders, or where a group of creditors has the same type of liens, such as mechanics' liens. If there is more than one creditor in a class, the class can exercise the option only if two-thirds in amount and a majority in number of allowed claims vote for such an election.[95] For example, in chapter 11 cases where most of the assets are pledged, very little may be available for unsecured creditors after administrative expenses are paid. Thus, the creditor might find it advisable to make the section 1111(b)(2) election. On the other hand, if there will be a payment to unsecured creditors of approximately 75 cents per dollar of debt, the creditor may not want to make this election. Note that the election is based on claims allowed, not just those voting. To be eligible for this election, the creditors must have allowed claims that are secured by a lien on property of the estate, and their interest in such property as holders of secured claims must not be of inconsequential value (§ 11.3). The election cannot be made if the holder has recourse against the debtor and property is sold under section 363 or is to be sold under the plan.

Often the secured creditor of a single-asset real estate case must decide if it is best to make the section 1111(b)(2) election and consider all of the claim secured. If the ratio of the value of the collateral to the amount of the debt is below a certain percentage point, making the election will result in the plan being nonconfirmable. For example, if the value of the security interest in a commercial building is $40 million and the amount of the note is $100 million, thus for the plan to be confirmed, the amount of the total payments must be equal to $100 million and the value of the payments must at least be $40 million. In order to generate these results at a current interest rate of 10 percent the payments period will have to be spread out over a period of 23 years. This period may be beyond the time in which property could be financed. As a result, the court may hold that the plan is not fair and equitable. However, if the value of the security was $75 million, a reasonable payment period exists and the plan would most likely be confirmed under the cramdown provisions if other conditions are satisfied.

The purpose of this election is to provide adequate protection to holders of secured claims where the holder is of the opinion that the collateral is undervalued. Also, if the treatment of the part of the debt that is accorded unsecured status is so unattractive, the holder may be willing to waive the unsecured deficiency claims.[96] The class of creditors that makes this election has the right to receive full payment for its claims over time. If the members of the class do not approve the plan, the court may confirm the plan as long as the plan provides

[95] 11 U.S.C. § 1111(b)(1)(A)(i).
[96] *Collier Bankruptcy Manual*, 3d ed., ¶ 1111.03(5).

that each member of the class receives deferred cash payments totaling at least the allowed amount of the claim. However, the present value of these payments as of the effective date of the plan must be at least equal to the value of the creditors' interest in the collateral.[97] Thus, although a creditor who makes the election under section 1111(b)(2) has the right to receive full payment over time, the value of that payment is required to only equal the value of the creditor's interest in the collateral.

Section 1111(b) does not specify when the election must be made. It should not, however, be required before the property is valued under section 506(a). Bankruptcy Rule 3014 provides that the election may be made at any time prior to the conclusion of the hearing on the disclosure statement, or within such later time as the court may fix. The election is to be made in writing and signed, unless made at the hearing on the disclosure statement. Also, Bankruptcy Rule 3014 states that if the election, where there is more than one creditor, is made by the majority, it "shall be binding on all members of the class with respect to the plan." The Advisory Committee Notes to Rule 3014 suggest that this election, once made and the disclosure statement approved, cannot be revoked unless the plan is not confirmed.

The bankruptcy court held that an undersecured creditor could not make the section 1111(b)(2) election on a conditional basis depending upon the court's determination of the confirmability of the plan.[98] The court held that a conditional election, or one made under protest, was binding. Generally an election can be withdrawn if the plan is materially altered. However, the court stated that there is no right to withdraw the section 1111(b)(2) election merely because the factual predicate of the plan has changed.

The bankruptcy court held, in *In re Overland Park Merchandise Mart*,[99] that it is technically improper to include in the same class the secured and unsecured parts of an undersecured claim.

DEVELOPING THE PLAN

The plan is the focal point of a chapter 11 reorganization. The function of the plan is to provide a description of the consideration each class of creditors and equity holders will receive. The plan may also be viewed as a document that satisfies the needs and objectives of the debtor and its stakeholders. It should be more of a settlement document than a document designed to satisfy the requirements of the Bankruptcy Code.

The use of chapter 11 and the development of a plan of reorganization is not limited to major businesses but is applicable as well to small businesses structured in the form of a corporation or individually owned through a proprietorship or a partnership. Although a large number of plans are filed by individuals, the focus in this section will be on those filed by corporations. A plan is often the result of intense negotiations between the debtor, its creditors, and equity holders. Often, plans for both large and small businesses deal with both revi-

---

[97] 11 U.S.C. § 1129(b)(2).
[98] *In re Paradise Springs Assocs.*, 165 B.R. 913 (Bankr. D. Ariz. 1993).
[99] 167 B.R. 647 (Bankr. D. Kan. 1994).

sions in financial structure and improvements in operations to make the business financially sound and economically viable. The terms of the plan not only must meet these objectives, but must be constructed to satisfy the requirements of the Bankruptcy Code.

The reorganization plan for a viable business is generally based on a business plan that has the blessings of the creditors' committee. With information from the business plan and knowledge about the value of the business (see Chapter 11), the debtor and its creditors are better equipped to negotiate a plan that will work and be in the best interest of the debtor, its creditors, and shareholders.

§ 6.17 Negotiating a Chapter 11 Plan

Bargaining between the debtor and its stakeholders can be both vigorous and delicate. The debtor bargains, perhaps, for a settlement that consists of a small percentage of the debt, one that demands only a small cash outlay now with payments to be made in the future. The debtor, early in the proceeding, in trying to convince the creditors that the business was viable prepared cash flow projections that were rather optimistic. Now the debtor wants a plan that does not overburden the business with future debt and interest payments and must now argue that the creditors will have to settle for less since the actual cash flow projections are going to be less than was anticipated. The creditors may argue that the optimistic cash flow projections are now capable of being realized, indicating that the value of the business is greater than anticipated, resulting in a large recovery. Whereas it may appear that the difference in the positions of the debtor and its creditors is becoming greater, there are several factors that tend to minimize the polarization of positions. All parties-in-interest see the need for the debtor with viable businesses to survive because they are generally better off if a plan can be developed. Liquidation is generally a less profitable option. Thus, the objective is to get the parties to focus on the solution that provides greater value.

The debtor may want the debts outstanding to be subordinated to new credit or may ask that the agreement call for partial payment in some form of equity. For example, the trade creditors want a settlement that represents a high percentage of the debt and consists of a larger cash down payment with the balance to be paid as soon as possible. If they demand too high a percentage, the company may be forced to liquidate, either immediately or at some future date, because it cannot make a large payment and still continue to operate. Creditors must not insist on more than the debtor has the ability to pay. The debtor needs to emerge from bankruptcy with a financial structure that allows the reorganized entity to obtain financing from trade creditors and other sources as working capital needed and provides the reorganized entity with sufficient cash from operations to sustain economic growth, generate a return to investors, and effectively compete in the market place.

In many cases the entity actually belongs to the creditors; thus any action that can be taken to increase the value of the reorganized entity will benefit all parties involved. In essence, the value of the reorganized debtor needs to be distributed among the interested parties—debtor, creditors, secured creditors, and shareholders. Creditors can demand that 90 percent of the value be represented by debt; however, this may significantly hamper the ability of the debtor to have enough working capital to sustain normal operations. A more workable solution may be to have a debt-to-equity ratio that is similar to the industry average. If the debtor does have a good basis for future profitable operations, the selection of the proper financial mix (debt-to-equity ratio) can significantly contribute to a successful reorganization.

If the creditors and the debtor can agree on the reorganization value of the entity that will emerge from chapter 11, the process of negotiating the terms of the plan will be much easier.

(a) Basic Rules

The success of the negotiations will, to some extent, depend on how well the parties involved agree on the valuation of the debtor and the long-term cash flow projections of the reorganized entity.

Fisher and Ury suggest four basic rules for negotiations:[100]

- *Separate the people from the problem*—do not allow ego and emotion to impact the economics of the decision. They should be dealt with separately.
- *Focus on interests, not positions*—attempt to satisfy each party's interests and not his or her negotiation position.
- *Invent options for mutual gains*—develop a range of potential solutions that advance shared interests and serve as catalysts for creatively reconciling conflicting interests.
- *Insist on using objective criteria*—rather than reaching an impasse, focus on objective criteria such as relative market value, etc.

(b) Factors Determining Success of the Plan

There are several factors that determine the extent to which a plan can be developed that will vary from one case to another. Most of these factors were discussed in other sections of this text. However, it is helpful to see them summarized in one location. A few of the many factors that influence the negotiations for the terms in a plan are described in 6.10 of Volume 2.

§ 6.18   Exclusivity Period

In cases where the debtor is allowed to operate the business as debtor-in-possession, the debtor has 120 days after the order for relief to file a plan and 180 days after the order of relief to obtain acceptance before others can file a plan.[101] The court may extend (or reduce) both time periods on request of any party after notice and hearing. For the average case, the time periods may be adequate, but for larger cases it will take more than 120 days to develop a plan. Even if a plan is put together in 120 days, it will take more than 60 days to obtain approval. After these time periods have expired, any party (debtor,

---

[100] *Getting to Yes* (Boston: Houghton Mifflin, 1981).
[101] 11 U.S.C., § 1121.

creditor, creditors' committee, equity security holder, and so forth) may file a plan.

If the debtor files the plan within the 120-day period or within an extension approved by the court, the debtor is given additional time (until 180 days after the order for relief or until the lapse of an extension approved by the court) to obtain the acceptance of all impaired classes of claims and interests. If the required acceptances are not obtained within the specified time period, the debtor's period of exclusivity ends. The acceptance by all impaired classes is required. Thus, the right that the debtor may have to cram down a class that did not accept the plan will not prevent the lapse of the debtor's exclusivity period. After the period of exclusivity ends, the court is required to consider plans submitted by other parties-in-interest, even if the debtor's plan was submitted first.[102]

If a trustee has been appointed, the time restrictions do not apply and any party-in-interest may file a plan. One approach that may be taken by the creditors to end the exclusivity period where the creditors desire the opportunity to submit a plan, may be to petition the court for a trustee to be appointed. Once the appointment has been approved, the creditors may elect a trustee or allow the U.S. trustee to appoint one, and thus obtain the right to file a plan because the appointment or election of a trustee ends the exclusivity period. It may be, however, that the motion to appoint a trustee may convince the court to end the exclusivity period and allow the creditors' plan to be submitted.

Once the exclusivity period ends, more than one plan may be filed. When multiple plans are submitted, the plan along with the applicable disclosure statement will be distributed by their proponent to the creditors and equity holders for voting. A creditor may vote for more than one of the plans. However, section 1129(c) provides that the court may confirm only one plan. Thus it is possible that more than one plan may be accepted by the required class of claims and interest and may satisfy the confirmation standards under the Bankruptcy Code. Section 1129(c) provides that under these conditions the court must decide which plan to confirm considering the relative preferences of creditors and stockholders in each of the plans. Although such consideration by the court is required, it would appear that it does not limit the court from considering other factors, such as the extent to which one of the plans required a cramdown on one or more of the impaired classes, the relative feasibility of the plans, and the relative preferences of the various classes of creditors and stockholders in each plan.

Initially courts were generally fairly lenient in extending the time period in which the debtor has exclusive right to develop a plan. However, *Timbers* (§ 5.27 and § 6.11) has resulted in a more careful review by the courts of requests to extend this exclusivity period. For example, in *In re Nicolet*,[103] the court required an affirmative showing by the debtor that good cause existed for the granting of the extension. In the largest bankruptcy case filed in 1988,[104] the court granted only a short extension of the exclusivity period, citing *Timbers* and stating that

---

[102] *In re Tranel*, 940 F 2d. 1168 (8th Cir. 1991).
[103] 80 B.R. 733 (Bankr. E.D. Pa. 1988).
[104] *In re Public Services Company of New Hampshire*, 88 B.R. 521 (Bankr. N.H. 1988).

"section 1121 was designed, and should be faithfully interpreted, to limit the delay that makes creditors the hostages of chapter 11 debtors."

The Bankruptcy Reform Act of 1994 modified section 158(a) of title 28 of the U.S. Code to provide for an immediate appeal to the district court from a bankruptcy court's order extending or reducing a debtor's exclusive period in which to file a plan. This change in title 28 will permit parties that feel they were harmed by an extension of or a failure to extend the exclusivity period to obtain possible recourse from the district court. This matter of right did not exist prior to this change under section 102 of the Bankruptcy Reform Act of 1994.

(a) Small Business

Earlier drafts of the changes to the Bankruptcy Code in 1994 contained a provision that would have created a new chapter 10 for small businesses. Congress decided not to add a new chapter but, instead, to modify the provisions of chapter 11 in order to expedite the process by which small businesses may reorganize under chapter 11. A small business is defined as one whose aggregate noncontingent, liquidated, secured, and unsecured debts are less than $2 million as of the date of the filing of the petition. A small business debtor that elects coverage under this provision can dispense with creditor committees. Section 1102(a) of the Bankruptcy Code was amended by the Bankruptcy Reform Act of 1994 to provide that, on request of a party in interest, the court may, in a case where the debtor is a small business, order that a committee of creditors not be appointed.

The Bankruptcy Reform Act of 1994 also modified section 1121 of the Bankruptcy Code to provide that only a debtor can file a plan during the first 100 days after the date of the order for relief and that all plans are to be filed within 160 days after the order for relief. On request of a party in interest, the court may reduce the 100-day period or the 160-day period for cause and may also increase the 100-day period if the debtor shows that the increase is needed because of circumstances for which the debtor should not be held accountable. The Bankruptcy Reform Act did not provide for an increase in the 160-day period in which a plan should be filed.

The Act amends section 1125 of the Bankruptcy Code to allow the bankruptcy court to conditionally approve a disclosure statement for a small business and to allow the debtor to solicit votes for the plan before the disclosure statement is approved, if the debtor provides adequate information to each holder of a claim or interest for which votes are solicited. The conditionally approved disclosure statement must be mailed at least 10 days prior to the confirmation hearing to those for whom votes were solicited. A hearing on the disclosure statement may be combined with a hearing on the confirmation of the plan.

§ 6.19   Classification of Claims

Section 1122 provides that claims or interests can be divided into classes, if each claim or interest is substantially similar to the others of such class. In *Matter of Bugg*,[105] the district court held that creditors holding liens on differ-

---

[105] 72 B.R. 781 (E.D. Pa. 1994).

ent properties do not have substantially similar claims and cannot be placed in the same class. In addition, a separate class of unsecured claims may be established consisting of claims that are below or reduced to an amount the court approves as reasonable and necessary for administrative convenience. For example, claims of less than $1,000, or those creditors who will accept $1,000 as payment in full of their claim, may be placed in one class and the claimants will receive the lesser of $1,000 or the amount of their claim. All creditors or equity holders in the same class are treated the same, but separate classes may be treated differently.

Generally, all unsecured claims, including claims arising from rejection of executory contracts or unexpired leases, will be placed in the same class except for administrative expenses. They may, however, be divided into different classes if separate classification is justified. The Bankruptcy Code does not require that all claims that are substantially the same be placed in the same class. Section 1122(a) does not require that all similarly situated claims be classified together. Thus the debtor has some discretion in classifying unsecured.[106]

There is considerable conflict among the courts regarding the extent to which claims that are similar must be placed in the same class or given similar treatment.

In *Barnes v. Whelan*,[107] the court stated that section 1122(a) "does not require that similar claims must be grouped together, but merely that any group created must be homogeneous." However, in *In re Mastercraft Record Plating, Inc.*, the court would not allow similar claims to be divided "to create a consenting class so as to permit confirmation."[108] If a group of unsecured claims was subordinated in favor of the other unsecured creditors and the holders of subordinated claims would receive less if the case were liquidated under chapter 7, the court would be required to consider the effect of this subordination and classify the claims separately.[109] In *In re Barney & Carey Co.*,[110] the bankruptcy court, relying upon *In re Tucson Self-Storage, Inc.*,[111] held that the unfair discrimination provision of section 1129(b)(1) of the Bankruptcy Code generally requires equal treatment of similarly situated creditors. Thus, similar classes cannot be treated in such disparate manner as to be unfair. In *In re Bloomingdale Partners*,[112] the bankruptcy court held that all claims that are substantially similar must be classified together. The court placed a tort claim in the same class with other unsecured creditors. However, in *In re EBP, Inc.*,[113] the bankruptcy court held that a tort claim that amounted to approximately 70 percent of the unsecured claims was considered dissimilar from the claims of unsecured trade creditors that were continuing to do business with the debtor, and thus could be classified separately. To further complicate the issues, some courts have held that whether claims are substantially similar for purposes of

---

[106] *In re One Times Square Associates Limited Partnership*, 41 F.3d 1502 (2d Cir. 1994), *cert. denied*, 513 U.S. 1153 (1995).

[107] 689 F.2d 193 (D.C. Cir. 1982).

[108] C.B.C.2d 1268 at 1270 (Bankr. Ct. S.D.N.Y. 1983).

[109] Collier, *supra note 96*, ¶ 1122.04(4).

[110] 170 B.R. 17 (Bankr. D. Mass. 1994).

[111] 166 B.R. 892 (Bankr. 9th Cir. 1994).

[112] 170 B.R. 984 (Bankr. N.D. Ill. 1994).

[113] 172 B.R. 241 (Bankr. N.D. Ohio 1994).

classification is a finding of fact and is reviewable only under the clearly erroneous standard.[114] However, other courts have held that the classification of claims is a matter of law.[115]

Deciding how to group claims becomes an important strategic decision whenever the debtor-in-possession has doubts as to whether the plan will be confirmed. A certain amount of gerrymandering of classes is acceptable as long as the claims that are grouped together are substantially similar. It is important to note that the substantial similarity test is based on the similarity of the claims, not the similarity of the creditors. In some situations, it is possible to group long-term suppliers with a strong interest in seeing the reorganization succeed with creditors who are pushing for liquidation. The limits to this are being explored in the courts and are somewhat uncertain. For example, in *In re Greystone Joint Venture III*,[116] the court refused to allow the debtor to put in separate classes a nonrecourse claim of $3.5 million and an unsecured trade creditor claim of less than $10,000. The Fifth Circuit rejected the debtor's argument that because the note was nonrecourse under state law, there was a sufficient distinction between the unsecured portion of the secured claim and that of the trade creditors to support separate classification. The court found that state law was irrelevant where the Bankruptcy Code, by the provisions of section 1111(b), allows the nonrecourse claim to be considered recourse. In this case, the trade creditors approved the plan, and Phoenix Mutual Life Insurance, holder of the large nonrecourse claim, voted against the plan. Because the trade creditors voted in favor of the plan, there was at least one class that voted for the plan, which was required for a "cram down." Courts continue to hold that, for purposes of the requirement in section 1129(a)(10) that at least one impaired class vote for the plan, the provision is not generally satisfied if the reason for the establishment of the class is to meet this requirement.[117]

Three other circuit courts have rejected this type of plan.[118] In a second circuit case that denied an attempt at gerrymandering classes, the circuit court refused to allow the debtor to separate two groups of claims. In *In re Boston Post Road Limited Partnership*,[119] the debtor attempted to separate the $5,000 trade creditor claim from a $500,000 deficiency claim filed by the FDIC. The court held that the claims must be grouped together under the substantial similarity requirements of section 1122(a).

---

[114] *See In re Johnson*, 21 F.3d 323 (9th Cir. 1994); *In re Patrician St. Joseph Partners, Ltd.*, 169 B.R. 669 (D. Ariz. 1994).

[115] *Texas Am. Oil Corp. v. U.S. Dep't of Energy*, 24 F.3d 210 (Fed. Cir. 1994); *In re Lumber Exch. Bldg. Ltd. Partnership*, 968 F.2d 647 (8th Cir. 1992).

[116] 948 F.2d 134 (5th Cir. 1991), *cert. denied*, 113 S. Ct. 72 (1992).

[117] *In re One Times Square Assocs. Ltd. Partnership*, 165 B.R. 773 (S.D.N.Y. 1994); *In re Dean*, 166 B.R. 949 (Bankr. D.N.M. 1994); *In re Daly*, 167 B.R. 734 (Bankr. D. Mass. 1994); *In re North Wash. Ctr. Ltd. Partnership*, 165 B.R. 805 (Bankr. D. Md. 1994); *In re Barakat*, 173 B.R. 672 (Bankr. C.D. Cal. 1994) (acceptance by a class that has no genuine interest in the reorganization does not satisfy the requirements of section 1129(a)(10) even when the class is technically impaired). *But see In re Rivers End Apartments, Ltd.*, 167 B.R. 470 (Bankr. S.D. Ohio 1994) (separate classification of artificial deficiency and trade creditors permitted).

[118] *John Hancock Mutual Life Insurance Co. v. Route 37 Business Park Associates*, 987 F.2d 154 (3d Cir. 1993); *In re Bryson Properties, XVIII*, 961 F.2d 496 (4th Cir. 1992), *cert. denied*, 113 S. Ct. 191 (1992); *In the matter of Lumber Exchange, Bldg. Ltd. Partnership*, 968 F.2d 647 (8th Cir. 1992); *In re Windsor on the River Assocs., Ltd.*, 7 F.3d 127 (8th Cir. 1994).

[119] 21 F.3d 477 (2d Cir. 1994).

Other bankruptcy and district court decisions have found similar plans to be improper.[120] Thus, a trend appears to be evolving against allowing a class with a comparatively small financial interest in the details of the plan from being the sole confirming class.

In *In re Stratford Associates Ltd. Partnership*,[121] the bankruptcy court held that unsecured claims may be separately classified where the notice for the separate classes is not improper, such as an attempt to gerrymander the voting. The court also noted that, in a cram-down situation, there is unfair discrimination if there is separate classification of unsecured claims and the plan provides less favorable treatment to one or more classes of unsecured claims. Several courts have held that the unsecured deficiency claim of an undersecured creditor may not be classified separately from other unsecured claims.[122] In *In re Channel Realty Associates*,[123] the bankruptcy court would not allow the debtor to unilaterally place the entire claim of an undersecured creditor into one secured class because it would be tantamount to make the section 1111(b)(2) election for the creditor.

Several courts have held that the deficiency claims of unsecured recourse creditors could not be separately classified from other unsecured claims when there is no legitimate reason for the separate classification.[124]

The Seventh Circuit[125] held that because the legal rights of a deficiency claim for an undersecured, nonrecourse deficiency claims under section 1111(b) of the Bankruptcy Code were substantially different from those of general unsecured creditors, separate classification was required for the deficiency claim.

§ 6.20   Claim Subordination

Subordination could occur by agreement or by order of the court. In fact, there are at least four types of subordination[126] that require consideration in developing a plan, as described here.

---

[120] *See, e.g., In re Briscoe Enterprises, Ltd.,* II, 138 B.R. 795 (Bankr. N.D. Tex. 1992); *In re Boston Post Road Ltd. Partnership,* 145 B.R. 745 (Bankr. D. Conn. 1992); *In re Willows Convalescent Centers Ltd. Partnership,* 1991 U.S. Dist. LEXIS 19430 (D. Minn. 1991); *In re Cantonwood Associates Ltd. Partnership,* 138 B.R. 648 (Bankr. D. Mass. 1992); *Piedmont Associates v. Cigna Property & Casualty Ins. Co.,* 132 B.R. 75 (N.D. Ga. 1991); *In re Valrico Square Ltd. Partnership,* 113 B.R. 794 (Bankr. S.D. Fla. 1990); *In re Waterways Barge Partnership,* 104 B.R. 776 (Bankr. N.D. Miss. 1989); *In re Ward,* 89 B.R. 998 (Bankr. S.D. Fla. 1988); *In re Caldwell,* 76 B.R. 643 (Bankr. E.D. Tenn. 1987). *But see In re Johnston,* 140 B.R. 526 (Bankr. 9th Cir. 1992); *In re Creekside Landing, Ltd.,* 140 B.R. 713 (Bankr. M.D. Tenn. 1992); *In re General Homes Corp.,* FGMC, 134 B.R. 853 (Bankr. S.D. Tex. 1991); *In re 11,111 Inc.,* 117 B.R. 471 (Bankr. D. Minn. 1990); *In re Mortgage Investment Co. of El Paso,* 111 B.R. 604 (Bankr. W.D. Tex. 1990).

[121] 145 B.R. 689 (Bankr. D. Kan. 1992).

[122] *In re Main Road Properties, Inc.* 144 B.R. 217 (Bankr. D. R.I. 1992); *In the matter of Boston Post Road Ltd.* Partnership, *supra* note 119.

[123] 142 B.R. 597 (Bankr. D. Mass. 1992).

[124] *See In re Baxter & Baxter, Inc.,* 172 B.R. 198 (Bankr. C.D.N.Y. 1994); *In re Barney & Carey Co.,* 170 B.R. 17 (Bankr. D. Mass. 1994).

[125] *In re Woodbrook Assocs.,* 19 F.3d 312 (7th Cir. 1994). *See In re Baldwin Park Towne Center, Ltd.,* 171 B.R. 374 (Bankr. C.D. Cal. 1994); *In re SM 104 Ltd.,* 160 B.R. 202 (Bankr. S.D. Fla. 1993); *In re Overland Park Merchandise Mart,* 167 B.R. 647 (Bankr. D. Kan. 1994).

[126] Daniel C. Cohn, "Subordinated Claims: Their Classification and Voting under Chapter 11 of the Bankruptcy Code," *American Bankruptcy Law Journal,* Vol. 56 (October 1982), pp. 295–301.

One problem that arises in all subordination provisions and has not been resolved deals with who has the right to vote in a plan—is it the senior or subordinated creditor? Section 1126(a) provides that the holder of a claim or interest may accept or reject a chapter 11 plan. However, it is not clear if the senior or subordinated creditor would be considered the holder of the claim. Generally, it is assumed by most plan proponents that the subordinated creditor has the right to vote on the plan's acceptance. To assume otherwise would most likely result in extensive litigation and delays. It would appear that this problem would be resolved if the subordination agreement provided that if the subordination results in all of the claim being transferred to the secured lender, the right to vote this claim in bankruptcy is transferred to the senior creditor.

(a) Contractual Subordination

Section 510(b) of the Bankruptcy Code provides that a subordination agreement is enforceable in bankruptcy to the same extent that such an agreement is enforceable under applicable nonbankruptcy law.

An agreement where a creditor agrees to give another superior rights to collect the debt is very common in chapter 11 cases. For example, in the case of an LBO, junior bonds were often issued that are subordinated to senior notes and other junior bonds. Some agreements forbid the subordination creditor from receiving any payment until the senior creditor is paid in full. For example, the bank may require this type—complete forbearance—where loans from the owner are subordinated. The more common type is "inchoate" forbearance where payments can be made to the subordinated creditor unless the debtor is in default on the senior debt.

Often the subordination apples only to institutional debt. Thus the subordination claim may be subordinated to a line of credit or term loan from a bank and not to the trade claims. Three types of creditors may be impacted by the subordination of a claim of one general unsecured creditor to a senior unsecured creditor and must be dealt with in the plan—senior creditor, subordinated creditor, and the other unsecured creditors. There is considerable uncertainty and debate over the best way to provide for the senior creditor to receive the consideration that it is entitled to receive from the subordinated creditor. One option is to put all claimants in one class and use treatment provisions to adjust consideration to the senior creditor from the subordinated creditor or provide for the same consideration and allow the senior creditor to use nonbankruptcy law for recovery from the subordinated creditor. A second option is to put the subordinated creditor in one class and the senior creditor and other unsecured creditors in another class and use treatment provisions to adjust the consideration the senior creditor receives from the subordinated class. A third option is to place the senior creditor, subordinated creditor, and other unsecured creditors in three separate classes. A large number of plans have used the third option—three separate classes—in developing the plan. Under this alternative the other unsecured creditors must be assured that the secured lender is not receiving a larger consideration that it is entitled to receive. To illustrate this concept, consider the following example where the senior creditor's claim has been subordinated to a bank's secured, term loan that was undersecured by $20,000:

Classes of Unsecured Claims	Claim Amount	Consideration	% Recovery
Senior creditor	$20,000	$17,000	85
Subordinated creditor	5,000	500	10
Other unsecured	40,000	20,000	50
Total	$75,000	$37,500	50

If all of the unsecured creditors were placed in one class and given the same treatment, the recovery would be 50 percent. Since the other unsecured are receiving 50 percent, it would be difficult for an objection to be raised by the other unsecured class on the basis that they are not fairly treated. In this particular case, the subordinated creditors were given $500 to obtain their approval of the plan. However, based on the loan agreement they are not entitled to any consideration unless the senior creditor is paid in full. The bank allowed this amount to be paid to obtain the subordinated creditor class's approval of the plan. In some cases the other unsecured creditors also agree to reduce their percent recovery to provide additional consideration to win the approval of the subordinated creditor's class.

(b) Co-Debtor Claims Subordination

Under section 509, the co-debtor who pays part of the claim of the primary creditor may have his or her claim against the debtor due to this payment subordinated to that of the primary creditor.

(c) Securities Fraud Claims Subordination

Under section 510(b), claims for fraud in the purchase of a security are subordinated to all claims or interests superior or equal to the security, except that if such claim is common stock, it has the same priority as common stock. For example, defrauded purchasers of common stock will have the same priority as other common stockholders but will be subordinated to all preferred stockholders and to general unsecured creditors. As with contractual subordination, it may be best to establish a separate class for the subordinated claim holders.

(d) Equitable Subordination

Section 510(c) provides that the court, after notice and a hearing, may apply principles of equitable subordination.

The legal test for establishing equitable subordination as defined in *Mobile Steel*[127] consist of three conditions:

1 The claimant must have engaged in inequitable conduct.
2 The misconduct must have resulted in injury to the creditors, or conferred an unfair advantage on the claimant.

---

[127] *In re Mobile Steel Co.*, 563 F.2d 692, 700 (5th Cir. 1977).

3 Equitable subordination must not be inconsistent with federal bankruptcy law.[128]

The *Mobile Steel* case was decided before the Bankruptcy Code became law and most likely is moot because section 510(c) incorporates the common law of equitable subordination into the Bankruptcy Code.[129] The Eleventh Circuit also concluded that claims could be subordinated only to the extent necessary to offset harm suffered by the debtor and the creditors because of the conduct.[130]

The standard of inequitable conduct that justifies subordination of a non-insider/non-fiduciary's claim generally provides that "unless the creditor has dominated or controlled the debtor to gain an unfair advantage, his claim will be subordinated, based upon inequitable conduct, only if the claimant has committed some breach of an existing, legally recognized duty arising under contract, tort or other area of law. In commercial cases, the proponent must demonstrate a substantial breach of contract and advantage-taking by the creditor."[131] In the absence of a contractual breach, the proponent must demonstrate fraud, misrepresentation, estoppel, or similar conduct that justifies the intervention of equity.[132] However, as noted in *Columbus Ave. Realty Trust*,[133] fraud and illegality constitute grounds for equitable subordination even where the creditor is not a fiduciary or insider or does not somehow control the debtor.

Cohn suggested that courts have relied on three basic kinds of unfairness as grounds for equitable subordination. The first is fraud, illegality, breach of fiduciary relationships, or other blatant wrongdoing. A second reason is undercapitalization.[134] It is not unusual for creditors to insist that insiders' claims be subordinated under the plan, or to object to insiders' claims on equitable grounds. For example, if the officers of an undercapitalized, closely held corporation made loans to the debtor and then sought to be paid on a par with other unsecured creditors, a court might be persuaded (on proper facts) that the funds should be deemed "capital contributions." Many factors might be considered, such as whether notes were executed under proper corporate authority and other aspects of how the debtor and the insider treated the transaction. A third ground for subordination, related to the second, relates to control over the debtor's operations. For example, in cases where a creditor controls another creditor for its own purposes and without regard to the debtor, the claim might be subordinated.

In the case of *In re Herby's Foods, Inc.*,[135] the insiders followed the practice of never injecting any equity capital into Herby's, electing instead to advance funds

---

[128] *In re Baker & Getty Financial Services, Inc.* 974 F.2d 712 (6th Cir. 1992).

[129] *In re 80 Nassau Associates*, 169 B.R. 832 (Bankr. S.D.N.Y. 1994).

[130] *In re Lemco Gypsum, Inc.* 911 F.2d 1553 (11th Cir. 1990), *reh'g denied* 930 F.2d 925 (11th Cir. 1991).

[131] *In re Kham & Nate's Shoes No. 2, Inc.*, 908 F 2d.1351, 1357 (7th Cir. 1990).

[132] *In re Boggy Boggs, Inc.*, 819 F.2d 574, 579 (5th Cir. 1987).

[133] 119 Bankr. at 377

[134] *Id.*, pp. 299–301.

[135] 2 F.3d 128 (5th Cir. 1993).

through tardily perfected secured loans made at times when no bona fide third-party lender would have done so. The funds were advanced with full knowledge that Herby's was undercapitalized and insolvent. The loans were not initially reflected on Herby's books and when finally booked, the debt was listed as an unsecured loan, and subsequently an effort was made to perfect the loans after interest payments ceased. Very few payments were made on the funds advanced and interest payments, when made, were not current. Based on these conditions the Fifth Circuit concluded that these actions constituted sufficient evidence of inequitable conduct to support equitable subordination of the debts. The Fifth Circuit refused to conclude that the ruling by the bankruptcy court that the insider claims "are hereby fully subordinated to those of the other unsecured creditors in this case" meant that the claims were reclassified as equity.

The Fifth Circuit also held in a earlier case that a creditor exercising its right to reduce the amount of money that it advanced in accordance with the loan agreement executed at arm's length and prior to the debtor's insolvency was not acting at a level of control necessary to invoke the doctrine of equitable subordination.[136] The failure of the bank to advance funds postpetition of no more than 25 percent of the maximum amount established where the bank reserved the right to cease making further advances was determined to be the bank's contractual privilege and did not justify the subordination of its claim.[137]

Equitable subordination may not be granted when a creditor takes reasonable actions to protect its interest, and when there has been no unfair advantage to the creditor or damage to other creditors.[138] Also, the claims of a disfavored subgroup may not be subordinated to other claims in the same category under section 510 (c) because the bankruptcy court lacks authority to take such action. The categorical reordering of priority must be done at the legislative level and is beyond the scope of judicial authority according to the Supreme Court.[139]

Although chapter 11 does not contain any specific provisions on how to handle postpetition penalty-type claims, bankruptcy courts generally favored such claims and disallowed them on equitable grounds where allowance might impact the effort to reorganize. Some courts subordinated these claims under the provisions of section 510(c) of the Bankruptcy Code.[140] However, the Supreme Court[141] concluded that postpetition tax penalties are administrative expense claims. The Supreme Court noted that because Congress did not deny noncompensatory, postpetition tax penalties the first priority given to other administrative expenses, the bankruptcy court may not make this determination under the guise of equitable subordination.

In *Stoubmos v. Kilimnik*,[142] the Ninth Circuit held that in determining whether an insider's claim should be subordinated under section 510(c), focus

---

[136] *In re Clark Pipe & Supply Co., Inc.* 893 F.2d 693 (5th Cir. 1990).

[137] *In re Kham & Nate's Shoes No. 2, Inc.*, 908 F 2d.1351 (7th Cir. 1990).

[138] *In re Castletons, Inc.*, 990 F.2d 551 (10th Cir. 1993).

[139] *United States v. Reorganized CF&I Fabricators of Utah, Inc.* 116 S. Ct. 2106 (1996).

[140] *In re Hillsborough Holdings Corp.*, 146 H.R. 1015 (Bankr. M.D. Fla. 1992).

[141] *United States v. Noland, Trustee for Debtor First Truck Lines, Inc.*, 116 S. Ct. 1524 (1996).

[142] 988 F.2d 949 (9th Cir. 1993); *see In re Fabricators, Inc.*, 926 F.2d 1458 (5th Cir. 1991); *In re N & D Properties*, 799 F.2d 726 (11th Cir. 1986).

should be on whether the conduct unfairly injured particular creditors or gave the insider an unfair advantage over particular creditors and not the extent to which creditors in general were harmed. The court also held that it makes no difference whether the claim is secured or unsecured and that subordination should only be applied to those creditors who were disadvantaged.

The bankruptcy court[143] held that if the creditors' misconduct resulted in harm to the entire creditor body, the party seeking equitable subordination need not identify the injured creditor or quantify the amounted by which they were injured. The party seeking the subordination must show only that the creditors were harmed in some general, concrete manner and then it is sufficient for that party to allege that the general creditors are less likely to collect their debts as a basis for the claim to be subordinated to all other claims.

§ 6.21 Secured Claim Classification

Generally, each secured claim with an interest in specific property will be in a separate class. However, the court has allowed creditors holding purchase money mortgages on different parcels of real property in a similar location to be placed in the same class.[144] Collier suggested that the classification of secured claims is determined on the basis of priority under state law, nature of the collateral, and agreement among creditors with respect to subordination.[145]

In the case of undersecured claim holders, only the secured part of the claim would be classified as a secured claim and the balance would be an unsecured claim under section 506 of the Bankruptcy Code unless the creditor elected to have the entire claim considered secured under section 1111(b)(2). Additionally, under certain conditions when the claim is undersecured, the debtor and creditor may agree on the consideration to be received in full settlement of the entire claim. Generally, in each situation described above the creditor will be in a separate class.

§ 6.22 Interest Classification

Interests will also be classified separately if the securities have different rights. For example, preferred stock is in a separate class from common stock, and one issue of preferred stock may be in a separate class from another if the rights are not the same.

§ 6.23 Content of the Plan

The items that may be included in the plan are listed in section 1123. The provisions are almost identical to those under Chapter X of prior law. Certain

---

[143] *In re 80 Nassau Associates,* 169 B.R. 832 (Bankr. S.D.N.Y. 1994).

[144] *See In re Palisades-on-the-Desplaines,* 89 F.2d 214 (7th Cir. 1937).

[145] Collier, *supra* note 96, ¶ 1122.04(6). Rather than classify the subordinated debt separately, it is possible, but not common, to assign the subordinated claim to the holder of the senior claims, who then votes the subordinated claim and receives all payments attributed to it until the senior claim is paid in full and the balance received is then attributed to the subordinated claim. See *In re Item-lab, Inc.,* 197 F. Supp. 194, 198 (E.D.N.Y. 1961).

items are listed as mandatory and others are discretionary. The mandatory provisions are:

1 Designate classes of claims and interests.
2 Specify any class of claims or interests that is not impaired under the plan.
3 Specify the treatment of any class of claims or interests that is impaired under the plan.
4 Provide the same treatment for each claim or interest in a particular class, unless the holders agree to less favorable treatment.
5 Provide adequate means for the plan's implementation, such as:
   a Retention by the debtor of all or any part of the property of the estate.
   b Transfer of all or any part of the property of the estate to one or more entities.
   c Merger or consolidation of the debtor with one or more persons.
   d Sale of all or any part of the property of the estate, either subject to or free of any lien, or the distribution of all or any part of the property of the estate among those having an interest in such property of the estate.
   e Satisfaction or modification of any lien.
   f Cancellation or modification of any indenture or similar instrument.
   g Curing or waiving any default.
   h Extension of a maturity date or a change in an interest rate or other term of outstanding securities.
   i Amendment of the debtor's charter.
   j Issuance of securities of the debtor, or of any entity involved in a merger or transfer of the debtor's business for cash, for property, for existing securities, or in exchange for claims or interests, or for any other appropriate purpose.
6 Include in the charter of the debtor, if the debtor is a corporation, or of any corporation referred to in provision 5 above, a provision prohibiting the issuance of nonvoting equity securities, and providing, as to the several classes of securities possessing voting power, an appropriate distribution of such power among such classes, including, in the case of any class of equity securities having a preference over another class of equity securities with respect to dividends, adequate provisions for the election of directors representing such preferred class in the event of default in the payment of such dividends.
7 Contain only provisions that are consistent with the interests of creditors and stockholders and with public policy with respect to the selection of officers, directors, or a trustee under the plan.

A plan that divests some shareholders of all shares and transfers completed ownership to another shareholder violated the equal treatment provisions of section 1123(a)(4).[146]

---

[146] *In re Modern Steel Treating Co.* 130 B.R. 60 (Bankr. N.D. Ill. 1991).

Effective for agreements entered into after October 22, 1994, the Bankruptcy Reform Act of 1994 added subsection (d) to section 1123 of the Bankruptcy Code. The new subsection provides that, notwithstanding subsection (a) and sections 506(b), 1129(a)(7), and 1129(b) of the Bankruptcy Code, if it is proposed in a plan to cure a default, the amount necessary to cure the default is to be determined in accordance with the underlying agreement and applicable nonbankruptcy law. This provision overrules the decision in *Rake v. Wade*,[147] in which the Supreme Court held that the Bankruptcy Code requires that interest be paid on mortgage arrearages paid by debtors curing defaults on their mortgages. Notwithstanding state law, this decision had the impact of requiring debtors to pay interest on interest *and* interest on late charges and other fees.

The plan filed by American Rice is presented as 6.11 in Volume 2 of *Bankruptcy and Insolvency Accounting*. Article IV (6.11(d)) satisfies the first man-datory provision—designation of claims and interests. Articles IV and V (6.11(d and e)) illustrates the second, third, and fourth mandatory provisions—specify those classes of claims that are not impaired, specify the treatment of any class of claim that is impaired, and provide for the same treatment for each class. Article V (6.11(e)) deals with equity interest. Article VIII (6.11(h)) contains items that fall under the fourth mandatory provision—provide adequate means to implement the plan.

Section 1124 describes what is meant by the impairment of a class of claims or interests (§ 6.25).

§ 6.24 Permissible Provisions

In addition to the requirements listed above, the plan according to section 1123 may:

1 Impair or leave unimpaired any class of unsecured or secured claims or interests.

2 Provide for the assumption, rejection, or assignment of executory contracts or leases.

3 Provide for settlement or adjustment of any claim or interest of the debtor or provide for the retention and enforcement by the debtor, the trustee, or by a representative of the estate appointed for such purpose, of any claim or interest.

4 Provide for the sale of all of the property of the debtor and the distribution of the proceeds to the creditors and stockholders.

5 Include any other provision not inconsistent with the provisions of the Bankruptcy Code.

In many cases it is not unusual for the plan to be confirmed before action is taken to recover preferences, fraudulent transfers, or other potential assets. The recovery action may be provided for in the plan under section 1123(b)(3). Two conditions exist for bringing postconfirmation preference action under

---

[147] 113 S. Ct. 2187 (1993).

section 1123(b)(3) by the debtor, trustee, or representative of the estate appointed for such purpose:

1 Any recovery must benefit the estate.
2 The plan must expressly retain the right to pursue such actions.[148]

A bankruptcy court held that benefits includes past benefits to the estate such as funding of a settlement agreement even though the recovery will benefit the new entity and not the estate.[149] An individual was considered as the representative of the estate for purposes of avoiding powers and recovery action when appointed by the debtor, both debtor and creditors agreed to the responsibilities of the individual, and the reorganization plan that was approved by the parties and confirmed by the court contained such agreement.[150]

Not covered in these requirements are the provisions for priority claims and administrative expenses. They are covered in the confirmation section of the Code, beginning at § 6.28.

In the plan filed by American Rice (see 6.11 of Volume 2), the first permissible provision allows the debtor to select between impaired or unimpaired classes of claims. Article VII (6.11(g)) deals with the rejection of executory contracts, Article XII (6.11(l)) covers retention of jurisdiction, and Article XI (6.11(k)) deals with the successors and assigns rights. These are all examples of items that may be classified as permissible provisions.

The provision that the debtor can arrange for the sale of all of the property and distribute the proceeds to the creditors and stockholders generally was not available under Chapter XI of prior law.[151] In fact, several large as well as small companies have decided in recent years to use chapter 11 for this purpose because of some of the advantages it offers. It is often easier to collect receivables when a company is in a chapter 11 proceeding rather than in chapter 7, and it results in a higher realization on these accounts. The debtor may avoid the appointment of a trustee and the related costs. The debtor knows the business and may be in a position to liquidate the business in a more orderly fashion than a trustee who is not familiar with the debtor's operations. The court may allow more time for the debtor to operate the business because it is possible that the creditors might not be placing as much pressure on the debtor to liquidate the business. It is easier, too, for a firm undergoing a chapter 11 liquidation to obtain going-concern values upon disposition of assets because management is in a better position to negotiate the sales transactions, if at least some of the current management is able to stay with the firm. Officers of the company will usually not receive salaries from a trustee unless they are retained as consultants, whereas they could be paid as employees of the debtor-in-possession in a chapter 11 proceeding. Also, the debtor has more flexibility in chapter 11. If a decision is made to continue the business, this may be easier to do if the debtor is already in a chapter 11 proceeding. The major advantage

---

[148] *In re Paramount Plastics, Inc.*
[149] *In re Churchfield Mangement & Investing Corp.*, 122 B.R. 76 (Bankr. S.D. N.Y. 1990).
[150] *In re Sweetwater*, 884 F.2d 1323 (10th Cir. 1989).
[151] *In re Pure Penn Petroleum Co.*, 188 F.2d 851 (2d Cir. 1951).

to the debtor of a chapter 11 liquidation plan over a liquidation under chapter 7 is that the debtor is able to maintain its control over the business; in chapter 7, the debtor would not have any control. There may also be tax benefits, although a liquidating corporation is ineligible for a discharge under section 1141(d)(3). The creditors may not always accept a liquidating chapter 11 proceeding, because they may have reservations about the debtor's management conducting a total liquidation without a trustee looking after the creditors' interest. Often, when a trustee is not appointed, there will be a change in management, or a professional liquidator will be retained to assist with the development of a plan of liquidation and with the eventual liquidation of the business.

The bankruptcy court noted that the provisions of section 1123 exist to accommodate financial restructuring and they are not intended as blanket authority for liquidation under chapter 11.[152]

§ 6.25 Impairment of Claims

In determining which classes of creditors' claims or stockholders' interests must approve the plan, it is first necessary to determine whether the class is impaired.[153] Section 1124 states that a class of claims or interests is impaired under the plan, unless the plan:

1 Leaves unaltered the legal, equitable, and contractual rights to which such claim or interest entitles the holder of such claim or interest.

2 Notwithstanding any contractual provision or applicable law that entitles the holder of such claim or interest to demand or receive accelerated payment of such claim or interest after the occurrence of a default—

    A cures any such default that occurred before or after the commencement of the case under this title, other than a default of a kind specified in section 365(b)(2) of this title [such as a bankruptcy or insolvency clause that would make the entire debt due];

    B reinstates the maturity of such claim or interest as such maturity existed before such default;

    C compensates the holder of such claim or interest for any damages incurred as a result of any reasonable reliance by such holder on such contractual provision or such applicable law; and

    D does not otherwise alter the legal, equitable, or contractual rights to which such claim or interest entitles the holder of such claim or interest.

Effective for petitions filed after October 22, 1994, the Bankruptcy Reform Act of 1994 amended section 1124 of the Bankruptcy Code to provide that the payment of a claim as of the effective date with cash equal to the allowed amount of the claim will result in the claim's being impaired. Prior to this amendment such claims were not impaired. As a result, creditors in a class that provides for the full payment of a claim with cash as of the effective date will be able to vote for or against the plan. If the debtor does not obtain the

---

[152] *In re Lyons Transportation Lines, Inc.,* 132 B.R. 526 (Bankr. W.D. Pa. 1991).
[153] 11 U.S.C. § 1129(a)(8).

votes needed for approval of the plan, the plan may be confirmed only if the "fair and equitable" cram-down provision of section 1129(b) of the Bankruptcy Code is satisfied. For the plan to be considered fair and equitable where the debtor is solvent, courts have held that the creditors must not only receive payment of their claim in full, but must also receive interest.[154] This provision overrules the decision in *New Valley*, where the bankruptcy court held that the requirements for confirmation were met without interest being paid because the claims were not impaired.[155]

Dealing with the 1994 amendments to the Bankruptcy Code, the bankruptcy court held that a class of creditors that is paid in full as of the effective date is impaired because the payment of the claim leaves the holder of such claim with no legal, equitable, or contractual rights.[156]

The Seventh Circuit noted that the standard for impairment is very lenient and that any alternation of rights constitutes impairment, even if the value of the rights is enhanced.[157] The bankruptcy court held that a class cannot be impaired by paying a rate of interest higher than that allowed by state law.[158] The Ninth Circuit allowed a bankruptcy court to approve a plan that permitted a debtor to pay prepetition interest rates even though the debtor was obligated to pay a higher postdefault rate and there was no acceleration of the debt.[159]

The Ninth Circuit Court held that a class providing for the payment of the amount required under section 502 of the Bankruptcy Code for the cancellation of lease is not considered impaired even though such payment is less than the amount that would have been received outside of bankruptcy.[160] (See 5.29.)

Item 8 of the confirmation requirements of section 1129(a) (see § 5.29) states that each class that is impaired must accept the plan. A class, as stated in this paragraph, is not impaired if the plan cures the defaults, reinstates the maturity of the claim or interest, compensates for certain damages suffered, and does not alter the legal, equitable, or contractual rights of each member of the class. Gitlin, Horwich, and Flaschen[161] made the following observations about this impairment provision, based on the authorities noted:

1 Cure and compensation payments must be made in cash prior to confirmation of the plan. *In re Jones*, 32 B.R. 951 (Bankr. D. Utah 1983).

2 As a matter of law, a class is not impaired if the plan cures defaults and reinstates the maturity of the mortgage—even when the then current

---

[154] *See, e.g., Consolidated Rock Products Co. v. Dubois*, 312 U.S. 510 (1941); *Debentureholders Protective Committee of Continental Inv. Corp.*, 679 F.2d 264 (1st Cir. 1982).

[155] *In re New Valley Corp.*, 168 B.R. 73 (Bankr. D.N.J. 1994).

[156] *In re Atlanta-Stewart Partners*, 193 B.R. 503 (Bankr. N.D. Ga. 1996).

[157] *In re Wabash Valley Power Association*, 72 F.3d 1305 (7th Cir. 1995), cert. denied, 117 S. Ct. 389 (1996).

[158] *See In re Windsor on the River Associates, Ltd.*, 7 F.3d 127 (8th Cir. 1993).

[159] *In re Boston Post Road Ltd. Partnership*, 145 B.R. 745 (Bankr. D. Conn. 1992).

[160] *In re Southeast Co.*, 868 F.2d 335 (9th Cir. 1989).

[161] Richard A. Gitlin, Harold S. Horwich, and Evan D. Flaschen, "Chapter 11 Plan Confirmation and the Real Estate Mortgage: 'Cramdown' and Other Unpalatable Alternatives," in Richard A. Gitlin, *Real Estate and the Bankruptcy Code*, 1986 (New York: Practising Law Institute, 1986), pp. 370–379.

market rate of interest exceeds the contract rate in the mortgage. *In re Victory Construction Co.*, 42 B.R. 145, 153 (Bankr. C.D. Cal. 1984).

3   Some courts have taken the position that a foreclosure judgment prevents deceleration of debt. *In re Celeste Court Apartments, Inc.*, 47 B.R. 470 (D. Del. 1985); *In re Monroe Park*, 18 B.R. 790 (Bankr. D. Del. 1982). *Contra, In re Madison Hotel Associates*, 749 F.2d 410 (7th Cir. 1984).

4   Damages suffered as a result of reasonable reliance on contractual provisions do *not* include the amount of the difference between interest on the loan at current market rates during the term of the plan and interest on the loan at a lower contractual rate. *In re Manville Forest Products Corp.*, 43 B.R. 293 (Bankr. S.D.N.Y. 1984); *In re Rolling Green Country Club*, 26 B.R. 729 (Bankr. D. Minn. 1982). However, damages have been held to include attorneys' fees and expenses in a prepetition foreclosure, and interest on unpaid mortgage installments at a market interest rate.

5   *In re Masnorth Corp.*, 28 B.R. 892 (Bankr. N.D. Ga. 1983), is also of note because it suggests that defaults in property maintenance covenants may have to be cured as well.

6   In *In re Barrington Oaks General Partnership*, 15 B.R. 952 (Bankr. D. Utah 1982), the court held that a transfer of mortgaged property from one mortgagor to another constituted impairment of the mortgagee's contractual rights even in the absence of a "due on transfer" provision in the mortgage. *Contra, In re Orlando Tennis World Development Inc.*, 34 B.R. 558 (Bankr. M.D. Fla. 1983).

7   In *In re Elijah*, 41 B.R. 348 (Bankr. W.D. Mo. 1984), the court held that a plan that proposed to cure defaults by surrender of collateral instead of payment of principal and interest altered the mortgagees' rights and thereby constituted impairment.

Thus, for a plan to leave unimpaired a class of claims or interests, the plan must leave unaltered the legal, equitable, and contractual rights of a class, cure defaults that led to acceleration of debts, or pay in cash the full amount of their claims.

§ 6.26 Disclosure Statement

A party cannot solicit the acceptance or rejection of a plan from creditors and stockholders affected by the plan unless they are given a written disclosure statement containing adequate information as approved by the court. Section 1125(b) requires that this disclosure statement must be provided prior to or at the time of the solicitation. The disclosure statement must be approved by the court, after notice and a hearing, as containing adequate information.

Adequate disclosure may also be important if the debtor wants to pursue causes of action against other parties. For example, in *Westland Oil Development v. Mcorp Management Solutions*,[162] the court held that the effect of the confirmation may be to bar the debtor for subsequently pursuing causes of action that were not adequately disclosed. The provisions of an order confirm-

---

[162] 157 B.R. 100 (S.D. Tex. 1993).

ing a plan have a binding, preclusive effect on issues that could have been raised at the time of confirmation, but that effect does not apply to the provisions of a disclosure statement.[163]

In *In re Kellogg Square Partnerships*,[164] the bankruptcy court held that a settlement of a claim that (1) was negotiated before the approval of the disclosure statement, (2) was a part of the plan, and (3) was to become effective upon confirmation of the plan, did not violate the prohibition against soliciting before the approval of the disclosure under section 1125 of the Bankruptcy Code. However, the distribution of a proposed disclosure statement and a notice of the hearing to a list of creditors before the court has approved the statement may subject the proponent to sanctions but will not result in disqualification from presenting a plan.[165]

(a) Adequate Information

Section 1125(a) states that adequate information means information of a kind, and in sufficient detail, as far as is reasonably practicable in light of the nature and history of the debtor and the condition of the debtor's books and records, that would enable a hypothetical reasonable investor typical of holders of claims or interests of the relevant class to make an informed judgment about the plan. This definition contains two parts. First it defines adequate information and then it sets a standard against which the information is measured. It must be the kind of information that a typical investor of the relevant class, not one that has special information, would need to make an informed judgment about the plan. Section 1125(a)(1) provides that adequate information need not include information about other possible proposed plans.

The bankruptcy court held that a disclosure statement does not meet the adequate information standard when the disclosure statement does not contain simple and clear language delineating the consequences of the plan on the claims of a class of unsecured creditors whom the court determined to be "average investors" without any sophisticated financial knowledge.[166]

(b) Objectives of Statement

The disclosure requirement is new under chapter 11, and the House Committee Report believed it to be the heart of the consolidation of Chapters X, XI, and XIII of prior law. Chapter XI did not contain any required disclosure. Chapter X, on the other hand, required the plan, once developed, to be sent to the SEC. The SEC would, within a few months, prepare an advisory report on the plan to inform the creditors and stockholders of the content of the plan and of the SEC's evaluation of its terms.

The objective of the disclosure statement provision is to require reasonable disclosure in all cases, but not necessarily to the extent required under Chapter X of prior law. The new law does provide for considerable flexibility in the

---

[163] *In re Outdoor Sports Headquarters, Inc.*, 161 B.R. 414 (Bankr. S.D. Ohio 1993).
[164] 160 B.R. 336 (Bankr. D. Minn. 1993).
[165] *In re Rock Broadcasting of Idaho, Inc.*, 154 B.R. 970 (Bankr. D. Idaho 1993).
[166] *In re Copy Crafters Quickprint, Inc.*, 92 B.R. 973 (Bankr. N.D.N.Y. 1988).

content of the disclosure statement, but it seems clear that Congress wanted to end the highly informal disclosure practices followed in Chapter XI proceedings under prior law, while avoiding the delay caused in obtaining SEC approval in Chapter X.

The disclosure statement must be approved by the court, after notice and hearing, before transmission to creditors or stockholders. The content of the disclosure statement is to be decided solely by the bankruptcy judge, and is not governed by any nonbankruptcy law, including the Securities Acts of 1933 and 1934. Any governmental agency, including the SEC, may be heard regarding the adequacy of the information disclosed, but such agency cannot appeal an order of the court approving the statement.[167] In cases where a large number of public security holders are affected by the proposed plan, it can be anticipated that the SEC will present its objection to any disclosure statements it believes do not contain adequate information or do contain misleading statements.

The district court held that under normal circumstances a disclosure statement need not comply with the disclosure standards of federal securities laws and the bankruptcy court is under no obligation to analogize to the securities laws.[168]

According to the House Committee Report, it was expected that the courts would take a practical approach to the question of what type of disclosure is necessary, taking into consideration the cost of preparing the statements, the need for speed in soliciting votes and confirming the plan, and the need for investor protection. Thus, precisely what constitutes adequate information in any given situation will develop on a case-by-case basis.

The Bankruptcy Code provides that the same disclosure statement must go to all members of a particular class, but it does allow different disclosures for different classes of creditors or stockholders.[169] This provision gives flexibility in the preparation and distribution of statements based on the needs of the various interest groups and should provide for lower printing and distribution costs. It is hoped that the information contained in the disclosure statement will, in most corporate cases, be based on an examination by an independent accountant. The Bankruptcy Code does, however, give the court the right to approve a disclosure statement without a valuation of the debtor or without an appraisal of the debtor's assets.[170]

(c) Prepetition Solicitation

Before filing a petition under chapter 11, some debtors may have already acquired the necessary votes to obtain approval of the plan. The information disclosure requirement of section 1125 will not apply if the solicitation of such acceptance or rejection was in compliance with any applicable nonbankruptcy law, rule, or regulation governing the adequacy of disclosure in connection with the solicitation.[171] If no nonbankruptcy law is applicable, then the solici-

---

[167] 11 U.S.C. § 1125(d).
[168] *Kirk v. Texaco Inc.*, 82 B.R. 678 (S.D.N.Y. 1988).
[169] *Id.*, § 1125(c).
[170] *Id.*, § 1125(b).
[171] *Id.*, § 1126(b).

tation must have occurred after the holder received adequate information as required under section 1125. The creditors' acceptance of an out-of-court agreement that would also carry over to a chapter 11 reorganization if a petition is filed should follow the provisions of section 1125 to avoid subsequent problems if the debtor ends up in chapter 11. (See § 4.11.)

(d) Content of Disclosure Statement

As noted above, the information disclosed in the statement should be adequate to allow the creditor or stockholder to make an informed judgment about the plan. Considerable difference in opinion exists as to the type of information that should be included in the disclosure statement. Phelan and Cheatham, for example, suggested that the best guides for drafting a disclosure statement are Form S-1 (used in connection with registration of securities under the 1933 Act), Form S-2 (used to register securities of new companies), and Form 10 (used for registration of securities under the 1934 Act).[172] They also suggested that some of the items required in these forms are not relevant to a bankruptcy proceeding; that the forms do constitute excellent evidence of the information the SEC believes to be the minimum required for the protection of the investors; and that to vary widely from such information may affect the ability of a person to satisfy the good faith requirement of section 1125(e).[173]

The bankruptcy court held, in *In re Malek*[174] that disclosure statements should at a minimum contain a description of the business, debtor's prepetition history, financial information, description of the plan and how it is to be executed, liquidation analysis, postpetition management and its compensation, projections of operations, litigation, transactions with insiders, and the tax consequence of the plan. Other information that might need to be disclosed includes the amount to be realized from the recovery of preferential payments and factors presently known to the debtor that might bear on the success or failure of the proposals contained in the plan.

The district court, in *Westland Oil Development v. Mcorp Management Solutions*,[175] held that a disclosure statement should include the events leading to the filing of the petition, a description of the assets and their value, the amount of claims, the estimated return to creditors in a chapter 7 liquidation, and the litigation likely to arise in a nonbankruptcy context.

Others feel that these requirements are more than would be necessary under most bankruptcy situations.[176] The Bankruptcy Code states in section 1125(d) that the requirements of the SEC are not applicable to reorganizations; indeed, that was one of the reasons to avoid the need to file the detailed information required by the securities laws.

It should also be remembered that the amount of disclosure required under Chapter X proceedings of prior law varied from one district to another, and

---

[172] Robin E. Phelan and Bruce A. Cheatham, "Issuing Securities under the New Bankruptcy Code: More Magic for the Cryptic Kingdom," *St. Mary's Law Journal*, Vol. 11 (1979), p. 426.

[173] *Id.*

[174] 35 B.R. 443 (Bankr. E.D. Mich. 1984).

[175] 157 B.R. 100 (S.D. Tex. 1993).

[176] See, for example, the disclosure statements filed in the Central District of California.

there will most probably be some differences in the amount of information that must be included in the disclosure statement. Information that might be included in the disclosure statement is discussed in the following paragraphs.

Introduction   The first part states that the proposed plan is enclosed, and defines the classes that must vote and the percentage of acceptance needed for approval. There should be a statement to the effect that no representations concerning the debtor, particularly regarding future operations, value of property, or value of securities to be issued under the plan, are authorized by the debtor other than as set forth in this disclosure statement. The introduction also indicates which information presented has been audited by a certified public accountant. The company and the nature of its operations are briefly described. Other information presented by the debtor should be designated as not warranted to be without any inaccuracies, although every effort has been made to see that it is accurate.[177]

Management   In order to evaluate the ability of the firm to continue as a going concern, the creditors need to know about the management of the company. If existing management is to be replaced, the disclosure statement should identify the new management. This is true even if a trustee is currently running the business. Included should be the list of all directors and key officers, their ages, their tenure with the company, and their prior business experience.

Summary of the Plan of Reorganization   The objective of this section of the disclosure statement is to have the debtor present the reasons why the creditors could expect more from the plan than from a liquidation of the business. It sets forth in summary form the major parts of the plan, including a description of the various classes of creditors and stockholders. In a sample form presented by Collier, the following paragraph was included in the disclosure statement:

> The Plan is based upon the Debtor's belief that the present forced liquidation value of his principal assets is so small as to offer the potential of only a minimal recovery to creditors. The Debtor believes that it is possible that some of his properties to be retained pursuant to the Plan will appreciate in value in the future, and debts secured by liens on certain of these properties will be reduced by sales of the properties and future earnings, thus permitting a more substantial recovery to creditors and thus offer the possibility that creditors will receive payment in full by way of extension. Further, certain obligations undertaken by the Debtor in the Plan will be guaranteed by trusts created some years ago for the benefit of his children.[178]

Reorganization Value   Included in the disclosure statement should be the reorganization value of the entity that will emerge from bankruptcy. One of the first, as well as the most difficult, steps in reaching agreement on the terms

---

[177] *Collier Forms Manual*, Form 11-721.
[178] *Id.*

of a plan is determining the value of the reorganized entity. Once the parties—debtor, unsecured creditors' committee, secured creditors, and shareholders—agree on the reorganization value, this value is then allocated among the creditors and equity holders. Thus, before it is determined what amount unsecured creditors, secured creditors, or equity holders will receive, the reorganization value must be determined. An unsecured creditors' committee or another representative of creditors or equity holders is generally unable, and often unwilling, to agree to the terms of a plan without any knowledge as to the reorganization value of the emerging entity. It would also appear that if this value is needed by the parties that must agree on the terms of a plan, it is also needed by each unsecured creditor to determine how to vote on the plan. Yet, many disclosure statements fail to disclose reorganization value. One method of presentation is to include these values in the pro forma balance sheet based on the assumption that the plan is confirmed. (See the discussion of pro forma statements below. The techniques that are used to determine reorganization value are discussed in Chapter 11.)

Financial Information   Several types of information could be of considerable benefit to the creditors and stockholders in assessing the potential of the debtor's business. Some of these are: audited reports of the financial position as of the date the petition was filed or as of the end of a recent fiscal year, and the results of operations for the past year; a more detailed analysis by the debtor of its properties, including a description of the properties, the current values, and other relevant information; and a description of the obligations outstanding with the material claims in dispute being identified. If the nature of the company's operations is going to change significantly as a result of the reorganization, historical financial statements for the past two to five years are of limited value.

In addition to the historical financial statements, the source of new capital and how the proceeds will be used, the postpetition interest obligation, lease commitments, financing arrangements, and so forth, a pro forma balance sheet showing the impact the proposed plan, if accepted, will have on the financial condition of the company may be included.

To provide the information needed by creditors and stockholders for effective evaluation of the plan, the pro forma statement should show the reorganization value of the entity. Thus, the assets would be presented at their current values and, if there is any excess of the reorganization value (going-concern value) over individual assets, this value would be shown. Liabilities and stockholders' equity should be presented at their discounted values, based on the assumption that the plan will be confirmed. If appraisals of the individual assets have not been made, it would appear appropriate to reflect the differences between the book value and reorganization value as an adjustment to the asset side of the pro forma balance sheet. (See § 8.18.)

If the plan calls for future cash payments, the inclusion of projections of future operations will help the affected creditors make a decision as to whether they believe the debtor will be able to make the required payments. Even if no future cash payments are called for in the plan, it may still be advisable to include in the disclosure statement the financial information that will allow the creditors and stockholders to see the potential the business has to operate profitably in the future. These projections must, of course, be based on reasonable assumptions, and the assumptions must be clearly set forth in the projections accompanying the disclosure statement.[179]

Liquidation   Included in the disclosure statement should be an analysis of the amount that creditors and equity holders would receive if the debtor was liquidated under chapter 7. To effectively evaluate the reorganization alternative, the creditor and equity holders must know what they would receive through liquidation. Also, the court, in order to confirm the plan, must ascertain, according to section 1129(a)(7), that each holder of a claim or interest who does not vote in favor of the plan must receive at least an amount that is equal to the amount that would be received in a chapter 7 liquidation.

Generally, it is not acceptable to state that the amount provided for in the plan exceeds the liquidation amount. Data must be presented to support this type of statement.

Special Risk Factors   In any securities that are issued pursuant to a plan in a chapter 11 proceeding, certain substantial risk factors are inherent in the issue. It may be advisable to include a description of some of the factors in the disclosure statement.[180]

Phelan and Cheatham indicated that the condition of the books and records of the debtor, the funds available for preparation of the disclosure statement, and other circumstances surrounding the rehabilitation may limit the amount of information that can reasonably be presented in the disclosure statement.[181] They recommended that the following should be included if the plan requires the issuance of securities:

1   A complete description of the capital structure of the rehabilitated debtor (including new infusions of capital and new funding agreements) and use of proceeds (if any).

2   A history of the business activities of the debtor (and the issuer in the case of a nondebtor issuer).

3   A list of parents, controlling persons, and subsidiaries of the issuer.

4   A complete description of the issuer's business, including, but not limited to, the following:

a   The competitive conditions in the industry or industries in which the issuer competes, and the issuer's competitive position in such industries.

b   The issuer's dependence on one or more customers.

c   The principal products produced or services rendered by the issuer and the methods of distribution of such products or services.

d   The current backlog of the issuer and comparable figures for the previous year.

e   The course and availability of raw materials essential to the issuer's business.

---

[179] *Collier Forms Manual,* Form 11-721.
[180] *Id.*
[181] Phelan and Cheatham, *supra* note 172, p. 426.

   f The importance of all patents, trademarks, licenses, franchises, and concessions held by the issuer.

   g Information regarding research and development.

   h The number of persons employed by the issuer.

   i Information regarding the seasonal nature of the issuer's business.

   j Information regarding foreign operations, regulatory problems, and working capital position. In addition, sales and revenue figures for each industry segment of the issuer and each class of similar products or services are required.

5 A description of all physical properties held by the issuer.

6 A complete description of major litigation involving the issuer.

7 Descriptions of each of the securities being issued.

8 Complete information regarding the officers and directors of the rehabilitated debtor.

9 Complete information regarding all remuneration to be paid or other transactions with insiders and controlling persons of the issuer or debtor.

10 A description of the major shareholders and controlling persons after the reorganization.

11 A description of any options or warrants to purchase securities of the issuer that remain outstanding.

12 A description of any pledges or other financing arrangements that conceivably could change control of the issuer at such date.

13 A complete description of the tax ramifications of the transaction.

14 Any attorneys' fees to be paid in connection with the proceeding.

15 The anticipated liquidity of the reorganized debtor.

The elimination of any one of the above items from the disclosure memorandum may constitute a material nondisclosure and subject all parties to securities law liabilities.[182]

U.S. Trustee Checklist   The U.S. trustee's office for the Central District of California has issued a checklist of items it believes should appear in the disclosure statement. However, the U.S. trustee for this district indicates that this list is neither exclusive nor exhaustive and, depending on the desire and nature of the debtor, the content may vary considerably. The checklist of 17 items is presented in 6.12 of Volume 2.

(e) U.S. Trustee Evaluation

Section 586(a) of title 28 of the U.S. Code provides that the U.S. trustee is to monitor plans and disclosure statements filed in chapter 11 cases and file with the court comments on the plans and statements. The objective, it would appear, is not to take a substantive legal position, but to point out at the hear-

---

[182] _Id._, pp. 426–428.

ing any discrepancies between the operating data and the data in the disclosure statements. For example, if the U.S. trustee believes that the projections of future operations in the disclosure statement are too high based on prior operating statements issued, this will be pointed out in the hearings. Once the statement is approved by the court, the U.S. trustee will not comment further on it.

(f) Safe Harbor Rule

Section 1125(e) provides that a person soliciting acceptance of a plan "in good faith" is not liable for violation of any applicable law, rule, or regulation governing the offer, issuance, sale, or purchase of securities. This provision codified the holdings in *Ernst and Ernst v. Hochfelder*.[183] The safe harbor rule provides that if the court has approved a disclosure statement indicating that it contains adequate information and meets the requirements of chapter 11, then the creditors, creditors' committee, counsel for committees, and others involved in the case are protected from potential civil and injunctive liability under the securities laws as a result of using the approved statement.

(g) Illustration of Content of Disclosure Statements

An example of a disclosure statement filed by the creditors' committee appears as 6.13 in Volume 2 of *Bankruptcy and Insolvency Accounting.* This example was chosen because it contains a good summary of the profit improvement actions that are needed to turn the business around (see 6.13(c)). Additional information about the reorganized debtor includes the reorganization value (6.13(c)), a summary of the plan of reorganization (6.13(d)), and selected federal income tax consequences of the plan (6.13(e)).

Selected data from the disclosure statement of General Homes Corporation are given in 6.14 of Volume 2. (An involuntary petition was filed against the corporation.) The activities of the company during the period before the order for relief was granted are shown in 6.14(b), and 6.14(c) summarizes the activities after the order for relief was granted. Presented in 6.14(d) through 6.14(g) is a summary of the company's plan, including the business plan and a summary of the reorganization value.

Other examples of selected sections of disclosure statements are presented in Chapters 11 and 16 of Volume 2.

Often, debtors will distribute the disclosure statement in a "package" that includes other data and will obtain court approval for the entire package. This may be common practice, but there is no requirement for the court to approve any additional data that are used in solicitation of the votes. The additional data should not contradict the information in the disclosure statement or misstate or falsely characterize material facts.[184]

---

[183] 425 U.S. 185 (1976).
[184] *In re Kellogg Square Partnerships*, 160 B.R. 336 (Bankr. D. Minn. 1993); *see Century Glove, Inc. v. First American Bank of New York*, 860 F.2d 94 (3d Cir. 1988).

§ 6.27 Modification of the Plan

Only the proponent of a plan may modify the plan at any time before confirmation, provided the plan as modified meets the plan content requirements of sections 1122 and 1123. The modified plan becomes the plan after it is filed with the court by the proponent. Also, section 1127(c) provides that the proponent of a plan must comply with the disclosure requirement of section 1125. As part of the bargaining process by which the debtor and various classes of creditors reach agreement on the terms of a plan, changes may be made affecting, for example, certain secured classes of claims. It is not uncommon for the holders of unsecured claims and interests to accept the terms of the proposed plan and any modifications that may be made thereafter, as long as the court determines that the rights of these classes are not materially and aversely affected by the modifications.

After confirmation, but before substantial consummation (see section 1101(2)), the plan may also be modified by the proponent or the reorganized debtor. The plan as modified must satisfy all of the statutory requirements and be confirmed by the court after notice and hearing.

Section 1127(b) of the Bankruptcy Code provides that once a plan has been substantially consummated, the plan cannot be modified. The requirements for consummation as stated in section 1101(2) of the Bankruptcy Code are:

1 All or substantially all of the property proposed by the plan has been transferred.
2 The debtor or the successor to the debtor assumes all or substantially all of the property dealt with under the plan.
3 Distribution under the plan has commenced.

The Bankruptcy Appeals Panel for the Ninth Circuit concluded that the transfer of all or substantially all of the property requirement does not refer to the distributions to be made to the creditors over time, but to the transfer of property, if any, to be made under the plan at or near the effective date. The court noted that such distributions need only commence.[185]

CONFIRMATION OF THE PLAN

§ 6.28 Acceptance of the Plan

Prior to the confirmation hearing on the proposed plan, the proponents of the plan will seek its acceptance. Once the results of the vote are known, the debtor or other proponent of the plan will request confirmation of the plan.

The holder of a claim or interest, as defined under section 502, is permitted to vote on the proposed plan. Voting is based on the classification of claims and interests. A major change from prior law is that the acceptance requirements are based on those actually voting and not the total value or number of claims or interests allowed in a particular class. The Secretary of the Treasury is

---

[185] *In re Antiquities of Nevada, Inc.*, 173 B.R. 926 (Bankr. 9th Cir. 1994).

authorized to vote on behalf of the United States when the United States is a creditor or equity security holder.

A class of claim holders has accepted a plan if at least two-thirds in amount and more than one-half in number of the allowed claims for that class that are voted are cast in favor of the plan. For equity interests, it is only necessary that votes totaling at least two-thirds in amount of the outstanding securities in a particular class that voted are cast for the plan. The majority in number requirement is not applicable to equity interests.[186]

The purchase of a claim for the purpose of preventing a cram down by the debtor was not by itself grounds on which to deny the creditor's right to vote on the plan, nor does it justify a classification separately from other unsecured creditors.[187]

Section 1126(e) excludes from the voting results computation any entity whose acceptance or rejection of a plan was not in good faith or was not solicited or procured in good faith. Subsection (f) provides that a class that is not impaired under the plan is presumed to have accepted the plan, and solicitation of acceptance is not required.

§ 6.29 Confirmation Hearing

After notice, the court will hold a hearing on confirmation of the plan. A party-in-interest may object to the confirmation.[188] It is also possible that the SEC may object to a plan's confirmation even though not a party-in-interest, because the SEC has the right to appear and be heard on any issue in a case under chapter 11.

If both a liquidation plan and a reorganization plan are confirmable, the court, in deciding which plan to confirm, should take into consideration the philosophy of the Bankruptcy Code that reorganization is preferable to liquidation.[189]

§ 6.30 Confirmation Requirements

The requirements that must be satisfied before the court will confirm a plan under chapter 11 are based partly on the requirements of prior law Chapters X and XI; the balance is new. Chapter XI required that the plan be in the best interest of creditors; namely, the creditors had to receive at least as much under the plan of arrangement as they would in liquidation. Chapter X required that the plan observe the "absolute priority" rule: all members of the senior class of creditors must have been satisfied in full before members of the next senior class could receive anything, and that class had to be satisfied before the third senior class, and so on. This meant, of course, that if the corporation was insolvent in the bankruptcy sense, the plan of reorganization did not have to make provision for the stockholders.

---

[186] 11 U.S.C. § 1126(c) and (d).
[187] *See In re Pleasant Hill Partners, Ltd. Partnership,* 163 B.R. 388 (Bankr. N.D. Ga. 1994); *In re Fairfield Associates,* 161 B.R. 595 (D.N.J. 1993).
[188] *Id.,* § 1128.
[189] *In re Oaks Partners, Ltd.,* 141 B.R. 453 (Bankr. N.D. Ga. 1992); *In re Nice Lite Inns,* 17 B.R. 367 (Bankr. S.D. Cal. 1982); *In re Consolidated Operating Partners L.P.,* 91 B.R. 113 (Bankr. D. Colo. 1988).

The new law partially codifies the absolute priority doctrine, but the rest of the test under section 1129(b) is new. In the same manner, the best-interest-of-creditors test is retained, but applied in a different way.

Section 1129(a), which contains the requirements that must be satisfied before a plan can be confirmed, is one of the most significant sections of the new Code. The first six requirements that must be satisfied before the plan can be confirmed are taken from Chapter X. They ensure, among other things, that the plan follows the plan requirements of sections 1122 and 1123 and that the court determines that disclosure was proper. Requirements 7, 8, and 9 are the provisions that require a valuation of the debtor's assets and business and determine how priority creditors are to be paid. They are described in more detail in §§ 6.31 through 6.34, along with the cram-down provision of section 1129(b). Requirements 10 and 11 contain two additional general provisions. The provisions are listed below:

1 *The plan complies with the applicable provisions of title 11.* Section 1122 concerning classification of claims and section 1123 on the content of the plan are two of the significant sections that must be followed.

2 *The proponents of the plan comply with the applicable provisions of title 11.* Section 1125 on disclosure is an example of a section that is referred to by this requirement.

3 *The plan has been proposed in good faith and not by any means forbidden by law.*

4 *Payments are disclosed.* Any payment made or to be made for services, costs, and expenses in connection with the case or plan has been approved by, or is subject to, the approval of the court as reasonable.

5 *Officers are disclosed.* The proponent of the plan must disclose those who are proposed to serve after confirmation as director, officer, or voting trustee of the reorganized debtor. Such employment must be consistent with the interests of creditors and equity security holders and with public policy. Names of insiders to be employed and the nature of their compensation must also be disclosed.

6 *The regulatory rate has been approved.* Any governmental regulatory commission that will have jurisdiction over the debtor after confirmation of the plan must approve any rate changes provided for in the plan.

7 *The best-interest-of-creditors test has been satisfied.* It is necessary for the creditors or stockholders who do not vote for the plan to receive as much as they would if the business were liquidated under chapter 7. This requirement is discussed in more detail in § 6.31.

8 *Acceptance by each class has been gained.* Each class of creditors or stockholders that is impaired under the plan must accept the plan. Section 1129(b) provides an exception to this requirement and is described in the "Cram Down" section in § 6.34.

9 *Treatment of priority claims is stated.* This requirement provides the manner in which priority claims must be satisfied unless the holders agree to a different treatment. (See § 6.32.)

10 *Acceptance by at least one class has been gained.* If a class of claims is impaired under the plan, at least one class that is impaired, other than a class of claims held by insiders, must accept the plan.

11 *The plan is feasible.* Confirmation of the plan is not likely to be followed by liquidation or the need for further financial reorganization unless such liquidation or reorganization is provided for in the plan. (See § 6.33.)

12 *Payment of fees.* The filing fees and quarterly fees must be paid or provided in the plan that they will be paid as of the effective date of the plan.

13 *Retiree benefit continuation.* The plan must provide, as of the effective date, for the continuation of all retiree benefits as defined under section 1114 and at the level established under section 1114.

The heart of section 1129, confirmation of the plan, is requirements 7, 8, and 9 (briefly mentioned above) of subsection (a) and subsection (b), which provide for a "cram-down." These requirements make it necessary under certain conditions to determine the value of the business via either liquidation or going-concern values. Because these requirements involve an evaluation of the business, it is important that the accountant fully understand them and the impact they can have. The techniques for determining the value of the business are discussed in Chapter 11.

§ 6.31   Best Interest of Creditors

The first part of requirement 7 is that each holder of a claim or interest in each class must accept the plan or will receive, as of the effective date of the plan, a value that is not less than the amount the holder would receive in a chapter 7 liquidation.[190] Note that the first alternative is that each holder must accept the plan. If any holder does not vote or votes against acceptance, then it is necessary for the liquidation values to be ascertained. This requirement, in fact, makes it necessary for the court to have some understanding of the liquidation value of the business in practically all chapter 11 cases; there will almost always be some creditors who do not vote. The extent to which the liquidation values will have to be applied to individual classes other than those of a large number of unsecured claims will depend on the manner in which the claims are divided into classes and whether there are any secured classes with a large number of claims.

The second part of the best-interest test applies to those holders of secured claims that elected under section 1111(b)(2) to have their entire claim, even though undersecured, considered a secured claim and have not accepted the plan. The best-interest test is satisfied here if the holder of such claim will receive under the plan property of value, as of the effective date of the plan, at least equal to the value of the creditors' interest in the debtor's property that secures the claim.[191]

---

[190] 11 U.S.C. § 1129(a)(7)(A).
[191] *Id.*, § 1129(a)(7)(B).

§ 6.32   **Priority Treatment**

Requirement 9 states that, unless the holder of a priority claim agrees to different treatment, the plan of reorganization must provide:

1 *Administrative expenses and involuntary gap claims.* Cash equal to the allowed amount of the claim must be paid on the effective date of the plan for administrative expenses and involuntary gap claims defined in section 507(a)(1) and (2). These claims are priorities 1 and 2 under the Bankruptcy Code. (See § 5.33.)

2 *Wages, employee benefits, and individual deposits.* Claims of wages up to $4,350 (rate to be adjusted April 30, 2001) per employee, employee benefits up to the extent of the unused wage priority, grain producers' and fishermen's claims not to exceed $4,350, and individual consumer deposits not to exceed $900 per individual as more specifically defined in section 507(a)(3–6) must receive deferred cash payments. These payments will have a present value as of the effective date of the plan equal to the allowed amount of the claim if the class has accepted the plan. If a class of these types of claims has not accepted the plan, they must receive cash on the effective date of the plan equal to the allowed amount of the claims. These claims are entitled to third, fourth, fifth, and sixth priority under the Bankruptcy Code.

3 *Taxes.* Tax claims that are entitled to seventh priority (sixth priority for bankruptcy petitions filed before October 8, 1984) in section 507(a)(7) must receive deferred cash payments, over a period not to exceed six years from the date of assessment of the claim, of a value as of the effective date of the plan equal to the allowed amount of the claim. (See § 5.33.)

The effective date of the plan should be stated in the plan. The date most likely used is that which is an established number of days after the plan is confirmed, provided there are no appeals from the confirmation hearing. If a plan does not state the effective date and there are objections to the confirmation, confusion may exist as to what should be the effective date. The way to avoid this problem is to set forth clearly in the plan what the effective date will be.

These tax priority claim provisions represent a major change from prior law, where deferred payments were allowed only if the taxing authority agreed to this provision. Under the Bankruptcy Code, tax payments can automatically be deferred. This provision, along with other changes, will mean that less cash will have to be deposited at the time of the confirmation. More immediate cash will then be available to the debtor at a time when operating cash is critical to the ability of the debtor to continue operating the business.

The district court held, in *In re Vkolle Electric, Inc.*,[192] that a seventh priority tax claim need not be amortized in equal installments over the six-year period from the date of assessment. Lower early payment together with a bal-

---

[192] 139 B.R. 451 (C.D. Ill. 1992).

loon payment at the end are permissible if the circumstances justify such terms. The court should balance the debtor's needs against the taxing agency's interest in receiving prompt payment.

A tax claim that is secured by the debtor's property is considered a secured lien and not a seventh-priority tax claim. As such, the claim can be crammed down under section 1129(b) of the Bankruptcy Code with the payment period in excess of the six-year limitation under section 1129(a)(9)(C).

The bankruptcy court held, in *In re Oaks Partners, Ltd.*,[193] that where there is a possibility that allowed administrative expenses might not be paid in full, the plan cannot be confirmed because it violates section 1129(a)(9)(A) of the Bankruptcy Code.

§ 6.33 Feasibility

Section 1129(a)(11) provides that confirmation of the plan is not likely to be followed by the liquidation or the need for further financial reorganization unless such liquidation or reorganization is a part of the plan. This require- ment, generally referred to as the feasibility test, means that the court must ascertain that the debtor has a reasonable chance of surviving once the plan is confirmed and the debtor is out from under the protection of the court. A well- prepared forecast of future operations based on reasonable assumptions, taking into consideration the changes expected as a result of the confirmation of the plan, is an example of the kind of information that can be very helpful to the court in reaching a decision on this requirement.

The court, if the issue of feasibility is raised, must be able to determine whether the debtor will be able to fund the debt requirements contained in the plan. For example, if the projected cash flows contained in the disclosure state- ment indicate that the debtor will not have enough cash to make the debt pay- ments, as required by the terms of the plan, the plan would not meet the feasibility requirement.

§ 6.34 Cram Down[194]

As noted in requirement 8, for a plan to be confirmed, a class of claims or interests must either accept the plan or not be impaired. However, subsection (b) of section 1129 allows the court under certain conditions to confirm a plan even though an impaired class has not accepted the plan.

However, as noted above, section 1129(a)(10) provides that at least one class that is impaired must accept the plan. See § 6.30 for a discussion of the need for at least one class to approve the plan. The Fifth Circuit held that a plan improperly classified creditors holding a general unsecured claim of an affiliate when it placed the claim in a separate class in order to obtain approval of one impaired class. The affiliate's claims were substantially similar to the other

---

[193] 141 B.R. 453 (Bankr. N.D. Ga. 1992).
[194] The author acknowledges the contributions of Kenneth N. Klee, Stutman, Treister & Glatt, Los Angeles, California, to this section and Chapter 11. For a more detailed discussion of the cram- down provision, see Kenneth N. Klee, "All You Ever Wanted to Know about Cram Down under the New Bankruptcy Code," *American Bankruptcy Law Journal*, Vol. 53 (Spring 1979), pp. 133–171.

unsecured creditors.[195] Security deposits that would have given rise to postpetition administrative expenses were not considered an impaired class for purposes of obtaining the approval of at least one class.[196]

The plan must not discriminate unfairly, and must be fair and equitable, with respect to each class of claims or interest impaired under the plan that has not accepted it. The Bankruptcy Code states conditions for secured claims, unsecured claims, and stockholder interests that would be included in the "fair and equitable" requirement. It should be noted that because the word "includes" is used, the meaning of fair and equitable is not restricted to these conditions.[197]

Widely disparate treatment of classes of the same legal priority may be considered unfair discrimination under section 1129(b)(1) of the Bankruptcy Code in situations where a class may not vote for the plan. In *In re Tucson Self-Storage, Inc.,*[198] the Ninth Circuit Bankruptcy Appeals Panel held that a plan that provided for trade creditors to be paid in full but only 10 percent paid for the unsecured part of a nonrecourse debt under section 1111(b) was not conformable because it failed to satisfy the "does not discriminate unfairly" requirement of section 1129(b)(1).

Section 1129(a)(10) provides that, in order for there to be a "cramdown," at least one class of claims that is impaired, other than a class of claims held by insiders, must accept the plan. The fact that a creditor is a proponent of a plan does not necessarily make that creditor an insider.[199]

(a) Modification of Secured Claims

The Ninth Cirucit held that the bankruptcy court had an affirmative duty to ensure that the Plan satisfied all 13 requirements for confirmation.[200] The bankruptcy court must confirm a chapter 11 debtor's plan of reorganization if the debtor proves by a preponderance of the evidence either that the Plan satisfies all 13 requirements of section 1129(a) or if the only condition not satisfied is the eighth requirement, the plan satisfies the *cramdown* alternative.[201] The cramdown alternative requires that the plan "does not discriminate unfairly" against and "is fair and equitable" toward each impaired class that has not accepted the plan.[202]

Section 1129(b) of the Bankruptcy Code indicates that, to be fair and equitable, the plan must provide for at least one of the following:

1 The holders of such claims must retain the lien securing such claims, whether the property subject to such lien is retained by the debtor or

---

[195] *In re T-H New Orleans Limited Partnership,* 10 F.3d 1099 (5th Cir. 1993), *cert. denied,* 511 U.S. 1083 (1994).
[196] *In re Boston Post Road Limited Partnership,* 21 F.3d 477 (2d Cir. 1994), *cert. denied,* 115 S. Ct. 897 (1994).
[197] See 11 U.S.C. § 102(3).
[198] 166 B.R. 892 (9th Cir. BAP 1994).
[199] *In re Union Meeting Partners,* 160 B.R. 757 (Bankr. E.D. Pa. 1993).
[200] *In re L & J Anaheim Assoc.,* 995 F.2d 940, 942 (9th Cir. 1993)
[201] *In re Ambanc La Mesa Limited Partnership,* 115 F.3d 650 (9th Cir. 1997).
[202] *Id. See In re Arnold and Baker Farms,* 177 B.R. 648 (9th Cir. BAP 1994), *aff'd,* 85 F.3d 1415 (9th Cir. 1996), *cert. denied* 117 S. Ct. 681 (1997).

transferred to another entity, to the extent of the allowed amount of such claims (see § 11.07). In addition, each holder of a claim of such class must receive on account of such claim deferred cash payments totaling at least the allowed amount of such claim, of a value, as of the effective date of the plan, of at least the value of such holder's interest in the estate's interest in such property.

2 For the sale, subject to section 363(k), of any property that is subject to the lien securing such claims, free and clear of such lien, with such lien to attach to the proceeds of such sale, and the treatment of such lien on proceeds under clause (1) or (3) of this subparagraph.

3 For the realization by such holders of the indubitable equivalent of such claims.[203]

It is only necessary to satisfy one of the above conditions. For example, it is not necessary to show that the creditor realized the indubitable equivalent of such claim if the debtor's plan provides for the creditor to retain the lien and make deferred payments equal to the amount of the claim with a value equal to the value of the collateral.[204] Priority tax claims are not considered an impaired class that can accept a plan.[205]

Related to the first alternative, the Ninth Circuit held that the value of the secured claim for the purposes of confirmation is the market value of real property plus the net amount of the rents collected postpetition and preconfirmation and subject to a deed of trust and assignment of rents. Because the debtor provided only for payments to equal the fair value of the property, the plan was not confirmable under the cramdown provisions of the Bankruptcy Code.[206]

To illustrate the treatment of secured claims, the following balance sheet based on reorganization values is shown (see §§ 11.3–11.7).

	X Corporation		
	Balance Sheet		
	Reorganization Values		
	(million dollars)		
Current assets	$ 1	Trade debt (unsecured)	$ 1
Real estate	4	Subordinated notes	2
Other Assets	5	Mortgage on real estate	6
		Stockholders' equity	1
Total	$10	Total	$10

All of the real estate is mortgaged. The plan proposes to pay the secured creditors $5 million in annual installments of $1 million per year at the beginning of each year. The holders of trade debt and the notes subordinated to trade debt have accepted the plan and the secured creditor has rejected the plan. The stockholders' interest was unaffected by the plan. The secured claim holder did not elect to

[203] 11 U.S.C. § 1129(b)(2)(A).
[204] *Wade v. Bradford*, 39 F.3d 1126 (10th Cir. 1994).
[205] *In re Bryson Properties, XVIII*, 961 F.2d 496 (4th Cir. 1992), *cert. denied*, 506 U.S. 866 (1992).
[206] *In re Ambanc La Mesa Limited Partnership*, 115 F.3d 650, 654 (9th Cir. 1997).

have the provisions of section 1111(b)(2) apply. The court determined that 20 percent was the appropriate discount rate to use to determine the present value of the payments as of the effective date of the plan. The total present value of the payments is $3.6 million. The judge would not confirm the plan, since none of the three standards is satisfied. The first is not satisfied, even though the amount received is greater than the value of the claim, because the present value of the payments of $3.6 million is less than the value of the creditors' interest in the property of $4 million. If the discount rate were 12 percent, then this requirement would be satisfied: the present value of the payments would equal $4 million. The second requirement is not applicable, because the collateral is not going to be sold. The third requirement would not be satisfied. The value of the payments is less than the claim and could not, thus, be the "indubitable" equivalent.

If the interest rate is changed to 12 percent and the creditor has elected to have the provision of section 1111(b)(2) apply, the judge would still not confirm the plan. The present value of the payments at the 12 percent rate does exceed the value of the property in which the creditor has an interest, but the total amount to be received is only $5 million, which is less than the $6 million claim. The total allowed amount of the claim of $6 million is considered secured because of the section 111(b)(2) election.

The third requirement states that the creditor must receive the indubitable equivalent.[207] Legislative history indicates that abandonment of the collateral to the creditor or acceptance of a lien on similar collateral would satisfy this requirement. However, the receipt of present cash payments less than the secured claims would not satisfy this standard because the creditor is deprived of an opportunity to gain from a future increase in the value of the collateral. Unsecured notes or equity securities of the debtor are not sufficient to constitute the indubitable equivalent of secured claims.[208]

The district court held, in *Matter of Bugg*,[209] that for the purpose of a secured claim, the interest rate to be used to determine the present value as of the effective date must be fixed unless both the creditor and debtor agree that an adjustable rate may be used.

(b) Unsecured Creditors' Test

For holders of unsecured claims, the Bankruptcy Code provides that one of the two following requirements must be satisfied for each class that is impaired and does not accept the plan:

1 The plan provides that each holder of a claim of such class receive or retain on account of such claim property of a value, as of the effective date of the plan, equal to the allowed amount of such claim.
2 The holder of any claim or interest that is junior to the claims of such class will not receive or retain on account of such junior claim or interest any property.[210]

---

[207] This last standard is derived from *In re Murel Holding Corp.*, 75 F.2d 241 (2d Cir. 1935).
[208] 124 Cong. Rec. H 11,103 (Sept. 28, 1978); S 17,420 (Oct. 6, 1978).
[209] 172 B.R. 781 (E.D. Pa. 1994).
[210] 11 U.S.C. § 1129(b)(2)(C).

Members of the class must, if they have not accepted the plan, receive or retain property that has a present value equal to the allowed amount of the claim. Alternatively, the plan can contain any provision for a distribution of less than full present value as long as no junior claim or interest will participate in the plan. Implicit in the concept of fairness is that senior classes will not receive more than 100 percent of their claims and any equal class will not receive preferential treatment.

The absolute priority rule is violated if creditors are not fully compensated under the plan, and the equity retains an interest in the reorganized debtor, even though creditors will control the operations and the plan forbids any distribution to equity interests before creditors are fully compensated.[211]

(c) Stockholders' Interest Test

The test for equity interests is very similar to the test for unsecured claims. Again, one of two standards must be satisfied for each class that is impaired and does not accept the plan:

1 The plan provides that each holder of an interest of such class receive, or retain on account of such interest, property of a value, as of the effective date of the plan, equal to the greatest of the allowed amount of any fixed liquidation preference to which such holder is entitled, any fixed redemption price to which such holder is entitled, and the value of such interest.

2 The holder of any interest that is junior to the interests of such class will not receive or retain under the plan on account of such junior interest in any property.[212]

(d) Value Exception

The Fifth Circuit in *Greystone*[213] ruled that the debtor could not arrange the classes in such a manner that at least one class will approve the plan. The court concluded that the *Greystone* plan impermissibly classified like creditors in different ways and manipulated classifications to obtain a favorable vote.

An exception to the absolute priority standard that is emerging as acceptable is the granting of new value. Under this new value corollary a party that is junior (often equity holders) to the senior creditor may receive an interest in the reorganized entity provided that interest resulted from the contribution of new value and not because of a current interest in value. With the Fifth Circuit having concluded that there is no "new value exception" to the absolute priority rule and then withdrew the opinion,[214] the circuit courts continued to be divided on this issue, as are the bankruptcy courts. The Seventh and Ninth Circuits has approve the "new value" exception, while the Second and Fourth Circuits have ruled against it.

While the Supreme Court's decision in *Bank of America v. 203 North*

---

[211] *In re Cantonwood Associates Ltd. Partnership,* 138 B.R. 648 (D. Mass. 1992).
[212] *Id.* § 1129(b)(2)C.
[213] *Supra* note 116.
[214] 1991 U.S. App. LEXIS 27096.

LaSalle Street Partnership [215] failed to decide if there is a place for new value, it held that one (or possibly both) of the following two conditions must exist for a plan to be confirmed:

1 The debtor must give up its exclusive right to propose a plan and give the creditors an opportunity to also propose a plan.

2 Any "new value" plan which is filed during the debtor's exclusivity period under section 1121(b) of the Bankruptcy Code is not confirmable unless it provides for the equity in the reorganized debtor to be subject to the competing bidding process. This process is designed to serve as a test to determine if the plan proponents of the debtor are paying the highest value for the equity.

The Supreme Court had granted certiorari in *In re Bonner Mall Partnership*,[216] to consider whether in a chapter 11 bankruptcy the new value exception to the absolute priority rule survived enactment of the Bankruptcy Code. Before the Supreme Court could hear the case the parties settled. The Ninth Circuit had held that the new value exception survives enactment. After settlement, the losing party mortgagee petitioned the Supreme Court to vacate the Ninth Circuit decision. The Supreme Court held that the Court had the power to vacate, but mootness by reason of settlement did not justify vacatur of judgment under review.[217] The Court, however, expressed no opinion on the survival of the new value exception.

As noted above, the new value exception relates to the extent to which the court may cram down a plan in a chapter 11 case if the shareholders or partners retain an ownership interest in the reorganized entity as a result of additional contributions of capital. Creditors have asserted that the Bankruptcy Code requires that either creditors' claims must be paid in full or the creditors must, by the requisite majorities, consent to the plan, before holders of equity interests may receive any distribution under a chapter 11 plan of reorganization. The Circuit Courts continued to be split as to whether the new value principle survives. Even within Circuits there was uncertainty as to the survival of the new value concept. For example, the Seventh Circuit seems internally divided on the question: In one case it analyzed a reorganization plan in light of the exception, while stating that the status of the doctrine is an open question after another panel criticized the exception and strongly hinted that it is moribund; and a third stopped just short of holding that the exception survives.[218] The Fourth Circuit has suggested that if the new value exception exists it is narrow in scope.[219]

---

[215] 526 U.S. 434 (1999). *See Kham & Nate's Shoes No. 2 v. First Bank*, 908 F.2d 1351 (7th Cir. 1990); *In re Anderson*, 913 F.2d 530, 532–33 (8th Cir. 1990); *In re U.S. Truck Co.*, 800 F.2d 581, 587–88 (6th Cir. 1986); *In re Dutlook/Century, Ltd.*, 127 B.R. 650, 656 (Bankr. N.D. Cal. 1991); *In re Lumber Exchange Ltd.*, 968 F.2d 647 (8th Cir. 1992).

[216] 2 F.3d 899 (9th Cir. 1993).

[217] *U.S. Bankcorp Mortgage Co. v. Bonner Mall Partnership*, 115 S. Ct. 386 (1994).

[218] *See In re Stegall*, 865 F.2d 140, 141–44 (7th Cir. 1989); *Kham & Nate's Shoes No. 2, Inc. v. First Bank of Whiting*, 908 F.2d 1351, 1359–62 (7th Cir. 1990); *Snyder v. Farm Credit Bank of St. Louis (In re Snyder)*, 967 F.2d 1126, 1128 (7th Cir. 1992).

[219] *Travelers Ins. Co. v. Bryson Properties, XVIII (In re Bryson Properties, Inc.*, XVIII, 961 F.2d 496, 503–05 (4th Cir. 1992), *cert'd denied*, 113 S. Ct. 191 (1992).

In *In re Trevarrow Lanes, Inc.*,[220] the bankruptcy court concluded that there is no new value exception to the absolute priority rule. However, under the fair and equitable standard, the court looked to *Los Angeles Lumber's* requirement that old equity's contribution must be essential to the success of the undertaking. The court concluded that the debtor did not establish that equity's proposed contribution was essential to the reorganization effort.

The bankruptcy court in *In re P.J. Keating Co.*[221] held that, for the purpose of a cramdown of the class of common stockholders under section 1129(b)(2)(C) of the Bankruptcy Code, the requirement that no one junior to the class receive interest in any property is automatically satisfied, because there is no class that is junior to the common stock. As a result, there is no need to determine the value of such interest. The court went on to note that the value should be the reorganization value of the debtor less the liabilities that exist following confirmation. The bankruptcy court also recognized that additional value may be attributed to a block of common stock that has the ability to control the corporation.

In *In re Bonner Mall Partnership*, the Ninth Cirucit stated that the new value corollary requires that former equity holders offer value under the plan that is (1) new, (2) substantial, (3) in money or money's worth, (4) necessary for successful reorganization, and (5) reasonably equivalent to the value or interest received.[222] In a Ninth Circuit case the 16 partners each contributed $20,000 payable over 10 years in annual increments of $2,000, resulting in an initial contribution of $32,000 and a total contribution of $320,000. The *new value* was not considered substantial. Courts generally consider current value only and not future value to be contributed in determining the adequacy of the new value contributed.

(e) Examples

In the example of X Corporation above, assume that the secured creditors have accepted a revised plan that provides for payments that have a present value of $5 million, and the holders of the subordinated notes agree to a settlement of $1.5 million. The trade creditors, who fare worse as the secured mortgagee renegotiates its position, now reject the revised plan as a class. They must receive full payment of their $1 million claim, because the holders of junior claims (subordinated notes) are receiving something in the plan. In addition, the debtor is solvent and the stockholders will still have their interest in the corporation.

Consider another example with the following changes in the reorganization values of the business:

---

[220] 183 B.R. 475 (Bankr. E.D. Mich. 1995).
[221] 168 B.R. 464 (Bankr. D. Mass. 1994).
[222] 2 F.3d 899, 908 (9th Cir. 1993).

Y Corporation
Balance Sheet
Reorganization Values
(million dollars)

Current assets	$0.5	Trade debt	$1.0
Real estate	4.0	Subordinate notes	2.0
Other assets	4.0	Mortgage on real estate	6.0
		Stockholders' equity	(0.5)
Total	$8.5	Total	$8.5

The plan provided: (1) the secured claim holder that had made an election under section 1111(b)(2) to be paid $5.2 million ($5 million present value); (2) subordinated holders to receive 25 percent of the stock of the company plus cash payments with a present value of $1 million; (3) the trade creditors to receive $0.8 million; and (4) the common stockholders to retain a 75 percent equity. In all, the plan provided for payments with a present value of $6.8 million plus 100 percent of the stock of the reorganized debtor.

Under these terms, the secured claim, trade debt, and subordinated note holders classes must each approve the plan before the court could confirm the plan. Secured and trade creditors are receiving less than the value of their claim. Because the stockholders are retaining value (75 percent interest in the corporation), the subordinated note holders must assent or receive values in property equal to their claim of $2 million. They are receiving only $1.425 million according to the following calculations (in millions):

Present value of cash			$1.000
Value of equity interest:			
Total equity after confirmation:			
Total reorganization value		$8.5	
Debt after confirmation:			
Trade	$0.8		
Subordinated notes	1.0		
Mortgage	5.0	6.8	
Total equity		1.7	
Percent allocated to subordinated claim holders		× 0.25	
Total value of equity interest			0.425
Total value of amount received by subordinated note holders			$1.425

Based on the above calculation, it would be necessary for the holders of the subordinated notes to receive approximately 60 percent ownership of the stock to meet the cram-down requirements.

Under the specified requirements for a fair and equitable plan of reorganization, it is not necessary that the stockholders receive anything, but a class of creditors should not receive more than 100 percent. If the secured creditors and trade creditors accept the plan as proposed and receive property valued at $5.8 million, leaving the balance of property having a present value of $1 million and 100 percent stock for the holders of the subordinate notes, the plan would not be confirmed. The subordinated note holders are receiving more than 100 percent, and this would not satisfy the general requirements of section 1129(b)(I), which states that the plan must not discriminate unfairly and must be fair and equitable. The court would most likely rule that granting the holders of subordinated claims more than 100 percent payment while giving stockholders nothing would not satisfy this requirement.[223]

In § 6.26 it was indicated that reorganization values should be included in the disclosure statement. Note that, in this example, unless the reorganized values are disclosed, it will be difficult for the subordinated note holder to decide how to vote on the plan.

Before any decision can be made about satisfying the cram-down requirements, it is necessary to determine the value of the debtor's business. The process used to determine these values is discussed in Chapter 11.

§ 6.35   Required Deposits

Under Chapter XI of prior law, it was necessary for the debtor to make a deposit equal to the amount of cash that was to be paid out under the plan of arrangement. The only claims that currently require cash payment at the date the plan of reorganization is confirmed are administrative expense and involuntary gap claims. Taxes (seventh priority) can be deferred, because the only requirement is that the present value of payments (not to exceed six years from date of assessment) must equal the amount of the claim (§ 6.32). The other priority claims can be deferred, although generally they are paid in full, provided the holders accept the plan; otherwise, full cash payment at the effective date of the plan will be required. The amount of cash required to be deposited (or paid at the effective date of the plan) is generally less under the new law. Viable businesses that, under prior law, were required to be liquidated because they could not raise the cash required for the deposit may now be allowed to continue operating.[224] Rule 3020(a) provides that the court may order the deposit of the consideration required to be distributed under the plan prior to the order confirming the plan. The money deposited is to be kept in a special account established for the purpose of making the distribution.

POSTCONFIRMATION

§ 6.36   Impact

The confirmation is binding on all creditors and stockholders, even though they did not accept the plan, were impaired under the plan, or were not dealt with in the plan. The confirmation of the plan, unless provided otherwise in

---

[223] If the stockholders retained the difference of the proposed consideration under the plan, namely 40 percent of their former interest in the corporation, or if they were given any interest and approved the plan, the court could confirm the plan. Section 1126(g) provides that a class receiving nothing cannot accept the plan.

[224] Trost, *supra* note 1, p. 1343.

the plan or order confirming the plan, vests all of the property of the estate in the debtor. All of the property is free and clear of all claims and interests of creditors, stockholders, and general partners in the debtor, unless the plan or order confirming the plan provides differently.[225]

Section 1141(c) of the Bankruptcy Code provides:

> (c) Except as provided in subsections (d)(2) and (d)(3) of this section and except as otherwise provided in the plan or in the order confirming the plan, after confirmation of a plan, the property dealt with by the plan is free and clear of all claims and interests of creditors, equity security holders, and of general partners in the debtor.

A problem has arisen with section 1141(c) because of the phrase "is free and clear of all claims and interests." *Claim* is defined in section 101(5) and is distinct from a *lien*, defined in section 101(37). However, the term *interest* is not defined in the Code. Thus, does the term *interest* mean "lien," or can it be interpreted to include a "lien"? Although *interest* is not defined to mean a lien, *lien* is specifically defined to mean "interest."

It should be noted that several sections of the Code use "interest," which is commonly understood to mean all property rights, including lien rights. For example, the term "interest" in section 361 of the Bankruptcy Code, setting forth procedures for adequate protection, has been judicially construed to encompass liens. Other sections of the Bankruptcy Code where interest is used to mean all property rights include sections 101(28), 363(f), 363(h), and 541.

In *Matter of Penrod*,[226] the court held that all liens not expressly preserved by the terms of the plan of reorganization are voided by the confirmation of that plan, and creditors are precluded from asserting or enforcing such void lien rights in later judicial proceedings. The court cited several cases in support of its conclusion.[227]

The creditor, Mutual Guaranty, relied upon *Relihan v. Exchange Bank*[228] and *Matter of Tarnow*[229] for the proposition that "pre-bankruptcy liens are unaffected by a debtor's Chapter 11 bankruptcy case unless the debtor takes affirmative steps to challenge the lien." The court in *Relihan v. Exchange Bank* held that section 1141 does not act to extinguish valid prepetition liens.

The court noted that *Tarnow* arose solely in the context of proof-of-claim litigation and extinguishment of a lien for failure to file a timely claim. In *Penrod*, the court noted that an active creditor, represented by competent counsel, filed a written acceptance to a plan that extinguished its lien. The plan was confirmed by the court and the creditor did not object or appeal the court's

---

[225] 11 U.S.C. § 1141.

[226] 169 B.R. 910 (Bankr. N.D. Ind. 1994).

[227] *See In re Johnson*, 139 Bankr. 208 (Bankr. D. Minn. 1992); *Matter of Depew*, 115 Bankr. 965 (Bankr. N.D. Ind. 1989); *In re Henderberg*, 108 Bankr. 407 (Bankr. N.D.N.Y. 1989); *In re Fischer*, 91 Bankr. 55 (Bankr. D. Minn. 1988); *In re Arctic Enters.*, Inc., 68 Bankr. 71 (D. Minn. 1986); *In re Pennsylvania Iron & Coal Co.*, 56 Bankr. 492 (Bankr. S.D. Ohio 1985); *In re American Properties*, 30 Bankr. 239 (Bankr. D. Kan. 1983).

[228] 69 Bankr. 122 (S.D. Ga. 1985).

[229] 749 F.2d 464 (7th Cir. 1984).

order confirming the plan. Mutual Guaranty also cited other cases that the court in *Penrod* distinguished for the reasons noted.[230]

The effect of section 1141 is far-reaching, according to *In re American Properties, Inc.,*[231] wherein the bankruptcy court noted that, after confirmation of a chapter 11 plan, a creditor's lien rights are only those granted in the confirmed plan. A creditor no longer can enforce its preconfirmation lien rights; a creditor must seek to enforce its lien rights granted in the plan rather than its pre-chapter 11 lien rights.

In a chapter 13 case, *Cen-pen Corp. v. Hanson,*[232] the Fourth Circuit, looking at section 1327 of the Bankruptcy Code (which is in all material respects identical to the provisions of section 1141), concluded that confirmation simply vested in the debtors the same interest in the property that they had before the filing of the chapter 13 petition. Thus, the lien rights survived the chapter 13 confirmation.

Once the plan has been confirmed, it is generally difficult to convince the court to consider other issues, including the issue related to the determination of taxes. For example, in *In re Wayne C. Callan,*[233] Wayne and Carol Callan filed a motion on January 6, 1992, pursuant to title 11, section 505 of the U.S. Code, for a determination that they were entitled to a postconfirmation federal tax refund.

The Callans had filed a chapter 11 petition on May 6, 1987, and their plan was confirmed on February 27, 1989. The property of the estate revested in the Callans upon confirmation of the plan, as provided by section 1141(b) of the Bankruptcy Code. The Callans applied to the IRS for a refund and requested abatement of taxes paid for heating fuel oil for the period from January 1, 1990, to September 18, 1990, in the amount of $58,944.40. Prior to 1990, the Callans had purchased heating fuel oil from a wholesale vendor for resale to the final consumers and had previously received the refund of the federal fuel tax and did not pass the tax burden to the ultimate consumer. A change in the tax law required the request for refund to be made by the end user.

The Callans argued that the inability to use the $58,944.40 from 1990 fuel taxes, which they had expected as a refund, hindered them in making their final plan payment. The tax refunds were not specifically mentioned in the plan as a source of funding, but the reorganization plan may have been devel-

---

[230] *General Elec. Credit Corp. v. Nardulli & Sons, Inc.,* 836 F.2d 184 (3d Cir. 1988) (plan expressly provided for retention of lien); *Estate of Lellock v. Prudential Ins.* Co., 811 F.2d 186 (3d Cir. 1987) (debtors filed petition for relief under chapter 7 of the Bankruptcy Code); *In re Eakin,* 153 Bankr. 59 (Bankr. D. Idaho 1993) (involved debtors in a chapter 7 bankruptcy case); *In re Howell,* 84 Bankr. 834 (Bankr. M.D. Fla. 1988) (case dealt with a debt that was nondischargeable under § 523(a)(6)); *In re Balogun,* 56 Bankr. 117 (Bankr. M.D. Ala. 1985) (plan required debtor to cure arrearages and make payments as they became due under the original agreement between the parties); *In re Ernst,* 45 Bankr. 700 (Bankr. D. Minn. 1985) (plan required payments to satisfy the allowed amount of a secured claim held by a creditor possessing a validly perfected mortgage); *In re Snedaker,* 39 Bankr. 41 (Bankr. S.D. Fla. 1984) (plan did not provide for payment of the creditor's secured claim or mention the property that was subject to garnishment debt; plan only dealt with the creditor's unsecured claim).

[231] 30 Bankr. 239 (Bankr. D. Kan. 1983).

[232] 58 F.3d 89 (4th Cir. 1995).

[233] (No. 3-87-00369-HAR) (Bankr. D. Alaska 1992).

oped on the assumption that the refund would be available. Thus, the problem had not even been foreseen by the Callans.

The IRS defended both on the merits and on the grounds that the court did not have jurisdiction. The jurisdictional argument was based on the premise that the portion of section 505 dealing with refunds refers to a refund by a "trustee." The term "trustee" no longer applied to the Callans, according to the argument of the IRS, because the plan had been confirmed and they were no longer debtors-in-possession. The court did not rule on the merits of the tax matter, but agreed that sovereign immunity was not waived in this contested proceeding, which involved postconfirmation taxes that were not specifically alluded to in the confirmed plan.

The bankruptcy court noted that the U.S. Supreme Court had recently held that "a waiver of federal sovereign immunity must be found in the statute itself. It is immaterial that there may be legislative history supporting a congressional intent for the federal waiver of sovereign immunity which might explain an imprecise statute."[234]

The bankruptcy court held that the taxes did not come from operations under the "estate" but with respect to activities of the postconfirmation or reorganized debtors. The trustee or debtor-in-possession was not seeking the refund. According to section 1107, the Callans were no longer chapter 11 debtors-in-possession, akin to trustees for many purposes. No waiver for a refund is granted in precise words for a reorganized debtor, and, under *Nordic Village*, none can be presumed.

The court retains jurisdiction over postconfirmation issues only to the extent provided for in the plan.[235] A plan provision that retains the bankruptcy court's jurisdiction to resolve disputes concerning the plan overrides a plan provision that all committees are to be dissolved as of the effective date.[236]

The court also noted that, when a debtor confirms a chapter 11 plan, it should begin cutting the ties with the bankruptcy process at the same time.[237]

After a plan has been confirmed, the debtor may not bring action to avoid a transfer where the transferee was not listed in the schedules and was not indicated in the disclosure statement.[238]

The Seventh Circuit held that amendments to a claim after a plan is confirmed under chapter 11 should be permitted rarely, if ever.[239]

Interest and penalties on taxes arising postpetition are considered administrative expenses. However, taxes or any other claims that arise after confirmation are not allowable against the estate.[240]

---

[234] *United States v. Nordic Village*, 112 S. Ct. 1011 (1992).

[235] *In re Johns-Manville Corp.*, 7 F.3d 32 (2nd Cir. 1993); *In re Jr. Food Mart of Arkansas, Inc.*, 161 B.R. 462 (Bankr. E.D. Ark. 1993).

[236] *In re Wedgestone Financial*, 152 B.R. 786 (Bankr. D. Mass. 1993).

[237] *Pettibone Corp. v. Easley*, 935 F.2d 120, 122 (7th Cir. 1991). See *In re Xonics, Inc.*, 813 F.2d 127, 130–32 (7th Cir. 1987); *In re Chicago, Rock Island & Pacific R.R.*, 794 F.2d 1182, 1186–87 (7th Cir. 1986). See also *Pacor, Inc. v. Higgins*, 743 F.2d 984, 994 (3d Cir. 1984); *Goodman v. Phillip R. Curtis Enterprises, Inc.*, 809 F.2d 228, 232–33 (4th Cir. 1987); *National City Bank v. Coopers & Lybrand*, 802 F.2d 990, 994 (8th Cir. 1986); *In re Gardner*, 913 F.2d 1515, 1518–19 (10th Cir. 1990).

[238] *Oneida Motor Freight v. United Jersey Bank*, 848 F.2d 414 (3d Cir. 1988); *In the matter of Freedom Ford, Inc.*, 140 B.R. 585 (Bankr. M.D. Fla. 1992).

[239] *Holstein v. Brill*, 987 F.2d 1268 (7th Cir. 1993).

[240] *In re Fullmer*, 962 F.2d 1463 (10th Cir. 1992).

If bankruptcy jurisdiction does not exist under 28 U.S.C. section 1334(b) or any other statute, a provision in a plan or in an order confirming the plan cannot create jurisdiction. For example, in *Zerand-Bernal Group, Inc. v. Cox*,[241] the Seventh Circuit held that the bankruptcy court did not have jurisdiction to enjoin products liability claims against the purchaser. The chapter 11 plan provided that the assets were to be sold free and clear of any liens, claims, or encumbrances of any nature, and reserved bankruptcy court jurisdiction to enjoin products liability claims against the purchaser. An action was brought, several years after the plan had been confirmed, by a third party who sustained personal injury from a machine made and sold by the debtor before the sale of the assets of the business. It was ruled that the bankruptcy court did not have jurisdiction.

§ 6.37 Distribution

Section 1143 provides that, if a plan requires presentment or surrender of a security or the performance of any other act as a condition to participation in the distribution, such action must be taken within five years after the order for confirmation. Any entity that fails to follow this provision may not participate in the distribution. For example, if it is determined that a junior lienholder has no secured claim because of the low value of the property pledged, it may be required that the lienholder deliver a release of the lien before that lienholder can receive a distribution as an unsecured creditor. The lien must be released within the five-year period in order for the lienholder to receive the distribution.

Rule 3021 states that the distribution to creditors whose claims are allowed and to holders of stock, bonds, debentures, notes, and other securities whose claims or equity security interests are allowed is to be made after the plan is confirmed.

§ 6.38 Discharge of Debts

The new law provides for the discharge of debts in a manner similar to the provisions in Chapter X of prior law. Unless the plan is a liquidating plan, all claims and interests of the corporate debtor are discharged (unless provided otherwise in the plan) whether or not a proof of claim was filed, whether or not the claim is allowed, and whether or not the holder of the claim has accepted the plan. Thus, the obtaining of credit by a corporation through the use of false financial statements will not result in the denial of a discharge. If, on the other hand, the debtor is an individual, all the provisions of section 523, including the use of false financial statements, that can prevent the debtor from obtaining a discharge of certain types of claims, apply in a chapter 11 case (§ 5.35).

The Fifth Circuit held, in *Matter of Christopher*,[242] that a person who extended postpetition credit to an individual chapter 11 debtor, with knowledge of the bankruptcy, had its claim discharged even though the claim was not scheduled and the lender did not receive the chapter 11 notices. Obviously, the debt was not scheduled because the creditor was not a creditor at the time the petition was filed. The court noted that due process does not

---

[241] 23 F.3d 159 (7th Cir. 1994).
[242] 28 F.3d 512 (5th Cir. 1994).

preclude discharge under these circumstances. The Fifth Circuit relied on *In re Sam*,[243] in which the court held that the claim of a prepetition creditor that had actual knowledge of the bankruptcy was held discharged despite the fact that the debt was not scheduled and the creditor did not receive formal notices.

§ 6.39 Postconfirmation Recovery

The debtor and the creditors' committee or other interested parties may agree to postpone any recovery actions such as avoiding power suits, including fraudulent transfers and preferences, until after the plan has been confirmed. Any recovery action that is to be taken after confirmation of the plan must be provided for in the plan. The Eighth Circuit held that although the bankruptcy court may have jurisdiction under section 1334(b) to hear avoiding power suits, unless the plan actually provides for the postconfirmation enforcement of such cause, the trustee, the debtor, or other representatives of the estate do not have standing to bring the suit.[244] Other courts have also held that representatives of the estate lack standing to bring such an action, including an action to recover preferences, unless such action was provided for in the plan.[245]

§ 6.40 Securities Law Exemption

Section 5 of the Securities Act of 1933 requires securities of publicly held companies to be registered with the SEC prior to their sale or offer for sale. The Bankruptcy Code provides for exemptions from section 5 of the 1933 Act for chapter 11 companies. Section 1145(a) states:

a Except with respect to an entity that is an underwriter as defined in subsection (b) of this section, section 5 of the Securities Act of 1933 (15 U.S.C. 77e) and any State or local law requiring registration for offer or sale of a security or registration or licensing of any issuer of, underwriter of, or broker or dealer in, a security does not apply to—
  1 the offer or sale under a plan of a security of the debtor, of an affiliate participating in a joint plan with the debtor, or of a successor to the debtor under the plan—
    A in exchange for a claim against, an interest in, or a claim for an administrative expense in the case concerning, the debtor or such affiliate; or
    B principally in such exchange and party for cash or property;
  2 the offer of a security through any warrant, option, right to subscribe, or conversion privilege that was sold in the manner specified in paragraph (1) of this subsection, or the sale of a security upon the exercise of such a warrant, option, right, or privilege;
  3 the offer or sale, other than under a plan, of a security of an issuer other than the debtor or an affiliate, if—
    A such security was owned by the debtor on the date of filing of the petition;

---

[243] 894 F.2d 778 (5th Cir. 1990).
[244] *Harstad v. First Am. Bank*, 39 F.3d 898 (8th Cir. 1994).
[245] *See In re Paramount Plastics, Inc.*, 172 B.R. 331 (Bankr. W.D. Wash. 1994); *In re Mako*, 120 B.R. 203 (Bankr. E.D. Okla. 1990).

    B the issuer of such security is—
        i required to file reports under Section 13 or 15(d) of the Securities
           Exchange Act of 1934 (15 U.S.C. 78m or 780(d)); and
        ii in compliance with the disclosure and reporting provision of such
           applicable section; and
    C such offer or sale is of securities that do not exceed—
        i during the two-year period immediately following the date of the
           filing of the petition, four percent of the securities of such class
           outstanding on such date; and
        ii during any 180-day period following such two-year period, one per-
           cent of the securities outstanding at the beginning of such 180-day
           period; or
4 a transaction by a stockbroker in a security that is executed after a trans-
    action of a kind specified in paragraph (1) or (2) of this subsection in such
    security and before the expiration of 40 days after the first date on which
    such security was bona fide offered to the public by the issuer or by or
    through an underwriter, if such stockbroker provides, at the time of or
    before such transaction by such stockbroker, a disclosure statement
    approved under section 1125 of this title, and, if the court orders, informa-
    tion supplementing such disclosure statement.

This exception is available only if the securities are not offered or sold by or through an underwriter. Note that the exchange must be *principally* for a claim against or an interest in the debtor or an affiliate. Thus, the issuance of securities in exchange for cash or some other form of consideration would not be exempted. The Bankruptcy Code does, however, allow for securities to be issued for administrative expenses in the case. An exchange by an interest holder involving stock plus cash when the debtor is insolvent may still be opposed by the SEC.[246] Subsection (2) of section 1145(a) also exempts the offering of a security through any warrant, option, right to subscribe, or conversion privilege sold in the manner described above. The Code also provides that the sale of a security upon the exercise of any warrant, option, right, or privilege is not subject to section 5 of the 1933 Act.

    Section 1145(a)(3) also exempts from section 5 of the Securities Act of 1933 the sale of portfolio securities owned by the debtor on the date the petition was filed. To be exempted, the distribution of securities within a two-year period subsequent to the date of the petition must not exceed 4 percent of the securities of that class outstanding at the date the petition was filed. Furthermore, subsequent distributions are allowed, provided they do not exceed 1 percent during any 180-day period. The exemption is limited to securities of a company that is required to file reports under sections 13 and 15(d) of the 1934 Act and is in compliance with the disclosure and reporting provisions of the appropriate section. SEC Rule 148 was issued prior to section 1145 becoming law, but it still provides guidance on the issuance of portfolio securities in situations not covered by section 1145(a)(3).

---

[246] Phelan and Cheatham, *supra* note 172, at p. 418. *See SEC v. Bloomberg*, 229 F.2d 315, 319 (1st Cir. 1962); Comment, "The Issuance of Securities in Reorganizations and Arrangements under the Bankruptcy Act and the Proposed Bankruptcy Act," *Ohio State Law Journal*, Vol. 36 (1975), pp. 380, 392.

Section 1145(a)(1) also provides that a successor to the debtor is exempted from the securities laws in the same manner that a debtor would be. Transactions of a stock during a 40-day period following the initial offer of the security under the plan are also exempt. Section 1145(a)(4) does provide that, as a condition for the exemption, the stockbroker must provide a copy of the disclosure statement required under section 1125 or other supplementary information that the court may require at the time of or before the transaction.

(a) Resale of Securities

Section 1145(b) specifies the standards under which a creditor, equity security holder, or other entities acquiring the securities under the plan of reorganization may resell them. Because the 1933 Act limits the sales by underwriters, section 1145(b) exempts from the definition of an underwriter those who receive securities in a reorganization, with four exceptions. A person who performs the following would be considered an underwriter:

1 Acquires a claim against, an interest in, or a claim for an administrative expense in the case concerning the debtor with a view to distribution.
2 Offers to sell securities offered or sold under the plan for the holder of the securities.
3 Offers to buy securities offered or sold under the plan for the holder of the securities, if the offer to buy is made with a view to distribution and under an agreement made in connection with the plan.
4 Is an issuer within the meaning of section 2(11) of the 1933 Act.

Section 1145(b)(1) provides that an entity is not an underwriter with respect to ordinary trading transactions of an entity that is not an issuer. Section 1145(b)(2) provides that an entity that issues stock for debt or for administrative expenses is not an underwriter.

Section 1145(c) makes an exempted offer or sale of securities under the chapter 11 plan a public offering to avoid its being characterized as a private placement that would result in restrictions under SEC Rule 144 on the resale of the securities.[247]

The last provision (subsection d) of section 1145 provides that the Trust Indenture Act of 1939 does not apply to a commercial note issued under the plan that matures within one year after the effective date of the plan.

§ 6.41 Final Decree

Rule 3022 of the Federal Rules of Bankruptcy Procedure provides that after an estate is fully administered in a chapter 11 case, the court on its own motion, or on motion of a party-in-interest, will enter a final decree closing the case. The 1991 Committee Note indicates that the court should not keep the case open only because of the possibility that the court's jurisdiction may be invoked in the future. It is further noted that the final decree does not deprive

---

[247] H.R. Rep. No. 95-595, 95th Cong., 1st Sess. 421 (1977).

the court of jurisdiction to enforce or interpret its own orders and does not prevent the court from reopening the case for cause under section 350(b) of the Bankruptcy Code.

§ 6.42 Conversion to Chapter 7

Section 1112(a) provides that a debtor may voluntarily convert a chapter 11 case to chapter 7 unless a trustee has been appointed, the case originally was commenced as an involuntary chapter 11, or the case was converted to a chapter 11 other than on the debtor's request. The court may also convert the case to chapter 7 after notice and a hearing. Section 1112(c) and (e) provides two exceptions to the general rule. Subsection (c) states that if the debtor is a farmer or a corporation that is not a moneyed, business, or commercial corporation, the debtor must consent to the conversion. As provided in subsection (e), the court could not convert a case unless the debtor may be a debtor under chapter 7. Thus, a railroad case could not be converted because a railroad cannot file under chapter 7.

The following ten reasons are stated in section 1112 as reasons why a court may convert a chapter 11 case to chapter 7:

  1 Continuing loss to or diminution of the estate and absence of a reasonable likelihood of rehabilitation.

  2 Inability to effectuate a plan.

  3 Unreasonable delay by the debtor that is prejudicial to creditors.

  4 Failure to propose a plan under section 1121 of title 11 within any time fixed by the court.

  5 Denial of confirmation of every proposed plan and denial of a request made for additional time for filing another plan or a modification of a plan.

  6 Revocation of an order of confirmation under section 1144 of title 11, and denial of confirmation of another plan or a modified plan under section 1129 of title 11.

  7 Inability to effectuate substantial consummation of a confirmed plan.

  8 Material default by the debtor with respect to a confirmed plan.

  9 Termination of a plan by reason of the occurrence of a condition specified in the plan.

10 No payment of filing, quarterly or other fees or charges.

In addition, a common ground for conversion is that there is a lack of good faith on the part of the debtor that constitutes an abuse of the court's jurisdiction.[248] There are also other grounds for conversion, such as the failure of the debtor to maintain business records.[249]

---

[248] *Collier Bankruptcy Manual*, 3d ed., ¶ 1112.04(2)(d)(ix).
[249] *In re Larmar Estates, Inc.*, 3 C.B.C.2d 218 (Bankr. E.D.N.Y. 1980).

Bankruptcy Rule 2002(a)(5) provides that all creditors, equity security holders, and indenture trustees must receive at least 20 days' notice by mail of a hearing to dismiss or to convert a chapter 11 case to chapter 7.

The conversion does not change the filing date of the bankruptcy case. The 60-day period for the decision to assume or reject a lease in a chapter 7 case begins on the date the order transferring the case is entered. The services of a trustee or examiner are terminated prior to conversion.[250] All claims incurred after the chapter 11 petition but before the conversion was filed that are not administrative expenses will be considered prepetition claims. Administrative expenses, including accounting fees, incurred after the conversion to chapter 7 have priority over those incurred during the period the debtor operated under chapter 11.

As a general rule, the amount and nature of a claim that is determined through the confirmation of a plan is binding even though the plan may subsequently be converted to chapter 7. For example, in *In re Pierce Packing Co.*,[251] the bankruptcy court held that confirmation of a chapter 11 plan binds a creditor to that plan's provisions even if the plan is not consummated and the case is converted to chapter 7. In *In re Laing*,[252] the Tenth Circuit held that, in a chapter 7 case that was converted from chapter 11, the creditor was not allowed to relitigate the dischargeability of a claim even if the claim was actually of a dischargeable type, because in the chapter 11 confirmed plan the debtor and creditor reached an agreement that the claim was not dischargeable.

The debtor's failure to file required tax returns before filing the chapter 13 petition, and his failure to bring himself into compliance with the tax laws during the period after filing and before the time of petition, was considered evidence of bad faith under section 1325(a)(3) of the Bankruptcy Code and the case was dismissed.[253]

§ 6.43   Advantages and Disadvantages of Chapter 11

Under certain conditions, chapter 11 proceedings may be more appropriate than informal settlements made out of court:

1   Rather than near-unanimous approval, majority approval in number and two-thirds in amount of allowed claims of creditors voting is sufficient to accept a plan of reorganization and bind dissenters.

2   Creditors bargain collectively with the debtor, which may result in more equitable treatment of the members of each class of claims or interest.

3   The debtor's assets are in the custody of the court and safe from attack when the petition is filed.

4   Executory contracts and leases can be canceled when such action benefits the debtor and can be assumed or assigned when this action benefits the debtor.

[250] 11 U.S.C. § 348(e).
[251] 169 B.R. 421 (Bankr. D. Mont. 1994).
[252] 31 F.3d 1050 (10th Cir. 1994).
[253] *Matter of Crayton*, 169 B.R. 243 (Bankr. S.D. Ga. 1994).

5 The creditors have an opportunity to investigate the debtor and its business affairs.

6 Certain preferential and fraudulent transfers can be avoided by the debtor-in-possession or trustee.

7 Proper protection can be provided to holders of public securities.

8 Certain tax advantages are available under the Bankruptcy Code.

9 Creditors are additionally protected by the requirements that to be confirmed by the court the plan must be in the best interests of creditors, be feasible, be fair and equitable to any impaired, dissenting classes, and provide for priority claims.

The major disadvantages of this method of rehabilitation are that it is more time-consuming and more costly, often resulting in smaller dividends to creditors.

CHAPTER 12: ADJUSTMENT OF DEBTS OF A FAMILY FARMER WITH REGULAR ANNUAL INCOME

§ 6.44 Purpose

To help farmers resolve some of their financial problems, Congress passed chapter 12 of the Bankruptcy Code. It became effective November 26, 1986, and was originally designed to last until October 1, 1993. Because chapter 12 relates to a specific class of debtors, Congress was to evaluate whether the chapter is serving its purpose and whether there is a need to continue this special chapter for the family farmer. After Congress makes this evaluation, it will be able to determine whether to make this chapter permanent. If Congress does not act, chapter 12 was scheduled to terminate on October 1, 1993. Public Law 103-65 extended the sunset date to October 1, 1998.

Under current law, a family farmer in need of financial rehabilitation may file either a chapter 11 or a chapter 13 petition. Most family farmers cannot file under chapter 13; they have too much debt to qualify and are limited to chapter 11. Many farmers have found chapter 11 needlessly complicated, unduly time-consuming, inordinately expensive, and, in many cases, unworkable.[254]

Chapter 12 is designed to give family farmers an opportunity to reorganize their debts and keep their land. According to legislative history, debtors under chapter 12 receive the protection from creditors that bankruptcy provides, while at the same time preventing abuse of the system and ensuring that farm lenders receive a fair repayment.[255]

§ 6.45 Requirements for Use

An individual or an individual and spouse engaged in farming operations whose total debt does not exceed $1.5 million and at least 80 percent of whose

---

[254] H.R. Rep. No. 99-958, 99th Cong., 2d Sess. 48 (1986).
[255] *Id.*

noncontingent, liquidated debts (excluding debt from principal residence, unless debt arose out of farming operations) on the date the petition is filed arose out of farming activities may file a chapter 12 petition. Additionally, more than 50 percent of the petitioner's gross income for the taxable year prior to the filing of the petition must be from farming operations.

A corporation or partnership in which more than 50 percent of the outstanding stock or equity is owned by a family may also file a chapter 12 petition if all of the following conditions are met:

1   More than 80 percent of the value of its assets consist of assets related to farming operations.
2   Total debts do not exceed $1.5 million and at least 80 percent of its noncontingent, liquidated debts on the date the case is filed arose out of farming operations.
3   The stock of a corporation is not publicly traded.

§ 6.46   Operation of Farm

Section 1204 allows the debtor to operate the farm unless the Bankruptcy Court orders otherwise. To operate the farm, it is necessary for the debtor to have control over its property. Section 1207(b) provides for this control by stating that the debtor remains in possession of all property of the estate. Section 1207(a) provides that the property of the estate includes, in addition to the property as of the date the petition is filed, all property acquired after the commencement of the case and earnings from services rendered before the case is closed.

Even though the debtor may be allowed to operate the business, a chapter 12 standing trustee will be appointed. The standing trustee is responsible for supervising the administration of the chapter 12 case. An example of a form letter that might be used by the chapter 12 trustee to inform a debtor-in-possession (DIP) of his or her responsibility in a chapter 12 case is shown as 6.15 in Volume 2. The sample letter sets forth the information, both financial and nonfinancial, that the chapter 12 trustee needs from the DIP, and other areas that should be of concern to the DIP.

Section 362 provides that the filing of a bankruptcy petition operates as an automatic stay against almost any action that the creditors may be taking, including any act to create, perfect, or enforce a lien against the property of the estate. In order for the secured creditor to proceed against the debtor, the stay must be removed. The basis primarily used by creditors to remove the stay is a lack of adequate protection under section 361 of the Bankruptcy Code.

At the time chapter 12 became law, two circuit court cases held that, in order to provide the creditor adequate protection, it was necessary for the debtor to compensate the secured creditor for opportunity cost, where the value of the collateral was less than the balance of the debt secured by the property pledged. These two cases were overturned by the Supreme Court decision in *Timbers* (see § 5.27 and § 6.11). Congress felt that the payment of this opportunity cost by family farmers—generally in the form of interest on the values of the collateral—is very difficult and may result in the loss of the farm. As a result, section

1205 of the Bankruptcy Code provides that a family farmer can provide protection by paying reasonable market rent.

The adequate protection issue in chapter 12 may not be very significant because these cases are being confirmed in most courts within (or close to within) the time period established (90 days for filing plan and 45 days thereafter for confirmation).

§ 6.47 Chapter 12 Plan

Only the debtor can file a plan in a chapter 12 case. The requirements for a plan in chapter 12 are more flexible and lenient than those in chapter 11. In fact, there are only three requirements set forth in section 1205 of the Bankruptcy Code that must be met. First, the debtor must submit to the supervision and control of the trustee all or such part of the debtor's future income as is necessary for the execution of the plan. Second, the plan must provide for full payment, in deferred cash payments, of all priority claims unless the creditors agree to a different treatment. Section 1222(a)(2) does not require that interest be included in deferred payments in all cases including tax claims.[256] Third, where creditors are divided into classes, the same treatment must apply to all claims in a particular class. The plan can alter the rights of secured creditors with an interest in real or personal property; however, there are a few restrictions. To alter the right of the secured claim holder, the debtor must satisfy one of the following three requirements:

1 Obtain acceptance of the plan.
2 Provide in the plan that the holder of such claim retain the lien and as of the effective date of the plan provide that the *value* of the payment to be made or property to be transferred is not less than the amount of the claim.
3 Surrender the property securing such claim.

Effective for agreements entered into after October 22, 1994, the Bankruptcy Reform Act of 1994 added subsection (d) to section 1222 of the Bankruptcy Code. It provides that, notwithstanding subsection (b)(2) and sections 506(b) and 1225(a)(5) of the Bankruptcy Code, if a plan proposes to cure a default, the amount necessary to cure the default is to be determined in accordance with the underlying agreement and applicable nonbankruptcy law. This provision overrules *Rake v. Wade*,[257] where the Supreme Court held that the Bankruptcy Code requires that interest be paid on mortgage arrearages paid by debtors curing defaults on their mortgages. Notwithstanding state law, this decision had the impact of requiring debtors to pay interest on interest *and* interest on late charges and other fees.

The Tenth Circuit Court of Appeals held that, in absence of special circumstances, such as market rate being higher than contract rate, bankruptcy courts should use current market rate of interest for similar loans in the Region when

---

[256] *See In re Herr*, 16 Bankr. Ct. Dec. (CRR) 1025 (Bankr. S.D. Iowa 1987).
[257] 113 S. Ct. 2187 (1993).

determining whether a chapter 12 plan proposes payment to creditors of value no less than the amount of the allowed claim.[258]

If a holder of an allowed unsecured claim does not accept the plan, the court may not approve the plan unless:

1   The value of the property to be distributed is equal to at least the amount of the claim;
2   The plan provides that all of the debtor's projected disposable income to be received within three years (or longer, if directed by the court) after the first payment is made will be a part of the payments under the plan.

To facilitate the operation of the business and the development of a plan, section 1206 of the Bankruptcy Code allows family farmers to sell assets not needed for the reorganization prior to confirmation without the consent of the secured creditor, provided the court approves such a sale.

Section 1221 provides that the debtor should file the plan within 90 days and that the court may extend this time period only if an extension is substantially justified. Section 1224 provides that the hearing for confirmation of the plan shall be concluded not later than 45 days after the plan is filed.

CHAPTER 13: ADJUSTMENT OF DEBTS OF AN INDIVIDUAL WITH REGULAR INCOME

§ 6.48   Nature

The Bankruptcy Reform Act of 1978 changed Chapter XIII of the Bankruptcy Act to make it more attractive for individual owners of small businesses. Prior to the new law, only employees (wage earners) were allowed to file according to the provisions of the Bankruptcy Act. In addition, some courts allowed pension fund or social security recipients and some self-employed individuals such as carpenters to seek relief under Chapter XIII. Other courts interpreted the act very narrowly, allowing only employees to file a petition. The objective of chapter 13 is to provide individuals with some alternative other than liquidation when in financial trouble. Chapter 13 allows the individual, with court supervision, to work out a plan that can provide for full or partial payment of debts over an extended period of time. The solution is similar in concept to a chapter 11 reorganization but on a less formalized and more practical scale.

§ 6.49   Filing of Petition

Section 109(e) provides that only an individual with regular income, who owes, at the time the petition is filed, noncontingent, liquidated, unsecured debts of less than $100,000 and noncontingent, liquidated, secured debts of less than $350,000 can file a petition under chapter 13. The definition of regular income requires that individuals filing the petition must have sufficient stable

---

[258] *Hardzog v. Federal Land Bank of Wichita,* 901 F.2d 858 (10th Cir. 1990).

and reliable income to enable them to make payments under the chapter 13 plan. The limit on amount of indebtedness will prevent some wage earners from filing a petition. However, the purpose of this limitation was to allow some small sole proprietors to file under this chapter, because the filing of a chapter 11 petition might be too cumbersome for them, and require the larger, individually owned, businesses to use chapter 11.

Effective for petitions filed after October 22, 1994, the Bankruptcy Reform Act of 1994 increased the debt limit for the filing of a chapter 13 petition for unsecured debts from $100,000 to $250,000; the limit for secured debt rose from $350,000 to $750,000. On April 1, 1998, and at each three-year interval thereafter, the dollar amounts for the debt limits for a chapter 13 petition are to be increased, beginning on April 1, to reflect the change in the Consumer Price Index for All Urban Consumers that occurred during the three-year period ending on December 31 of the immediately preceding year. The amounts are to be rounded to the nearest $25 multiple. An increase in the debt limits for chapter 13 will allow more debtors to file under chapter 13. The extent to which a small business will use chapter 13 will depend on several factors. Among them are a determination of the extent to which the debtor would be better off for tax purposes with a separate tax entity for the bankruptcy, as would be the case in chapter 7 or chapter 11, or with only one tax entity; the extent to which future disposable income must be included in the plan; and the extent to which the small business provisions of the Bankruptcy Reform Act of 1994 are effective.

Stockbrokers and commodity brokers are prohibited from filing under this chapter, as are partnerships and corporations. Individual partners may, however, file a petition. Section 302(a) provides that a joint petition can be filed by husband and wife. A small business owned by both husband and wife that is classified as a partnership would be excluded from filing a chapter 13 petition. It is also not necessary that there be a formal written partnership agreement between the husband and wife for the arrangement to be considered a partnership. The determination of the states of the husband and wife will to some extent depend on whether the assets of the business are for the benefit of all creditors of the debtor or only for business creditors. The mere fact that husband and wife are joint owners of property and joint obligers does not establish that they constitute a partnership.[259]

Cases have been split as to what property is in the bankruptcy estate when a debtor converts a petition from chapter 13 to another chapter. In a chapter 13 case, any property acquired after the petition is filed is property of the estate, at least until the confirmation of the plan. Some courts have held that if a chapter 13 case is converted, all property of the estate as of the date of the conversion is property of the chapter 7 estate. Other courts have held that the property of the estate consists only of the property as of the chapter 13 filing date. Effective for petitions filed after October 22, 1994, the Bankruptcy Reform Act of 1994 modified section 348 of the Bankruptcy Code to provide that, in a conversion from chapter 13 to another chapter, the property of the estate as of the date of the filing of the chapter 13 remains in the possession of the debtor as of the conversion date. Valuations of property and secured claims

---

[259] H.R. Rep. No. 95-595, 95th Cong., 1st Sess. 198 (1977).

in the chapter 13 case apply in the converted case. Allowed secured claims are reduced to the extent that they have been paid in accordance with the chapter 13 plan.

Section 348 of the Bankruptcy Code is, however, amended to provide that if the debtor converts a chapter 13 case to another chapter in bad faith, the property in the converted case will consist of the property as of the date of the conversion.

The debtor may voluntarily convert a case from chapter 13 to chapter 11 or chapter 7, and the creditors may petition a court to transfer a chapter 13 case to chapter 11 or chapter 7 for all businesses except for farmers.[260]

§ 6.50 Operation of Business

Section 1304 provides that the debtor in a chapter 13 case will be allowed to continue to operate the business unless the court orders otherwise. In addition, the debtor has the responsibility of an operating trustee to file the necessary reports and other required information with the appropriate taxing authorities (see § 5.45). To operate the business, it is necessary for the debtor to have control over its property. Section 1306(b) provides that the debtor remains in possession of all the property of the estate. The Bankruptcy Code also provides that the property of the estate includes, in addition to the property as of the date the petition was filed, all property acquired after the commencement of the case and earnings from services rendered before the case is closed.[261]

A trustee will be appointed in chapter 13 business cases. In districts that warrant it, a standing trustee may be appointed to handle all chapter 13 cases. Because of the amount of work that may be involved in the business cases, separate trustees may be appointed or the standing trustee may employ an accountant and attorney to assist in the performance of the required duties. As was mentioned above, the debtor remains in possession of the property and title is not transferred to the chapter 13 trustee. The principal function of the chapter 13 trustee is to collect payments under the plan and distribute them to the creditors. The duties were, however, expanded to include most of the functions of a trustee in a chapter 7 or chapter 11 case except reporting to taxing authorities and taking possession of the debtor's assets. The trustee will conduct an investigation into the acts, conduct, assets, liabilities, and financial condition of a business debtor and file a report with the court regarding the result of the examination.[262]

§ 6.51 The Plan

Only the debtor can file a plan in a chapter 13 case. The requirements for a plan in chapter 13 are much more flexible and lenient than those in chapter 11. In fact, only three requirements are set forth in the Bankruptcy Code that must

---

[260] 11 U.S.C. § 1307.
[261] Id., § 1306(a).
[262] Id., § 1302(c).

be met.[263] First, the debtor must submit to the supervision and control of the trustee all or such part of the debtor's future earnings as is necessary for the execution of the plan. Second, the plan must provide for full payment, in deferred cash payments, of all priority claims, unless the creditors agree to a different treatment. Third, where creditors are divided into classes, the same treatment must apply to all claims in a particular class.

The plan can alter the rights of secured creditors with an interest in real or personal property, but there are a few restrictions. A claim secured only by a security interest in real property that is the debtor's principal residence cannot be modified. Section 1325(a)(5) also provides that a lien secured by the debtor's property is to be retained by the holder of the secured claim in situations where the creditor does not approve the plan. Secured claims with liens on property of less value than the claim may be paid as a secured claim to the extent of the value of the property and as an unsecured claim for the balance. Once the amount set forth under the plan has been paid, it may be possible for the debtor to obtain an order from the court directing the lienholder to release the lien.[264] The Bankruptcy Code also permits the plan to provide for the curing of a default (such as payments on long-term mortgage debt) within a reasonable time and to make payments while the case is pending on any claim for which the last payment is due after the date when the last payment under the plan is due.

The trustee has the power to assume or reject any executory contracts or unexpired leases under section 365(d)(2) and, if no action is taken by the trustee, the debtor may include a provision in the plan for the assumption or rejection of such contracts.[265]

The plan cannot provide for payments that exceed three years unless the court, for cause, approves a longer time period. The court cannot, however, approve a time period for repayment that is longer than five years.[266] Section 1326(a) provides that, unless the court orders otherwise, the debtor is to start making payments under the proposed plan within 30 days after it is filed. The payments are to be retained by the trustee until the plan is confirmed. Upon confirmation, the trustee will distribute the payments in accordance with the plan. If the plan is not confirmed, the trustee is to return the payments to the debtor after deducting all unpaid priority claims, including administrative expenses.

(a) Confirmation of Plan

In order for the plan to be confirmed by the court, it must meet seven separate requirements.[267]

1 Provision must comply with chapter 13 and other applicable provisions of the Bankruptcy Code.

---

[263] *Id.*, § 1322(a).

[264] Joe Lee, "Chapter 13 née Chapter XIII," *American Bankruptcy Law Journal*, Vol. 53 (Fall 1979), p. 314.

[265] 11 U.S.C. § 1322(b)(7).

[266] *Id.*, § 1322(c).

[267] *Id.*, § 1325.

2   Required bankruptcy fees must be paid.

3   The plan must have been proposed in good faith.

4   Value, at the effective date, of property to be distributed under the plan to the unsecured creditors must not be less than the amount they would have received under a chapter 7 liquidation.

5   The holder of secured claims must (a) accept the plan or (b) retain the lien securing the property, and the value, as of the effective date of the plan, of property to be distributed on account of such claim must not be less than the allowed amount of the claim, or the debtor must surrender the property securing the claim to such holder.

6   The debtor must be able to make all payments under the plan and comply with the plan.

7   Under section 1325(b), if the trustee or a holder of an allowed unsecured claim objects to the confirmation of the plan, the court may not approve the plan unless, as of the effective date of the plan, the value of the property to be distributed to satisfy such claim is at least equal to the amount of this claim or the plan provides that the debtor's disposable income to be received during the three-year period following the due date of the first payment is to be applied to make payments under the plan. Disposable income includes income received by the debtor less the amount needed for the support of the debtor and his or her dependents plus, if engaged in business, the amount necessary for the continuation, preservation, and operation of the business.

The Bankruptcy Reform Act of 1994 provides that section 1325(a)(5) of the Bankruptcy Code is applicable to a situation where the final payment of a secured claim is due before the date on which final payment under the plan is due. This change overrules *First National Fidelity Corp. v. Perry*,[268] where the Circuit Court ruled that the payments could not be deferred under section 1325(a)(5) of the Bankruptcy Code as long as the value of the payments equals the amount of the debt. Under section 1322(b)(2) of the Bankruptcy Code, the delayed payments would constitute an impermissible modification of the mortgage holder's rights to immediate payment.

Section 1322 of the Bankruptcy Code was modified by the Bankruptcy Reform Act of 1994, effective for petitions filed after October 22, 1994, to allow a debtor to cure home mortgage defaults at least through a foreclosure sale and under applicable nonbankruptcy law. If the State provides the debtor more extensive "cure" rights, such as through some later redemption period, the debtor will enjoy those rights in bankruptcy.

Effective for agreements entered into after October 22, 1994, the Bankruptcy Reform Act of 1994 added subsection (e) to section 1322 of the Bankruptcy Code to provide that, notwithstanding subsection (b)(2) and sections 506(b) and 1325(a) of the Bankruptcy Code, if a plan is proposed to cure a default, the amount necessary to cure the default is to be determined in accordance with the underlying agreement and applicable nonbankruptcy law. This provision overrules the decision in *Rake v. Wade*,[269] where the Supreme Court held that

---

[268] 945 F.2d 61 (3d Cir. 1991).
[269] 113 S. Ct. 2187 (1993).

the Bankruptcy Code requires that interest be paid on mortgage arrearages paid by debtors curing defaults on their mortgages. Notwithstanding state law, this decision had the impact of requiring debtors to pay interest on interest *and* interest on late charges and other fees.

There are some major differences from chapter 11 in getting a plan confirmed under chapter 13. Note that the provisions above do not require that the creditors, either secured or unsecured, affirmatively approve the plan. Creditors may, however, object if their claim is not paid in full and the plan does not include disposable income of the debtor. The court must determine that the unsecured creditors will receive at least as much under the plan as they would in a chapter 7 liquidation. The unsecured creditors may, however, object to the confirmation of the plan under section 1324. Some possible reasons for their objection could be:

1   The plan was not proposed in good faith.
2   The plan as proposed is discriminatory in the way creditors' claims are classified.[270]
3   Creditors within the same class are unequally treated.
4   The plan does not satisfy the best-interest-of-creditors test.
5   Debtor's disposal income is not included in the plan.

If the holders of secured claims do not accept the plan as required by section 1325(9)(5)(A), the court must see that the creditors retain a lien securing the property and the value to be distributed must be at least equal to the allowed claim; or, the debtor must surrender the property as explained above. The amount of the allowed claim is determined as of the date of confirmation of the plan to ensure that the creditors' claims will not be affected by a decline in the value of the collateral during the period of consummation of the plan. (See § 11.5 for a discussion of the approaches used to value the property in a chapter 13 proceeding.)

In *Rake v. Wade*,[271] the court held that, in a case under chapter 13, oversecured creditors are entitled to preconfirmation and postconfirmation interest on any arrearages that are paid off under the debtor's plan. Therefore, the oversecured creditors' claims should be adjusted to reflect any such interest. It is important to note that this right to payment exists regardless of the terms of the original security agreement.

§ 6.52   Discharge of Debts

After completion of payments under the plan, the debtor is entitled to a discharge from all debts disallowed or provided for in the plan. The only exceptions are alimony, maintenance, or child support payments; certain long-term secured claims that will not be exhausted within the duration of the plan; and claims for postpetition consumer goods or services necessary for performance under the plan. This last exception would occur when the creditor failed to get

---

[270] Lee, *supra* note 264, p. 319.
[271] 113 S. Ct. 2187 (1993).

prior approval of the trustee for the obligation and as a result it was disallowed.[272] Thus, the use of chapter 13 can result in the debtor's obtaining discharge of debts that could not be obtained under a chapter 7 liquidation or a chapter 11 reorganization. (See § 5.50 and § 6.38.) Under a chapter 11 plan, the debtor is discharged upon confirmation; under chapter 13, the debtor will not earn a discharge until all payments are made under the plan.

The debtor can apply for a hardship discharge under certain conditions where payments required under the plan cannot be made. However, any discharge obtained is subject to the same exceptions to discharge in section 523 that apply to a chapter 7 liquidation.[273] In order for a hardship discharge to be granted, the court must determine that the failure of the debtor to complete payments was due to circumstances arising after confirmation for which the debtor was not responsible, each unsecured claim holder received at least as much as would have been received under a chapter 7 liquidation as of the effective date of the plan, and modification of the plan is impracticable.[274]

§ 6.53   Use of Chapter 13 by Business

Individuals owning businesses that can file in either chapter 13 or chapter 11 may find some advantages to using chapter 13. Merrick listed the following factors, which might cause chapter 13 to be more appealing:

1   Chapter 13 has much less creditor involvement. In chapter 11, creditors' committees have the right to consult the debtor regarding the administration of the estate; the creditors have the right to participate in the formulation of the plan, and they can request that a trustee or examiner be appointed; and the creditors and their committee have the right to raise any issue and appear and be heard in regard to it.

2   In chapter 11, the debtor runs the risk of a trustee's being appointed. In chapter 13, there is a standing trustee, but the debtor will operate the business.

3   A chapter 13 debtor must seek approval only from holders of secured claims; in chapter 11, approval from both secured and unsecured claim holders is necessary.

4   A disclosure statement containing adequate information is not required in chapter 13.

5   Confirmation of the plan may be more difficult in chapter 11. The section 1111(b) election is not available in chapter 13. Protection for unsecured creditors is not as inflexible in chapter 13 as in chapter 11 (section 1129(b)(2)).

6   Chapter 11 offers more chance that the debtor will become controlled by third parties. Under certain conditions, creditors can file plans in chapter 11 whereas only the debtor can file a chapter 13 plan. Chapter 13 offers greater opportunities for the debtor to make the critical decision to con-

[272] 11 U.S.C. § 1328.
[273] *Id.*, § 523.
[274] *Id.*, § 1328(b).

vert the case to liquidation and fewer reasons to allow a party-in-interest to request an involuntary dismissal of the case or conversion to liquidation.

7 Chapter 13 has a more comprehensive discharge provision (§ 6.52).[275]

An analysis of the first years of the new law in one district indicates that most small businesses are not using chapter 13 to the extent visualized by some. One of the problems with a chapter 13 case is that a fee of 10 percent of the payments under the plan must be paid to the standing trustee, even though the debtor continues to operate the business. In chapter 11, this fee would not be required, but a quarterly fee was subsequently added which made chapter 11 less of an advantage. Chapter 13 is, however, being used by small businesses where the unsecured creditors are not going to receive anything. In order to confirm a plan of this type, the judge needs only to ascertain that the creditors would not receive anything if the debtor were liquidated under chapter 7, providing it is determined that the plan was proposed in good faith. The Bankruptcy Amendments and Federal Judgeship Act of 1984 has made it more difficult for debtors to obtain a discharge in chapter 13 under these conditions, by allowing the creditors to object to the confirmation if the debtor's disposable income is not included in the plan (see § 5.50). The extent, of course, to which bankruptcy judges continue to confirm plans where the unsecured creditors receive nothing will determine how much chapter 13 will be used by businesses. A majority of the bankruptcy courts that have considered the good faith requirement have concluded that chapter 13 plans must offer substantial and meaningful payments.[276]

---

[275] Glenn Warren Merrick, "Chapter 13 of the Bankruptcy Reform Act of 1978," *Denver Law Journal*, Vol. 56 (1979), pp. 620–23.

[276] "News and Comments," *Bankruptcy Court Decisions*, Vol. 6 (July 17, 1980), p. A-65.

7

Retention of the Accountant and Fees

§ 7.1 Introduction

Because there are several ways of coping with financial difficulties and many different parties are involved, accountants and financial advisors have many avenues by which they may become involved in bankruptcy and insolvency proceedings. This chapter sets forth the ways in which the accountant or financial advisor may be retained and describes the procedures related to retention and to the determination of fees.

The retention of an accountant or financial advisor by the bankruptcy court, trustee, creditors' committee, or debtor-in-possession must be by order of the court, which also issues notice on the amount of fees or the rate to be used. The accountant or financial advisor prepares an affidavit setting forth the scope of the services to be rendered and the estimated time and costs required for such services. Based on this affidavit, the accountant or the counsel for the trustee, creditors' committee, or debtor-in-possession prepares an application for retention, along with a retention order for the judge to sign, and submits them to the court. Prior to the consideration of the order by the court, the U.S. trustee's office will review the application. If the court approves the retention, it will enter an order, confirm the scope of the services to be performed, and set the compensation for such services. An accountant may also be retained to render services for a debtor company that has not formally petitioned the court. In this situation, the accountant will obtain a signed engagement letter similar in format to the usual engagement letter; however, provision for a cash retainer and/or alternate sources of payment should be arranged if possible.

The accountant or financial advisor must keep adequate time and performance records while services are being rendered. Even in out-of-court settlements, the unexpected need to file a bankruptcy court proceeding should not find the accountant or financial advisor unprepared to justify his or her services. After the services have been rendered, the accountant files a petition for compensation in affidavit form with the bankruptcy court. The petition should contain enough information about the services rendered for the court to evaluate and compare them with the services authorized in the order of retention. After the hearings, if required, the judge will fix the exact compensation that the accountant or financial advisor will receive.

RETENTION OF THE ACCOUNTANT

§ 7.2 The Accountant or Financial Advisor's Role in the Proceedings

The accountant or financial advisor becomes a party to the proceedings through retention by the debtor-in-possession or trustee, if appointed, a creditors' committee, equity committee, other creditors' committees, secured lender, stockholder, or examiner. In a voluntary reorganization under chapter 11 of the Bankruptcy Code, the debtor normally remains in possession and has the right to retain an accountant for necessary accounting functions. The creditors' committee may desire the services of an accountant or financial advisor rather than using the information provided by the debtor's advisors to inquire into the affairs of the debtor prior to insolvency and to aid the committee in developing a plan. In a chapter 11 case, the accountant or financial advisor may also be retained as the examiner. In large cases, where several committees are formed, each committee of creditors and/or stockholders may retain its own financial advisors. The accountant or financial advisor may be appointed as the trustee in a chapter 7, chapter 11, or chapter 12 case.

§ 7.3 Obtaining the Engagement

Often an initial interview is scheduled where several accountants or financial advisors are invited to make a presentation to explain why your firm should be selected to represent your client. This process is often referred to as a "beauty contest." Since presentations are often held for different parties of interest—debtor, creditors' committee, etc.—it may be important that your firm not be disqualified from other possible engagements. Ground rules are often established that provide that participants in the first interview, for example, to represent the debtor, are not disqualified from subsequently representing another party, such as the creditors' committee. If such guidelines are not developed and there is a desire to be considered for subsequent engagements for the same client, an agreement should be prepared providing that no confidential information will be communicated during the initial interview. Additionally, the agreement may provide that in the event the accountant or financial advisor is not selected, he or she is free to be considered to represent another party in the filing.

§ 7.4 Retention Procedure—Formal

The retention of an accountant or financial advisor for the trustee must be by order of the court and is granted upon the application of the trustee, which must show, among other things, the necessity for such retention.

Section 327(a) of the Bankruptcy Code provides that the trustee "with the court's approval, may employ one or more attorneys, accountants, appraisers, auctioneers, or other professional persons . . . to represent or assist the trustee in carrying out the trustee's duties under this title." This requirement also applies to an accountant or financial advisor employed by a debtor-in-possession. An accountant or financial advisor who is not an employee cannot generally be employed by a trustee or debtor-in-possession except upon an order of the court expressly fixing the amount of the compensation or the rate by which it is to be measured. Thus, the accountant should not consider the engagement confirmed until the court has signed an order authorizing the retention. Because compensation must come from the debtor's estate, authorization must be given in advance, by written order of the court, and must fix the rate or measure of compensation. Section 1107(b) provides that accountants or other professionals are not disqualified for employment by a chapter 11 debtor solely because of such employment by or representation of the debtor prior to filing the petition. Section 327 provides that accountants and other professionals may be retained by the debtor-in-possession or the trustee, with court approval, if the professional does not hold or represent an interest adverse to the estate and is disinterested. Section 328(c) adds to the requirement by stating that the person must be a disinterested person. Section 328(c) provides that the court may deny allowance of compensation for services and reimbursement of expenses for a professional that is not disinterested or represents or holds an interest adverse to the interest of the estate. Under section 101(14), a creditor cannot be a disinterested person. This requirement might be interpreted to mean that if the accountant or financial advisor for the creditors' committee has unpaid fees as a result of rendering services for the debtor prior to the proceedings, such accountant or financial advisor is not disinterested and could be denied payment. In situations where this problem exists, the accountant should be sure the court is aware of the unpaid fees before the retention order is issued. In many bankruptcy courts, judges will not appoint the debtor's prior accountant or financial advisor if there are unpaid fees. There are, however, some judges who do object.

In recent years, the number of judges who have refused to appoint accountants or financial advisors where there are unpaid fees has increased significantly. In many regions, the U.S. trustee is also objecting to the appointment of accountants where there are unpaid accounting fees. If unpaid fees exist, the accountant should determine the prior practice of the judge who is handling the case and of the U.S. trustee, to determine their attitude toward unpaid fees. Where the judge will not appoint accountants and other professionals with unpaid fees, the unpaid fees must be forgiven before retention can be obtained.

The Third Circuit held that a debtor-in-possession may not retain an accountant that is one of the largest 20 creditors to assist in the execution of its postpetition duties.[1] And in another case the bankruptcy court denied employment for an accountant firm that was the eighth largest creditor.[2] However, in both of these cases the accounting firms did not waive the payment of their prepetition fees as a condition of employment.

A minority of courts have approved employment for attorneys and accountants in chapter 11 that are owed prepetition fees.[3] An accountant or financial advisor that is familiar with the nature of the debtor's operations would harm the debtor by not continuing as its accountant and would create unnecessary

---

[1] *U.S. Trustee v. Price Waterhouse*, 19 F.3d 138 (3d Cir. 1994).
[2] *In re Siliconix, Inc.* 135 B.R. 378 (N.D. Cal. 1991).
[3] *See In re Howard Smith, Inc.*, 207 B.R. 236t (Bankr. W.D. Okla. 1997); *In re Viking Ranches*, 89 B.R. 113 (Bankr. C.D. Cal. 1988); *In re Microwave Products of America, Inc.* 94 B.R. 971 (Bankr. W.D. Tenn. 1989).

administrative expenses for another advisor to obtain the desired understanding of the debtor's business. The court considers the extent to which the accountant or financial advisor could benefit unfairly from the appointment and whether the size of the prepetition claim is *de minimus* in relation to the total debts of the debtor.[4] In both *In re Howard Smith, Inc.* and *Textile Industries*, the court approved the employment because the prepetition claim was *de minimus* in relation to the total debts of the debtor.

The trustee or debtor-in-possession applies for the retention of an accountant or financial advisor by filing an application with the bankruptcy judge having jurisdiction. Included in the application are the facts of the case, reasons why an accountant or financial advisor is necessary, the name and address of the proposed advisor, a statement alleging that the particular accountant or financial advisor is qualified to perform such services and has no adverse interest in doing so, the hourly rates of the accountant and his or her associates, and an estimate of the total cost to the debtor's estate for his or her services.

Section 586(a) of title 28 of the U.S. Code provides that a function of the U.S. trustee is to monitor applications for fees filed with the court and submit to the court comments with respect to the approval of such applications. Thus, prior to obtaining approval of the fee application by the court, the application will need to be reviewed and approved by the U.S. trustee.

Section 327(b) provides that, if the trustee or debtor-in-possession is authorized to operate the business in a chapter 7 or chapter 11 proceeding and if the debtor has regularly employed attorneys, accountants, or other professional persons on salary, the trustee may retain or replace such professional persons if necessary to operate the business. The debtor-in-possession would have this same right in a chapter 11 proceeding. There is some uncertainty as to the extent that section 327(b) of the Bankruptcy Code would apply to the retention of independent accountants or financial advisors because the form of compensation is referred to as salary. Section 327(b) may allow an accountant, under restricted conditions, to receive payments for services rendered without an order from the court, but it is still advisable for the accountant to obtain court approval. The application for retention may state that the accountant is retained under the provision of section 327(b) to render periodic (monthly, quarterly, and so forth) accounting services. The application for retention may also request that the accountant be compensated at the firm's normal fee rates (current rates are then attached to the application) upon completion of each periodic assignment. According to section 327(d), the court may also authorize the trustee to act as attorney or accountant for the estate if such action is in the best interest of the estate.

§ 7.5 Creditors' Committee

Section 1103 grants the creditors' committee the right to employ, with court approval, accountants or other professionals to render services. This section

---

[4] Hon. Leslie Tchaikovsky, Linda Stanley, Molly Gallagher, and Margaret Sheneman, "Current Developments, Bankruptcy Review Commission, and Legislative Update," *14th Annual Bankruptcy and Reorganization Conference* (Medford, OR: Association of Insolvency and Restructuring Advisors, 1998), p. 28.

does not require that the accountants or other professionals employed or retained by the creditors' committee be totally disinterested persons as defined by section 158 of Chapter X of the former Bankruptcy Act. However, if the person employed is to be compensated for the services rendered, and reimbursed for expenses incurred, such person, according to section 328(c), must be a disinterested person as defined by section 101(14) and must not represent or hold an interest adverse to the interest of the estate during the period of employment. It was noted in § 7.4 that section 1107(b) provides a limited exception to this policy by stating that a professional person is not disqualified from employment by a debtor simply because the person represented the debtor prior to the commencement of the case. In order to reduce the costs of having two accountants, under prior law the debtor's accountant was, at times, appointed to represent the creditors' committee. This practice has generally ceased under the Bankruptcy Code. Bankruptcy judges may, however, allow the debtor's accountant to provide information for the creditors' committee, to avoid the cost of the committee having its own accountant, provided this procedure does not create a conflict-of-interest problem for the debtor's accountant. If a conflict of interest does arise, the court may at that time appoint an accountant for the creditors' committee.

Section 1103(b) provides that a person appointed to represent a creditors' committee may not at the same time represent any other entity having an adverse interest in connection with the case. This section further provides that representation of one or more creditors of the same class as represented by the committee does not per se constitute the representation of an adverse interest. If the accountant or financial advisor for a creditor of the debtor is asked to become the accountant or financial advisor for the creditors' committee, care must be taken to disclose the prior representations and to consider whether it is possible to serve as accountant to that creditor and comply with the requirement of section 1103(b) that the accountant or financial advisor for the creditors' committee may not represent any other entity having an adverse interest in connection with the case. As a matter of courtesy to the creditor, the accountant or financial advisor would want to discuss the appointment with the creditor prior to attempting to be engaged as the accountant or financial advisor for the committee.

§ 7.6   Source of Payment

The fees for professional services are paid out of the debtor's estate. As noted in Chapter 5, these expenses are considered administrative expenses and have a first priority. However, there must be unpledged assets to pay these expenses. If all assets of the debtor are pledged, the secured creditors must be willing to modify their security interest to provide for payment to accountants or financial advisors and attorneys who must render services in the case. Before an accountant or financial advisor agrees to work in a bankruptcy case, he or she would want to be sure there are unpledged assets or some other source of payment. It is common for attorneys to receive an advance before the petition is filed to cover part of the services to be rendered by them after the petition is filed. Accountants or financial advisors can also receive a retainer. In some cases, accountants or financial advisors have not requested advances when, if such request had been made, there was a good possibility it would have been granted.

If an advance is received by an accountant or financial advisor, this should be disclosed to the court. The nature of the disclosure will vary from district to district. For example, in the Central District of California, the accountant or financial advisor or other professional must disclose the total amount of prepetition payments received within a year prior to the petition date. Also, the accountant or financial advisor should disclose the amount of the prepetition services rendered, the expenses incurred during such year, and the funds that are remaining for postpetition services as of the date the petition is filed.

Generally, services that are rendered and are charged against the advance that existed as of the date the petition was filed must be reported in the same way as requests for payments for services rendered where there is no advance. A statement will be filed, often monthly, with the court disclosing the fees earned and expenses incurred along with the proper documentation to support these charges. The content of the form that is required in the Central District of California is described below (this form or one similar to it would most likely be required by other U.S. trustee offices).

Generally, any unearned portion of a prepetition or postpetition retainer that is an advance against fees must be deposited in a segregated trust account upon filing of the petition. If the prepetition retainer is earned upon receipt, the funds need not be segregated by the professional.

1. Any professional who has received a prepetition or postpetition retainer must submit to the United States Trustee a monthly Professional Fee Statement no later than the 20th day after the end of the month during which professional services were rendered, together with documentation supporting the charges for the professional services and expenses in the form required for professional fee applications in the "United States Trustee Guide to Applications for Professional Compensation." In addition, a copy of the Professional Fee Statement (without the supporting documentation) must be served on the official creditors' committee or, if no committee has been appointed, on the 20 largest unsecured creditors, and on those parties who have requested special notice. The Professional Fee Statement should include a statement that the supporting documentation can be obtained from the professional upon request.

2. The Professional Fee Statement must explicitly state that the fees and costs will be withdrawn from the trust account in the amount requested without further notice or hearing, unless an objection is filed with the clerk of the court and served upon the applicant(s) within 10 days after service of the Professional Fee Statement. If no objection is timely filed and served, the professional may withdraw the requested compensation without further notice, hearing, or order. If an objection is timely filed and served, the professional should refrain from withdrawing any funds until the objection has been resolved by the court.

3. Notwithstanding the submission of the Professional Fee Statement, as long as the professional is performing services covered by a retainer, the

professional must submit interim fee applications to the court every 120 days in the form and manner specified in the "Guide to Applications for Professional Compensation." Once the full amount of the retainer has been accounted for, no further Professional Fee Statements shall be filed.

4 Neither the United States Trustee nor any party in interest shall be stopped from raising objections to any charge or expense in any professional fee application filed with the court on the ground that no objection was lodged to the Professional Fee Statement.

5 *Special Note:* Some judges do not permit attorneys to draw down on retainers pursuant to the above procedures. Attorneys with retainers should thus make certain at the time of their employment what procedures are required by the judge to whom the case is assigned.

§ 7.7 Affidavit of Proposed Accountant

Once the accountant is selected, it is then necessary to obtain authorization by the court through an order for retention. This requires that the accountant make a preliminary survey of the debtor's operations, as well as the debtor's books and records, and use the survey's findings to compose a letter, under oath, addressed to the trustee or debtor-in-possession and containing the following information:

The firm's name and address, and, generally, the name of the specific accountant or financial advisor (normally a partner) asking to be retained

Nature of any relationship, connections, or business association of the accountant or financial advisor with the debtor, the creditors, the attorneys, or any other party to the proceedings (normally in the form of a disclaimer of any type of business association)

The qualifications, including any indication of past experience in bankruptcy and insolvency proceedings

A statement as to whether the accountant has already rendered services to the debtor or trustee and whether he or she has a claim against the estate

A statement that a preliminary survey of the bankrupt's books and records has been completed and that the accountant is familiar with their general contents (not necessary in all cases, especially when the accountant is not required to estimate the total cost of the services)

A description of the extent and nature of the services expected to be rendered

An estimate of the time to be expended on the audit, broken down by class of employee and hourly billing rate

A request for retention for a maximum amount based on the estimate of hours and the stated billing rates (some judges do not require a maximum amount)

The accountant's notarized signature (or executed under pains and penalty of perjury)

In addition to the above, some judges may require a statement that no other agreement exists between the accountant and any other party to share compensation awarded to the accountant. The information described above is the type of information normally found in the affidavit. It should, however, be realized that some judges will not require all of the information. For example, some judges will authorize the retention based on the billing rates only, without requiring a maximum amount. However, the Administrative Office of the United States Courts has requested that all orders authorizing the employment of accountants specifically state the hourly rates to be charged and a maximum allowance. The accountant or financial advisor should check with the debtor's counsel (or creditors' committee) if there is some question about the practices in the district where the retention is being requested.

In Volume 2 of *Bankruptcy and Insolvency Accounting*, 7.1 is an example of an affidavit of an accountant (the firm of Arthur Andersen & Co.) for the debtors (NextWave Personal Communications, Inc.) in a chapter 11 filing. In paragraphs 3–8, the accountant identifies the business association or connections that the accountant has had with the debtors. Item 4(b) indicates that the accounting firm was an unsecured creditor of the debtors for services, in the amount of $4,500, rendered prior to the filing of the petition.

The claim with the approval of the U.S. Trustee was transferred to a separate legal entity of which the accounting firm owned 45 percent of the interest with a 1 percent income distribution. Paragraph 10 describes the amount of the retainer received by Arthur Andersen. Rather than listing the services to be provided in the affidavit, reference was made to the application for retention. The application for retention is in 7.5 of Volume 2.

The accountant stated, in paragraph 11, that the billing rates are those customarily charged by the firm for such services. Paragraph 11 also indicates that the rates are revised at selected dates during the year and that the rates as revised will be used after those dates.

Another affidavit that was prepared by the debtor's financial advisors is included in 7.2 of Volume 2. Included with the affidavit is an engagement letter that was filed with the application for retention. The application for retention is in 7.6 of Volume 2. In Volume 2, 7.3 contains an affidavit for retention of the accountant by the trustee. The application for retention is in 7.7 of Volume 2.

In Volume 2, 7.4 contains an affidavit of an accountant for the creditors' committee. The application for retention based of the affidavit is in 7.8 of Volume 2.

(a) Connection

Rule 2014 of the Federal Rules of Bankruptcy Procedure requires that an application for approval of the employment of a professional person, including accountants, be accompanied by a verified statement of the professional describing the professional's connections, if any, with the debtor and parties-in-interest or their attorneys or accountants, the United States trustee or any person employed in the office of the U.S. trustee. This statement is included in the declaration or affidavit of the proposed accountant. While many declarations or affidavits of accountants already include a statement of this nature, the accountant or financial advisor must be sure that all possible connections are disclosed. Professional persons have a duty to disclose potential conflicts of interest and the failure to disclose due to mere negligence is not justified.[5] An accountant for the trustee or debtor is held to the same fiduciary standards as the trustee. A trustee, as well as the accountant, may not purchase property of the bankruptcy estate, even if the trustee or accountant previously resigned his or her position.[6] The bankruptcy court noted that possession of competitive information is not extinguished by resignation.[7]

Even a negligent or inadvertent failure to fully disclose relevant information may result in a denial of all fees requested by the professional.[8]

The accountant in *In re Thrifty Oil Co.*[9] did not disclose until the final fee application that it was the auditor for a major competitor that owed the debtor approximately $7 million. The bankruptcy court rejected the accountant's assertion that it is not required to perform a conflict check for major parties-in-interest that are not creditors. The court held that the accountant must disclose all of the connections with the debtor, creditors, or any other party-in-interest and that an interest adverse to the estate can arise from the representation of competitors or those in litigation with the debtor. However, the court in *In re Thrifty Oil* determined that because it did not appear that the audit performed by the accountant had any adverse impact on the bankruptcy estate or assisted the competitor (client) in its litigation dispute against the debtor, the objection to the fees was overruled. The bankruptcy court, in *In re Trust America Service Corp.*,[10] stated that a large accounting firm must conduct a conflict check among all departments and all locations of its partnership.

The failure to disclose all connections with parties-in-interest may result in fees being disallowed, including an order to disgorge all postpetition fees, and the professional being disqualified.[11]

Sections 327 and 328 apply only to professionals employed by a trustee and are not applicable to conflicts that occurred prior to the entry of the order for relief.[12]

(b) Service

Some judges do not require a detailed list of the services to be rendered, but only a general statement that the accountant will render normal accounting services, including the preparation of tax returns. (See 7.3, Volume 2).

If the affidavit or declaration that the CPA files with the court contains a list of specific services that will be rendered in the engagement, consideration should be given to adding a general statement indicating that other accounting

---

[5] *In re BH&P Inc.*, 949 F.2d 1300 (3d Cir. 1991).
[6] *In re Allied Gaming Management, Inc.*, 209 B.R. 201 (Bankr. W.D. La. 1997).
[7] *Id.*
[8] *In re Park-Helena Corp.*, 63 F. 3d 877 (9th Cir. 1995).
[9] 205 B.R. 1009 (Bankr. S.D. Cal. 1997).
[10] 175 B.R. 413 (Bankr. N.D. Fla. 1994).
[11] *See In re 245 Associates, LLC*, 188 B.R. 743 (Bankr. S.D. N.Y. 1995); *In re Basham*, 208 B.R. 926 (Bankr. 9th Cir. 1997); *In re Lewis*, 113 F.3d 1040 (9th Cir. 1997).
[12] *In the Matter of Wiredyne, Inc.*, 3 F.3d 1125 (7th Cir. 1993).

and tax services may also be rendered if such services are needed by the debtor-in-possession or trustee (creditors' committee, if retained by committee). Thus, any objections that might be raised because of an interpreted deviation from the retention order would fall under the last category. It is still advisable to obtain a modification in the original retention order for material deviations from the original order.

When authorized under applicable law to practice public accounting, it is possible for an accounting partnership, corporation, or professional association to be retained to render services in bankruptcy cases without identifying the particular accountants who will actually be working on the assignment; however, in most cases, the specific accountant is identified. In cases where a particular individual is identified in the order, Rule 2014(b) allows for another partner, member, or associate to act as the accountant without further order of the court.

§ 7.8 Survey of Work to Be Performed

As mentioned above, the accountant or financial advisor generally makes a preliminary survey of the work that is to be performed in order to include in the affidavit the scope of the services to be rendered or, in some cases, in order to make a presentation to obtain the engagement. If the accountant or financial advisor has performed audits for the debtor in the past, the condition of the records will be known and very little new information will be needed in order to prepare the affidavit.

Often, several accountants and financial advisors may be presentations to be retained as the accountant for the unsecured creditors' committee, other creditors' and equity holders' committees, or the trustee, if appointed. To make an effective presentation, the accountant or financial advisor must learn as much about the debtor's operations as possible. It is not uncommon for the accountant who can most effectively identify the debtor's problems and indicate the type of action and direction that the committee should pursue to be retained.

When a new accountant or financial advisor is selected, frequently at the request of the creditors or their committee, as much information as possible about the company must be gained in a very short time period. For example, the accountant or financial advisor may receive a call from an attorney who represents the creditors' committee, requesting services for the engagement. The attorney will then describe some of the background information about the debtor. After providing the accountant or financial advisor with this information, the attorney arranges, often the same day, to accompany the accountant or financial advisor to the office of the company to determine the nature of the debtor's operations. At the premises of the debtor, the accountant will make an inspection of the facilities, very briefly examine the records, and obtain copies of the most recent financial statements the company has issued. The accountant or financial advisor should ascertain directly from the controller whether the records are current, whether major impediments exist, and whether the key accounting personnel plan to stay with the company. The examination is very limited, with the accountant usually spending only part of a day at the debtor company. The accountant or financial advisor may be able to contact the debtor's independent accountant and obtain additional information.

It should be realized that the extent to which the accountant or financial advisor needs to investigate the nature of the debtor's operations depends on the type of information that must be included in the affidavit or declaration of the accountant or financial advisor. For example, if the court allows a general statement about the nature of the services and does not require a statement as to the maximum amount of fees necessary to perform the services specified, the preliminary survey of the debtor's books and records is not necessary. Accountants may still want to complete limited inquiries to be sure they want to be associated with this particular debtor.

In 7.1 of Volume 2, the accountant for the debtor made reference to the fact that he was familiar with the books, records, and financial information and data maintained by the debtor, as a result of the firm's prior engagements. In 7.2 of Volume 2, no reference was made to the extent to which the accountant for the creditors' committee was familiar with the debtor's operations.

§ 7.9 Application for Retention

The accountant or counsel for the trustee, debtor-in-possession, or creditors' committee uses the information in the accountant's affidavit on proposed services to prepare an application for retention of the accountant or financial advisor to be submitted to the bankruptcy court for its approval. Many accountants who actively render services in the bankruptcy area will prepare their own application for retention. By preparing their own application, these accountants are able to (1) include the information as well as the manner of presentation desired, (2) provide consistency in the content among engagements, and (3) be sure that the application is prepared and filed on a timely basis.

If the court approves the retention of the accountant or financial advisor it will enter the order, confirm the scope of the services to be performed, and set the rate or maximum compensation to be allowed for such services. As with the affidavit of the accountant, the amount of detail in the application for retention will vary depending on the requirements of the court or judge where the petition is filed. The application on behalf of the accountant or financial advisor must be made by either the trustee (debtor-in-possession) or committee and, according to Rule 2014(a), it must include the necessity for the employment, the name of the person to be employed, the reason for his or her selection, the professional services to be rendered, any proposed arrangement for compensation, and the applicant's connections with the debtor, creditors, or any other party-in-interest.

In Volume 2 of *Bankruptcy and Insolvency Accounting*, 7.5 offers an example of an application for retention that was prepared by the accountant and signed by the debtor. (The affidavit of the accountant, James Lukenda, for NextWave Personal Communications Inc. is in 7.1 of Volume 2.) As noted above, although counsel may prepare the application for the accountant, it is often advisable for the accountant to prepare the application for the debtor to sign. In the case of Next Wave Personal Communications Inc., the court would not allow the accountant to receive 100 percent of the fees for the audit engagement at the time of billing, as requested. Another example of an application for retention is given in 7.6 of Volume 2; this one, however, was prepared by the financial advisor for the debtor. (See 7.2 in Volume 2 for the corresponding affidavit of the financial advisor.)

An example of application for the employment of accountants and financial advisors for a chapter 7 trustee in the Southeast Banking Corporation is in 7.7 of Volume 2. The related affidavit of Soneet Kapila in the Southeast Banking Corporation is in 7.3 of Volume 2. Also, an example of the employment of accountants for the unsecured creditors' committee in Loewen Group International is in 7.8 of Volume 2. The related affidavit of Dewey Imhoff in Loewen Group International is in 7.4 of Volume 2.

Another example of an application for the retention of financial advisors to the creditors' committee, which appears as 7.9 in Volume 2, is drawn from the Public Service Company of New Hampshire's chapter 11 filing. Note that item 15 in 7.9 indicates that the financial advisor to the debtor is to be paid a set fee per month. A similar arrangement was approved by the financial advisor in Loewen Group International (see 7.6 of Volume 2). Accountants and attorneys are normally compensated for the services they render on a time basis, usually accounted for in six-minute intervals. Some courts have questioned the use of a flat fee per month and have refused to appoint financial advisors on this basis. Other judges have allowed the fees to be paid on a monthly basis, but have required the financial advisors to file with the court a statement indicating the time spent working on the engagement being billed. Thus, the financial advisors are required to file fee petitions similar to those filed by other professionals. In some chapter 11 filings, the services that are rendered by financial advisors from investment banking area are very similar to those rendered generally by financial advisors and accountants.

The Office of the United States Trustee for the region that includes the Central District of California has stated, in that an application to employ a professional person must include the following information:

1. The name and occupation of the person or firm to be employed.

2. Facts demonstrating the necessity for the employment and the specific services to be rendered.

3. The reason for the selection of the particular professional to be employed, including facts to substantiate that the proposed professional has attained a sufficient experience level to render the proposed services. The professional's personal and, if appropriate, firm resume should be attached. If a trustee proposes to retain his or her own firm as counsel, the application must show a compelling reason why appointment of outside counsel is not feasible.

4. A declaration under penalty of perjury setting forth, to the best of the professional's knowledge, all of the professional's connections with the debtor, creditors, or any other party in interest, their respective attorneys and accountants, the United States Trustee and any person employed by the office of the United States Trustee, and whether the professional holds any interest adverse to the estate of the debtor. The declaration must contain facts, not merely legal conclusions.

5. The terms and conditions of the employment agreement, including the hourly rate charged by each professional (including partners, associates, and paraprofessional persons employed by the professional) expected to render services to or for the benefit of the estate.

6. If the professional is an attorney, the application must state the amount
   and source of any fees, retainers or other compensation (including any
   contingency fee agreements) paid or agreed to be paid, including any fees,
   retainers or other compensation paid or agreed to be paid within one year
   of the filing of the petition, for services rendered or to be rendered in contemplation of or in connection with the case, whether the fees, retainers
   or other compensation has already been paid, whether the retainer is an
   advance against fees for services to be rendered or earned upon receipt,
   whether all or any portion of the retainer is refundable, the services, if
   any, the client is entitled to receive in exchange for the retainer, the facts
   justifying the amount of the retainer, and a declaration under penalty of
   perjury demonstrating the need for a retainer, including any unusual circumstances that would justify a postpetition retainer.

7. If the application is made more than thirty days after the date postpetition services commenced, it must include a declaration under penalty of
   perjury explaining the delay and stating the amount of fees and expenses
   that have accrued during the period between the date postpetition services were commenced and the date of the application.

8. If the application is made more than sixty days after the date postpetition
   services commenced, the Notice of Application required by Bankruptcy
   Local Rule 141(2)(b) must include a statement that retroactive employment is being requested and the date that services commenced. Normally only extraordinary facts will justify retroactive employment.

9. If more than one of a particular type of professional is being retained,
   each application must set forth the need for dual professionals, the services to be performed by each, a statement that there will be no duplication of services and an explanation of how duplication will be avoided.

In many regions of the U.S. trustee program, fee guidelines have been
enacted. Many of these guidelines are similar to the ones described above. The
ABI Report Steering Committee suggests that, although the guidelines may be
helpful to inexperienced bankruptcy professionals, they "clearly usurp the role
of Congress and the courts and result in the undesirable situation of a governmental body (the U.S. Department of Justice) both making the law and enforcing it. Guidelines also add a fifth potential level of governing authority to the
bankruptcy laws, following the bankruptcy statutes, the Bankruptcy Rules,
the local rules adopted in certain federal judicial districts, and the case law.
There is no statutory mandate for their existence, and their presence unduly
complicates the bankruptcy process, but has stepped beyond its statutory
authority through the use of fee Guidelines."[13]

However, the Bankruptcy Reform Act of 1994 provided that one of the duties
of the U.S. trustee is to review the petition for fee allowance in accordance with
procedural guidelines adopted by the Executive Office of the U.S. Trustee. The
Reform Act also provides that the guidelines shall be applied uniformly by the
U.S. trustee, except when circumstances warrant different treatment. On Janu-

---

[13] American Bankruptcy Institute, *National Report on Professional Compensation in Bankruptcy
Cases* (Washington, DC: American Bankruptcy Institute, 1991) pp. xiii–xiv.

ary 30, 1996, the Executive Office of the U.S. Trustee issued revised guidelines for reviewing fee applications for compensation and expenses reimbursement. These guidelines are included as Appendix D of this text.

§ 7.10 Retention Order

Based on the affidavit and application for retention filed with the court, the court will issue an order authorizing the accountant to be retained. The accountant (or counsel for the debtor or unsecured creditors' committee) will prepare the order that is submitted to the court for the judge's signature. Three examples of actual orders issued by the court are included in Volume 2. The first, issued in NextWave Personal Communications Inc. authorized the employment of accountants, appears as 7.10. Attached to the order is notice of the hearing for approval. For documents related to 7.10, the order authorizing the retention of the accountant by the debtor, see 7.1 and 7.5 in Volume 2. For documents related to 7.11, the order authorizing the retention of the accountant by the debtor in Loewen Group, see 7.2 and 7.6 of Volume 2. Each of these orders was prepared by the accountant or attorney for the debtor and submitted to the court for the bankruptcy judge's signature. Volume 2, 7.12 contains an order approving a financial advisor to the trustee (see 7.3 and 7.7 of Volume 2).

If counsel for the debtor or unsecured creditors' committee is preparing the application, the accountant must be sure the order is actually signed before spending a significant amount of time on the engagement.

An order issued by the bankruptcy court authorizing a debtor-in-possession to retain a financial advisory firm to perform professional services only establishes the nature and range of such services and does not bind the court to particular terms and conditions of employment, including the amount of fees to be awarded.[14]

In situations where the professional applications were approved after full disclosure, the professionals were allowed compensation for services rendered before the employment order was reversed on appeal.[15]

§ 7.11 Retention on a Retainer Basis

A retention order authorizing the accountant to render continuing accounting services is often required if the independent accountant assists the trustee, receiver, or debtor-in-possession in normal accounting duties, including the preparation of monthly, and sometimes weekly, operating statements for the court. This type of order is advantageous if the time period between commencement of the case and confirmation of a plan is of considerable length, in that payment for services is normally monthly under a retainer of this nature. In many chapter 11 proceedings, the time span covers several years. Accountants rendering normal periodic accounting services that would qualify under section 327(b) (see § 7.4) may state this in their affidavit or declaration. This procedure may increase the ability of the accountant to receive payments on a

---

[14] *Zolfo, Cooper & Co. v. Sunbeam-Oster Company, Inc.*, 50 F.3d 253 (3d Cir. 1995).
[15] *In re CIC Inv. Corp.*, 192 B.R. 549 (Bankr. 9th Cir. 1995).

monthly or other periodic basis. A sample of the accountant's affidavit requesting retention on a retainer basis as accountant for a debtor in New York is shown in 7.13 of Volume 2 of *Bankruptcy and Insolvency Accounting.* It is important that a retention order be obtained. The information filed with the court in the request to be retained may vary considerably because of local rules and practices and because of the nature of the engagement. An example of an application filed for retention as accountant for the debtor is given as 7.13 in Volume 2. Because the company involved was relatively small, the accountant not only assisted the debtor in developing a plan to emerge from chapter 11, but also compiled financial statements and assisted the debtor in record-keeping functions of the business. The complete documentation ((a) application for retention, (b) affidavit, (c) engagement letter, and (d) order for retention) needed to render services can be found in 7.14 of Volume 2.

§ 7.12 Deviations from Retention Order

The accountant should pay close attention to the scope of the accounting services to be rendered as they are described in the order for retention entered by the court. Deviation from the stated services will be closely scrutinized by the court and may not be included in the accountant's allowance for compensation. Likewise, if more time than the original estimate will be needed by the accountant, a supplemental court order must be obtained allowing additional compensation.

Once the retention orders are entered by the court, the accountant may begin rendering compensable services.

§ 7.13 Accountants as Consultants or Financial Advisors

Some accounting firms make it a policy to state on their application that they are accountants and consultants or financial advisors, if they anticipate providing assistance to the debtor or unsecured creditors' committee regarding the development or evaluation of a business plan, reorganization value, disclosure statement, or plan of reorganization. It should be realized by the court that the function of the accountant in today's bankruptcy environment includes much more than the preparation or reviewing of financial information, but some courts have questioned the rendering of these types of services by an accountant who is not also referred to as a consultant or financial advisor in the application for retention.

The function of the accountant or financial advisor is to assist the debtor in developing, including negotiating the terms of, a plan that will allow the debtor to emerge from chapter 11. To progress to the stage where a plan can be negotiated, the accountant may help the debtor develop a business plan, which would include analyzing the industry in which the debtor operates, determining the value of the business, determining the amount and nature of claims, and rendering other services. The performance of some of these services by members of the debtor's firm who are not CPAs or CIRAs should not suggest that the services are not to be rendered by the accountant or financial advisor in helping the debtor accomplish its objectives by developing a plan that will allow it to reorganize and operate profitably again.

Accountants and financial advisors for the unsecured creditors' committee or other creditors' or equity holders' committees perform a similar role, and the same policy should apply. For example, an accountant engaged to assist the creditors' committee in evaluating the debtor's plan may need to use its health care specialists, even though some of them may not be CPAs or CIRAs, to review the debtors' business plan and make suggestions as to how the plan should be changed. Performance of this service should not be considered outside of the range of services that the accountant might render. In an unreported decision by the bankruptcy court in the Central District of California, the court held that these types of services may be considered as services rendered by accountants and allowed as an administrative expense.

§ 7.14   Prepetition Retention

The debtor may need the services of an accountant or financial advisor just prior to filing the petition. For example, an accountant or financial advisor may be retained to help the debtor evaluate the alternatives that are available to pursue (for example, out-of-court settlement, chapter 11, find a buyer for business, and so forth) or to assist the debtor's counsel in gathering the information needed to file the petition. When engaged under these conditions, it is advisable for the accountant or financial advisor to obtain a retainer before rendering the services. If the accountant renders these services without a retainer and the debtor subsequently files a petition, the fees for these unpaid services will be considered a prepetition unsecured debt. It is customary practice for the debtor's counsel to receive a retainer and there is no reason why the accountant or financial advisor for the debtor could not also receive such a retainer.

§ 7.15   Retention Procedure—Informal

An accountant or financial advisor who is engaged to render services for a company in financial difficulty and who has not formally petitioned the court should obtain a signed engagement letter before any work is initiated. The format for the engagement letter is similar to that of the usual engagement letter; however, provision for alternate sources of payment should be arranged, in case the client elects to file a bankruptcy petition. Through this procedure, the accountant may avoid becoming a general creditor with a consequent reduction in claims. The alternate sources may consist of a guarantee of payment by one or more of the larger creditors or a personal guarantee by the principal officer or officers of the company. See 7.2 of Volume 2 for an example of an engagement letter prepared by the financial advisor for an engagement prior to the filing of the petition. The application for retention referenced this prior engagement letter.

In many cases, it is advisable for the accountant to obtain an advance before beginning the engagement. A large number of accounting firms have seen their claims for prepetition accounting services rendered for the debtor reduced to almost nothing when their claim is considered along with all of the other unsecured claims in bankruptcy proceedings. Obtaining an advance before starting the assignment eliminates this problem. The extent to which advances are obtained by accounting or financial advisory firms depends on the type of services being rendered, prior relationships with the client, the entity (for example, debtor or creditors' committee) that the accountant or financial advisor represents, and the policy and nature of the creditor community in the location where services are being rendered. Some firms will not start an engagement for a financially troubled debtor unless an advance is obtained. Advances are almost always common where certain types of wrongdoing are suspected and the accountant or financial advisor is engaged to do a special investigation.

It is also a good policy to have the client–debtor sign the engagement letter, even though the creditors may be requesting the services of the accountant or financial advisor. If the insolvent firm has other affiliates that are solvent, it is desirable to have them sign the engagement letter, deposit funds for the payment of fees, or guarantee payment.

§ 7.16   Accountants as Quasi-Officers of the Court

Appointment by order for retention through the bankruptcy court makes the accountant or financial advisor a quasi-officer of the court, owing a primary duty to the court. Normally, this duty involves reporting to and discussing problems with the trustee in the proceedings. Further, in all cases where persons seek compensation for services or reimbursement for expenses, they shall be held to fiduciary standards.[16] Such standards mean a special confidence has been imposed on the accountant who, in equity and good conscience, is bound to act in good faith and with due regard to the interest of the party imposing the confidence.[17]

In *In re Niover Bagels, Inc.,*[18] the bankruptcy court noted that in dealing with compensation for accountants there is also another factor that should not be overlooked. "By training and professional standards, accountants are different from attorneys. As certified public accountants, they must be independent, and are not bound by their professional canons, as lawyers are, to be zealous advocates for their clients. Indeed, accountants are *engaged* by their clients, and *do not represent* them. This is more than a term of art; it is an essential difference in professional training and orientation."

DETERMINATION OF ACCOUNTANT'S FEES

§ 7.17   Introduction

The accountant or financial advisor's fees are considered an administrative expense and receive first priority in payment. If the estate is not large enough to pay the administrative claims in full, the accountant shares in the balance available with others having administrative claims.

Even though the services of the accountant or financial advisor when retained by the court are a part of the cost of administering the estate, this pri-

---

[16] *Brown v. Gerdes,* 321 U.S. 178, 182 (1944).
[17] Chauncey Levy, "Creditors' Committees and Their Responsibilities," *Commercial Law Journal,* Vol. 74 (December 1969), p. 356n.
[18] 214 B.R. 291 (Bankr. E.D. N.Y. 1997).

ority may be reduced somewhat if the debtor is converted from chapter 11, chapter 12, or chapter 13 to chapter 7. If a company that originally filed under chapter 11 is subsequently converted to a chapter 7, the cost of administrative expenses claimed under the provisions of chapter 11 is secondary to administrative expense claims incurred under chapter 7.[19]

Under section 726(b) of the Bankruptcy Code, it appears that the restriction applies only to unpaid administrative expenses existing at the time of the distribution. Thus, the accountant or financial advisor should attempt to obtain court approval for these expenses prior to the conversion. This is especially a problem for an examiner who completes the investigation and recommends that the case be converted to chapter 7. The examiner is expected to issue an unbiased assessment of the debtor and its prospects for future operations; yet, a recommendation for the case to be converted to chapter 7 may result in the examiner's receiving less for his or her services than if the recommendation had been to continue operations. If this fact is pointed out to the judge at the time of the recommendation to convert to chapter 7, the judge may approve the chapter 11 administrative expense before conversion.

A separate claim must be filed for the services rendered in each phase of bankruptcy proceedings. To protect the fees involved, however, it is still important for the accountant to determine the condition of the debtor and the potential size of the debtor's estate.

§ 7.18   SEC May Object to Fees

Under prior law, the SEC was considered a party-in-interest under Chapter X and under some Chapter XI proceedings. In Chapter X or other proceedings where the SEC was involved, the judge was required to get an advisory report from the Washington office regarding fees. Under these conditions, it was an advisable practice of the accounting firm to review with district representatives of the SEC the entire application for fees before the time records were sent to the Washington office so that the SEC was aware of the type of work performed, the time worked, and the quality of the work.

The SEC often determines the average hourly rate for the entire engagement. It may therefore not only object to the hourly rates as established for partners, managers, seniors, and juniors, but may claim that partners and managers devoted too much time to the engagement. For example, the nature of the engagement may require that a considerable amount of time be spent on tax matters and settling litigation, and partners and managers may have to do most of the work. This should be pointed out to the SEC at the local level; a realistic awareness of some of the work involved and of the level of services required may prevent future reductions in the fees allowed. It is to the accountant's advantage to find out the SEC's views regarding the fees before the report is written. If the SEC evaluation is in error, the accountant then has an opportunity to try to answer its objections.

The SEC's role under the Bankruptcy Code has been altered. The SEC may appear and be heard on any issue arising in the case but may not appeal (section

---

[19] 11 U.S.C. § 726(b).

1109) as it could under prior law. Although the SEC still has the right to be heard regarding fees, the SEC may prefer to direct most of its efforts toward the appointment of a trustee when needed, an assessment of the adequacy of the disclosure statement, and the process confirming the plan. In fact, the SEC recently indicated that it will devote more attention to policy matters and less to specific aspects of a case (see § 8.28). This does not suggest, however, that the accountant should ignore the SEC in filing for compensation. Precautionary steps should continue to be followed. The SEC will continue to receive copies of business petitions under the Rules referred to in § 5.3.

§ 7.19 Compensation Reviewed by U.S. Trustee

Section 586 of title 28 of the U.S. Code states that one of the functions of the U.S. trustee is to monitor applications filed under section 327 of the Bankruptcy Code, which deals with the employment of professionals in a bankruptcy case, and, when deemed appropriate, to file with the court comments regarding the approval of such applications. Applications for the retention of accountants and petitions for the allowance of fees are reviewed by the U.S. trustee. In Volume 2 of *Bankruptcy and Insolvency Accounting*, 7.15 contains the guidelines for fees and disbursements for professionals in the Southern District of New York. Included in the guidelines are suggestions as to the type of records to keep to support the fee applications, the information to include in the fee application, and the expenses that may be reimbursed. Some of the guidelines should be followed in requesting reimbursements for selected expenses. For example, in the Southern District of New York, photocopying costs are reimbursable at the lesser of $.20 per page or actual costs.

§ 7.20 Compensation Must Be Approved by the Court

When retained by a trustee, the debtor-in-possession, or the creditors' committee, the accountant must receive remuneration from the debtor's estate. Payment can be made only when the accountant is engaged upon an order of the court that expressly fixes the amount or rate of compensation. A bankruptcy court, even in the absence of opposition, has an independent duty to review all fee requests.[20] As stated by another bankruptcy judge, the bankruptcy court has the ultimate responsibility to monitor the request for fees to be paid from the estate. The *reasonable compensation* standard must be applied to determine the allowed compensation to professionals that are providing services for the benefit of the estate.[21]

If an accountant renders services in bankruptcy cases without having a retention order, it is possible for the court to grant approval *nunc pro tunc*. The Fifth Circuit surveyed the case law and adopted the position that, except in special circumstances, *nunc pro tunc* relief would be allowed if a properly timed application would have been approved.[22] In another case, the bankruptcy court refused to approve the appointment of any accountant because the appli-

[20] *In re S.T.N. Enterprises, Inc.*, 70 Bankr. 823, 831 (Bankr. D. Vt. 1987).
[21] *See In re Fruits International, Inc.*, 87 B.R. 769, 770 (Bankr. D. Puerto 1988).
[22] *Fanelli v. Hensley*, 697 F.2d 1280 (5th Cir. 1983).

cation was not submitted until almost a year had passed after the services were completed and there had been no prior communication with the court.[23]

The Third Circuit, in *In re Arkansas Co.*,[24] adopted a two-part test to determine the propriety of retroactive approval of retention. First, the bankruptcy court must determine that the applicant satisfies the disinterestedness requirements of section 327(a). Second, the court must determine that the particular circumstances presented are so extraordinary as to warrant retroactive approval. In determining what constitutes extraordinary circumstances, the Third Circuit indicated that bankruptcy courts may consider several factors, including whether the applicant or some other person bore responsibility for applying for approval; whether the applicant was under time pressure to begin service without approval; the amount of delay after the applicant learned that initial approval had not been granted; [and] the extent to which compensation to the applicant will prejudice innocent third parties. The First Circuit[25] noted that while it did not regard this compendium of considerations as exhaustive, it was a useful checklist and it was commended to the bankruptcy courts. Retroactive approval was denied when it was determined that time pressures did not justify the failure to apply, but rather that the failure to file for retention was due simply to oversight. In *In re F/S Airlease II, Inc.*,[26] the Third Circuit also denied fees to a real estate broker that failed to become properly retained under section 327(a) prior to rendering services.

The First Circuit noted that "apart from the Seventh Circuit[27] which recently adopted a slightly more lenient 'excusable neglect' standard, . . . those courts of appeals that have considered the matter are consentient in their views" that in order to grant nunc pro tunc relief extraordinary circumstances must exist.[28] In *In re Singson* the Seventh Circuit noted that:

> Neither the Code nor the Rules of Bankruptcy Procedure suggest that lawyers and other professionals should take extraordinary care to ensure that authorization precedes the rendition of services. Ordinary care—that is, cost-justified precautions—ought to suffice. If the trustee and counsel have taken the appropriate precautions, and something nonetheless goes awry, authorization after the fact is proper. Which is exactly what Rule 9006(b)(1) says. This rule permits the court to permit a party or counsel to take a step, after the time for doing so has expired, "where the failure to act was the result of excusable neglect." Rule 9006(b)(2) says that the court may not enlarge the time specified by seven particular rules; Rule 2014(a) is not on the list. No other provision of the Code implies limits on belated approval. . . . We are not persuaded by, and do not follow, cases such as In re Land, 943 F.2d 1265 (10th Cir. 1991); In re Arkansas Co., 798 F.2d 645, 649 (3d Cir. 1986); and In re Kroeger Properties & Development, Inc., 57 Bankr. 821 (9th Cir. B.A.P. 1986), that adopt an "extraordinary circumstance" requirement. These opinions do not cite Rule 9006(b)(1).[29]

---

[23] *In Re Mork*, 6 C.B.C.2d 1334 (Bankr. D. Minn. 1982).
[24] 798 F.2d 645 (3d Cir. 1986).
[25] *In re Donald Jarvis*, 53 F.3d 416 (1st Cir. 1995).
[26] 844 F.2d 99 (3d Cir. 1988).
[27] *See In re Singson*, 41 F.3d 316, 318–19 (7th Cir. 1994).
[28] *In re Donald Jarvis*, 53 F.3d 416 (1st Cir. 1995).
[29] *See In re Singson*, 41 F.3d 316, 318–19 (7th Cir. 1994).

The Seventh Circuit concluded that it is possible to show "excusable neglect," as Rule 9006(b)(1) uses that term, without identifying any "extraordinary" circumstance. The Ninth Circuit[30] held that *nunc pro tunc* approval is justified when the failure to obtain prior approval is due to the need for services on an emergency basis and the professional relied on the debtor's representation that it would secure the required approval. A bankruptcy court refused to authorize a late-filed application by an attorney, but allowed a late-filed application by an accounting firm that was not experienced in the bankruptcy proceedings.[31]

Local rules often will establish a time period in which an application will not be considered late. For example, local rule for the bankruptcy court for the District of Rhode Island provides that "absent extraordinary circumstances, *nunc pro tunc.* Applications for appointment of professional persons pursuant to Sections 327 and 1103 of the Bankruptcy Code, and Bankruptcy Rule 2014, will not be considered. An Application is considered timely if it is filed within thirty (30) days of the date of the filing of the petition in bankruptcy or the date the professional commences rendering services, whichever occurs later."[32] The First Circuit held that these local rules are binding.[33]

In *In re Ibbetson*,[34] the court heard an appeal from an order of the bankruptcy court that denied full compensation to appellants' counsel because he failed to get an approval of employment at the beginning of the bankruptcy proceeding. The debtor filed a chapter 11 bankruptcy petition with the assistance of counsel on February 28, 1986. An application for employment of counsel was not filed at that time. On April 23, 1987, the bankruptcy court entered an order *nunc pro tunc* approving the employment of appellants' attorneys to February 28, 1986. Thereafter, on May 1, 1987, the U.S. trustee sought reconsideration of that order and requested that employment be made effective from the date of the entry of the order rather than retroactive to February 28, 1986, because counsels' neglect precluded retroactive approval. On May 22, 1987, the bankruptcy court granted the trustee's motion. Appellants' counsel then sought reconsideration of this order. On June 23, 1987, the bankruptcy court denied the motion for reconsideration. The bankruptcy court concluded that appellants' attorneys' argument that they were overworked and in turmoil did not constitute "extraordinary circumstances" such as would excuse them from compliance with the Bankruptcy Code's requirement of prior court approval of employment.

Ibbetson argued that extraordinary circumstances were present in the bankruptcy proceeding. It was noted that the combination of the "farm financial crisis" and "other pressures" along with the necessity of relying on "inexperienced, underpaid, and overworked young associates for details not affecting the welfare of clients" and the "confusion surrounding the departure of the young associate handling the details of the case" constituted such extraordinary circumstances.

---

[30] *In re Atkins*, 69 F.3d 970 (9th Cir. 1985).
[31] *In re Little Greek Restaurant, Inc.*, 206 B.R. 484 (Bankr. E.D. La. 1996).
[32] *In re Donald Jarvis*, 53 F.3d 416; (1st Cir. 1995).
[33] *Id.*
[34] 100 B.R. 548 (D.C. Kan. 1989).

The district court rejected this argument. The court noted that the failure to seek initial approval of employment was due to inadvertence and neglect and was not extraordinary. The district court in *Ibbetson* relied on the test that was developed in *In re Arkansas Co.*[35]—the court must determine that the particular circumstances are so extraordinary as to warrant retroactive approval.

In a survey conducted by the American Bankruptcy Institute,[36] it was reported that requests for retroactive appointment are not uncommon. Approximately one-tenth of the lawyers and judges report that professionals in chapter 11 always or frequently request retroactive appointment. Over 25 percent of the accountants reported that they always or frequently request retroactive appointment. Almost one-half of the judges report that they always or frequently approve such requests. Accountants and other professionals who depend on debtor's counsel to handle the application for employment receive more lenient treatment.

Although it is possible to find examples where courts have approved an order for the accountant to be engaged prior to the actual date the order is submitted and to receive payments for services rendered, it is advisable for the accountant to adopt the policy of obtaining the order before rendering services. For example, one bankruptcy judge requires the following attachment to any retention order:

> The order authorizing employment of the professional person to which this supplement is attached is granted upon the following conditions:
>
> (1) that the appointee shall receive no compensation from the debtor-in-possession until an application is filed requesting the same under Bankruptcy Rule 2016(a) and notice has been given to creditors as required by Bankruptcy Rule 2002,
>
> (2) that if the net income of the debtor-in-possession is insufficient to pay administrative costs, including fees to professional persons appointed by court order, interim payments on said fees will not be allowed unless it can be shown that there is a reasonable likelihood that the business will in the future generate sufficient income to pay all administrative expenses in full on the confirmation of a plan,
>
> (3) that all fee arrangements are subject to the provisions of 11 U.S.C. 328(a) stating, in part, . . . the court may allow compensation different from the compensation provided under the agreement and/or order after conclusion of such employment, if such terms and conditions prove to have been improvident . . .

To aid the court in setting the amount of compensation where the court requires that the application for retention contain a maximum amount, the accountant is required to make a preliminary survey of the debtor's books and records to estimate the extent of the services it will be necessary to perform (see § 7.8). The amount then fixed by the court is the maximum compensation the accountant will be given for services in the proceedings. Thus, if the accountant believes the value of these services will exceed the maximum

---

[35] *Supra* note 7.
[36] American Bankruptcy Institute, *supra* note 1, pp. 28–29.

amount provided for, there should be an immediate attempt to obtain an additional order increasing the maximum.

§ 7.21   Factors to Consider When Estimating Fees

The criteria used in setting reasonable fees prior to the Bankruptcy Reform Act are those given by the court in its decision concerning *Owl Drug Co.*[37] The factors to be weighed are:

The time spent in the proceedings

The complexity of the problems that arose

The relative size of the estate and the amount available for distribution

The quality of any opposition met

The results achieved, otherwise known as the *salvage theory* (rather than letting the time involved determine the remuneration, the fees are measured by the extent of success or accomplishments and benefits to the estate)[38]

The experience and standing of the accountant

The quality of skill necessary in the situation, and the amount of care and professional skill used

The fee schedule in the area

The ethics of the profession

Section 330 of the Bankruptcy Code as amended by the Bankruptcy Reform Act of 1994 provides that

1 The court may award to a trustee, an examiner or a professional person employed under section 327 or 1103 (a) reasonable compensation for actual, necessary services rendered by the trustee, examiner, professional person, or attorney and by any paraprofessional employed by any such person and (b) reimbursement for actual, necessary expenses.

2 The court may on its own motion or on the motion of the U.S. trustee, trustee for the estate, or any other party-in-interest, award compensation that is less than the amount of compensation that is requested.

3 In determining the reasonable compensation to be awarded, the court shall consider the nature, the extent, and the value of such services, taking into consideration all relevant factors, including:
   • Time spent on such services
   • Rate charged for such services
   • Whether the services were necessary to the administration of the case or beneficial at the time at which such services were rendered toward the completion of a case

---

[37] 16 F. Supp. 139, 142 (1936).
[38] William J. Rudin, "Fees and Allowances to Attorneys in Bankruptcy and Chapter XI Proceedings," *Fordham Law Review*, Vol. 34 (March 1966), p. 399.

- Whether the services were performed within a reasonable amount of time commensurate with the complexity, importance, and nature of the problem, issue, or task addressed
- Whether the compensation is reasonable based on the customary compensation charged by comparably skilled practitioners in cases other than those under this title

4 The court shall not allow compensation for unnecessary duplication of services, or services that were not reasonably likely to benefit the debtor's estate or necessary for the administration of the case. The court will, however, allow in a chapter 12 or 13 case where the debtor is an individual, reasonable compensation to the debtor's attorney for representing the interests of the debtor.

5 The court will reduce the amount of compensation awarded by the amount of interim compensation awarded under this section and may order the return of an interim compensation awarded that exceeds the amount of compensation awarded.

6 Any compensation awarded for the preparation of a fee application shall be based on the level and skill reasonably required to prepare the application.

Note that the 1994 amendments to the Bankruptcy Code acknowledged for the first time that the professional may receive compensation for the preparation of the fee petition. Courts often review the amount requested by the professional for the preparation of the fee application and have established limits as to the amount that will be allowed based on total fees requested. For example, some judges restrict the amount that will be paid to 3 percent, while other judges have allowed 5 percent of the total fee petition to be allocated to fee preparation. Regardless of the limits that might be placed on the time to prepare the fee application, such time must be clearly documented as would other time included in the fee application. Compensation for the time spent preparing a fee application in a bankruptcy case is allowed by some courts only for the actual time spent in providing the additional specificity required by the Bankruptcy Code and not provided to other clients.[39]

The applications for accountants' fees are held to the same strict guidelines as the ones for attorneys' fees. See *In re Sounds Distributing Corp*, 122 Bankr. 952, 956 (Bankr. W.D. Pa. 1991). The services rendered by the accountant or financial advisor retained in a bankruptcy case must, according to section 330, be reasonable and necessary. Services rendered for developing a creditors' committee plan for the purpose of creating bargaining leverage were disallowed because the plan developed was not confirmable.[40]

Often accountants will provide that current rates will apply and as rates are increased the court is notified. In *Thrifty Oil*,[41] the accountants were allowed to raise their rates during the middle of the case, provided the client was given at least 30 days' notice and there were no objections. The accounting firm

---

[39] *See In re WHET.*, 61 Bankr. 709 (Bankr. D. Mass. 1986).
[40] *In re Thrifty Oil Co.*, 205 B.R. 1099 (Bankr. S.D. Cal. 1997).
[41] *In re Thrifty Oil Co.*, 205 B.R. 1099 (Bankr. S.D. Cal. 1997).

demonstrated that all clients represented by the reorganization practice were charged the same hourly rates.

For large cases, it is often the practice for professionals to be paid 75 to 80 percent of their fees and 100 percent of their expenses on a monthly basis. The holdback may then be paid quarterly after a hearing, resulting in the professional being paid 100 percent during the cases. However, the professionals may be subject to potential disgorgement or disallowance of fees in a final petition for fees at the end of the case.[42]

Hon. Leslie Tchaikovsky, Linda Stanley, Molly Gallagher, and Margaret Sheneman[43] noted than in middle-market business cases, attorneys will usually receive a prepetition retainer of approximately 50 percent of the expected fees in the case. Accountants and financial advisors, however, often are engaged after the petition is filed and then only when it is realized by the attorney for the debtor or the creditors' committee that accounting work needs to be performed. Thus accountants and financial advisors often do not have an opportunity to obtain a retainer. In *In re Niover Bagels, Inc.,*[44] the bankruptcy court authorized the accountant to obtain monthly payments over the initial objection of the U.S. trustee. Often, as is the case for the middle-sized practitioner, the attorney had a retainer and the accountant did not. The U.S. trustee, ignoring the fact that the debtor's attorney had a retainer, objected to the monthly payments. However, the bankruptcy court, seeing the inequity involved and the need for accounting professionals, overruled the objection of the U.S. trustee.

In *In re Home Express,*[45] the bankruptcy court required accountants and attorneys for both the debtor and the committee to submit estimates of fees that would be incurred in the course of the case from the filing to plan confirmation and postconfirmation claims objection. The bankruptcy court used the estimated fees to establish a flat rate for the entire case and allowed the professionals to draw on the flat fees each month. The U.S. trustee did not object to the arrangement, but required quarterly time sheets to verify that the fees received were justified by the time spent.

The flat fees were subject to adjustment only upon a showing that they were "improvident in light of developments not capable of being anticipated" at the time the fee estimates were submitted. The fees were ultimately adjusted upward because of an unanticipated delay of a year in the reorganization process and the changes in four different sets of officers and company management during the two year-period that the company was in chapter 11.

The "loadstar" method used to determine the reasonableness of fees consists of the number of hours reasonably spent times a reasonable hourly rate. The total of this computation may then be adjusted taking into consideration other factors in order to certify the "reasonableness" of the amount to be paid.[46] Furthermore, only services rendered in benefit of the estate will be com-

---

[42] *See In re Knudsen Corp.,* 84 B.R. 668 (Bankr. 9th Cir. 1988).

[43] "Current Developments, Bankruptcy Review Commission, and Legislative Update," *14th Annual Bankruptcy and Reorganization Conference* (Medford, OR: Association of Insolvency and Restructuring Advisors, 1998), p. 28.

[44] 214 B.R. 291 (Bankr. E.D. N.Y. 1997).

[45] 213 B.R. 162 (Bankr. N.D. Ca. 1997).

[46] *Id.*

pensable from its funds. See *In re Reed,* 890 F.2d 104 (8th Cir. 1989), and *In re Plunkett,* 60 Bankr. 290 (Bankr. S.D.N.Y. 1986). In *In re Gillett Holdings, Inc.,* the bankruptcy court noted than any calculation of reasonable fees, based on services rendered and hours expended, "must be leavened with an assessment of benefit accruing to the estate."[47] The burden of establishing that the requested fees are reasonable is the responsibility of the applicant.[48]

The factors to consider upon adjusting the "loadstar" figure to ascertain the reasonableness of the fees as set forth in the Fifth Circuit decision are the following:[49]

1 The time and labor required
2 The novelty and difficulty of the questions
3 The skill requisite to perform the legal service properly
4 The preclusion of other employment by the attorney due to the acceptance of the case
5 The customary fee
6 Whether the fee is fixed or contingent
7 The time limitations imposed by the client or the circumstances
8 The amount involved and the results obtained
9 The experience, reputation, and ability of the attorneys
10 The "undesirability" of the case
11 The nature and length of the professional relationship with the client
12 Awards in similar cases

A bankruptcy court reasonableness assessment is not limited to only the factors listed in section 330. Three courts have held that the factors set forth in section 330(a) are not exhaustive and that bankruptcy courts may consider relevant factors beyond those listed in the statute.[50] In *In re Lan Associates* the court noted that in spite of the factors enumerated in section 330, many courts[51] continue to employ the twelve factors set forth in *Johnson v. Georgia Highway Express, Inc.*[52] to determine the reasonableness of professional fees. "Mindful of these cases and of the broad discretion bestowed on bankruptcy courts to determine appropriate trustee fees, we hold that the factors enumerated in section 330(a) are not all-inclusive."[53]

As discussed above, fees are generally based on a billing rate multiplied by the hours worked and are generally awarded at the end of the case unless the

---

[47] 137 Bankr. 462, 467 (Bankr. D. Colo. 1992).

[48] *In re Gillett Holdings, Inc.,* 137 Bankr. 462, 466 (Bankr. D. Colo. 1992); *In re S.T.N. Enterprises Inc.,* 70 Bankr. 823, 832 (Bankr. D. Vt. 1987).

[49] *Johnson v. Georgia Highway Express, Inc.,* 488 F.2d 714, 718 (5th Cir. 1974).

[50] *In re Greenley Energy Holdings of Pa., Inc.,* 102 B.R. 400, 405 (E.D. Pa. 1989); *In re Roco Corp.,* 64 B.R. 499, 502 (D.R.I. 1986); *In re Lan Associates,* 1999 U.S. App. LEXIS 24655 (3d Cir. 1999).

[51] *Garland Corp.,* 8 B.R. at 831; *Grant v. George Schumann Tire & Battery Co.,* 908 F.2d 874, 877–78 (11th Cir. 1990); *In re Permian Anchor Servs., Inc.,* 649 F.2d 763, 768 (10th Cir. 1981); *In re Malewicki,* 142 B.R. 353, 355 (Bankr. D. Neb. 1992); *Gillett Holdings,* 137 B.R. at 481 & n.10 (Bankr. D. Colo. 1992).

[52] 488 F.2d 714, 717–19 (5th Cir. 1974).

[53] *In re Lan Associates,* 1999 U.S. App. LEXIS 24655 (3d Cir. 1999).

court authorizes payment every 120 days (except in larger cases where fees may be paid monthly). Because of this delay, it may be appropriate for the bankruptcy court to award a bonus fee to the accountant or financial advisor. However, the bankruptcy court is not required to award such enhancement as a matter of law for the purposes of compensating the professional for the delay in payments.[54] The accountant should be aware, when estimating fees, that because of the nature of a bankruptcy court engagement, more seasoned personnel will be needed for this work than for normal accounting services.

§ 7.22   Compensation Based on Comparable Services

The court in the *Owl Drug* proceedings went on to note that any consideration of fee allowances must be according to the economy of administration principle, which requires that all unnecessary expenses be curtailed to a minimum in bankruptcy court proceedings. Thus, the courts should attempt to set the fees at the lowest amount that is reasonable, in order to maximize the distribution to creditors. Several accounting firms with considerable experience in bankruptcy proceedings estimate that, under the Bankruptcy Act, the accountant normally received about 75 percent of the "going rate" for services rendered under prior law Chapter XI arrangements and less than 50 percent in straight bankruptcy cases. In addition, the accountant often found it necessary to work a greater number of hours than was stipulated in the order of retention, for which no compensation was received.

In another case,[55] the judge set an arbitrary limit on fees payable, based on the amount of a district judge's salary. Other cases indicated that fees under the Bankruptcy Act were determined on the notions of conservation of the estate and economy of administration.

To overrule these standards developed from case law, Congress passed section 330, which provides that reasonable compensation to professionals is to be paid based on the time, the nature, the extent, and the value of such services, and the cost of comparable services other than in a case under the Bankruptcy Code. Legislative history indicates that if cases like these are allowed to stand, bankruptcy specialists, who enable the system to operate smoothly, efficiently, and expeditiously, will find higher income in other fields and will leave the bankruptcy field to those who cannot find other work or those who practice occasionally as a public service.[56] Thus, the policy of this section is to compensate accountants and other professionals serving in a bankruptcy proceeding at the same rate professionals would be compensated for performing comparable services other than in a bankruptcy case. Even with this law change, because of the nature of selected cases, the attitude of the bankruptcy judge, and the size of the estate, fees will not always be at normal private rates.

Section 330 of the Bankruptcy Code states that compensation is to be paid based on the cost of comparable services that are rendered for work performed outside the bankruptcy area. One issue that has created considerable discussion concerns whether the court should allow rates charged in the profes-

[54] *In re Music Merchants, Inc.*, 208 B.R. 944 (Bankr. 9th Cir. 1997).
[55] *In re Beverly Crest Convalescent Hospital, Inc.*, 548 F.2d 817 (9th Cir. 1976, as amended 1977).
[56] H.R. Rep. No. 95-595, 95th Cong., 1st Sess. 329–30 (1977).

sional's private practice or prevailing local rates. In *Baldwin United Corp.*,[57] the court held that, in cases that are complex, the rates charged by professionals in their private practice may be used rather than the prevailing local rates charged for like services. The court indicated that other considerations, including the reasonableness of the rate, difficulty of the case, and value of the services rendered to the debtor, may justify the rate charged.

In *In re Interstate United Electronic Sales Co.*,[58] the court held that, where adequate local representation was available and where there was no compelling need for special counsel, compensation beyond the local prevailing rate and compensation for travel should not be expected. The Tenth Circuit, in *Ramos v. Lamm*,[59] held that absent unusual circumstances, attorneys' fees would be based on rates prevailing in the area in which the court sits and would be calculated as of the time the court awards fees.

Reimbursement for actual, necessary expenses is also allowed under section 330.

Section 330 provides for the reimbursement of actual and necessary expenses, but accountants have experienced some difficulty in recovering their word-processing and communication costs. Generally, the courts will not allow the accountant to add a set percentage of the partners' and managers' fees or of the total fees at the end of the petition for fee allowance to cover these overhead costs. Thus, to be compensated for these costs, the accountant should itemize these expenses or include in the rates that are submitted to the court an allowance to cover these costs. In some areas, the problem arises because the attorneys have included these costs in their rates and the U.S. trustee or bankruptcy judge does not fully understand why these costs are a separate item on the petition for fees submitted by the accountant.

§ 7.23 Prepetition Fees

Accounting fees for services rendered prior to the filing of the petition are generally not subject to priority, as an administrative expense, in bankruptcy court proceedings.

(a) Debtor

If the accountant for the debtor wants to be assured of receiving compensation for work performed prior to the filing of the petition, payments should be received from financially troubled debtors in advance of rendering services or promptly upon the conclusion of the job. If the work extends over a fairly long time period, installment payments should be obtained. To be assured that fees will be received for work performed, it is advisable to obtain an advance prior to starting the job. The timing of the payments, the nature of the services rendered, and the manner in which the payment process is handled may be crucial. The accountant does not want the payment made by the debtor to be considered a preferential payment under section 547. If the payment is consid-

---

[57] 36 B.R. 40 (Bankr. S.D. Ohio 1984).
[58] 44 B.R. 784 (Bankr. S.D. Fla. 1984).
[59] 713 F.2d 546 (10th Cir. 1983).

ered preferential, then the trustee or debtor-in-possession has the right to recover all or part of the amount paid. For example, payments that are received subsequent to the time the services are rendered are payments on an antecedent debt. For these payments to be exempt, they must be for a debt incurred in the ordinary course of business and made in the ordinary course of business according to ordinary business terms. (See § 5.39.) To prevent at least some of the prepetition fees from being a preference, it is a good policy to make arrangements for the payments, as they are received, to be credited to one of the more recent bills.

(b) Creditors' Committee

When engaged by a creditor or some party other than the trustee or debtor, the accountant must rely on that person rather than on the debtor's estate for compensation if a bankruptcy court petition is filed (see § 7.15). Section 503(b)(4) does, however, provide for the allowance of prepetition accountants' fees by stating that reasonable compensation for professional services rendered by an attorney or an accountant of an entity described in paragraph (3) of section 503(b) is based on the time, the nature, the extent, and the value of such services, and the cost of comparable services. Also included would be reimbursement for actual, necessary expenses incurred by the attorney or accountant. As described in paragraph (3), the entities for whom the accountant may render services and possibly be reimbursed include a creditor that files an involuntary petition; a creditor that recovers property for the benefit of the estate; or a creditor, an indenture trustee, an equity security holder, or a committee representing creditors or equity security holders (other than a committee appointed in a chapter 11 case under the provisions of section 1102), when those entities are making a substantial contribution in a chapter 9 or chapter 11 case. Thus, for an accountant to be reimbursed by the bankruptcy court for services rendered for a creditors' committee prior to the date of the petition, it will be necessary to show that the committee's prepetition work made a substantial contribution to the case. If it can be shown that the actions of this committee led to a confirmation of the plan, this would be an example of a substantial contribution. It is not required, however, for the actions of the committee to lead to a confirmation. A substantial contribution may be made if the accountant discovers fraud that leads to a denial of confirmation of the plan.

TIME RECORDS

§ 7.24 Requirements

It is important for the accountant to keep adequate time and performance records while rendering services. When petitioning the court for a fee allowance, should the amount of the compensation be contested, such records would be vital. At the very least, the accountant should record the following information:

The date and a description and classification of the work that has been done

The time spent in the performance of the work

The name, classification, and per-diem billing rate of each staff member performing the work[60]

Most accounting firms use computerized forms for allocating time to their clients for services rendered. The court may not accept the computer runs unless there are authoritative records that support the work performed by the accountant. Computer records are often standardized for normal accounting services and generally show only a minimum amount of information: the employee–client's code number, the time spent, and, in some systems, only a code for a general classification of the type of work performed. In any accounting work performed for a bankruptcy case, it is advisable for the accounting firm to keep separate records that clearly show in detail the nature of the work performed. In awarding fees, the court also takes into consideration the quality of the services rendered by the accountant and the amount and types of reports issued. The accountant may need to spend a great deal of time looking for preferential payments and other types of irregularities. If none is discovered, the court may not understand the reason for the fees charged by the accountant. Thus, the accountant may need these detailed records to support the request for payment.

As a general rule, all time records should be kept in tenths of an hour, or six-minute intervals. Attorneys reflect their time in six-minute intervals, and most courts expect accountants to do the same. Thus, unless prior approval is obtained, time should be in six-minute intervals. If the accountant wants to use 15- or 30-minute intervals, it is advisable to obtain permission in advance from the court. The request for use of larger intervals may be made in the application for retention.

PETITION FOR FEE ALLOWANCE

§ 7.25   Court Discretion in Ruling on Fees

The requirement that the level of compensation be fixed in the court order of appointment has been held to be directory and not mandatory.[61] This means that, when ruling on fees, the court may exercise its discretion in light of all the circumstances surrounding the case.

The court also makes the final decision concerning compensation and the time when services were rendered. An accountant on loan to perform bookkeeping services for a debtor both before and after bankruptcy court proceedings can be allowed to recover for postpetition costs under an order continuing the debtor-in-possession and allowing employment of outside help. On the other hand, an accountant completing a special examination of the debtor's financial position begun before bankruptcy was not entitled to first priority for the expenses of the work done after bankruptcy because an order of the court

---

[60] Harold Gelb and Irving Goldberger, "Retention Order of the Accountant in Insolvencies and Bankruptcies and Petition for Compensation," *New York Certified Public Accountant*, Vol. 23 (October 1953), p. 634.

[61] *Littleton v. Kincaid*, 179 F.2d 848 (1950).

had not been obtained at the time of the commencement of the services.[62] Section 327(b) allows the trustee or debtor-in-possession to engage an accountant as a salaried employee, if necessary in the operation of the business.

The court may, for various reasons, elect to reduce the fees. Fees are often reduced if the court finds there has been duplication of effort or too much time has been spent on a particular project relative to the expected benefits. Fees have also been reduced where the court determines that functions, such as administrative duties, performed by a senior partner and billed at the senior partner's rate could have been performed by a less qualified staff member.

Courts have disallowed or reduced other selected costs related to the rendering of services, for example:

1 Courts have reimbursed travel at the subway rate when the subway, as a mode of transportation, should have been used rather than a taxi.

2 Time for local travel has been denied (some courts will allow local travel time, if it exceeds one hour).

3 Lunch money has been denied even when staff personnel spent ten hours a day on an assignment (another court allowed deduction only if the accountant spent ten hours on the case).

4 Travel costs at the first-class rate have been disallowed.

5 Some courts have allowed reimbursement of out-of-state professionals only for those costs that would have been incurred by local professionals.

6 Express mail costs have been allowed only if it can be shown that such service was necessary and that the need for the express service was not due to the delay of the professional in preparing the documents, and so on.

7 Long-distance phone charges must be justified as to their benefit to the estate or they will be disallowed.

8 Each item of expense, even if not in a prohibited class, must be specifically justified as necessary; in each instance, the applicant must show that a less expensive alternative was not reasonably available.

9 To receive reimbursement for telephone time, the professional must show purpose, length of conversation, and person called.

10 Comparisons have been made between times reported by accountants and by attorneys for phone calls or meetings between the two.

Some courts are reluctant to allow more than one person from the same firm attending meetings or participating in conference calls to receive fees for time devoted to meetings. Where more than one professional from the same firm participates, the reasons for attendance should be clearly documented.

There are many other examples of how courts have carefully scrutinized petitions for fee allowances and expense reimbursement. Thus, to avoid potential problems, the accountant should be familiar with the reimbursement policy of the local court and of the judge assigned to the case; avoid the incurrence of expenses that are unreasonable; and carefully document and justify all petitions submitted to the court for fees, allowances, and reimbursements.

---

[62] *Century Chemical Corp.*, 192 F. Supp. 205 (1961).

§ 7.26 Procedure for Filing the Petition

When the accountant has completed the engagement, a petition for compensation should be filed in affidavit form with the bankruptcy court having jurisdiction over the proceedings. The accountant or other professional should send the U.S. trustee a copy of the application for fees and expenses. The petition should contain enough information about the services the accountant has rendered so that the court may evaluate them and compare them with the services authorized in the order of retention. The application for compensation may include the following data:

The accountant's name, address, and firm affiliation

The source of the accountant's authorization to perform the services

The date when the accountant began the engagement

A list of the services the accountant rendered and the exhibits and schedules presented in the report

The total amount of compensation the accountant is requesting, accompanied by a schedule of the hours worked classified by the grade of accountant and the per-diem billing rate

The accomplishments believed to have resulted from the accountant's services, in light of the benefits that the estate has obtained from such services[63]

A sworn statement by the accountant concerning knowledge of the contents of the petition

The notarized signature of the accountant or signature under pains and penalty of perjury

An example of an affidavit applying for compensation is presented in 7.16 of Volume 2. The detail included in this example may not be required by some judges; in fact, in some districts, the affidavit consists of only a reference to the retention order, a brief summary of the services rendered, and the total amount of fees requested based on the hours worked and the approved billing rates for the various levels of services. This brief form may be acceptable for some bankruptcy judges, but others will require the detail shown in 7.16. Typically, attached to 7.16 would be the details of the assignment; identification of each staff person who rendered services, description of the services performed, and statement of the time required and the billing rate. Also enclosed with 7.16 would be a list of all of the expenses for which reimbursement was requested.

Other examples of petitions for fee allowance can be found in 7.17 through 7.20 of Volume 2. An example of a brief summary of the services rendered, by selected category, appears as 7.17, and 7.18 contains the detail of the work completed for an engagement for a small business. In some areas, the accountant would need to identify the class of work in addition to giving the description that is provided. Fee applications filed in the Southern District of Florida is in 7.19 of Volume 2 and the Southern District of Ohio is in 7.20 of Volume 2. Note the justifications for fees and reference to load star approach in 7.20.

---

[63] *Gelb and Goldberger, supra* note 19, p. 634.

Rule 2016 provides that a person seeking interim or final compensation for services or for reimbursement of expenses should include the following in the application:

1 The services rendered, the time expended, and the expenses incurred
2 The amount requested
3 A statement as to what payments have previously been made or promised to the applicant for services rendered in connection with the case
4 The source of the compensation paid or promised
5 The nature of any sharing of compensation except with an associate or member of an accounting or legal firm

The two guidelines that have been issued by the U.S. trustee for the Central District of California, and several examples that should be helpful to an accountant when completing a petition for fee allowance are included in 7.21 in Volume 2. The Billing instructions of "Fee Guide" describing those items that will be allowed as fees and those expenses that are not reimbursable, appear in 7.21. Part II of "Fee Guide," describes the general information required in the fee application, the billing format, and the activity code categories that should be used for accountants and other financial advisors in the Central District of California. (These categories may be required or used in other districts as well.) Examples of how the details for the fee application should be presented are reproduced in 7.21 also.

§ 7.27 Payment for Services Rendered

January 30, 1996, the Executive Office of the U.S. Trustee issued revised guidelines for reviewing fee applications for compensation and reimbursement of expenses under section 330 of the Bankruptcy Code. These guidelines apply to all fee petitions filed in cases that begin after October 22, 1994. Although these guidelines should not supersede any local rules, the U.S. trustees in the various regions in general expect the fee petitions to follow these guidelines. These guidelines are included in Appendix D of this text (Volume 1).

The Office of the United States trustee for the Central District of California, in indicated that the application for payment of professional fees and expenses should conform to a list of requirements that are in 7.21 of Volume 2.

The court will award compensation after notice and a hearing, pursuant to Bankruptcy Code section 330(a). The time the accountant will receive payment for the services rendered depends on the type of retention order. An accountant working under a retention order for special services normally receives payment of the time the case is completed. However, under some conditions, especially where the time period before a plan of arrangement or reorganization is accepted is of considerable length, the court may allow the accountant to receive payment, or at least partial payment, for services rendered. Section 331 provides that professionals, including accountants, may apply for interim compensation. Application can be submitted not more than once every 120 days, unless the court permits more frequent requests. The application must be for services rendered or expenses incurred prior to the date of the interim request and cannot pertain to future services or expenses. This section formalized the existing practice followed in some districts, which allowed accountants to apply for and receive interim compensation for services and expenses. Interim compensation may not be allowed where it appears that secured claims may cover all of the debtor's assets; when a case is converted to a chapter 7 case because administrative expenses in chapter 7 have priority over those previously incurred in chapter 11; when a cash shortage exists; or when large retainers were received before the petition was filed.

An example of a type of order that may be used to receive reimbursement for fees and expenses on a monthly basis, with a hearing at the end of each three-month period, is reproduced in 7.22 of Volume 2.

Accountants who are retained to perform accounting and management advisory services on a monthly basis should consider requesting at the time of their retention that they be allowed to apply monthly for compensation for completed services.

In some cases, the courts will allow professionals to be paid on an interim basis only on a set percentage, such as 75 percent, of the approved amount in the petition for fee allowance. The balance is paid at the conclusion of the estate, provided there are assets available to cover those fees. The procedure often applies to accountants as well as attorneys. However, some judges have made an exception to this procedure for accountants who are performing normal accounting work, such as an audit or a review of the financial records, and have allowed accountants to receive full payment for these services. For other accounting services rendered in relation to the reorganization, such as reviewing the reorganization plan, a percentage of the fees is held back. In order to not be subject to the fee "hold back" policy, the accountant should make a distinction between the types of service that will be rendered in the declaration or affidavit filed with the court prior to retention.

In a study conducted by the American Bankruptcy Institute (ABI),[64] it was determined that 46 percent of the courts generally hold back more than 20 percent of interim fee requests until the end of the chapter 11 case. The survey notes that, although holdbacks are a court-imposed practice under the Bankruptcy Code, effective November 1, 1979, they are not mentioned in the Code. According to the study, the primary reason that courts employ holdbacks is to protect professionals in the event of a fee disgorgement order at or prior to the conclusion of the case. However, the risk of disgorgement was found to be virtually nonexistent. The report issued by the Steering Committee appointed by the ABI to study professional compensation concludes that the "practice of requiring 'holdbacks' from interim compensation requests appears to be unnecessary absent extraordinary circumstances found to exist after notice and a hearing."[65]

The last recommendation of the Report Steering Committee was that the "ABI should attempt to better educate accountants concerning the legal requirements which must be met in order to succeed in obtaining requested fee awards and expense reimbursements."[66]

---

[64] *Supra* note 11.
[65] *Id.*
[66] *Id.*, p. xviii.

The need for the education of accountants was explained this way:

> The survey reveals, for example, that accountants encounter substantially greater payment delays than attorneys in chapter 11 cases. Presumably, many estate accountants rely on estate lawyers to tell them when they can file and how to file a fee application. These lawyers presumably are most acutely aware of the need to file their own fee applications, but have less concern for the fate of other estate professionals. Accountants also presumably possess less knowledge than lawyers of the legal standards applicable to compensation requests and the primary focus by estate lawyers on filing their own applications. Accountants, through increased education, can become more self-reliant in order to assure their prompt and full compensation as intended under the Bankruptcy Code.[67]

Some firms prepare their own affidavit and order for retention as well as the petition for fee allowance. By preparing their own orders, these accountants are able to include the information that they want in the petitions and, at the same time, be assured that they are filed with the court.

[67]*Id.*

8

Accounting and Financial Services for the Debtor-in-Possession or Trustee: Part 1

NATURE OF ACCOUNTING SERVICES

§ 8.1 Introduction

Bankruptcy proceedings are filled with various types of reports, emanating from the debtor-in-possession or trustee, to the bankruptcy judge, the creditors, and finally the Administrative Office of the U.S. Courts, in Washington. Because many of these reports deal with accounting information concerning the financial position of the debtor or estate, the projected profit or loss if the business continues, and other financial aspects of the debtor's operations, it is self-evident that the services of an accountant or financial advisor are essential in many of today's business reorganizations. This is especially true because of the complexities of modern business operations.

The unusual situations encountered in performing accounting or financial advisory services for a business involved in reorganization (chapter 11) or liquidation (chapter 7) often present several practical problems for the accountant or financial advisor. The unique aspects of this type of assignment require the accountant to be very resourceful in providing the additional information needed by the interested parties. This chapter and the next describe the nature of services that may be rendered by the accountant or financial advisor for the debtor-in-possession and the trustee. Chapter 10 discusses the services of the accountant or financial advisor as they relate to the creditors' committee and equity holders' committee. The services rendered for the trustee in a chapter 11 case are similar to those performed for the debtor-in-possession. The major difference is that the trustee may have a need for more investigative services. But even in a chapter 11 case where new management has been appointed, extensive investigative service may be performed for the debtor to determine—among other things—the extent to which possible preferential payments and fraudulent transfers were made. In chapter 11 cases where existing management is allowed to run the business, any preferences, fraudulent transfers, or other questionable transfers discovered by the accountant should be documented and discussed with debtor's counsel.

§ 8.2 Parties Retaining Accountants

An accountant may be engaged by any one of several parties in a chapter 11 case. The accountant may be retained:

- *By the debtor-in-possession.* The debtor in a chapter 11 proceeding will continue to require the same accounting and auditing services that were provided prior to the financial difficulties. Special services are also required. Examples of these services include:
  - Assisting in analyzing operational problems, designing a turnaround strategy, and implementing the strategy.
  - Performing financial consulting activities (management advisory services) that provide information to assist the debtor in making decisions, including the development of a business plan.
  - Assisting in determining the type of action to take to resolve financial problems.
  - Assisting in the management of the case, including claim processing.
  - Preparing information needed to file a bankruptcy petition, including schedules and statement of affairs.
  - Preparing operating statements.
  - Determining or assist in determining the reorganization value.
  - Providing information for disclosure statement.
  - Assisting in or formulating and negotiating the terms of a plan and evaluating the tax impact of the plan.
- *By the trustee.* In chapter 11 cases in which a trustee is appointed, an accountant or financial advisor may be retained by the trustee to provide any of the services that the debtor-in-possession may require.
- *As the examiner.* Accountants can serve as examiners. Thus, an accountant could be appointed to perform the investigative role of the examiner and other services as directed by the court. Accountants and financial advisors may also render services for the examiner.
- *By the creditors' committee.* Accountants or financial advisor are engaged by the creditors' committee to perform whatever services the committee feels are necessary to protect the creditors' interests. Some of the services commonly rendered include:
  - Reviewing the debtor's professional analysis of operational problems and strategy used to turn the business around or assisting the committee in the analysis.
  - Assisting the committee in managing the case.
  - Providing advice to the committee on the actions it should take to maximize return to creditors.
  - Assisting the committee in exercising adequate supervision over the debtor's activities.
  - Performing an investigation of the operations of the business, including preferences and fraudulent transfers.

- Assisting the committee in reviewing (or developing, in a creditors' plan) and determining the adequacy of information in a disclosure statement.
- Assisting the committee in evaluating (or developing the terms, in a creditors' plan) the proposed plan of reorganization. Accountants or financial advisors may also be retained by a committee of secured creditors or equity holders.

- *By the secured creditors.* Accountants may be retained by a major secured creditor to help that creditor evaluate the debtor's operations and financial condition and to provide advice on the course of action that should be pursued.
- *By the stockholders.* Accountants may be engaged by a major stockholder to perform services similar to those for secured creditors.

The term "accountant" is used in this chapter to refer to both the independent accountant engaged by the debtor and the internal accountant of the debtor. Many accounting services in a bankruptcy proceeding may be performed by the debtor's internal accountant, and the debtor's accounting staff often assists the independent accountant. Auditing services and the preparation of certain schedules and reports for the court require the engagement of an independent accountant. Under these circumstances, the accountant must refer to an independent accountant. The term "financial advisor" is used to refer to the many services that may be rendered in an out-of-court workout or in bankruptcy that assist in turning the business around, in solving operational problems, and in restructuring the financial aspects of the reorganized debtor.

There may be some advantages in having most of the accounting and financial services involved in the proceedings performed by an accountant or financial advisor because of the prior experience of these professionals and it allows the internal staff to focus on current operations.

§ 8.3   Summary of Services

Accountants may be involved in rendering services prior to the filing of the petition. Considerable planning by the debtor's accountant, attorney, and consultants may have an impact on the debtor's ability to reorganize and the time required for plan confirmation in chapter 11.

The services rendered by the accountant or financial advisor in bankruptcy and insolvency proceedings can be divided into over a dozen categories. The accountant or financial advisor:

1 Assists the debtor in analyzing operational problems, designing a turnaround strategy, and implementing the strategy.
2 Assists the debtor in determining the type of action to take to resolve financial problems.
3 Provides the debtor's counsel with the information needed to prepare the schedules, statement of affairs, and other forms necessary to file a petition.

4 Prepares special financial statements, including a balance sheet as of the date the petition is filed.

5 Provides the usual accounting services for the client.

6 Assists in the preparation of operating statements to be filed with the court.

7 Performs, if requested, several different types of consulting activities (management advisory services), which provide information that assists the debtor in making decisions necessary for the resumption of successful operations. The development of a business plan would be one of these activities.

8 Performs special investigative services, including an analysis of selected transactions, often to determine whether preferences or fraudulent transfers exist.

9 Reconciles and evaluates creditors' proofs of claims. After establishing the book balances for the unsecured creditors, these balances should be compared with the claims filed. If a claim has not been filed, the book balance is compared with the amount admitted on the debtor's schedules of liabilities, to determine its accuracy. Discrepancies are analyzed, and, if they are not reconcilable, this information is communicated to the trustee or counsel as well as to the creditors' committee. A proof of claim is filed on Bankruptcy Form 10. (A copy of Form 10 can be found in Appendix A of Volume 2 of *Bankruptcy and Insolvency Accounting*. The procedures to evaluate the proof of claims are discussed in Chapter 12.)

10 Assists in determining the value of the business. (Chapter 11 contains a discussion of the approaches used in determining the value of a business.)

11 Provides tax advice on several issues, including the impact that debt discharge and the terms of the plan will have on the debtor's tax liability. (Chapter 16 discusses these factors.)

12 Assists the client in formulating and negotiating the terms of a plan that will meet with the approval of creditors and at the same time allow the debtor to operate the business successfully.

13 Develops or assists in the preparation of the disclosure statement that must be issued prior to or at the time acceptance of the plan is solicited.

14 Renders other services, including assistance in finding sources of credit.

15 Serves as examiner in chapter 11 cases and trustee in chapter 7 and chapter 11 cases.

Accountants and financial advisors may render services in both chapter 11 and chapter 7 cases as well as in out-of-court situations. However, accountants and financial advisors have been more actively involved in chapter 11 cases than in chapter 7 cases. Most of the discussion in this chapter will relate to the work of the accountant or financial advisor in chapter 11 cases.

Discussion of the prefiling stage of reorganization cases is followed by a description of several services that may be rendered in chapter 11. Two major areas of service—operating statements and management advisory—and the role of computers in chapter 11 cases are found in Chapter 9. At the end of Chapter 9, a brief summary will describe how services rendered in a chapter 7 case and in an out-of-court engagement might differ from those in chapter 11. Accountants may also render services in chapter 12 cases.

PREFILING STAGE OF REORGANIZATION PROCEEDINGS

§ 8.4   Importance of Early Meeting

The accountant will often be the first to become aware that a client is headed toward financial difficulties and will be unable to continue profitable operations or pay liabilities as they become due. With accountants' and financial advisors' knowledge and experience, they can render valuable services for clients during this trying period.

It is difficult for debtors to admit that they cannot pay their debts and continue profitable operations. As a result, decisions to call a meeting of creditors or to file a petition under the Bankruptcy Code often are postponed until the last minute. This delay benefits no one, including the debtor. For several reasons, it is advisable to take action as soon as it becomes obvious that some type of relief is necessary. First, the debtor still has a considerable asset base. Second, there is a tendency for many of the key employees to leave when they see unhealthy conditions developing; early corrective action may encourage them to stay. Third, prompt action may make it possible for the debtor to maintain some of the goodwill that was developed during successful operating periods. If early action is taken, the debtor may be able to develop an out-of-court workout as described in Chapter 4 and avoid filing a bankruptcy petition. The fact remains that, in many cases, no kind of action is taken and the creditors force the debtor to call a meeting of the creditors or file a bankruptcy petition.

§ 8.5   Advice on Selection of Counsel

One of the first steps of a debtor faced with financial difficulties is to employ legal counsel. When a company realizes that it will be unable to continue profitable operations or pay liabilities as they become due, it should quickly seek a lawyer to work with the accountant in effecting a compromise or extension of the indebtedness, or to file a bankruptcy petition. The accountant should advise the debtor to select counsel who is qualified and who has considerable experience in bankruptcy work.

§ 8.6   Conference with Attorney

After the bankruptcy attorney has been selected, a meeting should be arranged among the debtor, the financial officer, the accountant or financial advisor, and the attorney. The accountant or financial advisor plays an important role in this conference. If the company's situation has not been closely followed, the accountant should determine the basic facts and gain a sound knowledge of the business, its history, and the causes of its present difficulties so that, at this meeting, the attorney can be given an overall view of the debtor's financial condition and the events that preceded it. To provide the attorney with this information, the accountant or financial advisor must analyze the activities of the debtor, compare the financial statements for the past three or four years, and determine what caused the cash shortage. For example, a comparison of the income statements for the past four years may show that, for the first three years, the gross profit percentage was fairly constant; however, during the last year it dropped 10 percent. What caused the change? This is the type of analysis that the accountant or financial advisor must make so that the major causes of the financial problem can be identified and possible corrective action can be discussed with the attorney. (See Chapter 2 for a discussion of the causes of business failure.) The accountant or financial advisor should discuss the company's financial condition with the members of the internal accounting staff. It is advisable to have the financial officer of the company present at this conference. In many initial conferences, the debtor's internal accountants are intimately involved.

(a) Information Required

The attorney will request certain information from the accountant or financial advisor, including the most recent balance sheet, an income statement, and an extensive list of the debtor's creditors. Each individual asset may be examined and an attempt will be made to determine the property's value. The nature and extent of the liabilities will be discussed, and it should be indicated whether they are secured, unsecured, contingent, or unliquidated. To initiate the reorganization proceedings, the attorney must have a complete and exact list of all creditors, including their addresses, the amounts due, the date incurred, the consideration for the debt, whether any security was given, and, if so, its nature and value. The information is needed because the debtor must file with the petition the list of the largest 20 unsecured creditors with the amount owed.

Under chapter 11 proceedings, the debtor is permitted to reject any executory contracts that will be burdensome. The accountant or financial advisor should furnish the debtor's attorney with a list of all executory contracts, including any contract that leaves something to be performed by either party, other than the obligation to pay money. Executory contracts may consist of employment contracts, long-term leases, commitments the company has made to produce goods for a specific customer at a set price over a long time period, construction contracts to expand the facilities, or agreements the company has signed for the purchase of a certain quantity of raw material. The accountant or financial advisor may also give an opinion as to which contracts will most likely be unprofitable and should be rejected.

It is important to discuss at this prefiling conference what caused the debtor's current problems, whether the company will be able to overcome its difficulties, and, if so, what measures will be necessary. The accountant or financial advisor may be asked to explain how the losses occurred and what can be done to avoid them in the future. To help with this determination, the accountant or financial advisor should project the operations for a 30-day period over at least the next three to six months and indicate the areas where steps will be necessary in order to earn a profit (see § 8.16).

Discussion of the debtor's past history, including a thorough examination of its business conduct, is essential. The attorney will want to know whether any financial statements have been issued, the nature of such statements, whether they can be substantiated, and whether they might be construed to be deceptive. Also investigated will be any preferential payments made to favored creditors or other transfers of property that are not in the regular course of business. Any unusually large purchases should be closely scrutinized, and the debtor should be able to account for all of the assets. Any other information concerning the debtor's activities, of which the attorney should be aware in order to anticipate problems that may arise in the course of the proceedings, should also be supplied. The debtor's counsel must have complete knowledge of the situation in order to work with the accountant or financial advisor to decide the best course of action to pursue. The accountant or financial advisor plays a crucial role in obtaining this information and in determining the course of action to follow.

One other area where the accountant's or financial advisor's services are indispensable is in the determination of insolvency and the exact date at which it occurred. The accountant or financial advisor may determine the debtor's financial condition (chapter 11), prepare worksheets, and compile supporting documents and records necessary to provide a preliminary indication of the client's condition. Later, the accountant or financial advisor may determine the value of the debtor. The proof of insolvency may be necessary where preferential payments or fraudulent transfers are involved (§ 11.4).

If at this preliminary meeting it is decided to file a petition to initiate reorganization proceedings, all parties involved must act quickly because a tax lien may be impending or a judgment sale or foreclosure of a mortgage may be threatening.

§ 8.7 Determine Alternatives

One of the first decisions that must be made at an early meeting of the debtor with bankruptcy counsel and accountants or financial advisors is whether it is best to liquidate (under provisions of state law or the Bankruptcy Code), to attempt an out-of-court settlement, to seek an outside buyer, or to file a chapter 11 petition. To decide which course of action to take, it is also important to ascertain what caused the debtor's current problems, whether the company will be able to overcome its difficulties, and, if so, what measures will be necessary. Accountants or financial advisors may be asked to explain how the losses occurrred and what can be done to avoid them in the future. To help with this determination, an ongoing projection of the operations for a 30-day period may be necessary for at least the next three to six months, to indicate the areas where remedies will be required in order to earn a profit.

For existing clients, the information needed to make a decision about the course of action to take may be obtained with limited additional work; however, for a new client, it will be necessary to perform a review of the operations to determine the condition of the business. Once the review has been completed, the client must normally decide to liquidate the business, attempt an informal settlement with creditors, or file a chapter 11 petition, unless additional funds can be obtained or a buyer for the business is located. For example, where the product is inferior, the demand for the product is declining, the distribution channels are inadequate, or other similar problems exist that cannot be corrected, either because of the economic environment or management's lack of ability, it is normally best to liquidate the company immediately.

The decision whether a business should immediately file a chapter 11 petition or attempt an out-of-court settlement depends on several factors. Among them are the following:

- Size of company
  - Public
  - Private
- Number of creditors
  - Secured
  - Unsecured
  - Public
  - Private
- Complexity of matter
  - Nature of debt
  - Prior relationships with creditors
- Pending lawsuits
- Executory contracts, especially leases
- Tax impact of alternative selected
- Nature of management
  - Competence
  - Mismanagement
  - Irregularities
- Availability of interim financing
- Severity of financial problems
  - Declining business
  - Substantial or continuing losses
  - Danger of failure

Regardless of the type of action that is to be taken (chapter 11 filing or out-of-court workout), several restructuring alternatives often need to be considered, such as:

- Issuance of equity to creditors
- Location of outside sources of capital
- Contribution of new equity by owners
- Disposal of a major part (segment) of the business

Because one or more of these alternatives might be relevant for a particular client, the accountant or financial advisor may prepare projected cash flows and operating results.

§ 8.8 Prebankruptcy Planning

Chapter 11 has become widely recognized and used as an effective means of rehabilitation for corporate debtors. However, the nature and importance of prebankruptcy planning for chapter 11 is often not fully understood or given adequate attention. Because planning prior to filing a petition largely determines the success of a reorganization, it is important to understand its nature and implementation. To accomplish this objective, it is useful to approach prebankruptcy planning by dividing it into five functional areas:

1 Cash management (accumulation)
2 Operations management
3 Legal requirements
4 Financial reporting and taxes
5 Public relations

There are several approaches to effective prebankruptcy planning in each of these areas. The appointment of planning teams is a method that has been very effective. In large cases, a separate planning team might be assigned to each of the five functional areas. In smaller cases, two or three teams might cover all five areas. Each planning team should consist of an attorney, an accountant or financial advisor, and a member of top management best able to oversee that area's function. Each team should prepare a plan of action, complete with timetables and a list of priority requirements. Initial priority is normally given to the identification of first-day orders (orders signed by the judge at the beginning of the case) that will be needed by the debtor to operate with minimal disruption.

(a) Cash Management (Accumulation)

The first and foremost concern of the debtor is cash accumulation to finance the reorganization. An immediate concern in many cases is how to obtain enough cash to operate for the first week or so. Although the automatic stay, which gives temporary release of prepetition obligations, will provide an influx of cash to the debtor, real success will depend on obtaining new accounts and financing throughout the reorganization process. The debtor must be able to operate the business without incurring excessive postpetition debt, or the court may order the case converted to a liquidation.

Responsibilities and concerns of the cash management team may include the following:

- Daily reporting and analysis of cash balances.
- Preparation of a plan to sweep cash accounts and effectively manage cash during the case.
- Location of financing during reorganization; if possible, inclusion of the nature of the financing agreement with the announcement of the filing of a bankruptcy petition. Major sources of financing that might need to be considered during the reorganization include:
  - DIP loan from existing lender.
  - Location of new DIP lender.
  - Sale and leaseback of assets.
  - Determination of ways to improve use of working capital.
  - Disposal of major segment of business or selected assets.

- Setup of new cash accounts. The debtor may need to move accounts to a bank where there will not be a problem with subsequent setoff or to the bank where DIP financing was obtained.
- Development of a cash management system for postpetition operations.
- Development of COD procedures for operating companies.
- Preparation of payroll account plan that may:
  - Pay in cash just before bankruptcy.
  - Issue cashier's checks to all employees.
  - Issue regular payroll checks and prepare an order to submit to the court, authorizing the bank to honor payroll checks outstanding at the petition date.
- Provision of operating cash for at least a few days after the petition is filed. There may not be enough time, for various reasons, to do the type of planning described above, but the debtor should at least consider moving any unencumbered cash to a bank that does not have claims against the debtor. If possible, before filing the petition, the debtor should negotiate with the bank to release cash collateral.

Where employee wages were not paid prior to filing, permission of the court can often be obtained to pay, on a date after the filing of the petition, employee's wages earned during the payroll period prior to the filing of the petition. The dichotomy of the prefiling debtor and the debtor-in-possession must not be underemphasized. The operating guidelines of the U.S. trustee for the various regions will most likely provide that all checking accounts of the debtor be closed upon the filing and that all outstanding checks be permitted to "bounce." In cases where the debtor has some flexibility in timing the filing of its petition, care may be taken to avoid the embarrassment resulting from the bank's not honoring payroll checks.

Examples of first-day orders that may be needed in this area include orders to:

- Use existing payroll accounts and honor employee payroll checks.
- Pay any back wages.
- Use existing bank accounts and honor drawn checks.
- Continue consolidated cash management system.
- Obtain postpetition financing.

While it is advisable to obtain an order from the court authorizing the debtor to use existing bank accounts, it may be possible to use the accounts even if such an order is not issued. However, it is advisable to file a first-day order requesting the use of existing bank accounts and honor drawn checks. In *In re Gold Standard Banking Inc.,*[1] the bankruptcy court held that the U.S. Trustee's requirement, that all checks issued by the debtor-in-possession be imprinted with a "Debtor-in-Possession" designation, was not authorized by the Bankruptcy Code provisions imposing reporting requirements. The bankruptcy court noted that, "[a]s a result of the absence of either an express or implied

[1] 179 B.R. 98 (Bankr. N.D. Ill. 1995).

statutory duty under the Bankruptcy Code or applicable rule among the Federal or Local Rules of Bankruptcy Procedure imposing such a duty on the debtor to imprint its checks, or a correlative enabling statute or rule, and in the absence of a federal regulation authorizing the UST to so require, the court concludes that the requirement . . . lacks the binding effect of law to be enforceable."

An example of an order for the debtor to maintain the existing cash management system, and the justification for the order, are shown as 8.1 of Volume 2 of *Bankruptcy and Insolvency Accounting*.

An example of an application for an order to pay prepetition wages to avoid the risk of massive resignations, discontent, or loss of morale among the essential employees, is shown as 8.2 in Volume 2. The order provided for (1) the payment of unpaid wages that accrued just prior to the filing of the petition and (2) the retention of the present payroll accounts and the payment of uncashed payroll checks drawn on this payroll account.

(b) Operations Management

Continuing operations are vital to a chapter 11 entity. Communications with suppliers, buyers, and employee representatives are therefore of utmost importance in a successful reorganization. Planning concerns can then be realized through interviews with operations members. Possible concerns may include the following:

- Review of purchasing procedures, including extra charges and pricing problems
- Study of vendor and supply problems, including an identification of critical vendors and alternate suppliers
- Development of a plan to handle and verify requests for reclaiming goods and to pay for goods that are properly reclaimed but are needed for continued operations
- Prepetition debt issues:
  - Establishing procedures to ensure that prepetition debt is not paid without proper authorization
  - Designating an individual to handle all requests for prepetition debt payments
  - Acquainting accounting personnel with techniques that might be used to obtain unauthorized prepetition debt payments.
- Development of procedures for handling warranty requests:
  - Obtaining permission to honor fully, including cash reimbursement.
  - Obtaining permission to honor with replacement goods (no cash).
  - Taking no action and allowing warranty to be paid with other unsecured claims.
- Employee relations:
  - Developing a plan to discuss chapter 11 filing with employees.
  - Developing a program of expense reimbursement.
  - Arranging a meeting to discuss modifications to collective bargaining agreements.

See the subsection on public relations for additional discussion regarding relations with employees.

Possible first-day orders that may be prepared in the operations management area include orders to:

- Continue honoring warranty claims.
- Pay prepetition wages, employee benefits, and business expenses paid by employees subject to reimbursement.
- Continue employee benefits, such as vacation pay, sick pay, and so on.
- Pay retiree benefits.
- Obtain assets in hands of third parties, including in-transit inventory.

Examples of "first-day orders" filed as of the filing date or shortly thereafter appear as 8.3 and 8.4 of Volume 2 of *Bankruptcy and Insolvency Accounting.* As shown in 8.3, warranty payments are allowed to retail customers for refund of overpayments on charge accounts, for return of unsatisfactory merchandise purchased prepetition (cash payments or credit), and for refund of prepetition deposits made for goods the customers no longer wanted. The application shown as 8.4 is requesting an order to honor accrued vacation days, sick leave, and other personnel policies. The application asks the court to grant the debtor the right to continue payroll policies on a day-to-day basis and to permit employees to utilize benefits such as vacation pay and sick leave that may have accrued prior to the filing of the petition.

(c) Legal Requirements

The legal team is responsible for overall planning of prefiling activity and preparation of court documents. Communication with other teams is crucial to ensure overall effectiveness. Activities of the legal team may include the following:

- Decisions needed in several areas, including whether subsidiaries should file or not file; corporate separateness; intermingled funds; cross-collateralization; extent of trade indebtedness; cash flow and prospects; location of operating assets; possibility of defraying costs of debtor's administration
- Selection of time to file:
  - Point in business cycle
  - Preferences and fraudulent transfers
  - Tax considerations
  - Importance of action of debtor before creditors act
  - Avoidance of separate closing of books
- Preparation of petitions
- Preparation of board resolutions
- Motions to extend time to file schedules of assets and liabilities, statement of affairs, and schedule of executory contracts, as required under section 1121(d)

- Evaluation of timing of filing with regard to preferences, operations, public relations, and so on
- Retention of necessary professionals for filing; compliance with Bankruptcy Rule 2014 and filing of necessary forms under section 327
- Preparation for adversary matters requiring early attention
- Preparation of list of employment and other executory contracts for acceptance/rejection, and plan for compliance with section 1114 (retiree benefits as administrative priority)
- Preparation of plan of reorganization
- Preparation of first-day orders (see above lists)

(d) Financial Reporting and Taxes

The financial reporting and tax team necessarily handles the accounting and disclosure aspects of chapter 11. Such duties may include:

- Preparing a list of the 20 largest creditors—Rule 1007(d) and Form 4.
- Preparing schedules of assets and liabilities, a statement of affairs, and a schedule of executory contracts—Rule 1007(a)(1).
- Compiling monthly operating reports for the court and creditors.
- Setting up new liability accounts.
- Setting up new asset accounts for selected items such as inventory and accounts receivable that might be pledged.
- Designing a claims processing plan.
- Monitoring the compliance reporting for the DIP financing agreement.
- Selecting a filing date:
  - Avoiding a separate closing by arranging for a filing date near month-end or, even better, at or near quarter-end or year-end.
- Tax considerations:
  - Withholding taxes or trust taxes under which responsible person may be personally liable under either section 6672 of the Internal Revenue Code (I.R.C.) or state laws.
  - If debtor is solvent or will become solvent as a result of debt discharge, then the filing of a bankruptcy petition has an advantage over out-of-court workout (I.R.C. section 108(a)).
  - If there is more than a 50 percent change of ownership under I.R.C. section 382, the bankruptcy exception of I.R.C. section 382(1) (available only to title 11 cases) may result in less of the net operating loss (NOL) being lost.

(e) Public Relations

The methods and timing of information disbursal can make a significant difference in the levels of cooperation received from creditors and others in the reorganization process. The public relations team has a particularly sensitive role and should be well prepared for the influx of questions that will occur after filing. All employees should be briefed to provide consistent answers to common questions asked.

For some medium-size and large companies, especially if they are public corporations, it may be advisable to retain a firm (or an individual) that specializes in public relations for companies in financial difficulty.

The public relations focus should be on both internal and external issues. From an internal perspective, it is important that all information regarding the potential filing be kept confidential. Facts regarding the filing should be known by as few individuals as possible, at the beginning of the preplanning process. Procedures for the handling of rumors should be developed. If the debtor is attempting an out-of-court workout, controlling rumors that may develop among the employees will be difficult. It may be necessary to schedule meetings with groups of employees to deal with the rumors, answer any questions, and provide any well-founded assurance that their jobs may not be in jeopardy.

The company's strategy for dealing with outside parties will be very important. Major customers, suppliers, key creditors and stockholders, and other interested parties, including the general public, need to be notified of the filing. The pros and cons of issuing a general press release must be considered. If the company does not issue a press release, it risks having information printed that conveys more negative connotations than might have appeared in a press release. However, once any contact is made with the press, additional questions and inquiries will follow. Listed below are some of the key issues that will need to be examined.

Planning steps include:

- Composing a statement describing the cause of the filing, for inclusion in letters, press releases, and so on.
- Scheduling dates for announcement to each category of interested parties within the communication matrix.
- Preparing press releases.
- Developing a program for communication to management, employees, key customers, and vendors.
- Identifying specific individuals within the company who are responsible for answering various types of questions with consistent answers.
- Identifying individual(s) who are to answer questions from the press.
- Estimating the impact the announcement may have on operations outside the United States. For example, bankruptcy, especially chapter 11, may have different meanings to workers in other countries than it would to U.S. workers.
- Preparing letters to announce the filing and a list of anticipated questions and answers from all interested parties:
  - Compiling a sample list of parties and areas of coverage.
- Informing all parties who need to be given notice of the bankruptcy filing: shareholders, customers, suppliers and other vendors, sales representatives, union officials, institutional creditors, public debt holders, regulatory agencies, community officials, news and financial press representatives.

- Communicating all needed information: cause of filing, nature of bankruptcy process, impact of filing on current operations, events that led to the filing, financial highlights, financing during bankruptcy, strategic action company is taking, and prospects for future profitable operations.

Employees will have their own questions and concerns. In 8.5 of Volume 2 are typical questions asked by employees in these circumstances, and some suggested answers that can be adapted as needed. It is critical in most bankruptcy filings that the employees fully understand the nature of the filing and are given satisfactory answers to any questions they may have regarding its effect on the company.

Proper prebankruptcy planning can reduce the time the debtor is in chapter 11 and result in fewer administrative expenses.

ACCOUNTING DATA RELATIVE TO THE PETITION

§ 8.9 Introduction

The accountant must supply the attorney with the following information, which, according to Rule 1007, is necessary for filing of a chapter 11 petition:

- *List of 20 largest creditors.* A list containing the names, addresses, and amounts of claims of the 20 largest unsecured creditors, excluding insiders, must be filed with the petition in a voluntary case. In an involuntary chapter 11 case, the list must be submitted within two days after an order of relief is entered. See Rule 1007 and Form 4.
- *List of creditors.* Rule 1007 provides that, unless the voluntary petition is accompanied by the schedules of liabilities or the court grants an extension, a list of the names and addresses of all creditors should be filed with the petition. In an involuntary petition, the debtor should file the list within 15 days unless the schedules of liabilities are filed.
- *List of equity security holders.* A list of each class of the debtor's equity security holders, showing the number and kinds of interests registered in the name of each holder and the last known address or place of business of each holder, should be filed within 15 days after the petition is filed, unless the court approves an extension of time.
- *Schedules of assets and liabilities.* See § 8.6.
- *Statement of executory contracts.* See § 8.8.
- *Statement of financial affairs.* See § 8.7.
- *Exhibit "A" to the petition.* This thumbnail sketch of the financial condition of the business should list total assets, total liabilities, secured claims, unsecured claims, information relating to public trading of the debtor's securities, and the identity of all insiders. See Appendix A of Volume 2 for an example of Exhibit A and Official Form 1. Also, 5.1 of Volume 2 contains an example of a petition.

The debtor must file additional reports or documents that may be required by local rules or by the U.S. trustee. For example, in the Central District of

California, the debtor must file with the U.S. trustee the following information and documents:

- Proof of establishment of new debtor-in-possession bank accounts:
  - General account
  - Payroll account
  - Tax account
- Declaration from the debtor, under penalty of perjury, verifying the closing of all prepetition bank accounts and stating the date each account was closed and the transfer of all monies to the new debtor-in-possession bank accounts
- A separate completed Real Property Questionnaire (Form UST-5) for each parcel of real property leased, owned, or in the process of being purchased by the debtor
- Proof of the following insurance coverage:
  - General comprehensive public liability insurance
  - Fire and theft insurance
  - Workers' compensation insurance
  - Vehicle insurance
  - Product liability insurance
  - Any other insurance coverage customary in the debtor's business
- Most recently filed state and federal payroll tax returns and state sales tax returns, with all schedules and attachments
- Most recently prepared audited and unaudited financial statements
- Projected operating statement for the first 30 days of operation under chapter 11
- Applications for compensation by principals, partners, officers, or directors of the debtor
- Copies of any trust agreements or conveyances (other than leases) to which the debtor is a party or under which the debtor holds, has possession of, or operates any personal or real property or business as a trustee or otherwise

Other U.S. trustee offices require similar information.

Often, the petition must be filed quickly to avoid pending legal proceedings, and the debtor's books are seldom up-to-date. In some circumstances, the accountant may be called on to assist the attorney in preparing a petition with only a few hours' notice. A so-called skeletal petition may be filed consisting principally of the petition, the exhibit "A," corporate minutes authorizing the filing, the list of 20 largest creditors, and a list of all claimants (with their addresses). After the petition is filed, the debtor has a brief automatic extension of time for the preparation of the remaining schedules and statements. Any additional extension of time may be granted only on application, for cause shown, and on notice to any committee, trustee, examiner, or other party identified by the court.

§ 8.10 Affidavit as to Projected Operations

Certain districts may require a sworn statement containing the data necessary to prove to the court that the debtor-in-possession will be able to operate the business at a profit. These projections, usually prepared in budget form and on a monthly basis, should be revised as new information becomes available and should indicate which areas, in the accountant's opinion, are unprofitable and which costs should be eliminated. The following data are illustrative of the type that may be included in the affidavit:

- The total amount of the payroll each week and the salaries paid to the officers of the corporation.
- All items that compose overhead.
- A statement of any litigation or levies pending on the debtor's property.
- The reasons why it is in the best interests of the creditors that the debtor remain in possession of the property. (It is important to show that they will receive more under reorganization proceedings than they would if the estate were to be liquidated.) (See § 6.31.)
- If there is reason to believe that the firm will not be able at least to break even, the accountant or financial advisor should consult with the debtor or the trustee, citing the reasons for this suspicion. At the end of each operating period, a statement of operations should be prepared and compared with the projection so that those interested may come to their own decisions about the future of the business and subsequent budgets may be modified. These budgets serve the dual function of controlling operations while the debtor remains in possession and guiding the preparation of the plan. See § 8.16 for comments relating to the preparation of the forecasts.

§ 8.11 Supporting Schedules

The schedules that must accompany the petition are sworn statements of the debtor's assets and liabilities as of the date the petition is filed under chapter 11, and other information about the debtor's operations and obligations. These schedules consist of the following:

Schedule A	Real Property
Schedule B	Personal Property
Schedule C	Property Claimed as Exempt
Schedule D	Creditors Holding Secured Claims
Schedule E	Creditors Holding Unsecured Priority Claims
Schedule F	Creditors Holding Unsecured Nonproperty Claims
Schedule G	Executory Contracts and Unexpired Leases
Schedule H	Codebtors
Schedule I	Current Income of Individual Debtor(s)
Schedule J	Current Expenditure of Individual Debtor(s)

Rule 1007 provides that the schedules should be filed within 15 days after the petition is filed, unless the bankruptcy court approves an extension. Copies of all schedules and of any extensions of time for filing the schedules should be filed with the U.S. trustee in the region where the petition was filed.

The schedules filed in a chapter 11 case can be extensive, as shown in 8.6 of Volume 2. (Some of the detailed data have been omitted in the Volume 2 example.) As is true in many of the larger bankruptcy cases, book values are used rather than market values as stated in the schedules. Form 6, which contains the format for all of the schedules, is reproduced in Appendix A of Volume 2.

It is crucial that this information be accurate and complete. The omission or incorrect listing of a creditor might result in a failure to receive notice of the proceedings; consequently, the creditor's claim could be exempted from a discharge when the plan is later confirmed. Omission of material facts may be construed as a false statement or concealment.

(a) Assets of the Debtor

Information concerning all interests of the debtor in property is provided in Schedules A, B, and C. These schedules indicate that the property is to be presented at market values. However, for most business reorganizations, the property is shown at book value. Market value as well as liquidation value may be needed for all or some of the debtor's property, but they are subsequently determined by investment bankers, appraisers, and similar parties. A statement of the real estate owned by the debtor, with an estimated value of its interest, is found on Schedule A.

Schedule B itemizes goods or personal property and tells where they are located: cash, negotiable instruments and securities, stock-in-trade, all motor vehicles and machinery, fixtures, equipment, patents, copyrights, and trademarks. One of the most important sections of this schedule for many businesses is the information regarding the debtor's stock-in-trade, to be computed from the actual inventory with a disclosure of the method of valuation used. The method used to value the inventory should be consistent with prior periods and should be a method that is in accordance with generally accepted accounting principles. If the method used to value inventory differs significantly (such as when LIFO is used) from the going-concern value of the inventory, the value of the inventory should be used instead of historical costs. The figures required in this schedule are totals for each classification, not individual values for each item. Information about accounts receivable, insurance policies, all unliquidated claims (such as from fire, storm damage, and water damage, as well as claims against insiders and other legal causes of action), and deposits of money made by the debtor is also included in Schedule B.

Property in reversion, remainder, or expectancy, including property held in trust for the debtor or subject to any power or right to dispose of or to charge should be included as real property on Schedule A or personal property on Schedule B. Schedule B also lists property not otherwise scheduled. Included in this schedule would be property transferred under assignment for benefit of creditors within 120 days prior to filing of the petition. Schedule C applies only to an individual debtor filing a petition and concerns all property that is exempt from the proceedings, such as household furniture, clothing, and so on. See § 5.34.

(b) Secured Creditors

Schedule D is provided for listing the holders of claims secured by a deposit or property of the debtor. Required on the schedule are: the name and address of each creditor; a description of the security being held and the date it was obtained; specification as to when each claim was incurred and the consideration therefore; indication as to whether the claim is contingent, unliquidated, or disputed; the amount of the claim; and the market value of the collateral.

(c) Priority Claims

All claims holding priority under the Bankruptcy Code must be listed on Schedule E. The most frequent of such claims are wages—salaries, contributions to employee benefit plans, and taxes. The name and address of each claimant to whom the debtor owes wages, commissions, salary, vacation pay, sick pay, or severance pay when the petition is filed must be listed. Each taxing authority must be listed separately. For the Internal Revenue Service, the District Director of the office where the debtor files its returns should be listed, and a breakdown of all federal taxes that are due should be prepared. For all other taxing authorities, the address of each agency and the amount owing must be listed. See § 5.33 for additional priority claims.

(d) Unsecured Creditors

A list of all unsecured creditors is required on Schedule F and must include their names and mailing addresses, when each claim was incurred and the consideration therefore, and the amount due each claimant. This information is generally taken from the books and records of the company. It is important to list all creditors and give the full name and correct address of each person. The exact amount due each creditor should be determined and the books posted so there is no doubt as to how much is owing. Unsecured creditors include not only general creditors, but also those who hold promissory notes; creditors with debt subject to setoff; judgment creditors; liabilities on notes or bills discounted that are to be paid by the drawers, makers, acceptors, or endorsers; creditors to whom the debtor is liable on accommodation paper; and officers or directors of the debtor who have loaned money to the company. It is important to list all claims that are disputed, contingent, or unliquidated, and indicate their status. Also listed should be claims incurred as partners or joint contractors; the partners or joint contractors should be specified.

When Schedules D, E, and F have been completed, all creditors who have or may have any interest in connection with the debtor's estate should have been listed. The accuracy of these schedules must again be emphasized. In reorganization proceedings, a claim admitted on the debtor's schedules is deemed filed under section 1111(a). See § 6.15.

A summary of debts and property taken from Schedules A–J is included on Form 6. A single oath for all of the schedules must be submitted, specifying the number of sheets included in the schedules and acknowledging that the affiant has read them. Separate forms of oath are provided for individuals, corporations, and partnerships. Form 6, which explains the information required on the schedules, summary, and oath, is shown in the Forms and Exhibits volume.

§ 8.12 Statement of Executory Contracts

This listing of unexpired leases and other unperformed agreements is provided to permit the trustee (or the debtor) to consider which of its obligations are burdensome to the estate and should be rejected under section 365. Rule 1007(b)(1) requires that a statement of executory contracts be filed with the court. Relevant particulars for each executory contract as required by Schedule G (Form 7) might consist of the following:

- Party contracting with debtor
- Address of party
- Concise characterization of contract (employment agreement, equipment lease, and so on)
- Date of contract
- Term of contract, expiration date, options, and so on
- Price or payment terms of contract
- Balance of any monies owed by the debtor or other condition(s) of default as of the petition date

Executory contracts were discussed in § 5.29. An example of Schedule G of Form 6, which lists the executory contracts and related information, appears in 8.8 of Volume 2.

§ 8.13 Statement of Financial Affairs

The statement of financial affairs, not to be confused with an accountant's usual use of the term, is a series of detailed questions about the debtor's property and conduct. The general purpose of the statement of financial affairs is to give both the creditors and the court an overall view of the debtor's operations. It offers many avenues from which investigations into the debtor's conduct may be begun.

The statement (Form 7 in Appendix A of Volume 2) consists of 21 questions to be answered under oath concerning the following areas:

1 Income from employment or operation of business
2 Income other than from employment or operation of business
3 Payments to creditors
4 Suits, executions, garnishments, and attachments
5 Repossessions, foreclosures, and returns
6 Assignments and receiverships
7 Gifts
8 Losses
9 Payments related to debt counseling or bankruptcy
10 Other transfers
11 Closed financial accounts
12 Safe deposit boxes

13 Setoffs

14 Property held for another person

15 Prior address of debtor

16 Nature, location, and name of business

17 Books, records, and financial statements

18 Inventories

19 Current partners, officers, directors, and shareholders

20 Former partners, officers, directors, and shareholders

21 Withdrawals from a partnership or distributions by a corporation

The statement of financial affairs must conform to the requirements set forth in Form 7. Note that the statement of financial affairs consists of numerous questions that deal with accounting information. In most bankruptcies, it is more appropriate for the accountant to answer these questions and complete the schedules than for this service to be performed by counsel. Often, the internal accountant and the debtor are too busy handling normal accounting problems to prepare this information. Thus, accountants or financial advisors are engaged to perform this function.

For an example of the statement of financial affairs filed in a chapter 11 case, see 8.7 of Volume 2. Some of the detailed data have been omitted, but the format and information segments are represented as a model.

ASSISTANCE IN FORMULATING PLAN

§ 8.14 Introduction

The accountant will be asked to advise and give suggestions to the debtor and attorney in drawing up a plan. (See the Forms and Exhibits volume for examples of plans filed under chapter 11.) Section 1121 of the Bankruptcy Code provides that only the debtor may file a plan of reorganization during the first 120 days of the case (unless a trustee has been appointed) or longer if the court grants an extension, which it often does. This breathing period is intended to permit the debtor to hold lawsuits and foreclosures in status quo, and to determine the economic causes of its financial predicament while developing a plan. Using the schedules of assets and liabilities, the statement of financial affairs, and post and projected financial statements, the debtor and its accountant will examine the liabilities of the debtor and the value of the business. They will explore sources of funding the plan, such as enhanced profitability, partial liquidation, issuance of debt securities, or outside capitalization. They will outline the classes of debt that cannot be deferred or reduced and negotiate with the rest.

The most important requirements are that the plan be approved by each class of claims and equity holders and that it be feasible. If the creditors or stockholders in any given class have not approved the plan, the class must receive at least as much as would be received if the debtor were liquidated under chapter 7. (This is the best-interest test discussed in § 6.31.) In situations where a class of creditors or stockholders has not approved the plan, the plan must be fair and equitable with respect to each of the classes impaired, as discussed in § 6.34. The accountant or financial advisor's help may also be essential to the preparation of an adequate disclosure statement, which must be issued at the time or before acceptance of the plan is solicited. (See § 8.20.)

§ 8.15   Liquidating Value of Assets

Section 1129(a)(7) provides that each holder of a claim must either accept the plan or receive or retain interest in property of a value that is at least equal to the amount that would have been received or retained if the debtor were liquidated under chapter 7. See §§ 11.10–11.11 for a description of the approaches used to determine liquidation values and 11.2 of Volume 2 for an example of a liquidation analysis.

The liquidation alternative often leaves the unsecured creditors with very little. For example, in one bankruptcy case where the debtor was a major retailer and had already closed several stores, an alternative being considered was to close all of the stores and liquidate the business. The accountant identified for the creditors the following reasons why liquidation value would be so low:

- Adverse impact of environment where the store is being liquidated:
  - Constrains selling prices.
  - Increases landlord settlements.
  - Leads to operating losses.
  - Lessens realization from liquidation of other assets.
- Administrative expenses unique to liquidation would be realized, although they had not been incurred in cities where stores were previously liquidated:
  - Additional administrative costs.
  - Breach of contract claims.
  - Materially higher settlement on pension costs, including probable additional assessments on already closed operations.
  - Higher landlord settlement costs because there would be no rehabilitation motive by the court.
  - Damages from personal property lease rejections, for example, computers and automobiles.
  - Operating losses for a minimum of 60 days until operational closing is complete.

§ 8.16   Projection of Future Operations

Section 1129(a)(11) contains the feasibility standard of chapter 11: Confirmation of the plan of reorganization is not likely to be followed by liquidation or further reorganization (unless contemplated). The accountant may assist the debtor or trustee to formulate an acceptable plan by projecting the ability of the debtor to carry out and perform the terms of the plan. To establish feasibility, the accountant or financial advisor must project the profitability potential of the business. Where the plan calls for installment payments, the accountant or financial advisor will be requested to prepare projected budgets, cash flow statements, and statements of financial position. The creditors must be assured by the projected income statement and cash flow statement that the debtor will be in a position to make the payments as they become due. The forecast of the results of operations and financial position should be prepared on the assumption that the proposed plan will be accepted and that the liability and asset accounts reflect the balance that would be shown after all adjustments are made relative to the debt forgiveness. Thus, interest expense is based on the liabilities that will exist after the discharge occurs. See the projected operating statement in 9.7 of Volume 2 for an example of the type of information presented in a forecast.

The forecast and the assumptions on which it is based originate with the debtor or trustee, who assumes the responsibility for them. However, the accountant would not want to be associated with the forecast in any way if the assumptions are believed to be incomplete or unreasonable. The assumptions on which the forecast is based should be clearly stated in the report. Any major changes in the operations of the business, such as the elimination of a division or a given product line, should be clearly set forth. If the forecast depends on the success of new products or markets, this should be stated. See § 9.7 for a more detailed discussion of projections. An example of cash flow and income projections, including a summary of the assumptions on which the projections are based, appears as 8.9 in Volume 2.

§ 8.17   Reorganization Value

Not only are cash projections needed for the feasibility test, as mentioned in the previous section, but they are an important part of the negotiation process. The creditors want to receive the maximum amount possible in any chapter 11 plan; often, they want the payment in cash as of the effective date of the plan. The creditors realize, however, that if their demands are beyond the ability of the debtor to make payments, the plan will not work and they will not receive the payments provided for in the plan. Cash flow projections assist both parties in developing reasonable conclusions regarding the value of the entity emerging from chapter 11. In some reorganizations, there is considerable debate over cash flow projections and the discount rate to be used in determining the value of the debtor's continuing operations, to which must be added the amount to be realized on the sale of nonoperating assets plus excess working capital. Once the debtor and its creditors' committee can agree on the basic value of the entity, it is easier to negotiate the terms of the plan.

Statement of Position (SOP) 90-7, *Financial Reporting by Entities in Reorganization under the Bankruptcy Code*, requires the reorganization value to be included in the disclosure statement. The techniques for determining the reorganization value are discussed in Chapter 11.

The accountant can be of considerable assistance to the debtor during the formulation of the plan by helping to determine the reorganization value of the debtor, or by helping the debtor to assess the valuation by an investment banker or other specialist. If the accountant develops the cash projections supporting the valuation, the accountant will be precluded from being independent for SEC purposes. Once the debtor has determined an estimate of the value of the entity that will emerge from bankruptcy, the accountant can provide assistance to the debtor in the negotiations with the creditor as to the terms of the plan.

§ 8.18   Pro Forma Balance Sheet

Of considerable help in evaluating a plan is a pro forma balance sheet showing how the balance sheet will look if the plan is accepted and all provisions of the plan are carried out. By using reorganization models or simulation models, the pro forma balance sheet may be prepared based on several possible courses of action that the debtor could take. The pro forma balance sheet illustrates what type of debt equity position would exist under different alternatives.

This pro forma balance sheet should reflect the debts at discounted values. For companies that must reflect fresh-start reporting, assets should be stated at their market values, according to SOP 90-7. If the debtor does not meet the requirements for fresh-start reporting, assets are presented at their historical cost values. However, a pro forma balance sheet that reflects the reorganized values of the entity would be of considerable benefit to the debtor in developing the terms for a plan.

Because current practice does not allow an entity that is emerging from bankruptcy but does not qualify for fresh-start reporting to adopt a new basis of accounting, there needs to be a reflection through pro forma statements of what the balance sheet, from an economic perspective, would look like upon emergence from bankruptcy. For example, if based on the discounted cash flows, the emerging entity could fund the issuance of debt equal to 60 percent of the unsecured debt. If this amount of debt would still leave the emerging entity with a deficit or very low balance in stockholder equity, the creditors may have to receive some form of equity, such as preferred stock, in order to have a balance sheet with positive stockholder equity. It can be argued that only the economic factors (i.e., the reorganization value is greater than debt, and the fact that the use of historical cost results in a deficit is irrelevant) should be used in determining the terms of the plan, but the fact remains that this is currently an issue in practice and plans are changed to provide for net positive stockholder equity on emergence.

It is also helpful, when developing a plan, if the debtor prepares a pro forma balance sheet based on the reorganization value of the entity even though the balance sheet will not be presented with these values after plan confirmation in cases where the debtor does not qualify for fresh-start reporting.

Once the terms of the proposed plan are finalized, the pro forma balance sheet based on the reorganization value reflecting the terms of the plan is generally included in the disclosure statement that must be submitted prior to or at the time when votes are solicited on the plan. The pro forma balance sheet reflecting reorganization values provides much more relevant information for the creditors and stockholders to make an informed judgment about how to vote on the plan. See § 6.26.

In Volume 2 of *Bankruptcy and Insolvency Accounting,* 8.9 contains: (a) an example of a pro forma balance sheet; (b) an explanation of the adjustments needed to convert the preconfirmation balance sheet to the pro forma postconfirmation balance sheet; (c) the cash flow and (d) the income projections for the next five years; (e) the projected balance sheet and (f) the projected statement of changes in cash as of the end of the next five fiscal years; and (g) the notes to the financial projections. The pro forma balance sheet does not include the adoption of fresh-start reporting because there was no change of ownership in this proposed plan.

Volume 2, at Chapter 14, contains an example of a pro forma balance sheet that does involve the adjustments to fresh start reporting. This pro forma statement is discussed in § 14.7.

§ 8.19   Formulating an Amended Plan

There is often a need for modified plans to be developed and submitted to the creditors (in an attempt to gain their approval, of course) as part of the negotiating process. Many factors can cover the need for a modified plan, including the discovery of additional claims, tax requirement changes, changes in financial condition, delays in obtaining plan approval, and changes in economic conditions.

Any amended plan of reorganization must make provision for taxes due at the time the petition was filed. At the time the initial petition was filed, the amount and nature of taxes may not have been known. Generally, taxes will not be compromised by taxing authorities, but installment payments are permissible. Section 1129(a)(9) provides that tax claims qualifying for the seventh priority must be satisfied with cash payments over a period not to exceed six years after the date of assessment of the claim. The cash payments must have a value, as of the effective date of the plan, equal to the allowed amount of the claim.

§ 8.20   Disclosure Statement

Before a proponent of a plan can solicit votes, a statement must be issued that contains adequate information. A large part of the information in this disclosure statement will be financial. Examples of (or excerpts from) disclosure statements issued in chapter 11 cases are presented in Chapters 6 and 14 of Volume 2.

The content of the disclosure statement was presented in § 6.26. The accountant or financial advisor for the debtor can assist the debtor in the preparation of this statement in several ways, such as helping the debtor decide whether the information disclosed would allow a creditor or stockholder to make an informed decision about how to vote on the plan. The financial data needed in the disclosure statement are discussed in § 14.7.

ACCOUNTANT OR FINANCIAL ADVISOR AS EXAMINER

§ 8.21   Nature of Service

The Bankruptcy Code provides for the appointment of an examiner to investigate the financial condition of the debtor, the operation of the business, and the potential for successful continuance of the business. This investigation will also include any allegations against the debtor of fraud, dishonesty, or mismanagement. Accountants and financial advisors are well-equipped to perform this function and provide the necessary report. Since the Bankruptcy Code, as originally passed, did not provide for the appointment of professionals to assist the examiner, accountants and financial advisors would be the most logical professionals to be retained where most of the investigation centers around the evaluation of financial information. In fact, a large number of accountants or other professionals with a business or financial background have been appointed, but the majority have been attorneys. Some judges have authorized the examiner to use professional persons already employed by creditors' or other committees appointed in the case. Some judges have allowed the examiner to retain professionals, such as accountants or financial advisors, to assist in the examination. See § 6.8 for a more detailed explanation of the role of the examiner.

Section 1106(b) of the Bankruptcy Code gives the court the right to assign any duty of the trustee to the examiner if the court does not want the debtor-in-possession to perform that function. In several cases, the courts have expanded the activities of accountants that have been appointed as examiners rather than appoint a trustee. One advantage to taking this action is that the accountant is already familiar with the debtor's operations and can easily expand his or her services. Section 321 of the Bankruptcy Code precludes an examiner in a case from being appointed the trustee, and section 327 provides that a trustee may not employ a person who has served as an examiner. Thus, to ensure that the creditors' interests are protected and to keep the cost of administering the estate as low as possible, the court may expand the role of the examiner in some cases. See § 6.8 for a discussion of the extent to which an examiner's role can be expanded.

ADDITIONAL OR OTHER SERVICES

§ 8.22   Introduction

This chapter and the next contain summaries of some of the services that the accountant may render for the debtor. The extent to which the accountant or financial advisor will assist the debtor can vary significantly, depending on several factors, including the size of the debtor, the nature of the debtor's debt, and the size and experience level of the debtor's internal accounting personnel. Often, the accountant may render normal accounting services for the debtor in addition to these special services.

§ 8.23   Normal Accounting Services

It is still necessary for the accountant to render the usual services that would be given any other client, and normal accounting procedures will be followed. However, it is important to realize that the debtor-in-possession is a new legal entity that must be distinguished from the debtor. The accountant must close the debtor's books as of the date the petition is filed and open new books for the new entity. In the opening entry, all of the prepetition liabilities are grouped into one account, usually labeled "prepetition debt." (See § 13.14.) None of the debtor's liabilities that existed at the date of the filing may be paid by the debtor-in-possession except upon specific order of the court.

Included in the normal accounting services is an audit of the chapter 11 company. The audit and investigation of the debtor's operations is described in Chapter 10.

§ 8.24   Special Investigation

In conducting an audit, the independent accountant will primarily examine the accounts and prepare the financial statements. This investigation will consist of examining any unusual transactions that occurred before bankruptcy proceedings were initiated, with utmost attention to any transactions that resulted in the dissipation of assets from factors other than losses in the ordinary course of the business. These normally include a transfer or concealment of assets; preferential payments to creditors; transactions with related parties not conducted at arm's length; major acquisitions, mergers, and investments that resulted in a loss; acquisitions of property at exorbitant prices; and any bulk sale of assets or of a part of the business. The independent accountant should describe these transactions in as much detail as is possible and analyze their effect on the financial position of the firm.[2] In many situations, the accountant is engaged to review selected aspects of the debtor's operation without performing an audit.

When retained by a trustee appointed in a chapter 11 reorganization, the accountant has the same responsibilities to the trustee as to a debtor-in-possession. When retained for the trustee, there is generally an audit and investigation of the debtor's activities. In fact, an investigation under these conditions is generally much more extensive than that required in a normal situation where the debtor retains possession. The extent of the examination depends on several factors, including the extent to which the debtor's management misused the company's assets. The independent accountant will generally conduct a thorough inquiry into the acts, conduct, property, financial condition, business transactions, history, and background of the debtor to determine whether the present management should be retained and whether a successful plan can be worked out. Everything that will help to establish the causes of the failure, including the conduct, attitudes, business judgment, and insight of the officers, directors, and managers, should be scrutinized. These audit and investigative services may also be needed by a nonaccountant examiner appointed by the court to perform an investigation. The extent to which an accountant can be retained by an examiner is uncertain (see § 8.21). It is possible for the accountant to be retained as the examiner.

Special studies may be made by accountants to analyze all transactions between the debtor and related parties, such as companies controlled, officers and directors, relatives of principal officers' families, and so on. Included in 8.10 of Volume 2 of *Bankruptcy and Insolvency Accounting* are some excerpts from a report issued by Price Waterhouse on the "Investigation of Related Party Transactions and Perquisites" for the creditors' committee of Food Fair Inc. and J. M. Fields, Inc. The total report was over 600 pages.

In performing an investigation of the acts and conduct of one company in bankruptcy, the accounting firm looked at the following factors in examining the financial condition of the debtor:

- *Return on equity and capital.* The debtor's operations were compared with other companies in the same industry and with all companies in a list prepared by *Forbes* magazine for a period of five years prior to the corporate reorganization.
- *Sales performance.* Again, the debtor's record was compared with companies in the same industry and other public companies.
- *Earnings performance.* The deteriorating trend in the debtor's earnings was emphasized by comparing it with companies in the same industry and other public companies. In this case, the company was 17th of 28, and 260th of 560. Four years later, the company had the second lowest growth in earnings compared to other companies in the same industry.
- *Business ratios and statistics.* The accountants determined the current ratio, quick ratio, and inventory/sales ratio for the year of the petition and for the previous four years. These ratios were compared with composite financial data of 17 leading competitors.
- *Long-term liquidity.* The accounting firm used a mathematical model to determine the nature of the year-to-year changes in liquidity of the debtor. The model computes the probability of the trend's continuing until a point is reached where available resources will be depleted. In this model, a ratio of 1 indicates that, unless the trend is altered, an illiquid position is probable within five years. The model indicated that this company was tending toward illiquidity during a year that ended four years prior to the date of the petition and continued to indicate this outcome in each of the subsequent years prior to bankruptcy.
- *Trade credit.* The ratio of inventory to payables was calculated for the fourth, fifth, and sixth years prior to bankruptcy, to show that an unfavorable trend was developing during this period. Compounding the effect during this time period were the increases in inventory with the increase in sales.
- *Other analysis.* Both long-term and short-term bank indebtedness was analyzed for the prior six years to detect the trends that developed. In addition, the growth in off-balance-sheet financing arrangements, along with the dividends paid, was disclosed and evaluated. See the ratio analysis discussion in § 2.22.

In all bankruptcy proceedings, the independent accountant's primary duty is to indicate the areas where there may have been wrongdoing, misconduct, or misappropriation. It is then the attorney's job to determine whether there has been a violation of the law.

§ 8.25 Accounting Services and the Granting of New Credit

The accountant may also assist the debtor in acquiring additional credit. Special schedules are prepared for the debtor in order to provide the credit grantors with the desired information.

Apart from the desire of the credit community to aid in the rehabilitation of a debtor, there are several business reasons for granting credit during a period of reorganization:

- Credit extended during the chapter 11 proceeding has priority over other unsecured debt and with court approval may have a priority over other administrative expenses. (See § 6.14.) Some banks actively review chapter 11 filings for opportunities to extend credit to companies that will most likely survive.
- Postpetition assets are unencumbered by prepetition liabilities during this period and hence there may be substantial asset value as a basis for the granting of new credit.
- Many creditors have obligations on bill-and-hold goods and on commitments. With proper credit lines, the liquidation of bill-and-hold goods and commitment position can be accomplished with minimum losses.
- Many creditors may be dealing with the debtor as an important customer and hence it is essential to keep this concern functioning as a user of their goods.
- A proper credit line will provide for earlier distributions to the creditors without undue risk. Controls will prevent a distribution if it is felt that it would have a detrimental effect in any way on new creditors.
- A debtor with credit lines should be able to operate the business in a more efficient fashion and thus maximize the payment to general creditors.

The debtor must not emerge from the reorganization as a credit risk. The company must be able to go to its creditors in the early stages of the reorganization period and receive the assistance it needs to reestablish itself in the business community and come out of the reorganization with the confidence of its creditors. During the reorganization period, the accountant can be of valuable assistance by helping the creditors understand the problem areas and the financial statements so that the groundwork for future credit granting can be established.

ROLE OF THE SEC

§ 8.26 Prior Law

Under prior law, the SEC had an interest in all Chapter X proceedings and an interest under other chapter proceedings if a public company was involved or if a considerable public interest was served by the company. Very frequently, the proceeding would be instigated as a result of an action brought by the SEC. The SEC adopted a policy of examining with greater scrutiny financial reports that contain qualified statements as to viability or uncertainties involving the determination of financial position and the results of operations. A flood of letters to the SEC from dissatisfied shareholders, or volatility in the stock—primarily declines, where shareholders may be hurt—often created immediate action from the SEC. Under these conditions, the SEC would hold an inquiry and often invite the accountant to explain the accounting treatment and position as to the statements. As a result of these hearings, the stock might drop even further and the debtor might then become aware of the need to file a petition in the bankruptcy court.

Procedurally, once the company filed the petition, the SEC's reorganization division would step in and assign an attorney and an analyst (who is often an accountant) to work on the case. If the company was a broker or dealer in securities, the SEC might assign someone from the broker-dealer section to the case. As a party to the proceedings, the SEC must be served with copies of all motions and all papers filed with the court. From a practical standpoint, if the case were one of significance, the SEC would work very closely with the other parties to the proceedings. Representatives might attend meetings held among counsel, trustees, and accountants, and participate in the discussion—at times, almost to the point of making management decisions.

The SEC also determined whether the action taken by the debtor-in-possession or the trustee was within what it believed to be the interpretation of the law. It would see that proper notices were given for property sales, payments to creditors, or payments to shareholders. The SEC is also a source of background information for the accountant, because it retains copies of all public documents filed. The accountants in an initial audit of a public company often spend the first week reviewing the documents that have been filed, collecting all published financial data, and obtaining copies of the statements filed with the SEC as a means of trying to determine what has happened. Also, the SEC might have subpoenaed records that the accountant needs to review. There is a need for close rapport and participation between the SEC and the accountants involved in the proceeding.

The SEC's chief role was to protect the public's interest. As a result, the accounting firm might find that, even though the payment of its fees was a priority item, it often came out second best. On the other hand, the SEC may not object to the principals' satisfying the demands of customers in order to avoid any criminal actions brought about by the dissatisfied customers.

The SEC played another role in keeping the proceedings moving. Very often, the attorneys for the debtor and creditors have a backlog of cases they are attempting to resolve. Consequently, after the initial impact, a slowdown of activities will occur. The SEC acted as a very welcome motivating influence to move things along.

§ 8.27 Bankruptcy Code Provisions

Section 1109 states:

a The Securities and Exchange Commission may raise and may appear and be heard on any issue in a case under this chapter, but the Securities and Exchange Commission may not appeal from any judgment, order, or decree entered in the case.

b A party-in-interest, including the debtor, the trustee, a creditors' committee, an equity security holders' committee, a creditor, an equity security holder, or any indenture trustee, may raise and may appear and be heard on any issue in a case under this chapter.

This section limits the extent to which the SEC can directly participate in the proceedings under chapter 11. The SEC may raise, appear, and be heard on any issue but does not have the right to appeal. The SEC is not considered a party-in-interest. The significance of the party-in-interest is summarized in Collier:

> . . . a party in interest may request an appointment of a trustee or examiner under section 1104(a) and (b); may request termination in a trustee's appointment under section 1105; may request conversion of the chapter 11 case to a case under chapter 7 or 13 of the Code pursuant to section 1112(b); may file a plan under section 1121(c) and may request an extension of the debtor's time to file a plan under section 1121(d); may object to confirmation of a plan under section 1128(b); and may request revocation of confirmation under section 1144 of the Code.[3]

§ 8.28   SEC Policy

The Bankruptcy Code does not contain any provisions that direct the SEC to perform any particular function in bankruptcy proceedings. Thus, the role of the SEC in bankruptcy cases is, in the opinion of some, optional rather than mandatory. The SEC, however, stated in Corporate Reorganization Release No. 331 (February 2, 1984) that the tradition of active SEC participation is almost as old as the agency itself. The release further stated that in cases involving significant public investor interest, the SEC has a commitment to the protection of public investors. In this release, the SEC stated that reorganization cases will have a new focus, based on three major concerns:

1 There should be less day-to-day SEC participation in reorganization cases, provided public investors are adequately represented by the committee process.
2 The SEC should work closely with the U.S. trustees.
3 The SEC should avoid partisan involvement in negotiations for a plan of reorganization.

Thus, as a general matter, the SEC will focus its participation in chapter 11 on legal and policy issues that are of concern to public investors generally and that may have an impact beyond the facts of a particular case.

The SEC stated that it would continue to address matters of its traditional expertise and interest relating to securities. For example, the SEC may comment, where appropriate, on the adequacy of the disclosure statement and participate where the SEC has a law enforcement interest.

The SEC has been primarily involved with five major issues (excluding enforcement issues) in chapter 11 cases:

1 Fee allowances
2 Appointment of shareholders, creditors, or other committees
3 Appointment of examiners or trustees
4 Loan, sale, or lease of property prior to confirmation of a plan
5 Adequacy of disclosure

---

[3] *Collier's Bankruptcy Manual*, 3d ed., ¶ 1109.03(3)n.

Corporate Reorganization Release No. 331 indicated that the SEC would be less concerned in the future about the first four issues unless they involve public policy in general. The SEC's role, according to the Bankruptcy Code and Release No. 331, is not to be determined by the size of the assets' or liabilities' balances in the case. However, by the nature of the SEC's role, it will appear in the larger cases. During the first four years following the adoption of the Bankruptcy Code, the SEC appeared in 75 cases where debtor assets totaled almost $14 billion.

Since the issuance of this release, the SEC has remained fairly active in bankruptcy cases, but, as suggested by the release, it is directing its attention primarily to the significant issues in the cases that affect investors. Its activity in cases has changed focus and declined, but its right to appear in cases to see that public investors are adequately represented still exists.

The Bankruptcy Code does not alter the continuing disclosure requirements of a publicly held debtor. The SEC has maintained for some time that the reporting obligations under the Securities Exchange Act of 1934 are not suspended by the filing of a bankruptcy court petition. It is not anticipated that the SEC will change its position. Reporting provisions may, however, on occasions be relaxed for trustees or debtors-in-possession while operating during the bankruptcy proceeding, but as soon as the conditions merit, the full requirements of the reporting procedures will apply. Modification by the SEC of its requirements will generally be made only if such modifications are consistent with the public protection purposes of federal securities laws.

The staff of the SEC has a high level of technical knowledge. They can very frequently offer the attorneys, and to some extent the accountants, guidance as to how procedural problems may be resolved. They are a fertile source of information.

PROFESSIONAL CONDUCT OF ACCOUNTANTS

§ 8.29 Introduction

As in any engagement, the accountant must be competent and ethical. The role of the accountant is crucial in the proceedings, especially to the bankruptcy judge, who must preserve and restore the business, protect the rights of creditors, and decide between rehabilitation or liquidation. In making these decisions, the bankruptcy judge relies on the accountant for objective and unbiased opinions. It is important to remember that the accountant is a quasi-officer of the court and owes primary responsibility to it.

§ 8.30 Personal Liability—Preparation of Financial Statements

The accountant should adhere to generally accepted accounting principles and procedures in statement presentation. Full disclosure is required, as well as clear and unambiguous language, in the report relating to any procedures not undertaken by the debtor's independent accountant. These may include observation of physical inventory, confirmation of accounts receivable or cash in banks, verification of potential or present legal liabilities of the debtor, or verification of security arrangements. Generous use of footnotes and comments to the financial statements is advisable.

Where the practice has been to issue unaudited financial statements for the use of management only, particular care must be given by the debtor's independent accountant in the preparation of these financial statements as well as those submitted to a creditors' committee or other interested third parties. The accountant should follow the appropriate guidelines in Statements on Standards for Accounting and Review Services or Attestation Standards in issuing any statement, even though it may be intended for use primarily by management when appropriate. As discussed in Chapter 15, most services rendered in bankruptcy fall under the litigation guidelines and are not subject to the attestation standards and guidelines in Statements on Standards for Accounting and Review Services.

Because the report of the debtor's accountant is being examined by and relied on by third parties, the accountant must be extremely careful about reliance on management's oral representations as to various transactions, and must insist on written documentation. This danger often lurks in noncash transactions such as the following:

- Accounts receivable–accounts payable setoffs, where the same party is a customer and a creditor
- Satisfaction of a trade liability by the transfer of fixed assets
- Private arrangement involving the collection of a customer's account but an oral representation that the account is uncollectible

§ 8.31   Professional Conduct of Debtor's Accountant—Toward Client

At the time the client recognizes that a bankruptcy petition is imminent, there often exist unpaid bills for services rendered by the accountant. The decision as to whether to liquidate or reorganize will depend to a great extent on the information that the debtor's accountant prepares for review by the client and the attorney. The accountant must decide whether these additional, usually time-consuming, services should be rendered when payment for them is very doubtful. Both ethical and practical considerations are involved. The resolution of the ethical aspects depends on the standards and the subjective motives of the individual practitioner. Some aspects of the practical side of this question that have bearing on the ethical issues should be considered.

The withdrawal of the accountant's services at this time will not prevent allegations from arising, however unjustified, regarding the failure of the accountant to exercise professional judgment prior to the withdrawal. It may be easier for the accountant to explain the basis of professional acts as an actively participating party in contact with the debtor's attorney, incoming creditors' accountant, or the creditors' committee, rather than as an outsider looking in while unjustified assumptions are being made. The creditors' committee is interested in finding as many recoveries as possible. One source is from the legal and professional staff of the debtor. If there is any indication, whether justified or unjustified, that the accountants of the debtor failed to exercise due care, this is often pursued by the legal staff of the committee.

Withdrawal at this time subjects the accountant's client to the findings of the accountant for the creditors' committee and to the assumptions drawn in the course of that review. The presence of the debtor's accountant and personal contact with the accountant representing the creditors' committee can explain or document various transactions that otherwise might be damaging to the client in negotiations with the creditors. If the debtor's accountant withdraws before the books and records are completed, treatment of individual items is left to the accountant for the creditors' committee. An example of this occurred where an accountant for a trustee in bankruptcy, working on the uncompleted books and records of a bankruptcy partnership, treated bank debit memos entered on the bank statements as an item of cost of goods sold. This resulted in a deficit gross profit on sales, which the trustee successfully used in court to deny the discharge in bankruptcy of the partnership and the individual partners on the basis of fraud. In reality, the debit memos represented insufficient-funds checks of customers; however, the damage had been done and no amount of oral testimony could correct the matter. Premature withdrawal of accounting services from an ailing business operation may result in a disservice not only to the client but to the accountant as well.

The debtor's accountant should appraise the client of what the creditors expect and what the debtor should or should not do during the interim period from the time of determination of an imminent bankruptcy proceeding to the actual negotiations with creditors. The accountant will want to identify for the client the prepetition acts that can result in criminal fraud charges, obviate the cooperation of creditors, or prevent a discharge of debts. The client should be aware of the fact that, if the company's integrity is questioned, very little cooperation can be expected from the creditors.

§ 8.32   Professional Conduct of Debtor's Accountant—Toward Creditors' Accountant

The most frequent complaints of incoming independent accountants for creditors involve the difficulties encountered in obtaining the necessary books of account of the debtor and various documentary evidence as the investigation proceeds. The duty of the incoming accountant is to the creditors and to the court. There is no room here for camaraderie between accountants but only for the fulfillment of professional, legal, and ethical responsibilities. The debtor's accountant, therefore, should undertake to do the following in order to facilitate the work of the accountant for the creditors' committee:

- Assist in locating all books of accounts and records.
- Explain the debtor's accounting system.
- Aid in obtaining documents requested by the creditors' committee accountant.
- Permit the accountant for the creditors' committee to review the debtor's accountant's workpapers as they relate to specific questions raised. There would appear to be no obligation for the debtor's accountant to release possession of the workpapers for a general review by the creditors' accountant.

- Make available copies of all requested tax returns of the debtor and discuss potential trouble areas in the event of an audit by a taxing agency. Any records or information given to the creditors' committee by the debtors' accountant should first be cleared by the debtor unless, of course, the debtors' accountant is directed by the court to provide such information. Even under these conditions, it may be advisable to review with the debtor the information that is being submitted.

In one instance, an arrangement with creditors failed because of a New York City business tax audit assessment which reduced the available assets below the agreed settlement percentage. The reason for this unnecessary occurrence was the debtor's accountant's failure to forward copies of the debtor's tax returns as requested by the creditors' accountant. These returns revealed that the debtor had used an incorrect gross sales base in calculating the New York City business tax. If the creditors' accountant had been aware of this error, the potential audit assessment would have been considered in determining the percentage creditors would receive.

A question frequently asked the creditors' accountant by the creditors' committee is: "Did the debtor's accountant fully cooperate with you?" A negative answer will often result in the adoption of a poor attitude by the creditors' committee toward the debtor.

§ 8.33   Direct Liability to Third Parties

The degeneration of the financial condition of a client's business operation creates natural alarm among creditors, credit agencies, bank loan officers, and various other financial institutions dealing with the debtor. The debtor's accountant, who previously had no direct contact with third parties, becomes very popular with them as they search for additional financial information relating to the debtor. The general integrity of the independent accountant will, no doubt, cause these very same third parties to rely on any oral assertions made by the debtor's accountant. With complete awareness of professional status as it relates to conduct and to personal legal liability under these conditions, the accountant:

- Should not engage in off-the-record conversation or written communication with third parties.
- Should, officially and on the record, discuss the debtor's financial position when called on by a proper third party, but only as to information reflected on the books and records of the client. It is advisable not to give personal opinions as to the future prospects of the client, whether they be good or poor, regardless of the sincerity of a personal opinion.
- Should not submit a tentative financial statement to any third party unless all the required auditing standards and procedures and statement presentation standards have been followed.
- Should seriously weigh the advisability of extending good offices in securing additional financing for the client where, in the accountant's judgment, repayment is highly doubtful.

- Should avoid unofficial or informal contact with the various national and local credit reporting agencies but submit, as requested, financial statements fully documented and prepared in accordance with generally accepted accounting principles.

§ 8.34   Other Professional Ethical Factors

Many ethical questions are raised when the accountant is involved in bankruptcy and insolvency proceedings. One question that deserves careful consideration arises when the accountant serves both the debtor and the creditors. As discussed in Chapter 7, the accountant may not be engaged by both the debtor and the creditors' committee, but, in order to keep accountants' fees as low as possible, the creditors' committee may use the debtor's accountant. This situation gives rise to some possible conflicts of interest, one of the largest involving the level of disclosure for which the accountant is responsible. The creditors will want to know as much as possible about the operations of the debtor. However, to reveal everything may prove misleading and unduly detrimental to the debtor. In this position, the accountant must find the correct point between adequate disclosure so that creditors may protect their interests and avoidance of excess disclosure that may injure the debtor.

To avoid potential problems, the debtor's accountant may operate with the creditors' committee under the policy that information requests will first be cleared with the debtor. As long as the debtor allows its accountant to answer the inquiries of the creditors' committee, the accountant may serve both parties and significantly reduce administrative expenses. Once the debtor objects to an inquiry of the creditors' committee, the committee may need to retain its own accountant.

Another area of potential conflict is in evaluating the plan proposed by the debtor. If the services of an accountant are needed by the creditors' committee to assist in the evaluation of the debtor's plan, the debtor's accountant will most likely be unable to assist the committee and it will be necessary for the committee to retain its own accountant at this point. This issue is discussed more fully in § 7.4.

The accountant is often required to assist the creditors' committee in exercising control over the assets of the debtor. The accountant's independence would appear to be impaired by performance of functions for the debtor that are generally performed by management. The Ethics Division of the AICPA has ruled that the following functions cannot be performed if the accountant is to remain independent:

- Cosign checks issued by the debtor corporation.
- Cosign purchase orders in excess of established minimum amounts.
- Exercise general supervision to ensure compliance with the budgetary controls and pricing formulas established by management, with the consent of the creditors, as part of an overall program aimed at the liquidation of deferred indebtedness.

See the discussion of creditors' committees and their accountants in § 5.6.

9

Accounting and Financial Services for the Debtor-in-Possession or Trustee: Part 2

§ 9.1 Introduction

The debtor in most bankruptcy proceedings needs assistance in order to effectively regain the position once occupied when operations were profitable. Many factors are responsible for business failures, but, as noted in Chapter 2, the major cause is inefficient management. Management may lack training or experience in basic business methods, such as interpreting financial data, managing funds, scheduling production and shipping, coordinating departmental activities, and a range of other management functions. In a common situation, a manager may be an expert in a technical field, such as designing, but have little managerial ability for directing the activities of the business.

There are several ways in which accountants can help debtors overcome financial problems caused by inefficient management or other factors, and carry out some of the procedural steps that are necessary for an agreement to be reached with creditors. These were mentioned in the previous chapter, and two of them are described in more detail in this chapter—issuance of operating statements and management advisory services. Also described in this chapter are the extent to which computers are helpful in bankruptcy and the services that an accountant may render in a chapter 7 case.

REPORTS ISSUED DURING CHAPTER 11 PROCEEDINGS

§ 9.2 Local Requirements

Several different types of reports are required while the debtor is operating the business in a chapter 11 reorganization proceeding. The nature of the reports and the time period in which they are issued depend to some extent on local rules, on the type of internal controls used by the debtor, and on the extent to which large losses are anticipated.

Because local rules will have impact on the nature of the reports required, they will be described before discussing the actual statements.

Districts establish local bankruptcy rules that generally apply to all cases filed in those particular districts. These rules cover some of the procedural matters that relate to the handling of a bankruptcy case, including appearance before the court, forms of papers filed with court, assignment of case, administration of case, employment of professionals, and operating statements. The rules for the filing of operating statements have become primarily the responsibility of the U.S. trustee; as a result, the specific procedures for these statements are those of the U.S. trustee. Examples of some of the local rules for the Central District of California, including the rules relating to employment of professionals, are in 9.1 of Volume 2 of *Bankruptcy and Insolvency Accounting*. Other regions have similar rules. Guideline No. 1 lists the nine documents that must be filed with the U.S. trustee:

1   Real Property Questionnaire
2   Proof of Insurance
3   Most recently filed state and federal payroll tax returns
4   Most recently filed state sales tax return
5   Most recently prepared audited and unaudited financial statements
6   Proof of establishment of debtor-in-possession bank accounts for general, payroll, and tax accounts and declaration that prepetition bank accounts have been closed
7   Projected operating statement for the first 30 days of operation
8   Applications for compensation for owners, officers, and directors
9   Copy of trust agreements or conveyances (other than leases) related to debtor's operations

A copy of the Real Property Questionnaire follows Guideline No. 2 in 9.1 of Volume 2. Guideline No. 5 refers to the operating reports for the Central District of California. A copy of the format for these reports can be found in 9.2 of Volume 2. The Professional Fee Statement referred to in Guideline No. 18 is reproduced immediately following the Guideline.

§ 9.3   U.S. Trustee's Requirements

The U.S. trustee, in some regions, likes to meet with the debtor and its counsel within a few days after the petition is filed. Under some pilot programs, the requirement was for a meeting within two days. The Central District of California initially required a meeting within two days after the petition was filed with the debtor, but has now changed to a meeting with the debtor and the largest 20 creditors within ten days. It might be helpful if the debtor has his or her accountant or chief financial officer attend this first informal meeting. In addition to the U.S. trustee or the assistant U.S. trustee, a bankruptcy analyst with an accounting orientation will also be present.

If there is an early meeting with the debtor, the debtor will describe the nature of the business and its problems to the U.S. trustee and the bankruptcy analyst, who will be attempting to learn as much about the business as possible. The U.S. trustee will find out about any filing problems and discuss certain procedures with the debtor. For example, provision will have to be made for wages earned during the payroll period just prior to the filing, in order to encourage the employees to stay with the company. The procedures to be followed in opening new bank accounts, closing prepetition records, and establishing new records will be discussed. Another important problem that must be resolved is compensation for officers. The U.S. trustee will determine what is thought to be an appropriate salary scale and will subsequently confirm by letter that the amount established is subject to review by the creditors' committee. The salaries of officers are generally reduced and are determined after evaluating what the company can afford and what the individual officers need to survive. In establishing the salaries, the U.S. trustee should also realize that it is important to keep the key personnel in order to provide for smoother operations during the rehabilitation period. The debtor, of course, has the right to contest the salaries established for officers and let the court rule on the amounts that should be paid.

Other topics discussed at this meeting center around the reasons for financial difficulty and the problem areas. The U.S. trustee will want to know whether there are any cash collateral problems, whether a prefiling creditors' committee was appointed, and any additional information about how the committee was formed. The U.S. trustee is interested in finding out the kinds of steps the debtor plans to take to correct the financial problems.

The U.S. trustee will establish with the debtor the type of operating reports that should be filed and the timing of such reports. Also requested will be a report on the verification of insurance coverage.

In Volume 2 of *Bankruptcy and Insolvency Accounting*, 9.2 shows a notice mailed to all attorneys for chapter 11 cases filed in the Central District of California, in which the U.S. trustee has set forth the requirements expected during the period of bankruptcy. Timely compliance with each of the requirements is expected by the U.S. trustee unless a supplemental notice modifying any of the requirements is executed and served on the debtor by the U.S. trustee. A request for the modification of any of the requirements should be made by letter addressed to the U.S. trustee. The written request for modification must explain in detail the reasons for making the request.

A request to modify the reporting requirements may also be made in writing. However, as is discussed below, it may be helpful to request a meeting with the representative of the U.S. trustee's office to discuss the form of the operating report that will be issued.

In the Central District of California, a form must be filed for approval of compensation for all insiders—owners, partners, officers, directors, shareholders, and relatives of any insider. The covering notice used by the U.S. trustee and the form in its entirety are reproduced as 9.3 in Volume 2 of *Bankruptcy and Insolvency Accounting*.

§ 9.4   Operating Statements

A complete periodic profit-and-loss statement and, often, a statement of cash receipts and disbursements must be filed with the court as required by the local rules or a specific order of the court.

The U.S. trustee for the region that includes the judicial districts in the states of Connecticut, New York (including the Southern District of New York), and Vermont has issued a statement that contains requirements based on the provisions found in Statement of Position (SOP) 90-7, *Financial Report-*

ing by Entities in Reorganization under the Bankruptcy Code, issued by the AICPA. For example, the instructions indicate that the statement of operations is to be based on the accrual method and that the debtor's revenues, cost of goods sold, and operating/administrative expenses are to be distinguished from reorganization items in arriving at a profit or loss.

Accountants should carefully study the guidelines issued by the Districts of New York, Connecticut, and Vermont. These guidelines allow the accountant to prepare the operating statements in accordance with generally accepted accounting principles (GAAP). Most of the other regions, such as those for the Central District of California, have schedules that do not conform with GAAP. At the time this edition was going to the printer, the U.S. trustee System was considering issuing one set of requirements for operating reports that would apply to all regions. Some of the proposals that were being considered did not conform to GAAP. Others, such as those that were being considered for the Northern District of California, were designed to follow the requirements in SOP 90-7. Any changes that are made in the operating report requirements will be included in the supplements that are issued annually.

The guidelines for the Districts of New York, Connecticut, and Vermont require:

- Opening of new bank accounts
- Proof of appropriate insurance coverage
- Monthly financial statements, issued in accordance with SOP 90-7, including a balance sheet, a statement of operations, a statement of cash flows, a schedule of federal, state, and local taxes collected and remitted, and a statement that insurance coverage is current
- Annual financial statements

It would be very helpful to accountants and financial advisors if all 20 regions had the same requirements. The guidelines in effect for the judicial districts of Connecticut, New York, and Vermont are presented as 9.4 in Volume 2 of *Bankruptcy and Insolvency Accounting.*

The Northern District of California, which is in Region 17, has adopted new operating report guidelines that are effective January 1, 1995. These guidelines are based on the provisions of SOP 90-7. Guidelines are provided for three types of cases:

1 General business
2 Real estate
3 Individual or small real estate

Based on authority from the U.S. trustee or the court, the debtor may use an internally generated report format other than the required Monthly Operating Report. However, the alternative report must provide the information requested in the guidelines, consisting, at least, of the following:

- Financial statements prepared in accordance with GAAP, including SOP 90-7

- Data requested in the schedules, including:
  - Aging schedule of accounts receivable
  - Aging schedule of accounts payable
  - Separate schedule of inventory, including valuation methods
  - Schedule of real and depreciable assets, showing cost and market values
- A statement of operations including current month, case to date, variance analysis, and next month forecast data

A debtor that has assets of less than $2 million may submit an abbreviated monthly report on the prescribed forms for "Small Real Estate or Individual Case." The report will consist of a summary of financial status, a simplified balance sheet, the summary of cash receipts and disbursements, and copies of current bank statements.

The forms and instructions for cases filed in the Northern District of California are presented in 9.5 in Volume 2 of *Bankruptcy and Insolvency Accounting.*

Information required to be filed with these operating reports is available in Word and Excel on diskettes that are distributed to chapter 11 debtors.

The operating reports for the Judicial Districts of New York, Connecticut, and Vermont and the Northern District of California have features that should serve as the basis for uniform operating reports for all regions because these operating reports are based on SOP 90-7.

It is important that the operating statement be carefully prepared because it is the court's and the creditors' and their committees' major source of information concerning the financial operations of the debtor-in-possession. It should be prepared on an accrual basis and must be signed by the debtor or trustee. However, for many small businesses, a cash receipts and disbursements statement may be used with a separate schedule of receivables and payables.

The income statement filed with the court differs somewhat from the typical statement. The accountant generally prepares the report based on an estimated gross profit figure because it is highly unlikely that a physical inventory will be taken every month. It may be necessary to have a physical inventory taken every 90 days. This would, of course, depend on the type of internal accounting control the debtor has, the nature of the business, and the materiality of the inventory. Depreciation and other expenditures that do not require future cash outlays should be clearly identified in the statements and, if practical, presented in a separate category. For manufacturing concerns, it is important to identify the amount of depreciation and other noncash expenditures in the cost of goods sold. In some businesses, depreciation expense can be viewed as a cash outlay, as would be the case in businesses that lease out a large amount of equipment with a relatively short life, such as automobiles. Under these conditions, depreciation expense is helpful in providing some indication of the future viability of the company. Also, nonrecurring expenses should be clearly labeled because the U.S. trustee and creditors' committee are primarily interested in the next period's projected income. All liabilities that become due after the petition is filed should be paid by the debtor in the regular course of the business, as should taxes that relate to the period after filing. However, taxes that accrued before the petition was filed should not be paid by the debtor as a normal business transaction.

The statement of operations (income statement) should be prepared in accordance with SOP 90-7. If the statement does not meet the requirements of SOP 90-7 (even though it meets the requirements of the U.S. trustee) and the accountant prepared the statement or was associated with the statement, the accountant should indicate that the statement has not been prepared in accordance with generally accepted accounting principles (GAAP). Chapter 13 contains a discussion of how the statement should be prepared to meet the requirements of SOP 90-7.

In addition to the revenue and expense statement that is usually required, local rules may necessitate that a cash receipts and disbursements statement or statement of cash flows be filed also. Again, the format is not generally specified, but the typical format for a statement of cash flows can be used. Chapter 13 discusses the techniques that should be followed to present the statement of cash flows in accordance with GAAP. As was true with the operating statement, some of the requirements of the U.S. trustee's office are not in accordance with GAAP. If the accountant issues a cash flow statement according to a specific format that does not follow the requirements of SOP 90-7, the accountant should indicate that the statement is not prepared in accordance with GAAP.

MANAGEMENT ADVISORY SERVICES

§ 9.5 Introduction

Until recently, most accountants and financial advisors actively involved in bankruptcy proceedings were primarily performing auditing and investigative services. There are, however, many opportunities for accountants to serve in a consultant capacity that can be of considerable benefit to management. Because of the many day-to-day problems the debtor has faced in the last few months prior to the time the petition is filed, the debtor spends most of its time trying to solve these problems and attempting to keep the corporation out of bankruptcy court in the short run. With this perspective the management of the business finds it very difficult to evaluate objectively the long-term prospects for the company.

The debtor needs direction in clearly defining its objectives and in preparing forecasts of future operations. Not only must these kinds of decisions be made, but they must be made in a relatively short time period if the company expects to regroup and resume profitable operations. For example, in a retail operation, a large number of stores may have to be closed, inventory that is obsolete must be liquidated, and the shelves must be restocked with inventory items that will sell. To make these kinds of short-run decisions and to evaluate carefully the available opportunities, if any, the debtor may find special studies and analyses made by accountants very helpful. Consultants may be retained by the debtor and/or creditors' committee to render services even before a decision is made as to whether the debtor can be rehabilitated. For example, in the W. T. Grant bankruptcy, a Chapter XI case, the finding by the consultants of an advanced state of deterioration in the retailing operations was a primary reason for the decision of the creditors' committee to recommend liquidation rather than rehabilitation under Chapter XI. Indeed, in this case, consultants were retained by both the debtor and the creditors' committee.[1]

The consulting activities discussed in this chapter are the business plan, forecast of future operations, and turnaround services.

§ 9.6 Business Plan

Many companies do not have any type of business or strategic plan at the time they attempt to work out some form of arrangement with creditors out of court or in a chapter 11 proceeding. Until the date the petition is filed, management personnel will have devoted most of their time to day-to-day problems, without analyzing the major financial problems faced by the business. They fail to ask questions that are most important for the survival of the business, such as:

- What products are most profitable?
- What are the strengths and weaknesses of the company?
- What areas should be expanded? liquidated?
- In what areas does the real potential for this business lie?
- What direction should this business take?

The greater the financial problems, the more time management devotes to day-to-day details; thus, almost no time is spent on providing direction for the company.

After the petition is filed, it is frequently left up to the bankruptcy court and the creditors to make strategic decisions that significantly influence the future of the business. They may decide which operations to eliminate and which products to discontinue. These decisions are made on a quasi-intuitive basis. For example, selected equipment may be sold or retained based on the influence of particular creditors rather than on the basis of an overall business plan.

In rendering advisory services to help develop a business plan, the accountant examines all the information that is available, analyzes it with a view toward future prospects, and develops recommendations. These recommendations may involve closing unprofitable units, replacing poor management, changing the information system, and revising the marketing approach. Some of the recommendations, such as closing some unprofitable operating units, are implemented while the company is in chapter 11 proceedings, and the effect is known immediately. Other strategic plans have a long-range effect, but they still have an impact on the nature of the company that comes out of

---

[1] See Bankruptcy Reform Act of 1978; Hearings on S. 2266 and H.R. 8200 before the Subcommittee on Improvements in Judicial Machinery, 95th Cong., 1st Sess. 587 (1977) (Statement of John J. Jerome).

the proceedings. A business plan allows all interested parties to have a better idea of what parts of the operations are salvageable, and it provides for better understanding of a plan proposed by the debtor.

The analysis required to make reasonable recommendations must involve an assessment of the environmental forces (past, present, and future) influencing the business and an evaluation of the strengths and weaknesses of the company. See Chapter 3 for a detailed discussion of those concepts.

(a) Illustration of Business Plan

Using a hypothetical example, 9.6 of Volume 2 of *Bankruptcy and Insolvency Accounting* contains some excerpts from a business plan developed for a fictitious company, Company ABC, in a chapter 11 case under the Bankruptcy Code. Two business plans were prepared by this company—one for retail operations and the other for nonretail operations. Included in this example are a management summary, three parts of operations review ((1) introduction, (2) manufacturing division summary, and (3) analysis of the beverage company), and part of an analysis of a division that was liquidated while keeping the centralized purchasing function for produce. The plan developed for each of the operating units consists of (1) an overview of the nature of this unit's activities, (2) past operating results, (3) operating capital requirement, (4) risks and alternatives, and (5) conclusions. The report issued was the result of a top-down review of all operations performed early in the case to identify operations that should be terminated or those that represented the potential to be a part of a "New Company ABC." There were specific criteria developed that the operation review summary attempted to follow to make judgments about each operation. Subsequent studies would be necessary to demonstrate the feasibility of the plan eventually proposed by Company ABC.

The kinds of services that accountants can render for businesses in financial difficulty provide for a more orderly rehabilitation of the business and result in benefit to all parties involved in the proceedings.

§ 9.7 Financial Projections

In § 8.16, it was pointed out how important it is to prepare projections of future operations to show that the reorganization plan is feasible. The benefits gained from projection of future operations go beyond whether the plan of reorganization is feasible. These projections are developed in conjunction with the development of an effective business plan and are crucial in determining the long-run prospects for the company. The projections are used to determine the value of the business as a going concern and to help determine the interest creditors and stockholders have in the reorganized company. Accountants often take an active role in helping to prepare financial projections and in evaluating the assumptions on which they are based. As an example of the projected financial information contained in a disclosure statement, 9.7 in Volume 2 presents the disclosure statement issued by Federated Department Stores. The principal assumptions used in the development of the projections are summarized.

COMPUTERS IN BANKRUPTCY

§ 9.8   Introduction

Many of the required services involved in a bankruptcy proceeding have been computerized. The use of computer models greatly reduces the amount of time involved and the risk of errors. In a complicated and drawn-out court situation, the use of computers can greatly facilitate arriving at an equitable agreement between debtors and creditors, while at the same time substantially reducing the administrative expenses incurred. Computers may be used to assist the debtors' or creditors' committee in managing the proceeding; to help process claims; to help develop the plan; to obtain relevant data for legal, accounting, or tax research; to develop simulation models; to evaluate various ways to solve the debtors' financial problems; and to develop cash forecasts, budgets, and other accounting systems and reports.

Models are available for both mainframe and microcomputer applications. Some systems are used to determine the best course of action for a debtor in a given scenario, and others will go as far as handling the actual processing and distribution of many of the forms, verifications, and notifications required by the Bankruptcy Code. This latter service was made possible by an August 1983 law that authorized the use of computer processing and mailings of various bankruptcy-related notices and documents.

§ 9.9   Proceeding Management and Claim Processing

One of the earliest and most comprehensive systems for managing the proceeding and for processing claims was developed by Itel Corporation during its management of the large chapter 11 reorganization that it went through in the 1970s. The Itel Corporation Bankruptcy Support Service (IBANK) allows debtors to process much of the information and to do the actual mailings of documents on their mainframe system. IBANK is most valuable to debtors involved in extensive proceedings that relate to large numbers of secured and unsecured creditors.

Underlying criteria such as interest rate trends, projected earnings, changes within a given industry, different alternatives available for financing, the amount of contingent claims, and the outcome of related lawsuits are used to set up the model. The computer system can then "crunch the numbers" and display potential results very rapidly. Through altering the assumptions, different scenarios can be run to see potential outcomes and to help management determine the best course of action to take. This kind of service is especially helpful when decisions must be made rapidly in the course of lengthy negotiations. Having access to information when it is needed can be a very powerful ally when dealing with a creditors' committee. The outcome of various alternatives can be evaluated and displayed immediately to the parties involved.

One of the major advantages offered by these proceeding management systems is that they can prepare and mail required documents automatically. For example, if the schedules of assets and liabilities have been posted and subsequent changes require their modification, the systems can update and post the new schedules. Certain time limitations that apply to the filing of claims, amendments, objections to claims, withdrawal, or settlement are built into the program. This helps management to avoid the negative consequences of missing dates that are specified by law, and ensures that the claims and modifications thereto of creditors, when not filed in a timely fashion, are not allowed.

For example, one system uses a multifield database to help debtors deal with the complexities of a bankruptcy. Creditors' files can be sorted in terms of classes of creditors, priorities of claims, and so on, and then arranged alphabetically within these categories. Notices sent to creditors include all the necessary information such as the amount of a claim and its current status. Ongoing information that changes over time is constantly updated. This could include the assessment of market values of collateral pledged as security, other assets that are not pledged as security, distributions made during the course of a chapter 11 case, and changes to or withdrawals of claims. Creditors are kept current on the proceedings of a case through the use of automatically prepared and mailed notices. Telephone inquiries are answered by the system as they are entered through automatic mailings.

In each bankruptcy case, a large number of reports and schedules must be prepared and submitted to the court, all of which have to be prepared and filed within a predetermined and properly sequenced schedule. For example, the disclosure statement must be submitted before the debtor can attempt to obtain approval of the plan. In some cases, it is very helpful to develop a PERT system to help manage the proceedings and to assist with the personnel and physical resources planning.

Several of the larger accounting firms have developed models to handle the claim processing of both large and small businesses. These claim processing models are run on both mainframe and microcomputers. For example, a model developed by one firm provides, among other features, the following:

- All the various formats of claims needed by the bankruptcy court
- Needed information for management to review and evaluate each claim
- Mailing lists and labels
- Creditor statements
- On-line update and inquiry capability
- Modeling and decision analysis capability, which enables management to evaluate settlement alternatives efficiently

Another area where computers can be of considerable value to the debtor in bankruptcy, or in trying to develop a settlement out of court, is in the evaluation of a plan of reorganization. A model can help the debtors' or creditors' committee assess the impact of various courses of action. For example, one firm has developed a system that will help in developing the terms of the plan, incorporating the speed and efficiency of computers and a menu-driven, user-friendly presentation. The system is based on the spreadsheet capabilities of Lotus 1-2-3, one of the most popular programs on the market for use with IBM or IBM-compatible personal computers. All of the necessary forms and schedules are accessed through the menu. As new or updated information arrives, the form that is required is brought up on the screen, and corrections and new entries are made. This program allows management to formulate plans of reorganization for chapter 11 proceedings and to keep the plan current with new information.

The outcome of a reorganization plan depends on a variety of assumptions. Some of these have been mentioned; others would include such things as the creditors' willingness to accept different mixes of cash and securities; economic trends; possible sources for financing continuing operations or acquisitions; and many other factors. These assumptions can be altered one at a time, with all else held constant, and the possible courses of action can be analyzed according to the needs of management. Using this technique, creditors or the debtor can identify potential problem areas and request clarifications. Once these have been received and entered into the system, a new set of comparisons is made and the process is repeated until both sides are satisfied that the most favorable course is being pursued.

Breakdowns of reorganization plans by computer models allow debtors and creditors to focus on the financial data that are most relevant to the case at hand. Time is not lost working on details that have little or no bearing on the final decision. Once these decisions have been made and a definitive plan has been formulated, computer-generated ballots will be sent to all of the creditors along with the disclosure statement, plan, and other information. Because the law requires that balloting take place over a specific period of time set by the bankruptcy judge, the voting process must be accomplished as efficiently as possible.

A number of other companies and individuals have developed or are working on systems for computer application that are designed to do part or all of the previously mentioned services. Some of these developed out of general applications; others were outgrowths of specific bankruptcy proceedings.

§ 9.10   Databases

The extensive databases established for the legal profession are of special use in bankruptcy situations. The LEXIS service of Mead Data Central and Westlaw's West Publishing Service are available for a subscription price. Using these services allows accountants and attorneys to review precedents that may affect the outcome of the cases they are working on. All of the cases decided during the past half-century (and more) by the district and appeals courts and the Supreme Court are available and can be searched for applications. A wealth of other data can also be accessed, such as chapter 11 of the Bankruptcy Code, manuals on bankruptcy proceedings, the actual forms that must be used, and other related materials. Cases can be accessed directly, the database can be searched by subject matter, and the decisions and history of particular judges can be reviewed. Much of this research can be done by support staff, which saves considerable expense.

In addition to databases described above additional information can be obtained through the Internet. For example several districts currently require bankruptcy petitions, motions and documents be filed through the Internet resulting in much easier access to this information. Eventually all of the bankruptcy courts will require that all documents be filed electronically. SEC filings, including 10K and 8K reports, are available from several sources including LEXIS/NEXIS and Edgar to provided financial and related information about public companies.

§ 9.11 Tracking Professional Costs

Other systems have been developed, including those that allow debtors to monitor the costs of outside and in-house professionals retained during chapter 7 or chapter 11 proceedings, and to evaluate the efficiency and effectiveness of these services. The system can also prepare calendars that include the appropriate schedules for filing of claims and stays; the dates for pleas; the timing of notices; and how the statutes of limitations will affect the case. Keeping track of the time and costs of professionals and support staff can be complex, and computers facilitate an efficient allocation of these resources. Having accurate and up-to-date records can be very important in a bankruptcy case where the judge is to determine the extent to which administrative claims are to be paid. The lack of good records may result in the judge's denying reimbursement for services rendered.

§ 9.12 Predicting Bankruptcy

Models have been developed that can predict the likelihood of an impending bankruptcy. For example, the Zeta score of Dr. Edward I. Altman can easily be applied through the use of a computer. Investors, lenders, creditors, and debtors can all benefit from these models when making decisions relating to their businesses. Other more complicated models have been developed which take into account different variables and can be applied to a longer-term analysis of the financial position of a company. Gamblers' Ruin, by Computer Aided Decisions, Incorporated, bases the prediction of bankruptcy on an analysis of the market net worth of a company versus the total liabilities. Another application is to make a study of corporate strategy and trends within an industry in order to make long-term predictions about the possibility of bankruptcy. This approach could prove especially valuable because it may give debtors enough time to take remedial action and avoid potential problems. See § 2.22.

The preceding discussion has covered a few of the applications of computers in bankruptcy situations. The listing of companies involved is intended to be demonstrative rather than comprehensive. There is a wide range of uses that can be of great value to the professional. As time passes and the use of computers increases, more applications will develop and new models will become popular.

ACCOUNTING SERVICES—CHAPTER 7 AND CHAPTER 11 LIQUIDATIONS

§ 9.13 Introduction

The remaining paragraphs of this chapter describe the procedures for liquidating a business under chapter 7. The services accountants render in a chapter 11 proceeding where a liquidation plan is adopted are similar to those in a chapter 7 liquidation case. Thus, the discussion here of services under chapter 7 is also applicable to a chapter 11 liquidation case.

§ 9.14 Items Requiring Immediate Attention

The importance of taking early action in a liquidation is very similar to that in a chapter 11 case where the accountant represents the creditors' committee. Even though a trustee is appointed in a chapter 7 case, it is still important that the accountant work with the trustee to see that the debtor's assets are not concealed. The types of items that need immediate attention are discussed in § 10.8. Among them are taking an inventory or obtaining possession of all of the debtor's books and records. Where fraud is suspected, the accountant may assist the trustee in securing all the debtor's books and records and transferring them to a suitable location. Speed is of the utmost importance in the removal process, for several reasons. Such records often disappear with no explanation as to their whereabouts. They may be disposed of innocently by persons who have no idea of their value. The trustee normally wants to vacate the premises as quickly as possible, to minimize rental expense. Thus, quick removal means greater assurance that the records will be adequately safeguarded. It is highly desirable that the accountants supervise this activity, because they are best able to determine which books are most useful and therefore should be preserved.

The accountant may assist the trustee in establishing controls over cash and other assets. The accountant also may be engaged to take a physical inventory and to inventory the property, plant, and equipment of the debtor.

§ 9.15 Performance of Audits and Other Special Investigations

The accountant may be engaged to investigate the past actions of the debtor. Transactions that could have resulted in the dissipation of the debtor's assets in a manner other than by loss in the ordinary course of business are examined closely. In the investigation, the accountant must be alert for irregular transfers, improper transactions with related parties, concealment of assets, false entries and statements, financing irregularities, or preferential payments. A comparison of the statements filed by the debtor with the company's records may reveal deliberate discrepancies, missing books or records, alterations, or fraud, as indicated by an inconsistent age of the records. In the audit of a liquidating business, attention is focused on the balance sheet; the statement of operations is of very little importance. (See Chapter 12 for a more detailed discussion of investigative services in bankruptcy situations.)

§ 9.16 Reconciliation of Debts with Proofs of Claims

Accountants frequently are engaged to reconcile the claims shown on the debtor's books with the proofs of claims that are filed with the court. This process can take considerable time.

§ 9.17 SIPC Liquidation

Accountants may be engaged to render services for the trustee in the liquidation of a stockbroker. Fees for administrative expenses (including accounting services) are paid out of the general estate of the stockbroker. However, if funds are not available from the estate to cover administrative expenses, they are covered by the Securities Investor Protection Corporation (SIPC).

In an SIPC liquidation, the accountant works directly with the trustee in helping to control the assets of the brokerage firm to satisfy customer accounts and to liquidate the brokerage firm. Accountants also prepare various types of financial statements, including liquidation statements for companies in chapter 7 and for SIPC liquidations. These statements are discussed in Chapter 13. See §§ 5.52–5.57 for a discussion of SIPC liquidations.

10

Accounting and Financial Services for the Creditors' Committee

NATURE OF CREDITORS' COMMITTEE

§ 10.1 Introduction

The creditors' committee is the representative and bargaining agent for the creditors. The committee often needs an accountant to assist them in protecting their interests. This chapter describes the aspects of the services rendered by the accountant that relate to the creditors' committee. The accountant or financial advisor, in order to adequately represent the creditors, must be thoroughly familiar with the manner in which the creditors' committee works. The services rendered by the accountant or financial advisor include providing a direction for the committee, helping the committee manage the case, assisting the committee in exercising adequate control over the debtor's activities, investigating the operations of the business, determining whether there is a basis for successful future operations, evaluating the debtor's business plan, and assisting the committee in evaluating or developing a proposed plan of out-of-court settlement or bankruptcy reorganization. Unless specified differently, the term "accountant" as used in this chapter refers to either an independent accountant or a financial advisor engaged by the creditors' committee.

Section 1102 of the Bankruptcy Code provides that a committee of unsecured creditors is to be appointed in a chapter 11 case. In addition, the section provides that other committees of creditors of other classes and committees of equity holders may be appointed. The conditions under which more than one committee may be appointed are discussed in § 6.6.

The creditors' committee may be an unofficial or official committee. It is known as an unofficial committee if it is formed without the authorization of the bankruptcy court. If the committee is appointed under the provisions of the Bankruptcy Code, it is known as an official committee. As was discussed in Chapter 4, there are no rigid rules governing the formation of the committee in out-of-court matters. However, the Bankruptcy Code (section 1102) provides that the U.S. Trustee shall appoint the committee and it will ordinarily consist of the seven largest unsecured creditors willing to serve. If a committee was established before the bankruptcy petition was filed, this committee may be allowed to continue provided the committee was fairly chosen and is representative of the different kinds of claims to be represented. Although the functions performed by the committee may vary depending on the particular case, the circumstances surrounding the case, and the type of remedy sought, the objective is basically the same: to provide the supervision and control essential to protect the interests of the creditors.

The creditors' committee is the "watchdog" over the activities of the debtor. The committee examines all aspects of the firm's operations, including an evaluation of the assets and liabilities. During the period while a plan is being formalized and the period immediately following the acceptance, the committee should closely and constantly supervise the debtor's business, in order to be sure that the assets do not continue to be diminished, wasted, or diverted.

The importance of the creditors' committee in chapter 11 proceedings cannot be overemphasized. The objective of the committee is similar to that of the SEC in Chapter X proceedings under prior law, in that it counterbalances the strong position of control given to the debtor by the Bankruptcy Act. Under prior law, the debtor alone could seek relief under Chapter XI,[1] had the right to petition for continuation in possession,[2] could solicit for acceptance of a proposed plan either before or after filing,[3] and was able to offer amendments or modifications to the plan.[4] Under these conditions, complete dominance by the debtor could be overcome only by active participation of the creditors' committee throughout all stages of the proceedings.

The new chapter 11 provisions give the creditors more opportunity to participate in the proceedings in selected areas. For example, the creditors can force the debtor into a chapter 11 reorganization proceeding and can, under certain conditions, file a plan. The debtor will still, in most cases, continue to operate the business, and actions of the creditors will be focused through the creditors' committee or committees. Thus, the importance of the creditors' committee has not been diminished by the new law.

The involvement of the bankruptcy judge has been changed by the Bankruptcy Code. Prior to this Code, the judge performed both administrative and judicial functions. In general, under the Bankruptcy Code the judge is restricted to judicial matters and will not be involved in the operations of the business except to resolve disputes in an adversary context. The Bankruptcy Reform Act of 1994 gave more power to bankruptcy judges to more effectively manage cases. Section 104(a) of the Act authorized bankruptcy judges to hold status conferences in bankruptcy cases and thereby manage their dockets in a more efficient and expeditious manner and to monitor the cases to see that all parties are moving toward agreeing on a plan of reorganization. The judge will not, however, preside over the meeting of creditors. The U.S. trustee is responsible for the administrative aspects of the case. The U.S. trustee appoints the unsecured creditors' committee and other creditors' or equity interests' committees when authorized by the court or when the U.S. trustee deems appropriate (section 1102). See § 6.4 and § 9.3. Even with the U.S. trustee responsible

---

[1] Bankruptcy Act, §§ 321–22.
[2] *Id.*, 342.
[3] *Id.*, 336.
[4] *Id.*, 363.

for the administrative functions of the case, the creditors' committee has greater responsibility under the Bankruptcy Code. Section 1103(c) provides that the tasks of the creditors' committee are:

- To conduct an investigation of the financial affairs of the debtor
- To determine whether the business should continue to operate
- To participate in the formulation and solicitation of a plan
- To request the appointment of a trustee or examiner if such appointment is considered necessary
- To consult with the trustee or debtor-in-possession concerning the administration of the case
- To perform other services that are in the best interests of the creditors represented by the committee

In summary, the role of the accountant for the creditors' committee is to provide direction for the committee and to help it accomplish the tasks listed above.

§ 10.2   Directing Activities of Committee

Some of the most important services the accountant can render for the committee involve providing direction for the committee. In some cases, members of the committee may have limited experience serving in this capacity and/or may be unfamiliar with the debtor's type of business. In other cases, the committee may be primarily composed of full-time workout specialists representing major banks and other financial lenders. Even in the latter situation, the committee needs direction from the accountant or financial advisor. The accountant plays a key role in helping the committee assess the causes of the debtor's problems, the parts of the business that have prospects for future profitable operations, and the extent to which management has the ability to turn the business around.

§ 10.3   Data

For the committee to be able to know the type of action that should be taken, a significant amount of data needs to be collected. The accountant or financial advisor can help the committee determine the type of information needed and when it is needed. Obtaining the information that the committee needs is not easy, especially when the debtor prefers to have the committee simply review the data that are provided to the committee through the debtor. The committee often needs to answer these critical questions at the beginning of the case: Should this business be liquidated or reorganized? What is the nature of the controls? What aspects of the debtor's operations demand the immediate attention of the committee?

To obtain the type of information needed by the committee, agreements should be worked out between the debtor and the committee to share information among the accountants or financial advisors and other professionals involved in the case.

§ 10.4   Bargaining Process

One of the basic functions performed by the creditors' committee is to negotiate a settlement and then make its recommendation to the other creditors.
An accountant who is familiar with the bargaining process that goes on
between the debtor and the creditors' committee in trying to reach a settlement can participate in the process and may even take the lead role. Bargaining can be both vigorous and delicate. The debtor bargains, perhaps, for a
settlement that consists of a small percentage of the debt, one that demands
only a small cash outlay now with payments to be made in the future. The
debtor may want the debts outstanding to be subordinated to new credit or
may ask that the agreement call for partial payment in preferred stock. The
creditors want a settlement that represents a high percentage of the debt and
consists of a larger cash down payment with the balance to be paid as soon as
possible. If the creditors demand too high a percentage, the company may be
forced to liquidate, either immediately or at some future date, because it cannot make a large payment and still continue to operate. Creditors must not
insist on more than the debtor has the ability to pay. However, creditors have
refused to accept a reasonable settlement that is very low because it establishes a bad example in the industry. In some trade areas, all parties involved
are almost of one large fraternity. Rutberg suggested:

> A meeting of creditors is like old home week. Everyone seems to know everyone
> else and there is much shaking of hands and slapping of backs and general good
> fellowship. It's something like the funeral of a lady who died at ninety-five after a
> full life and who left a great fortune to be divided up among the surviving rela-
> tives.[5]

The creditors do not want to establish a precedent with a settlement that is too
low. As a result, the creditors' committee may demand that the debtor be liquidated although they will receive less than would have been received from a
low out-of-court settlement or a plan of reorganization.

Some basic guidelines may be applicable in certain situations in the bargaining process. If a cash payment is called for in the proposal in full or partial
settlement, the down payment should at least be equal to the probable dividend to creditors if the business were liquidated. To offer this much is a strong
selling point for the debtor. Creditors may, in some cases, not accept anything
less. When a settlement calls for future payments, the creditors' committee
often insists that the payments be secured. The security may be in the form of
notes of the debtor endorsed by its officers or other individuals acceptable to
the committee. The creditors may also desire a mortgage on the debtor's real
estate, security interest in a patent or franchise right, a pledge of stock of a subsidiary, or other forms of security.

As another alternative, creditors may insist on the execution of a trust indenture and security agreement giving them a lien on all assets of the business as
security for the debtor's performance of the settlement or plan of reorganization.

In cases where very little cash is available for debt repayment on confirma-

[5] Sidney Rutberg, *Ten Cents on the Dollar* (New York: Simon & Schuster, 1973), p. 45.

tion, unsecured creditors may be interested in obtaining most of the outstanding stock of the company. Since the early 1980s, the creditors of public companies have received an increasing interest in the ownership of the debtor. It is not unusual for the creditors to own between 80 and 95 percent of the outstanding stock of the emerging equity. For example, Wickes's creditors received 84 percent ownership, and the existing equity of Emmons Industries retained only 3 percent interest while creditors received the balance. In some of the leveraged buyouts that have filed chapter 11, the stockholders received no equity in the reorganized entity, as was the case in Revco.

The debtor may be required to reduce expenses that the creditors consider excessive, such as travel and entertainment and officers' salaries.

§ 10.5 Role of Creditors' Accountant in the Bargaining Process

The services that the accountant may render for the creditors' committee in the negotiations with the debtor will vary significantly, depending on several factors—the size of the debtor, the experience of the members of the creditors' committee, the nature of the debtor's operations, and the confidence the creditors' committee has in the debtor and in the professionals, especially the attorneys and accountants, who are helping the debtor. The committee in most cases will, to varying degrees, depend on the accountant to help them evaluate the debtor's operations, the information provided about those operations, and the terms of a proposed plan. Some accountants are very effective at taking the lead role in negotiating with the debtor on behalf of the creditors. The business experience of these professionals and the knowledge they have gained in the process of collecting data about the debtor's operations provide them with the type of background that is needed to develop workable terms for a plan of reorganization.

The following paragraphs present the particular functions an accountant or financial advisor might perform in an out-of-court workout for a committee of unsecured creditors of a relatively small company. It is assumed that the accountant was first engaged to do a special investigation of the debtor's operations. (When following through in this example, readers should remember that the nature of the committee's activities and the accountant's services may vary considerably.)

A creditors' committee meeting may be called as soon as the accountant has completed the special investigation. If there is enough time, the report will be given in advance to all members of the committee. A copy may also be given to the debtor in advance; however, some committees request that the debtor not be given a copy of the report, other than the balance sheet, before the meeting. In an unofficial committee case, where time is crucial, especially in the textile industry, it is not unusual for the accountant to complete the special investigation only a day or two before the meeting. In other cases, the accountant sends the report to the committee members in advance of the meeting.

The first order of business is for the accountant to discuss the report orally with the committee. The highlights of the report should be pointed out, any irregularities discovered by the accountant should be described, and the reasons for the debtor's financial difficulty should be discussed. The creditors will generally want to know the type of cooperation the accountant received from the debtor in the investigation, and whether they are dealing with an "honest" debtor.

The accountant may, at this meeting, go over the statement of financial position in general. Then each item will be analyzed, and liquidating values will be assigned on the assumption that the business will be liquidated. (For an example of the type of statement of financial position that is issued, see Exhibits 13.1 and 13.2, on pages 526–528 and 530–531. Normally, the accountant does not use liquidation values in preparing this statement; it is based on the going-concern assumption. See §§ 15.12–15.17.) Liquidating values are established on the basis of the information gained from the accountant's examination and inquiries, the knowledge of the creditors at the meeting, and any appraisals that have been made (see § 8.6). If the company is very large, the accountant may prepare for the committee a statement of affairs, which would contain the liquidating values (§ 13.12). The accountant may be reluctant to prepare a statement of affairs for this meeting without performing additional auditing procedures and inquiries, but there is usually not enough time or funds available for this additional work. If the accountant prepares the statement of financial position in accordance with the format in Exhibit 13.2, where the assets are reduced by the amount of the obligation for which they are pledged, the statement will facilitate the discussion.

The committee, with the assistance of the accountant, will determine the amount that will be available from the sale of the assets after all priorities are paid. The administrative fees are estimated, and the balance represents the amount that would be available to unsecured creditors, a year or two hence.

After looking at the liquidation values, the committee reviews the value of the emerging entity as a going concern. The accountant may have prepared a cash flow projection for the committee for the next five years. Based on the cash flows and a selected discount rate, the committee attempts to ascertain the value of the business. Using this value, the creditors' committee then determines a range for the consideration it should receive. The form of this consideration, as discussed below, may vary, depending on several factors. In large cases, the creditors' committee may have an investment banker, an appraisal company consultant, an accountant, or financial advisor prepare an analysis indicating the value of the business. As discussed in § 8.17, the key to the bargaining process is the determination of the reorganization value of the emerging entity.

At this point, the debtor and debtor's counsel are brought into the meeting. The debtor's counsel will present the defense of the debtor's operations, and may point out the cause of the financial difficulty and the steps management is prepared to take to prevent the problem from recurring. The counsel then indicates, if the debtor is ready, the terms of the debtor's offer to the creditors. With the assistance of the accountant and the creditors' counsel, the committee will question the debtor about the plan. After considerable discussion about the proposed plan, the committee will send the debtor out of the room and discuss the plan with the accountant and counsel. Based on the proposal of the debtor, the creditors' committee can ascertain the value the debtor is placing on the emerging entity. If the creditors' committee thinks this value is too large, it may question the debtor as to how it was determined. Interested parties may need to resolve the issue of reorganization value before any type of agreement can be reached on the terms of the plan. Once the parties reach some type of consensus as to the value of the reorganization entity, discussion focuses on allocation of the debt and equity interests. The committee may reject the plan as it is and submit to the debtor a plan that is acceptable to them, or they may simply suggest that the plan be modified, such as by increasing the cash payment by $.15 per dollar of debt or by giving the creditors an additional 10 percent ownership of the emerging entity. The negotiations will continue until they come to a consensus, or until it is determined that a consensus cannot be obtained at this meeting. In a chapter 11 case, where time is not as critical, the committee will most likely want additional time to study the plan and compare, with the assistance of the accountant, the settlement amount with liquidation values.

The accountant for the creditors' committee will go over the plan with the committee and its counsel, make suggestions as to how it should be modified, and answer any questions the committee has about the plan. Revisions to the plan are developed and submitted to the committee for the next negotiating session.

§ 10.6 Form of Consideration

The form of consideration that is eventually given to the creditor will depend on many factors, including the amount of cash available on confirmation, the debtor's ability to obtain postpetition financing, the amount (if any) of unpledged assets, the nature of the business, cash flow projections, and the postconfirmation debt-to-equity relationship. However, the total amount of consideration will be related to the reorganization value of the emerging entity. For example, if (based on the reorganization value) the unsecured creditors decide they want at least 90 percent of that value, the 90 percent equity may be constituted in a number of ways. In such a case, the unsecured creditors may prefer to receive 80 percent of the value in the form of debt, and another 10 percent in the form of 50 percent of the common stock. However, emergence from bankruptcy with this much debt would make it difficult to obtain postpetition financing. Thus, the unsecured creditors might settle for 50 percent of the reorganized value in the form of debt, and 80 percent ownership of equity to ensure 90 percent of the reorganized value. In addition, the unsecured creditors might bargain for an extra 10 percent of stock ownership to compensate for the additional risk of owning stock rather than debt.

MONITORING DEBTOR'S ACTIVITIES

§ 10.7 Introduction

Services for the creditors' committee can be broken down into two categories: (1) a situation where the creditors' committee needs the accountant to assist it with immediate action, and (2) services that can be spread over several months.

§ 10.8   Areas Requiring Immediate Attention

The environment that the creditors' committee works under varies significantly. At one extreme, it is important in some cases that the creditors obtain control of the business as soon as possible, obtain all of the books and records, and take an inventory of the merchandise and other property. In other situations, it is necessary for the creditors to obtain only an understanding of the nature of the business and its problem areas and to be able to effectively evaluate the actions proposed by the debtor. As soon as the accountant or financial advisor for the creditors' committee is appointed, an immediate assessment must be made of the environment and the approach that should be taken. To make this assessment, the accountant or financial advisor should discuss the situation generally with both a representative of the creditors' committee and its counsel. In this discussion, the accountant or financial advisor must be satisfied that the necessary controls are in place to prevent the asset base from continuing to deteriorate. Often, it will be necessary for the accountant to make an immediate visit to the debtor's offices in order to observe the nature of the operations and the types of controls that exist for cash, inventory, and other property. At times, it is also helpful for the accountant to meet with the debtor's prior accountant and its new accountant or financial advisor, if one has been appointed.

In one case, the creditors' committee took very little action to evaluate the activities of the debtor during the first two months after the petition was filed. The debtor failed to pay administrative expenses associated with the postbankruptcy operations, and cash from postbankruptcy activities was diverted to other uses. Eventually, the creditors realized what was happening and petitioned the court for the appointment of a trustee. However, this action was not taken until the creditors had sustained additional material losses. Frequently, the smaller the case, the more important it will be for creditors to quickly ensure that proper controls are in place. A small asset base can be dissipated very quickly.

The areas requiring immediate attention will vary. For example, in one case, a debtor had several contracts to deliver products that would result in out-of-pocket losses to the debtor, and other contracts that would be profitable. The debtor, for various reasons, was not taking any action to reject the unprofitable contracts. The creditors' committee, which was actively involved, asked its accountants to evaluate the contracts, identifying those that were profitable and those that should be canceled. It was necessary to complete this evaluation within 48 hours because the debtor was about to honor some contracts that the creditors' committee thought should be rejected. The accountant identified several unfavorable contracts for rejection, resulting in substantial savings.

It should be realized that members of the creditors' committee may not be experienced in serving in this capacity. They may not know the types of action they should take. Under these conditions, the accountant should provide guidance to the committee by helping it to ask the right kinds of questions and by steering its activities in the right direction.

§ 10.9   Importance of Speed

When the creditors' committee retains an accountant or financial advisor, even if the environment is such that immediate action is not necessary, as discussed above, it usually wants the investigation including an analysis and resulting statements and reports to be completed as soon as possible so that a plan may be agreed on quickly. The committee asks for the accountant's report, including an analysis of the debtor's operations and suggested action needed to turn the business around, because it is impossible for the committee to take any type of action until it has examined the report and discussed the operations of the debtor with the accountant or financial advisor. As soon as the accountant or financial advisor accepts the engagement, he or she must begin the audit or special investigation. Accountants who are experienced representatives of creditors can complete the analysis and issue the report in a relatively short time. For example, a New York accounting firm frequently issues a detailed report on the financial position of a debtor within 10 to 14 days after the engagement is accepted, even though the companies involved have sales volumes in excess of several million dollars. However, in some complex circumstances, it takes months just to establish the financial position from the records and identify the cause of the debtor's financial problems and much longer to recommend a course of action to turn the business around and to restructure its debt.

It is advisable to seek a prompt settlement in order to halt the losses that the debtor may be incurring in the operation of its business and to block the possibility of misconduct by the debtor in the form of preferential payments, concealment of assets, or conversion of assets into property that is exempt from liquidation proceedings. In an out-of-court settlement, if there is an extended delay, some of the creditors may file suit for their claims, eventually forcing the debtor to file a petition under chapter 11, or may actually file an involuntary petition putting the debtor into chapter 7 or chapter 11.

§ 10.10   Establishment of Proper Controls

Supervision of the debtor and its activities is essential throughout the proceedings, beginning with negotiations concerning the settlement and ending only when the plan has been consummated. Control is normally aimed at conservation of the assets, and the creditors' committee holds an excellent position to perform such a function.

The importance of the supervisory function of the creditors' committee and of its representation of an unbiased viewpoint that protects the best interests of all the creditors was noted in the *Credit Service* case.[6] There, the judge stated that a complete review of the debtor's conduct must be made to ensure that the proposed arrangement is fair, equitable, and feasible, and this "should be made by a disinterested and competent committee for the information of and action thereon by the creditors."[7]

The two most crucial time periods during which control must be exercised are the period after the filing of the petition but before agreement on a plan, and the period when installment payments are pending if called for by the plan. One of the key functions performed by the accountant or financial advisor,

---

[6] *In re Credit Service, Inc.*, 31 F. Supp. 979 (D.C. Md. 1940).
[7] *Id.*

once the engagement for the creditors' committee has been accepted, is to preserve the assets through performance of an analysis of the status of the debtor's operations and records (Chapter 12). The first assignment of the accountant is to inventory the books and records (see §§ 12.10 and 12.11) and count the physical inventory. An accounting firm received a telephoned request for services from the attorney for a creditors' committee. The call came in the morning; that same afternoon, the accountants began and completed an inventory of the merchandise on the debtor's premises. The owner, unaware that the inventory had been taken, removed part of the inventory from the warehouse a few days later, hoping to conceal it from the assets of the estate. The owner was unsuccessful in the attempt. The accountant, at times, must move very fast in order to exercise adequate control. (See § 10.8.)

In addition to the special analysis, the accounting methods most frequently used to exercise control over the estate include some type of supervision or control over the receipts and disbursements and a statement of review of the debtor's operations. Whether such supervision is requested by the creditors' committee or U.S. trustee (see §§ 9.2–9.3), the objectives are the same.

§ 10.11 Investigation of Causes of Failure and Development of Controls to Limit Further Impairment of Assets

The creditors' committee needs to know, as early as possible after the petition is filed, what caused the debtor's current problems, whether the company will be able to overcome its difficulties, and, if so, what measures need to be taken in the future to avoid further losses. A brief review of the debtor's operations may not necessarily reveal the cause of failure, and it is the *cause* that must be identified by the accountant and eventually corrected; it is not enough just to correct the symptoms.

Once the underlying cause of failure has been identified, the accountant or financial advisor for the creditors' committee should develop procedures that will limit further impairment of assets. It is important during the early stages of the case to determine that proper controls are established over receipts and disbursements. The company may have had an adequate system at one time. However, during periods of financial difficulty, divisions of responsibility and other internal controls are often not enforced. Key accounting and financial personnel of the company may resign. Responsibilities must be reestablished, and proper control must be exercised over all receipts and disbursements.

Where there are unprofitable segments or divisions within the debtor's operations, the creditors' committee may insist that immediate action be taken to eliminate them. The accountant may monitor the results of the liquidation of unprofitable operations for the committee.

§ 10.12 Review of Receipts and Disbursements Control

Direct control can be exercised over all disbursements by having the accountant countersign all checks. It is not unusual for the creditors' committee to make such a request, and it was common practice, at one time, for accountants to sign the checks as part of their services for the creditors' committee. This practice is undesirable because of the ethical and legal implications associated with the signature. The ethical aspects are discussed in § 8.34. If the accountant's signature is on all checks, the inference may be made that the accountant is assuming responsibility for the disbursements. One accounting firm countersigned payroll checks for the debtor, but failed to make sure that the taxes withheld from employees were remitted to the Internal Revenue Service. The funds were used for other purposes for which the accountant had countersigned the checks. Officers, debtors-in-possession, and trustees may be held personally liable for failure to remit these taxes. Section 6672 of the Internal Revenue Code imposes a percentage penalty on a person required to collect and pay taxes who willfully fails to do so. In this situation, the Internal Revenue Service assumed that, because the accountant was responsible for signing the checks, he or she was also responsible for remitting the taxes withheld. The debtor did not have any funds to cover the taxes, so the accountant personally had to pay the amount due. Some accounting firms that formerly countersigned checks when requested to do so by creditors' committees have, at times, initialed all or selected checks before they were issued. Initialing all checks before they are issued still presents some legal and ethical problems associated with the cosigning of the checks.

(a) Receipts

Adequate records of all sales must be maintained, and the accountant must see that all cash received from sales and from collections of accounts receivable are deposited intact. Control must also be exercised over purchases, credit sales, returns, and payroll.

(b) Disbursements

The extent to which the accountant or financial advisor gets involved in the control of disbursements will vary, depending on the nature of the proceeding and the size of the debtor. In some cases, the accountant's involvement may be in the design of a system that will provide for control over the disbursements. In other situations, the accountant may review for the creditors' committee all disbursements in excess of a set dollar amount and advise the creditors' committee of any disbursements that are questionable or unusual. Examples of such disbursements are unauthorized postpetition payments and payments of prepetition obligations that have not been expressly authorized by the court. Accountants may also review with the creditors' committee chair or counsel the reports filed with the court for expense disbursement approval. At times, before any disbursement is made, the accountant may review all invoices supporting the disbursement and, in fact, try to justify the expenditure. Certain types of expenditures, such as travel and entertainment, professional fees, and other expenses of a personal nature, should be carefully examined by the accountant. The accountant and the creditors' committee must, however, be very careful in the way in which they exercise control over the debtor's operations (§ 10.14). The accountant will see that only those liabilities are paid which were incurred, in an out-of-court settlement, after the initial creditors' meeting. It is also important to make sure that all liabilities incurred for new services are paid promptly. An important part of the accountant's assistance in disbursement control is to evaluate the extent to which the debtor is enforcing and following the established controls.

(c) Review of Cash Flow Reports

By establishing a proper system of control, constantly monitoring the system to see that it is functioning properly, and frequently evaluating the cash flow, the accountant observes the day-to-day operations of the business during the time a settlement is being arranged. Cash flow receives a great deal of attention, primarily because the creditors do not want to see the assets of the business continue to diminish. Normally, the debtor's accountant will develop, with the cooperation of the debtor-in-possession, a forecast of the anticipated receipts and disbursements on a periodic basis (usually weekly) for a period of four to six months. At the end of each period, the debtor will submit a report comparing the actual results with the projected estimates. Exhibit 10-1 illustrates a statement of cash flow, and Exhibit 10-2 shows the actual and projected activity of a merchandise inventory account. The accountants for the creditors' committee will normally review these reports and discuss their analysis with the committee.

Exhibit 10-1 Cash Flow Statement

THOMAS MERCHANDISE, INC. (DEBTOR-IN-POSSESSION)
STATEMENT OF CASH FLOW

For the Week Ended August 28, 20XX
(In Thousands)

		Actual (Unaudited)		Projected
Receipts:				
Transferred from Stores		$ 814		$ 850
Income—Leased Departments		67		54
Miscellaneous		304		120
Adam Drugs, Inc.		930		—
		2,115		1,024
Disbursements:				
Merchandise	$242		$990	
Rents	22		—	
Payroll	136		139	
Other	263		155	
		663		1,284
Excess of Receipts over Disbursements		1,452		(260)
Cash—Beginning		2,793		2,793
Cash—End		$4,245		$2,533

Note: This statement is subject to the accompanying letter of transmittal.

JOHN X. DOE & COMPANY

Exhibit 10-2   Summary of Merchandise Inventory Account

THOMAS MERCHANDISE, INC. (DEBTOR-IN-POSSESSION)
MERCHANDISE DATA—APPAREL
Weekly: July–December 20XX
(In Thousands)

Week Ended	Sales Planned	Sales Actual	Orders Placed Retail	Orders Placed Cost	Orders Received Retail	Orders Received Cost	Open Orders—Cost	Cash in Banks	Payments on Purchases	Outstanding Debts to Vendors
20XX										
July 31	$ 650	$764	$4,166.0	$2,249.8	$ 360	$ 194.6	$2,055.2	$2,102	—	$ 195
Aug. 7	800	869	2,666.0	1,439.5	1,276	689.1	2,805.6	1,936	$ 11	872
14	800	817	3,276.0	1,768.9	1,940	1,047.6	3,526.9	2,378	87	1,833
21	800	883	956.5	516.5	2,026	1,093.8	2,949.6	2,793	118	2,808
28	850	800*	(752.8)	(406.5)	1,907	1,030.0	1,513.1	4,245	242	3,596
Sept. 4	850		1,100.0	600.0						
11	900		1,100.0	600.0						
18	900		1,100.0	600.0						
25	950		1,100.0	600.0						
Oct. 2	950		1,100.0	600.0						
9	950		1,100.0	600.0						
16	950		1,100.0	600.0						
23	950		1,100.0	600.0						
30	850		1,200.0	650.0						
Nov. 6	1,000		1,200.0	650.0						
13	1,000		1,200.0	650.0						
20	1,000		—	—						
27	1,050		—	—						
Dec. 4	1,150		900.0	500.0						
11	1,250		900.0	500.0						
18	1,450		900.0	500.0						
24	2,350		900.0	500.0						
31	1,200		—	—						

*Estimated.

The accountant for the creditors' committee must take whatever steps seem necessary to ensure that the assets do not continue to diminish because of mismanagement, or do not suspiciously disappear. The amount of control that must be exercised by the committee depends on such factors as its faith in the debtor's honesty and integrity and whether the debtor has an accountant.

An example of a report based on a detailed analysis of the operating statement appears as 10.1 in Volume 2 of *Bankruptcy and Insolvency Accounting.*

§ 10.13 Review of Debtor's Accounting System

In many bankruptcy cases, the amount of attention given to the accounting system and internal controls during the time when the debtor is facing financial difficulty is insignificant. Thus, although a good accounting system with proper controls may have existed a year or so prior to the filing of the petition, it may no longer be in place. Before placing any confidence in the reports issued by the debtor, the creditors' committee may ask its accountant to make a study of the accounting system. If it is inadequate, the accountant may be appointed by the court to devise an accounting system that would provide for the flow of accurate and timely financial information to the creditors' committee.

§ 10.14 "Insider" Problem

An insider as defined by section 101(31) includes, among others, a person in control of the debtor. An insider can be in a disadvantageous position in relation to other creditors regarding the content of the plan, avoidance of preferences, and other aspects of bankruptcy proceedings. Thus, in an attempted out-of-court settlement, the creditors and their committee must be very careful that they do not exercise a direct influence over the debtor's business that could result in the court's considering them insiders in case the debtor files a bankruptcy court petition. Any action taken by the accountant and the creditors' committee involving control over the debtor's operations must be taken only after consulting with the counsel for the creditors' committee. See § 5.6.

§ 10.15 Review of Weekly/Monthly Reporting

A key service that the accountant can render for the creditors' committee is to review the weekly or monthly reports issued by the debtor. Under conditions in which the debtor was not authorized to retain an independent accountant, or in situations in which the creditors do not trust the debtor's accountant, the accountant for the creditors' committee may actually prepare these reports. These reports generally include cash, key operating statistics, and operating statements. As discussed in § 10.12, the creditors' committee frequently requires cash-flow reports that compare actual with projected cash flows.

(a) Key Statistics

Accountants may work with the creditors' committee to identify key data that will help the committee to properly monitor the debtor's activities. What constitutes key data depends on the nature of the business. For example, in a retail operation, the key data might include inventory balances by type of product, sales, orders placed, orders received, open orders, merchandise payments, and outstanding debts. The members of the creditors' committee may not know the type of data that should be requested to effectively monitor the debtor's activities. In such situations, the accountant for the creditors' committee should take the lead and recommend key indicators to the committee. By working with the committee and the debtor, the accountant can develop projections for key areas and can recommend to the committee the weekly or monthly reports that should be prepared in order to compare the actual results with the projections.

(b) Operating Statements

As stated above, close supervision of the debtor's business operations is desirable to ensure that the assets do not continue to be diminished because of the management that originally caused the debtor's difficulties. Such control is also necessary to prevent the wasting or diversion of assets. To this end, the creditors' committee may require the debtor to furnish, in addition to periodic statements of cash receipts and disbursements, a monthly operating statement so that the committee may review the administration of the business, whether by the debtor or a receiver. In a chapter 11 proceeding, monthly operating statements must be filed with the court and the U.S. trustee (§§ 9.2–9.3). These will put the committee in a better position to reveal to the court what is actually occurring, and will enable it to halt any undesirable events much more quickly.

If the debtor attempts to prepare these statements, the reports may be inadequate and may give a misleading impression of the company's profitability. Under these conditions, it is desirable that the committee use its accountant to make an independent review of the debtor's records and prepare its own statements. Thus, in some proceedings, the accountant for the creditors, although not engaged directly by the debtor, may perform the necessary accounting services and prepare the required statements for the committee and the court. However, in most cases, the debtor's own independent accountant will prepare the required operating statements. The accountant for the creditors' committee will review the statements and advise the committee of the status of the company's operations. The operating statements are described and illustrated in § 9.4.

SPECIAL INVESTIGATIONS AND REVIEWS

§ 10.16 Audit and/or Investigation of Debtor's Books and Records

An important function performed by the accountant or financial advisor for the creditors' committee is a thorough examination of the debtor's past business transactions. The primary purpose of such an investigation is to ensure that all assets have been accounted for and any misconduct has been adequately explained. This work serves as a foundation from which the accountants or financial advisors will issue statements and reports and conduct any necessary investigations into the debtor's conduct. The creditors must have the results of any such examination to judge (1) whether a proposed plan is feasible and in their best interests before they decide whether to accept it, and (2) whether it will satisfy the Bankruptcy Code's fair and equitable requirements if they do not accept it. (See Chapter 12.)

(a) Discovery of Assets

It is crucial that the creditors have a knowledge of all the debtor's assets and their value. This includes all property that may be recovered because it was involved in a preferential transfer, assets that were concealed, and the like (§§ 12.12–12.29). The total assets available to creditors in liquidation must be determined, to ascertain the dividend the creditors would receive in a chapter 7 liquidation and to indicate whether a proposed plan is in their best interests.

(b) Discovery of Malfeasance

During the audit and/or investigation of the debtor, the accountant or financial advisor will be on the alert for any transactions believed to be questionable because of dishonesty, issuance of false financial statements, concealments, preferential payments, fraudulent transfers, and so forth (see Chapter 12). Any misconduct even merely suspected by the accountant should be reported to the creditors' committee because it will be taken into consideration by the committee when deciding whether the debtor should be rehabilitated. Such behavior may also influence the court in a decision to appoint a trustee and not allow the debtor to remain in possession or to require the debtor to furnish indemnity to protect the assets of the estate. The discovery of certain types of transactions may cause the debtor to be barred from a discharge of all or part of its debts or may, in the case of an out-of-court settlement, precipitate the filing of an involuntary chapter 7 or chapter 11 petition in order to further investigate the nature of the questionable transactions.

In chapter 7 liquidation proceedings, rather than emphasizing the future potential of the business as in a chapter 11 reorganization, creditors are concerned with the liquidation value of the debtor's assets and with discovery of any unusual transactions, including the transfer or concealment of assets. Examples of the types of unusual transactions the accountant would seek to discover through the audit are listed below:

- Preferential payments made within 90 days (one year for insiders) prior to the petition date
- Sales of inventory to vendors or other creditors
- Unjustified declines in inventory
- Fixed assets sold to creditors or others for less than their full value, sold to creditors as an account offset, or resold to the manufacturer as an account offset
- The misappropriation of receipts, especially advances from factors and unrecorded sales

- Liens given creditors prior to bankruptcy to enable them to obtain a greater percentage distribution than other creditors
- Any assets withdrawn by stockholders in the form of dividends, loans, transfer of assets, and so forth
- Potential assets, such as pending lawsuits, that might enlarge the size of the estate
- All other transactions that may have arisen outside of the ordinary course of the business

§ 10.17 Review of Debtor's Transactions

To assist the creditors' committee in its supervisory functions, the accountant or financial advisor for the committee may be asked to review the debtor's operations during the period when a plan is being formalized and immediately following its acceptance. This review generally concentrates on the major transactions of the debtor between the date the petition is filed and the date of review. In reviewing these transactions, accountants are looking for any indication that a trustee should be appointed. Emphasis is not solely on the discovery of irregularities that would indicate dishonesty on the part of management. The accountant also looks for indications of mismanagement of company resources or omission of the steps necessary to reverse the loss trend, which were developed prior to the filing of the petition. Another purpose of this review is to identify any payments on prefiling obligations that were made after the petition was filed, and any other payments that were not authorized by the court.

§ 10.18 Evaluation of Debtor's Projections

Of primary significance to a creditors' committee is whether the projections and forecasts submitted by the debtor are realistic. The representatives of the largest unsecured creditors on the committee typically are not accountants and thus may need assistance in evaluating the projections and other financial data prepared by the debtor. The accountant or financial advisor for the creditors' committee may be in a strong position to judge the debtor's evaluations and to make recommendations.

The intention is not to perform an audit of such data but rather to determine, through a review, whether the data in the projections can be supported to some extent by hard evidence. The level of involvement by the accountant or financial advisor for the creditors' committee will vary, depending on the sophistication of the company or of the financial people who prepared the data. The review of the data in some cases could be limited to a discussion with those who prepared the projections, to determine whether the figures submitted seem to make sense. The accountant for the committee may find that the preparation of this information has been somewhat loose or vague. In these circumstances, the accountant may need to get involved in the preparation or to perform a review of the appropriate accounting records to see whether the basic underlying data have some foundation in fact.

To a large extent, this task is similar to the kind of review that would be done in conjunction with reviewing quarterly unaudited financial statements of a business. The biggest difference is that, in quarterly reviews, the accountant is looking only at a historical period, whereas the projection data submitted by the debtor will involve future periods of time as well.

The most desirable way to communicate the results of the review to the creditors' committee is to discuss the projections with key members, in addition to submitting a written report. The accountant for the creditors' committee also may be asked to prepare projections for the committee. Frequently, creditors' committees will express concern over the level of the debtor's operations, the continuation of losses, and the required level of trade credit. To help the committee have a better understanding of the debtor's operations and the potential losses that could occur, comparative projections assuming varying levels of operation can be prepared.

(a) Reorganization Value

In some cases, accountants or financial advisors for the creditors' committees develop their own models of the debtor's operations. Cash flow projections can then be prepared for determining the reorganized entity's value. Operational changes made by the debtor are entered into the model, as are proposed sales or other major actions providing a basis for the committee response to the debtor's proposals. Evaluation by the creditors' committee focuses on the impact these actions will have on the value of the reorganized entity and on the amount of potential settlement. See § 8.17.

§ 10.19   Review of Plan of Reorganization and Disclosure Statement

As was noted in Chapter 8, the accountant for the debtor provides advice and assistance in the formulation of a plan of reorganization in a chapter 11 proceeding and a plan of settlement in an agreement out of court. An important function of an accountant employed by the creditors is to help evaluate the proposed plan of action. In a chapter 11 case where the debtor has not proposed a plan within 120 days, a proposed plan has not been accepted within 180 days after the petition was filed, or a trustee has been appointed, the accountant may assist the creditors in developing a plan to be submitted to the court. The accountant is able to provide valuable assistance to the committee because of his or her familiarity with the financial background, the nature of the operations, and the management of the company, as gained from the audit. In committee meetings, a great deal of time is spent in discussions between the committee members and the accountant concerning the best settlement they can expect and how it compares with the amount they would receive if the business were liquidated. The accountant or financial advisor also gives an opinion as to the debtor's future prospects for profit, assuming the business is not liquidated. (See §§ 8.16–8.18.)

The creditors are interested in receiving as much as possible under any reorganization plan. The accountant or financial advisor may work with the creditors' committee to see that the amount proposed under the plan is reasonable and fair, based on the nature of the debtor's business. First, it must be determined that the plan provides for at least as much as would be received in a chapter 7 liquidation. Second, the creditors must leave the debtor enough assets to operate the business after reorganization. If a reasonable basis does not exist for future operations, the judge may not confirm the plan because it is not feasible.

To help the creditors' committee with an evaluation of the plan, the accountant may need to perform an audit of the debtor's business or at least make a limited review of the debtor's operations and investigate any unusual transactions. Normally, the accountant focuses, at least in part, on the following areas in an evaluation of the plan:

- Because an attempt is being made to rehabilitate the business, the creditors will be interested in both prior years' operations and the future potential of the business. The accountant should attempt to provide information regarding the projected volume of the business and estimated gross and net profits. To determine the future success of the business, comparisons should be made of these figures with those typical of the industry.
- The causes of the debtor's past losses should be ascertained, and measures necessary to eliminate the problems must be determined to ensure that the debtor will be able to earn a profit in the future.
- The liquidation value of the debtor's assets should be fixed so that, while attempting to agree on a plan, creditors will know the smallest dividend acceptable to them and have a basis for judging a proposed plan.
- To determine whether the payments proposed under the plan are reasonable, the accountant may need to evaluate any valuations of the debtor that have been prepared or to prepare an estimate of the value of the debtor's business.
- To determine the size of the initial payment that it would be possible to make to creditors, it will be necessary to ascertain the status and extent of any liens existing on the debtor's property, any secured claims, and the amounts owed on priority claims.

In performing these services, the accountant for the creditors' committee must rely on the information contained in the disclosure statement and in other reports issued, if an audit has not been performed. Thus, the content of the disclosure statement may be most important. Because the disclosure statement serves as the basic report used by the creditors to evaluate the plan, it is critical that it be properly prepared and contain the type of information that would allow the creditors to effectively evaluate the proposed plan.

The accountant for the creditors' committee may be asked to evaluate the disclosure statement. If, in the accountant's opinion, it does not contain adequate information, the deficiencies may be conveyed to the debtor informally (normally, through creditors' committee counsel) prior to submission of the plan to the court, or an objection to the content of the statement may be raised at the disclosure hearing. If a trustee is appointed or if the 120-day period (including extensions) allowed for the debtor to develop a plan has expired, anyone may propose a plan. In this case, the accountant may assist the creditors' committee in developing a plan and in drafting the disclosure statement. Creditors' plans are becoming more common under chapter 11, and if bankruptcy judges, because of *Timbers*,[8] limit the time the debtor alone has to propose a plan, creditor plans may continue to increase. As a result, the accountant may

---

[8] *United Savings Assn. of Texas v. Timbers of Inwood Forests Associates, Ltd.*, 485 U.S. 365 (1988).

be involved much more in the development of a plan and the accompanying disclosure statement while serving as the accountant for the creditors' committee.

It is becoming more common for the creditors' committee to submit a proposed plan. A disclosure statement must be submitted to the court before the committee can solicit votes on the proposed plan. The accountant for the committee may help the committee prepare the disclosure statement or assist the committee in modifying the disclosure statement previously prepared by the debtor. The content of the disclosure statement is to be decided solely by the court and is not governed by nonbankruptcy law, including the Securities Acts of 1933 and 1934. It should be noted that SOP 90-7, issued by the AICPA, suggests that a disclosure statement cannot contain adequate information unless the reorganization value of the company is disclosed. The accountant for the committee may find that the best way to disclose the reorganization value of the debtor is to prepare a pro forma balance sheet using reorganization values.

In evaluating the information in the disclosure statement, the accountant for the creditors' committee may be asked to review the financial statements contained in the disclosure statement or others that were issued by the debtor. Special consideration must be made in reviewing pro forma and liquidation statements of financial condition. The pro forma statement provides the creditors with an indication of what the financial condition of the debtor will look like if the plan is accepted. This statement should show that the creditors will receive more if they accept the plan than would be received if the debtor were liquidated. The pro forma statement also should demonstrate that the plan is feasible in that, after satisfying the provisions of the plan, the debtor retains an asset base with which to operate. In reviewing the pro forma statement prepared by the debtor, special consideration must be given to the analysis of the assumptions used to prepare it and to the evaluation of the value of the assets (which may differ from book values). If the pro forma statement is based on historical costs, the accountant for the creditors' committee may want to restate them to reflect the reorganization values of the entity. The creditors' committee will be able to more effectively evaluate the terms of the plan if it can compare the terms to a pro forma statement that contains the reorganization value of the entity rather than historical values.

Liquidation statements are prepared to show what the unsecured creditors would receive if the business were liquidated. The assumptions used in the adjustments to book values must be evaluated carefully. The accountant or financial advisor for the creditors' committee may be asked to review statements of this nature and to provide advice as to the reasonableness of the analysis. There may be a tendency for the debtor to understate liquidation values in order to make the terms of the plan more appealing to the unsecured creditors.

OTHER ACCOUNTING SERVICES

§ 10.20 Introduction

An accountant or financial advisor may be retained by either a secured creditor or major stockholder or—under restricted conditions—may be retained by

the court to render services for a committee of secured creditors or stockholders. Under the latter arrangement, the fees are generally authorized by the
court and come out of the estate of the debtor. When engaged directly by a
secured creditor or stockholder, the accountant is normally paid by the client.

§ 10.21   Secured Creditor

An accountant can be engaged by a secured creditor to serve as its advisor
during the bankruptcy proceeding. Under this type of arrangement, the objective is to watch for anything that might be of interest to the secured creditor.
Work done in this capacity includes:

- Abstracting any financial data that could be related to the case
- Attending various creditor (and other) meetings with the secured creditors and providing them with information and insight during the meetings
- Reviewing reports issued by the debtor
- Helping the secured creditor make proposals for and an evaluation of the
  proposed plan

§ 10.22   Major Stockholder or Equity Committee

The services accountants or financial advisors can render to either a major
stockholder or an equity security holders' committee are similar to those performed for the creditors' committee or for a committee of secured creditors.
The equity holders generally are interested in the recovery of preferential
payments, fraudulent transfers, or other transfers that might increase the
value of the estate. Action for the recovery of these transfers generally is left
to the creditors' committee. However, if the creditors' committee is not taking necessary steps to preserve the estate for some reason, such as a conflict
of the interests of one of its members, the equity committee may take a more
active role.

For a major stockholder or an equity committee to be effective, they must
know what caused the debtor's financial difficulty and the nature of the
debtor's current activities. The accountant can assist by identifying the type of
information that should be obtained from the debtor. The accountant may
review operating reports and other financial information and advise the major
stockholder or equity committee of any potential problems in addition to giving an evaluation of the general status of the debtor's operations.

A major area in which the accountant can assist the client is in the evaluation of the plan. The extent to which the stockholders share in the plan of reorganization will depend to some extent on the solvency of the debtor. Thus, the
debtor needs assistance in estimating the prospects for successful future operations and the going-concern (reorganization) value of the business. A major
stockholder or equity committee is also interested in the tax consequences the
plan may have for future operations, especially the extent to which the net
operating loss can be preserved.

§ 10.23　Responsibilities of Creditors' Accountant or Financial Advisor

An accountant or financial advisor retained by the creditors has a primary duty to them and performs all work in their interest. One of the accountant's first concerns will be to inquire into the transactions that have occurred, which will require an analysis of the debtor's books and records. One of the purposes of this investigation will be to determine whether there have been any preferential or fraudulent transfers, unexplained losses, or other unusual and suspicious transactions. The creditors' accountant should, however, first ask the debtor about any questionable items rather than indiscriminately making accusations. In the same manner, the accountant will seek to establish the debtor's integrity and the soundness of the debtor's records and statements.

Another important function of an accountant employed by the creditors is to help them reach a conclusion about the proposed out-of-court settlement or plan of reorganization. This involves advising them as to the best settlement they can expect and comparing this with the distribution to be received if the business were liquidated. To accomplish this comparison, the forced sale value of the assets must be ascertained and the accountant must give an opinion as to the debtor's future earning power. The accountant should also contact the debtor to gain awareness of any situations that should be given consideration.

Finally, both the creditors and the accountant are concerned with closely supervising the debtor to protect the assets from being further diminished, wasted, or diverted, either before a plan is effected or after a settlement is reached. This supervision includes studying the financial statements issued by the debtor and being aware of all its actions.

The creditors' accountant is thus responsible to the creditors for making sure they know all the facts, investigating anything about which there may be a question, and helping them choose the most advantageous course of action. At the same time, there is a responsibility to the debtor to conduct all inquiries in a fair manner and to make sure the information given to the creditors is correct.

In situations where the creditors desire to develop a plan, the accountant may assist with the development process and may prepare most of the data for the disclosure statement. (Excerpts of a disclosure statement that was prepared by a creditors' committee appear as 6.13 in Volume 2 of *Bankruptcy and Insolvency Accounting*.) In addition to collecting the financial information to include in the disclosure statement, the accountant may determine the reorganization value and liquidation value of the entity.

Prior to the development of a disclosure statement, the creditors' committee will need to review and evaluate the debtor's business plan. The accountant should prepare an evaluation of the debtor's business plan and suggest any changes considered necessary in the plan. The accountant may be asked to prepare a complete business plan for use by the committee, but the more common situation is that the accountant will review the debtor's business plan and suggest changes that will serve as the basis for the reorganization plan. A summary of the changes to the business plan that are recommended by the creditors' committee may be included in the disclosure statement.

11

Valuation of a Business in Bankruptcy Proceedings

IMPORTANCE OF VALUATION

§ 11.1 Introduction

An additional service the accountant may be requested to render for the court, trustee, or debtor-in-possession is assistance in determining the value of the business. To be able to provide assistance, it is necessary to have some understanding of the various approaches that have been used in determining the value of businesses and some knowledge of the conditions that must exist before a particular approach can be used. As noted in Chapter 6, the liquidation value of a business must be determined to establish whether the plan is in the best interests of the creditors. The business must be valued also under the fair and equitable standards, to determine the extent to which a dissenting class will participate in a plan. In other words, before accepting a plan, the creditors need some understanding of the amount they would receive if the company were to be liquidated and the amount they will receive for their claims if the company is valued as a going concern. Related is the need to determine liquidating values of specific assets of the business for dissenting creditors in a given class. Section 1129(a)(7) of the Bankruptcy Code provides that, before the court can confirm the plan, it must be determined that these creditors will receive as much from the plan as they would receive if the business were to be liquidated under chapter 7.

Under prior law, Chapter X required that a going-concern value be placed on the business before a plan of reorganization could be confirmed. Chapter 11 requires only that the business be valued on a going-concern basis when an impaired class fails to approve a plan. This does not necessarily mean that a few businesses will have to be valued under the new law; rather, more emphasis will be placed on the going-concern value outside of the court's activities, to determine whether a class of creditors should accept or reject the plan. Some observers believe that arriving at a fair going-concern value for the business is even more important under the new law.

The objectives of this chapter are to summarize the situations mentioned in Chapters 5 and 6 where there is a need to determine the value of the business or the value of individual assets, and to describe the detailed procedures followed in determining the value of assets, individually and collectively.

Asset valuation is very critical in many chapter 11 proceedings and in chapter 7 proceedings. The discussion in this chapter will deal primarily with chapter 11 proceedings, but many of the Bankruptcy Code sections covered apply equally to chapter 7 proceedings and out-of-court settlements.

§ 11.2 Adequate Protection under Section 361

Section 361 of the Bankruptcy Code provides that the holders of secured claims, lessors, co-owners, conditional vendors, consigners, and similar parties, are entitled to adequate protection of their interest in a property when such holders request relief from the automatic stay. It is the value of the secured creditor's collateral and not the creditor's claim or even the creditor's rights in specific collateral that is protected.[1] When a creditor seeks adequate protection he is asking the court to ensure that the status quo will be maintained throughout the duration of the stay. The court has broad discretion in the method it chooses to remedy adequate protection problems.

Adequate protection may be required under three Bankruptcy Code sections:

1 *Section 362 dealing with the automatic stay.* For example, unless the security interest of the debtor is adequately protected, the court may remove the stay.

2 *Section 363 dealing with the use (including the use of cash collateral), sale, or lease of property of the debtor.* For example, the court may not approve the release of cash collateral until it has been determined that the impacted creditors are adequately protected.

3 *Section 364 dealing with the obtaining of credit.* For example, before the court might approve the granting of a senior or equal lien under the priming of a secured creditor, the court must ascertain that the creditor is adequately protected.

(a) Need for Valuation Services

If the court determines that the creditor is not adequately protected the court will grant the creditor relief from the automatic stay unless the debtor provides adequate protection in the form of cash payments, additional or replacement lien, or the indubitable equivalent as described above. Thus, determining if the creditor is adequately protected is important for both the debtor-in-possession and creditor. The creditor wants relief from the stay in order to take possession of the collateral that is securing the loan and the debtor-in-possession often wants to continue to have use of the property. In determining if a secured creditor is adequately protected not only must the current value of the collateral be determined, but an estimation must be made as to the extent the collateral may be currently or will in the future decline in

---

[1] *Wright v. Union Central Life Insurance Co.*, 311 U.S. 273 (1940).

value. Thus, the value that is assigned to the collateral is critical to the determination of whether the debtor-in-possession retains the use of the property or
the stay is removed giving the creditor access to the property.

(b) Valuation Approach

The Bankruptcy Code does not specify the method that is to be used to
determine the value of the creditor's interest in the property of the debtor, nor
does it define the time at which the value is to be determined. The legislative
history indicates that these matters are left to case-by-case interpretation and
development. It was expected that the courts would apply the concept in light
of facts in each case and generally equitable principles, and that no court
would develop hard and fast rules that would apply in every case. Legislative
history also indicates that an infinite number of variations is possible in dealing with debtors and creditors, that the law is continually developing, and that
new ideas are continually being implemented in this field. Thus, the drafters of
the Bankruptcy Code felt that flexibility is important to permit the courts to
adapt to varying circumstances and changing modes of financing.[2]

Legislative history also indicates that it is not expected that the courts will
construe value to mean, in every case, forced liquidation value or full going-
concern value. There is wide latitude between these two extremes. In any particular case, especially in a reorganization proceeding, the determination of
which entity should be entitled to the difference between the going-concern
value and the liquidation value must be based on equitable considerations
derived from the facts in the case. Negotiations between the parties will, in
most cases, determine the value, and only if the parties cannot agree will the
court become involved.[3]

It is expected that most valuations to determine adequate protection will be
based on the assumption that the business is a going concern. Several
approaches may be used to determine the value of collateral pledged as security for an allowed claim, including replacement costs, discounted cash flows
or earnings, earnings or cash flow multiples, and so on. Liquidating values
would be used for assets in businesses that are not expected to reorganize.

For individual assets the value will be determined based on the future cash
flows expected from that asset. Thus the value for accounts receivable pledged
as security under a floating lien arrangement might be based on the receivables
that are estimated to be collectible. In the case of inventory pledged where
there is an active market for the inventory, the first value generally considered
is replacement costs. Where the product is unique, the value may be based on
the amount expected to be realized from the sale of inventory after selling
costs and normal profit margins. The value of the stock of a subsidiary is based
on the projected cash flows from the business less interest-bearing debt.

As can be seen from the above examples, the approaches to the determination of value will vary depending on the circumstances in each case.

---

[2] H.R. Rep. No. 95-595, 95th Cong., 1st Sess. 338–40 (1977).
[3] *Id.*

As suggested by legislative history, courts have employed valuation standards on and between liquidation and going-concern values. In a recent paper, Bray summarized the broad range of decisions.[4] In determining value for the purpose of adequate protection under section 361 of the Bankruptcy Code, courts have generally held that the "commercial reasonableness" test applies. In *In re QPL Components, Inc.*,[5] the bankruptcy court defined "commercial reasonableness" as the "norm that a prudent businessman would employ to dispose of an asset through established commercial channels in an effort to realize its full economic value."

In *In re Demakes Enterprises, Inc.*,[6] the bankruptcy court held that liquidation values were to be used for the purpose of determining if the automatic stay should be lifted. The court noted that liquidating values should be used unless the business was to be sold as a going concern. The court rejected the use of fair market values noting that (1) no ready market exists and that it would take two to three years to sell the property, (2) fair market value is an artificial, theoretical estimate of what a willing buyer in an open market would pay and what a willing seller will accept, (3) the owner is not a willing seller, hopes to keep the property and the only foreseeable way the property will be sold, if at all, is through foreclosure.

In many situations the focal point in the determination of adequate protection is the extent to which an equity cushion is required. For a discussion of the issue of equity cushion see § 5.26.

§ 11.3 Claims Determination

Valuation issues need to be addressed in the determination of several types of claims. Among them are secured, recourses, and election to have all of the claim considered secured.

(a) Secured Claims

Section 506 provides that, if a creditor is undersecured, the claim will be divided into two parts. The first part is secured to the extent of the value of the collateral or to the extent of the amount of funds subject to setoff. The balance of the claim is considered unsecured. The value that is to be used to determine

---

[4] Gregory A. Bray, "Cash Collateral Valuation Issues in Bankruptcy," Association of Insolvency Accountants Valuation Conference (Westlake Village, Ca.: Association of Insolvency Accountants, October 27, 1994). p. 11. In support of going-concern values: *First Trust Union Bank v. Automatic Voting Mach. Corp. (In re Automatic Voting Mach. Corp.)*, 26 B.R. 970 (Bankr. W.D.N.Y. 1983); *In re QPL Components, Inc.*, 20 B.R. 342 (Bankr. E.D.N.Y. 1982); *First Nat'l Bank v. Shockley Forest Indus., Inc. (In re Shockley Forest Indus., Inc.)*, 5 B.R. 160 (Bankr. N.D. Ga. 1980); *Heritage Savs. & Loan Ass'n v. Rogers Dev. Corp. (In re Rogers Dev. Corp.)*, 2 B.R. 679 (Bankr. E.D. Va. 1980). In support of liquidating values: *American Bank & Trust Co. v. Ram Mfg., Inc. (In re Ram Mfg., Inc.)*, 32 B.R. 969 (Bankr. E.D. Pa. 1983); *In re C.F. Simonin's Sons, Inc.*, 28 B.R. 707 (Bankr. E.D.N.C. 1983). In support of values in between liquidation and going-concern: *In re Phoenix Steel Corp.*, 39 B.R. 218 (D. Del. 1984); *Margell v. Bouquet Invs. (In re Bouquet Invs.)*, 32 B.R. 988 (Bankr. C.D. Cal. 1983); *Lincoln Bank v. High Sky, Inc. (In re High Sky, Inc.)*, 15 B.R. 332 (Bankr. M.D. Pa. 1981).
[5] 20 B.R. 342 (Bankr. E.D.N.Y. 1982).
[6] 145 B.R. 362 (Bankr. D. Mass. 1992).

the amount of the claim that is secured is, according to section 506(a), to "be determined in light of the purpose of the valuation and of the proposed disposition or use of such property, and in conjunction with any hearing on such position or use or on a plan affecting such creditors' interest." The court in *In re Hotel Associates, Inc.*[7] held that prior to the determination of secured status and before a decision is made regarding the value of the security, the claim must first be allowed. Bankruptcy Rule 3012 provides that any party-in-interest may petition the court to determine the value of a secured claim.

Thus, the approach used to value property subject to a lien for a chapter 7 case may be different from that for a chapter 11 proceeding. Even within a chapter 11 case, property may be valued differently. For example, fixed assets that are going to be sold because of the discontinuance of operations may be assigned liquidation values, but assets that will continue to be used by the debtor may be assigned going-concern values. Furthermore, legislative history indicates that a valuation made early in a case under section 361 (§ 11.2) would not be binding on the debtor or creditor at the time the plan is confirmed. Courts will have to determine value on a case-by-case basis, but it is clear that the value is to be determined in light of the purpose of the valuation and the proposed disposition or use of the property.[8]

As an example, a machine that cost $10,000 two years ago could have several different values assigned, depending on the use of the machine and the nature of the debtor's operations. If it is the only machine the debtor uses to manufacture the products the debtor sells, the value to the debtor might be fairly high. On the other hand, if the debtor plans to sell the machine, which was specially made for the debtor's product, it may have only a very small scrap value. If the debtor has other, similar machines and plans to use the others and leave this one idle until volume increases, the machine probably has a lower value than in the first situation, but, hopefully, a higher value than in the second. To take the example further, if the debtor opposes a secured claimant's efforts to foreclose on the machine at the beginning of the case and, later, after the development of a business plan, decides to develop other product lines and sells the machine, the court could assign two different values to the very same machine.[9]

Also important in valuing the asset may be its benefit to the creditor. Consider an example where a debtor owns property that is surrounded by properties owned by a creditor who would like to remove the debtor's building and construct a new shopping center on the location. Without the debtor's property, the center could not be built. These two examples illustrate the problems with the determination of value of individual assets as collateral for secured claims.

When a chapter 11 reorganization will use the specific property being valued in its business, courts have determined the value by an archetypical valuation based on a simulated conversion into cash in the most commercially reasonable manner practicable in the circumstances.[10]

---

[7] 3 B.R. 340 (Bankr. E.D. Pa. 1980).

[8] S. Rep. No. 95-989, 95th Cong., 2d Sess. 68 (1978); see *Barash v. Public Finance Corp.*, 658 F.2d 504, 511 (7th Cir. 1981).

[9] Kenneth N. Klee, "All You Ever Wanted to Know about Cram Down under the New Bankruptcy Code," *American Bankruptcy Law Journal*, Vol. 53 (Spring 1979), p. 152.

[10] *In re Davis*, 14 B.R. 226 (Bankr. D. Maine 1981); see *Savloff v. Continental Bank (In re Savloff)*, 4 B.R. 285 (Bankr. E.D. Pa. 1980); *In the matter of Reynolds*, 5 C.B.C.2d 1578 (Bankr. N.D. Ga. 1981).

In a chapter 7 case under the Bankruptcy Code, the debtors (husband and wife) sought a section 506 valuation of their home, which secured the claims of four creditors. A year before the filing of their petitions, the debtors bought the home in Pennsylvania for $172,500, to which they made $35,000 worth of improvements. The debtors sought in this proceeding to establish a sheriff's sale value of $180,000, whereas creditors urged a value higher than $235,000, provided the property was advertised and an indefinite period was allowed in which to sell the property to the right buyer. The bankruptcy judge searched for guidance in valuing the collateral and adopted from the Bankruptcy Act a standard of commercial reasonableness for valuation of collateral based on the Uniform Commercial Code. The value is the amount that would be obtained by "the most commercially reasonable disposition under the circumstances," a quote from *In re American Kitchen Foods*.[11] The judge also quoted the Fifth Circuit Court of Appeals, which determined to value collateral under the Bankruptcy Act by "applying the norm that a prudent businessman would employ to dispose of an asset."[12] Applying these standards to the facts, the court considered the disparate appraisals, the inflationary spiral of our time, and the depressing effect of high interest rates on the real estate market; it concluded that the property was worth what the debtors paid for it plus the improvements they had made, or a total of $207,500.[13]

In *In re Monica Road Associates*[14] the bankruptcy court noted that in situations where prospects for reorganization appear good, going concern values should be used for the purpose of determining the value of the collateral under section 506(a). On the other hand, where the prospects appear dim, disposition or liquidation values should be used. In situations where the prospects are not clear, courts have greater difficulty. They must consider all material possibilities in determining which approach to follow.

(b) Date of Determination of Value

In determining the value for purposes of determining value of the collateral under section 506(a), the Fourth Circuit held that estimates of value made during a bankruptcy proceeding are binding only for the purpose of the specific hearing and do not have a *res judicata* on subsequent hearings.[15] Thus, a bankruptcy court faced with the need to revalue the collateral should not mechanically apply the value determined in the earlier proceeding, but should make an independent valuation of the collateral.[16]

In determining the value of the collateral for the purpose of classifying the debt in a plan, the value should be determined as of or close to the effective date of the plan.[17] *In the Matter of Seip*,[18] the bankruptcy court stated that the value should be in close proximity to the date of the confirmation of the plan.

---

[11] 2 Bankr. Ct. Dec. 715, 722 (N.D. Me. 1976).

[12] *In re Pennyrich, Inc. of Dallas*, 473 F.2d 417, 424 (5th Cir. 1973).

[13] *In re Savloff*, 4 B.R. 285 (Bankr. Pa. 1980).

[14] 147 B.R. 385 (Bankr. E.D. Va. 1992).

[15] *In re Midway Partners*, 995 F.2d 490 (4th Cir. 1993), *citing Dewsnup v. Timm*, 112 S. Ct. 773 (1992).

[16] *In re Snowshoe Co.*, 789 F.2d 1085 (4th Cir. 1986).

[17] *Matter of Savannah Gardens-Oaktree*, 146 B.R.306 (Bankr. S.D. Ga. 1992).

[18] 116 B.R. 709 (Bankr. D. Neb. 1990) *citing Ahlers v. Norwest Bank Worthington*, 794 F.2d 388 (8th Cir. 1986).

(c) Nonrecourse Considered Recourse

Section 1111(b) allows a secured claim to be treated as a claim with recourse against the debtor in chapter 11 proceedings (that is, where the debtor is liable for any deficiency between the value of the collateral and the balance due on the debt) whether or not the claim is nonrecourse by agreement or applicable law. This preferred status terminates if the property securing the loan is sold under section 363, is to be sold under the terms of the plan, or if the class of which the secured claim is a part elects application of section 1111(b)(2).

(d) Election to Have Entire Claim Considered Secured (Section 1111(b)(2))

Another election that is available under section 1111(b) is that certain classes of creditors can elect to have their entire claim considered secured. Such a class of creditors will normally be only one creditor. Multiple-member classes may, however, exist where there are publicly issued debentures, where an indenture trustee holds a lien on behalf of the debenture holders, or when there is a group of creditors that have the same type of liens, such as mechanics' liens. For example, in chapter 11 cases where most of the assets are pledged, very little may be available for unsecured creditors after administrative expenses are paid. Thus, the creditor might find it advisable to make the section 1111(b)(2) election. To be eligible for this election, the creditors must have allowed claims that are secured by a lien on property of the estate and their interest in such property as holders of secured claims must not be of inconsequential value.

Because the election for the holders of secured claims to consider all of the claims secured in a chapter 11 case is not available if their interest in the debtor's property is inconsequential value, valuation of collateral is important. Consider a creditor with a third mortgage of $400,000 on real estate in an excellent location. Because of a general decline in real estate values, the property is currently valued at $1 million with a first mortgage of $800,000 and a second of $200,000 outstanding. The value of the claim may appear to be inconsequential in this case; however, the creditor may want to make an election under section 1111(b), especially if the value is expected to go up and the amount to be paid to unsecured creditors is expected to be low. The courts will eventually determine, to some extent, the meaning of "inconsequential," but the accountant can provide information that can assist the courts in determining whether the value is significant in this context.

Other sections of the Bankruptcy Code, such as sections 522 and 554, also use an inconsequential value standard.

The election cannot be made if the holder has contractual recourse against the debtor or if the property is sold under section 363 or is to be sold under the plan. The purpose of this election is to provide adequate protection to holders of secured claims where the holder is of the opinion that the collateral is undervalued.

(e) Valuation Approach

In many of these transactions the asset to be valued is an individual asset such as a piece of equipment or a building. The value of equipment might be based on the replacement value or an appraised value of the equipment in its existing condition. In some cases the asset may be valued based on the cash flows that the asset will generate; discounted value of the future cash flows generated by the assets may be used.

§ 11.4 Recovery Action

Action may be taken by the trustee or debtor-in-possession to recover assets. Among the sources of recovery are preferences, fraudulent transfers, and requests for reclamation.

(a) Preferences (Section 547)

The provisions of section 547 grant the debtor-in-possession broad powers to recover transfers made immediately prior to the filing of the petition.

There are five elements that must be met for a transfer[19] to be characterized as a voidable preference:

1 The transfer must be made for the benefit of a creditor.
2 The transfer must be made for, or on account of, an antecedent debt owed by the debtor.
3 The transfer must be made while the debtor is insolvent. Insolvency is presumed if the transfer is made within 90 days prior to bankruptcy.
4 The transfer must have been made within 90 days prior to the filing of the petition. In the case of insiders the time period is extended to one year.
5 The transfer enables the creditor to receive more than it would receive in a liquidation or in a transfer made pursuant to an exception.

Exceptions to the general preference rule are found in section 547(c). The transferee has the burden of showing that a transfer fits within one of the following exceptions:

- Contemporaneous exchange for new value.
- Ordinary course of business and according to ordinary terms.
- A security interest incurred to finance purchased property.
- Preferential payments can be offset against subsequent new value granted to the debtor by the creditor.
- Creditors may receive a continuous interest in inventory and receivables to the extent that the creditor's position does not improve.

(b) Fraudulent Transfers (Sections 548 and 544)

Fraudulent conveyances may be attacked under the Bankruptcy Code or under state law according to section 544(b) of the Bankruptcy Code. Section

---

[19] Transfer is defined as "every mode, direct or indirect, absolute or conditional, voluntary or involuntary, of disposing of or parting with property, including retention of title as a security interest." Section 101(40). Using this definition, perfecting a security interest is a preference. *In re R & T Roofing Structural and Commercial Framing,* 79 B.R. 22 (D. Nev. 1987). Granting a change in status from unsecured to secured status is also considered a transfer.

548 of the Bankruptcy Code allows transfers within one year prior to filing of a petition to be avoided.

Action under sections 548 and 544 must be brought within two years after the order for relief or if a trustee is appointed in the second year within one year after the trustee is appointed.

(i) Bankruptcy Code   There are two separate grounds for finding a fraudulent transfer under section 548. The provisions found in section 548 act to restrain the debtor from entering into transactions that defraud the creditors. For a transfer to come under this section it must have occurred within one year prior to the date the petition was filed.

First, if the debtor entered into the transaction with the actual intent to hinder, delay, or defraud a creditor the transfer may be avoided. This section may be utilized by those who became creditors before the fraudulent transfer and those who became creditors after the fraudulent transfer. All that is relevant is the intent of the debtor; thus, it is unnecessary to determine the solvency or insolvency of the debtor.

The second section where valuation is important applies to transfers where the debtor conveys property or an interest in property for less than equivalent value and transfers where the debtor incurred an obligation for less than equivalent value. There is no need to show that the debtor intended to defraud the creditors. The transaction must have occurred when the debtor:

- Was insolvent, or completion of the transfer must have caused the debtor to become insolvent,
- Was engaged in a business or transaction, or was about to be engaged in business or transaction and was left with an unreasonably small capital, or
- Intended to incur debts beyond its ability to pay as they matured.

The nondebtor party to the transfer retains the right to recover to the extent that value was given to the debtor.

The term *transfer* is extremely broad under the Bankruptcy Code and has been used to cover a wide range of economic activity.[20] Two areas where this definition gains relevance are in foreclosure sales and leveraged buyouts. In a foreclosure sale, the court must look into whether reasonably equivalent value was obtained and in a leveraged buyout the corporation must receive reasonably equivalent value for pledging its assets to secure the debt used to fund the buyout.

(ii) State Law   State laws are generally based on one of three provisions:

1 *Uniform Fraudulent Conveyance Act (UFCA).* The UFCA is similar to Section 548. It has no "reach-back" provisions, but incorporates the state statutes of limitations that run from one to six years.

[20] Section 101(54) defines transfer as "every mode, direct or indirect, absolute or conditional, voluntary or involuntary, of disposing of or parting with property or with an interest in property, including retention of title as a security interest and foreclosure of the debtor's equity of redemption."

2 *Uniform Fraudulent Transfer Act (UFTA)*. The UFTA has a reach-back of four years.

3 *Statutory and Common Law*. For states without UFTA or UFCA, an American version of Statute of 13 Elizabeth has been adopted. The statute of limitations for fraud will most likely apply from one to six years.

Actions brought under UFCA, UFTA, or other state statutes are based on section 544(b) of the Bankruptcy Code, which allows action to be taken to recover transfers based on state fraudulent conveyance laws.

(c) Reclamation (Section 546)

Under U.C.C. 3-503(2)(a) and Bankruptcy Code section 546(c), a seller can require return of goods only if requested within 10 days of a transfer if the seller discovers the buyer is insolvent. A seller who transferred goods to the debtor in the ordinary course of business may reclaim the goods, if the seller demands reclamation, within 20 days after the debtor received the goods provided the goods were delivered within ten days before the petition was filed. The court may only deny the seller's reclamation rights if it either grants the seller administrative priority or a lien. Courts generally construe the 10-day requirement literally and do not allow extensions or exceptions.

(d) Need for Valuation Services

Generally most action taken to recover assets involves a determination that the debtor was insolvent at the time of the transfer. In order to establish if the debtor is solvent or insolvent, there must be a valuation of the business.

(e) Valuation Approach

Section 101(32)(A) of the Bankruptcy Code defines insolvent as:

> with reference to an entity other than a partnership and a municipality, financial condition such that the sum of such entity's debts is greater than all of such entity's property, at a fair valuation, exclusive of—
>
> (i) property transferred, concealed, or removed with intent to hinder, delay, or defraud such entity's creditors; and
> (ii) property that may be exempted from property of the estate under section 522 of this title;

The analysis is normally referred to as the "balance sheet test." Because a company's property (assets), at fair valuation, is compared to its debts (liabilities) as of a particular date; if its liabilities exceed its assets, it is insolvent. It is worth emphasizing that this definition explicitly excludes any assets (property) that the debtor may have transferred, concealed, or removed, with the intent to defraud, hinder or delay its creditors.

Before the balance sheet test can be conducted to determine solvency or insolvency, the appropriate premise must first be determined. The premise of value concept is often critical in insolvency-related valuations, because courts often require going concern values, unless clear and convincing evidence exists to the contrary. For example, in *Andrew Johnson Properties*,[21] the court said that if the bankrupt is a going concern at the time of the transfer of assets, the property must be valued as a going concern. While in *In re Mama D'Angelo*,[22] the court found the debtor not to be a viable going concern and stated:

> I believe [the debtor] was a going concern and solvent . . . until on or about July 4, 1989. *** [A]s of that date because the product could not be produced the company was dead on its feet, and was not a going concern. *** And thus it not being a going concern the liquidation values . . . must be used.

Case law generally interprets "fair valuation" for purposes of section 547 of the Bankruptcy Code to mean fair market value. In *Andrew Johnson Properties, Inc.*,[23] the court said fair value was the fair market value of the property between willing buyers and sellers or the value that can be made available to creditors within a reasonable period of time. While this case was based on the Bankruptcy Act, courts looking at the issue of the determination of insolvency for purposes of section 547 under the Bankruptcy code have applied the same standard. For example, the Fifth Circuit in *Lamar Haddox Contractors*,[24] noted that "[t]he fair value of property is not determined by asking how fast or by how much it has been depreciating on the corporate books, but by 'estimating what the debtor's assets would realize if sold in a prudent manner in current market conditions.' *Pennbroke Dev. Corp. v. Commonwealth Sav. & Laan Ass'n*, 124 B.R. 398, 402 (Bankr. S.D. Fl. 1991)."

In *In re Nextwave Personal Communications, Inc.*,[25] the bankruptcy court noted that for purposes of determining insolvency under section 548 the three general approaches used to determine value apply—(1) the replacement cost approach, (2) the market comparison approach, and (3) income stream or discounted cash flow analysis. In the bankruptcy court concluded that the market comparable analysis, subject to appropriate adjustments was the appropriate approach to use in this case. The court noted that discounted cash flow analysis "is widely if not universally used in the business and financial world as a tool to assist management in making decisions whether to invest in or dispose of business or major assets. It is generally not used as a tool for determining fair market value, particularly when that determination can be made using either replacement cost or market comparables."[26] In reaching this conclusion the bankruptcy courted cited *Keener v. Exxon Co.*[27] where the court noted that

---

[21] CCH Dec. ¶ 65,254 (D.C. Tenn. 1974).

[22] *In re Mama D'Angelo, Inc.*, 55 F.3d 552 (10th Cir. 1995).

[23] Andrew Johnson Properties, Inc., CCH Dec. ¶ 65,254 (D.C. Tenn. 1974).

[24] 40 F.3d 118 (5th Cir. 1994). *See also In re Roblin Industries, Inc.*, 78 F.3d. 30 (2d Cir. 1996) and *In re DAK Industries, Inc.*, 170 F.3d 1197 (9th Cir. 1999).

[25] 15 235 B.R. 277, 294 (Bankr. S.D.N.Y. 1999).

[26] Id. p. 294

[27] 32F.3d 127, 132 (4th Cir. 1994), *cert. denied*, 513 U.S. 1154. (1995). *See Amerada Hess Corp. v. Commissioner of Internal Revenue*, 517 F.2d 75, 83 (3d Cir. 1975); *Ellis v. Mobil Oil*, 969 F.2d 784, 786 (9th Cir. 1992); *BFP v. Resolution Trust Corp.*, 511 U.S.531, 548 (1994); *In re Grigonis*, 208 B.R. 950, 955 (Bankr. D.Mont. 1997).

"fair market value is, by necessity, best set by the market itself. An actual price, agreed to by a willing buyer and willing seller, is the most accurate gauge of the value the market places on a good. Until such an exchange occurs, the market value of an item is necessarily speculative."

The Seventh Circuit held that going-concern values should be used in determining the value of the inventory of a retail business for the purpose of determining solvency or insolvency for the recovery of a potential preferential transfer.[28] The Seventh Circuit in selecting the going concern standard, noted that while the going concern value is not the proper standard if the business is on its "deathbed" at the time of transfer, this business was not on its "deathbed." The Seventh Circuit noted that the "deathbed" and "death" came later and that caution should be taken not to consider property as "dead" simply because hindsight teaches that the debtor was on the road to financial disaster.

In determining the solvency of a partnership debtor in the context of a preference action against a nonrecourse creditor, section 101(32)(B) of the Bankruptcy Code requires that the net assets of a general partner be counted even though the debtor will not have access to the assets because the debt is nonrecourse.[29]

§ 11.5   Chapter 13 Secured Claims

If the holder of a secured claim does not accept the plan in a chapter 13 proceeding under the Bankruptcy Code, section 1325(a)(5) provides that the value of the property to be distributed as of the effective date of the plan must be at least equal to the amount of the secured claim. The amount of the secured claim would be determined according to the provisions of section 506(a), which would involve an evaluation of the collateral. In a chapter 13 case, it would be anticipated that going-concern values would be a factor in valuing property of secured creditors (§ 11.3).

In *Associates Commercial Corporation v. Rash,* 117 S. Ct. 1879 (1997), the Supreme Court held that in a chapter 13 cramdown under section 1325(a)(5), the debtor must provide the creditor with the equivalent of the present value of the replacement value of the collateral. The Court noted that "[a]pplying a foreclosure-value standard when the cram down option is invoked attributes no significance to the different consequences of the debtor's choice to surrender the property or retain it." On the other hand, the Court concluded that "the replacement-value standard . . . distinguishes retention from surrender and renders meaningful the key words 'disposition or use.'"

§ 11.6   Determining the Best Interest of Creditors and Stockholders under Chapter 11

Under section 1129(a)(7), each holder of a claim or interest must accept the plan or receive or retain under the plan property that is not less, as of the effective date of the plan, than the amount that would be received or retained if the

---

[28] *Matter of Taxman Clothing Co.,* 905 F.2d 166 (7th Cir. 1990).
[29] *In re Union Meeting Partners,* 169 B.R. 229 (Bankr. E. D. Pa. 1994).

debtor were liquidating under chapter 7. This protection is afforded to each member of a class of claims or interest, in contrast to other confirmation standards. As such, it is meaningful to those members of a class who voted to reject the plan but were overruled by a majority of the other members of the class or elected not to vote. If the claim is held by a secured creditor and an election is made by that class to have the entire claim secured under section 1111(b)(2), then the creditor must receive or retain property of a value, as of the effective date of the plan, that is at least equal to the value of the creditor's interest in the collateral.[30]

Section 1129(a)(7) incorporates the "best interest of creditors" test that was found in section 366(2) of Chapter XI under prior law, but sets forth what is intended. The new law also covers secured creditors and stockholders.

The amounts to consider when determining the values under a chapter 7 liquidation are liquidating values. The values used would most likely assume an orderly liquidation and not an immediate forced sale. In determining these values, there must be an evaluation of causes of action, such as avoiding powers that would be pursued in chapter 7, and costs of administration expenses. The value assigned to property pledged under the section 1111(b)(2) election would not necessarily be restricted to liquidation values but may depend on the possible disposition or retention of the collateral (§ 11.3).

§ 11.7   Determining Whether a Plan Is Fair and Equitable to a Dissenting Class in Chapter 11

Section 1129(b) permits the court to confirm a plan where creditors have not accepted the plan, provided the plan meets certain standards of fairness to dissenting classes of creditors or equity security holders. (See § 6.34.) Because the court can confirm the plan without creditor approval if these standards are met, the process is referred to as a "cram down." The standards of fairness to dissenting junior classes center around a modification of the "absolute priority" doctrine, where the dissenting class of creditors must be paid in full before any junior classes may share under the plan.

(a) Bankruptcy Act Provisions

As a basis for determining whether stockholders would participate in a Chapter X corporate reorganization under prior law, the court had to value the business and establish whether the debtor corporation was solvent or insolvent. According to section 179 of the Bankruptcy Act, if the debtor was insolvent, the plan of corporate reorganization completely terminated the interests of the existing stockholders without their approval. However, if the debtor was solvent, the stockholders had a vote to determine how the reorganization would be conducted, because their interests would be materially affected. Dissenting classes of stockholders were entitled to protection of their interests.

Section 221 of the Bankruptcy Act was the forerunner of section 1129(b) of

---

[30] 11 U.S.C. § 1129(a)(B). Note that the § 1111(b)(2) election requires approval by a class (§ 1111(b)(1)(A)), but generally each secured debt is in a separate class.

the Bankruptcy Code. It required that the Chapter X plan of corporate reorganization be "fair, equitable and feasible." For over a half a century, the words "fair and equitable" have been judicially interpreted to require the application of the "absolute priority" doctrine; that is, each class of creditors and stockholders is given its proper priority, and the legal and contractual rights of each party are considered. Essentially, the absolute priority doctrine requires a full realization of senior creditor claims before junior creditors are allowed to participate in the plan of reorganization; similarly, the claims of junior creditors must be satisfied before shareholders may participate. Given this requirement to satisfy all classes of creditors and stockholders strictly according to their order of priority, it is necessary to determine the amounts owed to each class and the value of the business. Thus, one of the purposes of the reorganization is to provide an equitable distribution of the debt claims (and equity claims, if there are any) to assets among both the creditors and the shareholders of the corporation. For this to be done, the court must assign a value to the securities issued to participants in the reorganization. Nothing except a speculative value can be assigned to the newly issued securities if no valuation has been made of the debtor's business on a going-concern basis. Hence, the corporate reorganization could hardly be deemed to be fair and equitable to everyone without a valuation and an allocation of those values to each class of creditors and interests designated by the plan.

(b) Bankruptcy Code Provisions

The relaxed absolute priority doctrine described in the following paragraphs requires valuation of a chapter 11 debtor's business if any class of secured creditors' claims, unsecured creditors' claims, or stockholders' interests does not approve the plan and is impaired under the plan.

(i) Secured Claims   For the courts to be able to force the acceptance of a plan on the holders of secured claims according to section 1129(b)(2)(A), the plan must provide for at least one of the following:

1   The holder retains the lien on the property up to the allowed amount of the claim. If the debtor elects to have section 1111(b)(2) apply (under which the entire debt is considered secured even though it exceeds the value of the collateral), the creditor is entitled to have the entire allowed amount of the debt secured by a lien even if the value of the collateral is less than the debt. In addition, the holder receives, on account of the allowed secured claims, payments, either present or deferred, of a principal face amount equal to the amount of the debt and of a present value equal to the value of the collateral.

2   The sale, subject to section 363(k) of the Bankruptcy Code, of any property that is subject to the claimants' lien securing such claims, free and clear of such lien, with the lien to attach to the proceeds of the sale and the subsequent treatment of the lien consistent with clause 1 (above) or 3 (below).

3   Realization by the holder of indubitable equivalent of the claim.

In provision 1 above, it is necessary to determine two values—one for the collateral and the other for the present value of future payments called for under the plan. To determine the value for this section of the Bankruptcy Code, it is generally not necessary to value the business; rather, the individual assets constituting the collateral are valued. The approaches used to determine the value for secured creditors in section 506 would also apply here; however, the creditor is not bound by any value placed on the property for the purpose of determining secured claims. The present value of future payments is determined by discounting to the present the value to be received in the future. The Bankruptcy Code does not provide any guidance as to what should be the basis for determining the rate to use in discounting future value. This does not, however, mean that the interest rate should be assumed to be the discount rate.

In determining the value for the purposes of a cram down of a secured lender, often the focus is on the interest rate to use to determine if the plan provides current and future payments that have a value equal to the value of the collateral. The declaration of an accountant regarding the interest rate to use is presented in 11.1 in Volume 2 of *Bankruptcy and Insolvency Accounting.*

(ii) Unsecured Claims   One of two standards must be satisfied before the plan can be confirmed where there is a dissenting class of impaired unsecured creditors. First, the plan may provide that the dissenting class receive or retain property that has a present value equal to the allowed amount of the claim. If the proposed property was a present cash payment, the claim would not be impaired under section 1124(3)(A). The value to be assigned to the property would, it appears, be based on the nature of the property (deferred cash, securities, and so on) and the conditions surrounding the transfer. The second standard states that the plan can provide for any fair type of treatment as long as junior creditors or stockholders do not participate in the plan and will not retain any claim against or interest in the debtor. The dissenting class has the right to prevent senior classes from receiving more than full compensation and to prevent equal classes from receiving preferential treatment. To determine whether any class has received more than full compensation, it will be necessary to determine the value of the consideration given. If any consideration is stock of the debtor corporation, it will be necessary to value the business on a going-concern basis.

The significance of this relaxed absolute priority doctrine lies in the flexibility and the leverage it may provide to creditors in the formulation of a plan of reorganization. If the principal creditors of W Corp. have security interests in all the assets of the business, it is possible that trade creditors will receive little and stockholders will receive nothing under the plan. If W Corp. has publicly traded securities and management hopes to preserve an opportunity for future equity capitalization, management may want very much to give up a little something to the old stockholders—or it may have another motive to do so. The holders of secured claims may agree and be willing to give up some of their compensation to be on good terms with or to bargain for the acceptance of the stockholder class. Such a proposed plan, which does not satisfy the absolute priority rule of Chapter X (the senior trade creditors are impaired but are not paid in full, and stockholders participate), could be confirmed if all classes accepted the plan. Hence, chapter 11 is more flexible than former Chapter X.

The ability of the impaired class of trade creditors to bar the payment (or retention) of any consideration to the stockholder class by invoking section 1129(b)(2)(B)(ii) may persuade the holders of secured claims against W Corp. to give up a little more to the trade creditors to bargain for their acceptance of the plan. Hence, certain classes of creditors may obtain an element of leverage (if only equal to nuisance value) in chapter 11 reorganizations as a result of the fair and equitable confirmation standards.

(iii) Stockholders' Interest   As with unsecured creditors, one of two standards must be met before a plan can be confirmed with a dissenting class of stockholders. The first standard states that each member of a class must receive or retain on account of such interest property of a value, as of the effective date of the plan, equal to the greatest of any liquidation preferences, redemption price, or the value of their interest. If the dissenting class consists of common stockholders, the plan must provide for them to receive property with a present value equal to the value of their ownership based on a going-concern valuation because the stock will not have a liquidation or redemption value. If the debtor is insolvent, the stockholders will not be entitled to any compensation. The second standard will allow any kind of fair treatment as long as junior interests do not receive any property or retain any interest in the debtor as analyzed above. This would appear to indicate that any kind of treatment for common stockholders would be acceptable because there are no interests junior to the common stockholder.

However, if there is any value, based on a going-concern valuation, to the common stockholders and the plan does not provide for their interest, and they then dissent to the plan, it would not be confirmed because, by necessity, some senior class is being provided for more than in full.[31] The approach used to determine the value of the business and the claims and interest of creditors and stockholders must be based on the assumption of the going concern.

Even if there seems to be no value for the common stockholders, the new chapter 11 is flexible enough to permit them to retain something under the plan of reorganization with everyone's acquiescence or approval. One practical reason for throwing a bone to the stockholders is explained this way. Stockholders whose equity interests are worthless cannot prevent the plan from providing that the stockholders will retain no property and that the creditors will receive all the debtor's stock. But the stockholders can insist on their day in court. The stock will be part of the consideration distributed under the plan, so a costly valuation of the business will be required to demonstrate that the stockholders have no interest in the business and that the unsecured creditors will not be overcompensated. Stockholders may be able to trade in the nuisance value of their fair and equitable protections by bargaining to give their consent to a plan that permits them to retain something.[32] (See § 6.34.)

To sum up the six cram-down permutations:

1 A class may be unimpaired and be deemed to have accepted the plan (section 1126(f)).

2 A class may receive nothing and be deemed to have rejected the plan (section 1126(g)); see item 6.

[31] Klee, *supra* note 10, p. 146.
[32] *Id.*, p. 145.

3 A holder may accept the plan but be overruled by a rejecting majority;
   see item 6.
4 A holder may accept the plan with a majority of its class.
5 A holder may reject the plan but be overruled by an assenting minority
   and either:
   a Receive treatment in the best interest of holders; or
   b Defeat confirmation.
6 A holder may reject the plan with a majority of its class and either:
   a Receive fair and equitable treatment; or
   b Defeat confirmation.

§ 11.8   Determining Feasibility

Under prior law, it was necessary for both Chapter X corporate reorganization
plans and Chapter XI arrangement plans to be feasible. This requirement also
concerned the question of value, because a condition of feasibility is equated to
the soundness of the proposed capital structure and the assurance of adequate
working capital. The SEC suggests that the enterprise must have sufficient cash,
working assets, and earning power to assure ample coverage of all financial obligations, including required capital expenditures as well as interest and principal
payments on its debt obligations when due.[33] The feasibility requirement thus
necessitates that the newly created entity have a reasonable prospect for successful business operations in the future. Because a debtor that remains insolvent
after the confirmation of the reorganization has very little opportunity for future
success, a reasonable and equitable valuation of assets was absolutely essential
to Chapter X and Chapter XI proceedings. Section 1129(a)(11) also contains a similar requirement stating that confirmation of the plan will not be given if the plan
is likely to be followed by the liquidation or the need for further financial reorganization of the business (unless the plan so proposes). Thus, the feasibility
requirement of Chapter X and Chapter XI of prior law extends to the new law.

§ 11.9   Codification of Value

Many provisions of the case law under the Bankruptcy Act have been added
to the statutory language of the Bankruptcy Code. Thus, value is mentioned
more frequently in the Code than in the prior Bankruptcy Act. Among the
other Code sections where a valuation is required are the following:

- *Section 101(18)*. Valuation problems may arise in determining whether
  an entity qualifies as a farmer as defined in this subsection.
- *Section 363(n)*. A trustee may avoid a sale if price was controlled (collu-
  sive bidding) and recover an amount to the extent that the *value* of the
  property sold exceeded the sales price.
- *Section 503(b)*. Compensation to be paid accountants and other professionals depends, among other factors, on the *value* of such services.
- *Section 506(b)*. To the extent that the *value* of property pledged as collateral exceeds the claim, prepetition interest, reasonable attorney's fees,
  and related costs may be allowed.

---

[33] 35 S.E.C. 290, 297–98 (1953). See also *Group of Institutional Investors v. Ch., M., St. P. & P.R.
Co.*, 318 U.S. 523, 539–41 (1943).

- *Section 506(c).* Here, *value* is associated with benefit in that the trustee may recover, from property securing an allowed secured claim, the reasonable costs of preserving or disposing of such property to the extent that it benefits the holder of the claim.
- *Section 522.* Subsection (a) states that *value*, when used in determining the property to be exempted from the estate of an individual, means "fair market value as of the date of filing of the petition."
- *Section 541(a)(6).* Earnings from services performed by an individual debtor after the petition is filed are exempt from the estate. In situations where the talents of the debtor represent the most important asset of the business, significant valuation problems can arise.
- *Section 542(a).* An entity must deliver to the trustee all property, or the *value* of such property, of the estate as of the date the petition was filed.
- *Section 547.* Contemporaneous exchanges must be for new *value*, as defined in subsection (a), for the transfer not to be considered a preference.
- *Section 548.* Subsection (a)(2) states that one possible condition for a fraudulent transfer is for the debtor to receive less than a reasonably equivalent *value* in exchange for such transfer. Subsection (d) defines *value* to mean "property, or satisfaction or securing of a present or antecedent debt of the debtor, but does not include an unperformed promise to furnish support to the debtor or to a relative of the debtor." Subsection (c) also requires the determination of *value*.
- *Section 549(b).* In an involuntary case, any transfer during the involuntary gap period is valid to the extent of *value* given for such transfer. Services are considered *value* given and will have to be valued.
- *Section 550(d).* A good faith transferee from whom the trustee may recover property transferred has a lien on the property to the extent of the lesser of the cost of any improvements made or the increase in *value* as a result of such improvements. The determination of value could be very difficult here. For example, if property goes down in value after the transfer is made but before improvements are made and improvements then increase the value, will the transferee have a lien on the total increase? The time period used to determine the increase in value is also very important.
- *Section 723.* Valuation problems will arise in assessing general partners for any deficiency of the partnership's estate to pay in full all claims.
- *Section 761. Net equity* and *value* are defined in subsection 17 for commodity broker liquidations and used in subsequent sections of the Bankruptcy Code dealing with the liquidation of commodity brokers. *Net equity* is also used in section 741.

There are other sections of the Bankruptcy Code that deal with value. The list above is presented to give the accountant some indication of the number of times value must be assigned to assets, liabilities, services, or the entire business.

LIQUIDATION VALUES

§ 11.10 Introduction

Liquidation values may have to be determined for several reasons. As noted in § 11.6, in order to confirm a plan of reorganization, the court must determine that each creditor or stockholder will receive an amount not less than the amount that would be received if the corporation was liquidated under chapter 7. Liquidation values do not necessarily mean the amount that would be obtained in a forced sale; most likely, they refer to the amount that could be obtained in an orderly liquidation. The liquidation values will, in most cases, be much less than going-concern values. For example, inventory in the garment industry is often worth no more than one-third of the cost in situations where the business is liquidated.

§ 11.11   Approaches

To determine the size of the payment that could be expected upon liquidation, the accountant must establish the value of all assets that remain in the estate. Several methods are used by accountants to determine the immediate market price for the assets. The accountant may have another client in the same type of business who may be able to supply information about the values of some of the assets, especially inventory. The accountant may be able to reasonably estimate the values of the assets through earlier experience with companies in the same industry. In order to determine the value of plant and equipment, the accountant may contact the manufacturer or a used equipment dealer. It is often necessary for the court or the creditors' committee to employ an auctioneer or appraiser to evaluate the assets. The assets listed will include not only the property on hand but also whatever may be recovered, such as assets concealed by the debtor, voidable preferences, any questionable transactions involving payments to creditors, returns of merchandise to vendors, sales of fixed assets, and repayment of loans to owners.

In determining liquidation values, certain outlays that would be necessary if the debtor's estate was liquidated under chapter 7 must be considered. Examples include expense of administration, priority claims, and costs of avoiding certain transfers and related costs associated with the recovery of assets for the benefit of the estate. The liquidation value of the business, therefore, is a projected evaluation of asset recoveries net of estimated expenses.

In Volume 2 of *Bankruptcy and Insolvency Accounting*, 11.2 is the liquidation analysis of Revco that was presented in the disclosure statement. The topics covered are:

- The description of the liquidation that appeared in the text of the disclosure statement
- The accountant's report issued on the liquidation analysis
- The liquidation values
- The notes to the liquidation analysis

The notes describe one of the major problems faced by accountants in determining liquidation values: What should be the time frame for determining liquidation values? For example, should the values be based on a "fire sale" approach using immediate liquidation values, or should it be an orderly liquidation spread over an expanded time period? It would appear that the largest liquidation value that can be obtained in a reasonable time period should be used. Thus, if it is possible to sell 20 drug stores as a block, that value should be used as the liquidation value rather than the value obtained by liquidating the inventory in the stores. The process illustrated in Volume 2 was used by Arthur Andersen in estimating the liquidation values for Revco.

GOING-CONCERN (REORGANIZATION) VALUATION[34]

§ 11.12   Introduction

This value is referred to as the reorganization value of the entity that emerges from bankruptcy. Several approaches have been used in practice, to determine the reorganization value of the new entity.

The appropriate method for valuing a business in Chapter X proceedings was established in 1941 by the U.S. Supreme Court's decision in *Consolidated Rock Products Co. v. DuBois.*[35] In regard to the importance of determining the value of the debtor's assets, the Court stated:

> A prediction as to what will occur in the future, an estimate, as distinguished from mathematical certitude, is all that can be made. But that estimate must be based on an informed judgment which embraces all facts relevant to future earning capacity and hence to present worth, including, of course, the nature and condition of the properties, the past earnings record and all circumstances which indicate whether or not that record is a reliable criterion of future performance.[36]

Thus, the proper method of valuation of the business as a going concern is the assessment based on future earning capacity, rather than the utilization of a procedure based on either the market value of outstanding stocks and bonds or the book value of the corporation's assets.

The objective of the balance of this chapter will be to discuss several methods used to determine the reorganization value of the emerging entity.

The bankruptcy court in *In re Melgar Enterprises, Inc.*[37] noted that there are three general appraisal techniques available to determine the fair market value of property. They are:

1   Market or sales comparison—based upon evidence of comparable sales.

2   Cost of land development—based upon the actual (theoretical) cost of construction less depreciation. This approach is also known as the replacement costs.

3   Capitalization of income—based on the capitalization for the net future income that the property is capable of producing. In *In re Southmark Storage Associates, Ltd.*[38] the court recognized two methods for determining the value base on capitalization of income: discounted cash flow analysis and the direct capitalization method. The court noted that the

---

[34] Part of this section is based on an article by Grant W. Newton and James J. Ward, Jr., which appeared in the *CPA Journal,* August 1976, pp. 26–32. Reprinted with permission of *The CPA Journal,* © 1976, New York State Society of Certified Public Accountants.

[35] 312 U.S. 510 (1941).

[36] *Id.,* p. 526.

[37] 151 B.R. 34 (Bankr. E.D.N.Y. 1993).

[38] 130 B.R. (Bankr. D. Conn. 1991).

discounted cash flow analysis is superior, and entitled to more weight in arriving at value, because the income projection is based on a longer time period than one year.

§ 11.13   Book Value

Under this approach, the assets are shown at book value. However, these amounts often have no relationship to the current value of the assets or of the entity as a whole. Book value is generally disregarded in determining the reorganization value of the entity.

§ 11.14   Appraisal Value or Replacement Cost

Another method is to adjust individual assets or groups of assets to reflect current values. Equipment is usually valued at its replacement cost less replacement depreciation. Identifiable intangibles such as proprietary processes are reflected at estimated values. Goodwill is usually shown at zero. This approach ignores the fact that the entity as a whole may be worth more than the individual components. Even when going-concern values are used to determine the reorganization value, appraisal values are still needed to allocate the going-concern value to individual assets in order to adjust the book values to reflect current costs.

There may be some situations where an appraisal of the assets is the best way to value a company, such as a nonprofit corporation where the principal assets owned by the debtor are the properties used by the debtor in rendering a service.

§ 11.15   Market Value of Securities

Despite the *Consolidated Rock Products* decision, the valuation of the holding or investment company at the time of reorganization is not based on the prospective future earnings of the entity, but on the present realizable market value of the securities on hand. This approach was selected even though the appellants argued that the going-concern value should be used to include matters such as increases in the value of securities held, increases in dividends, and "restoration of 'leverage' through the borrowing of money and the earnings of skilled management in the purchase and sale of securities."[39] It should be noted, however, that the securities held by the company in question did not represent a controlling interest in any company.

The rationale for the market approach is logical. The investment company has no fixed assets oriented to a particular function as would an industrial business; moreover, a specialized service is rendered only in the sense that the company offers diversification of investment and management of assets.[40] The market value is the fundamental valuation criterion used in the investment field when the debtor's shares comprise only a noncontrolling interest in

---

[39] *Central States Electric Corp. v. Austrian*, 183 F.2d 879, 884 (4th Cir. 1950), *cert. denied*, 340 U.S. 917 (1951).

[40] *Id.*

another entity. The situation, however, is substantially altered when the debtor's only assets consist of stock shares representing total control of other businesses. Under such circumstances, it is apparent that the debtor's financial outlook is completely dependent on the financial success or failure of the wholly owned entities. Accordingly, the debtor's valuation is based on the future earnings of those entities capitalized at the appropriate rate.[41]

§ 11.16 Discounted Cash Flows

The economic value of an entity is the sum of the value of its debts and its equity. This value is often called corporate or shareholder value.[42] For chapter 11 purposes, corporate value is the reorganization value. One approach that has been used to estimate the reorganization value of the new entity is to discount the cash flows by the cost of capital. The reorganization value is made of three components:[43]

1 The present value of cash flows from operations during the period in which cash flows are forecasted.
2 Residual or terminal values that represent the present value of the business attributable to the period beyond the forecast period.
3 The value of assets that will not be needed for operations by the reorganized entity. These assets may consist of excess working capital and assets that will be liquidated as part of the plan.

Reference to 11.3 in Volume 2, an example of how discounted cash flow may be used to calculate the reorganization value, may be helpful as this section is reviewed.

(a) Cash Flow from Operations

Cash flow from operations is the difference between the net cash inflows and outflows from operating activities plus additional capital expenditures and working capital investments. Depreciation and other noncash items are omitted. Interest and principal payments, including payments on capitalized lease obligations, are ignored, but the cash outlay for taxes is considered. The operating cash flows represent the amount that is available to compensate both debt and equity holders.

(b) Residual Value

The residual or terminal value represents the additional value the emerging entity will generate beyond the projection period. The residual value depends, among other factors, on the assumptions made about operations during the forecast projection and on the assessment of the competitive position of the emerging entity at the end of the projection period. For example, if the assump-

---

[41] *In re Equity Funding Corporation of America,* 391 F. Supp. 768 (C.D. Cal. 1975).
[42] Alfred Rappaport, *Creating Shareholder Value* (New York: The Free Press, 1986), pp. 50–51.
[43] *Id.,* p. 51.

tion is made that over the projection period the emerging entity will sell its highly technical divisions and keep only the division that operates in a very mature industry that will be declining over the next five years but will gener-ate a large amount of cash to fund the reorganized debt, the present value of the cash flows from operations will be very high and the residual value will be very low. On the other hand, if the assumption is made that the cash from the divi-sions in the mature industry will be used to fund research and development cost in the technical divisions, the present value of cash flows from operations will be low and there will be a large residual value.

Several techniques are used to estimate the residual value. In the example above, where a company was operating in a declining industry, liquidation values could be used. Other possible techniques are the perpetuity method, market-to-book ratio, and price–earnings ratio.

The perpetuity method is generally the preferred method for calculating the residual value because it is based on the competitive dynamics of the economy. For example, a company that is able to generate returns that are greater than the cost of capital will attract competitors that will eventually drive the returns down to the cost of capital. The perpetuity method assumes that, after the projection period, the emerging entity will earn, on average, only the cost of capital on its new investments.[44] Thus, once the rate of return on new investments is equal to the cost of capital, changes in future cash flows will not affect the value of the business. Thus, the residual value is equal to the annual cash flow at the end of the discount period divided by the cost of capi-tal. However, the cash flows into perpetuity may be represented by the new operating profit after taxes. Capital expenditures above the depreciation expense will not impact cash flows because, for the new investment, the returns will equal the cost of capital and not create any new value. Capital expenditures equal to the depreciation will be necessary to sustain continued operations at existing levels. Thus, the value of the perpetuity is:

$$\text{Residual value} = \frac{\text{Operating profit after taxes}}{\text{Cost of capital}}$$

The value of the perpetuity at the end of the projection period must be dis-counted. This method does not suggest that all cash flows after the projection period will be the same; rather, it suggests that cash flows from new invest-ments after this period will earn only the cost of capital and thus add no new value to the emerging entity.

Under the price–earnings ratio approach, the residual value is determined by multiplying the earnings at the end of the projection period by the estimated price–earnings ratio at that time. The use of the price–earnings ratio is described in § 11.17. Rappaport suggests that the following problems exist in the price–earnings approach.[45]

- It is based on the premise that value is driven by earnings. Earnings is not a good measure of economic value because alternative accounting meth-

[44] *Id.,* pp. 60–61.
[45] *Id.,* pp. 20, 63.

ods are used, risk is excluded, investment requirements are excluded, dividend policy is not considered, and the time value of money is ignored.

- An inherent inconsistency exists in commingling cash flows during the projection period with earnings after this period.
- The price–earnings approach does not explicitly take into account whether the business will be able to invest at, below, or above the cost of capital in the postprojection period.
- It is difficult to accurately forecast future price–earnings ratios. For example, the ratio for the Dow Jones Industrials for the past 20 years has ranged from 6 to 23.

Under the market-to-book approach, the residual value is determined by multiplying the book value of the equity times the ratio of market value to book value at the end of the projection period. This approach suffers from most of the same weaknesses that were discussed above for the price–earnings ratio method.

(c) Cost of Capital

The cost of capital represents the required return that must be earned if the value of the entity is to remain unchanged. Cash flows are discounted at the cost of capital to determine the value of the emerging entity. The cost of capital is normally determined by calculating the weighted average of the costs of debt and the cost of equity. Consider the following example, where the planned financial structure is 60 percent debt and 40 percent equity:

	Weight	Cost	Weighted Cost
Debt	60%	8%	4.8%
Equity	40%	18%	7.2%
Weighted average cost of capital			12.0%

The weights that are used should be those that are planned or targeted over the projection period. For a chapter 11 debtor, the weights should be based on the expected capital structure of the entity as it emerges from bankruptcy and on the expected changes during the projection period. Most financial texts suggest that the weights should be based on market values of equity rather than book values.

The rate that would generally be used for the cost of debt is the long-term yield currently being demanded by bondholders over the number of years in the projection period. In a bankruptcy case, this rate should be estimated according to the debt and equity structure that will emerge from bankruptcy, rather than the existing capital structure of the entity. Because interest is an expense for tax purposes, the rate should be reduced by the tax impact. The cost of debt is:

$$\text{Cost of debt} = \text{Long-term interest rate}(1 - \text{tax rate})$$

Preferred stock has been issued in a large number of chapter 11 cases. The calculation for the cost of preferred stock is similar to that of debt, except preferred stock does not generally have a maturity date and dividends are not deductible for tax purposes. The cost of preferred stock is:

$$\text{Cost of preferred stock} = \frac{\text{Annual dividend}}{\text{Proceeds (Value of preferred stock)}}$$

In most bankruptcy cases where preferred stock is issued, it is issued for debt. The proceeds would therefore be the value of the preferred stock at the time of issuance.

The cost of equity is not as easy to determine. In theory, it is the implicit rate of return necessary to attract investors to purchase the entity's stock. It is the return that must be earned on new projects to leave the value of the shareholders' equity unchanged. The approach generally used to estimate the cost of equity in chapter 11 proceedings is:

$$\text{Cost of equity} = \text{Risk-free rate} + \text{Equity risk premium}$$

The first component of the equation is the risk-free rate, which consists of the real interest rate plus an allowance for expected inflation. There are no "pure" risk-free securities issued in the United States. It may be claimed that there is no default risk in government securities, but long-term Treasury bonds are subject to capital losses if the interest rate rises. A pure risk-free rate cannot be found, and most practitioners use the rate on long-term Treasury bonds as a proxy for the risk-free rate.[46] Also included in the rate for Treasury bonds is the premium for expected inflation. The time period for the Treasury bonds should approximate that used for the projection period.

The second part of the equation for the cost of equity is the equity risk premium, which can be calculated by using several approaches. However, in a bankruptcy situation, it would appear that the most appropriate way to calculate the premium would be to base it on the following:

$$\text{Equity risk premium} = \text{Beta} \times (\text{Expected rate of return on the market} - \text{Risk-free rate})$$

Although it might be arguable whether the risk premiums should generally be based on forward-looking returns, forward-looking returns must be used in bankruptcy cases. The historical returns, hopefully, have limited value if the entity is to be successfully reorganized.

The first factor needed to calculate the equity risk premium is the beta coefficient—a measure of the stock's volatility relative to that of an average stock. Betas are generally determined by running a linear regression between past returns on the stock and past returns on some market index such as the Stan-

---

[46] Eugene F. Brigham and Louis C. Gapenski, *Intermediate Financial Management* (New York: Dryden Press, 1987), p. 118.

dard & Poor's 500. Betas determined in this manner are referred to as historical betas. They provide information about how risky the investment was in the past. Historical beta values may be of limited use in bankruptcy proceedings. Several approaches have been used to adjust historical betas. Rosenberg and Guy, and other researchers, have developed a "fundamental beta," suggesting that fundamental characteristics such as the industry in which the entity operates, the capital structure, and sales and earnings variability provide a better basis for estimating betas.[47]

For a bankrupt entity, any reliance on historical data in the development of the beta must be carefully evaluated; in many cases, betas based on historical data are of limited use. In some situations, the beta may best be determined by looking at betas of similarly sized companies within the industry of the debtor. For entities that have borrowed funds during the bankruptcy proceeding, or that will be obtaining new debt funds, the interest rate associated with those transactions in relation to the rate given to similar companies in the same industry might give some indication of the risk the market associates with the entity that will emerge from bankruptcy.

The cost of equity is also estimated in practice by adding together the Treasury bond rate and an estimate of the risk premium based on many of the factors discussed above.

The next factor needed to calculate the equity risk premium is the expected rate of return on the market. Merrill Lynch and other financial service firms regularly publish a forecast of the expected rate of return on the market, based on discounted cash flow models. From these data, the user can subtract the Treasury bond rate from the market forecast to determine the current market risk premium, which is then multiplied times the beta factor to determine the equity risk premium. The equity risk premium is added to the risk-free return to determine the cost of equity:

$$\text{Cost of equity} = \text{Risk-free rate} + \text{Beta(Expected rate of return on the market} - \text{Risk-free rate)}$$

(d) Special Troubled Business/Bankruptcy Considerations

On emergence from bankruptcy or from an out-of-court restructuring, the debt that issues or debt that continues may be greater than would normally exist. The stated rate of interest is often much less than the market rate. Thus, much of the debt may in fact have more characteristics of equity than of debt. Under these conditions the cost of equity may be used as the overall cost of capital.

(e) Discounts and Premiums

(i) Introduction In valuations in bankruptcy it is common for the ratio or related measure that has been determined from an analysis of firms in a similar business to be adjusted when applied to the specific business that is being

---

[47] Barr Rosenberg and James Guy, "Beta and Investment Fundamentals," *Financial Analysts Journal* (May–June 1976), pp. 60–72.

evaluated. For example, if in determining the cost of capital for a nonpublic trucking business, an estimate of the cost of capital might have been developed based on the beta factor for a large, public trucking business since these data are publically available. The cost might then be adjusted to allow for the fact that the chapter 11 company is smaller than the public company and that there is also a lack of marketability of the chapter 11 company. Additionally, if the stock being valued is held or will be held by a minority interest, the value should be discounted to account for a lack of control.

(ii) Discounts for Minority Interests   The minority discount is different from the discount for lack of marketability. The minority owner has no voice in the management, officers' compensation (or even the election of officers), declaration of dividends, mergers or disinvestments, or public offerings of stock. In situations where the holders of the interest in the company lack the ability to exercise control, the value of the interests held by the minority shareholder is worth less than the proportionate share of the company's reorganization value.

Several studies have been made that attempt to estimate the control premium and the inverse of the control premium, generally referred to as an implied discount for minority interest holdings.[48] Listed below are some of the studies and the results.

Control Premium Studies		
	Implied	
Study	Premium (%)	Discount (%)
Mergerstat[49]	37.1–38.3	27.4
Bolton, Trust & Estates, Dec. 1984	15–78	29.6
American Appraisal Association[50]	17.8–49.1	28.8
Merger & Acquisitions, Jan./Feb., 1991	27.5–49.1	29.7
Merger & Acquisitions, Jan./Feb., 1994	44.4–69.6	36.0
Merger & Acquisitions, Jan./Feb., 1994, 1995, 1996	43.2–65.0	32.4
Houlihan, Lokey & Zukin quarterly study	57–32	30.3

The average discount for minority interest was from 27.4 to 36 percent. The application tended to be between 30 and 35 percent.

In determining the discount to use some consideration should be given to the power that is associated with the control. Pratt lists the following factors as control prerogatives:

- Elect directors and appoint management.
- Determine management compensation and perquisites.
- Set policy and change the course of business.
- Acquire or liquidate assets.
- Select people with whom to do business and award contracts.

[48] James H. Schilt, *Business Valuation Review* (December 1996), p. 165.
[49] *Mergerstat Review,* published by Houlihan, Lokey & Zukin, Inc.
[50] Premium for Control Study, 1989.

- Make acquisitions.
- Liquidate, dissolve, sell out, or recapitalize the business.
- Sell or acquire treasury stock.
- Register the company's stock for public offering.
- Declare and pay dividends.
- Change the articles of incorporation or bylaws.[51]

The ability of a minority shareholder to block an acquisition or impact other control areas is much greater if there are a large number of shareholders that have control than if there is one individual that holds control.

The Tax Court cases have recognized the impact a minority interest ownership can have on the value of the stock. The discount has ranged from 20 to 40 percent (some have been as high as 60 percent) with the common application being between 30 and 35 percent.[52] The particular rate selected will depend, among other factors, on the impact of the control that can or cannot be exercised by the stockholders as described above.

(iii) Lack of Marketability The lack of marketability deals with how quickly and with what certainty the interest can be converted into cash with minimum transaction and administrative costs. The lack of marketability has been considered in a few bankruptcy cases and in many tax cases.

In *Gilliam v. Southern Cooperative Development Fund Investment Corporation*,[53] the bankruptcy court failed to examine the impact of lack of marketability. In determining the value of stock, the bankruptcy court did not consider whether a market for the stock existed. On appeal, the district remanded the case back to the bankruptcy court for further proceeding. The district court held that the findings of the bankruptcy court were incomplete and/or insufficient for the purpose of determining share value.

In *Minnelusa Company* the value of the shares were discounted by 35 percent for minority interest and 40 percent for lack of marketability. In this closely held business, the shares were pledged to a group of creditors as collateral for a promissory note provided to the debtor. Each creditor received 6 percent of the shares.

For many years, tax courts have also recognized the need for a discount for a lack of marketability. The discounts have ranged from 20 to 33 percent with the most common discounts being between 20 and 25 percent.[54]

Listed below are some of the marketability factors that will impact the amount of discount allowed:

1 *Time horizon.* In some cases it may take several years to complete a sale or a new stock offering. In other cases, the sales may take place in a few months.

---

[51] Pratt, Shannor, *Valuing a Business* (Homewood, IL: Dow Jones-Irwin, 1989), pp. 55–56.
[52] Black & Isom Associates, *Valuation Fundamentals, Techniques & Theory*, p. (1995), 7–3.
[53] 1994 WL 682659 (W.D. Tenn., 1994).
[54] 176 B.R. (Bankr. N.D. Fla., 1994).

2 *Cost to prepare for and execute the sale or stock offering.* Among the costs that should be considered are the following:

- Auditing and accounting fees.
- Legal costs.
- Administrative costs of management to deal with accountants and attorneys.
- Transaction and brokerage costs. For example: an equity offering (form S-18 registration) under $7.5 million could cost as much as 12 to 13 percent. As the amount of the offering declines, the percent generally increases.

3 *Risk.* A risk that the actual proceeds received may be less than the estimate, a risk that the business will not even sell, and a risk that the public offering will bring less than the estimated amount.

4 *Form of proceeds.* When businesses are sold in today's market, it is not uncommon for consideration other than cash to be a part of the sale price.

5 *Other factors:*

- Put rights
- Dividend payments
- Potential buyers
- Size of block
- Information access and reliability
- Restrictive transfer provisions[55]

(iv) Small Business Discount   Ibbotson Associates[56] report that the Capital Asset Pricing Model (CAPM) does not fully account for the higher returns of smaller stocks that are listed on the New York Stock Exchange. For example, market capitalization of companies at or below $195,375,000 have a long-term return of approximately 14 percent in excess of the riskless rate and have a CAPM return of 10.4 percent in excess of the riskless rate, or a difference of approximately 3.5 percentage points. In contrast, companies with a market capitalization between $3 billion and $755 million have a long-term return of approximately 9.5 percent in excess of the riskless rate and a CAPM return of 8.4 percent in excess of the riskless rate, for a difference of only one percentage point. For the smallest decile of New York Stock Exchange companies, the difference was almost 6 percent. The smallest company in the sample had a market capitalization of just under $94 million.

These results suggest that there are significant risk factors not considered by the CAPM that impact the returns of smaller companies. If these results are true for small companies listed on the New York Stock Exchange, the adjustment required for public non-listed companies or for companies that are not public may be much larger. These results also suggest that the adjustment to the cost of equity capital for small companies could be in excess of six percentage points or even twice that number.

---

[55] *Discounts for Lack of Marketability,* Chapter 15, pp. 351, 352, 358, and 359.
[56] Ibbotson Associates, *SBBI 1997 Yearbook,* p. 138.

(f) Asset Betas

The betas that are calculated (often by the use of linear regression) to measure the volatility or risk of an investment in relation to the volatility or risk of the market as a whole are equity betas. In order to estimate the risk of the business rather than the risk of the investment, an asset beta is calculated. The asset beta attempts to eliminate the financial risk of leverage.

The asset beta is calculated as follows:

$$\text{Beta asset} = [\text{Beta for debt}(1 - \text{Tax rate}) \times \text{Debt}/(\text{Debt} + \text{Equity})]$$
$$+ [\text{Beta for equity} \times \text{Equity}/(\text{Debt} + \text{Equity})]$$

Debt and equity are shown at market values. The marginal tax rate is used.

The capital asset pricing model (CAPM) cost of capital based on asset betas is calculated in the following manner:

$$\text{Cost of capital} = (\text{After-tax market premium} \times \text{asset beta})$$
$$+ \text{after-tax, risk-free rate.}$$

See 11.3 of Volume 2 of *Bankruptcy and Insolvency Accounting* for an example of value determined by using the above approach.

(g) Present Value of Nonoperating Assets

The present value of nonoperating assets is added to the value of the discounted cash flows for the projection period and the residual value. Included would be proceeds to be realized on the disposal of assets in segments of the business that will be eliminated and excess working capital.

(h) Uses

In summary, calculating the value of a debtor in bankruptcy is difficult because of changes that will be made in the debtor's operations as a result of the reorganization proceedings. Yet, a plan cannot be properly developed unless the interested parties have some indication of the value of the business. The discounted cash flow model is one approach that can be used to help estimate the reorganized value of the entity that will emerge from bankruptcy. This approach is used by both debtors and creditors as they attempt to develop the terms of the plan.

Bankruptcy courts have also accepted this approach. In *Equity Funding Corporation of America*,[57] the court allowed the use of discounted future profit flows as a basis to value part of the company on the argument that special factors may make the usual approach, which uses past earnings reports and future sales and expense projections, an unreliable guide. The court concluded that because the insurance companies (Bankers and Northern) owned by Equity Funding reported their earnings on the basis of statutory accounting as prescribed by state insurance departments, these records are "particularly unreliable indicators of future earning expectancy because both companies have substantially increased their new business production and have made signifi-

---

[57] 416 F. Supp. 132 (1975).

cant changes in the nature of their operations and types of insurance sold during the administration of the estate."[58]

The value for Bankers and Northern was then developed by looking at three separate income streams coming from their in-force business, their future sales capacity, and their income from assets not attributed to policy reserves. The court summarized the approach allowed as follows:

- The value of each company's existing business was determined by projecting profit flow from that business for 30 years and then discounting to present value at 15 percent.
- The value of each company's future sales capability was determined by capitalizing five times the present value of the future profits from one year's production of business.
- The value of the assets not attributed to policy reserves was determined by adjusting these assets to their market value. These assets are stocks, bonds, mortgages, and/or other investments that have a readily determinable market value. That market value is the appropriate measure of their value for reorganization purposes, because the value determined by investors in the marketplace is the best indicator of the present value of the future earnings of the assets.[59]

Although the court was very critical of the type of past earnings records made available by the companies, it is possible that the use of these data may provide for a more equitable valuation. Statutory accounting requires that a one-time payment be expensed in the first year of the policy, rather than spreading it over the life of the policy as allowed by GAAP. This is actually the type of information needed to estimate future cash flows. Other accounting requirements by state regulatory commissions are not in line with the actual cash flows. For example, most states require the buildup of reserves for new policies at a rate that is higher than experience would indicate is necessary. Another interesting aspect of this case is that cash projections were made for 13 years beyond the expected confirmation date. A period of 30 years was used to discount future "profit flows." It appears that the 13 years of cash flow projections could have served as the basis for 30 years of cash flow projections, thus allowing for cash flows to be discounted rather than profits.

Under the Bankruptcy Code, courts have accepted the valuation of a business based on the discounted cash flow method. For example, in *In re Johns-Manville*,[60] the court accepted a value of between $1.6 and $2.0 billion on a discounted cash flow basis, in determining whether the company was insolvent on a going-concern basis under the cram-down provisions of section 1129(b). The liabilities were estimated to be between $2.6 million and $4.3 million. Several other cases have also used a discounted cash flow approach in determining the value on a going-concern basis.[61]

[58] *Id.*, p. 142.
[59] *Id.*, p. 144.
[60] 68 B.R. 618 (Bankr. S.D. N.Y. 1986).
[61] *In re Beker Industries Corp.*, 58 B.R. 725 (Bankr. S.D. N.Y. 1986); *In re Wabash Valley Power Association, Inc.*, 77 B.R. 991 (Bankr. S.D. Ia. 1987): *In re Fiberglass Industries, Inc.*, 74 B.R. 738 (Bankr. N.D. N.Y. 1987).

Excerpts from Pullman Construction Industries' valuation are given in 11.4 of Volume 2 of *Bankruptcy and Insolvency Accounting*. The court eventually accepted the value that Pullman Construction developed. Included are a description of the statements of the debtor's expert and selected exhibits that the debtor's expert developed for the case. The approach used by the debtor follows the previous discussion of the discounted cash approach.

§ 11.17 Capitalization of Earnings

Another approach that has been used to estimate value in many cases is the capitalization of earnings. The discounted cash flow model is being widely accepted and is replacing the capitalization of earnings method as the generally accepted approach, but there are still several insights provided by a look at the capitalization of earnings model. The two factors needed to estimate the reorganized value using this model are future earnings and a capitalization rate.

(a) Prospective Earnings

No universal formula exists for a certain and accurate estimate of future earnings. Thus, courts have concluded that "valuation must be determined on a case-by-case basis, and all relevant factors must be taken into consideration in each case in determining going-concern values."[62] A survey of the literature and case law, however, reveals recurring factors that, although incapable of statement in concise formula fashion, will nevertheless prove instrumental in establishing valuation guidelines.

The logical first step to determine prospective future earnings is to evaluate "projected future sales and the estimated profit margin on those sales."[63] This evaluation of future sales may well be accomplished by means of a detailed analysis of the debtor's past operating history—information that may be of particular relevance to the court in its consideration of a plan of reorganization. Past history is relevant only insofar as it is indicative of the future earning power of a corporation. If it is shown that the record of past earnings is an unreliable criterion of future performance, the court must form an estimate of future performance by inquiring into all foreseeable factors that may affect future prospects.[64]

Section 172 of the Bankruptcy Act required the bankruptcy judge to submit any corporate reorganization plan of a debtor whose indebtedness exceeded $3 million to the SEC for examination and report. The role of the SEC under the Bankruptcy Code has been reduced, but its influence will be felt for some time. The SEC has taken the position that past records of earnings must be adjusted or weighted to take into account unusual past conditions and reasonably foreseeable changes in the future. As an example, adjustments have been made for expected surges of new business from customers who had previously been unwilling to deal with a debtor whose past operating losses failed to inspire

---

[62] *Moulded Products, Inc., v. Barry*, 474 F.2d 220, 226 (8th Cir. 1973).
[63] *In re Muskegon Motor Specialties*, 366 F.2d 522, 526 (6th Cir. 1966).
[64] *Protective Committee for Independent Stockholders of the TMT Trailer Ferry, Inc. v. Anderson*, 390 U.S. 414, 452 (1968).

confidence.[65] Other examples of unusual conditions for which adjustment must be made are: the stability and prospects of the industry, the rate of obsolescence of assets due to technical developments in the industry, the efficiency and integrity of future management, increased expenses, and possible alteration in competition within the debtor's industry.[66]

Closely allied to the problem of the weight to be assigned to past earnings is the difficulty in determining what year's earnings should be used as a base period. The SEC, in its analysis of corporate reorganization plans, has usually been inclined to eliminate—rather than adjust—abnormal years in the concern or industry and it has preferred to use earning trends instead of earning averages. Likewise, courts have steadfastly rejected estimates of future earnings based on unusual occurrences of prior years. In *In re Keeshin Freight Lines, Inc.*,[67] the court rejected the principal witness's estimates of earning expectancies because the two years in question had been subject to unusual events. In one of the two years, the company had purchased new machinery, thus significantly lowering its maintenance costs; in the other year, the company had received a 10 percent rate hike four months before its employees obtained their corresponding wage increase.[68] Predictions of future earnings based on war-year revenues have also been rejected by the courts,[69] as have estimates obtained by disregarding the high and low profit years when computing the average profit.[70]

In any given case, it is uncertain what years may ultimately be used as the base years. The SEC, in one instance, rejected a nine-year earnings period for a department store; in another, it accepted earnings for a one-year period, although the latter was the highest on record for department stores throughout the country.

Another litigious area concerns the appropriate interest payments, based on the corporate debt, to be deducted in estimating future earnings. In the case of *Moulded Products, Inc. v. Barry*,[71] the shareholders contended that utilization of the interest figure was inappropriate because the decision by management as to whether to capitalize the corporation through equity or debt was arbitrary. The court stated that interest payments on debt were to be deducted; not to do so would be "directly contrary to the basic approach courts have taken in the past to valuation of debtor corporations in reorganization proceedings."[72] The deduction from the estimated future earnings of 8 percent interest payments based on the corporate debt was affirmed in the case of *In re Imperial "400" National Inc.*[73]

The accountant, when assisting a chapter 11 debtor or trustee in the preparation of forecasts of future profits, should ensure that all assumptions used in preparing the projections are clearly set forth and that they appear reasonable.

---

[65] *Yale Express System, Inc.*, 44 S.E.C. 772, 780 (1972).

[66] *In re Chicago Rys. Co.*, 160 F.2d 59 (7th Cir. 1947).

[67] 86 F. Supp. 439 (N.D. Ill. 1949).

[68] *Id.*, p. 442.

[69] *In re Barlum Realty Co.*, 62 F. Supp. 81 (E.D. Mich. 1945).

[70] *Supra* note 37, p. 527.

[71] *Supra* note 36.

[72] *Supra* note 36.

[73] 374 F. Supp. 949 (D.N.J. 1974).

The trustee must be prepared to explain the logic of each assumption, especially any assumption that causes the forecast to deviate from past results. Any changes being implemented that will cause revenue to increase should be clearly identified for the judge. In addition, the projections should be adjusted for any changes to be caused by implementation of the plan of reorganization. For example, if debt is going to be reduced by 50 percent because of debt forgiveness and the issuance of equity securities, only the interest cost related to the remaining debt would be included. Finally, adjustments should be made for expenditure reductions from implementing cost efficiency measures.

It has been consistently recognized that nonproductive and nonoperating assets that do not contribute to earnings should be valued separately. This separate category includes excess cash or working capital, income tax loss carryover, excess plant and equipment, other nonproductive property held for liquidation, and investments that are not related to the business of the company.[74] In determining the value of the assets in the *Yale Express* Chapter X case, the court used four components: capitalized value of earnings, appraised value of buildings, excess working capital, and present value of tax loss carryover.[75]

(b) Appropriate Capitalization Rate

In general, deciding the appropriate rate of capitalization of future earnings and predicting future earnings both face the same problem: lack of mathematical certainty. Nevertheless, even though no precise formula has been developed to determine the rate, general agreement does exist concerning the basic principles of choosing an appropriate rate. Virtually all would agree that the capitalization rate should reflect the market free-interest rate (based on long-term government paper), to which is added an interest component that reflects the risk inherent in the enterprise and the industry. Thus, the basis for disagreement and uncertainty is provided by the assessment of the various factors contributing to the industry and enterprise risk.

As in forecasting future expected earnings, setting the rate of capitalization is best determined on a case-by-case basis, and any factors that appear relevant to a specific company's risk evaluation may be utilized to determine the rate of capitalization. Thus, when determining the appropriate rate of capitalization, courts have considered the cyclical nature of the industry; the number and character of the debtor's customers; the possible uncertainties in management; expenses and operations; the age and condition of the debtor's plant and equipment;[76] and the rate of technological progress in the industry.

Courts have also displayed a tendency to utilize in their calculations figures obtained from other companies within the industry, provided these companies are similar in nature to the debtor corporation. However, where the debtor has been compared to other concerns substantially differing in character, the

---

[74] Henry B. Gardner, Jr., "The SEC and Valuation under Chapter X," *University of Pennsylvania Law Review*, Vol. 91 (January 1943), p. 441.
[75] *Supra* note 39, p. 784 and 44 S.E.C. 886, 867 (1972).
[76] *Supra* note 37, p. 527.

courts have rejected the rate of capitalization so determined. As an example, in the case of *In re Muskegon Motor Specialties*, the expert witness had calculated the capitalization rate through utilization of the price–earnings ratio of 36 selected auto parts manufacturers listed on the stock exchange. Because the debtor was an unlisted company with no real market for its shares—and its sales varied from four times as great to only one one-hundredth as great as the sales of the companies whose capitalization rates had been computed—the court concluded that a comparison between such entities would yield little beneficial information.[77]

The estimated reorganized value of the company should be compared to the market value of the securities. These values will not necessarily agree. As a general rule, the estimated reorganized values will be greater than the market values of the securities for a short time after confirmation of the plan. However, if the assumptions underlying the calculations of the reorganized value turn out to be close to reality, then the securities' prices should approximate the reorganized value. The difference between the value of securities and the reorganized value should be evaluated to see whether it appears reasonable. Any party who advocates a value that differs materially should be prepared to justify the difference.

In summary, all factors that could conceivably be attributed to the riskiness of the company should be considered in determining the appropriate rate of capitalization.

The courts and the SEC have consistently valued companies by estimating the average earnings and multiplying them times a capitalization rate, but a strong argument can be made that the discounting of future earnings would be a better approach. The current approach can place a larger value on the company than is justified if the average earnings value used is much higher than the earnings in the first several years subsequent to the reorganization, as is typically the case. At other times, the value based on the capitalization of earnings approach can be too low. The process of determining the value of a business in chapter 11 reorganization needs to be reexamined, based on the developments of corporate finance in the past 30 years.

(c) Determining Value

Once the capitalization rate and average projected earnings have been determined, the value is assigned as follows:

$$V = \frac{E}{R}$$

where V = going-concern value of the business
E = average projected earnings for an indefinite time period
R = capitalization rate

Most court cases refer to the capitalization rate in terms of a multiple that is the reciprocal of the capitalization rate. The earnings normally represent the

---

[77] *Supra* note 37, p. 528.

net income after tax; net income before taxes and interest has been used on occasion, but not in recent years.

(d) SEC's Modified Approach

In reports issued by the SEC on a large number of Chapter X cases under prior law, the approach used above was modified and the courts on occasion accepted this modification. The value is determined on the basis of net income before interest but after taxes.

The following illustration of the calculation of the value of future earnings explains the procedure followed by the SEC in the *Yale Express* Chapter X corporate reorganization. This procedure was also adopted by the court.

In the *Yale Express*[78] case, the trustee estimated—based on the results of the first nine months—that the 1971 revenue of Yale Transport, the principal subsidiary of Yale Express, should be $10,902,000—an annual growth rate increase of 18 percent. For 1972, he selected a growth rate of 20 percent, because an increase in new business was anticipated, assuming that the approval of the plan of corporate reorganization would encourage companies that had previously refused to deal with Yale Express to do so now. Because the SEC had estimated that some of this increase would carry over into 1973, a 15 percent growth rate was selected for that year. For 1974, a rate of growth of 11 percent was selected. The 1974 estimate was based on an analysis of the growth in operating revenue for the region where Yale Transport operates and for 20 carriers comparable to Yale. The results of this analysis are shown in Exhibit 11-1.

The trustee estimated an operating profit of 8 percent for 1974, and this ratio was used by the SEC. The net profit from operations was reduced by the amount of income taxes at the rate of 48 percent. Although interest, in this case, was considered only to the extent that taxes were reduced, the court's decision in the previously noted case of *Moulded Products, Inc. v. Barry* requires that earnings be reduced by the interest. Exhibit 11-2 shows the calculations leading to the net amount that was to be capitalized. The 1974 projections were used as an estimated level of earnings on which to construct an approximate value for Yale Transport.

[78] *Supra* note 39, pp. 780, 782, 967.

Exhibit 11-1   Operating Revenues, 1966–1970

Year	New England Middle Atlantic* ($1,000)	Percent Increase	Trustee's Selected Carriers ($1,000)	Percent Increase
1966	$546,578	—	$246,985	—
1967	569,955	4.3	254,135	2.9
1968	606,812	6.5	297,783	17.2
1969	738,974	21.8	331,402	11.3
1970	806,352	9.1	375,433	13.3
Average		10.4		11.2

*Source: Trince's *Red Book of the Trucking Industry*, 1971 Edition.

Exhibit 11-2   Income Projections for Yale Transport

						($1,000)	
Year	Projected Revenues ($1,000)	Percent Increase	Operating Profit	Projected Interest	Net Profit before Income Taxes	Net Income after Income Taxes (48%)	Net Income plus Interest
1971	$10,902						
1972	13,082	20	$ 785	$162	$ 623	$324	$486
1973	15,044	15	1,053	159	894	466	625
1974	16,699	11	1,336	157	1,179	613	770

Note: Earnings value is determined by multiplying the earnings before interest and after taxes times the chosen multiple. For 1974, the equation would be $770,000 × 13 = $10,010,000.

As a basis for determining an appropriate capitalization rate, the SEC analyzed six publicly held motor carriers that in 1970 had revenues ranging from $23 million to $55 million. The average multiple for these six companies (derived by dividing the total market value of the equity plus the principal amount of debt by the income before interest and after taxes) was determined to be 13.9 for 1969–1971, as shown in Exhibit 11-3. For Yale Transport, a multiple of 13 was selected, taking into account primarily the company's past history and the fact that the earnings on which the valuation was based were not expected until 1974. Using the multiple of 13, the earnings value was determined to be $10,010,000 (see Exhibit 11-2).

The method used by the SEC to value Yale Transport attempts to follow the net operating income approach suggested by Modigliani and Miller.[79] Their theory implies that leverage can only distribute the business risk differently among the creditors and stockholders and that increasing the amount of borrowed funds does not increase the total risk. However, because interest is deductible for tax purposes, the larger the debt of Yale as it came out of bankruptcy, the higher the value that would be assigned to the transport division. A 100 percent increase in debt would result in an increased valuation of approximately $1 million.

Exhibit 11-4 contains the average price–earnings ratio (PER) for 1968, 1969, and 1970 for the same six comparable companies used by the SEC. Courts have frequently used these ratios, multiplying them times the net income after tax, to determine the value of the equity interest. Using this approach, the value of the business would be the value of the stockholders' equity plus debt. The earnings used to calculate the PER were net income after tax and interest but before extraordinary items. Note that the average PER was approximately 13, which is the multiple used by the SEC. Using the PER of 13, and including the

[79] F. Modigliani and M. Miller, "The Cost of Capital, Corporate Finance, and the Theory of Investment," *American Economic Review*, Vol. 48 (June 1958), pp. 261–97, and "Corporate Income Taxes and the Cost of Capital: A Correction," *American Economic Review*, Vol. 53 (June 1963), pp. 433–43.

Exhibit 11-3 Capitalization Multiples for Six Comparative Companies

(000s omitted)

	Market Value of Capitalization[a] as of December 31			Net Operating Profit after Income Taxes but before Interest			Multiples		
	1968[b]	1969[c]	1970[d]	1968	1969	1970	1968	1969	1970
Branch Motor Express Company	$15,119	$14,752	$28,015	$1,894	$1,251	$1,869	8.0	11.8	14.9
Eastern Freightways, Inc.	13,253	12,604	23,693	865	765	1,362	15.4	16.4	17.5
Hall's Motor Express, Inc.	23,789	17,471	24,854	2,044	1,310	1,362	12.5	13.3	18.2
Preston Trucking Co., Inc.	24,277	18,270	36,298	1,562	1,792	2,010	15.6	10.2	18.2
Smith's Transfer Corp.	22,841	25,784	61,994	1,894	2,400	3,804	12.0	10.7	16.4
Overnite Trucking Co.	32,386	32,220	55,818	2,449	2,644	4,284	13.1	12.2	13.0
Averages per year[e]							12.8	12.4	16.4

[a]Mean between high and low sale or bid prices of common stocks and debt at each year-end, taken at principal amounts.
[b]For year 1969.
[c]For year 1970.
[d]For period January 1 to October 31, 1971.
[e]Average multiple is 13.9 ((12.8 + 12.4 + 16.4) ÷ 3)

Exhibit 11-4 Price–Earnings Ratios for Six Comparative Companies

	1968	1969	1970
Branch Motor Express Co.	7.3	10.9	14.5
Eastern Freightways, Inc.	13.8	15.7	17.6
Hall's Motor Express, Inc.	11.9	11.6	31.7
Preston Trucking Co., Inc.	15.3	10.3	17.2
Smith's Transfer Corp.	9.8	8.3	6.3
Overnite Trucking Co.	10.3	11.6	18.8
Average per year	11.4	11.4	17.6
Average for three years			13.5

Value of stockholders' equity using multiple of 13 is $7,969,000 ($770,000 net income less interest of $157,000 times 13).

debt, the value of Yale Transport would be reasonably close to the value assigned to the business by the SEC.

In determining a value in the case of *Four Seasons Nursing Center of America*,[80] the trustee used a PER of six and the net income before taxes to determine the value in a prior law Chapter X proceeding. In reviewing the approach used by the trustee, the SEC reported that it preferred to use a single multiple to be applied to earnings after taxes but before interest. The SEC further noted that a multiple of 10.6 would yield approximately the same value as determined by the trustee. Because this multiple of 10.6 appeared to be reasonable, the SEC adopted it. One problem in selecting a multiple for *Four Seasons* was the great variability in multiples for other health care chains. For the 11 companies selected by the trustee, the price–earnings ratios varied from 57 to 700 in 1969. Four Seasons had a multiple of 184. For 1971, the range was from 13 to 93. The multiples were not available for two companies in 1969 or 1971. The SEC noted that the 1969 multiples did not reflect genuine investment values, but were symptoms of a dazzling euphoria that had gripped the market. The 1971 prices were some evidence of a return to some realism, although a skeptic may still discern some elements of lingering afterglow.[81]

The manner in which earnings and capitalization rate have been calculated and used by the SEC has varied from one case to another. For example, in some cases, the next year's earnings were used to determine the net income to multiply times the capitalization multiple. In other cases, the earnings expected in three or four years were used. An attempt was made, however, to justify each of these changes on the basis of economic conditions and other relevant environmental factors.

(e) Alternative Approach

The use of the price–earnings ratio (PER) valuation approach has the advantage of being easily explained to those in court who are not well trained in

---

[80] 44 S.E.C. 821 (1971).
[81] *Id.*, pp. 839–41.

finance. Several problems are associated with its use. For most firms in bankruptcy, prior ratios are often not a valid indication of future ratios. This is true for several reasons. Recent past years are not appropriate because the business sustained losses during this time period. Also, many business and operational changes may have resulted in a different type of operation, or major segments of the business may have been eliminated.

The bankruptcy courts have consistently used the PER of comparable companies. The net result is an average rate that may have little value. The rate in *Four Seasons*, as discussed above, was from 57 to 700. Many factors cause these ratios to be different among similar-size firms in the same industry. There is no indication that the business emerging from bankruptcy will have the characteristics to cause the PER to be the average of that of other companies. The assumption is also made that these firms are properly priced when, in fact, these ratios may contain temporary increases or decreases in earnings that distort the results. The PER for companies with the same type of operations and debt structure may differ because of the accounting methods used to report income. In pricing the stock, the market took into consideration these accounting differences; when a court simply uses the average PER, it is ignoring the adjustments made by the market. Finally, historical PERs are used and the value of the business must be in terms of the future.

(i) Estimating a Rate An alternative to using PER to determine the capitalization rate would be to estimate directly a required rate of return and use this to value the firm. The rate of return might consist of the yields of long-term corporate bonds plus an adjustment for ownership that reflects the systematic risk of the company. Ibbotson and Sinquefield[82] indicated that from 1926 to 1976 the average annual geometric return for long-term corporate bonds was 4.1 percent and the ownership premium was 4.9 percent for a common stock value of 9 percent. The systematic risk, which refers to the average relationship between the company's stock price and the market price, is measured for publicly traded companies using a beta coefficient. If, for example, the beta coefficient for a company is 1.2, this value would be multiplied times the 4.9 average percent ownership premium to arrive at a premium to add to the corporate bond rate to determine the total return.

Other adjustments may be necessary. In bankruptcy cases, when the plan calls for a debt–equity ratio that is higher than the industry average, an upward adjustment may be necessary to compensate for the high risk. For corporations privately held, a higher rate may be necessary to compensate for the lack of liquidity for owners. Likewise, adjustment must be made for situations where the corporation is controlled by owners and not diversified adequately.

The use of a rate developed apart from the PER of comparative companies may, in fact, accomplish the objective of selecting a rate that is representative of the risk inherent in a particular business. A rate based on risk identified by the beta coefficient should be as easily justified as using an average PER of companies in the same industry.

---

[82] Roger G. Ibbotson and Rex A. Sinquefield, *Stocks, Bonds, Bills and Inflation: The Past and the Future* (Charlottesville, VA: Financial Analysts Research Foundation, University of Virginia, 1982).

(ii) Using the Rate to Determine the Value   Once a decision has been made regarding a reasonable value for the rate of return, the next step is to use this rate to determine the value of the business. If the business has a limited life, the expected returns for the remaining life of the business could be discounted to the present, as described earlier. For a business expected to last indefinitely, the reciprocal of the rate of return could be multiplied times the expected average annual earnings, as used in most courts' decisions to date. Thus, the only change made is that the rate, rather than being determined by an average of comparable firms, is estimated directly.

§ 11.18   Determining Assets

Section 101(26) of the Bankruptcy Code provides the balance sheet definition of insolvency: the debtor's assets at fair valuation are insufficient to pay his or her debts. The only assets exempt from valuation under this section are fraudulently transferred or concealed assets and, in the case of individuals, those assets exempted from creditors of the estate under section 522. Under prior law, individual debtors were allowed to exempt these assets from the estate, but they were included in determining insolvency (except for purposes of fraudulent transfers). Fraudulent and concealed assets are excluded in the Bankruptcy Code definition even if they are discovered before insolvency or solvency is determined. For example, the cash surrender value of an insurance policy concealed by the debtor would be excluded.[83] Included in the property, however, would be intangibles such as patents, trade names, tort claims, and property rights.[84] Goodwill has generally been omitted from the assets, because it is considered in the accounting sense as the surplus arising from the difference between going-concern value and cost value.[85]

§ 11.19   Determining Liabilities

The finding of insolvency is determined by a comparison of assets with liabilities. Thus, a proper determination of insolvency would depend on the types of liabilities included. Under prior law, however, some uncertainty existed as to the types to be included in the balance sheet test of insolvency because section 1(14) of the Bankruptcy Act stated that "debt" shall include any debt, demand, or claim provable in bankruptcy. On the other hand, section 63 of the Act indicated that only provable debts share in the assets of the estate. The definition of debts as stated in section 1(14)—used in the determination of insolvency—conceivably extended the scope of potential beyond those listed in section 63. This is true because the use of the phrase "shall include" in section 1(14) suggested that liabilities other than provable claims could be included. This would mean that certain types of debts, such as contingent liabilities of guarantors and endorsers, could have been included for the purpose of determining the amount of liabilities, even though a likely default was not proved and, as a result, the contingent liability was not a provable debt.

[83] *Peterson v. Peterson,* 400 F.2d 336, 343 (8th Cir. 1968).
[84] *Collier on Bankruptcy,* 14th ed. 1.19(2).
[85] Thomas Burchfield, "The Balance Sheet Test of Insolvency," *University of Pittsburgh Law Review* (October 1961), p. 8n.

The Bankruptcy Code changed significantly the definition of liability. Section 101(12) defines a debt as a "liability or a claim." No reference is made in the Code to the concept of provability. A claim, as defined in section 101(4), means (1) right to payment, whether or not such right is reduced to judgment, liquidated, unliquidated, fixed, contingent, matured, unmatured, disputed, undisputed, legal, equitable, secured, or unsecured; or (2) right to an equitable remedy for breach of performance if such breach gives rise to a right to payment, whether or not such right to an equitable remedy is reduced to judgment, fixed, contingent, matured, unmatured, disputed, undisputed, secured, or unsecured.

A debt under the new law is broad enough to include all legal obligations of the debtor that give rise to payment, no matter how remote or contingent. Thus, the bankruptcy court can now deal with practically all types of debts and provide for the broadest possible relief. Debts that are contingent or unliquidated must be estimated under section 502(c).

No doubt one of the major problems associated with liabilities will be the amounts that are secured and unsecured for undersecured claims. This determination, however, depends on the value assigned to the collateral (see § 11.3).

In Volume 2 of *Bankruptcy and Insolvency Accounting*, 11.5 contains a description of the appraisals and valuation data that were used in the chapter 11 filing of Doskocil:

- The premises used in the valuation
- The enterprise or going-concern values
- The liquidation values that could be received from the liquidation of the individual assets in a liquidation in place
- The values of an orderly liquidation
- The assumptions and limiting conditions of the valuation

PART THREE

Auditing Procedures and Reports

12

Special Areas of Inquiry

NATURE OF AUDIT

§ 12.1 Introduction

Reporting on insolvent companies requires the application of audit procedures that vary somewhat from those utilized under normal conditions. Much more emphasis is placed on the balance sheet. The audit of a company in financial difficulty is very similar in many respects to the audit of a company that is in the process of being acquired by another. Emphasis is placed on selected accounts, and others are completely ignored. In a normal audit, the accountant searches for unrecorded liabilities and uses great care to see that the assets are not overstated; however, in a bankruptcy audit, the accountant must ascertain that there are no unrecorded or concealed assets.

The accountant must be on the alert for indications that occurrences out of the ordinary have taken place. Any transactions that could possibly result in the dissipation of the debtor's assets in a manner other than by loss in the ordinary course of business should be examined closely. These include irregular transfers, transactions with related parties, concealment of assets, false entries and statements, financing irregularities, or preferential payments. In the course of the investigation, the accountant may discover a more serious type of irregularity that constitutes fraud. A comparison of the statements filed by the debtor with the company's records may reveal deliberate discrepancies, or missing books or records, or erasures and alterations, or the age of the records may indicate that fraud exists.

The generally accepted standards and procedures that apply to the normal audit are also relevant to bankruptcy and insolvency proceedings under two conditions:

a Where there is an engagement to perform an audit or review under the attestations standards or a compilation under the Standards for Accounting and Review Services.

b Where an opportunity to analyze and challenge the work of the accountant does not exist. For example, when the CPA expresses a written conclusion about the reliability of a written assertion by another party, and the conclusions and assertions are for the use of others who will not have the opportunity to analyze and challenge the work, the professional standards would apply.

See Chapter 14 for a discussion of the reporting requirements when the reports issued are subject to the litigation guidelines. The financial statements should be presented in accordance with generally accepted accounting principles.

Most of the emphasis in this chapter is on audit procedures that differ from those utilized under normal conditions. The term "accountant" as used in this chapter refers to an independent accountant for either the debtor (or trustee, if appointed) or the creditors' committee.

The steps performed in an investigation of a company in financial difficulty are somewhat different from the normal audit designed to render an opinion. There are aspects of the investigation that are quite unique. Generally, more emphasis is placed on the balance sheet and, as the audit or investigation progresses, more modifications of the assignment are required in bankruptcy engagements than in normal engagements.

§ 12.2   Objectives

The purpose of the investigation in most bankruptcy and insolvency cases is to assist interested parties in determining what should be done with the "financially troubled debtor." Should the debtor reorganize and continue operations, or liquidate? Where this is the key issue, the accountant may do a limited investigation of the major aspects of the debtor's operations to ascertain whether the debtor can operate profitably again. In other cases, especially where there is an indication of possible fraud or mismanagement of the debtor's assets, there is a need for a complete investigation of the debtor's prior activities. The objective of the investigation is to determine the existence and extent of understated or undisclosed assets. The accountant searches for hidden bank accounts, assets in the name of the owner that were purchased with the debtor's funds, preferential payments, valuable assets written off or sold without adequate consideration, and any other unrecorded or concealed assets. Emphasis in the liability accounts is placed on the discovery of transactions that resulted in the reduction or modification of liabilities. The debtor may have granted invalid liens to secured creditors or overstated obligations to related companies. The accountant will search for executory contracts that may have been incorrectly recorded as actual liabilities. The claims filed by creditors will be examined to see whether they have been overstated. The equity accounts must be examined to determine whether there are any improprieties that would result in an increase in equity. The debtor may have purchased treasury stock illegally, received inadequate consideration for stock issues, or written off uncollected stock subscriptions.

In examining the income, the accountant looks for unrecorded sales, interest income, or other types of income where a failure to record may have resulted in an understatement of assets of considerable value. In the examination of the expense accounts, the accountant ascertains whether there were any payments for overstated or nonexistent expenses such as wage payments to fictitious employees or payments for purchases that were never delivered.

§ 12.3 Balance Sheet Emphasis

In the examination of a liquidating business, all attention is focused on the balance sheet; the statement of operations is of very little importance. Even in a chapter 11 proceeding, less emphasis is placed on the income statement. The creditors want to know the amount they would receive if the debtor were to be liquidated, so that they can compare it with the amount promised under a plan. This does not mean, however, that the income statement is not important. In fact, not enough attention is given to the income statement, and especially to projected statements, in many reorganization cases. An analysis of the income statements for the past few years is helpful in predicting future profits, and the success of the business in the long run will depend on its ability to make a profit. Over several years, the income statements provide information about the types of expenses that should be eliminated. They pinpoint the time period when the profits began to decline and often give some indication as to the causes of the company's failure. In most proceedings, both the creditors and the stockholders would be better off if the company could be successfully rehabilitated. Although the income statement does indicate areas where corrective action is needed, presenting historical statements is of little value if the nature of the debtor's operation has significantly changed. Of much more value are projected income statements and cash flows showing what future operations should look like with the debtor's changes.

The long-run profitability of the company often does not emerge clearly because long-range operating plans are not prepared or no analysis is made of the past operating results. One of the major reasons for this omission can be found in the background and attitude of the representatives of the creditors. Many banks, financial institutions, and other large credit grantors have a separate department that handles all accounts of debtors in financial difficulty. These specialists do not have the interest in the future of the company that the credit manager or a salesperson for the firm would have. Their primary interest is in obtaining the maximum amount from a particular account. It is immaterial that they may be able to keep a debtor in business, even when this means that an account that may have represented a large amount of sales for ten or 15 years is at stake. The performance of these specialists is measured by the size of the cash settlement. The accountant is frequently in a position to be of considerable benefit to the debtor by using the income statement—historical and forecasted—to help all parties involved consider the long-term prospects for the company. However, as noted in the previous paragraph, the projected statements are often more helpful.

§ 12.4 Modifications of Investigation

Examinations of companies involved in bankruptcy and insolvency could be extended endlessly. Throughout the investigation, a judgment has to be rendered by the accountant as to the extent of detailed work that must be performed. The accountant does not have a blank order to go in all directions and probe as deeply as seems necessary. If the accountant goes beyond the scope of the engagement as set forth in the retention order, payment for the extra work may not be authorized. (See § 7.12.)

If at any time major revisions in the scope of the investigation are required, it is a good policy for the accountant to discuss the changes with the party (or its counsel) that the accountant represents—that is, creditors' committee, trustee, or debtor-in-possession. The accountant should point out the initial findings and give an opinion on the direction that the investigation or review should take. With a consensus from the interested parties, the accountant will continue the investigation. The accountant should be very careful when selecting one or two areas to concentrate on and consequently making a judgment on the other areas that are not feasible to cover. A year or two later, the accountant may be open to criticism for not including certain areas that perhaps should have been examined. It takes a certain amount of experience and know-how to be able appropriately to tailor the scope of an investigation to particular situations. Restriction of time, fees, and various other influences often limits the scope of the engagement.

The priority of work assignments can also be affected by outside influences. The debtor may be faced with imminent foreclosure, and the conditions under which certain debts arose may have to be determined immediately. Very often, while the accountant is carrying out the work assignment in an orderly manner, the trustee may say, "Forget about everything else. Put four people on this problem and find out what happened." Or the trustee's attorney may demand that another problem area be examined. The interruptions may cause the progression of the scope of the audit to become disorderly, and the same phase of the examination may be reperformed a second or third time. The accountant may become resentful of this type of pressure, but these are the realities of bankruptcy and insolvency engagements. They are *not* all conducted in an orderly manner, nor are they the traditional type of examination. Pressure on the attorney for the debtor-in-possession or the trustee, or even the attorney for the creditors' committee, is transferred to the accountant. The orderliness and scope of an examination sometimes become completely uncontrollable, especially in the initial stages.

Because the investigation of a company involved in bankruptcy and insolvency proceedings is not the traditional type of engagement, the accountant's effectiveness will be measured in terms of creativity, imagination, and resourcefulness in finding out what really happened.

In many chapter 11 cases, the debtor does not need a complete examination. Resources available for professional fees are limited, and the accountant should generally focus on problems and opportunities that will be of the greatest benefit to the debtor and creditors. For example, a detailed search for preferences is very costly; however, an examination of payments to related parties, unusual payments, and payments over a preestablished dollar amount to suppliers and other creditors might be very helpful. Thus, the objective may be to investigate or evaluate selected events and opportunities that will best serve the needs of the debtor or creditors' committee (if representing such committee), rather than to complete an audit.

INTRODUCTION TO THE SPECIAL AREAS OF INQUIRY

The opportunity for manipulation of the books and transactions by the debtor means that the accountant must be on the alert for indications that occurrences out of the ordinary have taken place. Several types of transactions commonly found in insolvency cases demand extra attention on the part of the accountant.

§ 12.5 Irregularities

An irregularity is any transaction that is not in the ordinary course of business, and especially includes any transaction that results in the apparent dissipation of the debtor's assets in a manner other than by loss in the ordinary course of business. The period of time during which irregularities may have occurred is not limited to the 90-day period prior to the filing of the petition or the initiation of the out-of-court settlement. Instead, the time period covered during the audit may extend to a year or more, depending on the circumstances. The time period covered by the avoiding powers of the trustee is generally one year; however, it may extend beyond one year under section 544(b), which avails the trustees of remedies under state law.

Irregularities are of utmost importance in the accountant's investigation. The fundamental concern is with discovering transactions on the part of the debtor company that may result in the recovery of assets or provide information for a case for criminal prosecution. Recovered assets would enlarge the debtor's estate and make available a greater amount for distribution to creditors.

There are several common types of transactions that the accountant should carefully scrutinize as being suspect of irregularities. These will be briefly described here, and the important items will be more fully covered in the remainder of this chapter.

(a) Fraudulent Transfers

These primarily include transfers made or obligations incurred by the debtor company, without fair consideration and within one year prior to the bankruptcy petition, that render it insolvent, leave it with an unreasonably small amount of capital, or are accompanied by the intent to incur debts beyond the debtor's ability to pay such debts as they mature. Fraudulent transfers also include those transfers made with an actual intent to hinder, delay, or defraud the creditors. Thus, for sales of assets made within one year prior to the filing of a petition, the accountant must determine whether a reasonable equivalent value was received and the effect or intent of such transfer. See §§ 12.12–12.14.

(b) Transactions with Related Parties Such as Insiders, Officers, Employees, and Relatives

It is especially important to ascertain that such transactions were made at arm's length, that fair consideration was received for any transfer of assets, and that there are no paddings, incorrect cash expenses, misappropriated receipts, or improper purchases. The withdrawal of assets by stockholders as dividends, loans, transfers of assets, and so on, should all be very carefully examined for any manipulation or bad intent. See § 12.14.

(c) Concealment of Assets

This category usually includes an attempt to misappropriate property and hide the shortage. This is often difficult to prove because investigation must rely on records previously kept by the debtor. If it seems possible to show a concealment, turnover proceedings can be attempted, to regain possession of the property. See §§ 12.15–12.19.

(d) False Entries and Statements

Common examples of this irregularity are mutilation or alteration of the books, concealment or destruction of records, forgery of any document, and issuance of false statements. See §§ 12.20–12.23.

(e) Financing Irregularities

These include any schemes whereby the debtor attempts to obtain goods or money using methods outside the ordinary course of business. The most frequently manipulated accounts are receivables and inventory. See §§ 12.24–12.25.

(f) Preferential Payments

These are defined as irregularities by the Bankruptcy Code. Included are any transfers of property made by the debtor while insolvent, within 90 days (one year for insiders) prior to the filing of a petition, and in payment of an antecedent debt, when the effect of such payment was to cause one creditor to receive a greater percentage of debt than would have been received if the debtor had been liquidated under a chapter 7 proceeding. Transactions that should be carefully examined by the accountant include sales of inventory or other assets back to vendors as an account offset that would favor certain suppliers, liens given to creditors in contemplation of filing a petition, and repayment of loans to certain creditors in anticipation of filing a bankruptcy petition. See §§ 12.26–12.28.

(g) Other Types of Transactions

The types of transactions listed below should also be carefully examined by the accountant:

- Any major acquisition, merger, or investment that results in a loss.
- Bulk sales of assets or portions of the debtor's business.
- Indications that the debtor deliberately allowed liabilities to increase, causing hardship to the more recent creditors. An analysis of the accounts payable may indicate that, for several months prior to the filing of the petition, no payments were made on accounts even though new orders were being placed and some cash was received from sales.
- Attempts on the part of creditors to inflate their claims (§ 12.29).
- Any potential assets that may increase the size of the estate if settled favorably for the debtor, such as pending lawsuits or insurance claims.
- All other transactions that may have arisen outside the normal course of business.

The above list does not purport to include every type of irregularity possible in an insolvency case, but mentions only those most frequently encountered. Regardless of the reasons for any suspicions, the accountant's report should include any and all recoverable assets, such as assets involved in preferential payments, assets concealed by the debtor, certain assets that have been sold and are suspected of being involved in a fraudulent transfer, and any other assets relating to questionable transactions. It is crucial that the trustee's attorney is made aware of such irregularities, in order to initiate proceedings to recover such property for the estate.

§ 12.6 Fraud

A specific and somewhat more serious irregularity sometimes found in bankruptcy cases is fraud, or intentional deception in relinquishing some property or lawful right. This usually relates to the debtor's books and records (§§ 12.20–12.23) and may include the filing of false schedules and the giving of false testimony under oath.

The accountant normally attempts to discover fraud by comparing the schedules the debtor has filed and the company's statement of affairs with the amounts entered in the books for assets and liabilities. Indications that fraud may exist include missing books or records; erasures and alterations; computer runs without underlying support; and evidence that the accounting program was run at one point in time.

In addition to its own penalties under commercial law, fraud acts to bar an individual debtor from a discharge of all debts under chapter 7, according to section 727. Section 523(a)(2) of the Bankruptcy Code provides that a discharge for a debt shall be denied to an individual when it has been proven that the debtor obtained money or property on credit or as an extension, renewal, or refinance of credit by issuing a materially false statement, in writing, representing the financial condition of the debtor (or an insider of the debtor). It is also necessary for the creditor to have relied on the false statements and for the debtor to have issued the statements with the intent to deceive. This standard is strictly construed. Nevertheless, it may generally be stated that any attempt intentionally to deceive creditors and thereby gain money or property will mean that the debtor remains liable for the debts so incurred.

Section 523(a)(4) also provides that debts for embezzlement or larceny are exempted from discharge. Thus, a debt resulting from a willful and malicious taking of property of the debtor with the intention of returning the property or replacing it with actual value in a short time period, when injury is inflicted even though intent was not to do so, is nondischargeable.

§ 12.7 Proof of Fraud

To prove misrepresentation and thereby block a discharge of debt, the creditor must show the existence of three basic elements:

1 A fraudulent misrepresentation that is material (any substantial variation from the truth is considered material).
2 Moral depravity by the debtor in making the representation with the intent that it be relied on.
3 Reliance in fact by the creditor.

§ 12.8 Auditor's Responsibility for the Detection of Irregularities

In 1997 the Auditing Standards Board issued SAS No. 82 designed to clarify, but not increase, the auditor's responsibility to detect fraud. According to the AICPA "[t]he auditor has a responsibility to plan and perform the audit to obtain reasonable assurance about whether the financial statements are free of material misstatement, whether caused by error or fraud."[1]

The auditor's responsibility is still framed by the key concepts of materiality and reasonable assurance. It is the auditor's responsibility to detect material misstatements caused by fraud and is not directed to the detection of fraudulent activity per se. Thus, the auditor of financial statements must obtain reasonable assurance that the statements are free of material misstatements, whether caused by error or fraud. However, the Professional Standards also indicate that management is responsible for the prevention and detection of fraud. Management is responsible for adopting sound accounting policies and for establishing and maintaining internal control that will, among other things, record, process, summarize, and report transactions consistent with management's assertions embodied in the financial statements.

SAS No. 82

- Describes fraud and its characteristics
- Requires the auditor to specifically assess the risk of material misstatement due to fraud and provides categories of fraud risk factors to be considered in the auditor's assessment
- Provides guidance on how the auditor responds to the results of the assessment
- Provides guidance on the evaluation of audit test results as they relate to the risk of material misstatement due to fraud
- Describes related documentation requirements
- Provides guidance regarding the auditor's communication about fraud to management, the audit committee, and others

SAS No 82 describes two types of fraud that may result in financial statement misstatements

1. Fraudulent financial reporting. An example of fraudulent financial reporting is a company that ships customers goods that have not been ordered and then records the revenue as if it met all the criteria for revenue recognition. In other cases involving new high technology products, company personnel may have provided customers with a side agreement granting "right of return" for any reason or made payment for the goods contingent on receipt of funding or some other event. In such cases the side agreement typically is not disclosed to the auditor because the underlying transaction would not meet the criteria for revenue recognition under generally accepted accounting principles.

2. Misappropriation of assets. Examples of misappropriation of assets are thefts of cash, inventory or securities. Small practitioners specifically asked for guidance in this area because they were more likely to encounter misappropriations than fraudulent financial reporting. Audi-

---

[1] AICPA, Professional Standards, vol. 1, AU sec. 110, "Responsibilities and Functions of the Independent Auditor".

tors from larger firms were more concerned about fraudulent financial reporting from a materiality standpoint but also thought guidance on misappropriations would be helpful.

SAS no. 82 requires the auditor to specifically assess the risk of material misstatement of the financial statements due to fraud in every audit. The auditor must consider the following categories (as shown in paragraphs 16) of risk factors relating to fraudulent financial reporting

- Management's characteristics and influence over the control environment. These pertain to management's abilities, pressures, style, and attitude relating to internal control and the financial reporting process.
- Industry conditions. These involve the economic and regulatory environment in which the entity operates.
- Operating characteristics and financial stability. These pertain to the nature and complexity of the entity and its transactions, the entity's financial condition, and its profitability.

The auditor must asses the following risk factors that relate to misstatements arising from misappropriation of assets (paragraph 18):

- Susceptibility of assets to misappropriation. These pertain to the nature of an entity's assets and the degree to which they are subject to theft
- Controls. These involve the lack of controls designed to prevent or detect misappropriations of assets.
- The extent of the auditor's consideration of the risk factors in category 1 above is influenced by the degree to which risk factors in category 2 above are present.

Errors are basically defined as unintentional mistakes or omissions of amounts or disclosures in financial statements, and the term irregularities refers to intentional distortions of financial statements. The factor that most often distinguishes errors from irregularities is whether the underlying cause of a misstatement in financial statements is intentional or unintentional. It is often difficult to determine intent, especially in matters involving accounting estimates and application of accounting principles. Fraudulent financial reporting may involve acts such as:

- Manipulation, falsification, or alteration of accounting records or supporting documents from which financial statements are prepared
- Misrepresentation or intentional omission of events, transactions, or other significant information
- Intentional misapplication of accounting principles relating to amounts, classification, manner of presentation, or disclosure

§ 12.9   Methods of Discovering Irregularities and Fraud

The accountant's major source for the discovery of unusual transactions is the debtor's books and records. In a liquidation proceeding where it is believed that documents may be missing, the accountant may request the trustee to arrange to have all mail addressed to the debtor delivered to the trustee instead. In this manner, all checks received can be recorded and deposited, improprieties might be revealed by correspondence, and some of the gaps in the current records may be identified. An analysis of purchase returns may also reveal fraud.

The following is a list of schedules that, when prepared, may aid the accountant in the discovery of irregularities. Each worksheet includes those accounts most subject to manipulation:

> A schedule of all payments made by the debtor preceding the filing of the petition, to determine whether any preferential payments were made to creditors. Such a schedule should include all major payments made during the period from insolvency or during the ninety days preceding the filing of the petition.

> A worksheet of changes in major creditors' accounts, to indicate whether any payments were made to certain creditors for current or prior purchases and whether certain suppliers were being favored through substantial returns or other offsets.

> A report of all repayments of debt, to ascertain whether some creditors were paid in anticipation of the filing of the petition. Especially included should be repayments to officers, directors, stockholders, and other related parties.

> A schedule of the sale of fixed assets, to reveal any sales to creditors for less than full value, to creditors as an account offset, or back to the manufacturer for cash or as an account offset.

> A study of the trend of liabilities, purchases, and sales, to indicate the pattern by which debts grew, whether purchases were not being paid for even though sales were large, and whether this was occurring to the detriment of the debtor's more recent creditors. This report would be of value in establishing the intent of the debtor, always a difficult procedure.

> A reconciliation of the creditors' account balances per the debtor's books with the creditors' claims filed, including, if possible, explanation of any differences between the creditors' claims and the debtor's books.[2]

Even if the accountant harbors no suspicions about the debtor's actions, all transactions should be described in as much detail as possible, and their effect on the financial position of the business should be analyzed. Two different approaches have most commonly been used in reporting the debtor's history: (1) a chronological index, which is simply a schedule including a monthly chronology of all major inflows and outflows of cash and all major unusual transactions; and (2) a narrative description that outlines the sequence of events. Either approach, used as a normal audit procedure, would give indications of those areas where the accountant should conduct further inquiry.

An example of a report that is based on a special investigation of the debtor's operation and controls appears as 12.1 in Volume 2 of *Bankruptcy and Insolvency Accounting*.

---

[2] Edward A. Weinstein, "Accountants' Examination and Report in Bankruptcy Proceedings," *New York Certified Accountant*, Vol. 35 (January 1965), p. 38.

AVAILABILITY OF BOOKS AND RECORDS

§ 12.10 Locating and Obtaining Possession of the Records

After receiving the retention order, one of the first steps performed by the accountant is to take an inventory of the debtor's books and records and their condition. At the same time, examples of documents used by the business may be obtained. These are helpful in outlining the nature of the operations of the business, in determining how its systems operate and its procedures flow, and in identifying the responsible parties. For some types of audits—for example, where a broker or dealer in securities is involved—examinations of documents is absolutely essential. Ideally, management should prepare for the accountant the list of books and records and certify that the list is complete. If the records are turned over to the accountant, the list should be signed to indicate receipt of the records.

In a chapter 7 or other liquidation proceeding, or a situation where fraud is suspected, the accountant will assist the trustee or creditors' committee in securing all the debtor's books and records and transferring them to the accountant's office or other areas under the control of the accountant. Speed is of the utmost importance in the removal process, for several reasons. Such records often disappear with no explanation as to their whereabouts. They may be disposed of innocently by persons who have no idea of their value. The trustee normally wants to vacate the premises as quickly as possible, to minimize rental expense. Thus, quick removal means greater assurance that the records will be adequately safeguarded. It is highly desirable for the accountant to supervise this activity, because the accountant is best able to determine which books are most useful and therefore should be preserved.

In a proceeding where the debtor remains in possession, the debtor will retain the records but the auditor will ascertain that all records are accounted for. The books cannot be removed if the entity continues in existence. Even under these conditions, it is good practice to have management prepare a list of the books and records. The list should be signed by management and placed in the auditor's file for future reference.

It is important to realize that, as an appointee of the court, the accountant is correspondingly entitled to see all of the debtor's books and records.

§ 12.11 Scheduling the Books; Procedure Followed for Missing Records

The accountant is responsible for preparing a list of all the books and records turned over by the debtor, and for ascertaining whether any records are missing. Any such findings must be reported to the trustee's attorney. It is then the duty of the attorney to establish the existence and location of the missing books and initiate proceedings to recover them if such action is deemed necessary.

Again, speed is crucial. The shorter the time period between possession of the books by the trustee and proceedings to obtain missing records, the higher the probability that the books will be successfully recovered.

The trustee's attorney may employ turnover proceedings to obtain the debtor's books and records. The accountant's role in this process would be to reconstruct the debtor's bookkeeping system in order to show what books were kept in the system and what books are therefore missing. Once the books and records have been successfully located and obtained, they should be very carefully stored and made available only to those persons who are authorized to have access to them.

FRAUDULENT TRANSFERS

§ 12.12 Transfer of Assets Without Fair Consideration

Fraudulent transfers and obligations are defined in section 548 and include transfers that are presumed fraudulent regardless of whether the debtor's actual intent was to defraud creditors. A transfer may be avoided as fraudulent when made within one year prior to the filing of the bankruptcy petition, if the debtor made such transfer or incurred such obligation with actual intent to hinder, delay, or defraud existing or real or imagined future creditors. Also avoidable are constructively fraudulent transfers where the debtor received less than a reasonably equivalent value in exchange for such transfer or obligation and (1) was insolvent on the date when such transfer was made or such obligation was incurred, or became insolvent as a result of such transfer or obligation; (2) was engaged in business, or was about to engage in business or in a transaction for which any property remaining with the debtor was an unreasonably small capital; or (3) intended to incur, or believed that the debtor would incur, debts that would be beyond the debtor's ability to pay as such debts matured (see § 5.40).[3]

Section 548 of the Bankruptcy Code is based on section 67(d)(2) of the Bankruptcy Act. The trustee may avoid the transfers or obligations if they were made or incurred with the intent to hinder, delay, or defraud a past or future creditor. Transfers made without fair consideration are also avoidable if the debtor was or became insolvent, was engaged in business with an unreasonably small amount of capital, or intended to incur debts beyond the ability to repay such debts (even without proving the intent to defraud creditors).

Insolvency as employed in the determination of fraudulent transfers is defined in section 101(32) as occurring when the present fair salable value of the debtor's property is less than the amount required to pay its debts. The fair value of the debtor's property is also reduced by any fraudulently transferred property, and, for an individual, by the exempt property under section 522.

It is important to ascertain when a fraudulent transfer has in fact occurred because it represents a possible recovery that could increase the value of the estate. It can, under certain conditions, prevent the debtor from obtaining a discharge. To be barred from a discharge as the result of a fraudulent transfer, the debtor must be an individual and the proceedings must be under chapter 7 liquidation, or the trustee must be liquidating the estate under a chapter 11 proceeding.

---

[3] 11 U.S.C. § 548(a).

In ascertaining whether any fraudulent transfers have been made or fraudulent obligations incurred, the independent accountant would carefully examine transactions with related parties within the year prior to the petition (or other required period), look for the sale of large amounts of fixed assets, review liens granted to creditors, and examine all other transactions that appear to have arisen outside the ordinary course of the business.

§ 12.13   Sales of Assets Below Market Values

Upon realization that a business is in financial difficulty, those who are involved may attempt to minimize their personal losses by removing the company's assets. Or, the business may be a sham operation, meaning that the company was created solely for the purpose of obtaining personal gain at the expense of creditors. The methods used to accomplish such objectives normally involve the transfer of assets without fair consideration or for no consideration at all. The proceeds that are withheld from the business are kept by the owners and thereby concealed from the trustee.

The accountant should examine all sales of the debtor's assets for a period of at least one year before the petition was filed in order to determine whether any sales were made without adequate consideration. Any price discounts that are recorded should be investigated, for these may have been paid in cash to the owners. The accountant should also be on the alert for any price variations and compare sales of merchandise made to various customers.

§ 12.14   Transfer of Assets to Insiders, Officers, Employees, Relatives, and Others

Any payments made to those with a close relationship to the business, such as the owners, their relatives, employees, or other businesses controlled by these parties, should be closely investigated by the accountant. The usual question is whether fair consideration was received for the assets transferred. Assets may also be transferred to companies controlled by the debtor's owners in payment of various goods and services at highly inflated prices. For example, the owner of one corporation resolved to retire and sell his business to a senior employee. The amount received by the owner from the employee for the company's stock appeared to be reasonable. Upon closer inspection, however, the former owner (1) had substantially increased the rent that the business paid to an owner-controlled entity, (2) was paid a hefty stipend by the business for unrendered consulting services, and (3) received monthly payments from the business for a long-term covenant not to compete. These hidden costs for the transfer of the business rendered it insolvent within 24 months, and the former owner was the largest creditor of the estate.

(a) Analysis of Related Party Transactions

The term "related parties," as defined in Financial Accounting Standards Board (FASB) Statement No. 57, *Related Party Disclosures*, means the reporting entity; its affiliates; principal owners, management, and members of their immediate families; entities accounted for by equity method; and any other party with which the reporting entity deals, where one party has the ability to significantly influence the other to the extent that one party might be prevented from fully pursuing its own separate interests. Transactions indicative of the existence of related parties, according to Statement on Auditing Standards (SAS) No. 45, include borrowing or lending at interest rates below or above current market, selling real estate at a price significantly different from its appraised value, exchanging property in a nonmonetary transaction, and making loans with no repayment specifications.

Generally accepted accounting principles ordinarily do not require transactions with related parties to be accounted for in a manner different from that which would be appropriate if the parties were not related. Thus, within the framework of existing pronouncements, primary emphasis is placed on the adequacy of disclosure of such transactions and their significance in the financial statements.

In determining the scope of work to be performed with related parties, the accountant should, according to SAS No. 45, obtain an understanding of management responsibilities and the relationship of each component to the total entity, evaluate internal accounting controls over management activities, and consider the business purpose served by each component of the business. The business's structure and style of operating decisions should be based on management abilities and tax, legal, product, and geographical considerations; however, they are at times designed to obscure related party transactions. In auditing companies in financial difficulty, the accountant must carefully consider transactions with related parties. The following auditing procedures, set forth in SAS No. 45, represent the type of work the auditor should perform with respect to related party transactions:

Procedures to Determine Existence of Related Parties

1 Evaluate the company's procedures for identifying and properly accounting for related party transactions.
2 Obtain from management the names of all related parties and inquire whether any related party transaction existed during the period.
3 Review filings with SEC and other regulatory agencies for names of related parties and for other businesses in which officers and directors occupy directorship or management positions.
4 Determine names of all pension and other trusts established for the benefit of employees and the names of their officers and trustees.
5 Review stockholder listings of closely held companies to identify principal stockholders.
6 Review prior years' working papers for the names of known related parties.
7 Inquire of predecessor, principal, or other auditors of related entities as to their knowledge of existing relationships and extent of management involvement in material transactions.
8 Review material investment transactions to determine whether the nature and extent of investment created related parties.

Procedures to Identify Transactions with Related Parties

1 Provide audit personnel with names of known related parties so that they may become aware of transactions with such parties during their examination.

2 Review minutes of meetings of board of directors and executive or operating committees for information.

3 Review proxy and other material filed with SEC and any other regulatory agencies.

4 Review "conflict-of-interests" statements obtained by the company from its management.

5 Review the extent and nature of business transacted with major customers, suppliers, borrowers, and lenders for indications of previously undisclosed relationships.

6 Consider whether transactions are occurring but are not being given accounting recognition, such as receiving or providing management, accounting, or other services at no charge.

7 Review accounting records for large, unusual, or nonrecurring transactions or balances, particularly those at or near the end of reporting periods.

8 Review confirmations of compensating balance arrangements for indications that balances are or were maintained for or by related parties.

9 Review invoices from client's law firms for indications of the existence of related party transactions.

10 Review confirmations of loans receivable and payable for indications of guarantees. When guarantees are indicated, determine their nature and the relationships, if any, of the guarantors to the reporting entity.

Procedures to Examine Identified Related Party Transactions

1 Obtain an understanding of the business purpose of the transaction.

2 Examine invoices, executed copies of agreements, contracts, and other pertinent documents.

3 Determine whether the transaction has been approved by the authorized party.

4 Test for reasonableness of the compilation of amounts to be disclosed in the financial statements.

5 Arrange for the audits of intercompany account balances and for the examination of related party transactions by the auditors for each of the parties.

6 Inspect or confirm and obtain satisfaction as to the transferability and value of collateral.

Additional Procedures to Fully Understand a Particular Transaction

1 Confirm transaction amount and terms with the other party.

2 Inspect evidence in possession of the other party.

3 Confirm or discuss significant information with intermediaries.

4 Refer to financial publications, trade journals, credit agencies, and other sources when doubtful of lack of substance in any material transaction with an unfamiliar party.

5 Obtain information as to the financial capacity of the other party in cases of material uncollected balances, guarantees, and other obligations.

Information to Be Disclosed Concerning Material Related Party Transactions

• The nature of the relationship

• A description of the transactions for the reported period, including any necessary information revealing the effects on the financial statements

• The dollar volume of transactions and the effects of any change in the method of establishing terms from that used in the preceding period

• Amounts due to or from related parties and, if not otherwise apparent, the terms and meaning of the settlement

The accountant may not be able to determine whether related party trans-actions are on a basis equivalent to that which would have occurred in the absence of the relationship. Accordingly, representations to the effect that the related party transaction was recorded on the same basis as an equivalent arm's length transaction are difficult to substantiate. If such a representation is included in the financial statements and the auditor is unable to reach a con-clusion as to the propriety, he or she should include in the report a comment to that effect and express a qualified opinion or disclaim an opinion. If the audi-tor believes that the representation is misleading, he or she should express a qualified or adverse opinion, depending on materiality.

(b) Padding

There are several ways the debtor can transfer assets to related parties. Among them are padding, manipulation of cash expenses, abstraction of cash, and improper purchases (inventory or equipment), loans, and sales.

Padding, a form of payment of cash without fair consideration, attempts to obtain funds from the business by adding fictitious claims to expense accounts and then retaining the extra payment. The most common example is payroll padding: checks are prepared for employees who have been terminated or for fictitious employees who have been added to the payroll. It is very difficult to detect payroll padding that occurred in prior periods. The payroll records can be compared with the salaries reported to the Internal Revenue Service, but the tax records may agree with the payroll records because they also have been padded. One of the first steps usually taken by accountants is to compare the payroll for the period audited with prior periods. If there are any differences, the auditor will then attempt to determine what caused them. The payroll records are also examined for unusual names, addresses, and amounts. Confir-mation can be sent to past employees for verification that wages were actually received by the employee and that the employee really exists. The accountant should examine the files to see whether any W-2 mailings were returned. The supplies expense might be padded through the presentation of invoices for sup-plies that were never received; or, a repairs expense account could be enlarged by a claim for services never performed. The rent expense paid to a related party may be inflated by a substantial amount.

(c) Cash Expenses

Manipulation of cash expenses may be accomplished in the same ways as in the padding schemes described above. Other abstractions may be accomplished through improper petty cash withdrawals by using fictitious vouchers or increasing the amount of valid claims. Checks may be drawn to cash without the proper documentation. Individuals may have the corporation pay for large personal expenses, such as travel and entertainment. The methods of obtaining funds from a business through improper cash expenses are unlimited.

(d) Nondeposit or Diverting of Receipts

Individuals may abstract the cash from a sale or collection on an account and attempt to cover up the shortage in various ways. The sale may be recorded at a lower amount than is collected or may be unrecorded entirely.

(e) Improper Purchases

Invoices for amounts greater than the actual purchase price may be submitted for payment of assets purchased. Employees may submit for payment by the firm bills pertaining to merchandise bought for their own personal use. Assets may be purchased from a supplier connected to the debtor by common ownership, or some other arrangement, for a price well in excess of the product's value. In completing a review of the financial statements, one independent accountant noticed that paid invoices for the same type of equipment purchased for a dealership owned by the largest shareholder of the debtor company were different, depending on who financed the equipment. The correct amount was paid for equipment financed by the manufacturer but for purchases financed by banks, the amount paid was much higher.

Purchase discounts may be unrecorded and the resulting overpayment retained by an owner. Again, the methods of manipulating purchases are numerous and similar to those found in a business not experiencing financial difficulties.

(f) Improper Loans

Individuals may borrow funds in the company's name without recording the note on the books, and abstract the cash. During one audit, an accountant discovered sealed envelopes containing information about the notes the president had signed without authorization.

(g) Improper Sales of Merchandise

A less obvious method of transferring or diverting assets out of the debtor corporation is by selling merchandise at ridiculously low prices to a newly formed corporation is by selling merchandise at ridiculously low prices to a newly formed corporation or to a relative or friend. To uncover this possibility, the accountant usually examines the sales invoices for the months immediately preceding the filing, compares the prices charged thereon with prices charged at least six months prior to filing, and attempts to establish whether any substantial reduction occurred in the selling price of the bankrupt's merchandise.

(h) Sale and Leaseback Arrangements

Funds can be removed from the business in several different ways through the sale of assets under a sale and leaseback agreement with another company normally related in some manner. One company established an affiliate, with all of the stock owned by the company's own major stockholders, to purchase selected equipment and then lease it back to the company. The lease was then used by the new corporation as security to obtain funds from the bank to pay for the equipment. The lease was for a five-year term and was based on the value of the equipment and the amount of the payments; a provision in the lease that would allow the debtor to purchase the equipment for a nominal fee should have been added, but was not. Thus, after five years, the value of the equipment had been fully paid but the debtor had to continue the lease payments in order to use the equipment, which had a useful life of at least ten years.

CONCEALMENT OF ASSETS

§ 12.15 Merchandise

In an attempt to minimize their own personal losses, those involved with a debtor corporation may conceal the debtor's assets. Regardless of the type of assets involved, one basis for determining whether the assets on hand at the time of filing the petition were depleted by possible concealment is the financial statements prepared by the debtor. The accountant should closely examine these statements and supplement them with statements obtained from the files of the debtor's previous accountant.

Merchandise concealments or shortages must often be proven theoretically or technically—that is, through a reconstruction of the accounts rather than a physical count. The beginning inventory is ascertained from a financial statement or physical inventory, and the purchases to the date of the petition are added to it. From this total, the cost of sales is subtracted, which should yield the value of the merchandise in inventory as of the date of the petition. After a physical inventory is taken, if a lower figure results, the difference represents the amount of inventory that has been lost or concealed.

As an illustration of transfers of inventory by the bankrupt in a fraudulent matter, it was reported to a trustee that trucks had been seen loading up at the doors of the bankrupt's stores within a few days preceding the bankruptcy. The trustee obtained a copy of the auction inventory sheets for the accountant, in the hope that the missing inventory could be established. Unfortunately, the bankrupt had been operating five-and-dime stores that stocked and sold hundreds, if not thousands, of different items. The accountant could not make an actual unit count. Although the number of units purchased within the short period of time the debtor was in business could be established, it was impossible to determine how many units were sold, because the sales records consisted of only the register tapes. However, the accountant did pursue the following approach:

- The debtor was in business only a few months, so the total amount of purchases made by the debtor for its stores was established from the paid and unpaid bills.
- Because the debtor commenced its operations without any inventory, the only inventory available for sale was that which the purchase records clearly indicated had been procured.
- The auctioneer indicated (on an overall basis) that the merchandise brought at auction approximately 50 percent of the cost. Accordingly, the accountant doubled the auction proceeds, that is, the gross auction proceeds, to arrive at the approximate cost of the inventory on hand at the bankruptcy date. Therefore, the difference between the total purchases made and the inventory on hand for the auction at cost was the merchandise that had been used or consumed in the sales.
- The records then indicated what the sales were—that is, what the debtor reported as its sales—and by deducting the normal markup for this type of store from the sales, the cost of sales was determined. As might be expected, the inventory that evidently was consumed for the sales was far in excess of the indicated cost value of the sales. As a matter of fact, even if it were assumed that all sales were made at cost and that there was no markup on the sales, the merchandise consumed still far exceeded the sales, a clear indication that inventory was missing.

(a) Unrecorded Sales

Other assets may be concealed through unrecorded sales. Merchandise may be removed from the business with no consideration given or accounting entry made. The delivery of merchandise purchases may be diverted to the owners of the firm. Cash may be concealed by not recording the sale of scrap or waste or by recording a sale of good merchandise as a sale of scrap or waste with a lower value.[4]

Several methods may be employed to discover the diversion of assets by unrecorded sales. The gross profit earned in previous periods should be compared with that currently being received, and large drops in the amount should be investigated for possible uncompensated removal of merchandise. A schedule for the immediate period, including sales, purchases, and direct labor and production costs, should be prepared to uncover any unusual occurrences. Concealments might be discovered through a theoretical units merchandise audit, where a list is made by unit and dollar amount of the opening inventory, purchases, sales, and ending inventory. Individual, specific units of the merchandise might be traced through serial, style, or identification numbers. Purchase bills should be checked against receiving records. A schedule of all sales of scrap and waste materials should be prepared. An analysis should be made of

---

[4] Robert Bronsteen, "The Accountant's Investigation of Bankruptcy Irregularities," *New York Certified Public Accountant*, Vol. 37 (December 1967), p. 937.

all the processing and contracting bills to establish that all raw material purchased and not now in inventory has been incorporated into the finished product, and that all units that were processed were later accounted for either in sales or in the closing inventory.[5]

Merchandise may be held as collateral by creditors and not disclosed. Or, merchandise may never have been delivered by the supplier, although notes were issued in payment and the purchases are reflected on the books. Collateral may have been given for notes received by the debtor. The loans may have been entered on the books but the merchandise transferred or the collateral never recorded.

§ 12.16   Cash Surrender Value of Officers' Life Insurance Policies

Although the purchase of life insurance policies on the lives of corporate officers is not a deductible tax expense for the corporation, it is often deemed advisable to obtain life insurance on the officers of the corporation in order to provide the cash funds necessary to repurchase their capital stock from the surviving spouse or estate. Consequently, a large number of corporations own such life insurance policies. The asset is the cash surrender value of the policy. Because the corporation normally is in dire need of cash funds prior to the filing of the petition, loans have usually been taken by the corporation from the insurance company against the policies, either for payment of the premiums due or for other working capital needs. The accountant can uncover the existence of these policies by finding proper entries on the corporate books of account, by the discovery of the policies themselves, by premium notices found among the paid or unpaid bills, or by entries made on the books such as payments to life insurance companies for premiums.

The cash value can be determined by an examination of the policy itself or by direct communication with the insurance broker or the life insurance company in question. At the same time, the accountant must ascertain the loan, if any, outstanding against the policy either from entries on the books or from information received from the insurance company. The accountant must determine that all dividends receivable on the policies have been credited to the debtor corporation. Once this information is compiled, the equity in the policy is readily ascertainable. A judgment can then easily be made as to whether an offer made by a former officer of the debtor to repurchase the policy is equitable. Most corporate officers are well aware that these policies are a good buy for themselves and their families and they quite often will make an offer to repurchase the policies for the equity therein, whereas they may not as anxiously provide other information having a bearing on the administration of the debtor corporation.[6]

§ 12.17   Deposits and Security

Deposits and security are usually assets of the corporation arising from down payments made on the purchase of machinery or items of merchandise,

---

[5] *Id.,* pp. 937–38.
[6] Elliot G. Meisel, "Services Rendered by the Accountant to the Trustee" (accounting firm of Roberts & Leinwander Co.), p. 7 (mimeographed).

or security left with landlords for the performance of the terms of a lease. Where a complete set of books is available, these items are self-evident and present no problems to the auditor. However, many examinations have not uncovered such assets until more detailed searches were made of the records.

Among the records the accountant seeks are leases and receipts for deposits left with utilities. Naturally, the leases clearly indicate the security left with the landlord and the utility receipts likewise provide the information on utility deposits. Down payments on the purchase of machinery or equipment are a little more difficult to uncover and the accountant often relies on information provided by creditors. A search of correspondence is often helpful in uncovering deposits or security, if the debtor was a landlord or manufacturer of equipment for which such deposits are usually required.

§ 12.18   Investments and Real Estate

Investments in stocks or bonds can be uncovered from brokers' statements or payments to brokerage houses among the cash disbursements. Investments in real estate usually appear in the form of unusual cash disbursements, that is, disbursements that normally would not be made for the business under review. Again, examination of the correspondence files will often lead to the discovery of such investments, and a reading of the minute books of the corporation can be a lead to such assets. Included in this category is the ownership of subsidiary companies whose stock may have value (where the subsidiaries are solvent corporations). An abundance of transactions with another corporation, clearly not in the nature of normal purchases by the debtor corporation, usually indicates an affiliation with that corporation through holdings of common stock, or a relationship of parent and subsidiary companies. A debtor corporation is often found to be the parent company of a real estate corporation that owns the premises from which the debtor corporation had conducted its business. The real estate frequently turns out to be quite valuable, notwithstanding the fact that usually the mortgages are substantial in amount.[7] Ownership of real estate by a debtor corporation is apparent where tax payments are made to the local real estate taxing authorities or where payments of similar amounts are made to banks on a monthly or quarterly basis, indicating mortgage payments.

§ 12.19   Machinery and Equipment

The accountant's inventory or an auctioneer's report (in the case of a chapter 7 liquidation) will show the machinery and equipment located at the premises of the debtor, but the accountant will be more interested in reporting on the machinery and equipment *not* at the premises. The most common assets of this type are the automobiles used personally by the corporate officers. Although registered in the officers' own names, the cars are often purchased by the corporation, with all operating expenses completely paid by the corporation. Insurance brokers' bills will usually point out the existence of these assets as well as installment payments made on a monthly basis. Often, a letter will arrive, or will be discovered in the company's files, from an irate

---

[7] *Id.,* p. 9.

bailee wanting to know when someone is going to remove machinery from a warehouse or premises or who is going to pay for its storage cost. A review of the contracts file may uncover some assets that do not appear on the books of the corporation. Machinery or equipment usually does appear (at least in summary form) and the corporate tax returns ordinarily will have detailed schedules of the items included in this category.

Assets may also be concealed by the withdrawal of unusual receipts such as recovery of bad debts or insurance recoveries.

These investigations and determinations become the basis for a turnover proceeding to compel the debtor to surrender the property or its value that is unaccounted for and therefore presumably concealed by the debtor. Thus, the challenge to the accountant is to prove that certain assets exist, even though their physical existence is not immediately evident.

The concealment of assets when intended to hinder, delay, or defraud creditors is grounds for barring an individual debtor from the discharge of debts under a chapter 7 liquidation, as discussed in § 12.12.

FALSE ENTRIES AND STATEMENTS

§ 12.20 Mutilation and Alteration of Records

Any suspicion that the books have been tampered with should be quickly and carefully acted upon by the accountant and the trustee's attorney. There may be attempts on the part of the firm's owners or employees to conceal assets, make preferential payments, hide a fraudulent transfer, or effect some other irregularity. Indications of such activities include suspicious erasures, names or amounts that have been crossed out, and pages that have been rewritten. Documents that should receive the closest attention are checks, payroll records, deposit slips, and petty cash slips. The most reliable method of examining and investigating any unusual condition is to contact an independent third party to verify the debtor's records. An example of this procedure would be a comparison between the duplicate deposit tickets retained by the bank and the debtor's cash receipts journal. Other examples are given below:

- Examination of purchase bills and receiving records, to bring to light fictitious purchase bills used to siphon off business funds
- Examination of sales invoices and shipping documents, to reveal fictitious invoices used to obtain loans
- Review of loans received, to determine whether they were bona fide loans or disguised sales
- Analysis of receivable and payment subsidiary accounts, to see whether nonexistent or unusual accounts appear
- Audit of petty cash slips, to check for alterations

§ 12.21 Concealment and Destruction of Records

As previously discussed, locating and obtaining possession of the debtor's books and records is one of the accountant's first and most important tasks.

Should the investigation reveal that the debtor is withholding records, the attorney may initiate turnover proceedings to obtain possession of them. Intentional destruction of records, if proven, may give the attorney grounds for further legal actions. Section 727(a)(3) of the Bankruptcy Code explicitly states that a discharge of debts of an individual in a chapter 7 liquidation will be denied when it is proven that the bankrupt destroyed, mutilated, falsified, concealed, or failed to keep or preserve books of account or records from which the financial condition and transactions of the business might be ascertained. There is no similar provision in a chapter 11 reorganization unless the records are falsified for the purpose of obtaining credit.

§ 12.22   Forgery

Officers of the debtor may falsify a third party's signature for numerous reasons. The debtor may attempt to receive credit illegally by forging notes, mortgages, warehouse receipts, trust receipts, shipping documents, and other evidence often used as security. Forgery might also be used to endorse a check and divert the moneys to personal use. The proceeds from the sale of marketable securities might be misappropriated through forgery. Forgery is a form of deception and as such carries its own punishment under the federal laws.

§ 12.23   Issuance of False Statements

The following list explains how several accounts may be altered for financial statement purposes.

- Cash:
  - Kiting of receipts
  - Withdrawals not recorded
  - Deposits of worthless checks from insolvent affiliates
- Accounts receivable:
  - Worthless accounts not written off
  - Insufficient reserve for bad debts
  - Large returns and allowances in subsequent period
  - Fictitious sales
  - Invoices billed in advance of shipping dates
  - Fictitious accounts created to cover withdrawals to officers, other employees, and so on
  - Nondisclosure of hypothecation to banks or factors
- Notes receivable:
  - Worthless notes not written off
  - Insufficient reserve for bad debts
  - Forged or fictitious notes created to cover withdrawals
  - Contingent liability for discounted notes not shown
- Merchandise inventory:
  - Nondisclosure of liens
  - Inflated values and quantities

- Items billed in advance of shipping dates included in inventory
- Old obsolete inventory not disclosed
- Cash value—officers' life insurance:
  - Liability for loans not shown
  - Corporation not beneficiary
- Fixed and other assets:
  - Liens not disclosed
  - Inflated values by reappraisals and not shown
  - Inadequate reserve for depreciations
  - Leased equipment recorded as fixed assets
  - Personal assets (such as autos) not registered in corporate name but recorded as assets
  - Capitalized expenses that have no value
- Intercompany receivables:
  - From affiliates to cover withdrawals of officers
  - From affiliates that are insolvent
- Investments:
  - Worthless, but shown at original cost
  - Pledged and not recorded
  - Not registered in corporate name
  - To cover withdrawals to insolvent affiliates
- Liabilities:
  - Not recorded
  - Withdrawals of subordinated debts not shown
- Capital:
  - Notes and loans payable recorded as capital
  - False subordinations

The accountant discovers the issuance of false financial statements by comparing the statements the debtor has issued with the books and records. The comparison can be presented in tabular form, which reveals the difference between the statements and the records. Exhibits 12-1 and 12-3 present the statement of financial position and the statement of income and profit or loss, respectively, as originally issued by a debtor, a paint manufacturer that sold its products at retail. Exhibits 12-2 and 12-4 show the actual statements prepared by the accountant, comparing the debtor's statements with the records.

FINANCING IRREGULARITIES

§ 12.24 Receivables

Many schemes have been devised whereby the debtor attempts to receive goods or money using very confusing methods so that payment is delayed or the amount received is more than is actually due. The most common accounts manipulated to accomplish these goals are accounts receivable and inventory.

Exhibit 12-1 Statement of Financial Position, as Prepared by Debtor

A Retail Corporation
Statement of Financial Position
at December 31, 20XX

Assets

Current assets			
Cash in banks		$ 20,730	
Accounts receivable	$26,530		
Less: Allowance for doubtful accounts	3,500	23,030	
Merchandise inventory		131,810	
Prepaid expenses		4,470	
Total current assets			$180,040
Investments			
Common stock—Jones & Co.		4,760	
Preferred stock—Smith, Inc.		5,000	
Total investments			9,760
Fixed assets		49,530	
Less: Accumulated depreciation		22,720	
Net Fixed Assets			26,810
Other assets			
Deposits as security		8,500	
Goodwill		8,000	
Total other assets			16,500
Total assets			$233,110

Liabilities and Capital

Current liabilities			
Loan payable—bank		$ 20,000	
Accounts payable		80,560	
Taxes and accrued expenses		7,960	
Total liabilities			$108,520
Capital			
Capital stock issued		75,000	
Additional paid-in capital		35,000	
Accumulated earnings, January 1, 20XX	$ 5,170		
Profit for period [Exhibit 12-3]	9,420	14,590	
Total capital			124,590
Total liabilities and capital			$233,110

Many different types of abuses may be found in the financing of accounts receivable. Customers may be sent bills before the goods are shipped or the sale is consummated. Documents such as sales invoices or customers' signatures on financing agreements may be forged. Employees may fail to record merchandise that has been returned, thus showing an inflated accounts receivable total. Invoices may be padded so that, if the receivables were factored, the debtor would receive funds in excess of the actual costs.

In analyzing the receivables of the paint company, an auditor noticed that excessive amounts of returns were being made by customers, depreciating the value of the accounts receivable. Salespeople were inflating the receivables by making sales that would later be returned. This practice was encouraged because

Exhibit 12-2   Accountant's Comparative Statement of Financial Position, as Prepared from Debtor's Books

A Retail Corporation
Comparison of Issued Statement of Financial Position
with Books of Account
at December 31, 20XX

	Per Books	Per Financial Statement	Apparent Errors Assets Overstated	Apparent Errors Liabilities Understated
Assets				
Current assets				
Cash in banks	$ 2,730	$ 20,730	$18,000	
Accounts receivable—net	21,030	23,030	2,000	
Merchandise inventory	121,810	131,810	10,000	
Prepaid expenses	4,470	4,470		
Total current assets	150,040	180,040	30,000	
Investments				
Common stock—Jones & Co.	4,760	4,760		
Preferred stock—Smith, Inc.	-0-	5,000	5,000	
Total investments	4,760	9,760	5,000	
Fixed assets—net	26,810	26,810		
Other assets	16,500	16,500		
Total assets	$198,110	$233,110	$35,000	
Liabilities and Capital				
Current liabilities				
Loan payable—bank	$ 20,000	$ 20,000		
Notes payable—John Doe	6,000	-0-		$ 6,000
Accounts payable	103,560	80,560		23,000
Taxes and accrued expenses	7,960	7,960		
Total current liabilities	137,520	108,520		29,000
Due after one year				
Notes payable—John Doe	9,000	-0-		9,000
Total liabilities	146,520	108,520		$38,000
Capital				
Capital stock issued	75,000	75,000		
Additional paid-in capital	-0-	35,000		
Accumulated earnings (deficit)	(23,410)	14,590		
Total capital	51,590	124,590		
Total liabilities and capital	$198,110	$233,110		
Reconciliation of Capital				
Accumulated deficit per books	$(23,410)			
Accumulated earnings per statement		$ 14,590		
Total		$ 38,000		
Paid-in capital per statement		35,000		
Total to be accounted for		$ 73,000		
Assets apparently overstated		$ 35,000		
Liabilities apparently understated		38,000		
Total accounted for		$ 73,000		

Exhibit 12-3 Statement of Income and Profit or Loss, as Prepared by Debtor

A Retail Corporation
Statement of Income and Profit or Loss
for the Period from January 1 to December 31, 20XX

Net sales		$592,010
Cost of goods sold		
Merchandise inventory, January 1, 20XX	$ 98,490	
Net purchase	364,230	
Freight-in and other costs	10,510	
Available for sale	473,230	
Less: Merchandise inventory, December 31, 20XX	131,810	
Cost of goods sold		341,420
Gross profit		250,590
Expenses		
Sales salaries	101,790	
Administrative salaries	20,180	
Rent	53,890	
Advertising	19,850	
Taxes	8,790	
Utilities	10,040	
Depreciation	5,820	
Other expenses	20,810	
Total expenses		241,170
Net profit for period [Exhibit 12-1]		$ 9,420

the plant producer paid commissions on acceptance of the order, rather than after payment. Further analysis indicated that the salespeople were promising customers exclusive rights to the paint in their geographic area and then selling the same type of paint to a local competitor of the first customer. They camouflaged this action by placing a different trade name label on the cans of paint delivered to the second customer.

The business should have full ownership of its receivables, and there should be no liens outstanding against them nor any contingent liabilities for receivables that have been discounted. The total shown for accounts receivable should be the realizable cash value. Items that should be presented separately and not included in accounts receivable are:

- Shipments made on consignment
- Accounts for which there is indication that collection will not be possible because the customer was a bad credit risk
- Permanent investments of capital in or loans to affiliated or subsidiary businesses
- Receivables that resulted from transactions with officers, employees, or subsidiary companies
- Loans or advances to employees or officers
- Claims that will never be enforced, such as those resulting from transactions conducted under false pretenses

Exhibit 12-4 Accountant's Comparative Statement of Income and Profit or Loss, as Prepared from Debtor's Books

A Retail Corporation
Comparison of Issued Statement of Income and Profit
or Loss with Books of Account
for the Period from January 1, to December 31, 20XX

	Per Books		Per Financial Statement	
Net sales		$562,010		$592,010
Cost of goods sold				
Merchandise inventory,				
January 1, 20XX	$ 98,490		$ 98,490	
Net purchases	340,230		364,230	
Freight-in and other costs	10,510		10,510	
Available for sale	449,230		473,230	
Less: Merchandise inventory,				
December 31, 20XX	121,810		131,810	
Cost of goods sold		327,420		341,420
Gross profit		234,590		250,590
Expenses				
Sales salaries	111,790		101,790	
Administrative salaries	20,180		20,180	
Rent	53,890		53,890	
Advertising	24,850		19,850	
Taxes	8,790		8,790	
Utilities	10,040		10,040	
Depreciation	5,820		5,820	
Other expenses	27,810		20,810	
Total expenses		263,170		241,170
Net profit or (loss)		$(28,580)		$ 9,420

SUMMARY

	Sales	Gross Profit	Expenses	Net Profit
Per financial statement	$592,010	$250,590	$241,170	$ 9,420
Per books	562,010	234,590	263,170	(28,580)
Apparent misstatement	$ 30,000	$ 16,000	$ 22,000	$ 38,000

- Installment receivables
- Receivables arising from transactions other than the sale of merchandise—the sale of plant assets, insurance claims, and the like
- Credit balances in accounts receivable

To discover any of these irregularities, the most reliable procedure would be for the accountant to confirm the transactions with the third party involved. If there is a suspicion that merchandise was returned but not recorded, the customer should be contacted. Confirmation of a certain number of receivables is a normal audit procedure. If the receivables have been factored, they should be directly confirmed with the customer and all shipping documents, receipts, and the method and means of payment should be carefully examined to ensure the transactions are valid. If the accountant suspects that a shipment shown as a sale was actually made on consignment, the receiver of the goods should be contacted to see whether title did actually pass. Doubtful credit risks should be investigated and any transactions made with employees or officers should be carefully scrutinized. Many of the procedures followed in determining whether irregularities exist in accounts receivable are extensions of those found in a normal audit.

§ 12.25 Inventory

Inventories, the methods of financing purchases, and the use of inventories to obtain further credit are also subject to manipulation by the debtor. Signatures may be forged on receiving reports attesting that material was received and payment is therefore due the vendor. Subsequent payment may then be abstracted by the officers or employees. Other documents may be falsified to record a higher inventory value, cover up a shortage, and so forth. As with receivables, these transactions may best be verified through confirmation with outside parties.

A company with warehouses on its premises had a substantial amount of inventory subject to warehouse liens that were held by Lexington Warehouse Company. The accountant's investigation disclosed that items were not properly recorded in the warehouse receipts issued by Lexington Warehouse. As a result, in the recorded contents of certain lots there were variances from the description in the warehouse receipts, and inventory was overstated. Lot number 5589, for example, was on warehouse receipt number 36673 as 17,425 pounds headless shrimp at $.80 per pound for a value of $13,796. This lot actually contained fish that was valued at $.38 per pound for a total value of $6,621, or a difference of $7,175. It was determined that when the higher-quality shrimp came into the facilities of the company, it would be properly inventoried. A warehouse receipt would be prepared and sent to a New York bank for financing. The shrimp would then be taken out the front door and a lesser quality of shrimp—and in some cases, catfish—was substituted. The higher-quality shrimp were then taken to the back door and processed again.

The discrepancies were discovered by taking a detailed inventory. Also, the auditor discovered two black books which the company used to keep up with the changes it had made in the inventory placed in the warehouse.

Inventories may be financed through a technique known as kiting. This scheme uses the float period, or the time it takes for a check to clear the bank on which it is drawn. It is an attempt to prevent an overdraft from being detected by the bank; in effect, it uses the bank's credit without authorization or payment of interest. Kiting may also be tied in directly with the inventory. In the example of the shrimp, described above, the local warehouse was slow in notifying the Lexington Warehouse Company that the items had been sold. The company used the proceeds, which should have been directly applied to the payment of the loan because the inventory had been sold, until the bank in

New York received notice of the sale of the inventory. The company continued to list the item in inventory, although the sale was recorded.

Inventories may also be used as collateral to obtain credit. They may become security for new credit or outstanding obligations. If a debtor has inflated the inventory figure, the collateral is actually insufficient for the amount borrowed and the creditors have been deceived.

In a typical audit not involving insolvency, the accountant attempts to establish the correct quantity of items in inventory and the proper valuation of the goods. These are very important aspects of an audit involving a debtor in bankruptcy court, where it is necessary to ascertain whether the collateral is adequate and the amounts paid were for items that actually represented purchases. The correct quantity as shown in the inventory figure is determined through observation of a physical inventory and statistical sampling of the correspondence between the inventory records and actual goods. Valuation is tested by examining sales invoices, obtaining prices paid by other vendees, and questioning the seller as to how much was actually received. All these procedures must be conducted with a higher degree of suspicion on the part of the accountant than would normally be the case, because of the nature of the proceeding.

PREFERENTIAL PAYMENTS

§ 12.26 Introduction

A preferential payment as defined in section 547 of the Bankruptcy Code is a transfer of any of the property of a debtor to or for the benefit of a creditor, for or on account of an antecedent debt made or suffered by the debtor while insolvent and within 90 days before the filing of a petition initiating bankruptcy proceedings, when the effect of such transfer is to enable the creditor to receive a greater percentage of payment than would be received if the debtor were liquidated under chapter 7. Insolvency will be presumed during the 90-day period. A transfer of property to an insider between 90 days and one year before the filing of the petition is also considered a preferential payment. Preferences include the payment of money, a transfer of property, assignment of accounts receivable, or a mortgage of real or personal property (see § 5.39).

A preferential payment is not a fraud but rather a legitimate and proper payment of a valid antecedent debt. The voidability of preferences is created by law to effect equality of distribution among all the creditors. The 90-day period (one year for transactions with insiders) prior to filing the bankruptcy petition has been arbitrarily selected by Congress as the time period during which distributions to the debtor's creditors may be redistributed to all the creditors ratably. During this period, a creditor who accepts a payment is said to have been preferred and may be required to return the amount received and later participate in the enlarged estate to the pro rata extent of its unreduced claim.

§ 12.27 Recovery of Preferential Payments

The trustee will attempt to recover preferential payments, but not all payments are voidable. For a payment made to an insider between 91 days and one year prior to the petition to be voidable, the Bankruptcy Code, as originally passed, required that the insider who received payment had to have reasonable cause to believe that the debtor was insolvent at the time the transfer was made.[8] This requirement was eliminated by the Bankruptcy Amendments and Federal Judgeship Act of 1984, for petitions filed after October 8, 1984.

Section 547(f) provides that the debtor is presumed to be insolvent during the 90-day period prior to bankruptcy. This presumption does not apply to transfers to insiders between 91 days and one year prior to bankruptcy. This presumption requires the adverse party to come forth with some evidence to prove the presumption. The burden of proof, however, remains with the party in whose favor the presumption exists. Once this presumption is rebutted, insolvency at the time of payment is necessary, and only someone with the training of an accountant is in a position to prove insolvency. The accountant often assists the debtor or trustee in presenting evidence showing whether the debtor was solvent or insolvent at the time payment was made. In cases where new management is in charge of the business or where a trustee has been appointed, the emphasis is often on trying to show that the debtor was insolvent, in order to obtain the recovery of the previous payments and increase the size of the estate. The creditors' committee likewise wants to show that the debtor was insolvent at the time of payment, to provide a larger basis for payment to unsecured creditors. The specific creditor recovering the payment looks for evidence to indicate that the debtor was solvent at the time payment was made.

The accountant must note exceptions to the trustee's avoiding power, provided for in section 547. The exceptions, described in detail in § 5.39, are briefly mentioned here:

- Transfers intended as a contemporaneous exchange for new value.
- Transfers for business debts made in the ordinary course of business of both the debtor and creditor and made according to ordinary business terms.
- Giving of security in connection with an enabling lien to acquire property to the extent that the transferred interest is perfected within ten days.
- Giving in good faith future credit without security of any kind for property that becomes part of the debtor's estate when a preferential payment had previously been made. The amount of the new credit remaining unpaid at the time of the adjudication in bankruptcy may be set off against the amount that would otherwise be recoverable from the debtor. To establish the final amount of preferential payments to one creditor, it is necessary to set off all new credits against the prior preferential payments.
- Transfers where there is a perfected "floating" security interest in inventory or receivables or the proceeds of either, providing the creditors' position does not realize net improvement during the 90-day period (one year for insiders) prior to the petition date. Here, the accountant will be required to analyze the security interest and the account balance of each creditor in inventories and receivables 90 days prior to the petition date

---

[8] U.S.C. § 547(b)(4)(B).

and compare the results with the condition existing at the date the petition was filed.

- Fixing of a statutory lien that is not avoidable.
- Transfer by individual with consumer debt where value of all property transferred is less than $600.

§ 12.28 Search for Preferential Payments

Any payments made within the 90 days preceding the bankruptcy court filing and not in the ordinary course of business should be very carefully scrutinized. Additionally, transactions with insiders should be carefully reviewed to see whether any payments were preferences. Suspicious transactions would include anticipations of debt obligations, repayment of officers' loans, repayment of loans that have been personally guaranteed by officers, repayment of loans made to personal friends and relatives, collateral given to lenders, and sales of merchandise made on a contra account basis.

Sales that are unrecorded and result in the transfer and concealment of merchandise may result in benefit to preferred creditors in several ways. Collateral may be given to creditors but not recorded on the debtor's books. Merchandise may be concealed from the trustee by suppliers who send bills for undelivered merchandise under a "bill and hold" arrangement; or merchandise may be returned to creditors for a direct or indirect consideration. All these schemes are intended to prefer a certain creditor over another.

In seeking to find voidable preferences, the accountant has two crucial tasks: to determine the earliest date on which insolvency can be established within the 90-day period (one year for insiders), and to report to the trustee's or debtor's attorney all payments, transfers, or encumbrances made by the debtor after that date that may be subject to recovery. It is then the attorney's responsibility to determine which payments may be voidable and the type of recovery action to take. However, the accountant's role should not be minimized, for it is the accountant who initially determines those payments that are suspect.

The exact procedures to follow depend on several factors, including the honesty of the debtor and the desire of the creditors' committee to pursue and recover preferential payments. Examples of procedures that might be performed include:

- Preparation of a schedule of payments and other reductions of liabilities over an agreed-on amount, made within the 90-day period (one year for insiders) prior to the date of the petition, to determine possible preferential treatment to specific creditors. Included in this list are payments made to banks, affiliates, stockholders, management, directors, and other related parties.
- Preparation of a worksheet summarizing changes in major creditors' accounts for the 90-day period prior to the petition date, to ascertain that certain suppliers are not being favored by payments, returns, or offsets. In analyzing the accounts, the accountant would want to exclude those payments that come under the exclusions to preferences. One of the exclusions is payments made in the ordinary course of business according to

ordinary business terms. Ordinary business terms are not defined in the statute, and until the courts decide how to determine ordinary business terms, the accountant may want to schedule those payments as possible preferences if they were made after the term (30 days, 60 days, and so on) stated on the invoice.

- Preparation of a listing of all payments over an agreed-on amount made before due date, and credit memos issued for significant returns of inventory. For example, a return of inventory occurring within the 90-day period prior to the petition date may be a preference even if it is the same inventory that was delivered by the supplier.

For reports on the payments that should be scrutinized as possible preferences, there is no set format. The reports should, however, have a format that has been approved by the counsel for the debtors' or creditors' committee, whichever is appropriate, prior to the investigation. Generally, a report should state the agreed-on procedures that were performed and the result of the performance of these procedures.

If, as a result of the investigation by the accountant, a decision is made to attempt to recover the payment, counsel will file the necessary legal papers to begin the recovery. The balance of the recovery process is generally handled by the appropriate counsel. The potential value of the recovery should be greater than the cost to make the search. For example, if the percent recovery without the preference is 70 percent, the value to the estate of every dollar recovered is approximately $0.30.

§ 12.29   Inflated Claims

Just as it is important to minimize the priority and administration creditors in order to provide the maximum dividend to unsecured creditors, it is likewise important to limit the filing of the unsecured creditors to their proper amounts. Excessive amounts allowed for unsecured creditors will naturally diminish the dividend payable to those in that group.

After establishing the book balances for the unsecured creditors, the accountant compares these balances with the claims filed—or, if a claim is not filed, with the amount admitted on the debtor's schedules of liabilities—to determine their accuracy. Discrepancies are analyzed and, if they are not reconcilable, this information is communicated to the trustee or counsel and to the creditors' committee. Where the supplier has not given credit for payments made or credits allowed, the accountant locates the checks proving payments or the paperwork substantiating the allowance. In an interesting Chapter XI proceeding under prior law, the debtor (prior to the Chapter XI proceeding) had settled a claim with a supplier for $9,800, payable by adding $.10 to each item of goods purchased in the future until the $9,800 had been paid. This settlement was for an original invoice of approximately $60,000; however, the accounts payable records showed no liability at all to the creditor. Although the settlement preceded the filing of the arrangement petition and although there had been partial performance on the settlement, the creditor nonetheless presented a confirmation to the accountant showing the $60,000 balance as still due. Fortunately, the accountant noticed the $.10 additional payments on the invoices of the supplier (which aroused the accountant's suspicions) and the true facts were then uncovered. Consequently, instead of allowing a claim for $60,000, the statement reflected the true liability of $9,800 less partial payment thereon.

In any bankruptcy court proceeding, the accountant determines (by date of delivery as compared to the filing date of the petition) whether a claim is properly classified as administrative or nonadministrative. All the above verification naturally requires examination of the original documents, including receiving reports, purchase orders, and the actual supplier's invoices.

APPLICABILITY OF GENERALLY ACCEPTED AUDITING STANDARDS

§ 12.30   Auditing Standards

When the accountant states that an examination was conducted in accordance with generally accepted auditing standards (GAAS), this normally means that the examination performed was adequate to support an opinion on the financial statements and that it was performed with professional competence by properly trained persons. Such standards are really measures of an acceptable level of quality and are judged by the "prudent-person standard," or what other competent auditors would conclude to be necessary if given the same set of facts.

Two broad classifications of auditing standards are universally referred to:

1   *Personal* or *general standards*, which concern the auditor's training and experience and the quality of the work done
2   *Field work* and *reporting standards*, which refer to the evidence to be obtained and the means of reporting the results of the audit

These standards are obviously quite general in their applicability. This is necessary because no one set of auditing procedures can be applied in all situations. The accountant must select and apply the appropriate auditing procedures as required in particular circumstances.

Because of their generality, the auditing standards as set forth in the Statements on Auditing Standards certainly apply to the audit of a client involved in bankruptcy or insolvency proceedings. The auditor must have adequate technical training, maintain an independent mental attitude, and exercise due professional care. The work must be planned and supervised, internal control must be studied and evaluated, and sufficient competent evidential matter must be obtained. Finally, the financial statements must be presented in accordance with generally accepted accounting principles consistently applied. There must be adequate disclosures, and either an expression of an opinion or reasons why one cannot be given should be included in the report.

§ 12.31   Auditing Procedures

The nature of the bankruptcy and insolvency proceedings determines the specific procedures that will be followed. Because a liquidation proceeding allows for greater manipulation of the books and transactions, in many areas the accountant will need to scrutinize the records and supporting documents more closely than might otherwise be necessary. Special attention must be given to uncovering any irregularities—fraudulent transfers, preferential payments, false entries, concealment of assets, and the like. These investigations may necessitate greater reliance on sources outside the debtor's records than is normal, including confirmation with third parties. It may be necessary to reconstruct some accounts because of a lack of adequate data or the dubious nature of the debtor's information.

Other considerations arise because of the nature of the situation. For example, the question may be posed as to whether the auditor can represent the debtor and still be independent when supplying information for the creditors. Or, if the accountant helps devise a plan (settlement or reorganization) for rehabilitation and recommends its acceptance, can the same accountant later be independent when auditing the debtor's progress? Is it ever possible to rely on the system of internal control in insolvency proceedings, or should the examination be conducted as if there were no adequate safeguards? These and other specific questions arise when applying auditing standards to a bankruptcy court case.

The various audit steps that will be necessary must be individually determined for each case. Whether such procedures are adequate can only be measured by a consideration of what a reasonable person with the same training would do in a similar situation. But it still remains true that those standards that generally apply to all audit cases are also relevant to insolvency and bankruptcy proceedings.

The first generally accepted auditing standard of reporting requires that the auditor state whether the financial statements are presented in accordance with generally accepted principles of accounting. This means that any financial statements prepared by an accountant must not deviate from the standard presentation and treatment of accounts and transactions as commonly used by the profession.

No definitive list of accounting principles has been written down and may be referred to by auditors. Rather, the accountant must have a sound and thorough knowledge of accounting theory. It is also necessary to be aware of the pronouncements of the AICPA and FASB, areas covered in accounting literature, and current industry practice. Using these sources, the accountant must then apply personal judgment to determine whether a particular principle is generally accepted and appropriate in the circumstances.

The most common sources of accounting principles are the Accounting Research Bulletins and Opinions issued by the rule-making bodies of the AICPA, and Standards issued by the FASB. The principles set forth in AICPA and FASB publications are deemed to have substantial authoritative support and therefore are considered to be generally accepted accounting principles. Any departures from these pronouncements must be disclosed in a footnote to the financial statements or in a separate paragraph of the auditor's report. Such deviations are to be acceptable to the auditor only if they have substantial authoritative support and are acceptable practices. This decision is made by the accountant after examining all the relevant and authoritative sources of literature, and evaluating what is commonly done in such situations.

Chapter 15 presents a discussion of the application of the reporting standards to reports issued in bankruptcy and insolvency proceedings, and includes an analysis of the going-concern concept as it relates to entities facing financial difficulties.

The art of accounting is composed of the talent, training, experience, and knowledge that result in the accountant's judgment as to which auditing standards are appropriate and which accounting principles are applicable to a particular circumstance. Overriding these specific decisions are the general standards that apply to all cases, including bankruptcy and insolvency proceedings.

§ 12.32   Audit Program Guide

The audit program guide shown as 12.2 in Volume 2 of *Bankruptcy and Insolvency Accounting* has been prepared for the purpose of assisting accountants who are conducting audits of companies involved in bankruptcy and insolvency proceedings. By definition, it is designed to guide the auditor in preparing a customized program for each individual engagement; it is not intended to be used as a final program. Modification should and must be made, depending on the nature and characteristics of each situation, including the purpose of the audit. Emphasis for an audit designed to provide information to help management and the creditors in determining the type of corrective action needed for the company to be able to return to profitable operations would be different from emphasis for an investigative audit to determine the extent to which management has misused the company's resources.

13

Financial Reporting During Bankruptcy

§ 13.1 Introduction

The accountant will prepare not only current financial statements but supplementary statements that are helpful in evaluating the future prospects of the business. Three important questions must be answered in order to determine the direction in which the company's future will lie:

1 What is the current financial position of the business?
2 If the current position looks financially feasible, what about the future?
3 If, after projecting the company's operations, the future looks fairly promising, what financial methods can be employed to pump new, healthy financial "blood" into the business?

The report issued by the accountant states the results of operations, and, ideally, provides needed information about the possibility of the company's future existence.

Among the documents the accountant will submit, at the time the petition is filed or shortly thereafter, are the statement of affairs (sworn answers to 21 questions about the debtor's past operations; see Chapter 8); recent financial statements; schedules with detailed information about the assets and liabilities of the debtor, including the amount due each creditor; and a statement of the executory contracts of the debtor. Also, the accountant may prepare a statement of affairs showing realizable values, and other special-purpose statements to assist the debtor in securing additional funds. These various statements are discussed in detail in §§ 13.2–13.13.

The type of report that is issued with the financial statements will vary depending on the nature of the engagement. However, most of the services rendered on engagements with debtors in bankruptcy will not fall under the attestation standards or the guidelines to be followed under Standards for Accounting and Review Services. The nature and type of report that should be issued is described in Chapter 15. Chapter 14 describes how to account for the debtor on emergence from chapter 11.

FORM AND SUBSTANCE OF FINANCIAL STATEMENTS

§ 13.2 Financial Data Required at the Date of Filing of Petition in Chapter 11

Many of the statements and schedules the accountant is required to prepare in bankruptcy or insolvency proceedings are the same as those used by companies not experiencing financial difficulty. In insolvency proceedings, these reports are used in specific ways to provide the information needed to effect a fair and equitable settlement to all those involved.

When a petition is filed to initiate proceedings under chapter 11, certain documents must be filed at that time or shortly thereafter. Among the most important documents are the following:

- Statement of affairs. This consists of answers to 21 questions concerning the debtor's past operations, and should not be confused with the report titled "Statement of Affairs," to be discussed later, which shows the realizable value of the assets and the liabilities in the order in which they will be paid.
- Exhibit A to the petition, including:
  - A thumbnail sketch of the financial condition of the business listing total assets and total liabilities.
  - Listing of the amount of secured claims and unsecured claims.
  - Information regarding the public trading of the debtor's securities.
  - Identity of all insiders.
- List of 20 largest creditors that must be filed with the petition and list all creditors that must be filed within 15 days, unless an extension is granted.
- Schedules with detailed information about the assets of the debtor as of the date of the petition.
- Schedules with detailed information about the liabilities, including secured, unsecured, contingent, and unliquidated claims.
- Correct statement of the number and kind of interests of each equity security holder.
- Statement of all executory contracts.

The accountant or financial advisor obviously plays a very valuable role in obtaining the information required in these statements, and any attempt to file a petition and schedules without the aid of an accountant would reduce the reliability of the data accompanying the petition. A more detailed description of the schedules and other information filed with the petition appears in §§ 8.9–8.13.

§ 13.3 Balance Sheet

A balance sheet or statement of financial position must be prepared as of the date the bankruptcy petition is filed. In addition, for several reasons, the debtor will need to prepare this statement during the proceeding. Statement of Position (SOP) 90-7, *Financial Reporting by Entities in Reorganization under the Bankruptcy Code,* contains several suggestions that should be followed in preparing a balance sheet during a chapter 11 case.

(a) Petition Date

It is important to know the exact financial position of the debtor as of the date the petition was filed. This is necessary to determine the liabilities that should be classified as prepetition claims. Liabilities incurred operating the business in a chapter 11 case are considered administrative expenses, and those incurred prior to filing the petition, unless entitled to a priority or secured claim classification, will be general, unsecured claims.

The assets as of the petition date must be determined for several reasons. For example, where a floating lien exists on inventory and/or receivables, the actual balance in these accounts must be determined to establish the amount of the claim that is secured. These balances are also necessary to evaluate whether certain suppliers were given a preference over others. Preparation of a statement of financial position as of the petition date may help discover assets that were concealed prior to the filing of a petition.

One other area where accountants' or financial advisors' assistance may be needed is in the determination of insolvency and the exact date at which it occurred. Although the proof of solvency or insolvency is a function of attorneys, accountants determine the debtor's financial condition, prepare worksheets, and compile other supporting documents and records necessary to prove the client's condition. The proof of insolvency is necessary where preferential payments or fraudulent transfers are involved. Also, in a "cram down," the extent to which the stockholders participate in the plan depends on the solvency of the debtor. Normally, the first step in the determination of the solvency or insolvency of the debtor is the preparation of a balance sheet as of the date the petition was filed.

Often, a statement of income, showing the operating results for the year up to the date the bankruptcy petition was filed, is also prepared. To prepare a statement of financial position as of the petition date and a statement of income for the year up to the date the petition was filed, it may be necessary to use a cutoff date subsequent to the petition date and evaluate the transactions that occurred between the two dates, to establish the balance in the debtor's accounts as of the date the bankruptcy petition was filed.

(b) Issued to Creditors' Committee

Exhibit 13-1 shows the conventional balance sheet for the ABC Company as of December 31, 20XX, along with the notes to the balance sheet. Four months after the date of the balance sheet presented in Exhibit 13-1, the ABC Company appealed to its creditors for their assistance. Exhibit 13-2 shows the balance sheet as of April 28, 20XX; it is prepared in the normal manner except that all secured liabilities are subtracted from the assets to which they relate. In this balance sheet, the balance of accounts receivable is reduced to zero, because they are pledged to the First National Bank in the amount of $600,000, and the net realizable value is only $584,800. Priority claims are subtracted from the

Exhibit 13-1   Example of Standard Balance Sheet with Explanatory Notes, Showing Financial
Condition of ABC Company as of December 31, 20XX

ABC Company, Inc.
Balance Sheet
December 31, 20XX

Assets

Current assets

Cash				$ 35,295
Accounts receivable			$ 553,200	
Less: Allowance for discounts		$ 40,200		
Allowance for uncollectibles		92,300	132,500	420,700
Inventories				650,000
Tax refund receivable				294,673
Total current assets				1,400,668

Fixed and other assets

Property, plant, and equipment
(note 4)

Land			22,000	
Building	$1,150,000			
Less: Accumulated depreciation	510,000	640,000		
Fixtures and equipment	93,000			
Less: Accumulated depreciation	22,000	71,000	733,000	
Investment in XYZ Company			20,000	
Goodwill (notes 1 and 5)			10,250	763,250
TOTAL ASSETS				$2,163,918

Liabilities and Stockholders' Equity

Current liabilities

Accounts payable	$ 511,618
Salaries payable	100,500
Commissions payable	10,000
Taxes payable	100,000
Notes payable (note 3)	570,000
Payable to contractors	125,000
Reserve for liquidation losses (note 2)	200,000
Total current liabilities	1,617,118

Long-term liabilities

Mortgages payable (note 4)	487,500

Other liabilities

Notes payable—officer	36,000
Total liabilities	2,140,618

Stockholders' equity

Common stock ($10 par, 20,000
shares authorized,

18,000 shares outstanding; see note 5)	$ 180,000	
Additional paid-in capital	100,000	
Deficit	(256,700)	23,300
TOTAL LIABILITIES AND STOCKHOLDERS' EQUITY		$2,163,918

Exhibit 13-1   (*continued*)

ABC Company, Inc.
Notes to Balance Sheet

Note 1. Basis of Presentation and Summary of Significant Accounting Policies

Basis of Presentation:

ABC Company, Inc., had sustained losses from its operations during the four years ended December 31, 20XX, and based on subsequent unaudited financial information, losses have continued since December 31, 20XX. The accompanying financial statements have been prepared on a going-concern basis. Continuation of the Company's operations, realization of its assets, and liquidation of its liabilities are dependent on the ability of the Company to achieve a profitable level of operations and to obtain additional financing.

Summary of Significant Accounting Policies:

Inventories—The total merchandise inventory at December 31, 20XX, is stated at the lower of cost or market, determined by the FIFO method.

Property, Plant, and Equipment—Property, plant, and equipment are carried at cost. Additions and improvements are capitalized; maintenance and repairs are charged to operations as incurred. Depreciation is calculated using the straight-line method over the estimated useful lives of the assets.

Goodwill—The goodwill was transferred to the Company in 19XX (see note 5) and is being amortized at the rate of $1,000 per year.

Note 2. Operations to Be Discontinued and Estimated Liquidation Losses

On October 29, 20XX, the Board of Directors resolved to discontinue the operations of one division. A summary of the assets of this division is as follows:

Accounts receivable—net	$100,000
Inventories	225,000
Property, plant, and equipment	130,000
	$455,000

The liquidation of this division will probably result in liquidation losses. The Company had provided a reserve for estimated losses of $200,000; however, no determination can be made at this time as to the total amount of such losses.

Note 3. Notes Payable

The Company entered into a financing agreement in 20XX with the First National Bank of Boston wherein it applied for a revolving credit of $600,000. As security for the payment of the Company's debts to the bank, it granted and assigned to the bank a continuing security interest in all accounts receivable owned or created by the Company. The continuation of this agreement is conditioned on (1) a cash projection (unaudited) for the six months ending June 30, 20XX, furnished to the bank by the Company, (2) the ability of the Company to improve cash flow (including the program set forth in note 2), and (3) the assumption that there will be no material adverse changes in the Company's financial plans and projection on an overall basis.

Note 4. Mortgage Payable

Property, plant, and equipment are collateral for mortgages payable of $487,500. The mortgages payable mature in varying amounts to January 31, fifteen years from now, bearing interest from 5 percent to 9 percent per annum.

Exhibit 13-1   *(continued)*

Note 5. Stockholders' Equity

ABC Company, Inc., was incorporated under the laws of the State of New York on September 17, 20XX. Prior to that date, on April 6, 19XX, ABC Company, Inc., a wholly owned subsidiary of AF Industries, Inc., transferred certain assets to the new company, ABC Company, Inc., as follows:

Merchandise inventory	$296,000
Fixed assets (net of accumulated depreciation)	22,306
Goodwill	17,000
Cash surrender value of life insurance (net of loans thereon of $42,670)	5,775
Prepaid expenses	12,600
Other assets	4,500
	$358,181
Represented by:	
Capital stock (8,000 shares)	$80,000
Loans payable	278,181
	$358,181

On August 5, 20XX, ABC Company issued 10,000 shares of stock at $20 per share to the public. As of December 31, 20XX, AF Industries owned 30 percent of the outstanding stock and the President, Irving J. Stein, owned 10 percent.

total unpledged assets before arriving at the total book value of assets available to unsecured creditors. The general claim for the Employees' Profit Sharing Trust was for past benefits due more than 180 days prior to the date the petition was filed. If these benefits had been due within the 180-day period, it is possible that some part would have been considered a priority claim (§ 4.40). Also listed are factors that may create an increased capital deficit, such as additional losses that may be sustained on realization of assets, and administrative expenses or additional contingent or undisclosed liabilities.

This type of balance sheet is very useful in meetings with creditors' committees, in chapter 11 reorganization proceedings, or in out-of-court settlements. The final total represents the assets that are available for unsecured creditors. All assets are normally presented at book value less any necessary adjustments that should be made as a result of the audit. These are not liquidation values. It is assumed that the business will be rehabilitated and continue operations. The balance sheet differs from the statement of affairs in that the balance sheet is not prepared on the assumption that the business will be liquidated. The statement of affairs is described in detail in § 13.12.

This balance sheet is often prepared using book values. However, with Statement of Position (SOP) 90-7 now requiring entities to adopt fresh-start reporting where reorganization value is greater than liabilities and there is an ownership change, this balance sheet will be much more helpful to creditors and others if it is prepared using going-concern or reorganization values. Thus, the individual assets should be shown at their appraised values and, if the reorganization value is greater than the appraised values, the excess should be included in the balance sheet.

Although most debtors of this size that file a chapter 11 petition will not use fresh-start reporting because there will not be a change of ownership, a balance sheet prepared using reorganization values will be much more helpful to the creditors.

(c) Classification of Prepetition Liabilities

Paragraphs 23–26 of SOP 90-7 provide specific guidance for the preparation of the balance sheet during the reorganization. Liabilities subject to compromise should be separated from those that are not and from postpetition liabilities. Liabilities that are subject to compromise include unsecured claims, undersecured claims, and fully secured claims that may be impaired under a plan. Paragraph 23 indicates that if there is some uncertainty as to whether a secured claim is undersecured or will be impaired under the plan, the entire amount should be included with prepetition claims subject to compromise.

In view of the above, it is expected that most prebankruptcy claims will be reported initially as liabilities subject to compromise. There are a number of reasons for this. For example, at the time the balance sheet is prepared, the collateral may not have been appraised. Also, it might be determined as the case progresses that estimated cash flows from property are less than anticipated. All security interests may not have been fully perfected. Due to these and other factors, it is not unusual for claims that appeared fully secured at the onset of a case to be found to be compromised during the proceedings.

Paragraph 26 of SOP 90-7 also indicates that circumstances arising during the reorganization may require a change in the classification of liabilities between those subject to compromise and those not subject to compromise.

The principal categories (such as priority claims, trade debt, debentures, institutional claims, etc.) of the claims subject to compromise should be disclosed in the notes to the financial statements, as shown in Exhibit 13-3. Note that the focus of the reporting requirement is on providing information about the nature of the claims rather than on whether the claims are current or noncurrent.

Liabilities that are not subject to compromise consist of postpetition liabilities and liabilities not expected to be impaired under the plan. They are reported in the normal manner and thus should be segregated into current and noncurrent categories if a classified balance sheet is presented.

Prior to the issuance of SOP 90-7, there was considerable uncertainty as to how to classify prepetition liabilities.

The first part of paragraph 7 of Accounting Research Bulletin (ARB) No. 43, Chapter 3A, states:

> The term *current liabilities* is used principally to designate obligations whose liquidation is reasonably expected to require the use of existing resources properly classifiable as current assets, or the creation of other current liabilities. . . .

In all chapter 11 reorganization cases, it might be argued that all prepetition debts are not current liabilities because they are not going to be due within one year. At the time a chapter 11 petition is filed, there is an automatic stay that, with minor exceptions, prohibits any party from taking any action that will

Exhibit 13-2 Balance Sheet, or Statement of Financial Position, of ABC Company as of April 28, 20XX, after Appeal to Creditors for Assistance

ABC Company, Inc.
Balance Sheet
April 28, 20XX

Assets			
Current assets			
Cash			$ 7,327
Accounts receivable—assigned		$710,100	
Less: Allowance for discounts	$ 50,000		
Allowance for uncollectibles	75,200	125,300	
		584,800	
Less: Due to First National Bank			
of Boston (see contra)		$600,000	
Inventories		$795,000	
Less: Due to contractors		75,000	720,000
Tax refund receivable			7,673
Total unencumbered current assets			735,000
Fixed and other assets			
Property, plant, and equipment			
Land		22,000	
Building	$1,150,000		
Less: Accumulated depreciation	550,000	600,000	
Fixtures and equipment	93,000		
Less: Accumulated depreciation	25,000	68,000	
		690,000	
Less: Mortgage payable		487,500	202,500
Investment in XYZ Company			20,000
Goodwill		10,000	232,500
Total unencumbered assets			967,500
Less: Priority claims			247,500
Total assets available to			
unsecured creditors			$720,000

interfere with the debtor or its property until the stay is modified or removed. After a chapter 11 petition is filed, an unsecured creditor must generally wait until a plan has been developed before any payment will be received on pre-petition debt. The average time period needed to develop a plan and obtain its approval and confirmation is generally longer than one year.

 Most trade payables in a chapter 11 case will not be satisfied within a period of one year. FASB Statement No. 6, *Classification of Short-Term Obligations Expected to Be Refinanced,* was issued to attempt to eliminate the use of various ways to classify short-term obligations that will be refinanced. However, as with other FASB statements, the problems associated with chapter 11 reorganizations are not addressed. This statement provides that the refinancing of a short-term obligation on a long-term basis means either replacing it with a long-term obligation or with equity securities, or renewing, extending, or replacing it

Exhibit 13-2   *(continued)*

Liabilities, Less Capital Deficiency

Priority claims

Taxes payable	$100,000
Salaries payable	127,500
Commissions payable	20,000
Total priority claims	$247,500

Fully collateralized claims

Mortgages payable	$487,500
Contractors payable (see contra)	75,000
Total fully collateralized claims	$562,500

Partially collateralized claims

First National Bank of Boston

Notes payable	$500,000	
Accounts payable (see below)	100,000	
	600,000	
Less: Accounts receivable—assigned (see contra)	584,800	$ 15,200

General claims

Due to ABC Company, Inc.—Employees' Profit Sharing Trust		25,000	
Accounts payable	$ 682,000		
Less: Accounts payable—First National Bank of Boston (see above)	100,000	582,000	607,000
Notes payable—officer			36,000
Total unsecured liabilities			658,200
Reserve for liquidation losses			200,000
Capital deficiency			(138,200)

Subject to:

1. Additional losses that may be sustained on realization of assets and administrative expenses

2. Contingent and undisclosed liabilities

Total unsecured liabilities less capital deficiency	$720,000

with short-term obligations for an uninterrupted period extending beyond one year. According to this statement, short-term obligations that arise from transactions in the normal course of business and that are due in customary terms (such as trade payables, advance collections, and accrued expenses) are to be classified as current liabilities in all instances. Other short-term obligations are excluded from current liabilities under that statement only if the enterprise intends to refinance the obligation on a long-term basis and such intent is supported by an ability to consummate the refinancing, as demonstrated by either a financing agreement or the post-balance-sheet-date issuance of a long-term obligation or equity securities. It might be argued that FASB Statement No. 6 suggests that current liabilities should remain as such until a plan is developed

Exhibit 13-3   Liability Section of Balance Sheet

Liabilities and Shareholders' Equity (Deficit)

Liabilities Not Subject to Compromise

Current liabilities	
Short-term borrowings	xx
Accounts payable—trade	xx
Liability under warranty contracts	xx
Other current liabilities	xx
Total current liabilities	xx

Bonds payable, 6% fully secured		xx
Total liabilities not subject to compromise		xx
Liabilities subject to compromise (note A)		xx
Total liabilities		xx

Note A

Liabilities subject to compromise consist of the following:

Secured debt, 14%, secured by first mortgage on building	xx
Priority tax claims	xx
Senior subordinated secured notes, 15%	xx
Accounts payable (trade) and other miscellaneous claims	xx
Subordinated debentures, 17%	xx
Total	xx

[In this case, management has decided because of the low interest rate on the secured bonds to leave them unimpaired. Thus, they are listed as long-term liabilities that are not subject to compromise.]

because the intent requirement is not satisfied. This statement, however, does not address what happens at the time the chapter 11 petition is filed.

Upon the filing of a chapter 11 petition, the liability, to some extent, loses its distinct character. For example, nonsecured trade payables, notes payable, and other unsecured claims (with some exceptions) are frequently grouped into one class—unsecured claims. Thus, obligations arising from transactions in the normal course of business no longer have that specific characteristic. Because of the nature of chapter 11 proceedings, it seems inappropriate to apply the distinction made in FASB Statement No. 6. Also, at the time the petition is filed, unsecured liabilities likewise lose their specific term distinction. Obligations due within one year are often grouped with those that have a longer due date. These changes are accounted for in this manner by most debtors, with all unsecured prepetition debt shown in one account on balance sheets issued subsequent to the filing of the chapter 11 petition.

Provisions that make long-term obligations callable because the debtor violated provisions of a loan agreement create difficulties in deciding whether prepetition long-term liabilities should be reclassified. FASB Statement No. 78 amended paragraph 7 of Accounting Research Bulletin (ARB) No. 43, chapter 3A, by adding the following:

The current liability classification is also intended to include obligations that, by their terms, are due on demand or will be due on demand within one year (or operating cycle, if longer) from the balance sheet date, even though liquidation may not be expected within that period. It is also intended to include long-term obligations that are or will be callable by the creditor either because the debtor's violation of a provision of the debt agreement at the balance sheet date makes the obligation callable or because the violation, if not cured within a specified grace period, will make the obligation callable. Accordingly, such callable obligations shall be classified as current liabilities unless one of the following conditions is met:

a   The creditor has waived* or subsequently lost[†] the right to demand repayment for more than one year (or operating cycle, if longer) from the balance sheet date.
b   For long-term obligations containing a grace period within which the debtor may cure the violation, it is probable[‡] that the violation will be cured within that period, thus preventing the obligation from becoming callable.

If an obligation under (b) above is classified as a long-term liability (or, in the case of an unclassified balance sheet, is included as a long-term liability in the disclosure of debt maturities), the circumstances shall be disclosed. Short-term obligations that are expected to be refinanced on a long-term basis, including those callable obligations discussed herein, shall be classified in accordance with FASB Statement No. 6, *Classification of Short-Term Obligations Expected to Be Refinanced.*

* If the obligation is callable because of violations of certain provisions of the debt agreement, the creditor needs to waive its right with regard only to those violations.

[†] For example, the debtor has cured the violation after the balance sheet date and the obligation is not callable at the time the financial statements are issued.

[‡] *Probable* is defined in FASB Statement No. 5, *Accounting for Contingencies,* as "likely to occur" and is used in the same sense in this paragraph.

Because of the automatic stay, the creditor loses the right to demand repayment until the plan has been confirmed by the court. Thus, long-term obligations need not be reclassified, because one of the conditions (that is, the creditor has lost the right to demand payment for more than one year) necessary to prevent the reclassification of the callable obligations exists.

(d) Liability Amount

Liabilities that may be affected by the plan should be reported at the amount expected to be allowed even though they may be settled for a lesser amount. For example, once the allowed amount of an existing claim is determined or can be estimated, the carrying value of the debt should be adjusted to reflect that amount. Paragraph 25 of SOP 90-7 provides that debt discounts or premiums as well as debt issue costs should be viewed as valuations of the related debt. When the allowed claim differs from the net carrying amount of the debt, the discount or premium and deferred issue costs should be adjusted to the extent necessary to report the debt at the allowed amount of the claim. If these adjustments are not enough, then the carrying value of the debt will be adjusted. The gain or loss resulting from the entries to record these adjustments is to be reported as a reorganization item, as described in § 13.9.

Prepetition claims that become known after the petition is filed, such as a claim arising from the rejection of a lease, should also be reported on the basis of the expected amount of the allowed claim and not at an estimate of the settlement amount. Paragraph 48 of SOP 90-7 suggests that these claims should be reported at the amount allowed by the court because (1) that is the amount of the liability until it is settled, and (2) the use of the allowed amount is consistent with the amounts at which other prepetition liabilities are stated. See § 13.10.

Paragraph 24 of SOP 90-7 also indicates that FASB Statement No. 5, *Accounting for Contingencies,* applies to the process of determining the expected amount of an allowed claim. Claims that are not subject to reasonable estimation should be disclosed in the notes to the financial statements based on the provisions of FASB Statement No. 5. Once the accrual provisions of FASB Statement No. 5 are satisfied, the claims should be recorded. It is the intent of the SOP to require the recording of a liability once it can be estimated under the provisions of FASB Statement No. 5, so as not to delay the recording of claims until confirmation of the plan, as has been the practice in some situations.

In Volume 2 of *Bankruptcy and Insolvency Accounting,* 13.1 contains the financial statements issued by Allegheny International while in chapter 11; 13.1(b) is the balance sheet for 1989. The liabilities subject to compromise were labeled as prepetition liabilities. (The balance sheet for the end of 1990, reflecting the reorganization value, is presented as 14.1 in Volume 2.) Note 6 of 13.1(e) describes the prepetition liabilities.

The financial statements issued by Hills Department Stores during its chapter 11 filing appear in 13.2 of Volume 2. Of particular interest are the balance sheet (13.2(a)) and the contents of the liabilities subject to compromise (note 2 of 13.2(e)).

§ 13.4 Rejected Leases

According to FASB Statement No. 5, a claim must be "probable" and "reasonably estimable" before any amount is recorded. In this case, it would appear that almost all claims are probable. First, if the lease agreement was favorable to the debtor, it probably would not have been rejected. Generally, only the questionable or unfavorable agreements are rejected. Under these conditions, it generally can be assumed that there will be a legitimate claim. If that is not the case, there is no legitimate claim and no need to accrue a loss.

In considering accruals for rejected leases, three amounts are of concern:

1 The amount of the claim filed with the court. The amount of the allowed claim includes the unpaid rent that is due under the lease as of the earlier of the date the petition was filed or the date the lessor repossessed, or the lessee surrendered, the leased property, without acceleration, plus an amount allowed for damages resulting from the rejection of the lease. The claim for damages for rejection of a lease of real property is limited to the rent reserved by the lease for the greater of one year or 15 percent of the remaining terms of the lease. The amount calculated by taking 15 percent of the remaining terms of the lease may not exceed the rents for

the next three years. The calculation of damages begins as of the earlier of the date the petition was filed or the date the lessor repossessed, or the lessee surrendered, the leased property.

2 The amount of the claim allowed by the court. If the amount shown on the proof of claim is contested by the debtor, the court will fix the amount of the claim. Otherwise, the amount on the creditor's proof of claim stands.

3 The amount to be paid as provided for in the plan of reorganization. All claims for damages due to lease rejection are considered prepetition claims. The amount provided for in the plan may be less than the amount allowed by the court, as is the case with many unsecured claims.

Most liabilities that are on the books at the time the petition is filed are not reduced until the plan is approved, even though, in most cases, the probability of 100 percent of the claims being paid is low. Thus, because damages from lease rejection are considered prepetition claims, it appears that they should be booked at the amount of the claim. That amount would be the amount of the claim that is filed by the lessor, or, in the case where the debtor plans to challenge the claim, the amount management considers to be a reasonable estimate of the claim. The provisions of FASB Statement No. 5, *Accounting for Contingencies*, would apply when determining whether a liability should be recorded and, if so, at what amount. If part of this claim is subsequently discharged, the amount of discharge is income due to debt discharge.

There is, however, one key factor that makes some people question the above reasoning. The amount eventually paid as a result of a rejected lease is an obligation that was incurred because of the special provisions of the Bankruptcy Code. From this it might be reasoned that the amount of obligation to be booked from a lease rejection is the amount that the debtor eventually has to pay—that is, the amount provided for in the plan. If the lease rejection occurred outside of bankruptcy proceedings, the debtor would accrue an amount that represents an estimate of the damages from the lease cancellation, provided the claim is probable and reasonably estimable. The amount to be accrued, based on the above reasoning, would be an estimate of the amount that the debtor would eventually pay.

The above discussion deals with the "problem" requirement that is necessary before a claim can be recorded. The next requirement of FASB Statement No. 5 is that the amount must be reasonably estimable. As noted above, the maximum amount that will be paid for real property is limited to three years' rent. Based on the remaining life of the lease, the market for rental property, and the financial condition of the debtor, a reasonable estimate could be made of the potential liability. For other lease agreements, it would appear that the liability for damages could in most cases be estimated.

Paragraphs 23 and 24 of SOP 90-7 require the debtor to report the claims from lease rejections at an estimate of the amount that will be allowed, not at an estimate of the amount that will eventually be paid. The provisions of FASB Statement No. 5 should be followed in determining the amount to accrue. SOP 90-7 also requires that the debtor accrue the claim once it can be reflected in the accounts based on the provisions of FASB Statement No. 5 and not delay the recording of the claim until the plan is confirmed.

§ 13.5 Warranty Reserves and Similar Liabilities

The discussion here will be restricted to warranty claims; however, the concepts should apply to other similar liabilities. There are two types of warranty claims to consider: (1) claims that have been made against the company prior to the petition date for faulty, damaged, and otherwise unacceptable goods; and (2) claims that will be filed in the postpetition period for warranty guarantees on goods that were delivered prior to the filing of the petition. Both of these types of claims are prebankruptcy claims. All warranty claims arising from goods sold after the petition was filed are postpetition (administrative expense) claims. The first group of prepetition claims can generally be reasonably determined by reviewing all requests for refunds, exchanges, and other claims. However, the claims resulting from damages sustained by using the product are more difficult to estimate. An estimate of the prebankruptcy claims that will be filed during the proceeding may be even more difficult to determine. Prior experience can often provide the basis for a reasonable estimate. In fact, if the company has provided properly for this type of liability, the amount in the reserve account may be the most reasonable estimate of the potential liability available.

In estimating the amount to include in the prepetition liabilities, the FASB Statement No. 5 rules of "probable" and "reasonably estimable" apply. Thus, it would appear that the warranty claims estimated in accordance with FASB Statement No. 5 should be included with other prepetition liabilities. Once all of the warranty claims have been filed and approved by the court, the amount of the warranty claims in the prepetition liabilities can be adjusted. The warranty claims may, however, be handled in a more practical manner. In a chapter 11 reorganization, the objective is to come out of the proceedings with a viable and profitable operation. Thus, customer goodwill is important. Debtor's counsel may petition the court for, and receive, permission to honor all reasonable warranty claims for faulty or otherwise unacceptable products. Normally, a request of this nature would include authorization to cover refunds requested prior to, as well as those filed subsequent to, the petition date. The court may classify all of the payments of warranty claims as administrative expenses. Under these conditions, it would appear that the debtor would leave the provision of warranty expense as a liability, but not prepetition. As these claims are paid, they would be charged against the reserve account as normally required by generally accepted accounting principles.

Paragraphs 23 and 24 of SOP 90-7 require the debtor to report claims for warranties and other similar liabilities at an estimate of the amount that will be allowed and not at an estimate of the amount that will eventually be paid. The provisions of FASB Statement No. 5 should be used in determining the amount to accrue. SOP 90-7 also requires the debtor to accrue the claim once it can be reflected in the accounts based on the provisions of FASB Statement No. 5 and not delay the recording of the claim until the plan is confirmed.

As was discussed above, in order to maintain customer goodwill, the court may order the debtor to honor warranty claims from the sale of all goods including sales prior to the filing of the petition. In this situation, it would appear that the reserve for warranty claims should be reflected on the balance sheet as a liability not subject to compromise. The amount of the reserve would continue to be estimated in the normal manner based on the provisions of FASB Statement No. 5.

§ 13.6 Pension Liability

A claim is defined in the Bankruptcy Code (section 101(5)), as a:

> Right to payment, whether or not such right is reduced to judgment, liquidated, unliquidated, fixed contingent, matured, unmatured, disputed, undisputed, legal, equitable, secured or unsecured; or

> Right to an equitable remedy for breach of performance if such breach gives rise to a right to payment, whether or not such right to an equitable remedy is reduced to judgment, fixed, contingent, matured, unmatured, disputed, undisputed, secured or unsecured.

It would appear that any liability associated with pension plans could be a prepetition debt. Thus, the debtor should consider estimating and classifying such debt as a prepetition obligation. The court and the other creditors may agree to an arrangement in which the company will assume any liability from the provisions of a pension plan and will continue to make payments as though the bankruptcy plan had not been filed. However, this type of arrangement does not alter the fact that the liability is a prepetition debt.

(a) Nonvested Benefits

When a plan is terminated before or during bankruptcy and the conditions necessary for vesting—such as attainment of a specified age or minimum number of years of employment—have not occurred, claims for nonvested benefits are not allowed.

Under conditions where the plan is not terminated, it would appear that an employee with nonvested accrued benefits would have an allowable contingent claim for unfunded vested benefits.[1] The amount allowed would be the total amount of the employee's accrued benefits reduced by (1) the probability of such benefits vesting before the plan terminates and (2) the probability of the plan's terminating with insufficient assets to pay benefits.[2] The allowance of a claim for these benefits conflicts with the provisions of ERISA[3] and with the encouragement of the Internal Revenue Code to defer pension payments until retirement. Thus, the extent to which a bankruptcy court will allow this claim is very questionable. The claim, if allowed, would be for third priority to the extent of the amount accrued during the 90 days prior to the filing of the petition. All other claims would be unsecured. The accrued amount that is based on prior services will be an unsecured claim.

(b) Vested Benefits

At the time the plan is terminated, the employees have a claim only to the extent that the vested benefits are unfunded. The trust is responsible for the payment of benefits to the extent that they are funded. The amount of the claim

---

[1] 11 U.S.C. § 502(a).

[2] Sable, Eggertsen, and Bernstein, "Pension-Related Claims in Bankruptcy," *American Bankruptcy Law Journal*, Vol. 56 (1982), p. 160.

[3] ERISA requires that pensions be administered strictly in accordance with the provisions of the plan (29 U.S.C. § 1104(a)(1)(d)). Most plan agreements provide the payments are to be made only upon retirement or plan termination.

will be the present value of the nonforfeitable deferred benefits less the amount of the trust fund assets allocable to the employee. Allocations are made according to the guidelines stipulated in ERISA, section 4044.[4] A plan trustee may represent all prior claim holders and file a proof of multiple claims. Claims are unsecured except for the amount accrued within the 90 days prior to bankruptcy.

The liability to a plan trustee may be limited by contract to the amount of delinquent contributions. Thus, claims will be considered unsecured except for amounts that qualify as fourth priority. The fourth priority, consisting of contributions arising on account of service performed within 180 days prior to the filing of the petition, is limited to $2,000 times the number of employees covered by the plan less the extent to which covered employees have a third priority for wages due within 90 days prior to bankruptcy.

The Pension Benefit Guarantee Corporation (PBGC) is a guarantor of vested pension benefits. It may file a claim against the employer, because it must pay if the employer does not. It is not necessary for the PBGC to actually pay the benefits before it can file a claim. The PBGC guarantee is limited, however, to a maximum of $750 per month (adjusted annually in proportion to adjustments of the social security base). Benefit income made within the five-year period prior to termination of the plan is further limited. A claim can be filed for vested benefits to the extent that they are guaranteed and unfunded. PBGC can also file a claim for contributions that were not made under the plan. It has the power under ERISA to request a district court to appoint itself as trustee and to collect any amount due under the plan. Additionally, an employer can be liable for up to 30 percent of its net worth to PBGC for unfunded guaranteed benefits. Net worth for a chapter 11 case is based on going-concern concepts.

ERISA provides that the PBGC may place a lien on all the property of the debtor when an employer terminates a pension plan that does not have the assets to pay guaranteed benefits. The lien is to be treated in the same manner as a tax lien. If the lien is not perfected, it would not be valid to the bankruptcy court. In most cases, the plan is terminated after the petition is filed; if terminated earlier, notice may not have been filed.

Once it has been determined that all or part of the liability will be assumed by the PBGC, then the pension liability account should be reduced accordingly.

Generally, the only pension-related claim that is allowed when a plan is not terminated is a claim for delinquent contributions.

§ 13.7   Pro Forma Statement of Financial Position

Accountants are often asked to prepare pro forma statements of financial position as if the proposed plan has been approved. As discussed in § 6.26, the pro forma statement of financial position is often included in the disclosure statement.

Paragraph 37 of SOP 90-7 states that the pro forma statement of financial position should be prepared using reorganization values rather than historical costs. A debtor that does not qualify for fresh-start reporting would continue to use historical costs when emerging from chapter 11.

---

[4] 29 U.S.C. § 1344.

As noted in § 6.26, however, the statement would be of much more value if it was prepared using the going-concern or reorganized value of the entity that will emerge from bankruptcy.

§ 13.8   Notes to Statements

The notes to the balance sheet should receive greater attention than is conventional. The notes should explain the nature of the chapter 11 filing, including the impact the filing is having on operations. In Volume 2 of *Bankruptcy and Insolvency Accounting*, 13.1(e) and 13.2(e) are examples of selected notes to financial statements.

The notes, in the case of an audit or investigation of selected accounts, should explain the content of each account, include some of the major audit steps that were performed, and discuss any information that was not available during the examination and any deficiencies in the books and records. For example, a physical inventory might not have been taken at the date the petition was filed, and the accountant may wish to disclose the method used to satisfy the requirement that the inventory be correctly stated.

The balance sheet becomes the basis for the schedules of assets and liabilities that the debtor must file. These schedules consist of sworn statements of the debtor's assets and liabilities as of the date of filing the petition and include the same basic information found in the debtor's balance sheet. (For detailed discussion, see § 8.11.)

Rule 1007 requires that the debtor file its detailed schedules within 15 days after entry of the order for relief for an involuntary petition or within 15 days of filing a voluntary petition. An extension of time may be granted only on application for cause shown and after notice.

In addition to its conventional significance as a statement of position at one point in time, the balance sheet prepared as of the date of the petition derives greater importance because of the schedules for which it is the basis.

§ 13.9   Statement of Operations

The debtor is required to file with the court, usually on a monthly basis, a statement setting forth the results from operations. At times, the court may require operating or cash flow statements more frequently. Because of the complexities involved in preparing such a statement, an accountant's services usually prove to be necessary. For example, some statements must be prepared on an accrual basis (§ 9.4).

In addition to issuing the monthly income statement or statement of operations to the court, the debtor may issue operating statements to satisfy SEC requirements, or for other purposes, as part of the normal process of operating a business. Paragraphs 27–30 of SOP 90-7 explain how items are to be reported in the statement of operations issued during the period in which the debtor is reorganizing under chapter 11.

(a) Reorganization Items

The objective of reporting during the chapter 11 case is to present the results of operations of the reporting entity and to clearly separate those activities related to the normal operations of the business from those related to the reorganization. Thus, revenues, expenses (including professional fees), realized gains and losses, and provisions for losses resulting from the chapter 11 reorganization and restructuring of the business should be separately reported. According to paragraph 27 of SOP 90-7, items related to the reorganization (except for the reporting of discontinued operations, which are already reported separately) should be reported in a separate category within the income (loss) from operations section of the statement of operations. (See Appendix A of SOP 90-7 for an example of the form to use for operating statements issued during a chapter 11 case.) The part of the operating statement that relates to the reporting of reorganization items is as follows:

Earnings before reorganization items and income tax benefits	47
Reorganization items:	
Loss on disposal of facility	(60)
Professional fees	(50)
Provision for rejected executory contracts	(10)
Interest earned on accumulated cash resulting from	
chapter 11 proceeding	1
	(119)
Loss before income tax benefit and discontinued operations	(72)

Note that the reader of the statement of operations is able to determine the amount of income generated from continuing operations without the impact of the reorganization being reflected in these totals. Although some judgment on the part of management is involved to determine the part of income that relates to ongoing operations, a reasonable estimate of the segregation will be much more beneficial to the reader than including all items in this category, as is current practice.

A summary of the provisions relating to the operating statements follows:

- Gains or losses as a result of restructuring or disposal of assets directly related to the reorganization are reported as a reorganization item (unless the disposal meets the requirement for discontinued operations). The gains or losses include the gain or loss on disposal of the assets, related employee costs, and other charges related to the disposal of assets or restructuring of operations. Note that the reporting of a reduction in business activity does not result in reclassification of revenues or expenses identified with the assets sold or abandoned, unless the transaction is classified as a disposal of a business segment under APB Opinion No. 30.

- Professional fees are expensed as incurred and reported as a reorganization item.

- Interest income earned in chapter 11, which would not have been earned but for the proceeding, is reported as a reorganization item.

- Interest expense should be reported only to the extent that it will be paid during the proceeding or to the extent that it may be allowed as a priority, secured, or unsecured claim. The extent to which the reported interest expense differs from the contractual rate should be reflected in the notes to the operating statement or shown parenthetically on the face of the operating statement. The SEC prefers the latter.

SOP 90-7 contains an example of how the reorganization items are to be included in the statement of operations.

As noted earlier, 13.1 of Volume 2 of *Bankruptcy and Insolvency Accounting* contains the financial statements issued by Allegheny International while in chapter 11. The statement of operations for 1988, 1989, and 1990 is shown as 13.1(a). Selected entries in the reorganization items section of the statement of operations are described in more detail in Note 3 of 13.1(e). Reorganization items consist of administration costs, interest income, adjustments to estimated claims, and revaluation of assets and liabilities for fresh-start reporting in 1990. In 13.2 of Volume 2, the financial statement of Hills Department Stores, reorganization items in the statement of operations (13.2(b)) consists of store closing and reorganization costs, professional fees, and interest income.

Paragraph 28 of SOP 90-7 indicates that professional fees are to be expensed as incurred. The SOP concludes that professional fees and similar expenditures directly related to the chapter 11 proceeding do not result in assets or liabilities and should therefore be expensed as incurred as a reorganization item.

(b) Professional Fees

In many chapter 11 cases, professional fees are substantial in relation to the total assets of the debtor. For example, in a large number of cases, the professional fees have exceeded several million dollars. Services provided in chapter 11 reorganizations can be classified into at least the following five separate but related areas:

1 *Services required solely because the petition is filed.* Included would be the preparation of selected schedules that are filed with the petition, a statement of affairs, and special reports filed with the court, such as operating statements. Also included would be the time spent comparing proofs of claims with the debtor's records.

2 *Costs associated with discontinued operations.* Any accounting services rendered to help the debtor dispose of unprofitable operations should be charged to the discontinued operations.

3 *Costs associated with the reorganization of the ongoing business.* Included here are the costs associated with identifying the problem that created the financial difficulty in the first place, and developing a plan of action to correct the problem. Some of these costs are directly related to an analysis of business problems that, if addressed earlier, would have eliminated the need for the debtor to file a chapter 11 petition. However, the cost of professional fees necessary to correct the problem

is much greater if the debtor did not take early action and, as a result, files a petition.

4 *Normal legal and accounting services.* Certain professional services will continue during the proceedings; among them might be some types of management advisory services or an audit. It should be realized, however, that the filing of a petition may change the focus of the audit and, to some extent, the nature of the assignment.

5 *Costs associated with a temporary management team of workout specialists.* At times, in addition to salary and other costs, a large bonus might be paid at the conclusion of a successful reorganization of the company.

As can be seen, the expenditures for professional fees are related to both ongoing operations and chapter 11 proceedings. No doubt a significant amount of the costs related to chapter 11, such as evaluations of alternatives, should have been incurred even if a chapter 11 petition was not filed. According to SOP 90-7, only those fees directly related to the chapter 11 proceeding are reorganization items and should be expensed.

Prior to the issuance of SOP 90-7, there were at least three methods used to account for professional fees of a company in chapter 11.

First, it was argued that all professional fees (current and future) associated with an event (that is, the filing of a bankruptcy petition) should be accrued as of the occurrence of the event (that is, the date the petition is filed). There were several problems with this interpretation. An assumption was made that the filing of a petition was one event; all "probable" and "reasonably estimable" activities were to be accounted for as of the date the petition was filed. Thus, not only were expenses associated with the bankruptcy to be accrued, but income from debt discharge was also to be estimated. Although the total income from debt discharge could not be booked, income could be used to the extent of the estimated professional fees. It appeared that if professional fees were accrued, any other costs directly associated with the bankruptcy proceeding were also to be accrued.

Recording professional fees before the services are rendered is in fact recording a nonexistent liability. The services have not been rendered, so a claim does not exist. Although a loss contingency may be established for certain transactions or events, it is questionable whether this accrual would meet the requirements of FASB Statement No. 5.

The second method recognizes fees on the approval of a plan. Because a significant amount of debt is forgiven in most reorganizations, the professional fees were expenses until the plan was approved; they were then charged against the gain from debt discharge.

In theory, it appeared that the professional fees for direct bankruptcy services could be capitalized and charged against gain from debt discharge, assuming there was evidence to indicate that the gain from debt discharge would be large enough to offset the professional fees. The problem with this was that these costs were being capitalized as an asset on the books of a debtor whose prospects for successful future operations were highly questionable. In fact, the poorer the condition of the debtor, the greater was the prospect that the administrative expenses could be offset against a gain from debt discharge. It should be realized, however, that the debtor is incurring an expenditure that will eventually be paid by the creditors through their debt reduction; that is, the expenditure of company assets to pay administrative expenses is ultimately a reduction of assets that otherwise might have been distributed to creditors.

The third method, which recognizes professional fees as services are performed, was adopted by SOP 90-7. It was argued that this approach was the most theoretically viable alternative because these costs were generally period costs and should be charged against income in the period incurred. If this approach was used, nonexistent liabilities would not appear on the balance sheet (accrual at the beginning of the case) and assets would not be reflected where there was considerable uncertainty as to their realization (deferral of cost to confirmation of plan).

Even though most professional expenditures will provide substantial future benefits, they are, by their very nature, not of the type that would normally be capitalized; instead, they would generally be charged against the current period's revenue. Even when the policy is followed to expense items as incurred, specific costs related to the reorganization, in the form of stock issuance costs and so forth, would be charged against the proceeds or, in the case of stock for debt, against income from debt discharge. Some chapter 11 debtors have expensed all of the professional fees in years prior to confirmation and then, in the year of confirmation, they have reduced the gain from debt discharge by the amount of the professional fees incurred that year.

§ 13.10   Statement of Cash Flows

To abide by the requirement of FASB Statement No. 95, it may be necessary for the accountant to prepare the statement of cash flows. Examples of this statement are in the Forms and Exhibits volume.

In some instances, the court may require that a cash receipts and disbursements statement be filed weekly or bimonthly, although an order may be secured deleting this requirement for cause. The preparation of cash receipts and disbursements statements becomes extremely important where the debtor's plan calls for installment payments, and it is necessary for the accountant to show that such payments will be made. A statement of cash flows prepared in accordance with the provisions of FASB Statement No. 95 will in most cases satisfy these needs. As noted in § 9.4, the U.S. trustee's office in the Central District of California requires that monthly cash flow statements be filed. Other regions have similar requirements. See §§ 9.3 and 9.4.

Paragraph 31 of SOP 90-7 indicates that reorganization items should be disclosed separately within the operating, investing, and financing categories of the statement of cash flows. SOP 90-7 also indicates that reorganization items related to operating cash flows are better reflected if the direct method is used to prepare the statement of cash flows. An example of the statement of cash flows issued during a chapter 11 case is found in Appendix A to SOP 90-7. (See Appendix C.) The part of the statement related to the operations section of the statement of cash flows is presented below:

Cash flows from operating activities:

Cash received from customers	$2,220
Cash paid to suppliers and employees	(2,070)
Interest expense	(3)

Net cash provided by operating activities before reorganization items	147

Operating cash flows from reorganization items:

Interest received on cash accumulated because of the chapter 11 proceeding	1
Professional fees paid for services rendered in connection with the chapter 11 proceeding	(50)
Net cash used by reorganization items	(49)
Net cash provided by operating items	(98)

SOP 90-7 indicates that if the indirect method is used, the details of the operating cash receipts and payments resulting from the reorganization should be disclosed in a supplementary schedule or in the notes to the financial statement. The footnotes or supplementary schedule should include the information from the reorganization section of the statement of cash flows that is presented above.

It would also be acceptable to reflect this information in the cash flow statement, using the indirect approach, as shown below:

Net loss	$(118)

Adjustment to determine net cash provided by operating items before reorganization items:

Depreciation	20
Loss on disposal of facility	60
Provision for rejection of executory contracts	10
Loss on discontinued operations	56
Increase in postpetition liabilities and other liabilities	250
Increase in accounts receivable	(180)
Reorganization items	49

Net cash provided by operating activities before reorganization items	147

Reorganization items:

Interest received on cash accumulated because of the chapter 11 proceeding	1
Professional fees paid for services rendered in connection with the chapter 11 proceeding	(50)
Net cash provided by reorganization items	(49)
Net cash provided by operating activities	$ 98

Any reorganization items included in financing and investing activities should also be disclosed separately.

In 13.1 of Volume 2 (the financial statements issued by Allegheny International while in chapter 11), 13.1(c) contains the statement of cash flows for 1988, 1989, and 1990. Allegheny used the indirect method and included all of the reorganizations in one category. In 13.2 of Volume 2 (the financial statements of Hills Department Stores), 13.2(d) is an example of another cash flow statement. This cash flow statement identifies major categories of adjustments that need to be made to the net income using the indirect method.

§ 13.11   Statement of Capital Deficiency

A statement of capital deficiency is often prepared, setting forth in summary form the changes in the capital accounts for the last few years. This statement indicates the time period when the losses began to occur, any withdrawals by the owners, and all other major transactions dealing with the capital accounts.

§ 13.12   Statement of Affairs

A statement of affairs is quite commonly prepared when a business is experiencing financial difficulty and considering initiation of some type of remedy. This statement should not be confused with the statement of affairs that consists merely of answers to questions regarding the debtor's past operations (§ 8.13) and is filed under the Bankruptcy Code when a debtor files a petition. The statement of affairs, often prepared at the request of the bankruptcy judge or the creditors' committee in out-of-court proceedings, provides information that assists the creditors in deciding on the course of action they should take in their dealings with the insolvent debtor. The statement of affairs, developed from the balance sheet for the ABC Company as of April 28, 20XX (Exhibit 13-2), is shown in Exhibit 13-4.

The report prepared by the accountant is a statement of the debtor's financial condition as of a certain date, and presents an analysis of its financial position and the status of the creditors with respect to the debtor's assets. It has been termed "a statement of position from a 'quitting concern' point of view."

The statement of affairs is based on assumptions that differ quite clearly from those on which the balance sheet is based. Some of the major differences follow:

- It is hypothetical or pro forma; that is, it is an estimate of the probable outcome if the debtor's business should be liquidated.
- Liquidation is assumed to occur; therefore, it is necessary to establish a time period over which the assets will be sold, so that their value may be estimated. The shorter the time period, the smaller the proceeds that will be realized from sales.
- Correspondingly, the assumption of a going concern is abandoned and the emphasis is shifted from measuring periodic profit to establishing the debts and resources available to meet those obligations.
- The form used for the statement of affairs is one that will reveal the legal status of the several groups of creditors.

Exhibit 13-4   Statement of Affairs of ABC Company as of April 28, 20XX, the Date of Filing of Petition

ABC Company, Inc.
Statement of Affairs
April 28, 20XX

Book Value	Assets	Appraised	Estimated Amount Available	Loss or (Gain) on Realization
	Assets constituting collateral for holders of fully secured claims:			
$ 795,000	Inventories	$ 400,000		$395,000
22,000	Land	35,000		(13,000)
600,000	Building	650,000		(50,000)
68,000	Fixtures and equipment	20,000		48,000
	Total	1,105,000		
	Less: Fully secured claims (see contra)	562,500	$542,000	
	Assets constituting collateral for holders of partly secured claims:			
584,800	Accounts receivable	450,000		134,800
	Total	$ 450,000		
	Free assets (unencumbered):			
7,327	Cash	$ 7,327	7,327	
7,673	Tax refund receivable	7,673	7,673	
20,000	Investment in XYZ Company	20,000	20,000	
10,000	Goodwill	-0-		10,000
	Trademarks	5,000	5,000	(5,000)
	Estimated amount available		582,500	
	Liabilities with priority (see contra)		257,500	
	Estimated amount available for unsecured creditors (approximately 33¢ per dollar)		325,000	
	Estimated deficiency on unsecured liabilities		468,000	
	Reserve for liquidation losses established December 31, 19X6 (see contra)			(200,000)
$2,114,800	Totals		$793,000	$319,800

Exhibit 13-4   (*continued*)

Book Value	Liabilities and Stockholders' Equity		Amount Unsecured
	Liabilities with priority:		
$ -0-	Estimated liquidation costs	$10,000	
100,000	Taxes payable	100,000	
127,500	Salaries payable	127,500	
20,000	Commissions payable	20,000	
	Total liabilities with priority (deducted contra)	$257,500	
	Fully secured liabilities:		
75,000	Payable to contractors	$75,000	
487,500	Mortgages payable	487,500	
	Total fully secured liabilities (deducted contra)	$562,500	
	Partly secured liabilities: First National Bank of Boston		
500,000	Notes payable	$500,000	
100,000	Accounts payable	100,000	
	Total partly secured liabilities	600,000	
	Less: Accounts receivable assigned (see contra)	450,000	$150,000
	Unsecured liabilities: Due to ABC Company, Inc., Employees'		
25,000	Profit Sharing Trust		25,000
	Accounts payable	682,000	
582,000	Less Payable to First National Bank of Boston	100,000	582,000
36,000	Notes payable to officer		36,000
200,000	Reserve for liquidation losses (deducted contra)	$200,000	
	Stockholders' equity:		
180,000	Common stock		
100,000	Additional paid-in capital		
(418,200)	Deficit		
$2,114,800	Totals		$793,000

The normal procedure followed in constructing the statement of affairs consists of setting up the section headings; reporting each liability in the appropriate section, and, if the liability is secured, reporting the related asset in the appropriate section; listing all the remaining assets that should be the unencumbered assets; and summarizing the asset and liability data. Before the statement of affairs can be prepared, a balance sheet must be drawn up and additional data must be secured. In addition to the balance sheet, the following information is needed:

- Reliable estimates of the amount that can be expected to be realized from the sale of each asset
- All assets that are collateral for specific obligations
- Any obligations, including professional fees, that are expected to arise while liquidation is proceeding but are not currently found in the balance sheet

Several values may be shown on the statement of affairs for each asset, but the most important is the realizable value or the cash value of each asset in liquidation through forced sale. The column headings normally found for assets on the statement of affairs are:

- Book Value—the balance of each asset as it is found in the debtor's books and would appear on a balance sheet at that date.
- Appraised Value—the amount of cash expected to be realized upon sale of the asset.
- Estimated Amount Available—the proceeds that will be available for unsecured creditors as a result of the sale of the asset; obtained by subtracting the fully and partially secured claims and liabilities with priority from the total appraised value of assets.
- Estimated Loss or Gain on Realization of the Asset.

The basis of the classification scheme used for assets in the statement of affairs is the availability of assets to unsecured creditors, and this form is related to the liability classifications. It is important to include all those assets that will probably be accruing to the debtor. The groups and the order in which they are usually found are as follows:

- Assets constituting collateral for holders of fully secured claims, including all those assets with a realizable value expected to be at least equal to the claims against them
- Assets constituting collateral for holders of partly secured claims, including assets with a realizable value expected to be less than the claims against them
- Free assets—those available to meet the claims of general creditors

Liabilities and owners' equity are shown in the statement of affairs in the order in which the claims against the assets will be liquidated. The accountant should be careful to include all those liabilities expected to be incurred. Two columns are normally found for the liability section, one giving the book value or balance sheet amount of the claim and a second indicating the amount of the liability that is unsecured. They are classified in terms of their legal priority and secured status. The following groups are most commonly used:

- Liabilities with priority—creditors who, under the priority granted by the Bankruptcy Code, must be paid before anything is given to unsecured creditors.
- Fully secured liabilities—claims for which the collateral has a realizable value equal to or greater than the debt it is intended to secure.

- Partly secured liabilities—claims for which the collateral has a realizable value less than the debt it is intended to secure.
- Unsecured liabilities—liabilities with no legal priority and not secured by collateral; these claims must be satisfied by the unencumbered assets. Capital accounts.

The foregoing information readily gives an estimate of the amount the unsecured creditors may expect to receive. The percentage of each claim that will be paid is equal to the total realizable value of the free assets divided by the total amount of unsecured claims. Along with the statement of affairs, a deficiency statement is often prepared to show the source of the deficiency to unsecured creditors. Normally included are the estimated gain or loss on the realization of each asset and any additional costs associated with liabilities that have not been recorded, thus giving the total estimated loss from liquidation. The amount of this loss to be suffered by the owners and the deficiency to creditors are then shown. This statement is valuable in that it reveals how the capital contributed to the business was used and why it is not possible to pay all the creditors. Exhibit 13-5 presents the statement of deficiency to unsecured creditors for the ABC Company.

The preparation of a statement of affairs is virtually mandatory when a company is experiencing difficulty and attempting to decide which course of action would be best to follow. Its main advantage to the creditors is that it assists them in ascertaining what actions should be taken by setting forth the probable results from alternative policies.

§ 13.13   Special-Purpose Statements

If the accountant is conducting an investigation aimed at uncovering irregularities, the preparation of special schedules is crucial. It may be necessary to prepare a statement of all the payments made preceding the filing of the petition, to reveal any preferential payments; or, a schedule of all sales of assets may have to be devised to uncover fraudulent transfers.

The accountant will normally be asked to prepare, for a given time period following the filing of the petition, statements projecting the profit expectations of future operations. These statements provide a tool for working out a plan of reorganization and an out-of-court settlement, and should include budgets, cash flow statements, and profit projections.[5]

It is usually necessary to show why it would be in the best interests of the creditors for the debtor to remain in operation of the business. This involves proving that creditors would profit more from a plan of reorganization than from liquidation, and is usually accomplished with a schedule estimating the size of the dividend creditors would receive if the business were to be liquidated. To obtain such a figure, the forced-sale value of the assets must be determined and all those assets and causes of action that may be recovered for the debtor's estate must be included.

If a plan of reorganization providing for installment payments over a period of time is proposed, the accountant will be required to prepare a projected bud-

---

[5] Edward A. Weinstein, "Accountants' Examinations and Reports in Bankruptcy Proceedings," *New York Certified Public Accountant*, Vol. 35 (January 1965), p. 35.

Exhibit 13-5   Statement of Estimated Deficiency to Unsecured Creditors Filed by the ABC Company as of April 18, 20XX, the Date of Filing of Petition

ABC Company, Inc.
Statement of Estimated Deficiency
To Unsecured Creditors
April 28, 20XX

Estimated losses on realization		
On inventories	$395,000	
On fixtures and equipment	48,000	
On accounts receivable	134,800	
On goodwill	10,000	$587,800
Estimated gains on realization		
On land	13,000	
On buildings	50,000	
On trademarks	5,000	68,000
Net loss on realization		519,800
Unrecorded expenses		-0-
Liquidation expenses		
Legal fees and liquidation costs	7,000	
Accountants' liquidation fees	3,000	10,000
Total estimated losses and costs of liquidation		529,800
Less: Stockholders' equity		
Common stock	180,000	
Additional paid-in capital	100,000	
Less: Deficit	(418,200)	(138,200)
Estimated deficiency to unsecured creditors before adjustment		668,000
Less: Reserve for liquidation losses		200,000
Estimated deficiency to unsecured creditors		$468,000

get, a cash flow statement, and a balance sheet, to show that the debtor will be able to make the payments and that the plan is feasible.

Thus, the two main categories where special statements are found are in the search for irregular transactions and in drawing up a plan to effect rehabilitation. However, each insolvency proceeding is unique, and the individual situation will govern what additional reports the accountant must prepare so that the proceeding will provide complete and accurate information to all involved.

ACCOUNTING FOR A CHAPTER 11 FILING

§ 13.14   Use of New Accounts

The standard practice in a chapter 11 reorganization under the Bankruptcy Code will be for the debtor to remain in control of the business. The debtor's books and records retain their present form; however, some accounts will be closed and new ones added. Even where a trustee is appointed in a chapter 11 proceeding, the same books and records may be utilized.

The debtor cannot make payments on prefiling liabilities unless special approval is obtained from the court. Thus, it is necessary for the debtor's accountant to see that the liabilities prior to petition are clearly identified so they will not be paid during the normal course of business. One approach would be to transfer the prefiling unsecured debts to a separate account as of the date of the petition, and then to record and pay all liabilities incurred subsequent to the petition. Generally, secured liabilities are not transferred but rather are left in the account and clearly identified as prepetition debts. If there are current liabilities such as accounts payable when inventory or other assets were given as collateral, or other undersecured claims, it may be best to transfer these liabilities to a separate account to avoid confusion. Although undersecured claims may not be transferred to the prepetition claims account, these amounts should be shown with the prepetition claims in any statement of financial position that is issued. All claims that the debtor estimated would be impaired should be shown as prepetition claims because these claims will be voted on by the debtor. On the other hand, the debtor may transfer all liabilities, except those that the debtor thinks will not be impaired, to the prepetition liability account. If, during the proceeding, a valuation under section 506 indicates that a debt previously viewed as fully secured is actually undersecured, then this liability would be transferred to the prepetition liabilities. Likewise, if the debtor had estimated that a particular claim would be impaired and included it in the prepetition claims, and if the value of the security increases or if for other reasons the debtor decides under section 1124 of the Bankruptcy Code to leave this claim unimpaired, the debt would be transferred from the prepetition liability account.

Another approach that could be used in accounting for the liabilities would be not to make any formal entries in the accounts. The accountant might establish controls so that no debt incurred prior to the petition date can be paid without prior approval, and make a memorandum adjustment on all statements issued subsequent to the petition date so that the prepetition debts are presented separately. For large companies or companies with extensive computerized systems, this may be the best approach to take. Once the plan of reorganization has been confirmed, the debt will be reduced by the amount of forgiveness called for in the plan and by payments made under the provisions of the plan. One advantage of following this approach is that it reduces the future adjustments that have to be made in the accounts. Problems, such as whether this is a pre- or postpetition debt or whether it is fully secured and not impaired, will have to be resolved during the proceedings. Thus, it may be best to keep supplementary records regarding the prepetition liabilities. Once the issues are resolved and the plan is confirmed, the accounts can be properly adjusted.

It may also be desirable to establish new asset accounts. As of the petition date, it is necessary to establish the assets that existed and the extent to which they were pledged (see § 13.2). For example, in the case of pledged accounts receivable, it is necessary to know not only the balance of accounts receivable as of the petition date, but the individual accounts that make up this total. A common practice, however, is not to open new asset accounts but to prepare trial balances, as of the petition date, of both control and subsidiary accounts and to continue to use the existing asset accounts. The trial balances generally contain the information needed for the debtor to properly account for prebankruptcy assets.

Some systems allow the debtor to transfer the liabilities, as well as the assets, to a separate company (division). A separate account would be established that show the total prepetition debt. Any adjustments that have to be made will be recorded in the new company established with the net impact transferred to prepetition liability account. All post petition transactions would be recorded in the new accounts established.

At the time the petition is filed, it is not necessary to make any adjustments to the stockholder equity accounts.

§ 13.15 Illustration of Entries

For illustration of the types of entries that might be made as a result of the filing of a chapter 11 petition, readers should refer to the balance sheet in Exhibit 13-1 and consider this additional information:

1 On April 28, 20XX, ABC Company, Inc. filed a voluntary petition under chapter 11. The accountant elected to establish separate accounts for prepetition debts.

2 On May 31, 20XX, the First National Bank of Boston filed a secured claim for $520,000 and unsecured claims of $80,000. The net realizable value of the receivables was determined to be $520,000.

3 Jones Company shipped $50,000 in inventory to ABC Company, Inc. on April 20, 20XX, and the invoice was received April 27. The liability was recorded on that date, but the goods did not arrive until May 1.

4 On July 1, 20XX, the court confirmed a plan that provided for the following:
    a Debtor deposits $350,000 with escrow agent to cover priority claims and administrative costs.
    b All unsecured creditors except First National Bank receive $300,000. (Payment was subsequently made.) First National Bank receives 2,000 shares of common stock with an assigned value of $10 per share.
    c First National Bank agrees to extend the notes payable for two years. The interest rate is changed from 12 to 15 percent.
    d Debtor continues making normal payments on the mortgage.

During the period in which the debtor operates the business, there would be many more activities that were not mentioned, including the discontinuance of operations of selected unprofitable parts of the business. The following journal entries would be made to record the facts mentioned above:

1 Taxes payable	$100,000	
Salaries payable	127,500	
Commissions payable	20,000	
Priority claims		$247,500
Due to ABC Company, Inc., employees' profit-sharing trust	25,000	
Accounts payable	682,000	
Notes payable to office	36,000	
Prepetition claims		743,000

To transfer priority claims, unsecured claims, and secured accounts payable to the separate accounts.

2 No entry is necessary. Because the claim is impaired and must be dealt with in the plan, the entire amount should still be classified as a prepetition claim.

3 Prepetition claims	$ 50,000	
Accounts payable		$ 50,000

To correct an error where inventory purchased was incorrectly recorded as a prebankruptcy debt.

4a Escrow cash deposit	$350,000	
Cash		$350,000

To record deposit with escrow agent according to terms of plan.

4b Prepetition claims		$693,000
Cash		$300,000
Gain on debt forgiveness		373,000
Common stock		20,000

To record payment to unsecured creditors and First National Bank according to terms of plan.

4c 12 percent notes payable, due December 1, 20XX	$500,000	
15 percent notes payable, due December 1, 20XX		$500,000

4d No entry required.

Note that entry 1 assumed that the accountant had transferred the prepetition debts to a separate account. According to FASB Statement No. 15, the gain on debt forgiveness is an extraordinary item. If, however, the debtor elects (with proper approval) to eliminate the deficit through a quasi-reorganization or "mini" quasi-reorganization, the gain would be transferred to the paid-in capital account (see paragraphs 142–152). The entry, if an election is made just to eliminate the deficit, would be as follows:

Additional paid-in capital	$65,200	
Gain on debt forgiveness	373,000	
Retained earnings		$418,200

To eliminate the deficit in retained earnings.

§ 13.16   Accrued Interest

Accrued interest on a secured debt continues to run during the bankruptcy period when the assets securing the debt have a value greater than the amount of the debt. Technically, interest should not be accrued beyond the point where the accrued interest causes the amount of the debt to exceed the value of the assets. Any other reasonable fees, costs, or charges provided under the agreement should also be accrued according to section 506(b) of the Bankruptcy Code.

For an unsecured debt and the amount of debt classified as unsecured because it is undersecured, interest should be accrued to the date the petition was filed. Interest accruing subsequent to this date will not be allowed as a claim unless there is a surplus—that is, unsecured creditors will receive full payment for their claims. FASB Statement No. 15 (paragraph 13) states that the carrying amount of the payable is equal to the face amount, increased or decreased by applicable accrued interest and applicable unamortized premium, discount, finance charges, or issue costs. It has been suggested by some accountants that the carrying amount of the debt should include the accrued interest up to the effective date of the plan. Thus, the interest expense would be accrued during the proceedings and, because it would be disallowed by the bankruptcy court, the amount accrued (previously deducted as interest expense) would be reported as a gain on debt forgiveness along with the amount of debt and prebankruptcy accrued interest forgiven. This treatment is, however, questionable; the Bankruptcy Code (section 502) specifically disallows accrued postpetition interest on unsecured debt. It would appear that the applicable interest would include only that amount that could be paid under bankruptcy law. It should be realized that if the debtor's petition is subsequently dismissed, accrued postpetition interest would be an obligation of the debtor, as it would be if there were a surplus. In most situations, these two contingencies would not be sufficient to justify accruing the interest.

The fact that interest is not accrued during bankruptcy can have a significant impact on the results of operation. Often, companies in bankruptcy have a high debt–equity ratio with a large interest expense. The elimination of the interest payments and accruals can then cause the company to report a profit. Thus, many companies do report profits during bankruptcy and then show losses for the first full year of operations afterward, primarily because of interest payments on debt that was not paid or discharged. To keep the financial statements from being misleading, the interest that would have been accrued except for the bankruptcy petition should be at least disclosed. However, if the debtor has reached tentative agreement on a plan, disclosure of the interest associated with the debt existing after the confirmation of the plan is more meaningful.

Paragraph 29 of SOP 90-7 states that "[i]nterest expense should be reported only to the extent that it will be paid during the proceeding or that it is probable that it will be an allowed priority secured or unsecured claim." The SOP also indicates that the extent to which reported interest differs from the stated contractual interest should be disclosed. The staff of the SEC prefers that SEC registrants disclose the contractual interest parenthetically on the face of the statement of operations. Under the provisions of the SOP, interest expense is not considered a reorganization item. However, the SOP did consider that interest income earned by a debtor in chapter 11 only as a result of the proceeding should be reported as a reorganization item. In many cases, large amounts of cash accumulate during the proceeding because the debtor is not servicing any debt during reorganization. This interest is not an operating item and should be presented as a reorganization item.

14

Reporting Results of the Plan

§ 14.1   Introduction

Statement of Position (SOP) 90-7, *Financial Reporting by Entities in Reorganization under the Bankruptcy Code,* was issued by the Accounting Standards Executive Committee of the AICPA in November 1990. This Statement of Position affects how debtors in chapter 11 will report financial results during the reorganization and upon emergence from chapter 11. An important part of this Statement of Position is the requirement that all companies that emerge from chapter 11, where the reorganization value of the entity as a whole is less than the liabilities before confirmation and there is a more than 50 percent change in the shareholders of the new entity, adopt fresh-start reporting.

The provisions in SOP 90-7 relating to how the financial position and results of operations are reported during the proceeding are applicable to all companies that file chapter 11 and expect to reorganize.

The objective of this chapter is to discuss how companies emerging from chapter 11 report the results of the plan in conditions where fresh-start reporting applies and in conditions where fresh-start reporting does not apply. In addition, the chapter discusses the reporting of a plan developed in an out-of-court workout.

CHAPTER 11

§ 14.2   Requirements for Fresh-Start Reporting

Statement of Position (SOP) 90-7 requires debtors emerging from chapter 11 to adopt fresh-start reporting if the two conditions listed below are satisfied:

1 The reorganization value of the emerging entity immediately before the confirmation of the plan is less than the total of all postpetition liabilities and allowed prepetition claims.

2 Holders of existing voting shares immediately before confirmation retain less than 50 percent of the voting shares of the emerging entity.

The purpose of the first condition is to prevent the use of fresh-start reporting by solvent companies. For example, Texaco would not have been able to adopt fresh-start reporting even if a change of ownership had occurred (§ 5.10). Both of these requirements will prevent entities from filing a chapter 11 petition solely for the purpose of adopting fresh-start reporting in order to use current values for their assets.

With regard to the second requirement—holders of existing stock must retain less than 50 percent of the voting stock—paragraph 36 of SOP 90-7 indicates that the loss of control contemplated by the plan must be substantive and not temporary. Thus, the new controlling interest must not revert to the shareholders existing immediately before the plan was confirmed. For example, a plan that allows shareholders existing prior to the confirmation to reacquire control of the entity at a subsequent date may prevent an entity from adopting fresh-start reporting. On the other hand, a plan that allows the existing shareholders to regain control at the end of six years, and then only if selected operating profit targets are satisfied, most likely will not preclude the use of fresh-start reporting.

One factor that would need to be considered in determining whether there has been a loss of control is the intent of the owners involved. For example, a transfer of control to the creditors for the purpose of adopting fresh-start reporting might be viewed differently from a transfer where the creditors demanded control of the debtor's business until profits from the business resulted in an 80 percent recovery of their claims.

Disclosure of the reorganization values is required only where both conditions for fresh-start reporting are satisfied. For example, fresh-start reporting will not be used by most nonpublic entities because their plans generally do not provide for a change of ownership.

Chapter 11 entities that meet both of the above conditions should report the assets and liabilities at their going-concern or reorganization values and eliminate all prior earnings or deficits. Reorganization value is defined in SOP 90-7 as the "fair value of the entity before considering liabilities and approximates the amount that a willing buyer would pay for the assets of the entity immediately after the restructuring." The focus in determining the reorganization value is on the value of the assets, normally determined by discounted future cash flows. Reorganization value includes the sum of the value attributed to the reconstituted entity and the net realizable value of the disposition of assets not included in the reorganized firm, including any cash in excess of normal operating requirements. The reorganization value, however, is not generally determined by only one approach; several are used, depending on the circumstances. For example, in cases where discounted cash flows are used to determine reorganization value, the results may be reinforced by the use of an earnings multiple. See Chapter 11 for a discussion of how to determine reorganization values.

The amount the entity includes in the financial statements as the reorganization value is arrived at through negotiation among the debtor, creditors' and stockholders' committees, and other interested parties. Accountants serving as financial advisors to one or more of these parties, however, may play an integral part in the calculation and negotiation of reorganization value. As reflected by the debtor in the financial statements, reorganization value should be the value negotiated by the parties involved.

Whatever approaches are used in determining reorganization value, little reliance is placed on book values. Professionals involved in bankruptcy cases have been aware of the limited usefulness of book values for some time. For example, market values are required (even though book values are sometimes used) in the Schedules A, B, and C (dealing with assets) that are filed with the bankruptcy court at the time the petition is filed or shortly thereafter, and fair market values are used for assets pledged under section 506 of the Bankruptcy Code.

A major question that was left unanswered in SOP 90-7 deals with a situation where a shareholder who is also a creditor receives stock in exchange for the debt. As a general rule, it would appear that the receipt of stock for debt by a shareholder who is not in control of the corporation would be considered as received by a holder of debt and not be considered in determining the stock retained by existing shareholders. Thus, a transfer in which a 10 percent shareholder receives 60 percent of the stock of the reorganized company in exchange for funds loaned to the corporation would result in the adoption of fresh-start reporting, provided the first requirement was satisfied. If, on the other hand, the same shareholder owned 55 percent rather than 10 percent of the outstanding stock, fresh-start reporting would not be adopted because there has not been a loss of control by the preconfirmation shareholders.

§ 14.3 Allocation of Reorganization Value

Entities that meet the two conditions described in the preceding section should adopt fresh-start reporting and apply the following principles according to paragraph 38 of SOP 90-7.

(a) Asset Values

The reorganization value of the debtor is to be allocated to the entity's assets in conformity with Accounting Principles Board (APB) Opinion No. 16 for transactions reported based on the purchase method. Any part of the reorganization value that is not attributable to specific tangible assets or identifiable intangible assets should be reported as an intangible asset (reorganization value in excess of amounts allocable to identifiable assets) and amortized in accordance with the provisions of APB Opinion No. 17. SOP 90-7 indicates that the allocation period will generally be substantially less than 40 years. It is suggested that there are usually overriding pertinent factors that, when considered in determining the proper amortization period, will generally result in a life of less than 40 years for the reorganization value in excess of amounts allocable to identifiable assets. The SOP states that, at a minimum, "the same considerations used in determining the reorganization value should be applied in determining the period of amortization."

For public companies, the SEC is carefully reviewing the period selected for allocating the reorganization value in excess of amounts allocable to identifiable assets. In some filings, especially in the retail area, the SEC will not accept an allocation period in excess of 20 years.

(b) Liability Values

Liabilities that survive the reorganization should be shown at present value of amounts to be paid, determined at appropriate current interest rates. Thus, the same rules used to value liabilities in a purchase under APB Opinion No. 16 apply to fresh-start reporting. Under SOP 90-7, all liabilities will be shown at their discounted values. The practice of discounting debt has not always been followed in the past.

(c) Deferred Taxes

Deferred taxes are to be reported in conformity with FASB Statement No. 109, *Income Taxes.*

Deferred taxes must be reported when a difference exists between the fair market value and the tax basis of assets. For example, if the book basis as a result of the allocation of fair market value through fresh-start accounting is $80,000 and the tax basis is only $30,000, then deferred taxes must be recorded on the difference of $50,000. The impact of deferred taxes is discussed in § 14.6.

(d) Net Operating Loss

Benefits realized from preconfirmation net operating loss carryforwards should be used to first reduce reorganization value in excess of amounts allocable to identifiable assets and other intangibles. Once the remaining intangible assets are exhausted, the balance is reported as a direct addition to the additional paid-in capital. There was considerable debate over whether this balance should be added to operating profits or to additional paid-in capital. Both the SEC and the FASB preferred to add it to additional paid-in capital. The Accounting Standards Executive Committee (AcSEC) agreed to follow this method also, even though the AcSEC thought the excess was, conceptually, an operating profit item.

§ 14.4 Disclosures

The effects of the above adjustments on the reported amounts of individual assets and liabilities and the effects of the debt discharge resulting for the adoption of fresh-start reporting are to be made in the predecessor entity's financial statement of operations. Any gain due to the forgiveness of debt is an extraordinary item. This entry is made in the financial statements of the entity just prior to emergence from chapter 11. The adoption of fresh-start reporting results in the elimination of any prior retained earnings or deficits.

Paragraph 39 of SOP 90-7 indicates that, when fresh-start reporting is adopted, the notes to the initial financial statement should disclose the following:

- Adjustments to the historical amounts of individual assets and liabilities
- The amount of debt forgiven

- The amount of prior retained earnings or deficit eliminated
- Significant matters relating to the determination of reorganization value

The SOP indicates that among the matters relating to reorganization value that should be disclosed are the following:

- The method or methods used to determine reorganization value, and factors such as discount rates, tax rates, the number of years for which cash flows are projected, and the method of determining terminal value
- Sensitive assumptions (assumptions that involve a reasonable possibility of occurrence of a variation that would significantly affect measurement of reorganization value)
- Assumptions about anticipated conditions that are expected to be different from current conditions, unless otherwise apparent

In Volume 2 of *Bankruptcy and Insolvency Accounting*, 14.1 shows the balance sheet issued by Sunbeam-Oster after its adoption of fresh-start reporting. This model illustrates how a debtor might present the balance sheet resulting from fresh-start reporting, separate from prior balance sheets issued by the debtor.

Exhibit 14-2 of Volume 2 contains the statements issued by Wheeling-Pittsburgh Corporation, based on fresh-start reporting. These financial statements illustrate the procedures that need to be followed in making the entries to record fresh-start accounting and report the results of the plan.

§ 14.5   Recording the Adoption of Fresh-Start Reporting

The adoption of fresh-start reporting is reported in the last financial statement of operations issued by the predecessor entity. The entries that are made may be summarized in the following manner:

- Record the adjustments that are made to the liabilities, including prepetition claims and postpetition liabilities.
- Record the adjustments that are made to the equity interests as a result of issuance of new stock to prior shareholders.
- Record the adjustments to assets and to liabilities (not previously recorded) due to the adoption of fresh-start reporting.
- Record the entry to close the gain from debt discharge and the gain or loss on adoption of fresh-start accounting into the retained earnings (deficit) account and to eliminate the balance in the retained earnings (deficit) account and other equity accounts (of the predecessor entity) not previously eliminated.

Exhibit 14-1 is the preconfirmation balance sheet of a chapter 11 debtor and shows the appraised value of the assets. The reorganization value of the company is $80 million and the book value is equal to the tax value. The tax rate is 40 percent. The terms of the plan are as follows:

Exhibit 14-1   Preconfirmation Balance Sheet and Appraisal Values

	Book Value	Appraisal Value
	(Dollar values in thousands)	
Assets		
Cash	$ 4,000	$ 4,000
Inventory	25,000	27,000
Accounts receivable (net)	40,000	40,000
Other	4,000	-0-
Property, plant, and equipment (net)	3,000	4,000
Advance to related party	8,000	-0-
TOTAL	$84,000	$75,000
Current Liabilities		
Taxes	$ 2,500	
Accounts payable	5,000	
Administrative expenses	2,500	
Liabilities subject to compromise		
Trade payables	25,000	
Line of credit (Bank)	45,000	
Unsecured note payable	5,000	
Long-term debt (Bank)	10,000	
Total	95,000	
Stockholders' equity		
Common stock	3,500	
Retained earnings (deficit)	(14,500)	
TOTAL	$84,000	

- Trade debt—50 percent of the common stock (new issue).
- Bank—$20 million line of credit at prime plus 3 percentage points; $15 million, 10-year term loan with interest at 10 percent; 40 percent of the common stock (new issue).
- Unsecured note—$5 million, 10-year, 10 percent loan.
- Taxes—$2.5 million paid over 6 years with interest at 8 percent.
- Administrative expenses—$2.5 million paid as of effective date of the plan.
- Accounts payable (postpetition)—Paid in normal course of business after the plan is confirmed.
- Common shareholders—Old shares canceled; receive 10 percent of the new issue of common stock.

Exhibit 14-2 explains the recovery of each of the classes of claims and interests. The recovery analysis, in addition to providing a summary of the impact of the plan, assists in the determination of the entries that need to be made to record the implementation of the plan.

Exhibit 14-2 Recovery Analysis

				Plan		
	Preconfirmation	Cash	Debt	Stock Percent	Stock Value	Percent Recovered
Current Liabilities						
Taxes	$ 2,500		$ 2,500			100
Accounts payable	5,000		5,000			100
Administrative						
expense	2,500	$(2,500)				100
Liabilities subject						
to compromise						
Trade payables	25,000			50	$15,000	60
Line of credit						
(Long-term note)	55,000		35,000	40	12,000	85
Unsecured notes						
payable	5,000		5,000			100
Stockholders' equity						
Common stock	3,500			10	3,000	—
Retained earnings						
(deficit)	(14,500)					
TOTAL	$84,000	$(2,500)	$47,500	100%	$30,000	

The following entry (in $000) would be made to record the adjustments to liabilities and the payment of administrative expenses required by the plan:

Administrative expenses payable	$ 2,500	
Trade payables	25,000	
Line of credit (bank)	45,000	
Unsecured note payable	5,000	
Long-term debt (bank)	10,000	
Line of credit (new)		$20,000
Note (bank)		15,000
Unsecured note payable		5,000
Cash		2,500
Common stock (new)		27,000
Gain on settlement of debt		18,000

The entry (in $000) to record the issuance of new stock to existing shareholders and to retire old stock would be:

Common stock (old)	$3,500	
Common stock (new)		$3,000
Additional paid-in capital		500

The following entry (in $000) would record the adjustments to assets and liabilities as the result of the adoption of fresh-start reporting:

Inventory	$2,000	
Property, plant, and equipment	1,000	

Reorganization value in excess of amount allocable to identifiable assets	5,000	
Loss on revaluation of assets	4,000	
Other current assets		$4,000
Advance to related party		8,000

The entry (in $000) to close the gain from debt discharge to the retained earnings (deficit) account, in order to eliminate the retained earnings (deficit) and other equity accounts not previously eliminated, would be:

Additional paid in capital	$ 500	
Gain on settlement of debt	18,000	
Loss on revaluation of assets		$ 4,000
Retained earnings deficit		14,500

In 14.2 of Volume 2 of *Bankruptcy and Insolvency Accounting*, Note A to the financial statements of Wheeling-Pittsburgh Corporation for the year the company emerged from chapter 11 describes the reorganization. The entries made by the company are reflected in the Note. The first entry increases the liabilities to allow for additional claims. The second entry describes the distribution to creditors, the third entry records the issuance of stock for stock, and the fourth entry records the adoption of fresh-start accounting and the elimination of the deficit. Following the entries, the company summarizes the adjustments (for debt discharge and for the adoption of fresh-start reporting) that were made in the preconfirmation balance sheet to arrive at the postconfirmation balance sheet.

§ 14.6 Deferred Taxes[1]

In determining the reorganization value of an entity, an estimate of taxes that will actually be paid is used to calculate the value of future cash flows. The depreciation and amortization that will be allowed for tax purposes are used to determine the tax benefit from these non-cash-flow deductions. Any net operating loss that will survive the reorganization is considered in determining the future cash outflows for taxes. Thus, the reorganization value represents an economic value; it is the present value of the future cash flows after taxes.

It would appear to this author that as a result of the "purchase of the debtor by creditors," any difference between the value of the depreciable assets and the value for tax purposes becomes, in effect, a permanent difference. An adjustment should therefore not be made to allow for the deferred taxes.

Some would argue that future tax expenses should be based on book net income, even though the allocated taxes are ignored for valuation purposes. According to this line of reasoning, in calculating the future tax, depreciation and amortization should be based on allocation of the reorganization value to identifiable assets. Where this allocated value is greater than the value for tax purposes, the income tax expense calculated is less than the actual taxes due.

---

[1]Adapted from George F. Patterson and Grant W. Newton, "SOP 90-7, Financial Reporting by Entities in Reorganization under Bankruptcy Code," *Journal of Accountancy* (April 1993), pp. 46–53.

To allow the reorganized company to thus present income taxes based on book net income, a deferred tax liability has to be established at the time of the adoption of fresh-start reporting.

Unfortunately, the FASB advocated following the latter approach in FASB Statement No. 109. A deferred tax liability must be established, based on the difference between the tax values and the allocated value of assets. This deferred tax cannot be discounted even though several years will pass before the deferred tax is fully used. This deferred tax is reduced by any tax benefit from net operating losses that survive the reorganization and are carried forward.

The question therefore arises: What should be done with the debit (in cases where tax basis is less than the value of identifiable assets) or credit (in cases where tax basis is larger than the value of identifiable assets)? In most chapter 11 cases, it is expected that the tax basis will be less than the value of identifiable assets. The adjustment must be made, either to the assets or stockholders' equity, to provide for the recording of the deferred taxes. Neither of these alternatives is acceptable. If the adjustment is a debit and if the assets are increased, they are presented at a value that is greater than the reorganization value. If the reorganization value of the business is less than the value of individual assets, the increase in assets from the recording of the deferred tax is allocated to these assets. On the other hand, if the reorganization value is greater than the value of identifiable assets, the increase in assets from the recording of deferred taxes is added to "reorganization value in excess of amounts allocable to identifiable assets."

If the stockholders' equity is reduced, it is shown at a value that is less than the amount determined in the valuation of the business. Again, this is not a desirable result.

These adjustments are made to allow future net income after taxes to be presented based on book values. Any future use of this net income number will need to be adjusted because the actual taxes that must be paid will be greater than those shown.

FASB Statement No. 109 does not address the issue of how to reflect the adjustment that is required for the recognition of deferred taxes when fresh-start reporting is adopted. The statement does, however, suggest in an illustration of a purchase where the tax basis is different for the assigned value that the adjustment should be reflected in the goodwill account. Because the adoption of fresh-start accounting is similar to a purchase, it might be argued that the adjustment should be reflected in the same manner. However, FASB Statement No. 109 states that any benefit of a net operating loss that is left after goodwill has been reduced should be credited to operating income. The task forces and the AcSEC concluded that, in a fresh-start reporting, the deferred tax should be reflected in the same manner as a purchase. The FASB objected to this conclusion and stated that it should be handled like a quasi-reorganization and credited to stockholders' equity. Thus, it might be argued that the adjustment needed here should be reflected in the stockholders' equity rather than increasing the reorganization value in excess of amounts allocable to identifiable assets. On the other hand, with FASB Statement No. 109 silent on this topic, the conclusion might be that the approach used for a purchase should be adopted. In practice, companies are increasing the reorganization value to the extent that deferred taxes must be reported.

In many bankruptcy cases, the adjustment may be very large. The troubled company may have expanded operations during the 1980s, and a substantial part of the assets acquired during that period may be almost fully depreciated. Consider the following facts for a company emerging from chapter 11 and required to adopt fresh-start reporting (amounts are in millions of dollars):

	Reorganization Value	Tax Value
Assets		
Inventories and receivables	$ 6	$ 6
Property, plant, and equipment	19	6
Reorganization value in excess of amounts allocable to identifiable assets	5	0
Total	$30	$12

	Reorganization Value	Tax Value
Liabilities		
Current	$ 3	
Long-term	13	
Stockholders' equity	14	
Total	$30	

The company had a net operating loss of $1 million that will survive the reorganization and is reflected in "reorganization value in excess of amounts allocable to identifiable assets." The deferred taxes that will need to be recognized amount to $4.8 million (reorganization value of property, plant, and equipment and reorganization value in excess of amounts allocable to identifiable assets ($24 million) less tax value of $6 million times the 40 percent tax rate and less the tax benefit of the net operating loss of $.4 million).

To adjust the asset side of the balance sheet, the following journal entry (in millions) is needed:

Reorganization value in excess of amounts allocable to identifiable assets	$6.8	
Deferred taxes liability		$6.8

Since companies are allowed to amortize goodwill over a period of 15 years for income tax purposes, it appears that the goodwill account—reorganization value in excess of amounts allocable to identifiable assets—should also be considered in determining the difference between book and tax depreciation and amortization.

During the first year, net income before taxes is $3 million for book purposes and $4 million for tax purposes. The $1 million difference between tax net income and book net income is all attributable to the difference between depreciation and amortization of the reorganization value in excess of amounts allocable to identifiable assets based on the tax basis and based on reorganization (assigned) values. The deferred taxes should be increased by the amount of the tax benefit of the net operating loss that will be used in the current period. The following entry (in millions of dollars) will be made:

Income tax expense (.4 × $3)	$1.2		
Deferred taxes liability (.4 × $1)	.4		
Deferred taxes liability (.4 × $1)		$ .4	
Taxes payable (($4 − $1) × .4)		$1.2	

Assume the same net income before taxes and the same differences between tax and book depreciation for the second year. The following entry (in millions of dollars) would be made:

Income tax expense (.4 × $3)	$1.2	
Deferred taxes liability (.4 × $1)	.4	
Taxes payable ($4 × .4)		$1.60

Reorganization value in excess of amounts allocable to identifiable assets will be amortized over a period not to exceed 40 years. Generally, the SEC is not allowing public companies to automatically adopt a time period of 40 years. Paragraph 38 of SOP 90-7 suggests that there are pertinent factors that should be considered in determining the property amortization period for this asset, and that these factors would generally result in a useful life of less than 40 years. In this example, because almost half of the excess ($4.8 million from a total amount of $9.8 million) is attributable to the deferred taxes, the time required to recognize the difference between book and tax depreciation should be considered in selecting the amortization period.

All future tax benefits that arise from a net operating loss should be credited to the deferred taxes to the extent that deferred taxes were reduced by the tax benefits of the net operating loss at the time the company emerged from chapter 11. Next, the tax benefits should be used to reduce reorganization value in excess of amounts allocable to identifiable assets, and any remaining tax benefits should be reported as a direct addition to paid-in capital, according to paragraph 38 of SOP 90-7.

In Volume 2 of *Bankruptcy and Insolvency Accounting*, 14.2 contains excerpts from the Form 10-K filed by Wheeling-Pittsburgh when it emerged from chapter 11. Note E (14.2(h)) describes why Wheeling-Pittsburgh did not need to record any deferred taxes. Note E lists the tax impact of the differences that exist between book values resulting from fresh-start reporting and the tax basis of assets. This example is based on FASB Statement No. 96, but a schedule prepared using FASB Statement No. 109 would be similar.

§ 14.7   Disclosure Statement

Paragraph 37 of SOP 90-7 states that, although the court determines the adequacy of information in the disclosure statement, entities that expect to adopt fresh-start reporting should provide information about the reorganization value in the disclosure statement. The inclusion of this value should help creditors and shareholders to make informed judgments about the plan.

This provision probably has generated more controversy among attorneys than any other provision of SOP 90-7. The reluctance of debtor's counsel to disclose the reorganization value is understandable where there is considerable opposition to the plan for which the entity is seeking approval without the support of one or more committees of creditors. However, this type of information is precisely what is needed by the creditors and stockholders to make an informed decision about the plan. In cases where a consensual plan has not been achieved, careful scrutiny of the information in the disclosure statement is even more critical. It should be emphasized, however, that the reorganization value may not be nearly as essential as the disclosure of an entity's cash flow projections for the next five years or so. Once the cash flow projections are known, determining the reorganization value is often fairly easy.

SOP 90-7 suggests that the most logical place to report the reorganization value is in the pro forma balance sheet showing the projected financial position if the proposed plan is confirmed. Paragraph 37 states that the pro forma balance sheet should be prepared using reorganization values instead of historical costs.

Paragraph 37 also indicates that, if at the time the disclosure statement is issued the reorganization value has not been allocated to individual assets, a separate line item may be included in the pro forma balance sheet to reflect the difference between the total reorganization value of the emerging entity and the recorded amounts of individual assets.

In *In re Scioto Valley Co.,*[2] the court adopted a 19-point list of the types of information that may be required in a disclosure statement. Included in the list were "financial information, valuations or pro forma projections that would be relevant to the creditors' determination of whether to accept or reject the plan." Even in a case where an entity is proposing a plan without the support of the creditors' committee or other interested parties, creditors need to study an entity's cash projection and reorganization value to make an informed decision.

§ 14.8 Subsequent Events and Preconfirmation Contingencies

The acceptance by the creditors of an out-of-court settlement or the confirmation of a plan of reorganization after the fiscal year's end but before the issuance of statements is a subsequent event that may require recognition in the accounts. SAS No. 1, section 560.03, states that the first type of subsequent event that requires adjustment to the accounts consists of "those events that provide additional evidence with respect to conditions that existed at the date of the balance sheet and affect the estimates inherent in the process of preparing financial statements." This statement suggests that as of the date of the balance sheet, liabilities are overstated. These liabilities had not been adjusted downward because of the uncertainty surrounding the actual amount to be paid. The liabilities should, however, be adjusted downward as soon as the amount that must be paid is known. The events that created the need for debt forgiveness had to have occurred prior to the balance sheet date, because a petition was filed before this date and these events led to the need to file the chapter 11 petition.

Paragraph 57 of SOP 90-7 provides that "[f]inancial statements prepared as of a date after the parties in interest have approved a plan through the voting process, and issued after the plan has been confirmed by the court, should

---

[2] 88 B.R. 168 (Bankr. S.D. Ohio 1988).

report the effect of the plan if there are no material unsatisfied conditions." Paragraph 35 provides that the effects of a plan should be included in the entity's financial statements as of the date the plan is confirmed. SOP 90-7 provides guidance only in situations where the voting was completed before year-end and where the plan was confirmed before the financial statements were issued. Other situations are not directly addressed. For example, what is the status if the voting and plan confirmation were completed after year-end but before the financial statements were issued; or if the voting was approved before year-end but the plan has not yet been confirmed at the time the financial statements are issued?

A key question remains: Should the accounts be adjusted in situations other than the one exception provided for in paragraph 57? It should be noted that, in the exception provided, the plan had already been approved by the creditors and only the confirmation took place after year-end. Confirmation of the plan before the financial statements are issued eliminates a material uncertainty that may have existed at year-end in relation to an event that had already occurred—the creditors approved the plan. Thus, it is reasonable in this situation to reflect the results of the plan in the accounts.

It would appear that, in conditions where the voting took place after year-end and the financial statements were issued after the plan was confirmed, the approval of the plan by creditors and equity holders, or the confirmation of the plan, should not be reflected in the principal financial statements but should be disclosed in the notes or other supplementary schedules. The use of pro forma statements reflecting the terms of the proposed plan would be of considerable benefit to the reader of the financial statements.

Pro forma statements may also be presented to show what the operations for the year might have been if the reorganization had been confirmed at the beginning of the year. A statement of operations presented in this manner provides the reader with some indication of what future operations might be after the changes created by the chapter 11 reorganization are made. In Volume 2 of *Bankruptcy and Insolvency Accounting,* 14.2 contains excerpts from the Form 10-K filed by Wheeling-Pittsburgh when it emerged from chapter 11. An example of a pro forma operating statement issued on the assumption that the plan became effective as of the first day of the fiscal year is shown in 14.2(f).

Excerpts from the annual report filed by USG Corporation just prior to its emergence from chapter 11 are shown in 14.3 of Volume 2. USG filed a prepackaged chapter 11 plan; 14.3 consists of two Notes that describe the plan and show the impact the adoption of the plan and fresh-start reporting would have had on the balance sheet if the plan had become effective as of the last date of the year. The impact is shown in the form of a pro forma balance sheet. The preconfirmation balance to the accounts and the adjustments due both to restructuring and to fresh-start adjustments that are needed to prepare the pro forma balance sheet are stated.

Often there are contingencies that existing at the date fresh-start reporting is adopted that are subsequently resolved. SOP 90-7 does not describe how to account for these contingencies. The AICPA appointed a Task Force to draft a Practice Bulletin, *Accounting for Preconfirmation Contingencies in Fresh-Start Reporting.* The Financial Accounting Standards Board reviewed the Practice Bulletin and did not object to it being issued. Practice Bulletin 11 was issued by the AICPA and is effective for adjustments of preconfirmation contingencies made after March 31, 1994. Earlier application was encouraged. The Practice Bulletin provides that after the adoption of fresh-start reporting, adjustments that result from a preconfirmation contingency are to be included in the determination of net income in the period in which the adjustment is determined. These adjustments are to be included in the determination of income or loss from continuing operations and should be separately disclosed. Thus, adjustments are not to be made in the statements that were issued at the time fresh-start reporting was adopted.

The Practice Bulletin states that a preconfirmation contingencies include uncertainties as to:

- Amounts ultimately to be realized upon the disposition of assets designated for sale by the confirmed plan; proceeds upon disposition may vary from values estimated at confirmation.
- Nondischargable claims (e.g., environmental issues).
- Claims that are disputed, unliquidated or contingent and are unresolved at confirmation; these claims may be estimated for purposes of voting on the plan. The confirmed plan may provide for issuance of shares (or release of shares from escrow) in resolution of certain claims.

The Practice Bulletin states that preconfirmation contingencies do not include:

- Allocation of reorganization value to the entity's assets. Reorganization value includes the sum of the values attributed to the reconstituted entity (i.e., continuing business) and to other assets that will not be included in the reconstituted entity (e.g., assets designated for sale). The initial allocation of the value of the reconstituted entity to individual assets in conformity with the procedures specified by APB Opinion No. 16 may require the use of estimates. Those estimates may change when information the entity has arranged to obtain has been received, e.g., once appraisals of certain assets of the reconstituted business have been received.
- Deductible temporary differences or net operating loss and tax credit carryforwards that exist at confirmation. FASB Statement No. 109, *Accounting for Income Taxes*, and paragraph 38 of SOP 90-7 specify the accounting for those items.

Thus, if the value of individual assets have not been determined as of the date that fresh-start reporting is adopted, subsequent adjustments are to be made to the assets and are not to be reflected in the determination of net income in subsequent periods. According to FASB Statement No. 38, *Accounting for Preacquisition Contingencies of Purchased Enterprises*, the allocation could be made up to the end of the allocation period that occurs when the acquiring entity is no longer waiting for information that it has arranged to obtain and is known to be available or obtainable.

The Practice Bulletin does not fully describe how to account for the resolution of a contingency when a "pot" plan is adopted. In a "pot" plan the consideration that will be given, often in the form of stock, is determined. Once the amount of the claims are ascertained, the consideration that was set aside will be distributed to the creditors. It would appear that a plan of this nature would not be considered as a preconfirmation contingency.

In other situations the consideration that will be paid per dollar of debt is provided for in the plan based on an estimate of the amount of the allowed claims. If it is subsequently determined that the claims are different from the amount that was estimated, an adjustment it would appear based on the Practice Bulletin would be made to the net income for loss from continuing operations for the current period. The Practice Bulletin does not address the issue where the entire consideration is 100 percent of the stock and all of the stock is going to be distributed to the holders of allowed claims as subsequently determined. Based on this situation, it would appear that the only uncertainty is the number of shares that are going to be issued and that the creditors will own 100 percent of the reorganized entity and as a result this is not a preconfirmation contingency and no subsequent adjustment should be made.

§ 14.9 Reporting by Entities Not Qualifying for Fresh Start

Entities that do not meet both of the conditions for adopting fresh-start reporting are, according to paragraph 41 of SOP 90-7, required to discount any debt issued or compromised as a result of the reorganization.

Any forgiveness of debt is reported as an extraordinary item. According to SOP 90-7, quasi-reorganization accounting should not be used at the time of the reorganization in situations where the debtor does not qualify for fresh-start reporting. In situations where the debtor qualifies for fresh-start reporting, quasi-reorganization accounting would not be appropriate because the debtor is revaluing assets and liabilities under reorganization accounting.

SOP 90-7 does not preclude the reporting entity from subsequently adopting quasi-reorganization accounting where fresh-start accounting is not applicable. However, quasi-reorganization accounting may not be used to account for the confirmation of the plan on emerging from chapter 11.

§ 14.10 Comparison with Prior Periods

In filings with the SEC, comparative statements are required. However, because of the reorganization, a comparison of the operations subsequent to confirmation with the operations prior to and during chapter 11 proceedings should be made with careful consideration. Several factors limit the benefits that can be derived from such a comparison. As a result of the reorganization, the capital structure may be totally changed. A large amount of debt may have been converted to stock. Overhead costs may have been reduced in several areas. Selected operations (including entire product lines or divisions) may have been discontinued. Thus, any comparison of postconfirmation return on assets expressing per-share or similar performance-measuring devices with those of prepetition results will be of little value. The major benefit derived from the presentation of prepetition statements is that it serves as a historical record of what has happened and it gives the reader some indication of the changes that have been made in the asset and liability structure of the company. The problem the accountant faces in presenting these comparisons arises from the fact that conventional accounting standards of disclosure and presentation do not deal with special problems encountered by bankruptcy and insolvency proceedings.

It is, however, still common practice in many cases to present comparative data, especially for operating statements. For example, one auditor stated in the footnotes describing the reorganization proceedings that careful consideration had been given as to whether last year's financial statements should be presented for comparative purposes because the adjustments in connection with the plan and related reorganization were material. The auditor concluded that it would be beneficial for a reader of the financial statements to have comparative data. In the middle paragraph, the auditor commented that, although the reorganization adjustment materially affected the comparability of the balance sheets as of September 30, 20XX and 20XX, accounting principles were consistently applied during the two years ending on those dates.

Many chapter 11 companies have elected, especially in the issuance of balance sheets based on fresh-start reporting, to present the historical data without any attempt to give a comparative basis.

For example, 14.1 of Volume 2 of *Bankruptcy and Insolvency Accounting* contains the reorganization balance sheet for 1990. The balance sheet for 1989 was also presented in the Form 10-K, but not on a comparative basis with the preconfirmation balance sheet. A separate opinion was issued on the balance sheet reflecting the adoption of fresh-start reporting.

OUT-OF-COURT WORKOUTS

§ 14.11   Introduction

FASB Statement No. 15 provides that income arises when the carrying amount, including accrued interest before restructuring, is greater than the total future cash payments specified by the restructured liability terms. Total future cash payments include interest on the restructured debt. If the total future cash payments are greater than the carrying amount of debt before restructuring, no income is recorded, even if the revised interest rate is less than current market rates.

This statement clearly explains how to handle income from debt discharge when the transaction falls under its provisions. The problem faced is that in some out-of-court workouts FASB Statement No. 15 does not apply.

Its footnote 4 states that FASB Statement No. 15 does not apply ". . . if, under provisions of those Federal statutes or in a quasi-reorganization or corporate readjustment with which a troubled debt restructuring coincides, the debtor *restates its liabilities generally*" (emphasis added).

In an out-of-court workout where there is a corporate readjustment resulting in the debtor's "restating its liabilities generally," it would appear that FASB Statement No. 15 is not applicable. If FASB Statement No. 15 does not apply, two questions remain unanswered:

1 How should income from debt discharge—extraordinary item or equity adjustment—be classified?

2 How much income should be recognized, as determined by the extent to which the issuing debt is discounted?

Before looking at these two areas, the procedures to follow when FASB Statement No. 15 applies will be discussed.

§ 14.12   Debt Discharge under FASB Statement No. 15

When a company is liquidated and all its assets are sold, the business is dissolved and the books are permanently closed. In a reorganization proceeding or an out-of-court settlement, the debtor continues to use the same books and records, but the terms of the plan call for certain adjustments. The following sections discuss the most common entries made and the situations in which they are required under the assumption that FASB Statement No. 15 is applicable.

(a) Debt Forgiveness as an Extraordinary Item

FASB Statement No. 15 established standards of financial accounting and reporting by debtors and creditors for a troubled debt restructuring. The statement supersedes FASB Interpretation No. 2, *Interpreting Interest on Debt Arrangements Made under the Federal Bankruptcy Act,* and amends APB Opinion No. 26, *Early Extinguishment of Debt.* The statement applies to troubled debt restructurings consummated under reorganization or other provisions of the Bankruptcy Code, but does not apply if the debtor restates its liabilities generally in a quasi-reorganization or corporate readjustment.

A troubled debt restructuring may include, but is not necessarily limited to, one or a combination of the following:

- Transfer from the debtor to the creditor of receivables from third parties, real estate, or other assets, to satisfy fully or partially a debt (including a transfer resulting from foreclosure or repossession)
- Issuance or other granting of an equity interest to the creditor by the debtor to satisfy fully or partially a debt, unless the equity interest is granted pursuant to existing terms for converting the debt into an equity interest
- Modification of terms of a debt, such as one or a combination of:
  - Reduction (absolute or contingent) of the stated interest rate for the remaining original life of the debt
  - Extension of the maturity date or dates at a stated interest rate lower than the current market rate for new debt with similar risk
  - Reduction (absolute or contingent) of the face amount or maturity amount of the debt as stated in the instrument or other agreement
  - Reduction (absolute or contingent) of accrued interest[3]

---

[3] FASB, *Accounting Standards, Current Text* (Stamford, CT: FASB, 1993), § D22.105.

A debt restructuring is not necessarily a troubled debt restructuring, even if the debtor is experiencing some financial difficulties. For example, a troubled debt restructuring is not involved if:

- The fair value of cash, other assets, or an equity interest accepted by a creditor from a debtor in full satisfaction of its receivable at least equals the creditor's recorded investment in the receivable and the debtor's carrying amount of the payable.
- The creditor reduces the effective interest rate primarily to reflect a decrease in market interest rates in general, or a decrease in the risk, to maintain a relationship with a debtor that can readily obtain funds from other sources at the current interest rates.
- The debtor issues in exchange for its debt new marketable debt having an effective interest rate based on its market price that is at or near the current market interest rates of debt with similar maturity dates and stated interest rates issued by nontroubled debtors.[4]

FASB Statement No. 15 (paragraph 21) indicates that the gains on restructuring of payables are to be aggregated, included in measuring net income for the period of restructuring, and, if material, classified as extraordinary items, net of related income tax effect.

(b) Modification of Terms

When a restructuring involves only a modification of terms, the statement requires both the creditor and debtor to account for it on a prospective basis. No gain or loss would be recognized by debtors when only a modification of terms is involved, unless the carrying amount of the debt exceeds the total future cash payments specified by the new terms. If the carrying amount of the debt exceeds future cash payments, the debtor reduces the carrying amount of the debt, and all cash payments are recorded as reductions in the debt. Thus, the debtor recognizes a gain equal to the excess of the carrying amount of the payable over future cash payments, and no interest expended is recorded between the date of restructuring and the maturity date of the debt. The creditor recognizes an ordinary loss to the excess of the recorded investment in the receivable at the time of the restructuring over future cash receipts specified by the new terms, and such excess is not properly chargeable against a valuation allowance.

The following example illustrates the accounting for a debt restructuring as a result of a modification of terms.[5]

XYZ Company has the following debt at December 31, Year 10:

12% note payable, due December 31, Year 10 $10,000,000

Accrued interest payable on the 12% note   1,200,000

On December 31, Year 10, the debt is restructured as follows:

---

[4] *Id.,* § D22.107.

[5] The examples in this section were adapted from Ernst & Young, *Financial Reporting Developments, FASB Statements* (1978), pp. 239–80. (Used by permission.)

a $1,000,000 of the principal and $1,200,000 of accrued interest are forgiven by creditors.

b the maturity date is extended to December 31, Year 15.

c interest rate is reduced from 12% to 8%.

The total future cash receipts or payments under the new terms amount to $12,600,000 (principal of $9,000,000 and interest of $3,600,000) which exceeds the $11,200,000 carrying amount of the debt prior to the restructuring, and no gain or loss is recognized. The excess of the total payment over the carrying amount of the debt, $1,400,000 ($12,600,000 − $11,200,000 = $1,400,000) would be recognized as interest expense at a computed effective interest rate on the restructured amount of the debt. The computed interest rate will be 2.707 percent, the rate necessary to discount the future stream of cash payments to a present value equal to the remaining balance of the debt. The following amortization schedule shows the calculations:

Amortization Schedule

Date	Payment	Interest at Effective Rate of 2.707%	Payments of Principal	Bond Balance
12/31/Year 10				$11,200,000
12/31/Year 11	$ 720,000	$ 303,186	$ 416,814	10,783,186
12/31/Year 12	720,000	291,902	428,098	10,355,088
12/31/Year 13	720,000	280,314	439,686	9,915,402
12/31/Year 14	720,000	268,411	451,589	9,463,813
12/31/Year 15	9,720,000	256,187	9,463,813	-0-
	$12,600,000	$1,400,000	$11,200,000	

Excluding any related income tax effects, the creditor would record the debt restructuring and subsequent cash receipts as follows:

12/31/Year 11

Cash	$720,000	
Receivable from XYZ Company		$416,814
Interest income		303,186

To record receipt of first year's interest.

Similar journal entries would be made for each year through 12/31/Year 15. On that date, a journal entry would also be made to record receipt of principal:

Cash	$9,000,000	
Receivable from XYZ Company		$9,000,000

To record cash received for principal payment.

For the debtors, using a similar amortization schedule and excluding any related income tax effects, the following journal entries summarize the accounting for future cash payments under the structured terms:

12/31/Year 11
    Payable to creditors $416,814
    Interest expense   303,186
        Cash $720,000

To record first year's interest payment.

Similar entries would be made for each year through 12/31/Year 15, when an additional journal entry would be made to record payment of principal:

    Payable to creditors $9,000,000
        Cash $9,000,000

To record principal payment.

However, when the same facts as in the previous example are assumed, except that the interest rate is reduced to 3%, the total future cash payments under the new terms would be $10,350,000 (principal of $9,000,000 and interest of $270,000 for five years at 3%), which is $850,000 less than the $11,200,000 pre-restructuring carrying amount of the debt. In this case, the recorded investment in the receivable and the carrying amount of the payable would have to be reduced by $850,000. The debtor would recognize an extraordinary gain of $850,000. The creditor normally would offset the reduction against an allowance for uncollectible amounts. No interest income or expense would be recognized.

The creditor would record the debt restructuring and subsequent receipts as follows:

12/31/Year 10
    Allowance for uncollectible amounts $850,000
        Receivable from XYZ Company $850,000

To adjust recorded investment in receivable from XYZ Company due to modification of terms.

12/31/Years 11–15
    Cash $270,000
        Receivable from XYZ Company $270,000

To record annual receipts as reductions to the recorded investment in the receivable.

12/31/Year 15
    Cash $9,000,000
        Receivable from XYZ Company $9,000,000

To record receipt of payment from XYZ Company.

The debtor would record the debt restructuring and subsequent payments as follows:

12/31/Year 10
    Payable to creditors $850,000
        Gain on restructuring of debt $850,000

To adjust carrying amount of payable due to modification of terms.

12/31/Years 11–15
    Payable to creditors $270,000
        Cash $270,000

To record annual payment as reduction to carrying amount of payable.

12/31/Year 15
    Payable to creditors $9,000,000
        Cash $9,000,000

To record payment to creditors.

(c) Full Satisfaction through Transfer of Assets or Grant of Equity Interest

A debtor that transfers noncash assets (receivables, real estate, or other assets) or an equity interest to a creditor as full payment of a payable will recognize a gain on restructuring of payables. The gain is measured by the excess of the carrying value of the debt over the fair value of the assets or equity interest transferred.[6]

The fair value of the assets transferred is the amount on which a willing buyer and a willing seller would agree in a current sale. If an active market exists, fair value will be measured by the market value. If an active market does not exist, the selling prices for similar assets may be helpful in estimating fair value. If no market price is available, a forecast of expected cash flows may aid in estimating the fair value of assets transferred. The expected cash flows are to be discounted at a rate commensurate with the risk involved in holding that particular asset.[7]

For the creditors, the excess of the recorded investment in the receivable satisfied over the fair value of assets or equity interest transferred is a loss, and the creditors should normally charge the excess against an appropriate allowance account. After a troubled debt restructuring, the creditor should account for assets received in satisfaction of a receivable the same as if the assets had been acquired for cash.

Two examples are used to illustrate the procedures described above.

Example 1. Exchange of Debt for Real Estate under Construction

On December 31, 20XX, X Company owes Y Bank a debt of $10,000,000. The debt is restructured as follows:

a X Company transfers real estate under construction to Y Bank in full settlement of the debt.

b The carrying value of the real estate is $9,000,000.

c Current market prices are not available for either the transferred real estate or similar real estate.

d Both parties estimate that $6,000,000 incurred ratably over the next 12 months is required to complete construction.

e The completed property will be sold immediately for $16,000,000.

---

[6] FASB *supra* note 3, § D22.109.
[7] *Id.*

Assuming a discount factor of 12 percent, the fair value based on discounted future cash flows would be estimated as follows:

Estimated selling price of completed property		$16,000,000.0
Present value factor of 12 percent for 12 months		× 0.892857
		$14,285,712.0
Less present value of cost to complete:		
Estimated monthly cost $6,000,000/12 =	$500,000	
Present value of annuity factor of 1 percent per month for 12 months	× 11.255077	(5,627,538.5)
Estimated fair value		$ 8,658,173.5

X Company and Y Bank would make the following journal entries on December 31, 20XX:

X Company

Payable to bank	$10,000,000.0	
Loss on disposition of assets	341,826.5	
Real estate under construction		$9,000,000.0
Gain on restructuring		1,342,826.5

To record transfer of property in full settlement of debt.

Y Bank

Real estate received in restructuring	$8,658,173.5	
Allowance for loan losses	1,341,826.5	
Receivable from X Company		$10,000,000.0

To record receipt of property in full settlement of debt.

If at December 31, 20XX, the construction is completed at a cost of $6,500,000 and the property is appraised at an estimated current market value of $16,500,000, no adjustment should be made at December 31, 20XX, for the excess of market value of $16,500,000 over carrying value of $15,158,173.5 ($8,658,173.5 + $6,500,000).

Example 2. Exchange of Equity for Debt

Debt between B Company and C Bank is restructured as follows:

a B Company issues 1,000,000 shares of its common stock with $1.00 par value to C Bank in full settlement of debt totaling $3,000,000.
b Market price of the common stock is $1.00 per share.
c The shares issued to C Bank are restricted shares and cannot be sold without filing a registration statement.
d A 20 percent reduction from market price is estimated to reflect the restricted nature of these shares.

In accounting for the debt restructuring, B Company would recognize an extraordinary gain of $2,200,000 ($3,000,000 less $800,000, the estimated fair value of the shares issued), and C Bank would charge $2,200,000 against its allowance for loan losses.

(d) Partial Satisfaction

A troubled debt restructuring may involve receipt of assets or equity interests in partial satisfaction of a receivable and a modification of terms of the remaining receivable. Accounting for these restructurings should be the same as that for a modification of terms, and the fair value of assets transferred or equity interest granted should be accounted for as a partial cash payment.

The accounting required is as follows:

- The recorded receivable or the carrying amount of the payable should be reduced by the fair value of the assets or equity interest transferred.
- A debtor should recognize a gain or loss resulting from any disposition of assets.
- No gain or loss on restructuring should be recognized unless the remaining balance of the debt exceeds future cash payments specified by the new terms.
- Future interest income or expense should be determined using the interest method.[8]

(e) Contingent Interest

If a troubled debt restructuring involves contingent payables, those contingent amounts are to be recognized as a payable and as interest expense in future periods, in accordance with FASB Statement No. 5, *Accounting for Contingencies*.[9] For the debtor, at the time of restructuring, contingent cash payments should be included in the total future cash payments specified by the new terms. A debtor should not recognize a gain on a restructured debt involving contingent cash payments as long as the total future payments exceed the carrying amount. After the time of restructuring, the debtor should recognize interest expense and a payable for contingent payments when it is probable that a liability has occurred and the amount can be reasonably estimated.

For the creditors, contingent cash receipts should not be included in the total future cash receipts specified by the new terms, and the creditor should recognize a loss on restructuring unless subsequent realization is probable and the amount can be reasonably estimated. After the time of restructuring, contingent cash receipts should not be recognized as interest income until they become unconditionally receivable.

(f) Disclosure

A debtor should disclose the following four items of information about troubled debt restructurings that have occurred as of the date of each balance sheet:

---

[8] *Id.,* §§ D22.115 and D22.129.
[9] *Id.,* § D22.118.

1 For each restructuring, a description of the principal change in terms, the major features of settlement, or both

2 Aggregate gain on restructuring of payables and the related income tax effect

3 Aggregate net gain or loss on transfers of assets recognized during the period

4 Per-share amount of the aggregate gain on restructuring of payables, net of related income tax effect[10]

For periods after a troubled debt restructuring, a debtor should disclose the extent to which amounts contingently payable are included in the carrying amount of restructured payables. Total amounts that are contingently payable on restructured payables and the conditions under which those amounts would become payable or would be forgiven should be disclosed when it is reasonably possible that a liability will be incurred.

A creditor should disclose the following information about troubled debt restructurings as of the date of each balance sheet:

- For outstanding receivables whose terms have been modified in troubled debt restructuring by major category:
  - The aggregate recorded investment.
  - The gross interest income that would have been recorded in the period if those receivables had been current in accordance with the original terms and had been outstanding throughout the period or since origination, if held for part of the period.
  - The amount of interest income on those receivables that was included in net income for that period. A receivable whose terms have been modified need not be included in the disclosure if, subsequent to the restructuring, its effective interest rate is equal to or greater than the rate that the creditor was willing to accept for a new receivable.
- The amount of any commitments to lend additional funds to debtors owing receivables whose terms have been modified in troubled debt restructurings.[11]

§ 14.13 Reporting of Income from Debt Discharge When FASB Statement No. 15 Is Not Applicable

At least three alternatives are available for reporting income from debt discharge when there is a restructuring of liabilities and FASB Statement No. 15 does not govern the reporting procedure:

1 Extraordinary item

2 Paid-in capital

3 Income item—operating net income, one line below operating net income, or as an unusual item only

[10] *Id.*, § D22.121.
[11] *Id.*, § D22.136.

In the discussion of each of these procedures that follows, it is assumed that the debtor did not report the gain from debt discharge as a part of a quasi-reorganization. The procedures to follow when there is a quasi-reorganization are discussed in §§ 14.15 to 14.19.

(a) Extraordinary Item

A substantial amount of evidence exists to suggest that income from debts discharged should be classified as an extraordinary item even if FASB Statement No. 15 does not govern. It appears that, in most chapter 11 reorganizations, the income from debts discharged would meet both criteria stated in APB Opinion No. 30: *unusual nature* and *infrequency of occurrence*. FASB Statement No. 4 indicates in paragraph 8 that:

> Gains and losses from extinguishment of debt that are included in the determination of net income shall be aggregated and, if material, classified as an extraordinary item, net of related income tax effect. That conclusion shall apply whether an extinguishment is early or at scheduled maturity date or later. The conclusion does not apply, however, to gains or losses from cash purchases of debt made to satisfy current or future sinking-fund requirements. Those gains and losses shall be aggregated and the amount shall be identified as a separate item.

Paragraph 10 states that this classification shall be made without regard to the criteria of "unusual and infrequent" of APB Opinion No. 30. Additionally, the FASB used paragraph 8 of FASB Statement No. 4 as evidence that the income from debts discharged is an extraordinary item. Paragraph 21 of FASB Statement No. 15 states:

> Gains on restructuring of payables determined by applying the provisions of paragraphs 13–20 of this Statement shall be aggregated, included in measuring net income for the period of restructuring, and, if material, classified as an extraordinary item, net of related income tax effect, in accordance with paragraph 8 of FASB Statement No. 4, "Reporting Gains and Losses from Extinguishment of Debt."

In describing the basis for its conclusions, the FASB further stated, in paragraph 99, that "... a gain on restructuring of a payable in a troubled debt restructuring is indistinguishable from a gain or loss on other extinguishments of debt, and the same classification in financial statements is appropriate. Since FASB Statement No. 4 classifies a gain or loss on extinguishment of debt as an extraordinary item, the classification is appropriate for a gain on restructuring of a payable."

Paragraph 39 of SOP 90-7 indicates that any gain from debt discharge in a chapter 11 case where fresh-start reporting is required should be shown as an extraordinary item. Paragraph 41 indicates that debtors not qualified for fresh-start reporting should also follow the same practice. Although the SOP does not apply to out-of-court workouts, it will be difficult to justify a different approach.

Based on the above analysis, it would appear that income from debts discharged could logically be classified as an extraordinary item.

(b) Paid-In Capital

The difference between the amount of the liability and the amount that must be paid under the plan of reorganization is either a gift or an item of revenue. The definitions of revenue issued by authoritative bodies appear to indicate that income from debts discharged is a revenue item. In paragraph 12 of Statement No. 4, the APB defined revenue as:

> . . . a gross increase in assets or a gross decrease in liabilities recognized and measured in conformity with generally accepted accounting principles that results from those types of profit-directed activities of an enterprise that can change owners' equity. Revenue under present generally accepted accounting principles is derived from three general activities: (a) selling products, (b) rendering services and permitting others to use enterprise resources, which result in interest, rent, royalties, fees, and the like, and (c) disposing of resources other than products—for example, plant and equipment or investments in other entities. Revenue does not include receipt of assets purchased, proceeds of borrowing, investments by owners, or adjustments of revenue of prior periods.

The FASB, in Statement of Financial Accounting Concepts No. 3, has said:

> Revenues are inflows or other enhancements of assets of an entity or *settlements of its liabilities* (or a combination of both) during a period from delivering or producing goods, rendering services, or other activities that constitute the entity's ongoing major or central operations.

> Gains are increases in equity (net assets) from peripheral or incidental transactions of an entity and from all other transactions and other events and circumstances affecting the entity during a period except those that result from revenues or investments by owners.

> Gains and losses may be described or classified according to sources. Some gains or losses are net results of comparing the proceeds and sacrifices (costs) in peripheral or incidental transactions with other entities—for example, from sales of investments in marketable securities, from disposition of used equipment, or from *settlements of liabilities* at other than their carrying amounts. [emphasis added]

The American Accounting Association, in its 1948 statement dealing with concepts and standards, stated that revenue represents an inflow of assets or net assets into the firm as a result of sales of goods or services, and that revenue also includes gains from the sale or exchange of assets other than stock-in-trade and gains from *advantageous settlement of liabilities*.[12]

A gift is a voluntary transfer of property without any consideration being given for the transfer. If a gift is made to a debtor, its debts are canceled without any consideration on the part of the debtor. Gifts to the enterprise may be classified as capital or revenue. If the contributions are in the form of "conscience payment," they are normally considered revenue. Otherwise, gifts are normally considered a contribution to capital. The criteria to be used in determining how to classify the gift are the intent of the donor and the

---

[12] AAA Committee on Accounting Concepts and Standards, *Accounting and Reporting Standards for Corporate Financial Statements and Proceeding Statements and Supplements* (Columbus, OH: American Accounting Association, 1975), p. 15.

events surrounding the contribution. The philosophy underlying the enactment of the Bankruptcy Act and Bankruptcy Code was to allow the debtor to have a new start. The debtor came out of the proceedings without any commitments of any type directly related to the amount of debt forgiven. The cancellation may be viewed as a type of gift, in part directly from the creditors who agreed to the settlement and in part from Congress, which has imposed the discharge of indebtedness. However, it should be pointed out that one of the main reasons why creditors accept a plan is that they believe they will receive a greater return under the plan than under complete liquidation. Thus, the handling of the cancellation as a gift is, it would appear, in most cases very questionable.

Under the additional paid-in capital approach, the accounting entries made when the amount of the liability is reduced and the debt is paid off are as follows: the liability is debited for the full amount of the original indebtedness, cash is reduced by the amount actually paid out, and paid-in capital is increased by the difference. If any of the assets are subsequently written down, the contributed capital account must also be reduced by this amount.

There is very little support in practice for considering the gain from debt discharge as a component of paid-in capital, unless at the time of the discharge the entity adopts a quasi-reorganization. If the entity elects quasi-reorganization, the gain is used to reduce the deficit in retained earnings and the balance of the deficit is then charged to additional paid-in capital.

(c) Income Item

Based on the evidence indicating that income from debts discharged (provided the gain is considered to be revenue and not a capital item) is an extraordinary item, the reporting of the gain as operating income or on the line just below operating income—before extraordinary items—has very little support.

§ 14.14   Determining the Amount of Income from Debt Discharge When FASB Statement No. 15 Is Not Applicable

FASB Statement No. 15, paragraph 50, clearly indicates that debt issued in troubled debt restructuring is not discounted as long as the total amount to be paid (including interest) is less than the carrying value of the debt being restructured. However, the new debt will be discounted to the extent that the amount to be paid exceeds the carrying value of the old debt. If FASB Statement No. 15 does not apply, can the above procedures be followed?

Paragraph 38 of SOP 90-7 requires that, under the conditions where fresh-start reporting is adopted, liabilities, except for deferred taxes, should be stated at present values of the amounts to be paid, determined at appropriate current interest rates.

Paragraph 41 indicates that, in a chapter 11 case where fresh-start reporting is not adopted, liabilities compromised by confirmed plans should also be stated at present values of amounts to be paid.

Thus, the debtor will no longer have the option to elect to discount or not to discount debt issued in a chapter 11 case. These provisions apply only to chapter 11 cases. However, in out-of-court workouts where liabilities are generally restated, it will be difficult to justify accounting for issuance of new debt in a manner different from the discounting procedure described in this SOP.

(a) Arguments Against Discounting

The bases for the FASB's conclusions for limiting discounting, as set forth in FASB Statement No. 15, are as follows:

> The Board concluded that since a troubled debt restructuring involving modification of terms of debt does not involve transfers of resources or obligations (paragraph 77), restructured debt should continue to be accounted for in the existing accounting framework, on the basis of the recorded investment in the receivable or carrying amount of the payable before the restructuring.
>
> 147—The Board found persuasive the arguments that a creditor in a troubled debt restructuring is interested in protecting its unrecovered investment (represented in the accounts by the recorded investment in the receivable) and, if possible, obtaining a return. To the creditor, therefore, the effect of a restructuring that provides for recovery of the investment is to reduce the rate of return (the effective interest rate) between the restructuring and maturity. Similarly, the effect of that kind of restructuring to the debtor is to reduce the cost of credit (the effective interest rate) between the restructuring and maturity.
>
> 148—Thus, the Board concluded that no loss (creditor) or gain (debtor) should be recognized in a troubled debt restructuring if the total future cash receipts or payments (whether designated as interest or face amount) specified by the new terms at least equals the recorded investment or carrying amount of the debt before the restructuring.

The primary basis for the FASB's conclusion appears to be that a modification of terms is not an exchange of resources or obligations, but rather is a continuation of an existing debt. Thus, in an out-of-court workout where FASB Statement No. 15 does not apply and the transaction can be viewed as a modification of terms, it would appear that the new debt need not be discounted. The FASB also found persuasive the arguments (see the extract, paragraph 147 above) that the creditor is interested in protecting its unrecovered investment and the debtor in reducing the cost of debt between the restructuring and maturity. These same conditions exist in an out-of-court workout in which FASB Statement No. 15 does not apply.

It could also be argued that the principle of FASB Statement No. 15—debt is not discounted—is clearly developed. The statement was based on the assumption that a modification of terms does not involve an exchange. All exchanges of debt in a troubled debt restructuring in which the statement applies must follow the provisions of the statement. This is true even though the opinion may exist that a modification of terms is in fact an exchange. The fact that FASB Statement No. 15 does not apply because of footnote 4 (see § 14.11) should not prevent accounting for the restructure in accordance with the provisions of the statement when debt is exchanged for debt. By definition, the statement concludes that a modification of terms in a troubled debt restructuring is not an exchange. The restructuring should be accounted for in this manner even if liabilities are generally restated.

Those who favor not discounting also argue that if modification of terms that involve only 5 percent of the debt being discharged is not an exchange and FASB Statement No. 15 applies, then why should the same kind of transaction, except that it involves 40 percent of the debt being canceled, be handled differently? The transaction is subject to different treatment only because FASB Technical Bulletin No. 81-6 states that FASB Statement No. 15 would not apply to the latter modification.

(b) Arguments for Discounting

In an out-of-court workout where FASB Statement No. 15 does not apply, discounting may be considered appropriate for several reasons:

- The reason FASB Statement No. 15 does not apply is because there has been a major restructuring of the liabilities. The restructuring often involves much more than just a modification of terms. The underlying basis for not discounting—that an exchange of a resource or obligation has not occurred—is not applicable to an out-of-court workout that involves a major restructuring of its liabilities. Under these conditions, the discounting principles of APB Opinions No. 21 and No. 26 should apply. The FASB has stated in response to the suggestion that the content of the Exposure Draft conflicted with these opinions:

    . . . modifications of terms of continuing debt are different in substance from exchanges of resources or obligations and the Exposure Draft is consistent with the opinions.

  It would thus appear that if the modifications are in fact an exchange, the FASB would take the position that APB Opinion No. 20 applies and that discounting is necessary.

- The FASB must have realized, in adding footnote 4, that a restructuring of liabilities involves more than just a modification of terms and thus concluded that the provision for nondiscounting does not apply.

- The major provision in FASB Statement No. 15 that differs from prior practice or that is new is the provision for not discounting liabilities. Accounting for the issuance of stock or property, reporting gain on discharge, and disclosure requirements agree in general with prior practice. Thus, to claim that it is not necessary to discount liabilities has the effect of saying that the provisions of FASB Statement No. 15 apply even though footnote 4 and FASB Technical Bulletin No. 81-6 suggest otherwise.

- FASB Statement No. 15 in general violates the provisions of APB Opinion No. 21. Most modifications of terms are in fact exchanges of obligations. The arguments made by the FASB to justify the conclusions reached are very weak and should be used only in the limited requirements of FASB Statement No. 15. They should not be used in situations where the statement does not apply.

- Discounting is more in line with the economics of the transaction, and future balance sheets and income statements will more clearly reflect the financial position and results of operations.

The accountant still may receive considerable pressure for a client to either discount or not discount debt, depending on the goals of that particular debtor. For example, if the debtor needs a balance sheet with an improved debt–equity ratio, a position of discounting will be taken. On the other hand, if the debtor prefers to have future interest charges as low as possible, discounting will not be preferred. It appears that discounting should be used because it is more in line with the economics of the transaction.

QUASI-REORGANIZATION

§ 14.15 Introduction

A quasi-reorganization occurs when a company restates its accounts to provide the same effect that would result if a new corporate entity were created and acquired the business of the existing corporation. Neither the FASB nor any of its predecessors has dealt with the question of what is a quasi-reorganization and what conditions are necessary for a company to go through a quasi-reorganization. In 1953, the Committee on Accounting Procedures issued rules to be followed in making the adjustment, and the procedures to follow after the adjustment is made. Paragraph 3 of Accounting Research Bulletin (ARB) No. 43, Chapter 7A, indicates that the corporation should make a clear report to its shareholders of the restatements proposed to be made, and obtain their formal consent. Paragraph 4 indicates that, in general:

> . . . assets should be carried forward as of the date of readjustment at fair and not unduly conservative amounts, determined with due regard for the accounting to be employed by the company thereafter. If the fair value of any asset is not readily determinable a conservative estimate may be made, but in that case the amount should be described as an estimate and any material difference arising through realization or otherwise is not attributable to events occurring or circumstances arising after that date should not be carried to income or earned surplus.

Liabilities should also be restated to their value as a result of the readjustment. The other procedural requirement is that the retained earnings account should be dated after the quasi-reorganization.

No reference is made in ARB No. 43 to an adjustment that only eliminates the deficit and does not result in the adjustment of asset and liability accounts. The APB in an interpretation relating to income taxes did, however, recognize this practice of only charging deficits against capital when it stated: "The concepts described in the preceding paragraphs relative to quasi-reorganization apply equally to reorganizations under the bankruptcy laws where a deficit is written off to capital."

Several questions need to be analyzed when accounting for a quasi-reorganization. The first deals with which accounts the debtor should adjust and the second with what conditions must exist before the debtor can elect a quasi-reorganization. Quasi-reorganizations can be roughly classified into two types—"mini quasi" and "regular quasi."

§ 14.16   Adjustment of Equity Section Only ("Mini Quasi")

The deficit in retained earnings is eliminated by reducing the paid-in capital by the amount of the deficit. The deficit that is eliminated is generally the amount that is left after income from debt discharge has been credited to the deficit account. For example, the note to the financial statement of one company that used "mini quasi" was as follows:

Quasi-Reorganization:

In connection with the _____ and Asset Swap with its lending banks, the predecessor Trust effected a "Quasi-Reorganization" on May 31, 20XX resulting in a charge to shares of beneficial interest equal to the Trust's accumulated deficit. Net income since May 31, 20XX is reflected as retained earnings.

In another example of the deficit being eliminated, adjustment was not referred to as a quasi-reorganization. The note to the financial statements was worded this way:

For financial reporting purposes, as a result of the reorganization and to reflect the reorganized status of XYZ, the deficit as of June 4, 20XX, has been extinguished by a charge to capital in excess of par and earnings for the period June 4, 20XX, through September 27, 20XX, have been shown as retained earnings arising after the date of reorganization. Tax benefit realized during such period from utilization of the net operating loss carryforward has been credited to capital in excess of par and is not reflected as an extraordinary credit in the consolidated statement of income for the year ended September 27, 20XX.

Based on these two examples and on other companies' annual reports, the procedure whereby only the deficit is adjusted appears to be an acceptable accounting practice. There is, however, no official statement issued by the FASB or any of its predecessors. The SEC, in Staff Accounting Bulletin (SAB) No. 78, states that deficit reclassification alone is not an acceptable practice. See § 14.19.

§ 14.17   Adjustment of All Accounts

Using this approach, assets and liabilities are adjusted to reflect market values, and the retained earnings reflect only subsequent profit or loss.

Exhibit 14-3 shows a quasi-reorganization where assets and liabilities were restated. In this case, the gain from debt discharge was taken directly to the paid-in capital account, which differs from the practice followed by some accountants of reporting this gain as an extraordinary item when a quasi-reorganization is adopted. The footnote (note 1) describing the quasi-reorganization follows:

As of the date of confirmation . . . , the Company has undergone a quasi-reorganization whereby:

a. The stated value per share of common stock was reduced from $1.00 to $.10.

b. The accumulated deficit of the Company was eliminated by a charge to additional paid-in capital.

Exhibit 14-3 Quasi-Reorganization: Direct Adjustment to Paid-in Capital

Consolidated Statement of Shareholders' Equity (Deficiency in Assets)
Years Ended September 30, 20XX, 20XX, and 20XX
(In Thousands of Dollars, Except Share Data)

	Common Stock			Additional Paid-in Capital	Retained Earnings (Deficit)	Total
	Issued and Outstanding Shares	Issuable Shares	Amount			
Balance, September 30, 20XX	1,997,452		$1,997	$803	$(14,187)	$(11,387)
Net loss for year					(25,492)	(25,492)
Exercise of employee stock options	1,500		2	3		5
Balance, September 30, 20XX	1,998,952	—	1,999	806	(39,679)	(36,874)
Net loss for year					(173)	(173)
Balance, September 30, 20XX	1,998,952	—	1,999	806	(39,852)	(37,047)
Net earnings through April 4, 20XX					165	165
Effect of confirmation of plan and quasi-reorganization (note 1):						
Stock issued at date of confirmation	2,172,675		2,173			2,173
Stock issuable in lieu of cash payments on September 30, 20XX		4,345,326	4,345			4,345

Less treasury stock issuable to foreign subsidiary	(173,814)		(521)			(521)
Settlement of liabilities on discharge from bankruptcy		(347,626)		31,829		
Revaluation of property and plant				31,829		31,829
Change in stated value of common stock from $1.00 per share to $.10 per share			(7,196)	7,196		992
Deficit charged to additional paid-in capital				(39,687)	39,687	
Net earnings subsequent to April 4, 20XX					662	662
Tax benefit from use of net operating loss carryforward subsequent to April 4, 20XX				602		602
Balance, September 30, 20XX	3,997,813	3,997,700	$800	$1,738	$662	$3,200

[Notes to consolidated financial statements omitted]

c. The net result of settling the liabilities incurred prior to the commencement of [the bankruptcy] proceedings was credited to additional paid-in capital.

d. The fixed assets of the Company were increased by $992,000 to current fair market values and accumulated depreciation to the date of the quasi-reorganization was eliminated.

The issuance of shares of the Company's common stock has been recorded at the stated value of $.10 per share rather than the fair market value at the date of issuance. Any difference between the fair market value and the stated value would have no effect on shareholders' equity or the Company's results of operations.

Although SOP 90-7 would preclude the use of quasi-reorganization accounting today, the example illustrates how an out-of-court workout might be restructured.

The theory of quasi-reorganization should allow the assets to be revalued upward if they are stated below market values. The SEC has, over time, generally opposed a write-up in net assets and, in August 1988, clearly stated its objection to a write-up in net assets in SAB No. 78. See § 14.19. In general, it appears that the practice of adjusting all accounts of the debtor is more in line with the purpose of a quasi-reorganization.

§ 14.18   Conditions Necessary for Quasi-Reorganization

Prior to the issuance of SOP 90-7, there appear to have been more quasi-reorganizations associated with companies that had not filed a bankruptcy petition than with those that had filed a petition. Thus, quasi-reorganizations were not solely related to reorganization under bankruptcy law and will most likely continue to be used in out-of-court workouts. A chapter 11 reorganization should, however, contain the necessary requirements for a quasi-reorganization. Upon confirmation of the plan, the court grants the corporation the right to a "fresh start." In many cases, substantial amounts of debt are canceled. Also, the court will have determined that the new entity has the potential for successful future operations; that is, the plan is feasible. Because the court will have granted the corporation the right to a new start, it can be argued that the activities of the corporation should be accounted for, from this day forward, as a new entity—assets and liabilities should be stated at their market values, and the retained earnings balance should be zero. If the creditors make the same type of concessions out of court, it could also be argued that a quasi-reorganization is justified here also. The FASB (or its predecessors) has not decided to make the quasi-reorganization a mandatory requirement. The AICPA in SOP 90-7, concluded that fresh-start reporting should be used where the reorganization value exceeds prepetition claims and postpetition liabilities and there has been more than a 50 percent change in ownership. However, SOP 90-7 states that quasi-reorganization should not be used in chapter 11 where fresh-start reporting does not apply.

§ 14.19   Quasi-Reorganization and the SEC

The SEC's position concerning quasi-reorganization is explained in Accounting Series Release (ASR) No. 25 (FAR No. 210), issued in 1941, and in Staff Accounting Bulletin (SAB) No. 78, issued on August 25, 1988. FAR No. 210 states that, in a quasi-reorganization, the following conditions exist:

(1)   Earned surplus, as of the date selected, is exhausted;

(2)   Upon consummation of the quasi-reorganization, no deficit exists in any surplus account;

(3)   The entire procedure is made known to all persons entitled to vote on matters of general corporate policy and the appropriate consents to the particular transactions are obtained in advance in accordance with the applicable law and charter provisions;

(4)   The procedure accomplishes, with respect to the accounts, substantially what might be accomplished in a reorganization by legal proceedings—namely, the restatement of assets in terms of present conditions as well as appropriate modifications of capital and capital surplus, in order to obviate so far as possible the necessity of future reorganizations of like nature.

It is the view of the SEC that a quasi-reorganization may not be considered to have been effected unless all of the above conditions exist.

For some time now, the SEC has been opposed to a net write-up of assets in the quasi-reorganization. Thus, for assets to be increased above historical cost, there must be a reduction in the carrying value of other assets or an increase in the value of the liabilities by an amount at least equal to the increase over historical costs. In SAB No. 78, the SEC restated this position by stating:

> The staff believes that increases in the recorded values of specific assets (or reductions in liabilities) to fair value are appropriate providing such adjustments are factually supportable; however, the amounts of such increases are limited to offsetting adjustments to reflect decreases in other assets (or increases in liabilities) to reflect their new fair value. In other words, a quasi-reorganization should not result in a write-up of net assets of the registrant.

SAB No. 78 specifically precludes a net write-up in assets, but the SEC staff will consider previous write-downs in determining whether there has been an increase in net assets. The staff indicates that, in some cases, asset write-downs or similar losses recognized in income may be viewed as part of a quasi-reorganization if the timing and nature, relative to other revaluations reflected directly in equity, are such that they can be considered a single event. If the debtor desires to have a previous write-down considered to be part of a quasi-reorganization, the staff of the SEC should be consulted.

In SAB No. 78, the SEC stated that the deficit reclassification alone is not an acceptable practice:

> The staff believes a deficit reclassification of any nature is considered to be a quasi-reorganization. As such, a company may not reclassify or eliminate a deficit in retained earnings unless all requisite conditions set forth in Section 210 for a quasi-reorganization are satisfied.

Thus, unless the carrying value of all assets and liabilities approximate their fair values at the date of the quasi-reorganization, the SEC requires a revaluation of all assets and liabilities. However, there cannot be a write-up in net assets. This requirement applies to all entities involved in a quasi-reorganization, including those that are emerging from bankruptcy.

15

Reporting on an Insolvent Company

§ 15.1 Introduction

Analysis, reports, or schedules prepared or analyzed by the accountant or financial advisor and submitted have supreme importance in bankruptcy and insolvency proceedings. They are the chief source of information for all those who are interested in the debtor's operations and financial affairs.

Accountants often issue various types of reports and schedules as part of services rendered in the bankruptcy and insolvency area. These services include the evaluation or development of a business plan, valuation of the business, search for preferences, and the preparation of operating reports. Many of the reports or schedules produced would generally be classified as financial statements. Because financial statements are issued, the accountant must determine if a compilation, review, or audit report must be issued, or if the service that generated the statements is exempted from professional standards related to compilation of financial statements from the records and the attestation standards. This issue has involved considerable controversy among accountants that practice in the bankruptcy and insolvency area.

When the accountant begins an engagement involving bankruptcy or insolvency issues, a decision needs to be made as to application of the attestation standards. Section 9100.48 of *Attestation Engagements Interpretation*, "Applicability of Attestation Standards to Litigation Services," excludes litigation services that "involve pending or potential formal legal or regulatory proceedings before a trier of fact in connection with the resolution of a dispute between two or more parties. . . ." Guidance in this area is provided by the AICPA's Management Consulting Division, in *Consulting Services Special Report 93-1*, "Application of AICPA Professional Standards in the Performance of Litigation Services" (CSSR 93-1). This report concludes in paragraph 71/105.03 that "Bankruptcy, forensic accounting, reorganization, or insolvency services, as practiced by CPAs, generally are acceptable as forms of litigation services."

LITIGATION SERVICES

§ 15.2 Application of Litigation Services to Bankruptcy

CSSR 93-1 notes that the role of the accountant in a litigation engagement is different from the role in an attestation services engagement. When involved in an attestation engagement, the CPA firm expresses "a conclusion about the reliability of a written assertion of another party." In the performance of litigation services, the accountant helps to "gather and interpret facts and must support or defend the conclusions reached against challenges in cross-examination or regulatory examination and in the work product of others."

Appendix 71/B of CSSR 93-1 describes the delivery of reorganization services to include items such as the following:

- Preparing or reviewing valuations of the debtor's business
- Analyzing the profitability of the debtor's business
- Preparing or reviewing the monthly operating reports required by the bankruptcy court
- Reviewing disbursements and other transactions for possible preference payments and fraudulent conveyances
- Preparing or reviewing the financial projections of the debtor
- Performing financial advisory services associated with mergers, divestitures, capital adequacy, debt capacity, and so forth
- Consulting on strategic alternatives and developing business plans
- Providing assistance in developing or reviewing plans of reorganization or disclosure statements[1]

CSSR 93-1 then concludes that bankruptcy services, similar to those listed above, that are provided by CPAs generally are accepted as a form of litigation services. Appendix 71/B of CSSR 93-1 provides that:

> This acceptance is due to many fundamental and practical similarities between bankruptcy services and the consulting services associated with other forms of litigation. Bankruptcy law, as promulgated by the Bankruptcy Code and case law, is applied by bankruptcy judges and lawyers to resolve disputes between a debtor and its creditors (for example, distribution of the debtor's assets). Bankruptcy cases frequently include actions related to claims for preferential payments and fraudulent conveyances; negligence of officers, directors, or professionals engaged by the debtors; or other allegations common to commercial litigation. The bankruptcy court has the power and authority to value legal claims and resolve such common litigation as product liability, patent infringement, and breach of contract. The decisions of bankruptcy judges can be appealed as can the decisions of other courts.

The above guidelines according to CSSR 93-1 should also apply to services rendered in an out-of-court workout as described in the following paragraph from Appendix 71/B:

> Out-of-court restructuring holds the potential for litigation. Therefore, the settlement process is generally conducted with the same scrutiny, due diligence, and intense challenge as that of a formal court administered process. Furthermore, bankruptcy services provided by CPAs are typically not three-party attest services

---

[1] CSSR 93-1 notes that the words *review* and *reviewing* are not intended to have the same meaning as they do in the AICPA SSARSs.

(the three parties in attest services are the asserter, the attester, and the third party). Instead, affected parties have the opportunity to question, challenge, and provide input to the bankruptcy findings and process.

For services to be exempted, they must be rendered in connection with the litigation and the parties to the proceeding must have an opportunity to analyze and challenge the work of the accountant. For example, when the CPA expresses a written conclusion about the reliability of a written assertion by another party, and the conclusions and assertions are for the use of others who will not have the opportunity to analyze and challenge the work, the professional standards would apply. Also, when the CPA is specifically engaged to perform a service in accordance with the attestation standards or accounting services standards (SAARS), professional standards are applicable.

§ 15.3   Disclosure Requirements

If it is determined that the analysis or report that will be issued comes under the guidelines as a form of litigation services, it is advisable to explain both the association and the responsibility, if any, through a transmittal letter or a statement affixed to documents distributed to third parties. Appendix 71/B of CSSR 93-1 suggests the following format for a statement that would explain the association of the CPAs and their responsibility, if any:

> The accompanying schedules (projected financial information; debt capacity analysis; liquidation analysis) were assembled for your analysis of the proposed restructuring and recapitalization of ABC Company. The aforementioned schedules were not examined or reviewed by independent accountants in accordance with standards promulgated by the AICPA. This information is limited to the sole use of the parties involved (management; creditors' committee; bank syndicate) and is not to be provided to other parties.

If it is determined that the service does not qualify as litigation service, any financial statements that might be issued from the services rendered should be accompanied with an accountant's report based on the compilation of the financial statements. Prior to the issuance of a compilation report the format and nature of the report must be cleared with the Firm Administrator.

§ 15.4   Operating Reports

Another area where there is considerable uncertainty is in the issuance of operating reports. All regions of the U.S. Trustee require that monthly operating reports as well as annual operating reports be submitted to the court. Among those items that were listed in CSSR 93-1 that might fall under litigation services was the preparation or review of the monthly operating reports required by the bankruptcy court. These reports, especially for larger public companies, are often prepared in accordance with generally accepted accounting principles, including SOP 90-7. For example, in the region of New York, Connecticut, and Vermont, the U.S. Trustee has issued guidelines that require the statements to conform to SOP 90-7. Other U.S. Trustees have, on request by the accountant, allowed the statements to be prepared in the format that conforms to the manner in which the accountant normally prepares monthly financial statements. Additionally, the accountant is asked to prepare supplemental data not generally presented in monthly financial statements such as an aging schedule of post-petition payables and a schedule of postpetition taxes paid and accrued.

As noted above in CSSR 93-1, the professional standards would apply under two conditions:

1 When the CPA expresses a written conclusion about the reliability of a written assertion by another party, and the conclusions and assertions are for the use of others who will not have the opportunity to analyze and challenge the work
2 When the CPA is specifically engaged to perform a service in accordance with the attestation standards or accounting services standards (SAARS)

In most situations the second requirement, specifically engaged to perform attestation or compilation services, is not satisfied. Thus, based on this condition, the professional standards would not apply. CPAs are generally engaged to prepare the operating reports that the U.S. Trustee and the Bankruptcy Court require and not specifically to perform an audit or review of the financial records or even compile the financial statements in accordance with the professional standards.

It is the first requirement—expressing a written conclusion about the reliability of a written assertion by another party who will not have the opportunity to analyze and challenge the work—that needs further consideration by the profession. Whereas no specific hearing is scheduled to review the reports, creditors or other parties in interest might raise objections to the content of the reports. Objections to the operating reports have been raised, but rarely. The preparation or the review of monthly operating reports that are required by the court is one of the items listed in the services that are rendered by accountants in the performance of reorganization services. CSSR 93-1 notes that "Bankruptcy services provided by CPAs generally are accepted as a form of litigation services."

Since operating reports are considered a form of litigation services, a compilation report should not be issued on the reports. Rather, the following statement should be included in a transmittal letter or affixed to the operating reports.

The accompanying operating reports for the month of ____ were assembled for your analysis of the proposed restructuring of the ABC Company under chapter 11 of the Bankruptcy Code. The aforementioned operating reports were not examined or reviewed by independent accountants in accordance with the standards promulgated by the AICPA. This information is limited to the sole use of the parties in interest in this chapter 11 case and is not to be provided to other parties.

If on the other hand it is determined in a particular engagement that professional standards are applicable and the CPA is associated with the financial statements, then a compilation report should be issued based on the prescribed form as set forth in SAARS No. 3. As noted above, prior to the issuance of a compilation report, the format and nature of the report must be reviewed for conformity to applicable standards.

§ 15.5   Investigative Services

Preference analysis or other special investigative services performed in a bankruptcy proceeding, receivership, or out-of-court settlement, are considered a litigation service. As a result, the accountant is not required to issue an agreed-upon procedures report. This would not preclude the professional from issuing a report that describes the procedures performed and the results ascertained from the performance of the stated procedures. For example, using the above format, a report issued to a trustee based upon an analysis of preferences, might be worded as follows:

> The accompanying analysis of preferential payments was assembled (or prepared) for your analysis (or consideration) in conjunction with the proposed reorganization of ____ under chapter 11 of the Bankruptcy Code. The aforementioned analysis of preferential payments was not examined or reviewed by independent accountants in accordance with standards promulgated by the AICPA. This information is limited to the sole use of the trustee in this chapter 11 case and is not to be provided to other parties.

If it is desirable to include in the report a description of the procedures performed and the results ascertained from the performance of the stated procedures, the format of the report might be as follows:

Opening Paragraph

> The accompanying findings from the performance of selected procedures were assembled for your analysis of the reorganization of ____ under chapter 11 of the Bankruptcy Code. The aforementioned findings were not examined or reviewed by independent accountants in accordance with standards promulgated by the AICPA. This information is limited to the sole use of ____ and is not to be provided to other parties.

Procedures Performed and Findings

This is a description of the procedures performed and findings arranged by major categories or topics.

Conclusion

A paragraph dealing with the confidential nature may be included where it is determined that such a statement is needed, such as the following:

> The aforementioned report was prepared for ____. Because of the sensitive nature of the contents of the report, it should not be referred to, distributed, or communicated to others without our express consent.

§ 15.6   Financial Projections

Section 200.03 of the AICPA, *Statements on Standards for Attestation Engagements*, states that the standards for prospective financial statements do not apply for engagements involving prospective financial statements used solely in connection with litigation support services. CSSR 93-1 clearly indicates that prospective financial information qualifies as a litigation service. CSSR 93-1 states that parties-in-interest can challenge prospective financial information during negotiations or during bankruptcy court hearings often dealing with the plan's feasibility and adequacy of disclosure. Projections that are included in a disclosure statement would not be subject to the attestation standards since there is a hearing on the disclosure statement and the court must approve the disclosure statement before votes for the plan can be solicited. Parties-in-interest have an opportunity to challenge the prospective information included. Any projections provided for the debtor or for the creditors committee that are used in the negotiations of the plan would also not fall under the attestation standards.

CSSR 93-1 does, however, indicate that in situations where the users of the prospective financial information cannot challenge the CPA's work the attestation standards apply. CSSR 93-1 suggests that the attestation standard might apply in situations where exchange offers are made to creditors and stockholders with whom the company has not negotiated or who are not members of a creditor group represented by a committee. Section 200.03 of the AICPA, *Statements on Standards for Attestation Engagements*, indicates that if the prospective financial statements are used by third parties that do not have the opportunity to analyze and challenge the statements, the litigation exception does not apply.

Section 200.02 of the AICPA, *Statements on Standards for Attestation Engagements*, indicates that when an accountant submits, to his or her client or others, prospective financial statements that he or she has assembled (or assisted in assembling) or reports on prospective financial statements that might be expected to be used by third parties, a compilation, examination, or agreed-upon procedures engagement should be performed. Thus for prospective financial statements that do not qualify for the litigation exception, the engagement must be in the form of a compilation, examination, or agreed-upon procedures if the accountant is associated with the financial statements.

The determination of the reorganization or liquidation values to be included in the disclosure statement or to be used by the debtor or creditors' committee in the negotiations of the terms of a plan, as well as other services that involve financial projections, would fall under the litigation exception. If it is determined that the report regarding the issuance of financial projections would not fall under litigation services, the format and nature of the report must be reviewed for conformity to applicable standards.

The following wording might be in the transmittal letter or in a statement affixed to the documents:

> The accompanying projected financial statements (or information) were assembled for your analysis of the proposed restructuring and reorganization of ____ under chapter 11 of the Bankruptcy Code. The aforementioned statements were not examined or reviewed by independent accountants in accordance with standards promulgated by the AICPA. This information is limited to the sole use of ____ and is not to be provided to other parties.

ACCOUNTANT'S REPORT: NONLITIGATION SERVICES

§ 15.7 Introduction

The above analysis involved the issuance of a report that involved services that fall under the litigation guidelines. The balance of this chapter involves a discussion of the issues that arise when the litigation guidelines do not apply. Under these conditions, the attestation standards or the guidelines under SAARS would apply.

The reports issued by accountant's concerning companies in liquidation or rehabilitation proceedings in or out of court are very similar. The primary differences that arise relate mostly to the material covered rather than to the basic format. It is crucial for the accountant to realize, however, that liquidating proceedings involve audits of companies being liquidated, and the various debtor rehabilitation devices involve reorganization audits of going concerns.

The reports issued in bankruptcy and insolvency proceedings do differ significantly in certain respects from those issued as a result of a traditional audit. In reports on a going concern, the emphasis is on allocating costs into expired and unexpired portions to determine the results of operations. However, in reports on a firm involved in bankruptcy and insolvency proceedings, the concern shifts to the realizable value of the assets and the legally enforceable obligations that have been incurred by the debtor. Thus, the emphasis completely shifts from the income statement to the balance sheet in a chapter 7 case and partially shifts in a chapter 11 case. It may become desirable to disclose the fair market value of certain assets, when possible, and a comprehensive review of the assets is required to ensure that none is stated at a value significantly in excess of its realizable value. The examination would also be expanded to ensure that all liabilities are recorded, the requirements of all loan agreements have been met, and any deviations with their probable consequences have been disclosed. Included in the footnotes or elsewhere might also be management's appraisal of the situation.

§ 15.8   Limitations on Scope

The accountant's examination usually includes all the standard auditing procedures followed in a normal audit and conforms to generally accepted auditing standards. However, certain limitations do arise in the scope of the accountant's examination. The accountant's report is usually needed as soon as possible, to effect a plan, and the time necessary to perform the audit procedures is therefore not available. Or, the court or out-of-court creditors' committee may attempt to keep administrative expenses to a minimum and accordingly may restrict professional services to those deemed absolutely essential. The most common limitations in scope include an inability to confirm accounts receivable, to request vendors' statements, and to confirm deposits, prepaid expenses, and the like.

The scope of the examination may be limited further by certain obstacles and unusual situations that emerge during bankruptcy and insolvency proceedings. Examples of problems that may be encountered include poor, incomplete, or missing books and records; lack of written explanation for occurrences such as major investments, loan repayments to insiders, and other transactions with parent companies or stockholders; absence of employees familiar with the books and records; major transactions that have not been recorded; and executives who refuse to cooperate or are not familiar with major financial transactions.

When such situations arise, unusual audit procedures must frequently be employed. Alternative techniques, which are described in detail in Chapter 12,

- Interview people who might have knowledge of the unusual transactions being investigated.
- Review all available correspondence files.
- Review telephone call records and travel logs of key insiders.
- Examine the prior accountant's working papers.
- Inspect all documents held by the company's former attorneys.
- Confirm transactions, either orally or in writing, with second parties.
- Develop, chronologically, a list of all unusual transactions.
- Perform extensive tracing and retracing.

The obstacles and limitations in the scope of the examination and the subsequent employment of alternative procedures inevitably affect the type of report the accountant will be able to issue. Whether a qualified opinion or an actual disclaimer of opinion (compilation of review report for nonpublic company) should be given depends on the severity of the limitations. Other conditions prevalent in bankruptcy and insolvency proceedings must also be considered. These are discussed more fully in §§ 15.12–15.17.

Certain statements are normally found in an accountant's report concerning a company experiencing financial difficulty. Comparative balance sheets and income statements for a period of years may reveal the source of the debtor's problems. A statement of affairs or a balance sheet, with assets classified as free or secured and liabilities shown as priority, secured, and unsecured, may assist in deciding the best remedy to adopt. (See §§ 13.3 and 13.12.) It may also be advantageous to include a statement showing the debtor's capitalization with a schedule of all withdrawals of capital. For the statements to be presented in accordance with generally accepted accounting principles, a statement of cash flows must be included where an opinion is being expressed on the financial statements as a whole.

§ 15.9 Unique Disclosures in Report

The accountant's report covering these statements (and any additional ones prepared) contains some disclosures that are unique to bankruptcy and insolvency proceedings. Frequently, the following items are found:

- A brief history of the debtor, including a discussion of the reasons for filing a petition or seeking a settlement and any changes in management that have been made.
- If the accountant has disclaimed an opinion, the reasons for so doing.
- A discussion of any areas of the examination that were not completed and an indication as to why they were left undone. This includes disclosure of any books or records of the debtor that are withheld by an officer of the company.
- Documentation of sources used to obtain information for the report other than the debtor's books and records.
- Any corrections made to the book balances and the reasons for such changes.

- A detailed description of all unusual transactions, including a schedule of all possible preferential payments and a list of all discrepancies found between the debtor's books and records and the financial statements issued to the trade, bank, and credit agencies.
- An assessment of the probability of successfully continuing the business under a plan of settlement or a plan of reorganization.

The four standards of reporting established by the AICPA Committee on Auditing Procedures are to be followed by the auditor in presenting the report. The reporting standards are as follows:

> The report shall state whether the financial statements are presented in accordance with generally accepted accounting principles.
>
> The report shall identify those circumstances in which such principles have not been consistently observed in the current period in relation to the preceding period.
>
> Informative disclosures in the financial statements are to be regarded as reasonably adequate unless otherwise stated in the report.
>
> The report shall either contain an expression of opinion regarding the financial statements taken as a whole, or an assertion to the effect that an opinion cannot be expressed. When an overall opinion cannot be expressed, the reasons therefore should be stated. In all cases where an auditor's name is associated with financial statements, the report should contain a clear-cut indication of the character of the auditor's examination, if any, and the degree of responsibility being taken.[2]

§ 15.10 Full Disclosure

When writing the report, the accountant must decide the necessary and appropriate degree of disclosure about the debtor and its situation. In all cases, the third standard of reporting, adequacy of informative disclosure, must be followed. In order for the financial standards to be fairly presented in accordance with generally accepted accounting principles, adequate disclosure is required of all material matters.[3] Strengthening this requirement even further is the AICPA Code of Professional Ethics, Rule 202, which sets forth that a member shall not permit his or her name to be associated with financial statements in such a manner as to imply that he or she is acting as an independent public accountant unless he or she has complied with the applicable generally accepted auditing standards promulgated by the Institute. Thus, the failure to disclose adequate information violates the Code of Ethics.

The amount of disclosure required is more difficult for the accountant to determine in a situation involving companies having financial problems than in a normal audit. Thus, it might not be wise to reveal indiscriminately that a company is experiencing financial trouble. Knowledge of this fact might unjustifiably discourage customers from placing new orders, make credit more difficult for the debtor to obtain, or provide important information to competitors.

---

[2] *Auditing Standards* (New York: American Institute of Certified Public Accountants, 1993), §§ 410, 411, 431, 435, 504 and 508.
[3] *Id.,* § 431.02.

However, some disclosure is necessary (1) for the benefit of interested parties who lack the training to be able to discern the possibility of financial difficulty from the statements or (2) when this information is not readily apparent from a mere reading of the financial statements. The accountant is again limited because the need to remain independent places a restraint on any interpretation of the data or forecast of future events. Some suggestions that have been made for more adequate disclosure involve a clear statement in the footnotes that the company is headed toward financial trouble and may not be able to continue as a going concern, the conditions and events that gave rise to the problems, the possible resulting impact, and disclosure of management's plans to reverse the trend. However, if the enterprise is facing financial difficulty that may affect the continuance of general business operations, adequate disclosure of this fact is required in the opinion (§§ 15.12–15.17).

§ 15.11 Accountant's Responsibility for Disclosure

The accountant's responsibility for disclosure in a bankruptcy proceeding is greater than in a normal audit because the accountant is an appointee of the court. In *Food Town, Inc.*, it was ruled that when accountants are appointed by an order in such a proceeding, they become quasi-officers of the court and owe their primary duty to the court.[4] In *Brown v. Gerdes*, the court further decided that, in all cases, persons who seek compensation for services or reimbursement for expenses are held to fiduciary standards.[5] These standards imply that a special confidence has been imposed in another who, in equity and good conscience, is bound to act in good faith and with due regard to the person granting the confidence. These relationships and requirements mean that accountants must include in their report all those facts that come to their attention during the examination, even if detrimental to the debtor or its management. When preparing a report, the accountant must realize that the special proceedings impose additional requirements and responsibilities, beyond the normal considerations, as to the facts that must be disclosed.

The type of opinion that the accountant issues on the financial statements submitted with the report has a strong effect on the degree of confidence that other interested parties place in the statements. The accountant's report is often the only source of information available to those who are trying to decide the relationship they wish to have with the debtor in the future.

GOING-CONCERN CONCEPT

§ 15.12 Introduction

According to the first standard of reporting, "The report shall state whether the financial statements are presented in accordance with generally accepted accounting principles."[6] The accounting principle that presents the greatest

---

[4] 208 F. Supp. 139 (D.C. Maryland 1962).
[5] 321 U.S. 178, 182 (1944).
[6] *Auditing Standards, supra* note 1, § 410.01.

obstacle for the accountant who is examining a company facing financial difficulty is the going-concern concept, a concept that is basic to accounting theory
and one of the first concepts to gain general acceptance. Hatfield called it in
1909 a "general principle which with various applications, is now universally
accepted."[7]

§ 15.13   Going-Concern Concept Defined

The going-concern concept means continuance of a general enterprise situation. The assumption is made that assets are expected to have continuing usefulness for the general purposes for which they were acquired and that
liabilities are expected to be paid at maturity. Statement No. 4 of the Accounting Principles Board (APB) recognizes the going-concern concept as one of the
basic features of financial accounting, determined by the characteristics of the
environment in which financial accounting operates. It is described as follows:
"Going-concern—continuation of entity operations is usually assumed in
financial accounting in the absence of evidence to the contrary."[8]

The APB recognizes the following elements of modern economic organization as helping to provide an underlying continuity and stability to some
aspects of economic activity and hence to the task of measuring that activity:

1. Several forms of enterprise, especially the corporate form, continue to exist as
legal entities for extended periods of time.

2. The framework of law, custom, and traditional patterns of action provides a significant degree of stability to many aspects of the economic environment. In a
society in which property rights are protected, contracts fulfilled, debts paid, and
credit banking and transfer operations efficiently performed, the degree of uncertainty is reduced and the predictability of the outcome of many types of economic
activities is correspondingly increased.[9]

The going-concern concept was recognized by Moonitz in Accounting
Research Study (ARS) No. 1, and by Grady in ARS No. 7. The American
Accounting Association recognized "enterprise continuity" as an underlying
concept in its 1957 publication:

The "going concern" concept assumes the continuance of the general enterprise situation. In the absence of evidence to the contrary, the entity is viewed as remaining in operation indefinitely. Although it is recognized that business activities and
economic conditions are changing constantly, the concept assumes that controlling
environmental circumstances will persist sufficiently far into the future to permit
existing plans and programs to be carried to completion. Thus the assets of the
enterprise are expected to have continuing usefulness for the general purpose for
which they were acquired, and its liabilities are expected to be paid at maturity.

To the extent that termination of important activities can be predicted with
assurance, a partial or complete abandonment of the assumption of continuity is

---

[7] Henry Hatfield, *Modern Accounting* (New York: D. Appleton-Century Co., Inc., 1909), p. 80.
[8] American Institute of Certified Public Accountants, *Accounting Principles* (Chicago: Commerce
Clearing House, Inc., 1980), 1002.17(2).
[9] *Id.*, § 1023.16.

in order. Otherwise, the assumption provides a reasonable basis for presenting enterprise status and performance.[10]

§ 15.14　Absence of Evidence to the Contrary

The assumption is made that the entity's operations will continue "in the absence of evidence to the contrary." The problem for the accountant is to determine what constitutes evidence to the contrary. A business that has had profits for several years and is expanding its operations is clearly a going concern. An entity that is in the process of liquidating its assets is clearly not a going concern. However, what assumption should the accountant make for a business that has had losses for the past three years, or for an entity that is in a chapter 11 reorganization or attempting to work out an agreement with creditors out of court?

(a) Elements of Contrary Evidence

Before the issuance of a report, the accountant must be satisfied that evidence contrary to the going-concern assumption does not exist. Carmichael classified the elements of contrary evidence in the following manner:

a. Financing problems—difficulty in meeting obligations.
　1. Liquidity deficiency—the company's current liabilities exceed its current assets, which results in difficulty in meeting current obligations.
　2. Equity deficiency—the company's solvency is questionable because of a retained earnings deficit or, in more extreme cases, an excess of total liabilities over total assets.
　3. Debt default—the company has been unable to meet debt payment schedules or has violated one or more other covenants of its loan agreements.
　4. Funds shortage—the company has either limited or no ability to obtain additional funds from various capital sources.

b. Operating problems—apparent lack of operating success.
　1. Continued operating losses—no net profit has been earned for more than one past period.
　2. Prospective revenues doubtful—revenue is insufficient for day-to-day operating needs, or there have been cut-backs in operations, such as personnel reductions.
　3. Ability to operate is jeopardized—legal proceedings related to operations may severely curtail operations, or suppliers of operating materials may refuse to transact with the company.
　4. Poor control over operations—the company management has been unable to control operations, as evidenced by repetitive, uncorrected problems.[11]

---

[10] AAA Committee on Accounting Concepts and Standards, *Accounting and Reporting Standards for Corporate Financial Statements and Preceding Statements and Supplements* (Columbus, OH: American Accounting Association, 1957), p. 2.

[11] D. R. Carmichael, *The Auditor's Reporting Obligation: Auditing Research Monograph No. 1* (New York: American Institute of Certified Public Accountants, 1972), p. 94. Copyright © 1972 by the American Institute of Certified Public Accountants, Inc.

§ 15.15   Auditor's Responsibility for Evaluation

The AICPA issued, in the Spring of 1988, Statement on Auditing Standards (SAS) No. 59, *The Auditor's Consideration of an Entity's Ability to Continue as a Going Concern*, which repealed SAS No. 34. SAS No. 59 indicates that the auditor has a responsibility to evaluate whether there is substantial doubt about the entity's ability to continue as a going concern for a reasonable period of time, not to exceed one year beyond the date of the financial statements being audited. The statement further indicates that this evaluation is to be based on knowledge of relevant conditions and events that existed at or have occurred prior to the completion of the field work.

Paragraph 3 of SAS No. 59 indicates that the auditor should evaluate the ability of the entity to continue as a going concern for a reasonable period of time in the following manner:

a. The auditor considers whether the results of his procedures performed in planning, gathering evidential matter relative to the various audit objectives, and completing the audit identify conditions and events that, when considered in the aggregate, indicate there could be substantial doubt about the entity's ability to continue as a going concern for a reasonable period of time. In making that consideration, it may be necessary to obtain additional information about such conditions and events, and to obtain appropriate evidential matter to support information that mitigates the auditor's doubt.

b. If the auditor believes there is substantial doubt about the entity's ability to continue as a going concern for a reasonable period of time, he should (1) obtain information about management's plans that are intended to mitigate the effect of such conditions or events, (2) assess the likelihood that such plans can be effectively implemented, and (3) consider the need for disclosure.

c. If, after the auditor has evaluated management's plans, he concludes there is substantial doubt about the entity's ability to continue as a going concern for a reasonable period of time, the auditor should (1) consider the adequacy of disclosure about the entity's possible inability to continue as a going concern for a reasonable period of time, (2) modify his audit report to reflect his conclusion.

Paragraph 4 states that it is not the responsibility of the auditor to predict future conditions or events, and the fact that the entity may not continue as a going concern subsequent to receiving an unmodified report, even within one year following the date of the financial statements, does not, in itself, indicate inadequate performance by the auditor.

§ 15.16   Audit Procedures

SAS No. 59 indicates that the results of auditing procedures designed and performed to achieve other audit objectives should be sufficient to identify conditions and events that, when considered in the aggregate, indicate there could be substantial doubt about the ability of the entity to continue as a going concern for a reasonable time period. The statement lists the following as examples of procedures that may identify such conditions and events:

- Analytical procedures
- Review of subsequent events
- Review of compliance with the terms of debt and loan agreements
- Reading of minutes of meetings of stockholders, board of directors, and important committees of the board
- Inquiry of an entity's legal counsel about litigation, claims, and assessments
- Confirmation with related and third parties of the details of arrangements to provide or maintain financial support

§ 15.17 Consideration of Management's Plans

Paragraph 7 of SAS No. 59 indicates that if the auditor concludes after the identification of conditions and events in the aggregate that there is substantial doubt about the ability of the entity to continue as a going concern for a reasonable time period, he or she should consider management's plans for dealing with the adverse effects of the conditions and events. The auditor should consider whether it is likely that the adverse effects will be mitigated for a reasonable period of time and that such plans can be effectively implemented. The auditor's considerations relating to management's plans may include the following:

Plans to Dispose of Assets

- Restrictions on disposal of assets, such as covenants limiting such transactions in loan or similar agreements or encumbrances against assets
- Apparent marketability of assets that management plans to sell
- Possible direct or indirect effects of disposal of assets

Plans to Borrow Money or Restructure Debt

- Availability of debt financing, including existing or committed credit arrangements, such as lines of credit or arrangements for factoring receivables or sale-leaseback of assets
- Existing or committed arrangements to restructure or subordinate debt or to guarantee loans to the entity
- Possible effects on management's borrowing plans of existing restrictions on additional borrowing or the sufficiency of available collateral

Plans to Reduce or Delay Expenditures

- Apparent feasibility of plans to reduce overhead or administrative expenditures, to postpone maintenance or research and development projects, or to lease rather than purchase assets
- Possible direct or indirect effects of reduced or delayed expenditures

Plans to Increase Ownership Equity

- Apparent feasibility of plans to increase ownership equity, including existing or committed arrangements to raise additional capital

- Existing or committed arrangements to reduce current dividend requirements or to accelerate cash distributions from affiliates or other investors

Paragraphs 8 and 9 of SAS No. 59 describe additional steps the auditor
should take in evaluating management's plans. Paragraph 11 indicates that if,
after considering management's plans, the auditor concludes that the doubt
about the ability of the entity to continue as a going concern for a reasonable
time period is alleviated, he or she should consider the need for appropriate disclosure. If, on the other hand, the auditor concludes that there is substantial
doubt about the ability of the entity to continue as a going concern for a reasonable time period, the auditor should consider the possible effects on the
financial statements and the adequacy of the related disclosure. Paragraph 10
indicates that the information that might be disclosed includes the following:

- Pertinent conditions and events giving rise to the assessment of substantial doubt about the entity's ability to continue as a going concern for a
  reasonable period of time
- The possible effects of such conditions and events
- Management's evaluation of the significance of those conditions and
  events and any mitigating factors
- Possible discontinuance of operations
- Management's plans (including relevant prospective financial information)
- Information about the recoverability or classification of recorded asset
  amounts or the amounts or classification of liabilities

TYPES OF OPINIONS

§ 15.18   Unqualified Opinion

Four types of audit reports may be issued when going-concern problems
exist. These four types of reports are summarized below.

If, after considering identified conditions and events and management's
plans, the auditor concludes that substantial doubt about the ability of the
entity to continue as a going concern for a reasonable time period remains, the
audit report should include an explanatory paragraph (following the opinion
paragraph) to reflect that conclusion. Paragraph 12 of the AICPA's Auditing
Standards, section 341 (SAS No. 59 as amended by SAS No. 64) indicates that
the auditor's negative conclusions about the ability of the entity to continue as
a going concern should be expressed through the use of the phrase "substantial
doubt about the entity's ability to continue as a going concern," or similar
wording that uses both "substantial doubt" and "going concern."

In Volume 2 of *Bankruptcy and Insolvency Accounting*, 15.1 illustrates an
auditor's report that contains an explanatory paragraph describing an uncertainty about going concern. Note that the introductory, scope, and opinion
paragraphs are not changed from a standard unqualified auditor's report. An
explanatory paragraph, however, is added to the audit report to highlight the

going-concern problem. The explanatory paragraph must contain the phrases "substantial doubt" and "going concern" in order to indicate the severity of the problem.

In 15.2 of Volume 2, there is an example of an unqualified opinion issued with an explanatory paragraph in the case of Hills Department Stores.

§ 15.19 Qualified Opinion

A "qualified opinion" means that "except for" the effects of a particular situation, the financial statements are presented fairly in conformity with generally accepted accounting principles (GAAP). Qualified opinions are normally issued in one of the following situations: (a) the financial statements depart from GAAP, (b) management is unable to justify a change in accounting principles, or (c) the scope of the audit is limited.

For situations (a) and (b), the auditor must choose between a qualified opinion and an adverse opinion; for situation (c), the auditor must choose between a qualified opinion and a disclaimer of opinion. The choice of opinion depends on the materiality of the effect from the particular situation. When the effect is so material that a qualified opinion is unwarranted, an adverse opinion or disclaimer of opinion should be issued. Otherwise, a qualified opinion may be issued.

In situations where the auditor issues a qualified opinion, 15.3 of Volume 2 of *Bankruptcy and Insolvency Accounting* indicates the necessary paragraphs to be included in the auditor's report.

The accountant should also issue a qualified opinion if he or she is of the opinion that the entity's *disclosures* with respect to the ability of the entity to continue as a going concern for a reasonable period of time are inadequate. The qualification of the opinion is required, not because of the ability of the entity to continue as a going concern, but because of inadequate disclosures and, thus, a departure from generally accepted accounting principles. For example, the auditor may be of the opinion that the assets of the debtor are overvalued because of the debtor's financial problems. If the debtor refuses to write-down these assets, assuming they are material, the auditor would not want to issue an unqualified report with disclosures only about the uncertainty of the ability of the entity to continue. Any type of qualification must not be reported in the form of a "subject to" qualification, but rather in the form of an "except for" type of qualification.

§ 15.20 Disclaimer of Opinion

Prior to the effective date of SAS No. 59, the accountant often disclaimed an opinion of the statements issued during the bankruptcy or insolvency proceedings. Usually, this was because of the uncertainties surrounding the entity's continuation or because the auditor was unable to obtain sufficient competent evidential matter during the course of the examination. Also, audit obstacles may have been encountered that resulted in incomplete field work, or the scope of the examination may have been limited by the engagement letter or retention order. These situations clearly require that the accountant deny an opinion so that third parties will not rely on the financial statements when such reliance is not warranted. SAS No. 59 suggests that a disclaimer should no longer be issued solely because there is doubt about the ability of the debtor to continue as a going concern. However, a disclaimer would continue to be issued where the auditor, for various reasons, is unable to obtain sufficient competent evidential matter during the course of the examination to express an opinion.

It is important that the accountant state the reasons for disclaiming an opinion. These include disclosure of all areas of the examination that were not completed, limitations placed on the scope of the examination, and any other information that impacted the decision to disclaim an opinion.

An example of the type of disclaimer issued to creditors' committees and in chapter 11 reorganizations is shown in 15.4 of Volume 2 of *Bankruptcy and Insolvency Accounting.*

§ 15.21   Adverse Opinion

An adverse opinion means that the financial statements, as presented by management, do not present fairly the financial position, results of operations, or cash flows in conformity with GAAP. An adverse opinion is normally issued either when the financial statements contain a departure from GAAP or when management is unable to justify an accounting change, *and* the effect of either situation is considered so material that a qualified opinion is unwarranted. In addition, an adverse opinion may be issued when the entity's *disclosures* with respect to the ability of the entity to continue as a going concern are materially inadequate. The inadequacy of the disclosures constitutes a departure from GAAP. An adverse opinion may also arise in a situation when the entity's assets, even if it does continue, are in such a condition that it is impossible for them to be worth their book value. If the statements are not corrected, the accountant will be required to issue an adverse opinion.

In situations where the auditor issues an adverse opinion, 15.5 of Volume 2 of *Bankruptcy and Insolvency Accounting* indicates the necessary paragraphs to be included in the auditor's report.

§ 15.22   Reports Relating to the Results of Applying Agreed-on Procedures

It should be noted, again, that the concepts in this section apply to situations where the accountant's report does not fall under the litigation guidelines. In most bankruptcy and in some out-of-court engagements, the accountant will perform many of the services that are described in this section, but will not be required to follow the reporting procedures described here because the accountant's report falls under the litigation guidelines. Thus, reports that involve the equivalent of agreed-on procedures may be issued that involve financial statements.

In an audit of a debtor in a chapter 7, a chapter 11, or an out-of-court proceeding, the accountant may be engaged to apply agreed-on procedures to specific accounts or items in a financial statement. These procedures are generally not sufficient to enable the accountant to express an opinion on the specific accounts or items. Examples of this type of engagement would include the performance of selected procedures in connection with claims of creditors, or relating to inventory in a particular location. The standards that should be followed in an engagement of this nature were established in Statement on Auditing Standards (SAS) No. 35, *Special Reports*. Acceptance of an engagement of this nature is appropriate, according to SAS No. 14, only if:

- The parties involved have a clear understanding of the procedures to be performed.
- Distribution of the report is to be restricted to named parties involved.
- Financial statements of the entity are not to accompany the report.[12]

The report issued by the accountant should:

- Indicate the specified elements, accounts, or items to which the agreed-on procedures were applied.
- Indicate the intended distribution of the report.
- Enumerate the procedures performed.
- State the accountant's findings.
- Disclaim an opinion with respect to the specified elements, accounts, or items.
- State that the report should not be associated with the financial statements of the entity.[13]

If the accountant has no adjustments to propose to the specified elements, accounts, or items, he or she should include a comment to that effect in the report. The accountant may also wish to indicate that had additional procedures been performed with respect to the specified elements, accounts, or items, or had an examination of the financial statements been made in accordance with generally accepted auditing standards, other matters might have come to his or her attention that would have been reported.

The general standards and the first standard of field work are applicable to such engagements; however, the second and third standards of field work and the standards of reporting do not apply.

An example of a report based on comparison of the claims received from creditors with those listed in the records where agreed-on procedures were applied is given as 15.6 in Volume 2 of *Bankruptcy and Insolvency Accounting*. This report is a sample form issued by the AICPA. (The special provision for allowing claims without filing proofs of claim is discussed in § 6.19.)

Also in Volume 2, 15.7 contains the report issued where agreed-on procedures were applied in connection with a leveraged buyout transaction and relates to the solvency issued. The format of the report was suggested as part of the AICPA's conclusion that accountants should not issue solvency letters as described in § 15.29.

---

[12] *Auditing Standards, supra* note 1, § 622.01.
[13] *Id.*, § 622.04.

UNAUDITED FINANCIAL STATEMENTS

§ 15.23 Introduction

Accountants may encounter situations where they are associated with statements of a firm involved in insolvency proceedings, but no audit of the company is conducted. If the company is a public company, SAS No. 26 applies. For nonpublic companies, the accountant would follow the guidelines set forth in statements issued by the Accounting and Review Services Committee. A public entity is defined as "any entity (a) whose securities trade in a public market either on a stock exchange (domestic or foreign) or in the over-the-counter market, including securities quoted only locally or regionally, (b) that makes a filing with a regulatory agency in preparation for the sale of any class of its securities in a public market, or (c) subsidiary, corporate joint venture, or other entity controlled by an entity covered by (a) or (b)."[14]

§ 15.24 Public Entity Report

It is first necessary to ascertain when financial statements are unaudited. In 1967, the AICPA Committee on Auditing Procedures issued Statement on Auditing Procedures (SAP) No. 38. This statement was codified into SAS No. 1 and finally superseded by SAS No. 26. The second paragraph of (SAP) No. 38 stated that this situation arises if the accountant (a) has not applied any auditing procedures to the statements or (b) has not applied auditing procedures that are sufficient to permit the expression of an opinion concerning them. SAS No. 26 does not define unaudited financial statements, but states in the fourth paragraph that financial statements are audited if the accountant has applied auditing procedures sufficient to permit him or her to report on them. Financial statements that do not qualify as audited financial statements are presumed to be unaudited. According to SAS No. 26 (paragraph 3), accountants are considered to be associated with financial statements (1) when they consent to the use of their firm name in a report, document, or written communication setting forth or containing the statements, or (2) when they submit to the client or others financial statements that they have prepared or assisted in preparing, even if the firm name is not appended to the financial statements.

Prior to the issuance of SAP No. 38, the accountant could allow financial statements to be presented on plain paper without disclaiming an opinion. However, it is now required (SAS No. 26, paragraph 5) that whenever the accountant is associated with unaudited statements there must be a disclaimer of an opinion, making it clear that the accountant has not audited the statements and does not express an opinion on them. Furthermore, each page of the financial statements must be marked as unaudited. These steps are required so that anyone who becomes aware of the accountant's association with these statements will not place unwarranted reliance on them. The standard disclaimer report usually contains one paragraph similar to the following:

---

[14] Statement on Auditing Standards No. 26, *Associated with Financial Statements* (New York: American Institute of Certified Public Accountants, November 1979), para. 2n.

The accompanying balance sheet of X Company as of December 31, 20X1, and the related statements of income and retained earnings and changes in financial position for the year then added were not audited by us and accordingly we do not express an opinion on them.

(a) Required Procedures

Paragraph 5 of SAS No. 26 goes on to say that the accountant has no responsibility to apply any auditing procedures to unaudited financial statements beyond reading the statement for obvious material errors. If the accountant concludes on the basis of known facts that the statements are not in conformity with generally accepted accounting principles, the following steps should be taken:

- Insist upon appropriate revision; failing that,
- Set forth in the disclaimer the nature of the departure and, if practicable, state the effects on the financial statements or include the necessary information for adequate disclosures; failing that,
- Refuse to be associated with the statements and, if necessary, withdraw from the engagement.[15]

In certain situations, it may be necessary for the accountant to prepare, for the bankruptcy court or creditors' committees, financial statements that are unaudited and do not contain the footnotes necessary to meet the standard of full disclosure. Paragraph 12 of SAS No. 26 allows the accountant to issue a disclaimer of opinion where substantially all disclosures have been omitted. It is not necessary for the accountant to include in his or her report the disclosures omitted under these conditions, but the report should state that management has elected to omit substantially all of the disclosures. Because SAS No. 26 does not contain any suggestions as to how this statement should be worded, the accountant may refer to Statement on Standards for Accounting and Review Services (SSARS) No. 1 for some guidance.

Furthermore, the accountant should refuse to be associated with any unaudited financial statements that are believed to be false or intended to mislead.

The case involving *1136 Tenants' Corporation v. Max Rothenberg & Co.*[16] clearly points out how important it is for the accountant to be very careful in the issuance of unaudited statements. The accountant should have a written agreement with the client as to the nature and scope of the engagement. In addition, the manner in which the statements are to be used should be understood by both the accountant and the client, and this understanding should be confirmed in writing and signed by both parties.

(b) Comparative Statements

When unaudited statements for a prior year are presented with audited statements for the current year for comparative purposes, SAS No. 26 requires

---

[15] *Id.*, para. 11–13.
[16] 36 A.2d 802, 219 N.Y.S.2d 1007 (1st Dept. 1971); *aff'd* 30 N.Y.2d 585, 281 N.E.2d 846, 330 N.Y.S.2d 800 (Court of Appeals, 1972).

appropriate disclosure so that no opinion is expressed on the prior-year unaudited statements. When unaudited financial statements are presented in comparative form with audited financial statements in documents filed with the Securities and Exchange Commission, such statements should be clearly marked as "unaudited" but should not be referred to in the auditor's report. Paragraph 15 of SAS No. 26 states that when presented in any other document, the financial statements that have not been audited should be clearly marked to indicate their status, and either the report on the prior period should be reissued or the report on the current period should include as a separate paragraph an appropriate description of the responsibility assumed for the financial statements of the prior period. The accountant should also consider the current form and manner of presentation of the financial statements of the prior period in light of the information obtained during the current engagement.

An accountant for the creditors' committee may provide the committee with the information needed to reach an informed conclusion on the plan of settlement or reorganization. This normally requires only an investigatory audit, which does not constitute an examination sufficiently extensive to justify the accountant's expressing an opinion on the statements. However, if any type of report is issued by the accountant, it must be accompanied by a disclaimer of opinion, making it clear that the accountant has not audited the statements and does not express an opinion on them. The examination of a public company in bankruptcy court may not be sufficient to express an opinion, but the accountant may want to perform the procedures necessary to issue a review statement. Under these conditions, the auditor would follow the guidelines set forth in the standards issued by the Accounting and Review Services Committee for the review procedures and form of report applicable to such an engagement.

§ 15.25   Nonpublic Entity Reports

Accountants are faced with new reporting procedures when issuing unaudited statements in bankruptcy and insolvency proceedings for nonpublic companies. In issuing financial statements, an accountant must issue either a compilation report or a review report, according to SSARS No. 1, *Compilation and Review of Financial Statements*. The accountant should not issue any report on unaudited financial statements of a nonpublic entity or submit such financial statements to the client unless the provisions of SSARS No. 1 are followed regarding a compilation or review report. Thus, the accountant must know the meaning of financial statements in order to determine the applicability of SSARS No. 1.

(a) Financial Statements Defined

Financial statements are defined in paragraph 4 of SSARS No. 1 to consist of:

A presentation of financial data, including accompanying notes, derived from accounting records and intended to communicate an entity's economic resources or obligations at a point in time, or the changes therein for a period of time, in accordance with generally accepted accounting principles or a comprehensive basis of accounting other than generally accepted accounting principles.

Financial forecasts, projections and similar presentations, and financial presentations included in tax returns are not considered financial statements by SSARS No. 1. Tax returns, which are submitted to third parties in lieu of financial statements would, however, be considered financial statements. The following financial presentations were identified in SSARS No. 1 as being examples of financial statements:

- Balance sheet
- Statement of income
- Statement of retained earnings
- Statement of changes in financial position
- Statement of changes in owners' equity
- Statement of assets and liabilities (with or without owners' equity accounts)
- Statement of revenue and expenses
- Summary of operations
- Statement of operations by product lines
- Statement of cash receipts and disbursements

Many of the statements containing financial information issued to the court, the U.S. trustee, the creditors' committee, or the debtor by the accountant will be construed as financial statements and require issuance of a compilation or review report. This would include monthly cash receipts and disbursements reports or monthly operation statements. It would not, however, apply to any forecasts of future operations prepared or revised by the accountant and issued to the creditors' committee, debtor, U.S. trustee, or court, or included in a disclosure statement issued prior to the solicitation of the acceptance of a proposed plan of chapter 11 reorganization.

(b) Compilation of Financial Statements

A compilation of financial statements is defined as: "Presenting in the form of financial statements information that is the representation of management (owners) without undertaking to express any assurance on the statements."

There are four general standards and three reporting standards that apply to the compilation of financial statements. The general standards are:

1. The accountant should possess a level of knowledge of the accounting principles and practices of the industry in which the entity operates that will enable him or her to compile financial statements that are appropriate in form for an entity operating in that industry.

2. To compile financial statements, the accountant should possess a general understanding of the nature of the entity's business transactions, the form of its accounting records, the stated qualifications of its accounting personnel, the accounting basis on which the financial statements are to be presented, and the form and content of the financial statements.

3. The accountant is not required to make inquiries or perform other procedures to verify, corroborate, or review information supplied by the entity.

4 Before issuing the report, the accountant should read the compiled financial statements and consider whether such financial statements appear
to be appropriate in form and free from obvious material errors.

Although the third standard suggests that it is not necessary for the accountant to make inquiries and perform other procedures, most accountants
involved in rendering bankruptcy and insolvency services will have made
inquiries or performed other procedures. This does not, of course, prevent the
accountant from issuing a compilation report—or, if enough work was completed, from issuing a review or an audit report. In performing these inquiries
and procedures, the accountant may become aware that information supplied
by the entity is incorrect, incomplete, or misleading. Under these conditions,
the accountant should see that the deficiency in the financial statements is
corrected or that adequate disclosure, if appropriate, is made. Any other procedures performed before or during the compilation engagement should not be
described in the reports.

The reporting standards require that when financial statements are compiled
without audit or review they should be accompanied by a report stating that:

- A compilation has been performed.
- A compilation is limited to presenting in the form of financial statements information that is the representation of management (owners).
- The financial statements have not been audited or reviewed and, accordingly, the accountant does not express an opinion or any other form of
  assurance on them.

The date of completion of the compilation should be used as the date of the
accountant's report. Each page of the financial statement compiled by the
accountant should include a reference such as "See Accountants' Compilation
Report."

Paragraph 17 of SSARS No. 1 indicates that the following form of standard
report is appropriate for a compilation:

We have compiled the accompanying balance sheet of XYZ Company as of
December 31, 20XX, and the related statements of income, retained earnings, and
changes in financial position for the year then ended, in accordance with standards established by the American Institute of Certified Public Accountants.

A compilation is limited to presenting in the form of financial statements information that is the representation of management (owners). We have not audited
or reviewed the accompanying financial statements and, accordingly, do not
express an opinion or any other form of assurance on them.

It is also possible to issue a report without all of the footnotes necessary for
full disclosure. For example, the accountant may be requested to assist the
client in the preparation of operating statements. These statements could be
compiled for the client with substantially all disclosures omitted, provided the
omission is clearly indicated in the report and the omission is not, to the
accountant's knowledge, undertaken with the intention of misleading those
who are expected to use the financial statements. The following paragraph,

which would be added to the compilation report, is an illustration of the kind of explanation needed when substantially all disclosures are omitted:

> Management has elected to omit substantially all of the disclosures (and the statement of changes in financial position) required by generally accepted accounting principles. If the omitted disclosures were included in the financial statements, they might influence the user's conclusions about the company's financial position, results of operations, and changes in financial position. Accordingly, these financial statements are not designed for those who are not informed about such matters.

Although not required by SSARS No. 1, it is advisable for the accountant to maintain workpapers, which should describe, among other things, the steps taken by the client to ensure that the compilation standards have been followed and the action taken to satisfy any questions raised during the engagement. The workpapers are especially needed in bankruptcy and insolvency proceedings because of the special procedures that may be performed in addition to compiling financial statements.

(c) Review of Financial Statements

A review is defined as: "Performing inquiry and analytical procedures that provide the accountant with a reasonable basis for expressing limited assurance that there are no material modifications that should be made to the statements in order for them to be in conformity with generally accepted accounting principles or, if applicable, with another comprehensive basis of accounting." A review differs significantly from a compilation in that inquiry and analytical procedures are performed to provide the accountant with a reasonable basis for expressing limited assurance that there are no material modifications that should be made to the financial statements. A review does not, however, provide the basis for the expression of an opinion: it does not require a study and evaluation of internal accounting control or substantive testing.

The following guidelines (standards) apply to a review of financial statements:

- The accountant should possess a level of knowledge of the accounting principles and practices of the industry in which the entity operates and an understanding of the entity's business that will provide him or her, through the performance of inquiry and analytical procedures, with a reasonable basis for expressing limited assurance that there are no material modifications that should be made to the financial statements in order for the statements to be in conformity with generally accepted accounting principles.

- The requirement that the accountant possess a level of knowledge of the accounting principles and practices of the industry in which the entity operates does not prevent an accountant from accepting a review engagement for an entity in an industry with which the accountant has no previous experience. It does, however, place on the accountant a responsibility to obtain the required level of knowledge.

- The accountant's understanding of the entity's business should include a general understanding of the entity's organization, its operating characteristics, and the nature of its assets, liabilities, revenues, and expenses.
- The accountant's inquiry and analytical procedures should ordinarily consist of the following:
  - Inquiries concerning the entity's accounting principles and practices and the methods followed in applying them.
  - Inquiries concerning the entity's procedures for recording, classifying, and summarizing transactions, and accumulating information for disclosure in the financial statements.
  - Analytical procedures designed to identify relationships and individual items that appear to be unusual.
  - Inquiries concerning actions taken at meetings of the stockholders, the board of directors, the committees of the board of directors, or comparable groups, that may affect the financial statements.
  - After reading the financial statements, consideration, on the basis of information coming to the accountant's attention, of whether the financial statements appear to conform with generally accepted accounting principles.
  - Reports obtained from other accountants (if any) who have been engaged to audit or review the financial statements of significant components of the reporting entity, its subsidiaries, and other investees.
  - Inquiries of persons having responsibility for financial and accounting matters concerning (1) whether the financial statements have been prepared in conformity with generally accepted accounting principles consistently applied, (2) changes in the entity's business activities or accounting principles and practices, (3) matters as to which questions have arisen in the course of applying the foregoing procedures, and (4) events subsequent to the date of the financial statements that would have a material effect on the financial statements.

The Accounting and Review Services Committee did not specify the form or content of the workpapers that should be prepared in connection with a review of financial statements because of the different circumstances of individual engagements. In reviews where the client is in chapter 11, the workpapers will, in most cases, need to be more elaborate than in some other reviews because of the special demands placed on the accountant by the court or creditors' committee. At a minimum, paragraph 30 of SSARS No. 1 indicates that the workpapers should describe:

- The matters covered in the accountant's inquiry and analytical procedures
- Unusual matters that the accountant considered during the performance of the review, including their disposition

SSARS No. 1 also suggests that the accountant may wish to obtain a representation letter from the owner, manager, or chief executive officer and, if appropriate, the chief financial officer. In bankruptcy and insolvency reviews, a representation letter should, with rare exceptions, always be obtained.

The review of financial statements should be accompanied by a report that states:

- A review was performed in accordance with standards established by the American Institute of Certified Public Accountants.
- All information included in the financial statements is the representation of the management of the entity.
- A review consists principally of inquiries of company personnel and analytical procedures applied to financial data.
- A review has substantially less scope than an audit, the objective of which is the expression of an opinion regarding the financial statements taken as a whole; accordingly, no such opinion is expressed.
- The accountant is not aware of any material modifications that should be made to the financial statements in order for them to be in conformity with generally accepted accounting principles, other than those modifications, if any, indicated in the report.

The review report should be dated as of the date the inquiry and analytical procedures were completed, and each page of the financial statements should include a reference such as "See Accountant's Review Report."

The standard review report follows:

We have reviewed the accompanying balance sheet of XYZ Company as of December 31, 20XX, and the related statements of income, retained earnings, and changes in financial position for the year then ended, in accordance with standards established by the American Institute of Certified Public Accountants. All information included in these financial statements is the representation of the management (owners) of XYZ Company.

A review consists principally of inquiries of company personnel and analytical procedures applied to financial data. It is substantially less in scope than an examination in accordance with generally accepted auditing standards, the objective of which is the expression of an opinion regarding the financial statements taken as a whole. Accordingly, we do not express such an opinion.

Based on our review, we are not aware of any material modifications that should be made to the accompanying financial statements in order for them to be in conformity with generally accepted accounting principles.

The accountant should not issue a review report where substantially all disclosures are omitted from the financial statements. Any departures from generally accepted accounting principles should be disclosed in the report, including the effect of this departure if it has been determined. The accountant is not, however, required to determine the effects of a departure if management has not done so, provided the report discloses the fact that such determination has not been made.

In bankruptcy court proceedings, especially chapter 11, the basic financial statements may be accompanied by information presented for supplementary analysis purposes, such as a listing of general and administrative expenses or an analysis of the payroll and other taxes. (See Chapter 13 of this book.) The accountant should clearly indicate the degree of responsibility being taken with respect to supplementary information. Two alternatives are available to the accountant. One involves subjecting the supplementary information to the inquiry and analytical procedures applied to the review and report the procedures applied in the following manner:

> The other data accompanying the financial statements are presented only for supplementary analysis purposes and have been subjected to the inquiry and analytical procedures applied in the review of the basic financial statements, and the accountant did not become aware of any material modifications that should be made to such data.

Or, the accountant may elect not to assume any responsibility for the supplementary information and may inform the user of the financial statements in the following way:

> The other data accompanying the financial statements are presented only for supplementary analysis purposes and have not been subjected to the inquiry and analytical procedures applied in the review of the basic financial statements, but were compiled from information that is the representation of management, without audit or review, and the accountant does not express an opinion or any other form of assurance on such data.

The accountants, in bankruptcy court proceedings, will most likely review the supplementary information presented because of the effect this information may have on the decisions of the court, the U.S. trustee, or the creditors, or on the plan being formulated.

REPORTING ON A LIQUIDATION OF THE DEBTOR

§ 15.26   Introduction

A special type of report is required if the debtor has made a decision to file a plan of liquidation in chapter 11, has filed a chapter 7 petition, or has decided to liquidate the business without the assistance of the bankruptcy court. In an Interpretation of SAS No. 2, the staff of the Auditing Standards Board concluded that a liquidation basis of accounting may be considered generally accepted accounting principles if an entity is in liquidation or if liquidation appears imminent. Under these conditions, the auditor would issue an unqualified opinion on the liquidation statements if:

1   The liquidation basis of accounting has been properly applied.
2   Adequate disclosures are made in the financial statements.
3   The financial statements are not affected by a significant uncertainty.

An assessment of the impact that uncertainty (see item 3 above) can have on the liquidation statements may be difficult to make in some bankruptcy proceedings because of the difficulty in valuing some of the debtor's assets or segments of the business that may be sold intact as a viable, ongoing business. If the liquidation basis financial statements are going to be affected by uncertainties as to the realizability of the amounts at which the assets are presented and the amounts that creditors will agree to accept in settlement of their obligations, the auditor should consider the need to modify the report to reflect the uncertainty, as suggested in section 509.21–26 of Auditing Standards. In addition to qualifying the report as discussed above, the auditor may want to add the following sentence to the explanatory paragraph found in the reports presented:

> It is not presently determinable whether the amounts realizable from the disposition of the remaining assets or the amounts that creditors agree to accept in settlement of the obligations due them will differ materially from the amounts shown in the accompanying financial statements.

Note that, under these conditions, the report would generally be qualified because of the uncertainty concerning liquidation value of assets or concerning the amounts creditors will accept as settlement of their claim.

§ 15.27   Single-Year Report

The auditor may issue a single year's financial statement during the year the liquidation basis of accounting is adopted, or the current year's liquidation basis statements may be presented in conjunction with the going-concern statements of the prior year. The report for a single year should indicate, normally as a middle paragraph, that the debtor has changed its basis of accounting to the liquidation basis. An example of the report follows:

> We have audited the statement of net assets in liquidation of XYZ Company as of December 31, 20X2, and the related statement of changes in net assets in liquidation for the period from April 26, 20X2, to December 31, 20X2. In addition, we have audited the statements of income, retained earnings, and cash flows for the period from January 1, 20X2, to April 25, 20X2. These financial statements are the responsibility of the Company's management. Our responsibility is to express an opinion on these financial statements based on our audit.

> We conducted our audit in accordance with generally accepted auditing standards. Those standards require that we plan and perform the audit to obtain reasonable assurance about whether the financial statements are free of material misstatement. An audit includes examining, on a test basis, evidence supporting the amounts and disclosures in the financial statements. An audit also includes assessing the accounting principles used and significant estimates made by management, as well as evaluating the overall financial statement presentation. We believe that our audit provides a reasonable basis for our opinion.

> As described in Note X to the financial statements, the stockholders of XYZ Company approved a plan of liquidation on April 25, 20X2, and the company commenced liquidation shortly thereafter. As a result, the company has changed its basis of accounting for periods subsequent to April 25, 20X2 from the going-concern basis to a liquidation basis.

> In our opinion, the financial statements referred to above present fairly the net assets in liquidation of XYZ Company as of December 31, 20X2, the changes in

its net assets in liquidation for the period from April 26, 20X2, to December 31, 20X2, and the results of its operations and its cash flows for the period from January 1, 20X2, to April 25, 20X2, in conformity with generally accepted accounting principles.

§ 15.28   Comparative Financial Statements

As mentioned in the above paragraph, the debtor may present comparative financial statements for the year prior to adoption of the liquidation basis and the year subsequent to such adoption. In the explanatory paragraph to the report, the audit should indicate the change in accounting basis of the financial statements presented. A sample report that was presented in the Interpretation to SAS No. 2 follows:

> We have audited the balance sheet of XYZ Company as of December 31, 20X1, the related statements of income, retained earnings, and changes in financial position for the year then ended, and the statements of income, retained earnings, and cash flows for the period from January 1, 20X2, to April 25, 20X2. In addition, we have audited the statement of net assets in liquidation as of December 31, 20X2, and the related statement of changes in net assets in liquidation for the period from April 26, 20X2, to December 31, 20X2. These financial statements are the responsibility of the Company's management. Our responsibility is to express an opinion on these financial statements based on our audit.

> In our opinion, the financial statements referred to above present fairly the financial position of XYZ Company as of December 31, 20X1, the results of its operations and its cash flows for the year then ended and for the period from January 1, 20X2, to April 25, 20X2, its net assets in liquidation as of December 31, 20X2, and the changes in its net assets in liquidation for the period from April 26, 20X2 to December 31, 20X2, in conformity with generally accepted accounting principles applied on the bases described in the preceding paragraph.

If the auditor issues subsequent years' statements on the liquidation basis, the auditor may want to continue to put an explanatory paragraph in the report to emphasize that the financial statements are presented on a liquidation basis.

§ 15.29   Solvency Letters

CPAs have received requests from lenders, as a requisite to the closing of certain secured financing in connection with leveraged buyouts, recapitalizations, and other financial transactions, for written assurance regarding the solvency and related matters of the prospective borrower. The lenders are concerned that the financing arrangement not be considered a fraudulent transfer under the Bankruptcy Code or relevant state law. It is possible under section 548 of the Bankruptcy Code for a financing to be a fraudulent transfer if the borrower receives less than a reasonable equivalent value for the debt or for providing a security interest in its property and the borrower (1) is insolvent at the time the debt is incurred or would be rendered insolvent as a result of the transaction, (2) as a result of the transfer would be left with unreasonable small capital, or (3) as a result of the transfer would incur debts beyond its ability to pay as they mature.

If it is determined that the transfer is fraudulent, then the obligation to pay may be subordinated to the claims of other creditors and the security interest may be set aside. The Audit Standards Division of the AICPA has ruled in an Interpretation (of AU Section 2010) that the CPA may not provide any form of assurance, through examination, review, or agreed-on procedures engagements, that an entity is not insolvent at the time the debt is incurred, does not have unreasonably small capital, or has the ability to pay its debts as they mature. CPAs are also prohibited from using equivalent terms that may be defined as equivalents or substitutes for the terms listed above, such as fair salable value of assets exceeds liabilities.

Volume 2 of *Bankruptcy and Insolvency Accounting* presents, in 15.7, an example of the types of report that the accountant may issue.

§ 15.30 Reports on Prospective Financial Statements

An accountant who either (1) submits to clients or others prospective financial statements that the accountant has assembled or assisted in assembling or (2) reports on prospective financial statements, should compile, examine, or apply agreed-on procedures to the prospective financial statements, if those statements are or reasonably might be expected to be used by another (third) party. In many bankruptcy situations, the CPA may assist with forecasts or projections and, as a result, should consider the type of report to issue.

Volume 2 of *Bankruptcy and Insolvency Accounting* contains examples of five types of reports that the accountant may issue in connection with prospective financial statements. Each type is described briefly below (numbers in parentheses identify their locations in Volume 2):

- A report in which an opinion is expressed on the presentation of the projections (15.8).
- A report based on the compilation of projected financial statements (15.9).
- A report in which a client uses a computer to process the client's data (15.10).
- A disclaimer of opinion on prospective financial statements (15.11).
- A report on prospective financial statements for internal use only (15.12).

§ 15.31 Liquidation Analysis

Section 1129 of the Bankruptcy Code provides that when the creditors do not vote for the plan, but the class approves the plan, the creditors must receive as much under the plan as they would receive in a chapter 7 liquidation. As part of the disclosure statements, accountants may prepare and include a liquidation analysis to show that the creditors will receive more under the plan than under liquidation. Accountants may issue a compilation report on the liquidation analysis. For an example of a report that was issued in the Revco filing, see 11.2 of Volume 2 of *Bankruptcy and Insolvency Accounting*.

16

Tax Awareness

§ 16.1 Introduction

The income tax effect of certain transactions during the administration period and of tax assessments related to prebankruptcy periods can impose undue hardship on the bankrupt, who is already in a tenuous financial position. It is not uncommon for a bankrupt to realize substantial taxable income during the administration period, from the sale of all or part of the assets or from taxable recoveries. Net operating loss carryovers and other offsetting tax deductions are often unable to minimize the income tax effect. Therefore, in addition to ensuring that all statutory tax reporting and filing requirements are satisfied at the due dates, the accountant must be aware of those tax aspects that will permit the preservation and enlargement of the bankrupt's estate.

During the closing days of the 96th Congress, the Bankruptcy Tax Act of 1980 was passed as Public Law 96-589 and signed by President Carter on December 24, 1980. This Act eliminated a great deal of the uncertainty about handling debt forgiveness and other tax matters, because the Bankruptcy Code superseded the sections of Bankruptcy Act that contained provisions for nonrecognition of gain from debt forgiveness, and other related tax items. The Bankruptcy Code does not contain the same type of federal tax provisions. The new tax law was passed after some last-minute compromises were made. Congress adopted an amendment that delayed until January 1, 1982, the requirement that net operating losses and other tax attributes must be reduced by the amount of debt that is forgiven. The Deficit Reduction Act of 1984 contained provisions that subsequently modified the income from debt discharge provisions of section 108 of the Internal Revenue Code (I.R.C.).

The Tax Reform Act of 1986 significantly modified (1) how gain from debt discharge may be exempt from taxable income and (2) the extent to which net operating losses can now be preserved. The Technical and Miscellaneous Revenue Act of 1988 (TAMRA) modified I.R.C. section 382 and revised the rules for debt discharge by farmers. The Omnibus Budget Reconciliation Act of 1993 eliminated the stock-for-debt provision that did not require a title 11 or similar debtor to reduce tax attributes resulting from a gain on the transfer. Also, the Act expanded the attributes to be reduced under I.R.C. section 108.

The objective of this chapter is to identify items that the debtor and, to a limited extent, creditors and other interested parties should consider in developing a solution to problems faced by financially troubled companies. (For a more detailed discussion of the tax issues raised here, see Newton and Bloom's *Bankruptcy and Insolvency Taxation*, published by John Wiley & Sons and updated annually.)

NOTIFICATION OF PROCEEDINGS AND FILING OF RETURNS

§ 16.2 Notice to Governmental Agencies

Pursuant to section 6036 of the Internal Revenue Code (I.R.C.), every trustee in bankruptcy assignee for the benefit of creditors, other fiduciary, and executor must give notice of qualification to the Secretary of the Treasury or a delegated representative in the manner and within the time limit required by regulations of the Secretary or delegate.

Section 301.6036-1 of the Treasury Regulations requires that the individual in control of the assets of a debtor in any bankruptcy proceeding shall, within ten days of the date of an appointment or authorization to act, give notice in writing to the District Director of Internal Revenue for the district where the debtor is or was required to file returns. The notice shall not be required if, prior to or within ten days of the date of the fiduciary's appointment or authorization to act, any notice regarding the proceeding has been given under any provision of the Bankruptcy Code to the Secretary or other proper officer of the Treasury Department. In bankruptcy cases, Treasury Decision 8172[1] indicates that the Bankruptcy Rules requirements are sufficient and the notice need not be filed.

(a) Form of Notice

Where written notice is required, it may be made on Treasury Form 56 (Notice Concerning Fiduciary Relationship) and should include:

- The name and address of the person making such notice and the date of appointment or of taking possession of the assets
- The name, address, and employer identification number of the debtor or other person whose assets are controlled

Similar notices may be required by other governmental taxing authorities and should be filed in accordance with their prescribed procedures.

I.R.C. section 6903 requires that a fiduciary give to the Treasury Department a notice of relationship (a statement that any person is acting for another in a fiduciary capacity). This notice is filed on Treasury Form 56.

(b) Failure to Give Notice

If notice is not given as required by I.R.C. section 6036 in a situation where notification is necessary, the period of limitations on the assessment of taxes is suspended from the date the proceeding is instituted to the date notice is

---

[1] T.D. 8172 (January 1988).

received by the District Director and for an additional 30 days thereafter. However, the suspension in no case shall exceed two years.[2]

§ 16.3 Responsibility for Filing Income Tax Returns: Corporations

The receiver (under state law), trustee (under a title 11 case), or assignee having possession of or title to all or substantially all the property or business of a corporation shall file the income tax return for the corporation in the same manner and form as the corporation would be required to file the return.[3] The bankruptcy trustee, while acting on behalf of a bankrupt's estate, acts as a fiduciary. The trustee does not represent a separate taxable entity apart from the corporation. Treasury Regulations section 1.641(b)-2(b) provides that, in bankruptcy, a corporation is not a taxable entity separate from the person for whom the fiduciary is acting. Hence, income and expenses of a bankrupt corporation's trustee should be shown on the corporation's tax return. The identification number of the bankrupt corporation should be used by the trustee.[4] I.R.C. section 1399, which provides that no separate tax entity results from a corporation commencing a case under the Bankruptcy Code, was added to the Internal Revenue Code by the Bankruptcy Tax Act of 1980.

(a) Responsibility for Payment of Tax

When a tax payment is due, the person who is required to file the return is also responsible for paying the tax.[5] Thus, the trustee in bankruptcy, who is responsible for filing the corporate income tax return, must pay any tax that may be due. Failure to do so may result in personal liability on the part of the trustee. If a trustee has not been appointed, then the responsible official of the corporation operating as debtor-in-possession would be responsible.

When the bankruptcy estate is created, no tax is levied on the transfer of the debtor's assets to the estate, and there is no change in the tax basis of the assets transferred. Any gain realized on the disposition of the bankrupt's property results in an imposition of tax directly against the estate and indirectly against the creditors by the reduction of their bankruptcy dividend. Thus, the effect of bankruptcy is to shift the tax burden from the debtor to the creditors.[6]

(b) When to File a Corporate Tax Return

A corporate income tax return should be filed annually, regardless of whether the corporation has any income, as long as the corporation exists for tax purposes. A corporation in existence during any portion of the year must file a return. A corporation is not in existence after it ceases business and dissolves, retaining no assets, even though under state law it may thereafter be treated as continuing as a corporation for certain limited purposes connected

---

[2] I.R.C. § 6872; Treas. Reg. § 301.6872-1.
[3] I.R.C. § 6012(b)(3); Treas. Reg. § 1.6012-3(b)(4).
[4] Rev. Rul. 79-120, 1979-1 C.B. 382.
[5] I.R.C. § 6151(a).
[6] Sidney Krause and Arnold Kapiloff, "The Bankrupt Estate, Taxable Income, and the Trustee in Bankruptcy," *Fordham Law Review*, Vol. 34 (March 1966), p. 417.

with winding up its affairs, such as for purposes of suing and being sued.[7] If the corporation has valuable claims for which it will bring suit during this period, it has retained assets and therefore continues in existence. A corporation does not go out of existence if it is turned over to receivers or trustees who continue operations.

(c) Liquidating Trustee

The Supreme Court has held, in *Holywell Corporation v. Smith*,[8] that a liquidating trustee is required by the Internal Revenue Code to file income tax returns and pay taxes on the income attributable to the property of both the corporate debtors and an individual debtor.

Petitioner debtors (four affiliated corporate entities and Gould, an individual) filed chapter 11 bankruptcy petitions after one of them defaulted on a real estate loan. The bankruptcy court consolidated the cases and the debtors represented their own bankruptcy estates as debtors-in-possession. Creditors approved a chapter 11 plan that provided, inter alia, for placement of the debtors' property into a trust and appointment of a trustee to liquidate all of the trust property and to distribute it to the creditors of the various bankruptcy estates. The plan said nothing about whether the trustee had to file income tax returns or pay any income tax due, but the IRS did not object to the plan's confirmation. The plan took effect in October 1985. One of the corporate debtors filed a tax return for the fiscal year ending July 31, 1985, including as income capital gains earned in the postbankruptcy sale of certain properties in its estate, but requested respondent Smith, the appointed trustee, to pay the taxes owed. Neither the corporate debtors nor Smith filed income tax returns for succeeding fiscal years, in which there were capital gains and interest income. Over the objections of the IRS and the debtors, the bankruptcy court granted Smith's request for a declaratory judgment that he had no duty under the Internal Revenue Code to file income tax returns or pay income taxes. Both the district court and the court of appeals affirmed.

The Supreme Court held, however, that Smith is required by the Code to file income tax returns and pay taxes on the income attributable to the property of both the corporate debtors and Gould. The following excerpts are from the Court's decision:

(a) Smith is an "assignee" of "all" or "substantially all" of the "property . . . of a corporation" and therefore is required by section 6012(b)(3) of the Code to file returns that the corporate debtors would have filed had their property not been assigned to him. The plan transferred the corporate debtors' estates to Smith as trustee, and it is undisputed that he meets the usual definition of the word "assignee" in both ordinary and legal usage. Nothing in section 6012(b)(3) limits the definition of an "assignee" to persons who wind up a dissolving corporation or manage the day-to-day business of a distressed corporation.

(b) With respect to the income attributable to Gould's property, Smith is required by section 6012(b)(4) to make a return not, as the United States argues,

---

[7] Treas. Reg. § 1.6012-5.
[8] 112 S. Ct. 1021 (1992).

because he is the "fiduciary" of the "estate . . . of an individual," but because he is the "fiduciary" of a "trust." Since the plan declared and established a separate and distinct trust and vested the property of Gould's estate in Smith, it did not simply substitute Smith for Gould as the fiduciary of Gould's "estate." However, the trust here—which the plan described as a trust and created for the express purpose of liquidating Gould's estate and distributing it to creditors—clearly fits the description of a liquidating trust under Treas. Reg. 301.7701-4(d). Moreover, when the plan assigned the property of Gould's estate to Smith, it gave him powers consistent with the definition of "fiduciary" in section 7701(a)(6) of the Internal Revenue Code and Treas. Reg. 301.7701-6. Respondents' argument that it is Gould who must pay the trust's taxes under the Code's "grantor trust" rules is rejected. Also rejected is their contention that Smith lacked sufficient discretion in performing his duties under the plan to be a fiduciary, since the liquidating trust is a trust under the Code and Smith's duties satisfy the regulations' description of a fiduciary.

(c) Respondents also err in asserting that Smith may ignore the duties imposed by the Code because the plan does not require him to pay taxes. Section 1141(a) of the Bankruptcy Code—which states that "the provisions of a confirmed plan bind . . . any creditor"—does not preclude the United States from seeking payment of any taxes. Even if section 1141(a) binds creditors with respect to claims that arose before confirmation, it does not bind them with regard to post-confirmation claims.[9] Here, the United States is not seeking taxes due prior to Smith's appointment, but is merely asserting that Smith, after his appointment, must make tax returns in the same manner as the assignee of the property of any corporation or the trustee of any trust.

§ 16.4 Responsibility for Filing Income Tax Returns: Individual and Partnership

Whereas the procedure for corporations is well-established, much controversy existed in the past over the types of return to file for individuals and partnerships. To eliminate some of the uncertainty as to whether a separate entity was created, the Bankruptcy Tax Act added sections 1398 and 1399 to the Internal Revenue Code.

(a) Partnerships

I.R.C. section 1399 provides that no new entity is created when a case is filed by a partnership under the provisions of the Bankruptcy Code. The bankruptcy trustee would be required to file a partnership information return under I.R.C. section 6031 for the period(s) during which the trustee was operating the business. The Committee Reports indicate that it is the responsibility of the trustee to file the partnership return, although not specifically required by the statute. In a Private Letter Ruling,[10] the IRS held that a trustee of a partnership is responsible for filing Form 1065 only for the year during which the trustee was appointed and later years. No obligation exists to file Form 1065 for earlier partnership years. The trustee must, however, cooperate with the IRS by providing all relevant tax information he or she may have concerning prior years.

---

[9] *See* 11 U.S.C. § 101(10).
[10] Private Letter Ruling 8509038 (November 30, 1984).

(b) Individuals

When bankruptcy proceedings intervene into the affairs of an individual, a separate taxable entity is created:[11] the bankruptcy estate, consisting of the property belonging to the debtor before bankruptcy. After the petition has been filed, the bankruptcy estate can earn income and incur expenses. These transactions are administered by a trustee (or debtor-in-possession) for the benefit of the creditors. Concurrently, the individual debtor can also earn income, incur expenses, and acquire property, and these do not become part of the bankruptcy estate. The separate taxable entities for federal income tax purposes occur in bankruptcy cases under chapter 7 and chapter 11 of title 11 of the U.S. Code. No new taxable entity is created, however, under chapter 13 of the U.S. Code. Also, when a bankruptcy case involving an individual is dismissed by the bankruptcy court, the estate is not deemed to have been a separate taxable entity.

In cases where the individual and bankruptcy estate are separate entities, they are required to file separate returns. The estate must file Form 1041 and attach Form 1040, which is used to calculate the tax due for the estate based on the tax rates for married person filing separate return. The estate files Form 1041 (with Form 1040 attached) for the period beginning with the filing of the petition or for any subsequent year if gross income is equal to or greater than the amount of the exemption plus the basic standard deduction as required by I.R.C. section 6012(a)(9). The individual files his or her own Form 1040, as usual, and reports all income earned during the year. This includes income earned before bankruptcy proceedings, but not any income earned by the estate. I.R.C. section 6012(b)(4) requires that the fiduciary of the estate file the return. This would be the trustee, if appointed; otherwise, the debtor-in-possession must file the estate's return. A copy of Form 1041 appears as 16.1 in Volume 2 of *Bankruptcy and Insolvency Accounting.*

The new Act gives an individual debtor an election to close the taxable year as of the day before the date bankruptcy commences.[12] This election is available to individuals in either chapter 7 or chapter 11 proceedings. For a taxpayer who makes this election, the taxable year is divided into two "short" taxable years. The tax liability computed for the first short year is collectible from the bankruptcy estate. The tax is considered a liability before bankruptcy and thus payable by the estate. In the event the estate does not possess enough assets to pay the tax, the remaining liability is not discharged, but is collectible from the individual after the case.[13] This election must be made by the 15th day of the fourth month following bankruptcy, which is the due date for the return without an extension. Generally, the debtor would want to make the election for a short tax year if taxes are due as a result of income earned prior to filing the petition.

(c) Creation of a New Entity in Chapter 12

Because chapter 12 is patterned after chapter 13 and under chapter 13 no new entity is created, it might be concluded that under chapter 12 a new entity

---

[11] I.R.C. § 1398.
[12] I.R.C. § 1398(d)(3)(A).
[13] 11 U.S.C. § 523(a)(1).

is also not created. Also, I.R.C. section 1398 indicates that a new entity is created only in chapter 7 and chapter 11. However, section 1231 of the Bankruptcy Code allows the same state and local provisions for chapter 12 that apply for chapter 11. Section 1231 provides that the taxable year of the individual terminates on the date of the order for relief and that this termination marks the beginning of the tax period of the estate for state and local tax purposes. While it appears that the drafters of chapter 12 intended that the tax provisions of chapter 12 would follow chapter 11 and not chapter 13, practice suggests the opposite because section 1398 indicates that a separate estate is created only in chapters 7 and 11. The IRS has ruled that, in a chapter 12 case, a new entity is *not* created.[14]

SPECIAL RULES FOR INDIVIDUALS

§ 16.5 Introduction

With the addition of section 1398 to the Internal Revenue Code, different considerations must be given to individuals because a new estate is created when a chapter 7 or chapter 11 case is filed (see paragraph 16 of section 1398). Factors to be discussed include who—the individual or the estate—is required to report income and expense items in gross income, treatment of transfers between the debtor and the estate, carryover of the tax attribute to the estate and back to the debtor, and carryover and carryback of administration, liquidation, and reorganization expenses.

§ 16.6 Income and Deductions

I.R.C. section 1399 provides that the gross income of the estate for each taxable year includes the gross income of the debtor to which the estate is entitled under title 11 of the Bankruptcy Code. As noted in paragraph 20 of I.R.C. section 1399, this does not include any income earned by the individual prior to the commencement of the bankruptcy case. The gross income of the debtor (the individual as opposed to the estate) will include income earned prior to bankruptcy plus any item of income that is not included in the gross income of the estate.

The original bill passed by the House contained rules for dividing deductions and credits between the debtor and the estate. These provisions were subsequently modified to provide that if any item of deduction or credit of the debtor is treated under I.R.C. section 1398(e)(3) as a deduction or credit of the bankruptcy estate, that item is not allowable to the debtor.[15]

§ 16.7 Transfers between Debtor and Estate

A transfer (other than by sale or exchange) of an asset from the debtor to the estate is not treated as a disposition that would give rise to recognition of gain or loss, recapture of deductions or credits, or acceleration of income. Thus, a

---

[14] Private Letter Ruling 8928012 (April 7, 1989).
[15] S. Rep. No. 96-1035, 96th Cong. 2d Sess. 31 (1980).

transfer of an installment obligation is not treated as a disposition that would give rise to income under I.R.C. section 453(d).[16] The same provisions of nondisposition apply when assets are transferred (other than by sale or exchange) from the estate to the debtor.[17] In *In re McGowan*[18] and *In re Olson*,[19] the court held that the abandonment of property from the estate to the individual (often abandoned when there is no value in the property to the estate) is not a taxable event. Thus, the property will have the same holding period, basis, and so on, in the hands of the debtor as that of the estate at the time of the transfer. While, in *In re A.J. Lane & Co.*,[20] the bankruptcy court held that the transfer was taxable, a majority of courts have held and the Treasury has ruled[21] that such transfers are not taxable.

The following list provides several other cases that have dealt with various aspects of abandonment:

- In *In re Larry F. and Mary A. Layman*,[22] the district court would not allow the estate to abandon the property where the estate had already received $22,000 in the form of rental income before the request for abandonment.

- In the case of *In re Bentley*,[23] the Eighth Circuit held that if the property is sold and then the proceeds are subsequently abandoned the estate is responsible for the tax on the gain on the sale of the property.[24]

- In *In re Terjen*,[25] the district court held that the individual and not the bankruptcy estate was liable for taxes where the trustee abandoned property after creditors were afforded relief for the bankruptcy stay, but before a foreclosure sale was held.

- In *In re POPP*,[26] the bankruptcy court held that the trustee may only abandon property to the debtor because the debtor has a possessory interest in the assets that is superior to all third parties.

- In *In re Nevin*,[27] the bankruptcy court ordered, on motion from the IRS, the trustee to abandon to debtors their respective interests in the limited partnerships.

- Abandonment of property relates back to the inception of the case and revests title in the debtor as though the trustee never owned it.[28]

- Section 1398(f)(2) provides that in the termination of the estate, a transfer (other than by sale or exchange) of an asset of the estate from the estate to the debtor is not treated as a disposition for tax purposes. Pro-

[16] *Id.*
[17] I.R.C. § 1398(f)(2).
[18] 98 B.R. 104 (Bankr. N.D. Iowa 1988).
[19] 121 B.R. 346 (N.D. Iowa 1990); *aff'd,* unpublished opinion No. 90-2248 (8th Cir. Feb. 25, 1991).
[20] 133 B.R. 264 (Bankr. D. Mass. 1991).
[21] Treas Reg. § 1.1398-1.
[22] Civil No. 6-89-235; LEXIS, 88 TNT 240-17 (D.C. Minn. 1989).
[23] 916 F.2d 431 (8th Cir. 1990).
[24] See also *In re Perlman*, 188 B.R. 704 (Bankr. S.D. Fla. 1995).
[25] 154 B.R. 456 (E. D. Va. 1993).
[26] 166 B.R. 697 (Bankr. D. Neb. 1993).
[27] 135 B.R. 652 (Bankr. D. Hawaii, 1991).
[28] *Mason v. Commissioner*, 646 F. 2d 1309 (9th Cir. 1980).

ceeds from the sale of a claim was not considered a distribution form the
bankruptcy estate.[29]

- *In the matter of Donovan Feilmeier*[30] the bankruptcy court held that
  once property is no longer the property of the estate due to the release of
  the automatic stay in a chapter 11 case, any taxes arising from the sale of
  the debtor's property are the obligation of the debtor, not the obligation
  of the estate.

In a Private Letter Ruling,[31] the IRS reversed an earlier Private Letter[32] and
held that the estate is liable for all of the tax on the sale of property subject to
homestead exemption. A debtor had filed for bankruptcy under chapter 11 and
the case was later converted to chapter 7. The bankruptcy estate sold the
debtor's principal residence, which was subject to a $30,000 homestead exemp-
tion under California law. The IRS ruled that the gain realized on the sale of
the residence should be allocated between the estate and the debtor.

The IRS reconsidered this position and revoked it in the later Private Letter
Ruling, concluding that the estate is liable for the entire gain on the trustee's
sale of the debtor's residence and the individual is not liable for any of the tax.
The tax is an administrative expense of the estate.

Among the assets listed in the debtor's schedule of real property was the
debtor's principal residence. The debtor claimed a $30,000 homestead exemp-
tion in the residence pursuant to section 522 of the Bankruptcy Code. Under
California state law, the debtor receives this amount, free of the claims of creditors, out of the net proceeds of the sale of the residence. The trustee's sale of
the residence yielded X dollars, net of the costs of sale, and the debtor received
$30,000 out of the net proceeds as the homestead exemption amount.

The IRS noted that section 1398 of the Internal Revenue Code treats the
bankruptcy estate of an individual created in a chapter 7 or chapter 11 bankruptcy case as a separate taxable entity and provides that the transfer (other
than by sale or exchange) of an asset from the debtor to the estate is not treated
as a disposition for tax purposes, and that the estate is treated as the debtor
would be treated with respect to such asset. It should be noted that under
I.R.C. section 1398(g), the estate succeeds to the tax attributes the asset had in
the hands of the debtor, including its basis, holding period, and character.

The IRS also noted that under section 541 of the Bankruptcy Code, the
estate is comprised of all legal and equitable interests of the debtor's property,
including exempt property, and comes into being at the commencement of the
case. Section 522 of the Bankruptcy Code provides that the debtor may exempt
from property of the estate the property specified in section 522(d) or the property exempt under state law. Under California law, at the time this petition
was filed, the amount to be paid was $30,000.[33] Under California law, a home-
stead is exempt from sale if, at a court-ordered sale, the bid received at the sale

---

[29] *Susan Taylor Martin v. United States of America*, 97-2 USTC (CCH) P50,731, 80 A.F.T.R. 2d
(RIA) 6363 (E.D. La. 1977).
[30] No. BL85-2889 (Bankr. D. Nebr. Nov. 25, 1991).
[31] Private Letter Ruling 9122042 (March 4, 1991).
[32] Private Letter Ruling 9017075 (January 31, 1990).
[33] Cal. Civ. Proc. Code §§ 703.130 and 704.730 (West 1991).

does not exceed the amount of the homestead exemption plus any additional amount necessary to satisfy all liens and encumbrances on the property.[34]

The IRS noted that section 522(k) of the Bankruptcy Code provides that property that the debtor exempts under that section is not liable for payment of any administrative expense, except in cases that are not relevant here.

Two cases were referenced in support of this position. In *In re Duby*,[35] a chapter 7 bankruptcy trustee sold the debtor's real estate that was subject to an exemption and the court held "that the capital gains tax on the sale of the real property was an administrative expense under section 503(b) of the Bankruptcy Code and that pursuant to Bankruptcy Code section 522(k) could not impair the amount of the debtor's exemption. Therefore, the estate was liable for the capital gains tax on the sale of the exempt real property." The other case referenced was *In re Card*.[36]

In *Commissioner v. Bollinger*,[37] the IRS noted, the Supreme Court held that the capital gains tax on the sale of property is the tax liability of the owner of that property. The IRS concluded that, in this case, the owner of the property is the bankruptcy estate and, as a result, it is responsible for the tax.

The IRS indicated that, in states that allow the debtor a homestead exemption for the house itself (which is the case in California if the equity is less than the exemption amount), the house ceases to be property of the estate and ownership of the house revests in the debtor.[38] In situations where the property is transferred to the debtor, the debtor will be liable for the capital gains tax resulting from any subsequent sale of the house.

§ 16.8 Attribute Carryover to Estate

Under the Internal Revenue Code, the estate succeeds to the following income tax attributes of the debtor in a chapter 7 or chapter 11 case:[39]

- Net operating loss carryovers under I.R.C. section 172.
- Capital loss carryovers under I.R.C. section 1212.
- Recovery exclusion under I.R.C. section 111 (relating to bad debts, prior taxes, and delinquency amounts).
- Credit carryovers and all other items that, except for the commencement of the case, the debtor would be required to take into account with respect to any credit.
- Charitable contribution carryover under I.R.C. section 170(d)(1).
- The debtor's basis in and holding period for and the character in the debtor's hand of any asset acquired (other than by sale or exchange) from the debtor.

---

[34] *Id.*, §§ 704.720 and 704.800.
[35] 98 B.R. 126 (Bankr. D.R.I. 1989).
[36] 114 B.R. 228 (Bankr. N.D. Cal. 1990).
[37] 485 U.S. 340 (1988).
[38] See *In re Hahn*, 50 B.R. 69 (Bankr. D. Minn. 1985).
[39] I.R.C. § 1398(a).

- The debtor's method of accounting.
- Other tax attributes of the debtor to the extent provided by Treasury Regulations. For example, the Regulations could allow the estate the benefit of I.R.C. section 341 if the estate repays income the debtor received under claim of right.[40]

Two attributes were added to this list under Treas. Reg. section 1.1398-1 and -2. These regulations provide that the bankruptcy estate succeeds to the unused passive activity losses and credits under I.R.C. section 469 and to the unused losses from at-risk activities under I.R.C. section 465 of an individual debtor in a case under chapter 7 or chapter 11.

Under I.R.C. section 469, which was added to the code by the Tax Reform Act of 1986, passive activity losses and credits are disallowed and treated as deductions or credits allocable to the same activity in the next taxable year. Passive activity losses and credits are not among the attributes enumerated in I.R.C. section 1398(g) and (i).

I.R.C. section 465, added to the code by the Tax Reform Act of 1976, limits a taxpayer's deductible loss from an activity to the taxpayer's amount "at risk" (within the meaning of I.R.C. section 465(b)) in that activity. If a loss is not allowed under I.R.C. section 465, it is treated as a deduction allocable to the same activity in the next taxable year. Losses that are not allowed under I.R.C. section 465 are not among the attributes enumerated in I.R.C. section 1398(g) and (i).

§ 16.9 Attribute Carryover to Debtor

Upon termination of the estate in a chapter 7 or chapter 11 case, the debtor succeeds to the following:

- Net operating loss carryover.
- Capital loss carryover.
- Recovery exclusion.
- Credit carryover.
- Charitable contribution carryover.
- The estate's basis in and holding period for and the character in the estate's hand of any asset acquired (other than by sale or exchange) from the estate.
- Other tax attributes to the extent provided by Treasury Regulations.[41]

The unused passive activity losses and credits and the unused losses from at-risk activities will also revert back to the debtor on termination of the estate under Treas. Reg. § 1.1398-1.

---

[40] S. Rep. No. 96-1035, 96th Cong., 2d Sess. 28 (1980).
[41] I.R.C. § 1398(i).

§ 16.10 Carryback of Net Operating Losses and Other Credits Incurred Subsequent to Commencement of Case

I.R.C. section 1398(j)(2)(A) provides that, if the estate incurs a net operating loss (apart from the loss passing to the estate from the debtor, described in § 16.8), the estate can carry back its net operating loss to taxable years of the individual debtor prior to the years in which the bankruptcy proceeding commenced, as well as to previous taxable years of the estate. An individual incurring net operating losses cannot carry back these losses to the years that preceded the year in which the chapter 7 or chapter 11 case commenced. Similarly, section 1398 allows the bankruptcy estate to carry back excess credits, such as an investment tax credit, to the years prior to the commencement of the case; at the same time, it prohibits the individual from carrying back these credits to the prebankruptcy time period.

§ 16.11 Administrative Expenses

I.R.C. section 1398(h)(1) provides that any administrative expense allowed under section 503 of the Bankruptcy Code and any fees or charges assessed under chapter 123 of title 28 of the U.S. Code (court fee and costs) are deductible expenses of the estate. These expenses are allowed even though some of them may not be considered trade or business expenses. Administrative expenses are, however, subject to disallowance under other provisions, such as I.R.C. section 263 (capital expenditures), I.R.C. section 265 (expenses relating to tax-exempt interest), or I.R.C. section 275 (certain taxes), and it appears that the administrative expenses are subject to the disallowance of personal interest expense under I.R.C. section 163. With the 2 percent limitation on miscellaneous itemized deductions added by the Tax Reform Act of 1986, the amount of administrative expenses allowed could be reduced significantly if these costs are listed as itemized deductions. Administrative costs are not included in the list of exceptions to the 2 percent limitation.

Section 1398 allows any amount of administration, liquidation, and reorganization expenses not used in the current year to be carried back three years and carried forward seven years. The amount that is carried to any other taxable year is stacked after the net operating losses for that particular year. The unused administrative expenses can be carried back or carried over only to the taxable years of the estate. I.R.C. section 1398(h)(2)(D) also provides that expenses that are deductible solely because of the provision of I.R.C. section 1398(h)(1) are allowable only to the estate.

Often, administrative expenses are not paid until the end of bankruptcy proceedings, unless they were considered trade or business expenses. These costs are not deductible until paid and, frequently, there is no income during the last year of operating the estate to charge these expenses against, which means that no tax benefit is received from these expenses. To alleviate this problem, the 1986 law provided for the carryover and carryback provision.[42] Note that the restriction on carryback or carryover of administrative expenses to the estate applies only to those deductions that are allowed solely by reason of I.R.C. section 1398(h)(1). Thus, it would appear that an expense (even though it is an

---

[42] S. Rep. No. 96-1035, *supra* note 15, p. 29.

administrative expense in a bankruptcy case) that would normally be classified as an operating cost could be carried forward to the debtor, once the estate is terminated, as an item in the net operating loss carryover.

Some uncertainty exists as to how administrative expenses are classified by the bankruptcy estate on the Form 1040 that is attached to Form 1041. Items that are normally deducted, such as expenses on Schedule C, E, or F, should be handled in the normal manner. Administrative expenses that would not be allowed except for the fact that a bankruptcy petition was filed should be considered as deductions for adjusted gross income and reported as a negative value in the "Other Income" category on the front of Form 1040.

How should the estate handle payments that are made by the estate to the individual? Based on the prior discussion, it might be assumed that the payments would be either wages or income from consulting. As the result of a Private Letter Ruling,[43] there is now considerable uncertainty as to how to report these payments. The actual wording of I.R.C. section 1398(e)(3)(B) is as follows:

> *Ruling for making determinations with respect to deductions, credits, and employment taxes.* Except as otherwise provided in this section, the determination of whether or not any amount paid or incurred by the estate—
> A. is allowable as a deduction or credit under this chapter, or
> B. is wages for purposes of subtitle C,
> shall be made as if the amount were paid or incurred by the debtor and as if the debtor were still engaged in the trades and businesses, and in the activities, the debtor was engaged in before the commencement of the case.

In the same Private Letter Ruling, the IRS looked at the issue as to whether withdrawals by a debtor-in-possession are wages. In this situation, a farmer and his wife filed a chapter 11 petition. The farmer had been engaged to manage a farm for the bankruptcy estate as a debtor-in-possession as provided for in the Bankruptcy Code. As such, the bankruptcy estate treated the farmer as an employee of the estate and characterized amounts withdrawn from the estate for personal expenses as the payment of a manager's salary. The farmer requested to know whether, for federal employment tax purposes, a debtor-in-possession should be treated as an employee of the bankruptcy estate.

The IRS concluded that "[a]ccordingly, for purposes of determining whether the amounts withdrawn by you constitute wages for federal employment tax purposes, section 1398(e)(3)(B) of the Code requires such amounts to be treated as though they had been paid by you and as though you were still engaged in the business of operating your farm. Thus, we conclude that these amounts are not considered as wages paid you as an employee of the bankruptcy estate."

It might be assumed from this Private Letter Ruling that the IRS is stating that the amounts paid are not wages but distributions that are taxable to the individual and deductible by the estate, requiring Form 1099 to be filed. A careful review of the text would, however, also suggest that because the payments cannot be considered wages for employment tax purposes, they could not be considered a deduction because the same modification ("amount . . . paid . . . as if the debtor was still engaged in the trades and businesses") that applies to the wages also applies to the deduction.

---

[43] Private Letter Ruling 8728056 (April 15, 1987).

Legislative history suggests that the purpose of the modification was not to consider the issue of how wages paid to the owner are to be handled, but to deal with the problem of how to deduct expenses and handle wages if the trustee does not operate the debtor's trade or business, as shown in the following:

> Under present law, it is not clear whether certain expenses or debts paid by the trustee are deductible if the trustee does not actually operate the debtor's trade or business (and if such expenses are not incurred in a new trade or business of the estate.) To alleviate this problem, the bill provides that an amount paid or incurred by the bankruptcy estate is deductible or creditable by the estate to the same extent as that item would be deductible or creditable by the debtor had the debtor remained in the same trades, businesses, or activities after the case commenced as before and had the debtor paid or incurred such amount. The same test is applied to determine whether amounts paid by the estate constitute wages for purposes of Federal employment taxes (new Code sec 1398(e)(4)).[44]

In many cases, it would be to the advantage of the debtor to claim that amounts paid are not income (wages or a Form 1099 income item) but distributions of the assets of the estate. Often, the individual has no deductions because all of his or her property was transferred to the estate, and the individual will have to pay taxes on the income received from the estate. At the same time, the estate has the net operating losses of the individual that were acquired when the petition was filed, and does not need the wage deduction. This Private Letter Ruling might indicate that the amounts paid to the individual by the estate are withdrawals or distributions and not income. However, it is suggested here that the IRS has misapplied this section of the I.R.C. and that it will not be extended to apply to deductions as well.

§ 16.12 Change in Accounting Period

I.R.C. section 1398(j)(1) allows the estate to change its accounting period (taxable year) once without obtaining approval of the IRS, as is normally required under I.R.C. section 442. This rule allows the trustee to effect an early closing of the estate's taxable year prior to the expected termination of the estate, and then to submit a return for a "short year" for an expedited determination of tax liability as permitted under section 505 of the Bankruptcy Code.[45]

MINIMIZATION OF TAX AND RELATED PAYMENTS

There are several steps that a debtor in financial difficulty might take to reduce the cash outflow for taxes or to obtain tax refunds.

§ 16.13 Estimated Taxes

A company having financial problems may, after paying one or more installments of estimated taxes, determine that it should recompute its estimated tax liability. Downward recomputations may show that no additional payments are

---

[44] S. Rep. No. 96-1035, *supra* note 15, p. 30.
[45] *Id.*

necessary. If it is determined that too much tax was paid, a quick refund can be obtained by filing Form 4466 immediately after the taxable year ends.

§ 16.14 Prior Year Taxes

The IRS allows companies that owe taxes from the previous year to extend the time for payment to the extent that the tax will be reduced because of an expected net operating loss in the current year. This request is made on Form 1138. To obtain a quick refund of taxes previously paid, Form 1139 must be filed. This form must be filed within one year after the end of year in which the net operating loss occurred and can be filed only after Form 1120 for the loss year has been filed.

§ 16.15 Pension Funding Requirements

An employer may be able to obtain a funding waiver if it can show that substantial business hardship exists and that funding the pension would be adverse to the interests of the plan's participants in the aggregate. If the funding cannot be waived, payments may be deferred under Rev. Rul. 66-144.[46]

TREATMENT OF INCOME DURING BANKRUPTCY PERIOD

§ 16.16 Income Required to Be Reported

Generally, it is not thought that income would be a consideration during bankruptcy proceedings because insufficient profits have contributed to the insolvency. However, during the administration of the estate, transactions may occur that generate taxable income. Any income derived from the sale or operation of the debtor's assets must be reported as it is earned.

There may be many sources of income to a bankruptcy estate. Proceeds will be received from the sale or liquidation of assets. Rental income may be realized from real estate owned; royalties from patents or dividends from securities may be received; and interest may be accumulated on savings and other deposits of the debtor (or the trustee, who may deposit the bankruptcy estate's funds). In addition, if a debtor is solvent and not in a chapter 11 proceeding, then income will be recognized to the extent of the debts forgiven. An election cannot now be made to reduce the basis of assets.

§ 16.17 Deductions Allowed

In the determination of taxable net income, the trustee is allowed certain deductions. Most common are:

- The costs of administration in general.
- The costs of administration directly associated with the production of

---

[46] 1966-1 C.B. 91. See Rev. Rul. 84-18, 1984-1 C.B. 88.

income by the estate, provided that they are construed as ordinary and necessary business expenses.

- Payments made to priority and general unsecured creditors if such distributions are allocable to the debt associated with an item that would have been deductible by the bankrupt. It is necessary to realize, however, that debtors using an accrual basis may have already deducted the expense while actual payment is made by the trustee.
- Payments for priority tax claims incurred before filing the petition, which therefore would have been deductible by the debtor if paid prior to bankruptcy.
- Net operating loss carryovers.[47]

The taxpayer must, however, be very careful in deducting the general cost of administration. For example, the IRS stated in Rev. Rul. 77-204[48] that expenses connected with a reorganization are generally not deductible under I.R.C. section 162 because they are capital expenditures that will benefit the corporation in future years. However, all costs necessary to operate the business are deductible under I.R.C. section 162 in the same manner and to the extent they would have been had the bankruptcy proceeding not been instituted. A significant amount of professional fees is paid for help in operating the business profitably and not solely to reorganize the business. This ruling also held that, in a liquidation, the expenses incurred in connection with the sale of assets are not deductible under I.R.C. section 162, but must be offset against the proceeds of the sale in determining the gain or loss on the transaction.

There continues to be controversy over the extent to which the debtor can deduct administrative expenses. In general, costs incurred to defend the business are deductible under I.R.C. section 162.[49] Costs that provide long-term benefits must be capitalized, such as legal costs and officers' time incurred in friendly acquisition.[50] In Revenue Ruling 99-23[51] the IRS outlines its position in regard to an acquisition that might be considered startup costs. Costs incurred in a general search for, or an investigation of, an active trade or business in order to determine whether to enter a new business or which business to enter are eligible for amortization under I.R.C. section 195. Costs incurred in an attempt to acquire a specific business are acquisition costs subject to the capitalization rules under I.R.C. section 263. Applying these concepts to a chapter 11 reorganization, it would appear that legal fees related to the restructuring that provides long-term benefits should be capitalized under I.R.C. section 263.

§ 16.18 Discharge of Debts

One major source of income in most bankruptcy and insolvency proceedings comes from debt cancellation. I.R.C. section 61 lists discharge of debts as

---

[47] P.B. Chabrow, "Estates in Bankruptcy: Return Requirements, Rules Concerning Income and Deductions," *Journal of Taxation*, Vol. 31 (December 1969), pp. 365–66.

[48] Rev. Rul. 77-204, 1977-1 C.B. 40.

[49] *A. E. Staley Manufacturing Co. v. Commissioner*, 119 F.3d 482 (7th Cir. 1997), *rev'g* 105 T.C. 166 (1995).

[50] *Norwest Corporation v. Commissioner*, 112 T.C. No. 9 (1999).

[51] 1999-20 IRB 1.

one of the items subject to tax, and Treas. Reg. section 1.61-12(a) provides that the discharge of indebtedness may in whole or in part result in the realization of income. Taxable income, however, is not realized if a stockholder of a corporation cancels a debt that is owed without consideration. The amount canceled results in an additional contribution to capital by the stockholder who canceled the debt.

In selecting the form of financial relief, a debtor should consider the tax factors related to a gain on debt forgiveness. The rules for out-of-court proceedings are different from those for proceedings under the Bankruptcy Code.

In drafting the new bankruptcy tax law, one unresolved issue was how to handle the income from discharge of debt. If the income is taxed, it places a greater burden on the creditors, who are already, in most cases, receiving less than 100 percent of their claims. The amount going for taxes will reduce the amount creditors would receive. As initially passed by the House, H.R. 5043 provided that the gain from discharge of debt could be used to offset net operating losses and other tax credit carryovers (including the reduction of basis). An option was available: the debtor could elect to reduce the basis of depreciable property rather than reduce net operating loss carryovers. A compromise was reached—a delay for one year of the requirement to reduce net operating losses.

The Bankruptcy Tax Act amended I.R.C. section 108 to apply to bankruptcy proceedings as well as to out-of-court debt settlements. Prior to this amendment, I.R.C. section 108 applied only to discharge of debt out of court, and discharge of debt in bankruptcy proceedings was a part of the Bankruptcy Act. The Bankruptcy Code, however, contained no federal tax provisions for discharge of debt.

The amended I.R.C. section 108 provides that income from discharge of debt can be excluded from gross income under either one of the following conditions:

1   The discharge occurs in a Bankruptcy Code case.
2   The discharge occurs when the taxpayer is insolvent.[52]
3   The discharge occurs when the taxpayer is a solvent farmer.
4   The discharge occurs from qualified real property business indebtedness.

The amount excluded because of insolvency provisions, however, cannot exceed the amount by which the debtor is insolvent. Thus, in an out-of-court settlement where the debt outstanding is $10 million, the fair market value of the assets is $7 million, and $4 million of indebtedness is discharged, $3 million would fall under condition 2 (insolvent debtor) above and $1 million would be income.

In a 1944 Tax Court decision,[53] it was held that there was a gain on sale of property only to the extent that the debtor was insolvent after the transfer. The IRS, in a revised action on decision, has nonacquiesced the decision of the Tax Court in this case, on the grounds that insolvency of the taxpayer is irrelevant to income that is not discharge of indebtedness and that there is a gain in the full amount of the difference between the adjusted basis of the property and the fair market value of the property. The IRS in this action is also restating the

---

[52] I.R.C. § 108(a)(1).
[53] Texas Gas Distribution Co., 3 T.C. 57 (1944).

position that it has taken for some time now: a gain from debt discharge or transfer of property is determined by examining the nature of the transaction and not by looking at the solvency or insolvency of the taxpayer.

Once the nature of the gain is determined—transfer or debt discharge—the tax consequence of the gain is assessed. If the gain is from debt discharge, I.R.C. section 108 provides guidance as to how this gain is taxed, which depends on the solvency or insolvency of the taxpayer and on whether the taxpayer is in bankruptcy. If the gain is not from debt discharge but is capital gain or ordinary income from a sale or transfer of property, then the solvency, insolvency, or bankruptcy status of the debtor is generally irrelevant in determining the tax consequence of the transaction.

A modification of the debt generally does not have any tax impact, but an exchange may have adverse tax consequences. Normally, a modification involves altering the interest rate or the maturity date. However, the distinction between a modification and an exchange is not always clear. In Rev. Rul. 73-160 (1973-1 C.B. 365), the IRS held that an extension of the maturity date and subordination does not constitute an exchange. Also, an extension of the term and an increase in the interest rate on an installment debt is not a disposition of the debt under I.R.C. section 453, according to Rev. Rul. 68-419 (1968-2 C.B. 196: but see, Rev. Rul. 57-535, 1957-2 C.B. 513, and Rev. Rul. 73-160, 1973-1 C.B. 365, for a different position). The IRS ruled in Rev. Rul. 55-429 (1955-2 C.B. 252) that a reduction in the principal was not a disposition. In another ruling (Rev. Rul. 82-122, 1982-C.B. 80), the IRS held that a transfer to a third party or a change in the form of the note was a modification and not an exchange. Furthermore, according to the IRS, an increase in the interest rate that the parties bargained for is not a material change in the obligation. However, there is a limit, and in Rev. Rul. 82-188 (1982-2 C.B. 90) the IRS stated that modification of an installment note convertible into stock to increase the principal amount and to eliminate the conversion right was a disposition.

Generally, there will be no gain or loss because of debt modifications. Income from debt discharge will be recognized, however, to the extent the principal is reduced. In the case of an exchange of debt where the principal of the new is less than the principal of the old, income from debt discharge will be recognized. Original issue discount (OID) will be created if interest is less than rates under I.R.C. section 1274 and, if applicable, the imputed interest provisions of I.R.C. section 483 will be applied to the new debt to determine its adjusted principal amount.

In *Cottage Savings*,[54] the Supreme Court rejected the IRS's argument that there was a material modification because of an economic analysis and instead held that a material modification existed because the holder of the properties enjoyed legal entitlements that were materially different in kind and extent. *Cottage Savings* involved the exchange of mortgage portfolios by two savings and loan associations. This case has added considerable uncertainty as to what will now be considered a material modification. For example, changes to collateral might, under *Cottage Savings*, be considered a material modification or exchange.

An issue in many real estate workouts is whether the conversion of debt from nonrecourse to recourse or vice versa is a material modification. As noted above,

---

[54] 11 S. Ct. 1503 (1991).

a change in the collateral according to Rev. Rul. 73-160 was not considered a material modification. If the conversion is from recourse to nonrecourse, it might be argued that income from debt discharge should be realized to the extent that the debt exceeds the fair market value of the collateral. To claim this difference as income, it would appear that the IRS would have to show that the parties to the adjustment did not expect repayment. There was some concern that the IRS might use an anti-abuse argument to claim that, if the new or modified debt instrument is nonrecourse, the issue price of the new instrument should not exceed the fair market value of the debt instrument that was eliminated. Income from debt discharge would result if the value of the original debt instrument was less than the balance. The IRS has not taken this position as indicated in Proposed Treas. Reg. section 1.1274-4(g)(2)(iv), which provides that a potentially abusive situation does not include an exchange of a nonrecourse debt instrument for an outstanding debt instrument and a modification of a nonrecourse debt instrument treated as an exchange under Proposed Treas. Reg. section 1.1274-1(c).

Although a recourse–nonrecourse modification of a debt instrument may not result in income from debt discharge for a debtor partnership and eventually for the partner, the modification may result in a recognized gain for the individual partner. For example, if the modification alters the allocation of the debt between partners under I.R.C. section 752, gain may be recognized.

The Revenue Reconciliation Act of 1990 repealed I.R.C. section 1275(a)(4), which had provided that, if any debt instrument is issued in a reorganization in exchange for any other debt instrument and the issue price of the new debt instrument is less than the adjusted issue price of the old debt instrument, then the issue price of the new debt instrument shall be treated as equal to the adjusted issue price of the old debt instrument.

I.R.C. section 108(e)(11), as revised by the Revenue Reconciliation Act of 1990, provides that income will be created from debt discharge to the extent of the excess of the adjusted issue price of the old debt over the issue price of the new debt. In the case of exchanges of publicly traded debt, the issue price for the new debt will be its fair market value. The fair value will be determined under the rules of I.R.C. section 1273, resulting in a gain on debt discharge if the issue price of the new instrument is less than the adjusted issue price of the old debt. Under prior rules of I.R.C. section 1275(a)(4), no gain would be recognized. For debt instruments subject to interest on deferred payments under I.R.C. section 483 (rather than I.R.C. section 1274), the issue price, determined under I.R.C. section 1273(b)(4), is reduced to exclude unstated interest for purposes of determining income from cancellation of indebtedness.

If the new debt is not publicly traded, then its issue price would be its stated principal amount, unless it does not bear adequate stated interest, in which case the face amount would be discounted by the applicable federal rate as set forth in I.R.C. section 1274.

The IRS's effort to repeal I.R.C. section 1275(a)(4) increased significantly after the decision in _LTV_[55] by Judge Liftland. The OID rules were applied in determining the amount of the claim for bankruptcy purposes and resulted in the change being added to the 1990 tax legislation.

---

[55] _In re Chateaugay Corp._, 109 B.R. 51 (Bankr. S.D.N.Y. 1990), _reversed, LTV Corp. v. Valley Fidelity Bank & Trust Co._, 961 F.2d 378 (2d Cir. 1992).

It should be realized that these rules will apply to all cases where an old debt instrument is exchanged by the holder for a new debt instrument or in situations where the terms of the old instrument are modified to such an extent that they constitute an exchange.

The House Ways and Means Committee Report,[56] H.R. 5835, contains the following example to illustrate the exchange of public trade debt:

> A corporation issued for $1000 a bond that provided for annual coupon payments based on a market rate of interest. The bond is publicly traded. Some time later, when the old bond is worth $600, the corporation exchanges the old bond for a new bond that has a stated redemption price at maturity of $750. The exchange is treated as a realization event under section 1001. Under the bill, the new bond will have an issue price of $600 (the fair market value of the old bond) and deductible OID of $150 ($750 stated redemption price at maturity less $600 issue price) and the corporation will have COD of $400 ($1000 adjusted issue price of the old bond less $600 issue price of the new bond). Such results will occur whether or not the exchange qualifies as a reorganization.

(a) Bankruptcy or Insolvency Cases

Although the amount of debt discharged is not considered income, I.R.C. section 108(b) provides that the following tax attributes are to be reduced in the order listed (but see the election to reduce basis, item 5 below):

1 *Net operating losses.* Any net operating loss for the taxable year of discharge and any net operating loss carryover to the year of discharge.

2 *Research credit and general business credit.* Any carryover to or from the taxable year of discharge of a credit under the following I.R.C. sections:

   Section 30 (relating to credit for increasing research activities).

   Section 38[57] (relating to general business credit).

3 *Minimum tax credit.* Any minimum tax credit available under I.R.C. section 53(b) at the beginning of the taxable year immediately after discharge.

4 *Capital loss carryovers.* Any capital loss for the taxable years of the discharge and any capital loss carryover to the year of discharge under I.R.C. section 1212.

5 *Basis reduction.* The debtor's property reduced according to the provisions of I.R.C. section 1017, but not below liabilities immediately after discharge.

6 *Passive activity loss and credit carryovers.* Any passive activity loss or credit carryover of the taxpayer, under I.R.C. section 469(b), from the taxable year of the discharge.

7 *Foreign tax credit carryovers.* Any carryover to or from the taxable year of discharge of the credit allowed under Code section 33.[58]

---

[56] H.R. Rep. No. 810, 101st Cong., 2d Sess. 355 (1990).

[57] Any portion of a carryover that is attributable to the employee plan credit (within the meaning of I.R.C. § 48(o)(3)) is not considered in applying the provisions of I.R.C. § 108.

[58] I.R.C. § 108(b)(2).

Items 3 and 6 are effective for debt discharged in taxable years beginning after December 31, 1993.

The foreign tax credit carryover was added by the Senate to H.R. 5043 as originally passed by the House. Notice that this credit is reduced only after the basis of property is reduced. Also, the foreign tax credit and other credit carryovers (items 2 and 3, and passive activity credit in item 6 above) are reduced 33⅓ cents for each dollar of debt canceled. All other reductions are dollar-for-dollar.[59] The reductions are to be made after the determination of the tax for the year of discharge. For net operating and capital losses, the reductions shall be made first from the losses for the taxable year and then from the loss carryovers in the order of the taxable years for which the losses arose. The reduction of tax credits is to be made in the order the carryovers are considered for the taxable year of the discharge.[60]

Under situations where I.R.C. section 382 applies, the net operating loss remains even though it may not be possible to use all of it because of the restrictions of I.R.C. section 382(b)(1). However, under the bankruptcy exception, if I.R.C. section 382(1)(5) applies, then the net operation loss carryover that is reduced because of the adjustments required by I.R.C. section 382(1)(5) is not carried forward and would not be available to absorb future income from debt discharge that may arise when the corporation is in bankruptcy or is insolvent. The adjustments are interest earned during the past three years and 50 percent of the gain on the exchange of stock for debt for which tax attributes were not reduced because of the stock-for-debt exception. Under the revisions to I.R.C. section 382(1)(5) by the Omnibus Budget Reconciliation Act of 1993, the reduction originating from the stock-for-debt exception is no longer necessary because the exception was repealed for transactions after December 31, 1994, except for title 11 or similar cases filed before January 1, 1994.

(i) Election to Reduce Basis First   I.R.C. section 108(b)(5) allows the debtor to elect to apply any portion of the reduction required due to debt discharge to the reduction of the basis of depreciable property. The amount of the reduction cannot, however, exceed the aggregate adjusted basis of depreciable property held by the taxpayer as of the beginning of the first taxable year subsequent to the taxable year of discharge. This eliminates the reduction in the basis of property that was sold during the year of the discharge, as was allowed under prior law.

(b) Alternative Minimum Tax

I.R.C. section 56(g)(4)(B) provides that income from debt discharge under I.R.C. section 108 is not to be considered in determining the difference between adjusted current earnings of the corporation and the AMTI for purposes of calculating the alternative minimum tax.

A corporation with a net operating loss may still be required to pay an alternative minimum tax because only 90 percent of the net operating loss may be used in determining AMTI.

---

[59] I.R.C. § 108(b)(3).
[60] I.R.C. § 108(b)(4).

§ 16.19   Debt Discharge by Farmers

The Tax Reform Act of 1986 contained a special provision for handling debt discharge by farmers. I.R.C. section 108(g) provided that income from debt discharge by solvent farmers was to be handled as if the farmers were insolvent. Thus, tax attributes including the basis of property were reduced. Special rules applied to the procedure to follow in reducing property.

TAMRA of 1988 significantly changed the impact debt discharge can have on solvent farmers. To the extent that a farmer is insolvent or if the farmer has filed a bankruptcy petition, the rules for insolvent or bankrupt debtors would apply. Thus, these provisions apply only to out-of-court settlements where the farmer is solvent at the time debt is discharged or to the extent the farmer becomes solvent as a result of debt being discharged. The amount of income from debt discharge that can be excluded by a farmer who is solvent or becomes solvent as a result of debt being discharged, is limited. I.R.C. section 108(g)(3) states that the amount excluded cannot exceed the sum of tax attributes plus the aggregate adjusted basis of qualified property held by the taxpayer as of the beginning of the taxable year following the year in which the discharge occurred.

Tax attributes and the basis of qualified property are determined after any adjustments are made because of the insolvency of the farmer. Qualified property means any property used or held for use in a trade or business or for the production of income. Thus, the farmer would not be able to reduce the basis of personal use property, including the basis of the farmers' house.

I.R.C. section 108(b)(2) provides that the following tax attributes are to be reduced in the order listed:

1 Net operating losses carryover
2 General business credit carryover
3 Minimum tax credit under I.R.C. section 53(b)
4 Capital loss carryover
5 Basis reduction
6 Passive activity losses or credits
7 Foreign tax credit carryover

I.R.C. section 1017(b)(4) was modified by the TAMRA of 1988 to provide that, to the extent that qualified farm indebtedness is discharged, basis reduction that may be necessary because of the provisions of I.R.C. section 108(b)(2)(D) (basis reduction) shall be applied only to reduce the basis of qualified property in the following order:

1 Depreciable property
2 Land used or held for use in farming
3 Other qualified property

This reduction is to be made only after all other tax attributes (net operating losses, business credits, capital loss, and foreign tax credits) have been reduced.

For the special debt discharge provisions to apply, the debt must be qualified farm indebtedness. I.R.C. section 108(g)(2) provides that indebtedness will be qualified farm indebtedness if (1) the debt was incurred directly in connection with the operation by the taxpayer of the trade or business of farming and (2) 50 percent or more of the aggregate gross receipts of the taxpayer for the three taxable years immediately prior to the year the discharge occurred is attributable to the trade or business of farming. The TAMRA of 1988 makes it clear that the test is to be applied by dividing the gross receipts from farming for the three-year period by the farmer's gross receipts from all sources for the same period. The Tax Reform Act of 1986 uses the phrase "average annual gross receipts," which created some confusion as to its meaning.

For these debt discharge provisions to apply, the discharge must be made by a qualified person. A qualified person is one who is regularly engaged in the business of lending money, is not in any way related to the farmer, does not receive a fee with respect to the taxpayer's investment in the property, and was not the person from whom the farmer acquired the property. A federal, state, or local government or agency or instrumentality is a qualified person.

I.R.C. section 108(g) still provides some special relief to farmers who have a substantial amount of debt that is discharged out of court: income from debt discharge will not be taxed when the farmer becomes solvent, provided there still exists basis in property that can be reduced. However, many farmers have a very low basis in their property, especially land, and as a result may have a large tax liability resulting from the debt discharged. To avoid this liability, the farmer may find it necessary to at least consider the option of filing a bankruptcy petition.

The change in rules for debt discharge of farming indebtedness applies to discharges occurring after April 9, 1986, in tax years ending after that date.

§ 16.20   Cancellation of Real Property Business Indebtedness

The Omnibus Budget Reconciliation Act of 1993 allows individuals, partnerships, S corporations, and fiduciaries to exclude from gross income gain due to the discharge of qualified real property business indebtedness. Qualified real property business indebtedness is indebtedness that (1) is incurred or assumed in connection with real property used in a trade or business and (2) is secured by the real property. Qualified real property business indebtedness does not include qualified farm indebtedness. However, special rules under I.R.C. section 108(g) allow solvent farmers to make the election to reduce tax attributes. Debt incurred or assumed by the taxpayer after December 31, 1992, will qualify only if it was incurred or assumed in connection with the acquisition, construction, reconstruction, or substantial improvement of real property, or to finance the amount of any qualified real property business indebtedness.

The amount that is excluded cannot exceed the excess of the outstanding principal of the debt just prior to discharge over the fair market value of the business property that is the security for the debt. For the purposes of determining the fair market value of the property, the fair market value of the property is reduced by the outstanding principal amount of any other debt secured by the property.

Reduction in the basis of depreciable property may not exceed the adjusted basis of the depreciable real estate held by the taxpayer immediately before the discharge, determined after any reductions that might be required under I.R.C.

section 108(b) and (g). The basis is determined as of the first day of the next taxable year—or earlier, if the property is disposed of after the discharge occurs and before the end of the taxable year. Thus, basis in property other than the property that secures the debt that was discharged may be reduced under this provision. To some extent, this new legislation codifies the ruling in *Fulton Gold Corp. v. Commissioner.*[61] Fulton Gold held that the reduction of a nonrecourse debt was not income from debt discharge but should rather be reflected in basis reduction.

Consider the following example involving an S corporation that owns a building with a fair market value of $600,000 and a basis of $500,000. The building is pledged as security for a first mortgage for $530,000 and a second mortgage for $150,000. The corporation settles the second mortgage for a payment of $50,000 and has $100,000 of cancellation of debt income. If the debtor so elects, it may exclude from income $80,000—the amount by which the second mortgage exceeds the value of the property less the outstanding principal of any other debt securing the property [$150,000 − ($600,000 − $530,000)]. The basis of the property will be reduced by the amount of income from debt discharge that is excluded from current income, or $420,000 ($500,000 − $80,000). The corporation will be required to report as income $20,000 of the $100,000 of gain realized from debt discharge.

§ 16.21   Basis Adjustment

As noted above, there are three conditions under which the debtor may elect or be required to reduce the basis in assets:

1 Under I.R.C. section 108(b)(5), the debtor can elect to apply the gain from discharge to depreciable property before reducing net operating losses, capital losses, or other credits.
2 Under I.R.C. section 108(b)(2)(D), the debtor (whether in bankruptcy or insolvent) is required to reduce the basis in property if net operating and capital loss carryovers and certain tax credits do not absorb these losses.
3 Under I.R.C. section 108(g), an out-of-court solvent farmer debtor is required to reduce the basis of depreciable property after all other attributes have been reduced.

Treas. Reg. 1.1017-1, effective October 22, 1998, provides the general rules for basis reduction under I.R.C. section 108. The order of reduction under I.R.C. section 108(b)(2)(D) for COD income from debtors in bankruptcy or to the extent debtors in out-of-court settlements are insolvent is as follows:

1 Real property used in a trade or business or held for investment, other than real property described in section 1221(1), that secured the discharged indebtedness immediately before the discharge
2 Personal property used in a trade or business or held for investment, other than inventory, accounts receivable, and notes receivable, that secured the discharged indebtedness immediately before the discharge

[61] 31 B.T.A. 519 (1934).

3 Remaining property used in a trade or business or held for investment, other than inventory, accounts receivable, notes receivable, and real property described in section 1221(1)

4 Inventory, accounts receivable, notes receivable, and real property described in section 1221(1)

5 Property not used in a trade or business nor held for investment.

In the case of a reduction under I.R.C. section 108(b)(5) where the debtor makes the election to reduce first the basis of depreciable property, the basis reduction is to be made in the following order:

1 Depreciable real property used in a trade or business or held for investment, other than real property described in section 1221(1), that secured the discharged indebtedness immediately before the discharge

2 Depreciable personal property used in a trade or business or held for investment that secured the discharged indebtedness immediately before the discharge

3 Remaining depreciable property used in a trade or business or held for investment other than real property described in section 1221(1)

4 Real property described in section 1221(1) provided an election is made under section 108(f) to treat real property described in section 1221(1) as depreciable property

In the case of the reduction of the basis of qualified real property business indebtedness, the order of reduction is as follows:

1 Depreciable real property used in a trade or business or held for investment, other than real property described in section 1221(1), that secured the discharged indebtedness immediately before the discharge

2 Remaining depreciable property used in a trade or business or held for investment other than real property described in section 1221(1)

For the basis reductions under section 108(c) that deal with qualified real property business indebtedness, a taxpayer must reduce the adjusted basis of the qualifying real property to the extent of the discharged qualified real property business indebtedness before reducing the adjusted bases of other depreciable real property. The term *qualifying real property* means real property with respect to which the indebtedness is qualified real property business indebtedness within the meaning of section 108(c)(3).

The order for reduction of property of solvent farmers was discussed in § 16.19. In all cases, the reduction will take place on the first day of the taxable year following the year the discharge took place. The reduction of basis and other tax attributes is made on Form 982, a copy of which is in 16.2 of Volume 2 of *Bankruptcy and Insolvency Accounting.*

(a) Limitation on Deduction

The basis reduction for a bankruptcy case or an insolvent debtor is limited in that the amount of reduction cannot exceed the total of basis of the debtor's property over the total liabilities immediately after the discharge. This limitation does not apply if the debtor elected to first reduce the basis in property under I.R.C. section 108(b)(5).

(b) Individual's Estate

I.R.C. section 108(c)(7) provides that the basis adjustments, along with other attribute reductions due to debt discharge, are to be made by the estate as the taxpayer and not the individual. Thus, the election to reduce depreciable property and not tax attributes will be made by the trustee or debtor-in-possession. Basis adjustment is to be made as of the first day of the taxable year following the discharge. For example, consider a case where the estate files its final return for a period ending on September 15, 20XX, and basis adjustment is required. Should the individual reduce property as of September 16, 20XX—the beginning of a new taxable year of the estate (if it was required to file a return)—or as of January 1, 20XX—the first day of the individual's taxable year? The Senate Report[62] indicated that if basis reduction is required because of debt discharge in the final year of the bankruptcy estate, the reduction is to be made in the basis of assets acquired by the debtor from the estate and at the time acquired. Thus, it would appear that, in the example above, the basis should be reduced as of September 16, 20XX, and cannot include reduction of other property held by the debtor on September 16, 20XX. I.R.C. section 1017(c)(1) specifically states that basis of exempt property cannot be reduced. Attribute reductions other than basis reduction are to be made by the trustee or debtor-in-possession in the taxable year in which the discharge occurred.

(c) Recapture: Sections 1245 and 1250

I.R.C. section 1017(d) provides that any gain on subsequent disposition of reduced-basis property is subject to the recapture provisions of I.R.C. sections 1245 and 1250 (depreciable real property). The amount of reduction is treated as depreciation for the purpose of these sections, and the straight-line depreciation calculation under section 1250 is made as if there had been no reduction in basis resulting from debt forgiveness.

(d) Recapture: Investment Tax Credit

I.R.C. section 1017(c)(2) states that a reduction in basis is not considered a disposition of property. Thus, it will now not be necessary to recapture investment credit resulting from basis reduction.

Under prior law, if the basis of property on which investment tax credit was claimed was reduced because of debt cancellation, the credit was recaptured as if part of the property were disposed.[63] In Rev. Rul. 74-184,[64] the IRS held that a basis reduction, as a result of an election under I.R.C. sections 108 and 1017, amounted to the settlement of a claim for less than its fair value and in fact

---

[62] *Supra* note 15, p. 14.
[63] Treas. Reg. § 1.47-2(c)(1); Rev. Rul. 72-248, 1972-1 C.B. 16; Rev. Rul. 74-184, 1974-1 C.B. 8.
[64] *Id.*

was a disposition of property to the extent of the reduction. The ruling was questioned, especially where the debt reduction was unrelated to the cost of property, because the reduction in basis served only as a way authorized by Congress to postpone the taxability of income.

§ 16.22 Debt Discharge by Partnerships

Under I.R.C. section 108(d), the provisions applicable to the discharge of debt in a bankruptcy case or an out-of-court situation involving an insolvent debtor are to be applied at the partner level. The tax law in I.R.C. section 1017(b)(3)(c) provided that a partnership's interest in any partnership (whether or not that partnership's debt was discharged) may be treated as a depreciable asset only if there is a corresponding reduction in the partnership's basis in depreciable property with respect to such partner. The amount and nature of the reduction in the partner's basis in the partnership interest and in the assets of the partnership are to be determined by Treasury Regulations.

If a partner receives money from the partnership under an obligation to repay the money, this is a loan and not a distribution of property. If the partnership subsequently cancels the partner's debt, Treas. Reg. section 1.731-1(c)(2) requires the partner to realize income from debt discharge. In a liquidation of a partnership, the taxpayer must be able to present evidence that part of the amount received was related to debt canceled, in order to claim the income on liquidation was from debt discharge.[65]

§ 16.23 Debt Discharge by S Corporations

I.R.C. 108(d)(7) provides that debt discharged by an S corporation is reported at the corporate level if the S corporation is in bankruptcy or is insolvent (or to the extent that the S corporation is insolvent). Thus, income for the cancellation of debt is not recognized at the shareholder level. There is considerable uncertainty as to the impact of income from debt discharge on the basis of the stock in the S corporation. Most commentators have argued that the base is increased by the amount of the debt discharged. However, the IRS, in private letter rulings, has held that the shareholder did not get a stepped-up basis.[66]

§ 16.24 Exchange of Stock for Debt

The general rule developed by the courts where the exchange of stock for debt does not require the recognition of income was followed in I.R.C. section 108(e) of the Bankruptcy Tax Act of 1980 as it was finally approved. In addition to the fact that no income is recognized, the debtor was not required to reduce attributes. Also, this provision applied to all debts even though not evidenced by a security. The Deficit Reduction Act of 1984 codified the general rules developed by case law and restricted the exclusion to title 11 cases and to insolvent debtors. I.R.C. section 108(e) was amended to provide that, for purposes of determining income of a debtor from discharge of indebtedness, if a

---

[65] See Jack E. Zager, T.C. Memo. 1987-107.
[66] Private Letter Rulings 9423003 (Feb. 28, 1994) and 9541006 (July 5, 1995).

debtor corporation transfers stock to a creditor in satisfaction of its indebtedness, such corporation was treated as having satisfied the indebtedness with an amount of money equal to the fair market value of stock. In the case of a debtor in a title 11 case or to the extent the debtor is insolvent, the gain from the cancellation of debt was not included in taxable income and tax attributes were not reduced. Solvent corporations (fair market value of assets exceeds the amount of liabilities) are required to recognize income from debt discharge on an exchange of stock for debt.

The Omnibus Budget Reconciliation Act of 1993 repeals the exception that allowed any gain on the exchange of stock for debt to not be considered income and did not require the reduction of tax attributes for title 11 cases and out-of-court workout to the extent of the debtor's insolvency. As a result of this change, debtors will be required to reduce tax attributes, including net operating losses, to the extent that the basis of the debt exchange for stock exceeds the value of the stock and other consideration given. The revisions delete I.R.C. section 108(e)(10) and modify I.R.C. section 108(e)(8) to eliminate the *de minimis* rules and provide that, in the exchange of stock for debt, debt is satisfied with an amount of money equal to the fair market value of the stock. The repeal is effective for discharge occurring after December 31, 1994, except for title 11 and similar cases filed prior to January 1, 1994.

I.R.C. section 108 provides that, if the creditor receives stock for debt that was previously written off as an ordinary bad debt deduction, subsequent gain on the sale of the stock would be ordinary income to the extent of the loss previously taken. For example:

> Assume that corporation A made a $1,000 short-term loan to corporation B on July 1, 1980, and that corporation A, for its taxable year 1982, takes an $800 deduction for partially worthless bad debt under Code section 166(a). Assume further that on March 1, 1983, B satisfies the principal of the debt with B stock worth $500, resulting in a gain to A of $300. If A later disposes of the B stock for $1,500, $500 of A's gain will be treated as ordinary income ($800 bad debt deduction less $300 gain on receipt of the stock). In addition, if the stock is disposed of in a tax-free transaction (for example, by reason of secs. 354 or 1306), the potential recapture will carry over to the stock received.[67]

If the taxpayer is on a cash basis, any amount not taken into account by the method of accounting used is to be handled as a bad debt deduction.

§ 16.25 Purchase-Money Debt Reduction

When the debt arises out of the purchase of property, the discharge may be treated as a reduction of the purchase price. To be treated this way, the case must not be a chapter 11 case or the purchaser must not be insolvent; the reduction would otherwise be treated as income to the purchaser from a discharge of debt.

The Revenue Reconciliation Act of 1993 added new I.R.C. section 108(a)(1)(D). The new provision permits individuals and S corporations who own troubled business real estate to defer the tax that would otherwise be payable upon dis-

---

[67] S. Rep. No. 96-1035, *supra* note 15, p. 18.

charge of their indebtedness until they dispose of the related property. More precisely, the provision permits taxpayers other than C corporations to elect to exclude from gross income the income from a discharge, after December 31, 1992, of qualified real property business indebtedness. Indebtedness is "qualified real property indebtedness" if (1) it was incurred or assumed in connection with real property used in a trade or business, (2) it is secured by that real property, and (3) the taxpayer makes the appropriate election to invoke the provision. With minor exceptions, the term does not encompass an indebtedness incurred or assumed after January 1, 1993. Qualified acquisition indebtedness and refinancing indebtedness may qualify for the election even if incurred after January 1, 1993 as provided in I.R.C. § 108(c)(3) and (c)(4).

The amount excluded under I.R.C. section 108(a)(1)(D) may not exceed the basis of certain depreciable property of the taxpayer. In addition, the amount excluded (1) is treated as a reduction in basis of that property and (2) may not exceed the excess of the outstanding principal amount of the debt over the fair market value of the business real property that is security for the debt.

§ 16.26   Tax Planning

Consideration should be given to the tax consequences of the decision made by the debtor to resolve its financial problems. A chapter 11 petition may be better for a company that will be solvent after debt discharge than an out-of-court agreement. Also, the tax advantages of issuing some stock to pay obligations as opposed to only cash or notes should not be ignored. These tax differences and others suggest that the tax consequences of various possible decisions should be considered throughout the case.

CORPORATE REORGANIZATIONS

§ 16.27   Introduction

A corporation in bankruptcy or insolvency proceedings may find that one of the ways to provide for continued operations is to transfer all or part of its assets to another corporation. It is important for this transfer to be a tax-free exchange. To qualify for a tax-free exchange, the transfer must be made in connection with one of the types of tax-free reorganizations described in I.R.C. section 368(a)(1). For a transfer that qualifies as a tax-free reorganization, the new entity may be able to assume some of the tax attributes of the corporation in bankruptcy, such as unused net operating losses.

I.R.C. section 371, which provided for tax-free reorganization only for a Chapter X reorganization under the Bankruptcy Act, or a receivership or similar proceeding, no longer applies, and corporate reorganizations must now qualify under Code section 368(a)(1).

§ 16.28   Tax-Free G Reorganization

The Bankruptcy Tax Act of 1980 adds a new category of tax-free reorganization to I.R.C. section 168(a)(1). The new G reorganization includes certain transfers of all or part of the debtor's assets to another corporation pursuant to a court-approved reorganization plan in a bankruptcy case under the new title 11 of the U.S. Code, or in a receivership, foreclosure, or similar proceeding in federal or state court.

This new provision is designed to eliminate many of the requirements that have prevented financially troubled companies from utilizing the tax-free reorganizations included under the current law. The new G reorganization does not require compliance with state merger laws (as in A reorganizations), does not require that the financially distressed corporation receive solely stock of the acquiring corporation in exchange for its assets (C reorganization), and does not require that the former shareholders of the financially distressed corporation control the corporation receiving the assets (D reorganization).

(a) Requirements for G Reorganization

The G reorganization provision requires the transfer of assets by a corporation in a bankruptcy case and the distribution of stock or securities of the acquiring corporation in a manner that qualifies under I.R.C. section 354, 355, or 356.[68]

Under the general rule of I.R.C. section 354, stock or security holders recognize no gain or loss if stock or securities in a corporation in the reorganization are exchanged solely for stock or securities in that corporation or another corporation in the reorganization. Securities include stock and various long-term obligations such as bonds, debentures, and certain long-term notes. I.R.C. section 354 will not apply if the principal amount of securities received exceeds the principal amount of securities surrendered. It will also not apply if securities are received and none is surrendered.

The general rule of I.R.C. section 354 will not apply unless (1) the corporation to which the assets are transferred acquires substantially all the assets of the distributing corporation *and* (2) the stock, securities, and other properties received by the distributing corporation are distributed in pursuance of the plan of reorganization.

The "substantially all" test, as indicated in the Senate report, is to be interpreted in light of the underlying intent in adding the new G category. Thus, the need for the insolvent debtor to sell assets or divisions to raise cash or the need to pay off creditors is to be considered when determining whether a transaction qualifies as a G reorganization. This liberal application of the substantially all test does not apply to other reorganizations. Although I.R.C. section 368(a)(1)(G) requires only part of the assets to be distributed in the plan of reorganization, the additional requirements of the provisions of I.R.C. section 354, 355, or 356 may have the effect of reducing the flexibility of the intended liberal application of the substantially all test. For example, see the restrictions in I.R.C. section 354(b)(1) and (2), as discussed above. The extent to which I.R.C. section 354 will reduce the transfer of part of the assets is unclear. For example, if part of the assets are liquidated and distributed under section 363 of the Bankruptcy Code prior to the approval of a plan of reorganization, will a resulting reorganization qualify under the G reorganization?

---

[68] I.R.C. § 368(a)(1)(G).

(b) Additional Rules for G Reorganization

The Bankruptcy Tax Act of 1980 added to I.R.C. section 368(a) a subsection (3), which contained additional requirements for a G reorganization. The G reorganization can be used only in a case under title 11 of the U.S. Code or in a receivership, foreclosure, or similar proceeding. A bankruptcy case under title 11 or similar cases will be treated as such only if the corporation is under the jurisdiction of the court and the transfer is pursuant to a plan of reorganization approved by the court. A proceeding before a federal or state agency involving a financial institution to which I.R.C. section 585 or 593 applies is to be treated as a court proceeding.

A transaction that qualifies as a G reorganization is not to be treated as also qualifying as a liquidation under I.R.C. section 332, an incorporation under I.R.C. section 351, or another type of reorganization under I.R.C. section 368(a)(1). An exception is made so that a transfer may require the recognition of gain under I.R.C. section 357(c) if the liabilities assumed exceed the basis. It is also not necessary for a reorganization in bankruptcy proceedings to qualify for a G reorganization to receive tax-free treatment. Thus, an acquisition of the stock of a company in a chapter 11 case not covered by the G type of reorganization can still, for example, qualify for the nonrecognition treatment under I.R.C. section 368(a)(1)(B) or (E), for example.[69]

The continuity-of-interest requirement must be satisfied for the new G type of reorganization to qualify for nonrecognition treatment. Creditors receiving stock may be counted toward satisfying the continuity-of-interest rule.

(c) Triangular Reorganizations

The new law permits a triangular reorganization where a corporation is allowed to acquire a debtor corporation in a G reorganization by using the stock of the parent rather than its own stock. Also allowed is the purchase of an insolvent corporation by a "reverse merger," if the former creditors of the surviving corporation exchange their claim for voting stock that has a value equal to at least 80 percent of the value of the debts of the insolvent corporation. The 80 percent requirement restricts the extent to which this type of reorganization could work. In addition, the new law permits a corporation to transfer the assets of a debtor corporation, in a G reorganization by the acquiring corporation, to a controlled subsidiary without affecting the tax-free status of this reorganization.

(d) Transfer to Controlled Subsidiary

The new law allows a corporation that has acquired, in a G reorganization, substantially all the assets of a debtor corporation to transfer the assets to a controlled subsidiary without endangering the nonrecognition status of the reorganization.

(e) Treatment of Accrued Interest

Both the Senate and House reports indicate that a creditor exchanging securities in any corporate reorganization described in I.R.C. section 368 (including

---

[69] S. Rep. No. 96-1035, *supra* note 15, p. 36.

a G reorganization) is treated as receiving interest income on the exchange to the extent that the security holder receives new securities, stock, or any other property attributable to accrued but unpaid interest (including accrued original issue discount) on the securities surrendered. This provision, which reverses the so-called Carman rule,[70] applies regardless of whether the exchanging security holder realizes gain on the exchange overall. Under this provision, a security holder that had previously accrued the interest (including original issue discount) as income recognizes a loss to the extent that the interest is not paid in the exchange.[71]

§ 16.29 Personal Holding Company

The Bankruptcy Tax Act of 1980 exempts corporations in bankruptcy or similar proceedings from the personal holding company tax imposed by I.R.C. section 541. Section 5(a) of the Act provides a new paragraph (9) to I.R.C. section 542(c), listing specific exemptions from personal holding company status. New I.R.C. section 542(c)(9) states that a corporation in a title 11 or similar case is not subject to personal holding company rules unless the primary purpose of instituting or continuing these proceedings was to avoid the personal holding company tax.

AVAILABILITY OF NEW OPERATING LOSSES[72]

§ 16.30 Introduction

I.R.C. section 172 provides for the carryback and carryforward of net operating losses. Under this provision, a corporation is, in most cases, allowed to carry forward, for up to 20 years (nine years for regulated transportation companies), net operating losses sustained in a particular tax year and not carried back to prior years. The period was five years (seven for regulated transportation companies) for tax years ending before 1976 and 15 years between 1976 and 1997. Beginning with tax years ending in 1976, the taxpayer can elect not to carry losses back under I.R.C. section 172(b). Prior to that time, however, losses had to be carried back to the three preceding tax years first; if all of the loss was not used against income in prior years, it might then be carried forward. Effective for tax years beginning after 1997, the carryback time period was reduced to two years. The extent, however, to which the net operating loss can be preserved in bankruptcy and insolvency proceedings depends on the manner in which the debt is restructured.

The net operating loss, or at least part of it, is generally presumed where there is no change in ownership, except that some of the creditors may become stockholders as a result of the debt discharge and restructuring. The forgiveness of indebtedness does not affect the ability of the corporation to carry for-

---

[70] *Carman v. Commissioner*, 189 F.2d 363 (2d Cir. 1951); Rev. Rul. 59-98, 1959-1 C.B. 76.

[71] S. Rep. No. 96-1035, *supra* note 15, pp. 37–38; H.R. Rep. No. 96-833, 96th Cong., 2d Sess. 33 (1980).

[72] The author acknowledges the contribution of Gilbert D. Bloom, coauthor of *Bankruptcy and Insolvency Accounting* (New York: John Wiley & Sons, Inc., 1994), to this section.

ward prior net operating losses.[73] The loss carryover may, however, be reduced to the extent of the discharge of debt.

§ 16.31   Section 382 Limitation

The Tax Reform Act of 1986 includes the annual "section 382 limitation," which minimizes the effect of tax considerations on the decision to acquire loss corporations by placing a limit on potential loss carryovers equal to a hypothetical stream of income that would have been realized had the assets of the loss corporation been sold at their fair market value and the proceeds reinvested in high-grade securities. Further conditions for loss survival include the coverage of built-in losses, rules governing changes in ownership, and exceptions for bankrupt corporations.

Net operating loss limitations are considered only when there is a change in ownership of the corporation holding the carryovers. The new I.R.C. section 382 generally defines change in ownership as the situation where there has been a more than 50 percent change in ownership of the value of the loss corporation's stock. The use of any net operating loss resulting from operations before the ownership change in any period after the change would be subject to the section 382 limitation. The loss corporation acquired through a taxable purchase can no longer preserve net operating losses by simply continuing its historic business.

This limitation now restricts the absorption of any prechange net operating losses in a postchange taxable year to the fair market value multiplied by the "long-term tax-exempt rate." For example, X Corporation has a net operating loss of $4 million and stockholder A purchases 60 percent of the outstanding stock for $600,000. The long-term tax-exempt rate is 6 percent. The value of the loss corporation of $1 million ($600,000 ÷ .60) times the long-term tax-exempt rate of 6 percent results in a maximum use per year of the net operating loss of $60,000 ($1,000,000 × .06). The I.R.C. section 382 limitation not used in a given year because of insufficient taxable income is added to the limitation for a following year. The key factor in determining the use of net operating losses is the fair market value of the loss corporation. In the case of a taxable purchase of stock, this valuation will be relatively simple. However, in the situation where a change in control is the result of a reorganization in which the purchase price consists in part or in whole of stock of a corporation that is not publicly traded, this valuation will be much more difficult.

Some of the provisions of the new law seem inconsistent with the objectives of promoting certainty and reducing the role of tax considerations in acquisitions. There will be a reduction of carryovers in a case where there is no evident "continuity of business enterprise" or more than one-third of the loss corporation's assets are investment assets. I.R.C. section 269 contains a subjective test to further limit loss carryover survival. The separate return limitation year and the consolidated return change of ownership limitation under the consolidated return regulations are also maintained.

If the net unrealized loss on assets is greater than 25 percent of the fair market value of a corporation on the ownership change date, there will be a limi-

---

[73] Rev. Rul. 58-600, 1958-2 C.B. 29.

tation on the recognition of such "built-in" losses or deductions during the five taxable years after the ownership change. Within a taxable year, the recognizable amount of such losses or deductions will be added to prechange net operating losses and will be deductible only within the constraints of the I.R.C. section 382 limitation.

Tax compliance responsibilities arising out of corporate acquisitions, especially reorganizations accounted for as poolings, will be greatly expanded by extending the loss carryforward limitation to built-in deductions. In acquisitions priced at a discount from the net tax cost of assets resulting from depreciated assets or unrecognized liabilities, assets would need to be valued separately, unrecognized liabilities would have to be determined, and records would have to be carefully kept to ensure that any built-in losses in future periods can be isolated, in case they are subject to limitation.

§ 16.32 Special Rules for Corporations in Bankruptcy

The I.R.C. section 382 limitation would not apply if, immediately prior to the ownership change, the corporation was under the jurisdiction of a court in a federal bankruptcy proceeding (or similar case) and the historical creditors and shareholders of the loss corporation, after the change in ownership, own stock constituting 50 percent or more of the value of the loss corporation I.R.C. section 382(1)(5). Standard preferred stock will not be counted in this determination of continuity. Those creditors who held their claim for at least 18 months before the filing of the bankruptcy case or the claim arose during the ordinary course of the loss corporation's trade or business and is still held by the person who has at all times held the beneficial interest in the claim, are historical creditors.

Two special rules apply whenever the bankruptcy exception applies:

1 I.R.C. section 382(1)(5)(B) indicates that net operating losses will be reduced by any interest deducted during the three previous taxable years on the debt converted into stock.

2 Under I.R.C. section 382(1)(5)(D), after an ownership change that qualifies for the bankruptcy exception, any second ownership change within the following two years will result in the elimination of the net operating loss carryforwards that arose prior to the first ownership change.

If there is an ownership change under I.R.C. section 382 and the bankruptcy exception of I.R.C. section 382(1)(5) applies, the continuity of business requirement is not applicable as stated in Treas. Reg. section 1.382-3(b). However, in the absence of strong evidence to the contrary, a proposed amendment to Treas. Reg. section 1.269-3 would provide that an ownership change in bankruptcy, where I.R.C. section 382(1)(5) applies, is considered to be made for tax avoidance under I.R.C. section 269 unless the bankrupt corporation carries on more than an insignificant amount of an active trade or business during and subsequent to the bankruptcy case. It should be noted that a temporary cessation of activities will not be for tax avoidance if the corporation continues to utilize a significant amount of the historic business assets.

The proposed change to Treas. Reg. section 1.269-3 provides that the determination of whether the corporation carries on more than an insignificant amount of an active trade or business is based on all the facts and circumstances. The proposed change notes that the facts and circumstances may include the number of business assets that continue to be used or the number of employees in the work force who continue employment.

The Omnibus Budget Reconciliation Act of 1993 revised I.R.C. section 382(1)(5) to eliminate the need to make the 50 percent adjustment for the gain on stock for debt that would have been reported if the stock-for-debt exception did not affect transactions after December 31, 1994, except for title 11 or similar cases filed before January 1, 1994.

The debtor may elect not to have the bankruptcy exception under I.R.C. section 382(1)(5) apply. I.R.C. section 382(1)(6) provides that, if the debtor elects not to have the bankruptcy exception apply, the I.R.C. section 382 limitation is calculated based on the value of the equity of the corporation after the debt is discharged. This provision can be used in bankruptcy cases where the debtor elects not to apply the bankruptcy exception or where the debtor does not qualify for the bankruptcy exception. In cases where a large part of the outstanding debt is exchanged for stock, the value of the equity of the reorganized corporation will be much larger than the value before reorganization. As a result of this increase in value, in some cases, more of the net operating loss may be preserved under the I.R.C. section 382 limitation than by using the I.R.C. section 382(1)(5) exception.

The disclosure statement often contains a description of the tax impact of the plan, including a discussion of the extent to which the net operating loss may be preserved. An example of the content of a plan in the case of an S corporation is given in 16.3 of Volume 2 of *Bankruptcy and Insolvency Accounting*; a C corporation's plan appears as 16.4.

§ 16.33   Other Provisions

Pursuant to I.R.C. section 382(1)(5)(F), in the case of a G insolvency reorganization of a thrift institution, these rules will be liberalized in the following manner:

- Depositors will be treated as shareholders.
- The continuity percentage will be reduced to 20 percent or more.
- There will be no reduction in net operating losses by prior-year interest deductions or I.R.C. section 108 income.

Special limitations on unused business credits and research credits, capital loss carryforwards, and excess foreign tax credits under I.R.C. section 383 are amended. Regulations (to be defined) indicate that capital loss carryforwards will be limited to an amount determined on the basis of the tax liability attributable to the amount of the taxable income not in excess of the I.R.C. section 382 limitation for that taxable year, using the same ordering rules that have been in effect to date. The I.R.C. section 382 limitation that is applied to a prechange loss is reduced by any capital loss carryforward used in a postchange year. Also, there will be a limit on the amount of any excess credit used following an ownership change, under regulations, figured on the basis of the tax liability attributable to an amount of taxable income not in excess of the applicable I.R.C. section 382 limitation (after any excess foreign tax credits, capital loss carryforwards, and net operating loss carryforwards are taken into account). In the Conference Report to Accompany H.R. 3838,[74] passive activity losses and credits as well as minimum tax credits are included in I.R.C. section 383.

EFFECTS ON EARNINGS AND PROFITS

§ 16.34 Introduction

The earnings and profits of a corporation determine the extent to which corporate distributions are taxable. Also, in determining the personal holding company tax and the accumulated earnings tax, the earnings and profits must be considered. Two factors must be considered in analyzing the impact bankruptcy proceedings have on the earnings and profits account of a corporation. The first deals with the need to adjust the earnings and profits account by the amount that the canceled indebtedness exceeds the reduction in the basis of the assets. The second concerns the carryover of the earnings and profits balance, which is frequently a deficit to the reorganized corporation.

§ 16.35 Account Adjustment

A corporation in a chapter 11 proceeding must adjust its earnings and profits. Generally, the determination of the earnings and profits of a corporation for dividend purposes is based on generally accepted accounting principles that take into consideration the economic realities of the transaction as well as the tax impact of a given transaction. Thus, nontaxable income items, such as interest on state and municipal bonds, increase the earnings and profits available for dividends, and losses and expenses that are disallowed for tax purposes reduce the earnings and profits.

I.R.C. section 312 is amended to provide that, to the extent that the income from debt forgiveness is used to reduce the basis under I.R.C. section 1017, such basis reduction will not affect the earnings and profits account. This amount would eventually affect the earnings and profits account by reduced depreciation charges or an increase in the gain (reduction of the loss) when the asset is sold. The other income from debt forgiveness would be used to adjust the earnings and profits account.

The Senate added to the House bill a provision that any deficit in earnings and profits is reduced (but no provision was made to increase a positive earnings and profits balance) by the paid-in capital of any shareholder whose interest is terminated in a bankruptcy or similar case.

---

[74] H.R. Rep. No. 99-841, 99th Cong., 2d Sess. 194 (1986).

§ 16.36   Earnings and Profits Carryover

In general, if the plan of settlement or reorganization provides for debt forgiveness where the existing stockholders' interests are not eliminated, the earnings and profits account is preserved. This would be true even if there were a contribution of new capital or if the stockholders who held debt transferred it for stock.

In the case of a tax-free reorganization, the earnings and profits—or a deficit, as the case may be—will carry over. I.R.C. section 381(c)(2) provides for the preservation of the earnings and profits account for those tax-free reorganizations specified in I.R.C. section 381(a)(2). Deficits of one corporation cannot be used to reduce the amount of prereorganization earnings that any other corporation brings to the combination, but may be used only to offset future earnings. Again, these provisions would apply to chapter 11 and out-of-court proceedings.

One major problem arises in interpreting how the provisions of Code section 381 can be applied. If the creditors receive stock in the acquiring corporation and the interests of original stockholders of the acquired corporation are eliminated, will I.R.C. section 381 provide for the preservation of the earnings and profits? Or, should it be assumed that the earnings and profits were lost when the creditors, in fact, became the stockholders of the acquired corporation before the reorganization occurred? Revenue Ruling 77-204[75] might suggest that the earnings and profits are preserved, as would the amendment to I.R.C. section 382(b) provided by the Bankruptcy Tax Act (creditors receiving stock should be considered as stockholders before the reorganization). However, an amendment to I.R.C. section 312 (see § 16.35) eliminates part or most of the carryover of earnings and profits.

ADMINISTRATIVE ASPECTS OF TAXES

§ 16.37   Tax Priorities

Normally, secured debts are first satisfied and then unsecured debts are paid in the order of priority specified in I.R.C. section 507. (For a general discussion of the order of priority, see § 5.33.) In this section, the priorities are mentioned only to the extent they involve taxes.

(a) Administration Expenses

First priority given to unsecured debts is allowed for administrative expenses. Included in these expenses is any tax incurred during the administration of the estate while bankruptcy proceedings are in progress (I.R.C. section 503(b)). Examples of taxes that would qualify for first priority are income tax liabilities, most employees' withholding taxes and the employer's share of employment taxes, property taxes, excise taxes, recapture of investment tax

---

[75] Rev. Rul. 77-204, 1977-1 C.B. 49.

credit arising from property sales, and claims arising from excessive allowance of "quickie" refunds to the estate (such as the tentative net operating loss carrybacks allowed under I.R.C. section 6411).[76] Taxes on postpetition payment of prepetition wages would not be a first priority. I.R.C. section 503(b)(1)(C) provides that any fine or penalty or reduction in credit relating to a tax classified as an administrative expense is also given first priority.

The classification of a tax as an administrative expense or a seventh priority item is critical. For example, if a corporation, in an attempt to reach an out-of-court agreement with creditors, sells assets to make partial payments to creditors at a gain, a substantial tax liability may arise. Assume the corporation concludes that it cannot reach an out-of-court agreement and that it must file a bankruptcy petition. When should the petition be filed? Would it be best for the tax liability to be an administrative expense or a seventh priority item? If it is an administrative expense, the tax must be paid on or before the effective date of the plan, and interest and penalties must be paid on the tax. If it is a seventh priority item, it may be deferred up to six years, and interest and penalties will most likely not occur. In this case, it would be best to file the petition after the end of the taxable year in which the property was transferred. On the other hand, if this were an individual with no free assets, it might be better for the petition to be filed before any of the property was transferred and before a tax liability was created.

The bankruptcy court noted in *In the matter of Edward Lee Gobel*,[77] that section 503(b)(1)(B) of the Bankruptcy Code provides the postpetition taxes incurred by a bankruptcy estate are allowable as an administrative expense. Any penalties that might be assessed on these taxes are also an allowable administrative expense, pursuant to section 503(b)(1)(C).[78] Section 503 of the Bankruptcy Code does not specifically provide that interest on postpetition taxes is an administrative expense. However, prevailing case law almost universally recognizes that interest on these taxes is an appropriate administrative expense.[79]

Section 1399 provides that a new tax entity is not created for federal income tax purposes when the corporation files a bankruptcy petition. Thus, for federal income tax purposes the corporation in bankruptcy will determine the income tax liability in its normal manner for the entire year. However, this unresolved issue remains: how is the tax that relates to the period before the petition was filed handled for bankruptcy purposes? For example, in a year in which the petition is filed, is the tax for the entire year an administrative expense? Or should the tax liability be bifurcated—the tax liability for the period from the beginning of the taxable year to the day before the petition was filed and the tax liability for the period after the petition was filed until year-end? The tax liability for the period ending just before the petition was filed would be an eighth priority tax claim and in a chapter 11 case could be deferred over a period of six years from the date the tax was assessed. In contrast, the tax liability for the period after the petition is filed would be an administrative

---

[76] Richard L. Bacon and James L. Billinger, "Analyzing the Operation and Tax Effects of the New Bankruptcy Act," *Journal of Taxation*, Vol. 41 (February 1979), p. 76.

[77] 1991 Bankr. LEXIS 1638 (Bankr. N.D. Ind. 1991).

[78] See *U.S. v. Friendship College, Inc.* 737 F.2d 430 (4th Cir. 1984).

[79] See *In re Flo-Lizer, Inc.*, 916 F.2d 363 (6th Cir. 1990); *In re Allied Mechanical Service Inc.*, 885 F.2d 837, 879 (11th Cir. 1989); and *In re Mark Anthony Const., Inc.* 886 F.2d 1101 (9th Cir. 1989).

expense and thus must be paid during the administration of the case. The Service position is that the entire tax liability for a year ending after the petition is filed is an administrative expense.

The Eleventh Circuit, in *In re Hillsborough Holdings Corp.*,[80] Ninth Circuit, in *In re Pacific-Atlantic Trading Co.*,[81] and the Eighth Circuit, in *In re L.J. O'Neill Shoe Co.*,[82] held that the tax should be bifurcated between the prepetition and postpetition periods for the purpose of determining the priority of the tax liabilities. These courts focused on the language in section 507(a)(8)(A)(iii) describing taxes that were "not assessed before, but assessable under applicable law or by agreement, after the commencement of the case." All three courts concluded that this language includes taxes attributable to the prepetition period, because such taxes are not assessed before and do not become assessable until after the bankruptcy filing when the tax year closes; however, they realized that a literal interpretation of this phrase would also imply that postpetition taxes also fall under this section. Both circuit courts then concluded, based on legislative history and analysis, that section 507(a)(8) was only intended to deal with prepetition taxes. Thus, taxes based on income earned during the prepetition period are eighth priority.

(b) "Involuntary Gap" Claims

Creditors whose claims arise in the ordinary course of the debtor's business or financial affairs after any involuntary case is commenced, but before the appointment of a trustee or the order for relief is entered by the court, are granted second priority. Thus, any taxes arising during this period would receive second priority.

(c) Prepetition Wages

Claims for wages up to $4,300 per employee, earned within 90 days before the filing of the petition, receive third priority. Any taxes withheld on these wages would receive the same priority, according to I.R.C. section 346(f). Thus, withholding taxes on wages earned prior to the 90-day period and on wages earned by individuals in excess of the $4,300 limit would not receive any priority. These claims would be classified with other general unsecured claims. Claims that fall within the 90-day period and the $4,300 limit would receive third priority.

(d) Prepetition Taxes

Certain taxes are granted eighth priority. The Bankruptcy Code continues the policy of requiring the creditors of a bankrupt to pay the taxes owed by the debtor, because the payment of this tax reduces the amount that general unsecured creditors would otherwise receive. The Bankruptcy Code makes some modifications in the taxes that are granted priority status, and it attempts to solve some of the unresolved questions of the prior law.

---

[80] 116 F.3d 1391 (11th Cir. 1997).
[81] 64 F.3d 1292 (9th Cir. 1995).
[82] 64 F.3d 1146 (8th Cir. 1995).

(e) *Income and Gross Receipts Taxes*

Section 507(a)(8)(A) of the Bankruptcy Code contains several provisions granting priority to income and gross receipts taxes.

- Any tax on income or gross receipts for a taxable year ending on or before the date of the filing of the petition is given eighth priority, provided the date the return was last due, including extensions, is within three years before the petition was filed. Thus, any tax due for a taxable period that ended after the petition was filed is not granted eighth priority but would be considered an administrative expense (first priority).

  If a bankruptcy petition is filed on May 1, 20X8, any unpaid taxes due on a timely filed 20X4 tax return would not be a priority item. The return due date of April 15, 20X5, is more than three years prior to the petition date of May 1, 20X8. If the petition were filed on April 14, taxes would be an eighth priority. There has been some confusion because of the wording, "is last due including extensions, after three years before the date of the filing of the petition," for a year ending just before the petition is filed but where the return is due after the petition date. These taxes would be a eighth priority and, even though the return is not due until after the petition is filed, the return is still due for a time period that is less than three years before the petition was filed.

- Any income or gross receipts tax is to be assessed within 240 days before the petition was filed, even though the due date of the return does not fall within the three-year period discussed above. The purpose of the 240-day provision is to give the IRS time to take more drastic measures to collect the tax. If during this period an offer in compromise is made, the time from when the offer is made until it is accepted, rejected, or withdrawn is not counted. Furthermore, the tax will automatically be given priority if the petition is filed within 30 days after the offer was rejected or withdrawn or if the offer in compromise is still outstanding, provided the offer in compromise was made within 240 days after the assessment. If the petition is filed 240 days after the assessment, the tax does not have the priority unless it falls within the three-year period.

- Any income or gross receipts tax that has not been assessed but that is assessable is granted priority. Thus, even though a tax was due more than three years ago, it is still granted priority, provided the tax is assessable. Taxes that are nondischargeable under section 523a(1)(B) and (C) of the Bankruptcy Code are excluded from this provision. Examples of taxes that qualify under this provision are claims still being negotiated at the date of petition, previous years' taxes for which the taxpayer has extended the statute of limitations period, taxes in litigation where the tax authority is prohibited from assessing the tax, or any other unassessed taxes that are still open under the statute of limitations.

  A tax pending determination by the tax court at the date the petition is filed will be granted eighth priority. If the tax court has decided the issue against the taxpayer before a petition is filed and if no appeal is made, the tax will receive eighth priority even though no assessment has been made as of the petition date. The Bankruptcy Code ends the practice under prior law where, once the case was resolved in tax court and the assessment restriction was removed, the taxpayer could file a petition before the IRS could make the assessment and thus would avoid the tax's being considered as a priority claim. If the assessment is made before the petition is filed, the 240-day rule is in effect. Thus, tax claims due for petitions filed within 240 days after the assessment are eighth priority, and tax claims due where the petition is filed more than 240 days after would not receive priority unless the three-year period discussed above applies.[83]

(f) Property Taxes

Property taxes assessed and last payable without penalty within one year before the petition is filed are granted eighth priority. Note that the time period here is one year rather than the three-year period that applies to income and gross receipt taxes.

(g) Withholding Taxes

Section 507(a)(8)(C) of the Bankruptcy Code gives eighth priority to all taxes that the debtor was required to withhold and collect from others, for which the debtor is liable in any capacity. There is no time limit on the age of these taxes. Included in this category would be income taxes, state sales taxes, excise taxes, and withholdings on interest and dividends of nonresidents. Taxes withheld on wages will receive eighth priority, provided the wages were paid before the petition was filed. If not, then they will have the same priority as the wage claims. The part of the wages granted third priority will result in the related taxes being also granted third priority. Taxes that relate to the wages that are classified as unsecured claims (i.e., excess over $4,300 for each employee, or incurred more than 90 days before the petition was filed) will receive no priority.

To properly determine the priority of withholding taxes, the accountant must first determine when wages were paid (before or after petition date) for which withholdings were taken. If they were paid after the petition date, what is the priority of the wages? Withholding taxes on wages earned after the petition is filed are granted first priority.

Thus, withholding taxes can have first, third, eighth, or general creditor priority, depending on the status of the related payments.

The Supreme Court has issued its decision in two cases that involved trust funds. In the first case (*Begier, Trustee v. Internal Revenue Service*),[84] the Court held, without dissent, that trust fund taxes paid to the IRS by a company that later declared bankruptcy may not be recovered, whether the company paid the taxes out of a segregated trust fund or its general accounts.

American International Airlines, Inc. (AIA), became delinquent in remitting social security, withholding taxes, and passenger excise taxes. The IRS, under I.R.C. section 7512, ordered the company to deposit future taxes as collected into a separate bank account. The bank account was established by the company, but the funds deposited were insufficient to cover all of its tax obligations.

---

[83] *Supra* note 64, p. 77.
[84] 110 S. Ct. 2258, 110 L. Ed. 2d 46 (1990).

However, the company remained current on the obligations by paying part of them from the separate bank account and part from its general operating funds. After the company had filed its chapter 11 petition, the appointed bankruptcy trustee, Harry P. Begier, Jr., moved to recover AIA's trust fund payments made to the IRS during the 90 days before the bankruptcy filing.

The bankruptcy court held that AIA could not recover any tax payments made out of its segregated trust fund account. However, payments made out of the company's general accounts are "property of the debtor" and as a result they are subject to avoidance.[85]

The Third Circuit reversed the decision of the district court and held that any prepetition payment of trust fund taxes was a payment of funds that are not the debtor's property.[86]

Other courts have reached a conclusion different from the Third Circuit's in *Begier*. For example, see *R & T Roofing*[87] and *Drabkin v. District of Columbia*.[88]

The Supreme Court noted that "[e]quality of distribution among creditors is a central policy of the Bankruptcy Code. According to that policy, creditors of equal priority should receive pro rata shares of the debtor's property. See, e.g., 11 U.S.C. section 726(b) (1982 ed.). . . ." According to the Court, section 547(b) of the Bankruptcy Code furthers this policy by permitting a trustee in bankruptcy to avoid certain preferential payments made before the debtor files for bankruptcy that would have allowed the debtor to favor one creditor over others by transferring property shortly before filing for bankruptcy. However, the Court reasoned, that "if the debtor transfers property that would not have been available for distribution to his creditors in a bankruptcy proceeding, the policy behind the avoidance power is not implicated."

Begier argued that a trust was never created for the funds that were paid to the IRS, and thus the payment was made out of property of the debtor. The Court disagreed:

> The Internal Revenue Code directs "every person receiving any payment for facilities or services" subject to excise taxes to "collect the amount of the tax from the person making such payment." section 4291. It also requires that an employer "collec[t]" FICA taxes from its employees "by deducting the amount of the tax from the wages AS AND WHEN PAID." section 3102(a) (emphasis added). Both provisions make clear that the act of "collecting" occurs at the time of payment— the recipient's payment for the service in the case of excise taxes and the employer's payment of wages in the case of FICA taxes. The mere fact that AIA neither placed the taxes it collected in a segregated fund nor paid them to the IRS does not somehow mean that AIA never collected the taxes in the first place.

> The same analysis applies to taxes the Internal Revenue Code requires that employers "withhold." Section 3402(a)(1) requires that "every employer making payment of wages shall deduct and withhold UPON SUCH WAGES [the employee's federal income tax]." (Emphasis added.) Withholding thus occurs at the time of payment to the employee of his net wages. S. Rep. No. 95-1106, p. 33 (1978).

---

[85] *In re American International Airlines, Inc.*, 83 B.R. 324 (E.D. Pa. 1988). The district court affirmed.
[86] *Begier v. United States*, 878 F.2d 762 (1989).
[87] 887 F.2d 981 (9th Cir. 1989).
[88] 824 F.2d 1102 (9th Cir. 1987).

The Court noted that if "we were to read section 7501 to mandate segregation as a prerequisite to the creation of the trust, section 7512's requirement that funds be segregated in special and limited circumstances would become superfluous."

The Court concluded:

> We hold that AIA's payments of trust-fund taxes to the IRS from its general accounts were not transfers of "property of the debtor," but were instead transfers of property held in trust for the Government pursuant to section 7501. Such payments therefore cannot be avoided as preferences.

The other case involved the allocation of trust fund tax payments under a plan. In *United States v. Energy Resources Co., Inc.,*[89] the Supreme Court ruled that a bankruptcy court can direct the IRS to apply a debtor's payment to trust-fund employment taxes, even though doing so might leave the government at risk for non-trust-fund taxes.

Five circuit courts had looked at this issue. The Third Circuit, in *In re Ribs-R-Us,*[90] the Sixth Circuit, in *In re DuCharmes & Co.,*[91] and the Ninth Circuit, in *In re Technical Knockout Graphics, Inc.*[92] held that the payments were involuntary and could not be allocated.

On the other hand, the Eleventh Circuit held, in *In re A & B Heating and Air Conditioning,*[93] that the decision as to whether the taxes are voluntary (thereby allowing taxpayer allocation) is best made on a case-by-case basis with consideration of each bankruptcy plan as a whole. The Third Circuit held in *Energy Resources* that the payments may be made to trust funds first.

The Supreme Court in reaching this decision did not decide whether tax payments were voluntary or involuntary; rather, it held that a bankruptcy court's broad "authority to modify creditor–debtor relationships" entitled it to direct the debtor's payments toward withholding taxes, even though doing so might endanger the government's collection of other debtor liabilities.

The Court noted that the Bankruptcy Code does not explicitly authorize the bankruptcy courts to approve reorganization plans designating tax payments as either trust-fund or non-trust-fund. However, according to the Court, section 1123(b)(5) of the Bankruptcy Code grants the bankruptcy courts residual authority to approve reorganization plans, including any appropriate provision not inconsistent with the applicable provisions of the Code. Section 105 of the Bankruptcy Code also states that bankruptcy courts may "issue any order, process, or judgment that is necessary or appropriate to carry out the provisions" of the Act. The Court noted that these statutory directives are consistent with the traditional understanding that bankruptcy courts, as courts of equity, have broad authority to modify creditor–debtor relationships.[94]

The Court noted that the "government contends that the Bankruptcy Court's orders contravene section 6672 because, if the IRS cannot designate a

---

[89] 871 F.2d 223 (1st Cir. 1989), *aff'd,* 110 S. Ct. 2139 (1990).

[90] 828 F.2d 199 (3d Cir. 1987).

[91] 852 F.2d 194 (6th Cir. 1988).

[92] 833 F.2d 797 (9th Cir. 1987).

[93] 823 F.2d 462 (11th Cir. 1987).

[94] See *Pepper v. Litton,* 308 U.S. 295, 303–04 (1939); *United States National Bank v. Chase National Bank,* 331 U.S. 28, 36 (1947); *Katchen v. Landy,* 382 U.S. 323, 327 (1966).

debtor corporation's tax payments as nontrust fund, the debtor might be able to pay only the guaranteed debt, leaving the government at risk for nontrust fund taxes. This may be the case, but section 6672, by its terms, does not protect against this eventuality." The Court concluded that section 6672 "plainly does not require us to hold that the orders at issue here, otherwise wholly consistent with the bankruptcy court's authority under the Bankruptcy Code, were nonetheless improvident. . . . The Bankruptcy Court has not transgressed any limitation on its broad power. We therefore hold that it may order the IRS to apply tax payments to offset trust fund obligations where it concludes that this action is necessary for a reorganization's success."

As noted previously, in *In re Energy Resources Co., Inc. (United States v. Energy Resources Co.),*[95] the Supreme Court held that the bankruptcy court has the discretion to determine whether the interests of all the parties would best be served by allowing the debtor to set the order in which the trust fund taxes, interest, penalties, employer's taxes, and other taxes will be paid.

The case dealt with a chapter 11 reorganization. The question remained unanswered as to whether a debtor could allocate the trust fund taxes in a chapter 11 liquidation case. In *United States v. Kare Kemical, Inc.,*[96] Kare Kemical Co. proposed a plan of liquidation that required the IRS to first satisfy the principal portion of the firm's tax obligation and thereafter the accrued interest and penalties. The plan was approved by the bankruptcy court when it found sufficient elements of voluntariness to permit payment allocation. The district court affirmed. The Eleventh Circuit reversed the lower courts and held that the Supreme Court's reasons for allowing payment allocation in reorganizations are not present in liquidation cases.

The Third Circuit held that a chapter 7 trustee may not designate IRS tax payments. Keith Sorensen, an officer and director of Sorensen Industries, Inc., failed to pay withholding taxes in 1984, 1985, and 1986, and the corporation's own social security taxes. The IRS determined that Sorensen was a responsible person under I.R.C. section 6672.

Both Sorensen and Sorensen Industries filed a chapter 7 petition, and the same individual was appointed trustee in both cases. The trustee mailed a check for $34,000 for Sorensen Industries to the IRS and moved to have the bankruptcy court reduce Sorensen's responsible-person liability by the same amount. The bankruptcy court granted the trustee's motion and reduced Sorensen's liability under section 6672. The bankruptcy court based its decision on *United States v. Energy Resources Co.,*[97] which held that the bankruptcy court in a chapter 11 reorganization has the authority to direct the IRS to allocate tax payments.

The IRS appealed and the district court affirmed the bankruptcy court's reliance on *Energy Resources.* The Third Circuit reversed the district court and held that the bankruptcy court did not have the authority to designate Sorensen Industries' tax payment so as to reduce Sorensen's section 6672 liability. The Third Circuit found that the Supreme Court's holding in *Energy Resources* was based on the debtor's need for rehabilitation. A ruling in favor of rehabilitation loses its purpose in a chapter 7 liquidation case.[98]

---

[95] *Supra* note 74.
[96] 935 F.2d 243 (11th Cir. 1991).
[97] *Supra* note 89.
[98] *United States v. Lewis Pepperman,* 976 F.2d 123 (3d Cir. Sept. 3, 1992).

(h) Employer's Taxes

An employment tax on wages, salary, or commission earned before the petition was filed receives eighth priority, provided the date the last return was due, including extensions, is within three years before the filing date. Taxes due beyond this date are considered general claims, even though the individual responsible for submitting these taxes to the government is personally liable for these taxes under I.R.C. section 6672.

Businesses that are in financial trouble often delay paying employment taxes. Their intent is to submit the payments as soon as conditions improve. The problem is that conditions do not improve. Additional pressures are placed on the debtor by major creditors demanding payment. Again, the taxes withheld are not remitted. At the time the business files a bankruptcy petition, the unpaid tax withholdings are significant. At this stage, corporate officers often find out that they can be personally liable for their taxes. I.R.C. section 6672 provides:

> Any person required to collect, truthfully account for, and pay over any tax imposed by this title who willfully fails to collect such tax, or truthfully account for and pay over such tax, or willfully attempts in any manner to evade or defeat any such tax or the payment thereof, shall, in addition to other penalties provided by law, be liable to a penalty equal to the total amount of the tax evaded, or not collected, or not accounted for and paid over. No penalty shall be imposed under section 6653 for any offense to which this section is applicable.

The amount of the penalty is equal to 100 percent of the tax that should have been withheld and remitted to the IRS. For example, in the case of employment taxes, it includes the income taxes and the employee's share of social security taxes withheld. Any interest and penalties associated with these taxes are not subject to the 100 percent provision. Note that the penalty does not mean that the taxes are paid twice, but that the liability for these taxes may be transferred to responsible persons of the corporation.[99]

On wages not paid before the petition was filed, it was the intent of Congress to grant eighth priority only to the employer's share of the tax due on wages that receive third priority. The employee's tax on wages that are not granted priority would thus be a general claim, as would the wages.

(i) Excise Taxes

For an excise tax to qualify as a tax priority, the transaction creating the tax must have occurred before the petition was filed. In addition, if the excise tax is of the type that requires a tax return, to receive eighth priority the day the return is last due (including extensions) must be within three years before the petition was filed. If no return is required, the three-year limitation begins on the date the transaction occurred (section 507(a)(8)(E) of the Bankruptcy Code). This group of taxes includes sales taxes, estate and gift taxes, gasoline taxes, and any other federal, state, or local taxes defined by statute as excise taxes.

---

[99] For additional discussion of the 100 percent penalty, see Grant W. Newton and Gilbert Bloom's *Bankruptcy and Insolvency Accounting* (New York: John Wiley & Sons, Inc., 1994).

(j) Customs Duties

Sections 507(a)(8)(F) of the Bankruptcy Code provides that a customs duty arising from the importation of merchandise will receive priority if (1) entered for consumption within one year before the bankruptcy petition is filed, (2) covered by an entry liquidated or reliquidated within one year before the date the petition was filed, or (3) entered for consumption within four years before the petition date, but not liquidated by that date, if the Secretary of the Treasury certifies that the duties were not liquidated because of an investigation into assessment of antidumping or countervailing duties, fraud, or lack of information to properly appraise or classify such merchandise.

§ 16.38 Tax Penalty

The priority granted a tax penalty depends on its nature. A tax liability that is called a penalty but in fact represents a tax to be collected is granted eighth priority. These penalties are referred to in section 507(a)(8)(G) of the Bankruptcy Code as "compensation for actual pecuniary loss." Other prepetition penalties, including fines, forfeitures, and punitive damages, are not granted eighth priority, and in situations involving liquidations they are paid only after all unsecured debts have been satisfied (section 726(a)(4) of the Bankruptcy Code). Only amounts paid for postpetition interest and amounts paid to the debtor receive a lower priority in liquidation cases.

In *Burns*,[100] the Eleventh Circuit held that any tax penalty imposed with respect to a transaction or event that occurred more than three years before the date of the filing of a bankruptcy petition would be dischargeable under section 523(a)(8) of the Bankruptcy Code. The IRS, in developing a collateral agreement with the taxpayer, as reported in *In re William Thomas Plachter, Jr.*,[101] concluded that fraud penalties on taxes that were not dischargeable but were due more than three years before the petition was filed, were dischargeable as a result of the debtors' bankruptcy, in accordance with *Burns*.

In *Ronald Eugene Nye v. United States*,[102] the district court determined that fraud penalties, incurred on transactions ending more than three years before the filing of the petition, were dischargeable even though the tax to which the penalties related was not dischargeable.

§ 16.39 Interest

As under prior law, interest stops accruing when the petition is filed for purposes of determining prepetition liabilities. Interest that has accrued on prepetition taxes is considered part of the debt and would receive the same priority as the taxes received to which the interest applies. Interest that accrues during bankruptcy proceedings on a prepetition debt would, according to section 726(a)(5) of the Bankruptcy Code, receive payment only after all other creditors' claims have been satisfied.

---

[100] *Burns v. United States*, 887 F.2d 1541 (11th Cir. 1989).
[101] No. 88-02856-BKC-SMW (Bankr. S.D. Fla. 1991).
[102] No. 91-4009 (N.D. Ohio Mar. 19, 1992).

Postpetition interest will generally not be allowed in a chapter 11 case. There are, however, two exceptions. In the case of fully secured claims, postpetition interest will be allowed, but only up to the amount by which the value of the security interest exceeds the amount of the debt. For unsecured creditors, interest will only be allowed in situations where creditors are receiving full payment for all of their claims.

§ 16.40 Erroneous Refunds or Credits

Section 507 of the Bankruptcy Code provides that a claim from an erroneous refund or credit of a tax will be treated in the same manner as the claim for the tax to which the refund or credit applied. Thus, a refund received in error for income tax paid in 1977 will receive seventh priority if the tax liability incurred in 1977 would receive that priority. This provision would also apply to "quickie refunds" based on net operating loss carrybacks under I.R.C. section 6411.[103]

§ 16.41 Chapter 11 Reorganization

Section 1129(a)(9) of the Bankruptcy Code states that a plan must provide for the payment of all taxes with priority before the plan will be confirmed. Taxes classified as administration expenses and involuntary gap must be paid in full with cash on the effective date of the plan. Employees' withholding taxes on wages granted third priority are to be paid in full with cash on the effective date of the plan or, if the class has accepted the plan, with deferred cash payments that have a value equal to the claims. Claims for taxes granted eighth priority must be satisfied with deferred cash payment over a period not to exceed six years after the date of assessment of such claim; the value as of the effective date of the plan is equal to the allowed amount of the tax claims. These deferred payments include an amount for interest to cover the cost for not receiving payment as of the effective date of the plan. The Bankruptcy Code does not state whether the tax rate, market rate, or some other rate should be used to determine the value. Courts have, however, interpreted value to be determined by using market rates.

Other tax claims that do not qualify as tax priority items would receive treatment similar to that for other unsecured claims. Furthermore, the Bankruptcy Reform Act[104] contained a provision that exempts bankruptcy proceedings from section 3466 of the Revised Statutes of the United States.[105] In case of insolvency, debts due to the U.S. government must be satisfied before others are paid. This section does, however, continue to apply to common-law assignments for benefits of creditors and to equity receiverships under state laws.

§ 16.42 Chapter 12 and Chapter 13 Adjustments

A provision that applies to chapter 12 and chapter 13 proceedings is similar to Bankruptcy Code section 1129 (chapter 11 reorganization), requiring that

---

[103] *Supra* note 64, p. 78.
[104] P.L. 95-598, § 322.
[105] 31 U.S.C. 191.

priority items be provided for in the plan. Bankruptcy Code sections 1222 and 1322 state that the plan must provide for the full payment, in deferred cash payments, of all claims entitled to priority under section 507, unless the holder of a claim agrees to different treatment. Thus, all taxes with priority will be paid in full. Note that no interest is to be paid on these claims; it is not necessary that the present value of the future payments equal the claim, but only that the total future payments equal the debt. In chapter 11 proceedings, the present value of future payments is compared with the value of the claim.

Bankruptcy Code sections 1222 and 1322 provide that the time period for future payments must not exceed three years, unless the court approves a longer period, and in no case will the period exceed five years.

§ 16.43   Tax Discharge

The extent to which a tax is discharged depends on (1) whether the debtor is an individual or corporation, (2) the chapter under which the petition is filed, and (3) the nature and priority of the tax.

(a) Individual Debtors

Section 523(a) of the Bankruptcy Code provides that in a chapter 7 or chapter 11 proceeding involving an individual debt, all taxes that are entitled to priority (see chapter 3, paragraph 98) are exempt from a discharge. Also exempt from discharge are prepetition taxes due for a period when the debtor failed to file a return, filed the return late (exempt are late returns filed more than two years before petition date), or filed a fraudulent return or willfully attempted in any manner to evade or defeat the tax due. Any tax due that relates to a failure to file a return or to other misconduct of the debtor will automatically be considered nondischargeable if such tax qualifies for priority under section 507 of the Bankruptcy Code. Some question exists as to whether a return filed late due to a reasonable cause would be considered nondischargeable.

Taxes with priority are not exempt from a discharge under chapter 13, but Bankruptcy Code section 1322 provides that a plan must provide for the full payment of all claims with priority under section 507. The net effect of this provision is that the government will still receive payment in full for taxes due. It would, however, appear that priority taxes due because of a late return, a fraudulent return, or a failure to file a return would be dischargeable.

Section 1328(b) of the Bankruptcy Code provides for a later discharge of debts that were scheduled for payment in the plan if the debtor is, under certain conditions, unable to make these payments. The provisions of section 523(a) of the Bankruptcy Code are fully applicable to this subsequent discharge, which means that taxes with priority are exempt from discharge, as are taxes resulting from the misconduct of the debtor.

As a general rule, properly perfected tax liens are still valid even though an individual may be able to obtain a discharge from the tax.

In *Oliver J. Latour, Jr. v. IRS*,[106] the bankruptcy court held that tax liens do not attach to property acquired after the petition is filed. Oliver and Jane

---

[106] Adv. No. 91-0350 (Bankr. S.D. Ala. 1992).

Latour filed federal income tax returns for the years 1980 and 1985 through 1987. The IRS assessed deficiencies against the Latours for those years and filed notices of federal tax liens against the Latours' property. In September 1991, the Latours filed for bankruptcy under chapter 7 and listed the tax liabilities in their schedules filed with the court. They filed an adversary proceeding to determine the dischargeability of the tax liabilities and the validity of the tax liens. The bankruptcy court held that the tax liabilities were dischargeable. The tax claims were not subject to the exception to discharge set forth in section 523 of the Bankruptcy Code because the tax returns were filed more than two year before the date of the petition. The court also determined that the tax liens that attached to prepetition property and to any other property of the estate were valid and enforceable. However, the court ruled that the liens did not attach to any property acquired after the petition was filed and thus could not be enforced against such property.

(b) Corporate Debtors

Section 727 of the Bankruptcy Code prohibits the granting of a discharge to a corporation in a chapter 7 liquidation. Also, a corporation liquidating under a plan adopted in a chapter 11 case would not obtain a discharge. Because a corporation in effect goes out of business as a result of the liquidation, it might appear that the actual granting of a discharge is unimportant. A corporation, however, does not have to go out of existence, and shareholders have kept these shells alive so they could be reactivated at a later date for tax reasons or to avoid the costs of creating another corporation. A debtor will be reluctant to use these shells under the Bankruptcy Reform Act because any assets owned by the corporation are subject to attachment by the creditors for prebankruptcy debts.

Section 1141(d) of the Bankruptcy Code states that, unless otherwise provided, confirmation of the plan discharges the corporate debtor from any debt that arose before the date of confirmation. This would include all taxes that have not been paid, including taxes attributable to no return, a late return, or a fraudulent return. It should be noted, however, that, before a plan will be confirmed, taxes with priority must be paid or provided for in full. Thus, in reality, the only taxes that can be discharged in corporate reorganization are those that do not have priority. It should be noted that section 1106(a)(6) of the Bankruptcy Code provides that the trustee, in situations where the debtor did not file a tax return required by law, must furnish, without personal liability, the information that the government may require regarding prepetition liabilities arising from periods where the required returns were not filed. Also, the conference explanation indicates that the tax authority may disallow any tax benefit claimed subsequent to the reorganization if it results from a deduction, credit, or other item improperly reported prior to the filing of the petition.[107]

§ 16.44   Tax Preferences

The payment of a past due tax to a governmental unit can be considered a preferential payment under certain conditions. Section 547(b) of the Bankruptcy Code provides that any transfer made within 90 days before the petition

---

[107] 124 Cong. Rec. 5-17431. See Bacon and Billinger, *supra* note 64, p. 79.

is filed of property of the debtors, while insolvent, in payment of an antecedent debt owed by the debtor to an undersecured creditor may be avoided. The avoidance is based on the assumption that the creditor receive more as a result of the transfer than would have been received if the case were under chapter 7. A transfer is not, however, avoided if the payment was made within the ordinary course of business according to ordinary business terms. For tax purposes, it would appear that the date at which the payment must be received would be, according to section 547(a)(4) of the Bankruptcy Code, the day when such tax is last payable, including any extensions, without penalty. Thus, the trustee or debtor-in-possession could recover a tax paid within the last 90 days that was due more than three years ago. In a chapter 11 reorganization, the payment of a tax that has priority will, for all practical purposes, not be considered a preference, because the plan must provide for the payment of all priority debts.

Section 547(c)(6) of the Bankruptcy Code provides that the fixing of a statutory lien is not a preference. Thus, the creation of a tax lien is not a preference item unless the lien is not properly perfected (section 545).

§ 16.45 Tax Procedures

The provisions in the Bankruptcy Code changed the tax procedures to be followed in a bankruptcy case. The commencement of a bankruptcy case automatically stays assessment and collection of prepetition tax liabilities of the debtor until the tax is determined by the bankruptcy court.[108] The IRS may, however, issue a notice of deficiency to the debtor while the debtor is in bankruptcy.[109] Section 362(a)(8) of the Bankruptcy Code also provides for a stay of the commencement or continuation of a proceeding before the tax court at the time the petition is filed.

An attempt by a taxing unit to collect the tax and ignore the automatic stay can have adverse consequences. For example, in *In re Daniel Demos*,[110] the district court reversed an order of the bankruptcy court and held that the receipt of cash proceeds from insurance policies of the debtor in which the IRS had obtained a lien over two years earlier was in violation of the automatic stay. The court directed the IRS to turn over the proceeds to the debtor.

§ 16.46 State and Local Tax Provisions

The Bankruptcy Reform Act of 1978 contained some tax provisions for state and local governments. This law differs in some respects from the provisions in the Bankruptcy Tax Act of 1980. Until these differences are reconciled by technical amendments, the taxpayer will be required to report selected items differently, such as gain due to debt discharge. Sections 346, 728, 1146, and 1231 of the Bankruptcy Code contain the provisions for state and local taxes.

A substantial difference can exist between the federal taxes and the state and local taxes. For example, under I.R.C. section 1398, the estate has the option to elect a short taxable year, which ends on the day before the bank-

---

[108]11 U.S.C. §§ 362(a)(6) and 362(b)(8).
[109]11 U.S.C. § 362(b)(7).
[110]No. 85-C-1225 (E.D. Wis. July 22, 1987).

ruptcy petition is filed. Under section 346 of the Bankruptcy Code, no such election exists. Sections 728, 1146, and 1231 of the Bankruptcy Code provide that the taxable year of the individual terminates on the date of the order for relief in a chapter 7, chapter 11, or chapter 12 case. Under I.R.C. section 1398, the taxable year ends on the date before the petition was filed, if the taxpayer makes the short-tax year election.

I.R.C. section 1398 indicates that the estate is taxed as an individual filing separate returns, but under section 346 of the Bankruptcy Code the bankruptcy estate is taxed as an estate. I.R.C. section 1398 provides that a separate estate is created for individuals in a chapter 7 or chapter 11 case; section 346 of the Bankruptcy Code also provides that a separate estate is created in a chapter 12 case.

The provisions for state and local taxes, along with other tax issues, are discussed in more detail in Newton and Bloom's *Bankruptcy and Insolvency Taxation* 2nd edition (New York: Wiley, 1994, updated annually).

APPENDIX **A**

Title 11—Bankruptcy Code

CHAPTER 5.
CREDITORS, THE DEBTOR, AND THE ESTATE

SUBCHAPTER I. CREDITORS AND CLAIMS

SUBCHAPTER II. DEBTOR'S DUTIES AND BENEFITS

CHAPTER 7.
LIQUIDATION

SUBCHAPTER I. OFFICERS AND ADMINISTRATION

SUBCHAPTER II. COLLECTION, LIQUIDATION, AND
DISTRIBUTION OF THE ESTATE

CHAPTER 9.
ADJUSTMENT OF DEBTS OF A MUNICIPALITY

SUBCHAPTER I. GENERAL PROVISIONS

SUBCHAPTER II. ADMINISTRATION

CHAPTER 11.
REORGANIZATION

SUBCHAPTER I. OFFICERS AND ADMINISTRATION

SUBCHAPTER II. THE PLAN

SUBCHAPTER III. POSTCONFIRMATION MATTERS

CHAPTER 12.
ADJUSTMENTS OF DEBTS OF A FAMILY FARMER WITH REGULAR ANNUAL INCOME

SUBCHAPTER I. OFFICERS, ADMINISTRATION, AND THE ESTATE

SUBCHAPTER II. THE PLAN

CHAPTER 13.
ADJUSTMENT OF DEBTS OF AN INDIVIDUAL WITH REGULAR INCOME

SUBCHAPTER I. OFFICERS, ADMINISTRATION, AND THE ESTATE

SUBCHAPTER II. THE PLAN

1
GENERAL PROVISIONS

Sec. 101. *Definitions*

In this title [11 USCS §§ 101 et seq.]—

(1)   "accountant" means accountant authorized under applicable [applicable] law to practice public accounting, and includes professional accounting association, corporation, or partnership, if so authorized;

(2)   "affiliate" means—

(A)   entity that directly or indirectly owns, controls, or holds with power to vote, 20 percent or more of the outstanding voting securities of the debtor, other than an entity that holds such securities—

(i)   in a fiduciary or agency capacity without sole discretionary power to vote such securities; or

(ii)   solely to secure a debt, if such entity has not in fact exercised such power to vote;

(B)   corporation 20 percent or more of whose outstanding voting securities are directly or indirectly owned, controlled, or held with power to vote, by the debtor, or by an entity that directly or indirectly owns, controls, or holds with power to vote, 20 percent or more of the outstanding voting securities of the debtor, other than an entity that holds such securities—

       (i)   in a fiduciary or agency capacity without sole discretionary power to vote such securities; or

       (ii)   solely to secure a debt, if such entity has not in fact exercised such power to vote;

    (C)   person whose business is operated under a lease or operating agreement by a debtor, or person substantially all of whose property is operated under an operating agreement with the debtor; or

    (D)   entity that operates the business or substantially all of the property of the debtor under a lease or operating agreement;

  (4)   "attorney" means attorney, professional law association, corporation, or partnership, authorized under applicable law to practice law;

  (5)   "claim" means—

    (A)   right to payment, whether or not such right is reduced to judgment, liquidated, unliquidated, fixed, contingent, matured, unmatured, disputed, undisputed, legal, equitable, secured, or unsecured; or

    (B)   right to an equitable remedy for breach of performance if such breach gives rise to a right to payment, whether or not such right to an equitable remedy is reduced to judgment, fixed, contingent, matured, unmatured, disputed, undisputed, secured, or unsecured;

  (6)   "commodity broker" means futures commission merchant, foreign futures commission merchant, clearing organization, leverage transaction merchant, or commodity options dealer, as defined in section 761 of this title with respect to which there is a customer, as defined in section 761 of this title;

  (7)   "community claim" means claim that arose before the commencement of the case concerning the debtor for which property of the kind specified in section 541(a)(2) of this title [11 USCS § 541(a)(2)] is liable, whether or not there is any such property at the time of the commencement of the case;

  (8)   "consumer debt" means debt incurred by an individual primarily for a personal, family, or household purpose;

  (9)   "corporation"—

    (A)   includes—

       (i)   association having a power or privilege that a private corporation, but not an individual or a partnership, possesses;

       (ii)   partnership association organized under a law that makes only the capital subscribed responsible for the debts of such association;

       (iii)   joint-stock company;

       (iv)   unincorporated company or association; or

       (v)   business trust; but

    (B)   does not include limited partnership;

  (10)   "creditor" means—

    (A)   entity that has a claim against the debtor that arose at the time of or before the order for relief concerning the debtor;

    (B)   entity that has a claim against the estate of a kind specified in section 348(d), 502(f), 502(g), 502(h) or 502(i) of this title [11 USCS §§ 348(d), 502(f), (g), (h), (i)]; or

    (C)   entity that has a community claim;

  (11)   "custodian" means—

(A) receiver or trustee of any of the property of the debtor, appointed in a case or proceeding not under this title [11 USCS §§ 101 et seq.];

(B) assignee under a general assignment for the benefit of the debtor's creditors; or

(C) trustee, receiver, or agent under applicable law, or under a contract, that is appointed or authorized to take charge of property of the debtor for the purpose of enforcing a lien against such property, or for the purpose of general administration of such property for the benefit of the debtor's creditors;

(12)   "debt" means liability on a claim;

(12A)   "debt for child support" means a debt of a kind specified in section 523(a)(5) of this title for maintenance or support of a child of the debtor;

(13)   "debtor" means person or municipality concerning which a case under this title [11 USCS §§ 101 et seq.] has been commenced;

(14)   "disinterested person" means person that—

(A) is not a creditor, an equity security holder, or an insider;

(B) is not and was not an investment banker for any outstanding security of the debtor;

(C) has not been, within three years before the date of the filing of the petition, an investment banker for a security of the debtor, or an attorney for such an investment banker in connection with the offer, sale, or issuance of a security of the debtor;

(D) is not and was not, within two years before the date of the filing of the petition, a director, officer, or employee of the debtor or of an investment banker specified in subparagraph (B) or (C) of this paragraph; and

(E) does not have an interest materially adverse to the interest of the estate or of any class of creditors or equity security holders, by reason of any direct or indirect relationship to, connection with, or interest in, the debtor or an investment banker specified in subparagraph (B) or (C) of this paragraph, or for any other reason;

(15)   "entity" includes person, estate, trust, governmental unit, and United States trustee;

(16)   "equity security" means—

(A) share in a corporation, whether or not transferable or denominated "stock," or similar security;

(B) interest of a limited partner in a limited partnership; or

(C) warrant or right, other than a right to convert, to purchase, sell, or subscribe to a share, security, or interest of a kind specified in subparagraph (A) or (B) of this paragraph;

(17)   "equity security holder" means holder of an equity security of the debtor;

(18)   "family farmer" means—

(A) individual or individual and spouse engaged in a farming operation whose aggregate debts do not exceed $1,500,000 and not less than 80 percent of whose aggregate noncontingent, liquidated debts (excluding a debt for the principal residence of such individual or such individual and spouse unless such debt arises out of a farming operation), on the date the case is filed, arise out of a farming operation owned or operated by such individual or such individual and spouse, and such individual or such individual and spouse receive from such farming operation more than 50 percent of such individual's or such individual and spouse's gross income for the taxable year preceding the taxable year in which the case concerning such individual or such individual and spouse was filed; or

(B) corporation or partnership in which more than 50 percent of the outstanding stock or equity is held by one family, or by one family and the relatives of the members of such family, and such family or such relatives conduct the farming operation, and

(i) more than 80 percent of the value of its assets consists of assets related to the farming operation;

(ii) its aggregate debts do not exceed $1,500,000 and not less than 80 percent of its aggregate noncontingent, liquidated debts (excluding a debt for one dwelling which is owned by such corporation or partnership and which a shareholder or partner maintains as a principal residence, unless such debt arises out of a farming operation), on the date the case is filed, arise out of the farming operation owned or operated by such corporation or such partnership; and

(iii) if such corporation issues stock, such stock is not publicly traded;

(19) "family farmer with regular annual income" means family farmer whose annual income is sufficiently stable and regular to enable such family farmer to make payments under a plan under chapter 12 of this title;

(20) "farmer" means (except when such term appears in the term "family farmer") person that received more than 80 percent of such person's gross income during the taxable year of such person immediately preceding the taxable year of such person during which the case under this title concerning such person was commenced from a farming operation owned or operated by such person;

(21) "farming operation" includes farming, tillage of the soil, dairy farming, ranching, production or raising of crops, poultry, or livestock, and production of poultry or livestock products in an unmanufactured state;

(21A) "farmout agreement" means a written agreement in which—

(A) the owner of a right to drill, produce, or operate liquid or gaseous hydrocarbons on property agrees or has agreed to transfer or assign all or a part of such right to another entity; and

(B) such other entity (either directly or through its agents or its assigns), as consideration, agrees to perform drilling, reworking, recompleting, testing, or similar or related operations, to develop or produce liquid or gaseous hydrocarbons on the property;

(21B) "Federal depository institutions regulatory agency" means—

(A) with respect to an insured depository institution (as defined in section 3(c)(2) of the Federal Deposit Insurance Act) for which no conservator or receiver has been appointed, the appropriate Federal banking agency (as defined in section 3(q) of such Act);

(B)   with respect to an insured credit union (including an insured credit union for which the National Credit Union Administration has been appointed conservator or liquidating agent), the National Credit Union Administration;

(C)   with respect to any insured depository institution for which the Resolution Trust Corporation has been appointed conservator or receiver, the Resolution Trust Corporation; and

(D)   with respect to any insured depository institution for which the Federal Deposit Insurance Corporation has been appointed conservator or receiver, the Federal Deposit Insurance Corporation;

(22)   "financial institution" means a person that is a commercial or savings bank, industrial savings bank, savings and loan association, or trust company and, when any such person is acting as agent or custodian for a customer in connection with a securities contract, as defined in section 741 of this title, such customer;

(23)   "foreign proceeding" means proceeding, whether judicial or administrative and whether or not under bankruptcy law, in a foreign country in which the debtor's domicile, residence, principal place of business, or principal assets were located at the commencement of such proceeding, for the purpose of liquidating an estate, adjusting debts by composition, extension, or discharge, or effecting a reorganization;

(24)   "foreign representative" means duly selected trustee, administrator, or other representative of an estate in a foreign proceeding;

(25)   "forward contract" means a contract (other than a commodity contract) for the purchase, sale, or transfer of a commodity, as defined in section 761(8) of this title, or any similar good, article, service, right, or interest which is presently or in the future becomes the subject of dealing in the forward contract trade, or product or byproduct thereof, with a maturity date more than two days after the date the contract is entered into, including, but not limited to, a repurchase transaction, reverse repurchase transaction, consignment, lease, swap, hedge transaction, deposit, loan, option, allocated transaction, unallocated transaction, or any combination thereof or option thereon;

(26)   "forward contract merchant" means a person whose business consists in whole or in part of entering into forward contracts as or with merchants in a commodity, as defined in section 761(8) of this title, or any similar good, article, service, right, or interest which is presently or in the future becomes the subject of dealing in the forward contract trade;

(27)   "governmental unit" means United States; State; Commonwealth; District; Territory; municipality; foreign state; department, agency, or instrumentality of the United States (but not a United States trustee while serving as a trustee in a case under this title), a State, a Commonwealth, a District, a Territory, a municipality, or a foreign state; or other foreign or domestic government;

(28)   "indenture" means mortgage, deed of trust, or indenture, under which there is outstanding a security, other than a voting-trust certificate, constituting a claim against the debtor, a claim secured by a lien on any of the debtor's property, or an equity security of the debtor;

(29)   "indenture trustee" means trustee under an indenture;

(30)   "individual with regular income" means individual whose income

is sufficiently stable and regular to enable such individual to make payments under a plan under chapter 13 of this title [11 USCS §§ 1301 et seq.], other than a stockbroker or a commodity broker;

 (31) "insider" includes—

  (A) if the debtor is an individual—

   (i) relative of the debtor or of a general partner of the debtor;

   (ii) partnership in which the debtor is a general partner;

   (iii) general partner of the debtor; or

   (iv) corporation of which the debtor is a director, officer, or person in control;

  (B) if the debtor is a corporation—

   (i) director of the debtor;

   (ii) officer of the debtor;

   (iii) person in control of the debtor;

   (iv) partnership in which the debtor is a general partner;

   (v) general partner of the debtor; or

   (vi) relative of a general partner, director, officer, or person in control of the debtor;

  (C) if the debtor is a partnership—

   (i) general partner in the debtor;

   (ii) relative of a general partner in, general partner of, or person in control of the debtor;

   (iii) partnership in which the debtor is a general partner;

   (iv) general partner of the debtor; or

   (v) person in control of the debtor;

  (D) if the debtor is a municipality, elected official of the debtor or relative of an elected official of the debtor;

  (E) affiliate, or insider of an affiliate as if such affiliate were the debtor; and

  (F) managing agent of the debtor;

 (32) "insolvent" means—

  (A) with reference to an entity other than a partnership and a municipality, financial condition such that the sum of such entity's debts is greater than all of such entity's property, at a fair valuation, exclusive of—

   (i) property transferred, concealed, or removed with intent to hinder, delay, or defraud such entity's creditors; and

   (ii) property that may be exempted from property of the estate under section 522 of this title [11 USCS § 522];

  (B) with reference to a partnership, financial condition such that the sum of such partnership's debts is greater than the aggregate of, at a fair valuation—

   (i) all of such partnership's property, exclusive of property of the kind specified in subparagraph (A)(i) of this paragraph; and

   (ii) the sum of the excess of the value of each general partner's nonpartnership property, exclusive of property of the kind specified in subparagraph (A) of this paragraph, over such partner's nonpartnership debts; and

(C) with reference to a municipality, financial condition such that the municipality is—

    (i) generally not paying its debts as they become due unless such debts are the subject of a bona fide dispute; or

    (ii) unable to pay its debts as they become due;

(33) "institution-affiliated party"—

(A) with respect to an insured depository institution (as defined in section 3(c)(2) of the Federal Deposit Insurance Act), has the meaning given it in section 3(u) of the Federal Deposit Insurance Act; and

(B) with respect to an insured credit union, has the meaning given it in section 206(r) of the Federal Credit Union Act;

(34) "insured credit union" has the meaning given it in section 101(7) or the Federal Credit Union Act;

(35) "insured depository institution"—

(A) has the meaning given it in section 3(c)(2) of the Federal Deposit Insurance Act; and

(B) includes an insured credit union (except in the case of paragraphs (21B) and (33)(A) of this subsection);

(35A) "intellectual property" means—

(A) trade secret;

(B) invention, process, design, or plant protected under title 35;

(C) patent application;

(D) plant variety;

(E) work of authorship protected under title 17; or

(F) mask work protected under chapter 9 of title 17 [17 USCS §§ 901 et seq.]; to the extent protected by applicable nonbankruptcy law; and

(36) "judicial lien" means lien obtained by judgment, levy, sequestration, or other legal or equitable process or proceeding;

(37) "lien" means charge against or interest in property to secure payment of a debt or performance of an obligation;

(38) "margin payment" means, for purposes of the forward contract provisions of this title, payment or deposit of cash, a security or other property, that is commonly known in the forward contract trade as original margin, initial margin, maintenance margin, or variation margin, including mark-to-market payments, or variation payments; and

(39) "mask work" has the meaning given it in section 901(a)(2) of title 17.

(40) "municipality" means political subdivision or public agency or instrumentality of a State;

(41) "person" includes individual, partnership, and corporation, but does not include governmental unit, except that a governmental unit that—

(A) acquires an asset from a person—

    (i) as a result of the operation of a loan guarantee agreement; or

    (ii) as receiver or liquidating agent of a person;

(B) is a guarantor of a pension benefit payable by or on behalf of the debtor or an affiliate of the debtor; or

(C) is the legal or beneficial owner of an asset of—

    (i) an employee pension benefit plan that is a governmental plan, as defined in section 414(d) of the Internal Revenue Code of 1986; or

    (ii)   an eligible deferred compensation plan, as defined in section 457(b) of the Internal Revenue Code of 1986;

shall be considered, for purposes of section 1102 of this title, to be a person with respect to such asset or such benefit;

(42)   "petition" means petition filed under section 301, 302, 303, or 304 of this title, as the case may be, commencing a case under this title;

(42A)   "production payment" means a term overriding royalty satisfiable in cash or in kind—

    (A)   contingent on the production of a liquid or gaseous hydrocarbon from particular real property; and

    (B)   from a specified volume, or a specified value, from the liquid or gaseous hydrocarbon produced from such property, and determined without regard to production costs; and

(43)   "purchaser" means transferee of a voluntary transfer, and includes immediate or mediate transferee of such a transferee;

(44)   "railroad" means common carrier by railroad engaged in the transportation of individuals or property or owner of trackage facilities leased by such a common carrier;

(45)   "relative" means individual related by affinity or consanguinity within the third degree as determined by the common law, or individual in a step or adoptive relationship within such third degree;

(46)   "repo participant" means an entity that, on any day during the period beginning 90 days before the date of the filing of the petition, has an outstanding repurchase agreement with the debtor;

(47)   "repurchase agreement" (which definition also applies to a reverse repurchase agreement) means an agreement, including related terms, which provides for the transfer of certificates of deposit, eligible bankers' acceptances, or securities that are direct obligations of, or that are fully guaranteed as to principal and interest by, the United States or any agency of the United States against the transfer of funds by the transferee of such certificates of deposit, eligible bankers' acceptances, or securities with a simultaneous agreement by such transferee to transfer to the transferor thereof certificates of deposit, eligible bankers' acceptances, or securities as described above, at a date certain not later than one year after such transfers or on demand, against the transfer of funds;

(48)   "securities clearing agency" means person that is registered as a clearing agency under section 17A of the Securities Exchange Act of 1934 or whose business is confined to the performance of functions of a clearing agency with respect to exempted securities, as defined in section 3(a)(12) of such Act for the purposes of such section 17A [15 USCS § 78q-1];

(49)   "security"—

    (A)   includes—

        (i)   note;

        (ii)   stock;

        (iii)   treasury stock;

        (iv)   bond;

        (v)   debenture;

        (vi)   collateral trust certificate;

      (vii)   pre-organization certificate or subscription;

      (viii)   transferable share;

      (ix)   voting-trust certificate;

      (x)   certificate of deposit;

      (xi)   certificate of deposit for security;

      (xii)   investment contract or certificate of interest or participation in a profit-sharing agreement or in an oil, gas, or mineral royalty or lease, if such contract or interest is required to be the subject of a registration statement filed with the Securities and Exchange Commission under the provisions of the Securities Act of 1933, or is exempt under section 3(b) of such Act from the requirement to file such a statement;

      (xiii)   interest of a limited partner in a limited partnership;

      (xiv)   other claim or interest commonly known as "security"; and

      (xv)   certificate of interest or participation in, temporary or interim certificate for, receipt for, or warrant or right to subscribe to or purchase or sell, a security; but

(B)   does not include—

      (i)   currency, check, draft, bill of exchange, or bank letter of credit;

      (ii)   leverage transaction, as defined in section 761 of this title;

      (iii)   commodity futures contract or forward contract;

      (iv)   option, warrant, or right to subscribe to or purchase or sell a commodity futures contract;

      (v)   option to purchase or sell a commodity;

      (vi)   contract or certificate of a kind specified in subparagraph (A)(xii) of this paragraph that is not required to be the subject of a registration statement filed with the Securities and Exchange Commission and is not exempt under section 3(b) of the Securities Act of 1933 from the requirement to file such a statement; or

      (vii)   debt or evidence of indebtedness for goods sold and delivered or services rendered;

(50)   "security agreement" means agreement that creates or provides for a security interest;

(51)   "security interest" means lien created by an agreement;

(51A)   "settlement payment" means, for purposes of the forward contract provisions of this title, a preliminary settlement payment, a partial settlement payment, an interim settlement payment, a settlement payment on account, a final settlement payment, a net settlement payment, or any other similar payment commonly used in the forward contract trade;

(51B)   "single asset real estate" means real property constituting a single property or project, other than residential real property with fewer than 4 residential units, which generates substantially all of the gross income of a debtor and on which no substantial business is being conducted by a debtor other than the business of operating the real property and activities incidental thereto having aggregate noncontingent, liquidated secured debts in an amount no more than $4,000,000.

(51C)   "small business" means a person engaged in commercial or business activities (but does not include a person whose primary activity is the business of owning or operating real property and activities incidental thereto) whose aggregate noncontingent liquidated secured and unsecured debts as of the date of the petition do not exceed $2,000,000.

(52)   "State" includes the District of Columbia and Puerto Rico, except for the purpose of defining who may be a debtor under chapter 9 of this title [11 USCS §§ 901 et seq.];

(53)   "statutory lien" means lien arising solely by force of a statute on specified circumstances or conditions, or lien of distress for rent, whether or not statutory, but does not include security interest or judicial lien, whether or not such interest or lien is provided by or is dependent on a statute and whether or not such interest or lien is made fully effective by statute;

(53A)   "stockbroker" means person—

(A)   with respect to which there is a customer, as defined in section 741 of this title; and

(B)   that is engaged in the business of effecting transactions in securities—

(i)   for the account of others; or

(ii)   with members of the general public, from or for such person's own account;

(53B)   "swap agreement" means—

(A)   an agreement (including terms and conditions incorporated by reference therein) which is a rate swap agreement, basis swap, forward rate agreement, commodity swap, interest rate option, forward foreign exchange agreement, spot foreign exchange agreement, rate cap agreement, rate floor agreement, rate collar agreement, currency swap agreement, cross-currency rate swap agreement, currency option, any other similar agreement (including any option to enter into any of the foregoing);

(B)   any combination of the foregoing; or

(C)   a master agreement for any of the foregoing together with all supplements;

(56A)   "swap participant" means an entity that, at any time before the filing of the petition, has an outstanding swap agreement with the debtor;

(53D)   "term overriding royalty" means an interest in liquid or gaseous hydrocarbons in place or to be produced from particular real property that entitles the owner thereof to a share of production, or the value thereof, for a term limited by time, quantity, or value realized;

(53D)   "timeshare plan" means and shall include that interest purchased in any arrangement, plan, scheme, or similar device, but not including exchange programs, whether by membership, agreement, tenancy in common, sale, lease, deed, rental agreement, license, right to use agreement, or by any other means, whereby a purchaser, in exchange for consideration, receives a right to use accommodations, facilities, or recreational sites, whether improved or unimproved, for a specific period of time less than a full year during any given year, but not necessarily for consecutive years, and which extends for a period of more than three years. A "timeshare interest" is that interest purchased in a timeshare plan which grants the purchaser the right to use and occupy accommodations, facilities, or recreational sites, whether improved or unimproved, pursuant to a timeshare plan;

(54)*   "transfer" means every mode, direct or indirect, absolute or conditional, voluntary or involuntary, of disposing of or parting with property or with an interest in property, including retention of title as a security interest and foreclosure of the debtor's equity of redemption;

(55)*   "United States," when used in a geographical sense, includes all locations where the judicial jurisdiction of the United States extends, including territories and possessions of the United States;

Sec. 102. *Rules of Construction*

In this title—

(1)   "after notice and a hearing", or a similar phrase—

(A)   means after such notice as is appropriate in the particular circumstances, and such opportunity for a hearing as is appropriate in the particular circumstances; but

(B)   authorizes an act without an actual hearing if such notice is given properly and if—

(i)   such a hearing is not requested timely by a party in interest; or

(ii)   there is insufficient time for a hearing to be commenced before such act must be done, and the court authorizes such act;

(2)   "claim against the debtor" includes claim against property of the debtor;

(3)   "includes" and "including" are not limiting;

(4)   "may not" is prohibitive, and not permissive;

(5)   "or" is not exclusive;

(6)   "order for relief" means entry of an order for relief;

(7)   the singular includes the plural;

(8)   a definition, contained in a section of this title that refers to another section of this title, does not, for the purpose of such reference, affect the meaning of a term used in such other section; and

(9)   "United States trustee" includes a designee of the United States trustee.

Sec. 103. *Applicability of Chapters*

(a)   Except as provided in section 1161 of this title, chapters 1, 3, and 5 of this title apply in a case under chapter 7, 11, 12, or 13 of this title.

(b)   Subchapters I and II of chapter 7 of this title apply only in a case under such chapter.

(c)   Subchapter III of chapter 7 of this title applies only in a case under such chapter concerning a stockbroker.

(d)   Subchapter IV of chapter 7 of this title applies only in a case under such chapter concerning a commodity broker.

(e)   Except as provided in section 901 of this title, only chapters 1 and 9 of this title apply in a case under such chapter 9.

(f)   Except as provided in section 901 of this title, subchapters I, II, and III of chapter 11 of this title apply only in a case under such chapter.

(g)   Subchapter IV of chapter 11 of this title applies only in a case under such chapter concerning a railroad.

(h)   Chapter 13 of this title applies only in a case under such chapter.

(i)   Chapter 12 of this title applies only in a case under such chapter.

Sec. 104.   Adjustment of Dollar Amounts

(a)   The Judicial Conference of the United States shall transmit to the Congress and to the President before May 1, 1985, and before May 1 of every sixth year after May 1, 1985, a recommendation for the uniform percentage adjustment of each dollar amount in this title and in section 1930 of title 28.

(b) (1)   On April 1, 1998, and at each 3-year interval ending on April 1 thereafter, each dollar amount in effect under sections 109(e), 303(b), 507(a), 522(d), and 523(a)(2)(C) immediately before such April 1 shall be adjusted—

   (A)   to reflect the change in the Consumer Price Index for All Urban Consumers, published by the Department of Labor, for the most recent 3-year period ending immediately before January 1 preceding such April 1, and

   (B)   to round to the nearest $25 the dollar amount that represents such change.

(2)   Not later than March 1, 1998, and at each 3-year interval ending on March 1 thereafter, the Judicial Conference of the United States shall publish in the Federal Register the dollar amounts that will become effective on such April 1 under sections 109(e), 303(b), 507(a), 522(d), and 523(a)(2)(C) of this title.

(3)   Adjustments made in accordance with paragraph (1) shall not apply with respect to cases commenced before the date of such adjustments.

Sec. 105.   Power of Court

(a)   The court may issue any order, process, or judgment that is necessary or appropriate to carry out the provisions of this title. No provision of this title providing for the raising of an issue by a party in interest shall be construed to preclude the court from sua sponte, taking any action or making any determination necessary or appropriate to enforce or implement court orders or rules, or to prevent an abuse of process.

(b)   Notwithstanding subsection (a) of this section, a court may not appoint a receiver in a case under this title.

(c)   The ability of any district judge or other officer or employee of a district court to exercise any of the authority or responsibilities conferred upon the court under this title shall be determined by reference to the provisions relating to such judge, officer, or employee set forth in title 28. This subsection shall not be interpreted to exclude bankruptcy judges and other officers or employees appointed pursuant to chapter 6 of title 28 from its operation.

(d)   The court, on its own motion or on the request of a party in interest, may—

   (1)   hold a status conference regarding any case or proceeding under this title after notice to the parties in interest; and

(2)   unless inconsistent with another provision of this title or with applicable Federal Rules of Bankruptcy Procedure, issue an order at any such conference prescribing such limitations and conditions as the court deems appropriate to ensure that the case is handled expeditiously and economically, including an order that—

(A)   sets the date by which the trustee must assume or reject an executory contract or unexpired lease; or

(B)   in a case under chapter 11 of this title—

(i)   sets a date by which the debtor, or trustee if one has been appointed, shall file a disclosure statement and plan;

(ii)   sets a date by which the debtor, or trustee if one has been appointed, shall solicit acceptances of a plan;

(iii)   sets the date by which a party in interest other than a debtor may file a plan;

(iv)   sets a date by which a proponent of a plan, other than the debtor, shall solicit acceptances of such plan;

(v)   fixes the scope and format of the notice to be provided regarding the hearing on approval of the disclosure statement; or

(vi)   provides that the hearing on approval of the disclosure statement may be combined with the hearing on confirmation of the plan.

Sec. 106.   *Waiver of Sovereign Immunity*

(a)   Notwithstanding an assertion of sovereign immunity, sovereign immunity is abrogated as to a governmental unit to the extent set forth in this section with respect to the following:

(1)   Sections 105, 106, 107, 108, 303, 346, 362, 363, 364, 365, 366, 502, 503, 505, 506, 510, 522, 523, 524, 525, 542, 543, 544, 545, 546, 547, 548, 549, 550, 551, 552, 553, 722, 724, 726, 728, 744, 749, 764, 901, 922, 926, 928, 929, 944, 1107, 1141, 1142, 1143, 1146, 1201, 1203, 1205, 1206, 1227, 1231, 1301, 1303, 1305, and 1327 of this title.

(2)   The court may hear and determine any issue arising with respect to the application of such sections to governmental units.

(3)   The court may issue against a governmental unit an order, process, or judgment under such sections or the Federal Rules of Bankruptcy Procedure, including an order or judgment awarding a money recovery, but not including an award of punitive damages. Such order or judgment for costs or fees under this title or the Federal Rules of Bankruptcy Procedure against any governmental unit shall be consistent with the provisions and limitations of section 2412(d)(2)(A) of title 28.

(4)   The enforcement of any such order, process, or judgment against any governmental unit shall be consistent with appropriate nonbankruptcy law applicable to such governmental unit and, in the case of a money judgment against the United States, shall be paid as if it is a judgment rendered by a district court of the United States.

(5)   Nothing in this section shall create any substantive claim for relief or cause of action not otherwise existing under this title, the Federal Rules of Bankruptcy Procedure, or nonbankruptcy law.

(b)   A governmental unit that has filed a proof of claim in the case is deemed to have waived sovereign immunity with respect to a claim against such governmental unit that is property of the estate and that arose out of the same transaction or occurrence out of which the claim of such governmental unit arose.

(c)   Notwithstanding any assertion of sovereign immunity by a governmental unit, there shall be offset against a claim or interest of a governmental unit any claim against such governmental unit that is property of the estate.

Sec. 107. *Public Access to Papers*

(a)   Except as provided in subsection (b) of this section, a paper filed in a case under this title and the dockets of a bankruptcy court are public records and open to examination by an entity at reasonable times without charge.

(b)   On request of a party in interest, the bankruptcy court shall, and on the bankruptcy court's own motion, the bankruptcy court may—

(1)   protect an entity with respect to a trade secret or confidential research, development, or commercial information; or

(2)   protect a person with respect to scandalous or defamatory matter contained in a paper filed in a case under this title.

Sec. 108. *Extension of Time*

(a)   If applicable nonbankruptcy law, an order entered in a nonbankruptcy proceeding, or an agreement fixes a period within which the debtor may commence an action, and such period has not expired before the date of the filing of the petition, the trustee may commence such action only before the later of—

(1)   the end of such period, including any suspension of such period occurring on or after the commencement of the case; or

(2)   two years after the order for relief.

(b)   Except as provided in subsection (a) of this section, if applicable nonbankruptcy law, an order entered in a nonbankruptcy proceeding, or an agreement fixes a period within which the debtor or an individual protected under section 1201 or 1301 of this title may file any pleading, demand, notice, or proof of claim or loss, cure a default, or perform any other similar act, and such period has not expired before the date of the filing of the petition, the trustee may only file, cure, or perform, as the case may be, before the later of—

(1)   the end of such period, including any suspension of such period occurring on or after the commencement of the case; or

(2)   60 days after the order for relief.

(c)   Except as provided in section 524 of this title, if applicable nonbankruptcy law, an order entered in a nonbankruptcy proceeding, or an agreement fixes a period for commencing or continuing a civil action in a court other than a bankruptcy court on a claim against the debtor, or against an individual with respect to which such individual is protected under section 1201 or 1301 of this title, and such period has not expired before the date of the filing of the petition, then such period does not expire until the later of—

(1)   the end of such period, including any suspension of such period occurring on or after the commencement of the case; or

(2)   30 days after notice of the termination or expiration of the stay under section 362, 922, 1201 or 1301 of this title, as the case may be, with respect to such claim.

Sec. 109.   Who May Be a Debtor

(a)   Notwithstanding any other provisions of this section, only a person that resides or has a domicile, a place of business, or property in the United States, or a municipality, may be a debtor under this title.

(b)   A person may be a debtor under chapter 7 of this title only if such person is not—

(1)   a railroad;

(2)   a domestic insurance company, bank, savings bank, cooperative bank, savings and loan association, building and loan association, homestead association, small business investment company licensed by the Small Business Administration under subsection (c) or (d) of section 301 of the Small Business Investment Act of 1958, credit union, or industrial bank or similar institution which is an insured bank as defined in section 3(h) of the Federal Deposit Insurance Act; or

(3)   a foreign insurance company, bank, savings bank, cooperative bank, savings and loan association, building and loan association, homestead association, or credit union, engaged in such business in the United States.

(c)   An entity may be a debtor under chapter 9 of this title if and only if such entity—

(1)   is a municipality;

(2)   is specifically authorized, in its capacity as a municipality or by name, to be a debtor under such chapter by State law, or by a governmental officer or organization empowered by State law to authorize such entity to be a debtor under such chapter;

(3)   is insolvent;

(4)   desires to effect a plan to adjust such debts; and

(5)   (A)   has obtained the agreement of creditors holding at least a majority in amount of the claims of each class that such entity intends to impair under a plan in a case under such chapter;

(B)   has negotiated in good faith with creditors and has failed to obtain the agreement of creditors holding at least a majority in amount of the claims of each class that such entity intends to impair under a plan in a case under such chapter;

(C)   is unable to negotiate with creditors because such negotiation is impracticable; or

(D)   reasonably believes that a creditor may attempt to obtain a transfer that is avoidable under Section 547 of this title.

(d)   Only a person that may be a debtor under chapter 7 of this title, except a stockbroker or a commodity broker, and a railroad may be a debtor under chapter 11 of this title.

(e)   Only an individual with regular income that owes, on the date of the filing of the petition, noncontingent, liquidated, unsecured debts of less than $269,250 and noncontingent, liquidated, secured debts of less than $807,750, or an individual with regular income and such individual's spouse, except a stockbroker or a commodity broker, that owe, on the date of the filing of the petition, noncontingent, liquidated, unsecured debts that aggregate less than $269,250 and noncontingent, liquidated, secured debts of less than $807,750 may be a debtor under chapter 13 of this title.

(f)   Only a family farmer with regular annual income may be a debtor under chapter 12 of this title.

(g)   Notwithstanding any other provision of this section, no individual or family farmer may be a debtor under this title who has been a debtor in a case pending under this title at any time in the preceding 180 days if—

(1)   the case was dismissed by the court for willful failure of the debtor to abide by orders of the court, or to appear before the court in proper prosecution of the case; or

(2)   the debtor requested and obtained the voluntary dismissal of the case following the filing of a request for relief from the automatic stay provided by section 362 of this title.

Sec. 110.   Penalty for Persons Who Negligently or Fraudulently Prepare Bankruptcy Petitions

(a)   In this section—

(1)   "bankruptcy petition preparer" means a person, other than an attorney or an employee of an attorney, who prepares for compensation a document for filing; and

(2)   "document for filing" means a petition or any other document prepared for filing by a debtor in a United States bankruptcy court or a United States district court in connection with a case under this title.

(b) (1)   A bankruptcy petition preparer who prepares a document for filing shall sign the document and print on the document the preparer's name and address.

(2)   A bankruptcy petition preparer who fails to comply with paragraph (1) may be fined not more than $500 for each such failure unless the failure is due to reasonable cause.

(c) (1)   A bankruptcy petition preparer who prepares a document for filing shall place on the document, after the preparer's signature, an identifying number that identifies individuals who prepared the document.

(2)   For purposes of this section, the identifying number of a bankruptcy petition preparer shall be the Social Security account number of each individual who prepared the document or assisted in its preparation.

(3)   A bankruptcy petition preparer who fails to comply with paragraph (1) may be fined not more than $500 for each such failure unless the failure is due to reasonable cause.

(d) (1)   A bankruptcy petition preparer shall, not later than the time at which a document for filing is presented for the debtor's signature, furnish to the debtor a copy of the document.

(2)   A bankruptcy petition preparer who fails to comply with paragraph (1) may be fined not more than $500 for each such failure unless the failure is due to reasonable cause.

(e) (1)   A bankruptcy petition preparer shall not execute any document on behalf of a debtor.

(2)   A bankruptcy petition preparer may be fined not more than $500 for each document executed in violation of paragraph (1).

(f) (1)   A bankruptcy petition preparer shall not use the world "legal" or any similar term in any advertisements, or advertise under any category that includes the word "legal" or any similar term.

(2)   A bankruptcy petition preparer shall be fined not more than $500 for each violation of paragraph (1).

(g) (1)   A bankruptcy petition preparer shall not collect or receive any payment from the debtor or on behalf of the debtor for the court fees in connection with filing the petition.

(2)   A bankruptcy petition preparer shall be fined not more than $500 for each violation of paragraph (1).

(h) (1)   Within 10 days after the date of the filing of a petition, a bankruptcy petition preparer shall file a declaration under penalty of perjury disclosing any fee received from or on behalf of the debtor within 12 months immediately prior to the filing of the case, and any unpaid fee charged to the debtor.

(2)   The court shall disallow and order the immediate turnover to the bankruptcy trustee of any fee referred to in paragraph (1) found to be in excess of the value of services rendered for the documents prepared. An individual debtor may exempt any funds so recovered under section 522(b).

(3)   The debtor, the trustee, a creditor, or the United States trustee may file a motion for an order under paragraph (2).

(4)   A bankruptcy petition preparer shall be fined not more than $500 for each failure to comply with a court order to turn over funds within 30 days of service of such order.

(i) (1)   If a bankruptcy case or related proceeding is dismissed because of the failure to file bankruptcy papers, including papers specified in section 521(1) of this title, the negligence or intentional disregard of this title or the Federal Rules of Bankruptcy Procedure by a bankruptcy petition preparer, or if a bankruptcy petition preparer violates this section or commits any fraudulent, unfair, or deceptive act, the bankruptcy court shall certify that fact to the district court, and the district court, on motion of the debtor, the trustee, or a creditor and after a hearing, shall order the bankruptcy petition preparer to pay to the debtor—

(A)   the debtor's actual damages;

(B)   the greater of—

(i) $2,000; or

(ii)   twice the amount paid by the debtor to the bankruptcy petition preparer for the preparer's services; and

(C)   reasonable attorneys' fees and costs in moving for damages under this subsection.

(2)   If the trustee or creditor moves for damages on behalf of the debtor under this subsection, the bankruptcy petition preparer shall be ordered to

pay the movant the additional amount of $1,000 plus reasonable attorneys' fees and costs incurred.

(j) (1)   A debtor for whom a bankruptcy petition preparer has prepared a document for filing, the trustee, a creditor, or the United States trustee in the district in which the bankruptcy petition preparer resides, has conducted business, or the United States trustee in any other district in which the debtor resides may bring a civil action to enjoin a bankruptcy petition preparer from engaging in any conduct in violation of this section or from further acting as a bankruptcy petition preparer.

(2)   (A)   In an action under paragraph (1), if the court finds that—
(i)   a bankruptcy petition preparer has—
(I)   engaged in conduct in violation of this section or of any provision of this title a violation of which subjects a person to criminal penalty:
(II)   misrepresented the preparer's experience or education as a bankruptcy petition preparer, or
(III)   engaged in any other fraudulent, unfair, or deceptive conduct; and
(ii)   injunctive relief is appropriate to prevent the recurrence of such conduct, the court may enjoin the bankruptcy petition preparer from engaging in such conduct.

(B)   If the court finds that a bankruptcy petition preparer has continually engaged in conduct described in subclause (I), (II), or (III) of clause (i) and that an injunction prohibiting such conduct would not be sufficient to prevent such person's interference with the proper administration of this title, or has not paid a penalty imposed under this section, the court may enjoin the person from acting as a bankruptcy petition preparer.

(3)   The court shall award to a debtor, trustee, or creditor that brings a successful action under this subsection reasonable attorney's fees and costs of the action, to be paid by the bankruptcy petition preparer.

(k)   Nothing in this section shall be construed to permit activities that are otherwise prohibited by law, including rules and laws that prohibit the unauthorized practice of law.

3
CASE ADMINISTRATION

SUBCHAPTER I. COMMENCEMENT OF A CASE

Sec. 301.   Voluntary Cases

A voluntary case under a chapter of this title is commenced by the filing with the bankruptcy court of a petition under such chapter by an entity that may be a debtor under such chapter. The commencement of a voluntary case under a chapter of this title constitutes an order for relief under such chapter.

Sec. 302. *Joint Cases*

(a)   A joint case under a chapter of this title is commenced by the filing with the bankruptcy court of a single petition under such chapter by an
individual that may be a debtor under such chapter and such individual's
spouse. The commencement of a joint case under a chapter of this title constitutes an order for relief under such chapter.

(b)   After the commencement of a joint case, the court shall determine
the extent, if any, to which the debtors' estates shall be consolidated.

Sec. 303. *Involuntary Cases*

(a)   An involuntary case may be commenced only under chapter 7 or
11 of this title, and only against a person, except a farmer, family farmer, or a
corporation that is not a moneyed, business, or commercial corporation, that
may be a debtor under the chapter under which such case is commenced.

(b)   An involuntary case against a person is commenced by the filing
with the bankruptcy court of a petition under chapter 7 or 11 of this title—

(1)   by three or more entities, each of which is either a holder of a claim
against such person that is not contingent as to liability or the [subject on] subject of a bona fide dispute, or an indenture trustee representing such a holder,
if such claims aggregate at least $10,775 more than the value of any lien on
property of the debtor securing such claims held by the holders of such claims;

(2)   if there are fewer than 12 such holders, excluding any employee or
insider of such person and any transferee of a transfer that is voidable under
section 544, 545, 547, 548, 549, or 724(a) of this title, by one or more of such
holders that hold in the aggregate at least $10,775 of such claims;

(3)   if such person is a partnership—

(A)   by fewer than all of the general partners in such partnership; or

(B)   if relief has been ordered under this title with respect to all of
the general partners in such partnership, by a general partner in such
partnership, the trustee of such a general partner, or a holder of a claim
against such partnership; or

(4)   by a foreign representative of the estate in a foreign proceeding
concerning such person.

(c)   After the filing of a petition under this section but before the case
is dismissed or relief is ordered, a creditor holding an unsecured claim that is
not contingent, other than a creditor filing under subsection (b) of this section,
may join in the petition with the same effects as if such joining creditor were
a petitioning creditor under subsection (b) of this section.

(d)   The debtor, or a general partner in a partnership debtor that did not
join in the petition, may file an answer to a petition under this section.

(e)   After notice and a hearing, and for cause, the court may require the
petitioners under this section to file a bond to indemnify the debtor for such
amounts as the court may later allow under subsection (i) of this section.

(f)   Notwithstanding section 363 of this title, except to the extent that
the court orders otherwise, and until an order for relief in the case, any business of the debtor may continue to operate, and the debtor may continue to
use, acquire, or dispose of property as if an involuntary case concerning the
debtor had not been commenced.

(g)   At any time after the commencement of an involuntary case under chapter 7 of this title but before an order for relief in the case, the court, on request of a party in interest, after notice to the debtor and a hearing, and if necessary to preserve the property of the estate or to prevent loss to the estate, may order the United States trustee to appoint an interim trustee under section 701 of this title to take possession of the property of the estate and to operate any business of the debtor. Before an order for relief, the debtor may regain possession of property in the possession of a trustee ordered appointed under this subsection if the debtor files such bond as the court requires, conditioned on the debtor's accounting for and delivering to the trustee, if there is an order for relief in the case, such property, or the value, as of the date the debtor regains possession, of such property.

(h)   If the petition is not timely controverted, the court shall order relief against the debtor in an involuntary case under the chapter under which the petition was filed. Otherwise, after trial, the court shall order relief against the debtor in an involuntary case under the chapter under which the petition was filed, only if—

(1)   the debtor is generally not paying such debtor's debts as such debts become due unless such debts [that] are the subject of a bona fide dispute; or

(2)   within 120 days before the date of the filing of the petition, a custodian, other than a trustee, receiver, or agent appointed or authorized to take charge of less than substantially all of the property of the debtor for the purpose of enforcing a lien against such property, was appointed or took possession.

(i)   If the court dismisses a petition under this section other than on consent of all petitioners and the debtor, and if the debtor does not waive the right to judgment under this subsection, the court may grant judgment—

(1)   against the petitioners and in favor of the debtor for—

(A)   costs; or

(B)   a reasonable attorney's fee; or

(2)   against any petitioner that filed the petition in bad faith, for—

(A)   any damages proximately caused by such filing; or

(B)   punitive damages.

(j)   Only after notice to all creditors and a hearing may the court dismiss a petition filed under this section—

(1)   on the motion of a petitioner;

(2)   on consent of all petitioners and the debtor; or

(3)   for want of prosecution.

(k)   Notwithstanding subsection (a) of this section, an involuntary case may be commenced against a foreign bank that is not engaged in such business in the United States only under chapter 7 of this title and only if a foreign proceeding concerning such bank is pending.

Sec. 304.   *Cases Ancillary to Foreign Proceedings*

(a)   A case ancillary to a foreign proceeding is commenced by the filing with the bankruptcy court of a petition under this section by a foreign representative.

(b)   Subject to the provisions of subsection (c) of this section, if a party in interest does not timely controvert the petition, or after trial, the court may—

(1)   enjoin the commencement or continuation of

(A)   any action against—

(i)   a debtor with respect to property involved in such foreign proceeding; or

(ii)   such property; or

(B)   the enforcement of any judgment against the debtor with respect to such property, or any act or the commencement or continuation of any judicial proceeding to create or enforce a lien against the property of such estate;

(2)   order turnover of the property of such estate, or the proceeds of such property, to such foreign representative; or

(3)   order other appropriate relief.

(c)   In determining whether to grant relief under subsection (b) of this section, the court shall be guided by what will best assure an economical and expeditious administration of such estate, consistent with—

(1)   just treatment of all holders of claims against or interests in such estate;

(2)   protection of claim holders in the United States against prejudice and inconvenience in the possessing of claims in such foreign proceeding;

(3)   prevention of preferential or fraudulent dispositions of property of such estate;

(4)   distribution of proceeds of such estate substantially in accordance with the order prescribed by this title;

(5)   comity; and

(6)   if appropriate, the provision of an opportunity for a fresh start for the individual that such foreign proceeding concerns.

Sec. 305.   *Abstention*

(a)   The court, after notice and a hearing, may dismiss a case under this title, or may suspend all proceedings in a case under this title, at any time if—

(1)   the interests of creditors and the debtor would be better served by such dismissal or suspension; or

(2)   (A)   there is pending a foreign proceeding; and

(B)   the factors specified in section 304(c) of this title warrant such dismissal or suspension.

(b)   A foreign representative may seek dismissal or suspension under subsection (a)(2) of this section.

(c)   An order under subsection (a) of this section dismissing a case or suspending all proceedings in a case, or a decision not so to dismiss or suspend, is not reviewable by appeal or otherwise by the court of appeals under section 158(d), 1291, or 1292 of title 28 or by Supreme Court of the United States under section 1254 of title 28.

Sec. 306.   *Limited Appearance*

An appearance in a bankruptcy court by a foreign representative in connection with a petition or request under section 303, 304, or 305 of this title does not submit such foreign representative to the jurisdiction of any court in the United States for any other purpose, but the bankruptcy court may condition any order under section 303, 304, or 305 of this title on compliance by such foreign representative with the orders of such bankruptcy court.

Sec. 307.   United States Trustee

The United States trustee may raise and may appear and be heard on any issue in any case or proceeding under this title but may not file a plan pursuant to section 1121(c) of this title.

SUBCHAPTER II. OFFICERS

Sec. 321.   Eligibility to Serve as Trustee

(a)   A person may serve as trustee in a case under this title only if such person is—
    (1)   an individual that is competent to perform the duties of trustee and, in a case under chapter 7, 12, or 13 of this title, resides or has an office in the judicial district within which the case is pending, or in any judicial district adjacent to such district; or
    (2)   a corporation authorized by such corporation's charter or bylaws to act as trustee, and, in a case under chapter 7, 12, or 13 of this title, having an office in at least one of such districts.
(b)   A person that has served as an examiner in a case may not serve as trustee in the case.
(c)   The United States trustee for the judicial district in which the case is pending is eligible to serve as trustee in the case if necessary.

Sec. 322.   Qualification of Trustee

(a)   Except as provided in subsection (b)(1), a person selected under section 701, 702, 703, 1104, 1163, 1202, or 1302 of this title to serve as trustee in a case under this title qualifies if before five days after such selection, and before beginning official duties, such person has filed with the court a bond in favor of the United States conditioned on the faithful performance of such official duties.
(b) (1)   The United States trustee qualifies wherever such trustee serves as trustee in a case under this title.
    (2)   The United States trustee shall determine—
        (A)   the amount of a bond required to be filed under subsection (a) of this section; and
        (B)   the sufficiency of the surety on such bond.
(c)   A trustee is not liable personally or on such trustee's bond in favor of the United States for any penalty or forfeiture incurred by the debtor.
(d)   A proceeding on a trustee's bond may not be commenced after two years after the date on which such trustee was discharged.

Sec. 323.   Role and Capacity of Trustee

(a)   The trustee in a case under this title is the representative of the estate.

(b)   The trustee in a case under this title has capacity to sue and be sued.

Sec. 324. *Removal of Trustee or Examiner*

(a)   The court, after notice and a hearing, may remove a trustee, other than the United States trustee, or an examiner, for cause.

Sec. 325. *Effect of Vacancy*

A vacancy in the office of trustee during a case does not abate any pending action or proceeding, and the successor trustee shall be substituted as a party in such action or proceeding.

Sec. 326. *Limitation on Compensation of Trustee*

(a)   In a case under chapter 7 or 11, the court may allow reasonable compensation under section 330 of this title of the trustee for the trustee's services, payable after the trustee renders such services, not to exceed 25 percent on the first $5,000 or less, 10 percent on any amount in excess of $5,000 but not in excess of $50,000, 5 percent on any amount in excess of $50,000 but not in excess of $1,000,000, and reasonable compensation not to exceed 3 percent of such moneys in excess of $1,000,000, upon all moneys disbursed or turned over in the case by the trustee to parties in interest, excluding the debtor, but including holders of secured claims.

(b)   In a case under chapter 12 or 13 of this title, the court may not allow compensation for services or reimbursement of expenses of the United States trustee or of a standing trustee appointed under section 586(b) of title 28, but may allow reasonable compensation under section 330 of this title of a trustee appointed under section 1202(a) or 1302(a) of this title for the trustee's services, payable after the trustee renders such services, not to exceed five percent upon all payments under the plan.

(c)   If more than one person serves as trustee in the case, the aggregate compensation of such persons for such service may not exceed the maximum compensation prescribed for a single trustee by subsection (a) or (b) of this section, as the case may be.

(d)   The court may deny allowance of compensation for services or reimbursement of expenses of the trustee if the trustee failed to make diligent inquiry into facts that would permit denial of allowance under section 328(c) of this title or, with knowledge of such facts, employed a professional person under section 327 of this title.

Sec. 327. *Employment of Professional Persons*

(a)   Except as otherwise provided in this section, the trustee, with the court's approval, may employ one or more attorneys, accountants, appraisers, auctioneers, or other professional persons, that do not hold or represent an interest adverse to the estate, and that are disinterested persons, to represent or assist the trustee in carrying out the trustee's duties under this title.

(b)   If the trustee is authorized to operate the business of the debtor under section 721, 1202, or 1108 of this title, and if the debtor has regularly employed attorneys, accountants, or other professional persons on salary, the trustee may retain or replace such professional persons if necessary in the operation of such business.

(c)   In a case under chapter 7, 12, or 11 of this title, a person is not disqualified for employment under this section solely because of such person's employment by or representation of a creditor, unless there is objection by another creditor or the United States trustee, in which case the court shall disapprove such employment if there is an actual conflict of interest.

(d)   The court may authorize the trustee to act as attorney or accountant for the estate if such authorization is in the best interest of the estate.

(e)   The trustee, with the court's approval, may employ, for a specified special purpose, other than to represent the trustee in conducting the case, an attorney that has represented the debtor, if in the best interest of the estate, and if such attorney does not represent or hold any interest adverse to the debtor or to the estate with respect to the matter on which such attorney is to be employed.

(f)   The trustee may not employ a person that has served as an examiner in the case.

Sec. 328.   *Limitation on Compensation of Professional Persons*

(a)   The trustee, or a committee appointed under section 1102 of this title, with the court's approval, may employ or authorize the employment of a professional person under section 327 or 1103 of this title, as the case may be, on any reasonable terms and conditions of employment, including on a retainer, on an hourly basis, or on a contingent fee basis. Notwithstanding such terms and conditions, the court may allow compensation different from the compensation provided under such terms and conditions after the conclusion of such employment, if such terms and conditions prove to have been improvident in light of developments not capable of being anticipated at the time of the fixing of such terms and conditions.

(b)   If the court has authorized a trustee to serve as an attorney or accountant for the estate under section 327(d) of this title, the court may allow compensation for the trustee's services as such attorney or accountant only to the extent that the trustee performed services as attorney or accountant for the estate and not for performance of any of the trustee's duties that are generally performed by a trustee without the assistance of an attorney or accountant for the estate.

(c)   Except as provided in section 327(c), 327(e), or 1107(b) of this title, the court may deny allowance of compensation for services and reimbursement of expenses of a professional person employed under section 327 or 1103 of this title if, at any time during such professional person's employment under section 327 or 1103 of this title, such professional person is not a disinterested person, or represents or holds an interest adverse to the interest of the estate with respect to the matter on which such professional person is employed.

Sec. 329.   *Debtor's Transactions with Attorneys*

(a)   Any attorney representing a debtor in a case under this title, or in connection with such a case, whether or not such attorney applies for compensation under this title, shall file with the court a statement of the compensation paid or agreed to be paid, if such payment or agreement was made after one year before the date of the filing of the petition, for services rendered or to be rendered in contemplation of or in connection with the case by such attorney, and the source of such compensation.

(b)   If such compensation exceeds the reasonable value of any such services, the court may cancel any such agreement, or order the return of any such payment, to the extent excessive, to—

(1)   the estate if the property transferred—

(A)   would have been property of the estate; or

(B)   was to be paid by or on behalf of the debtor under a plan under chapter 11, 12, or 13 of this title; or

(2)   the entity that made such payment.

Sec. 330.   *Compensation of Officers*

(a) (1)   After notice to any parties in interest and the United States trustee and a hearing, and subject to sections 326, 328, and 329, the court may award to a trustee, an examiner, a professional person employed under section 327 or 1103—

(A)   reasonable compensation for actual, necessary services rendered by the trustee, examiner, professional person, or attorney, and by any paraprofessional person employed by any such person, and

(B)   reimbursement for actual, necessary expenses.

(2)   The court may, on its own motion or on the motion of the United States trustee, the United States trustee for the District or Region, the trustee for the estate, or any other party in interest, award compensation that is less than the amount of compensation that is requested.

(3)   (A)   In determining the amount of reasonable compensation to be awarded, the court shall consider the nature, the extent, and the value of such services, taking into account all relevant factors, including—

(A)   the time spent on such services;

(B)   the rates charged for such services;

(C)   whether the services were necessary to the administration of, or beneficial at the time at which the service was rendered toward the completion of, a case under this title;

(D)   whether the services were performed within a reasonable amount of time commensurate with the complexity, importance, and nature of the problem, issue, or task addressed; and

(E)   whether the compensation is reasonable based on the customary compensation charged by comparably skilled practitioners in cases other than cases under this title.

(4)   (A)   Except as provided in subparagraph (B), the court shall not allow compensation for—

(i)   unnecessary duplication of services; or

(ii)   services that were not—

(I)   reasonably likely to benefit the debtor's estate; or

(II)   necessary to the administration of the case.

(B)   In a chapter 12 or chapter 13 case in which the debtor is an individual, the court may allow reasonable compensation to the debtor's attorney for representing the interests of the debtor in connection with the bankruptcy case based on a consideration of the benefit and necessity of such services to the debtor and the other factors set forth in this section.

(5)   The court shall reduce the amount of compensation awarded under this section by the amount of any interim compensation awarded under section 331, and, if the amount of such interim compensation exceeds the amount of compensation awarded under this section, may order the return of the excess to the estate.

(6)   Any compensation awarded for the preparation of a fee application shall be based on the level and skill reasonably required to prepare the application.

(b) (1)   There shall be paid from the filing fee in a case under chapter 7 of this title $45 to the trustee serving in such case, after such trustee's services are rendered.

(2)   The Judicial Conference of the United States—

(A)   shall prescribe additional fees of the same kind as prescribed under section 1914(b) of title 28; and

(B)   may prescribe notice of appearance fees and fees charged against distributions in cases under this title; to pay $15 to trustees serving in cases after such trustees' services are rendered. Beginning 1 year after the date of the enactment of the Bankruptcy Reform Act of 1994, such $15 shall be paid in addition to the amount paid under paragraph (1).

(c)   Unless the court orders otherwise, in a case under chapter 12 or 13 of this title the compensation paid to the trustee serving in the case shall not be less than $5 per month from any distribution under the plan during the administration of the plan.

(d)   In a case in which the United States trustee serves as trustee, the compensation of the trustee under this section shall be paid to the clerk of the bankruptcy court and deposited by the clerk into the United States Trustee System Fund established by section 589a of title 28.

Sec. 331.   Interim Compensation

A trustee, an examiner, a debtor's attorney, or any professional person employed under section 327 or 1103 of this title may apply to the court not more than once every 120 days after an order for relief in a case under this title, or more often if the court permits, for such compensation for services rendered before the date of such an application or reimbursement for expenses incurred before such date is provided under section 330 of this title. After notice and a hearing, the court may allow and disburse to such applicant such compensation or reimbursement.

SUBCHAPTER III. ADMINISTRATION

Sec. 341.   Meetings of Creditors and Equity Security Holders

(a)   Within a reasonable time after the order for relief in a case under this title, the United States trustee shall convene and preside at a meeting of creditors.

(b)   The United States trustee may convene a meeting of any equity security holders.

(c)   The court may not preside at, and may not attend, any meeting under this section including any final meeting of creditors.

(d)   Prior to the conclusion of the meeting of creditors or equity security holders, the trustee shall orally examine the debtor to ensure that the debtor in a case under chapter 7 of this title is aware of—

　　(1)   the potential consequences of seeking a discharge in bankruptcy, including the effects on credit history;

　　(2)   the debtor's ability to file a petition under a different chapter of this title;

　　(3)   the effect of receiving a discharge of debts under this title; and

　　(4)   the effect of reaffirming a debt, including the debtor's knowledge of the provisions of section 524(d) of this title.

Sec. 342.   Notice

(a)   There shall be given such notice as is appropriate, including notice to any holder of a community claim of an order for relief in a case under this title.

(b)   Prior to the commencement of a case under this title by an individual whose debts are primarily consumer debts, the clerk shall give written notice to such individual that indicates each chapter of this title under which such individual may proceed.

(c)   If notice is required to be given by the debtor to a creditor under this title, any rule, any applicable law, or any order of the court, such notice shall contain the name, address, and taxpayer identification number of the debtor, but the failure of such notice to contain such information shall not invalidate the legal effect of such notice.

Sec. 343.   Examination of the Debtor

The debtor shall appear and submit to examination under oath at the meeting of creditors under section 341(a) of this title. Creditors, any indenture trustee, [or] any trustee or examiner in the case, or the United States trustee may examine the debtor. The United States trustee may administer the oath required under this section.

Sec. 344.   Self-incrimination; Immunity

Immunity for persons required to submit to examination, to testify, or to provide information in a case under this title may be granted under part V of title 18.

Sec. 345.   Money of Estates

(a)   A trustee in a case under this title may make such deposit or investment of the money of the estate for which such trustee serves as will yield the maximum reasonable net return on such money, taking into account the safety of such deposit or investment.

(b)   Except with respect to a deposit or investment that is insured or guaranteed by the United States or by a department, agency, or instrumentality of the United States or backed by the full faith and credit of the United States, the trustee shall require from an entity with which such money is deposited or invested—

(1)   a bond—

(A)   in favor of the United States;—

(B)   secured by the undertaking of a corporate surety approved by the United States trustee for the district in which the case is pending; and

(C)   conditioned on—

(i)   a proper accounting for all money so deposited or invested and for any return on such money;

(ii)   prompt repayment of such money and return; and

(iii) faithful performance of duties as a depository; or

(2)   the deposit of securities of the kind specified in section 9303 of title 31; unless the court for cause orders otherwise.

(c)   An entity with which such moneys are deposited or invested is authorized to deposit or invest such moneys as may be required under this section.

Sec. 346.   Special Tax Provisions

(a)   Except to the extent otherwise provided in this section, subsections (b), (c), (d), (e), (g), (h), (i), and (j) of this section apply notwithstanding any State or local law imposing a tax but subject to the Internal Revenue Code of 1986.

(b) (1)   In a case under chapter 7, 12, or 11 of this title concerning an individual, any income of the estate may be taxed under a State or local law imposing a tax on or measured by income only to the estate, and may not be taxed to such individual. Except as provided in section 728 of this title, if such individual is a partner in a partnership, any gain or loss resulting from a distribution of property from such partnership, or any distributive share of income, gain, loss, deduction, or credit of such individual that is distributed, or considered distributed, from such partnership, after the commencement of the case is gain, loss income, deduction, or credit, as the case may be, of the estate.

(2)   Except as otherwise provided in this section and in section 728 of this title, any income of the estate in such a case, and any State or local tax on or measured by such income, shall be computed in the same manner as the income and the tax of an estate.

(3)   The estate in such a case shall use the same accounting method as the debtor used immediately before the commencement of the case.

(c) (1)   The commencement of a case under this title concerning a corporation or a partnership does not effect a change in the status of such corporation or partnership for the purposes of any State or local law imposing a tax on or measured by income. Except as otherwise provided in this section and in section 728 of this title, any income of the estate in such case may be taxed only as though such case had not been commenced.

(2)   In such a case, except as provided in section 728 of this title, the trustee shall make any tax return otherwise required by State or local law to be filed by or on behalf of such corporation or partnership in the same manner and form as such corporation or partnership, as the case may be, is required to make such return.

(d)   In a case under chapter 13 of this title, any income of the estate or the debtor may be taxed under a State or local law imposing a tax on or measured by income only to the debtor, and may not be taxed to the estate.

(e)   A claim allowed under section 502(f) or 503 of this title, other than a claim for a tax that is not otherwise deductible or a capital expenditure that is not otherwise deductible, is deductible by the entity to which income of the estate is taxed unless such claim was deducted by another entity, and a deduction for such a claim is deemed to be a deduction attributable to a business.

(f)   The trustee shall withhold from any payment of claims for wages, salaries, commissions, dividends, interest, or other payments, or collect any amount required to be withheld or collected under applicable State or local tax law, and shall pay such withheld or collected amount to the appropriate governmental unit at the time and in the manner required by such tax law, and with the same priority as the claim from which such amount was withheld was paid.

(g) (1)   Neither gain nor loss shall be recognized on a transfer—

    (A)   by operation of law, of property to the estate;

    (B)   other than a sale, of property from the estate to the debtor; or

    (C)   in a case under chapter 11 or 12 of this title concerning a corporation, of property from the estate to a corporation that is an affiliate participating in a joint plan with the debtor, or that is a successor to the debtor under the plan, except that gain or loss may be recognized to the same extent that such transfer results in the recognition of gain or loss under section 371 of the Internal Revenue Code of 1986.

(2)   The transferee of a transfer of a kind specified in this subsection shall take the property transferred with the same character, and with the transferor's basis, as adjusted under subsection (j)(5) of this section, and holding period.

(h)   Notwithstanding sections 728(a) and 1146(a) of this title, for the purpose of determining the number of taxable periods during which the debtor or the estate may use a loss carryover or a loss carryback, the taxable period of the debtor during which the case is commenced is deemed not to have been terminated by such commencement.

(i) (1)   In a case under chapter 7, 12, or 11 of this title concerning an individual, the estate shall succeed to the debtor's tax attributes, including—

    (A)   any investment credit carryover;

    (B)   any recovery exclusion;

    (C)   any loss carryover;

    (D)   any foreign tax credit carryover;

    (E)   any capital loss carryover; and

    (F)   any claim of right.

(2)   After such a case is closed or dismissed, the debtor shall succeed to any tax attribute to which the estate succeeded under paragraph (1) of this subsection but that was not utilized by the estate. The debtor may utilize

such tax attributes as though any applicable time limitations on such utilization by the debtor were suspended during the time during which the case was pending.

(3)   In such a case, the estate may carry back any loss of the estate to taxable period of the debtor that ended before the order for relief under such chapter the same as the debtor could have carried back such loss had the debtor incurred such loss and the case under this title had not been commenced, but the debtor may not carry back any loss of the debtor from taxable period that ends after such order to any taxable period of the debtor that ended before such order until after the case is closed.

(j) (1)   Except as otherwise provided in this subsection, income is not realized by the estate, the debtor, or a successor to the debtor by reason of forgiveness or discharge of indebtedness in a case under this title.

(2)   For the purposes of any State or local law imposing a tax on or measured by income, a deduction with respect to a liability may not be allowed for any taxable period during or after which such liability is forgiven or discharged under this title. In this paragraph, "a deduction with respect to a liability" includes a capital loss incurred on the disposition of a capital asset with respect to a liability that was incurred in connection with the acquisition of such asset.

(3)   Except as provided in paragraph (4) of this subsection, for the purpose of any State or local law imposing a tax on or measured by income, any net operating loss of an individual or corporate debtor, including a net operating loss carryover to such debtor, shall be reduced by the amount of indebtedness forgiven or discharged in a case under this title, except to the extent that such forgiveness or discharge resulted in a disallowance under paragraph (2) of this subsection.

(4)   A reduction of a net operating loss or a net operating loss carryover under paragraph (3) of this subsection or of basis under paragraph (5) of this subsection is not required to the extent that the indebtedness of an individual or corporate debtor forgiven or discharged—

(A)   consisted of items of a deductible nature that were not deducted by such debtor; or

(B)   resulted in an expired net operating loss carryover or other deduction that—

(i)   did not offset income for any taxable period; and

(ii)   did not contribute to a net operating loss in or a net operating loss carryover to the taxable period during or after which such indebtedness was discharged.

(5)   For the purposes of a State or local law imposing a tax on or measured by income, the basis of the debtor's property or of property transferred to an entity required to use the debtor's basis in whole or in part shall be reduced by the lesser of—

(A)   (i)   the amount by which the indebtedness of the debtor has been forgiven or discharged in a case under this title; minus

(ii)   the total amount of adjustments made under paragraphs (2) and (3) of this subsection; and

(B)   the amount by which the total basis of the debtor's assets that were property of the estate before such forgiveness or discharge exceeds the debtor's total liabilities that were liabilities both before and after such forgiveness or discharge.

(6)   Notwithstanding paragraph (5) of this subsection, basis is not required to be reduced to the extent that the debtor elects to treat as taxable income, of the taxable period in which indebtedness is forgiven or discharged, the amount of indebtedness forgiven or discharged that otherwise would be applied in reduction of basis under paragraph (5) of this subsection.

(7)   For the purposes of this subsection, indebtedness with respect to which an equity security, other than an interest of a limited partner in a limited partnership, is issued to the creditor to whom such indebtedness was owed, or that is forgiven as a contribution to capital by an equity security holder other than a limited partner in the debtor, is not forgiven or discharged in a case under this title—

(A)   to any extent that such indebtedness did not consist of items of a deductible nature; or

(B)   if the issuance of such equity security has the same consequences under a law imposing a tax on or measured by income to such creditor as a payment in cash to such creditor in an amount equal to the fair market value of such equity security, than to the lesser of—

(i)   the extent that such issuance has the same such consequences; and

(ii)   the extent of such fair market value.

Sec. 347.   *Unclaimed Property*

(a)   Ninety days after the final distribution under section 726, 1226, or 1326 of this title in a case under chapter 7, 12, or 13 of this title, as the case may be, the trustee shall stop payment on any check remaining unpaid, and any remaining property of the estate shall be paid into the court and disposed of under chapter 129 of title 28.

(b)   Any security, money, or other property remaining unclaimed at the expiration of the time allowed in a case under chapter 9, 11, or 12 of this title for the presentation of a security or the performance of any other act as a condition to participation in the distribution under any plan confirmed under section 943(b), 1129, 1173, 1225 of this title, as the case may be, becomes the property of the debtor or of the entity acquiring the assets of the debtor under the plan, as the case may be.

Sec. 348.   *Effect of Conversion*

(a)   Conversion of a case from a case under one chapter of this title to a case under another chapter of this title constitutes an order for relief under the chapter to which the case is converted, but, except as provided in subsections (b) and (c) of this section, does not effect a change in the date of the filing of the petition, the commencement of the case, or the order for relief.

(b)   Unless the court for cause orders otherwise, in sections 701(a), 727(a)(10), 727(b), 728(a), 728(b), 1102(a), 1110(a)(1), 1121(b), 1121(c), 1141(d)(4), 1146(a), 1146(b), 1201(a), 1221, 1228(a), 1301(a), and 1305(a) of this title, "the order for relief under this chapter" in a chapter to which a case has been converted under section 706, 1112, 1208, or 1307 of this title means the conversion of such case to such chapter.

(c)   Sections 342 and 365(d) of this title apply in a case that has been converted under section 706, 1112, 1208, or 1307 of this title, as if the conversion order were the order for relief.

(d)   A claim against the estate or the debtor that arises after the order for relief but before conversion in a case that is converted under section 1112, 1208, or 1307 of this title, other than a claim specified in section 503(b) of this title, shall be treated for all purposes as if such claim had arisen immediately before the date of the filing of the petition.

(e)   Conversion of a case under section 706, 1112, 1208, or 1307 of this title terminates the service of any trustee or examiner that is serving in the case before such conversion.

(f) (1)   Except as provided in paragraph (2), when a case under chapter 13 of this title is converted to a case under another chapter under this title—

(A)   property of the estate in the converted case shall consist of property of the estate, as of the date of filing of the petition, that remains in the possession of or is under the control of the debtor on the date of conversion; and

(B)   valuations of property and of allowed secured claims in the chapter 13 case shall apply in the converted case, with allowed secured claims reduced to the extent that they have been paid in accordance with the chapter 13 plan.

(2)   If the debtor converts a case under chapter 13 of this title to a case under another chapter under this title in bad faith, the property in the converted case shall consist of the property of the estate as of the date of conversion.

Sec. 349.   *Effect of Dismissal*

(a)   Unless the court, for cause, orders otherwise, the dismissal of a case under this title does not bar the discharge, in a later case under this title, of debts that were dischargeable in the case dismissed; nor does the dismissal of a case under this title prejudice the debtor with regard to the filing of a subsequent petition under this title, except as provided in section 109(g) of this title.

(b)   Unless the court, for cause, orders otherwise, a dismissal of a case other than under section 742 of this title—

(1)   reinstates—

(A)   any proceeding or custodianship superseded under section 543 of this title;

(B)   any transfer avoided under section 522, 544, 545, 547, 548, 549, or 742(a) of this title, or preserved under section 510(c)(2), 522(i)(2), or 551 of this title; and

(C)   any lien voided under section 506(d) of this title;

(2)   vacates any order, judgment, or transfer ordered, under section 522(i)(1), 542, 550, or 553 of this title; and

(3)   revests the property of the estate in the entity in which such property was vested immediately before the commencement of the case under this title.

Sec. 350.   *Closing and Reopening Cases*

(a)   After an estate is fully administered and the court has discharged the trustee, the court shall close the case.

(b)   A case may be reopened in the court in which such case was closed to administer assets, to accord relief to the debtor, or for other cause.

SUBCHAPTER IV. ADMINISTRATIVE POWERS

Sec. 361.   *Adequate Protection*

When adequate protection is required under section 362, 363, or 364 of this title of an interest of an entity in property, such adequate protection may be provided by—

(1)   requiring the trustee to make a cash payment or periodic cash payments to such entity, to the extent that the stay under section 362 of this title, use, sale, or lease under section 363 of this title, or any grant of a lien under section 364 of this title results in a decrease in the value of such entity's interest in such property;

(2)   providing to such entity an additional or replacement lien to the extent that such stay, use, sale, lease, or grant results in a decrease in the value of such entity's interest in such property; or

(3)   granting such other relief, other than entitling such entity to compensation allowable under section 503(b)(1) of this title as an administrative expense, as will result in the realization by such entity of the indubitable equivalent of such entity's interest in such property.

Sec. 362.   *Automatic Stay*

(a)   Except as provided in subsection (b) of this section, a petition filed under section 301, 302, or 303 of this title, or an application filed under section 5(a)(3) of the Securities Investor Protection Act of 1970, operates as a stay, applicable to all entities, of—

(1)   the commencement or continuation, including the issuance or employment of process, of a judicial, administrative, or other action or proceeding against the debtor that was or could have been commenced before the commencement of the case under this title, or to recover a claim against the debtor that arose before the commencement of the case under this title;

(2)   the enforcement, against the debtor or against property of the estate, of a judgment obtained before the commencement of the case under this title;

(3)   any act to obtain possession of property of the estate or of property from the estate, or to exercise control over property of the estate;

(4)   any act to create, perfect, or enforce any lien against property of the estate;

(5)   any act to create, perfect, or enforce against property of the estate any lien to the extent that such lien secures a claim that arose before the commencement of the case under this title;

(6)   any act to collect, assess, or recover a claim against the debtor that arose before the commencement of the case under this title;

(7)   the setoff of any debt owing to the debtor that arose before the commencement of the case under this title against any claim against the debtor; and

(8)   the commencement or continuation of a proceeding before the United States Tax Court concerning the debtor.

(b)   The filing of a petition under section 301, 302, or 303 of this title, or of an application under section 5(a)(3) of the Securities Investor Protection Act of 1970, does not operate as a stay—

(1)   under subsection (a) of this section, of the commencement or continuation of a criminal action or proceeding against the debtor;

(2)   under subsection (a) of this section—

(A)   of the commencement or continuation of an action or proceeding for—

(i)   the establishment of paternity; or

(ii)   the establishment or modification of an order for alimony, maintenance, or support; or

(B)   of the collection of alimony, maintenance, or support from property that is not property of the estate;

(3)   under subsection (a) of this section, of any act to perfect, or to maintain or continue the perfection of, an interest in property to the extent that the trustee's rights and powers are subject to such perfection under section 546(b) of this title, or to the extent that such act is accomplished within the period provided under section 547(e)(2)(A) of this title;

(4)   under paragraph (1), (2), (3), or (6) of subsection (a) of this section, of the commencement or continuation of an action or proceeding by a governmental unit or any organization exercising authority under the Convention on the Prohibition of the Development, Production, Stockpiling and Use of Chemical Weapons and on Their Destruction, opened for signature on January 13, 1993, to enforce such governmental unit's or organization's police and regulatory power, including the enforcement of a judgment other than a money judgment, obtained in an action or proceeding by the governmental unit to enforce such governmental unit's or organization's police or regulatory power;

(5)   [Deleted]

(6)   under subsection (a) of this section, of the setoff by a commodity broker, forward contract merchant, stockbroker, financial institutions or securities clearing agency of any mutual debt and claim under or in connection with commodity contracts, as defined in section 761 of this title, forward contracts, or securities contracts, as defined in section 741 of this title, that constitutes the setoff of a claim against the debtor for a margin payment, as defined in section 101, 741, or 761 of this title, or settlement payment, as defined in section 101 or 741 of this title, arising out of commodity contracts, forward contracts, or securities contracts against cash, securities, or other property held by or due from such commodity broker, forward contract merchant, stockbroker, financial institution, financial institutions or securities clearing agency to margin, guarantee, secure, or settle commodity contracts, forward contracts, or securities contracts;

(7)   under subsection (a) of this section, of the setoff by a repo participant, of any mutual debt and claim under or in connection with repurchase

agreements that constitutes the setoff of a claim against the debtor for a margin payment, as defined in section 741 or 761 of this title, or settlement payment, as defined in section 741 of this title, arising out of repurchase agreements against cash, securities, or other property held by or due from such repo participant to margin, guarantee, secure or settle repurchase agreements;

(8)   under subsection (a) of this section, of the commencement of any action by the Secretary of Housing and Urban Development to foreclose a mortgage or deed of trust in any case in which the mortgage or deed of trust held by the Secretary is insured or was formerly insured under the National Housing Act and covers property, or combinations of property, consisting of five or more living units;

(9)   under subsection (a), of—

(A)   an audit by a governmental unit to determine tax liability;

(B)   the issuance to the debtor by a governmental unit of a notice of tax deficiency;

(C)   a demand for tax returns; or

(D)   the making of an assessment for any tax and issuance of a notice and demand for payment of such an assessment (but any tax lien that would otherwise attach to property of the estate by reason of such an assessment shall not take effect unless such tax is a debt of the debtor that will not be discharged in the case and such property or its proceeds are transferred out of the estate to, or otherwise revested in, the debtor).

(10)   under subsection (a) of this section, of any act by a lessor to the debtor under a lease of nonresidential real property that has terminated by the expiration of the stated term of the lease before the commencement of or during a case under this title to obtain possession of such property;

(11)   under subsection (a) of this section, of the presentment of a negotiable instrument and the giving of notice of and protesting dishonor of such an instrument;

(12)   under subsection (a) of this section, after the date which is 90 days after the filing of such petition, of the commencement or continuation, and conclusion of the entry of final judgment, of an action which involves a debtor subject to reorganization pursuant to chapter 11 of this title and which was brought by the Secretary of Transportation under section 31325 of title 46 (including distribution of any proceeds of sale) to foreclose a preferred ship or fleet mortgage, or a security interest in or relating to a vessel or vessel under construction, held by the Secretary of Transportation under section 207 or title XI of the Merchant Marine Act, 1936, or under applicable State law;

(13)   under subsection (a) of this section, after the date which is 90 days after the filing of such petition, of the commencement or continuation, and conclusion to the entry of final judgment, of an action which involves a debtor subject to reorganization pursuant to chapter 11 of this title and which was brought by the Secretary of Commerce under section 31325 of title 46 (including distribution of any proceeds of sale) to foreclose a preferred ship or fleet mortgage in a vessel or a mortgage, deed of trust, or other security interest in a fishing facility held by the Secretary of Commerce under section 207 or title XI of the Merchant Marine Act, 1936;

(14)   under subsection (a) of this section, of any action by an accrediting agency regarding the accreditation status of the debtor as an educational institution;

(15)   under subsection (a) of this section, of any action by a State licensing body regarding the licensure of the debtor as an educational institution;

(16)   under subsection (a) of this section of any action by a guaranty agency, as defined in section 435(j) of the Higher Education Act of 1965 or the Secretary of Education regarding the eligibility of the debtor to participate in programs authorized under such Act;

(17)   under subsection (a) of this section, of the setoff by a swap participant, of any mutual debt and claim under or in connection with any swap agreement that constitutes the setoff of a claim against the debtor for any payment due from the debtor under or in connection with any swap agreement against any payment due to the debtor from the swap participant under or in connection with any swap agreement or against cash, securities, or other property of the debtor held by or due from such swap participant to guarantee, secure or settle any swap agreement; or

(18)   under subsection (a) of the creation or perfection of a statutory lien for an ad valorem property tax imposed by the District of Columbia, or a political subdivision of a State, if such tax comes due after the filing of the petition.

(c)   Except as provided in subsections (d), (e), and (f) of this section—

(1)   the stay of an act against property of the estate under subsection (a) of this section continues until such property is no longer property of the estate; and

(2)   the stay of any other act under subsection (a) of this section continues until the earliest of—

(A)   the time the case is closed;

(B)   the time the case is dismissed; or

(C)   if the case is a case under chapter 7 of this title concerning an individual or a case under chapter 9, 11, 12, or 13 of this title, the time a discharge is granted or denied.

(d)   On request of a party in interest and after notice and a hearing, the court shall grant relief from the stay provided under subsection (a) of this section, such as by terminating, annulling, modifying, or conditioning such stay—

(1)   for cause, including the lack of adequate protection of an interest in property of such party in interest;

(2)   with respect to a stay of an act against property under subsection (a) of this section, if—

(A)   the debtor does not have an equity in such property; and

(B)   such property is not necessary to an effective reorganization; or

(3)   with respect to a stay of an act against single asset real estate under subsection (a), by a creditor whose claim is secured by an interest in such real estate, unless, not later than the date that is 90 days after the entry of the order for relief (or such later date as the court may determine for cause by order entered within that 90-day period)—

(A)   the debtor has filed a plan of reorganization that has a reasonable possibility of being confirmed within a reasonable time; or

(B)   the debtor has commenced monthly payments to each creditor whose claim is secured by such real estate (other than a claim secured by a judgment lien or by an unmatured statutory lien), which payments are in an amount equal to interest at a current fair market rate on the value of the creditor's interest in the real estate.

(e)   Thirty days after a request under subsection (d) of this section for relief from the stay of any act against property of the estate under subsection (a) of this section, such stay is terminated with respect to the party in interest making such request, unless the court, after notice and a hearing, orders such stay continued in effect pending the conclusion of, or as a result of, a final hearing and determination under subsection (d) of this section. A hearing under this subsection may be a preliminary hearing, or may be consolidated with the final hearing under subsection (d) of this section. The court shall order such stay continued in effect pending the conclusion of the final hearing under subsection (d) of this section if there is a reasonable likelihood that the party opposing relief from the stay will prevail at the conclusion of such final hearing. If the hearing under this subsection is a preliminary hearing, then such final hearing shall be concluded not later than thirty days after the conclusion of such preliminary hearing, unless the 30-day period is extended with the consent of the parties in interest or for a specific time which the court finds is required by compelling circumstances.

(f)   Upon request of a party in interest, the court, with or without a hearing, shall grant such relief from the stay provided under subsection (a) of this section as is necessary to prevent irreparable damage to the interest of an entity in property, if such interest will suffer such damage before there is an opportunity for notice and a hearing under subsection (d) or (e) of this section.

(g)   In any hearing under subsection (d) or (e) of this section concerning relief from the stay of any act under subsection (a) of this section—

(1)   the party requesting such relief has the burden of proof on the issue of the debtor's equity in property; and

(2)   the party opposing such relief has the burden of proof on all other issues.

(h)   An individual injured by any willful violation of a stay provided by this section shall recover actual damages, including costs and attorneys' fees, and, in appropriate circumstances, may recover punitive damages.

Sec. 363.   *Use, Sale, or Lease of Property*

(a)   In this section, "cash collateral" means cash, negotiable instruments, documents of title, securities, deposit accounts, or other cash equivalents whenever acquired in which the estate and an entity other than the estate have an interest and includes the proceeds, products, offspring, rents, or profits of property and the fees, charges, accounts or other payments for the use or occupancy of rooms and other public facilities in hotels, motels, or other lodging properties subject to a security interest as provided in section 552(b) of this title, whether existing before or after the commencement of a case under this title.

(b) (1)   The trustee, after notice and a hearing, may use, sell, or lease, other than in the ordinary course of business, property of the estate.

(2)   If notification is required under subsection (a) of section 7A of the Clayton Act in the case of a transaction under this subsection, then—

(A)   notwithstanding subsection (a) of such section, the notification required by such subsection to be given by the debtor shall be given by the trustee; and

(B)   notwithstanding subsection (b) of such section, the required waiting period shall end on the 15th day after the date of the receipt, by the Federal Trade Commission and the Assistant Attorney General in charge of the Antitrust Division of the Department of Justice, of the notification required under such subsection (a), unless such waiting period is extended—

(i)   pursuant to subsection (e)(2) of such section, in the same manner as such subsection (e)(2) applies to a cash tender offer;

(ii)   pursuant to subsection (g)(2) of such section; or

(iii)   by the court after notice and a hearing.

(c) (1)   If the business of the debtor is authorized to be operated under section 721, 1108, 1203, 1204, or 1304 of this title and unless the court orders otherwise, the trustee may enter into transactions, including the sale or lease of property of the estate, in the ordinary course of business, without notice or a hearing, and may use property of the estate in the ordinary course of business without notice or a hearing.

(2)   The trustee may not use, sell, or lease cash collateral under paragraph (1) of this subsection unless—

(A)   each entity that has an interest in such cash collateral consents;

or

(B)   the court, after notice and a hearing, authorizes such use, sale, or lease in accordance with the provisions of this section.

(3)   Any hearing under paragraph (2)(B) of this subsection may be a preliminary hearing or may be consolidated with a hearing under subsection (e) of this section, but shall be scheduled in accordance with the needs of the debtor. If the hearing under paragraph (2)(B) of this subsection is a preliminary hearing, the court may authorize such use, sale, or lease only if there is a reasonable likelihood that the trustee will prevail at the final hearing under subsection (e) of this section. The court shall act promptly on any request for authorization under paragraph (2)(B) of this subsection.

(4)   Except as provided in paragraph (2) of this subsection, the trustee shall segregate and account for any cash collateral in the trustee's possession, custody, or control.

(d)   The trustee may use, sell, or lease property under subsection (b) or (c) of this section only to the extent not inconsistent with any relief granted under section 362(c), 362(d), 362(e), or 362(f) of this title.

(e)   Notwithstanding any other provision of this section, at any time, on request of an entity that has an interest in property used, sold, or leased, or proposed to be used, sold, or leased, by the trustee, the court, with or without a hearing, shall prohibit or condition such use, sale, or lease as is necessary to provide adequate protection of such interest. This subsection also applies to property that is subject to any unexpired lease of personal property (to the exclusion of such property being subject to an order to grant relief from the stay under section 362).

(f)   The trustee may sell property under subsection (b) or (c) of this section free and clear of any interest in such property of an entity other than the estate, only if—

(1)   applicable nonbankruptcy law permits sale of such property free and clear of such interest;

(2)   such entity consents;

(3)   such interest is a lien and the price at which such property is to be sold is greater than the aggregate value of all liens on such property;

(4)   such interest is in bona fide dispute; or

(5)   such entity could be compelled, in a legal or equitable proceeding, to accept a money satisfaction of such interest.

(g)   Notwithstanding subsection (f) of this section, the trustee may sell property under subsection (b) or (c) of this section free and clear of any vested or contingent right in the nature of dower or curtesy.

(h)   Notwithstanding subsection (f) of this section, the trustee may sell both the estate's interest, under subsection (b) or (c) of this section, and the interest of any co-owner in property in which the debtor had, at the time of the commencement of the case, an undivided interest as a tenant in common, joint tenant, or tenant by the entirety, only if—

(1)   partition in kind of such property among the estate and such co-owners is impracticable;

(2)   sale of the estate's undivided interest in such property would realize significantly less for the estate than sale of such property free of the interests of such co-owners;

(3)   the benefit to the estate of a sale of such property free of the interests of co-owners outweighs the detriment, if any, to such co-owners; and

(4)   such property is not used in the production, transmission, or distribution, for sale, of electric energy or of natural or synthetic gas for heat, light, or power.

(i)   Before the consummation of a sale of property to which subsection (g) or (h) of this section applies, or of property of the estate that was community property of the debtor and the debtor's spouse immediately before the commencement of the case, the debtor's spouse, or a co-owner of such property, as the case may be, may purchase such property at the price at which such sale is to be consummated.

(j)   After a sale of property to which subsection (g) or (h) of this section applies, the trustee shall distribute to the debtor's spouse or the co-owners of such property, as the case may be, and to the estate, the proceeds of such sale, less the costs and expenses, not including any compensation of the trustee, of such sale, according to the interests of such spouse or co-owners, and of the estate.

(k)   At a sale under subsection (b) of this section of property that is subject to a lien that secures an allowed claim, unless the court for cause orders otherwise the holder of such claim may bid at such sale, and, if the holder of such claim purchases such property, such holder may offset such claim against the purchase price of such property.

(1)   Subject to the provisions of section 365, the trustee may use, sell, or lease property under subsection (b) or (c) of this section, or a plan under chapter 11, 12, or 13 of this title may provide for the use, sale, or lease of property, notwithstanding any provision in a contract, a lease, or applicable law that is conditioned on the insolvency or financial condition of the debtor, on the commencement of a case under this title concerning the debtor, or on the appointment of or the taking possession by a trustee in a case under this title or a custodian, and that effects, or gives an option to effect, a forfeiture, modification, or termination of the debtor's interest in such property.

(m)   The reversal or modification on appeal of an authorization under subsection (b) or (c) of this section of a sale or lease of property does not affect the validity of a sale or lease under such authorization to an entity that purchased or leased such property in good faith, whether or not such entity knew of the pendency of the appeal, unless such authorization and such sale or lease were stayed pending appeal.

(n)   The trustee may avoid a sale under this section if the sale price was controlled by an agreement among potential bidders at such sale, or may recover from a party to such agreement any amount by which the value of the property sold exceeds the price at which such sale was consummated, and may recover any costs, attorneys' fees, or expenses incurred in avoiding such sale or recovering such amount. In addition to any recovery under the preceding sentence, the court may grant judgment for punitive damages in favor of the estate and against any such party that entered into such an agreement in willful disregard of this subsection.

(o)   In any hearing under this section—

(1)   the trustee has the burden of proof on the issue of adequate protection; and

(2)   the entity asserting an interest in property has the burden of proof on the issue of the validity, priority, or extent of such interest.

Sec. 364.   *Obtaining Credit*

(a)   If the trustee is authorized to operate the business of the debtor under section 721, 1108, 1203, 1204, or 1304 of this title, unless the court orders otherwise, the trustee may obtain unsecured credit and incur unsecured debt in the ordinary course of business allowable under section 503(b)(1) of this title as an administrative expense.

(b)   The court, after notice and a hearing, may authorize the trustee to obtain unsecured credit or to incur unsecured debt other than under subsection (a) of this section, allowable under section 503(b)(1) of this title as an administrative expense.

(c)   If the trustee is unable to obtain unsecured credit allowable under section 503(b)(1) of this title as an administrative expense, the court, after notice and a hearing, may authorize the obtaining of credit or the incurring of debt—

(1)   with priority over any or all administrative expenses of the kind specified in section 503(b) or 507(b) of this title;

(2)   secured by a lien on property of the estate that is not otherwise subject to a lien; or

(3)   secured by a junior lien on property of the estate that is subject to a lien.

(d) (1)   The court, after notice and a hearing, may authorize the obtaining of credit or the incurring of debt secured by a senior or equal lien on property of the estate that is subject to a lien only if—

(A)   the trustee is unable to obtain such credit otherwise; and

(B)   there is adequate protection of the interest of the holder of the lien on the property of the estate on which such senior or equal lien is proposed to be granted.

(2)   In any hearing under this subsection, the trustee has the burden of proof on the issue of adequate protection.

(e)   The reversal or modification on appeal of an authorization under this section to obtain credit or incur debt, or of a grant under this section of a priority or a lien, does not affect the validity of any debt so incurred, or any priority or lien so granted, to an entity that extended such credit in good faith, whether or not such entity knew of the pendency of the appeal, unless such authorization and the incurring of such debt, or the granting of such priority or lien, were stayed pending appeal.

(f)   Except with respect to an entity that is an underwriter as defined in section 1145(b) of this title, section 5 of the Securities Act of 1933, the Trust Indenture Act of 1939, and any State or local law requiring registration for offer or sale of a security or registration or licensing of an issuer of, underwriter of, or broker or dealer in, a security does not apply to the offer or sale under this section of a security that is not an equity security.

Sec. 365.   *Executory Contracts and Unexpired Leases*

(a)   Except as provided in sections 765 and 766 of this title and in subsections (b), (c), and (d) of this section, the trustee, subject to the court's approval, may assume or reject any executory contract or unexpired lease of the debtor.

(b) (1)   If there has been a default in an executory contract or unexpired lease of the debtor, the trustee may not assume such contract or lease unless, at the time of assumption of such contract or lease, the trustee—

(A)   cures, or provides adequate assurance that the trustee will promptly cure, such default;

(B)   compensates, or provides adequate assurance that the trustee will promptly compensate, a party other than the debtor to such contract or lease, for any actual pecuniary loss to such party resulting from such default; and

(C)   provides adequate assurance of future performance under such contract or lease.

(2)   Paragraph (1) of this subsection does not apply to default that is a breach of a provision relating to—

(A)   the insolvency or financial condition of the debtor at any time before the closing of the case;

(B)   the commencement of a case under this title;

(C)   the appointment of or taking possession by a trustee in a case under this title or a custodian before such commencement; or

(D)   the satisfaction of any penalty rate or provision relating to a default arising from any failure by the debtor to perform nonmonetary obligations under the executory contract or unexpired lease.

(3)   For the purposes of paragraph (1) of this subsection and paragraph (2)(B) of subsection (f), adequate assurance of future performance of a lease of real property in a shopping center includes adequate assurance—

(A)   of the source of rent and other consideration due under such lease, and in the case of an assignment, that the financial condition and operating performance of the proposed assignee and its guarantors, if any, shall be similar to the financial condition and operating performance of the debtor and its guarantors, if any, as of the time the debtor became the lessee under the lease;

(B)   that any percentage rent due under such lease will not decline substantially;

(C)   that assumption or assignment of such lease is subject to all the provisions thereof, including (but not limited to) provisions such as a radius, location, use, or exclusivity provision, and will not breach any such provision contained in any other lease, financing agreement, or master agreement relating to such shopping center; and

(D)   that assumption or assignment of such lease will not disrupt any tenant mix or balance in such shopping center.

(4)   Notwithstanding any other provision of this section, if there has been a default in an unexpired lease of the debtor, other than a default of a kind specified in paragraph (2) of this subsection, the trustee may not require a lessor to provide services or supplies incidental to such lease before assumption of such lease unless the lessor is compensated under the terms of such lease for any services and supplies provided under such lease before assumption of such lease.

(c)   The trustee may not assume or assign any executory contract or unexpired lease of the debtor, whether or not such contract or lease prohibits or restricts assignment of rights or delegation of duties, if—

(1)   (A)   applicable law excuses a party, other than the debtor, to such contract or lease from accepting performance from or rendering performance to an entity other than the debtor or the debtor in possession [or an assignee of such contract or lease], whether or not such contract or lease prohibits or restricts assignment of rights or delegation of duties; and

(B)   such party does not consent to such assumption or assignment; or

(2)   such contract is a contract to make a loan, or extend other debt financing or financial accommodations, to or for the benefit of the debtor, or to issue a security of the debtor;

(3)   such lease is of nonresidential real property and has been terminated under applicable nonbankruptcy law prior to the order for relief; or

(4)   such lease is of nonresidential real property under which the debtor is the lessee of an aircraft terminal or aircraft gate at an airport at which the debtor is the lessee under one or more additional nonresidential leases of an aircraft terminal or aircraft gate and the trustee, in connection

with such assumption or assignment, does not assume all such leases or does not assume and assign all of such leases to the same person, except that the trustee may assume or assign less than all of such leases with the airport operator's written consent.

(d) (1)   In a case under chapter 7 of this title, if the trustee does not assume or reject an executory contract or unexpired lease of residential real property or of personal property of the debtor within 60 days after the order for relief, or within such additional time as the court, for cause, within such 60-day period, fixes, then such contract or lease is deemed rejected.

(2)   In a case under chapter 9, 11, 12, or 13 of this title, the trustee may assume or reject an executory contract or unexpired lease of residential real property or of personal property of the debtor at any time before the confirmation of a plan but the court, on the request of any party to such contract or lease, may order the trustee to determine within a specified period of time whether to assume or reject such contract or lease.

(3)   The trustee shall timely perform all the obligations of the debtor, except those specified in section 365(b)(2), arising from and after the order for relief under any unexpired lease of nonresidential real property, until such lease is assumed or rejected, notwithstanding section 503(b)(1) of this title. The court may extend, for cause, the time for performance of any such obligation that arises within 60 days after the date of the order for relief, but the time for performance shall not be extended beyond such 60-day period. This subsection shall not be deemed to affect the trustee's obligations under the provisions of subsection (b) or (f) of this section. Acceptance of any such performance does not constitute waiver or relinquishment of the lessor's rights under such lease or under this title.

(4)   Notwithstanding paragraphs (1) and (2), in a case under any chapter of this title, if the trustee does not assume or reject an unexpired lease of nonresidential real property under which the debtor is the lessee within 60 days after the date of the order for relief, or within such additional time as the court, for cause, within such 60-day period, fixes, then such lease is deemed rejected, and the trustee shall immediately surrender such nonresidential real property to the lessor.

(5)   Notwithstanding paragraphs (1) and (4) of this subsection, in a case under any chapter of this title, if the trustee does not assume or reject an unexpired lease of nonresidential real property under which the debtor is an affected air carrier that is the lessee of an aircraft terminal or aircraft gate before the occurrence of a termination event, then (unless the court orders the trustee to assume such unexpired leases within 5 days after the termination event), at the option of the airport operator, such lease is deemed rejected 5 days after the occurrence of a termination event and the trustee shall immediately surrender possession of the premises to the airport operator; except that the lease shall not be deemed to be rejected unless the airport operator first waives the right to damages related to the rejection. In the event that the lease is deemed to be rejected under this paragraph, the airport operator shall provide the affected air carrier adequate opportunity after the surrender of the premises to remove the fixtures and equipment installed by the affected air carrier.

(6)   For the purpose of paragraph (5) of this subsection and paragraph (f)(1) of this section, the occurrence of a termination event means, with

respect to a debtor which is an affected air carrier that is the lessee of an aircraft terminal or aircraft gate—

(A) the entry under section 301 or 302 of this title of an order for relief under chapter 7 of this title;

(B) the conversion of a case under any chapter of this title to a case under chapter 7 of this title; or

(C) the granting of relief from the stay provided under section 362(a) of this title with respect to aircraft, aircraft engines, propellers, appliances, or spare parts, as defined in section 40102 of title 49, except for property of the debtor found by the court not to be necessary to an effective reorganization.

(7) Any order entered by the court pursuant to paragraph (4) extending the period within which the trustee of an affected air carrier must assume or reject an unexpired lease of nonresidential real property shall be without prejudice to—

(A) the right of the trustee to seek further extensions within such additional time period granted by the court pursuant to paragraph (4); and

(B) the right of any lessor or any other party in interest to request, at any time, a shortening or termination of the period within which the trustee must assume or reject an unexpired lease of nonresidential real property.

(8) The burden of proof for establishing cause for an extension by an affected air carrier under paragraph (4) or the maintenance of a previously granted extension under paragraph (7)(A) and (B) shall at all times remain with the trustee.

(9) For purposes of determining cause under paragraph (7) with respect to an unexpired lease of nonresidential real property between the debtor that is an affected air carrier and an airport operator under which such debtor is the lessee of an airport terminal or an airport gate, the court shall consider, among other relevant factors, whether substantial harm will result to the airport operator or airline passengers as a result of the extension or the maintenance of a previously granted extension. In making the determination of substantial harm, the court shall consider, among other relevant factors, the level of actual use of the terminals or gates which are the subject of the lease, the public interest in actual use of such terminals or gates; the existence of competing demands for the use of such terminals or gates, the effect of the court's extension or termination of the period of time to assume or reject the lease on such debtor's ability to successfully reorganize under chapter 11 of this title, and whether the trustee of the affected air carrier is capable of continuing to comply with its obligations under section 365(d)(3) of this title.

(10) The trustee shall timely perform all of the obligations of the debtor, except those specified in section 365(b)(2), first arising from or after 60 days after the order for relief in a case under chapter 11 of this title under an unexpired lease of personal property (other than personal property leased to an individual primarily for personal, family, or household purposes), until such lease is assumed or rejected notwithstanding section 503(b)(1) of this title, unless the court, after notice and a hearing and based on the equities of the case, orders otherwise with respect to the obligations or timely performance thereof. This subsection shall not be deemed to affect the trustee's

obligations under the provisions of subsection (b) or (f). Acceptance of any such performance does not constitute waiver or relinquishment of the lessor's rights under such lease or under this title.

(e) (1)   Notwithstanding a provision in an executory contract or unexpired lease or in applicable law, an executory contract or unexpired lease of the debtor may not be terminated or modified, and any right or obligation under such contract or lease may not be terminated or modified, at any time after the commencement of the case solely because of a provision in such contract or lease that is conditioned on—

(A)   the insolvency or financial condition of the debtor at any time before the closing of the case;

(B)   the commencement of a case under this title; or

(C)   the appointment of or taking possession by a trustee in a case under this title or a custodian before such commencement.

(2)   Paragraph (1) of this subsection does not apply to an executory contract or unexpired lease of the debtor, whether or not such contract or lease prohibits or restricts assignment of rights or delegation of duties, if—

(A)   (i)   applicable law excuses a party, other than the debtor, to such contract or lease from accepting performance from or rendering performance to the trustee or to an assignee of such contract or lease, whether or not such contract or lease prohibits or restricts assignment of rights or delegation of duties; and

(ii)   such party does not consent to such assumption or assignment; or

(B)   such contract is a contract to make a loan, or extend other debt financing or financial accommodations, to or for the benefit of the debtor, or to issue a security of the debtor.

(f) (1)   Except as provided in subsection (c) of this section, notwithstanding a provision in an executory contract or unexpired lease of the debtor, or in applicable law, that prohibits, restricts, or conditions the assignment of such contract or lease, the trustee may assign such contract or lease under paragraph (2) of this subsection; except that the trustee may not assign an unexpired lease of nonresidential real property under which the debtor is an affected air carrier that is the lessee of an aircraft terminal or aircraft gate if there has occurred a termination event.

(2)   The trustee may assign an executory contract or unexpired lease of the debtor only if—

(A)   the trustee assumes such contract or lease in accordance with the provisions of this section; and

(B)   adequate assurance of future performance by the assignee of such contract or lease is provided, whether or not there has been a default in such contract or lease.

(3)   Notwithstanding a provision in an executory contract or unexpired lease of the debtor, or in applicable law that terminates or modifies, or permits a party other than the debtor to terminate or modify, such contract or lease or a right or obligation under such contract or lease on account of an assignment of such contract or lease, such contract, lease, right, or obligation may not be terminated or modified under such provision because of the assumption or assignment of such contract or lease by the trustee.

(g)   Except as provided in subsections (h)(2) and (i)(2) of this section, the rejection of an executory contract or unexpired lease of the debtor constitutes a breach of such contrast or lease—

(1)   if such contract or lease has not been assumed under this section or under a plan confirmed under chapter 9, 11, 12, or 13 of this title, immediately before the date of the filing of the petition; or

(2)   if such contract or lease has been assumed under this section or under a plan confirmed under chapter 9, 11, 12, or 13 of this title—

(A)   if before such rejection the case has not been converted under section 1112, 1208, or 1307 of this title, at the time of such rejection; or

(B)   if before such rejection the case has been converted under section 1112, 1208, or 1307 of this title—

(i)   immediately before the date of such conversion, if such contract or lease was assumed before such conversion; or

(ii)   at the time of such rejection, if such contract or lease was assumed after such conversion.

(h) (1)   (A)   If the trustee rejects an unexpired lease of real property under which the debtor is the lessor and—

(i)   if the rejection by the trustee amounts to such a breach as would entitle the lessee to treat such lease as terminated by virtue of its terms, applicable nonbankruptcy law, or any agreement made by the lessee, then the lessee under such lease may treat such lease as terminated by the rejection; or

(ii)   if the term of such lease has commenced, the lessee may retain its rights under such lease (including rights such as those relating to the amount and timing of payment of rent and other amounts payable by the lessee and any right of use, possession, quiet enjoyment, subletting, assignment, or hypothecation) that are in or appurtenant to the real property for the balance of the term of such lease and for any renewal or extension of such rights to the extent that such rights are enforceable under applicable nonbankruptcy law.

(B)   If the lessee retains its rights under subparagraph (A)(ii), the lessee may offset against the rent reserved under such lease for the balance of the term after the date of the rejection of such lease and for the term of any renewal or extension of such lease, the value of any damage caused by the nonperformance after the date of such rejection, of any obligation of the debtor under such lease, but the lessee shall not have any other right against the estate or the debtor on account of any damage occurring after such date caused by such nonperformance.

(C)   The rejection of a lease of real property in a shopping center with respect to which the lessee elects to retain its rights under subparagraph (A)(ii) does not affect the enforceability under applicable nonbankruptcy law of any provision in the lease pertaining to radius, location, use, exclusivity, or tenant mix or balance.

(D)   In this paragraph, "lessee" includes any successor, assign, or mortgagee permitted under the terms of such lease.

(2)   (A)   If the trustee rejects a timeshare interest under a timeshare plan under which the debtor is the timeshare interest seller and—

   (i) if the rejection amounts to such a breach as would entitle the timeshare interest purchaser to treat the timeshare plan as terminated under its terms, applicable nonbankruptcy law, or any agreement made by timeshare interest purchaser, the timeshare interest purchaser under the timeshare plan may treat the timeshare plan as terminated by such rejection; or

   (ii) if the term of such timeshare interest has commenced, then the timeshare interest purchaser may retain its rights in such timeshare interest for the balance of such term and for any term of renewal or extension of such timeshare interest to the extent that such rights are enforceable under applicable nonbankruptcy law.

  (B) If the timeshare interest purchaser retains its rights under subparagraph (A), such timeshare interest purchaser may offset against the moneys due for such timeshare interest for the balance of the term after the date of the rejection of such timeshare interest, and the term of any renewal or extension of such timeshare interest, the value of any damage caused by the nonperformance after the date of such rejection, of any obligation of the debtor under such timeshare plan, but the timeshare interest purchaser shall not have any right against the estate or the debtor on account of any damage occurring after such date caused by such nonperformance.

 (i) (1) If the trustee rejects an executory contract of the debtor for the sale of real property or for the sale of a timeshare interest under a timeshare plan, under which the purchaser is in possession, such purchaser may treat such contract as terminated, or, in the alternative, may remain in possession of such real property or timeshare interest.

  (2) if such purchaser remains in possession—

  (A) such purchaser shall continue to make all payments due under such contract, but may, offset against such payments any damages occurring after the date of the rejection of such contract caused by the non-performance of any obligation of the debtor after such date, but such purchaser does not have any rights against the estate on account of any damages arising after such date from such rejection, other than such offset; and

  (B) the trustee shall deliver title to such purchaser in accordance with the provisions of such contract, but is relieved of all other obligations to perform under such contract.

 (j) A purchaser that treats an executory contract as terminated under subsection (i) of this section, or a party whose executory contract to purchase real property from the debtor is rejected and under which such party is not in possession, has a lien on the interest of the debtor in such property for the recovery of any portion of the purchase price that such purchaser or party has paid.

 (k) Assignment by the trustee to an entity of a contract or lease assumed under this section relieves the trustee and the estate from any liability for any breach of such contract or lease occurring after such assignment.

 (l) If an unexpired lease under which the debtor is the lessee is assigned pursuant to this section, the lessor of the property may require a deposit or other security for the performance of the debtor's obligations under the lease substantially the same as would have been required by the landlord upon the initial leasing to a similar tenant.

(m) For purposes of this section 365 and sections 541(b)(2) and 362(b)(10), leases of real property shall include any rental agreement to use real property.

(n) (1) If the trustee rejects an executory contract under which the debtor is a licensor of a right to intellectual property, the licensee under such contract may elect—

(A) to treat such contract as terminated by such rejection if such rejection by the trustee amounts to such a breach as would entitle the licensee to treat such contract as terminated by virtue of its own terms, applicable nonbankruptcy law, or an agreement made by the licensee with another entity; or

(B) to retain its rights (including a right to enforce any exclusivity provision of such contract, but excluding any other right under applicable nonbankruptcy law to specific performance of such contract) under such contract and under any agreement supplementary to such contract, to such intellectual property (including any embodiment of such intellectual property to the extent protected by applicable nonbankruptcy law), as such rights existed immediately before the case commenced, for—

(i) the duration of such contract; and

(ii) any period for which such contract may be extended by the licensee as of right under applicable nonbankruptcy law.

(2) If the licensee elects to retain its rights, as described in paragraph (1)(B) of this subsection, under such contract—

(A) the trustee shall allow the licensee to exercise such rights;

(B) the licensee shall make all royalty payments due under such contract for the duration of such contract and for any period described in paragraph (1)(B) of this subsection for which the licensee extends such contract; and

(C) the licensee shall be deemed to waive—

(i) any right of setoff it may have with respect to such contract under this title or applicable nonbankruptcy law; and

(ii) any claim allowable under section 503(b) of this title arising from the performance of such contract.

(3) If the licensee elects to retain its rights, as described in paragraph (1)(B) of this subsection, then on the written request of the licensee the trustee shall—

(A) to the extent provided in such contract, or any agreement supplementary to such contract, provide to the licensee any intellectual property (including such embodiment) held by the trustee; and

(B) not interfere with the rights of the licensee as provided in such contract, or any agreement supplementary to such contract, to such intellectual property (including such embodiment) including any right to obtain such intellectual property (or such embodiment) from other entity.

(4) Unless and until the trustee rejects such contract, on the written request of the licensee the trustee shall—

(A)   to the extent provided in such contract or any agreement supplementary to such contract—

(i)   perform such contract; or

(ii)   provide to the licensee such intellectual property (including any embodiment of such intellectual property to the extent protected by applicable nonbankruptcy law) held by the trustee; and

(B)   not interfere with the rights of the licensee as provided in such contract, or any agreement supplementary to such contract, to such intellectual property (including such embodiment), including any right to obtain such intellectual property (or such embodiment) from another entity.

(o)   In a case under chapter 11 of this title, the trustee shall be deemed to have assumed (consistent with the debtor's other obligations under section 507), and shall immediately cure any deficit under, any commitment by the debtor to a Federal depository institutions regulatory agency (or predecessor to such agency), to maintain the capital of an insured depository institution, and any claim for a subsequent breach of the obligations thereunder shall be entitled to priority under section 507. This subsection shall not extend any commitment that would otherwise be terminated by any act of such an agency.

Sec. 366.   *Utility Service*

(a)   Except as provided in subsection (b) of this section, a utility may not alter, refuse, or discontinue service to, or discriminate against, the trustee or the debtor solely on the basis of the commencement of a case under this title or that a debt owed by the debtor to such utility for service rendered before the order for relief was not paid when due.

(b)   Such utility may alter, refuse, or discontinue service if neither the trustee nor the debtor, within 20 days after the date of the order for relief, furnishes adequate assurance of payment, in the form of a deposit or other security, for service after such date. On request of a party in interest and after notice and a hearing, the court may order reasonable modification of the amount of the deposit or other security necessary to provide adequate assurance of payment.

5
CREDITORS, THE DEBTOR, AND THE ESTATE

SUBCHAPTER I. CREDITORS AND CLAIMS

Sec. 501.   *Filing of Proofs of Claims or Interests*

(a)   A creditor or an indenture trustee may file a proof of claim. An equity security holder may file a proof of interest.

(b)   If a creditor does not timely file a proof of such creditor's claim, an entity that is liable to such creditor with the debtor, or that has secured such creditor, may file a proof of such claim.

(c)   If a creditor does not timely file a proof of such creditor's claim, the debtor or the trustee may file a proof of such claim.

(d)   A claim of a kind specified in section 502(e)(2), 502(f), 502(g), 502(h) or 502(i) of this title may be filed under subsection (a), (b), or (c) of this section the same as if such claim were a claim against the debtor and had arisen before the date of the filing of the petition.

Sec. 502. *Allowance of Claims or Interests*

(a)   A claim or interest, proof of which is filed under section 501 of this title, is deemed allowed, unless a party in interest, including a creditor of a general partner in a partnership that is a debtor in a case under chapter 7 of this title, objects.

(b)   Except as provided in subsections (e)(2), (f), (g), (h) and (i) of this section, if such objection to a claim is made, the court, after notice and a hearing, shall determine the amount of such claim in lawful currency of the United States as of the date of the filing of the petition, and shall allow such claim in such amount, except to the extent that—

(1)   such claim is unenforceable against the debtor and property of the debtor, under any agreement or applicable law for a reason other than because such claim is contingent or unmatured;

(2)   such claim is for unmatured interest;

(3)   if such claim is for a tax assessed against property of the estate, such claim exceeds the value of the interest of the estate in such property;

(4)   if such claim is for services of an insider or attorney of the debtor, such claim exceeds the reasonable value of such services;

(5)   such claim is for a debt that is unmatured on the date of the filing of the petition and that is excepted from discharge under section 523(a)(5) of this title;

(6)   if such claim is the claim of a lessor for damages resulting from the termination of a lease of real property, such claim exceeds—

(A)   the rent reserved by such lease, without acceleration, for the greater of one year, or 15 percent, not to exceed three years, of the remaining term of such lease, following the earlier of—

(i)   the date of the filing of the petition; and

(ii)   the date on which such lessor repossessed, or the lessee surrendered, the leased property; plus

(B)   any unpaid rent due under such lease without acceleration, on the earlier of such dates;

(7)   if such claim is the claim of an employee for damages resulting from the termination of an employment contract, such claim exceeds—

(A)   the compensation provided by such contract, without acceleration, for one year following the earlier of—

(i)   the date of the filing of the petition; or

(ii)   the date on which the employer directed the employee to terminate, or such employee terminated, performance under such contract; plus

(B)   any unpaid compensation due under such contract, without acceleration, on the earlier of such dates;

(8)   such claim results from a reduction, due to late payment, in the amount of an otherwise applicable credit available to the debtor in connec-

tion with an employment tax on wages, salaries, or commissions earned from the debtor; or

(9) proof of such claim is not timely filed, except to the extent tardily filed as permitted under paragraph (1), (2), or (3) of section 726(a) of this title or under the Federal Rules of Bankruptcy Procedure, except that a claim of a governmental unit shall be timely filed if it is filed before 180 days after the date of the order for relief or such later time as the Federal Rules of Bankruptcy Procedure may provide.

(c) There shall be estimated for purposes of allowance under this section—

(1) any contingent or unliquidated claim, the fixing or liquidation of which, as the case may be, would unduly delay the administration of the case; or

(2) any right to payment arising from a right to an equitable remedy for breach of performance.

(d) Notwithstanding subsections (a) and (b) of this section, the court shall disallow any claim of any entity from which property is recoverable under section 542, 543, 550, or 553 of this title or that is a transferee of a transfer avoidable under section 522(f), 522(h), 544, 545, 547, 548, 549, or 724(a) of this title, unless such entity or transferee has paid the amount, or turned over any such property, for which such entity or transferee is liable under section 522(i), 542, 543, 550, or 553 of this title.

(e) (1) Notwithstanding subsections (a), (b), and (c) of this section and paragraph (2) of this subsection, the court shall disallow any claim for reimbursement or contribution of an entity that is liable with the debtor on or has secured the claim of a creditor, to the extent that—

(A) such creditor's claim against the estate is disallowed;

(B) such claim for reimbursement or contribution is contingent as of the time of allowance or disallowance of such claim for reimbursement or contribution; or

(C) such entity asserts a right of subrogation to the rights of such creditor under section 509 of this title to

(2) A claim for reimbursement or contribution of such an entity that becomes fixed after the commencement of the case shall be determined, and shall be allowed under subsection (a), (b), or (c) of this section, or disallowed under subsection (d) of this section, the same as if such claim had become fixed before the date of filing of the petition.

(f) In an involuntary case, a claim arising in the ordinary course of the debtor's business or financial affairs after the commencement of the case but before the earlier of the appointment of a trustee and the order for relief shall be determined as of the date such claim arises, and shall be allowed under subsection (a), (b), or (c) of this section or disallowed under subsection (d) or (e) of this section, the same as if such claim had arisen before the date of the filing of the petition.

(g) A claim arising from the rejection, under section 365 of this title or under a plan under chapter 9, 11, 12, or 13 of this title, of an executory contract or unexpired lease of the debtor that has not been assumed shall be determined, and shall be allowed under subsection (a), (b), or (c) of this section or disallowed under subsection (d) or (e) of this section, the same as if such claim had arisen before the date of the filing of the petition.

(h)   A claim arising from the recovery of property under section 522, 550, or 553 of this title shall be determined, and shall be allowed under subsection (a), (b), or (c) of this section, or disallowed under subsection (d) or (e) of this section, the same as if such claim had arisen before the date of the filing of the petition.

(i)   A claim that does not arise until after the commencement of the case for a tax entitled to priority under section 507(a)(8) of this title shall be determined, and shall be allowed under subsection (a), (b), or (c) of this section, or disallowed under subsection (d) or (e) of this section, the same as if such claim had arisen before the date of the filing of the petition.

(j)   A claim that has been allowed or disallowed may be reconsidered for cause. A reconsidered claim may be allowed or disallowed according to the equities of the case. Reconsideration of a claim under this subsection does not affect the validity of any payment or transfer from the estate made to a holder of an allowed claim on account of such allowed claim that is not reconsidered, but if a reconsidered claim is allowed and is of the same class as such holder's claim, such holder may not receive any additional payment or transfer from the estate on account of such holder's allowed claim until the holder of such reconsidered and allowed claim receives payment on account of such claim proportionate in value to that already received by such other holder. This subsection does not alter or modify the trustee's right to recover from a creditor any excess payment or transfer made to such creditor.

Sec. 503.   Allowance of Administrative Expenses

(a)   An entity may timely file a request for payment of an administrative expense, or may tardily file such request if permitted by the Court for cause.

(b)   After notice and a hearing, there shall be allowed administrative expenses, other than claims allowed under section 502(f) of this title, including—

(1)   (A)   the actual, necessary costs and expenses of preserving the estate, including wages, salaries, or commissions for services rendered after the commencement of the case:

(B)   any tax—

(i)   incurred by the estate, except a tax of a kind specified in section 507(a)(8) of this title; or

(ii)   attributable to an excessive allowance of a tentative carryback adjustment that the estate received, whether the taxable year to which such adjustment relates ended before or after the commencement of the case; and

(C)   any fine, penalty, or reduction in credit relating to a tax of a kind specified in subparagraph (B) of this paragraph;

(2)   compensation and reimbursement awarded under section 330(a) of this title;

(3)   the actual, necessary expenses, other than compensation and reimbursement specified in paragraph (4) of this subsection, incurred by—

(A)   a creditor that files a petition under section 303 of this title;

(B)   a creditor that recovers, after the court's approval, for the benefit of the estate any property transferred or concealed by the debtor;

(C)   a creditor in connection with the prosecution of a criminal offense relating to the case or to the business or property of the debtor;

(D)   a creditor, an indenture trustee, an equity security holder, or a committee representing creditors or equity security holders other than a committee appointed under section 1102 of this title, in making a substantial contribution in a case under chapter 9 or 11 of this title;

(E)   a custodian superseded under section 543 of this title, and compensation for the services of such custodian; or

(F)   a member of a committee appointed under section 1102 of this title, if such expenses are incurred in the performance of the duties of such committee;

(4)   reasonable compensation for professional services rendered by an attorney or an accountant of an entity whose expense is allowable under paragraph (3) of this subsection, based on the time, the nature, the extent, and the value of such services, and the cost of comparable services other than in a case under this title, and reimbursement for actual, necessary expenses incurred by such attorney or accountant;

(5)   reasonable compensation for services rendered by an indenture trustee in making a substantial contribution in a case under chapter 9 or 11 of this title, based on the time, the nature, the extent, and the value of such services, and the cost of comparable services other than in a case under this title, and

(6)   the fees and mileage payable under chapter 119 of title 28.

Sec. 504.   *Sharing of Compensation*

(a)   Except as provided in subsection (b) of this section, a person receiving compensation or reimbursement under section 503(b)(2) or 503(b)(4) of this title may not share or agree to share—

(1)   any such compensation or reimbursement with another person; or

(2)   any compensation or reimbursement received by another person under such sections.

(b) (1)   A member, partner, or regular associate in a professional association, corporation, or partnership may share compensation or reimbursement received under section 503(b)(2) or 503(b)(4) of this title with another member, partner, or regular associate in such association, corporation, or partnership, and may share in any compensation or reimbursement received under such sections by another member, partner, or regular associate in such association, corporation, or partnership.

(2)   An attorney for a creditor that files a petition under section 303 of this title may share compensation and reimbursement received under section 503(b)(4) of this title with any other attorney contributing to the services rendered or expenses incurred by such creditor's attorney.

Sec. 505.   *Determination of Tax Liability*

(a) (1)   Except as provided in paragraph (2) of this subsection, the court may determine the amount or legality of any tax, any fine or penalty relating to a tax, or any addition to tax, whether or not previously assessed, whether or not paid, and whether or not contested before and adjudicated by a judicial or administrative tribunal of competent jurisdiction.

(2)   The court may not so determine—

(A)   the amount or legality of a tax, fine, penalty, or addition to tax if such amount or legality was contested before and adjudicated by a judicial or administrative tribunal of competent jurisdiction before the commencement of the case under this title; or

(B)   any right of the estate to a tax refund, before the earlier of—

(i)   120 days after the trustee properly requests such refund from the governmental unit from which such refund is claimed; or

(ii)   a determination by such governmental unit of such request.

(b)   A trustee may request a determination of any unpaid liability of the estate for any tax incurred during the administration of the case by submitting a tax return for such tax and a request for such a determination to the governmental unit charged with responsibility for collection or determination of such tax. Unless such return is fraudulent, or contains a material misrepresentation, the trustee, the debtor, and any successor to the debtor are discharged from any liability for such tax—

(1)   upon payment of the tax shown on such return, if—

(A)   such governmental unit does not notify the trustee, within 60 days after such request, that such return has been selected for examination; or

(B)   such governmental unit does not complete such an examination and notify the trustee of any tax due, within 180 days after such request or within such additional time as the court, for cause, permits;

(2)   upon payment of the tax determined by the court, after notice and a hearing, after completion by such governmental unit of such examination; or

(3)   upon payment of the tax determined by such governmental unit to be due.

(c)   Notwithstanding section 362 of this title, after determination by the court of a tax under this section, the governmental unit charged with responsibility for collection of such tax may assess such tax against the estate, the debtor, or a successor to the debtor, as the case may be, subject to any otherwise applicable law.

Sec. 506. *Determination of Secured Status*

(a)   An allowed claim of a creditor secured by a lien on property in which the estate has an interest, or that is subject to setoff under section 553 of this title, is a secured claim to the extent of the value of such creditor's interest in the estate's interest in such property, or to the extent of the amount subject to setoff, as the case may be, and is an unsecured claim to the extent that the value of such creditor's interest or the amount so subject to setoff is less than the amount of such allowed claim. Such value shall be determined in light of the purpose of the valuation and of the proposed disposition or use of such property, and in conjunction with any hearing on such disposition or use or on a plan affecting such creditor's interest.

(b)		To the extent that an allowed secured claim is secured by property the value of which, after any recovery under subsection (c) of this section, is greater than the amount of such claim, there shall be allowed to the holder of such claim, interest on such claim, and any reasonable fees, costs, or charges provided for under the agreement under which such claim arose.

(c)		The trustee may recover from property securing an allowed secured claim the reasonable, necessary costs and expenses of preserving, or disposing of, such property to the extent of any benefit to the holder of such claim.

(d)		To the extent that a lien secures a claim against the debtor that is not an allowed secured claim, such lien is void, unless—

(1)		such claim was disallowed only under section 502(b)(5) or 502(e) of this title; or

(2)		such claim is not an allowed secured claim due only to the failure of any entity to file a proof of such claim under section 501 of this title.

Sec. 507. *Priorities*

(a)		The following expenses and claims have priority in the following order:

(1)		First, administrative expenses allowed under section 503(b) of this title, and any fees and charges assessed against the estate under chapter 123 of title 28.

(2)		Second, unsecured claims allowed under section 502(f) of this title.

(3)		Third, allowed unsecured claims, but only to the extent of $4,300 for each individual or corporation, as the case may be, earned within 90 days before the date of the filing of the petition or the date of the cessation of the debtor's business, whichever occurs first, for—

(A)		wages, salaries, or commissions, including vacation, severance, and sick leave pay earned by an individual; or

(B)		sales commissions earned by an individual or by a corporation with only 1 employee acting as an independent contractor in the sale of goods or services for the debtor in the ordinary course of the debtor's business if, and only if, during the 12 months preceding that date, at least 75 percent of the amount that the individual or corporation earned by acting as an independent contractor in the sale of goods or services was earned from the debtor;

(4)		Fourth, allowed unsecured claims for contributions to an employee benefit plan—

(A)		arising from services rendered within 180 days before the date of the filing of the petition or the date of the cessation of the debtor's business, whichever occurs first; but only

(B)		for each such plan, to the extent of—

(i)		the number of employees covered by each such plan multiplied by $4,300; less

(ii)		the aggregate amount paid to such employees under paragraph (3) of this subsection, plus the aggregate amount paid by the estate on behalf of such employees to any other employee benefit plan.

(5) Fifth, allowed unsecured claims of persons—

(A) engaged in the production or raising of grain, as defined in section 557(b) of this title, against a debtor who owns or operates a grain storage facility, as defined in section 557(b) of this title, for grain or the proceeds of grain, or

(B) engaged as a United States fisherman against a debtor who has acquired fish or fish produce from a fisherman through a sale or conversion, and who is engaged in operating a fish produce storage or processing facility—but only to the extent of $4,300 for each such individual.

(6) Sixth, allowed unsecured claims of individuals, to the extent of $1,950 for each such individual, arising from the deposit, before the commencement of the case, of money in connection with the purchase, lease, or rental of property, or the purchase of services, for the personal, family, or household use of such individuals that were not delivered or provided.

(7) Seventh, allowed claims for debts to a spouse, former spouse, or child of the debtor, for alimony to, maintenance for, or support of such spouse or child, in connection with a separation agreement, divorce decree or other order of a court of record, determination made in accordance with State or territorial law by a governmental unit, or property settlement agreement, but not to the extent that such debt—

(A) is assigned to another entity, voluntarily, by operation of law; or otherwise; or

(B) includes a liability designated as alimony, maintenance, or support, unless such liability is actually in the nature of alimony, maintenance or support.

(8) Eighth, allowed unsecured claims of governmental units, only to the extent that such claims are for—

(A) a tax on or measured by income or gross receipts—

(i) for a taxable year ending on or before the date of the filing of the petition for which a return, if required, is last due, including extensions, after three years before the date of the filing of the petition;

(ii) assessed within 240 days, plus any time plus 30 days during which an offer in compromise with respect to such tax that was made within 240 days after such assessment was pending, before the date of the filing of the petition; or

(iii) other than a tax of a kind specified in section 523(a)(1)(B) or 523(a)(1)(c) of this title, not assessed before, but assessable, under applicable law or by agreement, after, the commencement of the case;

(B) a property tax assessed before the commencement of the case and last payable without penalty after one year before the date of the filing of the petition;

(C) a tax required to be collected or withheld and for which the debtor is liable in whatever capacity;

(D) an employment tax on a wage, salary, or commission of a kind specified in paragraph (3) of this subsection earned from the debtor before the date of the filing of the petition, whether or not actually paid before such date, for which a return is last due, under applicable law or under any extension, after three years before the date of the filing of the petition;

  (E) an excise tax on—

    (i) a transaction occurring before the date of the filing of the petition for which a return, if required, is last due, under applicable law or under any extension, after three years before the date of the filing of the petition; or

    (ii) if a return is not required, a transaction occurring during the three years immediately preceding the date of the filing of the petition;

  (F) a customs duty arising out of the importation of merchandise—

    (i) entered for consumption within one year before the date of the filing of the petition;

    (ii) covered by an entry liquidated or reliquidated within one year before the date of the filing of the petition; or

    (iii) entered for consumption within four years before the date of the filing of the petition but unliquidated on such date, if the Secretary of the Treasury certifies that failure to liquidate such entry was due to an investigation pending on such date into assessment of antidumping or countervailing duties or fraud, or if information needed for the proper appraisement or classification of such merchandise was not available to the appropriate customs officer before such date; or

  (G) a penalty related to a claim of a kind specified in this paragraph and in compensation for actual pecuniary loss.

  (9) Ninth, allowed unsecured claims based upon any commitment by the debtor to a Federal depository institutions regulatory agency (or predecessor to such agency), to maintain the capital of an insured depository institution.

  (b) If the trustee, under section 362, 363, or 364 of this title, provides adequate protection of the interest of a holder of a claim secured by a lien on property of the debtor and if, notwithstanding such protection, such creditor has a claim allowable under subsection (a)(1) of this section arising from the stay of action against such property under section 362 of this title, from the use, sale, or lease of such property under section 363 of this title, or from the granting of a lien under section 364(d) of this title, then such creditor's claim under such subsection shall have priority over every other claim under such subsection.

  (c) For the purpose of subsection (a) of this section, a claim of a governmental unit arising from an erroneous refund or credit of a tax has the same priority as a claim for the tax to which such refund or credit relates.

  (d) An entity that is subrogated to the rights of a holder of a claim of a kind specified in subsection (a)(3), (a)(4), (a)(5), (a)(6), (a)(7), (a)(8), or (a)(9) of this section if not subrogated to the right of the holder of such claim to priority under such subsection.

Sec. 508. *Effect of Distribution Other Than under This Title*

(a)   If a creditor receives, in a foreign proceeding, payment of, or a transfer of property on account of, a claim that is allowed under this title, such creditor may not receive any payment under this title on account of such claim until each of the other holders of claims on account of which such holders are entitled to share equally with such creditor under this title has received payment under this title equal in value to the consideration received by such creditor in such foreign proceeding.

(b)   If a creditor of a partnership debtor receives, from a general partner that is not a debtor in a case under chapter 7 of this title, payment of, or a transfer of property on account of, a claim that is allowed under this title and that is not secured by a lien on property of such partner, such creditor may not receive any payment under this title on account of such claim until each of the other holders of claims on account of which such holders are entitled to share equally with such creditor under this title has received payment under this title equal in value to the consideration received by such creditor from such general partner.

Sec. 509. *Claims of Codebtors*

(a)   Except as provided in section (b) or (c) of this section, an entity that is liable with the debtor on, or that has secured, a claim of a creditor against the debtor, and that pays such claim, is subrogated to the rights of such creditor to the extent of such payment.

(b)   Such entity is not subrogated to the rights of such creditor to the extent that—

(1)   a claim of such entity for reimbursement or contribution on account of such payment of such creditor's claim is—

(A)   allowed under section 502 of this title;

(B)   disallowed other than under section 502(e) of this title; or

(C)   subordinated under section 510 of this title; or

(2)   as between the debtor and such entity, such entity received the consideration for the claim held by such creditor.

(c)   The court shall subordinate to the claim of a creditor and for the benefit of such creditor an allowed claim, by way of subrogation under this section, or for reimbursement or contribution, of an entity that is liable with the debtor on, or that has secured, such creditor's claim, until such creditor's claim is paid in full, either through payments under this title or otherwise.

Sec. 510. *Subordination*

(a)   A subordination agreement is enforceable in a case under this title to the same extent that such agreement is enforceable under applicable non-bankruptcy law.

(b)   For the purpose of distribution under this title, a claim arising from rescission of a purchase or sale of a security of the debtor or of an affiliate of the debtor, for damages arising from the purchase or sale of such a security, or for reimbursement or contribution allowed under section 502 on account of such a claim, shall be subordinated to all claims or interests that are senior to or equal the claim or interest represented by such security, except that if such security is common stock, such claim has the same priority as common stock.

(c)   Notwithstanding subsections (a) and (b) of this section, after notice and a hearing, the court may—

(1)   under principles of equitable subordination, subordinate for purposes of distribution all or part of an allowed claim to all or part of another allowed claim or all or part of an allowed interest to all or part of another allowed interest; or

(2)   order that any lien securing such a subordinated claim be transferred to the estate.

SUBCHAPTER II. DEBTOR'S DUTIES AND BENEFITS

Sec. 521.   *Debtor's Duties*

The debtor shall—

(1)   file a list of creditors, and unless the court orders otherwise, a schedule of assets and liabilities, a schedule of current income and current expenditures, and a statement of the debtor's financial affairs;

(2)   if an individual debtor's schedule of assets and liabilities includes consumer debts which are secured by property of the estate—

(A)   within thirty days after the date of the filing of a petition under chapter 7 of this title or on or before the date of the meeting of creditors, whichever is earlier, or within such additional time as the court, for cause, within such period fixes, the debtor shall file with the clerk a statement of his intention with respect to the retention or surrender of such property and, if applicable, specifying that such property is claimed as exempt, that the debtor intends to redeem such property, or that the debtor intends to reaffirm debts secured by such property;

(B)   within forty-five days after the filing of a notice of intent under this section, or within such additional time as the court, for cause, within such forty-five day period fixes, the debtor shall perform his intention with respect to such property, as specified by subparagraph (A) of this paragraph; and

(C)   nothing in subparagraphs (A) and (B) of this paragraph shall alter the debtor's or the trustee's rights with regard to such property under this title.

(3)   if a trustee is serving in the case, cooperate with the trustee as necessary to enable the trustee to perform the trustee's duties under this title;

(4)   if a trustee is serving in the case, surrender to the trustee all property of the estate and any recorded information, including books, documents, records, and papers, relating to property of the estate, whether or not immunity is granted under section 344 of this title; and

(5)   appear at the hearing required under section 524(d) of this title.

Sec. 522.   *Exemptions*

(a)   In this section—

(1)   "dependent" includes spouse, whether or not actually dependent; and

(2)   "value" means fair market value as of the date of the filing of the petition or, with respect to property that becomes property of the estate after such date, as of the date such property becomes property of the estate.

(b)   Notwithstanding section 541 of this title, an individual debtor may exempt from property of the estate the property listed in either paragraph (1) or, in the alternative, paragraph (2) of this subsection. In joint cases filed under section 302 of this title and individual cases filed under section 301 or 303 of this title by or against debtors who are husband and wife, and whose estates are ordered to be jointly administered under Rule 1015(b) of the Federal Rules of Bankruptcy Procedure, one debtor may not elect to exempt property listed in paragraph (1) and the other debtor elect to exempt property listed in paragraph (2) of this subsection. If the parties cannot agree on the alternative to be elected, they shall be deemed to elect paragraph (1), where such election is permitted under the law of the jurisdiction where the case is filed.

Such property is—

(1)   property that is specified under subsection (d) of this section, unless the State law that is applicable to the debtor under paragraph (2)(A) of this subsection specifically does not so authorize; or, in the alternative,

(2)   (A)   any property that is exempt under Federal law, other than subsection (d) of this section, or State or local law that is applicable on the date of the filing of the petition at the place in which the debtor's domicile has been located for the 180 days immediately preceding the date of the filing of the petition, or for a longer portion of such 180-day period than in any other place; and

(B)   any interest in property in which the debtor had, immediately before the commencement of the case, an interest as a tenant by the entirety or joint tenant to the extent that such interest as a tenant by the entirety or joint tenant is exempt from process under applicable non-bankruptcy law.

(c)   Unless the case is dismissed, property exempted under this section is not liable during or after the case for any debt of the debtor that arose, or that is determined under section 502 of this title as if such debt had arisen, before the commencement of the case, except—

(1)   a debt of a kind specified in section 523(a)(1) or 523(a)(5) of this title;

(2)   a debt secured by a lien that is—

(A)   (i)   not avoided under subsection (f) or (g) of this section or under section, 544, 545, 547, 548, 549, or 724(a) of this title; or

(ii)   not void under section 506(d) of this title; or

(B)   a tax lien, notice of which is properly filed

(3)   a debt of a kind specified in section 523(a)(4) or 523(a)(6) of this title owed by an institution-affiliated party of an insured depository institution to a Federal depository institutions regulatory agency acting in its capacity as conservator, receiver, or liquidating agent for such institution.

(d)   The following property may be exempted under subsection (b)(1) of this section:

(1)   The debtor's aggregate interest, not to exceed $15,000 in value, in real property or personal property that the debtor or a dependent of the debtor uses as a residence, in a cooperative that owns property that the

debtor or a dependent of the debtor uses as a residence, or in a burial plot for the debtor or a dependent of the debtor.

(2)   The debtor's interest, not to exceed $2,575 in value, in one motor vehicle.

(3)   The debtor's interest, not to exceed $425 in value in any particular item or $8,625 in aggregate value, in household furnishings, household goods, wearing apparel, appliances, books, animals, crops, or musical instruments, that are held primarily for the personal, family, or household use of the debtor or a dependent of the debtor.

(4)   The debtor's aggregate interest, not to exceed $1,075 in value, in jewelry held primarily for the personal, family, or household use of the debtor or a dependent of the debtor.

(5)   The debtor's aggregate interest in any property, not to exceed in value $850 plus up to $8,075 of any unused amount of the exemption provided under paragraph (1) of this subsection.

(6)   The debtor's aggregate interest, not to exceed $1,625 in value, in any implements, professional books, or tools of the trade of the debtor or the trade of a dependent of the debtor.

(7)   Any unmatured life insurance contract owned by the debtor, other than a credit life insurance contract.

(8)   The debtor's aggregate interest, not to exceed in value $8,625 less any amount of property of the estate transferred in the manner specified in section 542(d) of this title, in any accrued dividend or interest under, or loan value of, any unmatured life insurance contract owned by the debtor under which the insured is the debtor or an individual of whom the debtor is a dependent.

(9)   Professionally prescribed health aids for the debtor or a dependent of the debtor.

(10) The debtor's right to receive—

(A)   a social security benefit, unemployment compensation, or a local public assistance benefit;

(B)   a veterans' benefit;

(C)   a disability, illness, or unemployment benefit;

(D)   alimony, support, or separate maintenance, to the extent reasonably necessary for the support of the debtor and any dependent of the debtor;

(E)   a payment under a stock bonus, pension, profit-sharing, annuity, or similar plan or contract on account of illness, disability, death, age, or length of service, to the extent reasonably necessary for the support of the debtor and any dependent of the debtor, unless—

(i)   such plan or contract was established by or under the auspices of an insider that employed the debtor at the time the debtor's rights under such plan or contract arose;

(ii)   such payment is on account of age or length of service; and

(iii)   such plan or contract does not qualify under section 401(a), 403(a), 403(b), or 408 of the Internal Revenue Code of 1986.

(11) The debtor's right to receive, or property that is traceable to—

(A)   an award under a crime victim's reparation law;

(B)   a payment on account of the wrongful death of an individual of whom the debtor was a dependent, to the extent reasonably necessary for the support of the debtor and any dependent of the debtor;

(C)   a payment under a life insurance contract that insured the life of an individual of whom the debtor was a dependent on the date of such individual's death, to the extent reasonably necessary for the support of the debtor and any dependent of the debtor;

(D)   a payment, not to exceed $16,150, on account of personal bodily injury, not including pain and suffering or compensation for actual pecuniary loss, of the debtor or an individual of whom the debtor is a dependent; or

(E)   a payment in compensation of loss of future earnings of the debtor of an individual of whom the debtor is or was a dependent, to the extent reasonably necessary for the support of the debtor and any dependent of the debtor.

(e)   A waiver of an exemption executed in favor of a creditor that holds an unsecured claim against the debtor is unenforceable in a case under this title with respect to such claim against property that the debtor may exempt under subsection (b) of this section. A waiver by the debtor of a power under subsection (f) or (h) of this section to avoid a transfer, under subsection (g) or (i) of this section to exempt property, or under subsection (i) of this section to recover property or to preserve a transfer, is unenforceable in a case under this title.

(f) (1)   Notwithstanding any waiver of exemptions but subject to paragraph (3), the debtor may avoid the fixing of a lien on an interest of the debtor in property to the extent that such lien impairs an exemption to which the debtor would have been entitled under subsection (b) of this section, if such lien is—

(A)   a judicial lien, other than a judicial lien that secures a debt—

(i)   to a spouse, former spouse, or child of the debtor, for alimony to, maintenance for, or support of such spouse or child, in connection with a separation agreement, divorce decree or other order of a court of record, determination made in accordance with State or territorial law by a governmental unit, or property settlement agreement; and

(ii)   to the extent that such debt—

(I)   is not assigned to another entity, voluntarily, by operation of law, or otherwise; and

(II)   includes a liability designated as alimony, maintenance, or support, unless such liability is actually in the nature of alimony, maintenance or support.

(B)   a nonpossessory, nonpurchase-money security interest in any—

(i)   household furnishings, household goods, wearing apparel, appliances, books, animals, crops, musical instruments, or jewelry that are held primarily for the personal, family, or household use of the debtor or a dependent of the debtor;

(ii)   implements, professional books, or tools, of the trade of the debtor or the trade of a dependent of the debtor; or

(iii)   professionally prescribed health aids for the debtor or a dependent of the debtor.

(2)   (A)   For the purposes of this subsection, a lien shall be considered to impair an exemption to the extent that the sum of—

(i)   the lien,

(ii)   all other liens on the property; and

(iii)   the amount of the exemption that the debtor could claim if there were no liens on the property; exceeds the value that the debtor's interest in the property would have in the absence of any liens.

(B)   In the case of a property subject to more than 1 lien, a lien that has been avoided shall not be considered in making the calculation under subparagraph (A) with respect to other liens.

(C)   This paragraph shall not apply with respect to a judgment arising out of a mortgage foreclosure.

(3)   In a case in which State law that is applicable to the debtor—

(A)   permits a person to voluntarily waive a right to claim exemptions under subsection (d) or prohibits a debtor from claiming exemptions under subsection (d); and

(B)   either permits the debtor to claim exemptions under State law without limitation in amount, except to the extent that the debtor has permitted the fixing of a consensual lien on any property or prohibits avoidance of a consensual lien on property otherwise eligible to be claimed as exempt property; the debtor may not avoid the fixing of a lien on an interest of the debtor or a dependent of the debtor in property if the lien is a nonpossessory, nonpurchase-money security interest in implements, professional books, or tools of the trade of the debtor or a dependent of the debtor or farm animals or crops of the debtor or a dependent of the debtor to the extent the value of such implements, professional books, tools of the trade, animals, and crops exceeds $5,000.

(g)   Notwithstanding sections 550 and 551 of this title, the debtor may exempt under subsection (b) of this section property that the trustee recovers under section 510(c)(2), 542, 543, 550, 551, or 553 of this title, to the extent that the debtor could have exempted such property under section (b) of this section if such property had not been transferred, if—

(1)   (A)   such transfer was not a voluntary transfer of such property by the debtor; and

(B)   the debtor did not conceal such property; or

(2)   the debtor could have avoided such transfer under subsection (f)(2)[(f) (1) (B)] of this section.

(h)   The debtor may avoid a transfer of property of the debtor or recover a setoff to the extent that the debtor could have exempted such property under subsection (g)(1) of this section if the trustee had avoided such transfer, if—

(1)   such transfer is avoidable by the trustee under section 544, 545, 547, 548, 549, or 724(a) of this title or recoverable by the trustee under section 553 of this title; and

(2)   the trustee does not attempt to avoid such transfer.

(i)   (1)   If the debtor avoids a transfer or recovers a setoff under subsection (f) or (h) of this section, the debtor may recover in the manner prescribed by, and subject to the limitations of section 550 of this title, the same as if the trustee had avoided such transfer, and may exempt any property so recovered under subsection (b) of this section.

(2) Notwithstanding section 551 of this title, a transfer avoided under section 544, 545, 547, 548, 549, or 724(a) of this title, under subsection (f) or (h) of this section, or property recovered under section 553 of this title, may be preserved for the benefit of the debtor to the extent that the debtor may exempt such property under subsection (g) of this section or paragraph (1) of this subsection.

(j) Notwithstanding subsections (g) and (i) of this section, the debtor may exempt a particular kind of property under subsections (g) and (i) of this section only to the extent that the debtor has exempted less property in value of such kind than that to which the debtor is entitled under subsection (b) of this section.

(k) Property that the debtor exempts under this section is not liable for payment of any administrative expense except—

(1) the aliquot share of the costs and expenses of avoiding a transfer of property that the debtor exempts under subsection (g) of this section, or recovery of such property, that is attributable to the value of the portion of such property exempted in relation to the value of the property recovered; and

(2) any costs and expenses of avoiding a transfer under subsection (f) or (h) of this section, or of recovery of property under subsection (i)(1) of this section, that the debtor has not paid.

(1) The debtor shall file a list of property that the debtor claims as exempt under subsection (b) of this section. If the debtor does not file such a list, a dependent of the debtor may file such a list, or may claim property as exempt from property of the estate on behalf of the debtor. Unless a party in interest objects, the property claimed as exempt on such list is exempt.

(m) Subject to the limitation in subsection (b), this section shall apply separately with respect to each debtor in a joint case.

Sec. 523. *Exceptions to Discharge*

(a) A discharge under section 727, 1141, 1228(a), 1228(b), or 1328(b) of this title does not discharge an individual debtor from any debt—

(1) for a tax or a customs duty—

(A) of the kind and for the periods specified in section 507(a)(2) or 507(a)(8) of this title, whether or not a claim for such tax was filed or allowed;

(B) with respect to which a return, if required—

(i) was not filed; or

(ii) was filed after the date on which such return was last due, under applicable law or under any extension, and after two years before the date of the filing of the petition; or

(C) with respect to which the debtor made a fraudulent return or willfully attempted in any manner to evade or defeat such tax;

(2) for money, property, services, or an extension, renewal, or refinancing of credit, to the extent obtained by—

(A) false pretenses, a false representation, or actual fraud, other than a statement respecting the debtor's or an insider's financial condition;

(B) use of a statement in writing—

(i) that is materially false;

(ii) respecting the debtor's of an insider's financial condition;

(iii) on which the creditor to whom the debtor is liable for such money, property, services, or credit reasonably relied; and

(iv) that the debtor caused to be made or published with intent to deceive; or

(C) for purposes of subparagraph (A) of this paragraph, consumer debts owed to a single creditor and aggregating more than $1,075 for "luxury goods or services" incurred by an individual debtor on or within 60 days before the order for relief under this title, or cash advances aggregating more than $1,075 that are extensions of consumer credit under an open end credit plan obtained by an individual debtor on or within 60 days before the order for relief under this title, are presumed to be nondischargeable; "luxury goods or services" do not include goods or services reasonably acquired for the support or maintenance of the debtor or a dependent of the debtor; an extension of consumer credit under an open end credit plan is to be defined for purposes of this subparagraph as it is defined in the Consumer Credit Protection Act;

(3) neither listed nor scheduled under section 521(1) of this title, with the name, if known to the debtor, of the creditor to whom such debt is owed, in time to permit—

(A) if such debt is not of a kind specified in paragraph (2), (4), or (6) of this subsection, timely filing of a proof of claim, unless such creditor had notice or actual knowledge of the case in time for such timely filing; or

(B) if such debt is of a kind specified in paragraph (2), (4), or (6) of this subsection, timely filing of a proof of claim and timely request for a determination of dischargeability of such debt under one of such paragraphs, unless such creditor had notice or actual knowledge of the case in time for such timely filing and request;

(4) for fraud or defalcation while acting in a fiduciary capacity, embezzlement, or larceny;

(5) to a spouse, former spouse, or child of the debtor, for alimony to, maintenance for, or support of such spouse or child, in connection with a separation agreement, divorce decree or other order of a court of record, determination made in accordance with State or territorial law by a governmental unit, or property settlement agreement, but not to the extent that—

(A) such debt is assigned to another entity, voluntarily, by operation of law, or otherwise (other than debts assigned pursuant to section 402(a)(26) of the Social Security Act, or any such debt which has been assigned to the Federal Government or to a State or any political subdivision of such State); or

(B) such debt includes a liability designated as alimony, maintenance, or support, unless such liability is actually in the nature of alimony, maintenance, or support;

(6)   for willful and malicious injury by the debtor to another entity or to the property of another entity;

(7)   to the extent such debt is for fine, penalty, or forfeiture payable to and for the benefit of a governmental unit, and is not compensation for actual pecuniary loss, other than a tax penalty—

    (A)   relating to a tax of a kind not specified in paragraph (I) of this subsection; or

    (B)   imposed with respect to a transaction or event that occurred before three years before the date of the filing of the petition;

(8)   for an educational benefit loan made, insured, or guaranteed by a governmental unit, or made under any program funded in whole or in part by a governmental unit or a non-profit institution, or for an obligation to repay funds received as an educational benefit, scholarship, or stipened, unless excepting such debts from discharge under this paragraph will impose an undue hardship on the debtor and the debtor's dependents;

(9)   for death or personal injury caused by the debtor's operation of a motor vehicle if such operation was unlawful because the debtor was intoxicated from using alcohol, a drug, or another substance;

(10)   that was or could have been listed as scheduled by the debtor in a prior case concerning the debtor under this title or under the Bankruptcy Act in which the debtor waived discharge, or was denied a discharge under section 727(a)(2), (3), (4), (5), (6), or (7) of this title, or under section 14c(1), (2), (3), (4), (6), or (7) of such Act;

(11)   provided in any final judgment, unreviewable order, or consent order or decree entered in any court of the United States or of any State, issued by a Federal depository institutions regulatory agency, or contained in any settlement agreement entered into by the debtor, arising from any act of fraud or defalcation while acting in a fiduciary capacity committed with respect to any depository institution or insured credit union;

(12)   for malicious or reckless failure to fulfill any commitment by the debtor to a Federal depository institutions regulatory agency to maintain the capital of an insured depository institution, except that this paragraph shall not extend any such commitment which would otherwise be terminated due to any act of such agency,

(13)   for any payment of an order of restitution under title 18, United States Code;

(14)   incurred to pay a tax to the United States that would be nondischargeable pursuant to paragraph (1);

(15)   not of the kind described in paragraph (5) that is incurred by the debtor in the course of a divorce or separation or in connection with a separation agreement, divorce decree or other order of a court of record, a determination made in accordance with State or territorial law by a governmental unit unless—

    (A)   the debtor does not have the ability to pay such debt from income or property of the debtor not reasonably necessary to be expended for the maintenance or support of the debtor or a dependent of the debtor and, if the debtor is engaged in a business, for the payment of expenditures necessary for the continuation, preservation, and operation of such business; or

(B)   discharging such debt would result in a benefit to the debtor that outweighs the detrimental consequences to a spouse, former spouse, or child of the debtor;

(16)   for a fee or assessment that becomes due and payable after the order for relief to a membership association with respect to the debtor's interest in a dwelling unit that has condominium ownership or in a share of a cooperative housing corporation, but only if such fee or assessment is payable for a period during which—

(A)   the debtor physically occupied a dwelling unit in the condominium or cooperative project; or

(B)   the debtor rented the dwelling unit to a tenant and received payments from the tenant for such period, but nothing in this paragraph shall except from discharge the debt of a debtor for a membership association fee or assessment for a period arising before entry of the order for relief in a pending or subsequent bankruptcy case;

(17)   for a fee imposed by a court for the filing of a case, motion, complaint, or appeal, or for other costs and expenses assessed with respect to such filing, regardless of an assertion of poverty by the debtor under section 1915(b) or (f) of title 28, or the debtor's status as a prisoner, as defined in section 1915(h) of title 28; or

(18)   owed under State law to a State or municipality that is—

(A)   in the nature of support, and

(B)   enforceable under part D of title IV of the Social Security Act (42 U.S.C. 601 et seq.).

(b)   Notwithstanding subsection (a) of this section, a debt that was excepted from discharge under subsection (a)(1), (a)(3), or (a)(8) of this section, under section 17a(1), 17a(3), or 17a(5) of the Bankruptcy Act, under section 439A of the Higher Education Act of 1965, or under section 733(g) of the Public Health Services Act in a prior case concerning the debtor under this title, or under the Bankruptcy Act, is dischargeable in a case under this title unless, by the terms of subsection (a) of this section, such debt is not dischargeable in the case under this title.

(c) (1)   Except as provided in subsection (a)(3)(B) of this section, the debtor shall be discharged from a debt of a kind specified in paragraph (2), (4), (6), or (15) of subsection (a) of this section, unless, on request of the creditor to whom such debt is owned, and after notice and a hearing, the court determines such debt to be excepted from discharge under paragraph (2), (4), (6), or (14), as the case may be, of subsection (a) of this section.

(2)   Paragraph (1) shall not apply in the case of a Federal depository institutions regulatory agency seeking, in its capacity as conservator, receiver, or liquidating agent for an insured depository institution, to recover a debt described in subsection (a)(2), (a)(4), (a)(6), or (a)(11) owed to such institution by an institution-affiliated party unless the receiver, conservator, or liquidating agent was appointed in time to reasonably comply, or for a Federal depository institutions regulatory agency acting in its corporate capacity as a successor to such receiver, conservator, or liquidating agent to reasonably comply, with subsection (a)(3)(B) as a creditor of such institution-affiliated party with respect to such debt.

(d)   If a creditor requests a determination of dischargeability of a consumer debt under subsection (a)(2) of this section, and such debt is discharged, the court shall grant judgment in favor of the debtor for the costs of, and a reasonable attorney's fee for, the proceeding if the court finds that the position of the creditor was not substantially justified, except that the court shall not award such costs and fees if special circumstances would make the award unjust.

(e)   Any institution-affiliated party of an insured depository institution shall be considered to be acting in a fiduciary capacity with respect to the purposes of subsection (a)(4) or (11).

Sec. 524.   Effect of Discharge

(a)   A discharge in a case under this title—

(1)   voids any judgment at any time obtained, to the extent that such judgment is a determination of the personal liability of the debtor with respect to any debt discharged under section 727, 944, 1141, 1228, or 1328 of this title, whether or not discharge of such debt is waived;

(2)   operates as an injunction against the commencement or continuation of an action, the employment of process, or an act, to collect, recover or offset any such debt as a personal liability of the debtor, whether or not discharge of such debt is waived; and

(3)   operates as an injunction against the commencement or continuation of an action, the employment of process, or an act, to collect or recover from, or offset against, property of the debtor of the kind specified in section 541(a)(2) of this title that is acquired after the commencement of the case, on account of any allowable community claim, except a community claim that is excepted from discharge under section 523, 1228(a)(1), or 1328(a)(1) of this title, or that would be so excepted, determined in accordance with the provisions of sections 523(c) and 523(d) of this title, in a case concerning the debtor's spouse commenced on the date of the filing of the petition in the case concerning the debtor, whether or not discharge of the debt based on such community claim is waived.

(b)   Subsection (a)(3) of this section does not apply if—

(1)   (A)   the debtor's spouse is a debtor in a case under this title, or a bankrupt or a debtor in a case under the Bankruptcy Act, commenced within six years of the date of the filing of the petition in the case concerning the debtor; and

(B)   the court does not grant the debtor's spouse a discharge in such case concerning the debtor's spouse; or

(2)   (A)   the court would not grant the debtor's spouse a discharge in a case under chapter 7 of this title concerning such spouse commenced on the date of the filing of the petition in the case concerning the debtor; and

(B)   a determination that the court would not so grant such discharge is made by the bankruptcy court within the time and in the manner provided for a determination under section 727 of this title of whether a debtor is granted a discharge.

(c)   An agreement between a holder of a claim and the debtor, the consideration for which, in whole or in part, is based on a debt that is dischargeable in a case under this title is enforceable only to an extent enforceable under applicable non-bankruptcy law, whether or not discharge of such debt is waived, only if—

(1)   such agreement was made before the granting of the discharge under section 727, 1141, 1228, or 1328 of this title;

(2)   (A)   such agreement contains a clear and conspicuous statement which advises the debtor that the agreement may be rescinded at any time prior to discharge or within sixty days after such agreement is filed with the court, whichever occurs later, by giving notice to rescission to the holder of such claim; and

(B)   such agreement contains a clear and conspicuous statement which advises the debtor that such agreement is not required under this title, under nonbankruptcy law, or under any agreement not in accordance with the provisions of this subsection;

(3)   such agreement has been filed with the court and, if applicable, accompanied by a declaration or an affidavit of the attorney that represented the debtor during the course of negotiating an agreement under this subsection, which states that—

(A)   such agreement represents a fully informed and voluntary agreement by the debtor;

(B)   such agreement does not impose an undue hardship on the debtor or a dependent of the debtor; and

(C)   the attorney fully advised the debtor of the legal effect and consequences of—

(i)   an agreement of the kind specified in this subsection; and

(ii)   any default under such an agreement;

(4)   the debtor has not rescinded such agreement at any time prior to discharge or within sixty days after such agreement is filed with the court, whichever occurs later, by giving notice of rescission to the holder of such claim;

(5)   the provisions of subsection (d) of this section have been complied with; and

(6)   (A)   in a case concerning an individual who was not represented by an attorney during the course of negotiating an agreement under this subsection, the court approves such agreement as—

(i)   not imposing an undue hardship on the debtor or a dependent of the debtor; and

(ii)   in the best interest of the debtor.

(B)   Subparagraph (A) shall not apply to the extent that such debt is a consumer debt secured by real property.

(d)   In a case concerning an individual, when the court has determined whether to grant or not to grant a discharge under section 727, 1141, 1228, or 1328 of this title, the court shall may hold a hearing at which the debtor shall appear in person. At any such hearing, the court shall inform the debtor that a discharge has been granted or the reason why a discharge has not been granted. If a discharge has been granted and if the debtor desires to make an agreement of the kind specified in subsection (c) of this section and was not represented by an attorney during the course of negotiating such agreement, then the courts shall hold a hearing at which the debtor shall appear in person and at such hearing the court shall—

    (1)   inform the debtor—

        (A)   that such an agreement is not required under this title, under nonbankruptcy law, or under any agreement not made in accordance with the provisions of subsection (c) of this section; and

        (B)   of the legal effect and consequences of—

            (i)   an agreement of the kind specified in subsection (c) of this section; and

            (ii)   a default under such an agreement; and

    (2)   determine whether the agreement that the debtor desires to make complies with the requirements of subsection (c)(6) of this [subsection] section, if the consideration for such agreement is based in whole or in part on a consumer debt that is not secured by real property of the debtor.

    (e)   Except as provided in subsection (a)(3) of this section, discharge of a debt of the debtor does not affect the liability of any other entity on, or the property of any other entity for, such debt.

    (f)   Nothing contained in subsection (c) or (d) of this section prevents a debtor from voluntarily repaying any debt.

    (g) (1)   (A) After notice and hearing, a court that enters an order confirming a plan of reorganization under chapter 11 may issue, in connection with such order, an injunction in accordance with this subsection to supplement the injunctive effect of a discharge under this section.

        (B)   An injunction may be issued under subparagraph (A) to enjoin entities from taking legal action for the purpose of directly or indirectly collecting, recovering, or receiving payment or recovery with respect to any claim or demand that, under a plan or reorganization, is to be paid in whole or in part by a trust described in paragraph (2)(B)(i), except such legal actions as are expressly allowed by the injunction, the confirmation order, or the plan of reorganization.

    (2)   (A)   Subject to subsection (h), if the requirements of subparagraph (B) are met at the time an injunction described in paragraph (1) is entered, then after entry of such injunction, any proceeding that involves the validity, application, construction, or modification of such injunction, or of this subsection with respect to such injunction, may be commenced only in the district court in which such injunction was entered, and such court shall have exclusive jurisdiction over any such proceeding without regard to the amount in controversy.

        (B)   The requirements of this subparagraph are that—

            (i)   the injunction is to be implemented in connection with a trust that, pursuant to the plan of reorganization—

                (I)   is to assume the liabilities of a debtor which at the time of entry of the order for relief has been named as a defendant in personal injury, wrongful death, or property-damage actions seeking recovery for damages allegedly caused by the presence of, or exposure to, asbestos or asbestos-containing products:

                (II)   is to be funded in whole or in part by the securities of 1 or more debtors involved in such plan and by the obligation of such debtor or debtors to make future payments, including dividends;

(III)   is to own, or by the exercise of rights granted under such plan would be entitled to own if specified contingencies occur, a majority of the voting shares of—

(aa)   each such debtor;

(bb)   the parent corporation of each such debtor; or

(cc)   a subsidiary of each such debtor that is also a debtor; and

(IV)   is to use its assets or income to pay claims and demands; and

(ii)   subject to subsection (h), the court determines that—

(I)   the debtor is likely to be subject to substantial future demands for payment arising out of the same or similar conduct or events that gave rise to the claims that are addressed by the injunction;

(II)   the actual amounts, numbers, and timing of such future demands cannot be determined;

(III)   pursuit of such demands outside the procedures prescribed by such plan is likely to threaten the plan's purpose to deal equitably with claims and future demands;

(IV)   as part of the process of seeking confirmation of such plan—

(aa)   the terms of the injunction proposed to be issued under paragraph (1)(A), including any provisions barring actions against third parties pursuant to paragraph (4)(A), are set out in such plan and in any disclosure statement supporting the plan; and

(bb)   a separate class or classes of the claimants whose claims are to be addressed by a trust described in clause (i) is established and votes, by at least 75 percent of those voting, in favor of the plan; and

(V)   subject to subsection (h), pursuant to court orders or otherwise, the trust will operate through mechanisms such as structured, periodic, or supplemental payments, pro rata distributions, matrices, or periodic review of estimates of the numbers and values of present claims and future demands, or other comparable mechanisms, that provide reasonable assurance that the trust will value, and be in a financial position to pay, present claims and future demands that involve similar claims in substantially the same manner.

(3)   (A)   If the requirements of paragraph (2)(B) are met and the order confirming the plan of reorganization was issued or affirmed by the district court that has jurisdiction over the reorganization case, then after the time for appeal of the order that issues or affirms the plan—

(i)   the injunction shall be valid and enforceable and may not be revoked or modified by any court except through appeal in accordance with paragraph (6);

(ii)   no entity that pursuant to such plan or thereafter becomes a direct or indirect transferee of, or successor to any assets of, a debtor or trust that is the subject of the injunction shall be liable with respect to any claim or demand made against such entity by reason of its becoming such a transferee or successor; and

(iii)   no entity that pursuant to such plan or thereafter makes a loan to such a debtor or trust or to such a successor or transferee shall, by reason of making the loan, be liable with respect to any claim or demand made against such entity, nor shall any pledge of assets made in connection with such a loan be upset or impaired for that reason;

(B)   Subparagraph (A) shall not be construed to—

(i)   imply that an entity described in subparagraph (A)(ii) or (iii) would, if this paragraph were not applicable, necessarily be liable to any entity by reason of any of the acts described in subparagraph (A);

(ii)   relieve any such entity of the duty to comply with, or of liability under, any Federal or State law regarding the making of a fraudulent conveyance in a transaction described in subparagraph (A)(ii) or (iii); or

(iii)   relieve a debtor of the debtor's obligation to comply with the terms of the plan of reorganization, or affect the power of the court to exercise its authority under sections 1141 and 1142 to compel the debtor to do so.

(4)   (A)   (i)   Subject to subparagraph (B), an injunction described in paragraph (1) shall be valid and enforceable against all entities that it addresses.

(ii)   Notwithstanding the provisions of section 524(e), such an injunction may bar any action directed against a third party who is identifiable from the terms of such injunction (by name or as part of an identifiable group) and is alleged to be directly or indirectly liable for the conduct of, claims against, or demands on the debtor to the extent such alleged liability of such third party arises by reason of—

(I)   the third party's ownership of a financial interest in the debtor, a past or present affiliate of the debtor, or a predecessor in interest of the debtor;

(III)   the third party's involvement in the management of the debtor or a predecessor in interest of the debtor, or service as an officer, director or employee of the debtor or a related party;

(III)   the third party's provision of insurance to the debtor or a related party; or

(IV)   the third party's involvement in a transaction changing the corporate structure, or in a loan or other financial transaction affecting the financial condition, of the debtor or a related party, including but not limited to—

      (aa)   involvement in providing financing (debt or equity), or advice to an entity involved in such a transaction; or

      (bb)   acquiring or selling a financial interest in an entity as part of such a transaction.

    (iii)   As used in this subparagraph the term "related party" means—

      (I)   a past or present affiliate of the debtor;

      (II)   a predecessor in interest of the debtor; or

      (III)   any entity that owned a financial interest in—

        (aa)   the debtor;

        (bb)   a past or present affiliate of the debtor; or

        (cc)   a predecessor in interest of the debtor.

(B)   Subject to subsection (h), if, under a plan of reorganization, a kind of demand described in such plan is to be paid in whole or in part by a trust described in paragraph (2)(B)(i) in connection with which an injunction described in paragraph (1) is to be implemented, then such injunction shall be valid and enforceable with respect to a demand of such kind made, after such plan is confirmed, against the debtor or debtors involved, or against a third party described in subparagraph (A)(ii), if—

    (i)   as part of the proceedings leading to issuance of such injunction, the court appoints a legal representative for the purpose of protecting the rights of persons that might subsequently assert demands of such kind, and

    (ii)   the court determines, before entering the order confirming such plan, that identifying such debtor or debtors, or such third party (by name or as part of an identifiable group), in such injunction with respect to such demands for purposes of this subparagraph is fair and equitable with respect to the persons that might subsequently assert such demands, in light of the benefits provided, or to be provided, to such trust on behalf of such debtor or debtors or such third party.

(5)   In this subsection, the term "demand" means a demand for payment, present or future, that—

(A)   was not a claim during the proceedings leading to the confirmation of a plan of reorganization;

(B)   arises out of the same or similar conduct or events that gave rise to the claims addressed by the injunction issued under paragraph (1); and

(C)   pursuant to the plan, is to be paid by a trust described in paragraph (2)(B)(i).

(6)   Paragraph (3)(A)(i) does not bar an action taken by or at the direction of an appellate court on appeal of an injunction issued under paragraph (1) or of the order of confirmation that relates to the injunction.

(7)   This subsection does not affect the operation of section 1144 or the power of the district court to refer a proceeding under section 157 of title 28

or any reference of a proceeding made prior to the date of the enactment of this subsection.

(h)   APPLICATION TO EXISTING INJUNCTIONS.—For purposes of subsection (g)—

(1)   subject to paragraph (2), if an injunction of the kind described in subsection (g)(1)(B) was issued before the date of the enactment of this Act, as part of a plan of reorganization confirmed by an order entered before such date, then the injunction shall be considered to meet the requirements of subsection (g)(2)(B) for purposes of subsection (g)(2)(A), and to satisfy subsection (g)(4)(A)(ii), if—

(A)   the court determined at the time the plan was confirmed that the plan was fair and equitable in accordance with the requirements of section 1129(b);

(B)   as part of the proceedings leading to issuance of such injunction and confirmation of such plan, the court had appointed a legal representative for the purpose of protecting the rights of persons that might subsequently assert demands described in subsection (g)(4)(B) with respect to such plan; and

(C)   such legal representative did not object to confirmation of such plan or issuance of such injunction; and

(2)   for purposes of paragraph (1), if a trust described in subsection (g)(2)(B)(i) is subject to a court order on the date of the enactment of this Act staying such trust from settling or paying further claims—

(A)   the requirements of subsection (g)(2)(B)(ii)(V) shall not apply with respect to such trust until such stay is lifted or dissolved; and

(B)   if such trust meets such requirements on the date such stay is lifted or dissolved, such trust shall be considered to have met such requirements continuously from the date of the enactment of this Act.

Sec. 525.   *Protection against Discriminatory Treatment*

(a)   Except as provided in the Perishable Agricultural Commodities Act, 1930, the Packers and Stockyards Act, 1921, and section 1 of the Act entitled "An Act making appropriations for the Department of Agriculture for the fiscal year ending June 30, 1944, and for other purposes," approved July 12, 1943, a governmental unit may not deny, revoke, suspend, or refuse to renew a license, permit, charter, franchise, or other similar grant to, condition such a grant to, discriminate with respect to such a grant against, deny employment to, terminate the employment of, or discriminate with respect to employment against, a person that is or has been a debtor under this title or a bankrupt or a debtor under the Bankruptcy Act, or another person with whom such bankrupt or debtor has been associated, solely because such bankrupt or debtor is or has been a debtor under this title or a bankrupt or debtor under the Bankruptcy Act, has been insolvent before the commencement of the case under this title, or during the case but before the debtor is granted or denied a discharge, or has not paid a debt that is dischargeable in the case under this title or that was discharged under the Bankruptcy Act.

(b)   No private employer may terminate the employment of, or discriminate with respect to employment against, an individual who is or has been a debtor under this title, a debtor or bankrupt under the Bankruptcy Act, or an individual associated with such debtor or bankrupt, solely because such debtor or bankrupt—

(1)   is or has been a debtor under this title or a debtor or bankrupt under the Bankruptcy Act;

(2)   has been insolvent before the commencement of a case under this title or during the case but before the grant or denial of a discharge; or

(3)   has not paid a debt that is dischargeable in a case under this title or that was discharged under the Bankruptcy Act.

(c) (1)   A governmental unit that operates a student grant or loan program and a person engaged in a business that includes the making of loans guaranteed or insured under a student loan program may not deny a grant, loan, loan guarantee, or loan insurance to a person that is or has been a debtor under this title or a bankrupt or debtor under the Bankruptcy Act, or another person with whom the debtor or bankrupt has been associated, because the debtor or bankrupt is or has been a debtor under this title or a bankrupt or debtor under the Bankruptcy Act, has been insolvent before the commencement of a case under this title or during the pendency of the case but before the debtor is granted or denied a discharge, or has not paid a debt that is dischargeable in the case under this title or that was discharged under the Bankruptcy Act.

(2)   In this section, "student loan program" means the program operated under part B, D, or E of title IV of the Higher Education Act of 1965 or a similar program operated under State or local law.

SUBCHAPTER III. THE ESTATE

Sec. 541.   *Property of the Estate*

(a)   The commencement of a case under section 301, 302, or 303 of this title creates an estate. Such estate is comprised of all the following property, wherever located and by whomever held:

(1)   Except as provided in subsections (b) and (c)(2) of this section, all legal or equitable interests of the debtor in property as of the commencement of the case.

(2)   All interests of the debtor and the debtor's spouse in community property as of the commencement of the case that is—

(A)   under the sole equal, or joint management and control of the debtor; or

(B)   liable for an allowable claim against the debtor, or for both an allowable claim against the debtor and an allowable claim against the debtor's spouse, to the extent that such interest is so liable.

(3)   Any interest in property that the trustee recovers under section 329(b), 363(n), 543, 550, 553, or 723 of this title.

(4)   Any interest in property preserved for the benefit of or ordered transferred to the estate under section 510(c) or 551 of this title.

(5)   Any interest in property that would have been property of the estate if such interest had been an interest of the debtor on the date of the filing of the petition, and that the debtor acquires or becomes entitled to acquire within 180 days after such date—

(A)   by bequest, device, or inheritance;

(B)   as a result of a property settlement agreement with debtor's spouse, or of an interlocutory or final divorce decree; or

(C)   as beneficiary of a life insurance policy or of a death benefit plan.

(6)   Proceeds, product, offspring, rents, or profits of or from property of the estate, except such as are earnings from services performed by an individual debtor after the commencement of the case.

(7)   Any interest in property that the estate acquires after the commencement of the case.

(b)   Property of the estate does not include—

(1)   any power that the debtor may exercise solely for the benefit of an entity other than the debtor;

(2)   any interest of the debtor as a lessee under a lease of nonresidential real property that has terminated at the expiration of the stated term of such lease before the commencement of the case under this title, and ceases to include any interest of the debtor as a lessee under a lease of nonresidential real property that has terminated at the expiration of the stated term of such lease during the case.

(3)   any eligibility of the debtor to participate in programs authorized under the Higher Education Act of 1965 (20 U.S.C. 1061 et seq; 42 U.S.C. 2751 et seq.), or an accreditation status or State licensure of the debtor as an educational institution;

(4)   any interest of the debtor in liquid or gaseous hydrocarbons to the extent that—

(A)   (i)   the debtor has transferred or is obligated to transfer such interest pursuant to a farmout agreement or any written agreement directly related to a farmout agreement; and

(ii)   but for the operation of this paragraph, the estate could include the interest referred to in clause (i) only by virtue of section 365 or 544(a)(3) of this title; or

(B)   (i)   the debtor has transferred such interest pursuant to a written conveyance of a production payment to an entity that does not participate in the operation of the property from which such production payment is transferred; and

(ii)   but for the operation of this paragraph, the estate could include the interest referred to in clause (i) only by virtue of section 542 of this title.

Paragraph (4) shall not be construed to exclude from the estate any consideration the debtor retains, receives, or is entitled to receive for transferring an interest in liquid or gaseous hydrocarbons pursuant to a farmout agreement; or

(5)   any interest in cash or cash equivalents that constitute proceeds of a sale by the debtor of a money order that is made—

(A)   on or after the date that is 14 days prior to the date on which the petition is filed; and

(B)   under an agreement with a money order issuer that prohibits the commingling of such proceeds with property of the debtor (notwithstanding that, contrary to the agreement, the proceeds may have been commingled with property of the debtor), unless the money order issuer had not taken action, prior to the filing of the petition, to require compliance with the prohibition.

(c) (1)   Except as provided in paragraph (2) of this subsection, an interest of the debtor in property becomes property of the estate under subsection (a)(1), (a)(2), or (a)(5) of this section notwithstanding any provision in an agreement, transfer instrument, or applicable nonbankruptcy law—

(A)   that restricts or conditions transfer of such interest by the debtor; or

(B)   that is conditioned on the insolvency or financial condition of the debtor, on the commencement of a case under this title, or on the appointment of or taking possession by a trustee in a case under this title or a custodian before such commencement, and that effects or gives an option to effect a forfeiture, modification, or termination of the debtor's interest in property;

(2)   A restriction on the transfer of a beneficial interest of the debtor in a trust that is enforceable under applicable nonbankruptcy law is enforceable in a case under this title.

(d)   Property in which the debtor holds, as of the commencement of the case, only legal title and not an equitable interest, such as a mortgage secured by real property, or an interest in such a mortgage, sold by the debtor but as to which the debtor retains legal title to service or supervise the servicing of such mortgage or interest, becomes property of the estate under subsection (a)(1) or (2) of this section only to the extent of the debtor's legal title to such property, but not to the extent of any equitable interest in such property that the debtor does not hold.

Sec. 542.   *Turnover of Property to the Estate*

(a)   Except as provided in subsection (c) or (d) of this section, an entity, other than a custodian, in possession, custody, or control, during the case, of property that the trustee may use, sell, or lease under section 363 of this title, or that the debtor may exempt under section 522 of this title, shall deliver to the trustee, and account for, such property or the value of such property, unless such property is of inconsequential value or benefit to the estate.

(b)   Except as provided in subsection (c) or (d) of this section, an entity that owes a debt that is property of the estate and that is matured, payable on demand, or payable on order, shall pay such debt to, or on the order of, the trustee, except to the extent that such debt may be offset under section 553 of this title against a claim against the debtor.

(c)   Except as provided in section 362(a)(7) of this title, an entity that has neither actual notice nor actual knowledge of the commencement of the case concerning the debtor may transfer property of the estate, or pay a debt owing to the debtor, in good faith and other than in the manner specified in subsection (d) of this section, to an entity other than the trustee, with the same effect as to the entity making such transfer or payment as if the case under this title concerning the debtor had not been commenced.

(d)   A life insurance company may transfer property of the estate or property of the debtor to such company in good faith, with the same effect with respect to such company as if the case under this title concerning the debtor had not been commenced, if such transfer is to pay a premium or to carry out a nonforfeiture insurance option, and is required to be made automatically, under life insurance contract with such company that was entered into before the date of the filing of the petition and that is property of the estate.

(e)   Subject to any applicable privilege, after notice and a hearing, the court may order an attorney, accountant, or other person that holds recorded information, including books, documents, records, and papers, relating to the debtor's property or financial affairs, to turn over or disclose such recorded information to the trustee.

Sec. 543.   *Turnover of Property by a Custodian*

(a)   A custodian with knowledge of the commencement of a case under this title concerning the debtor may not make any disbursement from, or take any action in the administration of, property of the debtor, proceeds, product, offspring, rents, or profits of such property, or property of the estate, in the possession, custody, or control of such custodian, except such action as is necessary to preserve such property.

(b)   A custodian shall—

(1)   deliver to the trustee any property of the debtor held by or transferred to such custodian, or proceeds, product, offspring, rents, or profits of such property, that is in such custodian's possession, custody, or control on the date that such custodian acquired knowledge of the commencement of the case; and

(2)   file an accounting of any property of the debtor, or proceeds, product, offspring, rents, or profits of such property, that, at any time, came into the possession, custody, or control of such custodian.

(c)   The court, after notice and a hearing, shall—

(1)   protect all entities to which a custodian has become obligated with respect to such property, or proceeds, product, offspring, rents, or profits of such property;

(2)   provide for the payment of reasonable compensation for services rendered and costs and expenses incurred by such custodian; and

(3)   surcharge such custodian, other than assignee for the benefit of the debtor's creditors that was appointed or took possession more than 120 days before the date of the filing of the petition, for any improper or excessive disbursement, other than a disbursement that has been made in accordance with applicable law or that has been approved, after notice and a hearing, by a court of competent jurisdiction before the commencement of the case under this title.

(d)   After notice and hearing, the bankruptcy court—

(1)   may excuse compliance with subsection (a), (b), or (c) of this section if the interests of creditors and, if the debtor is not insolvent, of equity security holders would be better served by permitting a custodian to continue in possession, custody, or control of such property, and

(2)   shall excuse compliance with subsections (a) and (b)(1) of this section if the custodian is an assignee for the benefit of the debtor's creditors

that was appointed or took possession more than 120 days before the date of the filing of the petition, unless compliance with such subsections is necessary to prevent fraud or injustice.

Sec. 544. Trustee as Lien Creditor and as Successor to Certain Creditors and Purchasers

(a)   The trustee shall have, as of the commencement of the case, and without regard to any knowledge of the trustee or of any creditor, the rights and powers of, or may avoid any transfer of property of the debtor or any obligation incurred by the debtor that is voidable by—

(1)   a creditor that extends credit to the debtor at the time of the commencement of the case, and that obtains, at such time and with respect to such credit, a judicial lien on all property on which a creditor on a simple contract could have obtained such a judicial lien, whether or not such a creditor exists;

(2)   a creditor that extends credit to the debtor at the time of the commencement of the case, and obtains, at such time and with respect to such credit, and execution against the debtor that is returned unsatisfied at such time, whether or not such a creditor exists; or

(3)   a bona fide purchaser of real property, other than fixtures, from the debtor, against whom applicable law permits such transfer to be perfected, that obtains the status of a bona fide purchaser and has perfected such transfer at the time of the commencement of the case, whether or not such a purchaser exists;

(b) (1)   Except as provided in paragraph (2), the trustee may avoid any transfer of an interest of the debtor in property or any obligation incurred by the debtor that is voidable under applicable law by a creditor holding an unsecured claim that is allowable under section 502 of this title or that is not allowable only under section 502(e) of this title.

(2)   Paragraph (1) shall not apply to a transfer of a charitable contribution (as that term is defined in section 548(d)(3)) that is not covered under section 548(a)(1)(B), by reason of section 548(a)(2). Any claim by any person to recover a transferred contribution described in the preceding sentence under Federal or State law in a Federal or State court shall be preempted by the commencement of the case.

Sec. 545. Statutory Liens

The trustee may avoid the fixing of a statutory lien on property of the debtor to the extent that such lien—

(1)   first becomes effective against the debtor—

(A)   when a case under this title concerning the debtor is commenced;

(B)   when an insolvency proceeding other than under this title concerning the debtor is commenced;

(C)   when a custodian is appointed or authorized to take or takes possession;

(D)   when the debtor becomes insolvent;

(E)   when the debtor's financial condition fails to meet a specified standard; or

(F)   at the time of an execution against property of the debtor levied at the instance of an entity other than the holder of such statutory lien;

(2)   is not perfected or enforceable at the time of the commencement of the case against a bona fide purchaser that purchases such property at the time of the commencement of the case, whether or not such a purchaser exists;

(3)   is for rent; or

(4)   is a lien of distress for rent.

Sec. 546. *Limitations on Avoiding Powers*

(a)   An action or proceeding under section 544, 545, 547, 548, or 553 of this title may not be commenced after the earlier of—

(1)   the later of—

(A)   2 years after the entry of the order for relief; or

(B)   1 year after the appointment or election of the first trustee under section 702, 1104, 1163, 1202, or 1302 of this title if such appointment or such election occurs before the expiration of the period specified in subparagraph (A); or

(2)   the time the case is closed or dismissed.

(b) (1)   The rights and powers of a trustee under section 544, 545, and 549 of this title are subject to any generally applicable law that—

(A)   permits perfection of an interest in property to be effective against an entity that acquires rights in such property before the date of perfection; or

(B)   provides for the maintenance or continuation of perfection of an interest in property to be effective against an entity that acquires rights in such property before the date on which action is taken to effect such maintenance or continuation.

(2)   If—

(A)   a law described in paragraph (1) requires seizure of such property or commencement of an action to accomplish such perfection, or maintenance or continuation of perfection of an interest in property; and

(B)   such property has not been seized or such an action has not been commenced before the date of the filing of the petition; such interest in such property shall be perfected, or perfection of such interest shall be maintained or continued, by giving notice within the time fixed by such law for such seizure or such commencement.

(c)   Except as provided in subsection (d) of this section, the rights and powers of a trustee under sections 544(a), 545, 547, and 549 of this title are subject to any statutory or common-law right of a seller of goods that has sold goods to the debtor, in the ordinary course of such seller's business, to reclaim such goods if the debtor has received such goods while insolvent, but—

(1)   such a seller may not reclaim any such goods unless such seller demands in writing reclamation of such goods—

(A)   before 10 days after receipt of such goods by the debtor; or

(B)   if such 10-day period expires after the commencement of the case, before 20 days after receipt of such goods by the debtor; and

(2)   the court may deny reclamation to a seller with such a right of reclamation that has made such a demand only if the court—

(A)   grants the claim of such a seller priority as a claim of a kind specified in section 503(b) of this title; or

(B)   secures such claim by a lien.

(d)   In the case of a seller who is a producer of grain sold to a grain storage facility, owned or operated by the debtor, in the ordinary course of such seller's business (as such terms are defined in section 557 of this title) or in the case of a United States fisherman who has caught fish sold to a fish processing facility owned or operated by the debtor in the ordinary course of such fisherman's business, the rights and powers of the trustee under sections 544(a), 545, 547, and 549 of this title are subject to any statutory or common law right of such producer or fisherman to reclaim such grain or fish if the debtor has received such grain or fish while insolvent, but—

(1)   such producer or fisherman may not reclaim any grain or fish unless such producer or fisherman demands, in writing, reclamation of such grain or fish before ten days after receipt thereof by the debtor; and

(2)   the court may deny reclamation to such a producer or fisherman with a right of reclamation that has made such a demand only if the court secures such claim by a lien.

(e)   Notwithstanding sections 544, 545, 547, 548(a)(2), and 548(b) of this title, the trustee may not avoid a transfer that is a margin payment as defined in section 101, 741, or 761 of this title, or settlement payment, as defined in section 101 or 741 of this title, made by or to a commodity broker, forward contract merchant, stockbroker, financial institution, or securities clearing agency, that is made before the commencement of the case, except under section 548(a)(1) of this title.

(f)   Notwithstanding sections 544, 545, 547, 548(a)(2), and 548(b) of this title, the trustee may not avoid a transfer that is a margin payment, as defined in section 741 or 761 of this title, or settlement payment, as defined in section 741 of this title, made by or to a repo participant, in connection with a repurchase agreement and that is made before the commencement of the case, except under section 548(a)(1) of this title.

(g)   Notwithstanding sections 544, 545, 547, 548(a)(2) and 548(b) of this title, the trustee may not avoid a transfer under a swap agreement, made by or to a swap participant, in connection with a swap agreement and that is made before the commencement of the case, except under section 548(a)(1) of this title.

(h)   Notwithstanding the rights and powers of a trustee under sections 544(1), 545, 547, 549, and 553, if the court determines on a motion by the trustee made not later than 120 days after the date of the order for relief in a case under chapter 11 of this title and after notice and a hearing, that a return is in the best interests of the estate, the debtor, with the consent of a creditor, may return goods shipped to the debtor by the creditor before the commencement of the case, and the creditor may offset the purchase price of such goods against any claim of the creditor against the debtor that arose before the commencement of the case.

Sec. 547. Preferences

(a)   In this section—

(1)   "inventory" means personal property leased or furnished, held for sale or lease, or to be furnished under a contract for service, raw materials, work in process, or materials used or consumed in a business, including farm products such as crops or livestock, held for sale or lease;

(2)   "new value" means money or money's worth in goods, services, or new credit, or release by a transferee of property previously transferred to such transferee in a transaction that is neither void nor voidable by the debtor or the trustee under any applicable law, including proceeds of such property, but does not include an obligation substituted for an existing obligation;

(3)   "receivable" means right to payment, whether or not such right has been earned by performance; and

(4)   a debt for a tax is incurred on the day when such tax is last payable without penalty, including any extension.

(b)   Except as provided in subsection (c) of this section, the trustee may avoid any transfer of an interest of the debtor in property—

(1)   to or for the benefit of a creditor;

(2)   for or on account of an antecedent debt owed by the debtor before such transfer was made;

(3)   made while the debtor was insolvent;

(4)   made—

(A)   on or within 90 days before the date of the filing of the petition; or

(B)   between ninety days and one year before the date of the filing of the petition, if such creditor at the time of such transfer was an insider; and

(5)   that enables such creditor to receive more than such creditor would receive if—

(A)   the case were a case under chapter 7 of this title;

(B)   the transfer had not been made; and

(C)   such creditor received payment of such debt to the extent provided by the provisions of this title.

(c)   The trustee may not avoid under this section a transfer—

(1)   to the extent that such transfer was—

(A)   intended by the debtor and the creditor to or for whose benefit such transfer was made to be a contemporaneous exchange for new value given to the debtor; and

(B)   in fact a substantially contemporaneous exchange;

(2)   to the extent that such transfer was—

(A)   in payment of a debt incurred by the debtor in the ordinary course of business or financial affairs of the debtor and the transferee;

(B)   made in the ordinary course of business or financial affairs of the debtor and the transferee; and

(C)   made according to ordinary business terms;

(3)   that creates a security interest in property acquired by the debtor—

(A)   to the extent such security interest secures new value that was—

(i)   given at or after the signing of a security agreement that contains a description of such property as collateral;

(ii)   given by or on behalf of the secured party under such agreement;

(iii)   given to enable the debtor to acquire such property; and

(iv)   in fact used by the debtor to acquire such property; and

(B)   that is perfected on or before 20 days after the debtor receives possession of such property;

(4)   to or for the benefit of a creditor, to the extent that, after such transfer, such creditor gave new value to or for the benefit of the debtor—

(A)   not secured by an otherwise unavoidable security interest; and

(B)   on account of which new value the debtor did not make an otherwise unavoidable transfer to or for the benefit of such creditor;

(5)   that creates a perfected security interest in inventory or a receivable or the proceeds of either, except to the extent that the aggregate of all such transfers to the transferee caused a reduction, as of the date of the filing of the petition and to the prejudice of other creditors holding unsecured claims, of any amount by which the debt secured by such security interest exceeded the value of all security interests for such debt on the later of—

(A)   (i)   with respect to a transfer to which subsection (b)(4)(A) of this section applies, 90 days before the date of the filing of the petition; or

(ii)   with respect to a transfer to which subsection (b)(4)(B) of this section applies, one year before the date of the filing of the petition; or

(B)   the date on which new value was first given under the security agreement creating such security interest;

(6)   that is the fixing of a statutory lien that is not avoidable under section 545 of this title;

(7)   to the extent such transfer was a bona fide payment of a debt to a spouse, former spouse, or child of the debtor, for alimony to, maintenance for, or support of such spouse or child, in connection with a separation agreement, divorce decree or other order of a court of record, determination made in accordance with State or territorial law by a governmental unit, or property settlement agreement, but not to the extent that such debt—

(A)   is assigned to another entity, voluntarily by operation of law, or otherwise; or

(B)   includes a liability designated as alimony, maintenance, or support, unless such liability is actually in the nature of alimony, maintenance or support; or

(8)   if, in a case filed by an individual debtor whose debts are primarily consumer debts, the aggregate value of all property that constitutes or is affected by such transfer is less than $600.

(d)   The trustee may avoid a transfer of an interest in property of the debtor transferred to or for the benefit of a surety to secure reimbursement of such a surety that furnished a bond or other obligation to dissolve a judicial lien that would have been avoidable by the trustee under subsection (b) of this section. The liability of such surety under such bond or obligation shall be discharged to the extent of the value of such property recovered by the trustee or the amount paid to the trustee.

(e) (1)   For the purposes of this section—

(A)   a transfer of real property other than fixtures, but including the interest of a seller or purchaser under a contract for the sale of real property, is perfected when a bona fide purchaser of such property from the debtor against whom applicable law permits such transfer to be perfected cannot acquire an interest that is superior to the interest of the transferee; and

(B)   a transfer of a fixture or property other than real property is perfected when a creditor on a simple contract cannot acquire a judicial lien that is superior to the interest of the transferee.

(2)   For the purposes of this section, except as provided in paragraph (3) of this subsection, a transfer is made—

(A)   at the time such transfer takes effect between the transferor and the transferee, if such transfer is perfected at, or within 10 days after, such time, except as provided in subsection (c)(3)(B);

(B)   at the time such transfer is perfected, if such transfer is perfected after such 10 days; or

(C)   immediately before the date of the filing of the petition, if such transfer is not perfected at the later of—

(i)   the commencement of the case; or

(ii)   10 days after such transfer takes effect between the transferor and the transferee.

(3)   For the purposes of this section, a transfer is not made until the debtor has acquired rights in the property transferred.

(f)   For the purpose of this section, the debtor is presumed to have been insolvent on and during the 90 days immediately preceding the date of the filing of the petition.

(g)   For the purposes of this section, the trustee has the burden of proving the avoidability of a transfer under subsection (b) of this section, and the creditor or party in interest against whom recovery or avoidance is sought has the burden of proving the nonavoidability of a transfer under subsection (c) of this section.

Sec. 548.   *Fraudulent Transfers and Obligations*

(1)   The trustee may avoid any transfer of an interest of the debtor in property, or any obligation incurred by the debtor, that was made or incurred on or within one year before the date of the filing of the petition, if the debtor voluntarily or involuntarily—

(A)   made such transfer or incurred such obligation with actual intent to hinder, delay, or defraud any entity to which the debtor was or became, on or after the date that such transfer was made or such obligation was incurred, indebted; or

(B)   (i)   received less than a reasonably equivalent value in exchange for such; and

(ii)   (I)   was insolvent on the date that such transfer was made or such obligation was incurred, or became insolvent as a result of such transfer or obligation;

(II)   was engaged in business or a transaction, or was about to engage in business or a transaction, for which any property remaining with the debtor was an unreasonably small capital; or

(III)   intended to incur, or believed that the debtor would incur, debts that would be beyond the debtor's ability to pay as such debts matured.

(2)   A transfer of a charitable contribution to a qualified religious or charitable entity or organization shall not be considered to be a transfer covered under paragraph (1)(B) in any case in which—

(A)   the amount of that contribution does not exceed 15 percent of the gross annual income of the debtor for the year in which the transfer of the contribution is made; or

(B)   the contribution made by a debtor exceeded the percentage amount of gross annual income specified in subparagraph (A), if the transfer was consistent with the practices of the debtor in making charitable contributions.

(b)   The trustee of a partnership debtor may avoid any transfer of an interest of the debtor in property, or any obligation incurred by the debtor, that was made or incurred on or within one year before the date of the filing of the petition, to a general partner in the debtor, if the debtor was insolvent on the date such transfer was made or such obligation was incurred, or became insolvent as a result of such transfer or obligation.

(c)   Except to the extent that a transfer or obligation voidable under this section is voidable under section 544, 545, or 547 of this title, a transferee or obligee of such a transfer or obligation that takes for value and in good faith has lien on or may retain any interest transferred or may enforce any obligation incurred, as the case may be, to the extent that such transferee or obligee gave value to the debtor in exchange for such transfer or obligation.

(d) (1)   For the purposes of this section, a transfer is made when such transfer is so perfected that a bona fide purchaser from the debtor against whom applicable law permits such transfer to be perfected cannot acquire an interest in the property transferred that is superior to the interest in such property of the transferee, but if such transfer is not so perfected before the commencement of the case, such transfer is made immediately before the date of the filing of the petition.

(2)   In this section—

(A)   "value" means property, or satisfaction or securing of a present or antecedent debt of the debtor, but does not include an unperformed promise to furnish support to the debtor or to a relative of the debtor;

(B)   a commodity broker, forward contract merchant, stockbroker, (financial institution,) financial institution or securities clearing agency that receives a margin payment, as defined in section 101, 741, or 761 of this title, or settlement payment, as defined in section 101 or 741 of this title, takes for value to the extent of such payment;

(C)   a repo participant that receives a margin payment, as defined in section 741 or 761 of this title, or settlement payment, as defined in section 741 of this title, in connection with a repurchase agreement, takes for value to the extent of such payment and;

(D)   a swap participant that receives a transfer in connection with a swap agreement takes for value to the extent of such transfer.

(3)   In this section, the term "charitable contribution" means a charitable contribution, as that term is defined in section 170(c)* of the Internal Revenue Code of 1986, if that contribution—

(A)   is made by a natural person; and

(B)   consists of —

(i)   a financial instrument (as that term is defined in section 731(c)(2)(C)** of the Internal Revenue code of 1986); or

(ii)   cash.

(4)   In this section, the term "qualified religious or charitable entity or organization" means—

(A)   an entity described in section 170(c)(1)*** of the Internal Revenue Code of 1986; or

* [*Editors' Note:* Internal Revenue Code section 170(c) states:
(c) Charitable contribution defined. —For purposes of this section, the term "charitable contribtuion" means a contribution or gift to or for the use of—
(1) A State, a possession of the United States, or any political subdivision of any of the foregoing, or the United States of the District of Columbia, but only if the contribution or gift is made for exclusively public purposes.
(2) A corporation, trust, or community chest, fund or foundation—
(A) created or organized in the United States or in any possession thereof, or under the law of the United States, any State, the District of Columbia, or any possession of the United States;
(B) organized and operated exclusively for religious, charitable, scientific, literary, or eductional purposes, or to foster national or international amateur sports competition (but only if no part of its activities involve the provision of athletic facilities or equipment), or for the prevention of cruelty to children or animals;
(C) no part of the net earnings of which inures to the benefit of any private shareholder or individual; and
(D) which is not disqualified for tax exemption under section 501(c)(3) by reason of attempting to influence legislation, and which does not participate in, or intervene in (including the publishing or distributing of statements), any political campaign on behalf of (or in opposition to) any candidate for public office.
A contribution or gift by a corporation to a trust, chest, fund, or foundation shall be deductible by reason of this paragraph only if it is to be used within the United States or any of its possessions exclusively for purposes specified in subparagraph (B). Rules similar to the rules of section 501(j) shall apply for purposes fo this paragraph.]

** [*Editors' Note:* Internal Revenue Code section 731(c)(2)(C) states:
(C) Financial instrument.—The term "financial instrument" includes stocks and other equity interests, evidences of indebtedness, options, forward or futures contracts, notional principal contracts, and derivatives.]

*** [*Editors' Note:* Internal Revenue Code section 170(c)(1) states:
(c) Charitable contribution defined.—For purposes of this section, the term "charitable contribution" means a contribution or gift to or for the use of—
(1)A State, a possession of the United States, or any political subdivision of any of the foregoing, or the United States or the District of Columbia, but only if the contribution or gift is made for exclusively public purposes.]

(B)   an entity or organization described in section 170(c)(2)* of the Internal Revenue Code of 1986.

Sec. 549. *Postpetition Transactions*

(a)   Except as provided in subsections (b) or (c) of this section, the trustee may avoid a transfer of property of the estate—

(1)   that occurs after the commencement of the case; or

(2)   (A)   that is authorized only under section 303(f) or 542(c) of this title; or

(B)   that is not authorized under this title or by the court.

(b)   In an involuntary case, the trustee may not avoid, under subsection (a) of this section, a transfer made after the commencement of such case but before the order for relief to the extent any value, including services, but not including satisfaction or securing of a debt that arose before the commencement of the case, is given after the commencement of the case in exchange for such transfer, notwithstanding any notice or knowledge of the case that the transferee has.

(c)   The trustee may not avoid under subsection (a) of this section a transfer of real property to a good faith purchaser without knowledge of the commencement of the case and for present fair equivalent value unless a copy or notice of the petition was filed, where a transfer of such real property may be recorded to perfect such transfer, before such transfer is so perfected that a bona fide purchaser of such property, against whom applicable law permits such transfer to be perfected, could not acquire an interest that is superior to the interest of such good faith purchaser. A good faith purchaser without knowledge of the commencement of the case and for less than present fair equivalent value has a lien on the property transferred to the extent of any present value given, unless a copy or notice of the petition was so filed before such transfer was so perfected.

(d)   An action or proceeding under this section may not be commenced after the earlier of—

(1)   two years after the date of the transfer sought to be avoided; or

(2)   the time the case is closed or dismissed.

Sec. 550. *Liability of Transferee of Avoided Transfer*

(a)   Except as otherwise provided in this section, to the extent that a transfer is avoided under section 544, 545, 547, 548, 549, 553(b), or 724(a) of this title, the trustee may recover, for the benefit of the estate, the property transferred, or, if the court so orders, the value of such property, from—

(1)   the initial transferee of such transfer or the entity for whose benefit such transfer was made; or

(2)   any immediate or mediate transferee of such initial transferee.

(b)   the trustee may not recover under subsection (a)(2) of this section from—

(1)   a transferee that takes for value, including satisfaction or securing of a present or antecedent debt in good faith, and without knowledge of the voidability of the transfer avoided; or

(2)   any immediate or mediate good faith transferee of such transferee.

(c)   If a transfer made between 90 days and one year before the filing of the petition—

(1)   is avoided under section 547(b) of this title; and

(2)   was made for the benefit of a creditor that at the time of such transfer was an insider;

the trustee may not recover under subsection (a) from a transferee that is not an insider.

(d)   The trustee is entitled to only a single satisfaction under subsection (a) of this section.

(e) (1)   A good faith transferee from whom the trustee may recover under subsection (a) of this section has a lien on the property recovered to secure the lesser of—

(A)   the cost, to such transferee, of any improvement made after the transfer, less the amount of any profit realized by or accruing to such transferee from such property; and

(B)   any increase in the value of such property as a result of such improvement, of the property transferred.

(2)   In this subsection, "improvement" includes—

(A)   physical additions or changes to the property transferred;

(B)   repairs to such property;

(C)   payment of any tax on such property;

(D)   payment of any debt secured by a lien on such property that is superior or equal to the rights of the trustee; and

(E)   preservation of such property.

(f)   An action or proceeding under this section may not be commenced after the earlier of—

(1)   one year after the avoidance of the transfer on account of which recovery under this section is sought; or

(2)   the time the case is closed or dismissed.

Sec. 551.   Automatic Preservation of Avoided Transfer

Any transfer avoided under section 522, 544, 545, 548, 549, or 724(a) of this title, or any lien void under section 506(d) of this title, is preserved for the benefit of the estate but only with respect to property of the estate.

Sec. 552.   Postpetition Effect of Security Interest

(a)   Except as provided in subsection (b) of this section, property acquired by the estate or by the debtor from the commencement of the case is not subject to any lien resulting from any security agreement entered into by the debtor before the commencement of the case.

(b) (1)   Except as provided in section 363, 506(c), 522, 544, 545, 547, and 548 of this title, if the debtor and an entity entered into a security agreement before the commencement of the case and if the security interest created by such security agreement extends to property of the debtor acquired before the commencement of the case and to proceeds, product, offspring, or profits of such property, then such security interest extends to such proceeds, product, offspring, or profits acquired by the estate after the commencement of the case to the extent provided by such security agreement and by applicable nonbankruptcy law, except to any extent that the court, after notice and a hearing and based on the equities of the case, orders otherwise.

(2)   Except as provided in sections 363, 506(c), 522, 544, 545, 547, and 548 of this title, and notwithstanding section 546(b) of this title, if the debtor and an entity entered into a security agreement before the commencement of the case and if the security interest created by such security agreement extends to property of the debtor acquired before the commencement of the case and to amounts paid as rents of such property or the fees, charges, accounts, or other payments for the use or occupancy of rooms and other public facilities in hotels, motels, or other lodging properties, then such security interest extends to such rents and such fees, charges, accounts, or other payments acquired by the estate after the commencement of the case to the extent provided in such security agreement, except to any extent that the court, after notice and a hearing and based on the equities of the case, orders otherwise.

Sec. 553.   Setoff

(a)   Except as otherwise provided in this section and in section 362 and 363 of this title, this title does not affect any right of a creditor to offset a mutual debt owing by such creditor to the debtor that arose before the commencement of the case under this title against a claim of such creditor against the debtor that arose before the commencement of the case, except to the extent that—

(1)   the claim of such creditor against the debtor is disallowed;

(2)   such claim was transferred, by an entity other than the debtor, to such creditor—

(A)   after the commencement of the case; or

(B)   (i)   after 90 days before the date of the filing of the petition; and

(ii)   while the debtor was insolvent; or

(3)   the debt owed to the debtor by such creditor was incurred by such creditor—

(A)   after 90 days before the date of the filing of the petition;

(B)   while the debtor was insolvent; and

(C)   for the purpose of obtaining a right to setoff against the debtor.

(b) (1)   Except with respect to a setoff of a kind described in section 362(b)(6), 362(b)(7), 362(b)(14), 365(h), 365(i)(2), or 546(h) of this title, if a creditor offsets a mutual debt owing to the debtor against a claim against the debtor on or within 90 days before the date of the filing of the petition, then the trustee may recover from such creditor the amount so offset to the extent that any insufficiency on the date of such setoff is less than the insufficiency on the later of—

(A)   90 days before the date of the filing of the petition; and

(B)   the first date during the 90 days immediately preceding the date of the filing of the petition on which there is an insufficiency.

(2)   In this subsection, "insufficiency" means amount, if any, by which a claim against the debtor exceeds a mutual debt owing to the debtor by the holder of such claim.

(c)   For the purposes of this section, the debtor is presumed to have been insolvent on and during the 90 days immediately preceding the date of the filing of the petition.

Sec. 554. *Abandonment of Property of the Estate*

(a)   After notice and a hearing, the trustee may abandon any property of the estate that is burdensome to the estate or that is of inconsequential value and benefit to the estate.

(b)   On request of a party in interest and after notice and a hearing, the court may order the trustee to abandon any property of the estate that is burdensome to the estate or that is of inconsequential value and benefit to the estate.

(c)   Unless the court orders otherwise, any property scheduled under section 521(1) of this title not otherwise administered at the time of the closing of a case is abandoned to the debtor and administered for purposes of section 350 of this title.

(d)   Unless the court orders otherwise, property of the estate that is not abandoned under this section and that is not administered in the case remains property of the estate.

Sec. 555. *Contractual Right to Liquidate a Securities Contract*

The exercise of a contractual right of a stockbroker, financial institution, or securities clearing agency to cause the liquidation of a securities contract, as defined in section 741 of this title, because of a condition of the kind specified in section 365(e)(1) of this title shall not be stayed, avoided, or otherwise limited by operation of any provision of this title or by order of a court or administrative agency in any proceeding under this title unless such order is authorized under the provision of the Securities Investor Protection Act of 1970 or any statute administered by the Securities and Exchange Commission. As used in this section, the term "contractual right" includes a right set forth in a rule or bylaw of a national securities exchange, a national securities association, or a securities clearing agency.

Sec. 556. *Contractual Right to Liquidate a Commodities Contract of Forward Contract*

The contractual right of a commodity broker or forward contract merchant to cause the liquidation of a commodity contract, as defined in section 761 of this title, or forward contract because of a condition of the kind specified in section 365(e)(1) of this title, and the right to a variation or maintenance margin payment received from a trustee with respect to open commodity contracts or forward contract, shall not be stayed, avoided, or otherwise limited by operation of any provision of this title or by the order of a court in any proceeding under this title. As used in this section, the term "contractual right" includes a right set forth in a rule or bylaw of a clearing organization or contract market or in a resolution of the governing board thereof and a right, whether or not evidenced in writing, arising under common law, under law merchant or by reason of normal business practice.

Sec. 557.   *Expedited Determination of Interests in, and Abandonment or Other Disposition of Grain Assets*

(a)   This section applies only in a case concerning a debtor that owns or operates a grain storage facility and only with respect to grain and the proceeds of grain. This section does not affect the application of any section of this title to property other than grain and proceeds of grain.

(b)   In this section—

(1)   "grain" means wheat, corn flaxseed, grain sorghum, barley, oats, rye, soybeans, other dry edible beans, or rice;

(2)   "grain storage facility" means a site or physical structure regularly used to store grain for producers, or to store grain acquired from producers for resale; and

(3)   "producer" means an entity which engages in the growing of grain.

(c) (1)   Notwithstanding sections 362, 363, 365, and 554 of this title, on the court's own motion the court may, and on the request of the trustee or an entity that claims an interest in grain or the proceeds of grain the court shall, expedite the procedures for the determination of interests in and the disposition of grain and the proceeds of grain, by shortening to the greatest extent feasible such time periods as are otherwise applicable for such procedures and by establishing, by order, a timetable having a duration of not to exceed 120 days for the completion of the applicable procedure specified in subsection (d) of this section. Such time periods and such timetable may be modified by the court, for cause, in accordance with subsection (f) of this section.

(2)   The court shall determine the extent to which such time periods shall be shortened, based upon—

(A)   any need of an entity claiming an interest in such grain or the proceeds of grain for a prompt determination of such interest;

(B)   any need of such entity for a prompt disposition of such grain;

(C)   the market for such grain;

(D)   the conditions under which such grain is stored;

(E)   the costs of continued storage or disposition of such grain;

(F)   the orderly administration of the estate;

(G)   the appropriate opportunity for an entity to assert an interest in such grain; and

(H)   such other considerations as are relevant to the need to expedite such procedures in the case.

(d)   The procedures that may be expedited under subsection (c) of this section include—

(1)   the filing of and response to—

(A)   a claim of ownership;

(B)   a proof of claim;

(C)   a request for abandonment;

(D)   a request for relief from the stay of action against property under section 362(a) of this title;

(E)   a request for determination of secured status;

(F)   a request for determination of whether such grain or the proceeds of grain—

      (i)   is property of the estate;

      (ii)   must be turned over to the estate; or

      (iii) may be used, sold, or leased; and

   (G) any other request for determination of an interest in such grain or the proceeds of grain;

  (2) the disposition of such grain or the proceeds of grain, before or after determination of interests in such grain or the proceeds of grain, by way of—

    (A) sale of such grain;

    (B) abandonment;

    (C) distribution; or

    (D) such other method as is equitable in the case;

  (3) subject to sections 701, 702, 703, 1104, 1202, and 1302 of this title, the appointment of a trustee or examiner and the retention and compensation of any professional person required to assist with respect to matters relevant to the determination of interests in or disposition of such grain or the proceeds of grain; and

  (4) the determination of any dispute concerning a matter specified in paragraph (1), (2), or (3) of this subsection.

(e) (1) Any governmental unit that has regulatory jurisdiction over the operation or liquidation of the debtor or the debtor's business shall be given notice of any request made or order entered under subsection (c) of this section.

  (2) Any such governmental unit may raise, and may appear to be heard on, any issue relating to grain or the proceeds of grain in a case in which a request is made, or an order is entered, under subsection (c) of this section.

  (3) The trustee shall consult with such governmental unit before taking any action relating to the disposition of grain in the possession, custody, or control of the debtor or the estate.

(f)   The court may extend the period for final disposition of grain or the proceeds of grain under this section beyond 120 days if the court finds that—

  (1) the interests of justice so require in light of the complexity of the case; and

  (2) the interest of those claimants entitled to distribution of grain or the proceeds of grain will not be materially injured by such additional delay.

(g)   Unless an order establishing an expedited procedure under subsection (c) of this section, or determining any interest in or approving any disposition of grain or the proceeds of grain, is stayed pending appeal—

  (1) the reversal or modification of such order on appeal does not affect the validity of any procedure, determination, or disposition that occurs before such reversal or modification, whether or not any entity knew of the pendency of the appeal; and

  (2) neither the court nor the trustee may delay, due to the appeal of such order, any proceeding in the case in which such order is issued.

(h) (1) The trustee may recover from grain and the proceeds of grain the reasonable and necessary costs and expenses allowable under section 503(b) of this title attributable to preserving or disposing of grain or the proceeds of grain, but may not recover from such grain or the proceeds of grain any other costs or expenses.

  (2) Notwithstanding section 326(a) of this title, the dollar amounts of

money specified in such section include the value, as of the date of disposition, of any grain that the trustee distributes in kind.

(i)   In all cases where the quantity of a specific type of grain held by a debtor operating a grain storage facility exceeds ten thousand bushels, such grain shall be sold by the trustee and the assets thereof distributed in accordance with the provisions of this section.

Sec. 558.   *Defenses of the Estate*

The estate shall have the benefit of any defense available to the debtor as against any entity other than the estate, including statutes of limitation, statutes of frauds, usury, and other personal defenses. A waiver of any such defense by the debtor after the commencement of the case does not bind the estate.

Sec. 559.   *Contractual Right to Liquidate a Repurchase Agreement*

The exercise of a contractual right of a repo participant to cause the liquidation of a repurchase agreement because of a condition of the kind specified in section 365(e)(1) of this title shall not be stayed, avoided, or otherwise limited by operation of any provision of this title or by order of a court or administrative agency in any proceeding under this title, unless, where the debtor is a stockbroker or securities clearing agency, such order is authorized under the provisions of the Securities Investor Protection Act of 1970 or any statute administered by the Securities and Exchange Commission. In the event that a repo participant liquidates one or more repurchase agreements with a debtor and under the terms of one or more such agreements has agreed to deliver assets subject to repurchase agreements to the debtor, any excess of the market prices received on liquidation of such assets (or if any such assets are not disposed of on the date of liquidation of such repurchase agreements, at the prices available at the time of liquidation of such repurchase agreements from a generally recognized source or the most recent closing bid quotation from such a source) over the sum of the stated repurchase prices and all expenses in connection with the liquidation of such repurchase agreements shall be deemed property of the estate, subject to the available rights of setoff. As used in this section, the term "contractual right" includes a right set forth in a rule or bylaw, applicable to each party to the repurchase agreement, of a national securities exchange, a national securities association, or a securities clearing agency, and a right, whether or not evidenced in writing, arising under common law, under law merchant or by reason of normal business practice.

Sec. 560.   *Contractual Right to Terminate a Swap Agreement*

The exercise of any contractual right of any swap participant to cause the termination of a swap agreement because of a condition of the kind specified in section 365(e)(1) of this title or to offset or net out any termination values or payment amounts arising under or in connection with any swap agreement shall not be stayed, avoided, or otherwise limited by operation of any provision of this title or by order of a court or administrative agency in any proceeding under this title. As used in this section, the term 'contractual right' includes a right, whether or not evidenced in writing, arising under common law, under law merchant, or by reason of normal business practice.

7
LIQUIDATION

SUBCHAPTER I. OFFICERS AND ADMINISTRATION

Sec. 701.   Interim Trustee

(a) (1)   Promptly after the order for relief under this chapter, the United States trustee shall appoint one disinterested person that is a member of the panel of private trustees established under section 586(a)(1) of title 28 or that is serving as trustee in the case immediately before the order for relief under this chapter to serve as interim trustee in the case.

(2)   If none of the members of such panel is willing to serve as interim trustee in the case, then the United States trustee may serve as interim trustee in the case.

(b)   The service of an interim trustee under this section terminates when a trustee elected or designated under section 702 of this title to serve as trustee in the case qualifies under section 322 of this title.

(c)   An interim trustee serving under this section is a trustee in a case under this title.

Sec. 702.   Election of Trustee

(a)   A creditor may vote for a candidate for trustee only if such creditor—

(1)   holds an allowable, undisputed, fixed, liquidated, unsecured claim of a kind entitled to distribution under section 726(a)(2), 726(a)(3), 726(a)(4), 752(a), 766(h), or 766(i) of this title;

(2)   does not have an interest materially adverse, other than an equity interest that is not substantial in relation to such creditor's interest as a creditor, to the interest of creditors entitled to such distribution; and

(3)   is not an insider.

(b)   At the meeting of creditors held under section 341 of this title, creditors may elect one person to serve as trustee in the case if election of a trustee is requested by creditors that may vote under subsection (a) of this section, and that hold at least 20 percent in amount of the claims specified in subsection (a)(1) of this section that are held by creditors that may vote under subsection (a) of this section.

(c)   A candidate for trustee is elected trustee if—

(1)   creditors holding at least 20 percent in amount of the claims of a kind specified in subsection (a)(1) of this section that are held by creditors that may vote under subsection (a) of this section vote; and

(2)   such candidate receives the votes of creditors holding a majority in amount of claims specified in subsection (a)(1) of this section that are held by creditors that vote for a trustee.

(d)   If a trustee is not elected under this section, then the interim trustee shall serve as trustee in the case.

Sec. 703.   Successor Trustee

(a)   If a trustee dies or resigns during a case, fails to qualify under section 322 of this title, or is removed under section 324 of this title, creditors may elect, in the manner specified in section 702 of this title, a person to fill the vacancy in the office of trustee.

(b)   Pending election of a trustee under subsection (a) of this section, if necessary to preserve or prevent loss to the estate, the United States trustee may appoint an interim trustee in the manner specified in section 701(a).

(c)   If creditors do not elect a successor trustee under subsection (a) of this section or if a trustee is needed in a case reopened under section 350 of this title, then the United States trustee—

(1)   shall appoint one disinterested person that is a member of the panel of private trustees established under section 586(a)(1) of title 28 to serve as trustee in the case; or

(2)   may, if none of the disinterested members of such panel is willing to serve as trustee, serve as trustee in the case.

See. 704. *Duties of Trustee*

The trustee shall—

(1)   collect and reduce to money the property of the estate for which such trustee serves, and close such estate as expeditiously as is compatible with the best interests of parties in interest;

(2)   be accountable for all property received;

(3)   ensure that the debtor shall perform his intention as specified in section 521(2)(B) of this title;

(4)   investigate the financial affairs of the debtor;

(5)   if a purpose would be served, examine proofs of claims and object to the allowance of any claim that is improper;

(6)   if advisable, oppose the discharge of the debtor;

(7)   unless the court orders otherwise, furnish such information concerning the estate and the estate's administration as is requested by a party in interest;

(8)   if the business of the debtor is authorized to be operated, file with the court, with the United States trustee, and with any governmental unit charged with responsibility for collection or determination of any tax arising out of such operation, periodic reports and summaries of the operation of such business, including a statement of receipts and disbursements, and such other information as the United States trustee or the court requires; and

(9)   make a final report and file a final account of the administration of the estate with the court and with the United States trustee.

Sec. 705. *Creditors' Committee*

(a)   At the meeting under section 341(a) of this title, creditors that may vote for a trustee under section 702(a) of this title may elect a committee of not fewer than three, and not more than eleven, creditors, each of whom holds an allowable unsecured claim of a kind entitled to distribution under section 726(a)(2) of this title.

(b)   A committee elected under subsection (a) of this section may consult with the trustee or the United States trustee in connection with the administration of the estate, make recommendations to the trustee or the United States trustee respecting the performance of the trustee's or the United

States trustee's duties, and submit to the court or the United States trustee any question affecting the administration of the estate.

Sec. 706. Conversion

(a)   The debtor may convert a case under this chapter to a case under chapter 11, 12, or 13 of this title at any time, if the case has not been converted under section 1112, 1208, or 1307 of this title. Any waiver of the right to convert a case under this subsection is unenforceable.

(b)   On request of a party in interest and after notice and a hearing, the court may convert a case under this chapter to a case under chapter 11 of this title at any time.

(c)   The court may not convert a case under this chapter to a case under chapter 12 or 13 of this title unless the debtor requests such conversion.

(d)   Notwithstanding any other provision of this section, a case may not be converted to a case under another chapter of this title unless the debtor may be a debtor under such chapter.

Sec. 707. Dismissal

(a)   The court may dismiss a case under this chapter only after notice and a hearing and only for cause, including—

(1)   unreasonable delay by the debtor that is prejudicial to creditors; [or]

(2)   nonpayment of any fees or charges required under chapter 123 of title 28; and

(3)   failure of the debtor in a voluntary case to file, within fifteen days or such additional time as the court may allow after the filing of the petition commencing such case, the information required by paragraph (1) of section 521, but only on a motion by the United States trustee.

(b)   After notice and a hearing, the court, on its own motion or on a motion by the United States trustee, but not at the request or suggestion of any party in interest, may dismiss a case filed by an individual debtor under this chapter whose debts are primarily consumer debts if it finds that the granting of relief would be a substantial abuse of the provisions of this chapter. There shall be a presumption in favor of granting the relief requested by the debtor. In making a determination whether to dismiss a case under this section, the court may not take into consideration whether a debtor has made, or continues to make, charitable contributions (that meet the the definition of "charitable contribution" under section 548(d)(3)) to any qualified religious or charitable entity or organization (as that term is defined in section 548(d)(4)).

SUBCHAPTER II. COLLECTION, LIQUIDATION, AND DISTRIBUTION OF THE ESTATE

Sec. 721. Authorization to Operate Business

The court may authorize the trustee to operate the business of the debtor for a limited period, if such operation is in the best interest of the estate and consistent with the orderly liquidation of the estate.

Sec. 722. *Redemption*

An individual debtor may, whether or not the debtor has waived the right to redeem under this section, redeem tangible personal property intended primarily for personal, family, or household use, form a lien securing a dischargeable consumer debt, if such property is exempted under section 522 of this title or has been abandoned under section 554 of this title, by paying the holder of such lien the amount of the allowed secured claim of such holder that is secured by such lien.

Sec. 723. *Rights of Partnership Trustee against General Partners*

(a)   If there is a deficiency of property of the estate to pay in full all claims which are allowed in a case under this chapter concerning a partnership and with respect to which a general partner of the partnership is personally liable, the trustee shall have a claim against such general partner to the extent that under applicable nonbankruptcy law such general partner is personally liable for such deficiency.

(b)   To the extent practicable, the trustee shall first seek recovery of such deficiency from any general partner in such partnership that is not a debtor in a case under this title. Pending determination of such deficiency, the court may order any such partner to provide the estate with indemnity for, or assurance of payment of, any deficiency recoverable from such partner, or not to dispose of property.

(c)   Notwithstanding section 728(c) of this title, the trustee has a claim against the estate of each general partner in such partnership that is a debtor in a case under this title for the full amount of all claims of creditors allowed in the case concerning such partnership. Notwithstanding section 502 of this title, there shall not be allowed in such partner's case a claim against such partner on which both such partner and such partnership are liable, except to any extent that such claim is secured only by property of such partner and not by property of such partnership. The claim of the trustee under this subsection is entitled to distribution in such partner's case under section 726(a) of this title the same as any other claim of a kind specified in such section.

(d)   If the aggregate that the trustee recovers from the estates of general partners that subsection (c) of this section is greater than any deficiency not recovered under subsection (b) of this section, the court, after notice and a hearing, shall determine an equitable distribution of the surplus so recovered, and the trustee shall distribute such surplus to the estates of the general partners in such partnership according to such determination.

Sec. 724. *Treatment of Certain Liens*

(a)   The trustee may avoid a lien that secures a claim of a kind specified in section 726(a)(4) of this title.

(b)   Property in which the estate has an interest and that is subject to a lien that is not avoidable under this title and that secures an allowed claim for a tax, or proceeds of such property, shall be distributed—

(1)   first, to any holder of an allowed claim secured by a lien on such property that is not avoidable under this title and that is senior to such tax lien;

(2)   second, to any holder of a claim of a kind specified in section 507(a)(1), 507(a)(2), 507(a)(3), 507(a)(4), 507(a)(5), 507(a)(6), or 507(a)(7) of this title, to the extent of the amount of such allowed tax claim that is secured by such tax lien;

(3)   third, to the holder of such tax lien, to any extent that such holder's allowed tax claim that is secured by such tax lien exceeds any amount distributed under paragraph (2) of this subsection;

(4)   fourth, to any holder of an allowed claim secured by a lien on such property that is not avoidable under this title and that is junior to such tax lien;

(5)   fifth, to the holder of such tax lien, to the extent that such holder's allowed claim secured by such tax lien is not paid under paragraph (3) of this subsection; and

(6)   sixth, to the estate.

(c)   If more than one holder of a claim is entitled to distribution under a particular paragraph of subsection (b) of this section, distribution to such holders under such paragraph shall be in the same order as distribution to such holders would have been other than under this section.

(d)   A statutory lien the priority of which is determined in the same manner as the priority of a tax lien under section 6323 of the Internal Revenue Code of 1986 shall be treated under subsection (b) of this section the same as if such lien were a tax lien.

Sec. 725.   Disposition of Certain Property

After the commencement of a case under this chapter, but before final distribution of property of the estate under section 726 of this title, the trustee, after notice and a hearing, shall dispose of any property in which an entity other than the estate has an interest, such as a lien, and that has not been disposed of under another section of this title.

Sec. 726.   Distribution of Property of the Estate

(a)   Except as provided in section 510 of this title, property of the estate shall be distributed—

(1)   first, in payment of claims of the kind specified in, and in the order specified in, section 507 of this title, proof of which is timely filed under section 501 of this title or tardily filed before the date on which the trustee commences distribution under this section;

(2)   second, in payment of any allowed unsecured claim, other than a claim of a kind specified in paragraph (1), (3), or (4) of this subsection, proof of which is—

(A)   timely filed under section 501(a) of this title;

(B)   timely filed under section 501(b) or 501(c) of this title; or

(C)   tardily filed under section 501(a) of this title, if—

(i)   the creditor that holds such claim did not have notice or actual knowledge of the case in time for timely filing of a proof of such claim under section 501(a) of this title; and

(ii)   proof of such claim is filed in time to permit payment of such claim;

(3)   third, in payment of any allowed unsecured claim proof of which is tardily filed under section 501(a) of this title, other than a claim of the kind specified in paragraph (2)(C) of this subsection;

(4)   fourth, in payment of any allowed claim, whether secured or unsecured, for any fine, penalty, or forfeiture, or for multiple, exemplary, or punitive damages, arising before the earlier of the order for relief or the appointment of a trustee, to the extent that such fine, penalty, forfeiture, or damages are not compensation for actual pecuniary loss suffered by the holder of such claim;

(5)   fifth, in payment of interest at the legal rate from the date of the filing of the petition, on any claim paid under paragraph (1), (2), (3), or (4) of this subsection; and

(6)   sixth, to the debtor.

(b)   Payment on claims of a kind specified in paragraph (1), (2), (3), (4), (5), (6), (7), or (8) of section 507(a) of this title, or in paragraph (2), (3), (4), or (5) of subsection (a) of this section, shall be made pro rata among claims of the kind specified in each such particular paragraph, except that in a case that has been converted to this chapter under section 1009, 1112, 1208 or 1307 of this title, a claim allowed under section 503(b) of this title incurred under this chapter after such conversion has priority over a claim allowed under section 503(b) of this title incurred under any other chapter of this title or under this chapter before such conversion and over any expenses of a custodian superseded under section 543 of this title.

(c)   Notwithstanding subsections (a) and (b) of this section, if there is property of the kind specified in section 541(a)(2) of this title, or proceeds of such property, in the estate, such property or proceeds shall be segregated from other property of the estate, and such property or proceeds and other property of the estate shall be distributed as follows:

(1)   Claims allowed under section 503 of this title shall be paid either from property of the kind specified in section 541(a)(2) of this title, or from other property of the estate, as the interest of justice requires.

(2)   Allowed claims, other than claims allowed under section 503 of this title shall be paid in the order specified in subsection (a) of this section, and, with respect to claims of a kind specified in a particular paragraph of section 507(a) of this title or subsection (a) of this section, in the following order and manner:

(A)   First, community claims against the debtor or the debtor's spouse shall be paid from property of the kind specified in section 541(a)(2) of this title, except to the extent that such property is solely liable for debts of the debtor.

(B)   Second, to the extent that community claims against the debtor are not paid under subparagraph (A) of this paragraph, such community claims shall be paid from property of the kind specified in section 541(a)(2) of this title that is solely liable for debts of the debtor.

(C)   Third, to the extent that all claims against the debtor including community claims against the debtor are not paid under subparagraph (A) or (B) of this paragraph such claims shall be paid from property of the estate other than property of the kind specified in section 541(a)(2) of this title.

(D)   Fourth, to the extent that community claims against the debtor or the debtor's spouse are not paid under subparagraph (A), (B), or

(C) of this paragraph, such claims shall be paid from all remaining property of the estate.

Sec. 727. *Discharge*

(a)   The court shall grant the debtor a discharge, unless—

(1)   the debtor is not an individual;

(2)   the debtor, with intent to hinder, delay, or defraud a creditor or an officer of the estate charged with custody of property under this title, has transferred, removed, destroyed, mutilated, or concealed, or has permitted to be transferred, removed, destroyed, mutilated, or concealed—

(A)   property of the debtor, within one year before the date of the filing of the petition; or

(B)   property of the estate after the date of the filing of the petition;

(3)   the debtor has concealed, destroyed, mutilated, falsified, or failed to keep or preserve any recorded information, including books, documents, records, and papers, from which the debtor's financial condition or business transactions might be ascertained, unless such act or failure to act was justified under all of the circumstances of the case;

(4)   the debtor knowingly and fraudulently, in or in connection with the case—

(A)   made a false oath or account;

(B)   presented or used a false claim;

(C)   gave, offered, received, or attempted to obtain money, property, or advantage, or a promise of money, property, or advantage, for acting or forbearing to act; or

(D)   withheld from an offer of the estate entitled to possession under this title, any recorded information, including books, documents, records, and papers, relating to the debtor's property or financial affairs;

(5)   the debtor has failed to explain satisfactorily, before determination of denial of discharge under this paragraph, any loss of assets or deficiency of assets to meet the debtor's liabilities;

(6)   the debtor has refused, in the case—

(A)   to obey any lawful order of the court, other than an order to respond to a material question or to testify;

(B)   on the ground of privilege against self-incrimination, to respond to a material question approved by the court or to testify, after the debtor has been granted immunity with respect to the matter concerning which such privilege was invoked; or

(C)   on a ground other than the properly invoked privilege against self-incrimination, to respond to a material question approved by the court or to testify;

(7)   the debtor has committed any act specified in paragraph (2), (3), (4), (5), or (6) of this subsection, on or within one year before the date of the filing of the petition, or during the case, in connection with another case, under this title or under the Bankruptcy Act, concerning an insider;

(8)   the debtor has been granted a discharge under this section, under section 1141 of this title, or under section 14, 371, or 476 of the Bankruptcy Act, in a case commenced within six years before the date of the filing of the petition;

(9)   the debtor has been granted a discharge under section 1328 of this title, or under section 660 or 661 of the Bankruptcy Act, in a case commenced within six years before the date of the filing of the petition, unless payments under the plan in such case totaled at least—

      (A)   100 percent of the allowed unsecured claims in such case; or

      (B)   (i)   70 percent of such claims; and

          (ii)   the plan was proposed by the debtor in good faith, and was the debtor's best effort; or

(10)   the court approves a written waiver of discharge executed by the debtor after the order for relief under this chapter.

(b)   Except as provided in section 523 of this title, a discharge under subsection (a) of this section discharges the debtor from all debts that arose before the date of the order for relief under this chapter, and any liability on a claim that is determined under section 502 of this title as if such claim had arisen before the commencement of the case, whether or not a proof of claim based on any such debtor or liability is filed under section 501 of this title, and whether or not a claim based on any such debt or liability is allowed under section 502 of this title.

(c) (1)   The trustee, a creditor, or the United States trustee may object to the granting of a discharge under subsection (a) of this section.

    (2)   On request of a party in interest, the court may order the trustee to examine the acts and conduct of the debtor to determine whether a ground exists for denial of discharge.

(d)   On request of the trustee, a creditor, or the United States trustee, and after notice and a hearing, the court shall revoke a discharge granted under subsection (a) of this section if—

    (1)   such discharge was obtained through the fraud of the debtor, and the requesting party did not know of such fraud until after the granting of such discharge;

    (2)   the debtor acquired property that is property of the estate, or became entitled to acquire property that would be property of the estate, and knowingly and fraudulently failed to report the acquisition of or entitlement to such property, or to deliver or surrender such property to the trustee; or

    (3)   the debtor committed an act specified in subsection (a)(6) of this section.

(e)   The trustee, a creditor, or the United States trustee may request a revocation of a discharge—

    (1)   under subsection (d)(1) of this section within one year after such discharge is granted; or

    (2)   under subsection (d)(2) or (d)(3) of this section before the later of—

      (A)   one year after the granting of such discharge; and

      (B)   the date the case is closed.

Sec. 728.   *Special Tax Provisions*

(a)   For the purposes of any State or local law imposing a tax on or measured by income, the taxable period of a debtor that is an individual shall terminate on the date of the order for relief under this chapter, unless the case was converted under section 1112 or 1208 of this title.

(b)   Notwithstanding any State or local tax imposing a tax on or measured by income, the trustee shall make tax returns of income for the estate of an individual debtor in a case under this chapter or for a debtor that is a corporation in a case under this chapter only if such estate or corporation has net taxable income for the entire period after the order for relief under this chapter during which the case is pending. If such entity has such income, or if the debtor is a partnership, then the trustee shall make and file a return of income for each taxable period during which the case was pending after the order for relief under this chapter.

(c)   If there are pending cases under this chapter concerning a partnership and a case under this chapter concerning a partner in such partnership, a governmental unit's claim for any unpaid liability of such partner for a State or local tax on or measured by income, to the extent that such liability arose from the inclusion in such partner's taxable income of earnings of such partnership that were not withdrawn by such partner, is a claim only against such partnership.

(d)   Notwithstanding section 541 of this title, if there are pending a case under this chapter concerning a partnership and a case under this chapter concerning a partner in such partnership, then any State or local tax refund or reduction of tax of such partner that would have otherwise been property of the estate of such partner under section 541 of this title—

(1)   is property of the estate of such partnership to the extent that such tax refund or reduction of tax is fairly apportionable to losses sustained by such partnership and not reimbursed by such partner; and

(2)   is otherwise property of the estate of such partner.

SUBCHAPTER III. STOCKBROKER LIQUIDATION

Sec. 741. Definitions for This Subchapter

In this subchapter—

(1)   "Commission" means Securities and Exchange Commission;

(2)   "customer" includes—

(A)   entity with whom a person deals as principal or agent and that has a claim against such person on account of a security received, acquired, or held by such person in the ordinary course of such person's business as a stockbroker from or for the securities account or accounts of such entity—

(i)   for safekeeping;
(ii)   with a view to sale;
(iii)   to cover a consummated sale;
(iv)   pursuant to a purchase;
(v)   as collateral under a security agreement; or
(vi)   for the purpose of effecting registration of transfer;

and

(B)   entity that has a claim against a person arising out of—

(i)   a sale or conversion of a security received, acquired, or held as specified in subparagraph (A) of this paragraph; or

(ii)   a deposit of cash, a security, or other property with such person for the purpose of purchasing or selling a security;

(3)   "customer name security" means security—

(A)   held for the account of a customer on the date of the filing of the petition by or on behalf of the debtor;

(B)   registered in such customer's name on such date or in the process of being so registered under instructions from the debtor; and

(C)   not in a form transferable by delivery on such date;

(4)   "customer property" means cash, security, or other property, and proceeds of such cash, security, or property, received, acquired, or held by or for the account of the debtor, from or for the securities account of a customer—

(A)   including—

(i)   property that was unlawfully converted from and that is the lawful property of the estate;

(ii)   a security held as property of the debtor to the extent such security is necessary to meet a net equity claim of a customer based on a security of the same class and series of an issuer;

(iii)   resources provided through the use or realization of a customer's debit cash balance or a debit item includible in the Formula for Determination of Reserve Requirement for Brokers and Dealers as promulgated by the Commission under the Securities Exchange Act of 1934; and

(iv)   other property of the debtor that any applicable law, rule, or regulation, requires to be set aside or held for the benefit of a customer, unless including such property as customer property would not significantly increase customer property; but

(B)   not including—

(i)   a customer name security delivered to or reclaimed by a customer under section 751 of this title; or

(ii)   property to the extent that a customer does not have a claim against the debtor based on such property;

(5)   "margin payment" means payment or deposit of cash, a security, or other property, that is commonly known to the securities trade as original margin, initial margin, maintenance margin, or variation margin, or as a mark-to-market payment, or that secures an obligation of a participant in a securities clearing agency;

(6)   "net equity" means, with respect to all accounts of a customer that such customer has in the same capacity—

(A)   (i)   aggregate dollar balance that would remain in such accounts that the liquidation, by sale or purchase, at the time of the filing of the petition, of all securities positions in all such accounts, except any customer name securities of such customer; minus

(ii)   any claim of the debtor against such customer in such capacity that would have been owing immediately after such liquidation; plus

(B)   any payment by such customer to the trustee, within 60 days after notice under section 342 of this title, of any business related claim of the debtor against such customer in such capacity;

(7)   "securities contract" means contract for the purchase, sale, or loan of a security, including an option for the purchase of sale of a security, cer-

tificate of deposit, or group or index of securities (including any interest therein or based on the value thereof), or any option entered into on a national securities exchange relating to foreign currencies, or the guarantee of any settlement of cash or securities by or to a securities clearing agency;

(8)   "settlement payment" means a preliminary settlement payment, a partial settlement payment, an interim settlement payment, a settlement payment on account, a final settlement payment, or any other similar payment commonly used in the securities trade; and

(9)   "SIPC" means Securities Investor Protection Corporation.

Sec. 742. Effect of Section 362 of This Title in This Subchapter

Notwithstanding section 362 of this title, SIPC may file an application for a protection decree under the Securities Investor Protection Act of 1970. The filing of such application stays all proceedings in the case under this title unless and until such application is dismissed. If SIPC completes the liquidation of the debtor, then the court shall dismiss the case.

Sec. 743. Notice

The clerk shall give the notice required by section 342 of this title to SIPC and to the Commission.

Sec. 744. Executory Contracts

Notwithstanding section 365(d)(1) of this title, the trustee shall assume or reject, under section 365 of this title, any executory contract of the debtor for the purchase or sale of a security in the ordinary course of the debtor's business, within a reasonable time after the date of the order for relief, but not to exceed 30 days. If the trustee does not assume such a contract within such time, such contract is rejected.

Sec. 745. Treatment of Accounts

(a)   Accounts held by the debtor for a particular customer in separate capacities shall be treated as accounts of separate customers.

(b)   If a stockbroker or a bank holds a customer net equity claim against the debtor that arose out of a transaction for a customer of such stockbroker or bank, each such customer of such stockbroker or bank shall be treated as a separate customer of the debtor.

(c)   Each trustee's account specified as such on the debtor's books, and supported by a trust deed filed with, and qualified as such by, the Internal Revenue Service, and under the Internal Revenue Code of 1986, shall be treated as a separate customer account for each beneficiary under such trustee account.

Sec. 746. Extent of Customer Claims

(a)   If, after the date of the filing of the petition, an entity enters into a transaction with the debtor, in a manner that would have made such entity a customer had such transaction occurred before the date of the filing of the petition, and such transaction was entered into by such entity in good faith and before the qualification under section 322 of this title of a trustee, such entity shall be deemed a customer, and the date of such transaction shall be deemed to be the date of the filing of the petition for the purpose of determining such entity's net equity.

(b)   An entity does not have a claim as a customer to the extent that such entity transferred to the debtor cash or a security that, by contract, agreement, understanding, or operation of law, is—

(1)   part of the capital of the debtor; or

(2)   subordinated to the claims of any or all creditors.

Sec. 747.   Subordination of Certain Customer Claims

Except as provided in section 510 of this title, unless all other customer net equity claims have been paid in full, the trustee may not pay in full or pay in part, directly or indirectly any net equity claim of a customer that was, on the date the transaction giving rise to such claim occurred—

(1)   an insider;

(2)   a beneficial owner of at least five percent of any class of equity securities of the debtor, other than—

(A)   nonconvertible stock having fixed preferential dividend and liquidation rights; or

(B)   interests of limited partners in a limited partnership;

(3)   a limited partner with participation of at least five percent of the net assets or net profits of the debtor; or

(4)   an entity that, directly or indirectly, through agreement or otherwise, exercised or had the power to exercise control over the management or policies of the debtor.

Sec. 748.   Reduction of Securities to Money

As soon as practicable after the date of the order for relief, the trustee shall reduce to money, consistent with good market practice, all securities held as property of the estate, except for customer name securities delivered or reclaimed under section 751 of this title.

Sec. 749.   Voidable Transfers

(a)   Except as otherwise provided in this section, any transfer of property that, but for such transfer, would have been customer property, may be avoided by the trustee, and such property shall be treated as customer property, if and to the extent that the trustee avoids such transfer under section 544, 545, 547, 548, or 549 of this title. For the purpose of such sections, the property so transferred shall be deemed to have been property of the debtor and, if such transfer was made to a customer or for a customer's benefit such customer shall be deemed, for the purposes of this section, to have been a creditor.

(b)   Notwithstanding sections 544, 545, 547, 548, and 549 of this title, the trustee may not avoid a transfer made before five days after the order for relief if such transfer is approved by the Commission by rule or order, either before or after such transfer, and if such transfer is—

(1)   a transfer of a securities contract entered into or carried by or through the debtor on behalf of a customer, and of any cash, security, or other property margining or securing such securities contract; or

(2)   the liquidation of a securities contract entered into or carried by or through the debtor on behalf of a customer.

Sec. 750.   Distribution of Securities

The trustee may not distribute a security except under section 751 of this title.

Sec. 751.   Customer Name Securities

The trustee shall deliver any customer name security to or on behalf of the customer entitled to such security, unless such customer has a negative net equity. With the approval of the trustee, a customer may reclaim a customer name security after payment to the trustee, within such period as the trustee allows, of any claim of the debtor against such customer to the extent that such customer will not have a negative net equity after such payment.

Sec. 752.   Customer Property

(a)   The trustee shall distribute customer property ratably to customers on the basis and to the extent of such customers' allowed net equity claims and in priority to all other claims, except claims of the kind specified in section 507(a)(1) of this title that are attributable to the administration of such customer property.

(b) (1)   The trustee shall distribute customer property in excess of that distributed under subsection (a) of this section in accordance with section 726 of this title.

(2)   Except as provided in section 510 of this title, if a customer is not paid the full amount of such customer's allowed net equity claim from customer property, the unpaid portion of such claim is a claim entitled to distribution under section 726 of this title.

(c)   Any cash or security remaining after the liquidation of a security interest created under a security agreement made by the debtor, excluding property excluded under section 741(4)(B) of this title, shall be apportioned between the general estate and customer property in the same proportion as the general estate of the debtor and customer property were subjects to such security interest.

SUBCHAPTER IV. COMMODITY BROKER LIQUIDATION

Sec. 761.   Definitions for This Subchapter

In this subchapter—
(1)   "Act" means Commodity Exchange Act;
(2)   "clearing organization" means organization that clears commodity contracts made on, or subject to the rules of, a contract market or board of trade;
(3)   "Commission" means Commodity Futures Trading Commission;
(4)   "commodity contract" means—

(A)   with respect to a futures commission merchant, contract for the purchase or sale of commodity for future delivery on, or subject to the rules of, a contract market or board of trade;

(B)   with respect to a foreign futures commission merchant, foreign future;

(C)   with respect to a leverage transaction merchant, leverage transaction;

(D)   with respect to a clearing organization, contract for the purchase or sale of a commodity for future delivery on, or subject to the rules of, a contract market or board of trade that is cleared by such clearing organization, or commodity option traded on, or subject to the rules of, a contract market or board of trade that is cleared by such clearing organization; or

(E)   with respect to a commodity options dealer, commodity option;

(5)   "commodity option" means agreement or transaction subject to regulation under section 4c(b) of the Act;

(6)   "commodity options dealer" means person that extends credit to, or that accepts cash, a security, or other property from, a customer of such person for the purchase or sale of an interest in a commodity option;

(7)   "contract market" means board of trade designated as a contract market by the Commission under the Act;

(8)   "contract of sale," "commodity," "future delivery," "board of trade," and "futures commission merchant" have the meanings assigned to those terms in the Act;

(9)   "customer" means—

(A)   with respect to a futures commission merchant—

(i)   entity for or with whom such futures commission merchant deals and that holds a claim against such futures commission merchant on account of a commodity contract made, received, required, or held by or through such futures commission merchant in the ordinary course of such futures commission merchant's business as a futures commission merchant from or for the commodity futures account of such entity; or

(ii)   entity that holds a claim against such futures commission merchant's arising out of—

(I)   the making, liquidation, or change in the value of a commodity contract of a kind specified in clause (i) of this subparagraph;

(II)   a deposit or payment of cash, a security, or other property with such futures commission merchant for the purpose of making or margining such a commodity contract; or

(III)   the making or taking of delivery on such a commodity contract;

(B)   with respect to foreign futures commission merchant—

(i)   entity for or with whom such foreign futures commission merchant deals and that holds a claim against such foreign futures commission merchant on account of a commodity contract made, received, acquired, or held by or through such foreign futures commission merchant in the ordinary course of such foreign futures commission merchant's business as a foreign futures commission merchant from or for the foreign futures account of such entity; or

(ii)   entity that holds a claim against such foreign futures commission merchant arising out of—

(I)   the making, liquidation, or change in the value of a commodity contract of a kind specified in clause (i) of this subparagraph;

(II)   a deposit or payment of cash, a security, or other property with the debtor for the purpose of making or margining such a commodity contract; or

(III)   the making or taking of delivery on such a commodity contract;

(C)   with respect to a leverage transaction merchant—

(i)   entity for or with whom such leverage transaction merchant deals and that holds a claim against such leverage transaction merchant on account of a commodity contract engaged in by or with such leverage transaction merchant in the ordinary course of such leverage transaction merchant's business as a leverage transaction merchant from or for the leverage account of such entity; or

(ii)   entity that holds a claim against such leverage transaction merchant arising out of—

(I)   the making, liquidation, or change in value of a commodity contract of a kind specified in clause (i) of this subparagraph;

(II)   a deposit or payment of cash, a security, or other property with such foreign futures commission merchant for the purpose of entering into or margining such a commodity contract; or

(III)   the making or taking of delivery on such a commodity contract;

(D)   with respect to a clearing organization, clearing member of such clearing organization with whom such clearing organization deals and that holds a claim against such clearing organization on account of cash, a security, or other property received by such clearing organization to margin, guarantee, or secure a commodity contract in such clearing member's proprietary account or customers' account; or

(E)   with respect to a commodity options dealer—

(i)   entity for or with whom such commodity options dealer deals and that holds a claim on account of a commodity contract made, received, acquired, or held by or through such commodity options dealer in the ordinary course of such commodity options dealer's business as a commodity options dealer from or for the commodity options account of such entity; or

(ii)   entity that holds a claim against such commodity options dealer arising out of—

(I) the making of, liquidation of, exercise of, or a change in value of, a commodity contract of a kind specified in clause (i) of this subparagraph; or

(II) a deposit or payment of cash, a security, or other property with such commodity options dealer for the purpose of making, exercising, or margining such a commodity contract;

(10) "customer property" means cash, a security, or other property, or proceeds of such cash, security, or property, received, acquired, or held by or for the account of the debtor, from or for the account of a customer—

(A) including—

(i) property received, acquired, or held to margin, guarantee, secure, purchase, or sell a commodity contract;

(ii) profits or contractual or other rights accruing to a customer as a result of a commodity contract;

(iii) an open commodity contract;

(iv) specifically identifiable customer property;

(v) warehouse receipt or other document held by the debtor evidencing ownership of or title to property to be delivered to fulfill a commodity contract from or for the account of a customer;

(vi) cash, a security, or other property received by the debtor as payment for a commodity to be delivered to fulfill a commodity contract from or for the account of a customer;

(vii) a security held as property of the debtor to the extent such security is necessary to meet a net equity claim based on a security of the same class and series of an issuer;

(viii) property that was unlawfully converted from and that is the lawful property of the estate; and

(ix) other property of the debtor that any applicable law, rule, or regulation requires to be set aside or held for the benefit of a customer, unless including such property as customer property would not significantly increase customer property; but

(B) not including property to the extent that a customer does not have a claim against the debtor based on such property;

(11) "foreign future" means contract for the purchase or sale of a commodity for future delivery on, or subject to the rules of, a board of trade outside the United States;

(12) "foreign futures commission merchant" means entity engaged in soliciting or accepting orders for the purchase or sale of a foreign future or that, in connection with such a solicitation or acceptance, accepts cash, a security, or other property, or extends credit to margin, guarantee, or secure any trade or contract that results from such a solicitation or acceptance;

(13) "leverage transaction" means agreement that is subject to regulation under section 19 of the Commodity Exchange Act, and that is commonly known to the commodities trade as a margin account, margin contract, leverage account, or leverage contract;

(14) "leverage transaction merchant" means person in the business of engaging in leverage transactions;

(15) "margin payment" means payment or deposit of cash, a security, or other property, that is commonly known to the commodities trade as original margin, initial margin, maintenance margin, or variation margin, including market-to-market payments, settlement payments, variation payments, daily settlement payments and final settlement payments made as adjustments to settlement prices;

(16) "member property" means customer property received, acquired, or held by or for the account of a debtor that is a clearing organization, from or for the proprietary account of a customer that is a clearing member of the debtor; and

(17) "net equity" means, subject to such rules and regulations as the Commission promulgates under the Act, with respect to the aggregate of all of a customer's accounts that such customer has in the same capacity—

(A) the balance remaining in such customer's account immediately after—

(i) all commodity contracts of such customer have been transferred, liquidated, or become identified for delivery; and

(ii) all obligations of such customer in such capacity to the debtor have been offset; plus

(B) the value, as of the date of return under section 766 of this title, or any specifically identifiable customer property actually returned to such customer before the date specified in subparagraph (A) of this paragraph; plus

(C) the value, as of the date of transfer, of—

(i) any commodity contract to which such customer is entitled that is transferred to another person under section 766 of this title; and

(ii) any cash, security, or other property of such customer transferred to such other person under section 766 of this title to margin or secure such transferred commodity contract.

Sec. 762. *Notice to the Commission and Right to Be Heard*

(a) The clerk shall give the notice required by section 342 of this title to the Commission.

(b) The Commission may raise and may appear and be heard on any issue in a case under this chapter.

Sec. 763. *Treatment of Accounts*

(a) Accounts held by the debtor for a particular customer in separate capacities shall be treated as accounts of separate customers.

(b) A member of a clearing organization shall be deemed to hold such member's proprietary account in a separate capacity from such member's customers' account.

(c) The net equity in a customer's account may not be offset against the net equity in the account of any other customer.

Sec. 764. *Voidable Transfers*

(a) Except as otherwise provided in this section, any transfer by the debtor of property that, but for such transfer, would have been customer property, may be avoided by the trustee, and such property shall be treated as customer property, if and to the extent that the trustee avoids such transfer under section 544, 545, 547, 548, 549, or 724(a) of this title. For the purpose of such sections, the property so transferred shall be deemed to have been property of the debtor, and, if such transfer was made to a customer or for a customer's benefit, such customer shall be deemed, for the purposes of this section, to have been a creditor.

(b)   Notwithstanding sections 544, 545, 547, 548, 549, and 724(a) of this title, the trustee may not avoid a transfer made before five days after the order for relief, if such transfer is approved by the Commission by rule or order, either before or after such transfer, and if such transfer is—

(1)   a transfer of a commodity contract entered into or carried by or through the debtor on behalf of a customer, and of any cash, securities, or other property margining or securing such commodity contract; or

(2)   The liquidation of a commodity contract entered into or carried by or through the debtor on behalf of a customer.

Sec. 765. *Customer Instructions*

(a)   The notice required by section 342 of this title to customers shall instruct each customer—

(1)   to file a proof of such customer's claim promptly, and to specify in such claim any specifically identifiable security, property, or commodity contract; and

(2)   to instruct the trustee of such customer's desired disposition, including transfer under section 766 of this title or liquidation, of any commodity contract specifically identified to such customer.

(b)   The trustee shall comply, to the extent practicable, with any instruction received from a customer regarding such customer's desired disposition of any commodity contract specifically identified to such customer. If the trustee has transferred, under section 766 of this title, such a commodity contract the trustee shall transmit any such instruction to the commodity broker to whom such commodity contract was so transferred.

Sec. 766. *Treatment of Customer Property*

(a)   The trustee shall answer all margin calls with respect to a specifically identifiable commodity contract of a customer until such time as the trustee returns or transfers such commodity contract, but the trustee may not make a margin payment that has the effect of a distribution to such customer of more than that to which such customer is entitled under section (h) or (i) of this section.

(b)   The trustee shall prevent any open commodity contract from remaining open after the last day of trading in such commodity contract, or into the first day on which notice of intent to deliver on such commodity contract may be tendered, whichever occurs first. With respect to any commodity contract that has remained open after the last day of trading in such commodity contract or with respect to which delivery must be made or accepted under the rules of the contract market on which such commodity contract was made, the trustee may operate the business of the debtor for the purpose of—

(1)   accepting or making tender of notice of intent to deliver the physical commodity underlying such commodity contract;

(2)   facilitating delivery of such commodity; or

(3)   disposing of such commodity if a party to such commodity contract defaults.

(c)   The trustee shall return promptly to a customer any specifically identifiable security, property, or commodity contract to which such customer is entitled, or shall transfer, on such customer's behalf, such security, property, or commodity contract to a commodity broker that is not a debtor under this title, subject to such rules or regulations as the Commission may prescribe, to the extent that the value of such security, property, or commodity contract does not exceed the amount to which such customer would be entitled under subsection (h) or (i) of this section if such security, property, or commodity contract were not returned or transferred under this subsection.

(d)   If the value of a specifically identifiable security, property, or commodity contract exceeds the amount to which the customer of the debtor is entitled under subsection (h) or (i) of this section, then such customer to whom such security, property, or commodity contract is specifically identified may deposit cash with the trustee equal to the difference between the value of such security, property, or commodity contract and such amount, and the trustee then shall—

(1)   return promptly such security, property, or commodity contract to such customer; or

(2)   transfer, on such customer's behalf, such security, property, or commodity contract to a commodity broker that is not a debtor under this title, subject to such rules or regulations as the Commission may prescribe.

(e)   Subject to subsection (b) of this section, the trustee shall liquidate any commodity contract that—

(1)   is identified to a particular customer and with respect to which such customer has not timely instructed the trustee as to the desired disposition of such commodity contract;

(2)   cannot be transferred under subsection (c) of this section; or

(3)   cannot be identified to a particular customer.

(f)   As soon as practicable after the commencement of the case, the trustee shall reduce to money, consistent with good market practice, all securities and other property, other than commodity contracts, held as property of the estate, except for specifically identifiable securities or property distributable under subsection (h) or (i) of this section.

(g)   The trustee may not distribute a security or other property except under subsection (h) or (i) of this section.

(h)   Except as provided in subsection (b) of this section, the trustee shall distribute customer property ratably to customers on the basis and to the extent of such customers' allowed net equity claims, and in priority to all other claims, except claims of a kind specified in section 507(a)(1) of this title that are attributable to the administration of customer property. Such distribution shall be in the form of—

(1)   cash;

(2)   the return or transfer, under subsection (c) or (d) of this section, of specifically identifiable customer securities, property, or commodity contracts; or

(3)   payment of margin calls under subsection (a) of this section.

Notwithstanding any other provisions of this subsection, a customer net equity claim based on a proprietary account, as defined by Commission rule, regulation, or order, may not be paid either in whole or in part, directly or indirectly, out of customer property unless all other customer net equity claims have been paid in full.

(i)   if the debtor is a clearing organization, the trustee shall distribute—

(1)   customer property, other than member property, ratably to customers on the basis and to the extent of such customers' allowed net equity claims based on such customers' accounts other than proprietary accounts, and in priority to all other claims, except claims of a kind specified in section 507(a)(1) of this title that are attributable to the administration of such customer property; and

(2)   member property ratably to customers on the basis and to the extent of such customers' allowed net equity claims based on such customers' proprietary accounts, and in priority to all other claims, except claims that are attributable to the administration of member property or customer property.

(j) (1)   The trustee shall distribute customer property in excess of that distributed under subsection (h) or (i) of this section in accordance with section 726 of this title.

(2)   Except as provided in section 510 of this title, if a customer is not paid the full amount of such customer's allowed net equity claim from customer property, the unpaid portion of such claim is a claim entitled to distribution under section 726 of this title.

9
ADJUSTMENT OF DEBTS OF A MUNICIPALITY

SUBCHAPTER I. GENERAL PROVISIONS

Sec. 901.   Applicability of Other Sections of This Title

(a)   Sections 301, 344, 347(b), 349, 350(b), 361, 362, 364(c), 364(d), 364(e), 364(f), 365, 366, 501, 502, 503, 504, 506, 507(a)(1), 509, 510, 524(a)(1), 524(a)(2), 544, 545, 546, 547, 548, 549(a), 549(c), 549(d), 550, 551, 552, 553, 557, 1102, 1103, 1109, 1111(b), 1122, 1123(a)(1), 1123(a)(2), 1123(a)(3), 1123(a)(4), 1123(a)(5), 1123(b), 1124, 1125, 1126(a), 1126(b), 1126(c), 1126(e), 1126(f), 1126(g), 1127(d), 1128, 1129(a)(2), 1129(a)(3), 1129(a)(8), 1129(a)(10), 1129(b)(1), 1129(b)(2)(A), 1129(b)(2)(B), 1142(b), 1143, 1144, and 1145 of this title apply in a case under this chapter.

(b)   A term used in a section of this title made applicable in a case under this chapter by subsection (a) of this section or section 103(e) of this title has the meaning defined for such term for the purpose of such applicable section, unless such term is otherwise defined in section 902 of this title.

(c)   A section made applicable in a case under this chapter by subsection (a) of this section that is operative if the business of the debtor is authorized to be operative in a case under this chapter.

Sec. 902. Definitions for This Chapter

In this chapter—

(1) "property of the estate", when used in a section that is made applicable in a case under this chapter by section 103(e) or 901 of this title, means property of the debtor;

(2) "special revenues" means—

(A) receipts derived from the ownership, operation, or disposition of projects or systems of the debtor that are primarily used or intended to be used primarily to provide transportation, utility, or other services, including the proceeds of borrowings to finance the projects or systems;

(B) special excise taxes imposed on particular activities or transactions;

(C) incremental tax receipts from the benefited area in the case of tax increment financing;

(D) other revenues or receipts derived from particular functions of the debtor, whether or not the debtor has other functions; or

(E) taxes specifically levied to finance one or more projects or systems, excluding receipts from general property, sales, or income taxes (other than tax-increment financing) levied to finance the general purposes of the debtor;

(3) "special tax payer" means record owner or holder of legal or equitable title to real property against which a special assessment or special tax has been levied the proceeds of which are the sole source of payment of an obligation issued by the debtor to defray the cost of an improvement relating to such real property;

(4) "special tax payer affected by the plan" means special tax payer with respect to whose real property the plan proposed to increase the proportion of special assessments or special taxes referred to in paragraph (2) of this section assessed against such real property; and

(5) "trustee", when used in a section that is made applicable in a case under this chapter by section 103(e) or 901 of this title, means debtor, except as provided in section 926 of this title.

Sec. 903. Reservation of State Power to Control Municipalities

This chapter does not limit or impair the power of a State to control, by legislation or otherwise, a municipality of or in such State in the exercise of the political or governmental powers of such municipality, including expenditures for such exercise, but—

(1) a State law prescribing a method of composition of indebtedness of such municipality may not bind any creditor that does not consent to such composition; and

(2) a judgment entered under such a law may not bind a creditor that does not consent to such composition.

Sec. 904. Limitation on Jurisdiction and Powers of Court

Notwithstanding any power of the court, unless the debtor consents or the plan so provides, the court may not, by any stay, order, or decree, in the case or otherwise, interfere with—

(1)   any of the political or governmental powers of the debtor;
(2)   any of the property or revenues of the debtor; or
(3)   the debtor's use or enjoyment of any income-producing property.

SUBCHAPTER II. ADMINISTRATION

Sec. 921.   *Petition and Proceedings Relating to Petition*

(a)   Notwithstanding sections 109(d) and 301 of this title, a case under this chapter concerning an unincorporated tax or special assessment district that does not have such district's own officials is commenced by the filing under section 301 of this title of a petition under this chapter by such district's governing authority or the board or body having authority to levy taxes or assessments to meet the obligations of such district.

(b)   The chief judge of the court of appeals for the circuit embracing the district in which the case is commenced shall designate the bankruptcy judge to conduct the case.

(c)   After any objection to the petition, the court, after notice and a hearing, may dismiss the petition if the debtor did not file the petition in good faith or if the petition does not meet the requirements of this title.

(d)   If the petition is not dismissed under subsection (c) of this section, the court shall order relief under this chapter.

(e)   The court may not, on account of an appeal from an order for relief, delay any proceeding under this chapter in the case in which the appeal is being taken; nor shall any court order a stay of such proceeding pending such appeal. The reversal on appeal of a finding of jurisdiction does not affect the validity of any debt incurred that is authorized by the court under section 364(c) or 364(d) of this title.

Sec. 922.   *Automatic Stay of Enforcement of Claims against the Debtor*

(a)   A petition filed under this chapter operates as a stay, in addition to the stay provided by section 362 of this title, applicable to all entities, of—

(1)   the commencement or continuation, including the issuance or employment of process, of a judicial, administrative, or other action or proceeding against an officer or inhabitant of the debtor that seeks to enforce a claim against the debtor; and

(2)   the enforcement of a lien on or arising out of taxes or assessments owed to the debtor.

(b)   Subsections (c), (d), (e), (f), and (g) of section 362 of this title apply to a stay under subsection (a) of this section the same as such subsections apply to a stay under section 362(a) of this title.

(c)   If the debtor provides, under section 362, 364, or 922 of this title, adequate protection of the interest of the holder of a claim secured by a lien on property of the debtor and if, notwithstanding such protection such creditor has a claim arising from the stay of action against such property under section 362 or 922 of this title or from the granting of a lien under section 364(d) of this title, then such claim shall be allowable as an administrative expense under section 503(b) of this title.

(d)   Notwithstanding section 362 of this title and subsection (a) of this section, a petition filed under this chapter does not operate as a stay of application of pledged special revenues in a manner consistent with section 927 of this title to payment of indebtedness secured by such revenues.

Sec. 923.   Notice

There shall be given notice of the commencement of a case under this chapter, notice of an order for relief under this chapter, and notice of the dismissal of a case under this chapter. Such notice shall also be published at least once a week for three successive weeks in at least one newspaper of general circulation published within the district in which the case is commenced, and in such other newspaper having a general circulation among bond dealers and bondholders as the court designates.

Sec. 924.   List of Creditors

The debtor shall file a list of creditors.

Sec. 925.   Effect of List of Claims

A proof of claim is deemed filed under section 501 of this title for any claim that appears in the list filed under section 924 of this title, except a claim that is listed as disputed, contingent, or unliquidated.

Sec. 926.   Avoiding Powers

(a)   If the debtor refuses to pursue a cause of action under section 544, 545, 547, 548, 549(a), or 550 of this title, then on request of a creditor, the court may appoint a trustee to pursue such cause of action.

(b)   A transfer of property of the debtor to or for the benefit of any holder of a bond or note, on account of such bond or note, may not be avoided under section 547 of this title.

Sec. 927.   Limitation on Recourse

The holder of a claim payable solely from special revenues of the debtor under applicable nonbankruptcy law shall not be treated as having recourse against the debtor on account of such claim pursuant to section 1111(b) of this title.

Sec. 928.   Postpetition Effect of Security Interest

(a)   Notwithstanding section 552(a) of this title and subject to subsection (b) of this section, special revenues acquired by the debtor after the commencement of the case shall remain subject to any lien resulting from any security agreement entered into by the debtor before the commencement of the case.

(b)   Any such lien on special revenues, other than municipal betterment assessments, derived from a project or system shall be subject to the necessary operating expenses of such project or system, as the case may be.

Sec. 929.   Municipal Leases

A lease to a municipality shall not be treated as an executory contract or unexpired lease for the purposes of section 365 or 502(b)(6) of this title solely by reason of its being subject to termination in the event the debtor fails to appropriate rent.

Sec. 930. *Dismissal*

(a)   After notice and a hearing, the court may dismiss a case under this chapter for cause, including—

(1)   want of prosecution;

(2)   unreasonable delay by the debtor that is prejudicial to creditors;

(3)   failure to propose a plan within the time fixed under section 941 of this title;

(4)   if a plan is not accepted within any time fixed by the court;

(5)   denial of confirmation of a plan under section 943(b) of this title and denial of additional time for filing another plan or a modification of a plan; or

(6)   if the court has retained jurisdiction after confirmation of a plan—

(A)   material default by the debtor with respect to a term of such plan; or

(B)   termination of such plan by reason of the occurrence of a condition specified in such plan.

(b)   The court shall dismiss a case under this chapter if confirmation of a plan under this chapter is refused.

SUBCHAPTER III. THE PLAN

Sec. 941. *Filing of Plan*

The debtor shall file a plan for the adjustment of the debtor's debts. If such plan is not filed with the petition, the debtor shall file such a plan at such later time as the court fixes.

Sec. 942. *Modification of Plan*

The debtor may modify the plan at any time before confirmation, but may not modify the plan so that the plan as modified fails to meet the requirements of this chapter. After the debtor files a modification, the plan as modified becomes the plan.

Sec. 943. *Confirmation*

(a)   A special tax payer may object to confirmation of a plan.

(b)   The court shall confirm the plan if—

(1)   the plan complies with the provisions of this title made applicable by sections 103(e) and 901 of this title;

(2)   the plan complies with the provisions of this chapter;

(3)   all amounts to be paid by the debtor or by any person for services or expenses in the case or incident to the plan have been fully disclosed and are reasonable;

(4)   the debtor is not prohibited by law from taking any action necessary to carry out the plan;

(5)   except to the extent that the holder of a particular claim has agreed to a different treatment of such claim, the plan provides that on the effective

date of the plan each holder of a claim of a kind specified in section 507(a)(1) of this title will receive on account of such claim cash equal to the allowed amount of;

(6)   any regulatory or electoral approval necessary under applicable nonbankruptcy law in order to carry out any provision of the plan has been obtained, or such provision is expressly conditioned on such approval; and

(7)   the plan is in the best interests of creditors and is feasible.

Sec. 944   Effect of Confirmation

(a)   The provisions of a confirmed plan bind the debtor and any creditor, whether or not—

(1)   a proof of such creditor's claim is filed or deemed filed under section 501 of this title;

(2)   such claim is allowed under section 502 of this title; or

(3)   such creditor has accepted the plan.

(b)   Except as provided in subsection (c) of this section, the debtor is discharged from all debts as of the time when—

(1)   the plan is confirmed;

(2)   the debtor deposits any consideration to be distributed under the plan with a disbursing agent appointed by the court; and

(3)   the court has determined—

(A)   that any security so deposited will constitute, after distribution, a valid legal obligation of the debtor; and

(B)   that any provision made to pay or secure payment of such obligation is valid.

(c)   The debtor is not discharged under subsection (b) of this section from any debt—

(1)   excepted from discharge by the plan or order confirming the plan; or

(2)   owed to an entity that, before confirmation of the plan, had neither notice nor actual knowledge of the case.

Sec. 945.   Continuing Jurisdiction and Closing of the Case

(a)   The court may retain jurisdiction over the case for such period of time as is necessary for the successful implementation of the plan.

(b)   Except as provided in subsection (a) of this section, the court shall close the case when administration of the case has been completed.

Sec. 946.   Effect of Exchange of Securities before the Date of the Filing of the Petition

The exchange of a new security under the plan for a claim covered by the plan, whether such exchange occurred before or after the date of the filing of the petition, does not limit or impair the effectiveness of the plan or of any provision of this chapter. The amount and number specified in section 1126(c) of this title include the amount and number of claims formerly held by a creditor that has participated in any such exchange.

11
REORGANIZATION

SUBCHAPTER I. OFFICERS AND ADMINISTRATION

Sec. 1101.   Definitions for This Chapter

In this chapter—
  (1)   "debtor in possession" means debtor except when a person that has qualified under section 322 of this title is serving as trustee in the case;
  (2)   "substantial consummation" means—
    (A)   transfer of all or substantially all of the property proposed by the plan to be transferred;
    (B)   assumption by the debtor or by the successor to the debtor under the plan of the business or of the management of all or substantially all of the property dealt with by the plan; and
    (C)   commencement of distribution under the plan.

Sec. 1102.   Creditors' and Equity Security Holders' Committees

(a) (1)   Except as provided in paragraph(s), as soon as practicable after the order for relief under chapter 11 of this title, the United States trustee shall appoint a committee of creditors holding unsecured claims and may appoint additional committees of creditors or of equity security holders as the United States trustee deems appropriate.
  (2)   On request of a party in interest, the court may order the appointment of additional committees of creditors or of equity security holders if necessary to assure adequate representation of creditors or of equity security holders. The United States trustee shall appoint any such committee.
  (3)   On request of a party in interest in a case in which the debtor is a small business and for cause, the court may order that a committee of creditors not be appointed.
(b) (1)   A committee of creditors appointed under subsection (a) of this section shall ordinarily consist of the persons, willing to serve, that hold the seven largest claims against the debtor of the kinds represented on such committee, or of the members of a committee organized by creditors before the commencement of the case under this chapter, if such committee was fairly chosen and is representative of the different kinds of claims to be represented.
  (2)   A committee of equity security holders appointed under subsection (a)(2) of this section shall ordinarily consist of the persons, willing to serve, that hold the seven largest amounts of equity securities of the debtor of the kinds represented on such committee.

Sec. 1103.   Powers and Duties of Committees

(a)   At a scheduled meeting of a committee appointed under section 1102 of this title, at which a majority of the members of such committee are present, and with the court's approval, such committee may select and authorize the employment by such committee of one or more attorneys, accountants, or other agents, to represent or perform services for such committee.

(b)   An attorney or accountant employed to represent a committee appointed under section 1102 of this title may not, while employed by such committee, represent any other entity having an adverse interest in connection with the case. Representation of one or more creditors of the same class as represented by the committee shall not per se constitute the representation of an adverse interest.

(c)   A committee appointed under section 1102 of this title may—

(1)   consult with the trustee or debtor in possession concerning the administration of the case;

(2)   investigate the acts, conduct, assets, liabilities, and financial condition of the debtor, the operation of the debtor's business and the desirability of the continuance of such business, and any other matter relevant to the case or to the formulation of a plan;

(3)   participate in the formulation of a plan, advise those represented by such committee of such committee's determinations as to any plan formulated, and collect and file with the court acceptances or rejections of a plan;

(4)   request the appointment of a trustee or examiner under section 1104 of this title; and

(5)   perform such other services as are in the interest of those represented.

(d)   As soon as practicable after the appointment of a committee under section 1102 of this title, the trustee shall meet with such committee to transact such business as may be necessary and proper.

Sec. 1104.   Appointment of Trustee or Examiner

(a)   At any time after the commencement of the case but before confirmation of a plan, on request of a party in interest or the United States trustee, and after notice and a hearing, the court shall order the appointment of a trustee—

(1)   for cause, including fraud, dishonesty, incompetence, or gross mismanagement of the affairs of the debtor by current management, either before or after the commencement of the case, or similar cause, but not including the number of holders of securities of the debtor or the amount of assets or liabilities of the debtor; or

(2)   if such appointment is in the interest of creditors, any equity security holders, and other interests of the estate, without regard to the number of holders of securities of the debtor or the amount of assets or liabilities of the debtor.

(b)   Except as provided in section 1163 of this title, on the request of a party in interest made not later than 30 days after the court orders the appointment of a trustee under subsection (a), the United States trustee shall convene a meeting of creditors for the purpose of electing one disinterested person to serve as trustee in the case. The election of a trustee shall be conducted in the manner provided in subsections (a), (b), and (c) of section 702 of this title.

(c)   If the court does not order the appointment of a trustee under this section, then at any time before the confirmation of a plan, on request of a party in interest or the United States trustee, and after notice and a hearing, the court shall order the appointment of an examiner to conduct such an investigation of the debtor as is appropriate, including an investigation of any allegations of fraud, dishonesty, incompetence, misconduct, mismanagement, or irregularity in the management of the affairs of the debtor of or by current or former management of the debtor, if—

(1)   such appointment is in the interests of creditors, any equity security holders, and other interests of the estate; or

(2)   the debtor's fixed, liquidated, unsecured debts, other than debts for goods, services, or taxes, or owing to an insider, exceed $5,000,000.

(d)   If the court orders the appointment of a trustee or examiner, if a trustee or an examiner dies or resigns during the case or is removed under section 324 of this title, or if a trustee fails to qualify under section 322 of this title, then the United States trustee, after consultation with parties in interest shall appoint, subject to the court's approval, one disinterested person other than the United States trustee to serve as trustee or examiner, as the case may be, in the case.

Sec. 1105.   *Termination of Trustee's Appointment*

At any time before confirmation of a plan, on request of a party in interest or the United States trustee, and after notice and a hearing, the court may terminate the trustee's appointment and restore the debtor to possession and management of the property of the estate and of the operation of the debtor's business.

Sec. 1106.   *Duties of Trustee and Examiner*

(a)   A trustee shall—

(1)   perform the duties of a trustee specified in sections 704(2), 704(5), 704(7), 704(8), and 704(9) of this title;

(2)   if the debtor has not done so, file the list, schedule, and statement required under section 521(1) of this title;

(3)   except to the extent that the court orders otherwise, investigate the acts, conduct, assets, liabilities, and financial condition of the debtor, the operation of the debtor's business and the desirability of the continuance of such business, and any other matter relevant to the case or to the formulation of a plan;

(4)   as soon as practicable—

(A)   file a statement of any investigation conducted under paragraph (3) of this subsection, including any fact ascertained pertaining to fraud, dishonesty, incompetence, misconduct, mismanagement, or irregularity in the management of the affairs of the debtor, or to a cause of action available to the estate; and

(B)   transmit a copy or a summary of any such statement to any creditors' committee or equity security holders' committee, to any indenture trustee, and to such other entity as the court designates;

(5)   as soon as practicable, file plan under section 1121 of this title, file a report of why the trustee will not file plan, or recommend conversion of the case to a case under chapter 7, 12 or 13 of this title or dismissal of the case;

(6)   for any year for which the debtor has not filed a tax return required by law, furnish, without personal liability, such information as may be

required by the governmental unit with which such tax return was to be filed, in light of the condition of the debtor's books and records and the availability of such information; and

(7)   after confirmation of a plan, file such reports as are necessary or as the court orders.

(b)   An examiner appointed under section 1104(d) of this title shall perform the duties specified in paragraphs (3) and (4) of subsection (a) of this section, and, except to the extent that the court orders otherwise, any other duties of the trustee that the court orders the debtor in possession not to perform.

Sec. 1107.   Rights, Powers, and Duties of Debtor in Possession

(a)   Subject to any limitations on a trustee serving in a case under this chapter, and to such limitations or conditions as the court prescribes, a debtor in possession shall have all the rights, other than the right to compensation under section 330 of this title, and powers, and shall perform all the functions and duties, except the duties specified in sections 1106(a)(2), (3), and (4) of this title, of a trustee serving in a case under this chapter.

(b)   Notwithstanding section 327(a) of this title, a person is not disqualified for employment under section 327 of this title by a debtor in possession solely because of such person's employment by or representation of the debtor before the commencement of the case.

Sec. 1108.   Authorization to Operate Business

Unless the court, on request of a party in interest and after notice and hearing, orders otherwise, the trustee may operate the debtor's business.

Sec. 1109.   Right to Be Heard

(a)   The Securities and Exchange Commission may raise and may appear and be heard on any issue in a case under this chapter, but the Securities and Exchange Commission may not appeal from any judgment, order, or decree entered in the case.

(b)   A party in interest, including the debtor, the trustee, a creditors' committee, an equity security holders' committee, a creditor, an equity security holder, or any indenture trustee, may raise and may appear and be heard on any issue in a case under this chapter.

Sec. 1110.   Aircraft Equipment and Vessels

(a) (1)   The right of a secured party with a security interest in equipment described in paragraph (2) or of a lessor or conditional vendor of such equipment to take possession of such equipment in compliance with a security agreement, lease, or conditional sale contract is not affected by section 362, 363, or 1129 or by any power of the court to enjoin the taking of possession unless—

(A)   before the date is 60 days after the date of the order for relief under this chapter, the trustee, subject to the court's approval, agrees to perform all obligations of the debtor that become due on or after the date of the order under such security agreement, lease, or conditional sale contract; and

(B)   any default, other than a default of a kind specified in section 365(b)(2), under such security agreement, lease, or conditional sale contract—

(i)   that occurs before the date of the order is cured before the expiration of such 60-day period; and

(ii)   that occurs after the date of the order is cured before the later of—

(I)   the date that is 30 days after the date of the default; or

(II)   the expiration of such 60-day period.

(2)   Equipment is described in this paragraph if it is—

(A)   an aircraft, aircraft engine, propeller, appliance, or spare part (as defined in section 40102 of title 49) that is subject to a security interest granted by, leased to, or conditionally sold to a debtor that is a citizen of the United States (as defined in 40102 of title 49) holding an air carrier operating certificate issued by the Secretary of Transportation pursuant to chapter 447 of title 49 for aircraft capable of carrying 10 or more individuals or 6,000 pounds or more of cargo; or

(B)   a documented vessel (as defined in section 30101(1) of title 46) that is subject to a security interest granted by, leased to, or conditionally sold to a debtor that is a water carrier that holds a certificate of public convenience and necessity or permit issued by the Interstate Commerce Commission.

(3)   Paragraph (1) applies to a secured party, lessor, or conditional vendor acting in its own behalf or acting as trustee or otherwise in behalf of another party.

(b)   The trustee and the secured party, lessor, or conditional vendor whose right to take possession is protected under subsection (a) may agree, subject to the court's approval, to extend the 60-day period specified in subsection (a)(1).

(c)   With respect to equipment first placed in service on or prior to the date of enactment of this subsection, for purposes of this section—

(1)   the term "lease" includes any written agreement with respect to which lessor and the debtor, as lessee have expressed in the agreement or in a substantially contemporaneous writing that the agreement is to be treated as a lease for Federal income tax purposes; and

(2)   the term "security interest" means a purchase-money equipment security interest.

Sec. 1111.   Claims and Interests

(a)   A proof of claim or interest is deemed filed under section 501 of this title for any claim or interest that appears in the schedules filed under section 52(1) or 1106(a)(2) of this title, except a claim or interest that is scheduled as disputed, contingent, or unliquidated.

(b) (1)   (A)   A claim secured by a lien on property of the estate shall be allowed or disallowed under section 502 of this title the same as if the holder of such claim had recourse against the debtor on account of such claim, whether or not such holder has such recourse, unless—

(i)   The class of which such claim is a part elects, by at least two-thirds in amount and more than half in number of allowed claims of such class, application of paragraph (2) of this subsection; or

(ii)   such holder does not have such recourse and such property is sold under section 363 of this title or is to be sold under the plan.

(B)   A class of claims may not elect application of paragraph (2) of this subsection if—

(i)   the interest on account of such claims of the holders of such claims in such property is of inconsequential value; or

(ii)   the holder of a claim of such class has recourse against the debtor on account of such claim and such property is sold under section 363 of this title or is to be sold under the plan.

(2)   If such an election is made, then notwithstanding section 506(a) of this title, such claim is a secured claim to the extent that such claim is allowed.

Sec. 1112.   *Conversion or Dismissal*

(a)   The debtor may convert a case under this chapter to a case under chapter 7 of this title unless—

(1)   the debtor is not a debtor in possession;

(2)   the case originally was commenced as an involuntary case under this chapter; or

(3)   the case was converted to a case under this chapter other than on the debtor's request.

(b)   Except as provided in subsection (c) of this section, on request of a party in interest or the United States trustee or bankruptcy administrator, and after notice and a hearing, the court may convert a case under this chapter to a case under chapter 7 of this title or may dismiss a case under this chapter, whichever is in the best interest of creditors and the estate, for cause, including—

(1)   continuing loss to or diminution of the estate and absence of a reasonable likelihood of rehabilitation;

(2)   inability to effectuate a plan;

(3)   unreasonable delay by the debtor that is prejudicial to creditors;

(4)   failure to propose a plan under section 1121 of this title within any time fixed by the court;

(5)   denial of confirmation of every proposed plan and denial of a request made for additional time for filing another plan or a modification of a plan;

(6)   revocation of an order of confirmation under section 1144 of this title, and denial of confirmation of another plan or a modified plan under section 1129 of this title;

(7)   inability to effectuate substantial consummation of a confirmed plan;

(8)   material default by the debtor with respect to a confirmed plan;

(9)   termination of a plan by reason of the occurrence of a condition specified in the plan; or

(10) nonpayment of any fees or charges required under chapter 123 of title 28.

(c)   The court may not convert a case under this chapter to a case under chapter 7 of this title if the debtor is a farmer or, a corporation that is not a moneyed, business, or commercial corporation, unless the debtor requests such conversion.

(d)   The court may convert a case under this chapter to a case under chapter 12 or 13 of this title only if—

(1)   the debtor requests such conversion;

(2)   the debtor has not been discharged under section 1141(d) of this title; and

(3)   if the debtor requests conversion to chapter 12 of this title, such conversion is equitable.

(e)   Except as provided in subsections (c) and (f), the court, on request of the United States trustee, may convert a case under this chapter to a case under chapter 7 of this title or may dismiss a case under this chapter, whichever is in the best interest of creditors and the estate if the debtor in a voluntary case fails to file, within fifteen days after the filing of the petition commencing such case or such additional time as the court may allow, the information required by paragraph (1) of section 521, including a list containing the names and addresses of the holders of the twenty largest unsecured claims (or of all unsecured claims if there are fewer than twenty unsecured claims), and the approximate dollar amounts of each of such claims.

(f)   Notwithstanding any other provision of this section, a case may not be converted to a case under another chapter of this title unless the debtor may be a debtor under such chapter.

Sec. 1113. *Rejection of Collective Bargaining Agreements*

(a)   The debtor in possession, or the trustee if one has been appointed under the provisions of this chapter, other than a trustee in a case covered by subchapter IV of this chapter and by title I of the Railway Labor Act, may assume or reject a collective bargaining agreement only in accordance with the provisions of this section.

(b) (1)   Subsequent to filing a petition and prior to filing an application seeking rejection of a collective bargaining agreement, the debtor in possession or trustee (hereinafter in this section "trustee" shall include a debtor in possession), shall—

(A) make a proposal to the authorized representative of the employees covered by such agreement, based on the most complete and reliable information available at the time of such proposal, which provides for those necessary modifications in the employees' benefits and protections that are necessary to permit the reorganization of the debtor and assures that all creditors, the debtor and all of the affected parties are treated fairly and equitably; and

(B) provide, subject to subsection (d)(3), the representative of the employees with such relevant information as is necessary to evaluate the proposal.

(2)   During the period beginning on the date of the making of a proposal provided for in paragraph (1) and ending on the date of the hearing provided for in subsection (d)(1), the trustee shall meet, at reasonable times, with the authorized representative to confer in good faith in attempting to reach mutually satisfactory modifications of such agreement.

(c)   The court shall approve an application for rejection of collective bargaining agreement only if the court finds that—

(1)   the trustee has, prior to the hearing, made a proposal that fulfills the requirements of subsection (b)(1);

(2)   the authorized representative of the employees has refused to accept such proposal without good cause; and

(3)   the balance of the equities clearly favors rejection of such agreement.

(d) (1)   Upon the filing of an application for rejection the court shall schedule a hearing to be held not later than fourteen days after the date of the filing of such application. All interested parties may appear and be heard at such hearing. Adequate notice shall be provided to such parties at least ten days before the date of such hearing. The court may extend the time for the commencement of such hearing for a period not exceeding seven days where the circumstances of the case, and the interests of justice require such extension, or for additional periods of time to which the trustee and representative agree.

(2)   The court shall rule on such application for rejection within thirty days after the date of the commencement of the hearing. In the interests of justice, the court may extend such time for ruling for such additional period as the trustee and the employees' representative may agree to. If the court does not rule on such application within thirty days after the date of the commencement of the hearing, or within such additional time as the trustee and the employees' representative may agree to, the trustee may terminate or alter any provisions of the collective bargaining agreement pending the ruling of the court on such application.

(3)   The court may enter such protective orders, consistent with the need of the authorized representative of the employee to evaluate the trustee's proposal and the application for rejection, as may be necessary to prevent disclosure of information provided to such representative where such disclosure could compromise the position of the debtor with respect to its competitors in the industry in which it is engaged.

(e)   If during a period when the collective bargaining agreement continues in effect, and if essential to the continuation of the debtor's business, or in order to avoid irreparable damage to the estate, the court, after notice and a hearing, may authorize the trustee to implement interim changes in the terms, conditions, wages, benefits, or work rules provided by a collective bargaining agreement. Any hearing under this paragraph shall be scheduled in accordance with the needs of the trustee. The implementation of such interim changes shall not render the application for rejection moot.

(f)   No provision of this title shall be construed to permit a trustee to unilaterally terminate or alter any provisions of a collective bargaining agreement prior to compliance with the provisions of this section.

Sec. 1114. *Payment of Insurance Benefits to Retired Employees*

(a)   For purposes of this section, the term "retiree benefits" means payments to any entity or person for the purpose of providing or reimbursing payments for retired employees and their spouses and dependents, for medical, surgical, or hospital care benefits, or benefits in the event of sickness, accident, disability, or death under any plan, fund, or program (through the purchase of insurance or otherwise) maintained or established in whole or in part by the debtor prior to filing a petition commencing a case under this title.

(b) (1)   For purposes of this section, the term "authorized representative" means the authorized representative designated pursuant to subsection (c) for persons receiving any retiree benefits covered by a collective bargaining agreement or subsection (d) in the case of persons receiving retiree benefits not covered by such an agreement.

(2)   Committees of retired employees appointed by the court pursuant to this section shall have the same rights, powers, and duties as committees appointed under sections 1102 and 1103 of this title for the purpose of carrying out the purposes of sections 1114 and 1129(a)(13) and, as permitted by the court, shall have the power to enforce the rights of persons under this title as they relate to retiree benefits.

(c) (1)   A labor organization shall be, for purposes of this section, the authorized representative of those persons receiving any retiree benefits covered by any collective bargaining agreement to which that labor organization is signatory, unless

(A)   such labor organization elects not to serve as the authorized representative of such persons, or

(B)   the court, upon a motion by any party in interest, after notice and hearing, determines that different representation of such persons is appropriate.

(2)   In cases where the labor organization referred to in paragraph (1) elects not to serve as the authorized representative of those persons receiving any retiree benefits covered by any collective bargaining agreement to which that labor organization is signatory, or in cases where the court, pursuant to paragraph (1) finds different representation of such persons appropriate, the court, upon a motion by any party in interest, and after notice and a hearing, shall appoint a committee of retired employees if the debtor seeks to modify or not pay the retiree benefits or if the court otherwise determines that it is appropriate, from among such persons, to serve as the authorized representative of such persons under this section.

(d)   The court, upon a motion by any party in interest, and after notice and a hearing, shall appoint a committee of retired employees if the debtor seeks to modify or not pay the retiree benefits or if the court otherwise determines that it is appropriate, to serve as the authorized representative, under this section, of those persons receiving any retiree benefits not covered by a collective bargaining agreement.

(e) (1)   Notwithstanding any other provision of this title, the debtor in possession, or the trustee if one has been appointed under the provisions of this chapter (hereinafter in this section "trustee" shall include a debtor in possession), shall timely pay and shall not modify any retiree benefits, except that—

(A)   the court, on motion of the trustee or authorized representative, and after notice and a hearing, may order modification of such payments, pursuant to the provisions of subsections (g) and (h) of this section; or

(B)   the trustee and the authorized representative of the recipients of those benefits may agree to modification of such payments; after which such benefits as modified shall continue to be paid by the trustee.

(2)   Any payment for retiree benefits required to be made before a plan confirmed under section 1129 of this title is effective has the status of an allowed administrative expense as provided in section 503 of this title.

(f) (1)   Subsequent to filing a petition and prior to filing an application seeking modification of the retiree benefits, the trustee shall—

(A)   make a proposal to the authorized representative of the retirees, based on the most complete and reliable information available at the time of such proposal, which provides for those necessary modifications in the retiree benefits that are necessary to permit the reorganization of the debtor and assures that all creditors, the debtor and all of the affected parties are treated fairly and equitably; and

(B)   provide, subject to subsection (k)(3), the representative of the retirees with such relevant information as is necessary to evaluate the proposal.

(2)   During the period beginning on the date of the making of a proposal provided for in paragraph (1), and ending on the date of the hearing provided for in subsection (k)(1), the trustee shall meet, at reasonable times, with the authorized representative to confer in good faith in attempting to reach mutually satisfactory modifications of such retiree benefits.

(g)   The court shall enter an order providing for modification in the payment of retiree benefits if the court finds that—

(1)   the trustee has, prior to the hearing, made a proposal that fulfills the requirements of subsection (f);

(2)   the authorized representative of the retirees has refused to accept such proposal without good cause; and

(3)   such modification is necessary to permit the reorganization of the debtor and assures that all creditors, the debtor, and all of the affected parties are treated fairly and equitably, and is clearly favored by the balance of the equities; except that in no case shall the court enter an order providing for such modification which provides for a modification to a level lower than that proposed by the trustee in the proposal found by the court to have complied with the requirements of this subsection and subsection (f): *Provided, however,* That at any time after an order is entered providing for modification in the payment of retiree benefits, or at any time after an agreement modifying such benefits is made between the trustee and the authorized representative of the recipients of such benefits, the authorized representative may apply to the court for an order increasing those benefits which order shall be granted if the increase in retiree benefits sought is consistent with the standard set forth in paragraph (3); and: *Provided further,* That neither the trustee nor the authorized representative is precluded from making more than one motion for a modification order governed by this subsection.

(h) (1)   Prior to a court issuing a final order under subsection (g) of this section, if essential to the continuation of the debtor's business, or in order to avoid irreparable damage to the estate, the court, after notice and a hearing, may authorize the trustee to implement interim modifications in retiree benefits.

(2)   Any hearing under this subsection shall be scheduled in accordance with the needs of the trustee.

(3)   The implementation of such interim changes does not render the motion for modification moot.

(i)   No retiree benefits paid between the filing of the petition and the time a plan confirmed under section 1129 of this title becomes effective shall be deducted or offset from the amounts allowed as claims for any benefits which remain unpaid, or from the amounts to be paid under the plan with respect to such claims for unpaid benefits, whether such claims for unpaid benefits are based upon or arise from a right to future unpaid benefits or from any benefits not paid as a result of modifications allowed pursuant to this section.

(j)   No claim for retiree benefits shall be limited by section 502(b)(7) of this title.

(k) (1)   Upon the filing of an application for modifying retiree benefits, the court shall schedule a hearing to be held not later than fourteen days after the date of the filing of such application. All interested parties may appear and be heard at such hearing. Adequate notice shall be provided to such parties at least ten days before the date of such hearing. The court may extend the time for the commencement of such hearing for a period not exceeding seven days where the circumstances of the case, and the interests of justice require such extension, or for additional periods of time to which the trustee and the authorized representative agree.

(2)   The court shall rule on such application for modification within 90 days after the date of the commencement of the hearing. In the interests of justice, the court may extend such time for ruling for such additional period as the trustee and the authorized representative may agree to. If the court does not rule on such application within 90 days after the date of the commencement of the hearing, or within such additional time as the trustee and the authorized representative may agree to, the trustee may implement the proposed modifications pending the ruling of the court on such application.

(3)   The court may enter such protective orders, consistent with the need of the authorized representative of the retirees to evaluate the trustee's proposal and the application for modification, as may be necessary to prevent disclosure of information provided to such representative where such disclosure could compromise the position of the debtor with respect to its competitors in the industry in which it is engaged.

(l)   This section shall not apply to any retiree, or the spouse or dependents of such retiree, if such retiree's gross income for the 12 months preceding the filing of the bankruptcy petition equals or exceeds $250,000, unless such retiree can demonstrate to the satisfaction of the court that he is unable to obtain health, medical, life, and disability coverage for himself, his spouse, and his dependents who would otherwise be covered by the employer's insurance plan, comparable to the coverage provided by the employer on the day before the filing of a petition under this title.

SUBCHAPTER II. THE PLAN

Sec. 1121.   Who May File a Plan

(a)   The debtor may file a plan with a petition commencing a voluntary case, or at any time in a voluntary case or an involuntary case.

(b)   Except as otherwise provided in this section, only the debtor may file a plan until after 120 days after the date of the order for relief under this chapter.

(c)   Any party in interest, including the debtor, the trustee, a creditors' committee, an equity security holders' committee, a creditor, an equity security holder, or any indenture trustee, may file a plan if and only if—

(1)   a trustee has been appointed under this chapter;

(2)   the debtor has not filed a plan before 120 days after the date of the order for relief under this chapter; or

(3)   the debtor has not filed a plan that has been accepted, before 180 days after the date of the order for relief under this chapter, by each class of claims or interests that is impaired under the plan.

(d)   On request of a party in interest made within the respective periods specified in subsections (b) and (c) of this section and after notice and a hearing, the court may for cause reduce or increase the 120-day period or the 180-day period referred to in this section.

(e)   In a case in which the debtor is a small business and elects to be considered a small business—

(1)   only the debtor may file a plan until after 100 days after the date of the order for relief under this chapter;

(2)   all plans shall be filed within 160 days after the date of the order for relief; and

(3)   on request of a party in interest made within the respective periods specified in paragraphs (1) and (2) and after notice and a hearing, the court may—

(A)   reduce the 100-day period or the 160-day period specified in subparagraph (1) or (2) for cause, and

(B)   increase the 100-day period specified in paragraph (1) if the debtor shows that the need for an increase is caused by circumstances for which the debtor should not be held accountable.

Sec. 1122.   Classification of Claims or Interests

(a)   Except as provided in subsection (b) of this section, a plan may place a claim or an interest in a particular class only if such claim or interest is substantially similar to the other claims or interests of such class.

(b)   A plan may designate a separate class of claims consisting only of every unsecured claim that is less than or reduced to an amount that the court approves as reasonable and necessary for administrative convenience.

Sec. 1123.   Contents of Plan

(a)   Notwithstanding any otherwise applicable nonbankruptcy law, a plan shall—

(1)   designate, subject to section 1122 of this title, classes of claims, other than claims of a kind specified in section 507(a)(1), 507(a)(2), or 507(a)(8) of this title, and classes of interests;

(2)   specify any class of claims or interests that is not impaired under the plan;

(3)   specify the treatment of any class of claims or interests that is impaired under the plan;

(4)   provide the same treatment for each claim or interest of a particular class, unless the holder of a particular claim or interest agrees to a less favorable treatment of such particular claim or interest;

(5)   provide adequate means for the plan's implementation, such as—

(A)   retention by the debtor of all or any part of the property of the estate;

(B)   transfer of all or any part of the property of the estate to one or more entities; whether organized before or after the confirmation of such plan;

(C)   merger or consolidation of the debtor with one or more persons;

(D)   sale of all or any part of the property of the estate, either subject to or free of any lien, or the distribution of all or any part of the property of the estate among those having an interest in such property of the estate;

(E)   satisfaction or modification of any lien;

(F)   cancellation or modification of any indenture or similar instrument;

(G)   curing or waiving of any default;

(H)   extension of a maturity date or a change in an interest rate or other term of outstanding securities;

(I)   amendment of the debtor's charter; or

(J)   issuance of securities of the debtor, or of any entity referred to in subparagraph (B) or (C) of this paragraph, for cash, for property, for existing securities, or in exchange for claims or interests or for any other appropriate purpose;

(6)   provide for the inclusion in the charter of the debtor, if the debtor is a corporation, or of any corporation referred to in paragraph (5)(B) or (5)(C) of this subsection, of a provision prohibiting the issuance of nonvoting equity securities, and providing, as to the several classes of securities possessing voting power, an appropriate distribution of such power among such classes, including, in the case of any class of equity securities having a preference over another class of equity securities with respect to dividends, adequate provisions for the election of directors representing such preferred class in the event of default in the payment of such dividends; and

(7)   contain only provisions that are consistent with the interests of creditors and equity security holders and with public policy with respect to the manner of selection of any officer, director, or trustee under the plan and any successor to such officer, director, or trustee.

(b)   Subject to subsection (a) of this section, a plan may—

(1)   impair or leave unimpaired any class of claims, secured or unsecured, or of interests;

(2)   subject to section 365 of this title, provide for the assumption, rejection, or assignment of any executory contract or unexpired lease of the debtor not previously rejected under such section;

(3)   provide for—

(A)   the settlement or adjustment of any claim or interest belonging to the debtor or to the estate; or

(B)   the retention and enforcement by the debtor, by the trustee, or by a representative of the estate appointed for such purpose, of any such claim or interest;

(4)   provide for the sale of all or substantially all of the property of the estate, and the distribution of the proceeds of such sale among holders of claims or interests;

(5)   modify the rights of holders of secured claims, other than a claim secured only by a security interest in real property that is the debtor's principal residence, or of holders of unsecured claims, or leave unaffected the rights of holders of any class of claims; and

(6)   include any other appropriate provision not inconsistent with the applicable provisions of this title.

(c)   In a case concerning an individual, a plan proposed by an entity other than a debtor may not provide for the use, sale, or lease of property exempted under section 522 of this title, unless the debtor consents to such use, sale, or lease.

(d)   Notwithstanding subsection (a) of this section and sections 506(b), 1129(a)(7), and 1129(b) of this title, if it is proposed in a plan to cure a default the amount necessary to cure the default shall be determined in accordance with the underlying agreement and applicable nonbankruptcy law.

Sec. 1124.   *Impairment of Claims or Interests*

Except as provided in section 1123(a)(4) of this title, a class of claims or interests is impaired under a plan unless, with respect to each claim or interest of such class, the plan—

(1)   leaves unaltered the legal, equitable, and contractual rights to which such claim or interest entitles the holder of such claim or interest; or

(2)   notwithstanding any contractual provision or applicable law that entitles the holder of such claim or interest to demand or receive accelerated payment of such claim or interest after the occurrence of a default—

(A)   cures any such default that occurred before or after the commencement of the case under this title, other than a default of a kind specified in section 365(b)(2) of this title;

(B)   reinstates the maturity of such claim or interest as such maturity existed before such default;

(C)   compensates the holder of such claim or interest for any damages incurred as a result of any reasonable reliance by such holder on such contractual provision or such applicable law; and

(D)   does not otherwise alter the legal, equitable, or contractual rights to which such claim or interest entitles the holder of such claim or interest.

Sec. 1125.   *Postpetition Disclosure and Solicitation*

(a)   In this section—

(1)   "adequate information" means information of a kind, and in sufficient detail, as far as is reasonably practicable in light of the nature and history of the debtor and the condition of the debtor's books and records, that would enable a hypothetical reasonable investor typical of holders of claims or interests of the relevant class to make an informed judgment about the plan, but adequate information need not include such information about any other possible or proposed plan; and

(2)   "investor typical of holders of claims or interests of the relevant class" means investor having—

    (A)   a claim or interest of the relevant class;

    (B)   such a relationship with the debtor as the holders of other claims or interests of such class generally have; and

    (C)   such ability to obtain such information from sources other than the disclosure required by this section as holders of claims or interests in such class generally have.

(b)   An acceptance or rejection of a plan may not be solicited after the commencement of the case under this title from a holder of a claim or interest with respect to such claim or interest unless, at the time of or before such solicitation, there is transmitted to such holder the plan or a summary of the plan, and a written disclosure statement approved, after notice and a hearing, by the court as containing adequate information. The court may approve a disclosure statement without a valuation of the debtor or an appraisal of the debtor's assets.

(c)   The same disclosure statement shall be transmitted to each holder of a claim or interest of a particular class, but there may be transmitted different disclosure statements, differing in amount, detail, or kind of information, as between classes.

(d)   Whether a disclosure statement required under subsection (b) of this section contains adequate information is not governed by any otherwise applicable nonbankruptcy law, rule, or regulation, but an agency or official whose duty is to administer or enforce such a law, rule, or regulation may be heard on the issue of whether a disclosure statement contains adequate information. Such an agency or official may not appeal from, or otherwise seek review of, an order approving a disclosure statement.

(e)   A person that solicits acceptance or rejection of a plan, in good faith and in compliance with the applicable provisions of this title, or that participates, in good faith and in compliance with the applicable provisions of this title, in the offer, issuance, sale, or purchase of a security, offered or sold under the plan, of the debtor, of an affiliate participating in a joint plan with the debtor, or of a newly organized successor to the debtor, or of a newly organized successor to the debtor under the plan, is not liable, on account of such solicitation or participation, for violation of any applicable law, rule, or regulation governing solicitation of acceptance or rejection of a plan or the offer, issuance, sale, or purchase of securities.

(f)   Notwithstanding subsection (b), in a case in which the debtor has elected under section 1121(e) to be considered a small business—

    (1)   the court may conditionally approve a disclosure statement subject to final approval after notice and a hearing;

    (2)   acceptances and rejections of a plan may be solicited based on a conditionally approved disclosure statement as long as the debtor provides adequate information to each holder of a claim or interest that is solicited, but a conditionally approved disclosure statement shall be mailed at least 10 days prior to the date of the hearing on confirmation of the plan; and

    (3)   a hearing on the disclosure statement may be combined with a hearing on confirmation of a plan.

Sec. 1126.　Acceptance of Plan

(a)　The holder of a claim or interest allowed under section 502 of this title may accept or reject a plan. If the United States is a creditor or equity security holder, the Secretary of the Treasury may accept or reject the plan on behalf of the United States.

(b)　For the purposes of subsections (c) and (d) of this section, a holder of a claim or interest that has accepted or rejected the plan before the commencement of the case under this title is deemed to have accepted or rejected such plan, as the case may be, if—

　　(1)　the solicitation of such acceptance or rejection was in compliance with any applicable nonbankruptcy law, rule, or regulation governing the adequacy of disclosure in connection with such solicitation; or

　　(2)　if there is not any such law, rule, or regulation, such acceptance or rejection was solicited after disclosure to such holder of adequate information, as defined in section 1125(a) of this title.

(c)　A class of claims has accepted a plan if such plan has been accepted by creditors, other than any entity designated under subsection (e) of this section, that hold at least two-thirds in amount and more than one-half in number of the allowed claims of such class held by creditors, other than any entity designated under subsection (e) of this section, that have accepted or rejected such plan.

(d)　A class of interest has accepted a plan if such plan has been accepted by holders of such interests, other than any entity designated under subsection (e) of this section, that hold at least two-thirds in amount of the allowed interests of such class held by holders of such interests, other than any entity designated under subsection (e) of this section, that have accepted or rejected such plan.

(e)　On request of a party in interest, and after notice and a hearing, the court may designate any entity whose acceptance or rejection of such plan was not in good faith, or was not solicited or procured in good faith or in accordance with the provisions of this title.

(f)　Notwithstanding any other provision of this section, a class that is not impaired under a plan, and each holder of a claim or interest of such class, are conclusively presumed to have accepted the plan, and solicitation of acceptances with respect to such class from the holders of claims or interests of such class is not required.

(g)　Notwithstanding any other provision of this section, a class is deemed not to have accepted a plan if such plan provides that the claims or interests of such class do not entitle the holders of such claims or interests to receive or retain any property under the plan on account of such claims or interests.

Sec. 1127.　Modification of Plan

(a)　The proponent of a plan may modify such plan at any time before confirmation, but may not modify such plan so that such plan as modified fails to meet the requirements of sections 1122 and 1123 of this title. After the proponent of a plan files a modification of such plan with the court, the plan as modified becomes the plan.

(b)   The proponent of a plan or the reorganized debtor may modify such plan at any time after confirmation of such plan and before substantial consummation of such plan, but may not modify such plan so that such plan as modified fails to meet the requirements of section 1122 and 1123 of this title. Such plan as modified under this subsection becomes the plan only if circumstances warrant such modification and the court, after notice and a hearing, confirms such plan as modified, under section 1129 of this title.

(c)   The proponent of a modification shall comply with section 1125 of this title with respect to the plan as modified.

(d)   Any holder of a claim or interest that has accepted or rejected a plan is deemed to have accepted or rejected, as the case may be, such plan as modified, unless, within the time fixed by the court, such holder changes such holder's previous acceptance or rejection.

Sec. 1128.   Confirmation Hearing

(a)   After notice, the court shall hold a hearing on confirmation of a plan.

(b)   A party in interest may object to confirmation of a plan.

Sec. 1129.   Confirmation of Plan

(a)   The court shall confirm a plan only if all of the following requirements are met:

(1)   The plan complies with the applicable provisions of this title.

(2)   The proponent of the plan complies with the applicable provisions of this title.

(3)   The plan has been proposed in good faith and not by any means forbidden by law.

(4)   Any payment made or to be made by the proponent, by the debtor, or by a person issuing securities or acquiring property under the plan, for services or for costs and expenses in or in connection with the case, or in connection with the plan and incident to the case, has been approved by, or is subject to the approval of, the court as reasonable.

(5)   (A)   (i)   The proponent of the plan has disclosed the identity and affiliations of any individual proposed to serve, after confirmation of the plan, as a director, officer, or voting trustee of the debtor, an affiliate of the debtor participating in a joint plan with the debtor, or a successor to the debtor under the plan; and

(ii)   the appointment to, or continuance in, such office of such individual, is consistent with the interests of creditors and equity security holders and with public policy; and

(B)   the proponent of the plan has disclosed the identity of any insider that will be employed or retained by the reorganized debtor, and the nature of any compensation for such insider.

(6)   Any governmental regulatory commission with jurisdiction, after confirmation of the plan, over the rates of the debtor has approved any rate change provided for in the plan, or such rate change is expressly conditioned on such approval.

(7) With respect to each impaired class of claims or interests—

  (A) each holder of a claim or interest of such class—

    (i) has accepted the plan; or

    (ii) will receive or retain under the plan on account of such claim or interest property of a value, as of the effective date of the plan, that is not less than the amount that such holder would so receive or retain if the debtor were liquidated under chapter 7 of this title on such date; or

  (B) if section 1111(b)(2) of this title applies to the claims of such class, each holder of a claim of such class will receive or retain under the plan on account of such claim property of a value, as of the effective date of the plan, that is not less than the value of such holder's interest in the estate's interest in the property that secures such claims.

(8) With respect to each class of claims or interests—

  (A) such class has accepted the plan; or

  (B) such class is not impaired under the plan.

(9) Except to the extent that the holder of a particular claim has agreed to a different treatment of such claim, the plan provides that—

  (A) with respect to a claim of a kind specified in section 507(a)(1) or 507(a)(2) of this title, on the effective date of the plan, the holder of such claim will receive on account of such claim cash equal to the allowed amount of such claim;

  (B) with respect to a class of claims of a kind specified in section 507(a)(3), 507(a)(4), 507(a)(5), 507(a)(6), or 507(a)(7) of this title, each holder of a claim of such class will receive—

    (i) if such class has accepted the plan, deferred cash payments of a value, as of the effective date of the plan, equal to the allowed amount of such claim; or

    (ii) if such class has not accepted the plan, cash on the effective date of the plan equal to the allowed amount of such claim; and

  (C) with respect to a claim of a kind specified in section 507(a)(8) of this title, the holder of such claim will receive on account of such claim deferred cash payments, over a period not exceeding six years after the date of assessment of such claim, of a value, as of the effective date of the plan, equal to the allowed amount of such claim.

(10) If a class of claims is impaired under the plan, at least one class of claims that is impaired under the plan has accepted the plan, determined without including any acceptance of the plan by any insider.

(11) Confirmation of the plan is not likely to be followed by the liquidation, or the need for further financial reorganization, of the debtor or any successor to the debtor under the plan, unless such liquidation or reorganization is proposed in the plan.

(12) All fees payable under section 1930 of title 28, as determined by the court at the hearing on confirmation of the plan, have been paid or the plan provides for the payment of all such fees on the effective date of the plan.

(13) The plan provides for the continuation after its effective date of payment of all retiree benefits, as that term is defined in section 1114 of this title, at the level established pursuant to subsection (e)(1)(B) or (g) of section

1114 of this title, at any time prior to confirmation of the plan, for the duration of the period the debtor has obligated itself to provide such benefits.

(b) (1)   Notwithstanding section 510(a) of this title, if all of the applicable requirements of subsection (a) of this section other than paragraph (8) are met with respect to a plan, the court, on request of the proponent of the plan, shall confirm the plan notwithstanding the requirements of such paragraph if the plan does not discriminate unfairly, and is fair and equitable, with respect to each class of claims or interests that is impaired under, and has not accepted, the plan.

(2)   For the purpose of this subsection, the condition that a plan be fair and equitable with respect to a class includes the following requirements:

(A)   With respect to a class of secured claims, the plan provides—

(i)   (I)   that the holders of such claims retain the liens securing such claims, whether the property subject to such liens is retained by the debtor or transferred to another entity, to the extent of the allowed amount of such claims; and

(II)   that each holder of a claim of such class receive on account of such claim deferred cash payments totaling at least the allowed amount of such claim, of a value, as of the effective date of the plan, of at least the value of each holder's interest in the estate's interest in such property;

(ii)   for the sale, subject to section 363(k) of this title, of any property that is subject to the liens securing such claims, free and clear of such liens, with such liens to attach to the proceeds of such sale, and the treatment of such liens on proceeds under clause (i) or (iii) of this subparagraph; or

(iii)   for the realization by such holders of the indubitable equivalent of such claims.

(B)   With respect to a class of unsecured claims—

(i)   the plan provides that each holder of a claim of such class receive or retain on account of such claim property of a value, as of the effective date of the plan, equal to the allowed amount of such claim; or

(ii)   the holder of any claim or interest that is junior to the claims of such class will not receive or retain under the plan on account of such junior claim or interest any property.

(C)   With respect to a class of interests—

(i)   the plan provides that each holder of an interest of such class receive or retain on account of such interest property of a value, as of the effective date of the plan, equal to the greatest of the allowed amount of any fixed liquidation preference to which such holder is entitled, and fixed redemption price to which such holder is entitled, or the value of such interest; or

(ii)   the holder of any interest that is junior to the interests of such class will not receive or retain under the plan on account of such junior interest any property.

(c)   Notwithstanding subsection (a) and (b) of this section and except as provided in section 1127(b) of this title, the court may confirm only one plan, unless the order of confirmation in the case has been revoked under section

1144 of this title. If the requirements of subsection (a) and (b) of this section are met with respect to more than one plan, the court shall consider the preferences of creditors and equity security holders in determining which plan to confirm.

(d)   Notwithstanding any other provision of this section, on request of a party in interest that is a governmental unit, the court may not confirm a plan if the principal purpose of the plan is the avoidance of taxes or the avoidance of the application of section 5 of the Securities Act of 1933. In any hearing under this subsection, the governmental unit has the burden of proof on the issue of avoidance.

SUBCHAPTER III. POSTCONFIRMATION MATTERS

Sec. 1141.   *Effect of Confirmation*

(a)   Except as provided in subsection (d)(2) and (d)(3) of this section, the provisions of a confirmed plan bind the debtor, any entity issuing securities under the plan, any entity acquiring property under the plan, and any creditor, equity security holder, general partner in the debtor, whether or not the claim or interest of such creditor, equity security holder, or general partner is impaired under the plan and whether or not such creditor, equity security holder, or general partner has accepted the plan.

(b)   Except as otherwise provided in the plan or the order confirming the plan, the confirmation of a plan vests all of the property of the estate in the debtor.

(c)   Except as provided in subsection (d)(2) and (d)(3) of this section and except as otherwise provided in the plan or in the order confirming the plan, after confirmation of a plan, the property dealt with by the plan is free and clear of all claims and interests of creditors, equity security holders, and of general partners in the debtor.

(d) (1)   Except as otherwise provided in this subsection, in the plan, or in the order confirming the plan, the confirmation of a plan—

(A)   discharges the debtor from any debt that arose before the date of such confirmation, and any debt of a kind specified in section 502(g), 502(h) or 502(i) of this title, whether or not—

(i)   a proof of the claim based on such debt is filed or deemed filed under section 501, of this title;

(ii)   such claim is allowed under section 502 of this title; or

(iii)   the holder of such claim has accepted the plan; and

(B)   terminates all rights and interests of equity security holders and general partners provided for by the plan.

(2)   The confirmation of a plan does not discharge an individual debtor from any debt excepted from discharge under section 523 of this title.

(3)   The confirmation of a plan does not discharge a debtor if—

(A)   the plan provides for the liquidation of all or substantially all of the property of the estate;

(B)   the debtor does not engage in business after consummation of the plan; and

(C)   the debtor would be denied a discharge under section 727(a) of this title if the case were a case under chapter 7 of this title.

(4)   The court may approve a written waiver of discharge executed by the debtor after the order for relief under this chapter.

Sec. 1142.   *Implementation of Plan*

(a)   Notwithstanding any otherwise applicable nonbankruptcy law, rule, or regulation relating to financial condition, the debtor and any entity organized or to be organized for the purpose of carrying out the plan shall carry out the plan and shall comply with any orders of the court.

(b)   The court may direct the debtor and any other necessary party to execute or deliver or to join in the execution or delivery of any instrument required to effect a transfer of property dealt with by a confirmed plan, and to perform any other act, including the satisfaction of any lien, that is necessary for the consummation of the plan.

Sec. 1143.   *Distribution*

If a plan requires presentment or surrender of a security or the performance of any other act as a condition to participation in distribution under the plan, such action shall be taken not later than five years after the date of the entry of the order of confirmation. Any entity that has not within such time presented or surrendered such entity's security or taken any such other action that the plan requires may not participate in distribution under the plan.

Sec. 1144.   *Revocation of an Order of Confirmation*

On request of a party in interest at any time before 180 days after the date of entry of the order of confirmation, and after notice and a hearing, the court may revoke such order if and only if such order was procured by fraud. An order under this section revoking an order of confirmation shall—

(1)   contain such provisions as are necessary to protect any entity acquiring rights in good faith reliance on the order of confirmation; and

(2)   revoke the discharge of the debtor.

Sec. 1145.   *Exemption from Securities Laws*

(a)   Except with respect to an entity that is an underwriter as defined in subsection (b) of this section, section 5 of the Securities Act of 1933 and any State or local law requiring registration for offer or sale of a security or registration or licensing of an issuer of, underwriter of, or broker or dealer in, a security do not apply to—

(1)   the offer or sale under a plan of a security of the debtor, of an affiliate participation in a joint plan with the debtor, or of a successor to the debtor under the plan—

(A)   in exchange for a claim against, an interest in, or a claim for an administrative expense in the case concerning, the debtor or such affiliate; or

(B)   principally in such exchange and partly for cash or property;

(2)   the offer of a security through any warrant, option, right to subscribe, or conversion privilege that was sold in the manner specified in paragraph (1) of this subsection, or the sale of a security upon the exercise of such a warrant, option, right, or privilege;

(3) the offer or sale, other than under a plan, of a security of an issuer other than the debtor or an affiliate, if—

(A) such security was owned by the debtor on the date of the filing of the petition;

(B) the issuer of such security is—

(i) required to file reports under section 13 or 15d of the Securities Exchange Act of 1934; and

(ii) in compliance with the disclosure and reporting provision of such applicable section; and

(C) such offer or sale is of securities that do not exceed—

(i) during the two-year period immediately following the date of the filing of the petition, four percent of the securities of such class outstanding on such date; and

(ii) during any 180-day period following such two-year period, one percent of the securities outstanding at the beginning of such 180-day period; or

(4) a transaction by a stockbroker in a security that is executed after a transaction of a kind specified in paragraph (1) or (2) of this subsection in such security and before the expiration of 40 days after the first date on which such security was bona fide offered to the public by the issuer or by or through an underwriter, if such stockbroker provides, at the time of or before such transaction by such stockbroker a disclosure statement approved under section 1125 of this title, and, if the court orders, information supplementing such disclosure statement.

(b) (1) Except as provided in paragraph (2) of this subsection and except with respect to ordinary trading transactions of an entity that is not an issuer, an entity is an underwriter under section 2, of the Securities Act of 1933 if such entity—

(A) purchases a claim against, interest in, or claim for an administrative expense in the case concerning, the debtor, if such purchase is with a view to distribution of any security received or to be received in exchange for such a claim or interest;

(B) offers to sell securities offered or sold under the plan for the holders of such securities;

(C) offers to buy securities offered or sold under the plan for the holders of such securities, if such offer to buy is—

(i) with a view to distribution of such securities; and

(ii) under an agreement made in connection with the plan, with the consummation of the plan, or with the offer of sale of securities under the plan; or

(D) is an issuer, as used in such section 2(11), with respect to such securities.

(2) An entity is not an underwriter under section 2(11) of the Securities Act of 1933 or under paragraph (1) of this subsection with respect to an agreement that provided only for—

(A) (i) the matching or combining of fractional interests in securities offered or sold under the plan into whole interests; or

(ii) the purchase or sale of such fractional interests from or to entities receiving such fractional interests under the plan; or

(B) the purchase or sale for such entities of such fractional or whole interests as are necessary to adjust for any remaining fractional interests after such matching.

(3) An entity other than an entity of the kind specified in paragraph (1) of this subsection is not an underwriter under section 2(11) of the Securities Act of 1933 with respect to any securities offered or sold to such entity in the manner specified in subsection (a)(1) of this section.

(c) An offer of sale of securities of the kind and in the manner specified under subsection (a)(1) of this section is deemed to be a public offering.

(d) The Trust Indenture Act of 1939 does not apply to a note issued under the plan that matures not later than one year after the effective date of the plan.

Sec. 1146.   *Special Tax Provisions*

(a) For the purpose of any State or local law imposing a tax on or measured by income, the taxable period of a debtor that is an individual shall terminate on the date of the order for relief under this chapter, unless the case was converted under section 706 of this title.

(b) The trustee shall make a State or local tax return of income for the estate of an individual debtor in a case under this chapter for each taxable period after the order for relief under this chapter during which the case is pending.

(c) The issuance, transfer, or exchange of a security, or the making or delivery of an instrument of transfer under a plan confirmed under section 1129 of this title, may not be taxed under any law imposing a stamp tax or similar tax.

(d) The court may authorize the proponent of a plan to request a determination, limited to questions of law, by a State or local governmental unit charged with responsibility for collection or determination of a tax on or measured by income, of the tax effects, under section 346 of this title and under the law imposing such tax, of the plan. In the event of an actual controversy, the court may declare such effects after the earlier of—

(1) the date on which such governmental unit responds to the request under this subsection; or

(2) 270 days after such request.

SUBCHAPTER IV. RAILROAD REORGANIZATION

Sec. 1161.   *Inapplicability of Other Sections*

Sections 341, 343, 1102(a)(1), 1104, 1105, 1107, 1129(a)(7), and 1129(c) of this title do not apply in a case concerning a railroad.

Sec. 1162.   *Definition*

In this subchapter, "Commission" means Interstate Commerce Commission.

Sec. 1163.   *Appointment of Trustee*

As soon as practicable after the order for relief the Secretary of Transportation shall submit a list of five disinterested persons that are qualified and willing to serve as trustees in the case. The United States trustee shall appoint one of such persons to serve as trustee in the case.

Sec. 1164.   Right to Be Heard

The Commission, the Department of Transportation, and any State or local commission having regulatory jurisdiction over the debtor may raise and may appear to be heard on any issue in a case under this chapter, but may not appeal from any judgment, order, or decree entered in the case.

Sec. 1165.   Protection of the Public Interest

In applying sections 1166, 1167, 1169, 1170, 1171, 1172, 1173, and 1174 of this title, the court and the trustee shall consider the public interest in addition to the interests of the debtor, creditors, and equity security holders.

Sec. 1166.   Effect of Subtitle IV of Title 49 and of Federal, State, or Local Regulations

Except with respect to abandonment under section 1170 of this title, or merger, modification of the financial structure of the debtor, or issuance of sale of securities under a plan, the trustee and the debtor are subject to the provisions of subtitle IV of title 49 that are applicable to railroads, and the trustee is subject to orders of any Federal, State, or local regulatory body to the same extent as the debtor would be if a petition commencing the case under this chapter had not been filed, but—

(1)   any such order that would require the expenditure, or the incurring of an obligation for the expenditure, of money from the estate is not effective unless approved by the court; and

(2)   the provisions of this chapter are subject to section 601(b) of the Regional Rail Reorganization Act of 1973.

Sec. 1167.   Collective Bargaining Agreements

Notwithstanding section 365 of this title, neither the court nor the trustee may change the wages or working conditions of employees of the debtor established by a collective bargaining agreement that is subject to the Railroad Labor Act except in accordance with section 6 of such Act.

Sec. 1168.   Rolling Stock Equipment

(a) (1)   The right of a secured party with a security interest in or of a lessor or conditional vendor of equipment described in paragraph (2) to take possession of such equipment in compliance with an equipment security agreement, lease, or conditional sale contract is not affected by section 362, 363, or 1129 or by any power of the court to enjoin the taking of possession, unless—

(A)   before the date that is 60 days after the date of commencement of a case under this chapter, the trustee, subject to the court's approval, agrees to perform all obligations of the debtor that become due on or after the date of commencement of the case under such security agreement, lease, or conditional sale contract; and

(B)   any default, other than a default of a kind described in section 365(b)(2), under such security agreement, lease, or conditional sale contract—

(i)   that occurs before the date of commencement of the case and is an event of default therewith is cured before the expiration of such 60-day period; and

(ii)   that occurs or becomes an event of default after the date of commencement of the case is cured before the later of—

(I)   the date that is 30 days after the date of the default or event of default; or

(II)   the expiration of such 60-day period.

(2)   Equipment is described in this paragraph if it is rolling stock equipment or accessories used on such equipment, including superstructures and racks, that is subject to a security interest granted by, leased to, or conditionally sold to the debtor.

(3)   Paragraph (1) applies to a secured party, lessor, or conditional vendor acting in its own behalf or acting as trustee or otherwise in behalf of another party.

(b)   The trustee and the secured party, lessor, or conditional vendor whose right to take possession is protected under subsection (a) may agree, subject to the court's approval, to extend the 60-day period specified in subsection (a)(1).

(c)   With respect to equipment first placed in service on or prior to the date of enactment of this subsection, for purposes of this section—

(1)   the term "lease" includes any written agreement with respect to which the lessor and the debtor, as lessee, have expressed in the agreement or in a substantially contemporaneous writing that the agreement is to be treated as a lease for Federal income tax purposes; and

(2)   the term "security interest" means a purchase-money equipment security interest.

(d)   With respect to equipment first placed in service after the date of enactment of this subsection, for purposes of this section, the term "rolling stock equipment" includes rolling stock equipment that is substantially rebuilt and accessories used on such equipment.

Sec. 1169.   *Effect of Rejection of Lease of Railroad Line*

(a)   Except as provided in subsection (b) of this section, if a lease of a line of railroad under which the debtor is the lessee is rejected under section 365 of this title, and if the trustee, within such time as the court fixes, and with the court's approval, elects not to operate the leased line, the lessor under such lease, after such approval, shall operate the line.

(b)   If the operation of such line by such lessor is impracticable or contrary to the public interest, the court, on request of such lessor, and after notice and a hearing, shall order the trustee to continue operation of such line for the account of such lessor until abandonment is ordered under section 1170 of this title, or until such operation is otherwise lawfully terminated, whichever occurs first.

(c)   During any such operation, such lessor is deemed a carrier subject to the provisions of subtitle IV of title 49 that are applicable to railroads.

Sec. 1170. *Abandonment of Railroad Line*

(a)   The court, after notice and a hearing, may authorize the abandonment of all or a portion of a railroad line if such abandonment is—
   (1)   (A)   in the best interest of the estate; or
         (B)   essential to the formulation of a plan; and
   (2)   consistent with the public interest.

(b)   If, except for the pendency of the case under this chapter, such abandonment would require approval by the Commission under a law of the United States, the trustee shall initiate an appropriate application for such abandonment with the Commission. The court may fix a time within which the Commission shall report to the court on such application.

(c)   After the court receives the report of the Commission, or the expiration of the time fixed under subsection (b) of this section, whichever occurs first, the court may authorize such abandonment, after notice to the Commission, the Secretary of Transportation, the trustee, any party in interest that has requested notice, any affected shipper or community, and any other entity prescribed by the court, and a hearing.

(d) (1)   Enforcement of an order authorizing such abandonment shall be stayed until the time for taking an appeal has expired, or, if an appeal is timely taken, until such order has become final.

   (2)   If an order authorizing such abandonment is appealed, the court, on request of a party in interest, may authorize suspension of service on a line or a portion of a line pending the determination of such appeal, after notice to the Commission, the Secretary of Transportation, the trustee, any party in interest that has requested notice, any affected shipper or community, and any other entity prescribed by the court, and a hearing. An appellant may not obtain a stay of the enforcement of an order authorizing such suspension by the giving of a supersedeas bond or otherwise, during the pendency of such appeal.

(e) (1)   In authorizing any abandonment of a railroad line under this section, the court shall require the rail carrier to provide a fair arrangement at least as protective of the interests of employees as that established under section 11347 of title 49.

   (2)   Nothing in this subsection shall be deemed to affect the priorities or timing of payment of employee protection which might have existed in the absence of this subsection.

Sec. 1171. *Priority Claims*

(a)   There shall be paid as an administrative expense any claim of an individual or of the person representative of a deceased individual against the debtor or the estate, for personal injury to or death of such individual arising out of the operation of the debtor or the estate, whether such claim arose before or after the commencement of the case.

(b)   Any unsecured claim against the debtor that would have been entitled to a priority if a receiver in equity of the property of the debtor had been appointed by a Federal court on the date of the order for relief under this title shall be entitled to the same property in the case under this chapter.

Sec. 1172.   *Contents of Plan*

(a)   In addition to the provisions required or permitted under section 1123 of this title, a plan—

(1)   shall specify the extent to and the means by which the debtor's rail service is proposed to be continued, and the extent to which any of the debtor's rail service is proposed to be terminated; and

(2)   may include a provision for—

(A)   the transfer of any or all of the operating railroad lines of the debtor to another operating railroad; or

(B)   abandonment of any railroad line in accordance with section 1170 of this title.

(b)   If, except for the pendency of the case under this chapter, transfer of, or operation of or over, any of the debtor's rail lines by an entity other than the debtor or a successor to the debtor under the plan would require approval by the Commission under a law of the United States, then a plan may not propose such a transfer or such operation unless the proponent of the plan initiates an appropriate application for such a transfer or such operation with the Commission and, within such time as the court may fix, not exceeding 180 days, the Commission, with or without a hearing, as the Commission may determine, and with or without modification or condition, approves such application, or does not act on such application. Any action or order of the Commission approving, modifying, conditioning, or disapproving such application is subject to review by the court only under sections 706(2)(A), 706(2)(B), 706(2)(C), and 706(2)(D) of title 5.

(c) (1)   In approving an application under subsection (b) of this section, the Commission shall require the rail carrier to provide a fair arrangement at least as protective of the interests of employees as that established under section 11347 of title 49.

(2)   Nothing in this subsection shall be deemed to affect the priorities or timing or payment of employee protection which might have existed in the absence of this subsection.

Sec. 1173.   *Confirmation of Plan*

(a)   The court shall confirm a plan if—

(1)   the applicable requirements of section 1129 of this title have been met;

(2)   each creditor or equity security holder will receive or retain under the plan property of a value, as of the effective date of the plan, that is not less than the value of property that each such creditor or equity security holder would so receive or retain if all of the operating railroad lines of the debtor were sold, and the proceeds of such sale, and the other property of the estate, were distributed under chapter 7 of this title on such date;

(3)   in light of the debtor's past earnings and the probable prospective earnings of the reorganized debtor, there will be adequate coverage by such prospective earnings of any fixed charges, such as interest on debt, amortization of funded debt, and rent for leased railroads, provided for by the plan; and

(4)   the plan is consistent with the public interest.

(b)   If the requirements of subsection (a) of this section are met with respect to more than one plan, the court shall confirm the plan that is most likely to maintain adequate rail service in the public interest.

Sec. 1174.   Liquidation

On request of a party in interest and after notice and a hearing, the court may, or, if a plan has not been confirmed under section 1173 of this title before five years after the date of the order for relief, the court shall, order the trustee to cease the debtor's operation and to collect and reduce to money all of the property of the estate in the manner as if the case were a case under chapter 7 of this title.

12
ADJUSTMENTS OF DEBTS OF A FAMILY FARMER WITH REGULAR ANNUAL INCOME*

SUBCHAPTER I. OFFICERS, ADMINISTRATION, AND THE ESTATE

Sec. 1201.   Stay of Action against Codebtor

(a)   Except as provided in subsections (b) and (c) of this section, after the order for relief under this chapter, a creditor may not act, or commence or continue any civil action, to collect all or any part of a consumer debt of the debtor from any individual that is liable on such debt with the debtor, or that secured such debt, unless—
    (1)   such individual became liable on or secured such debt in the ordinary course of such individual's business; or
    (2)   the case is closed, dismissed, or converted to a case under chapter 7 of this title.
(b)   A creditor may present a negotiable instrument, and may give notice of dishonor of such an instrument.
(c)   On request of a party in interest and after notice and a hearing, the court shall grant relief from the stay provided by subsection (a) of this section with respect to a creditor, to the extent that—
    (1)   as between the debtor and the individual protected under subsection (a) of this section, such individual received the consideration for the claim held by such creditor;
    (2)   the plan filed by the debtor proposes not to pay such claim; or
    (3)   such creditor's interest would be irreparably harmed by continuation of such stay.
(d)   Twenty days after the filing of a request under subsection (c)(2) of this section for relief from the stay provided by subsection (a) of this section, such stay is terminated with respect to the party in interest making such request, unless the debtor or any individual that is liable on such debt with the debtor files and serves upon such party in interest a written objection to the taking of the proposed action.

*Note: Chapter 12 is repealed as of October 1, 1993.

Sec. 1202. *Trustee*

(a)   If the United States trustee has appointed an individual under section 586(b) of title 28 to serve as standing trustee in cases under this chapter and if such individual qualifies as a trustee under section 322 of this title, then such individual shall serve as trustee in any case filed under this chapter. Otherwise, the United States trustee shall appoint one disinterested person to serve as trustee in the case or the United States trustee may serve as trustee in the case if necessary.

(b)   The trustee shall—

(1)   perform the duties specified in sections 704(2), 704(3), 704(5), 704(6), 704(7), and 704(9) of this title;

(2)   perform the duties specified in section 1106(a)(3) and 1106(a)(4) of this title if the court, for cause and on request of a party in interest, the trustee, or the United States trustee, so orders;

(3)   appear to be heard at any hearing that concerns—

(A)   the value of property subject to a lien;

(B)   confirmation of a plan;

(C)   modification of the plan after confirmation; or

(D)   the sale of property of the estate;

(4)   ensure that the debtor commences making timely payments required by a confirmed plan; and

(5)   if the debtor ceases to be a debtor in possession, perform the duties specified in sections 704(8), 1106(a)(1), 1106(a)(2), 1106(a)(6), 1106(a)(7), and 1203.*

Sec. 1203. *Rights and Powers of Debtor*

Subject to such limitations as the court may prescribe, a debtor in possession shall have all the rights, other than the right to compensation under section 330, and powers, and shall perform all the functions and duties, except the duties specified in paragraphs (3) and (4) of section 1106(a), of a trustee serving in a case under chapter 11, including operating the debtor's farm.

Sec. 1204. *Removal of Debtor as Debtor in Possession*

(a)   On request of a party in interest, and after notice and a hearing, the court shall order that the debtor shall not be a debtor in possession for cause, including fraud, dishonesty, incompetence, or gross mismanagement of the affairs of the debtor, either before or after the commencement of the case.

(b)   On request of a party in interest, and after notice and a hearing the court may reinstate the debtor in possession.

Sec. 1205. *Adequate Protection*

(a)   Section 361 does not apply in a case under this chapter.

(b)   In a case under this chapter, when adequate protection is required

---

*Subsections 1202(c) and 1202(d) were repealed by Pub. L. No 99-554 (1986) with delayed effective dates. These subsections are currently only applicable to federal districts in states of Alabama and North Carolina.

under section 362, 363, or 364 of this title of an interest of an entity in property, such adequate protection may be provided by—

(1)   requiring the trustee to make a cash payment or periodic cash payments to such entity, to the extent that the stay under section 362 of this title, use, sale, or lease under section 363 of this title, or any grant of a lien under section 364 of this title results in a decrease in the value of property securing a claim of an entity's ownership interest in property;

(2)   providing to such entity an additional or replacement lien to the extent that such stay, use, sale, lease, or grant results in a decrease in the value of property securing a claim or of an entity's ownership interest in property;

(3)   paying to such entity for the use of farmland the reasonable rent customary in the community where the property is located, based upon the rental value, net income, and earning capacity of the property; or

(4)   granting such other relief, other than entitling such entity of compensation allowable under section 503(b)(1) of this title as an administrative expense, as will adequately protect the value of property securing a claim or of such entity's ownership interest in property.

Sec. 1206.   Sales Free of Interests

After notice and a hearing, in addition to the authorization contained in section 363(f), the trustee in a case under this chapter may sell property under section 363(b) and (c) free and clear of any interest in such property of an entity other than the estate if the property is farmland or farm equipment, except that the proceeds of such sale be subject to such interest.

Sec. 1207.   Property of the Estate

(a)   Property of the estate includes, in addition to the property specified in section 541 of this title—

(1)   all property of the kind specified in such section that the debtor acquires after the commencement of the case but before the case is closed, dismissed, or converted to a case under chapter 7 of this title, whichever occurs first; and

(2)   earnings from services performed by the debtor after the commencement of the case but before the case is closed, dismissed, or converted to a case under chapter 7 of this title, whichever occurs first.

(b)   Except as provided in section 1204, a confirmed plan, or an order confirming a plan, the debtor shall remain in possession of all property of the estate.

Sec. 1208.   Conversion or Dismissal

(a)   The debtor may convert a case under this chapter to a case under chapter 7 of this title at any time. Any waiver of the right to convert under this subsection is unenforceable.

(b)   On request of the debtor at any time, if the case has not been converted under section 706 or 1112 of this title, the court shall dismiss a case under this chapter. Any waiver of the right to dismiss under this subsection is unenforceable.

(c)   On request of a party in interest, and after notice and a hearing, the court may dismiss a case under this chapter for cause, including—

(1)   unreasonable delay, or gross mismanagement, by the debtor that is prejudicial to creditors;

(2)   nonpayment of any fees and charges required under chapter 123 of title 28;

(3)   failure to file a plan timely under section 1221 of this title;

(4)   failure to commence making timely payments required by a confirmed plan;

(5)   denial of confirmation of a plan under section 1225 of this title and denial of a request made for additional time for filing another plan or a modification of a plan;

(6)   material default by the debtor with respect to a term of a confirmed plan;

(7)   revocation of the order of confirmation under section 1230 of this title, and denial of confirmation of a modified plan under section 1229 of this title;

(8)   termination of a confirmed plan by reason of the occurrence of a condition specified in the plan; or

(9)   continuing loss to or diminution of the estate and absence of a reasonable likelihood of rehabilitation.

(d)   On request of a party in interest, and after notice and a hearing, the court may dismiss a case under this chapter or convert a case under this chapter to a case under chapter 7 of this title upon a showing that the debtor has committed fraud in connection with this case.

(e)   Notwithstanding any other provision of this section, a case may not be converted to a case under another chapter of this title unless the debtor may be a debtor under such chapter.

SUBCHAPTER II. THE PLAN

Sec. 1221.   *Filing of Plan*

The debtor shall file a plan not later than 90 days after the order for relief under this chapter, except that the court may extend such period if the need for an extension is attributable to circumstances for which the debtor should not justly be held accountable.

Sec. 1222.   *Contents of Plan*

(a)   The plan shall—

(1)   provide for the submission of all or such portion of future earnings or other future income of the debtor to the supervision and control of the trustee as is necessary for the execution of the plan;

(2)   provide for the full payment, in deferred cash payments, of all claims entitled to priority under section 507 of this title, unless the holder of a particular claim agrees to a different treatment of such claim; and

(3)   if the plan classifies claims and interests, provide the same treatment for each claim or interest within a particular class unless the holder of a particular claim or interest agrees to less favorable treatment.

(b)   Subject to subsections (a) and (c) of this section, the plan may—

(1)   designate a class or classes of unsecured claims, as provided in section 1122 of this title, but may not discriminate unfairly against any class so

designated; however, such plan may treat claims for a consumer debt of the debtor if an individual is liable on such consumer debt with the debtor differently than other unsecured claims;

(2)   modify the rights of holders of secured claims, or of holders of unsecured claims, or leave unaffected the rights of holders of any class of claims;

(3)   provide for the curing or waiving of any default;

(4)   provide for payments on any unsecured claim to be made concurrently with payments on any secured claim or any other unsecured claim;

(5)   provide for the curing of any default within a reasonable time and maintenance of payments while the case is pending on any unsecured claim or secured claim on which the last payment is due after the date on which the final payment under the plan is due;

(6)   subject to section 365 of this title, provide for the assumption, rejection, or assignment of any executory contract or unexpired lease of the debtor not previously rejected under such section;

(7)   provide for the payment of all or part of a claim against the debtor from property of the estate or property of the debtor;

(8)   provide for the sale of all or any part of the property of the estate or the distribution of all or any part of the property of the estate among those having an interest in such property;

(9)   provide for payment of allowed secured claims consistent with section 1225(a)(5) of this title, over a period exceeding the period permitted under section 1222(c);

(10)   provide for the vesting of property of the estate, on confirmation of the plan or at a later time, in the debtor or in any other entity; and

(11)   include any other appropriate provision not inconsistent with this title.

(c)   Except as provided in subsections (b)(5) and (b)(9), the plan may not provide for payments over a period that is longer than three years unless the court for cause approves a longer period, but the court may not approve a period that is longer than five years.

(d)   Notwithstanding subsection (b)(2) of this section and sections 506(b) and 1225(a)(5) of this title, if it is proposed in a plan to cure a default, the amount necessary to cure the default, shall be determined in accordance with the underlying agreement and applicable nonbankruptcy law.

Sec. 1223.   *Modification of Plan before Confirmation*

(a)   The debtor may modify the plan at any time before confirmation, but may not modify the plan so that the plan as modified fails to meet the requirements of section 1222 of this title.

(b)   After the debtor files a modification under this section, the plan as modified becomes the plan.

(c)   Any holder of a secured claim that has accepted or rejected the plan is deemed to have accepted or rejected, as the case may be, the plan as modified, unless the modification provides for a change in the rights of such holder from what such rights were under the plan before modification, and such holder changes such holder's previous acceptance or rejection.

Sec. 1224.   *Confirmation Hearing*

After expedited notice, the court shall hold a hearing on confirmation of the plan. A party in interest, the trustee, or the United States trustee may object to the confirmation of the plan. Except for cause, the hearing shall be concluded not later than 45 days after the filing of the plan.

Sec. 1225.   *Confirmation of Plan*

(a)   Except as provided in subsection (b), the court shall confirm a plan if—

(1)   the plan complies with the provisions of this chapter and with the other applicable provisions of this title;

(2)   any fee, charge, or amount required under chapter 123 of title 28, or by the plan, to be paid before confirmation, has been paid;

(3)   the plan has been proposed in good faith and not by any means forbidden by law;

(4)   the value, as of the effective date of the plan, of property to be distributed under the plan on account of each allowed unsecured claim is not less than the amount that would be paid on such claim if the estate of the debtor were liquidated under chapter 7 of this title on such date;

(5)   with respect to each allowed secured claim provided for by the plan—

(A)   holder of such claim has accepted the plan;

(B)   (i)   the plan provides that the holder of such claim retain the lien securing such claim; and

(ii)   the value, as of the effective date of the plan, of property to be distributed by the trustee or the debtor under the plan on account of such claim is not less than the allowed amount of such claim; or

(C)   the debtor surrenders the property securing such claim to such holder; and

(6)   the debtor will be able to make all payments under the plan and to comply with the plan.

(b) (1)   If the trustee or the holder of an allowed unsecured claim objects to the confirmation of the plan, then the court may not approve the plan unless, as of the effective date of the plan—

(A)   the value of the property to be distributed under the plan on account of such claim is not less than the amount of such claim; or

(B)   the plan provides that all of the debtor's projected disposable in come to be received in the three-year period, or such longer period as the court may approve under section 1222(c), beginning on the date that the first payment is due under the plan will be applied to make payments under the plan.

(2)   For purposes of this subsection, "disposable income" means income which is received by the debtor and which is not reasonably necessary to be expended—

(A)   for the maintenance or support of the debtor or a dependent of the debtor; or

(B)   for the payment of expenditures necessary for the continuation, preservation, and operation of the debtor's business.

(c)   After confirmation of a plan, the court may order any entity from whom the debtor receives income to pay all or part of such income to the trustee.

Sec. 1226.   Payments

(a)   Payments and funds received by the trustee shall be retained by the trustee until confirmation or denial of confirmation of a plan. If a plan is confirmed, the trustee shall distribute any such payment in accordance with the plan. If a plan is not confirmed, the trustee shall return any such payments to the debtor, after deducting—

(1)   any unpaid claim allowed under section 503(b) of this title; and

(2)   if a standing trustee is serving in the case, the percentage fee fixed for such standing trustee.

(b)   Before or at the time of each payment to creditors under the plan, there shall be paid—

(1)   any unpaid claim of the kind specified in section 507(a)(1) of this title; and

(2)   if a standing trustee appointed under section 1202(c) of this title is serving in the case, the percentage fee fixed for such standing trustee under section 1202(d) of this title.

(c)   Except as otherwise provided in the plan or in the order confirming the plan, the trustee shall make payments to creditors under the plan.

Sec. 1227.   Effect of Confirmation

(a)   Except as provided in section 1228(a) of this title, the provisions of a confirmed plan bind the debtor, each creditor, each equity security holder, and each general partner in the debtor, whether or not the claim of such creditor, such equity security holder, or such general partner in the debtor is provided for by the plan, and whether or not such creditor, such equity security holder, or such general partner in the debtor has objected to, has accepted, or has rejected the plan.

(b)   Except as otherwise provided in the plan or the order confirming the plan, the confirmation of a plan vests all of the property of the estate in the debtor.

(c)   Except as provided in section 1228(a) of this title and except as otherwise provided in the plan or in the order confirming the plan, the property vesting in the debtor under subsection (b) of this section is free and clear of any claim or interest of any creditor provided for by the plan.

Sec. 1228.   Discharge

(a)   As soon as practicable after completion by the debtor of all payments under the plan, other than payments to holders of allowed claims provided for under section 1222(b)(5) or 1222(b)(10) of this title, unless the court approves a written waiver of discharge executed by the debtor after the order for relief under this chapter, the court shall grant the debtor a discharge of all debts provided for by the plan allowed under section 503 of this title or disallowed under section 502 of this title, except any debt—

    (1)   provided for under section 1222(b)(5) or 1222(b)(10) of this title; or

    (2)   of the kind specified in section 523(a) of this title.

  (b)   At any time after the confirmation of the plan and after notice and a hearing, the court may grant a discharge to a debtor that has not completed payments under the plan only if—

    (1)   the debtor's failure to complete such payments is due to circumstances for which the debtor should not justly be held accountable;

    (2)   the value, as of the effective date of the plan, of property actually distributed under the plan on account of each allowed unsecured claim is not less than the amount that would have been paid on such claim if the estate of the debtor had been liquidated under chapter 7 of this title on such date; and

    (3)   modification of the plan under section 1229 of this title is not practicable.

  (c)   A discharge granted under subsection (b) of this section discharges the debtor from all unsecured debts provided for by the plan or disallowed under section 502 of this title, except any debt—

    (1)   provided for under section 1222(b)(5) or 1222(b)(10) of this title; or

    (2)   of a kind specified in section 523(a) of this title.

  (d)   On request of a party in interest before one year after a discharge under this section is granted, and after notice and a hearing, the court may revoke such discharge only if—

    (1)   such discharge was obtained by the debtor through fraud; and

    (2)   the requesting party did not know of such fraud until after such discharge was granted.

  (e)   After the debtor is granted a discharge, the court shall terminate the services of any trustee serving in the case.

Sec. 1229. *Modification of Plan after Confirmation*

  (a)   At any time after confirmation of the plan but before the completion of payments under such plan, the plan may be modified, on request of the debtor, the trustee, or the holder of an allowed unsecured claim, to—

    (1)   increase or reduce the amount of payments on claims of a particular class provided for by the plan;

    (2)   extend or reduce the time for such payments; or

    (3)   alter the amount of the distribution to a creditor whose claim is provided for by the plan to the extent necessary to take account of any payment of such claim other than under the plan.

  (b) (1)   Sections 1222(a), 1222(b), and 1223(c) of this title and the requirements of section 1225(a) of this title apply to any modification under subsection (a) of this section.

    (2)   the plan as modified becomes the plan unless, after notice and a hearing, such modification is disapproved.

  (c)   A plan modified under this section may not provide for payments over a period that expires after three years after the time that the first payment under the original confirmed plan was due, unless the court, for cause, approves a longer period, but the court may not approve a period that expires after five years after such time.

Sec. 1230.   Revocation of an Order of Confirmation

(a)   On request of a party in interest at any time within 180 days after the date of the entry of an order of confirmation under section 1225 of this title, and after notice and a hearing, the court may revoke such order if such order was procured by fraud.

(b)   If the court revokes an order of confirmation under subsection (a) of this section the court shall dispose of the case under section 1207 of this title, unless, within the time fixed by the court, the debtor proposes and the court confirms a modification of the plan under section 1229 of this title.

Sec. 1231.   Special Tax Provisions

(a)   For the purpose of any State or local law imposing a tax on or measured by income, the taxable period of a debtor that is an individual shall terminate on the date of the order for relief under this chapter, unless the case was converted under section 706 of this title.

(b)   The trustee shall make a State or local tax return of income for the estate of an individual debtor in a case under this chapter for each taxable period after the order for relief under this chapter during which the case is pending.

(c)   The issuance, transfer, or exchange of a security, or the making or delivery of an instrument of transfer under a plan confirmed under section 1225 of this title, may not be taxed under any law imposing a stamp tax or similar tax.

(d)   The court may authorize the proponent of a plan to request a determination, limited to questions of law, by a State or local governmental unit charged with responsibility for collection or determination of a tax or measured by income, of the tax effects, under section 346 of this title and under the law imposing such tax, of the plan. In the event of an actual controversy, the court may declare such effects after the earlier of—

(1)   the date on which such governmental unit responds to the request under this subsection; or

(2)   270 days after such request.

13
ADJUSTMENT OF DEBTS OF AN INDIVIDUAL WITH REGULAR INCOME

SUBCHAPTER I. OFFICERS, ADMINISTRATION, AND THE ESTATE

Sec. 1301.   Stay of Action against Codebtor

(a)   Except as provided in subsections (b) and (c) of this section, after the order for relief under this chapter, a creditor may not act, or commence or continue any civil action, to collect all or any part of a consumer debt of the debtor from any individual that is liable on such debt with the debtor, or that secured such debt, unless—

(1)   such individual became liable on or secured such debt in the ordinary course of such individual's business; or

(2)   the case is closed, dismissed, or converted to a case under chapter 7 or 11 of this title.

(b)   A creditor may present a negotiable instrument, and may give notice of dishonor of such an instrument.

(c)   On request of a party in interest and after notice and a hearing, the court shall grant relief from the stay provided by subsection (a) of this section with respect to a creditor, to the extent that—

(1)   as between the debtor and the individual protected under subsection (a) of this section, such individual received the consideration for the claim held by such creditor;

(2)   the plan filed by the debtor proposes not to pay such claim; or

(3)   such creditor's interest would be irreparably harmed by continuation of such stay.

(d)   Twenty days after the filing of a request under subsection (c)(2) of this section for relief from the stay provided by subsection (a) of this section, such stay is terminated with respect to the party in interest making such request, unless the debtor or any individual that is liable on such debt with the debtor files and serves upon such party in interest a written objection to the taking of the proposed action.

Sec. 1302.   Trustee

(a)   If the United States trustee appoints an individual under section 586(b) of title 28 to serve as standing trustee in cases under this chapter and if such individual qualifies under section 322 of this title, then such individual shall serve as trustee in the case. Otherwise, the United States trustee shall appoint one disinterested person to serve as trustee in the case or the United States trustee may serve as a trustee in the case.

(b)   The trustee shall—

(1)   perform the duties specified in sections 704(2), 704(3), 704(4), 704(5), 704(6), 704(7), and 704(9) of this title;

(2)   appear to be heard at any hearing that concerns—

(A)   the value of property subject to a lien;

(B)   confirmation of a plan; or

(C)   modification of the plan after confirmation;

(3)   dispose of, under regulations issued by the Director of the Administrative Office of the United States Courts, moneys received or to be received in a case under chapter XII of the Bankruptcy Act;

(4)   advise, other than on legal matters, and assist the debtor in performance under the plan; and

(5)   ensure that the debtor commences making timely payments under section 1326 of this title.

(c)   If the debtor is engaged in business, then in addition to the duties specified in subsection (b) of this section, the trustee shall perform the duties specified in sections 1106(a)(3) and 1106(a)(4) of this title.

Sec. 1303.   Rights and Powers of Debtor

Subject to any limitations on a trustee under this chapter, the debtor shall have, exclusive of the trustee, the rights and powers of a trustee under sections 363(b), 363(d), 363(e), 363(f), and 363(l), of this title.

Sec. 1304. Debtor Engaged in Business

(a)   A debtor that is self-employed and incurs trade credit in the production of income from such employment is engaged in business.

(b)   Unless the court orders otherwise, a debtor engaged in business may operate the business of the debtor and, subject to any limitations on a trustee under sections 363(c) and 364 of this title and to such limitations or conditions as the court prescribes, shall have, exclusive of the trustee, the rights and powers of the trustee under such sections.

(c)   A debtor engaged in business shall perform the duties of the trustee specified in section 704(8) of this title.

Sec. 1305. Filing and Allowance of Postpetition Claims

(a)   A proof of claim may be filed by any entity that holds a claim against the debtor—

(1)   for taxes that become payable to a governmental unit while the case is pending; or

(2)   that is a consumer debt, that arises after the date of the order for relief under this chapter, and that is for property or services necessary for the debtor's performance under the plan.

(b)   Except as provided in subsection (c) of this section, a claim filed under subsection (a) of this section shall be allowed or disallowed under section 502 of this title, but shall be determined as of the date such claim arises, and shall be allowed under section 502(a), 502(b), or 502(c) of this title, or disallowed under section 502(d) or 502(e) of this title, the same as if such claim had arisen before the date of the filing of the petition.

(c)   A claim filed under subsection (a)(2) of this section shall be disallowed if the holder of such claim knew or should have known that prior approval by the trustee of the debtor's incurring the obligation was practicable and was not obtained.

Sec. 1306. Property of the Estate

(a)   Property of the estate includes, in addition to the property specified in section 541 of this title—

(1)   all property of the kind specified in such section that the debtor acquires after the commencement of the case but before the case is closed, dismissed, or converted to a case under Chapter 7, 11, or 12 of this title whichever occurs first; and

(2)   earnings from services performed by the debtor after the commencement of the case but before the case is closed, dismissed, or converted to a case under chapter 7, 11, or 12 of this title, whichever occurs first.

(b)   Except as provided in a confirmed plan or order confirming a plan, the debtor shall remain in possession of all property of the estate.

Sec. 1307. Conversion or Dismissal

(a)   The debtor may convert a case under this chapter to a case under chapter 7 of this title at any time. Any waiver of the right to convert under this subsection is unenforceable.

(b)   On request of the debtor at any time, if the case has not been converted under section 706, 1112, or 1208 of this title, the court shall dismiss a case under this chapter. Any waiver of the right to dismiss under this subsection is unenforceable.

(c)   Except as provided in subsection (e) of this section, on request of a party in interest or the United States trustee and after notice and a hearing, the court may convert a case under this chapter to a case under chapter 7 of this title, or may dismiss a case under this chapter, whichever is in the best interests of creditors and the estate, for cause, including—

(1)   unreasonable delay by the debtor that is prejudicial to creditors;

(2)   nonpayment of any fees and charges required under chapter 123 of title 28;

(3)   failure to file a plan timely under section 1321 of this title;

(4)   failure to commence making timely payments under section 1326 of this title;

(5)   denial of confirmation of a plan under section 1325 of this title and denial of a request made for additional time for filing another plan or a modification of a plan;

(6)   material default by the debtor with respect to a term of a confirmed plan;

(7)   revocation of the order of confirmation under section 1330 of this title, and denial of confirmation of a modified plan under section 1329 of this title;

(8)   termination of a confirmed plan by reason of the occurrence of a condition specified in the plan other than completion of payments under the plan;

(9)   only on request of the United States trustee, failure of the debtor to file, within fifteen days, or such additional time as the court may allow, after the filing of the petition commencing such case, the information required by paragraph (1) of section 521; or

(10)   only on request of the United States trustee, failure to timely file the information required by paragraph (2) of section 521.

(d)   Except as provided in subsection (e) of this section, at any time before the confirmation of a plan under section 1325 of this title, on request of a party in interest or the United States trustee and after notice and a hearing, the court may convert a case under this chapter to a case under chapter 11 or 12 of this title.

(e)   The court may not convert a case under this chapter to a case under chapter 7, 11, or 12 of this title if the debtor is a farmer, unless the debtor requests such conversion.

(f)   Notwithstanding any other provision of this section, a case may not be converted to a case under another chapter of this title unless the debtor may be a debtor under such chapter.

SUBCHAPTER II. THE PLAN

Sec. 1321.   *Filing of Plan*

The debtor shall file a plan.

Sec. 1322. Contents of Plan

(a)   The plan shall—

(1)   provide for the submission of all or such portion of future earnings or other future income of the debtor to the supervision and control of the trustee as is necessary for the execution of the plan;

(2)   provide for the full payment, in deferred cash payments, of all claims entitled to priority under section 507 of this title, unless the holder of a particular claim agrees to a different treatment of such claim; and

(3)   if the plan classifies claims, provide the same treatment for each claim within a particular class.

(b)   Subject to subsections (a) and (c) of this section, the plan may—

(1)   designate a class or classes of unsecured claims, as provided in section 1122 of this title, but may not discriminate unfairly against any class so designated; however, such plan may treat claims for a consumer debt of the debtor if an individual is liable on such consumer debt with the debtor differently than other unsecured claims;

(2)   modify the rights of holders of secured claims, other than a claim secured only by a security interest in real property that is the debtor's principal residence, or of holders of unsecured claims, or leave unaffected the rights of holders of any class of claims;

(3)   provide for the curing or waiving of any default;

(4)   provide for payments on any unsecured claim to be made concurrently with payments on any secured claim or any other unsecured claim;

(5)   notwithstanding paragraph (2) of this subsection, provide for the curing of any default within a reasonable time and maintenance of payments while the case is pending on any unsecured claim or secured claim on which the last payment is due after the date on which the final payment under the plan is due;

(6)   provide for the payment of all or any part of any claim allowed under section 1305 of this title;

(7)   subject to section 365 of this title, provide for the assumption, rejection, or assignment of any executory contract or unexpired lease of the debtor not previously rejected under such section;

(8)   provide for the payment of all or part of a claim against the debtor from property of the estate or property of the debtor;

(9)   provide for the vesting of property of the estate, on confirmation of the plan or at a later time, in the debtor or in any other entity; and

(10)   include any other appropriate provision not inconsistent with this title.

(c)   Notwithstanding subsection (b)(2) and applicable nonbankruptcy law—

(1)   a default with respect to, or that gave rise to, a lien on the debtor's principal residence may be cured under paragraph (3) or (5) of subsection (b) until such residence is sold at a foreclosure sale that is conducted in accordance with applicable nonbankruptcy law; and

(2)   in a case in which the last payment on the original payment schedule for a claim secured only by a security interest in real property that is the debtor's principal residence is due before the date on which the final pay-

ment under the plan is due, the plan may provide for the payment of the claim as modified pursuant to section 1325(a)(5) of this title.

(d)   The plan may not provide for payments over a period that is longer than three years, unless the court, for cause, approves a longer period, but the court may not approve a period that is longer than five years.

(e)   Notwithstanding subsection (b)(2) of this section and sections 506(b) and 1325(a)(5) of this title, if it is proposed in a plan to cure a default, the amount necessary to cure the default shall be determined in accordance with the underlying agreement and applicable nonbankruptcy law.

Sec. 1323.   *Modification of Plan before Confirmation*

(a)   The debtor may modify the plan at any time before confirmation, but may not modify the plan so that the plan as modified fails to meet the requirements of section 1322 of this title.

(b)   After the debtor files a modification under this section, the plan as modified becomes the plan.

(c)   Any holder of a secured claim that has accepted or rejected the plan is deemed to have accepted or rejected, as the case may be, the plan as modified, unless the modification provides for a change in the rights of such holder from what such rights were under the plan before modification, and such holder changes such holder's previous acceptance or rejection.

Sec. 1324.   *Confirmation Hearing*

After notice, the court shall hold a hearing on confirmation of the plan. A party in interest may object to confirmation of the plan.

Sec. 1325.   *Confirmation of Plan*

(a)   Except as provided in subsection (b), the court shall confirm a plan if—

(1)   the plan complies with the provisions of this chapter and with the other applicable provisions of this title;

(2)   any fee, charge, or amount required under chapter 123 of title 28, or by the plan, to be paid before confirmation, has been paid;

(3)   the plan has been proposed in good faith and not by any means forbidden by law;

(4)   the value, as of the effective date of the plan, of property to be distributed under the plan on account of each allowed unsecured claim is not less than the amount that would be paid on such claim if the estate of the debtor were liquidated under chapter 7 of this title on such date;

(5)   with respect to each allowed secured claim provided for by the plan—

(A)   the holder of such claim has accepted the plan;

(B)   (i)   the plan provides that the holder of such claim retain the lien securing such claim; and

(ii)   the value, as of the effective date of the plan, of property to be distributed under the plan on account of such claim is not less than the allowed amount of such claim; or

(C) the debtor surrenders the property securing such claim to such holder; and

(6) the debtor will be able to make all payments under the plan and to comply with the plan.

(b) (1) If the trustee or the holder of an allowed unsecured claim objects to the confirmation of the plan, then the court may not approve the plan unless, as of the effective date of the plan—

(A) the value of the property to be distributed under the plan on account of such claim is not less than the amount of such claim; or

(B) the plan provides that all of the debtor's projected disposable income to be received in the three-year period beginning on the date that the first payment is due under the plan will be applied to make payments under the plan.

(2) For purposes of this subsection, "disposable income" means income which is received by the debtor and which is not reasonably necessary to be expended—

(A) for the maintenance or support of the debtor or a dependent of the debtor; and

(B) if the debtor is engaged in business, for the payment of expenditures necessary for the continuation, preservation, and operation of such business.

(c) After confirmation of a plan, the court may order any entity from whom the debtor receives income to pay all or any part of such income to the trustee.

Sec. 1326. *Payments*

(a) (1) Unless the court orders otherwise, the debtor shall commence making the payments proposed by a plan within 30 days after the plan is filed.

(2) A payment made under this subsection shall be retained by the trustee until confirmation or denial of confirmation of a plan. If a plan is confirmed, the trustee shall distribute any such payment in accordance with the plan. If a plan is not confirmed, the trustee shall return any such [payments] payment to the debtor, after deducting any unpaid claim allowed under section 503(b) of this title as soon as practicable.

(b) Before or at the time of each payment to creditors under the plan, there shall be paid—

(1) any unpaid claim of the kind specified in section 507(a)(1) of this title; and

(2) if a standing trustee appointed under section 586(b) of title 28 is serving in the case, the percentage fee fixed for such standing trustee under section 586(e)(1)(B) of title 28.

(c) Except as otherwise provided in the plan or in the order confirming the plan, the trustee shall make payments to creditors under the plan.

Sec. 1327. *Effect of Confirmation*

(a) The provisions of a confirmed plan bind the debtor and each creditor, whether or not the claim of such creditor is provided for by the plan, and whether or not such creditor has objected to, has accepted, or has rejected the plan.

(b)   Except as otherwise provided in the plan or the order confirming the plan, the confirmation of a plan vests all of the property of the estate in the debtor.

(c)   Except as otherwise provided in the plan or in the order confirming the plan, the property vesting in the debtor under subsection (b) of this section is free and clear of any claim or interest of any creditor provided for by the plan.

Sec. 1328. *Discharge*

(a)   As soon as practicable after completion by the debtor of all payments under the plan, unless the court approves a written waiver of discharge executed by the debtor after the order for relief under this chapter, the court shall grant the debtor a discharge of all debts provided for by the plan or disallowed under section 502 of this title, except any debt—

(1)   provided for under section 1322(b)(5) of this title;

(2)   of the kind specified in paragraphs (5), (8), or (9) of section 523(a) of this title; or

(3)   for restitution, or a criminal fine, included in a sentence on the debtor's conviction of a crime.

(b)   At any time after the confirmation of the plan and after notice and a hearing, the court may grant a discharge to a debtor that has not completed payments under the plan only if—

(1)   the debtor's failure to complete such payments is due to circumstances for which the debtor should not justly be held accountable;

(2)   the value, as of the effective date of the plan, of property actually distributed under the plan on account of each allowed unsecured claim is not less than the amount that would have been paid on such claim if the estate of the debtor had been liquidated under chapter 7 of this title on such date; and

(3)   modification of the plan under section 1329 of this title is not practicable.

(c)   A discharge granted under subsection (b) of this section discharges the debtor from all unsecured debts provided for by the plan or disallowed under section 502 of this title, except any debt—

(1)   provided for under section 1322(b)(5) of this title; or

(2)   of a kind in section 523(a) of this title; or

(d)   Notwithstanding any other provision of this section, a discharge granted under this section does not discharge the debtor from any debt based on an allowed claim filed under section 1305(a)(2) of this title if prior approval by the trustee of the debtor's incurring such debt was practicable and was not obtained.

(e)   On request of a party in interest before one year after a discharge under this section is granted, and after notice and a hearing, the court may revoke such discharge only if—

(1)   such discharge was obtained by the debtor through fraud; and

(2)   the requesting party did not know of such fraud until after such discharge was granted.

Sec. 1329. *Modification of Plan after Confirmation*

(a)   At any time after confirmation of the plan but before the completion of payments under a plan, the plan may be modified, upon request of the debtor, the trustee, or the holder of an allowed unsecured claim, to—

(1)   increase or reduce the amount of payments on claims of a particular class provided for by the plan;

(2)   extend or reduce the time for such payments; or

(3)   alter the amount of the distribution to a creditor whose claim is provided for by the plan to the extent necessary to take account of any payment of such claim other than under the plan.

(b) (1)   Sections 1322(a), 1322(b), and 1323(c) of this title and the requirements of section 1325(a) of this title apply to any modification under subsection (a) of this section.

(2)   the plan as modified becomes the plan unless, after notice and a hearing, such modification is disapproved.

(c)   A plan modified under this section may not provide for payments over a period that expires after three years after the time that the first payment under the original confirmed plan was due, unless the court, for cause, approves a longer period, but the court may not approve a period that expires after five years after such time.

Sec. 1330. *Revocation of an Order of Confirmation*

(a)   On request of a party in interest at any time within 180 days after the date of the entry of an order of confirmation under section 1325 of this title, and after notice and a hearing, the court may revoke such order if such order was procured by fraud.

(b)   If the court revokes an order of confirmation under subsection (a) of this section, the court shall dispose of the case under section 1307 of this title, unless, within the time fixed by the court, the debtor proposes and the court confirms a modification of the plan under section 1329 of this title.

APPENDIX **B**

Federal Rules of Bankruptcy Procedure

CONTENTS
Rule

PART I.
COMMENCEMENT OF CASE; PROCEEDINGS RELATING TO PETITION AND ORDER FOR RELIEF

PART II.
OFFICERS AND ADMINISTRATION; NOTICES; MEETINGS; EXAMINATIONS; ELECTIONS; ATTORNEYS AND ACCOUNTANTS

PART III.
CLAIMS AND DISTRIBUTION TO CREDITORS AND EQUITY INTEREST HOLDERS; PLANS

PART IV.
THE DEBTOR: DUTIES AND BENEFITS

PARTS V, VI, VII, VIII, AND IX, COVERING RULES 5001–9032, ARE NOT INCLUDED IN THIS APPENDIX.

Rule 1001. Scope of Rules and Forms; Short Title

The Bankruptcy Rules and Forms govern procedure in cases under title 11 of the United States Code. The rules shall be cited as the Federal Rules of Bankruptcy Procedure and the forms as the Official Bankruptcy Forms. These rules shall be construed to secure the just, speedy, and inexpensive determination of every case and proceeding.

PART I
COMMENCEMENT OF CASE; PROCEEDINGS RELATING TO PETITION AND ORDER FOR RELIEF

Rule 1002. Commencement of Case

(a) **Petition.** A petition commencing a case under the Code shall be filed with the clerk.

(b) **Transmission to United States Trustee.** The clerk shall forthwith transmit to the United States trustee a copy of the petition filed pursuant to subdivision (a) of this rule.

Bankruptcy Code References: §§ 301, 302, 303, 304 and 362

Rule 1003. Involuntary Petition

(a) **Transferor or Transferee of Claim.** A transferor or transferee of a claim shall annex to the original and each copy of the petition a copy of all documents evidencing the transfer, whether transferred unconditionally, for security, or otherwise, and a signed statement that the claim was not transferred for the purpose of commencing the case and setting forth the consideration for and terms of the transfer. An entity that has transferred or acquired a claim for the purpose of commencing a case for liquidation under chapter 7 or for reorganization under chapter 11 shall not be a qualified petitioner.

(b) **Joinder of Petitioners After Filing.** If the answer to an involuntary petition filed by fewer than three creditors avers the existence of 12 or more creditors, the debtor shall file with the answer a list of all creditors with their addresses, a brief statement of the nature of their claims, and the amounts thereof. If it appears that there are 12 or more creditors as provided in § 303(b) of the Code, the court shall afford a reasonable opportunity for other creditors to join in the petition before a hearing is held thereon.

Bankruptcy Code References: §§ 303, 304 and 362

Rule 1004.   Partnership Petition

(a) Voluntary Petition. A voluntary petition may be filed on behalf of the partnership by one or more general partners if all general partners consent to the petition.

(b) Involuntary Petition; Notice and Summons. After filing of an involuntary petition under § 303(b)(3) of the Code, (1) the petitioning partners or other petitioners shall cause forthwith a copy of the petition to be sent to or served on each general partner who is not a petitioner; and (2) the clerk shall issue forthwith a summons for service on each general partner who is not a petitioner. Rule 1010 applies to the form and service of the summons.

Bankruptcy Code References: §§ 301, 303 and 723

Rule 1005.   Caption of Petition

The caption of a petition commencing a case under the Code shall contain the name of the court, the title of the case, and the docket number. The title of the case shall include the name, social security number and employer's tax identification number of the debtor and all other names used by the debtor within six years before filing the petition. If the petition is not filed by the debtor, it shall include all names used by the debtor which are known to petitioners.

Bankruptcy Code References: § 301, 302, 303 and 304

Rule 1006.   Filing Fee

(a) General Requirement. Every petition shall be accompanied by the filing fee except as provided in subdivision (b) of this rule. For the purpose of this rule, "filing fee" means the filing fee prescribed by 28 U.S.C. section 1930(a)(1)-(a)(5) and any other fee prescribed by the Judicial Conference of the United States under 28 U.S.C. section 1930(b) that is payable to the clerk upon the commencement of a case under the Code.

(b) Payment of Filing Fee in Installments.

(1) *Application for Permission to Pay Filing Fee in Installments.* A voluntary petition by an individual shall be accepted for filing if accompanied by the debtor's signed application stating that the debtor is unable to pay the filing fee except in installments. The application shall state the proposed terms of the installment payments and that the applicant has neither paid any money nor transferred any property to an attorney for services in connection with the case.

(2) *Action on Application.* Prior to the meeting of creditors, the court may order the filing fee paid to the clerk or grant leave to pay in installments and fix the number, amount and dates of payment. The number of installments shall not exceed four, and the final installment shall be payable not later than 120 days after filing the petition. For cause shown, the court may extend the time of any installment, provided the last installment is paid not later than 180 days after filing the petition.

(3) *Postponement of Attorney's Fees.* The filing fee must be paid in full before the debtor or chapter 13 trustee may pay an attorney or any other person who renders services to the debtor in connection with the case.

Bankruptcy Code References: § 301, 302, 303, 304, 707, 1112, 1208 and 1307

Rule 1007. *Lists, Schedules and Statements; Time Limits*

(a) List of Creditors and Equity Security Holders.

(1) *Voluntary Case.* In a voluntary case, the debtor shall file with the petition a list containing the name and address of each creditor unless the petition is accompanied by a schedule of liabilities.

(2) *Involuntary Case.* In an involuntary case, the debtor shall file within 15 days after entry of the order for relief, a list containing the name and address of each creditor unless a schedule of liabilities has been filed.

(3) *Equity Security Holders.* In a chapter 11 reorganization case, unless the court orders otherwise, the debtor shall file within 15 days after entry of the order for relief a list of the debtor's equity security holders of each class showing the number and kind of interests registered in the name of each holder, and the last known address or place of business of each holder.

(4) *Extension of Time.* Any extension of time for the filing of the lists required by this subdivision may be granted only on motion for cause shown and on notice to the United States trustee and to any trustee, committee elected pursuant to § 705 or appointed pursuant to § 1102 of the Code, or other party as the court may direct.

(b) Schedules and Statements Required.

(1) Except in a chapter 9 municipality case, the debtor, unless the court orders otherwise, shall file schedules of assets and liabilities, a schedule of current income and expenditures, a schedule of executory contracts and unexpired leases, and a statement of financial affairs, prepared as prescribed by the appropriate Official Forms.

(2) An individual debtor in a chapter 7 case shall file a statement of intention as required by § 512(2) of the Code, prepared as prescribed by the appropriate Official Form. A copy of the statement of intention shall be served on the trustee and the creditors named in the statement on or before the filing of the statement.

(c) Time Limits. The schedules and statements, other than the statement of intention, shall be filed with the petition in a voluntary case, or if the petition is accompanied by a list of all the debtor's creditors and their addresses, within 15 days thereafter, except as otherwise provided in subdivisions (d), (e), and (h) of this rule. In an involuntary case the schedules and statements, other than the statement of intention, shall be filed by the debtor within 15 days after entry of the order for relief. Schedules and statements previously filed in a pending chapter 7 case shall be deemed filed in a superseding case unless the court directs otherwise. Any extension of time for the filing of the schedules and statements may be granted only on motion for cause shown and on notice to the United States trustee and to any committee elected pursuant to § 705 or appointed pursuant to § 1102 of the Code, trustee, examiner, or other party as the court may direct. Notice of an extension shall be given to the United States trustee and to any committee, trustee, or other party as the court may direct.

(d) List of 20 Largest Creditors in Chapter 9 Municipality Case or Chapter 11 Reorganization Case. In addition to the list required by subdivision (a) of this rule, a debtor in a chapter 9 municipality case or a debtor in a voluntary chapter 11 reorganization case shall file with the petition a list containing the name, address and claim of the creditors that hold the 20 largest unsecured claims, excluding insiders, as prescribed by the appropriate Official Form. In an involuntary chapter 11 reorganization case, such list shall be filed by the debtor within 2 days after entry of the order for relief under § 303(h) of the Code.

(e) List in Chapter 9 Municipality Cases. The list required by subdivision (a) of this rule shall be filed by the debtor in a chapter 9 municipality case within such time as the court shall fix. If a proposed plan requires a revision of assessments so that the proportion of special assessments or special taxes to be assessed against some real property will be different from the proportion in effect at the date the petition is filed, the debtor shall also file a list showing the name and address of each known holder of title, legal or equitable, to real property adversely affected. On motion for cause shown, the court may modify the requirements of this subdivision and subdivision (a) of this rule.

(f) [Abrogated]

(g) Partnership and Partners. The general partners of a debtor partnership shall prepare and file the schedules of the assets and liabilities, schedule of current income and expenditures, schedule of executory contracts and unexpired leases, and statement of financial affairs of the partnership. The court may order any general partner to file a statement of personal assets and liabilities within such time as the court may fix.

(h) Interests Acquired or Arising after Petition. If, as provided by § 541(a)(5) of the Code, the debtor acquires or becomes entitled to acquire any interest in property, the debtor shall within 10 days after the information comes to the debtor's knowledge or within such further time the court may allow, file a supplemental schedule in the chapter 7 liquidation case, chapter 11 reorganization case, chapter 12 family farmer's debt adjustment case, or chapter 13 individual debt adjustment case. If any of the property required to be reported under this subdivision is claimed by the debtor as exempt, the debtor shall claim the exemptions in the supplemental schedule. The duty to file a supplemental schedule in accordance with this subdivision continues notwithstanding the closing of the case, except that the schedule need not be filed in a chapter 11, chapter 12, or chapter 13 case with respect to property acquired after entry of the order confirming a chapter 11 plan or discharging the debtor in a chapter 12 or chapter 13 case.

(i) Disclosure of List of Security Holders. After notice and hearing and for cause shown, the court may direct an entity other than the debtor or trustee to disclose any list of security holders of the debtor in its possession or under its control, indicating the name, address and security held by any of them. The entity possessing this list may be required either to produce the list or a true copy thereof, or permit inspection or copying, or otherwise disclose the information contained on the list.

(j) Impounding of Lists. On motion of a party in interest and for cause shown the court may direct the impounding of the lists filed under this rule, and may refuse to permit inspection by any entity. The court may permit inspection or use of the lists, however, by any party in interest on terms prescribed by the court.

(k) Preparation of List, Schedules, or Statements of Default of Debtor. If a list, schedule, or statement, other than a statement of intention, is not prepared and filed as required by this rule, the court may order the trustee, a petitioning creditor, committee, or other party to prepare and file any of these papers within a time fixed by the court. The court may approve reimbursement of the cost incurred in complying with such an order as an administrative expense.

(l) Transmission to United States Trustee. The clerk shall forthwith transmit to the United States trustee a copy of every list, schedule, and statement filed pursuant to subdivision (a)(1), (a)(2), (b), (d), or (h) of this rule.

Bankruptcy Code References: §§ 107, 303, 342, 343, 365, 521, 522, 523, 723, 727, 1102, 1104, 1106, 1109 and 1112.

Rule 1008.   Verification of Petitions and Accompanying Papers

All petitions, lists, schedules, statements and amendments thereto shall be verified or contain an unsworn declaration as provided in 28 U.S.C. § 1746.

Bankruptcy Code References: §§ 301, 302, 303, 304, 523 and 727

Rule 1009.   Amendments of Voluntary Petitions, Lists, Schedules, and Statements

(a) General Right to Amend. A voluntary petition, list, schedule, or statement may be amended by the debtor as a matter of course at any time before the case is closed. The debtor shall give notice of the amendment to the trustee and to any entity affected thereby. On motion of a party in interest, after notice and a hearing, the court may order any voluntary petition, list, schedule, or statement to be amended and the clerk shall give notice of the amendment to entities designated by the court.

(b) Statement of Intention. The statement of intention may be amended by the debtor at any time before the expiration of the period provided in § 521(2)(B) of the Code. The debtor shall give notice of the amendment to the trustee and to any entity affected thereby.

(c) Transmission to United States Trustee. The clerk shall forthwith transmit to the United States trustee a copy of every amendment filed pursuant to subdivision (a) or (b) of this rule.

Bankruptcy Code References: §§ 301, 302, 303, 521, 522, 523, 727 and 1112

Rule 1010.   Service of Involuntary Petition and Summons; Petition Commencing Ancillary Case

On the filing of an involuntary petition or a petition commencing a case ancillary to a foreign proceeding the clerk shall forthwith issue a summons for service. When an involuntary petition is filed, service shall be made on the debtor. When a petition commencing an ancillary case is filed, service shall be made on the parties against whom relief is sought pursuant to § 304(b) of the Code and on any other parties as the court may direct. The summons shall be served with a copy of the petition in the manner provided for service of a summons and complaint by Rule 7004(a) or (b). If service cannot be made, the court may order that the summons and petition be served by mailing copies to the party's last known address, and by at least publication in a manner and form directed by the court. The summons and petition may be served on the party anywhere. Rule 7004(f) and Rule 4(g) and (h) F.R.Civ.P. apply when service is made or attempted under this rule.

Bankruptcy Code References: §§ 303 and 324

Rule 1011. *Responsive Pleading or Motion in Involuntary and Ancillary Cases*

(a) **Who May Contest Petition.** The debtor named in an involuntary petition or a party in interest to a petition commencing a case ancillary to a foreign proceeding may contest the petition. In the case of a petition against a partnership under Rule 1004(b), a nonpetitioning general partner, or a person who is alleged to be a general partner but denies the allegation, may contest the petition.

(b) **Defenses and Objections; When Presented.** Defenses and objections to the petition shall be presented in the manner prescribed by Rule 12 F.R.Civ.P. and shall be filed and served within 20 days after service of the summons, except that if service is made by publication on a party or partner not residing or found within the state in which the court sits, the court shall prescribe the time for filing and serving the response.

(c) **Effect of Motion.** Service of a motion under Rule 12(b) F.R.Civ.P. shall extend the time for filing and serving a responsive pleading as permitted by Rule 12(a) F.R.Civ.P.

(d) **Claims Against Petitioners.** A claim against a petitioning creditor may not be asserted in the answer except for the purpose of defeating the petition.

(e) **Other Pleadings.** No other pleadings shall be permitted, except that the court may order a reply to an answer and prescribe the time for filing and service.

Bankruptcy Code References: §§ 303 and 304

Rule 1012. *[Abrogated]*

Rule 1013. *Hearing and Disposition of a Petition in an Involuntary Case*

(a) **Contested Petition.** The court shall determine the issues of a contested petition at the earliest practicable time and forthwith enter an order for relief, dismiss the petition, or enter any other appropriate order.

(b) **Default.** If no pleading or other defense to a petition is filed within the time provided by Rule 1011, the court, on the next day, or as soon thereafter as practicable, shall enter an order for the relief requested in the petition.

Bankruptcy Code Reference: § 303

Rule 1014. *Dismissal and Change of Venue*

(a) **Dismissal and Transfer of Cases.**

(1) *Cases Filed in Proper District.* If a petition is filed in a proper district, on timely motion of a party in interest, and after hearing on notice to the petitioners, the United States trustee, and other entities as directed by the court,

the case may be transferred to any other district if the court determines that the transfer is in the interest of justice or for the convenience of the parties.

(2) *Cases Filed in Improper District.* If a petition is filed in an improper district, on timely motion of a party in interest and after hearing on notice to the petitioners, the United States trustee, and other entities as directed by the court, the case may be dismissed or transferred to any other district if the court determines that transfer is in the interest of justice or for the convenience of the parties.

(b) Procedure When Petitions Involving the Same Debtor or Related Debtors are Filed in Different Courts. If petitions commencing cases under the Code are filed in different districts by or against (1) the same debtor, or (2) a partnership and one or more of its general partners, or (3) two or more general partners, or (4) a debtor and an affiliate, on motion filed in the district in which the petition filed first is pending and after hearing on notice to the petitioners, the United States trustee, and other entities as directed by the court, the court may determine, in the interest of justice or for the convenience of the parties, the district or districts in which the case or cases should proceed. Except as otherwise ordered by the court in the district in which the petition filed first is pending, the proceedings on the other petitions shall be stayed by the courts in which they have been filed until the determination is made.

Bankruptcy Code References: §§ 349, 707, 1112, 1208 and 1307.

Rule 1015.   Consolidation or Joint Administration of Cases Pending in Same Court

(a) Cases Involving Same Debtor. If two or more petitions are pending in the same court by or against the same debtor, the court may order consolidation of the cases.

(b) Cases Involving Two or More Related Debtors. If a joint petition or two or more petitions are pending in the same court by or against (1) a husband and wife, or (2) a partnership and one or more of its general partners, or (3) two or more general partners, or (4) a debtor and an affiliate, the court may order a joint administration of the estates. Prior to entering an order the court shall give consideration to protecting creditors of different estates against potential conflicts of interest. An order directing joint administration of individual cases of a husband and wife shall, if one spouse has elected the exemptions under § 522(b)(1) of the Code and the other has elected the exemptions under § 522(b)(2), fix a reasonable time within which either may amend the election so that both shall have elected the same exemptions. The order shall notify the debtors that unless they elect the same exemptions within the time fixed by the court, they will be deemed to have elected the exemptions provided by § 522(b)(1).

(c) Expediting and Protective Orders. When an order for consolidation or joint administration of a joint case or two or more cases is entered pursuant to this rule, while protecting the rights of the parties under the Code, the court may enter orders as may tend to avoid unnecessary costs and delay.

Bankruptcy Code Reference: § 302

Rule 1016.   Death or Incompetency of Debtor

Death or incompetency of the debtor shall not abate a liquidation case under chapter 7 of the Code. In such event the estate shall be administered and the case concluded in the same manner, so far as possible, as though the death or incompetency had not occurred. If a reorganization, family farmer's debt adjustment, or individual's debt adjustment case is pending under chapter 11, chapter 12, or chapter 13, the case may be dismissed; or if further administration is possible and in the best interest of the parties, the case may proceed and be concluded in the same manner, so far as possible, as though the death or incompetency had not occurred.

Bankruptcy Code References: §§ 348, 349, 707, 1113, 1208 and 1307.

Rule 1017.   *Dismissal or Conversion of Case; Suspension*

(a) Voluntary Dismissal; Dismissal for Want of Prosecution or Other Cause. Except as provided in §§ 707(a)(3), 707(b), 1208(b), and 1307(b) of the Code and in Rule 1017(b), (c) and (e), a case shall not be dismissed on motion of the petitioner or for want of prosecution or other cause or by consent of the parties, before a hearing on notice as provided in Rule 2002. For the purpose of the notice, the debtor shall file a list of all creditors with their addresses within the time fixed by the court unless the list was previously filed. If the debtor fails to file the list, the court may order the debtor or another entity to prepare and file it.

(b) Dismissal for Failure to Pay Filing Fee.

(1)   For failure to pay any installment of the filing fee, the court may after hearing on notice to the debtor and the trustee dismiss the case.

(2)   If the case is dismissed or the case closed without full payment of the filing fee, the installments collected shall be distributed in the same manner and proportions as if the filing fee had been paid in full.

(c) Dismissal of voluntary chapter 7 or chapter 13 case for failure to timely file list of creditors, schedules, and statement of financial affairs. The court may dismiss a voluntary chapter 7 or chapter 13 case under section 707(a)(3) or section 1307(c)(9) after a hearing on notice served by the United States trustee on the debtor, the trustee, and any other entities as the court directs.

(d) Suspension. The court shall not dismiss a case or suspend proceedings under section 305 before a hearing on notice as provided in Rule 2002(a).

(e) Dismissal of an individual debtor's chapter 7 case for substantial abuse. The court may dismiss an individual debtor's case for substantial abuse under section 707(b) only on motion by the United States trustee or on the court's own motion and after a hearing on notice to the debtor, the trustee, the United States trustee, and any other entities as the court directs.

(1)   A motion to dismiss a case for substantial abuse may be filed by the United States trustee only within 60 days after the first date set for the meeting of creditors under section 341(a), unless, before the time has expired, the court for cause extends the time for filing the motion. The United States trustee shall set forth in the motion all matters to be submitted to the court for its consideration at the hearing.

(2)   If the hearing is set on the court's own motion, notice of the hearing shall be served on the debtor no later than 60 days after the first date set for the meeting of creditors under section 341(a). The notice shall set forth all matters to be considered by the court at the hearing.

(f)   Procedure for dismissal, conversion, or suspension.

(1)   Rule 9014 governs a proceeding to dismiss or suspend a case, or to

convert a case to another chapter, except under sections 706(a), 1112(a), 1208(a) or (b), or 1307(a) or (b).

(2)   Conversion or dismissal under sections 706(a), 1112(a), 1208(b), or 1307(b) shall be on motion filed and served as required by Rule 9013.

(3)   A chapter 12 or chapter 13 case shall be converted without court order when the debtor files a notice of conversion under sections 1208(a) or 1307(a). The filing date of the notice becomes the date of the conversion order for the purposes of applying section 348(c) and Rule 1019. The clerk shall promptly transmit a copy of the notice to the United States trustee.

Bankruptcy Code References: §§ 303, 305, 348, 349, 350, 706, 707, 1112, 1208 and 1307.

Rule 1018.   Contested Involuntary Petitions; Contested Petitions Commencing Ancillary Cases; Proceedings to Vacate Order for Relief; Applicability of Rules in Part VII Governing Adversary Proceedings

The following rules in Part VII apply to all proceedings relating to a contested involuntary petition, to proceedings relating to a contested petition commencing a case ancillary to a foreign proceeding, and to all proceedings to vacate an order for relief; Rules 7005, 7008–7010, 7015, 7016, 7024–7026, 7028–7037, 7052, 7054, 7056, and 7062, except as otherwise provided in Part I of these rules and unless the court otherwise directs. The court may direct that other rules in Part VII shall also apply. For the purposes of this rule a reference in the Part VII rules to adversary proceedings shall be read as a reference to proceedings relating to a contested involuntary petition, or contested ancillary petition, or proceedings to vacate an order for relief. Reference in the Federal Rules of Civil Procedure to the complaint shall be read as a reference to the petition.

Bankruptcy Code References: §§ 303 and 304

Rule 1019.   Conversion of Chapter 11 Reorganization Case, Chapter 12 Family Farmer's Debt Adjustment Case, or Chapter 13 Individual's Debt Adjustment Case to Chapter 7 Liquidation Case

When a chapter 11, chapter 12, or chapter 13 case has been converted or reconverted to a chapter 7 case:

(1)   *Filing of Lists, Inventories, Schedules, Statements.*

(A)   Lists, inventories, schedules, and statements of financial affairs theretofore filed shall be deemed to be filed in the chapter 7 case, unless the court directs otherwise. If they have not been previously filed, the debtor shall comply with Rule 1007 as if an order for relief had been entered on an involuntary petition on the date of the entry of the order directing that the case continue under chapter 7.

(B)   If a statement of intention is required, it shall be filed within 30 days after entry of the order of conversion or before the first date set for the meeting of creditors, whichever is earlier. The court may grant an extension of time for cause only on written motion filed, or oral request made during a hearing, before the time has expired. Notice of an extension shall be given to the United States trustee and to any committee, trustee, or other party as the court may direct.

(2) *New Filing Periods.* A new time period for filing claims, a complaint objecting to discharge, or a complaint to obtain a determination of dischargeability of any debt shall commence pursuant to Rules 3002, 4004, or 4007, provided that a new time period shall not commence if a chapter 7 case had been converted to a chapter 11, 12, or 13 case and thereafter reconverted to a chapter 7 case and the time for filing claims, a complaint objecting to discharge, or a complaint to obtain a determination of the dischargeability of any debt, or any extension thereof, expired in the original chapter 7 case.

(3) *Claims Filed in Superseded Case.* All claims actually filed by a creditor in the superseded case shall be deemed filed in the chapter 7 case.

(4) *Turnover of Records and Property.* After qualification of, or assumption of duties by the chapter 7 trustee, any debtor in possession or trustee previously acting in the chapter 11, 12, or 13 case shall, forthwith, unless otherwise ordered, turn over to the chapter 7 trustee all records and property of the estate in the possession or control of the debtor in possession or trustee.

(5) *Filing Final Report and Schedule of Postpetition Debts.*

(A) *Conversion of Chapter 11 or Chapter 12 Case.* Unless the court directs otherwise, if a chapter 11 or chapter 12 case is converted to chapter 7, the debtor-in-possession or, if the debtor is not a debtor-in-possession, the trustee serving at the time of conversion, shall:

(i) not later than 15 days after conversion of the case, file a schedule of unpaid debts incurred after the filing of the petition and before conversion of the case, including the name and address of each holder of a claim; and

(ii) not later than 30 days after conversion of the case, file and transmit to the United States trustee a final report and account;

(B) *Conversion of Chapter 13 Case.* Unless the court directs otherwise, if a chapter 13 case is converted to chapter 7,

(i) the debtor, not later than 15 days after conversion of the case, shall file a schedule of unpaid debts incurred after the filing of the petition and before conversion of the case, including the name and address of each holder of a claim; and

(ii) the trustee, not later than 30 days after conversion of the case, shall file and transmit to the United States trustee a final report and account;

(C) *Conversion After Confirmation of a Plan.* Unless the court orders otherwise, if a chapter 11, chapter 12, or chapter 13 case is converted to chapter 7 after confirmation of a plan, the debtor shall file:

(i) a schedule of property not listed in the final report and account acquired after the filing of the petition but before conversion, except if the case is converted from chapter 13 to chapter 7 and § 348(f)(2) does not apply;

(ii) a schedule of unpaid debts not listed in the final report and account incurred after confirmation but before the conversion; and

(iii) a schedule of executory contracts and unexpired leases entered into or assumed after the filing of the petition but before conversion.

(D) *Transmission to United States Trustee.* The clerk shall forth-with transmit to the United States trustee a copy of every schedule filed pursuant to Rule 1019(5).

(6) *Postpetition Claims; Preconversion Administrative Expenses: Notice.* A request for payment of an administrative expense incurred before conversion of the case is timely filed under § 503(a) of the Code if it is filed before conversion or a time fixed by the court. If the request is filed by a governmental unit, it is timely if it is filed before conversion or within the later of a time fixed by the court or 180 days after the date of the conversion. A claim of a kind specified in § 348(d) may be filed in accordance with Rules 3001(a)–(d) and 3002. Upon the filing of the schedule of unpaid debts incurred after commencement of the case and before conversion, the clerk, or some other person as the court may direct, shall give notice to those entities listed on the schedule of the time for filing a request for payment of an administrative expense and, unless a notice of insufficient assets to pay a dividend is mailed in accordance with Rule 2002(e), the time for filing a claim of a kind specified in § 348(d).

Bankruptcy Code References: §§ 341, 348, 365, 501, 502, 521, 523, 542, 701, 702, 704, 706, 726, 727, 1111, 1112, 1208 and 1307.

Rule 1020. Election to Be Considered a Small Business in a Chapter 11 Reorganization Case

In a chapter 11 reorganization case, a debtor that is a small business may elect to be considered a small business by filing a written statement of election not later than 60 days after the date of the order for relief.

Bankruptcy Code References: §§ 1102, 1121 and 1125.

PART II
OFFICERS AND ADMINISTRATION; NOTICES; MEETINGS; EXAMINATIONS; ELECTIONS; ATTORNEYS AND ACCOUNTANTS

Rule 2001. Appointment of Interim Trustee before Order for Relief in a Chapter 7 Liquidation Case

(a) **Appointment.** At any time following the commencement of an involuntary liquidation case and before an order for relief, the court on written motion of a party in interest may order the appointment of an interim trustee under § 303(g) of the Code. The motion shall set forth the necessity for the appointment and may be granted only after hearing on notice to the debtor, the petitioning creditors, the United States trustee, and other parties in interest as the court may designate.

(b) **Bond of Movant.** An interim trustee may not be appointed under this rule unless the movant furnishes a bond in an amount approved by the court, conditioned to indemnify the debtor for costs, attorney's fee, expenses, and damages allowable under § 301(i) of the Code.

(c) **Order of Appointment.** The order directing the appointment of an interim trustee shall state the reason the appointment is necessary and shall specify the trustee's duties.

(d) **Turnover and Report.** Following qualification of the trustee selected under § 702 of the Code, the interim trustee, unless otherwise ordered, shall (1) forthwith deliver to the trustee all the records and property of the estate in possession or subject to control of the interim trustee, and (2) within 30 days thereafter file a final report and account.

Bankruptcy Code References: §§ 303, 542, 701, 702 and 704.

Rule 2002.   Notices to Creditors, Equity Security Holders, United States, and United States Trustee

(a) **Twenty-Day Notices to Parties in Interest.** Except as provided in subdivisions (h), (i) and (l) of this rule, the clerk, or some other person as the court may direct, shall give the debtor, the trustee, all creditors and indenture trustees at least 20 days notice by mail of (1) the meeting of creditors under § 341 or § 1104(b) of the Code; (2) a proposed use, sale, or lease of property of the estate other than in the ordinary course of business, unless the court for cause shown shortens the time or directs another method of giving notice; (3) the hearing on approval of a compromise or settlement of a controversy other than approval of an agreement pursuant to Rule 4001(d), unless the court for cause shown directs that notice not be sent; (4) in a chapter 7 liquidation, a chapter 11 reorganization case, and a chapter 12 family farmer's debt adjustment case, the hearing on the dismissal of the case or the conversion of the case to another chapter, unless the hearing is under § 707(a)(3) or § 707(b) or is on dismissal of the case for failure to pay the filing fee; (5) the time fixed to accept or reject a proposed modification of a plan; (6) hearings on all applications for compensation or reimbursement of expenses totalling in excess of $500; (7) the time fixed for filing proofs of claims pursuant to Rule 3003(c); and (8) the time fixed for filing objections and the hearing to consider confirmation of a chapter 12 plan.

(b) **Twenty-Five-Day Notices to Parties in Interest.** Except as provided in subdivision (1) of this rule, the clerk, or some other person as the court may direct, shall give the debtor, the trustee, all creditors and indenture trustees not less than 25 days notice by mail of (1) the time fixed for filing objections and the hearing to consider approval of a disclosure statement; and (2) the time fixed for filing objections and the hearing to consider confirmation of a chapter 9, chapter 11, or chapter 13 plan.

(c) **Content of Notice.**

(1) *Proposed Use, Sale, or Lease of Property.* Subject to Rule 6004 the notice of a proposed use, sale, or lease of property required by subdivision (a)(2) of this rule shall include the time and place of any public sale, the terms and conditions of any private sale and the time fixed for filing objections. The notice of a proposed use, sale, or lease of property, including real estate, is sufficient if it generally describes the property.

(2) *Notice of Hearing on Compensation.* The notice of a hearing on an application for compensation or reimbursement of expenses required by subdivision (a)(7) of this rule shall identify the applicant and the amounts requested.

(d) **Notice to Equity Security Holders.** In a chapter 11 reorganization case, unless otherwise ordered by the court, the clerk, or some other person as the court may direct, shall in the manner and form directed by the court give notice to all equity security holders of (1) the order for relief; (2) any meeting of equity security holders held pursuant to § 341 of the Code; (3) the hearing on the proposed sale of all or substantially all of the debtor's assets; (4) the hearing on the dismissal or conversion of a case to another chapter; (5) the time fixed for filing objections to and the hearing to consider approval of a disclosure statement; (6) the time fixed for filing objections to and the hearing to consider confirmation of a plan; and (7) the time fixed to accept or reject a proposed modification of a plan.

(e) **Notice of No Dividend.** In a chapter 7 liquidation case, if it appears from the schedules that there are no assets from which a dividend can be paid, the notice of the meeting of creditors may include a statement to that effect; that it is unnecessary to file claims; and that if sufficient assets become available for the payment of a dividend, further notice will be given for the filing of claims.

(f) **Other Notices.** Except as provided in subdivision (1) of this rule, the clerk, or some other person as the court may direct, shall give the debtor, all creditors, and indenture trustees notice by mail of (1) the order for relief; (2) the dismissal or the conversion of the case to another chapter or the suspension of proceedings under § 305; (3) the time allowed for filing claims pursuant to Rule 3002; (4) the time fixed for filing a complaint objecting to the debtor's discharge pursuant to § 727 of the Code as provided in Rule 4004; (5) the time fixed for filing a complaint to determine the dischargeability of a debt pursuant to § 523 of the Code as provided in Rule 4007; (6) the waiver, denial, or revocation of a discharge as provided in Rule 4006; (7) entry of an order confirming a chapter 9, 11, or 12 plan; and (8) a summary of the trustee's final report and account in a chapter 7 case if the net proceeds realized exceed $1,500. Notice of the time fixed for accepting or rejecting a plan pursuant to Rule 3017(c) shall be given in accordance with Rule 3017(d).

(g) **Addresses of Notices.** All notices required to be mailed under this rule to a creditor, equity security holder, or indenture trustee shall be addressed as such entity or an authorized agent may direct in a filed request; otherwise, to the address shown in the list of creditors or the schedule whichever is filed later. If a different address is stated in a proof of claim duly filed, that address shall be used unless a notice of no dividend has been given.

(h) **Notices to Creditors Whose Claims Are Filed.** In a chapter 7 case, after 90 days following the first date set for the meeting of creditors under § 341 of the Code, the court may direct that all notices required by subdivision (a) of this rule be mailed only to the debtor, the trustee, all indenture trustees, creditors that hold claims for which proofs of claim have been filed, and creditors, if any, that are still permitted to file claims by reason of an extension granted pursuant to Rule 3002(c)(1) or (c)(2). In a case where notice of insufficient assets to pay a dividend has been given to creditors pursuant to subdivision (e) of this rule, after 90 days following the mailing of a notice of the time for filing claims pursuant to Rule 3002(c)(5), the court may direct that notices be mailed only to the entities specified in the preceding sentence.

(i) **Notices to Committees.** Copies of all notices required to be mailed under this rule shall be mailed to the committees elected pursuant to § 705 or appointed pursuant to § 1102 of the Code or to their authorized agents. Notwithstanding the foregoing subdivisions, the court may order that notices required by subdivision (a)(2), (3) and (7) of this rule be transmitted to the

United States trustee and be mailed only to the committees elected pursuant to § 705 or appointed pursuant to § 1102 of the Code or to their authorized agents and to the creditors and equity security holders who serve on the trustee or debtor in possession and file a request that all notices be mailed to them. A committee appointed pursuant to § 1114 shall receive copies of all notices required by subdivisions (a)(1), (a)(6), (b), (f)(2), and (f)(7), and such other notices as the court may direct.

(j) **Notices to the United States.** Copies of notices required to be mailed to all creditors under this rule shall be mailed (1) in a chapter 11 reorganization case to the Securities and Exchange Commission at any place the Commission designates if the Commission has filed either a notice of appearance in the case or a written request to receive notices; (2) in a commodity broker case, to the Commodity Futures Trading Commission at Washington, D.C.; (3) in a chapter 11 case to the District Director of Internal Revenue for the district in which the case is pending; (4) if the papers in the case disclose a debt to the United States other than for taxes, to the United States attorney for the district in which the case is pending and to the department, agency, or instrumentality of the United States through which the debtor became indebted; or if the filed papers disclose a stock interest of the United States, to the Secretary of the Treasury at Washington, D.C.

(k) **Notices to United States Trustee.** Unless the case is a chapter 9 municipality case or unless the United States trustee otherwise requests, the clerk, or some other person as the court may direct, shall transmit to the United States trustee notice of the matters described in subdivisions (a)(2), (a)(3), (a)(5), (a)(9), (b), (f)(1), (f)(2), (f)(4), (f)(6), (f)(7), and (f)(8) of this rule and notice of hearings on all applications for compensation or reimbursement of expenses. Notices to the United States trustee shall be transmitted within the time prescribed in subdivision (a) or (b) of this rule. The United States trustee shall also receive notice of any other matter if such notice is requested by the United States trustee or ordered by the court. Nothing in these rules shall require the clerk or any other person to transmit to the United States trustee any notice, schedule, report, application or other document in a case under the Securities Investor Protection Act, 15 U.S.C. § 78aaa et seq.

(l) **Notice by Publication.** The court may order notice by publication if it finds that notice by mail is impracticable or that it is desirable to supplement the notice.

(m) **Orders Designating Matter of Notices.** The court may from time to time enter orders designating the matters in respect to which, the entity to whom, and the form and manner in which notices shall be sent except as otherwise provided by these rules.

(n) **Caption.** The caption of every notice given under this rule shall comply with Rule 1005. The caption of every notice required to be given by the debtor to a creditor shall include the information required to be in the notice by § 342(c) of the Code.

(o) **Notice of Order for Relief in Consumer Case.** In a voluntary case commenced by an individual debtor whose debts are primarily consumer debts, the clerk or some other person as the court may direct shall give the trustee and all creditors notice by mail of the order for relief within 20 days from the date thereof.

Bankruptcy Code References: §§ 301–304, 326, 327, 328, 329–331, 341, 363, 501, 502, 504, 523, 706, 707, 726, 727, 944, 1102, 1111, 1112, 1125, 1126, 1127, 1128, 1129, 1144, 1206, 1208, 1223, 1228, 1229, 1230, 1307, 1323, 1324, 1328, 1329 and 1330.

Rule 2003.   *Meeting of Creditors or Equity Security Holders*

(a) **Date and Place.** In a chapter 7 liquidation or a chapter 11 reorganization case, the United States trustee shall call a meeting of creditors to be held no fewer than 20 and no more than 40 days after the order for relief. In a chapter 12 family farmer's debt adjustment case, the United States trustee shall call a meeting of creditors to be held no fewer than 20 and no more than 35 days after the order for relief. In a chapter 13 individual's debt adjustment case, the United States trustee shall call a meeting of creditors to be held no fewer than 20 and no more than 50 days after the order for relief. If there is an appeal from or a motion to vacate the order for relief, or if there is a motion to dismiss the case, the United States trustee may set a later [time] date for the meeting. The meeting may be held at a regular place for holding court or at any other place designated by the United States trustee within the district convenient for the parties in interest. If the United States trustee designates a place for the meeting which is not regularly staffed by the United States trustee or an assistant who may preside at the meeting, the meeting may be held not more than 60 days after the order for relief.

(b) **Order of Meeting.**

(1) *Meeting of Creditors.* The United States trustee shall preside at the meeting of creditors. The business of the meeting shall include the examination of the debtor under oath and, in a chapter 7 liquidation case, may include the election of a trustee or of a creditors' committee. The presiding officer shall have the authority to administer oaths.

(2) *Meeting of Equity Security Holders.* If the United States trustee convenes a meeting of equity security holders pursuant to § 341(b) of the Code, the United States trustee shall fix a date for the meeting and shall preside.

(3) *Right To Vote.* In a chapter 7 liquidation case, a creditor is entitled to vote at a meeting if, at or before the meeting, the creditor has filed a proof of claim or a writing setting forth facts evidencing a right to vote pursuant to § 702(a) of the Code unless objection is made to the claim or the proof of claim is insufficient on its face. A creditor of a partnership may file a proof of claim or writing evidencing a right to vote for the trustee for the estate of a general partner notwithstanding that a trustee for the estate of the partnership has previously qualified. In the event of an objection to the amount or allowability of a claim for the purpose of voting, unless the court orders otherwise, the United States trustee shall tabulate the votes for each alternative presented by the dispute and, if resolution of such dispute is necessary to determine the result of the election, the tabulation for each alternative shall be reported to the court.

(c) **Record of Meeting.** Any examination under oath at the meeting of creditors held pursuant to § 341(a) of the Code shall be recorded verbatim by the United States trustee using electronic sound recording equipment or other means of recording, and such record shall be preserved by the United States trustee and available for public access until two years after the conclusion of the meeting of creditors. Upon request of any entity, the United States trustee shall certify and provide a copy or transcript of such recording at the entity's expense.

(d) Report of Election and Resolution of Disputes in a Chapter 7 Case.

(1) Report of undisputed election. In a chapter 7 case, if the election of a trustee or a member of a creditors' committee is not disputed, the United States trustee shall promptly file a report of the election, including the name and address of the person or entity elected and a statement that the election is undisputed.

(2) Disputed election. If the election is disputed, the United States trustee shall promptly file a report stating that the election is disputed, informing the court of the nature of the dispute, and listing the name and address of any candidate elected under any alternative presented by the dispute. No later than the date on which the report is filed, the United States trustee shall mail a copy of the report to any party-in-interest that has made a request to receive a copy of the report. Pending disposition by the court of a disputed election for trustee, the interim trustee shall continue in office. Unless a motion for the resolution of the dispute is filed no later than 10 days after the United States trustee files a report of a disputed election for trustee, the interim trustee shall serve as trustee in the case.

Bankruptcy Code References: §§ 341, 343, 701, 702, 705, 723, 901, 1102, 1103 and 1161

(e) Adjournment. The meeting may be adjourned from time to time by announcement at the meeting of the adjourned date and time without further written notice.

(f) Special Meetings. The United States trustee may call a special meeting of creditors on request of a party in interest or on the United States trustee's own initiative.

(g) Final Meeting. If the United States trustee calls a final meeting of creditors in a case in which the net proceeds realized exceed $1,500, the clerk shall mail a summary of the trustee's final account to the creditors with a notice of the meeting, together with a statement of the amount of the claims allowed. The trustee shall attend the final meeting and shall, if requested, report on the administration of the estate.

Rule 2004. *Examination*

(a) Examination on Motion. On motion of any party in interest, the court may order the examination of any entity.

(b) Scope of Examination. The examination of an entity under this rule or of the debtor under § 343 of the Code may relate only to the acts, conduct, or property or to the liabilities and financial condition of the debtor, or to any matter which may affect the administration of the debtor's estate, or to the debtor's right to a discharge. In a family farmer's debt adjustment case under chapter 12, an individual's debt adjustment case under chapter 13, or a reorganization case under chapter 11 of the Code, other than for the reorganization of a railroad, the examination may also relate to the operation of any business and the desirability of its continuance, the source of any money or property acquired or to be acquired by the debtor for purposes of consummating a plan and the consideration given or offered therefor, and any other matter relevant to the case or to the formulation of a plan.

(c) Compelling Attendance and Production of Documentary Evidence. The attendance of an entity for examination and the production of documentary evidence may be compelled in the manner provided in Rule 9016 for the attendance of witnesses at a hearing or trial.

(d) Time and Place of Examination of Debtor. The court may for cause shown and on terms as it may impose order the debtor to be examined under this rule at any time or place it designates, whether within or without the district wherein the case is pending.

(e) Mileage. An entity other than a debtor shall not be required to attend as a witness unless lawful mileage and witness fee for one day's attendance shall be first tendered. If the debtor resides more than 100 miles from the place of examination when required to appear for an examination under this rule, the mileage allowed by law to a witness shall be tendered for any distance more than 100 miles from the debtor's residence at the date of the filing of the first petition commencing a case under the Code or the residence at the time the debtor is required to appear for the examination, whichever is the lesser.

Bankruptcy Code References: §§ 341, 343 and 521

Rule 2005. *Apprehension and Removal of Debtor to Compel Attendance for Examination*

(a) Order to Compel Attendance for Examination. On motion of any party in interest supported by an affidavit alleging (1) that the examination of the debtor is necessary for the proper administration of the estate and that there is reasonable cause to believe that the debtor is about to leave or has left the debtor's residence or principal place of business to avoid examination, or (2) that the debtor has evaded service of a subpoena or of an order to attend for examination, or (3) that the debtor has willfully disobeyed a subpoena or order to attend for examination, duly served, the court may issue to the marshal, or some other officer authorized by law, an order directing the officer to bring the debtor before the court without unnecessary delay. If, after hearing, the court finds the allegations to be true, the court shall thereupon cause the debtor to be examined forthwith. If necessary, the court shall fix conditions for further examination and for the debtor's obedience to all orders made in reference thereto.

(b) Removal. Whenever any order to bring the debtor before the court is issued under this rule and the debtor is found in a district other than that of the court issuing the order, the debtor may be taken into custody under the order and removed in accordance with the following rules:

(1) If the debtor is taken into custody under the order at a place less than 100 miles from the place of issue of the order, the debtor shall be brought forthwith before the court that issued the order.

(2) If the debtor is taken into custody under the order at a place 100 miles or more from the place of issue of the order, the debtor shall be brought without unnecessary delay before the nearest available United

States magistrate judge, bankruptcy judge, or district judge. If, after hearing, the magistrate judge, bankruptcy judge, or district judge finds that an order has issued under this rule and that the person in custody is the debtor, or if the person in custody waives a hearing, the magistrate judge, bankruptcy judge, or district judge shall order removal and the person in custody shall be released on conditions ensuring prompt appearance before the court that issued the order to compel the attendance.

(c) Conditions of Release. In determining what conditions will reasonably assure attendance or obedience under subdivision (a) of this rule or appearance under subdivision (b) of this rule, the court shall be governed by the provisions and policies of title 18, U.S.C., § 3146(a) and (b).

Bankruptcy Code References: §§ 341 and 343

Rule 2006. *Solicitation and Voting of Proxies in Chapter 7 Liquidation Cases*

(a) Applicability. This rule applies only in a liquidation case pending under chapter 7 of the Code.

(b) Definitions.

   (1) Proxy. A proxy is a written power of attorney authorizing any entity to vote the claim or otherwise act as the owner's attorney in fact in connection with the administration of the estate.

   (2) Solicitation of Proxy. The solicitation of a proxy is any communication, other than one from an attorney to a regular client who owns a claim or from an attorney to the owner of a claim who has requested the attorney to represent the owner, by which a creditor is asked, directly or indirectly, to give a proxy after or in contemplation of the filing of a petition by or against the debtor.

(c) Authorized Solicitation.

   (1) A proxy may be solicited only by (A) a creditor owning an allowable unsecured claim against the estate on the date of the filing of the petition; (B) a committee elected pursuant to § 705 of the Code; (C) a committee of creditors selected by a majority in number and amount of claims of creditors (i) whose claims are not contingent or unliquidated, (ii) who are not disqualified from voting under § 702(a) of the Code and (iii) who were present or represented at a meeting of which all creditors having claims of over $500 or the 100 creditors having the largest claims had at least five days notice in writing and of which meeting written minutes were kept and are available reporting the names of the creditors present or represented and voting and the amounts of their claims; or (D) a bona fide trade or credit association, but such association may solicit only creditors who were its members or subscribers in good standing and had allowable unsecured claims on the date of the filing of the petition.

   (2) A proxy may be solicited only in writing.

(d) Solicitation Not Authorized. This rule does not permit solicitation (1) in any interest other than that of general creditors; (2) by or on behalf of any custodian; (3) by the interim trustee or by or on behalf of any entity not qualified to vote under § 702(a) of the Code; (4) by or on behalf of an attorney at law; or (5) by or on behalf of a transferee of a claim for collection only.

(e) Data Required from Holders of Multiple Proxies. At any time before the voting commences at any meeting of creditors pursuant to § 341(a) of the Code, or at any other time as the court may direct, a holder of two or more proxies shall file and transmit to the United States trustee a verified list of the proxies to be voted and a verified statement of the pertinent facts and circumstances in connection with the execution and delivery of each proxy, including:

(1) a copy of the solicitation;

(2) identification of the solicitor, the forwarder, if the forwarder is neither the solicitor nor the owner of the claim, and the proxyholder, including their connections with the debtor and with each other. If the solicitor, forwarder, or proxyholder is an association, there shall also be included a statement that the creditors whose claims have been solicited and the creditors whose claims are to be voted were members or subscribers in good standing and had allowable unsecured claims on the date of the filing of the petition. If the solicitor, forwarder, or proxyholder is a committee of creditors, the statement shall also set forth the date and place the committee was organized, that the committee was organized in accordance with clause (B) or (C) of paragraph (c)(1) of this rule, the members of the committee, the amounts of their claims, when the claims were acquired, the amounts paid therefor, and the extent to which the claims of the committee members are secured or entitled to priority;

(3) a statement that no consideration has been paid or promised by the proxyholder for the proxy;

(4) a statement as to whether there is any agreement and, if so, the particulars thereof, between the proxyholder and any other entity for the payment of any consideration in connection with voting the proxy, or for the sharing of compensation with any entity, other than a member or regular associate of the proxyholder's law firm, which may be allowed the trustee or any entity for services rendered in the case, or for the employment of any person as attorney, accountant, appraiser, auctioneer, or other employee for the estate;

(5) if the proxy was solicited by an entity other than the proxyholder, or forwarded to the holder by an entity who is neither a solicitor of the proxy nor the owner of the claim, a statement signed and verified by the solicitor or forwarder that no consideration has been paid or promised for the proxy, and whether there is any agreement, and, if so, the particulars thereof, between the solicitor or forwarder and any other entity for the payment of any consideration in connection with voting the proxy, or for sharing compensation with any entity, other than a member or regular associate of the solicitor's or forwarder's law firm which may be allowed the trustee or any entity for services rendered in the case, or for the employment of any person as attorney, accountant, appraiser, auctioneer, or other employee for the estate;

(6) if the solicitor, forwarder, or proxyholder is a committee, a statement signed and verified by each member as to the amount and source of any consideration paid or to be paid to such member in connection with the case other than by way of dividend on the member's claim.

(f) Enforcement of Restrictions on Solicitation. On motion of any party in interest or on its own initiative, the court may determine whether there has been a failure to comply with the provisions of this rule or any other impropriety in connection with the solicitation or voting of a proxy. After notice and a hearing the court may reject any proxy for cause, vacate any order entered in consequence of the voting of any proxy which should have been rejected, or take any other appropriate action.

Bankruptcy Code References: §§ 702 and 705

Rule 2007. Review of Appointment of Creditors' Committee Organized before Commencement of the Case

(a) **Motion to Review Appointment.** If a committee appointed by the United States trustee pursuant to § 1102(a) of the Code consists of the members of a committee organized by creditors before the commencement of a chapter 9 or chapter 11 case, on motion of a party in interest and after a hearing on notice to the United States trustee and other entities as the court may direct, the court may determine whether the appointment of the committee satisfies the requirements of § 1102(b)(1) of the Code.

(b) **Selection of Members of Committee.** The court may find that a committee organized by unsecured creditors before the commencement of a chapter 9 or chapter 11 case was fairly chosen if:

(1) it was selected by a majority in number and amount of claims of unsecured creditors who may vote under § 702(a) of the Code and were present in person or represented at a meeting of which all creditors having unsecured claims of over $1,000 or the 100 unsecured creditors having the largest claims had at least five days notice in writing, and of which meeting written minutes reporting the names of the creditors present or represented and voting and the amounts of their claims were kept and are available for inspection;

(2) all proxies voted at the meeting for the elected committee were solicited pursuant to Rule 2006 and the lists and statements required by subdivision (e) thereof have been transmitted to the United States trustee; and

(3) the organization of the committee was in all other respects fair and proper.

(c) **Failure to Comply with Requirements for Appointment.** After a hearing on notice pursuant to subdivision (a) of this rule, the court shall direct the United States trustee to vacate the appointment of the committee and may order other appropriate action if the court finds that such appointment failed to satisfy the requirements of § 1102(b)(1) of the Code.

Bankruptcy Code References: §§ 702, 705 and 1102

Rule 2007.1. Appointment of Trustee or Examiner in a Chapter 11 Reorganization Case

(a) **Order to Appoint Trustee or Examiner.** In a chapter 11 reorganization case, a motion for an order to appoint a trustee or an examiner pursuant to § 1104(a) or § 1104(c) of the Code shall be made in accordance with Rule 9014.

(b) **Election of Trustee.**

(1) *Request for an Election.* A request to convene a meeting of creditors for the purpose of electing a trustee in a chapter 11 reorganization case

shall be filed and transmitted to the United States trustee in accordance with Rule 5005 within the time prescribed by § 1104(b) of the Code. Pending court approval of the person elected, any person appointed by the United States trustee under § 1104(d) and approved in accordance with subdivision (c) of this rule shall serve as trustee.

(2) *Manner of Election and Notice.* An election of a trustee under § 1104(b) of the Code shall be conducted in the manner provided in Rules 2003(b)(3) and 2006. Notice of the meeting of creditors convened under § 1104(b) shall be given as provided in Rule 2002. The United States trustee shall preside at the meeting. A proxy for the purpose of voting in the election may be solicited only by a committee of creditors appointed under § 1102 of the Code or by any other party entitled to solicit a proxy pursuant to Rule 2006.

(3) *Report of Election and Resolution of Disputes.*

(A) *Report of Undisputed Election.* If the election is not disputed, the United States trustee shall promptly file a report of the election, including the name and address of the person elected and a statement that the election is undisputed. The United States trustee shall file with the report an application for approval of the appointment in accordance with subdivision (c) of this rule. The report constitutes appointment of the elected person to serve as trustee, subject to court approval, as of the date of entry of the order approving the appointment.

(B) *Disputed Election.* If the election is disputed, the United States trustee shall promptly file a report stating that the election is disputed, informing the court of the nature of the dispute, and listing the name and address of any candidate elected under any alternative presented by the dispute. The report shall be accompanied by a verified statement by each candidate elected under each alternative presented by the dispute, setting forth the person's connections with the debtor, creditors, any other party-in-interest, their respective attorneys and accountants, the United States trustee, and any person employed in the office of the United States trustee. Not later than the date on which the report of the disputed election is filed, the United States trustee shall mail a copy of the report and each verified statement to any party-in-interest that has made a request to convene a meeting under § 1104(b) or to receive a copy of the report, and to any committee appointed under § 1102 of the Code. Unless a motion for the resolution of the dispute is filed not later than 10 days after the United States trustee files the report, any person appointed by the United States trustee under § 1104(d) and approved in accordance with subdivision (c) of this rule shall serve as trustee. If a motion for the resolution of the dispute is timely filed, and the court determines the result of the election and approves the person elected, the report will constitute appointment of the elected person as of the date of entry of the order approving the appointment.

(c) **Approval of Appointment.** An order approving the appointment of a trustee elected under § 1104(b) or appointed under § 1104(d), or the appointment of an examiner under § 1104(d) of the Code, shall be made on application of the United States trustee. The application shall state the name of the person appointed and, to the best of the applicant's knowledge, all the person's connections with the debtor, creditors, any other parties-in-interest, their respective attorneys and accountants, the United States trustee, and persons employed in the office of the United States trustee. Unless the person has been elected under § 1104(b), the application shall state the names of the parties-in-interest with whom the United States trustee consulted regarding the appointment. The application shall be accompanied by a verified statement of the person appointed setting forth the person's connections with the debtor, creditors, any other party-in-interest, their respective attorneys and accountants, the United States trustee, and any person employed in the office of the United States trustee.

Bankruptcy Code Reference: § 1104

Rule 2008. Notice to Trustee of Selection

The United States trustee shall immediately notify the person selected as trustee how to qualify and, if applicable, the amount of the trustee's bond. A trustee that has filed a blanket bond pursuant to Rule 2010 and has been selected as trustee in a chapter 7, chapter 12, or chapter 13 case that does not notify the court and the United States trustee in writing of rejection of the office within five days after receipt of notice of selection shall be deemed to have accepted the office. Any other person selected as trustee shall notify the court and the United States trustee in writing of acceptance of the office within five days after receipt of notice of selection or shall be deemed to have rejected the office.

Bankruptcy Code Reference: §§ 321, 322, 701–703, 1104 and 1163

Rule 2009. Trustees for Estates When Joint Administration Ordered

(a) Election of Single Trustee for Estates Being Jointly Administered. If the court orders a joint administration of two or more estates pursuant to Rule 1015(b), creditors may elect a single trustee for the estates being jointly administered.

(b) Right of Creditors to Elect Separate Trustee. Notwithstanding entry of an order for joint administration pursuant to Rule 1015(b) the creditors of any debtor may elect a separate trustee for the estate of the debtor as provided in § 702 of the Code.

(c) Appointment of Trustees for Estates Being Jointly Administered.

(1) *Chapter 7 Liquidation Cases.* The United States trustee may appoint one or more interim trustees for estates being jointly administered in chapter 7 cases.

(2) *Chapter 11 Reorganization Cases.* If the appointment of a trustee is ordered, the United States trustee may appoint one or more trustees for estates being jointly administered in chapter 11 cases.

(3) *Chapter 12 Family Farmer's Debt Adjustment Cases.* The United States trustee may appoint one or more trustees for estates being jointly administered in chapter 12 cases.

(4) *Chapter 13 Individual's Debt Adjustment Cases.* The United States trustee may appoint one or more trustees for estates being jointly administered in chapter 13 cases.

(d) Potential Conflicts of Interest. On a showing that creditors or equity security holders of the different estates will be prejudiced by conflicts of interest of a common trustee who has been elected or appointed, the court shall order the selection of separate trustees for estates being jointly administered.

(e) **Separate Accounts.** The trustee or trustees of estates being jointly administered shall keep separate accounts of the property and distribution of each estate.

Bankruptcy Code Reference: §§ 302, 322, 701, 702, 704, 723, 926, 1104, 1202 and 1302

Rule 2010.   Qualification by Trustee; Proceeding on Bond

(a) **Blanket Bond.** The United States trustee may authorize a blanket bond in favor of the United States conditioned on the faithful performance of official duties by the trustee or trustees to cover (1) a person who qualifies as trustee in a number of cases, and (2) a number of trustees each of whom qualifies in a different case.

(b) **Proceeding on Bond.** A proceeding on the trustee's bond may be brought by any party in interest in the name of the United States for the use of the entity injured by the breach of the condition.

Bankruptcy Code Reference: §§ 322, 549, 701–703, 1104 and 1163

Rule 2011.   Evidence of Debtor in Possession or Qualification of Trustee

(a) Whenever evidence is required that a debtor is a debtor in possession or that a trustee has qualified, the clerk may so certify and the certificate shall constitute conclusive evidence of that fact.

(b) If a person elected or appointed as trustee does not qualify within the time prescribed by § 322(a) of the Code, the clerk shall so notify the court and the United States trustee.

Bankruptcy Code Reference: §§ 1101, 1105 and 1107

Rule 2012.   Substitution of Trustee or Successor Trustee; Accounting

(a) **Trustee.** If a trustee is appointed in a chapter 11 case or the debtor is removed as debtor in possession in a chapter 12 case, the trustee is substituted automatically for the debtor in possession as a party in any pending action, proceeding, or matter.

(b) **Successor Trustee.** When a trustee dies, resigns, is removed, or otherwise ceases to hold office during the pendency of a case under the Code (1) the successor is automatically substituted as a party in any pending action, proceeding, or matter; and (2) the successor trustee shall prepare, file, and transmit to the United States trustee an accounting of the prior administration of the estate.

Bankruptcy Code Reference: §§ 322, 324, 325, 701, 703, 704, 1104, 1202 and 1302

Rule 2013.   Public Record of Compensation Awarded to Trustees, Examiners, and Professionals

(a) **Record to Be Kept.** The clerk shall maintain a public record listing fees awarded by the court (1) to trustees and attorneys, accountants, appraisers, auctioneers and other professionals employed by trustees, and (2) to examiners. The record shall include the name and docket number of the case, the name of the individual or firm receiving the fee and the amount of the fee awarded. The record shall be maintained chronologically and shall be kept current and open to examination by the public without charge. "Trustees," as used in this rule, does not include debtors in possession.

(b) **Summary of Record.** At the close of each annual period, the clerk shall prepare a summary of the public record by individual or firm name, to reflect total fees awarded during the preceding year. The summary shall be open to examination by the public without charge. The clerk shall transmit a copy of the summary to the United States trustee.

Bankruptcy Code References: §§ 322, 326, 328, 701, 703, 1104, 1163, 1202 and 1302

Rule 2014. *Employment of Professional Persons*

(a) **Application for an Order of Employment.** An order approving the employment of attorneys, accountants, appraisers, auctioneers, agents, or other professionals pursuant to § 327, § 1103, or § 1114 of the Code shall be made only on application of the trustee or committee. The application shall be filed and, unless the case is a chapter 9 municipality case, a copy of the application shall be transmitted by the applicant to the United States trustee. The application shall state the specific facts showing the necessity for the employment, the name of the person to be employed, the reasons for the selection, the professional services to be rendered, any proposed arrangement for compensation, and, to the best of the applicant's knowledge, all of the person's connections with the debtor, creditors, any other party in interest, their respective attorneys and accountants, the United States trustee, or any person employed in the office of the United States trustee. The application shall be accompanied by a verified statement of the person to be employed setting forth the person's connections with the debtor, creditors, any other party in interest, their respective attorneys and accountants, the United States trustee, or any person employed in the office of the United States trustee.

(b) **Services Rendered by Member or Associate of Firm of Attorneys or Accountants.** If, under the Code and this rule, a law partnership or corporation is employed as an attorney, or an accounting partnership or corporation is employed as an accountant, or if a named attorney or accountant is employed, any partner, member, or regular associate of the partnership, corporation or individual may act as attorney or accountant so employed, without further order of the court.

Bankruptcy Code Reference: §§ 327, 328, 329, 504, 703, 1102 and 1103

Rule 2015. *Duty to Keep Records, Make Reports, and Give Notice of Case*

(a) **Trustee or Debtor in Possession.** A trustee or debtor in possession shall (1) in a chapter 7 liquidation case and, if the court directs, in a chapter 11 reorganization case file and transmit to the United States trustee a complete inventory of the property of the debtor within 30 days after qualifying as a trustee or debtor in possession, unless such an inventory has already been filed; (2) keep a record of receipts and the disposition of money and property received; (3) file the reports and summaries required by § 704(8) of the Code which shall include a statement, if payments are made to employees, of the amounts of deductions for all taxes required to be withheld or paid for and in behalf of employees and the place where these amounts are deposited; (4) as soon as possible after the commencement of the case, give notice of the case to every entity known to be holding money or property subject to withdrawal or order of the debtor, including every bank, savings or building and loan association, public utility company, and landlord with whom the debtor has a deposit, and to every insurance company which has issued a policy having a cash surrender value payable to the debtor, except that notice need not be given to any entity who has knowledge or has previously been notified of the case; (5) in a chapter 11 reorganization case, on or before the last day of the month after each calendar quarter until a plan is confirmed or the case is converted or dismissed, file and transmit to the United States trustee a statement of disbursements made during such calendar quarter and a statement of the amount of the fee required pursuant to 28 U.S.C. § 1930(a)(6) that has been paid for such calendar quarter.

(b) Chapter 12 Trustee and Debtor in Possession. In a chapter 12 family farmer's debt adjustment case, the debtor in possession shall perform the duties prescribed in clauses (2)–(4) of subdivision (a) of this rule and, if the court directs, shall file and transmit to the United States trustee a complete inventory of the property of the debtor within the time fixed by the court. If the debtor is removed as debtor in possession, the trustee shall perform the duties of the debtor in possession prescribed in this paragraph.

(c) Chapter 13 Trustee and Debtor.

(1) *Business Cases.* In a chapter 13 individual's debt adjustment case, when the debtor is engaged in business, the debtor shall perform the duties prescribed by clauses (2)–(4) of subdivision (a) of this rule, and if the court directs, shall file and transmit to the United States trustee a complete inventory of the property of the debtor within the time fixed by the court.

(2) *Nonbusiness Cases.* In a chapter 13 individual's debt adjustment case, when the debtor is not engaged in business, the trustee shall perform the duties prescribed by clause (2) of subdivision (a) of this rule.

(d) Transmission of Reports. In a chapter 11 case the court may direct that copies or summaries of annual reports and copies or summaries of other reports shall be mailed to the creditors, equity security holders, and indenture trustees. The court may also direct the publication of summaries of any such reports. A copy of every report or summary mailed or published pursuant to this subdivision shall be transmitted to the United States trustee.

Bankruptcy Code References: §§ 343, 521, 704, 1104, 1106, 1107, 1108, 1163, 1202, 1204, 1302 and 1304

Rule 2016. *Compensation for Services Rendered and Reimbursement of Expenses*

(a) Application for Compensation or Reimbursement. An entity seeking interim or final compensation for services, or reimbursement of necessary expenses, from the estate shall file an application setting forth a detailed statement of (1) the services rendered, time expended and expenses incurred, and (2) the amounts requested. An application for compensation shall include a statement as to what payments have theretofore been made or promised to the applicant for services rendered or to be rendered in any capacity whatsoever in connection with the case, the source of the compensation so paid or promised, whether any compensation previously received has been shared and whether an agreement or understanding exists between the applicant and any other entity for the sharing of compensation received or to be received for services rendered in or in connection with the case, and the particulars of any sharing of compensation or agreement or understanding therefor, except that details of any agreement by the applicant for the sharing of compensation as a member or regular associate of a firm of lawyers or accountants shall not be required. The requirements of this subdivision shall apply to an application for compensation for services rendered by an attorney or accountant even though the application is filed by a creditor or other entity. Unless the case is a chapter 9 municipality case, the applicant shall transmit to the United States trustee a copy of the application.

(b) Disclosure of Compensation Paid or Promised to Attorney for Debtor. Every attorney for a debtor, whether or not the attorney applies for compensation, shall file and transmit to the United States trustee within 15 days after the order for relief, or at another time as the court may direct, the statement required by § 329 of the Code including whether the attorney has shared or agreed to share the compensation with any other entity. The statement shall include the particulars of any such sharing or agreement to share by the attorney, but the details of any agreement for the sharing of the compensation with a member or regular associate of the attorney's law firm shall not be required. A supplemental statement shall be filed and transmitted to the United States trustee within 15 days after any payment or agreement not previously disclosed.

Bankruptcy Code References: §§ 326, 327, 328, 329–331 and 504

Rule 2017.   Examination of Debtor's Transactions with Debtor's Attorney

(a) Payment or Transfer to Attorney before Order for Relief. On motion by any party in interest or on the court's own initiative, the court after notice and a hearing may determine whether any payment of money or any transfer of property by the debtor, made directly or indirectly and in contemplation of the filing of a petition under the Code by or against the debtor or before entry of the order for relief in an involuntary case, to an attorney for services rendered or to be rendered is excessive.

(b) Payment or Transfer to Attorney after Order for Relief. On motion by the debtor, the United States trustee, or on the court's own initiative, the court after notice and a hearing may determine whether any payment of money or any transfer of property, or any agreement therefor, by the debtor to an attorney after entry of an order for relief in a case under the Code is excessive, whether the payment or transfer is made or is to be made directly or indirectly, if the payment, transfer, or agreement therefor is for services in any way related to the case.

Bankruptcy Code References: §§ 329 and 504

Rule 2018.   Intervention; Right to Be Heard

(a) Permissive Intervention. In a case under the Code, after hearing on such notice as the court directs and for cause shown, the court may permit any interested entity to intervene generally or with respect to any specified matter.

(b) Intervention by Attorney General of a State. In a chapter 7, 11, 12, or 13 case, the Attorney General of a State may appear and be heard on behalf of consumer creditors if the court determines the appearance is in the public interest, but the Attorney General may not appeal from any judgment, order, or decree in the case.

(c) Chapter 9 Municipality Case. The Secretary of the Treasury of the United States may, or if requested by the court shall, intervene in a chapter 9 case. Representatives of the state in which the debtor is located may intervene in a chapter 9 case with respect to matters specified by the court.

(d) Labor Unions. In a chapter 9, 11, or 12 case, a labor union or employees' association, representative of employees of the debtor, shall have the right to be heard on the economic soundness of a plan affecting the interests of the employees. A labor union or employees' association which exercises its right to be heard under this subdivision shall not be entitled to appeal any judgment, order, or decree relating to the plan, unless otherwise permitted by law.

(e) Service on Entities Covered by This Rule. The court may enter orders governing the service of notice and papers on entities permitted to intervene or be heard pursuant to this rule.

Bankruptcy Code Reference: §§ 1109 and 1164

Rule 2019. *Representation of Creditors and Equity Security Holders in Chapter 9 Municipality and Chapter 11 Reorganization Cases*

(a) Data Required. In a chapter 9 municipality or chapter 11 reorganization case, except with respect to a committee appointed pursuant to § 1102 or 1114 of the Code, every entity or committee representing more than one creditor or equity security holder and, unless otherwise directed by the court, every indenture trustee, shall file a verified statement setting forth (1) the name and address of the creditor or equity security holder; (2) the nature and amount of the claim or interest and the time of acquisition thereof unless it is alleged to have been acquired more than one year prior to the filing of the petition; (3) a recital of the pertinent facts and circumstances in connection with the employment of the entity or indenture trustee, and, in the case of a committee, the name or names of the entity or entities at whose instance, directly or indirectly, the employment was arranged or the committee was organized or agreed to act; and (4) with reference to the time of the employment of the entity, the organization or formation of the committee, or the appearance in the case of any indenture trustee, the amounts of claims or interest owned by the entity, the members of the committee or the indenture trustee, the times when acquired, the amounts paid therefor, and any sales or other disposition thereof. The statement shall include a copy of the instrument, if any, whereby the entity, committee, or indenture trustee is empowered to act on behalf of creditors or equity security holders. A supplemental statement shall be filed promptly, setting forth any material changes in the facts contained in the statement filed pursuant to this subdivision.

(b) Failure to Comply; Effect. On motion of any party in interest or on its own initiative, the court may (1) determine whether there has been a failure to comply with the provisions of subdivision (a) of this rule or with any other applicable law regulating the activities and personnel of any entity, committee, or indenture trustee or any other impropriety in connection with any solicitation and, if it so determines, the court may refuse to permit that entity, committee, or indenture trustee to be heard further or to intervene in the case; (2) examine any representation provision of a deposit agreement, proxy, trust mortgage, trust indenture, or deed of trust, or committee or other authorization, and any claim or interest acquired by any entity or committee in contemplation or in the course of a case under the Code and grant appropriate relief; and (3) hold invalid any authority, acceptance, rejection, or objection given, procured, or received by an entity or committee who has not complied with this rule or with § 1125(b) of the Code.

Bankruptcy Code References: §§ 1102 and 1103

Rule 2020. Review of Acts by United States Trustee

A proceeding to contest any act or failure to act by the United States trustee is governed by Rule 9014.

Bankruptcy Code Reference: § 586

PART III
CLAIMS AND DISTRIBUTION TO CREDITORS AND EQUITY INTEREST HOLDERS; PLANS

Rule 3001. Proof of Claim

(a) **Form and Content.** A proof of claim is a written statement setting forth a creditor's claim. A proof of claim shall conform substantially to the appropriate Official Form.

(b) **Who May Execute.** A proof of claim shall be executed by the creditor or the creditor's authorized agent except as provided in Rules 3004 and 3005.

(c) **Claim Based on a Writing.** When a claim, or an interest in property of the debtor securing the claim, is based on a writing, the original or a duplicate shall be filed with the proof of claim. If the writing has been lost or destroyed, a statement of the circumstances of the loss or destruction shall be filed with the claim.

(d) **Evidence of Perfection of Security Interest.** If a security interest in property of the debtor is claimed, the proof of claim shall be accompanied by evidence that the security interest has been perfected.

(e) **Transferred Claim.**

(1) *Transfer of Claim Other Than for Security Before Proof Filed.* If a claim has been transferred other than for security before proof of the claim has been filed, the proof of claim may be filed only by the transferee or an indenture trustee.

(2) *Transfer of Claim Other Than for Security After Proof Filed.* If a claim other than one based on a publicly traded note, bond, or debenture has been transferred other than for security after the proof of claim has been filed, evidence of the transfer shall be filed by the transferee. The clerk shall immediately notify the alleged transferor by mail of the filing of the evidence of transfer and that objection thereto, if any, must be filed within 20 days of the mailing of the notice or within any addition time allowed by the court. If the alleged transferor files a timely objection and the court finds, after notice and a hearing, that the claim has been transferred other than for

security, it shall enter an order substituting the transferee for the transferor. If a timely objection is not filed by the alleged transferor, the transferee shall be substituted for the transferor.

(3) *Transfer of Claim for Security Before Proof Filed.* If a claim other than one based on a publicly traded note, bond, or debenture has been transferred for security before proof of the claim has been filed, the transferor or transferee or both may file a proof of claim for the full amount. The proof shall be supported by a statement setting forth the terms of the transfer. If either the transferor or the transferee files a proof of claim, the clerk shall immediately notify the other by mail of the right to join in the filed claim. If both transferor and transferee file proofs of the same claim, the proofs shall be consolidated. If the transferor or transferee does not file an agreement regarding its relative rights respecting voting of the claim, payment of dividends thereon, or participation in the administration of the estate, on motion by a party in interest and other notice and a hearing, the court shall enter such orders respecting these matters as may be appropriate.

(4) *Transfer of Claim for Security After Proof Filed.* If a claim other than one based on a publicly traded note, bond, or debenture has been transferred for security after the proof of claim has been filed, evidence of the terms of the transfer shall be filed by the transferee. The clerk shall immediately notify the alleged transferor by mail of the filing of the evidence of transfer and that objection thereto, if any, must be filed within 20 days of the mailing of the notice or within any additional time allowed by the court. If a timely objection is filed by the alleged transferor, the court, after notice and a hearing, shall determine whether the claim has been transferred for security. If the transferor or transferee does not file an agreement regarding its relative rights respecting voting of the claim, payment of dividends thereon, or participation in the administration of the estate, on motion by a party in interest and after notice and a hearing, the court shall enter such orders respecting these matters as may be appropriate.

(5) *Service of Objection or Motion; Notice of Hearing.* A copy of an objection filed pursuant to paragraph (2) or (4) or a motion filed pursuant to paragraph (3) or (4) of this subdivision together with a notice of a hearing shall be mailed or otherwise delivered to the transferor or transferee, whichever is appropriate, at least 30 days prior to the hearing.

(f) **Evidentiary Effect.** A proof of claim executed and filed in accordance with these rules shall constitute prima facie evidence of the validity and amount of the claim.

(g) To the extent not inconsistent with the United States Warehouse Act or applicable State law, a warehouse receipt, scale ticket, or similar document of the type routinely issued as evidence of title by a grain storage facility, as defined in section 557 of title 11, shall constitute prima facie evidence of the validity and amount of a claim of ownership of a quantity of grain.

Bankruptcy Code References: §§ 501, 502 and 506

Rule 3002. *Filing Proof of Claim or Interest*

(a) **Necessity for Filing.** An unsecured creditor or an equity security holder must file a proof of claim or interest in accordance with this rule for the claim or interest to be allowed, except as provided in Rules 1019(3), 3003, 3004, and 3005.

(b) Place of Filing. A proof of claim or interest shall be filed in accordance with Rule 5005.

(c) Time for Filing. In a chapter 7 liquidation, chapter 12 family farmer's debt adjustment, or chapter 13 individual's debt adjustment case, a proof of claim shall be filed within 90 days after the first date set for the meeting of creditors called pursuant to § 341(a) of the Code, except as follows:

(1)   A proof of claim filed by a governmental unit is timely filed if it is filed not later than 180 days after the date of the order for relief. On motion of a governmental unit before the expiration of such period and for cause shown, the court may extend the time for filing of a claim by the governmental unit.

(2)   In the interest of justice and if it will not unduly delay the administration of the case, the court may extend the time for filing a proof of claim by an infant or incompetent person or the representative of either.

(3)   An unsecured claim which arises in favor of an entity or becomes allowable as a result of a judgment may be filed within 30 days after the judgment becomes final if the judgment is for the recovery of money or property from that entity or denies or avoids the entity's interest in property. If the judgment imposes a liability which is not satisfied, or a duty which is not performed within such period or such further time as the court may permit, the claim shall not be allowed.

(4)   A claim arising from the rejection of an executory contract or unexpired lease of the debtor may be filed within such time as the court may direct.

(5)   If notice of insufficient assets to pay a dividend was given to creditors pursuant to Rule 2002(e), and subsequently the trustee notifies the court that payment of a dividend appears possible, the clerk shall notify the creditors of that fact and that they may file proofs of claim within 90 days after the mailing of the notice.

Bankruptcy Code References: §§ 341, 502, 506 and 726.

Rule 3003. Filing Proof of Claims or Equity Security Interest in Chapter 9 Municipality or Chapter 11 Reorganization Cases

(a) Applicability of Rule. This rule applies in chapter 9 and 11 cases.

(b) Schedule of Liabilities and List of Equity Security Holders.

(1)   *Schedule of Liabilities.* The schedule of liabilities filed pursuant to § 521(1) of the Code shall constitute prima facie evidence of the validity and amount of the claims of creditors, unless they are scheduled as disputed, contingent, or unliquidated. It shall not be necessary for a creditor or equity security holder to file a proof of claim or interest except as provided in subdivision (c)(2) of this rule.

(2)   *List of Equity Security Holders.* The list of equity security holders filed pursuant to Rule 1007(a)(3) shall constitute prima facie evidence of the validity and amount of the equity security interests and it shall not be necessary for the holders of such interests to file a proof of interest.

(c) Filing Proof of Claim.

(1)   *Who May File.* Any creditor or indenture trustee may file a proof of claim within the time prescribed by subdivision (c)(3) of this rule.

(2) *Who Must File.* Any creditor or equity security holder whose claim or interest is not scheduled or scheduled as disputed, contingent, or unliquidated shall file a proof of claim or interest within the time prescribed by subdivision (c)(3) of this rule; any creditor who fails to do so shall not be treated as a creditor with respect to such claim for the purposes of voting and distribution.

(3) *Time for Filing.* The court shall fix and for cause shown may extend the time within which proofs of claim or interest may be filed. Notwithstanding the expiration of such time, a proof of claim may be filed to the extent and under the conditions stated in Rule 3002(c)(2), (c)(3), and (c)(4).

(4) *Effect of Filing Claim or Interest.* A proof of claim or interest executed and filed in accordance with this subdivision shall supersede any scheduling of that claim or interest pursuant to § 521(1) of the Code.

(5) *Filing by Indenture Trustee.* An indenture trustee may file a claim on behalf of all known or unknown holders of securities issued pursuant to the trust instrument under which it is trustee.

(d) Proof of Right to Record Status. For the purposes of Rules 3017, 3018, and 3021 and for receiving notices, an entity who is not the record holder of a security may file a statement setting forth facts which entitle that entity to be treated as the record holder. An objection to the statement may be filed by any party in interest.

Bankruptcy Code References: §§ 501, 502, 521, 925 and 1111

Rule 3004. *Filing of Claims by Debtor or Trustee*

If a creditor fails to file a proof of claim on or before the first date set for the meeting of creditors called pursuant to § 341(a) of the Code, the debtor or trustee may do so in the name of the creditor, within 30 days after expiration of the time for filing claims prescribed by Rule 3002(c) or 3003(c), whichever is applicable. The clerk shall forthwith mail notice of the filing to the creditor, the debtor and the trustee. A proof of claim filed by a creditor pursuant to Rule 3002 or Rule 3003(c), shall supersede the proof filed by the debtor or trustee.

Bankruptcy Code References: §§ 341, 501, 502 and 111

Rule 3005. *Filing of Claim, Acceptance, or Rejection by Guarantor, Surety, Indorser, or Other Codebtor*

(a) Filing of Claim. If a creditor has not filed a proof of claim pursuant to Rule 3002 or 3003(c), an entity that is or may be liable with the debtor to that creditor, or who has secured that creditor, may, within 30 days after the expiration of the time for filing claims prescribed by Rule 3002(c) or 3003(c) whichever is applicable, execute and file a proof of claim in the name of the creditor, if known, or if unknown, in the entity's own name. No distribution shall be made on the claim except on satisfactory proof that the original debt will be diminished by the amount of distribution. A proof of claim filed by a creditor pursuant to Rule 3002 or 3003(c) shall supersede the proof of claim filed pursuant to the first sentence of this subdivision.

(b) Filing of Acceptance or Rejection; Substitution of Creditor. An entity which has filed a claim pursuant to the first sentence of subdivision (a) of this rule may file an acceptance or rejection of a plan in the name of the creditor, if known, or if unknown, in the entity's own name but if the creditor files a proof of claim within the time permitted by Rule 3003(c) or files a notice prior to confirmation of a plan of the creditor's intention to act in the creditor's own behalf, the creditor shall be substituted for the obligor with respect to that claim.

Bankruptcy Code References: §§ 501, 502, 509 and 1111

Rule 3006.   Withdrawal of Claim; Effect on Acceptance or Rejection of Plan

A creditor may withdraw a claim as of right by filing a notice of withdrawal, except as provided in this rule. If after a creditor has filed a proof of claim an objection is filed thereto or a complaint is filed against that creditor in an adversary proceeding, or the creditor has accepted or rejected the plan or otherwise has participated significantly in the case, the creditor may not withdraw the claim except on order of the court after a hearing on notice to the trustee or debtor in possession, and any creditors' committee elected pursuant to § 705(a) or appointed pursuant to § 1102 of the Code. The order of the court shall contain such terms and conditions as the court deems proper. Unless the court orders otherwise, an authorized withdrawal of a claim shall constitute withdrawal of any related acceptance or rejection of a plan.

Bankruptcy Code References: §§ 501, 502, 705, 1102 and 1111

Rule 3007.   Objections to Claims

An objection to the allowance of a claim shall be in writing and filed. A copy of the objection with notice of the hearing thereon shall be mailed or otherwise delivered to the claimant, the debtor or debtor in possession and the trustee at least 30 days prior to the hearing. If an objection to a claim is joined with a demand for relief of the kind specified in Rule 7001, it becomes an adversary proceeding.

Bankruptcy Code References: §§ 502, 506, 704, 1202 and 1302

Rule 3008.   Reconsideration of Claims

A party in interest may move for reconsideration of an order allowing or disallowing a claim against the estate. The court after a hearing on notice shall enter an appropriate order.

Bankruptcy Code References: §§ 350 and 502

Rule 3009.   Declaration and Payment of Dividends in a Chapter 7 Liquidation Case

In a chapter 7 case, dividends to creditors shall be paid as promptly as practicable. Dividend checks shall be made payable to and mailed to each creditor whose claim has been allowed, unless a power of attorney authorizing another entity to receive dividends has been executed and filed in accordance with Rule 9010. In that event, dividend checks shall be made payable to the creditor and to the other entity and shall be mailed to the other entity.

Bankruptcy Code References: § 704

Rule 3010.   Small Dividends and Payments in Chapter 7 Liquidation, Chapter 12 Family Farmer's Debt Adjustment, and Chapter 13 Individual's Debt Adjustment Cases

(a) **Chapter 7 Cases.** In a chapter 7 case no dividend in an amount less than $5 shall be distributed by the trustee to any creditor unless authorized by local rule or order of the court. Any dividend not distributed to a creditor shall be treated in the same manner as unclaimed funds as provided in § 347 of the Code.

(b) **Chapter 12 and Chapter 13 Cases.** In a chapter 12 or chapter 13 case no payment in an amount less than $15 shall be distributed by the trustee to any creditor unless authorized by local rule or order of the court. Funds not distributed because of this subdivision shall accumulate and shall be paid whenever the accumulation aggregates $15. Any funds remaining shall be distributed with the final payment.

Bankruptcy Code References: §§ 347, 704, 726, 1202, 1226, 1302 and 1326

Rule 3011.   Unclaimed Funds in Chapter 7 Liquidation, Chapter 12 Family Farmer's Debt Adjustment, and Chapter 13 Individual's Debt Adjustment Cases

The trustee shall file a list of all known names and addresses of the entities and the amounts which they are entitled to be paid from remaining property of the estate that is paid into court pursuant to § 347(a) of the Code.

Bankruptcy Code References: §§ 347, 704, 1202, 1226, 1302 and 1326

Rule 3012.   Valuation of Security

The court may determine the value of a claim secured by a lien on property in which the estate has an interest on motion of any party in interest and after a hearing on notice to the holder of the secured claim and any other entity as the court may direct.

Bankruptcy Code References: §§ 361, 506, 1124 and 1129

Rule 3013.   Classification of Claims and Interests

For the purposes of the plan and its acceptance, the court may, on motion after hearing on notice as the court may direct, determine classes of creditors and equity security holders pursuant to §§ 1122, 1222(b)(1), and 1322(b)(1) of the Code.

Bankruptcy Code References: §§ 1122, 1222 and 1322

Rule 3014.   Election Pursuant to § 1111(b) by Secured Creditor in Chapter 9 Municipality and Chapter 11 Reorganization Cases

An election of application of § 1111(b)(2) of the Code by a class of secured creditors in a chapter 9 or 11 case may be made at any time prior to the conclusion of the hearing on the disclosure statement or within such later time as the court may fix. If the disclosure statement is conditionally approved pursuant to Rule 3017.1, and a final hearing on the disclosure statement is not held, the election of application of § 1111(b)(2) may be made not later than the date fixed pursuant to Rule 3017.1(a)(2) or another date the court may fix. The election shall be in writing and signed unless made at the hearing on the disclosure statement. The election, if made by the majorities required by § 1111(b)(1)(A)(i), shall be binding on all members of the class with respect to the plan.

Bankruptcy Code References: § 1111

Rule 3015. Filing, Objection to Confirmation, and Modification of a Plan in a Chapter 12 Family Farmer's Debt Adjustment or a Chapter 13 Individual's Debt Adjustment Case

(a) **Chapter 12 Plan.** The debtor may file a chapter 12 plan with the petition. If a plan is not filed with the petition, it shall be filed within the time prescribed in § 1221 of the Code.

(b) **Chapter 13 Plan.** The debtor may file a chapter 13 plan with the petition. If a plan is not filed with the petition, it shall be filed within 15 days thereafter, and such time may not be further extended except for cause shown and on notice as the court may direct. If a case is converted to chapter 13, a plan shall be filed within 15 days thereafter, and such time may not be further extended except for cause shown and on notice as the court may direct.

(c) **Dating.** Every proposed plan and any modification thereof shall be dated.

(d) **Notice and Copies.** The plan or a summary of the plan shall be included with each notice of the hearing on confirmation mailed pursuant to Rule 2002. If required by the court, the debtor shall furnish a sufficient number of copies to enable the clerk to include a copy of the plan with the notice of the hearing.

(e) **Transmission to United States Trustee.** The clerk shall forthwith transmit to the United States trustee a copy of the plan and any modification thereof filed pursuant to subdivision (a) or (b) of this rule.

(f) **Objection to Confirmation; Determination of Good Faith in the Absence of an Objection.** An objection to confirmation of a plan shall be filed and served on the debtor, the trustee, and any other entity designated by the court, and shall be transmitted to the United States trustee, before confirmation of the plan. An objection to confirmation is governed by Rule 9014. If no objection is timely filed, the court may determine that the plan has been proposed in good faith and not by any means forbidden by law without receiving evidence on such issues.

(g) **Modification of Plan After Confirmation.** A request to modify a plan pursuant to § 1229 or 1329 of the Code shall identify the proponent and shall be filed together with the proposed modification. The clerk, or some other person as the court may direct, shall give the debtor, the trustee, and all creditors not less than 20 days notice by mail of the time fixed for filing objections and, if an objection is filed, the hearing to consider the proposed modification, unless the court orders otherwise with respect to creditors who are not affected by the proposed modification. A copy of the notice shall be transmitted to the United States trustee. A copy of the proposed modification, or a summary thereof, shall be included with the notice. If required by the court, the proponent shall furnish a sufficient number of copies of the proposed modification, or a summary thereof, to enable the clerk to include a copy with each notice.

Any objection to the proposed modification shall be filed and served on the debtor, the trustee, and any other entity designated by the court, and shall be transmitted to the United States trustee. An objection to a proposed modification is governed by Rule 9014.

Bankruptcy Code References: § 1321

Rule 3016. Filing of Plan and Disclosure Statement in Chapter 9 Municipality and Chapter 11 Reorganization Cases

(a) **Identification of Plan.** Every proposed plan and any modification thereof shall be dated and, in a chapter 11 case, identified with the name of the entity or entities submitting or filing it.

(b) **Disclosure Statement.** In a chapter 9 or 11 case, a disclosure statement under § 1125 or evidence showing compliance with § 1126(b) of the Code shall be filed with the plan or within a time fixed by the court.

Bankruptcy Code References: §§ 941, 1121, 1125, 1126 and 1161

Rule 3017. Court Consideration of Disclosure Statement in Chapter 9 Municipality and Chapter 11 Reorganization Cases

(a) **Hearing on Disclosure Statement and Objections.** Except as provided in Rule 3017.1, after a disclosure statement is filed in accordance with Rule 3016(c), the court shall hold a hearing on not less than 25 days notice to the debtor, creditors, equity security holders and other parties in interest as provided in Rule 2002 to consider such statement and any objections or modifications thereto. The plan and the disclosure statement shall be mailed with the notice of the hearing only to the debtor, any trustee or committee appointed under the Code, the Securities and Exchange Commission and any party in interest who requests in writing a copy of the statement or plan. Objections to the disclosure statement shall be filed and served on the debtor, the trustee, any committee appointed under the Code and such other entity as may be designated by the court, at any time prior to approval of the disclosure statement or by such earlier date as the court may fix. In a chapter 11 reorganization case, every notice, plan, disclosure statement, and objection required to be served or mailed pursuant to this subdivision shall be transmitted to the United States trustee within the time provided in this subdivision.

(b) **Determination on Disclosure Statement.** Following the hearing the court shall determine whether the disclosure statement should be approved.

(c) **Dates Fixed for Voting on Plan and Confirmation.** On or before approval of the disclosure statement, the court shall fix a time within which the holders of claims and interests may accept or reject the plan and may fix a date for the hearing on confirmation.

(d) **Transmission and Notice to United States Trustee, Creditors and Equity Security Holders.** On approval of a disclosure statement, unless the court orders otherwise with respect to one or more unimpaired classes of creditors or equity security holders, the debtor in possession, trustee, proponent of the plan, or clerk as ordered by the court shall mail to all creditors and equity security holders, and in a chapter 11 reorganization case shall transmit to the United States trustee, (1) the plan, or a court approved summary of the plan;

(2) the disclosure statement approved by the court; (3) notice of the time within which acceptances and rejections of such plan may be filed; and (4) such other information as the court may direct including any opinion of the court approving the disclosure statement or a court approved summary of the opinion. In addition, notice of the time fixed for filing objections and the hearing on confirmation shall be mailed to all creditors and equity security holders pursuant to Rule 2002(b), and a form of ballot conforming to the appropriate Official Form shall be mailed to creditors and equity security holders entitled to vote on the plan. In the event the opinion of the court is not transmitted or only a summary of the plan is transmitted, the opinion of the court or the plan shall be provided on request of a party in interest at the expense of the proponent of the plan. If the court orders that the disclosure statement and the plan or a summary of the plan shall not be mailed to any unimpaired class, notice that the class is designated in the plan as unimpaired and notice of the name and address of the person from whom the plan or summary of the plan and disclosure statement may be obtained upon request and at the plan proponent's expense, shall be mailed to members of the unimpaired class together with the notice of the time fixed for filing objections to and the hearing on confirmation. For the purposes of this subdivision, creditors and equity security holders shall include holders of stock, bonds, debentures, notes, and other securities of record at the date the order approving the disclosure statement is entered or another date fixed by the Court, for cause, after notice and a hearing.

(e) Transmission to Beneficial Holders of Securities. At the hearing held pursuant to subdivision (a) of this rule the court shall consider the procedures for transmitting the documents and information required by subdivision (d) of this rule to beneficial holders of stock, bonds, debentures, notes and other securities and determine the adequacy of such procedures and enter such orders as the court deems appropriate.

Bankruptcy Code References: §§ 901, 1125, 1126, 1128 and 1161

Rule 3017.1.   Court Consideration of Disclosure Statement in a Small Business Case

(a) Conditional Approval of Disclosure Statement. If the debtor is a small business and has made a timely election to be considered a small business in a chapter 11 case, the court may, on application of the plan proponent, conditionally approve a disclosure statement filed in accordance with Rule 3016(b). On or before conditional approval of the disclosure statement, the court shall:

(1)   fix a time within which the holders of claims and interests may accept or reject the plan;

(2)   fix a time for filing objections to the disclosure statement;

(3)   fix a date for the hearing on final approval of the disclosure statement to be held if a timely objection is filed; and

(4)   fix a date for the hearing on confirmation.

(b) Application of Rule 3017. Rules 3017(a), (b), (c), and (e) do not apply to a conditionally approved disclosure statement. Rule 3017(d) applies to a conditionally approved disclosure statement, except that conditional approval is considered approval of the disclosure statement for the purpose of applying Rule 3017(d).

(c) Final Approval.

(1)　*Notice.* Notice of the time fixed for filing objections and the hearing to consider final approval of the disclosure statement shall be given in accordance with Rule 2002 and may be combined with notice of the hearing on confirmation of the plan.

(2)　*Objections.* Objections to the disclosure statement shall be filed, transmitted to the United States trustee, and served on the debtor, the trustee, any committee appointed under the Code, and any other entity designated by the court at any time before final approval of the disclosure statement or by an earlier date as the court may fix.

(3)　*Hearing.* If a timely objection to the disclosure statement is filed, the court shall hold a hearing to consider final approval before or combined with the hearing on confirmation of the plan.

Rule 3018.　*Acceptance or Rejection of Plan in a Chapter 9 Municipality or a Chapter 11 Reorganization Case*

(a) Entities Entitled to Accept or Reject Plan; Time for Acceptance or Rejection. A plan may be accepted or rejected in accordance with § 1126 of the Code within the time fixed by the court pursuant to Rule 3017. Subject to subdivision (b) of this rule, an equity security holder or creditor whose claim is based on a security of record shall not be entitled to accept or reject a plan unless the equity security holder or creditor is the holder of record of the security on the date the order approving the disclosure statement is entered. For cause shown, the court after notice and hearing may permit a creditor or equity security holder to change or withdraw an acceptance or rejection. Notwithstanding objection to a claim or interest, the court after notice and hearing may temporarily allow the claim or interest in an amount which the court deems proper for the purpose of accepting or rejecting a plan.

(b) Acceptances or Rejections Obtained before Petition. An equity security holder or creditor whose claim is based on a security of record who accepted or rejected the plan before the commencement of the case shall not be deemed to have accepted or rejected the plan pursuant to § 1126(b) of the Code unless the equity security holder or creditor was the holder of record of the security on the date specified in the solicitation of such acceptance or rejection for the purposes of such solicitation. A holder of a claim or interest who has accepted or rejected a plan before the commencement of the case under the Code shall not be deemed to have accepted or rejected the plan if the court finds after notice and hearing that the plan was not transmitted to substantially all creditors and equity security holders of the same class, that an unreasonably short time was prescribed for such creditors and equity security holders to accept or reject the plan, or that the solicitation was not in compliance with § 1126(b) of the Code.

(c) Form of Acceptance or Rejection. An acceptance or rejection shall be in writing, identify the plan or plans accepted or rejected, be signed by the creditor or equity security holder or an authorized agent, and conform to the appropriate Official Form. If more than one plan is transmitted pursuant to Rule 3017, an acceptance or rejection may be filed by each creditor or equity security holder for any number of plans transmitted and if acceptances are filed for more than one plan, the creditor or equity security holder may indicate a preference or preferences among the plans so accepted.

(d) Acceptance or Rejection by Partially Secured Creditor. A creditor whose claim has been allowed in part as a secured claim and in part as an unsecured claim shall be entitled to accept or reject a plan in both capacities.

Bankruptcy Code References: §§ 502, 1126, 1128, 1129 and 1325

Rule 3019. Modification of Accepted Plan before Confirmation in a Chapter 9 Municipality or a Chapter 11 Reorganization Case

In a chapter 9 or chapter 11 case, after a plan has been accepted and before its confirmation, the proponent may file a modification of the plan. If the court finds after hearing on notice to the trustee, any committee appointed under the Code, and any other entity designated by the court that the proposed modification does not adversely change the treatment of the claim of any creditor or the interest of any equity security holder who has not accepted in writing the modification, it shall be deemed accepted by all creditors and equity security holders who have previously accepted the plan.

Bankruptcy Code References: § 942, 1127, 1223 and 1323

Rule 3020. Deposit; Confirmation of Plan in a Chapter 9 Municipality or a Chapter 11 Reorganization Case

(a) Deposit. In a chapter 11 case, prior to entry of the order confirming the plan, the court may order the deposit with the trustee or debtor in possession of the consideration required by the plan to be distributed on confirmation. Any money deposited shall be kept in a special account established for the exclusive purpose of making the distribution.

(b) Objection to and Hearing on Confirmation in a Chapter 9 or Chapter 11 Case.

(1) *Objection.* An objection to confirmation of the plan shall be filed and served on the debtor, the trustee, the proponent of the plan, any committee appointed under the Code, and any other entity designated by the court, within a time fixed by the court. Unless the case is a chapter 9 municipality case, a copy of every objection to confirmation shall be transmitted by the objecting party to the United States trustee within the time fixed for filing objections. An objection to confirmation is governed by Rule 9014.

(2) *Hearing.* The court shall rule on confirmation of the plan after notice and hearing as provided in Rule 2022. If no objection is timely filed, the court may determine that the plan has been proposed in good faith and not by any means forbidden by law without receiving evidence on such issues.

(c) Order of Confirmation. The order of confirmation shall conform to the appropriate Official Form and notice of entry thereof shall be mailed promptly as provided in Rule 2002(f) to the debtor, the trustee, creditors, equity security holders, and other parties in interest. Except in a chapter 9 municipality case, notice of entry of the order of confirmation shall be transmitted to the United States trustee as provided in Rule 2002(k).

(d) Retained Power. Notwithstanding the entry of the order of confirmation, the court may issue any other order necessary to administer the estate.

(e) Stay of Confirmation Order. An order confirming a plan is stayed until the expiration of 10 days after the entry of the order, unless the court orders otherwise.

Bankruptcy Code References: §§ 105, 541, 944, 1128, 1129, 1141, 1142, 1224, 1322, 1324, 1327.

Rule 3021.   Distribution under Plan

Except as provided in Rule 3020(e), after a plan is confirmed, distribution shall be made to creditors whose claims have been allowed, to interest holders whose interests have not been disallowed, and to indenture trustees who have filed claims under Rule 3003(c)(5) that have been allowed. For purposes of this rule, creditors include holders of bonds, debentures, notes, and other debt securities, and interest holders include the holders of stock and other equity securities, of record at the time of commencement of distribution, unless a different time is fixed by the plan or the order confirming the plan.
Bankruptcy Code References: § 1143

Rule 3022.   Final Decree in Chapter 11 Reorganization Case

After an estate is fully administered in a chapter 11 reorganization case, the court, on its own motion or on motion of a party in interest, shall enter a final decree closing the case.
Bankruptcy Code References: §§ 350 and 1143

PART IV
THE DEBTOR: DUTIES AND BENEFITS

Rule 4001.   Relief from Automatic Stay; Prohibiting or Conditioning the Use, Sale, or Lease of Property; Use of Cash Collateral; Obtaining Credit; Agreements

(a) **Relief from Stay; Prohibiting or Conditioning the Use, Sale, or Lease of Property.**

(1) *Motion.* A motion for relief from an automatic stay provided by the Code or a motion to prohibit or condition the use, sale, or lease of property pursuant to § 363(e) shall be made in accordance with Rule 9014 and shall be served on any committee elected pursuant to § 705 or appointed pursuant to § 1102 of the Code or its authorized agent, or, if the case is a chapter 9 municipality case or a chapter 11 reorganization case and no committee of unsecured creditors has been appointed pursuant to § 1102, on the creditors included on the list filed pursuant to Rule 1007(d), and on such other entities as the court may direct.

(2) *Ex Parte Relief.* Relief from a stay under § 362(a) or a request to prohibit or condition the use, sale, or lease of property pursuant to § 363(e) may be granted without prior notice only if (A) it clearly appears from specific facts shown by affidavit or by a verified motion that immediate and irreparable injury, loss, or damage will result to the movant before the adverse party or the attorney for the adverse party can be heard in opposition, and (B) the movant's attorney certifies to the court in writing the efforts, if any, which have been made to give notice and the reasons why notice should not be required. The party obtaining relief under this subdivision and § 362(f) or § 363(e) shall immediately give oral notice thereof to the trustee or debtor in possession and to the debtor and forthwith mail or otherwise transmit to

such adverse party or parties a copy of the order granting relief. On two days notice to the party who obtained relief from the stay without notice or on shorter notice to that party as the court may prescribe, the adverse party may appear and move reinstatement of the stay or reconsideration of the order prohibiting or conditioning the use, sale, or lease of property. In that event, the court shall proceed expeditiously to hear and determine the motion.

(3) *Stay of Order.* An order granting a motion for relief from an automatic stay made in accordance with Rule 4001(a)(1) is stayed until the expiration of 10 days after the entry of the order, unless the court orders otherwise.

(b) Use of Cash Collateral.

(1) *Motion; Service.* A motion for authorization to use cash collateral shall be made in accordance with Rule 9014 and shall be served on any entity which has an interest in the cash collateral, on any committee elected pursuant to § 705 or appointed pursuant to § 1102 of the Code or its authorized agent, or, if the case is a chapter 9 municipality case or a chapter 11 reorganization case and no committee of unsecured creditors has been appointed pursuant to § 1102, on the creditors included on the list filed pursuant to Rule 1007(d), and on such other entities as the court may direct.

(2) *Hearing.* The court may commence a final hearing on a motion for authorization to use cash collateral no earlier than 15 days after service of the motion. If the motion so requests, the court may conduct a preliminary hearing before such 15 day period expires, but the court may authorize the use of only that amount of cash collateral as is necessary to avoid immediate and irreparable harm to the estate pending a final hearing.

(3) *Notice.* Notice of hearing pursuant to this subdivision shall be given to the parties on whom service of the motion is required by paragraph (1) of this subdivision and to such other entities as the court may direct.

(c) Obtaining Credit.

(1) *Motion; Service.* A motion for authority to obtain credit shall be made in accordance with Rule 9014 and shall be served on any committee elected pursuant to § 705 or appointed pursuant to § 1102 of the Code or its authorized agent, or, if the case is a chapter 9 municipality case or a chapter 11 reorganization case and no committee of unsecured creditors has been appointed pursuant to § 1102, on the creditors included on the list filed pursuant to Rule 1007(d), and on such other entities as the court may direct. The motion shall be accompanied by a copy of the agreement.

(2) *Hearing.* The court may commence a final hearing on a motion for authority to obtain credit no earlier than 15 days after service of the motion. If the motion so requests, the court may conduct a hearing before such 15 day period expires, but the court may authorize the obtaining of credit only to the extent necessary to avoid immediate and irreparable harm to the estate pending a final hearing.

(3) *Notice.* Notice of hearing pursuant to this subdivision shall be given to the parties on whom service of the motion is required by paragraph (1) of this subdivision and to such other entities as the court may direct.

(d) Agreement Relating to Relief from the Automatic Stay, Prohibiting or Conditioning the Use, Sale, or Lease of Property, Providing Adequate Protection, Use of Cash Collateral, and Obtaining Credit.

(1) *Motion; Service.* A motion for approval of an agreement (A) to provide adequate protection, (B) to prohibit or condition the use, sale, or lease

of property, (C) to modify or terminate the stay provided for in § 362, (D) to use cash collateral, or (E) between the debtor and an entity that has a lien or interest in property of the estate pursuant to which the entity consents to the creation of a lien senior or equal to the entity's lien or interest in such property shall be served on any committee elected pursuant to § 705 or appointed pursuant to § 1102 of the Code or its authorized agent, or, if the case is a chapter 9 municipality case or a chapter 11 reorganization case and no committee of unsecured creditors has been appointed pursuant to § 1102, on the creditors included on the list filed pursuant to Rule 1007(d), and on such other entities as the court may direct. The motion shall be accompanied by a copy of the agreement.

(2) *Objection.* Notice of the motion and the time within which objections may be filed and served on the debtor in possession or trustee shall be mailed to the parties on whom service is required by paragraph (1) of this subdivision and to such other entities as the court may direct. Unless the court fixes a different time, objections may be filed within 15 days of the mailing of notice.

(3) *Disposition; Hearing.* If no objection is filed, the court may enter an order approving or disapproving the agreement without conducting a hearing. If an objection is filed or if the court determines a hearing is appropriate, the court shall hold a hearing on no less than five days' notice to the objector, the movant, the parties on whom service is required by paragraph (1) of this subdivision and such other entities as the court may direct.

(4) *Agreement in Settlement of Motion.* The court may direct that the procedures prescribed in paragraphs (1), (2), and (3) of this subdivision shall not apply and the agreement may be approved without further notice if the court determines that a motion made pursuant to subdivisions (a), (b), or (c) of this rule was sufficient to afford reasonable notice of the material provisions of the agreement and opportunity for a hearing.

Bankruptcy Code References: §§ 361, 362, 363, 364, 365, 1201 and 1301

Rule 4002.   Duties of Debtor

In addition to performing other duties prescribed by the Code and rules, the debtor shall (1) attend and submit to an examination at the times ordered by the court; (2) attend the hearing on a complaint objecting to discharge and testify, if called as a witness; (3) inform the trustee immediately in writing as to the location of real property in which the debtor has an interest and the name and address of every person holding money or property subject to the debtor's withdrawal or order if a schedule of property has not yet been filed pursuant to Rule 1007; (4) cooperate with the trustee in the preparation of an inventory, the examination of proofs of claim, and the administration of the estate, and (5) file a statement of any change of the debtor's address.

Bankruptcy Code References: §§ 341, 343 and 521

Rule 4003.   Exemptions

(a) **Claim of Exemptions.** A debtor shall list the property claimed as exempt under § 522 of the Code on the schedule of assets required to be filed by Rule 1007. If the debtor fails to claim exemptions or file the schedule within the time specified in Rule 1007, a dependent of the debtor may file the list within 30 days thereafter.

(b) Objections to Claim of Exemptions. The trustee or any creditor may file objections to the list of property claimed as exempt within 30 days after the conclusion of the meeting of creditors held pursuant to Rule 2003(a) or the filing of any amendment to the list or supplemental schedules unless, within such period, further time is granted by the court. Copies of the objections shall be delivered or mailed to the trustee and to the person filing the list and the attorney for such person.

(c) Burden of Proof. In any hearing under this rule, the objecting party has the burden of proving that the exemptions are not properly claimed. After hearing on notice, the court shall determine the issues presented by the objections.

(d) Avoidance by Debtor of Transfers of Exempt Property. A proceeding by the debtor to avoid a lien or other transfer of property exempt under § 522(f) of the Code shall be by motion in accordance with Rule 9014.

Bankruptcy Code References: § 522

Rule 4004. *Grant or Denial of Discharge*

(a) Time for Filing Complaint Objecting to Discharge; Notice of Time Fixed. In a chapter 7 liquidation case a complaint objecting to the debtor's discharge under § 727(a) of the Code shall be filed not later than 60 days following the first date set for the meeting of creditors held pursuant to § 341(a). In a chapter 11 reorganization case, such complaint shall be filed not later than the first date set for the hearing on confirmation. At least 25 days' notice of the time so fixed shall be given to the United States trustee and all creditors as provided in Rule 2002(f) and (k) and to the trustee and the trustee's attorney.

(b) Extension of Time. On motion of any party in interest, after hearing on notice, the court may for cause extend the time for filing a complaint objecting to discharge. The motion shall be filed before such time has expired.

(c) Grant of Discharge.

(1) In a chapter 7 case, on expiration of the time fixed for filing a complaint objecting to discharge and the time fixed for filing a motion to dismiss the case pursuant to Rule 1017(e), the court shall forthwith grant the discharge unless:

(A) the debtor is not an individual,

(B) a complaint objecting to the discharge has been filed,

(C) the debtor has filed a waiver under § 727(a)(10),

(D) a motion to dismiss the case pursuant to Rule 1017(e) is pending,

(E) a motion to extend the time for filing a complaint objecting to discharge is pending, or

(F) the debtor has not paid in full the filing fee prescribed by 28 U.S.C. § 1930(a) and any other fee prescribed by the Judicial Conference of the United States under 28 U.S.C. § 1930(b) that is payable to the clerk upon the commencement of a case under the Code.

(2) Notwithstanding Rule 4004(c)(1), on motion of the debtor, the court may defer the entry of an order granting a discharge for 30 days and, on motion within that period, the court may defer entry of the order to a date certain.

(d) Applicability of Rules in Party VII. A proceeding commenced by a complaint objecting to discharge is governed by Part VII of these rules.

(e) Order of Discharge. An order of discharge shall conform to the appropriate Official Form.

(f) Registration in Other Districts. An order of discharge that has become final may be registered in any other district by filing a certified copy of the order in the office of the clerk of that district. When so registered the order of discharge shall have the same effect as an order of the court of the district where registered.

(g) Notice of Discharge. The clerk shall promptly mail a copy of the final order of discharge to those specified in subdivision (a) of this rule.

Bankruptcy Code References: §§ 341, 524, 727, 1141, 1228 and 1328

Rule 4005.   Burden of Proof in Objecting to Discharge

At the trial on a complaint objecting to a discharge, the plaintiff has the burden of proving the objection.

Bankruptcy Code References: § 727

Rule 4006.   Notice of No Discharge

If an order is entered denying or evoking a discharge or if a waiver of discharge is filed, the clerk, after the order becomes final or the waiver is filed, shall promptly give notice thereof to all creditors in the manner provided in Rule 2002.

Bankruptcy Code References: § 727, 1144, 1228, 1230, 1328 and 1330

Rule 4007.   Determination of Dischargeability of a Debt

(a) Persons Entitled to File Complaint. A debtor or any creditor may file a complaint to obtain a determination of the dischargeability of any debt.

(b) Time for Commencing Proceeding Other Than Under § 523(c) of the Code. A complaint other than under § 523(c) may be filed at any time. A case may be reopened without payment of an additional filing fee for the purpose of filing a complaint to obtain a determination under this rule.

(c) Time for Filing Complaint Under § 523(c) in Chapter 7 Liquidation, Chapter 11 Reorganization, and Chapter 12 Family Farmer's Debt Adjustment Cases; Notice of Time Fixed. A complaint to determine the dischargeability of any debt pursuant to § 523(c) of the Code shall be filed not later than 60 days following the first date set for the meeting of creditors held pursuant to § 341(a). The court shall give all creditors no less than 30 days' notice of the time so fixed in the manner provided in Rule 2002. On motion of any party-in-interest, after hearing on notice, the court may for cause extend the time fixed under this subdivision. The motion shall be made before the time has expired.

(d) Time for Filing Complaint Under § 523(c) in Chapter 13 Individuals Debt Adjustment Case; Notice of Time Fixed. On motion by a debtor for a discharge under § 1328(b), the court shall enter an order fixing a time for the filing of a complaint to determine the dischargeability of any debt pursuant to § 523(c) and shall give no less than 30 days' notice of the time fixed to all creditors in the manner provided in Rule 2002. On motion of any party-in-interest after hearing on notice the court may for cause extend the time fixed under this subdivision. The motion shall be made before the time has expired.

(e) **Applicability of Rules in Part VII.** A proceeding commenced by a complaint filed under this rule is governed by Part VII of these rules.

Bankruptcy Code References: §§ 341, 523, 1141, 1228 and 1328

Rule 4008. *Discharge and Reaffirmation Hearing*

Not more than 30 days following the entry of an order granting or denying a discharge, or confirming a plan in a chapter 11 reorganization case concerning an individual debtor and on not less than 10 days notice to the debtor and the trustee, the court shall hold a hearing as provided in § 524(d) of the Code. A motion by the debtor for approval of a reaffirmation agreement shall be filed before or at the hearing.

Bankruptcy Code References: §§ 524, 727 and 1141

Statement of Position

Statement of Position

90-7

Financial Reporting by Entities in Reorganization Under the Bankruptcy Code

November 19, 1990

**Prepared by the AICPA Task Force
on Financial Reporting
by Entities in Reorganization
Under the Bankruptcy Code**

**American Institute of
Certified Public Accountants**

AICPA

NOTE

This statement of position presents recommendations of the AICPA Task Force on Financial Reporting by Entities in Reorganization Under the Bankruptcy Code on reporting for entities that have filed petitions with the Bankruptcy Court and expect to reorganize as going concerns under Chapter 11 of title 11 of the United States Code. It represents the considered opinion of the AICPA Accounting Standards Executive Committee on the best practice for such financial reporting and is considered to be consistent with existing standards and principles covered by rule 203 of the AICPA Code of Professional Conduct. AICPA members should be prepared to justify departures from this statement of position.

TABLE OF CONTENTS

SUMMARY

This statement of position provides guidance for financial reporting by entities that have filed petitions with the Bankruptcy Court and expect to reorganize as going concerns under Chapter 11 of title 11 of the United States Code.

It recommends that all such entities report the same way while reorganizing under Chapter 11, with the objective of reflecting their financial evolution. To do that, their financial statements should distinguish transactions and events that are directly associated with the reorganization from the operations of the ongoing business as it evolves.

The statement recommends that, on emergence from Chapter 11, entities meeting specified criteria adopt fresh-start reporting. It also recommends how entities not meeting those criteria should report their liabilities.

FINANCIAL REPORTING BY
ENTITIES IN REORGANIZATION
UNDER THE BANKRUPTCY CODE

Introduction

1. This statement of position (SOP) was prepared by the Task Force on Financial Reporting by Entities in Reorganization Under the *Bankruptcy Code* to provide guidance on financial reporting by entities that have filed petitions with the *Bankruptcy Court* and expect to reorganize as going concerns under *Chapter 11* of title 11 of the Unites States Code ("Chapter 11").[1]

Petition, Proceeding, and Plan

2. An entity enters reorganization under Chapter 11 by filing a petition with the Bankruptcy Court, an adjunct of the United States District Courts. The filing of the *petition* starts the *reorganization proceeding*. The goal of the proceeding is to maximize recovery by creditors and shareholders by preserving it as a viable entity with a going concern value. For that purpose, the entity prepares a *plan of reorganization* intended to be confirmed by the court. The plan provides for treatment of all the assets and liabilities of the debtor, which might result in forgiveness of indebtedness. For the plan to be confirmed and the reorganization proceedings thereby concluded, the consideration to be received by parties in interest under the plan must exceed the consideration they would otherwise receive on liquidation of the entity under *Chapter 7* of the Bankruptcy Code. The court may confirm a plan even if some classes of creditors or some of the stockholders have not accepted it, provided that it meets standards of fairness required by Chapter 11 to the dissenting class of creditors or the dissenting stockholders.

3. The plan is the heart of every Chapter 11 reorganization. The provisions of the plan specify the treatment of all creditors and equity holders upon its approval by the Bankruptcy Court. Moreover, the plan shapes the financial structure of the entity that emerges.

4. Chapter 11 provides that, unless a *trustee* is appointed, the debtor has the exclusive right to file a plan for the first 120 days of the case, or such longer or shorter time as the Bankruptcy Court decrees, for cause. If a plan is filed within the exclusive period, additional time is provided to allow the debtor to obtain plan acceptance. The appointment of the trustee immediately terminates the debtor's exclusive right to file a plan, and any party in interest may then do so.

5. Except to the extent that specific debts are determined by the Bankruptcy Court not to be discharged by the plan, the provisions of a *confirmed plan* bind the debtor, any entity issuing securities under the plan, any entity acquiring assets under the plan, and any creditor, equity security holder, or general partner in the debtor, regardless of whether the *claim* is impaired under

---

[1] A glossary of defined terms, which are in italics when they first appear in the text, begins on page 923.

the plan and whether such creditor, equity security holder, or general partner has accepted the plan. A claim is impaired if, subject to certain rights to cure defaults, its legal rights are affected adversely by the plan.

6. In general, except as provided in the plan or in the order confirming the plan, confirmation of the plan discharges the debtor from all preconfirmation claims and terminates all rights and interest of equity security holders or general partners as provided for in the plan.

7. The Bankruptcy Court confirms a plan if it finds all of the following:

- The plan and the plan proponent have complied with various technical requirements of the Bankruptcy Code.
- Disclosures made in soliciting acceptance of the plan have been adequate.
- Dissenting members of *consenting classes of impaired claims* would receive under the plan at least the amount they would have received under a Chapter 7 proceeding.
- Claims entitled to priority under the Bankruptcy Code will be paid in cash.
- Confirmation of the plan is not likely to be followed by liquidation or further reorganization.
- At least one class of impaired claims, apart from insiders, has accepted the plan.
- The plan proponent has obtained the consent of all impaired classes of claims or equity securities, or the plan proponent can comply with the *cram-down provisions* of the Bankruptcy Code. (Under the cram-down provisions, the court may confirm a plan even if one or more classes of holders of impaired claims or equity securities do not accept it, as long as the court finds the plan does not discriminate unfairly and is fair and equitable to each *nonconsenting class* impaired by the plan.)

8. In general, a *secured claim* is deemed to be treated fairly and equitably if it remains adequately collateralized and will receive a stream of payments whose discounted value equals the amount of the secured claim on the effective date of the plan. In general, an *unsecured claim* is deemed to be treated fairly and equitably if it receives assets whose discounted value equals the allowed amount of the claim, or if the holder of any claim or equity security interest that is junior to the dissenting class will not receive or retain any assets under the plan. Similarly, an equity security interest is deemed fairly and equitably treated if that interest receives assets whose discounted value equals the greatest of any fixed liquidation preference, any fixed redemption price, or the value of such interest, or if no junior equity security interest will receive any assets under the plan.

Reorganization Value

9. An important part of the process of developing a plan is the determination of the *reorganization value* of the entity that emerges from bankruptcy. Reorganization value generally approximates fair value of the entity before

considering liabilities and approximates the amount a willing buyer would pay for the assets of the entity immediately after the restructuring. The reorganization value of an entity is the amount of resources available and to become available for the satisfaction of postpetition liabilities and *allowed claims* and interest, as negotiated or litigated between the *debtor-in-possession* or trustee, the creditors, and the holders of equity interests. Reorganization value includes the sum of the value attributed to the reconstituted entity and other assets of the debtor that will not be included in the reconstituted entity. Reorganization value and the terms of the plan are determined only after extensive arms-length negotiations or litigation between the interested parties. Before the negotiations, the debtor-in-possession, creditors, and equity holders develop their own ideas on the reorganization value of the entity that will emerge from Chapter 11. Several methods are used to determine the reorganization value; however, generally it is determined by discounting future cash flows for the reconstituted business that will emerge from Chapter 11 and from expected proceeds or collections from assets not required in the reconstituted business, at rates reflecting the business and financial risks involved.

The Disclosure Statement

10.   A *disclosure statement* approved by the court is transmitted to all parties entitled to vote on the plan at or before the time their acceptance of the plan is solicited. The disclosure statement provides information that enables them to make informed judgments about the plan.

11.   No postpetition solicitation of acceptance of a plan may be made unless by the time of the solicitation a disclosure statement previously approved by the Bankruptcy Court has been sent to those whose acceptance is required. The disclosure statement must contain adequate information, which is defined in the Bankruptcy Code as information that would enable a hypothetical reasonable investor typical of holders of claims or interests of the relevant class to make an informed judgment about the plan, as far as it is reasonably practicable to provide in light of the nature and history of the *emerging entity* and the condition of the emerging entity's records. Examples of the kinds of items that may be included in disclosure statements to provide such information include a summary of the reorganization plan, historical and prospective financial information, and a pro forma balance sheet reporting the reorganization value and the capital structure of the emerging entity.

12.   What constitutes adequate information depends on the circumstances of the entity in Chapter 11, the nature of the plan, and the sophistication of the various classes whose acceptance is required. Although a valuation is not required for a Bankruptcy Court's approval of a disclosure statement, the instances in which valuations are not made are generally restricted to those in which the reorganization value of the emerging entity is greater than the liabilities or in which holders of existing voting shares retain more than 50 percent of the emerging entity's voting shares when the entity emerges from reorganization.

13.   After reorganization proceedings have started, acceptances of a plan may not be solicited by any person without a disclosure statement approved by

the court, but acceptances obtained before the proceedings started may be counted if (a) they were solicited in compliance with applicable nonbankruptcy law governing the adequacy of disclosure or (b) there is not any applicable nonbankruptcy law but there was in fact adequate information provided at the time of the prebankruptcy solicitation of acceptances of the plan.

Current Literature and Reporting Practices

14.   The current financial reporting literature provides no specific guidance for financial reporting by entities in reorganization proceedings. Entities generally continue to apply the financial reporting principles they applied before filing petitions; these principles usually do not adequately reflect all changes in the entity's financial condition caused by the proceeding. The financial statements prepared while entities are in Chapter 11 reorganization are therefore not as useful to users of financial statements as they should be. For example, the Bankruptcy Code allows the debtor to reject executory contracts such as leases and take-or-pay contracts. Some entities report the resulting claims at the estimated amounts of the allowed claims, while others report them at the estimated amounts at which they will be settled.

15.   Another area in which reporting is diverse during the Chapter 11 reorganization is the classification of liabilities. Some entities report all *prepetition liabilities* as current, whereas others report them as long-term debt or as a separate item between current and long-term liabilities. Financial Accounting Standards Board (FASB) Statement No. 6, *Classification of Short-Term Obligations Expected to Be Refinanced*, states that all short-term obligations resulting from transactions in the normal course of business that are due in customary terms, such as trade payables, advance collections, and accrued expenses, are to be classified as current liabilities. However, FASB Statement No. 6 does not address reporting by entities in Chapter 11 reorganization whose unsecured debt may not be paid without approval of the Bankruptcy Court and therefore may neither be paid within one year, or the operating cycle, if longer, nor satisfied with current assets.

16.   Further, the financial reporting literature provides no specific guidance for financial reporting by entities emerging from Chapter 11 reorganization under confirmed plans. As a result, practice is diverse. For example, FASB Statement No. 15, *Accounting by Debtors and Creditors for Troubled Debt Restructurings*, in footnote 4, and FASB Technical Bulletin No. 81-6, *Applicability of Statement 15 to Debtors in Bankruptcy Situations*, indicate that Statement No. 15 does not apply to troubled debt restructurings in which debtors restate their liabilities generally under the purview of the Bankruptcy Court. A majority of reorganizations of businesses result in general restructuring of liabilities, and considerable confusion exists on how to report the restructured liabilities. FASB Interpretation No. 2 states that Accounting Principles Board (APB) Opinion No. 21, *Interest on Receivables and Payables*, should apply to cases under the Bankruptcy Code. However, that interpretation was superseded by FASB Statement No. 15. An analysis of reporting by entities emerging from bankruptcy indicates that some report their debt at discounted amounts and others follow the guidelines in FASB Statement No. 15.

17. There is no specific guidance on whether an emerging entity should restate assets. For example, some restate their assets—though there generally is no net write-up—through quasi-reorganizations, and others do not. An analysis of reporting by emerging entities indicates that some eliminate deficits in their retained earnings by reducing additional paid-in capital while others retain such deficits.

Scope

18. This statement of position applies to financial reporting both by entities that have filed petitions with the Bankruptcy Court and expect to reorganize as going concerns under Chapter 11 and by entities that have emerged from Chapter 11 (emerging entities) under confirmed plans.

19. It does not apply to entities that restructure their debt outside Chapter 11, to governmental organizations, or to entities that liquidate or adopt plans of liquidation under the Bankruptcy Code.

Conclusions

20. The following is a summary of the conclusions reached by the Accounting Standards Division. They should be read in conjunction with the discussion of conclusions, which follows this summary and explains the basis for the conclusions.

Financial Reporting During Reorganization Proceedings

21. Entering a reorganization proceeding, although a significant event, does not ordinarily affect or change the application of generally accepted accounting principles followed by the entity in the preparation of its financial statements. However, the needs of financial statement users change, and thus changes in the reporting practices previously followed by the entity are necessary.

22. An objective of financial statements issued by an entity in Chapter 11 should be to reflect its financial evolution during the proceeding. For that purpose, the financial statements for periods including and subsequent to filing the Chapter 11 petition should distinguish transactions and events that are directly associated with the reorganization from the ongoing operations of the business.

Balance Sheet

23. The balance sheet of an entity in Chapter 11 should distinguish prepetition liabilities subject to compromise from those that are not (such as fully secured liabilities that are expected not to be compromised) and *postpetition liabilities.* Liabilities that may be affected by the plan should be reported at the amounts expected to be allowed, even if they may be settled for lesser amounts. If there is uncertainty about whether a secured claim is *undersecured,* or will be impaired under the Plan, the entire amount of the claim should be included with prepetition claims subject to compromise; such a claim should not be reclassified unless it is subsequently determined that the claim is not subject to compromise.

24. Prepetition liabilities, including claims that become known after a petition is filed, should be reported on the basis of the expected amount of the allowed claims in accordance with FASB Statement No. 5, *Accounting for Contingencies,* as opposed to the amounts for which those allowed claims may be settled. Claims not subject to reasonable estimation should be disclosed in the notes to the financial statements based on the provisions of FASB Statement No. 5. Once these claims satisfy the accrual provisions of FASB Statement No. 5, they should be recorded in the accounts in accordance with the first sentence of this paragraph.

25. Debt discounts or premiums as well as debt issue costs should be viewed as valuations of the related debt. When the debt has become an allowed claim and the allowed claim differs from the net carrying amount of the debt, the recorded amount should be adjusted to the amount of the allowed claim (thereby adjusting existing discounts or premiums, and deferred issue costs to the extent necessary to report the debt at this allowed amount). The gain or loss resulting from the entries to record the adjustment should be classified as *reorganization items,* as discussed in paragraph 27. Premiums and discounts as well as debt issuance cost on debts that are not subject to compromise, such as fully secured claims, should not be adjusted.

26. Liabilities subject to compromise should be segregated from those that are not subject to compromise on the balance sheet. The principal categories of the claims subject to compromise should be disclosed in the notes to the financial statements. Circumstances arising during reorganization proceedings may require a change in the classification of liabilities between those subject to compromise and those not subject to compromise. Liabilities not subject to compromise should be further segregated into current and noncurrent classifications if the entity presents a classified balance sheet.

Statement of Operations

27. The statement of operations should portray the results of operations of the reporting entity while it is in Chapter 11. Revenues, expenses (including professional fees), realized gains and losses, and provisions for losses resulting from the reorganization and restructuring of the business should be reported separately as reorganization items, except for those required to be reported as discontinued operations and extraordinary items in conformity with APB Opinion 30, *Reporting the Results of Operations.*

28. Some entities defer professional fees and similar types of expenditures until the plan is confirmed and then reduce gain from debt discharge to the extent of the previously deferred expenses. Others accrue professional fees and similar types of expenditures upon the filing of the Chapter 11 petition. Still others expense professional fees and similar types of expenditures as incurred. The task force concluded that professional fees and similar types of expenditures directly relating to the Chapter 11 proceeding do not result in assets or liabilities and thus should be expensed as incurred and reported as reorganization items.

29.   Interest expense should be reported only to the extent that it will be paid during the proceeding or that it is probable that it will be an allowed priority, secured, or unsecured claim. Interest expense is not a reorganization item. The extent to which reported interest expense differs from stated contractual interest should be disclosed. The task force understands that the staff of the Securities and Exchange Commission (SEC) prefers that SEC registrants disclose this parenthetically on the face of the statement of operations.

30.   Interest income earned by an entity in Chapter 11 that it would not have earned but for the proceeding (normally all interest income) should be reported as a reorganization item.

Statement of Cash Flows

31.   Reorganization items should be disclosed separately within the operating, investing, and financing categories of the statement of cash flows. This presentation can be better accomplished by the use of the direct method of presenting the statement. If the indirect method is used, details of operating cash receipts and payments resulting from the reorganization should be disclosed in a supplementary schedule or in the notes to the financial statements.

Condensed Combined Financial Statements

32.   Consolidated financial statements that include one or more entities in reorganization proceedings and one or more entities not in reorganization proceedings should include condensed combined financial statements of the entities in reorganization proceedings. The combined financial statements should be prepared on the same basis as the consolidated financial statements.

33.   Intercompany receivables and payables of entities in reorganization proceedings should be disclosed in the condensed combined financial statements. In addition, the propriety of the carrying amounts of intercompany receivables from entities in Chapter 11 should be evaluated.

Earnings Per Share

34.   Earnings per share should be reported, when required, in conformity with APB Opinion 15, *Earnings Per Share*. If it is probable that the plan will require the issuance of common stock or common stock equivalents, thereby diluting current equity interests, that fact should be disclosed.

Financial Reporting When Entities Emerge From Chapter 11 Reorganization

35.   Entities whose plans have been confirmed by the court and have thereby emerged from Chapter 11 should apply the reporting principles in the following paragraphs as of the confirmation date or as of a later date when all material conditions precedent to the plan's becoming binding are resolved.

Fresh-Start Reporting

36.   If the reorganization value of the assets of the emerging entity immediately before the date of confirmation is less than the total of all postpetition liabilities and allowed claims, and if holders of existing voting shares immediately before confirmation receive less than 50 percent of the voting shares of the emerging entity, the entity should adopt fresh-start reporting upon its emergence from Chapter 11. The loss of control contemplated by the plan must be substantive and not temporary. That is, the new controlling interest must not revert to the shareholders existing immediately before the plan was filed or confirmed.

37.   While the court determines the adequacy of the disclosure statement, entities that expect to adopt fresh-start reporting should report information about the reorganization value in the disclosure statement, so that creditors and stockholders can make an informed judgment about the plan. The most likely place to report the reorganization value is in the pro forma balance sheet that is commonly part of the disclosure statement. Because reorganization value may not have been allocated to individual assets concurrently with the preparation of the pro forma balance sheet included in the disclosure statement in some cases, it may be necessary to include in the pro forma balance sheet a separate line item to reflect the difference of the total reorganization value of the emerging entity over recorded amounts. When possible, reorganization value should be segregated into major categories.

38.   Entities that adopt fresh-start reporting in conformity with paragraph 36 should apply the following principles:

- The reorganization value of the entity should be allocated to the entity's assets in conformity with the procedures specified by APB Opinion 16, *Business Combinations*, for transactions reported on the basis of the purchase method. If any portion of the reorganization value cannot be attributed to specific tangible or identified intangible assets of the emerging entity, such amounts should be reported as the intangible asset identified as "reorganization value in excess of amounts allocable to identifiable assets." This excess should be amortized in conformity with APB Opinion 17, *Intangible Assets*. There usually are overriding pertinent factors that should be considered in determining the proper amortization period of this asset that would generally result in a useful life of substantially less than forty years. At a minimum, the same considerations used in determining the reorganization value should be applied in determining the period of amortization.

- Each liability existing at the plan confirmation date, other than deferred taxes, should be stated at present values of amounts to be paid determined at appropriate current interest rates.

- Deferred taxes should be reported in conformity with generally accepted accounting principles. Benefits realized from preconfirmation net operating loss carryforwards should first reduce reorganization value in excess of amounts allocable to identifiable assets and other intangibles until exhausted and thereafter be reported as a direct addition to paid-in capital.

- Changes in accounting principles that will be required in the financial statements of the emerging entity within the twelve months following the adoption of fresh-start reporting should be adopted at the time fresh-start reporting is adopted.

39.   The financial statements of the entity as of and for the period immediately preceding the date determined in conformity with the guidance in paragraph 35 should reflect all activity through that date in conformity with the guidance in paragraphs 21 through 34. Additionally, the effects of the adjustments on the reported amounts of individual assets and liabilities resulting from the adoption of fresh-start reporting and the effects of the forgiveness of debt should be reflected in the predecessor entity's final statement of operations. Forgiveness of debt, if any, should be reported as an extraordinary item. Adopting fresh-start reporting results in a new reporting entity with no beginning retained earnings or deficit. When fresh-start reporting is adopted, the notes to the initial financial statements should disclose the following:

- Adjustments to the historical amounts of individual assets and liabilities
- The amount of debt forgiveness
- The amount of prior retained earnings or deficit eliminated
- Significant matters relating to the determination of reorganization value, such as—
  - The method or methods used to determine reorganization value and factors such as discount rates, tax rates, the number of years for which cash flows are projected, and the method of determining *terminal value*
  - Sensitive assumptions—that is, assumptions about which there is a reasonable possibility of the occurrence of a variation that would have significantly affected measurement of reorganization value
  - Assumptions about anticipated conditions that are expected to be different from current conditions, unless otherwise apparent

Comparative Financial Statements

40.   Chapter 2A of Accounting Research Bulletin (ARB) No. 43, *Restatement and Revision of Accounting Research Bulletins*, states the following in paragraph 1:

> The presentation of comparative financial statements in annual and other reports enhances the usefulness of such reports and brings out more clearly the nature and trends of current changes affecting the enterprise.

Paragraph 3 of that chapter requires comparative financial statements that are presented to be comparable from year to year, with any exceptions to comparability being clearly disclosed. Fresh-start financial statements prepared by entities emerging from Chapter 11 will not be comparable with those prepared before their plans were confirmed because they are, in effect, those of a new entity. Thus, comparative financial statements that straddle a confirmation date should not be presented.[2]

Reporting by Entities Not Qualifying for Fresh Start

41. Entities emerging from Chapter 11 that do not meet the criteria in paragraph 36 do not qualify for a fresh start. Liabilities compromised by confirmed plans should be stated at present values of amounts to be paid, determined at appropriate current interest rates. Forgiveness of debt, if any, should be reported as an extraordinary item.

42. Because this statement of position applies to financial reporting for entities that enter and intend to emerge from Chapter 11 reorganization, quasi-reorganization accounting should not be used at the time of the reorganization.

Discussion of Conclusions

Reporting Prepetition Liabilities

43. The task force believes that entities in Chapter 11 reorganization should segregate liabilities subject to compromise from those that are not subject to compromise. Therefore, prepetition liabilities that may be impaired by a plan and that are eligible for compromise because they are either unsecured or undersecured should be separately classified and designated in the balance sheet as prepetition liabilities subject to compromise, because that provides the most meaningful presentation while in Chapter 11 reorganization.

44. The financial reporting literature does not specifically address the balance sheet classification issues that result from filing a petition. Guidance for classifying liabilities as current in a classified balance sheet is provided in paragraph 7 of ARB 43, chapter 3A, which states the following:

> The term *current liabilities* is used to designate obligations whose liquidation is reasonably expected to require the use of existing resources properly classified as current assets, or the creation of other current liabilities. . . .

Trade payables that are incurred in the normal course of business are usually classified as current in classified balance sheets because they meet the ARB 43 criteria cited above. However, filing a petition generally causes the payment of unsecured or undersecured prepetition liabilities to be prohibited before the plan is confirmed. The Chapter 11 reorganization ending in confirmation of a plan typically takes more than one year or one operating cycle, if longer.

45. It might be argued that prepetition liabilities classified as current in a classified balance sheet, such as trade payables, should retain that classification under the provisions of FASB Statement No. 6, *Classification of Short-*

---

[2]The SEC and other regulatory agencies may require the presentation of predecessor financial statements. However, such presentations should not be viewed as a continuum because the financial statements are those of a different reporting entity and are prepared using a different basis of accounting, and, therefore, are not comparable. Attempts to disclose and explain exceptions that affect comparability would likely result in reporting that is so unwieldy it would not be useful.

Term Obligations Expected to Be Refinanced. That Statement requires all short-term liabilities incurred in the normal course of business and due in customary terms to be classified as current. Other short-term liabilities are excluded from the current liability classification under FASB Statement No. 6 if the entity intends to refinance the obligations on a long-term basis and such intent is supported by the facts. However, FASB Statement No. 6 does not address what occurs when a petition is filed.

46. FASB Statement No. 78, *Classification of Obligations That Are Callable by the Creditor,* amended paragraph 7 of ARB 43, chapter 3A, by requiring current liabilities classification in a classified balance sheet for long-term liabilities that, by their terms, are due on demand or will be due on demand within one year, or the operating cycle, if longer. This definition also includes long-term liabilities that are or will be callable by the creditor because of a violation of a provision of the debt agreement. The *automatic stay provisions* of Chapter 11 make it unnecessary to reclassify prepetition long-term liabilities even though prepetition creditors might demand payment or there is a violation of a covenant in the debt agreement.

47. Prepetition liabilities should be reported at the amounts of allowed claims—that is, at the amount allowed by the court, even though such liabilities may not be paid in full.

48. When prepetition claims become known after a petition is filed (for example, a claim resulting from the rejection of an operating lease), they should be reported at the estimated amounts of the allowed claims. Some believe that such prepetition claims should be reported at estimates of the settlement amounts. However, these prepetition claims should be reported at an amount allowed by the court because that is the amount of the liability until it is settled and the use of allowed amounts is consistent with the amounts at which other prepetition liabilities are stated and thereby provides comparability among the various kinds of claims.

Statement of Operations

49. Losses as a result of restructuring or disposal of assets directly related to reorganization proceedings are best included as reorganization items to the extent that they are not otherwise reported as part of the results of discontinued operations in conformity with APB Opinion 30, *Reporting the Results of Operations.* That does not result in reclassification of revenues and expenses from operations sold or abandoned, except those that meet the criteria in APB Opinion 30. Rather, gains or losses classified as reorganization items might include a gain or loss on disposal of assets plus related employee costs and charges or other assets directly related to the assets disposed of or the operations restructured. Also, income, expenses, realized gains, and losses that can be directly associated with the proceeding are best segregated and presented as reorganization items in the statement of operations. Examples include interest income (as indicated in paragraph 30), professional fees, and losses on executory contracts.[3]

---

[3]Appendix A illustrates a statement of operations that includes reorganization items.

50.   The task force believes that segregation of reorganization items provides meaningful disclosure and is consistent with APB Opinion 30, paragraph 26, which states the following:

> A material event or transaction that is unusual in nature or occurs infrequently but not both, and therefore does not meet both criteria for classification as an extraordinary item, should be reported as a separate component of continuing operations.

Interest Expense

51.   Certain provisions of the Bankruptcy Code may relieve the entity from its obligation to pay interest. Generally, interest on secured claims accrues only to the extent that the value of underlying collateral exceeds the principal amount of the secured claim. In addition, interest on unsecured claims does not accrue during the proceeding if the entity is insolvent; therefore, disclosure of contractual interest is considered useful because it may differ from interest actually being reported.

Interest Income

52.   An entity in reorganization typically accumulates cash during the proceeding because it is not paying its obligations currently. The cash ultimately is distributed to creditors or others in conformity with the plan. The amount of cash accumulated does not reflect the entity's prepetition activities, and it is not expected that such an accumulation would recur in the reorganized entity. The interest income earned during the proceeding on cash accumulated during the proceeding, therefore, is a reorganization item. To the extent that management can reasonably estimate that portion of interest income applicable to normal invested working capital, it should be reported as an operating item in the ordinary manner.

Statement of Cash Flows

53.   FASB Statement No. 95, *Statement of Cash Flows*, requires information on the cash activity of reporting entities. The task force believes that such information is the most beneficial information that can be provided in the financial statements of an entity in Chapter 11. It also believes the direct method is the better method to provide such information by such entities.

54.   Paragraph 27 of FASB Statement No. 95 lists the operating items that should be reported separately when the direct method is used. That paragraph encourages further breakdown of those operating items if the entity considers such a breakdown meaningful and it is feasible to do so. Further identification of cash flows from reorganization items should be provided to the extent feasible. For example, interest received might be segregated between estimated normal recurring interest received and interest received on cash accumulated because of the reorganization. Appendix A illustrates a statement of cash flows for an entity operating under Chapter 11.

Fresh-Start Reporting

55.   The effects of a plan should be included in the entity's financial statements as of the date the plan is confirmed. However, inclusion should be delayed to a date not later than the effective date if there is a material unsatisfied condition precedent to the plan's becoming binding on all the parties in interest or if there is a stay pending appeal. That might occur, for example, if obtaining financing for the plan or for the transfer of material assets to the debtor by a third party is a condition to the plan's becoming effective.

56.   Financial statements prepared as of the date after the parties in interest have approved a plan through the voting process, and issued after the plan has been confirmed by the court, should report the effects of the plan if there are no material unsatisfied conditions.

57.   An essential element in negotiating a plan with the various classes of creditors and equity interests is the determination of reorganization value by the parties in interest. The plan provides for allocating the reorganization value among the parties in interest in accordance with their legal priorities: first to secured claims to the extent of the value of the collateral securing the claims, then to claims entitled to priority under the Bankruptcy Code, and then to the various classes of unsecured debt and equity interests in accordance with their legal priorities or as the parties may otherwise agree. In the event that the parties in interest cannot agree on the reorganization value and presumably the plan of reorganization, the court may be called upon to determine the reorganization value of the entity before a plan of reorganization can be confirmed.

58.   The task force concluded that reorganization value can be a more objective measure of fair value than a purchase price in a business combination. This view is based on two factors. First, a purchase price in a nonbankruptcy business combination may exceed the fair value of the acquired entity, because such determinations may be influenced by a variety of factors unrelated to that entity. Second, in the reorganization process, extensive information available to the parties in interest, the adversarial negotiation process, the involvement of the Bankruptcy Court, the use of specialists by one or more of the parties in interest, and the fact that all elements of the determination are focused solely on the economic viability of the emerging entity result in an objective and reliable determination of reorganization value.

59.   If, based on reorganization value, the parties in interest allow the entity to survive as a going concern and emerge from Chapter 11, the financial reporting should reflect that fact. The ability to reflect reorganization value would enhance the representational faithfulness of the emerging entity's financial statements.

60.   Under the *absolute priority doctrine* of the Bankruptcy Code, if the amount of postpetition liabilities and allowed claims exceeds the reorganization value of the emerging entity, existing shareholders lose their legal right to any economic interest without the consent of creditors. Therefore, any equity interest in the emerging entity ultimately held by existing shareholders is given to them by the creditors. Among the reasons the creditors might give

such shareholders equity interests in the emerging entity are to avoid the expensive and time-consuming legal proceedings necessary to implement the cram-down provisions of the Bankruptcy Code or to preserve continuity of management.

61. Based on the factors described in paragraphs 57, 58, and 60, some would conclude that the combination of change in majority ownership and voting control—that is, loss of control by the existing shareholders, a court-approved reorganization, and a reliable measure of the entity's fair value—results in a fresh start, creating, in substance, a new reporting entity. Others believe that a change in control and the exchange of debt and equity based on reorganization value is in substance an acquisition at fair value by new shareholders in exchange for extinguishing their debt. Although the former shareholders can receive a portion of the new equity, they have lost their rights to any equity interest in the reorganized entity and receive such interest only with the consent of the real stakeholders, the creditors who will become the new shareholders. The task force concluded that under each view a new reporting entity is created and assets and liabilities should be recorded at their fair values. That is, assets should be recorded on the basis of reorganization value and liabilities should be recorded at fair value.

62. Some believe that the recognition of reorganization value in the balance sheet of an emerging entity that meets the criteria for fresh-start reporting should be limited to no net write-up of assets, similar to the SEC staff's interpretation of FRR Section 210 (ASR 25). That view is a combination of the notion that assets and liabilities should be reported at fair value in a fresh start and the belief that assets cannot be written up in a historical cost transaction-based accounting model. The task force did not accept that view for the reasons stated in paragraph 61.

Fair Value of Liabilities

63. In a typical Chapter 11 reorganization, there is a general restructuring of liabilities. FASB Statement No. 15, *Accounting by Debtors and Creditors for Troubled Debt Restructurings*, does not apply in a general restructuring of liabilities.

64. A general restructuring of liabilities involves negotiation between the parties in interest. The negotiation and distribution under the confirmed plan constitutes an exchange of resources and obligations. By analogy, the guidance provided by APB Opinion 16 for recording liabilities assumed in a business combination accounted for as a purchase should be applied in reporting liabilities by an entity emerging from Chapter 11.

Analogous Literature

65. The task force believes that the principles of quasi-reorganization accounting are not applicable to Chapter 11 reorganizations. Some argue that such a requirement would conflict with ARB 43 because it would prohibit adopting an accounting procedure that is now generally accepted. The task force does not believe that is the case. ARB 43 relates to a procedure called a

quasi-reorganization. Webster's dictionary defines *quasi* as "having some resemblance." The task force interprets ARB 43 to apply to situations that resemble but are not reorganizations under Chapter 11. There is no specific guidance for a legal reorganization, so practice has sometimes looked to ARB 43 when reporting a legal reorganization. The task force believes that is the case with many emerging entities. This statement of position provides specific guidance for all reorganizations under Chapter 11, and an analogy to ARB 43 is not appropriate.

Effective Date and Transition

66. This entire statement of position shall become effective for financial statements of enterprises that have filed petitions under the Bankruptcy Code after December 31, 1990. Additionally, for enterprises that file petitions prior to January 1, 1991, and that have plans of reorganization confirmed after June 30, 1991, paragraphs 35 through 42 of this SOP shall be applied to their financial statements. Earlier application by entities in reorganization is encouraged.

APPENDIX A

Illustrative Financial Statements and Notes to Financial Statements for an Entity Operating Under Chapter 11

A-1. XYZ Company is a manufacturing concern headquartered in Tennessee, with a fiscal year ending on December 31. On January 10, 19X1, XYZ filed a petition for relief under Chapter 11 of the federal bankruptcy laws. The following financial statements (balance sheet and statements of operations and cash flows) are presented as of and for the year ended December 31.

XYZ Company
(Debtor-in-Possession)
Balance Sheet
December 31, 19X1

	(000s)
Assets	
Current Assets	
Cash	$ 110
Accounts receivable, net	300
Inventory	250
Other current assets	30
Total current assets	690
Property, plant and equipment, net	430
Goodwill	210
Total Assets	$1,330

Liabilities and Shareholders' Deficit   (000s)

Liabilities Not Subject to Compromise

 Current Liabilities:

  Short-term borrowings $ 25

  Accounts payable-trade   200

  Other liabilities   50

   Total current liabilities   275

Liabilities Subject to Compromise   1,100(a)

  Total liabilities   1,375

Shareholders' (deficit):

 Preferred stock   325

 Common stock   75

 Retained earnings (deficit)   (445)

                       (45)

   Total Liabilities & Shareholders' (Deficit) $1,330

(a) Liabilities subject to compromise consist of the following:

  Secured debt, 14%, secured by first

   mortgage on building $ 300,000(b)

  Priority tax claims   50,000

  Senior subordinated secured notes, 15%   275,000

  Trade and other miscellaneous claims   225,000

  Subordinated debentures, 17%   250,000

                 $ 1,100,000

(b) The secured debt in this case should be considered, due to various factors, subject to compromise.

The accompanying notes are an integral part of the financial statements.

XYZ Company
(Debtor-In-Possession)
Statement of Operations
For the Year Ended December 31, 19X1
(000s)

	19X1
Revenues:	
Sales	$ 2,400
Cost and expenses:	
Cost of goods sold	1,800
Selling, operating and administrative	550
Interest (contractual interest $5)	3
	2,353
Earnings before reorganization items and income tax benefit	47
Reorganization items:	
Loss on disposal of facility	(60)
Professional fees	(50)
Provision for rejected executory contracts	(10)
Interest earned on accumulated cash resulting from Chapter 11 proceeding	1
	(119)
Loss before income tax benefit and discontinued operations	(72)
Income tax benefit	10
Loss before discontinued operations	(62)
Discontinued operations:	
Loss from operations of discontinued products segment	(56)
Net loss	$ (118)
Loss per common share:	
Loss before discontinued operations	$ (.62)
Discontinued operations	(.56)
Net loss	$ (1.18)

The accompanying notes are an integral part of the financial statements.

XYZ Company
(Debtor-in-Possession)
Statement of Cash Flows
For the Year Ended December 31, 19X1
Increase in Cash and Cash Equivalents
(000s)

	19X1
Cash flows from operating activities:	
Cash received from customers	$ 2,220
Cash paid to suppliers and employees	(2,070)
Interest paid	(3)
Net cash provided by operating activities before reorganization items	147
Operating cash flows from reorganization items:	
Interest received on cash accumulated because of the Chapter 11 proceeding	1
Professional Fees paid for services rendered in connection with the Chapter 11 proceeding	(50)
Net cash used by reorganization items	(49)
Net cash provided by operating activities	98
Cash flows from investing activities:	
Capital expenditures	(5)
Proceeds from sale of facility due to Chapter 11 proceeding	40
Net cash provided by investing activities	35
Cash flows used by financing activities:	
Net borrowings under short-term credit facility (post petition)	25
Repayment of cash overdraft	(45)
Principal payments on prepetition debt authorized by court	(3)
Net cash provided by financing activities	(23)
Net increase in cash and cash equivalents	110
Cash and cash equivalents at beginning of year	—
Cash and cash equivalents at end of year	$ 110
Reconciliation of net loss to net cash provided by operating activities	
Net loss	$ (118)
Adjustments to reconcile net loss to net cash provided by operating activities	
Depreciation	20
Loss on disposal of facility	60
Provision for rejected executory contracts	10
Loss on discontinued operations	56
Increase in postpetition payables and other liabilities	250
Increase in accounts receivable	(180)
Net cash provided by operating activities	$ 98

The accompanying notes are an integral part of the financial statements.

XYZ Company Notes to Financial Statements
December 31, 19X1

Note X—Petition for Relief Under Chapter 11

On January 10, 19X1, XYZ Company (the "Debtor") filed petitions for relief under Chapter 11 of the federal bankruptcy laws in the United States Bankruptcy Court for the Western District of Tennessee. Under Chapter 11, certain claims against the Debtor in existence prior to the filing of the petitions for relief under the federal bankruptcy laws are stayed while the Debtor continues business operations as Debtor-in-possession. These claims are reflected in the December 31, 19X1, balance sheet as "liabilities subject to compromise." Additional claims (liabilities subject to compromise) may arise subsequent to the filing date resulting from rejection of executory contracts, including leases, and from the determination by the court (or agreed to by parties in interest) of allowed claims for contingencies and other disputed amounts. Claims secured against the Debtor's assets ("secured claims") also are stayed, although the holders of such claims have the right to move the court for relief from the stay. Secured claims are secured primarily by liens on the Debtor's property, plant, and equipment.

The Debtor received approval from the Bankruptcy Court to pay or otherwise honor certain of its prepetition obligations, including employee wages and product warranties. The Debtor has determined that there is insufficient collateral to cover the interest portion of scheduled payments on its prepetition debt obligations. Contractual interest on those obligations amounts to $5,000, which is $2,000 in excess of reported interest expense; therefore, the debtor has discontinued accruing interest on these obligations. Refer to note XX [see appendix B, note X] for a discussion of the credit arrangements entered into subsequent to the Chapter 11 filings.

Fresh-Start Accounting and Illustrative Notes to Financial Statements

B-1.   The Bankruptcy Court confirmed XYZ's plan of reorganization as of June 30, 19X2. It was determined that XYZ's reorganization value computed immediately before June 30, 19X2, the date of plan confirmation, was $1,300,000, which consisted of the following:

Cash in excess of normal operating requirements generated by operations	$ 150,000
Net realizable value of asset dispositions	75,000
Present value of discounted cash flows of the emerging entity	1,075,000
Reorganization value	$1,300,000

XYZ Company adopted fresh-start reporting because holders of existing voting shares immediately before filing and confirmation of the plan received less than 50% of the voting shares of the emerging entity and its reorganization value is less than its postpetition liabilities and allowed claims, as shown below:

Postpetition current liabilities	$ 300,000
Liabilities deferred pursuant to Chapter 11 proceeding	1,100,000
Total postpetition liabilities and allowed claims	1,400,000
Reorganization value	(1,300,000)
Excess of liabilities over reorganization value	$ 100,000

B-2.   The reorganization value of the XYZ Company was determined in consideration of several factors and by reliance on various valuation methods, including discounting cash flow and price/earnings and other applicable ratios. The factors considered by XYZ Company included the following:

- Forecasted operating and cash flow results which gave effect to the estimated impact of
  - Corporate restructuring and other operating program changes
  - Limitations on the use of available net operating loss carryovers and other tax attributes resulting from the plan of reorganization and other events
- The discounted residual value at the end of the forecast period based on the capitalized cash flows for the last year of that period

- Market share and position
- Competition and general economic considerations
- Projected sales growth
- Potential profitability
- Seasonality and working capital requirements

B-3.   After consideration of XYZ Company's debt capacity and other capital structure considerations, such as industry norms, projected earnings to fixed charges, earnings before interest and taxes to interest, free cash flow to interest, and free cash flow to debt service and other applicable ratios, and after extensive negotiations among parties in interest, it was agreed that XYZ's reorganization capital structure should be as follows:

Postpetition current liabilities	$ 300,000
IRS note	50,000
Senior debt	275,000 (1)
Subordinated debt	175,000
Common stock	350,000
	$1,150,000 (2)

(1) Due $50,000 per year for each of the next four years, at 12% interest, with $75,000 due in the fifth year.
(2) See paragraph B-5 for the balance sheet adjustments required to reflect XYZ Company's reorganization value as of the date of plan confirmation.

B-4.   The following entries record the provisions of the plan and the adoption of fresh-start reporting:

Entries to record debt discharge:

Liabilities subject to compromise	1,100,000	
Senior debt—current		50,000
Senior debt—long-term		225,000
IRS note		50,000
Cash		150,000
Subordinated debt		175,000
Common stock (new)		86,000
Additional paid-in capital		215,000
Gain on debt discharge		149,000

Entries to record exchange of stock for stock:

Preferred stock	325,000	
Common stock (old)	75,000	
Common stock (new)		14,000
Additional paid-in capital		386,000

Entries to record the adoption of fresh-start reporting and to eliminate
the deficit:

Inventory	50,000	
Property, plant, and equipment	175,000	
Reorganization value in excess of amounts allocable to identifiable assets	175,000	
Gain on debt discharge	149,000	
Additional paid-in capital	351,000	
Goodwill		200,000
Deficit		700,000

B-5. The effect of the plan of reorganization on XYZ Company's balance sheet, as of June 30, 19X2, is as follows:

	Pre-confirmation	Adjustments to Record Confirmation of Plan — Debt Discharge	Adjustments to Record Confirmation of Plan — Exchange of Stock	Adjustments to Record Confirmation of Plan — Fresh Start	XYZ Company's Reorganized Balance Sheet
Assets:					
Current Assets					
Cash	$ 200,000	$ (150,000)			$ 50,000
Receivables	250,000				250,000
Inventory	175,000			$ 50,000	225,000
Assets to be disposed of valued at market, which is lower than cost	25,000				25,000
Other current assets	25,000				25,000
	675,000	(150,000)		50,000	575,000
Property, plant, and equipment	175,000			175,000	350,000
Assets to be disposed of valued at market, which is lower than cost	50,000				50,000
Goodwill	200,000			(200,000)	
Reorganization value in excess of amounts allocable to identifiable assets				175,000	175,000
	$ 1,100,000	$ (150,000)		$ 200,000	$1,150,000
Liabilities and Shareholders' Deficit:					
Liabilities Not Subject to Compromise					
Current liabilities					
Short-term borrowings	$ 25,000				$ 25,000
Current maturities of senior debt		$ 50,000			50,000
Accounts payable trade	175,000				175,000
Other liabilities	100,000				100,000
	300,000	50,000			350,000
Liabilities Subject to Compromise					
Prepetition liabilities	1,100,000	(1,100,000)			
IRS note		50,000			50,000
Senior debt, less current maturities		225,000			225,000
Subordinated debt		175,000			175,000
Shareholders' deficit:					
Preferred stock	325,000		$ (325,000)		
Additional paid-in capital		215,000	386,000	$ (351,000)	250,000
Common stock—old	75,000		(75,000)		
Common stock—new		86,000	14,000		100,000
Retained earnings (deficit)	(700,000)	149,000		700,000 (149,000)	
	(300,000)	450,000	0	200,000	350,000
	$ 1,100,000	$ (150,000)	$ 0	$ 200,000	$ 1,150,000

B-6.   The following illustrative footnote disclosure discusses the details of XYZ Company's confirmed plan of reorganization. In this illustration a tabular presentation entitled "Plan of Reorganization Recovery Analysis" is incorporated in the footnote. The plan of reorganization recovery analysis may alternatively be presented as supplementary information to the financial statements.

Note X—Plan of Reorganization

On June 30, 19X2, the Bankruptcy Court confirmed the Company's plan of reorganization. The confirmed plan provided for the following:

Secured Debt—The Company's $300,000 of secured debt (secured by a first mortgage lien on a building located in Nashville, Tennessee) was exchanged for $150,000 in cash and a $150,000 secured note, payable in annual installments of $27,300 commencing on June 1, 19X3, through June 1, 19X6, with interest at 12% per annum, with the balance due on June 1, 19X7.

Priority Tax Claims—Payroll and withholding taxes of $50,000 are payable in equal annual installments commencing on July 1, 19X3, through July 1, 19X8, with interest at 11% per annum.

Senior Debt—The holders of approximately $275,000 of senior subordinated secured notes received the following instruments in exchange for their notes: (*a*) $87,000 in new senior secured debt, payable in annual installments of $15,800 commencing March 1, 19X3, through March 1, 19X6, with interest at 12% per annum, secured by first liens on certain property, plant, and equipment, with the balance due on March 1, 19X7; (*b*) $123,000 of subordinated debt with interest at 14% per annum due in equal annual installments commencing on October 1, 19X3, through October 1, 19X9, secured by second liens on certain property, plant, and equipment; and (*c*) 11.4% of the new issue of outstanding voting common stock of the Company.

Trade and Other Miscellaneous Claims—The holders of approximately $225,000 of trade and other miscellaneous claims received the following for their claims: (*a*) $38,000 in senior secured debt, payable in annual installments of $6,900 commencing March 1, 19X3, through March 1, 19X6, with interest at 12% per annum, secured by first liens on certain property, plant, and equipment, with the balance due on March 1, 19X7; (*b*) $52,000 of subordinated debt, payable in equal annual installments commencing October 1, 19X3, through October 1, 19X8, with interest at 14% per annum; and (*c*) 25.7% of the new issue of outstanding voting common stock of the Company.

Subordinated Debentures—The holders of approximately $250,000 of subordinated unsecured debt received, in exchange for the debentures, 48.9% of the new issue outstanding voting common stock of the Company.

Preferred Stock—The holders of 3,250 shares of preferred stock received 12% of the outstanding voting common stock of the new issue of the Company in exchange for their preferred stock.

Common Stock—The holders of approximately 75,000 outstanding shares of the Company's existing common stock received, in exchange for their shares, 2% of the new outstanding voting common stock of the Company.

The Company accounted for the reorganization using fresh-start reporting. Accordingly, all assets and liabilities are restated to reflect their reorganization value, which approximates fair value at the date of reorganization. The following table ("Plan of Reorganization Recovery Analysis") summarizes the adjustments required to record the reorganization and the issuance of the various securities in connection with the implementation of the plan.

XYZ Company
Plan of Reorganization
Recovery Analysis

	Elimination of Debt and Equity		Surviving Debt	Recovery						Total Recovery	
				Cash	IRS Note	Senior Debt	Subordinated Debt	Common Stock* %	Common Stock* Value	$	%
Postpetition liabilities	$ 300,000		$ 300,000							$ 300,000	100%
Claim/Interest											
Secured debt	300,000			$ 150,000		$ 150,000				300,000	100
Priority tax claim	50,000				$ 50,000					50,000	100
Senior debt	275,000	$ (25,000)				87,000	$ 123,000	11.4%	$ 40,000	250,000	91
Trade and other miscellaneous claims	225,000	(45,000)				38,000	52,000	25.7	90,000	180,000	80
Subordinated debentures	250,000 1,100,000	(79,000)						48.9	171,000	171,000	68
Preferred stockholders	325,000	(283,000)						12.0	42,000	42,000	
Common stockholders	75,000	(68,000)						2.0	7,000	7,000	
Deficit	(700,000)	700,000									
Total	$ 1,100,000	$ 200,000	$ 300,000	$ 150,000	$ 50,000	$ 275,000	$ 175,000	100.0%	$ 350,000	$ 1,300,000	

*The aggregate par value of the common stock issued under the plan is $100,000.

Absolute priority doctrine. A doctrine that provides that if an impaired class does not vote in favor of a plan, the court may nevertheless confirm the plan under the cram-down provisions of the Bankruptcy Code. The absolute priority doctrine is triggered when the cram-down provisions apply. The doctrine states that all members of the senior class of creditors and equity interests must be satisfied in full before the members of the second senior class of creditors can receive anything, and the full satisfaction of that class must occur before the third senior class of creditors may be satisfied, and so on.

Administrative expenses (claims). Claims that receive priority over all other unsecured claims in a bankruptcy case. Administrative claims (expenses) include the actual, necessary costs and expenses of preserving the estate, including wages, salaries, or commissions for services rendered after the commencement of the case. Fees paid to professionals for services rendered after the petition is filed are considered administrative expenses.

Allowed claim(s). The amount allowed by the Court as a claim against the Estate. This amount may differ from the actual settlement amount.

Automatic stay provisions. Provisions causing the filing of a petition under the Bankruptcy Code to automatically stay virtually all actions of creditors to collect prepetition debts. As a result of the stay, no party, with minor exceptions, having a security or adverse interest in the debtor's property can take any action that will interfere with the debtor or the debtor's property, regardless of where the property is located or who has possession, until the stay is modified or removed.

Bankruptcy Code. A federal statute, enacted October 1, 1979, as title 11 of the United States Code by the Bankruptcy Reform Act of 1978, that applies to all cases filed on or after its enactment and that provides the basis for the current federal bankruptcy system.

Bankruptcy Court. The United States Bankruptcy Court is an adjunct of the United States District Courts. Under the jurisdiction of the District Court, the Bankruptcy Court is generally responsible for cases filed under Chapters 7, 11, 12, and 13 of the Bankruptcy Code.

Chapter 7. A liquidation, voluntarily or involuntarily initiated under the provisions of the Bankruptcy Code, that provides for liquidation of the business or the debtor's estate.

Chapter 11. A reorganization action, either voluntarily or involuntarily initiated under the provisions of the Bankruptcy Code, that provides for a reorganization of the debt and equity structure of the business and allows the business to continue operations. A debtor may also file a plan of liquidation under Chapter 11.

Claim. As defined by Section 101(4) of the Bankruptcy Code, (a) a right to payment, regardless of whether the right is reduced to judgment, liquidated, unliquidated, fixed, contingent, matured, unmatured, disputed, undisputed, legal, secured, or unsecured, or (b) a right to an equitable remedy for breach of performance if such breach results in a right to payment, regardless of whether the right is reduced to a fixed, contingent, matured, unmatured, disputed, undisputed, secured, or unsecured right.

Confirmed plan. An official approval by the court of a plan of reorganization under a Chapter 11 proceeding that makes the plan binding on the debtors and creditors. Before a plan is confirmed, it must satisfy eleven requirements in section 1129(a) of the Bankruptcy Code.

Consenting classes.   Classes of creditors or stockholders that approve the proposed plan.

Cram-down provisions.   Provisions requiring that for a plan to be confirmed, a class of claims or interests must either accept the plan or not be impaired. However, the Bankruptcy Code allows the Court under certain conditions to confirm a plan even though an impaired class has not accepted the plan. To do so, the plan must not discriminate unfairly and must be fair and equitable to each class of claims or interests impaired under the plan that have not accepted it. The Code states examples of conditions for secured claims, unsecured claims, and stockholder interests in the fair and equitable requirement.

Debtor-in-possession.   Existing management continuing to operate an entity that has filed a petition under Chapter 11. The debtor-in-possession is allowed to operate the business in all Chapter 11 cases unless the court, for cause, authorizes the appointment of a trustee.

Disclosure statement.   A written statement containing information approved as adequate by the court. It is required to be presented by a party before soliciting the acceptance or rejection of a plan of reorganization from creditors and stockholders affected by the plan. Adequate information means information of a kind, and in sufficient detail, as far as is reasonably practicable in light of the nature and history of the debtor and the condition of the debtor's records, that would enable a hypothetical reasonable investor typical of holders of claims or interests of the relevant class to make an informed judgment about the plan.

Emerging entity (reorganized entity).   An entity that has had its plan confirmed and begins to operate as a new entity.

Impaired claims.   In determining which class of creditors' claims or stockholders' interests must approve the plan, it is first necessary to determine if the class is impaired. A class of creditors' claims or stockholders' interests under a plan is not impaired if the plan (a) leaves unaltered the legal, equitable, and contractual right of a class, (b) cures defaults that lead to acceleration of debt or equity interest, or (c) pays in cash the full amount of the claim, or for equity interests, the greater of the fixed liquidation preference or redemption price.

Nonconsenting class.   A class of creditors or stockholders that does not approve the proposed plan.

Obligations subject to compromise.   Includes all prepetition liabilities (claims) except those that will not be impaired under the plan, such as claims where the value of the security interest is greater than the claim.

Petition.   A document filed in a court of bankruptcy, initiating proceedings under the Bankruptcy Code.

Plan (plan of reorganization).   An agreement formulated in Chapter 11 proceedings under the supervision of the Bankruptcy Court that enables the debtor to continue in business. The plan, once confirmed, may affect the rights of undersecured creditors, secured creditors, and stockholders as well as those of unsecured creditors. Before a plan is confirmed by the Court, it must comply with general provisions of the Code. Those provisions mandate, for example, that (a) the plan is feasible, (b) the plan is in the best interest of the creditors, and, (c) if an impaired class does not accept the plan, the plan must be determined to be fair and equitable before it can be confirmed.

Postpetition liabilities. Liabilities incurred subsequent to the filing of a petition that are not associated with prebankruptcy events. Thus, these liabilities are not considered prepetition liabilities.

Prepetition liabilities. Liabilities that were incurred by an entity prior to its filing of a petition for protection under the Code, including those considered by the Bankruptcy Court to be prepetition claims, such as a rejection of a lease for real property.

Reorganization items. Items of income, expense, gain, or loss that are realized or incurred by an entity because it is in reorganization.

Reorganization proceeding. A Chapter 11 case from the time at which the petition is filed until the plan is confirmed.

Reorganization value. The value attributed to the reconstituted entity, as well as the expected net realizable value of those assets that will be disposed before reconstitution occurs. Therefore, this value is viewed as the fair value of the entity before considering liabilities and approximates the amount a willing buyer would pay for the assets of the entity immediately after the restructuring.

Secured claim. A liability that is secured by collateral. A fully secured claim is one where the value of the collateral is greater than the amount of the claim.

Terminal value. Reorganization value calculated based on the discounting of cash flows normally consists of three parts: (a) the discounted cash flows determined for the forecast period, (b) residual value or terminal value, and (c) the current value of any excess working capital or other assets that are not needed in reorganization. Terminal or residual value represents the present value of the business attributable to the period beyond the forecast period.

Trustee. A person appointed by the Bankruptcy Court in certain situations based on the facts of the case, not related to the size of the company or the amount of unsecured debt outstanding, at the request of a party in interest after a notice and hearing.

Undersecured claim (liability). A secured claim whose collateral is worth less than the amount of the claim.

Unsecured claim (liability). A liability that is not secured by collateral. In the case of an undersecured creditor, the excess of the secured claim over the value of the collateral is an unsecured claim, unless the debtor elects in a Chapter 11 proceeding to have the entire claim considered secured. The term is generally used in bankruptcy to refer to unsecured claims that do not receive priority under the Bankruptcy Code.

Accounting Standards Executive Committee

(1989–1990)

JOHN L. KREISCHER, *Chairman*	MARJORIE B. MARKER
PETER S. DYE	JAMES C. MEEHAN
ANDREW D. FINGER	FRANCIS J. O'BRIEN
WILLIAM W. HOLDER	BARRY P. ROBBINS
WILLIAM J. IHLANFELDT	WALTER SCHUETZE
PAUL KARR	JERRY SNOW
GREGORY D. KOSCHINSKA	REVA STEINBERG
RAY L. KRAUSE	

Task Force on Financial Reporting by Entities in Reorganization Under the Bankruptcy Code

Members	Advisers
JOHN J. ROBBINS, *Chairman*	ALAN JACOBS
PETER J. GIBBONS	GEORGE F. PATTERSON, JR.
GRANT W. NEWTON	KEITH ROWDEN
RONALD S. ORR	CLARENCE STAUBS
WARREN W. PETRAGLIA	

AICPA Staff

PAUL ROSENFIELD, *Director Accounting Standards*	AL GOLL, *Technical Manager Accounting Standards*

About the Task Force

In addition to the chairman, John Robbins of Kenneth Leventhal & Company, Warren Petraglia and Alan Jacobs of Ernst & Young, and Peter Gibbons of Price Waterhouse specialize in reorganizations. Grant Newton is professor of accounting at Pepperdine University and author of a book on bankruptcy and insolvency accounting practice and procedures. Ron Orr specializes in bankruptcy proceedings with the law firm of Gibson, Dunn & Crutcher, Keith Rowden was on the FASB staff as an accounting fellow until returning to Coopers & Lybrand, and Clarence Staubs was on the SEC staff until his retirement. George F. Patterson, Jr. of Kenneth Leventhal & Company did most of the drafting.

Guidelines for Reviewing Applications for Compensation and Reimbursement of Expenses Under 11 U.S.C. Section 330

Fee Guidelines

GUIDELINES FOR REVIEWING APPLICATIONS FOR COMPENSATION AND REIMBURSEMENT OF EXPENSES FILED UNDER 11 U.S.C. § 330

Effective January 30, 1996

(a) General Information.

(1) The Bankruptcy Reform Act of 1994 amended the responsibilities of the United States Trustees under 28 U.S.C. 586(a)(3)(A) to provide that, whenever they deem appropriate, United States Trustees will review applications for compensation and reimbursement of expenses under section 330 of the Bankruptcy Code, 11 U.S.C. 101, et seq. ("Code"), in accordance with procedural guidelines ("Guidelines") adopted by the Executive Office for United States Trustees ("Executive Office"). The following Guidelines have been adopted by the Executive Office and are to be uniformly applied by the United States Trustees except when circumstances warrant different treatment.

(2) The United States Trustees shall use these Guidelines in all cases commenced on or after October 22, 1994.

(3) The Guidelines are not intended to supersede local rules of court, but should be read as complementing the procedures set forth in local rules.

(4) Nothing in the Guidelines should be construed:

(i) To limit the United States Trustee's discretion to request additional information necessary for the review of a particular application or type of application or to refer any information provided to the United States Trustee to any investigatory or prosecutorial authority of the United States or a state;

(ii) To limit the United States Trustee's discretion to determine whether to file comments or objections to applications; or

(iii) To create any private right of action on the part of any person enforceable in litigation with the United States Trustee or the United States.

(5) Recognizing that the final authority to award compensation and reimbursement under section 330 of the Code is vested in the Court, the Guidelines focus on the disclosure of information relevant to a proper award under the law. In evaluating fees for professional services, it is relevant to consider various factors including the following: the time spent; the rates charged; whether the services were necessary to the administration of, or beneficial towards the completion of, the case at the time they were rendered; whether services were performed within a reasonable time commensurate with the complexity, importance, and nature of the problem, issue, or task addressed; and whether compensation is reasonable based on the customary compensation charged by comparably skilled practitioners in non-bankruptcy cases. The Guidelines thus reflect standards and procedures articulated in section 330 of the Code and Rule 2016 of the Federal Rules of Bankruptcy Procedure for awarding compensation to trustees and to professionals employed under section 327 or 1103. Applications that contain the information requested in these Guidelines will facilitate review by the Court, the parties, and the United States Trustee.

(6) Fee applications submitted by trustees are subject to the same standard of review as are applications of other professionals and will be evaluated according to the principles articulated in these Guidelines. Each United States Trustee should establish whether and to what extent trustees can deviate from the format specified in these Guidelines without substantially affecting the ability of the United States Trustee to review and comment on their fee applications in a manner consistent with the requirements of the law.

(b) Contents of Applications for Compensation and Reimbursement of Expenses.
All applications should include sufficient detail to demonstrate compliance with the standards set forth in 11 U.S.C. § 330. The fee application should also contain sufficient information about the case and the applicant so that the Court, the creditors, and the United States Trustee can review it without searching for relevant information in other documents. The following will facilitate review of the application.

(1) *Information about the Applicant and the Application.* The following information should be provided in every fee application:

(i) Date the bankruptcy petition was filed, date of the order approving employment, identity of the party represented, date services commenced, and whether the applicant is seeking compensation under a provision of the Bankruptcy Code other than section 330.

(ii) Terms and conditions of employment and compensation, source of compensation, existence and terms controlling use of a retainer, and any budgetary or other limitations on fees.

(iii) Names and hourly rates of all applicant's professionals and paraprofessionals who billed time, explanation of any changes in hourly rates from those previously charged, and statement of whether the compensation is based on the customary compensation charged by comparably skilled practitioners in cases other than cases under title 11.

(iv) Whether the application is interim or final, and the dates of previous orders on interim compensation or reimbursement of expenses along with the amounts requested and the amounts allowed or disallowed, amounts of all previous payments, and amount of any allowed fees and expenses remaining unpaid.

(v) Whether the person on whose behalf the applicant is employed has been given the opportunity to review the application and whether that person has approved the requested amount.

(vi) When an application is filed less than 120 days after the order for relief or after a prior application to the Court, the date and terms of the order allowing leave to file at shortened intervals.

(vii) Time period of the services or expenses covered by the application.

(2) *Case Status.* The following information should be provided to the extent that it is known to or can be reasonably ascertained by the applicant:

(i) In a chapter 7 case, a summary of the administration of the case including all moneys received and disbursed in the case, when the case is expected to close, and, if applicant is seeking an interim award, whether it is feasible to make an interim distribution to creditors without prejudicing the rights of any creditor holding a claim of equal or higher priority.

(ii) In a chapter 11 case, whether a plan and disclosure statement have been filed and, if not yet filed, when the plan and disclosure statement are expected to be filed; whether all quarterly fees have been paid to the United States Trustee; and whether all monthly operating reports have been filed.

(iii) In every case, the amount of cash on hand or on deposit, the amount and nature of accrued unpaid administrative expenses, and the amount of unencumbered funds in the estate.

(iv) Any material changes in the status of the case that occur after the filing of the fee application should be raised, orally or in writing, at the hearing on the application or, if a hearing is not required, prior to the expiration of the time period for objection.

(3) *Summary Sheet.* All applications should contain a summary or cover sheet that provides a synopsis of the following information:

(i) Total compensation and expenses requested and any amount(s) previously requested;

(ii) Total compensation and expenses previously awarded by the court;

(iii) Name and applicable billing rate for each person who billed time during the period, and date of bar admission for each attorney;

(iv) Total hours billed and total amount of billing for each person who billed time during billing period; and

(v) Computation of blended hourly rate for persons who billed time during period, excluding paralegal or other paraprofessional time.

(4) *Project Billing Format.*

(i) To facilitate effective review of the application, all time and service entries should be arranged by project categories. The project categories set forth in Exhibit A should be used to the extent applicable. A separate project category should be used for administrative matters and, if payment is requested, for fee application preparation.

(ii) The United States Trustee has discretion to determine that the project billing format is not necessary in a particular case or in a particular class of cases. Applicants should be encouraged to consult with the United States Trustee if there is a question as to the need for project billing in any particular case.

(iii) Each project category should contain a narrative summary of the following information:

(A) a description of the project, its necessity and benefit to the estate, and the status of the project including all pending litigation for which compensation and reimbursement are requested;

(B) identification of each person providing services on the project; and

(C) a statement of the number of hours spent and the amount of compensation requested for each professional and paraprofessional on the project.

(iv) Time and service entries are to be reported in chronological order under the appropriate project category.

(v) Time entries should be kept contemporaneously with the services rendered in time periods of tenths of an hours. Services should be noted in detail and not combined or "lumped" together, with each service showing a separate time entry; however, tasks performed in a project which total a de minimis amount of time can be combined or lumped together if they do not exceed .5 hours on a daily aggregate. Time entries for telephone calls, letters, and other communications should give sufficient detail to identify the parties to and the nature of the communication. Time entries for court hearings and conferences should identify the subject of the hearing or conference. If more than one professional from the applicant firm attends a hearing or conference, the applicant should explain the need for multiple attendees.

(5) *Reimbursement for Actual, Necessary Expenses.* Any expense for which reimbursement is sought must be actual and necessary and supported by documentation as appropriate. Factors relevant to a determination that the expense is proper include the following:

(i) Whether the expense is reasonable and economical. For example, first class and other luxurious travel mode or accommodations will normally be objectionable.

(ii) Whether the requested expenses are customarily charged to non-bankruptcy clients of the applicant.

(iii) Whether applicant has provided a detailed itemization of all expenses including the date incurred, description of expense (e.g., type of travel, type of fare, rate, destination), method of computation, and, where relevant, name of the person incurring the expense and purpose of the expense. Itemized expenses should be identified by their nature (e.g., long distance telephone, copy costs, messengers, computer research, airline travel, etc.) and by the month incurred. Unusual items require more detailed explanations and should be allocated, where practicable, to specific projects.

(iv) Whether applicant has prorated expenses where appropriate between the estate and other cases (e.g., travel expenses applicable to more than one case) and has adequately explained the basis for any such proration.

(v) Whether expenses incurred by the applicant to third parties are limited to the actual amounts billed to, or paid by, the applicant on behalf of the estate.

(vi) Whether applicant can demonstrate that the amount requested for expenses incurred in-house reflect the actual cost of such expenses to the applicant. The United States Trustee may establish an objection ceiling for any in-house expenses that are routinely incurred and for which the actual cost cannot easily be determined by most professionals (e.g., photocopies, facsimile charges, and mileage).

(vii) Whether the expenses appear to be in the nature nonreimbursable overhead. Overhead consists of all continuous administrative or general costs incident to the operation of the applicant's office and not particularly attributable to an individual client or cases. Overhead includes, but is not limited to, word processing, proofreading, secretarial and other clerical services, rent, utilities, office equipment and furnishings, insurance, taxes, local telephones and monthly car phone charges, lighting, heating and cooling, and library and publication charges.

(viii) Whether applicant has adhered to allowable rates for expenses as fixed by local rule or order of the Court.

EXHIBIT A

PROJECT CATEGORIES

Here is a list of suggested project categories for use in most bankruptcy cases. Only one category should be used for a given activity. Professionals should make their best effort to be consistent in their use of categories, whether within a particular firm or by different firms working on the same case. It would be appropriate for all professionals to discuss the categories in advance and agree generally on how activities will be categorized. This list is not exclusive. The application may contain additional categories as the case requires. They are generally more applicable to attorneys in chapter 7 and chapter 11, but may be used by all professionals as appropriate.

ASSET ANALYSIS AND RECOVERY: Identification and review of potential assets including causes of action and non-litigation recoveries.

ASSET DISPOSITION: Sales, leases (§ 365 matters), abandonment and related transaction work.

BUSINESS OPERATIONS: Issues related to debtor-in-possession operating in chapter 11 such as employee, vendor, tenant issues and other similar problems.

CASE ADMINISTRATION: Coordination and compliance activities, including preparation of statement of financial affairs; schedules; list of contracts; United States Trustee interim statements and operating reports; contacts with the United States Trustee; general creditor inquiries.

CLAIMS ADMINISTRATION AND OBJECTIONS: Specific claim inquiries; bar date motions; analyses, objections and allowances of claims.

EMPLOYEE BENEFITS/PENSIONS: Review issues such as severance, retention, 401K coverage and continuance of pension plan.

FEE/EMPLOYMENT APPLICANTS: Preparations of employment and fee applications for self or others; motions to establish interim procedures.

FEE/EMPLOYMENT OBJECTIONS: Review of and objections to the employment and fee applications of others.

FINANCING: Matters under §§ 361, 363 and 364 including cash collateral and secured claims; loan document analysis.

LITIGATION: There should be a separate category established for each matter (e.g., XYZ Litigation).

MEETINGS OF CREDITORS: Preparing for and attending the conference of creditors, the § 341(a) meeting and other creditors' committee meetings.

PLAN AND DISCLOSURE STATEMENT: Formulation, presentation and confirmation; compliance with the plan confirmation order, related orders and rules; disbursement and case closing activities, except those related to the allowance and objections to allowance of claims.

RELIEF FROM STAY PROCEEDINGS: Matters relating to termination or continuation of automatic stay under § 362.

The following categories are generally more applicable to accountants and financial advisors, but may be used by all professionals as appropriate.

ACCOUNTING/AUDITING: Activities related to maintaining and auditing books of account, preparation of financial statements and account analysis.

BUSINESS ANALYSIS: Preparation and review of company business plan; development and review of strategies; preparation and review of cash flow forecasts and feasibility studies.

CORPORATE FINANCE: Review financial aspects of potential mergers, acquisitions and disposition of company or subsidiaries.

DATA ANALYSIS: Management information systems review, installation and analysis, construction, maintenance and reporting of significant case financial data, lease rejection, claims, etc.

LITIGATION CONSULTING: Providing consulting and expert witness services relating to various bankruptcy matters such as insolvency, feasibility, avoiding actions; forensic accounting, etc.

RECONSTRUCTION ACCOUNTING: Reconstructing books and records from past transactions and bringing accounting current.

TAX ISSUES: Analysis of tax issues and preparation of state and federal tax returns.

VALUATION: Appraise or review appraisals of assets.

Exhibit B: *Sample Summary Sheet*

In re _____ :

                 : CHAPTER

                 : Case No.

  Debtor. :

FEE APPLICATION

NAME OF APPLICANT:

ROLE IN THE CASE:

Fees Previously Requested	$
Fees Previously Awarded	$
Expenses Previously Requested	$
Expenses Previously Awarded	$
Retainer Paid	$

CURRENT APPLICATION

Fees Requested	$
Expenses Requested	$

NAMES OF PROFESSIONALS/ PARAPROFESSIONALS	YEAR ADMITTED TO PRACTICE	Hours Billed CURRENT APPLICATION	RATE	TOTAL FOR APPLICATION
PARTNERS				
ASSOCIATES				
PARAPROFESSIONALS				
				TOTAL BLENDED HOURLY RATE

Glossary

Absolute priority doctrine Section 1129(b) of the Bankruptcy Code allows the court under certain conditions to confirm a plan even though an impaired class has not accepted the plan. For the court to confirm the plan under these conditions it must determine that the plan satisfies the absolute priority requirement—that is, the plan must not discriminate unfairly with respect to each class of claims or interests impaired under the plan that has not accepted it. The Bankruptcy Code states conditions for secured claims, unsecured claims, and stockholder interests according to the "absolute priority doctrine" that would be included in the "fair and equitable" requirement. For example, a class of unsecured creditors that did not accept the plan must receive 100 percent of their claim, or if less is received, then a class junior to them could not receive any value. See *Cram down.*

Accountant An accountant, as used in the Bankruptcy Code (section 101(1)) means an accountant authorized under applicable law to practice public accounting, and includes professional accounting associations, corporations, or partnerships, if so authorized.

Administrative expenses The actual, necessary costs of preserving the estate, including wages, salaries, and commissions for services rendered after the commencement of the case. Compensation awarded a professional person, including accountants and attorneys, for postpetition services is also an expense of administration.

Adequate protection Holders of secured claims, lessors, co-owners, conditional vendors, consignors, and so forth, are entitled to adequate protection of their interest in the property when such holders request relief from the automatic stay. Adequate protection is also required before the debtor or trustee can use, sell, or lease certain kinds of collateral or before a lien that is prior to or equal to the creditor's lien can be granted.

Allowed claim The amount of the claim that the court allows against the bankruptcy estate. The amount may differ from the amount reflected in the books and records.

Assignment A remedy available under state insolvency laws, many of which provide for judicial proceedings. The debtor voluntarily transfers title to assets to an assignee who then liquidates them and distributes the proceeds among the creditors. The debtor will not be discharged of any unpaid indebtedness.

Attorney An attorney as used in the Bankruptcy Code (section 101(4)), means attorney, professional law association, corporation, or partnership, authorized under applicable law to practice law.

Automatic stay A petition, filed under the Bankruptcy Code, that automatically stays virtually all actions of creditors to collect prepetition debts. As a result of the stay, no party, with minor exceptions, having a security or adverse interest in the debtor's property can take any action that will interfere with the debtor or the debtor's property, regardless of where the property is located or who has possession, until the stay is modified or removed.

Bankruptcy The proceedings initiated voluntarily by a financially troubled debtor, or involuntarily by creditors when the debtor is generally not paying debts as they become due. The filing of a petition in a federal court under the Bankruptcy Code is involved.

Bankruptcy Act A federal statute enacted July 2, 1898, as title 11 of the United States Code and amended more than 90 times; applicable to all cases filed before October 1, 1979, the date the Bankruptcy Reform Act of 1978 became law.

Bankruptcy Code A federal statute, enacted October 1, 1979, as title 11 of the United States Code by the Bankruptcy Reform Act of 1978; applicable to all cases filed on or after its enactment. Provides the basis for the federal bankruptcy system in effect today.

Bankruptcy Court The United States Bankruptcy Court of trial jurisdiction that is a unit of the district court. Responsible for all cases filed under chapters 7, 11, 12, and 13 of the Bankruptcy Code.

Bankruptcy judge The judge of the court of bankruptcy where a bankruptcy case is pending.

Bankruptcy Reform Act of 1978 The Act passed by and signed by the President on November 6, 1978, which provided for the new Bankruptcy Code, established the U.S. trustee system in ten districts or groups of districts, and revised the bankruptcy court system. Subsequent modifications extended the U.S. trustee system throughout the United States and revised other sections of the Act.

Bankruptcy Rules Section 2075 of title 28, chapter 131 of the United States Code provides that the Supreme Court shall have the power to prescribe the general rules, the forms to be used, and procedures to follow as long as these do not conflict with the provisions of the Bankruptcy Code. On April 25, 1983, the United States Supreme Court prescribed Federal Rules of Bankruptcy Procedure that were reported to Congress and became effective on August 1, 1983. The Rules have been modified several times.

Best-interest-of-creditors test Under the best-interest-of-creditors requirement, it is necessary for the creditors or stockholders who do not vote or who voted against the plan to receive as much under the plan as they would if the business were liquidated under chapter 7.

Business bankrupt/debtor   A bankrupt/debtor whose financial problems result from some type of business activity.

Cash collateral   Cash collateral is cash, negotiable instruments, documents of title, securities, deposit accounts, or other cash equivalents where the estate and someone else have an interest in the property. Also included would be the proceeds of noncash collateral, such as inventory and accounts receivable, if converted to proceeds of the type defined as cash collateral, provided the proceeds are subject to the prepetition security interests.

Chapter X proceeding   A corporate reorganization taken under Chapter X of the Bankruptcy Act (filed before October 1, 1979). Used mostly by large corporations with complex debt structures and with widely held public securities. Replaced by chapter 11 of the Bankruptcy Code.

Chapter XI proceeding   An arrangement under Chapter XI of the Bankruptcy Act. Used mostly by businesses for the purpose of working out a settlement, with court approval, providing for creditors to agree to accept partial payment in satisfaction of their claims and/or an extension of the time for repayment. The provisions of Chapter XI applied only to unsecured creditors. Replaced by chapter 11 of the Bankruptcy Code.

Chapter 7 proceeding   A liquidation voluntarily or involuntarily initiated under the provisions of the Bankruptcy Code on or after October 1, 1979; provides for an orderly liquidation of the business or debtor's estate.

Chapter 11 proceeding   A reorganization action, either voluntary or involuntary, initiated under the provisions of the Bankruptcy Code on or after October 1, 1979; provides for a reorganization of the debt structure of the business and allows the business to continue operations. The business may also liquidate under chapter 11.

Chapter 12 proceeding   A reorganization, voluntarily initiated under the Bankruptcy Code, for family farmers with regular income.

Chapter 13 proceeding   A voluntary action initiated under the provisions of the Bankruptcy Code on or after October 1, 1979; provides for the settlement of debts of individuals with regular income. Some small, individually owned businesses may also file a petition under chapter 13.

Claim   Section 101(4) of the Bankruptcy Code defines a claim as (1) a right to payment, whether or not such right is reduced to judgment, liquidated, unliquidated, fixed, contingent, matured, unmatured, disputed, undisputed, legal, secured, or unsecured, or (2) a right to an equitable remedy for breach of performance if such breach gives rise to a right to payment, whether or not such right to an equitable remedy is reduced to judgment, fixed, contingent, matured, unmatured, disputed, undisputed, secured, or unsecured.

Committee case   A nonjudicial endeavor by the debtor and an unofficial creditors' committee to effect a voluntary agreement, out of court, wherein the debtor normally remains in business but secures an extension of time for payment, or a reduction in amount, or both, of all or part of its unsecured debts.

Composition (informal)   An out-of-court agreement between a debtor and its creditors whereby the debtor normally remains in business but provides for full satisfaction of claims by partial payment, and for cancellation of remaining indebtedness.

Confirmation An official approval by a court of a plan of reorganization under chapter 11 proceedings; makes the plan binding on the debtor and creditors. Before a plan is confirmed, it must satisfy thirteen requirements stated in section 1129(a) of the Bankruptcy Code. Plans may also be confirmed in chapter 12 and chapter 13, but the requirements for confirmation differ in some respects from the confirmation requirements under chapter 11.

Consenting classes Classes of creditors or shareholders that vote in favor of the plan of reorganization.

Corporate reorganization Used to refer to the proceedings under Chapter X of the Bankruptcy Act.

Cram down For a plan to be confirmed, a class of claims or interests must either accept the plan or not be impaired. However, the Bankruptcy Code allows the court, under certain conditions, to confirm a plan even though an impaired class has not accepted the plan. The plan must not discriminate unfairly, and must be fair and equitable with respect to each class of claims or interests impaired under the plan that has not accepted it. The Bankruptcy Code states conditions for secured claims, unsecured claims, and stockholder interests that would be included in the fair and equitable requirement. It should be noted that, because the word "includes" is used, the meaning of "fair and equitable" is not restricted to these conditions.

Creditor An entity that has a claim against the debtor that arose before the order for relief or that is treated under the provisions of the Bankruptcy Code as though it arose before the petition was filed.

Creditors' committee In a chapter 11 case, a committee of creditors holding unsecured claims is appointed as soon as practicable after the order for relief is granted. The U.S. trustee has the responsibility for appointing the committee without any authorization from the court. The committee will ordinarily consist of the seven largest creditors willing to serve or, if a committee was organized before the order for relief, such committee may continue provided it was fairly chosen and is representative of the different kinds of claims to be represented.

Date of bankruptcy Date when a petition in bankruptcy is filed with the bankruptcy court.

Debt Defined in section 101(12) of the Bankruptcy Code to mean liability on a claim.

Debtor A person or municipality that has commenced a case under the Bankruptcy Code.

Debtor-in-possession Refers to a debtor in a chapter 11 case unless a trustee has been appointed. The debtor will remain in possession of its assets in a chapter 11 case unless a trustee is appointed.

Discharge An order entered in a bankruptcy court proceeding; releases the debtor from debts (except those exempt from discharge) remaining due after nonexempt assets are distributed, or upon confirmation of a plan under chapter 11.

Disclosure of adequate information   Disclosure of information of a kind and in sufficient detail, as far as is reasonably practicable in light of the nature and history of the debtor and the condition of the debtor's books and records, that would enable a hypothetical reasonable investor typical of holders of claims or interests of the relevant class to make an informed judgment about a plan of reorganization under chapter 11 of the Bankruptcy Code. The statement containing adequate information is referred to as the disclosure statement.

Disinterested person   A disinterested person is anyone other than a:

1 Creditor
2 Stockholder
3 Insider
4 Investment banker for any outstanding security of the debtor
5 Investment banker, or an attorney for the investment banker, in connection with the offer, sale, or issuance of a security of the debtor within three years prior to filing of the petition
6 Director, officer, or employee of the debtor or investment banker within two years prior to filing of the petition
7 Person who has an interest adverse to the interest of the estate, creditors, or stockholders because of any direct or indirect relationship to the debtor or investment banker

Accountants, attorneys, or other professionals must be disinterested persons in order to be retained to render professional services in connection with the bankruptcy proceedings.

Entity   Defined in section 101(15) to include person, estate, trust, governmental unit, and United States trustee.

Equity security   A share in a corporation (whether or not transferable or denominated stock) or similar security; interest of a limited partner in a limited partnership; or warrant or right (other than a right to convert) to purchase, sell, or subscribe to a share or interest.

Estate   The commencement of a case under the Bankruptcy Code creates an estate comprised of the property of the debtor.

Examiner   An official appointed by the bankruptcy court in a chapter 11 reorganization, if no trustee is serving, to conduct an investigation of the debtor as is appropriate, including an investigation of any allegations of fraud, dishonesty, incompetence, misconduct, mismanagement, or irregularity in the management of the affairs of the debtor of or by current or former management of affairs of the debtor of or by current or former management of the debtor, if (1) such appointment is in the interests of creditors, any equity security holders, and other interests of the estate, or (2) the debtor's fixed, liquidated, unsecured debts, other than debts for goods, services, or taxes, or owing to an insider, exceed $5 million.

Executory contract   A contract in which something other than payment itself must be performed wholly or in part to complete the original agreement. Unexpired leases or purchase commitments are examples of executory contracts typically found in cases under the Bankruptcy Code.

Exempt assets   Property of an estate which by federal or state laws is not liable for any debt of the debtor that arose before the commencement of the case. The debtor may maintain possession of exempt assets.

Fair and equitable test   Section 1129(b) of the Bankruptcy Code allows the court under certain conditions to confirm a plan even though an impaired class has not accepted the plan. For the court to confirm the plan it must determine that the plan must not discriminate unfairly, and must be fair and equitable, with respect to each class of claims or interest impaired under the plan that has not accepted it. The Bankruptcy Code states conditions for secured claims, unsecured claims, and stockholder interests according the "absolute priority doctrine" that would be included in the "fair and equitable" requirement. For example, courts have determined that a plan that provides only for the payment of the claim in full with cash and not interest to a class that has voted against the plan where the owners retain their interest is not "fair and equitable."

Family farmer   Section 101(18) of the Bankruptcy Code defines a family farmer. See Appendix A.

Family farmer with regular income   A family farmer with annual income that is sufficiently stable and regular to enable the farmer to make payments under a chapter 11 plan.

Farming operation   Includes farming, tillage of the soil, dairy farming, ranching, production or raising of crops, poultry, or livestock, and production of poultry or livestock products in an unmanufactured state.

Feasibility test   A plan of reorganization will not be confirmed unless it is feasible—that is, confirmation of the plan is not likely to be followed by liquidation or the need for further financial reorganization unless such liquidation or reorganization is provided for in the plan. This requirement means that the court must ascertain that the debtor has a reasonable chance of surviving once the plan is confirmed and the debtor is out from under the protection of the court. A well-prepared forecast of future operations based on reasonable assumptions, taking into consideration the changes expected as a result of the confirmation of the plan, is an example of the kind of information that can be very helpful to the court in reaching a decision on this requirement.

Fraudulent transfer   A transfer of an interest or an obligation incurred by the debtor, within one year prior to the date the petition was filed, with the intent to hinder, delay, or defraud creditors or whereby the debtor received less than fair equivalent value and the debtor (1) was insolvent before or became insolvent as the result of such transfer, (2) was left with unreasonably small business capital, or (3) intended to incur debts beyond the ability to pay such debts as they matured. Fraudulent transfers may be voided. Certain transfers considered fraudulent under state law may be avoided even if the transfer occurred more than one year before the petition was filed.

Fresh start   Under SOP 90-7, debtors emerging from chapter 11 are required to adopt fresh start reporting under two conditions:

1   The reorganized value of the emerging entity immediately before the confirmation of the plan is less than the total of all postpetition liabilities and allowed claims.
2   Holders of existing voting shares immediately before confirmation retain less than 50 percent of the voting share of the emerging entity.

Fresh start reporting requires the debtor to use current values (going concern or reorganization values) in its balance sheet for both assets and liabilities and to eliminate all prior earnings or deficits.

Impairment   In determining which classes of claims or stockholders' interest must approve the plan, it is first necessary to determine whether the class is impaired. Section 1124 of the Bankruptcy Code provides that a class of claims or interests is impaired under the plan, unless the plan: (1) leaves unaltered the legal, equitable, and contractual rights to which such claim or interest entitles the holder of such claim or interest, or (2) notwithstanding any contractual provision or applicable law that entitles the holder of such claim or interest to demand or receive accelerated payment of such claim or interest after the occurrence of a default (a) cures any such default that occurred before or after the commencement of the case under this title, other than a default of a kind specified in section 365(b)(2) of this title [such as a bankruptcy or insolvency clause that would make the entire debt due]; (b) reinstates the maturity of such claim or interest as such maturity existed before such default; (c) compensates the holder of such claim or interest for any damages incurred as a result of any reasonable reliance by such holder on such contractual provision or such applicable law; and (d) does not otherwise alter the legal, equitable, or contractual rights to which such claim or interest entitles the holder of such claim or interest.

Individual with regular income   An individual other than a stockholder or a commodity broker whose income is sufficiently stable and regular to enable such individual to make payments under a plan under chapter 13 of the Bankruptcy Code (in a case filed on or after October 1, 1979).

Insider   Includes director, officer, person in control, relative, partner, affiliate, and managing agent.

Insolvency   (1) In the equity sense, the inability of the debtor to pay obligations as they mature. (2) In the bankruptcy sense, a condition where the liabilities of the debtor exceed the fair valuation of its assets.

Insolvency proceeding   Action undertaken in a state court or otherwise under state insolvency laws.

Involuntary petition   A petition filed under chapter 7 or chapter 11 by creditors forcing the debtor into bankruptcy court.

Irregularities   Any transactions that are not in the ordinary course of business, especially those transactions that resulted in the apparent dissipation of the debtor's assets in a manner other than by loss in the ordinary course of business.

Judicial lien   A lien obtained by judgment, levy, sequestration, or other legal or equitable process or proceeding.

Lien   A charge against or interest in property to secure payment of a debt or performance of an obligation.

Liquidation   Used to refer to proceedings under chapter 7 of the Bankruptcy Code filed on or after October 1, 1979; also generally used to refer to the cessation of business and sale of all assets of the debtor. A business may also liquidate under chapter 11.

New value exception   In a situation where the debtor is attempting to obtain confirmation of a plan over the objection of a class of creditors that did not approve the plan and when the equity holders retained control of the company due to the contribution of new value rather than prior equity. The court may allow the confirmation if it is determined that other parties-in-interest had the right to submit a competing plan or had the right to "overbid" the price paid by the existing owners.

Nonbusiness bankrupt/debtor   A bankrupt whose financial difficulties are unrelated to any type of business operations.

Nonconsenting class   A class of creditors or shareholders that does not vote in favor of the plan or reorganization.

Obligations subject to compromise   Used in Statement of Position (SOP) 90-7 as a classification of liabilities consisting of all prepetition liabilities (claims) except those that are expected not to be impaired under the plan, such as fully secured liabilities that the debtor does not anticipate will be compromised. For example, the debtor might be expected to leave unimpaired a long-term over-secured note with a very low interest rate.

Order for relief   An order, whether by decree or by position of law in a case with the Bankruptcy Code (filed on or after October 1, 1979) granting relief to (or against) the debtor. In a voluntary case, the entry of the order for relief is the filing of the petition. The court must enter the order or relief in an involuntary case if the petition is uncontested or if the court determines that (1) the debtor is generally not paying debts as they become due or (2) within 120 days before the petition was filed, a custodian was appointed for substantially all of the debtor's property.

Person   As defined by the Bankruptcy Code (section 101(41)), includes individual, partnership, and corporation, but does not include governmental unit.

Petition   A document filed in a court of bankruptcy, initiating proceedings under the Bankruptcy Code.

Plan   An agreement that, when confirmed by the bankruptcy court, provides for the rehabilitation or liquidation of the debtor in a bankruptcy case under chapter 11, chapter 12, or chapter 13. The plan may affect secured creditors and stockholders as well as unsecured creditors' interests.

Postpetition liabilities   Used in Statement of Position (SOP) 90-7 to refer to liabilities incurred subsequent to the filing of the petition and not associated with prebankruptcy events. Postpetition liabilities are reflected on the balance sheet of a company in chapter 11 as "liabilities not subject to compromise."

Preference A transfer of property on account of a past debt within 90 days (one year for insiders) prior to filing the petition, while the debtor is insolvent, to a creditor who receives more than would be received if the debtor's estate were liquidated under chapter 7. The Bankruptcy Code provides exceptions for certain transactions that are substantially contemporaneous or in the ordinary course of business.

Prepetition liabilities Liabilities that were incurred prior to the filing of a bankruptcy petition, including those that may arise after the filing of the petition but are considered prepetition claims by the Bankruptcy Code—for example, damages associated with the rejection of a lease. Prepetition liabilities are included in the "liabilities subject to compromise" unless the claim is expected not to be impaired in balance sheets prepared during the chapter 11 case.

Priority claim A claim or expense paid after secured claims and before unsecured claims are satisfied, in accordance with statutory categories. The discharge is a privilege and the bankruptcy laws provide exceptions to discharge, in whole or in part, for certain wrongdoing, such as concealment of assets, or certain types of debt, such as alimony. Under the Bankruptcy Code (cases filed after October 1, 1979), a corporation that liquidates all (or substantially all) of its assets is ineligible for a discharge.

Proof of claim The Bankruptcy Code permits a creditor or indenture trustee to file a proof of claim and an equity holder to file a proof of interest. The filing of the proof is not mandatory in a chapter 11 case, and the debtor may obtain a discharge for debts that were listed on the schedules filed with the court, even though a proof of claim is not filed. The debtor or trustee has the power to file a claim on behalf of the creditor, if the creditor did not file a timely claim. Thus, for debts that are nondischargeable, the debtor may file a proof of claim to cause the creditor to receive some payment from the estate and avoid having to pay all of the debt after the bankruptcy proceedings are over.

Receiver An individual appointed by the bankruptcy court under the Bankruptcy Act (cases filed before October 1, 1979) to receive and preserve the property of the estate, to operate its business legally or represent the estate until a trustee can be elected or appointed. Also, an official appointed by any court of equitable jurisdiction as its agent for almost any proper purpose, which may include the liquidation of a business.

Relative An individual related by affinity or consanguinity within the third degree as determined by the common law; includes individuals in a step or adoptive relationship. Included would be spouse, son, daughter, brother, sister, father, and mother.

Reorganization Proceedings under chapter 11 of the Bankruptcy Code (cases filed on or after October 1, 1979) where a debtor attempts to reach an agreement with creditors, secured and unsecured, and continue in business.

Reorganization Items Items of income, expense, gain, or loss that are realized or incurred as a result of the reorganization and restructuring of the business.

Reorganization items are reflected in a separate category in the statement of operations.

Reorganization value   The value attributed to the reconstituted entity plus the expected net realizable value of those assets that will not be used by the reconstituted entity. Under Statement of Position (SOP) 90-7, this value is viewed as the fair value of the entity before considering liabilities and it approximates the amount that a willing buyer would pay for the assets of the entity immediately after the restructuring.

Schedules   The detailed lists of debts and assets that the debtor is required to file with a petition in bankruptcy court or shortly thereafter.

Secured claim   A claim against a debtor that is secured by collateral which may be used to satisfy the debt in the event the debtor defaults. Under the Bankruptcy Code, a creditor's claim is secured only to the extent of the value of the collateral unless the creditor selects in a chapter 11 proceeding (section 1111(b)(2)) to have the entire debt considered secured.

Setoff   The right that exists between two parties to net their respective debts where each party, as a result of unrelated transactions, owes the other an ascertained amount. The creditor has the right to offset a mutual debt, provided both the debt and the credit arose before the commencement of the case.

Single-asset real estate   Real property that constitutes a single property or project (other than residential real property with fewer than four residential units) that generates substantially all of the gross income of a debtor and where no substantial business other than operating the real property and related activities is conducted. The debtor's noncontingent, liquidated secured debts must not exceed $4 million.

Small business   A person engaged in commercial or business activities (excluding owning and operating real property and related activities) whose aggregate noncontingent, liquidated secured and unsecured debts as of the petition date do not exceed $2 million.

Statement of affairs   A report filed with a petition under chapter 11; consists of answers to 21 questions concerning the debtor's past operations. Also used to refer to a statement of a debtor's financial condition as of a certain date, based on the assumption that the business will be liquidated. The statement consists of an analysis of the debtor's financial position and the status of the creditors with respect to the debtor's assets.

Statutory lieu   A lien arising solely by force of a statute on specified circumstances or conditions or line of distress for rent, whether or not statutory. Statutory lien does not include security interest or judicial regardless of how such security interest or lien arose.

Transfer   Every mode, direct or indirect, absolute or conditional, voluntary or involuntary, of disposing of or parting with property or with an interest in property, including retention of title as a security interest and foreclosure of the debtor's equity of redemption. See *Fraudulent transfer.*

Trust indenture and security agreement   An agreement between the debtor and creditors, in the nature of an out-of-court extension agreement, that provides creditors with a lien on all the debtor's assets as security for the debtor's performance of its obligations to them under the agreement. Such agreements may also be used in connection with a chapter 11 case under the Bankruptcy Code.

Trustee   The Bankruptcy Code refers to four categories of trustees—U.S. trustee, interim trustee, trustee under a chapter 7, 11, 12, or 13 petition, and standing trustee.

1   *U.S. trustee*—A trustee appointed by the Attorney General in 21 regions to establish, maintain, and supervise a panel of private trustees who are eligible and available to serve as trustees in cases under chapters 7, 11, 12, or 13 of the Bankruptcy Code. The U.S. trustee is responsible for the administrative aspects of the bankruptcy case. Among other duties, the U.S. trustee approves fee applications, appoints trustees and committees, and reviews operating statements.

2   *Interim trustee*—As soon as the order for relief has been entered in a chapter 7 case, the court will appoint a disinterested person from a panel of private trustees to serve as the interim trustee.

3a   *Chapter 7 trustee*—At a meeting of creditors called under section 341, a trustee may be elected if an election is requested by at least 20 percent in amount of qualifying claims. The interim trustee will continue to serve if a trustee is not elected.

3b   *Chapter 11 trustee*—The Bankruptcy Code provides in chapter 11 cases that a trustee can be appointed in certain situations based on the facts of the case and not related to the size of the company or the amount of unsecured debt outstanding. The trustee is appointed only at the request of a party-in-interest after a notice and hearing.

3c   *Chapter 12 or 13 trustee*—The U.S. trustee may appoint an individual trustee to a chapter 12 or chapter 13 case where a standing trustee has not been appointed.

4   *Standing trustee*—In districts where warranted, the U.S. trustee may appoint one or more individuals to serve as standing trustees for cases filed under chapter 12 or chapter 13. In addition to most of the duties of a trustee in a chapter 7 or chapter 11 case, the standing trustee collects payments under the plan and distributes them to the creditors. A percentage fee based on payments under the plan will be collected by the standing trustee to cover trustee's costs.

Turnover order   An order by a bankruptcy judge directing that property or proceeds from sale of property be turned over to a trustee as part of the debtor's estate.

Undersecured claim   A secured claim where the value of the collateral is less than the amount of the claim.

Unsecured claim   A claim that is not secured by any collateral. In the case of an undersecured creditor, the excess of the secured claim over the value of the collateral is an unsecured claim, unless the debtor elects in a chapter 11 proceeding to have the entire claim considered secured. The term is generally used in bankruptcy and insolvency proceedings to refer to unsecured claims that do not receive priority under the Bankruptcy Code.

U.S. trustee   See *Trustee*.

Voluntary petition (bankruptcy)   A petition filed by a debtor of its own free will, initiating proceedings under the Bankruptcy Code.

Statutes Citations

Section 1145(b), § 6.40(a)
Section 1145(b)(1), § 6.40(a)
Section 1145(b)(2), § 6.40(a)
Section 1145(c), § 6.40(a)
Section 1146, § 16.46
Section 1204, § 6.46
Section 1206, § 6.47
Section 1207(a), § 6.46
Section 1222, §§ 6.47, 16.42
Section 1222(a)(2), § 6.47
Section 1224, § 6.47
Section 1225(a)(5), § 6.47
Section 1225(b)(2), § 6.47
Section 1304, § 6.50
Section 1306(b), § 6.50
Section 1322, §§ 16.42, 16.42(a)
Section 1322(b)(2), §§ 5.50(a), 6.51(a)
Section 1322(e), § 6.51(a)
Section 1324, § 6.51(a)
Section 1325(9)(5)(A), § 6.51(a)
Section 1325(a), § 6.51(a)
Section 1325(a)(3), § 6.42
Section 1325(a)(5), §§ 6.51, 6.51(a), 11.5
Section 1326(a), § 6.51
Section 1328(b), § 16.42(a)
Section 1334(b), § 6.39
Section 1398, § 16.4
Section 1399, § 16.4
Section 3466, § 5.16
Section 5457(f), § 5.39(a)
Section 6703(c)(1), § 5.43

Internal Revenue Code:

Section 56(g)(4)(B), § 16.18(b)
Section 61, § 16.18
Section 108, §§ 16.1, 16.18, 16.18(b), 16.21, 16.21(d), 16.24
Section 108(a), § 8.8(d)
Section 108(a)(1)(D), § 16.25
Section 108(b), § 16.18(a)
Section 108(b)(2), § 16.19
Section 108(b)(5), §§ 16.18(a)(i), 16.21
Section 108(b)(D), § 16.21
Section 108(c), § 16.21
Section 108(c)(3), §§ 16.21, 16.25
Section 108(c)(7), § 16.21(b)
Section 108(d), § 16.22
Section 108(d)(7), § 16.23
Section 108(e), § 16.24
Section 108(e)(8), § 16.24
Section 108(e)(10), § 16.24
Section 108(e)(11), § 16.18
Section 108(g), § 16.19
Section 108(g)(2), § 16.19
Section 108(g)(3), § 16.19

Section 111, § 16.8
Section 122(1), § 16.21
Section 162, § 16.17
Section 168(a)(1), § 16.28
Section 170(d)(1), § 16.8
Section 172, §§ 16.8, 16.30
Section 172(b), § 16.30
Section 263, § 16.11
Section 265, § 16.11
Section 269, §§ 16.31, 16.32
Section 312, §§ 16.35, 16.36
Section 341, § 16.8
Section 346(f), § 16.37(c)
Section 351, § 16.28(b)
Section 354, § 16.28(a)
Section 354(b)(1), § 16.28(a)
Section 354(b)(2), § 16.28(a)
Section 368, § 16.28(e)
Section 368(a)(1), §§ 16.27, 16.28(b)
Section 368(a)(1)(B), § 16.28(b)
Section 368(a)(1)(E), § 16.28(b)
Section 368(a)(1)(G), § 16.28(a)
Section 371, § 16.27
Section 381, § 16.36
Section 381(a)(2), § 16.36
Section 381(c)(2), § 16.36
Section 382, §§ 16.1, 16.18(a), 16.31[n]16.33
Section 382(1), § 8.8(d)
Section 382(1)(5), §§ 16.18(a), 16.32
Section 382(1)(5)(B), § 16.32
Section 382(1)(5)(D), § 16.32
Section 382(1)(5)(F), § 16.33
Section 382(1)(6), § 16.32
Section 382(b), § 16.36
Section 382(b)(1), § 16.18(a)
Section 383, § 16.33
Section 408(f), § 5.36(c)
Section 453(d), § 16.7
Section 465(b), § 16.8
Section 469, § 16.8
Section 469(b), § 16.18(a)
Section 483, § 16.18
Section 503(b), § 16.37(a)
Section 503(b)(1)(C), § 16.37(a)
Section 507, § 16.37
Section 541, § 16.29
Section 542(c), § 16.29
Section 542(c)(9), § 16.29
Section 585, § 16.28(b)
Section 593, § 16.28(b)
Section 752, § 16.18
Section 1017, §§ 16.21(d), 16.35
Section 1017(b)(3)(c), § 16.22
Section 1017(b)(4), § 16.19
Section 1017(c)(2), § 16.21(d)
Section 1017(d), § 16.21(c)
Section 1212, § 16.8
Section 1245, § 16.21(c)

Section 1250, § 16.21(c)
Section 1273, § 16.18
Section 1273(b)(4), § 16.18
Section 1274, § 16.18
Section 1275(a)(4), § 16.18
Section 1398, §§ 16.4(c), 16.5, 16.7, 16.11, 16.46
Section 1398(e)(3), § 16.6
Section 1398(e)(3)(B), § 16.11
Section 1398(e)(4), § 16.11
Section 1398(f)(2), § 16.7
Section 1398(g), § 16.8
Section 1398(h)(1), § 16.11
Section 1398(h)(2)(D), § 16.11
Section 1398(i), § 16.8
Section 1398(j)(1), § 16.12
Section 1398(j)(2)(A), § 16.10
Section 1399, §§ 16.3, 16.6
Section 3402(a)(1), § 16.37(g)
Section 4291, § 16.37(g)
Section 6012(a)(9), § 16.4(b)
Section 6012(b)(3), § 16.3(c)
Section 6012(b)(4), § 16.3(c)
Section 6031, § 16.4(a)
Section 6036, § 16.2(b)
Section 6411, §§ 16.37(a), 16.40
Section 6672, §§ 8.8(d), 10.12, 16.37(g), 16.37(h)
Section 6903, § 16.2(a)
Section 7501, § 16.37(g)
Section 7512, § 16.37(g)

Treasury Regulations:

1.61[n]12(a), § 16.18
1.269[n]3, § 16.32
1.382[n]3(b), § 16.32
1.641(b)-2(b), § 16.3
1.731[n]1(c)(2), § 16.22
1.1017[n]1, § 16.21
1.1274[n]1(c), § 16.18
1.1274[n]4(g)(2)(iv), § 16.18
1.1398[n]1, §§ 16.8, 16.9
301.6036[n]1, § 16.2
301.7701[n]4(d), § 16.3(c)
301.7701[n]6, § 16.3(c)

Uniform Commercial Code:

Section 1[n]201(23), § 5.5
Section 2[n]702, § 5.38
Section 2[n]705, § 5.29(a)
Section 3[n]503(2)(a), § 11.4(c)

United States Code, Title 28:

Section 158(b), § 5.18
Section 473, § 6.8
Section 586(a), §§ 5.19(a), 6.26(e), 7.4
Section 2412(d)(2)(a), § 5.20

Case Index

Name Index

Subject Index